The Liberal Lexicon:

A Socialistic, Spiritualistic Encyclodictionary

VOL. 2

Dr. Gary Joseph Pasieka, Ph.D.

(Revised, Expanded, Enhanced Edition)

CDXLIV

ISBN: 978-1-966615-26-2 (Paperback)
ISBN: 978-1-966615-27-9 (HardBack)
ISBN: 978-1-966615-28-6 (Ebook)

Table of Contents

E

E – (*EE*) The 5th letter in the English alphabet, a vowel. In physics, the letter E symbolizes energy.

EARBUD – (*EER*-bud) A tiny ear-phone, actual telephone, comparable in size to a hearing aid. Like a hearing aid, an earbud is hardly perceptible. Therefore, when a person is talking on this *micro*-phone, she looks quite insane, talking to herself. As with all portable phones, it's a rude social faux pas to impose your personal conversations on we who don't give a damn. Earbuds can cause chaos. For instance, Mike (of Fargo, Michigan) happened to be standing at a urinal in a restaurant restroom. A gentleman entered and engaged the next fixture. *"How are you?"* the gentleman inquired. *"Fine thanks,"* Mike replied politely. Then the gentleman propositioned: *"Maybe we can get together later, honey."* Mike exploded: *"Are you some kind of fuckin' pervert!?!"* The astonished gentleman backed away in perplexity. He had been talking to his wife on his earbud.

EARLY CHILDHOOD EDUCATION – (*ER*-lee *CHILD*-hood ed-jew-*KAY*-shun) Schooling from infancy to age eight (3rd grade). Ideally, Early Childhood Education is divided into three subgroups: 1. Infant / Toddler Programs serve children from birth to age two years. 2. Preschool / Kindergarten serves children from three to five years of age. 3. Primary School serves children from Kindergarten (five years) to age eight (3rd grade). In all this time, students have been learning to socialize and later how to read. Fourth grade (Elementary School, age 9) the emphasis shifts from learning to read, to reading to learn. Post Script: The best investment a government can make in its people and nation is free education – including Early Childhood.

EARLY RUM – (*ER*-lee *RUM*) A Jamaican colloquialism (*Jamaicanism*), a suggested remedy for *veisalgia* (hangover). Early rum by different names is practiced the world over, and has been from time immemorial. It is having a stiff drink or two the morning after the bender. Using alcohol to mitigate the alcohol-induced illness is taking *"A bit of the hair from the dog that bit you."* Early rum works – temporarily. One will quickly get high, or drunk again. One is afforded immediate relief when your head feels like a football. But alas, it is only a delaying tactic. The hangover will return. The piper must be paid. With veisalgia, the only way out is through.

EARMARK – (*EER*-mahrk) Originally an identification tag stapled to the ear of an animal to show ownership. In the political lexicon, an earmark is a provision in a piece of Congressional legislation that directs specified federal funds to specific projects, programs, organizations, or individuals. As a verb, to earmark is to set aside funds for a specified purpose, use, or recipient.

EARNED BENEFITS – (*ERND BEN*-ne-fits) An alternate name for government entitlements. Earned benefits include Social Security, Medicare, Medicaid, Unemployment Insurance, Welfare Payments, Food

Stamps, School Lunched, all the government programs to help those in need. American citizens get a fraction of the benefits awarded to citizens of other industrialized nations. Eliminating earned benefits is the Republican wet dream. Being rich, and representing the rich, the Republicans don't need the benefits, so they do not want to pay for them. (*"I got mine, to hell with you."* – Republican Credo.) As a U.S. citizens and human beings, we earned our benefits. It's not charity, but compensation. We are indeed *"entitled"* to these government programs. However Republican propaganda has managed to equate the term *"entitlement"* with *"handout."* Therefore, the alternative term, earned benefits is used in its stead.

EARTH – (*ERTH*) Our cosmic home, 3rd planet from the Sun, largest of the terrestrial planets. Earth is the densest planet in the solar system. It weighs about 6,000 million, million tons. Earth is about 4.54 billion years old (c. 1.5 trillion days). The only planet we know of with all the ingredients for life, (as we know it) is Earth. Earth has been serendipitously (or divinely) blessed in scores of ways to make the planet a comfortable home for all creatures, plant and animal. This has been called the *"Goldilocks Effect."* Earth is not too hot, not too cold, but just right. We are perfectly places, just over 93 million miles from the Sun. Indeed, the earth's temperature varies from the frigid poles to the torrid tropics. But the average temperature is about 580 degrees Fahrenheit. In fact, Earth is not too extreme in any respect, be that luck or providence. The rotating molten nickel-iron core of the planet creates a magnetic field that deflects dangerous ultraviolet light and solar winds. The gravitational force of our one large Moon provides our seasons, and assures a steady rotation. Otherwise, a wobbling Earth would produce climatic calamities.

EARTH – (*ERTH*) As an element (along with fire, water, and air) in classical Western philosophy, Earth is associated with the physical body and material abundance. The energy of Earth is considered to be cool, dry and is feminine in nature. Ergo, *"Mother Earth,"* *"Mother Nature."*

EARTH JURISPRUDENCE – (*ERTH JUR*-ris-proo-dens) Jurisprudence is the philosophy of law. Earth jurisprudence is a philosophy of law and human governance of the planet. It was introduced in 2007 by *"Ecotheologian"* Fr. Thomas Berry (1914 – 2009). Earth jurisprudence is anti-anthropocentric meaning man is not the center of the universe. It recognizes that humans are indeed the highest evolved species on Earth, but not the only lifeform. All living creatures, fauna and flora have a legal right to live and thrive on this planet. This is called the *"Rights of Nature."* Because of Homo sapiens' predominant status in the animal hierarchy, Homo sapiens have the predominant responsibility as the righteous, compassionate stewards on our common home planet. Earth jurisprudence does not give special privilege to private property. No one can really own any part of the planet – land, sea, air, sunshine – anyway. No one has the right to defile any part of the environment – not even if you *"own"* it. All creatures have a right to their unique habitats, even if they do not benefit man capitalistically. Earth jurisprudence does not give man total jurisdiction over everything. Environmental protection is a categorical imperative. All life is inherently valuable and constitutionally protected according to the jurisprudence of the Earth.

EARTHKIND – (*ERTH*-kyhd) In the Cosmic scheme of existence, Earthkind refers to all the living creatures, animals and plants that inhabit this planet. The inference in the term *Earthlings* seems to be confined only to humans. Earthkind takes in all life. Too, the term implies that the Earth is an infinitesimal granule in the mountainous Cosmos. There are infinite other kinds in the universe.

EARTHLING – (*ERTH*-ling) A human [read: *"humus"*] being. The words human and humus are cognates (cousin words). Humus is Latin for *"earth, soil."* An earthling or human being is literally from the earth or soil. The etymology of the words earthling or earth being is the Proto-Indo-European term *"dhghomon,"* which also gives us <u>human</u> and <u>humus</u>. In the Biblical story of creation, *"The Lord God formed the man of the dust from the ground...."* – Genesis 2:7. That man was named Adam, the name coming from the Hebrew *"adamah"* meaning ground, (or by extension, earth, humus). Incidentally: When we meet our extraterrestrial cousins, out intergalactic name is sure to be Earthlings.

EARTHQUAKE – (*ERTH*-kwake) The natural movement of the planet's tectonic plates, bringing disastrous damage and death to the inhabitants living on the crustal surface. The Earth is constantly quaking. In fact, about a million earthquakes occur annually, the vast majority going unnoticed. About 95% of earthquakes occur along the boundaries of tectonic plates. About 435 miles into the Earth is the limit of the deepest earthquake. About 80% of the planet's earthquakes are along the Pacific rim, and 15% in the Mediterranean region. Earthquake is the planet's most catastrophic natural disaster. The most powerful earthquake that can be reasonably expected would register 9.6 on the Richter Scale. Rock simply cannot withstand any greater pressure to trigger a more powerful quake. It is estimate that several faults, 600 miles long, would have to erupt to produce a point 10 earthquake. If a fault stretching clear around the world erupted, the quake would register 10.6 in magnitude. A powerful earthquake in a large urban area would kill more people than any other natural disaster. On average, 3 killer earthquakes strike the planet every year.

EARTH TONES – (*ERTH* tohns) Natural colors as found in the soils of the Earth. Earth tones are muted and flat colors, usually various shades of brown, like the good Earth. Too, shades of green are included in Earth tones, provided they are not too glaringly bright. Earth tones are warm, soothing to view. They present a relaxed, nature-friendly atmosphere.

EAST ASIA – (*EEST AY*-sha) A region that includes China, Japan, Mongolia, Taiwan, North Korea, and South Korea. All of these nations comprise the Orient.

EASTER – (*EES*-ter) Christian Feast of the Resurrection. Easter is the most important Christian Holyday. After all, the Resurrection of Jesus, which presages the Resurrection of man, is the foundation of Christianity. The Crucifixion was the sacrifice, and prerequisite for the Resurrection, the promise.

EASTERN EUROPE – (*EES*-turn *YOUR*-up) A region that includes Albania, Bosnia and Herzegovina, Bulgaria, Croatia, the Czech Republic, Hungary, Macedonia, Poland, Romania, Slovakia, and Yugoslavia (Serbia). Western Russia, west of the Ural Mountains is geographically in Europe. But culturally, European Russia is not part of the East European family. Russia has always been unique. Russia did not participate in any of the historical epochs of European History: The Renaissance, Reformation, Counter-Reformation, or Renaissance. The Russians were a Slavic Caucasian, Orthodox Christian people isolated from Europe. It's totally autocratic Czardom was more Oriental than European. In fact, the Imperial Russian flag featured the double-headed eagle, looking west to Europe, but also east to Asia (Siberia). Russia's forced Europeanization or Westernization by Peter (1672 – 1725) and Catherine (1729 – 1796) The Great were veneer, widow-dressing. Russia was, and perhaps still is a semi- Asian/European hybrid.

EASTERN MEDITERRANEAN – (*EES*-turn med-it- ter-*RAY*-nee-an) A region that includes Lebanon, Syria, Jordan, and Israel. This beautiful and historic region is a political powder keg. Though overwhelmingly Islamic, the Jewish population of Israel, and Christian additive to Lebanon creates perpetual turmoil.

EASTERN PHILOSPHY – (*EES*-turn fil-*LOS*-so-fee) A varied set of ideas, beliefs, and values from the Far, Middle, and Near East that stress inner peace, tranquility, attitudinal development, and mysticism. Eastern philosophy is very spiritual, whereas Western philosophy is much more materialistic. Eastern philosophy has its roots in Hinduism, Buddhism, Jainism, and mysticism. These theologies have influenced Islam, also from the East. Incidentally: Where Western Religious Theology looks up for God, Eastern Religious Theology looks within.

EAT – (*EET*) (Eating, Eaten, Eater, Ate) To devour nourishment. Eating is an energy transfer system. All sentient, living organisms, simple and sophisticated must eat to sustain life. Plants eat inorganic minerals along with sunlight to survive. Animals eat plants and other animals. So it is not incorrect to say that *"the first animal was a plant that turned cannibal."* When animals (including man, of course) eat, they rob the energy collected by other sentient, living beings – plants and animals. The creature eaten sacrifices its life in the process of surrendering its energy. Life feeds on life which demands death. Life is sacrificial. *"Everything eaten is killed. Every meal is a sacrifice."* – Adi Dad (1939 – 2008). Some must die so others may live. If this were not so, the planet would be choked by its own life, resulting in the death of all life. Conversely, if there were not enough creatures to serve as sacrifice, this too would bring life to death. That is why plants far outnumber animals, and plant eaters (herbivores) far outnumber animal eaters (carnivores) by 10 to 1. Therefore, eating entails sacrifice. We give thanks for our food, and the creatures sacrificed in becoming food. We also give thanks that we are not the sacrifice, among the eaten. (In *"nature red in tooth and claw,"* we sometimes are.). The sacrifice to sustain our life was made by others, physically and spiritually. *"Now as they were eating, Jesus took bread, gave thanks, and gave it to the disciples, saying: 'Take, eat; this is my body'."* – Matthew 26:26.

EAT CAKE – (eet *KAYK*) (*"Let Them Eat Cake"*.) The infamous, cold-blooded jeer attributed to heartless (later *headless*) French Queen Marie Antoinette (1755 – 1793). She made this sarcastic, discompassionate suggestion to her finance minister when he told her that the people had no bread. Historians debate the validity of the statement, but certainly not the cold indifferent attitude of the crown and aristocracy to the poverty. This was on the eve of the French Revolution (July 14, 1789). Incidentally, the Queen did not mean *"cake,"* as we understand it. She did not suggest that the breadless poor somehow obtain a sweet dessert of cake. The urban peasants used communal baking ovens. The cake the Queen referred to was the hard, burnt crud that caked-up on the inside oven walls. *"Ou'ils mangent de la brioche,"* translates to *"Let them eat cake."* This statement has been immortalized as the epitome of arrogant callousness, insensitivity, pitilessness of the *"Haves,"* toward the *"Have Nots."* Let them eat cake exemplifies the attitude of the billionaires that make up the Trump Administration, and the 0.1% of the American population that controls 90% of the national wealth. Queen Marie Antoinette, King Louis XVI (1754 – 1793) and a good part of the French aristocracy lost their heads in the Revolution. They should have been more concerned with distributive justice. *"Those who forget their history are condemned to relive it."* – Philosopher George Santayana (1863 – 1952).

EAT CROW – (eet *KROW*) (Crow eating) An embarrassing concession, an argumentative capitulation, a humiliating admission that one was wrong. Eat crow is a colloquial idiom used in English-speaking countries, especially the USA. Politicians are often said to have eaten crow when after an acrimonious polemic, the facts prove them incorrect. So eating crow is a sort of act of contrition after suffering an intellectual defeat. Eating crow is a distasteful proposition, figuratively and literally. A crow, like a vulture, rat, any carrion- eating scavenger does not offer delectable meat to eat. The Biblical *Book of Leviticus* forbids the eating of scavenging animals for religious [read: *health*] reasons. Since the Middle Ages, such creatures as crows have been considered off-limits as far as a food source, even illegal at times. So to eat crow is traditionally abominable and therefore a humiliation. The present-day figurative meaning of *"eat crow"* dates back to the mid-19th century. On November 2, 1850, the *Saturday Evening Post* published a popular story that was circulating about a Lake Mahopac, New York farmer. The article was entitled *"Can You Eat Crow?"* The story tells of a farmer who took in boarders. However, the food he served his guests was unsatisfactory. The boarders often complained. The farmer accused his guests of being fussy city dandies. *"I kin eat anything,"* the farmer boasted. So one of his guests jokingly suggested that he eat a crow. *"I kin eat a crow!"* the farmer bellowed. So a crafty urbanite trapped a crow and prepared it for cooking. However, the crow was stuffed with snuff – chewing tobacco. Indeed, the farmer ate the crow, but had to admit: *"I kin eat a crow, but I be darned if I hanker after it."* Though this story might elicit a weak smile today, it was a knee-slapper by 19th century standards.

EBB – (*EB*) (Ebbed, Ebbing) The outflowing of the tide as the water returns to the sea – the ebb tide. Therefore, the term ebb has come to mean falling away or declining. The ebbing moon descended below the horizon.

EBIONITES – (*EB*-bon-nyts) Ancient Jews who accepted Jesus (c. 7-2 BCE – c. 30- 33 CE) as the longed-for Messiah. In every other respect they were Jewish. Some Ebionites were Hebraic Christians (Judaisers) followers of St. Peter. They were also known as *"God fearers."* This was the condition that St. Peter expected all Christians to follower. However, St. Peter lost out to St. Paul, the *"Apostle to the Gentiles."* In fact, it's amusing but true that: *"Roses are red, violets are bluish. If it wasn't for Paul, we'd all be Jewish."*

EBONICS – (ee-*BON*-nics) The Afro-American patois or dialect, sometimes condescendingly called *"Black English,"* or more disparagingly *"ghetto talk."* In the evolution of this dialect, West African Pigeon English refined into Gullah, which evolved into Plantation Creole, which produced Ebonics. Ebonics became a Liberal social issue in the 1970s, part of a culture war. It was exclaimed to be a legitimate, respectable dialect of AmerEnglish. Ebonics was taught in some Progressive schools. It did not catch-on or survive. *"I axed you a question,"* and *"He be going to school"* remained poor English.

E-BOOK – (*EE*-book) (<u>E</u>lectronic <u>Book</u>) A book accessible on a computerized screen in digital form. E-books are taking a big bite out of the hardcopy publishing business. For example, between 2008 and 2010, e-book sales jumped 1,260%. E-books cannot, will not be accepted by traditional scholars, both Liberal and conservative. They cannot be annotated or physically highlighted. Where is the marginalia in an e-book? E-books cannot be <u>man</u>handled, <u>man</u>ually <u>man</u>ipulated as a <u>man</u>uscript. E-book just float about, somewhere in cyber space.

EBULLIENT – (eb-*BULE*-lee-ent) (Ebullition) Exuberant. Overflowing with enthusiasm, bubbling over with excitement and joy!

ECCENTRIC – (ek-*SEN*-trik) (Eccentricism, Eccentrically) A unique character, independent of social mores or conventions. An eccentric is one with the courage to march at the beat of his own drummer. He needs not to disguise his idiosyncrasies. All great, inventive minds are eccentric. A Caveat: Take care not to confuse an eccentric with an eclectic, which is one who prefers variety.

ECCENTRIC ARTICRAFTS – (ek-*SENT*-trik *ART*-ah-krafts) An online company selling a variety of small sculptures of all types. These art presentations are created from every available material, especially natural elements like stone, rocks, shells, pinecones, nuts, wood, whatever. Any artifact like jewelry, hardware, bottles, metals, wax, toys, glass shards, antiques, figurines, old machine parts may be incorporated into the collage of these eclectic aesthetic creations. The sculptor/artists of *"ECCENTRIC ARTICRAFTS"* is the author of this book, Dr. Gary J. Pasieka. Displays of his work can be viewed and purchased on *"ESTY,"* at www.esty.com. Dr. Pasieka can be contacted via the company address: eccart444@gmail.com, or his personal address: gp0444@aol.com. If one is interested in an unique, extraordinary, idiosyncratic gift for that unique individual, chances are that you'll find it at *"ECCENTRIC ARTICRAFTS."*

ECCE SIGNUM – (*EK*-keh *SIG*-num) Latin for *"here is the proof."* Very many of our legal terms and law jargon is taken directly from Latin.

ECCHYMOSIS – (ek-uh-*MO*-sis) A bruise. The discoloration of the skin due to bruising. The black and blue bruise is caused by subcutaneous bleeding.

ECCLESIOPHOBIA – (ek-clee-see-o-*Fo*-bee-a) Phobic fear of churches.

ECHELON – (*ESH*-el-lon) A general term for a level of command, authority, or rank. On a hierarchical scale of power, one may be in the lower, middle, or upper echelon.

ECHELON – (*ESH*-el-lon) One of the levels, steps, or grades in a hierarchical organization, and the group of individuals occupying such a level. The term derives from the Old French *"eschele"* meaning a *"stepped ladder."* A military command, authority or rank is organized in an echelon. For example, a colonel is a high echelon officer, while a lieutenant is a low echelon officer. In fact, echelon has been applied to just about any structure or formation that resembles a series of steps.

ECHO – (*EK*-oh) (Echoes, Echoed, Echoing) A repetition of a sound produced by the reflection of sound waves from a wall, mountain, or other hard, obstructing surface. An echo is best produced in an enclosed area like a hall, canyon, or cave. Lining the hard walls with soft and perforated material will absorb the sound, denying the reverberation or echo. The sound cannot be bounced off. This is soundproofing.

ECHO CHAMBER – (*EK*-oh *CHAYM*-ber) A large space (room, hallway, cave) where sound reverberates off the walls, ceiling and floor, (an echo), and is heard over again. In political parlance, an echo chamber refers to several media outlets that repeat or echo the same news or propaganda. This is particularly true of right-wing media. A segment of the populations watches FOX NEWS, then NEWSMAX, then any number of fascist propaganda outlets. Together, these show produce the right-wing echo chamber. The views hear the same lies and conspiracy theories, over and over. The only information they ever hear is from the fascist echo chamber. This is how Donald Trump (b. 1946) and his *"MAGAmagots"* captured the allegiance of 30% of the U.S. population. *"Tell a big lie often enough, and the people will begin to believe it, and so will you."* – Nazi Propaganda Minister Joseph Goebbels (1897 – 1945).

ECHOIC – (e-*KOH*-ik) Imitative, resembling an echo. An onomatopoeic word is echoic. For example: the words *"bark," "meow,"* or *"moo,"* imitates or echoes the animals that make those sounds.

E-CIGARETTES – (*EE*-sig-ar-*ETS*) (<u>E</u>lectronic <u>Cigarette</u>) A devise to satisfy a nicotine addict's craze. An e-cigarette is a gadget resembling a cigarette-holder, which simulates the experience of smoking. It contains a cartridge with a heater that vaporizes liquid nicotine instead of burning tobacco. There is no actual combustion or burning. The capitalist tobacco industry hoped that this would be a socially acceptable way for nicotine addicts to get their fix in public. Today, smoking is banned in most places. The e-cigarette produces vapor, not smoke, the industry claims. But smoke is vapor. Too, nicotine vapor is discharged into the public air at any rate. So the e-cigarette ruse is a corporate capitalist failure. Incidentally: With e-cigarettes, the vile, capitalist tobacco industry has discovered a novel way to addict a new generation to nicotine. In April, 2018, it was revealed that e-cigarette use by high school students had jumped 90%. We now need a public *"No Vaporizing"* law. Update: By late September, 2019, 8 deaths had been attributed to vaping with e-cigarettes. The deaths were caused by respiratory disorders. After all, nicotine is toxic. Several stores had discontinued provision of the products.

ECLECTICISM – (ek-*LEK*-ti-siz-um) (Eclectic) Diversity in tastes. Selecting from a variety of different sources making a novel whole. Not confined to a single method or style. Eclecticism is choosing ideas, concepts, doctrines, beliefs from a variety of systems of thought in the process of constructing one's own system. A Caveat: Take care not to confuse an eclectic with an eccentric, which is an oddly unique individual.

ECLIPSE – (*EE*-clips) When one planetary body passes through the shadow of another. A dark shade drifts across the eclipsed body. It becomes dark, no longer visible. Incidentally: In an astounding coincidence, the sun is 400 times bigger in circumference than the moon. Furthermore, the sun is 400 times farther from the Earth than the moon. Therefore, both celestial bodies appear to be the same size to us on Earth. Because of these amazingly similar dimensions, the moon is able to block out the light of the sun completely, in a total eclipse.

ECOANXIETY – (ee-co-ang-*ZY*-et-tee) Alarm caused by the dread of environmental perils, especially climate change. Ecoanxiety is also a feeling of helplessness over the potential consequences today, and even more so for future generations.

ECOCENTRISM – (ee-co-*SENT*-tris-um) (Ecocentrists) Literally, *"nature centered."* Ecocentrism is an ethical belief that man does not govern the natural environment, but is a part of it. Natural entities like wildlife, biodiversity, natural landscapes, clean air and water are primary, and man's artificial constructions secondary. The ecosystem takes precedence over the highway system in ecocentrism. Indeed, like all animals, man must use the environment, but not abuse the environment. Ecocentrists view man as but one link in the chain of life.

ECO-HAZARDOUS – (*EE*-coh *HAZ*-erd-dus) (Eco-Hazard) Anything, anyone, dangerous to the environment. *Eco-hazardous* is a new word to the dictionary (2023) but an old problem. People and corporations that are eco-hazardous are <u>careless</u> – they could not <u>care less</u> about our habitat, if it prevents them from making money. Capitalists, by their very nature are eco-hazardous. They are money driven. Money is their first priority. Regulations to protect the ecology cost money. Therefore, one of their primary demands of their Republican lackeys is deregulation – give us a free hand to do what we wish, and to hell with nature. It is far more profitable to pollute the air, water, and dump on the land than to be eco-friendly. Conscientiousness can be expensive. As long as free-wheeling, free enterprise capitalism is tolerated, eco-hazards will continue to poison us. *"If the environmentalists get in our way, we will simple destroy the environment."* – Capitalist Industrialist and Eco-Hazard Ross Perot (1930 – 2019).

ECOLOGIST'S CREDO – (ee-*COL*-la-jists *CRAY*-dow) *"Everything in Nature has its purpose."*

ECOLOGY – (ee-*COL*-la-jee) (also Bionomics) A branch of biology which concerns the relationship and interaction of living creatures and their environment. Human ecology s a branch of sociology which studies the interdependence of people, their institutions and environment.

ECONOMIC EASTER – (*EE*-kon-nom-mik *EES*-ter) A foolish, capricious declaration by President Donald Trump (b. 1946), that America will be safe enough from the Coronavirus in one month, to get back to work. After all, the Republican capitalist credo is: *"Time is money, and business is our business."* This prediction was made at the end of March, 2020. Trump's aspiration is that the contagion will have run its course by Easter Sunday, April 12, 2020. The Trump prognosis was based on no science, no data, no medical research, but on a Presidential hunch, Trump's desperate hope. Due to his ineptitude, incompetence, and self-centeredness the COVID-19 Virus has become the *"Trump Virus."* The Trump Virus has caused the *"Trump Depression."* The depression will result in Trump's defeat at the polls in November, 2020. With no Presidential deference, immunity, or protection, Trump will ultimately be convicted and imprisoned for his multiple concealed corruptions and crimes. So Trump is franticly gambling on an *"Economic Easter,"* to end his troubles. Though Trump had declared: *"I am not responsible,"* irresponsible Trump cannot shirk this responsibility. Trump's Economic Easter is an attempt to arouse a miraculous Wall Street Resurrection. Choosing this occasion was symbolic. It is hoped to incite a self-fulfilling prophecy, to resuscitate the dead economy, in a Lazarus-like fashion. But as Trump's mimesis, Epidemiologist Dr. Anthony Fauci (b. 1940) reminded us and Trump: *"The disease sets the timetable."* This Easter Sunday, Trump anticipates an economic resurrection. But the virus, rather than business will be resurrected. Rev. Al Sharpton (b. 1954) had reminded: *"Trump missed the part of what happened on Good Friday."* Indeed, every resurrection is preceded by a crucifixion. The slow torturous viral crucifixion will continue to torment and kill long after Easter. At this writing, there is no end in sight. The abatement of precautions for economic stimulation is suicidal, murderous, criminal. Trump's Economic Easter is a farce, as is Trump himself. Newsflash: On March 29, 2020, perplexed President Trump walked back his Easter Economic revival date. Trump's *"aspiration"* when society will be well enough for capitalist enterprise to resume is now April 30, 2020. Temporarily, the doctors and scientists have captured Trump's attention over the businessmen and economists. A Caveat: nothing is certain in the Trump Administration. Like a child, Donald Trump is influenced by the last person who had his ear.

ECONOMIC DISPARITY – (ee-kon-*NOM*-mik dis-*PAR*-ri-tee) The unfair distribution of wealth. Nowhere is economic disparity more glaring than in the United States of America. Today, less than 1% of the population controls 96% of the American wealth. Jesus must have anticipated this injustice when he said: *"For to the one who has, more will be given. And from the one who has not, even what he has will be taken away."* America today resembles Rome before the fall. Legislation and taxation established by capitalist Republicans have made the rich richer and the middleclass poorer. The poor have become absolutely destitute. Never before has home ownership dropped so low. The middleclass is residing in trailers, and the working class is residing in dumpsters. Never before have so few people owned shares of stock in America. The wealth, like cream, is rising to the top. The rising Dow-Jones average of the stock market is a measurement of economic disparity (D.O.W. = Disparity Of Wealth). *"If a free society cannot help the many who are poor, they cannot save the few who are rich,"* warned President John F. Kennedy (1917 – 1963). The only solution to economic disparity is Socialism, the fair distribution of the wealth to all.

ECONOMIC GROWTH – (ee-kon-*NOM*-mik *GROWTH*) The expansion of a nation's wealth production. Politicians, economists, investors, brokers, bankers, CEOs are always anxious about economic growth, hoping that the economy gets bigger. That's understandable if the population is also getting bigger. Ideally, economic growth must match population growth in order to care for more people. It is natural for the economic growth to stall when the population stalls. Today, the population is falling. So why must we insist that the economy grows when the population is not? The only people who desire a growing economy in a shrinking population are the greedy few who control the economy. The rich never have enough. Corporate capitalists fear a shrinking population as much as they fear a shrinking economy. Fewer people means fewer consumers, customers, means fewer dollars in profit. Actually, a drop in population is a blessing. Fewer people will share the planet's limited resources. Presently, our economy produces much more than enough, providing the wealth is distributed equitably. That requires a move away from capitalist hoarding to Socialist sharing. In a well-managed government with a Socialist economy, perpetual growth is not required or necessary. Incidentally: The Bubonic Plague, or Black Death of the 12th century killed a third of Europe's population. The calamitous population drop did not destroy Europe. On the contrary, Europe was rejuvenated – like the pruning of a plant. After the plague, fewer people had more to share. Labor became more valuable benefiting workers. Wealth was distributed more fairly. Feudalism was weakened. Living conditions improved for the peasantry. The losers where the aristocracy that hoped to hoard the wealth and power. A similar condition applies today with the reduction of population. The only losers will be the aristocracy again, the oligarchic capitalists. They desire population increases so that more workers will be competing for lower wages, and more hungry consumers.

ECONOMIC HITMAN – (ee-kon-*NOM*-mik *HIT*-man) C.I.A. field operative employed abroad to protect American corporate capitalist interests by corrupting government officials. Bribery and death threats are the tools of the economic hitman's trade. The economic hitman is the first stage in C.I.A. meddling in foreign nations. It is followed by fomenting riots, assassinations, revolt, revolution, or military invasion by the U.S.A. It is customary for the economic hitman to present a foreign leader with a choice: in one had a stack of money, in the other a bullet. Not a word need be said. The policy of using economic hitmen is another answer to the naïve question: *"Why do they hate us?"* Incidentally: It's ironic that the Americans were upset with Russian electoral meddling. The Russians simply took a page out of the C.I.A. handbook.

ECONOMIC IMPERIALISM – (ee-kon-*NOM*-mik im-*PEER*-ree-al-is-um) Gaining authority and control over a weaker nation by usurping its wealth, a form of neo-colonialism. Economic imperialism is exploitation of an underdeveloped country by extractive industries of a powerful nation. Unlike the British and French Empires of old, the United States does not conquer territory, but rather natural resources (oil, minerals, timber) and the finest farmland. Like traditional colonialism, economic imperialism depletes a region's wealth, but without any responsibility for the native population's welfare, like colonial imperialism. Economic imperialism consists of ruling the economy. American capitalist corporations seize the country's riches. Forests are denuded.

Mountains are leveled for minerals, leaving a lunar landscape. The ecology is rapaciously raped. The most productive food-producing land is commandeered by huge foreign agri-corporations for plantations. Wall Street gets richer, while the native populations grow poorer. Small farmers become serfs – dependent peasant laborers. Capitalist greed generates visceral anti-American hate. So the CIA installs pro-American fascist dictators in these countries to protect corporate interests. The dictator oppresses his own people, and is richly rewarded by the U.S. Government. But Socialist revolution is inevitable, as the people rise against their brutal tyrant, the American puppet. The CIA supports the dictator by organizing terrorist death squads. If the Socialist revolution gains momentum that the dictator can't handle, U.S. troops invade to suppress the people and save corporate profits. Economic imperialism is preserved. This is why America maintains an astounding 800 military bases in 177 countries throughout the world! Economic imperialism is another answer to the naïve question: *"Why do they hate us?"*

ECONOMICS – (ee-kon-*NOM*-miks) The study of *"who gets what and how much."* Economics involves how we intend to distribute our limited national wealth. Economics used to be called *"political economy."* It still should be, for no discipline is more political than economics. With capitalist economics, the wealth is hoarded at the top. With Socialist economics, the wealth is shared among *ALL*. The great Socialist scholar, Michael Harrington (1928 – 1989) correctly insisted that *"Economic power is political power."* That is certainly the reason why a recent German Finance Minister told the Greek Socialist scholar Yanis Varoufakis (b. 1961) that: *"Elections cannot be allowed to change economic policy."* Incidentally: Economics is one of the Social Sciences. Actually, as a science, it is more like meteorology in accuracy.

ECONOMIC TIGER – (ee-kon-*NOM*-mik *TY*-ger) A country with rapid economic growth due to cheap labor, high technology, and aggressive exports. The beneficiaries of the economic tiger are the wealthy capitalists, the industrialists and manufacturers, not the child and slave labor that suffer the cheap wages and unhuman working conditions.

ECONOMISTS – (ee-*KON*-nom-mists) Social Scientists who study the production, distribution, and consumption of goods and services, or the material, financial welfare of mankind. Economists make projections on the future financial condition of the state. They seem to be the only professional scholars who can be wrong all the time, yet not be held accountable or considered disreputable. This is partially true because economics is an imprecise pseudo-science. Playwright and philosopher George Bernard Shaw

(1856 – 1950) said that *"If all the economists were laid end to end, they would not reach a conclusion."* John Maynard Keynes (1883 – 1946), a great economist himself, maintained that *"Economists should be humble, like dentists."* An economics Professor once told his students: *"Taking my economics class may not keep you off the welfare line, but at least you'll know why you are there."*

ECONOMY OF SIZE – (ee-*KON*-na-mee uhv *SYZ*) A bargain. Economy of size refers to the fact that the larger the size of the container, the less the cost of the contents, than would be a smaller size. For example: You get more cereal for less money in a big box, than you would get in a small box.

E CONTRARIO – (ee kon-*TRAR*-ree-o) Latin for *"On the contrary."*

ECSOMATIC – (ex-so-*MAT*-tik) (Ecsomatically) Out-of-body. An ecsomatic experience is an out-of-body experience. It involves perceiving the world from a position different from the one occupied by one's physical body. During ecsomatic episodes, people often have the experience of leaving their bodies and then viewing them as if from the outside. In near-death experiences, people testify to hovering ecsomatically above their bodies as medical personnel frantically try to revive them. Astralprojection or teleportation, in which one spiritually travels about through time and space is also an ecsomatic experience. *"There are stranger things in heaven and earth, than are dreamt of in your philosophy."* – William Shakespeare (1564 - 1616) <u>Hamlet</u>.

ECOSYSTEM – (*EE*-co-sis-tem) An interdependent community of plants and animals, and the environment they inhabit. An ecosystem exists in a delicate balance. Introduction of a disruptive factor like an oil spill or an invasive species can upset the balance and destroy the ecosystem. An ecosystem is a world within our world.

ECOTERRORISM – (ee-co-*TEAR*-or-is-um) (Ecoterrorists) Terrorize the ecology by declaring war on nature. Ecoterrorism is wanton destruction of the natural environment for political, economic, or military ends, or just for spite. The quickest, easiest way to conduct Ecoterrorism is starting a forest fire. Century- old trees and countless animal perish. Toxic chemicals dumped in a creek will poison a river. Trash discarded in the wilderness is ecoterrorism. Capitalist extractive industries like strip-mining, and clear-cut logging are corporate ecoterrorists. Footnote: Iraqi Dictopresident Saddam Hussein (1937 – 2006) conducted ecoterrorism in the Gulf War of 1990 – 1991. As his forces retreated from Kuwait, Saddam ordered the oilwells set ablaze. This was an environmental disaster, a case of ecoterrorism.

ECOTHEOLOGY – (ee-co-thee-*OL*-la-jee) (Ecotheologist, Ecotheological) The melding or incorporating ecology with spirituality. Ecotheologists consider all of God's creations as sacred, including the environment. Ecotheologists see divinity in Nature.

ECO-TOURISM – (*EE*-co *TOUR*-is-um) Visitors intent on observing nature, interested in flora and fauna, rather than beer and bikinis. Eco-tourism developed in the small volcanic islands of the Eastern Caribbean, like Dominica, Saint Lucia, Martinique. These mountains jutting out of the sea are not blessed with pearly beaches. They don't attract low-brow tourists seeking sea, sand and sin. They depend on eco-tourism. The wildlife is in the misty rainforest, not at the hotel jamboree. Sightseeing, hiking, camping, mountain climbing, breathtaking geology, appreciation of natural beauty is all part of eco-tourism.

ECOWAS – (*EC*-coe-wahs) An acronym for <u>E</u>conomic <u>C</u>ommunity <u>O</u>f <u>W</u>est <u>A</u>frican <u>S</u>tates. ECOWAS is a 17-nation association of primarily former French African colonies. Membership includes: Benin, Burkina Faso, Cabo Verde, Cote D'Ivoire, Gambia, Ghana, Guinea, Guinea Bissau, Liberia, Mali, Niger, Nigeria, Senegal, Sierra Leone, and Togo. As of June 29, 2019, the ECOWAS nations had adopted a single currency, the ECO (*EC*-coe). This will mark an end to French economic imperialism in West Africa, particularly over its former colonies. The one trepidation of the member states is domination by giant Nigeria. Nigeria, with about 50% of the population, generates about 66% of the GDP of the ECOWAS union. This represents far greater influence than Germany asserts on the EU (European Union).

ECSTASY – (*EX*-stas-see) (Ecstatic) A state of rapture, exaltation, overpowering joy. Ecstasy has been experiences by some mystic and saints who have had a Divine encounter. This is genuine, rapturous ecstasy. People have tried to imitate this mental state pharmaceutically with mind-altering drugs.

ECTOMORPH – (*EK*-tow-morf) In the study of morphology, an ectomorph is a thin-bodied individual.

ECTOTHERMIC – (ek-tow-*THERM*-mic) (Ectothermal) Literally *"heated from without."* Ectothermal animals are cold-blooded, so to speak. Reptiles are ectothermal creatures. They are largely dependent on the environment to warm their bodies to enable them to perform their normal functions. The opposite of ectothermal is *endothermal,* or warm-blooded animals like mammals. Incidentally: endothermic (warm-blooded) animals use much of their energy keeping warm. Ectothermic (cold-blooded) creatures use much of their energy growing larger to conserve heat.

ECUMENICALISM – (ek-yoo-*MEN*-i-cal-is-um) (Ecumenical) Universal, general, concerning all. In a religious context, ecumenicalism refers to the respect, honor, and validity of all religions. An ecumenical will find spiritual truth in every faith. *"There are many roads to heaven, each man need not take the same path."* Ecumenicalism celebrates diversity and is totally tolerant of every faith. The most ecumenical religion is Buddhism. Early in its history, Buddhists would traverse the mountain passes connecting India, China, Nepal, and Tibet. On meeting a stranger they would ask: *"And what sublime spiritual path do you walk?"* That is ecumenicalism. *"I have learned so much from God that I can call myself a Christian, a Hindu, a Muslim, a Buddhist, a Jew."* – Persian Mystic, Poet Hafez (c. 1325 – 1390). *"He who does reverence to his own sect, while disparaging the sects of others with intent to enhance the glory of his own sect, by such conduct inflicts the severest injury on his own sect."* – *"May the partisans of all doctrines in all countries unite and live in a common fellowship. For all alike profess mastery to be attained over oneself and purity of the heart."* – Ashoka (303 – 232 B.C.E.).

ECUMENICAL PATRIARCHATE – (ek-yoo-*MEN*-i-cal *PAY*-tree-are-kayt) The titular head of the Eastern Orthodox Christian Church. This Archbishop, Patriarch, or Metropolitan is seated in Istanbul, Turkey (a Muslim country). However for centuries this was Christian Byzantium, with its capital at Constantinople (today's Istanbul). Bartholomew the First (b. 1940) is still called the Ecumenical Patriarch of Constantinople. This makes him the official leader of the Eastern Orthodox Christian Church. His Western counterpart is Pope Francis the First (b. 1936) in Rome. However, the Ecumenical Patriarch has far less authority over his Patriarchs, than the Pope has over his Bishops. Orthodox Patriarchs are granted much autocephaly (independence) over their dioceses. Incidentally: There had been 270 Patriarchs of Constantinople, and 266 Popes of Rome.

ECZEMA – (*EK*-suh-muh) Also known as *dermatitis,* eczema is a group of inflammatory skin diseases. Symptoms of eczema are itchy red skin, rash, and blisters. The cause of the variety of eczema conditions cannot yet be ascertained. A combination of genetic and environmental factors may be responsible. The most common form of eczema is *Atopic Dermatitis.* Over 30 million Americans suffer from the disease. Eczema is unsightly but not contagious. It can appear anywhere on the body, but most commonly invades the hands, wrists, feet, ankles, the inside bend of the elbow and behind the knees. Symptoms flare-up then die-down. The propensity for eczema is thought to be hereditary. An outbreak may be due to allergens, chemical irritants, and stress/anxiety. There is no known cure for eczema at this time. Topical ointments of hydrocortisone helps to relieve the itchy rash.

E.D. – (ee-*DEE*) An abbreviation and initialism for erectile dysfunction which is impotence. It is a condition making it hard to get a hard on. ED is the difficulty or inability of a man to attain and maintain an erect penis, prohibiting sexual intercourse. Of course, erectile dysfunction is emasculating. There are a number of medical causes of ED. Excessive anxiety and stress will cause a fellow to go limp as well. Erectile dysfunction to some degree is a natural symptom of aging. Men in their 60's are 4 times more likely to suffer from ED [read: *limberdick*], than men in their 40's. Capitalists have capitalized on the phallic pliability problem. A multi-billion dollar industry as arisen to help guys get it up. It can't be coincidence that the popular ED drug *Viagra,* rhymes with *Niagara.* Incidentally: Comedian George Burns (1896 – 1996) commented that: *"Sex at 90 is like trying to shoot pool with a rope."*

EDACIOUS – (ed-*DAY*-shush) (Edaciously) Greedily devouring, voracious, consuming. The very nature of capitalism is edacious. Devour your competitors, devour the market, devour the consumers, devour the government, devour all the profit.

ED.D. – (ee-dee *DEE*) An *"Academic Eddie,"* or Education Doctorate. An Ed.D. is a professional degree in Education, originally intended for school administration. The Ed.D. is not a research degree requiring a laborious doctoral dissertation. Though called *"doctor,"* in America, the Education Doctorate (Ed.D.) is not recognized internationally as the Ph.D. Incidentally: A tempest in a teapot was ignited in December, 2020, when First Lady Jill Biden (b. 1951) continued to flaunt her *"Doctorate Degree,"* insisting on being addressed as *"Dr. Jill."* Mrs. Biden owns an Ed.D. in Educational Leadership, the field that trains school administrators. Jill never clarified the fact that she owns an Ed.D. as opposed to a Ph.D. She let the credentials confusion linger. Too, political commentators wrongly refer to Jill's Ph.D. To add to the hilarity, Fox TV's Tucker Carlson (b. 1969) referred to Dr. Jill as *"Dr. Pepper."* Certainly, this may all sound merely academic to most. However, it is a sensitive issue to those who had to travel, investigate, research, experiment, and write a book called the *"Doctor Dissertation,"* then publicly defend it, in order to earn a Ph.D. (a Doctorate of Philosophy). Perhaps it is equivalent to calling a nurse a physician, or a security guard a police officer, or a fast-food cook, a 5-star chef. Furthermore, failing to distinguish between an Ed.D. and a Ph.D. is like equating an *"Online Doctorate,"* from a virtual *"electronical correspondence course,"* with a Ph.D. from an established University.

EDENIC – (ee-*DEN*-ik) An adjective that refers to the Biblical Garden of Eden. What is edenic is paradisiacal. One may be in an edenic location, or an edenic frame of mind.

EDENTATES – (e-*DEN*-tayts) An order of New World (American) mammals including armadillos, sloths, and South American anteaters. Edentates do not possess incisor and canine teeth.

EDEOMANIA – (ed-dee-o-*MAY*-nee-a) (Edeomaniac) A neurotic, erotic obsession with genitals. An edeomaniac's private thoughts are on the private parts.

EDGE PLAY – (*EJ PLAY*) Daring, adventurous, exploratory sexual experiences. Edge play is dropping all inhibitions and setting one's fantasies free. It is consensually pushing one's boundaries beyond that which one would ordinarily submit. Edge play goes beyond bisexual to *"trisexual,"* game to try anything.

EDIFYING – (*ED*-di-fy-ing) (Edification) Any influence (like Socialism) that makes one a more compassionate, benevolent, humane person. Missionary service is edifying. An edifying experience as feeding, healing, protecting the helpless is approaching saintliness.

EDITORIAL REFERENCE – (ed-di-*TOR*-ree-al *REF*-er-rans) An opinionated fact book. A reference book (encyclopedia, dictionary, or encyclodictionary) that is a factual, academic presentation of information, worthy of being referred to when needed. An editorial is a commentary of a particular point of view. Combine the two and you have an editorial reference book. All the information included in this type of book is valid, albeit with a spin. An editorial reference presents a biased interpretation, conclusion of the actual facts. It is not propaganda, for it is perfectly candid about its purpose. The purpose of an editorial reference is to *"open eyes, move minds, and sway hearts."* That is the ultimate goal of this editorial reference book, the <u>LIBERAL LEXICON: *A Socialistic, Spiritualistic Encyclodictionary.*</u>

ED SCHOOL – (*ED SKOOL*) The College of Education in a university. Ed School is the teacher training institution. Ed School is essential for society and civilization. Teaching is a craft, with qualities of art and science. Teaching therefore must be taught. The remarkable Roman educator Quintilian (35 - 100 CE) testified that *"There are many details in our art which the unskilled critic will never notice."* As far back as the 14th century, the great Muslim scholar, Ibn Khaldoun (1332 – 1406) realized that *"Instruction itself has become a part of the arts."* Centuries later, Jean-Jacques Rousseau (1712 – 1778) had asked: *"How can a child be properly educated by one who has not been properly educated himself?"* Ed School is often the largest college on campus, because of society's need of teachers. This means many tuition-paying customers for the university. Compared to the Colleges of Physics, Chemistry, or Medicine, the College of Education is low tech (as is teaching). It does not require expensive equipment or machinery. Therefore, Ed School is a real money-maker for the university writ-large, a virtual milch-cow. Ed Profs in Ed School are not miracle workers. All that can be expected of Ed School is to produce legally qualified, minimally competent, potentially great teachers. As educationist Susan Ohanian stated: *"Students need real teachers, and real teachers must be trained."*

EDUCATED PERSON – (*ED*-jew-kay-ted *PER*-son) An individual well-schooled, who has cultivated the faculties and powers of the mind and heart. She is learned in knowledge and understanding in a variety of social settings. He is comfortable and displays appropriate behavior among all socio-economic groups.

The educated person is cosmopolitan, experienced, tolerant and respectful of all foreign cultures. That is because he is Progressive, Liberally- minded, a Socialist at work and heart. The educated person is a *generalist.* She is informed, knowing something about everything. This is a Liberal education – an education for a good life. Too, the educated person is a *specialist.* He is skilled, trained, qualified, knowing everything about something. This is a professional or vocational education – an education for making a good living. An educated person *"Progressively thinks globally, acts locally."* Post Script: Apply this description to one Donald J. Trump (b. 1946). Indeed, the clown, albeit rich, does not even approach the state of educated.

EDUCATION – (ed-jew-*KAY*-shun) Acquiring general knowledge, developing the powers of reasoning and judgment, preparing for an intellectually mature life. A true education makes one a better person, otherwise it is classed as miseducation. Education serves three major purposes. *Societal education* concerns the citizen. *Economic education* concerns the worker. *Personal education* concerns the man. Free, universal education should be mandatory, obligatory, for everyone, everywhere. Like vaccination is provided by the government to prevent disease, education should be provided by the government to prevent ignorance. Education is mental nutrition. Education is on the same crucial level as food, shelter, clothing, and medical care. A *"dog- eat-dog"* economic society like capitalism will never consider education in this manner. Capitalism regards education as the privilege of the rich, a symbol of their wealth. Only in a Socialist society, will all be educated, and attain their God-given potential. *"The walls of the educational system must come down. Education should not be a privilege, so the children of these who have money can study"* – Che Guevara (1928 – 1967).

EDUCATION – (ed-jew-*KAY*-shuhn) (The Etymology) Derives from *"Educatio,"* (Latin) meaning *"all means of learning."* Furthermore, education derives from *"Educere,"* (Greek) meaning *"to draw out of, to educe [the best]."* Lastly, education derives from *"Educare,"* (Greek) meaning *"to rear, to bring up [children]."* Education changes people, changes them for the better. Education is liberating and liberalizing. That's why Trumpublican fascists fear education. They try to portray the educated as aloof elites. The more educated a person become, the more liberal they are until they embrace Socialism. That's why Republicans-cum Trumpublicans are against free education.

EDUCATIONAL DIVIDE – (ed-jew-*KAY*-shuhn-uhl dee-*VYD*) The gulf, the partition between the Educated Liberals (Democrats, Socialists) and the uneducated conservatives (Republicans, fascists). Does education make for better informed decision-making, for discernment? If not, then education is a wasteful fraud. We know its not! Demographically, Liberal Democrats are better educated than conservative Republicans. It therefore stands to reason that the Liberals make better decisions and so are correct on the issues and candidates. The uneducated Republicans are not. Uneducated Republican voters are mistaken, and on the wrong side of history. They lack discernment and an understanding of the consequences of their choices, because of their lack of education. Most of these people are rural Southerners and Westerners from so-called red states. Its not surprising that these states lag towards the bottom in educational statistics. Lowly educated people are gullible, easily duped and manipulated. They have difficulty discerning the truth from a lie. The uneducated poor are goaded by the clever rich (Fox News) to vote against their own economic interests, and vote for fascists like Donald Trump (b. 1946). Phenomenally, uneducated conservatives, on becoming educated become Liberal. Education is enlightenment. That's why in the reddest, most conservative, poorly educated Republican states, the blue islands of Liberalism are the educated college towns.

EDUCATIONAL 4C's – (ed-jew-*KAY*-shuhn-uhl for *SEES*) The 4 basic indispensables that must be taught at school: Litera<u>c</u>y, Ora<u>c</u>y, Numera<u>c</u>y, and Courte<u>s</u>y. The Educational 4C's are presented to the child early, in elementary school. That's because they are elemental skills or *"tool subjects,"* needed to investigate advanced knowledge.

EDUCATIONAL GOALS – (ed-jew-*KAY*-shuhn-uhl) What citizens or policy makers want formal educational institutions (schools and colleges) to accomplish, expressed in terms of characteristics of people who have been educated. Capitalist educational goals are to maintain the class structure dominated by the rich. The goal is also to create an army of docile, subservient, submissive workers who will promote capitalism against their own economic interests. Socialist educational goals are the fair distribution of wealth, and the advancement of all segments of society. This is attained by universally free, quality education.

EDUCATIONAL PSYCHOLOGY – (ed-jew-*KAY*-shuhn-uhl sy-*COL*-lo-jee) The scientific study of the teaching/learning process.

EDUCATIONAL RESULTS – (ed-jew-*KAY*-shuhn-uhl ree-*SULTS*) What you've developed into, because of what you've learned. The educational results testify if the educational goals were successful. Educational results determine how the material learned in school has improved or educated one as a better human being. Often, educational results are on a delayed fuse. It may take years for the learning to solidify and take hold. A sincere education will not only make one competent, but also compassionate. Education had somehow failed if it produced the brilliant evil scientist, or the sadistic, serial-killing surgeon. Education can result in a *"Dr. Jekyll"* or *"Mr. Hyde."* Despite the transfer of tremendous knowledge, an education that produces a social monster is a *"miseducation,"* as Dr. John Dewey (1859 – 1952) had taught. Education can result in great wealth and brilliant accomplishments within a soulless individual. The heartless, fascistic Elon Musk (b. 1971) is a case in point.

EDUCATIONISTS – (ed-jew-*KAY*-shuhn-ists) Professors serving in the university's College of Education. Educationists serve in 3 capacities: *Disciplinists, Generalists,* and *Pedagogists. Disciplinists* are the academicians who perform at teaching and research. They teach Educational Foundations, History, Philosophy, Sociology, and Psychology. *Generalists* are the professionals who perform at teaching and service. These are the Professors of Educational Administration, Curriculum, Counseling, and Higher Education. *Pedagogists* are the clinicians who perform at teaching and teacher training. They are teaching models who instruct the methods courses and instructional techniques. Pedagogists supervise student teachers in the classrooms. All three types of Ed Professors are necessary in the College of Education, if Ed School proves to be successful.

EDUCATION PROFESSORS – (ed-jew-*KAY*-shuhn pro-*FES*-sors) Educationist; Ed Profs; Teacher trainers. College level teachers of teachers. Education professors should be master teachers, dedicate to providing the nation with legally qualified, minimally competent, but potentially great educators. Publishing research to bolster the pride of the college should be of no concern to the Professor of Education. Ed Profs must have years of practical experience in the classroom themselves. How else can they be effective? However, research reveals that about 17% of Education Professors have never been in a school classroom, and about 51% have not actually taught in a public school for 16 years. As Jesus admonished: *"Physician, heal thyself."*

EDUCATOR'S OATH – (*ED*-jew-kay-tors *OHTH*) *"I solemnly pledge to dedicate my life to the craft of teaching. I will give to those who are or have been my teachers the respect and gratitude which is their due. I will practice my profession with conscience and dignity; the wellbeing of my students will always be my primary concern. I will honor the position of parents and uphold public trust. I will maintain by all the means in my power the honor of my profession. I will respect the privacy of students. I will teach toward meeting the individual needs and abilities of students. I will accept all engaged in education as my colleagues. I will not permit considerations of religion, nationality, ethnicity, race, party politics, social standing, or monetary rewards received from my labors to intervene between my duty and my students. I will maintain utmost respect for human dignity and human values, and I will hold human caring and consideration as the fundamental in the student-teacher relationship. I make this promise solemnly, freely, and upon my oath for as long as I am engaged in education."*

EDUMETRICS – (ed-jew-*MET*-rics) The common sense conviction that all tests should be related to instruction. Edumetrics insist that you *"test what you teach."* The concept of edumetric flies in the face of the state mandated standardized test. The opposite of an edumetric test is a psychometric test, (intelligence test) which tests what it is assumed you should know. An edumetric test can be the only valid test.

EDUTAINMENT – (ed-jew-*TAYN*-ment) A misunderstood and maligned term which simply means making learning fun. Although learning is work, it need not be laborious. However, a reasonable balance must be maintained. A classroom is, after all, a workshop not a carnival. Both teacher and students are workers. *"Entertainment and learning are not opposites; entertainment may be the most effective mode of learning."* – Philosopher Herbert Marcuse (1898 – 1979).

E.E.A. – (ee ee *AY*) (Environment of Evolutionary Adaptation) The time in the late *Pleistocene Era* (c. 2.6 million to 11,700 BCE) when the human brain was hard-wired to reflect its present characteristics and capacities. At this time, Homo sapient was evolving into *Homo sapien sapien*. The psycho-emotional differences between men and women (*Mars* and *Venus, Yin and Yang*) were established in the brain during the Environment of Evolutionary Adaptation. At this time, the final touches were being tweaked on the male and female brain, which makes men and women so different. The great psychoanalyst Sigmund Freud (1856 – 1939) declared that he did not know what women wanted. *"Women are a complete mystery,"* declared Dr. Steven Hawking (1942 - 2018), theoretical astrophysicist. Indeed. What occurred during the E.E.A. is directly responsible for arguments between husbands and wives today. The distinction between male and female is apparent in little children. A group of little boys in go-carts will rambunctiously try to ram into each other (aggression, competition). A group of little girls will meticulously try to avoid bumping into each other (nurturance, cooperation). The children are too young to have learned that behavior (nurture, sociology). It was hard-wired in their brain from birth (nature, biology). This all occurred in the E.E.A. (Environment of Evolutionary Adaptation).

EERIE – (*EAR*-ree) A ghostly, spooky, atmosphere, inspiring superstitious fear. A graveyard or a haunted house is an eerie environment.

EFFECT/AFFECT – (ef-*FECT AF*-fect) (Effected, Effecting; Affected, Affecting) Two English words that confuse even the most learned and scholarly. Both words can have different meanings and uses depending on the context. The basic difference is that affect is usually a verb, meaning to influence or produce a change in something. Effect is usually a noun, meaning the result or consequence of something. For example: *"The weather affected ny mood."* Conversely, *"The weather had an effect on my mood."* Effect is the outcome. Something that is produced by a cause. An effect is a result or consequence. The *effect* is the result that is produced by an *affect* or influence. An *effect* or change is established by an *affect* or motivation. In conclusion: *"The affect of the storm had a major effect on our travel plans."* Is that clear now? I didn't think so.

EFFECTIVENESS – (ef-*FEC*-tiv-ness) The extent to which goals are accomplished. Effectiveness involves producing the intended results. Effectiveness is *"doing the right thing."* (In contrast, efficiency is *"doing the thing right."*)

EFFEN – (*EF*-fin) A euphemism for *"fuck'en ."* The syllable *"ef"* stands for the letter F in the F-word, Fucking. Effen is a great example of a euphemism, which is a word you use, when you can't use the word you really want.

EFFETE – (e-*FEET*) Weak, lacking vigor, stamina, and ambition, due to overindulgence. *"Cornucopia Kids"* are effete snobs. They tend to be helpless for having everything done for them.

EFFICACY – (*EF*-fi-ca-see) (Efficacious) Being effective, able to produce the desired effect or results. An efficacious plan is successful.

EFFICIENCY – (ef-*FISH*-shen-see) The extent to which goals are realized with minimal waste of time, effort, and resources. Efficiency is *"doing the thing right."* (In contrast, effectiveness is *"doing the right thing."*)

EFFIGY – (*EF*-fih-jee) A three-dimensional image created to resemble a specific person or entity. Effigies are usually created to be destroyed. An effigy may be created and then destroyed as a magical act to banish an individual or spirit, or cause them harm. In modern times, effigies are often fashioned in caricature of political figures, to be mocked, hanged, and burned as a form of protest to show the peoples' displeasure with the individual. Voodoo dolls are miniature effigies that are subjected to torture and dismemberment or burning in the casting of a curse on the person they represent. The doll, the effigy holds no inherent power. It serves as a prop to help intensify the emotion, and therefore the power of the spell or curse caster which is psychic.

EFFLORESCENT – (ef-floor-*ES*-sent) (Effloresced, Efflorescing) A fabulous flowering, blossoming, bursting into spectacular bloom. *"After two days of steady rain, the efflorescent garden shown brilliantly."*

EFFULGENCE – (ef-*FULL*-jens) (Effulgent) The shining forth of a brilliant radiance. *"The effulgent supernova mesmerized the cosmologists."*

EFFUSION – (ef-FEW-shun) Effusive) An unrestrained pouring forth of a liquid, words, or emotions.

E.G. – (ee *JEE*) (e. g. = *"exempli gratia"*) An abbreviated initialism meaning for example; for the sake of example; as such.

EGALITARIANISM – (ee-gal-lit-*TER*-ee-an-is-um) (Egalitarian) Equalitarianism. The view that all humans are equal and should be treated equally in liberties, rights, respect, acceptance, and opportunities. Egalitarianism is a Socialistic concept. A genuine egalitarian would insist on economic equality of all people as well.

EGESTA – (ee-*JES*-tah) (also Excreta) Bio-matter egested or excreted from the body as excrement, urine, vomit, or sweat. A Caveat: Egesta is not to be confused with *"ejecta,"* which is geo-matter ejected, as from a volcanic eruption.

EGG – (*AYG*) A primitive, self-contained uterus, lower on the evolutionary scale than is the case with mammals. An egg is a roundish reproductive body produced by female birds and reptiles. It consists of an ovum that is enveloped in albumen, jelly, membranes, and the hard shell. The egg is micro- environment, housing a pond with nutrients for the development of the embryo/fetus. The reptiles improved the amphibian gelatinous egg by providing a hard shell that holds water. This cut the final tie animals had to the sea. Now, animals could populate the land, and reproduce away from water. Incidentally: On rare occasions, a fowl's egg may backtrack up the reproductive canal. Another egg, shell will form around the egg. The result is a giant egg within an egg.

EGGNOG – (*AYG*-nog) A rich, high-caloric dessert drink made from milk, cream, egg whites, sugar, nutmeg, cinnamon, and an alcoholic beverage like whiskey, bourbon, especially brandy or rum. The origin of eggnog cannot be definitively discerned. That's because for a long time, many concoctions that included eggnog ingredients have been mixed and consumed. In the mid-1600s, *"nog"* was a strong beer brewed in East Anglia, England. Beers were often mixed with other ingredients. Chances are that the eggnog we enjoy today dates back to late colonial America, circa 1775. In *The Passage to Burlington* (c. 1790), American poet Philip Freneau (1752 – 1832) wrote: *"And Bryan O'Buster made love to egg nog, And pester'd the ladies to taste of his grog; Without it (said Bryan) I never can dine, 'Tis better by far than your balderdash wine…."*

EGG ON – (ayg *ON*) (Egged on) To encourage or urge one forward. The egg in *"egg on"* has nothing to do with an ovum, omelet, or eggs from birds or any other oviparous creature. The term *"egg"* was a 13th century English word, a variant and synonym of *"edge"* or *"urge,"* as to edge or urge one forward. This usage of egg entered the British Isles with the Viking invasions, for both edge and egg derives from the Old Norse *"eddja".* So egg has been used as a verb in English since around the 13th century, where it appeared in the Trinity College rendition of Homer, in the form of *"eggede,"* circa 1200. Later, in 1566, the term *"egg on"* appears in Thomas Drant's (c. 1540 – 1578) translation of Horace (65 – 8 BCE): *Horace his arte of poetrie, pistles and satyrs englished*: *"Ile egge them on to speak some thing, whiche spoken may repent them."*

EGGS BENEDICT – (*AYGS BEN*-nuh-dikt) A dish consisting of toast or toasted halves of English muffin covered with a thin slice of fried or broiled ham, poached eggs, and a topping of hollandaise sauce. Incidentally: In a 1942 interview with *The New Yorker*, retired stock broker Lemuel Benedict (d. 1943) claimed credit for inspiring the eggs Benedict dish. Benedict testified that in 1884, he entered the Waldorf Hotel restaurant one morning with a horrible hangover. He ordered what he thought he could tolerate. Benedict ordered *"buttered toast, poached eggs, crisp bacon, and a hooker of hollandaise."* Oscar Tschirky (1866

– 1950) the maître d'hôtel was impressed with the dish so he put it on the menu. Tschirky substituted ham for bacon and a toasted English muffin for bread toast. Eggs Benedict was born.

EGO – (*EE*-go) The I, me, my physical body. The ego is the temporal, corporeal self, as contrasted with the spiritual self. The Buddha (c. 563 – c. 483 BCE) called the ego *"The false self."* We project our fear, hate, and hurt on people who remind us of our inner demon – the ego. Pride, envy, jealousy, greed, all negative attributes are of the ego. *"The true enemy is inside. The maker of trouble, the source of all our suffering, the destroyer of our joy, and the destroyer of our virtue is inside. It is Ego. I call it, 'I, the most precious one.'"* – Lama Gehlek Rimpoche (b. 1939). *"The ego is your enemy, not your friend. It is the ego that gives you wounds and hurts you. It is the ego that makes you violent, angry, jealous, competitive. It is the ego that is continuously comparing and feeling miserable."* – Rajneesh (1931 – 1990). *"The ego is an exquisite instrument. Enjoy it, use it – just don't get lost in it."* – Ram Dass (b. 1931). *"Ego is a social institution with no physical reality. The ego is simply your symbol of yourself."* – Shunryu Suzuki (1904 – 1971).

EGOCENTRIC – (ee-go-*SEN*-tric) (Egocentricity) Seeing oneself at the social center. Having an exaggerated estimation of oneself. Extreme conceit.

EGOISM – (*EE*-go-is-um) (Egoistic) Egotism. In general, excessive self-love and preoccupation with oneself. In a philosophical sense, egoism is self- gratification. It is the belief that the aim in life is to procure for oneself pleasure. Egoism insists that humans are by nature selfish, self-seeking, self- interested creatures. It is therefore natural to be self-centered. Capitalism has its spiritual roots in egoism. Capitalist egoism expounds that: *"I got mine, to hell with you!"*

EGOISTIC HEDONISM – (ee-go-*TIS*-tic *HEE*-dom-is-um) The psycho-philosophical theory that all human actions should be motivated by the desire to secure one's own pleasure, and avoid pain. This is the same as psychological hedonism, but with one major difference. Egoistic hedonism has no compunction about causing others pain and suffering in the search for one's own pleasure.

EGOT – (*EE*-got) An acronym for *Emmy, Grammy, Oscar, Tony,* the 4 big show business awards. If someone wins one of these prestigious talent awards, she or he is an EGOT.

EGOTESTICLE – (ee-go-*TES*-ti-cal) To be phallocentric, having a chauvinistic belief in male superiority. An egotesticle personality is egotistically machismo. An egotesticle male subscribes to Sigmund Freud's (1856 – 1939) theory of female *"penis envy."*

EGOTISM – (*EE*-go-tis-um) (Egotistical) Egoism. Egotism revels in self-conceit, self-adulation, self-praise offensive. Egotism is a quality of dedicated capitalists. Egotism has no compunction about using other people for self-aggrandizement. *"What's in it for me?"* is an egotistical maxim.

EGREGIOUS – (eh-*GREE*-jus) Flagrantly bad, heinous, horrible, like an egregious lie, blunder, or egregious brutality.

EID AL-ADHA – (eed al-a-*DA*) One of two Islamic holidays called Eid (pronounced *eed*). Eid al-Adha is the greater *Bairam* or feast, celebrated 70 days after Ramadan, marking the end of the Islamic calendar year. The term Adha means *"Holiday of Harm."* Eid al-Adha commemorates Abraham's willingness to sacrifice his son Isaac, an expression of absolute submission (or Islam) to Allah (or God). Too, Eid al-Adha marks the conclusion of the Hajj, the annual pilgrimage to Mecca.

EID AL-FITR – (eed al-*FEET*-ra) One of two Islamic holiday called Eid (pronounce *eed*). Eid al-Fitr is the lesser *Bairam* or feast. It is a celebration feast after fasting during Ramadan.

EIGHT – (*ATE*) In spiritual numerology the appearance of 3 eights (888) refers to *newlife*. A phase in your life is coming to an end. A new, better life is before you. Be prepared. Do not procrastinate. Let go of the past.

EIGHTFOLD PATH – (*ATE*-fold *PATH*) Buddhism's formulation of the 8 steps necessary for *"awakening."* They are: 1. Right views or understanding; 2. Right purpose or aspiration; 3. Right speech; 4. Right conduct; 5. Right livelihood; 6. Right effort; 7. Right kind of awareness, mindfulness; 8. Right concentration, meditation.

EIGHTY-SIX'D – (*AY*-tee *SIKS'D*) (86'd) To be 86'd is to be eliminated or terminated. To be fired or cut from the squad is to be 86'd. Originally, the term was a gangland reference for murder. 86'd stood for "80 miles out, and 6 feet under." It is said that the mob would drive a victim 80 miles out of town, make him dig his own 6-foot grave. The mileage and depth amounted to 86. With such people we must share this planet!

EIGHTY/TWENTY PARADOX – (*AY*-tee *TWEN*-tee *PAIR*-a-dox) An irony, absurdity that affects married couples. Research shows that most married couples are 80% satisfied with their mate. However, it's the 20% that they dislike about each other that may ignite a divorce. They set out on a quest to find a partner who doesn't exhibit those 20% of bad habits, and often succeed. However, the new mate is also an 80/20, with at least 20% of other bad habits you can't stand. Too, you are an 80/20 to your mate. The solution is not divorce but patience, endurance, toleration, and communication. *"Don't sweat the small stuff, and most of it is small stuff."*

EINKORN – (*EYN*-corn) A wild wheat-grass native to southeastern Turkey. Einkorn was domesticated over 10,600 years ago, but wild grain was gathered much earlier. Einkorn was grown in cooler climates than emmer wheat, the other ancient variety. Both varieties were cultivated in the Near East. Einkorn is still grown in parts of Europe and Asia as animal fodder. Emmer has evolved into bread wheat. Grains of einkorn were found on *Otzi* (c. 3300 BCE) *"The Iceman,"* found in the Alps (1991).

EINSATZGRUPPEN – (*EYN*-shotz-*GROOP*-en) German Nazi murder squads during World War Two. The Einsatzgruppen numbered about 3,000 SS and Gestapo operating in the conquered Eastern countries. They were divided into sub- groups of 5 called *"Einsatzkommandos."* They followed the *Wehrmacht* (army) working behind the lines, searching for Nazi state enemies to exterminate. Their primary victims were Polish intellectuals, Communists, Romani (Gypsies) and especially Jews. The Einsatzgruppen and their kommandos are synonymous with brutal war criminality.

EINSTEINIUM – (ahyn-*STEYN*-nee-um) (Es) A transuranic (beyond uranium) element (#99) named after the Austrian theoretical physicist, Albert Einstein (1879 – 1955). Einsteinium was discovered in

1952. These exotic elements like einsteinium were created in experiments. Many exist for seconds before disintegrating. Their only use is in further experiments.

EINSTEIN VISA – (*EYEN*-steyn *VEE*-sa) (EB-1) A rare U.S. visa issued to rare people. Named after the great physicist Albert Einstein (1879 – 1955), this permit for American citizenship is reserved for *"Individuals with extraordinary ability."* *"Recipients are supposed to be the best of the best,"* according to immigration lawyer Rita Sostrin. In 2016, only 5,530 Einstein visas had been issued, and not all of those recipients passed the interview. In 2001, Melania Knav (b. 1970) from Sevnica, Slovenia was issued an Einstein visa. She had married New York real estate mogul and *"sugar daddy"* Donald Trump (b. 1946) (24 years her senior). Melania was a fashion model. Immigration lawyer Chris Wright had said: *"When it's a glamorous model and pictures show cleavage rather than research, people assume there is something underhanded going on."* Einstein awardees are supposed to contribute to America in a special way. Immigration lawyer David Soloway believes that: *"Most people would readily say that it makes sense for someone who is extraordinarily skilled in the sciences to be admitted to this country. But in modeling? Really?"* Though Melania Trump is no Madame Curie (1867 – 1934), it doesn't take an Einstein to see that she possesses special gifts. Perhaps she contributes by keeping up the President's morale. It's still mystifying how Melania Trump, Einstein recipient, is helping to *"Make America Great Again."*

EJACULATION – (ee-jack-yoo-*LAY*-shun) (Ejaculating, Ejaculator) Ejaculation has different meanings in discourse and in intercourse. In discourse it refers to a sudden abrupt utterance. In intercourse it refers to the abrupt discharge of semen from the erect penis during sex. It is literally a *"seminal moment."* Ejaculation provides the male with the rewarding orgasm. It is the climax of arousal, of excitation from phallic stimulation. It is the act of *"cuming,"* in the vulgar vernacular. Ejaculation may result from autoerotic manipulation (masturbation), as well as intercourse, of course. It may occur during sleep as a result of erotic *"wet dreams."* Ejaculation results in a tremendous release of stress, tension, pressure. It is like a tightly would spring that has suddenly been released, relaxed. Incidentally: The relief felt after ejaculation is one of nature's best anxiety relievers. Furthermore, ejaculation by any means releases semen, forcing the testes to manufacture more. This is important for older men, for it stimulates testosterone production, which slows aging.

EJECTA – (ee-*JECT*-tah) Debris blasted out of a planet after a collision with a great cosmic body. The rings of Saturn may be the ejecta from the collision of a moon with the planet. Our moon is ejecta from the collision of the rogue planet *Theia* (or *Orpheus*) and the young planet Earth.

EJECTA – (ee-*JECT*-tah) Geo-matter ejected as from a volcanic eruption. Ejecta is not to be confused with *"egesta,"* which is bio-matter excreted from the body, such as excrement, urine, vomit or sweat.

EL AL-KITAB – (el al ki-*TOB*) (also Ahl al-Kitab) *"People of the Book"* (Bible). Muslim term for Jews and Christians. Being monotheistic, Jews and Christians are considered *"semi-infidel,"* and are therefore afforded preferential treatment among non-Muslims. Judaism and Christianity are Abrahamic religions like Islam. Both rely on The Book, the Bible, which is also the basis for much of the Koran. Muslim men may marry el al-Kitab women, provided that they convert. Muslim women cannot marry Non-Muslim men. The el al-Kitab are treated with a deference not afforded to polytheists or atheists. Incidentally: Christianity emerged from Judaism, and Islam emerged from Judaism and Christianity.

ELAN – (ay-*LON*) French for dashing spirit, flair, panache. To possess élan is to have a combination of style and vigor. A sparking white knight on horseback may very well display élan.

ELAN VITAL – (ay-*LON* vy-*TELL*) In philosophy, the life force, the basic creative principle of all living things. The philosopher Henri Bergson (1859 – 1941) introduced the concept. The elan vital is the driving force propelling life on to higher and higher levels of structure and organization. It is likened to a flow or current of consciousness, with which all the universe is imbued, and which determine the direction of evolution. Bergson spoke of elan vital as a supraconsciousness, a nonempirical, intangible, invisible, nonverifiable acting force. Elan vital sounds like an aspect of Divine will.

ELASTIC CLAUSE – (el-*LAS*-tic *CLAWS*) (Also called the *"Necessary and Proper"* clause) Article I, Section 8, Clause 18 of the U.S. Constitution that grants Congress *"implied power."* The elastic clause reads: *"Congress shall have the power to make all laws necessary and proper...."* This provision legally enables Congress to pass laws to meet unexpected contingencies that are not mentioned in the Constitution. These are the implied power. Liberals love the elastic clause, conservatives hate it. Conservatives are *"strict constructionists."* They want Congress to exercise only the powers delegated in the Constitution, nothing implied. They oppose stretching the Constitution through the elastic clause. Conservatives fear that Congress will one day redistribute their wealth fairly with implied powers. Liberals or Progressives are *"loose constructionists."* They commend the elastic clause and implied powers as an avenue to distributive justice.

ELBOW BUMP – (*EL*-bow buhmp) A silly, albeit necessary salutation during a contagion outbreak. The elbow bump is an awkward greeting on meeting that avoids the handshake. Obviously, the hands are the germiest part of the body. In order to avoid the transmission of bacteria or viruses, people must not clasp each other's hands. The elbow bump is a way to satisfy gregarious human's need to engage in safe physical contact. The elbow bump became widespread during the Coronavirus Pandemic which commenced in 2020. Footnote: Sillier than the elbow bump was the *"footsie brush."* Hope we don't adopt the *"rump- bump."* Incidentally: The most charming, warm, sacred and safest greeting is the ancient Hindu *"Namaste"* (nam-*OS*-tee). This is the traditional Hindu expression on meeting or parting, used by the speaker, holding hands together in front of the bosom in a prayerful fashion. This Sanskrit word and gesture speaks volumes. It means *"I honor the truth, the light, the peace, the love in you. I salute your divine qualities. The God (ness) in me greets and honors the God (ness) in you. My soul bows to your soul. We are one in God."*

ELDER – (*EL*-der) (Elderly) Of greater age, an older person. Usually with age comes experience and wisdom. Therefore, elders are usually is positions of authority and power, as tribal chiefs, for instance. They command high esteem. They are honored for their lifelong contributions to the society and culture. Eastern Oriental culture pays far more esteem to their elders than does Western, Occidental culture. Incidentally: What is the age limit for our governing elders? In this election year 2024, the Democratic candidate, Joe Biden (b. 1942) is 81, while the Republican candidate, Donald Trump (b. 1946) is 77 years old. This accounts for the lack of enthusiasm for either candidate.

ELECTION DAY – (el-*LEK*-shun *DAY*) The Presidential Election Day is the special day 0n which Americans vote for their *"Commander-in-Chief,"* the President. The entire House of Representatives, 1/3 of the Senate, as well as Governors, Mayors, Judges, all the state officials are up for election as well. By law (1845) Presidential Election Day comes the Tuesday after the first Monday in November, every 4 years, on an even-numbered year. Tuesday was chosen because farmers in the 19th century often needed a full day to travel by horse to vote at the county seat. Too, Tuesday did not interfere with Sunday church, or traditional market day, which was Wednesday. According to the calendar, the earliest possible Election Day is November 2nd, the latest November 8th. November was chosen because it wouldn't interfere with spring or summer farming chores. Too, November is usually not freezing cold in the north, yet. Presidential Election Day is a hallowed occasion, our only celebration of democracy. Why isn't it an official holiday? The Republicans won't have it! If Election Day were a holiday, laboring people would not have to go to work. More common folk would vote. This the Republicans fear. Republicans represent the wealthy capitalists. They certainly do not want to make it easier for the poor and working citizens to vote. That may endanger the privileged status of the rich.

ELECTION DENIERS – (el-*LEK*-shun dee-*NY*-yers) (Election Denial) Stubborn stupids who have embraced *"Trump's Big Lie."* Election deniers refuse to acknowledge that American elections are fair, not corrupted. In fact, the only elections that may be corrupt are those corrupted by Trumpublicans who are disappointed with the results (the Big Liars). Election deniers refuse to acknowledge the legitimacy of elections they lose. Only if they win do they accept the results as fair. This is flagrantly undemocratic and anti-American. Trumpublican election deniers, like Donald Trump (b. 1946) are fascists. They lust power, which means denying power to their opponents. Incidentally: Not all election deniers believe the Big Lie. Some know it is not true, but so wish that it was. Nevertheless, they use election denial to suppress democratic elections by suppressing the vote. Of course, election denial, the Big Lie, all of Trump's and QAnon's crazy conspiracies are used by the plutocracy, the oligarchy, the Republican rich to preserve their wealth and hegemony. *"Who do you think controls the Republican Party? Big money controls the Republican Party. This is where their campaign contributions come from."* – Socialist Senator Bernie Sanders (b. 1941). After Thought: Why don't Trumpublican sports fans became *"Scoreboard Deniers?"* If the score or count doesn't go their team's way, why don't they simply fantasize that they won?

ELECTION FRAUD – (el-*LEK*-shun *FRAWD*) Not *"voter"* fraud, but rather *"voting"* fraud. Election fraud is voting fraud on a grand scale. Election fraud is cheating at the polling place, the voting station, not by the voter, but by the election administrator. Voting machines are rigged, ballots not counted or destroyed, results are padded. Ironically, the Republicans who scream the loudest about voter fraud by the citizens, are most guilty of election fraud by Republican election administrators. Dictators are masters of election fraud. Joseph Stalin (1878 – 1953) admitted that *"He who casts the vote decides nothing. He who counts the vote decides everything."*

ELECTION INTEGRITY ACT – (el-*LEK*-shun in-*TEG*-rit-tee *AKT*) The pernicious voter suppression law enacted in the state of Georgia in 2021. It is a Republican reaction to the loss in the presidential and senatorial elections in 2020. The law is also called the *"Georgia Senate Bill 202."* The Election Integrity Act would more accurately be called the *"Election Inequity Act."* It is a common ploy of Republicans to name a law or program the opposite of its nefarious intended effect. Cheating is not an act of integrity. The law is designed to eliminate Democratic votes, especially among African-American citizens. It is purely, unabashedly *"neo-Jim Crowism."* It makes voting a burden, a hardship, especially on the poor (Democrats). It reduces the time to request an absentee ballot. It requires voter identification on an absentee ballot. It reduces the number of ballot drop boxes in Black populated areas. It allows challenges to voter eligibility aimed at the poor. It replaces the Secretary of State as Chair of the Election Board by legislators (Republicans) enabling them to adjust the results by defrauding the election. The law is intended to create long uncomfortable lines of voters who would have to stand for hours, after work, suffering the elements. The most absurd absurdity is that the law criminalizes Good Samaritans who would bring food and drink to the weary voters. The Election Integrity Act would be ludicrous if it wasn't so dangerous. It is so nakedly, shamelessly corrupt that it is funny – though no laughing matter. This legislative atrocity, absurdity is a model for other Republican controlled states. As in a tin-horn dictatorship or a banana republic, the Election Integrity Act turns the election into mere window dressing. This law is a fatal blow to democracy. It is a giant leap toward fascism. *"The person who casts the vote determines nothing. The person who counts the vote determines everything."* – Joseph Stalin (1878 – 1953). Footnote: In order to highlight the absurdities of Republican voter-suppression laws, a Democratic legislator should propose that voter be mandated to stand on one foot in the line at the voting poll.

ELECTIONS – (el-*LEK*-shuns) (Elect, Elected, Electorate) To choose or elect by popular assent, representatives, leaders, and policies. An election is the sacred sacrament of democracy. Elections are decided by the counting of votes. Elections are at the heart of democracy, the soul of self-government. Elections should proclaim majority rule, assuring government of the people, by the people, for the people. Election tampering should be treated as treason. If elections become fraudulent, and the electorate loses faith in elections, liberty is lost. Incidentally: Elections are a nuisance and often a threat to the rich and powerful. Capitalism leans against democracy toward fascism. Elections jeopardize wealth. A German Finance Minister told Greek Socialist scholar Yanis Varoufakis (b. 1961) that: *"Elections cannot be allowed to change economic policy."*

ELECTIVE ASTROLOGY – (el-*LEK*-tiv as-*TROL*-lo-jee) That branch of astrology that determines the right and wrong dates and times for crucial events. Though Adolf Hitler banned astrology in the Nazi empire, he maintained his own secret astrologer. The First Lady Nancy Reagan (1921 – 2016) consulted with President Ronald Reagan's (1911 – 2004) White House Astrologer every morning. The first thing the late sleeping (c. 9:00 a.m.) President heard each morning was wife Nancy's elective astrology report. Yes, Reagan was a movie star, and ran the nation by the stars.

ELECTORAL CHAOS – (el-*LEK*-tor-al *KAY*-os) In a U.S. Presidential election, if no candidate wins at least 270 electoral votes, in the Electoral College, the election is thrown into the House of Representatives. All the Representatives of both parties meet as state delegations in secret caucus to vote for a President. One state, one vote. (This happened once, in 1828. Though Andrew Jackson (1767 – 1845) got most of the popular and electoral votes, the House elected John Quincy Adams (1767 – 1848) President.) In the case of no electoral victory, the Senate elects the Vice-President. So we can end up with a President from one party, and a Vice-President from the other. If the House cannot decide on a President, but the Senate has chosen a Vice-President, the Vice-President becomes acting President, until the House makes up its mind. Now, if neither the House nor the Senate can decide on the President or Vice-President, the Speaker of the House becomes acting President, until the House and Senate can decide on our leaders.

ELECTORAL COLLEGE – (el-*LEK*-tor-al *COL*-lej) An anti-democratic vestigial remain designed to obfuscate presidential elections. The Electoral College was established by the plutocratic Founding Fathers, the Constitution drafters as a firewall to protect their wealth. Election by popular vote would be too difficult to manipulate and fraudulate. Therefore the Electoral College was instituted by the aristocracy to enable them to reject a legitimately elected presidential candidate who threatened their wealth. This would be accomplished by manipulating the state's electors. Each state is portioned as many electors as it has members in Congress. In other words, the more people in the state, the more electors. When citizens vote, they are not voting for the President directly, but for a team of electors. Your vote is request to a group of people already in place, to elect the President for you. The electors are *"outstanding"* citizens who will decide who is the best candidate for the Presidency. They do not have to take into consideration the people's will. Initially, the anti- democratic Founding Fathers defined *"outstanding"* as capitalist and aristocratic. The archaic Electoral College makes a mockery of democracy and majority rule. The Electoral College is a *"winner take all"* proposition. The candidate who wins the popular vote in the state (even by one vote), gets all of that state's electoral votes. That presents a problem. The problematic formula is: *"If you win big in the small states, but lose small in the big states,"* you will get millions more votes than your opponent, but <u>NOT</u> be elected President. (For example, win 99% of the popular votes in Wyoming or Montana (small states), but get only 3 electoral votes from each state. However, win 49% of the votes in both California and Texas (big states), but get none of the combined 90 electoral votes.) Incidentally: Democrat Al Gore (b. 1948) won thousands of more votes than Republican George W. Bush (b. 1946), but lost the Presidency to Bush in 2000. Democrat Hillary Clinton (b. 1947) won three million more votes than Republican Donald Trump (b. 1946), but lost the Presidency to Trump. The Electoral College was responsible for the injustice. Incidentally: A Constitutional crisis is brewing now in late November, 2020, which involves the Electoral College. *"The Constitution is just a gentlemen's agreement made by rich gentlemen."* So said Professor Jason Johnson (Morgan State University) on MSNBC News. Johnson is absolutely correct. The loser of the 2020 Presidential Election, President Donald Trump (b. 1946) has the Constitutional right to manipulate the Electoral College, and steal the Presidency away from the people. The Electoral College was established just for that purpose – to serve a last-ditch *"safety-valve,"* to cancel the will of the people. Certainly, the Founding Fathers never fathomed, in their wildest nightmares, a vile Trump. But they did anticipate the day when the people would democratically elect a Socialistic Presidential Candidate who would fairly redistribute theirs, and their decedent's wealth. In this case, the Electors in the Electoral College could be coaxed, bribed, or threatened to ignore the will of the people, and install a *"rational,"* *"reasonable,"* *"favorable"* candidate in the White House. Today, Trump is just exploiting the oligarchic mechanism that the Founding Fathers had installed in the Constitution.

ELECTORAL PARITY – (el-*LEK*-tor-al *PAIR*-ri-tee) Equal protection, equal justice under the election laws. This can only be achieved if all states abide by the same election rules, under Federal authority. The states cannot be trusted with voting administration. They are too partisan and corrupt. The voting laws have to be coordinated, harmonized, integrated to assure integrity. Across the states, a *"Uniformed Code of American Voting"* must be formalized. Federal Marshals must serve as election watchdogs. Voting is the most fundamental participation in democracy. It is ludicrous to tolerate the chaotic, unjust helter- skelter employed by the various states.

ELECTORATE – (el-*LEK*-tor-rate) The voting public. Those citizens eligible and registered to vote. Electorate should not be confused with *constituency.* Constituents are all people represented by an elected official, whether eligible to vote or not. Everyone, even children are some officials' constituent. The Democratic electorate tends to be Liberal, Progressive, Socialistic. The Republican electorate tends to be conservative, reactionary, capitalistic.

ELECTRICITY – (el-lek-*TRIS*-si-tee) (Electronics) The greatest most influential discovery of modern times. One of the basic properties of elementary particles of matter giving rise to all electric and magnetic forces and interactions. An electrical charge can be positive or negative. As a power source, electricity is fundamental to modern civilization. It would take 150 slaves to equal the work done by electrical appliances for the average American. Citizens of modern societies are totally dependent on electricity in their daily lives. *"Mysterious affair, electricity."* – Samuel Beckett (1906 – 1989). *"Those who live by electronics die by electronics."* – Kurt Vonnegut (1922 – 2007). Incidentally: All of our modern, work-saving, time-saving appliances run on electricity. It has been estimated that it would require 150 slaves to provide the services that our electrical appliances do for us today.

ELECTROLYTE – (el-*LEK*-tro-lite) Any of certain inorganic compounds that dissociate in biological fluids into ions capable of conducting electrical currents and constituting a major force in controlling fluid within the body. Electrolytes, regulate blood pressure, and revive fatigued muscles due to vigorous exercise. Electrolyte loss occurs from dehydration due to illness (diarrhea, vomiting), or profuse sweating as when exercising. An electrolyte is a scientific term for sodium chloride (table salt). A small glass of salt water is recommended during vigorous exercise. Iodized salt is preferable.

ELECTROMAGNETIC RADIATION – (el-lek-tro-mag-*NET*-tic ray-dee-*AY*-shun) Light waves. Energy that moves in the form of disturbances in electrical and magnetic fields. Light (electromagnetic radiation) exists in various wave-lengths. The shorter, more compact the wave-length, the greater its penetrative power. From shortest, strongest to longest, weakest they are: Gamma Rays -> X-Rays -> Ultra-Violet Rays -> Visible Light Ray -> Infrared Rays -> Microwaves -> Radio Frequency Waves.

ELECTROMETEORS – (el-*LEKT*-tro-meet-tee-ors) In meteorology, a visible or audible manifestation of atmospheric electricity such as lightning or thunder.

ELECTRON – (el-*LEK*-tron) A negatively charged elementary particle that is a fundamental constituent of matter, and orbits the nucleus of the atom. An electron is 2,000 times smaller than the proton it orbits. In fact, to count a line of electrons an inch long would take 19 million years.

ELECTRONIC CLOUD – (el-lec-*TRON*-nic *CLOWD*) In physics, the region of space around the nucleus of an atom in which the electrons dance.

ELECTRUM – (el-*LEK*-trum) An amber-colored alloy of gold and silver. Why would anyone adulterate gold with a less valuable mental creating an alloy? For strength. Gold is so soft, even too soft for ornaments and jewelry.

ELECTUARY – (el-*LEK*-chew-air-ree) A medicine sweetened with sugar, honey, or sweet syrup to make it more palatable. Electuaries are usually prepared for children or animals.

ELEEMOSYNARY – (el-ee-*MOS*-sin-air-ree) Charitable, concerned with or dependent on charity. Eleemosynary relates to alms giving. A compassionate, Liberal eleemosynary is a generous giver.

ELEGY – (*EL*-le-jee) A melancholy, mournful poem, especially a funeral song or a lament for the dead. A Caveat: Don't confuse elegy with eulogy, a praise- worthy speech for a deceased person.

ELEMENTARY SCHOOL – (el-le-*MEN*-tar-ree) America's primary school, first established in Massachusetts Bay Colony (17th century), then spreading throughout New England then America. The elementary school teaches the *"tool subjects"*: reading, writing, spelling, counting (arithmetic) and behaving (socialization). Today's *traditional* elementary school proceeds through 8 grades with student ages ranging from 5 to 14 years. A *kindergarten* (pre- school) often precedes grade one. Intermediate schools (junior highs and middle schools) have lifted the burden of grades 6, 7, and 8 from the elementary school in many locales.

ELEMENTAL SPITITS – (el-le-*MENT*-tal *SPEER*-rits) Ghostly entities associated with each of the 4 elements – air water, earth, fire. Elemental spirits were first described in alchemical works written by Paracelsus (1493 – 1541) in the 16th century. The name of the spirit creatures varies by tradition but the most common are: earth elements – gnomes; water elements – undines or nymphs; air elements – sylphs; fire elements – salamanders.

ELEMENTS – (*EL*-le-ments) Matter. Actually, different vibrational excitations of a string of light. The elements are the 118 pure, uncombined chemicals listed on the Periodic Table, from which all matter is created. The first 25 simpler elements up to iron are created by stars like our sun. Once a very large star begins to produce iron, it will explode into a supernova. As a result of the explosion, all the other natural elements more complex than iron are spewed throughout the universe. The first 92, ending with uranium are natural. The final 26 are artificially man-made, many surviving for a mere fraction of a fraction of a second. An element cannot be broken down into simpler constituents by chemical means, because all its atoms have the same atomic number, meaning the same unique number of protons in its nucleus. That's what makes it a unique substance or chemical. The number of protons determines the identity of the element. The atoms of all the elements are constructed of about 20 sub-atomic particles. Again, all the elements (all of matter) are simply different vibrational excitations of a string of light.

ELEPHANT – (*EL*-uh-fahnt) A huge pachyderm with a long prehensile trunk formed of the nose and upper lip and long ivory tusks. It is a herbivore and the largest land animal in the world. Elephants must eat at least 150 lbs. of foliage a day. They kill about 500 people a year worldwide. No animal can wreak more carnage than a rampaging elephant. Different species inhabit the savannah, jungle, and desert. Elephant herds are the closest faunal social group. Elephants dwell in Africa, India, and Southeast Asia. The African elephant is larger, more aggressive, with bigger floppy ears. Indian (Asian) elephants are smaller, more tamable, with ivory tusks borne only by the males. The African and Asian elephants have distinct immune systems, and will sicken each other if kept together. Unlike his African cousin, the Indian elephant has long been used for work and entertainment. The African elephant, like the zebra, cannot be tamed. Elephants have the closest social familial bonds of all animals. Only man holds family dearer than elephants.

ELEPHANT IN ROOM – (EL-uh-fahnt in room) Not your fat Republican cousin, but an English metaphoric idiom for a crucial topic, critical question, or compelling controversy that is obvious to all, but all are afraid to confront. An elephant is the largest land animal on Earth. If you can't see the elephant, it's because you don't want to see the elephant. It's a case of avoidance. The elephant in the room (like his companion, the 800-pound gorilla), may be too scary and uncomfortable to see. The metaphoric pachyderm may be personally, socially, or politically too embarrassing to see, or too inflammatory and threatening to see. So human nature represses the actual existence of the problematic issue. In 1814, Russian poet and fabulist Ivan Krylov (1769 – 1844) wrote a fable entitled *"The Inquisitive Man."* Krylov wrote of a man who visited a museum, noticing all sorts of things except a huge elephant in the room. The phrase became proverbial. In 1872, Fyodor Dostoevsky (1821 – 1881) wrote in his novel <u>Demons</u>: *"Belinsky was just like Krylov's Inquisitive Man, who didn't notice the elephant in the museum."* The <u>Oxford English Dictionary</u> gives the first recorded use of the phrase, as a simile, in <u>The New York Times</u> on June 20, 1959: *"Financing schools has become a problem about equal to having an elephant in the living room. It's so big you just can't ignore it."* Incidentally: Concerning the issue of women's reproductive rights, the Republican Elephant could not see the elephant in the room.

ELEVATOR – (*EL*-le-vay-tor) A moving platform, cage, or compartment for carrying passengers or freight from one level of a building to another. Simple and complex hoists for elevating cargo or people are ancient. The Roman Colosseum for instance had elevators that brought vicious animals up from the cellars to the killing arena. Credit for inventing the modern elevator goes to Elisha Otis (1811 – 1861) back in 1854. Before the elevator, no building would surpass 5 stories. Without the elevator, major cities would not be recognizable. The elevator made the skyscraper possible. Footnote: The skyscraper was an American contribution to architecture.

ELEVATION – (el-le-*VAY*-shun) Height of the terrain above sea level, as contrasted with altitude which is height in the atmosphere. A mountain rises in elevation. An airplane climbs in altitude. Incidentally: For every 1,000 feet up in elevation, the temperature drops 3.5 degrees Fahrenheit. That's why mountain peaks are snow covered. This is comparable to traveling 300 miles north in latitude.

ELI LAMA SABACHTHANI – (*EE*-lie la-*MA* sa-bach-*THON*-nee) Aramaic for *"My God, My God, Why Hath Thou Forsaken Me?"* These were among the last words of Jesus, before he expired on the cross (c. 30 – 33 CE). It is the most enigmatic, controversial utterance attributed to Jesus in all the four approved Gospels. This may be the most human pronouncement that Jesus had ever made. Though it's impossible to say what Jesus was actually thinking, it certainly reveals his humanness in weakness. Writhing in such agony, it is excusable that any man would question God's mercy. Perhaps Jesus was delirious, which is equally understandable. In any case, the cry *"Eli, Eli, Lama Sabachthani"* reveals the image of a Son of

Man, rather than the Son of God. Incidentally: Jews have difficulty with Jesus' divinity, while Christians have difficulty with Jesus' humanity.

ELITES – (el-*LEETS*) The highest class, the ruling group, the most powerful and richest segment of society. Affluent and flatulent President Donald Trump (b. 1946) is a member of the elite and represents the interests of the wealthy elite. Nevertheless, Trump twists this term to describe his political opponents, the educated class. That's because his base of supporters who are uneducated, believe they recognize an enemy in educated citizens. Trump's strategy seems to work. It draws attention away from the fact that the rich are the actual elites, and the real enemy of the poor (Trump supporters). Propagating this deception is one of the primary goal of FOX [read: *TRUMP*] News.

ELIXIR – (el-*LICKS*-er) A vitalizing concoction or health potion. Alchemists long sought the *"Elixir of Life,"* that would provide youth, longevity, perhaps immortality. The alchemists experimented with the 4 elements, *air, water, fire,* and *earth* in their search for the elixir. In a sense, they were right. *Air* represents deep breathing. *Water* represents adequate hydration. *Fire* represents burning energy or exercise. *Earth* represents healthy food. *Air water, fire,* and *earth* are the Elixir of Life, providing youth and longivity.

ELK – (*ELK*) A huge deer, but signifying different species to Europeans and Americans. In Europe, the Elk is what Americans call the Moose. There is a European Elk, that they call the Red Deer. The Moose to Americans is unmistakable. The American Elk is called a Wapiti.

ELLIPSIS – (ill-*LIP*-sis) (Plural, Ellipses = ill-*LIP*-seez.) A line of period points (3 or 4), inserted in a sentence, to omit a phrase, sentence, or paragraph. A fourth ellipsis mark is used to serve as a period, ending the sentence. For example: *"Donald Trump is the most corrupt ... and despicable individual to occupy the White House ...."*

ELLIPTICAL – (ee-*LIP*-ti-kuhl) (Elliptically) In speech or writing, communication expressed with extreme or excessive economy, relieved of all irrelevant matter. In other words, concisely, to the point. Elliptically also means ambiguously, cryptically. To communicate elliptically is to jump between thoughts, ideas, or expressions without sufficient transition or logical connection.

ELLIPTICAL – (ee-*LIP*-ti-kuhl) Concerning physical fitness, an elliptical is an exercise machine with rotating or sliding peddles, as well as handlebars that move forward and backward. An elliptical exercises both arms (upper body) and legs (lower body), in the same amount of time. The caloric cost (burning of calories) is substantial. An elliptical machine may be a stand-up appliance, or a sit-down stationary bike. There are very many styles of ellipticals in very many price ranges. Some are light and simple, others are big, heavy, complicated with useless bells-and-whistles. Some ellipticals are chain-driven, others are propelled by belts. The simplest chain-driven bike is the best buy.

EL NINO – (el *NEEN*-yoh) A weather pattern created by the warming of the Pacific Ocean off the west coast of South America. This occurs in late December (near Christmas) every 5 to 10 years. El Nino has caused catastrophic weather conditions. The warmer ocean current pushes water and heavy rains toward the Americas, resulting in flooding. In Australia and Asia, drought conditions prevail. No nation is affected more adversely from El Nino than Peru. Its rains causes catastrophic floods and mudslides. Too, El Nino decreases the important fish supply along the Pacific Coast of South America.

ELOCUTION – (el-lo-*KEW*-shun) The art of public speaking. Elocution includes oral delivery, utilization of voice, gesticulation, expression – the entire package.

EMACIATE – (ee-*MAY*-see-ayt) (Emaciated, Emaciation) To waste away. To make abnormally lean or thin by a gradual disintegration of the flesh. A starving person is emaciated. Dreadfully, people had been emaciated to death in dungeons, sucked dry of blood by lice!

EMAIL – (*EE*-mail), <u>E</u>lectronic <u>Mail</u>. A system for sending and receiving typed messages electronically over a computer network, virtually instantly. Email is asynchronous (one operation at a time). Email correspondence does not require the receiver of the message to be online at the time the message is sent or received. Email also allows a user to distribute messages to many recipients simultaneously. The first email was sent with the invention of the internet in 1969. Today, over 100 billion emails are sent daily. Too, 40% of humanity, the world's population has used email. That's over a dozen for each human being on Earth. A Caveat: The Downside of the email is the person who fails to check her mail.

EMANATION – (em-an-*AY* shun) (Emanate, Emanating) To emit, flow out, issue forth. *The river emanated from a subterranean cave.*

EMANCIPATION – (ee-man-sip-*PAY*-shun) (Emancipate, Emancipating, Emancipated) Manumission, liberation. Emancipation is freedom from bondage or physical, emotional, or economic slavery. In law, emancipation is the legal release from another's control (as with married child from parents). Eighteen is usually the legal age of emancipation from parental control.

EMANCIPATION PROCLAMATION – (ee-man-sip-PAY-shun proc-la-*MAY*-shun) An executive order issued by President Abraham Lincoln (1809 – 1865) on January 1, 1863, freeing the slaves in those states *still in rebellion* against the United States. The Proclamation did not free the slaves in the border states no longer fighting the Union. These were Delaware, Maryland, Kentucky, and Missouri. For this reason, amateur historians (and moralists) have called Lincoln hypocritical. Actually, he was compassionately sincere, but politically pragmatic. If the four states mentioned above had seceded as well, the balance of power may have tipped to the Confederacy. The war would be lost, and no slaves would be emancipated anywhere. Lincoln proved to be correct. Too, the Emancipation Proclamation changed the war from a political struggle to a moral crusade. Up till then, Britain and France flirted with the idea of supporting the South for economic reasons. They actually supplied the South with weapons, and a battleship. Britain and France hoped to cripple the United States as a commercial competitor. The Proclamation made this move morally impossible.

EMANCIPATORS – (ee-*MAN*-sip-pay-tors) (Emancipation, Emancipate) Those with the authority to free slaves, serfs, or liberate people in bondage. The two great historic emancipators in recent times have been the Liberal Czar Alexander III of Russia (1818 – 1881), and the Liberal President Abraham Lincoln (1809 – 1865) of the United States. Alexander liberated the serfs in the Russian Empire in 1861, Lincoln liberated the slaves in America in 1863. Incredibly, both emancipators were assassinated, Lincoln in 1865, Alexander in 1881.

EMASCULATION – (ee-mas-kyoo-*LAY*-shun) Male castration. Castration can pertain to both male and female (male testicles and female ovaries). Usually, emasculation involves only males and includes both testicles and penis. To emasculate is to rob a man of his manhood. It is surgical sexual sterilization. Without testicles to produce sperm, and a penis to deliver it, the man cannot sire children. Too, the testicles produce testosterone, the hormone that keeps men male, virile. To lose the testicles and testosterone will make a male physically and emotionally docile because he has no balls. Incidentally: In Medieval Europe, orphan boys were often brought off the streets to live in monasteries, and trained as choir singers. Inorder to keep their sweet boyish voices into adulthood, they would be castrated. Sexually, they were made perpetually pre-pubic. The Turkish Ottoman Sultans created eunuchs by castrating the bodyguards of their harems. Without balls to produce sperm and a penis to penetrate, the body guards were not erotically interested in the nude female bodies.

EMBALMER'S GRAY – (em-*BAHLM*-ers *GRAY*) A livid pallor that comes over the face of a corpse following an improperly performed embalmment. Embalmer's gray makes the corps resemble an old manikin.

EMBARGO – (em-*BAR*-go) In economics and international relations, a refusal to trade. An embargo is an order of a government prohibiting the movement of merchant ships into or out of its ports. The embargo can be a general stoppage of commerce with some nation, or just the prohibition on the export or import of certain products. For example, ivory is embargoed for the protection of elephants. In some cases, embargos are dangerous. Oil and copper were embargoed to Benito Mussolini (1883 – 1945) for invading Ethiopia in 1936. So Italian-Americans enamored with Mussolini at that time mailed about 400 tons of copper to Italy, all in copper postcards. The United States embargoed oil and iron to Japan in the 1930's because of Japan's invasion of China. This led to the Japanese attack on Pearl Harbor (1941). American (and her dependent nations) embargoed arms to Fidel Castro's (1926 – 2016) Socialist Cuba in 1959. After the Cuban Missile Crisis (1962) the U.S. and others placed a general embargo on Cuba. In 2017 President Barack Obama (b. 1961) rescinded the travel band on Cuba. But the Republican Congress refuses to lift the economic embargo. The cruel, vindictive embargo has crippled little Cuba for decades. In 2015, Raul Castro (b. 1931) reported to the United that since 1962, the American led embargo had cost Cuba Nations $833.7 billion dollars. During the 1973 Arab Oil Embargo, President Richard Nixon (1913 – 1994) was planning to invade Saudi Arabia, Kuwait, and the Arab Emirates, and seize the oil fields. The plans were discussed with the British.

EMBARRASSMENT – (em-*BEAR*-ass-ment) (Embarrass, Embarrassing) To feel humiliated, shamed, naked to the world (em-*BARE-ASS*-ed). In fact, embarrassment is a uniquely personal emotion. What embarrasses one person will not embarrass another. It is therefore silly to say that someone embarrassed you. They may have said or done something, and then you chose to feel embarrassed by it. In that, you've empowered them over you. *"What you think of me is none of my business."* – Pastor Terry Cole-Whittaker (b. 1939). Incidentally: In *"The Gospel of Thomas,"* the Disciples asked Jesus: *"When will you appear to us, and when will we see you?"* Jesus replied: *"When you undress without being ashamed and take your clothe and put them under your feet like little children and trample on them, then you will see the Son of the Living One, and you will not be afraid."*

EMBEDDED – (em-*BED*-ed) (In Bed) To be in bed with another means to be in cooperation with him. Embedded is being under control, as are news correspondence in combat zones. Embedded is being censored, edited, manipulated by the generals to tell the public what the military wishes it to know. The *"Fourth Estate"* has become *"For the State."* An em*bed*ded journalist is in *bed* with the government. They have become *"lapdogs with laptops."* Embedding journalism is part of the *"Vietnam Syndrome."* Freedom of access made Vietnam the first television war. The military had difficulty exaggerating or lying about the war's progress. Too, the atrociousness of war was brought right into America's homes. Secretary of State Dean Rusk (1909 – 1994) lamented: *"Vietnam is the first struggle fought on television in everyone's living room every day. What would have happened in World War Two if Guadalcanal, and the Anzio beachhead, and the Battle of the Bulge or the Diep Raid were on television? And the other side was not doing the same thing? Whether ordinary people can sustain their war effort under that kind of daily hammering is a very large question."* TV, freedom of the press helped turn public opinion against the Vietnam War and military. The generals vowed that in future wars, they would control the news. The result: embedded journalists. The first conflict in which the military controlled the press was the gruesome Panama Invasion (December 1989 to January 1990). The U.S. Government still denies the atrocities, and there was no press coverage to prove the truth. That's how the military likes it. *"Television brought the brutality of war into the comfort of the living room. Vietnam was lost in the living rooms of American – not on the battlefields of Vietnam."* – Marshall McLuhan (1911 – 1980).

EMBELLISH – (em-*BEL*-lish) (Embellishment) To adorn, to exaggerate. In a literary narrative, an embellishment is a fictitious addition, to excite interest. In the 19th century, biographies were often absurdly embellished to create heroes. Concerning his biography, mountain man and scout, Kit Carson (1809 – 1868) said: *"It may be true, but I don't got any recollection of it."* Likewise, frontiersman Davy Crocket (1786 – 1836) said of his biography: *"Some of that may be fact, but I think he laid it on a bit too thick."*

EMBEZZLEMENT – (em-*BEZ*-zel-ment) (Embezzler, Embezzling) Denotationally, the fraudulent appropriation of property or money placed in one's care. Connotationally, embezzlement bears two perspectives. When executives, managers, banksters, and other corporate capitalists embezzle out of greed, it is *whitewashed* as *"white collar crime."* When workers embezzle out of need, they are fired, fined, and jailed. The bankster embezzles to concentrate the wealth. The bank teller embezzles to redistribute the wealth. Like looting, embezzlement on the part of the poor is not a moral crime, because it is the exercise of distributive justice. Embezzlement is a vital contributor to the *"underground economy,"* when the capitalist economy is closed to the poor.

EMBLEMATICALS – (em-ble-*MAT*-ti-cals) (Also called Enigmaticals, Problematicals, Ceremonials.) Native artifacts that have no discernable purpose. Most emblematicals were shamanistic, magical articles.

EMBOUCHURE – (am-boo-*CHUR*) A French term: geographically the mouth of a river or valley where the water or terrain widens-out. In a musical context an embouchure is the mouthpiece of a wind instrument. Furthermore, embouchure refers to the adjustments the musicians must make with their mouths to accommodate the mouthpiece.

EMBOURGEOISEMENT – (em-booz-*WA*-ment) The development of a propertied merchant class, prosperous, though below the aristocratically rich. Embourgeoisement also refers to the develop a false consciousness in the working class, against their own economic interests in support of capitalist hegemony. Embourgeoisement attempts to deceive the working class, that they too can join the middle class if they support the capitalist agenda. The depleted *"American Dream"* is an example of Embourgeoisement.

EMBROCATION – (em-broh-*KAY*-shuhn) (Embrocate, Embrocating) A liniment. A medical preparation, usually an oily liquid, topically applied to the skin and rubbed into the muscles. Embrocations sooth the pain of sprains, bruises, arthritis, and sore muscles. They usually contain alcohol, camphor, balms, and herbal oils. Adding capsicum (the ingredient in hot peppers) will produce a heat rub. The verb form, embrocate entered English in the 1610s from the Latin *"embrocatus,"* meaning *"a lotion that soaks in."*

E=MC2 – (Energy equals mass multiplied by the speed of light, squared.) Albert Einstein's (1879 – 1955) famous Mass-Energy Equation, which provided the *"Relativity Theory."* It means the amount of energy when mass is annihilated is the speed of light in empty space. Matter is transformed into energy when an atom is split. This is the basis of nuclear fission, power stations, and the atomic bomb. E=MC2 declares that matter and energy are interchangeable, therefore related or relative. Ergo, the Relativity Theory. Incidentally: Einstein, a Theoretical Physicist was a dreamer who never excelled at math. Einstein had declared that *"Since the mathematicians have invaded the theory of relativity, I do not understand it myself anymore."* Incidentally: In a light moment, Professor Einstein defined relativity thusly: *"When a man sits with a pretty girl for an hour, it seems like a minute. But let him sit on a hot stove for a minute – and it's longer than any hour. That's relativity."* A Conficta: *"There was a young lady named Bright. Whose speed was faster than light. She went out one day, in a relative way, and came back the previous night!"*

E-MEET – (*EE*-meet) In internet etiquette, to make one's acquaintance online. One might say: *"I'm very glad to e-meet you."*

EMERALD – (*EM*-er-ald) A rare variety of beryl that is colored green by chromium and highly valued as a gemstone. Emeralds are discovered in Columbia, Brazil, and other parts of South America. Where such gems are deposited is a mere geological accident. As with all minerals, the right chemical elements came together under the right condition to create the bounty. It was purely serendipitous. It could have happened anywhere if geology had permitted.

EMERGENCY – (ee-*MER*-jen-see) A crisis. The sudden emergence of an urgent, unexpected occurrence, requiring immediate action. Most emergencies are bad happenings. Being unforeseen, it is difficult to be prepared for an emergency. A breakdown, accident, injury, or disaster are emergencies. The trauma center of a hospital is equipped to handle most emergencies. Incidentally: A medical professor told his students: *"For the first 6 months I will teach you how to perform heart surgery. Then for the next three-and-a-half years, I will teach you what to do when something goes wrong."*

EMERGENCY MANAGERSHIP – (ee-*MER*-jen-see *MAN*-a-jer-ship) In partisan politics, a Republican strategy to emasculate Democratic districts. Bankrupt communities (poor, black, Democratic) are seized by the Republican governor. A Republican manager [read: *dictator*] is appointed to dismiss all elected officials, seize and sell all remaining public assets. The citizens are left as impotent serfs. The most egregious example of emergency managership has occurred in Michigan. This rendition of dictatorial government had resulted in the poisoned-water tragedy of Flint, Michigan.

EMERITUS – (e-*MER*-i-tus) A honorary designation for a retired professional (college professor) who is no longer active, though retaining his title – Professor Emeritus.

EMETOPHOBIA – (e-met-o-*FO*-bee-a) (Emetophobic) Phobic fear of vomiting. Any normal person would fear embarrassing the prospect of vomiting in public. Unless one was poisoned. Vomiting is a defense mechanism to instantly ride the body of ingested toxins. However, an emetophobic is a neurotic who is obsessed with the haunting fear.

EMIGRATION – (em-mi-*GRAY*-shun) Means both departing and entering a country. In 1789, the Americans invented the word *"immigration,"* to specifically mean entering the United States of America. This reflects, early on, an arrogance displayed by Americans, a sense of exceptionalism. Therefore to Americans, emigration means leaving a country, while immigration means entering a country (specifically, the U.S.A.). Other societies use the term emigration doing both ways.

EMINENCE GRISE – (*Ay*-mee-nahs *GREEZ*) Literally, *"gray eminence"* in French. Eminence grise means the power behind the throne. It refers to the person who wields de facto authority and influence, albeit unofficially, behind the scenes. The term was used to describe the wily French Capuchin friar, Pere Joseph (1577 – 1638), agent and confidant of Cardinal Richelieu (1585 – 1642), chief minister to King Louis XIII (1601 – 1643). Pere Joseph influenced Cardinal Richelieu, who influenced King Louis XIII. Being a Capuchin, the eminent monk, Pere Joseph wore a gray habit. Ergo, the *"Gray Eminence,"* or *"Eminence Grise,"* (the power behind the throne). Incidentally: No American President was ever more mesmerized by eminence grise than Donald Trump (b. 1946). Right-wing commentators Sean Hannity (b. 1961), Rush Limbaugh (b. 1951), Ann Coulter (b. 1961), Laura Ingraham (b. 1963) and many others have power over Trump. Fox News Network dictates governmental policy to Trump. In fact, the last person to have Trump's ear is his eminence grise.

EMINENT DOMAIN – (*EM*-min-ent do-*MAYN*) The right of government to expropriate *private* property for the *public* good. Without eminent domain, we would have no public facilities. Eminent domain is a form of *"nationalization,"* a Socialistic concept. It is a necessary procedure providing the property owner is fairly compensated, and the property goes to *public,* not *private* use. The injustice arises when the government takes a citizen's home or store and gives the land to Walmart. If the government can nationalize the little man's property for the public good, than it can nationalize the big corporations for the public good as well. Eminent domain is the legal precedent for the government's nationalization of all capitalist corporations – banks, insurance companies, corporations, utilities, transportation, agri-businesses everything. Eminent domain grants the government the right to Socialize the nation, for all the people.

EMISSARY – (*EM*-uh-sair-ree) A special envoy or representative sent on a errand, mission, or meeting, representing another. Often, the emissary's mission is confidential. Unlike an envoy who is a governmental official, an emissary can represent anyone.

EMISSARY/ENVOY – (*EM*-uh-ser-ee *ON*-voi) An envoy is a diplomatic agent of the second rank, next in status after an ambassador. An emissary is any agent sent on a mission to represent the interests of another. An envoy is a governmental agent. An emissary not necessarily so. Therefore, an envoy is a more important, prestigious position than an emissary.

EMMENTALER – (*EM*-men-tal-er) A small Swiss village, original home of Swiss cheese. In fact, *Emmentaler* is the official name for *Swiss cheese.*

EMMER – (*EM*-mer) A wild wheat-grass that grows along with einkorn wheat in the Near East. (Einkorn grows in cooler climate, farther north.) Both were among the first grains domesticated by man. Through a serendipitous cross- breeding with goat grass, emmer wheat evolved into precious bread wheat.

EMO – (*EE*-moh) (Emos) A truncation of the word <u>Emo</u>tion. Emo is a vague subcultural movement most prominent among white, middleclass suburban youth. Emo encompasses a distinctive music, dress, and attitudes. Emo emerged in the mid-1980s from the hardcore punk music culture. Its music came to be known as *"Emotional Hardcore,"* or *"Emocore."* The chief <u>emo</u>tion that governs Emo is depression. Emo music, like its devotees is pensive, cathartic, emphasizing <u>emo</u>tional expression, often with confessional lyrics. Though doleful and melancholy, Emo adherents are not necessarily always despondent. Emos display a distinctive style. They are reminiscent of the Hippies, minus the vitality, poverty, and strong convictions. Emos wear long, dyed hair that partially overs their eyes and faces. They like hoodie sweatshirts, skinny fit jeans, and skate shoes. You will notice them wearing many bracelets and wristbands. Emos portray a picture of angst, ennui, and drama. Many seem to be crying out for help, at least for answers. They are <u>emo</u>tionally fragile, seeking psycho-emotional catharsis. Although they certainly don't know it, Emos subscribe to the philosophy of Existentialism. *"We are condemned to be free,"* Existentialist Philosopher Jean Paul Sartre (1905 – 1980) lamented. "Often, being in awareness and being in despair coincide." – Existentialist Philosopher Aman Tiwari, in <u>*Memoir: The Cathartic Night*</u> (2020).

EMOJI – (ee-*MOH*-jee) In digital technology, a small digital or pictorial ideogram or symbol that represents a thing, concept, emotion, whatever. Emojis are used in text messages and other electronic communications and usually part of a standardized set. There are an infinite number of emojis and new ones popping up all the time. Emojis are intended to enhance the understanding, the meaning of a correspondence. For example: *"I am so very happy,"* would be accompanied by a grinning-face emoji ☺. Emoji is a Japanese term meaning *"pictograph."* The letter *"e"* refers to *"picture, drawing,"* and the term *"moji"* means *"written."* The word and usage gained popularity between 1990 – 95. Emojis should be used casually, for fun, not seriously, and never be invested with too much importance, authority. This can lead to grave misunderstandings. People have been sued and jailed for the lazy habit of substituting emojis for explanatory texts, thinking that the recipient will understand the message. An emoji is not appropriate in a contract or legal document. An obscene emoji can be interpreted as sexting which can be a crime. *"Whenever someone invents something good, someone else will come along and push it too far."* – Philosopher George Santayana (1863 – 1952).

Incidentally: According to artist and intellectual Rebecca Hanna Pasieka (b. 1996), of Bristol, England, *"Emojis are culturally specific. They are far more meaningful to the Japanese (who invented them), than to Westerners. The Japanese read significance into emojis that Westerners do not."*

EMOLLIENT – (em-*MOL*-lee-ent) Having the power of softening or relaxing. An emollient is soothing, as lotion is to the skin.

EMOLUMENT – (ee-*MOL*-yu-ment) Payment, fees, salary from office or employment. Emolument is honest compensation for services rendered.

EMOLUMENT CLAUSE – (em-*MOL*-you-ment *CLAWS*) Forty-nine words in Article I, Section 9, Clause 8, of the Constitution that prohibits public officials (including the President) from profiteering from the office. It reads: *"No Title of Nobility shall be granted by the United States: And no Person holding any Office of Profit or Trust under them, shall without the Consent of the Congress, accept of any present, Emolument, Office, or Title, of any kind whatever, from any King, Prince, or foreign State."* The Emolument Clause forbids putting the U.S. Government, officials, or policy up for sale. The Emolument Clause has been enforced throughout American History, *Until Now!* Actually, there has been little reason to enforce the Clause, *Until Now!* That's because there has never been a more blatantly corrupt, covetous, piggish gang in the White House than the Trumps. The Family Trump are the fattest most gluttonous swine, in Presidential History. The White House has become the *"Trump Trough."* There is no slimy sheik, or odious dictator, or vile tycoon who the Trumps won't suck- up to, in order to get richer. They peddle influence, take bribes, and alter U.S. Foreign Policy for self-enrichment. Formerly, Donald Trump (b. 1946), Donald Trump Jr. (b. 1977), Ivanka Trump (b. 1981), Eric Trump (b. 1984), and Jared Kushner (b. 1981) would be behind bars for violating the Emolument Clause. The shameless Republican Congress has given the Trumps tacit permission and encouragement to ignore the Constitution. If the Trumps were Democrats, they'd be in jail. But the vile Republican Congressmen do not want to lose their Republican *"sugar daddy"* to prison. *"Emolumentum ad absurdum!"* Incidentally: In early January, 2020, it was revealed that the shameless Trump has at least 300 known conflicts of interest, emolument violations, from which he profits. No President in American History has milked the office for personal gain as had Trump.

EMOTE – (ee-*MOHT*) The verb form of emotion. To emote is to express emotion or deep, passionate feelings. *"I can't help but to emote in a natural disaster."*

EMOTICONS – (ee-*MOHT*-ti-con) A digital icon or a sequence of keyboard symbols that serve to represent a facial expression, as :-) for a sideways smiling face. Emoticons are related to, but different from *emojis*, which are fully fashioned pictures. Emoticons are created by the writer. They are used in a digital (computer) message like emojis, to convey the writer's emotions or clarify intent – (emotion conveyers). ></))))*> something's fishy.

EMOTIONAL BANK ACCOUNT – (ee-*MOH*-shuhn-uhl *BANK* ak-*KOWNT*) The accumulation of love one has stored in her/his heart for another. Like a financial bank account, the emotional bank account is not infinite. There is a limit to how much love one can dole out to another. When someone is kind they make an emotional deposit into the account. But when someone is cruel, they make a withdrawal from the emotional bank account.

EMOTIONAL GENDER – (ee-*MOH*-shuhn-uhl *JEN*-der) Psychosexual role switching. One's psychological sex or mental sexual status. Emotional gender is the sexual fantasy one plays while engaged in sex. One's actual gender is decisively male or female. But one's emotional gender is who you imagine to be while making love. It is perfectly normal for a man to fantasize that he is the woman to whom he is love making. Conversely, it is not an aberration for a woman to imagine that she is the male partner through the intercourse. Embracing one's emotional gender is much more common than most are willing to admit. It is the exercise of our instinctive bisexual nature, and essential to mental health. Being the product of a father and mother, the average man is 60% male and 40% female. Likewise, the average woman is 60% female and 40% male. Of course, differences vary in individuals. Nevertheless, it is personally imperative that we uninhibitly acknowledge, accept, and celebrate our natural emotional gender. In *"The Gospel of Thomas,"* Jesus said: *"When you make the two into one, and when you make the inside like the outside and the outside like the inside and the above like below – that is, to make the male and the female into a single one, so that the male will not be male and the female will not be female… then you will enter the kingdom."*

EMOTIONAL HEMOPHILIACS – (ee-*MOH*-shuhn-uhl hee-mo-*FEE*-lee-aks) A sardonic term coined by comedian and social commentator Bill Mahar (b. 1956). Mr. Mahar is a pragmatic Progressive realist who becomes frustrated with bleeding-heart Liberals. He views them as emotional hemophiliacs. The slightest social bump, scratch, or bruise and they begin to bleed, so to speak. The extreme extent of their political correctness make dialogue with them impossible. They are super-sensitive. Their pain threshold is so shallow that they scream about every misplaced word. Freedom of speech is lost on them, according to Mr. Mahar. This is particularly troublesome for a comedian as is he. Emotional hemophiliacs cannot take a joke, unless it's directed against the conservative opposition.

EMOTIONS – (ee-*MOH*-shuhns) Mental, psychological <u>E</u>nergy in <u>MOTION</u>. Emotions are a state of feelings: happy, sad, worried, or fearful. Emotions govern moods, which affect attitudes, and drives behaviors. Physiologically, emotions are sensations brought on by neurotransmitters (brain chemicals). Enjoyable and distressful occurrences will trigger the neurotransmitters that will reinforce our emotions.

EMP – (ee em *PEE*) <u>E</u>lectro<u>M</u>agnetic <u>P</u>ulse bomb. A weapon delivered by an intercontinental ballistic missile, that when detonated would emit rapid and invisible bursts of electromagnetic energy, creating a devastating geomagnetic storm. This would jam a nation's or continent's entire power grid. Everything electrical would be fried. This means lights out, refrigeration down, phones dead, computers quit, vehicles stall, elevators halt, trains stop, planes drop from the sky. Modern civilization would cease. It is an ideal capitalist bomb, for it does minimal damage to private property. Nevertheless, an EMP would hurl society back 200 years in time. These bombs exist, and may be in the possession of volatile North Korea. With an ElectroMagnetic Pulse attack, death would come slowly for most. Starvation, dehydration, exposure (to heat or cold), isolation, lack of medication, depression would all take their toll. Only survivalists, trained to live in harmony with nature, rather than dependent on technology would endure. They would have to live off the Earth as our pioneer ancestors had, in order to survive an ElectroMagnetic Pulse (EMP) attack.

"If you worry about disaster all the time, that's what you're going to get." – Chuck Palahniuk (b. 1962). *"He who lives by electricity, will die by electricity."* – Kurt Vonnegut (1922 – 2007). *"Those dependant ob man-made technology are doomed. Those familiar with nature-made survival technology will prevail."* – Italian King Victor Emmanuel II (1820 – 1878).

EMPATH – (*EM*-path) (A Psychic Empath.) A person with the metaphysical power of psychic empathy. An empath is spiritually aware of another's thoughts, emotions, and supernaturally knows of another's life experiences. They can feel another's pain. Empaths can therefore diagnose medical problems and serve as healers. Police forces utilize the abilities of empaths in crime solving. They are sometimes called *"mentalists."*

EMPATHY – (*EM*-path-thee) (Empathetic, Empathetically) The Compassionate ability to feel another's despair. An empathetic person can relate to another's misery. Empathy is more than mere sympathy. To be empathetic is to act on ones feelings. That's because empathy is rooted in love. An empathetic person would never be a passive witness to another's pain. Empathy is cultivated through experience. Having suffered, I commiserate with those who suffer. As it is difficult for a camel to pass through the eye of a needle, so it is difficult for a rich man to empathize. British journalist Walter Bagehot (1826 – 1877) wrote: *"Poverty is an anomaly to rich people; it is very difficult to make out why people who want dinner do not ring the bell."* *"Empathy is seeing with the eyes of another, listening with the ears of another, and feeling with the heart of another."* – Psychiatrist Alfred Adler (1870 – 1937).

EMPIRE – (*Em*-pie-er) A number of underdeveloped territories, countries, regions ruled by a powerful imperial nation for economic exploitation. The imperial power of a colonial empire is always vastly more technologically advanced that the colonials. The British Empire is the classic example. Archaic colonial empires were ruled by a king of kings called an emperor. *"I have often before now been convinced that a democracy is incapable of empire."* – Thucydides (c. 460 – c. 400 BCE). This is true, but a capitalist democracy may create economic empires by usurping the invaded territory's natural resources. This is what America had done.

EMPIRICAL QUESTION – (em-*PEER*-ri-cal *KWEST*-shun) An inquiry or question that requires integration or analysis of remembered or given information to supply a predictable answer. For example: *"What marked the decline of the American middle class?"* *"The Reagan election of 1980 which shifted wealth from the middle class to the rich."*

EMPIRICISM – (em-*PEER*-ri-siz-um) A sub-philosophy of pragmatism, maintaining that all knowledge is derived from experience. Empirical means experiential, or through experience. Empiricists maintain that no knowledge is innate or a priori.

EMPORIATRICS – (em-por-ree-*AT*-riks) The field of medicine that studies the health of travelers. Jet lag, dietary diversity, water qualities, the stress of travel are all considered.

EMPORIUM – (em-*POR*-ree-um) A large retail store selling a vast variety of merchandise. Any large department store like Walmart qualifies as an emporium.

EMPTY CALORIES – (*EMP*-tee *CAL*-lor-rees) A non-nutritional energy source. The term empty calories applies to foods and drinks composed primarily or solely of sugar, fats, oils, or alcoholic beverages. Though these edibles provide energy, they lack nutritionals like vitamins, minerals, protein, fiber, or essential fatty acids. Candy, cake, cookies, softdrinks, potato chips, snacks, treats, beer, wine, whisky all supply empty calories. Empty calories will provide a quick boost, a temporary sugar high. That's great, providing it's employed occasionally, and is not the dietary staple. Empty calories will keep the machine running, albeit inefficiently, but will result in eventual breakdown. Incidentally: Poor people are often fat. Their obesity does not indicate prosperity, but rather poverty. Poor people rely on cheap empty caloric foods. Their poor diets consist of sweets, sodas, chips, cakes, liquor, inexpensive processed foods high in sugar and fats. The result is obesity, and all the health problems related to that condition. The condition is empty calories. The problem is poverty. The cause is capitalism. The solution is Socialism.

EMPYREAN – (em-puh-*REE*-uhn) (Empyreal) The firmament, the highest heaven. The ancients supposed that the empyrean contained the pure element of fire. The term "empyrean" derives from the Latin *"empyreus,"* that was taken from the Greek *"empyos,"* meaning *"fiery."* The etymological sense is *"formed of pure fire or light."* The ancient Greek cosmology of a fiery heaven was later replaced with a Christian sense of *"abode of God and the angels."*

EMULATION – (em-yoo-*LAY*-shun) (Emulate, Emulous) The desire or effort to equal or excel others. Emulation is competitive and is rooted in envy. To emulate is to imitate with the desire to equal or surpass.

EMULSION – (em-*MUL*-shun) Droplets dispersed in another liquid that will not mix into a solution, like oil in water. An emulsion is a colloid of liquid suspended within liquid.

EN BANC – (on *BONK*) (*In the bench.*) In law, a proceeding in which all judges of a court participate in the decision. The full panel of judges assigned to a court sit to hear a case *en banc*, usually a case of special significance. The U.S. Supreme Court sits en banc.

EN BLOC – (on *BLAWK*) French for *"as a whole."*

ENCEINTE – (en-*SAINT*) Pregnant with child.

ENCHILADA – (en-chuh-*LAH*-duh) In Mexican cooking, a tortilla wrap. An enchilada is a cornmeal flatbread tortilla roll filled with a seasoned mixture of meats, beans, potatoes, cheese, and various vegetables, drenched in a chili- based hot sauce. The term enchilada was first recorded about 1885. In Spanish it means *"spiced with chili."*

ENCLAVE – (*ON*-klayv) (also Exclave) A part of a country that is separated from the rest of the country by a foreign territory. This geopolitical situation can spell trouble. East Prussia, separated from Germany proper by the Polish Corridor provided an excuse for the German invasion of Poland in 1939, starting World War Two. Bangladesh (East Pakistan) separated from Pakistan proper by India resulted in a bloody war of independence won by Bangladesh (1971). Alaska is a huge enclave, separated from the U.S. proper by Canada. Europe's dangerous enclave is Russian Kaliningrad, on the Baltic Sea between Poland and Lithuania. Hawaii cannot be considered an enclave, because the Pacific Ocean is not a nation. It appears that the terms *"enclave"* and *"exclave"* are virtually synonymous. The only difference is that an enclave may be part of a nation within itself. For example, The city of Hamtramck is an enclave within the city of Detroit, Michigan.

ENCLOSURES – (en-*CLO*-shurs) (Also called the Clearances.) The 18th century practice of Scottish landlords to evict the peasants and turn the farms into sheep pastures. The people were cleared-out, the land was enclosed for the animals. Families who rented a hut and plot of land for generations were put out in the cold. Woolen blankets were in great demand as a trade item with the American Indians. Valuable furs were gained in return, especially beaver. The capitalistic gentry could not pass-up this lucrative opportunity, despite the hardship of the peasants. Thousands of poor people died due to the enclosures. *"The last capitalist we hang, will be hanged with the rope he sold to us."* – Dr. Karl Marx (1818 – 1883).

ENCRYPTION – (en-*KRIP*-shun) (Encrypt) To encipher, make secret. Encryption is the process of encoding a message or information, in such a way that only authorized parties can access it and those who are not authorized cannot. Encryption is used in computer cryptography.

ENCULTURATION – (en-cul-chur-*RAY*-shun) The sociological process of learning the cultural norms of one's group or society. Even the young native-born citizens must learn their culture or be encultured. That's what differentiates enculturation from acculturation, which involves immigrates adopting the entirely new culture of their new homes. Socialization is a part of greater enculturation.

ENCYCLODICTIONARIAN – (en-syk-lo-dik-shun-*AIR*-ee-an) A scholar who comprises encyclodictionaries. The author of this LIBERAL LEXICON: *A Socialistic, Spiritualistic Encyclodictionary* is an encyclodictionarian.

ENCYCLODICTIONARY – (en-syk-lo-*DIC*-shun-air-ree) An editorial reference book. A lexicon of encyclopedic nature. A dictionary/encyclopedia hybrid. This type of reference book contains the denotations of a conventional dictionary, with the implied connotations as well. Technical grammatical information, as found in a conventional dictionary is not included. Too, an encyclodictionary provides commentary and interesting anecdotes not found in a conventional dictionary. This very text is an encyclodictionary. Incidentally: This massive tome, the LIBERAL LEXICON: *A spiritualistic, Socialistic Encyclodictionary*, is an example.

ENCYCLOPEDIA – (en-syk-lo-*PEE*-dee-a) A book containing articles on various topics, usually in alphabetical order, covering all branches of knowledge, or all aspects of a subject. In a sense, an encyclopedia is an expanded type of dictionary. Even moreso is the hybrid encyclodictionary. *"Dictionary: The universe in alphabetical order."* – Anatole France (1844 – 1924).

ENCYCLOPEDIEST – (en-syk-lo-*PEE*-dist) A scholar who comprises encyclopedias.

ENDEMIC – (en-*DEM*-mic) When a plant or animal is found here, and nowhere else on Earth.

ENDLOSUNG – (*END*-lay-sung) German for *"final solution."* The fateful decision to exterminate Europe's Jews, made at the Wannsee Conference in Germany, January, 1942.

ENDOGAMY – (en-*DOG*-uh-mee) (Endogamy) The term *"gamy"* comes from the Greek *"gamia"* meaning *"marriage."* The prefix "en" is Greek for *"in."* Endogamy is marrying within the in group. It is a social expectation that one will marrry a partner of the same tribe, ethnic or religious group.

ENDOMORPH – (*EN*-do-morf) The body type of an obese person.

ENDONYM – (*EN*-doe-nim) A self-assigned name by the locals of a place, a pet name. For example: New York City's *"Hell Kitchen,* or *"Little Italy,"* or Detroit's *"Corktown,"* or *"Paradise Valley."*

ENDORPHINS – (en-*DOR*-fins) (<u>ENDO</u>genous Mo<u>RPHIN</u>e) A group of peptides occurring in the brain and other tissues of vertebrates resembling opiates. They react with the brain's opiate receptors to raise the pain threshold. In this way endorphins act as natural pain killers.

ENDOTHERMIC – (en-do-*THER*-mic) (Endothermal) Literally *"heat from within."* Warm-blooded animals like mammals and birds are endothermic. They generate their own body heat. Body temperature remains constant, between 98 degrees and 112 degrees Fahrenheit, depending on the animal, despite the environment. The smaller the animal, the higher the body temperature must be. The opposite of endothermic is *ectothermic* or cold-blooded animals, dependent largely on the environment to regulate their body temperatures. Generally speaking, endothermic (warm-blooded) animals use much of their energy keeping warm. Ectothermic (cold-blooded) creatures use much of their energy growing larger to conserve heat.

ENDUE – (en-*DOO*) (Endued) To invest or endow with some gift, quality, or faculty. *"But suddenly, he was endued with courage."*

ENDURING PATTERNS – (en-*DUR*-ring *PAT*-turns) Ancient cultural traditions still practiced, though the origins and meanings are lost in the mist of time. For instance, christening a new ship by smashing it with a bottle of champagne. Champagne was substituted for fast staining red wine. Red wine was a substitute for red blood of a human sacrifice. The pattern endures with no reason why.

ENEMY – (*EN*-nem-mee) Anyone who is perceived as a dangerous threat in any way. An enemy is someone who generates fear. Fear is the anxiety that comes with perceived loss. Therefore, an enemy represents the fear of loss: of life, property, loved-ones, prestige, whatever is cherished. Eliminate the fear and you eliminate the enemy.

ENEMY'S ENEMY – (*EN*-ne-mees *EN*-ne-mee) *"My enemy's enemy is my friend."* Enemy's enemy is a policy to support someone you loath, because your enemy loaths them more. A great example from the 20th century is Winton Churchill's (1874 – 1965) relationship with Joseph Stalin (1878 – 1953) and the Soviet Union. Churchill, as an aristocrat and imperialist feared and hated Communism. Socialist Russia was a long-term threat to the British rich and the British Empire. Too, Churchill despised and distrusted perfidious Stalin, (it takes one to know one). Nevertheless, Churchill allied and supported Russia during World War Two, because Britain's enemy, Nazi Germany, was a bigger enemy to Russia. Russia ceased to be an enemy, until Germany was defeated. *"I would make a pact with the devil, if it would help me defeat Germany,"* Churchill explained. A more subtle example exists today in America. Donald Trump (b.

1946) is immoral, dishonest, criminal, the antithesis of Jesus, an anti-Christ figure in fact. Nevertheless, Fundamentalist Evangelical Christians admire, support, revere Trump. Why? Because their enemy's enemy is their friend. The enemy of Fundamentalist Christians are Liberal Progressives. For the longest time, the Fundamentalists felt scorned, insulted, humiliated, by the Liberals. Fundamentalists hate the Liberals, and the Liberals hate Trump. Conversely, Trump hates the Liberals. That is the conscious or subconscious reason why Fundamentalists love Trump. Fundamentalists know that Trump is a cad, a lout, an immoral Godless heathen. However, they love how the Liberals disdain Trump. Therefore, the Fundamentalists will sacrifice their morals in order to savor their disdain for the left.

ENERGY – (*EN*-ner-jee) Power, force, heat. Energy is loosely compacted matter. Conversely, matter is tightly compressed energy. The two, energy and matter are inter-convertible. Actually, energy is one of several vibratory frequencies of light. Light energy vibrating at a very low frequency congeals into matter. So when matter is dense, its energy level is low. When energy is intense, the matter is diffuses or spread-out widely. Burning converts matter into energy slowly. A nuclear reaction converts matter into energy rapidly.

ENERGY WORK – (*EN*-ner-jee *WERK*) Any activity that involves changes in the human energy field or subtle body. Energy work is commonly used as part of a holistic healing regimen or alternative medicine. The practitioner makes adjustments to the flow of life energy at the 7 chakras. She may use various techniques including acupuncture, acupressure, or may use crystals or their energy through Reiki or Laying of Hands.

ENERVATE – (*EN*-ner-vate) To weaken, exhaust, draw out the strength and wear out the will of a fighting force or competitor. Europeans in the tropics and semi- tropical New World were soon enervated by the heat. So they imported African slaves to work their plantations.

ENGINE – (*EN*-jin) Any mechanical contrivance or machine, with moving parts. As such, an engine is an advanced, complicated, sophisticated tool (a machine). Engines today are usually fuel-powered, as the internal-combustion engine in a car, boat, or plane. However historic engines simply required moving parts, as the hand-operated cotton gin or en<u>gi</u>ne. The term engine is inaccurately used interchangeably with motor. A motor is a comparatively small and powerful electrically-powered engine. It converts electrical energy into mechanical energy or work. A <u>motor</u>boat is actually powered by an engine.

ENGINEER – (en-jin-*NEER*) A professionally trained person, skilled in the design, construction, and use of engines or machines, usually mechanical or electrical, and in any of various branches related to those machines. Engineers occupy a higher technical grade than technicians. Engineers create, whereas technicians merely maintain.

ENGINEERING DISASTERS – (en-jin-*NEER*-ing dis-*AS*-ters) The failure of some infrastructural creation resulting in extreme damage and often tragic loss of life. Buildings topple, bridges collapse, dams burst, planes crash, factories explode. As a general rule, 3 things must go wrong in order to trigger an engineering disaster. Ordinarily, the bad luck (and engineering) of 3 mishaps must occur, compounding each other. Often, one of the 3 factors may not be man-made, but rather nature related. Wind, rain, lightning, earthquake is often a contributing factor. In fact, 40% of airline accidents are weather related. However, nature must be taken into account when engineering a structure. Research shows that the cascade of failures that result in engineering disasters often begin in connecting joints of a structure. Use of superior (albeit more expensive) materials will avert tragedies. So will increased governmental safety regulations. Both suggestions are vehemently opposed by corporate capitalists.

ENGINEER'S CREDO – (en-jin-*NEERS CRAY*-dow) *"One test is worth a thousand expert opinions."*

ENGLISH – (*ING*-lish) A Teutonic- based language that broke away from High German about 1,800 to 1,700 years ago. Middle English began as a Saxon/Danish hybrid dialect. Later with the Norman Conquest, English was fortified with a great admixture of Franco-Latin words. English is the most widespread and influential language in the world. It has a greater vocabulary than any other language. It is the language of science, diplomacy, and air travel. Most of the world's publications, radio and television broadcasts are in English. English is the *lingua franca* of planet Earth. No one will rise to any level of prominence, anywhere on Earth without a knowledge of English.

ENGLISH CARIBBEA – (*ING*-lish car *RIB*-bee-a) The former English colonials of the Caribbean Basin who speak a dialect of English. They include the citizens of Jamaica, Barbados, Trinidad and Tobago, Guyana, Belize, Grenada, Dominica, Montserrat, Anguilla, St. Lucia, The Bahamas, Cayman Islands, Virgin Islands, Antigua and Barbuda, St. Kitts and Nevis, Turks and Caicos Islands, St. Vincent and the Grenadines. English-speaking Caribbeans are primarily Black, being of African heritage.

ENGLISHED – (*ING*-lish'd) The verb form of the noun English. *"To English"* is to change an awkwardly foreign word into a word easier for English speakers. This is a form of convenient corruption. The spelling of the new word is Anglofied. For example: the Mongol capital *Shag-tu* was Englished into *Xanadu*.

ENHANCED INTERROGATION – (en-*HANS'D* in-ter-ro-*GAY*-shun) To inflict physical torment or psychological anguish in an attempt to extract information from *detainees*. Enhanced interrogation is predicated on the twisted premise that the ends justify the means. Enhanced interrogation is merely a euphemism for torture. Water-boarding, terrorizing with dogs, sensory deprivation, Confining individuals in coffins, freezing and over-heating prisoners are preferred procedures. Unlike burning, cutting, whipping, they do not leave marks as evidence. Religious and sexual humiliation has been found to break devout Muslims. Torture is unreliable for people will say anything in agonizing delirium. *"American Exceptionalists"* insist the U.S. does not torture. Nevertheless, the U.S. has been placed on an *"International Torture Watch List."* Yale History Professor John Merriman (b. 1946) said: *"Torture had hurt the United States gravely. Being put on the Torture List had really hurt America.... America had lost so much prestige, endearment, clout, and respect."* Former French Minister of Foreign Affairs and Socialist, Bernard Kouchner (b. 1939) lamented for the U.S.A.: *"The magic is gone. The magic is over. Things will never be the same again [for America]."*

ENIGMA – (en-*NIG*-ma) (Enigmatic) An inexplicable, bewildering occurrence or personality.

ENIGMA MACHINE – (en-*NIG*-ma *MA*-sheen) A German typewriter-like cryptographic message transmitter used during World War Two. The electro- mechanical rotor cipher machine coded and decoded diplomatic and military correspondence. Poland was the center of cryptology between the World Wars. A trio of Polish mathematicians turned cryptologists broke the Enigma Machine's secrets. It was the most complex code the world had ever seen. The task was statistically impossible. The number of different combinations the German system could theoretically produce was cosmic: 3 x 10 to the 114th power! (That is 3 followed by 114 zeros.) Consider that statistical impossibility is agreed to be 10 to the 50th power! The number of possibilities the machine could produce was 158 million, million! (The number of atoms estimated in the visible universe is 10 to the 80th power!) Nevertheless, the Poles succeeded. Furthermore, a Polish radio manufacturer (secretly working for Polish Intelligence) built an Enigma Machine, simply from mathematical equations! They turned the machine over to British Intelligence. It provided a treasure trove of crucial secret intelligence on the war. The Enigma Machine shortened the war by at least a year, maybe two, and thus saved countless lives. The actual information provided by the Enigma Machine was code-named *"Ultra"* by the British.

ENIGMATICALS – (en-ig-*MA*-ti-cals) (Also called Problematicals, Emblematicals, and Ceremonials.) Ancient artifacts that anthropologists cannot explain. They serve no discernible utilitarian purpose. Enigmaticals are probably magical, shamanistic implements. There practical usage cannot be determined with any certainty. They therefore stand as an enigma.

ENJOIN – (en-*JOYN*) In law to require an individual by writ of injunction to perform or refrain from a certain act.

ENLARGED HEART – (en-*LARJD HART*) (Cardiomegaly) Enlargement of the heart is a critical medical condition. It may have several causes. It is usually the result of morbid obesity. High blood pressure or coronary artery disease may also result in cardiomegaly. Being enlarged, the heart may not pump blood effectively, which can lead to congestive heart failure. Some symptoms are: Shortness of breath; Leg swelling; Palpitations or skipped heartbeats; and Tired feeling. Athletes are not exempt from cardiomegaly. Bodybuilders can be particularly at risk. The heart must do much more work to feed a bigger body. This is dangerous if the cardiovascular system is not aerobically conditioned. The heart itself will enlarge to accommodate the enlarged body. That seems good, but it's not, if the heart is weak. Now the heart has to work even harder to feed its enlarged self as well. Too, the coronary arteries that crown and feed the heart, cannot accommodate the enlarged organ. The best assurance against cardiomegaly is to become cardiovascularly fit, through aerobic exercise.

ENLIGHTENMENT – (en-*LITE*-ten) Literally *"Being in the Light,"* or Divine Grace. Enlightenment is balancing your biology with your spirituality, your human and divine natures. A key to enlightenment is tolerance. In Buddhism, enlightenment is experiencing of one's own essential or true nature and therefore awakening to the nature of all existence, as in the Buddha's *"awakening"* under the sacred Bodhi Tree. Enlightenment in Buddhism is somewhat equivalent to transformation in Hinduism, and salvation in Christianity. The 3 essential aspects of enlightenment are: Nonresistance, Nonattachment, and Nonjudgment. In *The Gospel of Thomas* Jesus said: *"If someone becomes like God, he will become full of light. But if he becomes one, separated from God, he will become full of darkness."* Incidentally: The spiritual teacher Ram Dass (b. 1931) asked his teacher, Hindu Guru Neem Karoli Baba (c. 1900 – 1973): *"How can I best be enlightened?"* Guru Baba replied: *"Love people."* *"Enlightenment is not about becoming divine. Instead it's about becoming more fully human. It is the end of ignorance."* – Surya Das (b. 1950). *"The person who says, 'I'm enlightened' probably isn't. If you think you are enlightened, spend two weeks with your parents."* – Ram Dass (b. 1931).

"Enlightenment is ego's ultimate disappointment." "It's possible to be completely enlightened — except with your family." – Chogyam Trungpa (1939 – 1987).

ENLIGHTENMENT – (en-*Lite*-ten-ment) In European History, the *"Child of the Renaissance,"* the *Age of Reason.* The Enlightenment was the period of Western thought, beginning in the late 17th century and driven by the *Scientific Revolution,* in which the power of reason was elevated over the authority of religion and tradition. The culmination, the crowning achievement of the Enlightenment was the *French Revolution* (1789 – 1799). Unlike the American Revolution, the French Revolution introduced the concept of distributive justice with *"Liberty, Equality, and Fraternity."*

EN MASSE – (on *MAS*) French for *"In mass."* In a large body.

ENNUI – (on-*WEE*) A profound boredom. A feeling of utter weariness and discontent. Ennui is a lack of interest, purposelessness, adrift without a goal. Life seems meaningless. Ennui often arises from overindulgence and satiety. The individual lacks the capacity to be stimulated. An often sought avenue for stimulation is drugs. Too, people suffering from ennui are vulnerable to manipulation by messianic demagogues. The despair of ennui is fertile ground for the ascendency of fascist dictators. Many of the *"stupids"* who support charlatan Donald Trump (b. 1946) suffer from ennui.

ENOCHLOPHOBIA – (en-ock-lo-*Fo*-bee-a) (also Ochlophobia) Phobic fear of crowds.

ENOUGH – (ehn-*NUHF*) Having an adequate amount. Possessing a sufficient amount to fulfill a want or need. One who is not greedy is satisfied with enough. *"Enough is abundance to the wise."* – Euripides (c. 480 – c. 406 BCE). *"He who knows enough is enough will always have enough."* – Lao Tzu (c. 604 – c. 531 BCE).

ENOUGH IS ENOUGH – (ehn-*NUHF* iz ehn-*NUHF*) An awkward, tiresome cliché that is ubiquitously used in all social strata. The word *"enough"* means adequate for the want or need; sufficient for the purpose or to satisfy desire. However the two usages of enough in this phrase bear different meanings. In this redundant cliché, the first term means *"much,"* while the second means *"too much."* Enough is enough is a cry of despair, frustration, exasperation. It means *"I'm fed-up!" "I've had a bellyful!" "Let's do something!"* This phrase is applied in situations of profound disappointment, gross inaction, and negligent neglect. For example, with every new mass-murder in America, every other conscientious politician cries: *"ENOUGH is ENOUGH!"* Today, gun control is the recipient of *"enough is enough"* ad nauseum. Incidentally: *"Enough is enough"* is not a recent annoyance. It was a popular cliché in England before John Heywood (c. 1497 – c. 1580) recorded it in his book of proverbs in 1546. *"Enough with enough is enough!" "He who knows enough is enough will always have enough."* – Lao Tzu (c. 604 – c. 531 BCE).

ENQUIRIZATION – (en-kwy-er-eye-*ZA*-shun) The floating of false news stories in the hope that reputable news agencies will report them, and therefore be set up for ridicule. The term *"Enquirization"* is taken from the *National Enquirer,* a sensational scandal publication, read by the most hopelessly stupid. The Trump presidency had taken a page out of the National Enquirer and has disseminated *"fake news,"* in order to damage the credibility of the press, and dupe the electorate. Enquirization is used as a trap to defame respected reporters critical of the Trump regime. It is hoped that the public will lose faith in the free press reporting of the multiple Trump scandals and crimes.

ENRONIZATION – (en-ron-eye-*ZAY*-shun) A term for all that is corrupt about corporate capitalism. Enron was a Houston-based corporation that traded in energy. It was the 7th largest corporation in the U.S.A. Its leadership lied about its earnings, hid its debt, and collapsed the company. Many investors lost everything including retirement savings. Many Enron executives got very rich. When the bubble burst, several were convicted of criminal fraud. But capitalism is inherently fraud. Enron epitomized capitalist greed. The Enronization of big business is proof that corporate capitalism is a ticking time bomb. It must be replaced by state [read: *people*] controlled Socialism.

ENSEMBLE – (on-*SAHM*-bo) French for all the parts of a thing taken together, so that each part is considered only in relations to the whole. In an ensemble, all units are mutually dependent, like a choir or orchestra. Too, an ensemble is the entire attire or costume, with all matching pieces.

ENSHA ALLAH – (*En*-sha *A*-la) Arabic for *"The Will of God."* Ensha Allah expresses the Muslim faith in God's goodness, submission and surrender to God's care.

ENTAIL – (*EN*-tail) Law that restricted the descent of an estate to a specified line of heirs. Entail decreed that great lordly estates could not be divided and subdivided. Partition the gentry's land, and you destroy the landed gentry. So the wealth was kept in the family. The entire estate was bequeathed to the eldest son (primogeniture) who became the lord. Entail, like primogeniture, was a means of maintaining aristocratic power.

ENTANGLED SKEIN – (en-*TANG*-guld *SKINE*) A skein is a length of yarn or thread wound around a reel. If the skein becomes entangled, it is knotted, disordered, confused, putting a stop to further progress. An entangled skein may be used to describe an issue, project, or organization that is in chaotic disarray. The Trump White House is a political, administrative entangled skein, for instance.

ENTHEOGENS – (en-*THEE*-oh-jens) (Entheogenic, Entheomania) Holy hallucinogens. Entheogens are psychoactive substances that induce alterations in perception, mood, consciousness, cognition, and behavior. Entheogens are mind-altering plant chemicals. Some can be synthesized in a lab. The primary purpose of partaking in entheogens is to enhance spiritual development.

Shamans worldwide have used entheogens from time immemorial in divination, spiritual healing, and communion with God. In fact, the *"theo"* in en<u>theo</u>gens means *"God"* in Greek.

ENTHEOMANIA – (en-*THEE*-o-may-nee-a) Neurotic belief that one is divinely inspired. Entheomania is induced by smoking or ingesting enthegenic plant chemicals, as do tribal shamans.

ENTHUSIASM – (en-*THOOS*-see-as-um) *En Theos*, literally *"God in you."* Enthusiasm is zealous devotion, fervor, interest in a task, a key to success. Nothing great was ever accomplished without an abundance of enthusiasm. Enthusiasm is a reflection of fun, excitement, joy for the job.

ENTITLEMENT REFORM – (en-*TIE*-till-ment ree-*FORM*) The hard-hearted, cold-blooded Republican intent to cancel, eliminate, destroy, the social safety net, to which non-affluent Americans are entitled. The term *"reform"* is a Republican euphemism for *"replace"* or *"destroy."* They must disguise their real motives in order to maintain the support of uninformed people, to vote against their own economic interests, which are the entitlements. The capitalist Republicans have campaigned to denigrate the term *"entitlement."* They are trying to conflate entitlement with *"mooching,"* or *"freeloading."* Republicans hope to stigmatize entitlement reception with shame. Actually, we are indeed entitled to Social Security, Medicare, Medicaid, welfare, unemployment payments – all the entitlements – as American citizens and children of God. Entitlement Reform is a Republican ruse to undo 130 years of Socialistic progress toward distributive justice.

ENTITLED – (en-*TY*-tuld) (Entitle, Entitling, Entitlement). Originally, in the mid- 15th century, to be entitled meant to be bestowed with a rank or office, along with a title (Sir), as in knighthood. Too, to be entitled meant to be granted the title, or legal rights to estates or property. Therefore, entitled came to mean a right, qualification, claim, or something deserved. Today, civilized societies maintain that the poor are entitled to support from the state. So welfare or government assistance programs have come to be called entitlements. By 2019, the term entitled acquired another meaning, quite the opposite from the poor. Entitled came to refer to the arrogant rich. The wealthy who feel they deserve a special, privileged position in society are called the entitled.

ENTITLEMENTS – (en-*TY*-till-ments) Earned Benefits. Programs and benefits using established eligibility requirements to provide health, nutritional, or income supplements to needy citizens. Conservatives have created a pejorative image for Social Security, welfare, Medicare, Medicaid, social survival benefits. Conservative Republicans consider entitlements handouts, and the recipients freeloaders. Actually, we are indeed *entitled* to our *entitlements* as citizens, human beings, and children of God. Social entitlements benefit not just the recipients, but all citizens. The Republicans have slandered, denigrated the word entitlement. Therefore the term *"Earned Benefits"* is used in its stead. *"Effective defense demands better nutrition, better housing, better day-to-day medical care, better education, better recreation for every age."* – Eleanor Roosevelt (1884 – 1962). Incidentally: In China, 500 years before Jesus, Confucius (551 – 479 BCE), *"The Patron Saint of Government Administrators"* decreed that children and the elderly were entitled to be fed at State expense. Too, universal education was free for all.

ENTITY – (*EN*-tit-tee) A real thing that has a real existence. The term entity describes a non-specific being with an independent existence and personality. In other words, a conscious thing with a self-contained existence. In metaphysical circles, the term entity is used to refer to non-corporeal, ethereal, or cryptozoological beings, or ordinary material beings as well.

ENTOMOLOGY – (on-tom-*MOL*-lo-jee) A bug scientist. A branch of zoology that studies insects. Caveat: Don't confuse entomology with etiology, the investigation of causes; or etymology, the study of word origins.

ENTOMOPHOBIA – (on-tom-o-*FO*-bee-a) Phobic fear of bugs, insects.

ENTOURAGE – (*ON*-tour-roj) Retinue, hangers-on. A group of attendants or associates that accompany a celebrity or V.I.P. To be trailed by an entourage is a status symbol for celebrities. The retinue feeds on the celebrity's fame.

ENTRAPMENT – (en-*TRAP*-ment) To be snared, perhaps unfairly, by police in some illegal activity. To be lured by a law-enforcement agent to commit a crime. Is a *"bait car,"* placed in a poor neighborhood a trap to snare desperate youths? After all, the temptation is screaming out: *"Take me, I'm yours."* So does a gorgeous woman. The police will use a female undercover cop acting as a prostitute. Perhaps the gentleman never had criminal solicitation in mind until approached by the *"hooker-cum-cop."* Other times, the victim may be set- up in a situation that appears to be criminal. This is an illegal, unethical *"sting operation."* FBI Director J. Edgar Hoover (1895 – 1972) was a guilt-ridden gay. He was a prurient who loved to victimize celebrities and politicians with sexual entrapment. Hoover considered author John Steinbeck (1902 – 1968) a Communist and the most dangerous man in America. This was due to Steinbeck's book, <u>The Grapes of Wrath</u> (1939). A sympathetic sheriff had warned Steinbeck to stay out of motel rooms. He was told *"The Boys"* [read: FBI] planned to frame him. A frantic woman would burst into the room, rip-off her clothes, scratch herself, and scream *"RAPE!"* Hoover attempted a similar stunt on Rev. Martin Luther King (1929 – 1968) and had dossiers on all the Kennedy brothers. Incidentally: Entrapment may occur outside of law enforcement. It can occur in the office. A female co-worker may savor dressing as a salacious seductress. She may enjoy the sexual tension she creates in the atmosphere. But when the gentlemen engage in the game and make propositions, they are penalized with sexual harassment. Entrapment? In this example, Sociology is pitted against Biology. In too many cases, Biology is the victor for, *"An erect penis has no conscience."*

ENTREAT – (en-*TREET*) To beg, implore or beseech. One may entreat for mercy.

ENTRÉE – (*ON*-tray) The dish served as the main course of the meal. In America, it is usually some sort of meat, fish, animal flesh. Ironically, entrée is French for *"entry."* Originally, the entrée was an appetizer, a starter at the entrance of the meal. With time, meals simplified. Though the entree dish was often eliminated, the entrée term was not. It was passed on to the main course, which today is the entrée.

ENTREMETS – (*ON*-tre-may) French for a side dish. A dish or dishes served at dinner between or after the main course. An entremets is an opulent gluttony of the self-indulgent capitalist/aristocratic rich.

ENTREPRENEUR – (on-tray-pren-*NEUR*) An economic risk taker. An entrepreneur is an imaginative, enterprising, innovating, idea-monger. Unfortunately, capitalism turns entrepreneurs into greedy, self-serving exploiters, bent on private profit rather than service to mankind. Capitalist entrepreneurs cheat and deceive their way to the top, destroying all weaker obstacles in their path. A textbook example is *"His Swindleness,"* President Donald Trump (b. 1946).

ENTREPRENEURIAL DELUSION – (on-tray-pren-*NEUR*-ree-al dee-*LOOSH*-shun) The favorite American capitalist lie that everyone has the opportunity to be a capitalist, to become rich, and to join the plutocracy. The delusional entrepreneurial credo is: *"You too can become a millionaire."* The entrepreneurial delusion is part of the equally delusional and deceptive concept of *"American Exceptionalism."* The entrepreneurial delusion has been employed to suppress the Socialist movement in America. The American poor were persuaded not to pull down the rich, but instead to join them, while suppressing the leveler. Entrepreneurial delusion is a pipe dream.

ENTREPRENEURIAL INCLUSIONISM – (on-tray-pren-*NEUR*-ree-al in-*KLOO*-shuhn- iz-uhm) Part of the fictitious American Dream that under capitalism: *"In the U.S.A., you too can become a millionaire."* For about 150 years capitalists have been tempting citizens away from Socialism with greedy acquisition rather than generous redistribution. The entrepreneurial inclusionist argument is that free enterprise frees everyone to get rich. *Fat chance!* This proposal is false and a lie. The entrepreneurial geniuses among us are few and far between. It takes a special person with special talents to join the plutocracy. It requires unique intelligence, cleverness, ruthlessness, even heartlessness to win the capitalist rat race. Match all that with damned good luck and you too can become a millionaire. Actually, the American Dream today has been reduced to winning the lottery.

ENTROPY – (*EN*-tro-pee) The nature of energy to dissipate, of motion to slow and stop, of all things to age, wear-out, to fall apart. Entropy is the natural movement toward decay, chaos, disorganization, death. Entropy is the result of time. Entropy is a breakdown, preceding a recycling, resulting in a buildup. *"And I will die, and you will die, and we all will die, and even the stars will fade out one after another in time."* – Jack Kerouac (1922 – 1969).

ENTRUMPMENT – (en-*TRUMP*-ment) (Entrump, Entrumped, Entrumpified) Trumpistic entrapment. Entrumpment is being trapped by Trump in Donald's ideological dungeon. This is the fate of Republican politicians, particularly Congressmen. Entrumpment occurs in conservative red states and in Republican gerrymandered Congressional districts. These polities are homogeneously single-minded and simple-minded (like Trump). Too, they have been highjacked by Donald Trump's (b. 1946) vile Svengali spell. These regions have therefore been Trumpified. The Republican politicians who hope to represent these regions must also Trumpify. They must surrender their independence, intellect, and integrity and succumb to Trump's shameless demands in order to hold office. They have been politically and morally emasculated. These Republicans are servile victims of Entrumpment.

ENUNCIATION – (en-nun-see-*AY*-shun) Articulation. The proper and distinct pronunciation of words. When enunciated accurately, speech is clear and understandable. Foreign accents play havoc on enunciation.

ENURESIS – (en-yuh-*REE*-sis) Bed-wetting; nighttime urinary incontinence; lack of control over urination, especially during sleep. Ordinarily, enuresis afflicts the very young and the very old. There are several causes of enuresis, both physical and psycho-emotional. Physically, bladder disorders like infections nay cause bed-wetting. Emotional stress with induce children to wet their bed during sleep. Enuresis is apparent in children who are abused in any number of ways. Incidentally: Enuresis is part of the *"Macdonald Triad,"* which identifies troubled children capable of becoming sociopaths or even psychopaths. Enuresis, along with arson and zoosadism (animal cruelty) are common factors, indicators, of children in danger of growing up to be psychopathic serial killers. Sexual abuse of a child generates stress that will cause enuresis, which serves as a sign of later psychopathy, according to research.

ENVIRONMENTAL DNA – (en-vy-ron-*MENT*-tal *DEE EN AY*) (eDNA) Deoxyribonucleic acid collected from our surroundings. Environmental DNA samples may be taken from the soil, water, snow, even the air. Samples of eDNA can be deposited by saliva, feces, urine, mucus, gametes hair, skin cells, and carcasses. Such samples can be analyzed by high-throughtput DNA sequencing methods, known as metagenomics, metabarcoding, and single- species detection for rapid monitoring and measurement of biodiversity.

ENVIRONMENTALISM – (en-vy-ron-*MENT*-tal-is-um) Prudential environmentalism is concerned with the preservation of natural resources to assure long-term exploitation. It is a conservative approach, characteristic of capitalism. Ethical environmentalism is concerned with protecting nature for nature's sake, believing that all life is precious as well as their habitat. This is the Liberal, Socialistic approach to environmentalism. Environmentalism was vital to Native American survival. A Cree Indian prophecy declares: *"When all the trees have been cut down, when all the animals have been hunted, when all the waters have been dirtied, when all the air is unsafe to breathe, only then will you discover you cannot eat money."*

ENVISION – (en-*VIZH*-uhn) (Envisioned, Envisioning) To imagine, to picture mentally, especially some future event. One must first envision before one can create.

ENVOY – (*ON*-voi) An envoy is a diplomatic agent of the second rank, next in status after an ambassador. A special emissary or representative sent on an important errand, mission, or meeting for the government. Often, the envoy's mission is of a confidential diplomatic nature.

ENVOY/EMISSARY – (*ON*-voi *EM*-uh-ser-ee) An envoy is a diplomatic agent of the second rank, next in status after an ambassador. An emissary is any agent sent on a mission to represent the interests of another. An envoy is a governmental agent. An emissary not necessarily so. Therefore, an envoy is a more important, prestigious position than an emissary.

ENVY – (en-*VEE*) The covetous feeling that *"I want what's yours."* Envy tends to create a sense of false competition. Envy is always confused with jealousy which is the fearful belief that *"you want what's mine."* *"Our envy always lasts longer than the happiness of those we envy."* – Heraclitus (535 – 475 BCE). *"Envy creates the beginning of strife."* – Democritus (c. 460 – c. 370 BCE).

EON – (*EE*-on) (Also Aeon) A billion year period. The universe is estimated to be 13.7 eons old.

EONISM – (*EE*-on-is-um) Male Transvestism. A neurotic compulsion in a man to adopt a woman's clothing and mannerisms.

EPHEBOPHILIA – (ep-heh-boh-*FEE*-lee-ah) (Ephebophiliac) (also Hebephilia) A neurotic paraphilial disorder in which one is sexually attracted to adolescents.

EPHEMERAL – (ef-*FEM*-er-al) Transitory, temporary, impermanent. Anything ephemeral is short lived, not long lasting.

EPHEMERAL LITERATURE – (ef-*FEM*-er-al *LIT*-ter-ra-chur) Temporary print as with newspapers, magazines, billboards, advertisements, commercial literature.

EPI – (*EP*-pee) A prefix loanword from Greek meaning *"upon, on, over, near, at, before, after."*

EPICANTHUS – (e-pi-*CAN*-thus) A fold of skin from the eyelid over the inner canthus (corner) of the eye, characteristic of Oriental people. The epicanthic fold produced the *"slant-eyed"* appearance. It is thought to have evolved in their ancient Mongolian ancestors as a defense mechanism from blizzards, snow blindness, and sandstorms.

EPICENTER – (*EP*-pee-sen-ter) The point on the Earth's surface that corresponds to the location in the Earth where an earthquake originates. The epicenter is ground zero.

EPICURE – (*EP*-pi-cur) (Epicurean) A self-indulgent gourmet. A connoisseur of fine food and wine. An epicure cultivates a discriminating palate for the enjoyment of the very best cuisine. An epicure always insists on the highest quality of exotic ingredients. The dishes must be impeccably prepared. An epicure's kitchen is an art studio of cookery, in which lavish specialties are created. Expense can never be a consideration. That's why only rich capitalists can afford to be epicures. Eating becomes an orgasmic experience. Presentation to the epicure is as important as taste. An epicurean is usually a pig, one self-indulgent in luxury and sensual pleasures.

EPICUREANISM – (e-pi-*CUR*-ree-an-is-um) (Epicure) Today, an epicurean is a gourmet at best, a glutton at worst. He is fond of luxury and indulging in sensual pleasures, especially in eating and drinking. However, the original Epicurean philosophers of classical Greece simply believed that the goal of life was happiness, achieved by a life of moderation, simplicity, and friendship. The founder of the philosophical school was Epicurus (341 – 270 BCE). He taught that the contemplative pleasures were preferred over the sensuous pleasures. Nevertheless, the definition has mutate to mean one who is appetite oriented.

EPIDEMIC – (ep-pi-*DEM*-mic) Prevalent, widespread. An epidemic is affecting many persons at the same time in a *locality*, as does a contagious disease.

EPIGENETICS – (ep-pi-jen-*NET*-tics) The branch of genetics that studies how heritable traits can be modified by environmental influences or other mechanisms without a change to the DNA sequence. Epigenetics is the victory of sociology over biology, of nurture over nature. In a sense, epigenetics represents the triumph of the will.

EPIGRAM – (*EP*-pi-gram) (Epigrammatic) A witticism or quip. A very clever, pointed saying tersely expressed, is epigrammatic.

EPIGRAPH – (*Ep*-pi-graf) An inscription, especially on a monument, statue, or building. An epigraph is also an appropriate quotation at the heading of a book or chapter.

EPILEPSY – (*EP*-uh-lep-see) (Epileptic) A neurological brain disorder effecting the entire nervous system of the body. An epileptic episode may be mild (*petit mal*) or severe (*grand mal*). A petit mal seizure is characterized by dizziness, sleepiness, and loss of attention. A grand mal seizure will result in severe convulsions, foaming at the mouth, falling about, with loss of consciousness. Till this day, epilepsy remains a mystery. No single definitive cause has been isolated. A victim experiences uncontrolled electrical firing of the brain neurons, a lightning storm in the head. Seizures seem to be triggered by stress. Sufferers tend to see a halo of light, as a warning that a seizure if imminent. There are over 50 million known epileptics worldwide. Deaths from seizures is usually confined to the elderly who cannot take the physical stress. Accidents during seizures may break bones and take lives. It is easy to see how the ancients could have interpreted an epileptic episode as a spiritual or demonic possession. Incidentally: The term epilepsy derives from the Greek *"epilepsis"* meaning *"seizure." "The lightning flashes through my skull; mine eyeballs ache and ache; my whole beaten brain seems as beheaded, and rolling on some stunning ground."* – Herman Melville (1819 – 1891).

EPIPHANY – (e-*PIFF*-fan-nee) (Epiphanal) A sudden re-awakening, positive paradigm shift, change of heart. An epiphany is not necessarily as profound as a divine *metanoia*. Nevertheless, it can be a life-changing occurrence. With an epiphany, one's attitude, consciousness, and life are transformed. *"Most spiritual experience begin with suffering. They begin with groundlessness. They begin when the rug has been pulled out from under us."* – Buddhist Nun Pema Chodron (b. 1936).

EPIPHENOMENALISM – (ep-pi-fen-*OM*-men-al-is-um) A philosophical theory of the relationship of body and mind. It is the belief that consciousness is an aftereffect, a by-product (epiphenomenon) caused by certain cerebral processes. Consciousness is to the brain, what a shadow is to the body. The body causes the shadow, but the shadow has no effect on the body. Likewise, the brain causes consciousness, but consciousness has no effect on the brain. So goes epiphenomenalism.

EPIPHENOMENON – (ep-pi-fen-*OM*-men-on) A by-product of an earlier event, incident, or episode. An epiphenomenon is a secondary phenomenon, a spin- off of the first. In medicine, an epiphenomenon is an unexpected secondary condition arising during the course of a disease or treatment. For example, a person contracts pneumonia while in the hospital for hip replacement surgery.

EPIPHYTE – (*EP*-pi-fite) A aerophyte or air plant. A plant that grows above the ground, supported nonparasitically by another plant or structure, deriving its nutrients and water from rain, air, dust. An orchid or bromeliad are epiphytes. Epiphytes are also called pneumatophores.

EPISCOPALIAN – (ep-piss-co-*PAY*-lee-an) American Anglican. A major Christian denomination, the American branch of the Anglican or Church of England. American Anglicans had to change the name of their church after the American Revolution (1789), for they rebelled against the authority of King George III, they also rebelled against the head of the Anglican Church, the same king.

EPISODIC MEMORY – (ep-pi-*SOD*-dic *MEM*-mor-ree) Concerns reminiscences of one's personal past, one's life history. Personal experiences are recalled in detail, including time and place they occurred. Often with dementia, the victim cannot recall immediate, present-day occurrences. However episodic memory stays intact.

EPISTEMIC PRIVACY – (ep-pi-*SOD*-dic *PRY*-va-see) Private knowledge. The content of consciousness that is inaccessible to anyone except the contemplator. Epistemic knowledge is personal information like feelings, emotions, pains, pleasures, fantasies, desires, lusts that cannot be known be others, never made public. The polar opposite of epistemic privacy is epistemic publicity.

EPISTEMIC PUBLICITY – (ep-pis-*TEM*-mic pub-*BLIS*-si-tee) Common knowledge that is accessible, shared, communicated to the public. Popular news is epistemic publicity. This is information made privy to all. It is not personal, but universal. The polar opposite of epistemic publicity is epistemic privacy.

EPISTEMOLOGY – (ep-is-tem-*OL*-lo-jee) The philosophical study of knowledge.

EPISTLE – (ep-*PISS*-sal) A Greco-Roman literary model of an essay in the form of a mock letter to be published. Ironically, St. Paul's epistles are not true epistles. They were actual letters, sent to one person or community, never intended for reproduction or publication.

EPITAPH – (*EP*-i-taf) A brief statement or poem written in praise of a deceased person. A commemorative inscription on a tomb or mortuary monument about the person buried at the site. For example, *"Forgive a sinner, and wink your eye at a homely girl."* – H. L. Mencken's (1880 – 1956) epitaph. Occasionally, one writes his own epitaph shortly before death, to be inscribed on his headstone. For instance: *"When I'm dead, I hope it's said, 'His sins were scarlet, but his books were read'."* Graveyard humor overflows on Boot Hill Arizona. For example, Lester Moore was a Wells Fargo station agent killed in a robbery. His epitaph reads: *"Here below lies Lester Moore. He took four slugs from a .44. No Less no more."*

EPITHET – (*EP*-i-thet) A sobriquet or nickname. A word or phrase applied to a person, usually associated with some personal attribute. Good examples are King Richard *the Lionhearted,* King Louis *the Fat,* and Czar Ivan *the Terrible.*

EPONYM – (*EP*-i-nim) A person's proper name that becomes a word, like Caesar or Quisling. These words are of eponymous origin.

EPROCTOPHILIA – (ep-prok-toh-FEE-lee-ah) (Eproctophiliac) A neurotic paraphilial disorder in which one is sexually excited by flatulence. An eproctophiliac has a fart fetish.

EPSOM SALT – (*EP*-sum *SAWLT*) (also Epsomite) Magnesium sulfate heptahydrate ($MgSO_4.7H_2O$). Epsom salt is a chemical compound with multiple usages. Medicinally, Epsom salt is administered externally and internally. It serves as a soothing hot bath for sore muscles and injury pain. Soaking the feet in an Epsom salt bath is especially effective. Mixed in water it can be taken orally. In this application, Epsom salt serves as an analgesic (pain killer) for migraines, and is used to treat asthma. Epsom salt is an essential fertilizer. Magnesium is an essential part of chlorophyll (plant blood). Chlorophyll is responsible for photosynthesis (plant growth). Epsom salt is used in brewing beer, and as a coagulant for tofu. It is added to bottled water to add minerals and taste. Epsom salt can be used as a substitute for table salt. Incidentally: The tern Epsom salt entered English in 1770. Its name derives from Epsom, a town in Surrey, England. There, the mineral spring provided Epsom water, known for its medicinal properties since Elizabethan times. The place name Epsom was recorded back about 973 as *"Ebbesham,"* meaning *"Ebbi's homestead." Ebbi* was some forgotten Anglo-Saxon. The Epsom water from the spring was exhausted in the 19th century.

EQUABLE – (*EK*-wuh-bul) Uniform, unvarying. Equable also means placid and even-tempered. *He displays an equable demeanor.*

EQUALITY – (ee-*KWAL*-li-tee) (Equal) Everyone is created equally, the same way, through conception and birth. Every human being is equally helpless in infancy, and dependent in childhood. However we are not equal in regards to our talents, abilities, and luck [read: *economic circumstances*]. Nevertheless, we are duty-bound to treat everyone equally, despite their exterior circumstances. As we are all born equally, we shall all die equally. In death, we will all become equal again. The Italian proverb teaches us that *"After the game is over, both the king and pawn are dropped into the same box."* Equality is sameness, though not fairness (or kindness). Equity strives to assure common access, opportunity, and accountability. The Progressive President Theodore Roosevelt (1858 – 1919) had declared that *"I do intend to see that the rich man is held to the same accountability as the poor man."* However, *"What is fair is equal, but what is equal is not always fair."* – Spartan Greek Proverb. The Athenian Philosopher Aristotle (384 – 322 BCE) added: *"There is no worst injustice than to treat unequal causes equally."* Social economic justice is arrived at through *equity*, rather than equality. *"Equality is the result of human organization. We are not born equal."* – Philosopher Hannah Arendt (1906 – 1975).

EQUAL JUSTICE – (*EE*-kwal *JUS*-tis) Equal justice is guaranteed under the law. It's mere window dressing. The laws are not made to equalize justice. On the contrary, the law (like the tax code) is skewed against the poor to benefit the rich. Laws are designed to protect wealth, and suppress the poor who need it. After all, *"The majestic equality of the law…forbids the rich as well as the poor to sleep under bridges, to beg in the streets, and to steal bread."* – Anatole France (1944 – 1924) <u>Le Lys Rouge</u> (1894) (<u>The Red Lily</u>).

EQUAL PROTECTION – (*EE*-kwal pro-*TEK*-shun) (Equal protection of the law.) A guarantee that no person or class of persons shall be denied the same protection of the laws that is enjoyed by other persons or classes in similar circumstances. Denial of this right is prohibited by the 14th Amendment. Despite the rhetoric, in a capitalist system, capital talks, while poverty walks.

EQUATOR – (*EE*-kway-tor) The imaginary line that encircles the globe, diving the Earth into Northern and Southern Hemispheres. The Equator is equal distance between the North and South Poles. Because of the Earth's tilt on its axis, the sun always strikes the Earth directly at the equator. That makes the equatorial region the hottest part of our planet. There are no seasonal changes on the equator. Too, day and night are always equal, 12 hours each. Incidentally: Because of the equal hours of darkness and light, lands along the equator have almost no twilight period at dawn and dusk. It almost seems like day turns to night, and night turns to day as if someone threw a switch.

EQUILIBRATE – (ee-*KWIL*-li-brayt) To balance out equally, to keep in equipoise or equilibrium.

EQUINOX – (*EE*-kwee-noks) Times when the sun crosses the equator. One of two times each year (March 21 and September 21) when the Earth's polar axis is not pointed toward or away from the sun, but is at a 90-degree angle to the sun. On each of these two days, the amount of daylight and darkness are equal in length. The equinox marks the beginning of spring and autumn.

EQUIPAGE – (*EC*-kwa-paj) Equipment. The outfitting of a ship, an army, a soldier. Too, an equipage is a horse-drawn carriage attended by servants.

EQUIPOISE – (*EC*-kwa-pois) (Equipoised) An even balance or equilibrium. A counter balance or poise.

EQUITIES – (*EC*-kwi-tees) (Equity) In economics, stocks that represent ownership shares in a corporation. In present day capitalist America, never had few people owned equities. Conversely, never had few people owned more equities (at the economic apex).

EQUITY – (*EC*-kwi-tee) Treating different people differently, in order to attain true fairness and justice. Equity and equality are not equal, because people are not equal. People have vastly different genetic, intelligence, talents, abilities, and family backgrounds. Equality strives for the same or equal opportunity. Equity strives to assure common provision and results. With equity, unequal people are not treated equally, but fairly, in order to make them equal. That's the premise behind *Affirmative Action*. In Progressive Finland, not equal but equitable justice prevails. For example, traffic fines in Finland are not equal [read: *unfair*] but equitable. Fines are progressive according to income. Therefore, when a millionaire Nokia CEO got a speeding ticket in his expensive sports car, his fine was $100,000 dollars. Distributive justice in action. Incidentally: In Progressive, Socialistically-inspired Finland, everyone's income is public record. Take that Mr. Trump.

EQUITY – (*EC*-kwi-tee) In economics, equity is the monetary values of a property or business beyond any amounts owed on it in mortgages, claims, liens, and so on.

EQUITY LAW – (*EC*-kwi-tee *LAW*) Fairness law. The name of a type of court originating in England to handle legal problems when the existing laws did not cover some situations in which a person's rights were violated by another person. In the United States, civil courts have the powers of both law and equity. If only money is represented in a case, the court is acting as a law court and will give only monetary relief. If something other than money is requested – injunction, declaratory judgment, specific performance of a contractual agreement, etc. – then the court takes jurisdiction in equity and will grant a decree ordering acts to be done or not done. There is no jury in an equity case. Action at law and suits in equity involve civil cases, not criminal.

EQUIVOCATE – (ee-*KWIV*-vo-kayt) (Equivocal, Equivocation) To prevaricate. To use vague, ambiguous expressions in order to mislead. Politicians are equivocal masters. They hedge or avoid controversial issues through the obfuscation of equivocation.

ERBFEINDSCHAFT – (*ERB*-fahynd-shaft) A German word for hatred passed on from generation to generation. Erbfeindschaft is traditional or hereditary enmity and hostility. The term originally, specifically referred to the vindictive relationship between Germany and France. The antagonistic rivalry goes back to the wars of the French King Louis XIV (1643 – 1715), to the Napoleonic Wars (1803 – 1815), to the Franco-Prussian War (1870 – 1871) to the First World War (1914 – 1918), to World War Two (1939 – 1945). The European Union (EU) (1993) was established largely as a consequence of erbfeidschaft. Incidentally: Erbfeidschaft can be applied throughout the world. It is particularly evident in the Balkans, the historic *"Powderkeg of Europe."* That's why Yugoslavia self- destructed.

ERBIUM – (*ER*-bee-um) (Er) The element was a name given by its discoverer, the Swedish chemist Carl Gustaf Mosander (1797 – 1858) in 1843. The 68 protons in its nucleus give erbium its atomic number. Erbium is a soft malleable silvery- white element of the rare-earth group. Erbium is used in special alloys and in room-temperature lasers. Too, erbium's pink salts are used in color pigments.

ERECTILE DYSFUNCTION – (er-*REC*-tie-ill *DIS*-func-shun) (abbreviated to ED) Erectile dysfunction is impotence. It is a condition making it hard to get a hard on. ED is the difficulty or inability of a man to attain and maintain an erect penis, prohibiting sexual intercourse. Of course, erectile dysfunction is emasculating. There are a number of medical causes of ED. Excessive anxiety and stress will cause a fellow to go limp as well. Erectile dysfunction to some degree is a natural symptom of aging. Men in their 60's are 4 times more likely to suffer from ED [read: *limberdick*], than men in their 40's. Capitalists have capitalized on the phallic pliability problem. A multi-billion dollar industry as arisen to help guys get it up. It can't be coincidence that the popular ED drug *Viagra,* rhymes with *Niagara.* *"Why can't sex be as easy as eating?"* – Ralph Robert Moore. Incidentally: Comedian George Burns (1896 – 1996) commented that: *"Sex at 90 is like trying to shoot pool with a rope."*

ERECTILE EXERCISE – (er-*REC*-tie-ill *EKS*-er-syz) Bringing the penis to erection in order to assure optimal penile performance. Coitus or masturbation serves as cock calisthenics. The dick desires a regular workout. For the love muscle, like any muscle: *"if you don't use it you lose it."* Dr. Tobias Kohler is Professor of Urology at Southern Illinois University School of Medicine, and the Mayo Clinic. He claims that *"It is important to keep your penis in shape. It has to be essentially exercised."* Cuming to *"erection maintains a healthy tone. The smooth muscles of the penis must be periodically enriched with oxygen by the rush of blood that engorges the penis and makes it erect,"* Dr. Kohler contends. *"If they don't do anything to maintain normal erections, they will get shortening of the penis. Without regular erections, penile tissue can become less elastic and shrink, making the penis 1 centimeter* [0.4 inches] *to 2 centimeters* [0.8 inches] *shorter,"* Dr. Kohler warns. Post Script: Wow! I had a feeling this was true, and I'm not a doctor of medicine.

ERECTION – (ih-*REK*-shun) (Erect, Erected, Erecting) To erect is to buildup. To stand erect is to be straight, stiff, and tall. In physiology, an erection is when a gut gets a hard on. It is the distention of the male penis when sexually aroused. The sexually stimulated brain through the nervous system orders the circulatory system to engorge the penis and clitoris with blood, making them hard and erect. This is an erection, getting a hard on. Once erected, ejaculation and orgasm occurs, enabling procreation. *"Is that a gun in your pocket, or are you just happy to see me?"* – Mae West (1893 – 1980). Incidentally: Republican Senatorial candidate and baboon, Herschel Walker (b. 1962) had stated on a Fox TV interview: *"The election is not about Herschel walker. The ERECTION is about the people."* Republican Senators Ted Cruz (b. 1970) and Lindsey Graham (b. 1955) flanked Walker and nodded approvingly to his erection. *"Men have only two emotions: hungry and horny. So if you see him without an erection, make him a sandwich."* – Adi Da (1939 – 2008). *"The way to a man's heart, is through his penis."* – Chloe Thurlow. *"For some reason I start getting an erection. They follow their own tide tables."* – Ralph Robert Moore.

ERETHISM – (*ER*-reth-is-um) (also *Erethismus Mercurialis*) Popularly known as Mad Hatter disease. Erethism is a neurological disorder affecting the entire nervous system caused by mercury poisoning. Mercury is a highly toxic chemical, the only metal that is liquid at room temperature. Emotional symptoms of erethism include depression, anti-social behavior, mood swings from timidity to aggressiveness, irritability, apathy, low self-confidence. Physical symptoms include general body pain, headaches, tremors, weakness, irregular heartbeat, and ultimately, death. Erethism is generally caused by the inhalation of mercury vapors. Certainly, those most at risk are those who must work with mercury. Mercury was formerly used in the manufacture of hats. Therefore hat makers or hatters often suffered from erethism. Before long, people were accused of being *"as mad as a hatter."* The phrase appeared in *Blackwood's Edinburgh Magazine* (January-June, 1829): *"He's raving."* *"Dementit."* *"Mad as a hatter."* Lewis Carroll (1832 – 1998) popularized the *"Mad Hatter"* in his 1865 novel, *Alice's Adventures in Wonderland.*

ERETZ ISRAEL – (*ER*-retz *IS*-ray-al) Literally means the land of Israel. Eretz Israel implies a land with undefined borders. Eretz Israel is a concept dear to Jewish or Israeli *"irredentists,"* or imperialists. They regard the present State of Israel as *"unredeemed."* The most extreme Israeli irredentists would not be satisfied until the State of Israel reached its greatest pre-Roman extent, from the Nile to the Euphrates Rivers.

ERGO – (*AIR*-go) Latin meaning *"Therefore."* Ergo also means *"hence." "Ergo, Trump is a criminal and traitor, as well as being a horrible human being."*

ERGONOMICS – (ur-guh-*NOM*-iks) (also known as HFE, *"Human Factors Engineering"*) The scientific study of efficiency in the workplace. Ergonomics involves the application of psychological and physiological principles to the engineering and design of products, processes, and systems. Ergonomics is a method of engineering, particularly in the workplace, making the environment more conducive to wellbeing and health. The primary goals of human factors engineering are to reduce human error, increase productivity and system availability, and enhance safety, health and comfort with a specific focus on the interaction between the human and equipment. Ergonomics seeks to conform the device to man, not man to the device. The human and mechanical machines are thus harmonized. Spaces, appliances, tools, instruments, machines, vehicles, utensils of every kind are designed to conform to the anatomical, physical, and psychological demands of the person. Incidentally: The term *"ergonomics"* was coined in the 1950s. It was devised from the Greek words *"ergon,"* meaning *"work,"* and *"oikonomia,"* meaning *"household management."*

ERGOT – (*ER*-got) A fungus on rye, barley, and other grains with hallucinogenic properties. Ergot can kill. In the Middle Ages, it was called *"St. Anthony's Fire."* Entire villages were poisoned by ergot infested bread and went mad. We can only speculate how many executions for witchcraft were ergot induced insanity. The hallucinations that culminated with the witch trials at Salem, Massachusetts (1692 – 1693) and elsewhere are now attributed to ergot poisoning. LSD is made from ergot.

ERGS – (*URGS*) Sandy deserts in contrast to *regs* (rocky deserts).

ERIE CANAL – (*EE*-ree can-*NAL*) (1817 – 1825) One of mankind's greatest engineering feats, some say the greatest construction project in the Western World in the past 4,000 years! The grand plan was to connect the port of New York City with the Great Lakes and the Midwest. The project was the brainchild of New York Governor DeWitt Clinton (1769 – 1828). Considered to be an impossible task, naysayers called the Erie Canal proposal *"Clinton's Folly."* The project entailed digging a 360 mile canal between Albany and Buffalo, linking the Hudson River with Lake Erie. In 8 years, 50,000 men with picks and shovels excavated 11 million cubic yards of rock, at a cost of $7 million dollars. Nearly 1,000 men (primarily Irish and German immigrants) were killed during construction. They had to cut through the Niagara Escarpment, a 60-foot-high wall of solid limestone, 30 miles thick, all the way to Lake Erie. The Erie Canal brought the bounty of the Midwest to NYC, and traded to Europe. Immediately, New York City surpassed New Orleans as the nation's top seaport.

ERISTIC – (er-*RIS*-tic) Argumentation through spurious reasoning. A manipulation of language and ideas, not to arrive at truth, but to win the verbal dispute. Political *"spin doctors"* excel at eristical debate. Eristic is a sophistic propaganda technique. The phrase *"eristic dialectic"* is sometimes used pejoratively, specifically to refer to the Sophists' claim to debate in such a way as to make the worse appear the better and the better appear the worse.

EROGENOUS ZONES – (er-*ROJ*-jen-us *ZONES*) Parts of the body especially sensitive to sexual stimulation and attraction. Included in the erogenous zone are the genitals or reproductive organs, breasts, nipples, buttocks, anus, and mouth. Actually, a skilled lover can arouse sexual desire from any part of the body, not only the erogenous zone. Too, erogenous zones are sensitive because they are meant to be stimulated for sexual pleasure. God did not bless the inhibited with sexual gratification.

EROS – (*ER*-roas) The ancient Greek God of Love. Eros refers to sensual, sexual, erotic love. Physical attraction, desire are attributed to eros. Too, according to psychoanalyst Sigmund Freud (1856 – 1939), eros refers to the life wish, the desire to survive. So there is a vital relationship between sexuality and survival, both personally, and as a species.

EROSION – (ee-*ROW*-shun) The result of weathering on the geology by the action of wind, water, ice, or gravity. Over time, erosion radically alters landscapes, wearing down mountains into plains.

EROTICA – (ih-*ROT*-ti-kuh) (Erotic, Eroticism) Relating to human sexuality in art, sexual enjoyments, games, and lovemaking. The term erotica is taken from the Greek *"erotikos,"* meaning *"amatory"* – (relating to love, lovers, lovemaking). Erotica, though sexy, is distinguished from pornography. Erotica is seductive, not exploitative, as is pornography. Erotica is actual art, sexual art, whereas pornography is performance. *"No nude, however abstract, should fail to arouse in the spectator some vestige of erotic feeling, even if it be only faintest shadow – and if it does not do so it is bad art and false morals."* – Art Historian, Sir Kenneth Clark (1903 – 1983). *"Art can never exist without naked beauty displayed."* – Poet William Blake (1757 – 1827).

EROTIC HUMILIATION – (ih-*ROT*-tic hu-mil-lee-*AY*-shun) Consensual psychological shame, abasement, indignity performed and endured in order to experience erotic excitement and sexual arousal. Erotic humiliation is most satisfying before an audience, in public. It includes nudity [read: being *emBARE-ASSed*] collar and leash, crawling, spanking, whipping, boot and body licking, bondage, mild tortures, a variety of submissive, subservient sexual and beastly behaviors. Most would agree that this extreme of gratifying degradation is beyond the pale of normality. Psychiatrically, most erotic humiliation would be considered a masochistic neurosis. Like all forms of masochism, there is a desire to be punished, which is generated by some conscious or subconscious shame or guilt. Perhaps an unremitted transgression exists from a past existence, a Karmic debt that is being paid through erotic humiliation. Perhaps that compels the individual to suffer public punishment. Whatever the reason, the best venue for displaying public performances of erotic humiliation is *"The Folsom Street Fair"* each September, in San Francisco's Market District. The lascivious, licentious is licensed. Deviance is deified. What is normally considered to be indecent exposure is considered decently exposed. *"Folsom"* is a convention of BDSM (Bondage Dominance SadoMasochism) practioners and aficionados. This event is a carnival of uninhibited sexual fantasies, bizarre unrestrained libertinism, a walk on the wild side. It is Fundamentally *"Sodom and Gomorrah"* revisited. The Folsom Fair of Erotic Humiliation could only take place in libertarian San Francisco, California. One could not fathom the event occurring in repressed Muskogee, Oklahoma. *"The only unnatural sex act is that which you cannot perform."* – Sexologist Alfred Kinsey (1894 – 1956). *"There is something very liberating about public humiliation."* – Actor Joaquin Phoenix (b. 1974).

EROTICISM – (ih-*ROT*-ti-sis-um) (Erotic) Art that is sexually stimulating. Erotic art can be displayed in stone, on canvass, on stage, or in film. Eroticism excites sexual passion. It exalts sexuality, whereas pornography demeans sexuality. The erotic is associated with love, whereas the pornographic is associated with aggression. Eroticism glorifies sex, whereas pornography prostitutes sex. It's safe to exposed children to the erotic, but not to the pornographic. Incidentally: Sometimes, the difference between eroticism and pornography may be attitudinal and perceptual. The artist Henri de Toulouse-Lautrec (1864 – 1901) attended an exhibition of his paintings at the Louvre in Paris. Not knowing the artist was standing near, a prudish aristocratic lady began to rebuke one of his paintings. *"Look at that filth,"* the woman exclaimed. *"A half-naked woman, removing her clothes with a man seated on her bed. Disgusting pornography!"* Hearing this, the angry Lautrec approached the woman and asserted: *"You are mistaken, Madame. The lady is not undressing, she is dressing. It is not her bedroom, but their bedroom. The man seated on the bed is her husband. They are preparing to attend their son's 20th wedding anniversary. Furthermore Madame, I would thank you to take your filthy eyes off my lovely paintings."*

EROTOGRAPHOMANIA – (er-rot-tow-graf-o-*MAY*-nee-ah) (Erotographomamiac) A neurotic interest in erotic, pornographic literature. One addicted to pornographic literature and pictures.

EROTOLOGY – (er-rot-*TOL*-lo-jee) (Erotologist = er-rot-*TOL*-lo-jist) The study of satisfying sex. An erotologist is a skilled love-maker. She/he has mastered the art of intercourse. An erotologist is not a scientist, like a sexologist. He is not a specialist in the clinic, but a specialist in the bed. Incidentally: At a wedding, an erotological bridesmaid was overheard to say to another bridesmaid concerning the groom: *"Give me 5 minutes with him, and he'll forget all about this wedding."*

EROTOMANIA – (er-rot-tow-*MAY*-nee-a) (also Aphrodisiomania = af-ro-dy-see- o-*MAY*-nee-a) An abnormally powerful sex drive. An eroto<u>maniac</u> is <u>mania</u>cally obsessed with sex.

EROTOPHOBIA – (air-rot-toh-*FOH*-bee-ah) (Erotophobiac) One suffering from a neurotic, abnormal fear of sex – masturbation, intercourse, or any sexual feelings. An erotophobiac is not accurately an asexual who has no interest or need for sex. Erotophobia is a fear, like a phobic fear of fire, heights, or being on the water. Religious fanatics who were conditioned [read: *brainwashed*] to believe that sex is an evil sin, of the devil, warranting eternal punishment in hell, were erotophobia candidates. In the Middle Ages, such people, especially crazed monks, castrated themselves. Specific aspects of erotophobia are *"gymnophobia"* – a fear of nudity; and *"genophobia"* – a fear of sexual intercourse. All of these phobias require psychiatric intervention.

ERRANT – (*ER*-rant) Erring, going astray, deviating from the proper course. An errant arrow is off course, flying aimlessly, for example.

ERRATIC – (er-*RAT*-tic) Deviating from the usual or proper course of conduct or expectation. To be erratic is to wander, with no fixed course. That's why in geology, an erratic is a huge boulder displaced by a glacier. It is a mineralogical foreigner that had been transported from afar. The mineral composition of an erratic is often totally foreign to its geologic placement. Glacial erratics are called *"drop stone."* Good examples are visible in Central Park, New York City.

ERRATUM – (er-*ROT*-tum) (also a *Corrigendum* = cor-ree-*JEN*-dum) The term is taken from the Latin *"errata corrige"* meaning *"mistakes corrected."* An erratum (or corrigendum) is a correction of a published text. As a general rule, publishers issue an *erratum* for a production error or <u>publishing mistake</u>, and a *corrigendum* for an <u>author's mistake</u>. Sometimes, the terms erratum or corrigendum are loosely used to mean the error itself. An errata sheet or slip may take the form of a loose list of corrections inserted at the beginning of the book, by the Table of Contents. For example: In Peter Ustinov's (1921 – 2004) publication, <u>My Russia</u> (1983), a small *"errata slip"* is inserted on the 4th page. Eleven errors were detected in the work, after publication. For instance: *"Page 26, Line 41, 'Caspian' should read 'Volga'"; "Page 182, Line 2, 'four million ethnic 'Russians' should read 'Ukrainians.'"*

ERSE – (*URS*) An alternative name for any of the old Goidelic languages. Erse (also Erische) has been used as another name for Irish Gaelic. From the 16th through the 19th centuries, the term Erse was applied to Scottish Gaelic.

ERSTWHILE – (U*RST*-why-al) Formerly, previously, in the bygone past, once upon a time. The term originated in Old English (West Saxon), and referred to an early space in time. Today, one may refer to erstwhile friends.

ERUCT – (ih-*EUHKT*) (Eructation) Acid reflux. To belch forth, as gas and acid from the stomach. Eructation is a symptom of heartburn. Too, eruct is also applied to the violent emission of fumes from a volcano.

ERYTHROCYTES – (e-*RITH*-ro-sites) Red blood cells that carry oxygen throughout the body. Erythrocytes give blood its red color. That's because they carry oxygen fixing iron in the compound, hemoglobin.

ERYTHROPHOBIA – (e-rith-ro-*FO*-bee-a) Phobic fear of blushing, (and the color red).

ERYTHROPOIETIN – (ih-rith-roh-*POY*-it-tin) A hormone that stimulates the production of red blood cells (erythrocytes) and hemoglobin in the bone marrow. The reaction of this hormone is to produce more oxygen for the bodily tissues. A synthetic form of erythropoietin is illegally administered to athletes as a performance-enhancing drug. This banned procedure is called *"blood doping."*

ESBAT – (*ES*-bat) A day for spiritual gatherings of a witch's coven or circle group or observation by a solo practitioner. Esbats are special days set aside for worship and spellwork. It may take place on either the full moon or the new moon or both, depending on tradition.

ESCAPE VELOSITY – (vel-*LOS*-si-tee) The speed that an object needs to be traveling to break free from a planet's or moon's gravity. At 17,500 miles per hour, a space vehicle will enter and remain in Earth's orbit. A spacecraft leaving the surface of Earth needs to be going 7 miles per second, or 25,020 miles per hour to leave without falling back to the surface or falling into orbit.

ESCARPMENT – (es-*KARP*-ment) In topography, a steep slope with a nearly flat plateau on top.

ESCHATOLOGY – (es-chat-*Ol*-lo-jee) The philosophical/theological concern with finality, as with death, divine judgment, cosmic destruction, and so on. Concerning the universe, cosmogony, the birth of the

Cosmos is the opposite of eschatology. Both eschatology and cosmogony are the meeting places of physics and metaphysics, of science and Spirituality.

ESCARGOT – (es-car-*GO*) (Helix pomatia) Escargot is French for *"edible snails."* Escargot is usually eaten with a sauce made of melted butter and garlic. The commercial raising of snails primarily for food is called *"heliciculture."*

E-SCOOTER – (*EE-SKOO*-ter) An Electric Scooter. An e-scooter is an example of a non-polluting, *"micromobility machine."* It is a simple, lightweight vehicle propelled by a small motor powered by rechargeable batteries. Unlike a motorized bicycle, an e-scooter has no seat. One stands, one foot before the other on a floorboard. A long vertical headtube attaches the floorboard to the handlebars. The entire device is collapsible, folding into one manageable piece. There are adult and child models. They are priced in the range of bicycles. The speed and range vary greatly depending on the sophistication of the machine. Therefore, one may travel from 12 to 75 mph, for 2 to 137 miles on one electrical charge. Obviously, like motorcycles, these machines can be dangerous. It has always been the case that technology outruns the law to regulate it. To date (March 2023), Only California requires a driver's license to operate an e-scooting on a public road, like a motorcycle. Too, the speed cannot surpass 15 mph, which prohibits it from most thoroughfares. All other states consider the e-scooter to be in the class of a motorized bicycle. Paris France is considering banning e-scooters (called *"trottinettes"* because the French hate English words). There have been several accidents and deaths related to e-scooters in Paris.

ESCOVEITCHED FISH – (*ES*-co-veechd *FISH*) The term Escoveitch is a corruption of the Spanish *"escabeche"* meaning *"pickled."* Escoveitched Fish is one of Jamaica's oldest European cuisines. It was brought to the island by the first Spanish explorers. More accurately, *escoveitching* (marinating) was brought to Jamaica by Spanish Jews, who passed themselves off as Portuguese. The fish is lightly fried and drained. It is then put in a marinade of vinegar which was boiled with onions, carrots, chocho (a squash), very hot peppers (*Scotch bonnets*), and pimento grains. It is left to marinade overnight. The shredded vegetables and picked juice is served on the fish. The pickling process works as a preservative, so Escoveitch fish was very popular before refrigeration. It was a favorite of Catholics on meatless holydays, and of Jamaican Jews. Today, Escoveitched Fish is a seaside delicacy, eaten with *bammy* (fried cassava bread) right on the beach.

ESCROW – (*ES*-crow) A legal contract deposited with a third party instructing him to hold money, property, or goods for another, pending fulfillment of some conditions. Property held in escrow.

ESCUTCHEON – (es-*CUTCH*-en) A shield on which a coat of arms is depicted. More commonly today, an escutcheon is an ornamental plate decorating a keyhole, door handle, drawer pull, or light switch.

ESKER – (*ES*-ker) A serpentine ridge of gravelly and sandy drift, formed by streams under or in glacial ice.

ESOTERIC – (es-o-*TER*-ric) (Esoterica, Esoterically) Covert. Secret knowledge, reserved for the initiated few. Spycraft is an esoteric profession.

ESOTERICISM – (es-o-*TER*-ri-siz-um) Being in a cryptic, mysterious state or quality. Esotericism is exhibited by spies. Too, a secret or highly complicated concept understood by a select few qualifies as an esotericism.

ESP – (ee es *PEE*) (Extra Sensory Perception) This initialism refers to apprehension, cognition, communication that goes beyond the physical 5 senses into the metaphysical, "extra" [read: *spiritual*] realm. ESP relies on intuition and inspiration in order to practice telepathy, clairvoyance, the mystic arts. Extra sensory abilities are vestigial, dormant aptitudes, capabilities that were surrendered when human beings gained the large cerebrum, or thinking brain. (We traded reasoning for instinctive ESP.) ESP practices can be regained or fortified with practice. On the other hand, advanced metaphysical talents are God-given to deserving prophets and saints.

ESPERANTO – (es-per-*RON*-toe) An artificial language invented in 1887 by Ludwik Lejzer Zamenhof (1859 – 1917), a Polish physician and philologist, and intended for international use. Esperanto is based on word roots common to major European languages. Esperanto is a Pan-European lingua franka. Esperanto utilizes the Latin script (alphabet). The vocabulary is primarily from Germanic and Romance languages. The grammar is adopted primarily from the Slavic languages. Today, there may be as many as 2 million Esperanto speakers. Incidentally: Dr. Zamenhof published the first book on Esperanto in 1887. It was entitled <u>Unua Libre</u>, meaning *"First Book."* Dr. Zamenhof reasoned that if the people of Europe could communicate, they would not be quick to go to war. Dr. Zamenhof used the pseudonym, Dr. Esperanto. The word Esperanto translates into English as *"one who hopes."*

ESPIONAGE – (*ES*-pee-on-nozh) Spying. Secretly stealing information from a rival or enemy. Governments employ espionage to gather military, political, commercial, or industrial secrets. Capitalist corporations spy on each other as well, stealing trade and technical secrets. Espionage may be conducted by secret agents who infiltrate a foreign government, or by technology like video cameras, listening devices, and aerial drones or satellites. Incidentally: During World War Two, the Manhattan Project which created the atomic bomb was totally compromised by American and British scientists working for Russia. Joseph Stalin (1878 – 1953) knew about the atomic bomb before President Harry Truman (1884 – 1972). The stolen information gave the Russians the atomic bomb 2 years earlier than expected. In fact, the Manhattan Project was the greatest espionage victory in history.

ESPLANADE – (*ES*-pluh-nod) A long open walkway, designed for pedestrians, especially along the seashore. Esplanades are gratefully off-limits to motorized vehicles.

ESPN – (ee-es-pee-*EN*) An initialism for <u>E</u>ntertainment and <u>S</u>ports <u>P</u>rogramming <u>N</u>etwork. ESPN is an American international cable sports channel established in 1979, headquartered in Bristol, Connecticut. ESPN was founded by sports director William F. Rasmussen (b. 1932), his son Scott W. Rasmussen (b. 1956), and Ed Eagan. ESPN is owned by The Walt Disney Company (80%) and Hearst Communications (20%). ESPN has 13 sister channels including ABC (<u>A</u>merican <u>B</u>roadcasting <u>C</u>ompany), that covers all major sporting events. ESPN also operates in Latin America, Brazil, Canada, Australia, and the United Kingdom.

ESPRESSO – (es-*PRES*-so) A strong dark coffee prepared by forcing live steam under pressure, or boiling water through ground dark-roast coffee beans. Espresso is a thicker liquid than ordinary coffee, with more caffeine. Espresso is of Italian origin.

ESQUE – (*ESK*) An adjective suffix indicating style, manner, resemblance, or a distinctive character. Examples are: Roman<u>esque</u> (Roman like), pictur<u>esque</u> (picture like), Lincoln<u>esque</u> (Lincoln like), and so on.

ESQUIRE – (*ESK*-kwy-er) (abbreviated Esq. or Esqr.) The Medieval shield bearer of a knight. The esquire was often subsequently knighted. Today, esquire is an empty, unofficial title of respect, having no precise significance. It is written in abbreviated form after a man's surname (e.g. Thomas C. Pasieka, Esq.). In the U.S., this tradition is applied to lawyers, women included. In Britain, esquire is applied to a commoner considered to have attained the social position of a *"gentleman."*

ESSENCE – (*ES*-sens) In philosophy, the distinctive nature of a thing. That which makes a thing what it is. Essence is that which is necessary and unchanging about a thing. Essence and existence are identical. The essence of the body is matter. The essence of the soul is Spirit. Both matter and Spirit are light energy – a part of God who is the Light of the World, of all worlds.

ESSENTIAL MAXIMS – (es-*SEN*-shuhl *MAX*-ims) Resentment, remorse, and regret are three viruses that could ravage one's life. But there are three maxims on human nature that can help one cope and survive. 1. *"Adults are merely children in aging skin."* 2. *"The heart has its reasons that reason does not know."* – Blaise Pascal (1623 – 1662). 3. *"We did the best we could, with who we were, and what we knew, at that point in time, space, and life."* – Gary J. Pasieka (b. 1951). Bear these maxims in mind and heart. One will cope with life infinitely better.

ESSENTIAL OIL – (es-*SEN*-shuhl *OIL*) (also Volatile oil) Fragrant oils extracted from a plant into a concentrated oil that is said to contain the *"essence"* or *"soul"* of the plant. In alchemical philosophy, essential oil is the soulful principle of the plant. Essential oils are used in magic potions and in medicinal substances. Essential oils evaporated into the air make a pine forest the healthiest area on Earth.

ESSENTIAL WORKERS – (es-*SEN*-shuhl *WERK*-ers) Those who work jobs vital to the safe functioning of society. Essential workers include healthcare employees, firefighters, just police officers, educators, food providers, trash collectors, utilities operators, and others. Essential workers are essential for the community's health and wellbeing. In a sense, every worker in directly or indirectly an essential worker. The complexity of society and the division of labor have made everyone's contribution essential.

ESSENTIALISM – (es-*SEN*-shuhl-is-um) An educational perspective rooted in conservative Realism that holds that there is a common core of information and skills that an educated person must have. Furthermore, the school should be organized to transmit this core of essential material to everyone. Essentialists demand the same ultra-rigorous education for all, regardless of aptitude, despite ability or proclivity. This is both true and false. It is admirable for all to read Shakespeare. But Shakespeare will not produce better plumbers, mechanics, carpenters or surgeons, for that matter.

ESTABLISHMENT CLAUSE – (es-*TAB*-lish-ment *CLAWS*) The pronouncement in the First Amendment to the U.S. Constitution stating: *"Congress shall make no law respecting an establishment of religion, or prohibiting the free exercise thereof.…"* The establishment Clause mandates the separation of church and state. So, it is leagally established, as the basic law of the land, that religion must be kept out of the public school. Period.

ESTIVATE – (*ES*-tuh-vayt) This verb means *"to spend the summer,"* as at some vacation location. The term entered English in 1620s from the Latin *"aestivatus,"* meaning *"to reside during the summer."* *"Aestus"* in Latin means *"heat,"* and *"aestas"* in Latin means *"the hot season,* or *"summer."* So, an estivate residence is a summer home for the indulgent rich. *"I estivate in cool Northern Michigan."*

ESTRANGEMENT – (es-*STRANJ*-ment) The term is taken from the Latin *"extraneare,"* meaning *"to treat or regard something as a stranger."* Estrangement is the act of keeping something at a distance. It is withdrawing and withholding one's emotions and confidence in things, usually do to unfriendliness. A divorced couple experiences mutual estrangement.

ESTROGEN – (*Es*-tro-jen) Female sex hormone, keeps women feminine. Estrogen is the *"tend-and-befriend"* hormone. It is the polar opposite of the male testosterone, the *"fright-or-flight"* hormone. Incidentally: Only one hydrogen atom and the configuration of its bond (the bent of its hook) makes the difference between estrogen and testosterone, and therefore between male and female. Furthermore, generally speaking, the average woman is 60% estrogen, 40 % testosterone. Conversely, the average man is 60% testosterone, and 40% estrogen. Indeed, after all, our parents were male and female.

ESTRUS – (*Es*-trus) The period of maximum sexual receptivity in females. In animals, this is the period when they are in "heat," or being in "rut." Female animals in estrus emit sex pheromones that excite the males, inducing them to "rut." Human females are sexually active all the time. However, they may be even more stimulated, amorous when ovulating and are fertile. This may be regarded as being in estrus. Incidentally: The erogenous zone, the genital regions of both males and females emit sexually stimulated pheromones. This is particularly true of females. The scents excite sexual passion.

ESTUARY – (*Es*-chew-air-ree) A broadened seaward end of a river, where the river's currents meet the ocean's tides. A wide, shallow bay forms where the ocean water submerges the mouth of the river and where salt water and freshwater mix. This brackish environment is rich in marine life like clams, oysters, crabs. An unpolluted estuary is a seafood cornucopia.

ET AL. – (et *AUL*) Latin for *"and others."* One may write: *"The entire family was present: brother, sisters, cousins, nieces, nephews, et al."* In law, when the words *el al.* are used in an opinion, the court is thereby indicating that there are unnamed parties, either plaintiffs or defendants, also before the court in the case.

ETC. – (et-*SET*-er-ah) (etc. = *"et cetera"*) Means, *"and others; so forth; so on."* Et cetera is used to indicate that more of the same sort or class might have been mentioned, but for brevity have been omitted.

ETCH-A-SKETCH – The phrase etch-a-sketch was coined in 1960, by the *Ohio Art Company.* It is the name of a popular mechanical drawing toy, the screen of which is wiped totally clean by shaking. The term etch-a-sketch has entered the American political lexicon. A Republican spokesman likened the Romney campaign strategy in the 2012 presidential election to the Etch-A-Sketch. Willard Mitt Romney (b. 1947) came on as ultra-conservative during the primary election in order to please the ultra-conservative Republican base, just to win the nomination. But Romney intended to sing a moderate song during the general election in order to win moderate votes. Like the etch-a-sketch toy, Romney intended to wipe the screen clean for the general election. In other words, every conservative promise, commitment, declaration, and policy statement made during the Republican primary election season would be considered void, invalid come the general election. The *"ETCH-A-SKETCH moment"* revealed the deceit and duplicity of the conservative Republican Party, and their candidate, Willard Mitt Romney.

ETERNAL – (ee-*TURN*-nal) Everlasting, forever, perpetual, immortal, of infinite duration. The eternal exhibits continuation in time without beginning or end. Soul, spirit, God are eternal. All have no succession, but existing all at once, an unchanging timeless present One.

ETERNAL NOW – (ee-*TURN*-al) Buddhist teaching about *"living in the moment."* The contemporary metaphysician and Spiritualist, Eckhart Tolle (b. 1948) concurred: *"Life is now. There was never a time when your life was not now, nor will there ever be."*

ETERNAL QUESTION – (ee-*TURN*-al *KWES*-chun) *"What's in it for me?"* This is the question that capitalists eternally ask. It reflects a sense of insecurity even desperation. It says, *"I must get mine before it's all gone!"* This is *scarcity thinking* – the false belief that there is not enough to go around. The eternal question is an aberration of higher human nature. It represents the erroneous notion that we stand alone and can survive independently. *"No man is an island entire of itself. Every man is a piece of the continent, a part of the main."* – John Donne (1573 – 1631). Socialism substitutes *"WE"* thinking, for *"ME"* thinking. The authentic eternal question is: *"How can we all prosper together?"*

ETERNAL RECURRENCE – (ee-*TURN*-al ree-*CUR*-rans) The philosophical belief in the repetition of general cyclic patterns in the universe. Examples are the planetary cycles, changing seasons, day and night, birth and death, plant growth and decay. Eternal recurrence maintains that all events in the universe have occurred an infinite number of times in the past, and will occur again an infinite number of times in the future. The universe itself has imploded and exploded in several Big Bangs, and shall continue to do so.

ETERNAL REGRET – (ee-*TURN*-al ree-*GRET*) A poem. *"Words I wish I had not said; Deeds I did that now I dread; Hurt me so in heart and head; There's no amends with our beloved dead."* – Gary J. Pasieka (b. 1951) October 15, 2015.

ETERNAL REUNION – (ee-*TURN*-al ree-*YOUN*-yon) The spiritual conviction of life after death, accompanied by a reunification of deceased loved-ones. Most religions subscribe to an eternal reunion. It is one of the most comforting and consoling doctrines espoused by religion. Eternal reunion takes the bitter sting out of death. The sense of finality and oblivion is dissipated. Many who have had near-death experiences testify that deceased loved-ones had welcomed them (or their souls) beyond the veil, into the eternal. The belief in eternal reunion transforms death from a terror to an adventure. Mormon leader John

Taylor (1808 – 1887) wrote: *"While we are mourning the loss of our friend, others are rejoicing to meet him behind the veil."*

ETERNAL VERITIES – (ee-*TURN*-al *VER*-ri-tees) Truths or ideas that are true, have been forever true, and will remain true everlastingly. The Philosophy of Idealism is predicated on absolutes, eternal verities.

ETERNITY – (ee-*TUR*-nit-tee) (Eternal) Timeless, endless, infinite, everlasting, forever. *"Eternity is the now that does not pass away."* – St. Augustine (354 – 430 CE). The term eternity derives from the Latin *"aeternus,"* meaning *"enduring, permanent."* God is eternal, without beginning or end. All religions insist that man's true being is the eternal soul. Being created in the image and likeness of God, the soul, like God is immortal – ergo eternal. Death is foreign to the eternal soul. So it is. *"Eternity is a long time, especially towards the end."* – Astrophysicist Stephen Hawking (1942 – 2018).

ETHANOL – (*ETH*-uh-nawl) Consumption alcohol. Ethanol is a chemical compound (CH_3CH_2OH) obtained from the fermentation of sugars and starches or by chemical synthesis (distillation). Ethanol is the intoxicating ingredient of alcoholic beverages. Related to ether, ethanol numbs the brain [read: gets you high]. Any vegetation can be converted into alcohol through fermentation or distillation. But all alcohols are not drinkable. Ethanol has many uses other than partying. It is an excellent solvent, used in explosives, and as an additive to or replacement for petroleum-based fuels (gasohol). A Caveat: Do not confuse *ethanol* with *ethenol*, vinyl alcohol (CH_2CHOH) or *ethynol*, an alkyne alcohol (C_2H_2O), or *ethanal*, which is acetaldehyde (CH_3CHO). *Ethenol* and *ethynol* will blind, then kill you! *Ethanol* is a toxin produced in the gut when *ethanol* is exposed to oxygen. *Ethanal* is a hangover inducer. *Ethanal* may not kill you, but you may wish you were dead!

ETHEREAL – (ee-*THER*-ree-al) (also Aethereal) Being light, airy, delicately cloud- like. The term ethereal derives from the Latin *"ether"* meaning the upper regions of the atmosphere or the heavens. Therefore, ethereal had come to mean heavenly, celestial, spiritual as well.

ETHERIALIZE – (ee-*THER*-ree-al-yz) (Etherialization) According to Historian Arnold Toynbee (1889 – 1975) in *A Study of History* (1934 – 1961), etherialization is the process of overcoming material obstacles which releases the energies of a society to respond to internal, spiritual challenges. Professor Toynbee believed that: *"A society that is declining materially, may be advancing spiritually."* This is etherialization.

ETHICAL EGOISM – (*ETH*-thi-cal *EE*-go-is-um) In philosophy, the theory that one ought to act so as to secure the greatest possible good for oneself. Of course, this is self-indulgent greediness. Ethical egoism is at the heart of capitalism.

ETHICAL HEDONISM – (*ETH*-thi-cal *HEE*-don-is-um) In philosophy, the theory that acts are right insofar as they contribute to happiness or pleasure and wrong insofar as they contribute to unhappiness or suffering. Ethical hedonism is self- indulgent, if not selfish in nature. Too, the pleasure that it seeks is usually of a carnal nature. Is a missionary being ethically hedonistic by feeding and healing poor natives?

ETHICAL RELATIVISM – (*ETH*-thi cal *REL*-la-tiv-is-um) In philosophy, the theory that the rightness and wrongness of acts are relative to, functions of, the attitudes of the person judging the acts. Therefore, morality is subjective. A good argument in the defense of cannibalism.

ETHICS – (*ETH*-ics) Branch of axiology (philosophy) that examines moral values and the rules of right and wrong. Ethics is concerned with edifying rules, which govern edifying behaviors, which are morals. It is the search for the morally good life. To be ethical is to exhibit high moral standards. Criminals are generally considered to be unethical. However, abject poverty creates criminals. It brings forth the very worst in people, as they fall victim to despair and desperation. This is why crime is highest in capitalist societies. The ancient Chinese proverb attests that *"Only when you have food, clothing, and shelter will you have ethics."* Mark Twain (1835 – 1910) rightly observed that *"Principles* [read: *ethics*] *have no real force except when one is well-fed."* Indeed. That is why *"The first step in the evolution of ethics is a sense of solidarity with other human beings."* – Dr. Albert Schweitzer (1875 – 1965). That means a Socialist society.

ETHNIC CLEANSING – (*ETH*-nic *CLEN*-sing) The violent removal of an ethnic group from a community or society. A region can be *"cleansed"* of a people by forced deportation (A Trail of Tears) or by genocide (A Holocaust). Ethnic cleansing has resulted in mass murder on a national scale.

ETHNIC GROUP – (*ETH*-nic *GROOP*) (Ethnicity) A group of people who share a common language, customs, religion, and heritage or history. Ethnicity is tribalism. Members of an ethnic group, or their ancestors share a national origin (that is, a specific country or area in the world). Ethnic groups must feel a sense of common tribalism, solidarity, and destiny. One's ethnic heritage cannot be escaped. You can change your name, you can change your spouse, you can change your address, but you can't change your grandfather.

ETHNICITY – (*ETH*-nis-si-tee) The historic, cultural, biological background of one's ancestry. Ethnicity (blood) is not to be confused with nationality (citizenship).

ETHNIC NATIONALISM – (*ETH*-nik *NA*-shun-al-is-um) Ethnic nationalism goes beyond ethnic pride. There's an element of exclusivity involved. With ethnic nationalism, the central theme pivots on having a shared heritage stemming from a common language, faith, or ancestry. For example, Spanish speaking Americans with Latin American ancestry might feel a greater comradery to one another, than to other groups of American. Likewise, an Italian-American may ask another person, *"Paesano?"* enquiring if he too is Italian. This too is an indication of ethnic nationalism. Incidentally: The term *"paesano"* is short for *"compaesano,"* meaning *"same village,"* the implication being familiarity.

ETHNIC SLURS – (*ETH*-nik *SLERS*) Ethnophaulisms. Hate-speech of people from different cultural, national, or racial groups. Ethnic slurs are aimed at the *"other,"* the outsider, not in our tribe. Ethnic slurs involve insults, epithets, mockery. Sometimes, a slur becomes legitimized as the name *"Eskimo,"* which means *"raw meat eaters."* This name was pinned on the Inuit by their southern cousins the Cree Indians of Canada. Following is a brief list of common ethnic slurs: <u>Africans</u>: Nigger, Coon, Jiggs, Spook; <u>Asians</u>: Chink, Gook; <u>Arabs</u>: Camel Jockey, Sand Nigger; <u>Latinos</u>: Spic, Grease Ball; <u>Native Americans</u>: Redskin, Squaw; <u>European</u>: Whitey, Honky, Gringo. Furthermore, individual ethnics were/are targeted: <u>Italians</u>:

Dago; <u>Irish</u>: Paddy, Mick; <u>Jews</u>: Kike; <u>Polish</u>: Polack; <u>French</u>: Frog; <u>British</u>: Limey; <u>Japanese</u>: Nip; <u>Germans</u>: Kraut, Square Head. Hate is rooted in fear. That's why people's ethnicity is slurred.

ETHNOBOTANY – (eth-no-*BOT*-tan-nee) The science of collecting traditional health plants, and interviewing shamans for *"materia medica"* knowledge. Over 80% of the people on Earth use plants as their medicine. An estimated 4,000 known medical plants in Africa, over 80,000 worldwide have been identified. Still, only 1% of the flowering plants on Earth have been tested for their medicinal qualities. The Amazon Rainforest is the great, untapped, ethnobotanical treasure trove. On average 3 new species are discovered in the Amazon rainforest daily. We can't imagine what magical galenicals they may yield. Ethnobotany is part pharmacology, part anthropology. Native shamans, medicinemen, bush doctors must be studied. They must act as teachers sharing their ancient knowledge to add to our Western medical knowledge. *"The universities do not teach all things so a doctor must seek out old wives, gypsies, sorcerers, wandering tribes, old robbers, and such outlaws and take lessons from them. A doctor must be a traveler. Knowledge is experience."* – Paracelsus (1493 – 1541) The Alchemist.

ETHNOCENTRISM – (eth-no-*SEN*-tris-um) Small-minded belief in the superiority of one's familiar culture and the denigration of all others. Ethnocentrism escalated to its insane maximum resulting in the Nazi *"master race"* madhouse. Incidentally: Starting in 2016, the vile fascist racist, Donald Trump (b. 1946) had opened America's *"Pandora's Box"* of ethnocentrism. Through Trumpublicans, QAnon Nuts, MAGAmaniacs, White Supremacists, Christian Nationalists, Nazi Militias, Trump had stoked the embers of hatred and divisiveness in our country.

ETHNOGRAPHY – (eth-*NOG*-graf-fee) The scientific study of human culture through observation, collection, and analysis of anecdotal field notes. Ethnography is an anthropological methodology.

ETHNOHISTORY – (eth-no-*HIS*-tor-ree) Branch of anthropology that collects oral history from non-literate cultures. The few remaining non-literate tribes rely of history memorizers to keep their culture intact.

ETHNOLOGY – (eth-*NOL*-luh-jee) (Ethnologist, Ethnological) In anthropology, ethnology is the study of cultures, especially in regard to their historical development and the similarities and dissimilarities between them. A Caveat: Do not confuse <u>ethno</u>logy with <u>etho</u>logy, which is the study of animal behavior.

ETHNOPHAULISM – (eth-no-*FALL*-is-um) An ethnic or racial slur typically utilizing the caricature of some identifiable feature of the group being derided, often physical features. For example, *"nigger"* is an offensive word for Africans, originally referring to their dark (black) skin (negro). The German Nazis depicted Jews with comically big noses. In America, racist publications always depicted Negroes with over-sized lips.

ETHOLOGY – (eth-*OL*-luh-jee) The branch of zoology that studies animal behavior. The term "ethology" derives from the Greek *"ethos"* meaning *"character,"* and *"logia"* meaning *"study of."* A Caveat: Do not confuse <u>etho</u>logy with <u>ethno</u>logy, which is the study of human cultural development.

ETHOS – (*EE*-thos) The organizational soul. The deepest held convictions of an institution. An organization's spirit as enunciated in its mission statement is its ethos.

ETIOLATE – (*EE*-tee-uh-late) (etiolated, Etiolating) To cause a plant to weaken, whiten, grow pale, by depriving light. The term etiolate has expanded to include anything that is made sickly, drained of vitality, color, and vigor.

ETIOLOGY – (ay-tee-*Ol*-lo-jee) The investigation of causes, causation, causality, applied to science or philosophy. A Caveat: Don't confuse etiology with etymology, the study of word origins; or entomology, the study of bugs.

ETIQUETTE – (*ET*-ti-ket) Artificially prescribed code of social behavior, conventional customs, primarily for appearance, like dinner table utensil usage. An estimated 90% of etiquette rules are meaningless, made arbitrarily at some point in the past. Incidentally: On her death bed, etiquette high priestess, Emile Post (1872 – 1960) sighed: *"What difference does it make what fork you use at dinner!?"*

ETRUSCANS – (et-*TRUS*-cans) An advanced ancient people from Etruria (roughly modern Tuscany) in west-central Italy. The Etruscans dominated the fledgling Romans until the Romans rebelled and conquered them about 264 BCE. Powerful Etruscan families remained influential in early Rome. The early Etruscans spoke an enigmatic non-Indo-European language, yet to be deciphered. The Etruscans were a liberal, tolerant people, the most erotic in antiquity. Their women were totally liberated. They were not at all sexually inhibited. The Etruscans were quite superstitious though. The Etruscans later adopted the Greek alphabet, altered it, and passed it on to the Romans. The Greeks also taught them how to grow grapes and make wine. The Etruscans passed this knowledge down to Romans and Gauls. The gladiatorial games were bequeathed to the Romans by the Etruscans. Much of Roman culture rests on an Etruscan foundation.

ET SEQ. – (et SEEK) (Abbreviated form of *et sequens*.) A Latin term, *et seq.* means *"and those following,"* or *"the following item."*

ETYMOLOGY – (et-ti-*MOL*-lo-jee) The research and study of word origins. Where a definition tells what a word means, an etymology tells where a word came from. So, if definition is comparable to your name, etymology is comparable to your ethnic background and nationality. A Caveat: Don't confuse etymology with etiology, the investigation of causes; or entomology, the study of bugs.

ETYMON – (*ET*-ti-mon) (Etyma, Etymology, Etymological) The etymology of etymon is the Greek *"etymos,"* meaning *true, real, actual.* An etymon is a linguistic form of a word from which the modern form is historically derived. It is a word origin. Take for example the word theology. The etymons creating the word are taken from the Greek words *"theo,"* meaning *God,* and *"logia,"* meaning *study of.* The Greek *"theologia"* was adopted into Latin, then transferred into French as *"theologie."* The French term was bequeathed to English as theology. Incidentally, the study of etymons is etymology.

EUCHARIST – (*YOU*-car-rist) The consecrated bread, shared at the Holy Communion of the Lord's Supper. The Eucharistic Banquet is a Holy Sacrament of the Catholic Church. The distribution and consumption of the Holy Eucharist is the center piece and purpose of the Catholic Mass. The term Eucharist derives from the Latin *"eucharistia,"* and the Greek *"eukharistia,"* meaning *"thanksgiving, gratitude."* In the Catholic Mass, the Eucharist is more than symbolic. Through the doctrine of *"Transubstantiation,"* the priest transmutes the bread into the actual body of Jesus Christ. Likewise, the wine is transmuted into Christ's blood. This is performed spiritually, not physically. Faith is absolved of proof.

EUDAEMONISM – (you-*DAY*-mon-is-um) In philosophy, the theory that acts are right insofar as thy contribute to man's well-being and happiness. The emphasis in eudaemonism is not upon pleasure, as in hedonistic ethics, but upon the way of life most suited to man's nature.

EUGENICS – (you-*JEN*-nix) The scientific breeding of people with specific racial, physical traits deemed superior. Eugenics is designed to preserve racial purity (an oxymoronic concept). The Nazis elevated eugenics to a serious and murderous national policy. Still, to the wealthy, eugenics is a viable solution to poverty.

EUGLENA – (yoo-*GLEE*-na) A green unicellular organism with a reddish eyespot found in stagnant freshwater pools. The euglena has a long tail called a flagellum with which it navigates like an animal. However, like an alga, its body contains chlorophyll which produces sugar from sunlight like a plant. Therefore, the euglena is a cross between a plant and animal. Perhaps sentient organisms like the euglena made the transition from plant to animal about 1.5 billion years ago. Today euglenas are classed as protists (protoctist), along with algae, molds, fungi, protozoans simple bacteria, organisms between the plant animal kingdoms. Footnote: The first animal was a plant that turned cannibal.

EULOGY – (*YOO*-la-jee) A praise-worthy speech for a deceased person, even if he is not worthy of praise. According to St. Augustine (354 – 430 CE) *"No eulogy is due to him who simply does his duty and nothing more."* Seldom if ever is the truth spoken in a eulogy. Death seems to exonerate or at least mitigate the sins, crimes, absurdities of the person-turned-carcass. Some may fear antagonizing the liberated spirit. Or perhaps it's because we subconsciously imagine being the defenseless corps inevitably, and hope that undeserved kindness will be cast upon us. As baseball great, and dugout philosopher Yogi Berra (1925 – 2015) asserted: *"You got to go to peoples' funerals, or when you die, they won't come to yours."* Be that as it may, the safest policy is to *"Live your eulogy."* Incidentally: In May, 2018, Senator John McCain (b. 1936), dying of brain cancer announced that he invites former Presidents George W. Bush (b. 1946) and Barrack Obama (b. 1961) to his inevitable funeral. McCain made it known that he does not want President Donald Trump (b. 1946) in attendance. McCain despised Trump! A Caveat: Don't confuse eulogy with elegy, a melancholy, mournful poem, especially a funeral song or lament for the dead.

EUNUCH – (*YU*-nuk) A castrated, sexless man. A eunuch is a male rendered more docile and sexually inert by the removal of his genitals. Eunuchs served as guards in the harems of powerful sheiks. Being sexless, eunuchs would not be tempted to taste the forbidden fruit.

EUPHEMISM – (*Yu*-fem-is-um) (Euphemistically) A word you use when you can't use the word you really mean or want. Euphemisms are a form of hypocrisy, falsetalk. A popular euphemism used by hunters is *"harvest,"* rather than kill. Therefore, one does not shoot the deer in the heart, but rather *"harvests"* the deer in the heart. In January 2017, President Trump's (b. 1946) Press Secretary Sean Spicer (b. 1971) and the President's Counselor Kellyanne Conway (b. 1967) rattled-off a litany of lies, that they euphemistically called *"alternative facts."* Euphemisms are readily used by the military to sanitize a rotten situation. For example, an invasion becomes an *"incursion."* People are not killed but *"neutralized."* A bodybag is a *"remains past human."* Torture is *"enhanced interrogation."* At the U.S. Guantanamo Bay Prison Camp in Cuba, a suicide by a detainee is called a *"manipulative self-injurious behavior."*

EUPHONY – (*YOO*-fone-nee) (Euphonious) Pleasant sounding. A harp is euphonious, a cymbal is not.

EUPHORIA – (you-*FOR*-ree-a) (Euphoric) An ecstatic state of joy, almost manic happiness, frenzied exaltation. Mystic saints who survive their *"Dark Night of the Soul"* enter rhapsodic euphoria in their enlightenment or atonement [read: *at-one-ment*] with God. On the mundane, temporal, carnal realm, a powerful orgasm is as euphoric as it gets.

EUPHORIATE – (you-*FOR*-ree-ate) Any route to euphoria. A euphoriate can be a drug, potion, chant, dance, orgasm, prayer or meditation. As long as an ecstatic, rhapsodic condition is produced, the process qualifies as a euphoriate. For some, alcohol serves as a euphoriate, initially. It mimics serotonin, the *"feel good"* neurotransmitter (brain chemical). But alcohol is a heinous deceiver, for soon, depression sets in followed by veisalgia (hangover). Footnote: A recovered drug addict testified that the immediate sensation from smoking crack cocaine can only be described as *"a total body orgasm."*

EURASIA – (your-*AISH*-sha) The combined continental landmass of Europe plus Asia. Eurasia is geographically separated by the Ural Mountains in far Eastern Russia.

EURASIAN UNION – (your-*AISH*-she-an *YOON*-yon) A revived version of the Union of Soviet Socialist Republics, as planned by Russian Dictopresident Vladimir Putin (b. 1952). Putin's grand strategy is to reassert Russian hegemony over the former Soviet states that had gained independence. The plan is to establish a confederation of the former states, re-integrating their economies and foreign policies with Russia's. Unlike the Union of Soviet *Socialist* Republics, the new Eurasian Union will not be *Socialist.* There is nothing Communistic [read: *Socialist*] about President Putin. He is thoroughly, greedily, capitalist. He has privatized all the government controlled, Socialist industries. Of course, a percentage of these industries are owned by Putin. With a net worth of over 200 billion dollars, Vladimir Putin is one of the richest men in the world, and one of the most powerful. *"Indeed, Putin has been corrupted by the blessings of capitalism!"* Communists are egalitarian comrades, not capitalist oligarchs. Putin is not about to Socialistically share his wealth with his Russian comrades. (Of course, Russia has a homeless population now, another capitalist blessing.) The Eurasian Union will begin as the Russian counterpart to the EU (<u>E</u>uropean <u>U</u>nion) and NATO (<u>N</u>orth <u>A</u>tlantic <u>T</u>reaty <u>O</u>rganization). But this is a mere prelude to future political domination, occupation, and incorporation. The list of nations that Putin is targeting are: Belarus, Moldova, Georgia, Armenia, Azerbaijan, Turkmenistan, Uzbekistan, Kyrgyzstan, and Tajikistan. If all goes well, perhaps the Ukraine, and even the 3 Baltic States of Lithuania, Latvia, and Estonia will be re-incorporated. Poland, Romania, Bulgaria, and old Yugoslavia better be alert. News Flash: It is now March, 2022. Putin has commenced his Euroasian project with a devastating invasion of the Ukraine. Prayerfully, the righteous world democracies will be able to stop him. *"The only way Russia can defend its borders is to expand them."* – Empress Catherine the Great (1729 – 1796).

EURO – (*YOUR*-roh) Name of the currency used by most of the members of the <u>E</u>uropean <u>U</u>nion (EU): France, Germany, Spain, Portugal, Belgium, Italy, Finland, Ireland Austria, Greece, Netherlands, Slovenia,

Estonia, Latvia, Luxembourg, Andorra, Monaco, Guadeloupe, Martinique, French Guiana, Vatican, and other micro-states.

EUROAMERICANS – (your-roh-am-*MER*-ri-cans) Caucasians, generally British, Irish, French, Dutch, Spanish, Polish, Italian, and others in America, as well as all Americans of U.S. citizenship. After all, every white American had European ancestry. The term Euroamericans is used to distinguish them from Afro-Americans and Native Americans.

EUROCENTRISM – (your-roh-*SENT*-tris-um) (Eurocentric) Literally means Europe front-and-center. Eurocentrism is a weltanschauuug or world view that makes Europe and Caucasian values supreme in the world. It is ethnocentric and even racist as it elevates European-based Western Civilization above all other cultures. Nations like America, Canada, Australia, New Zealand that were established and populated by Europeans share in the Eurocentric bias. History from a white man's perspective prevails. According to the *"Center for InterAmerican Studies"* at Germany's Bielefeld University, A Eurocentric approach to history and geopolitics often disregards the colonial violence and exploitation inflicted by Europe on much of the world. Too, Eurocentrism implies that Caucasian perspectives are dominant and Christian values are superior and the only reliable narratives.

EUROCRATS – (*YOUR*-roh-crats) Europeans who support the European Union (EU).

EUROPEAN UNION – (your-roh-*PEE*-an *YOON*-yon) (EU) An economic association, made up of several European countries, whose ultimate goal is for Europe to be a unified economic region. (The covert intention of organizing the EU was to restrain German economic dominance by tying its economy to the rest of Europe. So the EU's hidden agenda is to keep Germany in, and keep Russia out.) Economic interdependence will nullify the need for war. Hopefully, the EU will be the first step toward a U.S.E. (United States of Europe) or U.N.E. (United Nations of Europe). Unfortunately, the European Union absorbed a tremendous blow when a key member, Britain, abandoned the Union in 2016. The withdrawal campaign was called *"BrExit,"* for British Exit.

EUROPIUM – (your-roh-*POR*-ree-um) (Eu) The element is named after Europe. The 63 protons in its nucleus give Europium its atomic number. Europium is a soft, ductile, reactive, silvery-white element of the rare-earth metals. Europium produces light pink salts. It is used as the red phosphor in color televisions and lasers.

EUROPOID – (*YOUR*-row-poyd) (Europoidal) Bearing the physical characteristics of Caucasian Europeans. Europoid is a general term. Eurpoidal individuals have white skin, with long, narrow noses. They are generally tall with elongated faces. They have round, almond-shaped eyes. Their hair is relatively straight to wavy, colored black, brown, blonde, reddish, gray, and sometimes white. The males display moderate to heavy body hair. People genetically originating from the Germanic, Scandinavian, Slavonic and Mediterranean populations are included in the Europoid classification.

EUROZONE – (*YOUR*-row-zoan) Those member states of the European Union that have adopted the euro as the national currency. They are considered as a single economic entity. The Eurozone includes: Austria, Belgium, Cyprus, Estonia, Finland, France, Germany, Greece, Ireland, Italy, Latvia, Lithuania,

Luxembourg, Malta, Netherlands, Portugal, Slovakia, Slovenia, and Spain. Incidentally: Andorra, Monaco, San Marino, and The Vatican accept the euro, as well as their own currency. Too, Kosovo and Montenegro have adopted the euro exclusively, but are not European Union members.

EUSTATIUS – (you-*STAY*-shus) (Actually, St. Eustatius.) Small volcanic island (7 sq. miles) in the Netherlands Antilles (Caribbean). Known by its citizens as Statia (*STAY*-sha), St. Eustatius is a semi-autonomous part of Holland. It has been called *"The Golden Rock of the Caribbean."* It is 3.3 times bigger than Central Park, New York. St. Eustatius played an important role in the American War of Independence. The island's Dutch warehouses became a vast depot for guns and powder (largely French), shipped to the Americans during the Revolutionary War (1775 – 1783). Furthermore, on November 16, 1776, the American warship *Andrew Doria,* flying the new U.S. flag sailed to the island. The governor fired a cannonade symbolic of official recognition. This was the historic *"First Salute."* By doing so, St. Eustatius had become the first state to recognize American independence, and the birth of the United States.

EUSTRESS – (*YOU*-stress) Healthy stress, (as opposed to unhealthy distress). *Eus*-tress is *use*-full stress. It keeps us stimulated, alert, enthused. Like exercise or pressure on muscles and bones, eustress helps keep us fit, physical and mentally. A little tension keeps us from becoming mentally, emotionally flabby.

EUTHENASIA – (you-then-*AY*-sha) Inducing a painless death. Euthanasia is employed to put a sufferer out of misery. It should be the personal privilege of those suffering a terminal illness, to decide whether they wish languish in anguish, or pass to Paradise. Euthanasia involves assisted suicide or mercy killing. Dr. Jack Kevorkian (1928 – 2011) (University of Michigan) was persecuted as *"Doctor Death"* and imprisoned for helping terminal, pain-ridden people undergo a painless, peaceful, dignified departure. Incidentally: A Jamaican friend, Carlene, has dramatic and eloquent plans for her peaceful departure. Carlene insisted that she would not lose her mind, would not writhe in pain, and would not bankrupt her family in her last days. She will call together her family and close friends with plenty of champagne. After the farewells, she will go to bed with a full bottle of sleeping pills. *"Death is not the greatest of evils. It is worse to want to die, and not be able to."* – Sophocles (c. 497 – 406 BCE). *"Thank Heaven! The crisis, the danger is past, and the lingering illness, is over at last, and the fever called 'Living' is conquered at last."* – Edgar Allan Poe (1809 – 1849).

EVACUATION VILLAGES – (ee-vac-kew-*AY*-shun *VIL*-la-jes) A hypothetical plan that would save tens-of-thousands of lives in a meteorological or seismic emergency. The great natural peril to Florida and other coastal regions are hurricanes and tsunamis. The Socialist solution is a series of evacuation villages. Up and down the Florida Peninsula, in the center of the state, refugee centers would be constructed. Several thousand small units of reinforced concrete would be built. They would be simply furnished but livable, like a spartan motel room. Standard emergency clothing and plenty of non-perishable food would be provided. Superhighways from all surrounding population centers would lead to the villages. Too, Fast mass-transit trains would also run to these safe havens. Evacuation villages would create thousands of federally funded jobs. This would revitalize the economy. Nothing good comes cheaply. The rich and their corporations would pay for the project through fair taxation (as they did for the Interstate Highway System in the 1950's).

EVALUATOR'S CREDO – (ee-*VAL*-you-ate-tors *C*RAY-dow) *"Whatever exists, exists in some amount, and it can be measured."* – Psychologist Edward Thorndike (1874 – 1949).

EVALUATION – (ee-*VAL*-you-a-shun) An appraisal, a diagnostic determination to judge the value of an examination, performance, or personality. Formative evaluation is part of the teaching-learning process. Summative evaluation determines pass or fail.

EVALUATIVE QUESTION – (ee-*VAL*-you-a-tiv *KWES*-chun) An inquiry or question that requires that a judgement be made or a value be put on something. For Example: *"What economic system conforms with the Social Gospel preached by Jesus?" "Socialism, of course."*

EVANGELICALISM – (ev-*VAN*-jel-is-um) (Evangelists, Evangelize, Evangelicals) Evangelicalism is Biblical Fundamentalism. Evangelicalism accepts the Scriptures as the word of God, fundamentally. That means being fundamentally in compliance with Jesus' Social Gospel, and evangelizing it universally. Biblical Evangelism proselytizes the feeding, clothing, and housing of the poor, despite the cost. Jesus said: *"If you love me, feed my lambs, feed my sheep,"* (John 21:15). But present day Evangelicals don't subscribe to these Scriptural fundamentals. They have become Political Fundamentalists. Political issues concerning the conservative Republican agenda (anti-abortion, anti-gay marriage, school prayer, low taxes, voter suppression) is what they proselytize. A true, Christocentric Evangelical would never excuse and support a lying, cheating, lecherous, treacherous heathen like Donald Trump (b. 1946). This is not Biblical Evangelicalism. It is theological heresy to say so. It's conservative political manipulation of Evangelicalism. True Scriptural Evangelicalism is as compassionate and Socialistic as was Jesus. Footnote: Much in the Old Testament (first 4/5ths of the Bible) is time contingent – meant for a particular people, in a particular place, for a specific reason, at a specific time. Furthermore, much is also ancient Hebrew mythology.

EVANGELICALS – (ee-van-*JEL*-lih-cahls) (Evangelists, Evangelize, Evangelicalism) Technically, an Evangelical is one who Evangelizes, or preaches/teaches the Bible, and the word of Jesus, as written in the Gospels. That is far from their present-day profile. Evangelicals primarily occupy the entire arch of the South, from Virginia down to Florida, west along the Gulf Coast, through Texas, up into Arkansas, Oklahoma, and Nebraska. This is the *"Bible Belt."* Evangelicals are strongest in the rural regions. Evangelicals have always been a paradoxical population. Despite their boastful Christian sanctimoniousness, it was they who owned the slaves. Despite their boastful patriotism, it was they who turncoat, rebelled, and made war against the United States in the Civil War (1861 – 1865). Evangelicals organized the Ku Klux Klan (KKK) and lynched their Black neighbors. Evangelicals were the segregationists, who prevented Blacks from voting with *"Jim Crow"* laws. Holy Evangelicals fought the Civil Rights Bills, and when they lost, joined the Republican Party en masse. After the Evangelical Republicans lost the 2020 presidential election, they established *"neo-Jim Crow"* laws to suppress the Black vote. Evangelicals are racists, at best, bigots. They have substituted the Gospel of Trump for the Gospel of Jesus. Incidentally: Evangelicals need a *"Great Awakening,"* a revival of the fundamental teachings of Jesus, especially his *"Social Gospel,"* as written in Matthew 25: 35-40. *"Jesus is too woke for today's Evangelicals."* – Traditional Republican Michael Steele (b. 1958).

EVANGENITALS – (ee-van-*JEN*-nit-tuhls) Lascivious Evangelicals. Hypocritical pastors, who preach sexual restraint and decency, but practice sexual decadence. Some Evangenitals are high profile TV personalities.

They are profiled even higher when they are caught in extra-marital affairs, or even in homosexual liaisons. Some of the most prominent Evangenitals are Pastor Jimmy Swaggart (b. 1935); Pastor Jim Baker (b. 1940); Pastor Ted Haggard (b. 1956); Pastor Jerry Falwell Jr. (b. 1962).

EVAPORITES – (ee-*VAP*-por-ites) In geology, sedimentary rocks formed from minerals left after water evaporated.

EVAPORATION – (ee-vap-por-*RAY*-shun) Conversion of a liquid into a gas. Water heated into vapor, steam or gas is evaporation. Evaporation produces clouds. Evaporating water carries heat away with it. That is why sweating cools the body. The drier the air, the cooler you'll be because dry air holds more water, resulting in more evaporation, resulting in more heat loss from your body. Conversely, when the relative humidity is high, the saturated air cannot hold much body evaporation. The wet sweat remains on the skin surface holding the body heat against the body.

EVEREST – (*EV*-ver-rest) (Sagarmatha in Nepali, Chomolungma in Tibetan.) Himalayan Mountain on the Tibet-Nepal border, the tallest in the world. Mt. Everest is 29,028 feet above sea level, or five-and-a-half miles high. About 10% of Everest's climbers die in the attempt. Everest was born 50 million years ago when the Indian subcontinent slammed into Asia. The Indian plate subducted under the Asian plate uplifting the Earth. India is still moving northward under Asia at 2 inches a year. So the Himalayas and Mt. Everest are still growing. But the geological giant will not grow indefinitely. Eventually, it will have to collapse under the force of its own weight. The top of Everest is sedimentary limestone. The middle of the mountain is composed of metamorphic marble, the base and root (*pluton*) is igneous granite. Remarkably, ocean marine fossils are found in the limestone rock atop Mt. Everest, proof of the uplift. Footnote: Trying to breathe atop Mt. Everest, is like trying to breathe at a height outside a commercial airliner. Incidentally: Mt. Everest was named after Sir George Everest (1790 – 1866), the Surveyor-General of India, who never climbed the mountain.

EVERGLADES – (*EV*-er-glayds) A huge subtropical swampland in southern Florida that covers about one-and-a half million acres, or 4,000 square miles of wetlands. It is therefore 25% larger than Rhode Island and Delaware combined. Thirty different species of snake inhabit the Everglades, 4 of which are venomous. The Everglades is now home to scores of animals, invasive species, in particular the Burmese python. Today, over 50,000 pythons inhabit the marshland. In the battle for dominance, the python will replace the alligator as the apex predator. The Miami metropolis is only 18 miles away from the glades. Incidentally: The everglades are the last refuge in the U.S.A. for the rare American crocodile, about 2,000 surviving.

EVICTION – (ee-*VIK*-shun) (Evict, Evicted) To be ousted, dispossessed of one's home. To legally expel a tenant along with family from land, a building, or lodging, usually for nonpayment of rent to a landlord. Eviction is a cruel, heartless, inhumane capitalist practice. Poverty, tragedy, and adversity may make the rent payment impossible. A poor family may have to choose among food, medicine, clothing, or rent. To the lord of the land or property, his rent takes priority. If not, the family is evicted, made homeless, furniture and meager belongings cast out on the street in the rain and snow. Of all the animals on Earth, only man must pay rent for a spot on this planet to lay his head. Even Jesus lamented: *"Foxes have holes, and birds of the air have nests, but the Son of Man has nowhere to lay his head,"* – Matthew 8:20. The landlord has his legal right, for the law is on the capitalist's side. Of course, that's because landlords, property owners make the law. *"The majesty equality of the law forbids the rich, as well as the poor to sleep under bridges, to beg in the street, and to steal bread,"* – Anatole France (1844 – 1924). Eviction is indifferent to pain and should be illegal, like the debtor's prison. Decent housing should be a constitutional right. Those who are unable to purchase a domicile should be awarded a respectable government owned dwelling, rent free. No one should be evicted and compelled to sleep in a dumpster or cardboard box. *"Live in my heart and pay no rent."* – Irish Proverb.

EVIDENCE – (*EV*-vi-dens) (Evidential, Evidentiary, Evidently) In a court of law, artifacts, documents, photographs, video tape, witness testimony all constitute evidence. Truth, and therefore justice are arrived at through evidence. In his impeachment and Senatorial trial, President Donald Trump (b. 1946) withheld every type of evidence from Congress. Trump and his Republican sycophants [read: *ass-likers*] feared the truth. More so, they fear that the American people would learn the truth. The truth would result in imprisonment for Trump and his enablers, co-conspirators. That's why they were hiding and denying the evidence. Incidentally: *"The absence of evidence is not evidence of absence"* – Archeologist's Credo.

EVIDENT – (*EV*-vi-dent) Plain or clear to sight or understanding. *"Trump's guilt was clearly evident."*

EVIDENTIARY – (ev-vi-*DENT*-chee-air-ree) (Evidential, Evidently, Evidence) Of or relating to physical or testimonial proof or evidence. *"Evidentiary proof condemned Trump as a fraud, criminal, and traitor."*

EVIL – (*EE*-vil) A state of separation from God (Good). Evil is having fallen out of atonement (*at-one-ment*) with God. As there is no such thing as darkness, but an absence of light, and there is no such thing as cold, but an absence of heat, there is no such thing as evil but an absence of Good or God. In a less theological context, evil is a subjective concept that varies greatly according to culture, tradition, time frame, and circumstance. For example, one may agree that murder is evil. Too, Adolf Hitler was evil. The murders that Hitler had ordered were evil. But the order to murder Hitler was not evil, but good. *"Where's evil? It's that large part of every man that wants to hate without limit, that wants to hate with God on its side."* – Kurt Vonnegut (1922 – 2007). *"There are three all-powerful evils: lust, anger, and greed."* – Tulsidas (c. 1511 – 1623).

EVIL DIVIDER – (*EE*-vil div-*VY*-der) One who maliciously attempts to sow discord within a family, organization, nation, or among a population to weaken the target for personal gain. Evil divider was the role the *"Contra-President"* Donald Trump (b. 1946) performed. Trump is justifiably called a <u>Contra</u>-President because his actions were (and continue to be) <u>contra</u>dictory, <u>contra</u>ry to the moral responsibility of a President to unite the people. Trump has demonstrated that he has no convictions, ethics, or morals. His only core value is himself, his ego, fed by self-indulgence and self-aggrandizement. Trump learned from the *"Tea Party,"* and *"The Birthers,"* that he can divide and conquer. By stoking the flames of bigotry, racism, fear, and hate, Trump was able to muster just enough support to hijack the Presidency. Trump behaved like a vengeful Mafia don, enriching his family, and punishing his enemies. Trump intentionally made more enemies. An evil divider needs enemies to keep his devotees frightened and angry enough to continue supporting him. The *"culture war"* was contrived to serve as red meat, to satisfy the bloodlust of Trump's troops. The evil divider turns liberals against conservatives, the religious against the secular, pro-life against pro-choice, whites against blacks, native born against immigrants, urban against rural, educated against the unschooled – in other words, to create the *"Disunited States of America."* Civil strife, civil disorder, civil war are all in Trump's plans. The most frightful auspice is that the calamitous national divide will long out-live the evil divider. *"Every kingdom divided against itself is laid waste, and no city or house divided against itself will stand."* – Jesus, in Matthew 12:25.

EVIL EMPIRE – (*EE*-vil *EM*-py-yer) President Ronald Reagan's (1911 – 2004) insulting depiction of the Soviet Union and Russians, that derailed détente and heated-up the cold war (1980). Russian Premier Yuri Andropov (1914 – 1984) called Reagan *"Insane."* Russian Premier Mikhail Gorbachev (b. 1931) called Reagan *"A caveman and a dinosaur."* In his 1988 visit to Moscow, President Reagan recanted his *"Evil Empire"* slur in the Kremlin.

EVIL EYE – (*EE*-vil *AHY*) A look that is thought capable of inflicting injury or bad luck on the person at whom it is directed. The evil eye is a curse at a glance. Some are thought to possess the power to inflict bad luck or harm with a stare. Many cultures maintain a belief in the evil eye. Envy, jealousy, revenge are common motives for retaliating with the evil eye.

EVIL ISMS – (*EE*-vil *IZ*-ums) The evil isms are three in number. They are the cause of all man-made strife and misery on Planet Earth. They are *Fascism, Racism,* and *Capitalism.* The governmental evil is Fascism, the social evil is Racism, the economic evil is Capitalism. Fascism is the source of domination, dictatorship. Racism is the source of hate, injustice. Capitalism is the source of greed, want. Fascism, Racism, and Capitalism is Satan's destructive agenda for mankind. These are the raw materials with which Satan creates sin. Every human atrocity has been instigated by these evil isms. Poverty, persecution, prejudice would not exist, if not for Fascism, Racism, and Capitalism. Remove these evil isms from the equation of human relations, and we have removed the cause of war itself. Eliminate Fascism, Racism, and Capitalism and we eliminate the possibility of genocide ever more. The abundance of Planet Earth is unimaginable. Yet, there is hunger and starvation among us. Eradicate Fascism, Racism, and Capitalism, and we will eradicate famine, worldwide, as well. The three evil isms are a curse, a plague on our species, and on all life on Earth. Incidentally: The solution, the salvation from Fascism, Racism, and Capitalism is Democracy, Brotherhood, and Socialism.

EVIL TRINITY – (*EE*-vil *TRIN*-nit-ee) The three scourges of the human race: <u>Fascism</u> (persecution), <u>Capitalism</u> (exploitation), and <u>Racism</u> (hate). Together, these 3 vices are responsible for all the misery suffered by humanity. Fascism is government by dictatorship. Personal freedom is supplanted by oppression. Fascism robs people of their dignity and humanity. Most wars are commenced by fascist regimes. Life in a fascist state is lived in fear of arrest, torture, and imprisonment. Much of humanity suffers the lash of fascism. Capitalism is the economics of greed. It is the reason why most of the world lives in poverty. Wealth, the Earth's bounty, is hoarded by a small minority of individuals at the very apex of the food chain. *"I got mine, to hell with you"* is the credo of capitalism. It is estimated that about 7,000 people in the world own everything! That amounts to about 0.00009% of the planetary population. This is due to capitalism. Capitalism is the perpetrator of illness, starvation, and death. Racism is the hatred of people who do not resemble the racist. Color is the primary criterion for considering some people as inferior. Racism, like fascism and capitalism dehumanizes people. It deprives others of a fair chance to succeed in life. In extreme cases, as with the German Hitlerite Nazis, racism turned people into animals, or rather into things. Like debris in a trash dump, racism victims were incarnated in death camps. Incidentally: The Evil Trinity of fascism, capitalism, and racism united in the Nazi movement. The salvation of civilizations depends on substituting Democracy for Fascism; Socialism for Capitalism; and Brotherhood for Racism.

EVINCE – (ee-*VINS*) (Evincing) To prove, show clearly, manifest or make perfectly certain a point of view or emotion.

EVISCERATE – (ev-*VIS*-er-rate) (Eviscerated, Evisceration) Disembowel, to cut and pull out the entrails or intestines from a creature. Animals are eviscerated when butchered for meat. Incidentally: In Medieval England, public evisceration was one of the execution steps for treason by a commoner. He would be partially hanged, eviscerated, and then quartered (torn limbs from body by 4 horses). This was the fate of the Scottish rebel/patriot, William Wallace (c. 1270 – 1305), *"Braveheart."* Footnote: Noble, aristocratic traitors were neatly, quickly, painlessly beheaded for treason.

EVOCATIVE – (ee-*VOK*-ka-tiv) (Evoke, Evocation) Tending to arouse, incite, inflame, stimulate, cause, or summon. An evocative statement or behavior elicits strong emotional reactions. It evokes an intense response. An evocative person is forever controversial and often in conflict. No American politician and influencer has been more evilly evocative than vile Donald Trump (b. 1946).

EVOKE – (ee-*VOHK*) (Evoked, Evocation, Evocative) To call up, summon, elicit, cause to appear. In metaphysics and witchcraft, to evoke a spirit is to call it up, to summon it forth, to bring it into your environment, particularly in hopes of gathering its favor and services. Both benevolent and malevolent spirits can be evoked. A Caveat: Don't confuse *"evoke," "call up"* a spirit, with *"invoke,"* which is to *"call in"* a spirit. Invocation is an invitation for possession. The spirit is drawn into one's body.

EVOLUTION – (ev-vo-*LOO*-shun) A slow, gradual change in the phylogeny of a species, adapting to changing environmental conditions, becoming more complex, advanced and sophisticated. Evolution progresses from the simple to the increasingly complex and advanced. Human evolution simplistically followed the progression from ape to ape-man to man-ape to man. Our humanoid ancestors left the trees for the African savanna about 7 million years ago. Proto-human Australopithecines stood erect about 4 million years ago. They evolved into Homo habilis and began to fashion crude tools 2.5 million years ago. Homo habilis (1st tool maker) evolved into Pithecanthropine Homo erectus (the 1st fire maker). About 700,000 years ago, Homo erectus migrated throughout the Old World. Homo erectus spawned 2 human-like species. Denisovans evolved deep in Asia. In the Middle East and Europe, Homo erectus evolved into Homo neanderthalis (c. 500,000 years ago). Therefore, Neanderthal Man was in Europe 100,000 years before Homo sapien (modern man) about 50,000 years ago. Homo sapien also evolved from Homo erectus long after the Neanderthals had. Homo sapien evolved into our present day condition about 200,000 years ago. In Europe, modern man and Neanderthals coexisted and mated for at least 5,000 years. Too, Homo sapiens and Homo erectus may have met in Asia. Incidentally: It took at least 2 million years for man to change from the little dark creature with the stone in his hand, Australopithecus in Central Africa, to the modern form, Homo sapiens. That is the pace of biological evolution – even though the biological evolution of man has been faster than that of any other animal. *"If man came from monkeys, how come we still have monkeys?"* – Herschel Walker (b. 1962), Footballer turned Trumpublican Politician. The ancient Greek Philosopher Empedocles (490 – 430 BCE) suggested both reincarnation and evolution when he said: *"For before this, I was born once a boy, and a maiden, and a plant, and a bird, and a darting fish in the sea."*

EWER – (*YOO*-er) A large jug or pitcher with a wide spout.

EX – (*EKS*) A prefix or word-forming element, in English meaning *"out of, from,"* but also *"upwards, completely, deprived of, without,"* and *"former."* The word *"ex"* derives from Latin. In Latin it can mean: *"out of, from within; from which time, since; according to; in regard to."*

EX ANIMO – (eks a-*NEE*-mo) Latin for sincerely, *"from the heart."*

EXACTING – (eks-*ACK*-ting) Rigid, or severe in demand, sacrifice, hardship. *"Travel in the days of the Apostolic missionaries was indeed exacting."*

EX CATHEDRA – (eks ca-*THEE*-dra) Latin for *"From the chair."* Ex cathedra means with authority by virtue of one's office. In the Catholic Church, Ex Cathedra refers to the Papal encyclical of 1870 which created the doctrine of *"Papal Infallibility."* It states that as Head of the Church, the Pope cannot be wrong when speaking on ecclesiastical issues.

EXCEPTIONAL LEARNER – (eks-*SEP*-shun-al *LERN*-ner) A student officially identified as handicapped, disabled, challenged. Exceptional learners have special learning needs and require special instruction. Cost should never be an issue when serving these special children. You judge the righteousness of a nation in how it treats its least, and mot needy, helpless citizens. The Democrats (Socialists) will, the Republicans (capitalists) won't.

EXCEPTIONALISM (eks-*SEP*-shun-al-is-um) (American) – The arrogant notion that America is somehow special among nations with a divinely ordained manifest destiny. American exceptionalism is chauvinistic, ethnocentric nationalism mixed with mysticism. It proclaims Americans as the new *"chosen people"*. America is exceptional for its distributive injustice, lack of universal healthcare, and miserly social programs for the needy. America experiences all the virtues and vices displayed by every other country. In February, 2017, President Trump told political analyst Joe Scarborough (b. 1963) *"Well I think that our country does plenty of killing too, Joe."* Trump candidly went on to tell political analyst Bill O'Reilly (b. 1949): *"There are a lot of killers. We've got a lot of killers. Well, you think our country is so innocent."* Trump spoke the truth for a change. So much for American Exceptionalism. Philosopher Henry David Thoreau (1817 – 1862) had admonished: *"They are to be men first, and Americans only at a late and convenient hour."*

EXCHANGE JEW – (eks-*CHAYNJ JEW*) During the insanity which was the Nazi regime, exchange Jews were Jewish families with a member who was a citizen of a foreign nation at war with Germany. These Jews were not sent to the concentration camps. They were exchanged to that foreign nation for German P.O.W.'s (Prisoners Of War), if that nation bought into the bargain.

EXCISION – (eks-*SISZ*-on) Means cutting out, as opposed to *incision* which is cutting into. A surgeon must first make an incision, in order to make an excision of a tumor.

EXCLAVE – (*EKS*-klayv) (also Enclave) A part of a country that is separated from the rest of the country by a foreign territory. This geopolitical situation can spell trouble. East Prussia, separated from Germany proper by the Polish Corridor provided an excuse for the German invasion of Poland in 1939, starting World War Two. Bangladesh (East Pakistan) separated from Pakistan proper by India resulted in a bloody war of independence won by Bangladesh (1971). Alaska is an exclave, separated from the U.S. proper by Canada. Technically, Hawaii cannot be considered an exclave, because the Pacific Ocean is not a nation. The exclave of Kaliningrad is a Russian exclave sandwiched between Poland and Lithuania, totally separated from the Russian mainland. It may be the most politically precarious territory in the world.

EXCLUSIONARY RULE – (eks-*CLU*-shun-air-ree *ROOL*) In law a procedure in search-and-seizure cases seeking to suppress the use of evidence which has been improperly obtained.

EXCOMMUNICATION – (eks-com-mun-ni-*KAY*-shun) (Excommunicated, Excommunicating, Excommunicant) To be cut-off from membership, participation, communion with the Church. An excommunicant is denied all sacraments of the Church by ecclesiastical sentence. To Catholic believers, excommunication is a sentence to hell. It was a powerful weapon used by Popes against political enemies – kings, Masons, and Communists.

EXCORIATE – (eks-*COR*-ree-ate) (Execration) To denounce vehemently, to brutally berate, to censure severely. To excoriate also refers to stripping or skinning an animal. So to be excoriated is to be verbally skinned, tongue- lashed, flayed, stripped of all dignity.

EXCREMENT – (EKS-kruh-ment) (Excremental, Excrementally) Solid or semi-solid waste matter discharged from the body as feces. Excrement in the vulgar vernacular is *"shit,"* and excremental means *"shitty." "Donald Trump's excremental ravings are worthy of his cultists."*

EXCRESCENCE – (eks-*KRES*-sens) A projection or protuberance, an outgrowth from some part of an animal or vegetable body. A tumor is an excrescence, as well as a gall on a tree. Hair, horns, and antlers are included as excrescences.

EXCRETA – (eks-*SKREE*-tuh) (also Egesta) Excreted bio-matter such as feces, urine, vomit, saliva, or sweat.

EXCRETION – (eks-*CREE*-shun) (Excrete, Excretory, Excrement) Elimination or expulsion of waste products from the body. All living creatures have some sort of excretory system. The process of excretion is essential for life. Human beings excrete sweat, urine, and feces. Urination and defecation are toiletry requirements. They are performed in absolute privacy, secrecy by adults. (Babies are free from this inhibition.) Elimination or excretion of bodily wastes in public is considered dreadful, abnormal, immoral, shameful, and illegal. One will be convicted as a *"sex offender,"* (as if there is anything sexy about peeing or crapping). Why the great taboo surrounding excretion? After all, every animal does it. That may be the answer. Excretion, like procreation, reminds us that we are still animals, with all the animalistic requirements, needs. It's an affront to our sense of superiority and hubris to be reminded that, despite all our accomplishments, we are still mammals.

EXCRUCIATING – (eks-*SKROO*-shee-ay-ting) (Excruciate, Excruciatingly) Torturously painful, causing unbearable suffering. Excruciating is the present- participle of excruciate (1560s). The term excruciating entered English in the 1590s. Ex*cruci*ate is taken from the Latin *"excruciatus,"* meaning to *"torment by torture."* It implies the infliction of pain comparable to cruci_fixion, for *"crusis"* is Latin for *"cross."*

EXCULPATE – (*EKS*-cul-payt) (Exculpation, Exculpatory) To vindicate, exonerate, declare free from blame. Exculpation is to clear a person of guilt or fault.

EXECRABLE – (*EKS*-ec-ra-bahl) Utterly detestable, abominable, absolutely abhorrent. *"The mercenary soldier is the most abject and execrable human being."* – Philosopher Desiderius Erasmus (1466 – 1536).

EXCUSE/EXPLANATION – (eks-*KEWS* ex-plan-*NAY*-shun) Both terms involve a justification of some act. But there is a difference. An excuse is an alibi, a rationalization in search of a pardon. An excuse precedes an apology. An explanation, on the other hand, is an account of what happened. Guilt is not suggested. An explanation is a commentary on the cause of the incident. It is a description providing information and evidence. A wife may say: *"Don't give me any excuses."* The husband may respond: *"This is not an excuse, but an explanation."*

EXECUTIVE ORDER – (eks-*EC*-kew-tiv *OR*-der) A written command by the President to the executive branch of government of which he is chief. The sprawling executive branch includes the cabinet departments as well as the military. As C.E.O. of the executive branch, the President can issue mandates, directives for action. Of course, the executive orders must be legal or constitutional. The legislative nature of executive orders sometimes conflicts with Congress, the legislative branch. All Presidents had issued directives, but Theodore Roosevelt (1858 – 1919) was first to designate them *"executive orders."* It happened that the capitalist Congress had allocated money to mine the Grand Canyon. Appalled by their greed and environmental disregard, Teddy issued what he called an *"executive order"* protecting the majestic site from capitalist corporations. No President had issued more executive orders quicker than President Donald Trump (b. 1946) in 2017. With these orders, Trump hoped to fulfill silly campaign promises made to his *low-information* supporters. Trump's edicts recall the *ukases* delivered by the Czars. Most of Trump's executive orders are deregulations. They rescind protections of the environment and benefit great capitalist corporations.

EXECUTIVE PRIVILEGE – (eks-*EC*-kew-tiv *PRIV*-lej) The right claimed by the President for the executive branch of the U.S. Government, of withholding information in the public (not private) interest. The term emerged in the 1950's, though the prerogative dates back to President George Washington (1732 – 1799). Executive Privilege maintains that the President can preserve confidential communications within the executive branch under certain circumstances. This includes resisting some subpoenas and other oversight by the legislative and judicial branches of government. This right comes into effect when revealing information would impair governmental functions. Executive Privilege is not explicitly mentioned in the Constitution. (Neither is Congressional Oversight.) However, the Supreme Court has ruled that they must exist as a consequence of the doctrine of separation of powers. Executive Privilege is abused when the President tries to employ it for private, personal gain or protection. Richard Nixon (1913 – 1994) attempted to employ Executive Privilege to escape the Watergate scandal charges (1972 – 1974). But no President has abused Executive Privilege as *"His Insidiousness,"* President Donald Trump (b. 1946). In an attempt to cover-up his multiple illegalities, criminalities, and corruptibilities, Trump has twisted Executive Privilege into nefarious *"stonewalling."* Trump has withheld information from Congress, and has coached and threatened witnesses to illegally ignore Congressional Oversight responsibility. Incidentally: Executive Privilege was first employed in 1792 by President Washington. He hoped to suppress details of the disastrous expedition of General Arthur St. Clair (1737 – 1818) against the Indian tribes on the Ohio-Indiana border, the *"Battle of the Wabash"* (1791). Secretary of State Thomas Jefferson (1743 – 1826) recorded that the President: *"Ought to communicate such papers as the public good would permit & ought to refuse those the disclosure of which would injure the public."*

EXECUTIVE TIME – (eks-*EC*-kew-tiv *TYM*) Normally, unscheduled time set aside by a CEO, or any leader, that does not involve the work of managing and governing. For the President of the United States, executive time is a small fraction of the day, for the Chief Executive to unwind. But the Trump Administration is not normal, and neither is Donald Trump (b. 1946). Trump's employees secretly despise him. That's why they leak information to the press about what really transpires in the White House. To Trump, executive time dominates the day. At least 60% of President Trump's time is watching television, or tweeting invectives. That's when he is not playing golf. Intelligence briefings on international crisis cannot take more than a few minutes, and the information must corroborate his (or Putin's) agenda, or Trump explodes in a rage. The Intelligence Community calls Trump's attitude and behavior *"willful ignorance."* It has been calculated that for every hour Trump devotes to national security meetings, 7 hours (86%) are wasted on his executive [read: *personal*] time. Disillusioned Trump supporter, Ann Coulter (b. 1961) called Trump *"An incompetent lunatic and lazy."*

EXECUTOR – (eks-*EC*-you-tor) One who has been officially assigned to execute the laws, enforce the rules, or accomplish the conditions, as of a contract or will. It is imperative that the executor be a *"Fair Broker,"* especially when concerning a will. He or she must never, ever be a beneficiary of the will as well. That creates a conflict of interest. An executor with a vested interest may be tempted to *"put her thumb on the scale."* Holding both positions can trigger human greed. Rare is the person endowed with the level of enlightenment, who will not take advantage of his power for self-indulgence, self-enrichment. An executor-cum-beneficiary will almost always declare *"Executive Privilege"* and commit an abuse of power. A judge cannot preside over her own trial. Likewise, an executor of a will cannot be a beneficiary as well. Parents be warned, that when you make a sibling the executor of your will, for you may be planting the seeds of the family's destruction. *"For where your treasure is, there your heart will be as well."* – Jesus in Matthew 6:21. Incidentally: A female executor is technically an *executrix.*

EXEGESIS – (eks-e-*JEE*-sis) The explanation or critical interpretation of a text, especially a Biblical Scripture. An exegesis is a theological hermeneutic.

EXERCISE – (*EKS*-er-syz) Systematic physical exertion is expending muscular energy for better health, bodily performance and function. Exercise involves motion. The body, like a mechanical devise, is a machine, in that it is composed of moving parts. If the moving parts become static, motionless, they will eventually seize, lockup, breakdown, or die. In the long run, exercising is as vital as breathing, drinking, eating, and excreting to maintain life. Exercise can also serve as a tonic for the soul. Dedicate the workout as an offering, a sacrifice. Make the physical exercise an exercise in prayer. This is called a *"kinhin"* by Buddhists. *"Remember that bodily exercise, when it is well ordered, is also prayer by means of which you can please God the Lord."* – St. Ignatius of Loyola (1491 – 1556). *"Long exercise, my friend, inures the mind; and what we once disliked we pleasing find."* – Ancient Greek Poet Hesiod (fl. 750 to 650 BCE).

EXFOLIATION – (eks-fo-*LEE*-ay-shun) In geology, the process in which sheets of rock peel or flake as a result of weathering. Like pages falling from an old book, the fossil record can be easily read, due to exfoliation. In medical care, an *exfoliate* is a substance, liquid, cream, or ointment that softens hard dead skin, as on callused feet, so it can be flaked or peeled away.

EXHIBITIONISM – (eks-hib-*BISH*-shun-is-um) (Exhibit, Exhibitionist) The desire to show-off, to display one's talents, abilities or body. In psychiatry, exhibitionism is defined as a neurotic paraphilial disorder in which one is sexually aroused by exposing one's genitals to an unsuspecting person. In the culture of exotic erotica, exhibitionism is a compulsion, a powerful sex drive to be seen naked. Too, an exhibitionist is erotically stimulated by performing sex acts in view of others. Exhibitionism is permissible when regulated as in strip clubs, a nude beach, porn movie sets, or in private sex groups among like-minded people. But *private* is counterintuitive to the *public* obsession of exhibitionism. Regardless, public nudity is illegal, especially when children are present. One may even be branded as a *"sex offender."* What motivates one to exhibitionism? People are complex and very unique. However exhibitionism may be an erotic fetish, a psychological defense mechanism, of a form of gambling. As an erotic fetish, it reveals a sense of masochism, a need to be shamed as a pleasurable punishment. Exhibitionism serving as a defense mechanism is a stress reliever that draws subconscious attention away from some deeper more painful problem, like early child abuse. Like bungee jumping, exhibitionism may provide some with an adrenaline rush, as well as a sexual high. Taking the chance of getting caught is profoundly stimulating. *"The exhibitionist loves to flirt with shame,"* as Professor Mason Cooley (1927 – 2002) maintained. Of course, there are those with such exquisite bodies that they simply love to display their art. How is a living work of art different from a beautiful nude statue, painting, or photo? Exhibitionism is a rebellious act. It challenges our sense of morality, the social mores. The exhibitionist relishes the shock element when exposing his/her wares. As society changes, so does the degree of exhibitionism that is publicly tolerated. A woman in a bikini would be scandalous in 1901. Furthermore, *"If modesty disappeared, so would exhibitionism."* – Mason Cooley.

EXIGENT – (*EKS*-i-jent) (Exigency) Urgent, urgently. Requiring immediate attention.

EXISTENCE – (eks-*SIS*-tens) (Exist, Exists, Existing, Existed, Existential) In a state of being. Who or what exists, is. *"To be or not to be, that is the question."* This is Prince Hamlet's famous soliloquy in William Shakespeare's (1564 – 1616) <u>Hamlet</u> (1600). An entity may exist as an animate or an inanimate being. A rabbit, fly, person, or tree are all alive and exist. A rock, car, pencil, or computer are not alive, but also exist.

These eight arbitrary examples are material entities. They are visible, tangible, tactile. Existence is usually confined to the physical world. But what about existence on the metaphysical, spiritual plane? All religions and most of the people on Earth believe is spiritual existence as well. This involves the spirit or soul within the corporeal body. When the animate becomes inanimate (dies), does it still exist? Like the existence of God, this is a question of faith, which is belief beyond the requirement of proof. Most people now, and always had believed that there is life after death, or post-life existence. Some even include non-human creatures, believing they too are endowed with souls. (*"All Dogs Go to Heaven."* A 1989 animated musical movie.) *"The purpose of existence is to exist. It is too fantastic to have a meaning."* – Guru Jaggi Vasudev (b. 1957). Incidentally: *"Cogito, ergo sum."* (*"I think therefore I am."*) This is Philosopher Rene Descartes' (1596 – 1650) *"First Principle,"* in his *Discourse on the Method* (1637). A contemporary rendition of Descartes may be: *"I receive texts, therefore I am."*

EXISTENTIAL – (eks-is-*TEN*-chee-ahl) Pertaining to existence. To vividly experience varied dimensions of reality in the present. Existential is being aware that one is, and that one is an acting, choosing, being creating and expressing one's self-identity in the process of acting and choosing responsibly.

EXISTENTIAL ANXIETY – (eks-is-*TEN*-chee-ahl anx-*EYE*-et-tee) The fear of the loss of meaning in life. When ennui (lack of interest) and anomie (lack of values) sets in, existential anxiety can take grip. Psychiatrist and Holocaust survivor, Viktor Frankl (1905 - 1997) maintained that those who survived the death camps possessed a reason to live, even if it was revenge. *"He who has a why to live can bear almost any how,"* – Philosopher Friedrich Nietzsche (1844 - 1900).

EXISTENTIAL DEPRESSION – (eks-is-*TEN*-chee-ahl dee-*PRESH*-shun) Emotional despair brought on by all the misery in the world, and one's helplessness to assuage it. Existential depression is a malady of the heart suffered by sensitive, compassionate souls. It is a neurotic condition that can become psychotic, leading to madness. In German, existential depression is called *"weltschmerz"* meaning suffering the pain of the world. In *The Gospel of Thomas* Jesus said: *"Blessed are those who have been persecuted in their heart. They are the ones who have truly come to know the Father." "It is impossible for one to live without tears who considers things exactly as they are."* – Gregory of Nyssa (c. 335 – c. 395).

EXISTENTIALISM – (eks-is-*TEN*-chee-ahl-is-um) Youngest of the 4 major philosophies predicated on personal choice. Existentialism propounds the liberal or radical contention that truth is whatever I say it is. An existentialist will punctuate her discussion with *"I choose to…"* or *"I feel that…."* An existentialist would argue that she did not ask to be born. She (her *essence*) was thrust into this world (*existence*), without her consent. Her existence preceded her essence. Now she must create her essence. She was placed in the world, so she's obliged to make that world and herself, in order to exist harmoniously. That is accomplished through her essential choices.

EXISTENTIALIST'S CREDO – (eks-is-*TEN*-chee-ahl-ists *CRAY*-dow) *"Existence precedes essence."* – Jean Paul Sartre (1905 – 1980). This means that man was born into a world he did not create. So now he must reshape that world with his personal choices. In *Existentialism is a Humanism*, (1946), Sartre explained: *"What is meant by existence precedes essence? It means man exists, turns up, appears on the scene, and, only afterwards, defines himself."*

EXISTENTIAL PSYCHOLOGY – (eks-is-*TEN*-chee-ahl sy-*COL*-lo-jee) (also Phenomenology) The school of psychology that maintains that individuals are constantly making choices that determine the kind of person they become. Existential psychology is opposed to all determinisms, including behaviorism. Prominent existential psychologists were: Carl Rogers (1902 – 1987), Viktor Frankl (1905 – 1997), Abraham Maslow (1908 – 1970), Rollo May (1909 – 1994), T.S. Szasz (1920 – 2012).

EXISTENTIAL THREAT – (eks-is-*TEN*-chee-al *THRET*) A life-terminating danger. An existential threat is a threat to existence. Death, genocide, extinction are existential threats. Some existential threats are nuclear war, global warming, a viral pandemic, an asteroid collision. Intelligent life on Earth would be extinguished. Furthermore: The fascist megalomaniac, Donald J. Trump (b. 1946) is an existential threat to Democracy, and the United States of America as we know it. God help America and humanity if that Son of Satan ever regains power.

EXIT POLL – (*EKS*-it *POLE*) A survey of voters on election day as they leave the voting station or exit the polling place. To professional political scientists and statisticians, this information may give an early indication of how the election will swing.

EXIT VELOCITY – (*EKS*-it vel-*LOS*-si-tee) A speed of at least 25,000 mph. Exit velocity is the speed required of a spacecraft to break free of Earth's gravitational pull and venture into interplanetary space.

EX MORE – (eks *MOR*-ray) Latin for *"according to custom."*

EXOBIOLOGY – (eks-o-by-*OL*-lo-jee) (also Astrobiology) The study and search for extraterrestrial lifeforms or beings. Exobiology is related to alienology and ufology. It is estimated that over 50 billion stars in our galaxy may have planets with some form of life. *"The universe would not be complete without intellectual creatures."* – Thomas Aquinas (1225 – 1274).

EXODUS – (*EKS*-a-dus) A mass departure of people. The first great Exodus was the deliverance of the Israelites from Egyptian bondage led by Moses (c. 1273 BCE). The account is recorded in the second book of the Bible of the same name, Exodus. The second Exodus occurred in 1945 after World War Two. This entailed the deliverance of the surviving Jews from Nazi bondage to Palestine (Israel). They were conducted by the leaders of the Zionist Movement. This Exodus triggered an anti-British insurgency; a civil war with the Palestinians; and actual wars with Arab neighbors. Nevertheless, against all odds, the Jews succeeded in establishing the Nation of Israel in 1948.

EX OFFICIO – (eks o-*FISH*-she-o) Latin for *"From office."* Ex officio means officially, by virtue of holding office.

EXOGENESIS – (eks-o-jen-*NEE*-sis) Developing a *"test-tube baby."* Exogenesis is creating an embryo outside the mother's womb. The mother, of course, can be any mammal, including a woman. Exogenesis raised a plethora of bioethical issues. Just because we could, does that mean we should? Is man playing God?

EXOGAMY – (eks-*OG*-gam-mee) (Exogamous) The term *"gamy"* comes from the Greek *"gamia"* meaning "marriage." The Greek prefix *"ex"* means *"out."* Exogamy is marrying outside of one's tribe or specific socio-cultural unit. In small, isolated, communities, exogamy may be a social taboo. One may be shunned or ostracized for breaking this expectation. Exogamy is not prevalent is a large diverse nation like the U.S.A. However, family disapproval may follow interracial marriage. Jewish people too are very exclusive, and usually marry within the religio-culture.

EXONUMIA – (eks-oh-*NOO*-mee-uh) Items as tokens or medals that resemble coins, but are not intended to circulate as money. Metallic coins as subway, bus, or casino tokens qualify as exonumia. Religious medals and Alcoholic Anonymous awards are also examples.

EXONYM – (*EKS*-soh-nim) Literally an *"out name,"* or *"outside name."* A name we use for someone or someplace that they don't use for themselves. An exonym is a name that foreigners use for a place, nation, or group of people that the indigenous people do not use. For example, Poland is the exonym for *Polska*; Germany for *Deutschland*; Finland for *Suomi*; Hungary for *Magyarorszag;* Eskimos is the exonym for *Inuits;* and *Amerykanski* for American.

EXOPLANET – (*EKS*-oh-plan-net) A distant heavenly body, a satellite orbiting a star. An exoplanet is a planet outside our home solar system.

EXORBITANT – (eks-*ORB*-bi-tant) Unreasonably excessive, extravagant, beyond all bounds of propriety, especially concerning price and cost. Capitalism is inherently exorbitant in what it charges the customer, and what it rakes-in as profit. Military spending is the absolute worst, exorbitantly obscene.

EXORCISM – (*EKS*-or-siz-um) The ritualistic casting-out of negative energy or evil spirits from a place, object, animal or person. Exorcisms are performed by religious authorities like shamans, witch doctors, priests, ministers and rabbis. Exorcism is the last resort when medicine and psychiatry fail. Exorcism may possess a degree of efficacy. An excessively religious person needs an excessively religious rite to free him of his possession. This is fighting fire with fire, using exorcism as a sort of placebo. On the other hand, it cannot be proved that demonic possession is not real, and that exorcism does not work. *"Absence of evidence is not evidence of absence,"* as archeologists say. *"A young man had become possessed by a devil. The thing within him burst into loud lamentation and departed from the man. At once the youth's eye fell out of his cheek, and the whole of the pupil which had been black became white."* – St. Augustine (354 – 430 CE).

EXORCIST'S CREDO – (*EKS*-or-sists *CRAY*-dow) The mantra or credo of the Catholic exorcist is: *"By the power of Christ I command you! Be gone evil spirit!"*

EXHORT – (eks-*ZAWRT*) (Exhortation) To urge, advise, caution earnestly, admonish urgently. *"I exhort you to dump your dumb Trump idolatry into the dumpster."*

EXOSPHERE – (*EKS*-o-sfeer) Highest, last layer of the atmosphere, almost airless. The exosphere is above the *ionosphere,* and merges into interplanetary space.

EXOTERIC – (eks-o-*TER*-ric) The term is taken from the Greek *"exoterikos,"* meaning *"being outside, exterior."* Exoteric is the opposite of esoteric. Exoteric means open to everyone. It pertains to that which is not secret, but is readily comprehended by the public. Exoteric information is easily understood by the educated and unschooled alike.

EXOTHERMIC REACTION – (eks-o-*THER*-mik ree-*AK*-shuhn) A chemical reaction that gives off heat. For example, the fermentation of a compost pile or the drying of concrete produces exothermic reactions.

EXOTIC EROTICA – (eks-*OT*-tic ih-*ROT*-tik-ka) Sex as recreation. Having *"fuck'en fun!"* literally and figuratively. Exotic erotica refers to all the sexual positions, techniques, games, that arouses erotic excitation, climaxing in orgasm. Exotic erotica may be confined to partners or group sex. It may be heterosexual or homosexual. There are no taboos in exotic erotic performances, as long as it is practiced among consenting adults, and does not involve criminality (e.g. serious harm or homicide). Bondage, whipping, humiliation, anything that will turn one on qualifies as exotic erotica. *"Sex is as important as eating or drinking and we ought to allow the one appetite to be satisfied with as little restraint or false modesty as the other."* – Marquis de Sade (1740 – 1814), Exotic Erotica Connoisseur. *"The only unnatural sex act is that which you cannot perform."* – Sexologist Dr. Alfred Kinsey (1894 – 1956). *"I am different. Let this not upset you."* – The Alchemist Paracelsus (c. 1493 – 1541).

EXOTIC RIVER – (eks-*OT*-tic *RIV*-ver) A river that flows from a humid environment (the tropics) across a dry desert into a sea. The obvious example is the Nile River. It originates at misty tropical Lake Victoria (Tanzania, Uganda, Kenya), flows north through the parched Sahara Desert, and empties into the Mediterranean in Egypt.

EX PARTE – (eks par-*TAY*) In law, with only one side present. An *ex parte* judicial proceeding involves only one party without notice to, or contestation by, any person adversely affected.

EXPATIATE – (eks-*PAY*-shee-ate) To elaborate, or enlarge on a topic or theme in detail or length. *"Let us expatiate this incident in more detail."*

EXPATRIATE – (eks-*PAY*-tree-it, ex-*PAY*-tree-ate) As a verb, to expatriate is to leave one's nation for another. As a noun, an expatriate is one who gives up his citizenship, for that of another country. So an expatriate is a patriot who exited her country to live in another.

EXPATRIATE TAX – (eks-*PAY*-tree-it *TAX*) A tariff or tax on products made by expatriate businesses. Corporations that abandon their employees to manufacture abroad should have to pay for the damage done by their move. These expatriate companies relocate overseas to take advantage of de- unionized child and slave labor. They pay their foreign workers a pittance with no health benefits whatsoever. They make a mint and can afford to pay the tax for their perfidy. These funds could go to pay the unemployment benefits made necessary by the fugitive factories relocation. The tax will also offset the revenue loss from sales and income tax no longer generated by the jobless. The expatriate tax should encourage domestic industries to stay put.

EXPECTANCY – (eks-*PEC*-tan-see) (Expect, Expectation) In metaphysics, to anticipate a positive result, to look forward to a victorious outcome. Expectancy is an exercise in faith. It is activating the *Law of Attraction* for our benefit (so we in turn can benefit others). Expect the healing, and the good fortune. Pray expectantly in the past tense as if the prayer was already answered, and answered it shall be. However, our hopes and plans must be in accord with God's will for us.

EXPECTATION – (eks-spect-*TAY*-shun) (Expect, Expecting, Expectancy) To look forward to a likely occurrence. To anticipate the occurrence of a future outcome. The term derives from the Latin *"expectare,"* meaning *"desire, anticipation, hope"* and *"long for."* It has been in English usage since the 1550s. Expectation can be a set-up for disappointment. *"Expectation is the root of all heartache,"* William Shakespeare (1564 – 1616) declared. Therefore, *"Expect nothing. Live frugally on surprise."* – Poet, Author, Alice Walker (b. 1944). This advice is corroborated by spiritual teacher Ram Dass (b. 1931): *"It is important to expect nothing, to take every experience, including the negative ones, as merely steps on the path and to proceed."* Optimists expect a positive, favorable future. Pessimists expect a negative, unfavorable future. Mystics teach that the *"Law of Attraction"* is based on positive expectation. It maintains that belief, confidence, faith will bring about the expected outcome. A Caveat: Expectation, expectancy presents a contradiction. Much of life is a contradiction. *"So, you say I contradict myself. Very well, I contradict myself. I am large. I contain multitudes."* – Poet Walt Whitman (1819 – 1892).

EXPERIENCE – (eks-*PEER*-ree-ens) A personal encounter. Accumulating knowledge over time from a great amount of practice. Trite but true, practice makes perfect. Experience is living through events, feelings, emotions, sufferings, happenings, and various states of consciousness. Experience (good or bad) results in gained knowledge. Experience consists of both successes and failures which leads to wisdom. The experienced practitioner is the best performer. Miguel de Cervantes (1547 – 1616) declared that: *"Experience is the universal mother of sciences."* Experience requires participation, an action taken. *"However much you are read in theory, if thou hast no practice thou art ignorant."* – Persian Poet Saadi (1210 – 1292). The knowledge or information gained through experience can be epiphanal, a life-changing experience. A natural byproduct of experience, over time, is wisdom. Quality of workmanship is enhanced through experience. As the old adage goes: *"There is no substitute for the Brewmeister's nose,"* – German Proverb. Hands-on participation is the best mode of leaning. As English lexicographer, Samuel Johnson (1709 – 1784) declared: *"All the reading and study in the world will not teach a man to make a shoe."* Experience is often loaded with surprises. The C.E.O. of I.T.&T., Harold Geneen (1910 – 1997) asserted that *"Experience is what you get when you get what you didn't expect."* *"Experience is a truer guide than the words of others."* – Leonardo da Vinci (1452 – 1519). Wise Ben Franklin (1706 – 1790) appreciated the power of experience. Ben warned us to *"Beware of young doctors and old barbers."* *"Experience is always a trustworthy guide; it may not tell you everything, but it never lies."* – Writer George Sand (1804 – 1876).

EXPERIENTIALISM – (eks-peer-ree-*EN*-chal-is-um) A philosophical theory that immediate concrete experience is the only source of knowledge and the only method of testing the value and truth of knowledge, theories, hypotheses, and so on.

EXPERIENTIALISM – (eks-peer-ee-*EN*-chee-al-is-um) An educational perspective rooted in the Liberal Philosophy of Pragmatism. In experientialism, the student experiences learning through the *Discovery Approach.* Hands-on experiments and field trips are utilized. Experientialism is part of Progressive Education.

EXPERT – (*EKS*-pert) A highly trained specialist or authority, with extraordinary knowledge and skill in some particular field. The field of expertise may be professional, vocational, artistic, academic, athletic, whatever. Formal education, but more importantly time, drill, practice, rehearsal, experience, makes an expert. In fact, research indicates that it takes about 10,000 hours of study and hard work to become an expert at anything. *"An expert is someone who knows some of the worst mistakes that can be made in his subject and how to avoid them."* – Physicist Werner Heisenberg (1901 – 1976). *"The duty of a politician for me is to be a representative: a politician is not an expert, experts are experts, hired for their expertise and so on."* – Philosopher Slavoj Zizek (b. 1949).

EXPIATE – (*EKS*-pee-ayt) To atone for some wrongdoing, to make amends or reparations.

EXPLANATION/EXCUSE – (eks-plan-*NAY*-shun ex-*KEWS*) Both an explanation and excuse are interpretative attempts at clarification. But a major distinction is in order. An explanation is a statement that enhances understanding by presenting the facts of the matter. An explanation is an honest account of what had occurred. It is not an apology or an admittance of guilt. An explanation is a reconciliation of the truth. An excuse, on the other hand, is an alibi. It is an attempt to escape guilt. An excuse is often a lie. It seeks to avoid blame through rationalization [read: *rationing lies*]. Wives often confuse an explanation for an excuse. This results in much frustration on the part of husbands. His persistent attempt to explain is interpreted as a litany of excuses. The wife, convinced of his guilt, expects nothing less than an apology, a *mea culpa*. Often, the husband will falsely incriminate himself for peace sake. Otherwise, communication breaks down, and a vexatious mood grips the home. Even when upset, women must recognize the difference between an explanation and an excuse. *"Come, now let us reason together."* – Isaiah 1:18. Incidentally: *"Nothing makes a husband unhappier, than an unhappy wife."*

EXPLETIVE – (*EKS*-slit-tiv) A curse word. An expletive is an interjectory word or expression, frequently profane; an exclamatory oath. For example: *"Oh fuck!"* or *"Holy shit!"* *"His tirade was punctuated with expletives."*

EXPLICATION – (eks-pli-*KAY*-shun) The term is taken from the Latin *"explicare,"* meaning *"to unfold."* An explication is a precise explanation. It is making obvious (explicit) what is implied or implicit in a statement.

EXPLICATORY – (eks-*PLIK*-a-tor-ree) A teaching method that utilizes demonstration, modeling, coaching. Training is explicatory.

EXPLOIT – (*EKS*-ployt or eks-*PLOYT*) Exploit is an unusual word known as a *"homograph."* This is 2 words that are spelled the same, pronounced differently, with different meanings. As a noun, an exploit (*EKS*-ployt) is a great, heroic feat, a notable deed. We admire the exploits of brave Socialist champions. As a verb, to exploit (eks-*PLOYT*) is to take cruel advantage of a weaker party by a stronger oppressor. We disdain how greedy capitalists exploit the poor. The noun form of the contemptuous act of exploiting is exploitation.

EXPLOITATION – (eks-ploy-*TAY*-shun) (Exploit, Exploiting, Exploited, Exploiter) The act of the strong, taking advantage of the weak. Exploitation is the selfish utilization for profit, generated by greed, inherent in capitalism. Profit, despite the consequences, is the purpose of exploitation (and capitalism). Exploitation involves get rich quick, use it and use it up. Corporate capitalism exploits people at home and abroad. Multinational corporations, the World Bank, the I.M.F. (International Monetary Fund) exploit undeveloped nations, keeping them subservient and underdeveloped. *"Do not hold grain waiting for higher prices when people are hungry."* – Zoroaster (d. 583 BCE).

EXPLOITATION FILMS – (eks-ploy-*TAY*-shun *FILMS*) A nasty genre of the American cinema, consisting of low-budget movies meant to disgust, shock, enrage, terrify and titillate the audience. Exploitation films are characterized by extreme violence, excessive gore, vulgar nudity, gratuitous sex, torture scenes, and plenty of explosions. Revenge movies and slasher films fall into this genre. Exploitation films often glorify monsters. They exploit the cruelest instincts, the dark side in human beings. They are inherently misogynous. You can be sure that the exploitation film will include a bloody, half-naked woman, running for her life through the woods. Exploitation films appeal to bullies who enjoy sadistic exploitation, and to weak masochists, the exploited, victims who lust for revenge. The *"Texas Chainsaw Massacre"* (1974) and the *"I Spit on Your Grave"* (1978) series are exploitation examples. There are no social redeeming qualities, no edifying benefits in exploitation films. On the contrary, they may encourage sociopaths to cross the line into psychopathology.

EXPLORATORY REFERENDUM – (eks-*PLOR*-uh-tor-ree ref-fer-*REN*-dum) To explore is to investigate, examine, study, discover for information, to become knowledgeable. Referendum is Latin meaning *"that which must be referred."* So an exploratory referendum is referring any law, policy, issue to the voters to discover the peoples' will. Representing the public will is the essence of democracy. The House of Representatives is elected to represent the peoples' will. The same applies to all legislators, executives, even judges. However, all government officials must be educated as to what the public wills. Polls are handy but not precise or official enough. That's why we need occasional exploratory referendums. Controversial issues should be clearly, simply recoded at the bottom of every voting ballot. Questions concerning abortion, poverty, guns, immigration, taxing the rich, wealth redistribution, should be put to the people for the benefit of the politicians. Perhaps corporate lobbyists would lose some of their influence if the politicians knew what the voters desired. Too, passing the hot issue off to the people takes the politicians off the hook. Politicians can justify their vote to the lobbyists and party leadership by declaring their responsibility to represent the popular will.

EXPLOSION – (eks-*PLOH*-shun) (Explode, Explosive) A violent outburst usually caused by rapid oxidation (combustion or burning). An explosion is a flash ignition of some volatile fuel source. An explosion produces a sudden, powerful release and expansion of gas, heat, and demolished debris, along with a forceful shock wave and thunderous noise, blast. An explosion can be a destructive event causing great damage and death. A bomb blast is an explosion. It will disintegrate structures, ignite fires, and flatten property with its shock wave. Spontaneous combustion is not the only cause of explosions. An explosion can be caused by contained pressure that can no longer hold, as in an exploding water heater. In nature, a volcanic eruption works on the same principle. Unchecked nuclear fission (atom splitting) and fusion (atom bonding) can produce Earth-shattering explosions. The power of explosive energy can serve us or slaughter us. Explosive force can move mountains, or eradicate civilizations. Incidentally: Only 20% of the American wounds in World War Two (1941 – 1945) were due to rifle fire. About 80% were due to some form of explosive – bomb, shell, grenade, or torpedo.

EXPONENTIALLY – (eks-po-*NEN*-chee-al-lee) Rising or expanding at a steady and rapid rate. Bacteria for instance, multiply exponentially. An exponential increase involves multiplication, rather than addition. The increase is on a geometrical scale. An arithmetic increase would be 1, 2, 3, 4, 5…. An exponential increase would be 1, 2, 4, 8, 16, 32…. Incidentally: *"If you want to improve incrementally, be competitive. If you want to improve exponentially be cooperative."* – Gary J. Pasieka (b. 1951).

EXPORT REVOLUTION – (*EKS*-port rev-vo-*LOO*-shun) A favorite term used by pro- capitalist government officials. Actually, export revolution is a pejorative euphemism for oppose capitalist exploitation, stand up for the oppressed people abroad.

EXPOSITORY METHOD – (eks-*POS*-si-tor-ree) The traditional didactic approach to teaching, with the teacher as expert. Expository or didactic method is rooting in the philosophies of Idealism and Realism. In an expository setting, the student's mindset is *"Tell me, I want to know."*

EX POST FACTO – (eks post *FAC*-tow) Latin for *"after the fact,"* often thought of in terms of a law making an act illegal after someone has committed the act. Article 1, section 10 of the U.S. Constitution prohibits retroactive *ex post facto* laws. So, if the law was not enacted when the action took place, the perpetrator cannot be convicted ex post facto.

EXPOSTULATE – (eks-*POS*-chew-late) (Expostulation) To remonstrate. To earnestly reason with someone against something that person has done or intends to do. To expostulate is to persuade or dissuade a person from taking some action. The White House Staff has ineffectually expostulated with President Donald Trump (b. 1946) to stop his childish, unpresidential tweeting to the public.

EXPRESS – (eks-*PRES*) Literally, *"to press out."* To express is to utter a thought, set forth an opinion, make clear one's feelings. To express emotion [read: *energy in motion*] is an abreaction. It serves as a psychological purgative, to expel the stressful poison within.

EXPROPRIATION – (eks-pro-pree-*AY*-shun) The Socialistic maneuver of the popular government confiscating private, foreign-owned property for the public weal. Unlike nationalization which pays the foreign capitalists for their loss, expropriation gives them *NOTHING,* but an order to leave. After all, decades of exploitation of the natural resources and cheap labor had compensated them several times over. The native populations had paid the foreign capitalist imperialists with their treasure, sweat, and blood. History has shown that righteous expropriation has been met with assassinations, terrorism, coups, military intervention, and fascist dictatorship from the expropriated capitalist foreigner. The primary purpose of the C.I.A. and the military for that matter, is to protect corporate capitalist investments abroad. When blowback occurs, naïve Americans ask: *"Why do they hate us?"*

EXPULSION – (eks-*PAUL*-shun) In education, to be permanently expelled or excluded from school, a grievous disciplinary measure. Expulsion is summative, whereas suspension is formative or temporary.

EXPUNGE – (eks-*PUNJ*) Blot out. In law for example, a court order requesting that a student's record be expunged of any references to disciplinary action during such and such a time means that the references are to be *"wiped off the books."*

EXPURGATE – (*EKS*-pert-gayt) (Expurgated, Expurgation) To censor. To Expurgate is to amend a literary piece by removing words, passages, or pictures that are deemed offensive or objectionable. By the 2020s, the Republican Party had thoroughly morphed into the Trumpublican Party. The hardcore base of this party were the Christen Fundamentalists, today the Christian Nationalists. Though still a minority, these fanatics gained control of many local governments, including schoolboards. They expurgated books and purged libraries of anything they deemed salacious, controversial, or unpatriotic. This was a great blow to freedom of speech, press, and expression. Expurgation is fascist practice. *"The dirtiest book of all is the expurgated book."* – Walt Whitman (1819 – 1892).

EX REL. – (eks *REL*) Latin for *"on behalf of."* In law, *ex rel.* designates a private individual on whose behalf the state is acting in a legal proceeding. When a case is titled *State ex rel. Thomas v. Rebecca,* it means that the state is bringing a lawsuit against Thomas on behalf of Rebecca.

EXSICCATE – (EK-si-kayt) (Exsiccating, Exsiccated, Exsiccation) To dry out to dry up. To remove moisture or wetness by absorption or evaporation. *"Exsiccate"* entered English in the 1540s from the Latin *"exsiccatus,"* meaning *"to make dry." "The water hole exsiccates every summer."*

EX TEMPORE – (eks *TEM*-por) From Latin meaning *"on the spur of the moment, off hand, without preparation."*

EXTENSIONALITY – (eks-ten-shun-*AL*-li-tee) The deepest expression of love, when you see yourself in other people. Extensionality involves enhancing each other without greedy envy or fearful jealousy. One elevated to the extensionality level finds joy in other's joyfulness. Extensionality cannot be arrived at in a competitive, *dog-eat-dog,* capitalist environment. Only in Socialism can people extend themselves beyond their selfish egos. Capitalism encourages *"individuality"* whereas Socialism encourages *"extensionality."*

EXTERNAL DISECONOMIES – (eks-*TUR*-nal dis-*CON*-nom-mees) The detrimental by-product of economic interaction. For example, pollution and distributive injustice [read: *poverty*], corruption, crime are external diseconomies created by capitalism.

EXTERNAL ECONOMIES – (eks-*TUR*-nal ee-*CON*-nom-mees) The beneficial by- products of economic interaction. For example, artistic buildings, safe neighborhoods, clean streets, prosperity, full employment, free education are external economies created by Socialism.

EXTERNALITY – (eks-turn-*NAL*-li-tee) The pedagogical concept that everyone gains from an educated citizenry. Education is not just for the internal benefit of the individual, but for the external benefit of society. A good argument for the concept of externality is to ask: *"Would you rather live next door to an educated family (schooled in culture) or an uneducated family (unschooled but street-smart)?"* Martin Luther (1483 – 1546) a powerful proponent of education lamented: *"There are some who have no children, and therefore feel no interest in them."* Luther recognized the detriment to society generated by such selfish apathy. Incidentally: In his <u>Notes on Virginia</u> (1781 – 1783) Thomas Jefferson (1743 – 1826) wrote: *"An amendment of our constitution must here come in aid of the public education."*

EXTINCTION – (eks-*TINK*-shun) The demise of a species of animal or plant from the face of the Earth. Extinction is the re-shuffling of the deck so that new species may emerge. There have been at least 5 great extinctions in the Earth's history, when most lifeforms have been wiped-out. The average lifespan of a species has been about 600,000 years. The Chicxulub asteroid that collided into the Mexican Yucatan 65 million years ago doomed over 10 billion dinosaurs to extinction. This cleared a path for mammals that eventually led to man. Incidentally: It has been determined that 800 is the minimal number for a population to procreate successfully and avoid extinction.

EXTINCTION REBELLION – (eks-*TINK*-shun ree-*BELL*-yon) (abbreviated XR) A global environmental movement founded in the United Kingdom in May 2018. XR is a grassroots organization established by environmental activists Julian Roger Hallam (b. 1966) and Gail Marie Bradbrook (b. 1972). The stated aim of the Extinction Rebellion is nonviolent disobedience and rebellion against extinction of life on Earth. The existential threat comes from global warming, climate chaos, biodiversity decrease, ecological and social collapse. The existential enemies are the corporate capitalists. Rapacious capitalist corporations put private profit before people, polluting the planet. This is the cause of the worldwide emergency and the reaction from the Extinction Rebellion. Incidentally: Capitalist governments always collude on the side of capitalist corporations. On January 10, 2020, The British Counter-Terrorist Police had declared the Extinction Rebellion an *"extremist ideology."* This puts XR on the radical terrorist list alongside Neo-Nazism and Islamic incendiaries. *"The state is a pillar of capitalism, and it is ridiculous to expect any redress from it."* – Anarchist Emma Goldman (1869 – 1940).

EXTIRPATE – (*EKS*-ter-pate) To exterminate. To totally remove or completely destroy.

EXTORTION – (eks-*TOR*-shun) (Extort, Extorting, Extorted) The crime of wresting or wringing money, information, or anything of values from a person by violence, intimidation, blackmail, threat, torture, or abuse of authority. Gangs and organized crime use extortion techniques to squeeze money out of small businesses. Governments use extortion such as blackmail to force individuals to become spies.

EXTRACTIVE INDUSTRIES – (eks-*TRAC*-tiv *IN*-dus-trees) The capitalist exploitative industries: mining, oiling, lumbering, fracking. Extractive industries take what is valuable and leave a raped landscape. Corporate capitalists connive with fascist dictators to robe peasants of their nation's natural resources. The government euphemistically calls the extractive industries *"American interests abroad."*

EXTRA CURRICULUM – (*EKS*-tra cur-*RIC*-kew-lum) In education, the planned experiences outside the formal curriculum. Extra-curricular activities are not formal school subjects, they are voluntary and cater to student's interests. However, the hidden curriculum is heard in the extra curriculum. Lessons about competition, cooperation, teammanship, and sportsmanship are transmitted in the extra curriculum.

EXTRADITION – (eks-truh-*DISH*-shun) (Extradite, Extradited) The process of transferring between states and nations a person wanted for criminal prosecution and imprisonment. Fugitives from the law are extradited from one civilized polity to another. The states of the United States are expected to extradite suspected criminals to the state of their crime. However the *"culture war"* between the right and left may hamper some extraditions. For example, will Florida's Governor, Ron DeSantis (b. 1978) a Trump devotee extradite Donald Trump (b. 1946) to New York or Georgia to stand trial for Trump's criminal actions there? Civilized nations too have mutual extradition treaties. However, a fugitive from injustice may seek political asylum in a democratic foreign country. In this case, extradition would be a miscarriage of justice and denied.

EXTRAJUDICIAL – (eks-tra-joo-*DISH*-suhl) Beyond the law, extralegal. An extrajudicial controversy is adjudicated outside the court and the law. Vigilantism is extrajudicial as is a kangaroo court.

EXTRALEGAL ENTREPRENEURSHIP – (*EKS*-tra-*LEE*-guhl on-truh-pruh-*NUR*-ship) A banned business; an illegal enterprise. An extralegal entrepreneur is a capitalist [read: *money generator*] who accumulates wealth surreptitiously, free from governmental oversight and regulation. Therefore, extralegal entrepreneurships do not contribute any taxation. What makes them illegal is the product or service they offer. They provide the consuming public with banned commodities like drugs. Drug cartels are the most obvious extralegal entrepreneurships. They must operate illicitly because the drugs they sell are deemed dangerous to public health – which they are. The government has the responsibility to prohibit, outlaw the sale of dangerous products. Then why doesn't the government prohibit the sale of guns, cigarettes, alcohol, or automobiles, for that matter? Recall that the government did prohibit the sale of alcohol from 1920 to 1933. This resulted in the creation of extralegal entrepreneurships in the form of the gangster syndicates. Ironically, if the government, or its capitalist proxies control the illegal commodity, it is no longer illegal. *"All I did was to give the people what they wanted. And for that, I became a hunted man."* – Extralegal Entrepreneur, Al Capone (1899 – 1947).

EXTRA MILE – (*EKS*-tra *MYHL*) (Go the Extra Mile.) An expression meaning to serve beyond the norm or expected. A mile is a measurement of distance. It originated as the distance a Roman soldier could traverse in a thousand double- steps (5,280 feet). It was the custom in Roman-held provinces that a Roman soldier could command a civilian to carry his equipment for one mile. That prompted Jesus to say: *"If anyone forces you to go one mile, go with him two miles. Give to the one who begs from you, and do not refuse the one who would borrow from you."* – Matthew 5: 41,42.

EXTRAPOLATE – (eks-*TRAP*-po-late) To conjecture. Extrapolate is to infer an unknown from something that is known. For example, considering his *"Social Gospel,"* it's logical to extrapolate that Jesus was a Socialist.

EXTRATERRESTRIALS – (eks-tra-ter-*REST*-ree-als) (ET is the initialism for ExtraTerrestrial.) Literally, other than Earthlings, alien creatures not of our world. People from another planet. At best, extraterrestrials are our intelligent Cosmic brothers and sisters, in whatever form God has bestowed on them. A pattern has emerged among witnesses and abductees concerning the appearance of extraterrestrials. They have been described as either *"Grays"* or *"Nordics."* Grays are the little gray-toned creatures with huge heads, with large almond-shaped eyes. They are tiny with thin bodies the size of young children. They have long skinny arms with long thin fingers. The Grays have come to represent the stereotypical ETs. The Nordics are physically human-looking. They are tall (around 6 foot 2 inches) pale complected with blonde hair, closely resembling a Scandinavia, ergo, Nordics. It has been suggested that advanced beings can *"shape-shift,"* change form to suit the occasion. For a long time extraterrestrials were considered a joke. People had to prove that they saw a UFO. Today, the government must prove that the aircraft is not a UFO. Extraterrestrials usually refer to corporeal beings, rather than spiritual. Too, we tend to imagine extraterrestrials as intelligent creatures, rather than microbes. It is astronomically arrogant to think that we are the only intelligent creatures in this unthinkably vast cosmos. *"The universe would be incomplete without intellectual creatures,"* insisted philosopher/theologian St. Thomas Aquinas (1225 – 1274). Some have suggested that extraterrestrials are actually angels. In 1600, the Italian philosopher and monk, Giordano Bruno (1548 – 1600) was burned alive by the Catholic Church for proclaiming that the Earth was not the only world God had made. Indeed the Earth is an insignificant speck, in an unspectacular galaxy, which is lost in the cosmic sea, like a single grain of sand in the Sahara. The naïve who believe that we are alone simply lack imagination. Though we have not yet contacted extraterrestrials does not mean that they are unaware of us. The great naturalist, David Attenborough (b. 1926) reported that he had sliced off the roof of a termite mound. He watched the thousands of insects going about their duty, oblivious of his observation. It dawned on him how superior extraterrestrials may likewise be watching, studying us at this moment. The environment of planet Earth is responsible for our physical evolution. Extraterrestrials from alien environments will have evolved quite differently. They may not look like us. Furthermore, they may not share our sense of morality. Perhaps we may represent a simple resource to them. Theoretical physicist and cosmologist Stephen Hawking (1942 – 2018) warned about extraterrestrial encounters: *"If aliens came to visit us, the outcome may be just like when Christopher Columbus came to America – which didn't turn out too well for the Native Americans."* The Nazi SS rocket scientist turned American rocket scientist, Wernher von Braun (1912 – 1977) warned: *"World War Three will be with the extraterrestrials."* *"Am I a spaceman? Do I belong to a new race on earth, bred by men from outer space in embraces with earth women?"* – Psychiatrist Wilhelm Reich (1897 – 1957). *"My Kingdom is not of this world "* – Jesus, in John 18:36.

EXTRATROPICAL – (eks-tra-*TROP*-pi-cal) A misleading meteorological term which means *"not tropical."* The term extratropical is a negative, used to describe a positive. An extratropical cyclonic depression is simply a temperate zone storm. This sort of communication confusion is the result of esoteric professional nomenclature.

EXTRA-VIRGIN – (*EKS*-tra *VER*-jin) Not a reference to a hopelessly celibate maiden, but to a grade of olive oil. The oil from pressed olive fruit has played a major role in the development of Mediterranean and Middle Eastern societies for thousands of years. Ancient and present economies have been, and are dependent on olive oil. The trade in olive oil had stimulated commerce, exploration, and cultural interactions. Olive oil has been used as a cooking staple, condiment, medicine, soap, lubricant, lighting fuel. Till this day, while Northern Europe is the land of butter (and beer), Southern Europe remains the land of olive oil (and wine). Olive oil is processed in two major grades: regular and extra-virgin. Extra-virgin oil is unrefined, (not processed with chemicals or heat, therefore untouched, as are virgins). Ergo, the name. Extra-virgin olive oil has far less *oleic acid* ($C_{18}H_{34}O_2$), a fatty by-product. Oleic acid detracts from the preferred taste. Regular olive oil is light yellow, whereas extra-virgin olive oil is darker in color. Therefore extra-virgin olive oil is superior for human consumption. *"The peoples of the Mediterranean began to emerge from barbarism when they learned to cultivate the olive and vine."* – Thucydides (c. 460 – c. 400 BCE).

EXTREME VETTING – (eks-*TREEM VET*-ting) Donald Trump's euphemism for *"War on Islam."* Extreme vetting involves bans on Muslims from selected countries that Trump claims pose a threat to America.

The nations targeted are Syria, Somalia, Sudan, Yemen, Libya, Iraq, and Iran. Ironically, not one of these nations has produced a terrorist who had killed Americans. Oil-rich Saudi Arabia was responsible for the 9/11 attacks, but it is not on the hit list. Can Trump's family business ties with the Saudis have something to do with this? Trump makes Lady Liberty into a liar.

EXTREMOPHILES – (eks-*TREEM*-o-fy-als) Creatures that live in incredibly harsh, unlikely environments. Some extremophiles live deep in the Earth, in totally dark caves. Others live in glacial ice, or parched deserts. Still other extremophiles live is the ocean abyss around the scalding water from hydrothermal vents. Bacteria comprise the most likely form of extremophiles. Microbial life has been found in hot sulfur springs, in glacial ice, steaming geysers, on radioactive nuclear fuel rods, even in space on our satellites.

EXTRINSIC – (eks-*TRIN*-sic) From without. Needing external influences to motivate behavior. An extrinsic personality must be leaned-on, in order to perform. The opposite of extrinsic is intrinsic, meaning from within. An intrinsic person is self-motivated.

EXTRINSIC EDUCATION – (eks-*TRIN*-sic ed-jew-*KAY*-shun) *"Useful"* learning, meaning learning to make a living. Extrinsic education assures a meal ticket. It has been called learning that *"bakes bread."* Extrinsic education is job-training, vocational ed. It is strictly utilitarian, practical. Its goal is external gain by learning a profitable skill. Its counterpart is *intrinsic education* which is for self- improvement, personal edification.

EXTRINSIC MOTIVATION – (eks-*TRIN*-sic mo-ti-*VAY*-shun) In education, when students exert effort not to learn, but to gain a reward, or avoid a punishment. The extrinsic motivation may be a grade, to please parents, or avoid trouble.

EXTROVERT – (*EKS*-tro-vert) An outgoing, gregarious person, in extreme cases a show-off. An extrovert is more concerned with his external social environment, than his inner thoughts and feelings. She is the life of the party. An extrovert tends to be boisterous, assertive, brash. Extroversion is not a neurotic condition, but a personality type. The opposite of extrovert is introvert – quiet, contemplative, meditative, inwardly-directed. Both were introduced by psychiatrist Carl Gustav Jung (1875 – 1961).

EXTRUDE – (eks-*TROOD*) (Extruding, Extrusion) To squeeze or press out. Juice is extruded from and orange.

EXUBERANCE – (ig-*ZOO*-ber-antz) (Exuberant, Exuberantly) Effusively and almost uninhibitedly enthusiastic. Exuberance can also refer to an overflow, a lavish abundance. *"Exuberance is beauty."* – William Blake (1757 – 1827).

EXUDE – (eks-*YOOD*) (Exudation) To ooze out, as sap from a tree, or sweat from a hot body.

EXURBINITES – (eks-*ERB*-bin-yts) Prosperous people who move to the freshly constructed exurbs (affluent gated-communities beyond the suburbs). Suburbia was the product of *"white flight,"* those escaping the racial diverse cities. Exurbia is the product of *"wealth flight,"* those desiring to be among *"their own kind."* Exurbanites are people who flee suburbia to dwell among rich, conservative, unapologetic bigots like themselves.

EXURB – (*EKS*-urb) A small prosperous, gated-community, located beyond the suburbs in what was recently rural.

EYE CARE – (*AHY KER*) The terms used for the eye care professionals is confusing. An <u>Ophthalmologist</u> (of-thuhl-*MOL*-uh-jist) (Ophthalmology) is an eye doctor, a physician. An <u>Optometrist</u> (op-*TOM*-i-trist) (Optometry) is an eye examiner. An *Optician* (op-TISH-uhn) is an eyeglasses maker and seller.

EYE ROLLING – (*AHY ROE*-ling) In Western culture, a passive-aggressive response to an undesirable situation, statement, or person. The gesture is used to disagree or dismiss the targeted person without physical contact or comment. Eye rolling was used by American slaves, especially females, against their oppressors. It was a way to preserve some dignity in the face of an insult or humiliation, without risking life or limb – in most cases. If the slavocrat was wise to the defiance, punishment was sure to come. Often in the bad Old South, cayenne pepper would be rubbed into the offenders eyes as punishment. Eye rolling has been passed on, especially in the black community, to this day. Incidentally: Young black girls will employ eye rolling against teachers. In order to de-escalate a crisis, a white teacher can ignore the defiance by playing dumb. But a black teacher cannot. It's not uncommon to hear a black teacher demand: *"Don't you go rolling those eyes to me, girl!"*

EYRIE – (*AIR*-ee) (also Aerie) The nest of a bird of prey (eagle, hawk, falcon), built in a high inaccessible place.

F

F – (*EF*) The 6th letter in the English alphabet, a consonant. In traditional educational evaluation, an F grade represents Failure. Too, F is the chemical symbol for the element Fluorine, as indicated on the Periodic Table of Chemical Elements.

FAANG – (*FANG*) An acronym for the 5 monstrous tech company behemoths: Facebook, Apple, Amazon, Netflix, Google. FAANG is corporate capitalism on steroids. FAANG constitutes a *"corpocracy,"* a government run by corporations. The wealth and power concentrated in this cabal is the greatest danger to democracy today. As the wise Supreme Court Justice Lewis Brandies (1856 – 1941) warned us: *"We either have a great amount of wealth concentrated in the hands of a few, or democracy. We can't have both."* Consider the wealth of these leviathans: Facebook > $104 billion; Apple > $226 billion; Amazon > $233 billion; Netflix > $17 billion; Google > $715 billion. Together, FAANG controls over one trillion, three hundred and thirty-five billion dollars in wealth ($1,335,000,000,000). The United States of FAANG is richer than the 79 poorest countries in the world combined! In financial power it ranks 18th in the world, out of 187 nations, above Australia! FAANG has a higher GNP (Gross National Product) than Norway, Denmark, Finland and Ireland Combined! FAANG controls almost 7% of the wealth in America! Such economic power can buy elections and candidates, dictate legislation and governmental policy, influence popular opinion through its social media outlets. It can run the country. This corporate beast has the claws and FAANGs to tear away our liberty. A capitalist corpocracy is a fascist dictatorship. As Vladimir Lenin (1870 – 1924) warned: *"Fascism is capitalism in decay."* Democratic Senator Elizabeth Warren (b. 1949) proposes the break-up of these colossal companies. That's good for a start. But they must be nationalized, taken over by the government, for the welfare and profit of the people. As always, the problem is capitalism, the solution is Socialism.

FACE – (*FAYS*) (Facial) The front part of the head from the forehead to the chin. One's face is one's recognizable identity. Personality shines forth from one's face. The face reflects one's moods, emotions, attitudes, and character. The compassionate missionary, Rev. Dr. Albert Schweitzer (1875 – 1965) asserted that: *"At 20 everyone has the face that God gave them, at 40 the face that life gave them, and at 60 the face they earned."* Indeed, time and life carves our facial features to reflect our hearts and expose our souls. Abraham Lincoln (1809 – 1865) was correct when he insisted that you can judge a man by his face. *"Every man over forty is responsible for his face,"* Lincoln said. This has never been more true than in the case of Donald Trump (b. 1946). Trump's miserable bloated face is dripping with virulent venom, vicious vengeance, and vile vituperation. Indeed, *"The eyes are the windows to the soul."* Notice Trump's squinting pig eyes, almost closed. This is a subliminal defense mechanism of liars. It screams out: *"Don't look me in the eyes and recognize my lies!"* A face-to-face meeting with Trump will immediately expose his heart of darkness and malicious soul. Behind Trump stands the *"Ass-Licker General,"* Vice-President Mike Pence (b. 1959). His glum, dour face indicate shame, humiliation, and em*BARE-ASS*ment. Fundamentalist Pence' face is lined with guilt for having to lie for Trump. Too, Pence perpetually blinks his eyes. Every police interrogator will tell you that is an indication of lying. Incidentally: Magnanimous faces are not necessarily attractive. Lincoln's face was worn by depression, responsibility, stress and anguish. Once, an opponent called Lincoln *"two-faced."* Lincoln self-effacedly replied: *"If I had two faces, do you think I'd be wearing this one?" "I ain't much baby, but I'm all I got."* – Jess Lair (1927 – 2000).

FACEBOOK – (*FAYS* book) Rebranded *Meta* in 2022. Facebook (Meta) is a worldwide social media networking service founded in Cambridge, Massachusetts (2004). One of its 5 founders and present Chairman and CEO is Mark Zuckerberg (b.1984). Facebook is headquartered in Menlo Park, California. Facebook (Meta) employs over 66,185 people. It total assets amount to over $187.73 billion dollars. Astoundingly, over 2.895 billion people subscribe to Facebook (Meta) globally. Only in totalitarian countries where free speech is banned, will Facebook be banned as well. So Facebook (Meta) is a rich and powerful global social entity, and intends to keep it that way. The company allocates over $20 million dollars annually to pay 80 lobbyists to bribe (lobby) lawmakers. Facebook's generosity is reserved for the business-hearted Republicans who work to keep the industry deregulated [free of government guard rails]. Like the two-faced Roman god *Janus,* Facebook (Meta) and all unregulated social media networks can be both, a blessing and a curse, for good or for evil. Millions of people can be enlightened by truth, or corrupted by lies. Information can be communicated to entire nations in moments. Millions of people can be mobilized to foment revolutionary change – defending a righteous cause, or establishing a fascist dictatorship. Furthermore, the liberties presented by the social media is a double-edged sword. It seems impossible to keep nefarious foreign powers from disseminating lies and propaganda, injurious to our society and democracy. This was the case with the *"Russian meddling,"* which commenced with the 2016 Presidential Election, and concluded with the curse of Trump. In fact, whistleblower accusations, governmental investigation and lawsuits are what led Facebook to reboot as Meta.

FACE MASKS – (*FAYS* masks) (Face Masking) In sports and industry, a face mask serves as a protective device of steel and plastic that guards the face from injury. Baseball catchers and hockey goalies were face masks. So do welders and other industrial workers. Equipment to mask the face comes in various forms. In the medical field, cloth and fortified paper masks have long been employed by surgeons during operations. This protects the vulnerable patient from bacterial infection. With the Coronavirus pandemic of 2020, prudent people began to mask in public, and governments soon made it mandatory. This was medically imperative to arrest the spread of the outbreak. Face masks protect an individual in a contaminated environment. Too, face masks protect the community from an infected individual. During the viral calamity, what can be more sensible and considerate than wearing face masks? Who can possibly object to their universal application? President Donald J. Trump (b. 1946) can. In the irrational time of Trump, wearing protective face masks became a political statement. Face masks indicate the severity of the viral crisis, and served as a reminder of Trump's gross mishandling of the disaster. Despite contamination in the White House, Trump discouraged the wearing of face masks, and refused to wear one himself. *"It makes me look stupid,"* Trump declared. (Actually, Trump does not need a face mask to look stupid.) Diehard supporters of Trump also refused to wear face masks in public. Being unmasked became a symbol of Trump loyalty among his cultists. (Anecdotally, perhaps 70% of Americans wear masks in public, 30% do not. Comparatively, about 99% of Jamaicans wear masks.) Furthermore, Trump must revive the economy by opening society, despite the danger of death. A depressed economy translates into electoral defeat, which would ultimately translate into Trump's well- deserved imprisonment. Face masks are symbolic of society's unreadiness to reopen. Incidentally: One is 18 times safer from viral contagion when wearing a mask. Too, it requires 9 out of 10 people in an area wearing masks, for masks to be effective in subduing the outbreak.

FACEPLANT – (*FAYS*-plant) (Faceplanted) To fall on your face. To inadvertently plant your face in the dirt. Originally, the term faceplant referred to a skateboarding and biking accidents, in which one hit the ground face first. The term was adopted into popular parlance to mean any disastrous occurrence, failure, some grave mistake. *"Trump's interview on fascist Fox TV was a faceplant!"*

FACESITTING – (*FAYS*-sit-ting) (Facesitter) To rest one's bare derriere on the front part of another's head, from the forehead to the chin. The nose and mouth will be lodged between the ass cheeks and gooch (*perineum*). This is the area between the vulva and anus in females, and between the scrotum and anus in males. *"The ass is the face of the soul in sex,"* philosopher Charles Bukowski declared. (1920 – 1994). Facesitting is a fetish among some exotic erotic connoisseurs. It can serve as an arousing foreplay performance. Facesitting will provide the recipient with the fragrance of pussy, a taste of testes, and the essence of ass. This is an erotic aroma to facesitting enthusiasts. These pheromones serve as a stimulating aphrodisiac. The sitter must be cautious. Sitting on another's face requires a gentle balancing act. A careless flop with all one's weight may result in injury. Too, one's human tushie-cushion can asphyxiate (suffocate). For professional, career facesitting couples, special small stools can be purchased to take much of the weight off the ass-licker's mug. It is constructed similarly to a toilet seat, which is understandably and appropriate. *"The only unnatural sex act is that which you cannot perform."* – Sexologist Dr. Alfred Kinsey (1894 – 1956). A Caveat: I am a messenger. As such, I am reporting, not supporting.

FACETIOUS – (fas-*SET*-tee-us) (Facetiously) Not meant to be taken literally or seriously. A facetious statement lacks serious intent. It may be said amusingly or frivolously. Hyperbole (exaggeration for effect) is being facetious. For instance, *"A million people wanted my ticket!"*

FACIAL RECOGNITION – (*FAY*-shul rek-kog-*NISH*-shun) Remembering a face. A technology capable of matching a human face from a digital image or a video frame against a data base of faces. Facial recognition systems are typically employed to authenticate users through ID verification services. It works by pinpointing and measuring facial features from a given image. Facial recognition is like high-tech fingerprinting. It is not fail-proof as of yet.

FACIAL SIGHT – (*FAY*-shul *SYT*) The mysterious way that blind people can sense, feel objects in their path, as if they can detect the vibrations from the atoms that comprise the objects. It seems that people who had been blind all their lives develop a mysterious radar warning them of objects in their path. This is facial sight.

FACIUM EST – (fa-*SEE*-um *EST*) Latin for *"It is done."*

FACSIMILE – (fak-*SIM*-muh-lee) An exact copy, as of a book, painting, or manuscript. A perfect replica of a vehicle, building, anything is a facsimile.

FACT – (*FAKT*) (Factual) A simple, proven bit of truth, accepted by all. A fact must be the description of a real occurrence, happening, in order to be factual. A fact is a truth. But truth, on the temporal plane is pragmatic or changeable. What is true today, may not be true tomorrow, and neither will its facts. It is a fact that St. Paul (c. 5 – c. 67 CE) could not have flown from Corinth to Rome. Yet the laws of aerodynamics where the same then as now. It is also a fact that today, St. Paul could have made that flight. The facts changed because the truth changed. A fact is a single brick of data, which, built upon others creates concepts, which, combined with others erects philosophies. Facts are assumed to be true. A false fact, as disseminated by the Trump Administration is oxymoronic, as is the moronic ox Donald Trump (b. 1946). *"Facts cannot be altered by a wish, but they can destroy the wisher."* – Ayn Rand (1905 – 1982).

FACTIONALISM – (*FAK*-shun-uhl-iz-uhm) (Factions, Factional, Factionalization) A condition in which a group, organization, government, or nation splits into two or more smaller groups with differing and often opposing opinions, interests, loyalties, and goals. Factionalism is fractionalism. Factionalism is a poisonous paralytic form of political polarization. Citizens align into mutually hateful factions. In the book, <u>How Civil Wars Start</u> (2020), Dr. Barbara F. Walter (b. 1964) explained: *"Civil wars ignite and escalate in ways that are predictable; they follow a script. Countries that factionalize have political parties based on ethnic, religious, or racial identity rather than ideology, and these parties then seek to rule at the exclusion and expense of others."* Indeed, factionalism is a leap toward insurrection, revolution, civil war, and dismemberment. Presently (January 2022) it appears that factionalism is affecting the *"Disunited States of America."* Incidentally: Another term for factionalism is *"Balkanization."* This term was created because of the factioning and fractioning of Yugoslavia on the Balkan Peninsula into 7 hostile states.

FACTIOUS – (*FAK*-shus) Divisive, dissentious, tending to break up or fracture into factions.

FACTITIOUS – (fac-*TISH*-ee-us) Unnatural, artificial, not genuine. Factitious laughter, crying, approval is contrived, not spontaneous or sincere.

FACT MASSAGING – (*FAKT* muh-*SAHZH*-ing) A fact is an article of truth. A massage is a manipulation of the body to relieve uncomfortable tension. Fact massaging is manipulating an article of truth to relieve the tension of uncomfortable perception. Fact massaging goes beyond spinning facts to changing them. It is pure deceit, lying about the truth. Like a vigorous body massage, the truth is battered in a fact massage. In 2021, the Republicans-cum- Trumpublicans maliciously, ridiculously massaged the facts about the 2020 Presidential election (*"The Big Lie"*) and the attempted coup of January 6, 2021. They insisted that Donald Trump (b. 1946) won the election which was stolen from him. Too, they presented the deadly violent attack on the Capitol Building as a tourist excursion. American politics had never experienced such a degree of fact massaging until the emergence of *"His Fraudulency,"* Donald Trump. *"Everyone is entitled to their own opinion, but no one is entitled to their own facts."* – Daniel Patrick Moynihan (1927 – 2003).

FACTORY – (*FAC*-tor-ree) An industrial building used for the manufacture and assembly of goods. But long before the Industrial Revolution (c. 1760), the factory had been the temple of capitalist exploitation for private profit. After all, the term *"factory"* is taken from *"factor,"* a slave agent and trader who managed the freshly captured human merchandise in Africa. The holding-pens on the West African *"Slave Coast"* came to be called *"factories."* With slave labor, sugarcane became the world's first agricultural product to undergo an industrial process before marketing. The Jamaican boiling houses of sugar juice came to be called *"factories."* The Industrial Revolution broke forth in mid-18th century Britain. Cottage industry gave way to factory production. The new evil that made the factory ghastly was different. It was the domination of men by the pace of the machines. The workers for the first time were driven by an unhuman clockwork: the power first of water and then of steam. The underlying purpose of the factory was not to make a product, but to make a profit. The factory was the embodiment of evil capitalism, as the stock market is today. Therefore, the capitalist factory had devoured human lives throughout history. Incidentally: For the first 16 and a half months of World War Two, over 5 times more American died in factories (64,000) than in battle (12,000).

FACTOTUM – (fak-*TOW*-tuhm) A skillful handyman, jack-of-all-trades, a *"Mr. Fixit."* A factotum is employed to do all kinds of work. He is an indispensable *"Man Friday."*

FACTUAL QUESTION – (*FAC*-chew-al *KWES*-chun) An inquiry or question that requires the recall of information through the mental processes of recognition and rote memory. For example*: "Who was the first Socialist to make a serious bid for the U.S. Presidency?" "Senator Bernie Sanders of Vermont in 2016."*

FACULTY PSYCHOLOGY – (*FAC*-kwal-tee sy-*COL*-lo-jee) Unsubstantiated 19th century educational belief that all formal education was based on the training of the mind. The mind was considered to be like a muscle, which is strengthened through mental exercise. The harder the subject, the stronger became the mind (like lifting heavier weights). Studying Hebrew for instance, was considered beneficial because it gave the mind a good workout. Though keeping mentally active is important, faculty psychology is erroneous.

FAD/TREND – (*FAD TREND*) A fad is defined as a temporary fashion, notion, style, or craze. A trend is defined as a general course or prevailing tendency, style, or fashion. The terms are used interchangeably. In both cases, some sort of movement has been set in motion. But there is a difference. Whereas a fad is top down, a trend is bottom up. A fad initiates in the upper-class and percolates down to the masses. A trend develops in the grassroots, and rises up through society. Fads are whimsical, trends are lasting.

FAIENCE – (fy-*ONS*) Glazed pottery or earthenware, especially a fine variety with highly colored designs.

FAILSAFE – (*FAYL*-sayf) Foolproof. Literally safe from failure, free from error. Failsafe is a built-in safety contingency in case of a malfunction emergency. In machinery, to be failsafe is to be equipped with a secondary system that insures continued operation even if the primary system fails.

FAILURE – (*FAYL*-your) To fall short of your goal. Failure is an event, not a character trait – you may have failed, but you are not a failure. Failure is a step toward ultimate success. Furthermore, failure is not living up to your personal standards, not the world's standards.

FAINEANT – (*FAY*-nee-uhnt) Idle, indolent or being a lazy idler, a do-nothing. *President Donald Trump (b. 1946) had become even more fainéant to his duties. Since losing the election, Trump had retired on the job."*

FAIR – (*FARE*) Concerning morality, to be far is to be just. Fair is free from dishonesty, impartiality, bias, and discrimination. It has been said time and again that life is not fair. True enough. But that doesn't mean that we shouldn't strive to make it so. Capitalism encourages rugged individualism, unfair competition, every man for himself. This means the strong get stronger, the rich get richer, the powerful oppress the weak. That is not fair. Socialists believe in true fairness. Under Socialism, it is unfair to treat unequal people equally. This is the rationalization underpinning affirmative action.

FAIR – (*FARE*) (Fairness, Unfairness) Ethically speaking, fair is being free from bias, not dishonest, exhibiting true justice. It's a cliché that *"Life is not fair,"* but that doesn't mean we should want it to be so. Life is not fair when the people in power are not fair. Fairness is a moral concept. It is morally unfair, or immoral that some people should have millions and billions, while others are homeless, hungry, and ill, the circumstances notwithstanding. Life is only unfair in a capitalist regime, predicated on the conviction that *"I got mine, to hell with you!"* *"Rugged individualism,"* *"Dog-eat-dog"* economics creates unfairness. Do you believe in your heart that Jesus would consider 21st century America fair? Of course not, because Jesus was a Socialist. Every religious avatar in history were Socialists. Society will become fair when Socialism is adopted.

FAIR – (*FARE*) Meteorologically speaking, in fair weather, clouds should cover no more than 40% of the sky. No fog likely in a fair forecast.

FAIR VALUE – (fair *VAL*-yoo) The honest, equitable, actual worth of any item, property, commodity, or asset. On Wall Street at the stock market, fair value refers to a company's stock worth as determined by a willing seller and buyer – how much one will accept, how much one will pay. The fair value becomes "unfair" when the Federal Reserve Bank (*The Fed*) interferes in the stock market with vast infusions of money. When the The Fed lowers interest rates, or stimulates the banks with billions of dollars, the banks lend more money to companies. Both the banks and companies get richer. The company's stock prices go up, which is reflected by a rise in the DOW average (the stock market goes up). Stock holders get richer too (on paper). This is not fair value of the stock. It is the worth of the stock on Federal Reserve "steroids." Free enterprise horse trading produces the fair value. Federal Reserve support puts the thumb on the scale, in support of capitalism – banks, companies, stock market, shareholders. In a sense, The Fed is using command economy tactics [read: *Socialism*] to support the free market [read: *capitalism*]. In another sense, it is welfare for the rich.

FAIT ACCOMPLI – (*FATE* a-*COM*-ply) Latin for an accomplished fact, a done deed, a situation beyond alteration.

FAITH – (*FAYTH*) Blind trust. Faith is belief not requiring proof, belief plus expectation. Faith is intuitive certainty, conviction in that which is not seen. Indeed, faith sees the invisible, feels the intangible, and achieves the impossible. Classical Historian Edith Hamilton (1867 – 1963) maintained that: *"Faith is not belief. Belief is passive. Faith is active."* Too, faith goes beyond hope, for faith is hope, minus any doubt. Hope is for gamblers. Faith is for believers. The great Church Father and scholar, St. Thomas Aquinas (1225 – 1274) wrote: *"Faith has to do with things that are not seen and hope with things that are not at hand."* The faithful give thanks while the miracle is still in progress. *"Faith is the substance of things hoped for, the evidence of things not seen."* – Hebrews 11:1. Therefore, the opposite of faith is fear, for those who have faith should fear not. Of course, in order to have faith, one must believe. Faith is not scientific but metaphysical. Psychologist William James (1842 – 1910) said: *"My will to believe is stronger than the cool logic of the intellect."* The blessed St. Bernard of Clairvaux (1090 – 1153) admitted: *"I believe though I do not comprehend, and I hold by faith what I cannot grasp with the mind."* That's what faith is all about.

FAJITAS – (fah-*HEE*-tuhs) A *"Tex-Mex"* dish of thin strips of marinated and grilled meat, usually beef. Fajitas is usually served with tortillas, salsa, and refried beans. The term fajita was first recorded in about 1975. In Spanish it literally means *"little sash,"* a sash being a belt or strip, as are the cuts of the meat.

FAKE ELECTORS – (*FAYK* el-*LEK*-tors) A plot to hijack the 2020 presidential election by Donald Trump (b. 1946) and a cast of state, federal, and congressional conspirators. The *"Fake Electors Plot"* was conceived by Trump's attorney Kenneth Chesebro (b. 1961) and propagated by disgraced Trump lawyer John Eastman (b. 1960). The electors in this controversy are a congregation of representatives that comprise the Electoral College (or assembly). Their duty has come to be to *"rubber-stamp"* the will of the voters in their states. Who wins the majority of the popular vote in a presidential election, automatically receives all that state's electoral votes. Who wins at least 270 electoral votes nationally is elected president. The Democratic candidate, Joe Biden (b. 1942) won the 2020 presidential election over Republican candidate Donald Trump. But Trump and his fascist followers attempted to stage a coup and usurp the presidency. They plotted with Republican parties in 7 states: Arizona, Georgia, Michigan, Nevada, New Mexico, Wisconsin, and Pennsylvania to gather groups of *"Fake Electors,"* who would disregard the will of the people, and cast their votes for Donald Trump as president. Obviously, this is anti-democratic, unethical, but at the time, not strictly *"extra-legal,"* (a flaw, perhaps intentional, in the Constitution). It wasn't until months later (July 6, 2020), that the Supreme Court dictated that Electoral College electors must abide by the will of the voters. At this writing, (July 2023), the Fake Electors Plot is still being investigated, awaiting adjudication. However, what the Trump conspirators did was not, at that time, unconstitutional. The Constitution does not say that it cannot be done. The ability to manipulate the Electoral College was not an oversight on the part of the Founding Fathers, but their plan. In fact, the Founding Father of the Constitution wanted this vague, uncertainty to exist, just in case they needed to subvert a presidential election themselves. That's right. The Founding Father were wealthy merchants and plantation owners. They distrusted democracy, always fearing the common people would elect a president who would redistribute their wealth, or that of their descendant's – [read: A Socialist]. That's why they created the awkward, undemocratic Electoral College in the first place. It stands as an anti-democratic *"safety valve"* to protect the rich and powerful few, from the will of the great common hoard. The Founders figured that their class could always persuade the electors to change their votes, or change the electors. Therefore, the Trump fascists used the Electoral College in the very way the Founding Fathers had designed it, in case of an overly- democratic emergency. In this case, the emergency was Trump's defeat. Hopefully, the Fake Electors abuse may provide the impetus to abandon the archaic, anti-democratic Electoral College. *"The election is not determined by those who cast the vote, but rather by those who count the vote."* – Joseph Stalin (1878 – 1953). *"The trouble with free elections is that you never know how they are going to turn out."* – Vyacheslav Molotov (1890 – 1986).

FAKE NEWS – (*FAYK NOOZ*) Bogus, dishonest charge made by Donald Trump (b. 1946) and his underlings that professional, reputable news agencies are fabricating stories, falsifying information, to discredit him and his presidency. This is an outrageous, delusional, paranoid assertion. Fake news is literally *"Trumped-up"* news. It is uncertain whether Trump neurotically believes his falsehoods or is a hopeless pathological liar. To Donald Trump, fake news is any news that does not conform to his wishes, and that does not flatter him personally. President Trump's persistent accusations of fake news-casting are an ominous portent for America's future. At the same time, Trump is the master of fake/false news. MSNBC researchers have calculated that Trump had uttered no less than 400 lies in his first 100 days (an astounding 4 lies a day!). The New York Times had calculated 30,573 lies and misrepresentations made by Trump in his four years in office. All of Trump's Trumpublican asslickers spread the fake news like fertilizer. Steve Bannon (b. 1953) for instance advised: *"The way to deal with the press is to flood the zone with shit,"* [read: fake news]. The only fake news is that the U.S. has a competent, authentic President. Indeed the capstone of Trump's fake news was that he had actually won the 2020 presidential election, *"The BIG LIE."* *"The greatest enemy of truth is very often not the lie, deliberate, contrived, and dishonest, but the myth, persistent, persuasive, and unrealistic."* – President John F. Kennedy (1917 – 1963). *"Everyone is entitled to his own opinion, but not his own facts."* – Senator Daniel Patrick Moynihan (1927 – 2003). Incidentally: It is a common practice of the C.I.A. to spread fake news to discredit Socialists. They will try to demonize the Socialist president and his regime with outrageous atrocities. Be aware that this is a prelude to a U.S. military invasion to overthrow the Socialist government, in favor of a pro-capitalist, fascist dictator. This is occurring presently (2018) with the Socialist government of Venezuela. American capitalists want their oil. *"When regard for the truth has been broken down or even slightly weakened, all things will remain doubtful."* – St. Augustine of Hippo (354 – 430 CE). *"When lies have been accepted for some time, the truth always astounds with an air of novelty."* – Clement of Alexandria (c. 150 – c. 215). *"Till the false is seen as the false, truth is not."* – Rajneesh (1931 – 1990).

FALAISE GAP – (fal-*LAY GAP*) Also Falaise Pocket. Falaise is a large town in Normandy, in northwestern France on the Ante River. Falaise was the site of the decisive engagement of the Battle of Normandy in the Second World War. From August 12 to 21, 1944, three German army corps were surrounded by allied forces consisting of Americans, British, Canadians, Poles, and French troops. Over 10,000 Germans were killed, 50,000 taken prisoner. The Germans called the Falaise Gap their *"French Stalingrad."* The way was now clear to Paris and the German border.

FALCON – (*FEL*-kon) Fastest animal on Earth (*Peregrines*), with a dive speed of over 200 mph. Falcons attack prey on the wing, while their cousins, hawks, attack prey on the ground.

FALKLAND ISLANDS – (*FAULK*-land *EYE*-lands) (The Argentinean Malvinas Islands.) A group of small islands in the South Atlantic, 300 miles off the coast of Argentina. The total land area is only 4,700 square miles, (smaller than Connecticut) much being barren rock. The population stands at about 3,140 islanders. They are rabidly British, as colonials displaced from the motherland tend to be. Though geographically Argentinean, the British refuse to relinquish the islands. In the days between sail and oil powered vessels, coaling stations throughout the globe were essential to maritime nations. Despite Argentinean claims, the imperialist British occupied the Falkland Islands in 1833. This was 10 years after the U.S. declared the

Monroe Doctrine (1823) closing the Western Hemisphere to further European colonization. The U.S. did not react to Britain's seizure. British control of the Falklands has vexed Argentina ever since. In 1982, Argentinean troops occupied the islands. In the brief 2-month war, the British won back the colony. It cost Britain 255 dead plus 3 civilians killed accidentally by British shelling. When added to the 775 wounded, total British casualties amounted to over a third of the colony's total population. The war cost Britain 2.778 billion pounds (over 9 billion today). It made conservative Prime Minister Margaret Thatcher (1925 – 2013) a war hero, and guaranteed her re-election.

FALLACY – (*FEL*-la-see) A falsehood. A deceptive, misleading, erroneous belief. The Trump administration's *"fake news"* stands as fallacies. In philosophy, a fallacy is an unsound argument or an error in reasoning. It is a logical error. A fallacy is reasoning that does not follow the rules of inference or violates them. It is an erroneous argument in which the conclusion is not justified by the statements supporting it.

FALLACY OF COMPOSITION – (*FEL*-la-see of *COM*-po-si-shun) In philosophy, arguing that what is true of each part of a whole is also true of the whole itself. For example: *"Some male hairdressers and fashion designers are gay. Therefore, all male hairdressers and fashion designers are gay."* This is a false assertion of the fallacy of composition.

FALLACY OF DIVISION – (*FEL*-la-see of div-*VIZ*-on) In philosophy, arguing that what is true of the whole, is also true of its parts, or some of its parts. For Example: *"Oakland County Michigan is a wealthy county. Therefore, Stella the 'Bag Lady' from Oakland County must be very rich."* This is a false assertion of the fallacy of division.

FALLEN TIMBERS – (*FAWL*-len *TIM*-bers) (1794) Decisive battle in U.S. History, fought near present day Toledo Ohio called *"America's Second Yorktown."* By defeating the Indians, General Anthony Wayne (1745 – 1796) and Colonel John Francis Hamtramck (1756 – 1803) secured the Northwest Territories (Ohio, Indiana, Michigan) for the U.S., and not for British Canada.

FALL LINE – (*FAWL* lyne) A linear region in the Eastern United States along which the Coastal Plain meets the foot of the Appalachian Mountains (the Piedmont). The fall line exhibits waterfalls and rapid rivers that indicate the rise in elevation.

FALLOUT – (*FAWL*-owt) An early atomic-age term referring to the deadly dispersion of radioactive waste particles after an atomic blast. Fallout has entered the political lexicon. It refers to damaging publicity that follows a political disaster. Political strategists [read: *spin doctors*] frantically attempt to contain the fallout, the rain of bad news. Incidentally: The Trump White House is perpetually fighting the fallout from President Donald Trump's (b. 1946) ignorance and malevolence.

FALLOW – (*FAL*-low) Unused farmland. Give the field a rest about every 4th year. Allow it to remain fallow so it can rejuvenate its fertility.

FALSE – (*FAWLS*) (Falsity) Not true. An idea, belief, proposition, opinion is false when the fact to which it refers does not exist. There is no evidence supporting a falsity. The opposite of false is true. Facts are true or false. However, what is true today may be proven false tomorrow, and vice-versa.

FALSE BRAVADO – (fawls bruh-*VAH*-doh) Fake bravery. False bravado is a pretentious, swaggering display of false courage. False bravado is over- compensated defensiveness. It often is accompanied by boisterous trash talk. Frightened bullies utilize false bravado.

FALSE CONSCIOUSNESS – (*FAWLS CON*-chess-ness) A ruse perpetrated by the rich to distract the poor from realizing their true class consciousness. Patriotism, racism, bigotry, greed, fundamentalism have all served to block working class solidarity. The poor must develop the true consciousness that the real enemy is corporate capitalism, not each other. By spreading the false consciousness of racism, the wealthy have prevented poor whites from uniting with poor blacks. As a result, the South is still un-unionized, keeping both the whites and blacks poor, the corporate capitalists richer. It was the employment of false consciousness by conservatives, capitalists, and Republicans that resulted in the disastrous Trump electoral victory of 2016.

FALSE EQUIVALENCY – (*FAWLS* ee-*KWIV*-va-lan-see) Equivalent means equal, the same. What is false is invalid, untrue. So a false equivalence is an invalid comparison. It is suggesting that two unequals are actually equal. A false equivalency attempts to commensurate incomparable incidents, occasions, or personalities. To say that Republican Donald Trump (b. 1946) is a new Republican Ronald Reagan (1911 – 2004) is a false equivalency. Too, equating Liberal Civil Rights protesters (*Black Lives Matter*) with neo-Nazis militiamen (*Proud Boys*) as Trump had, is also false equivalency. Incidentally: Now that Donald Trump is facing judicial peril, his Republican sycophants are trying to establish the false equivalence between Hillary Clinton's (b. 1947) legal emails, and Trump's illegal stolen secret documents. Furthermore, the Republicans- cum-Trumpublicans are desperately trying to impeach President Joe Biden (b. 1942) on anything, just to create a false equivalency with the twice impeached Trump.

FALSE FLAG – (fawls *FLAG*) A deceptive set-up. A covert operation or propaganda to deceive. To false flag is to create the appearance that a person, group, political party, or nation was responsible for some loathsome act, disguising the actual source of responsibility. The term derives from pirate culture. The unscrupulous buccaneers would falsely fly a peaceful nation's flag while approaching a targeted ship. Being deceived, the victim would neither flee nor fire. With surprise on their side, the pirates would attack. Sometimes the false flag would remain hoisted planting the blame on some innocent nation. Some nations had despicably painted the Red Cross on military vehicles, a most noxious false flag. During the Cuban Missile Crisis (October 1962), the U.S. Air Force painted war planes to look like those of the Cuban Air Force. Too, the C.I.A. often bombed Socialist Revolutionaries with unmarked planes (a form of false flagging) in support of fascist capitalist regimes (especially in Latin America). Private and political organizations also false flag. In October, 2018, a violent Trump supporter, (inspired by Trump's vile, virulent vituperations), sent 14 pipe bombs to prominent Democratic leaders and Trump critics. The right wing hate media, led by perfidious Fox News and Rush Limbaugh (1951 – 2021) hoisted several fraudulent false flags. The gist of their ridiculous assertions was that anti-Trump Democrats mailed the pipe bombs in order to discredit Trump and the Republicans before the midterm election.

FALSEHOOD – (*FAWLS*-hood) False means untrue. Hood means a state of being, in this case. A falsehood is a lie. So why don't you just say it? Why sanitize the word *"lie"* with *"falsehood."* A falsehood may be a mistake. But a lie is a naked deception. At the interview, Donald Trump (b. 1946) did not make 27 falsehoods. He lied 27 fuckin' times! Don't try to preserve his dignity, because he is wholly devoid of dignity. When you try, you are committing a falsehood.

FALSE NARRATIVE – (*FAWLS NAR*-ra-tiv) A preposterous euphemism for a *LIE*. A false narrative is a phony story or explanation consisting of *"alternate facts,"* (another preposterous Trump Administration euphemism).

FALSE POSITIVE/NEGATIVE – (*FAWLS POS*-si-tiv *NEG*-ga-tiv) In both cases, a mistaken test result. A false positive is incorrect data that indicates a particular condition or attribute is present, when it's not. A test that indicates cancer but is wrong, is a false positive. The opposite error is a false negative, when the test fails to indicate a condition or attribute.

FALSE SCARCITY – (fawls *SKAIR*-si-tee) (also fake scarcity) Scarcity is a dearth, lack of something, anything that is needed. A fake or false scarcity is a contrived shortage of a dire commodity for selfish, self-indulgent reasons. Capitalism is predicated on the law of supply and demand. When the demand is greatest, the supply is most valuable. Therefore, when a commodity is most needed, the capitalist in control is free to raise the price the highest. This is free enterprise. In a catastrophe like a natural disaster, emergency, accident, war, capitalists will try to profiteer on the calamity, the suffering of the population. The cost or price of scarce food, water, medicine, or fuel will be raised sky-high. The capitalist law of supply and demand is against the law of love. The perfidious corporate capitalists don't need a traumatic experience to profiteer. They will create an artificial scarcity in order to hike prices just out of greed. They will blame a hurricane for the high price of gasoline, or inflation for the prohibitive cost of bread, milk, eggs, or meat. It is a lie! It is a conspiracy hatched in the corporate capitalist boardrooms. In some cases they will intentionally hold back production that creates the scarcity that hikes prices and profits. The less milk in the supermarket, the more consumers will pay for what's available, whatever the cost. When the supply increases, the cost never goes down. The higher prices remain perpetually. Planet Earth is blessed with abundance. There is more than enough to go around for everyone. This applies to food, water, land, shelter – everything. The inherent greed which is capitalism creates scarcity. Understand that only about 7,000 people on Earth own everything, control everything! The only solution, the only salvation for humanity is Socialism.

FALSETALK – (*FAWLS*-talk) Double-speak. Using an Orwellian code to confuse and obfuscate an issue. Falsetalk employs verisimilitude and euphemistic language to convince people to support policies against their own interests. Falsetalk is indeed successful with the simple minded and bigots, as *Fox News Network* demonstrates. The Nazi propagandists were masters of falsetalk. They used the term *"Socialist"* in the name of their organization (National *Socialist,* or Nazis), to attract workers. In fact, the National Socialist Nazis murdered the Socialists. The architect of the Russian Revolution, Vladimir Lenin (1870 – 1924) said that capitalism uses *"Falsehood and deception to hoodwink the masses of workers and peasants to stultify their minds."* Today, the champion of falsetalk is Donald Trump (b. 1946). MSNBC television has calculated that Trump had spouted no less than 400 lies in his first 100 days (an astonishing 4 lies a day!) 2,000 by year's end! After four years, the Prince of Liars tried to deceive us 30,573 times, at least. *"Beware of false knowledge; it is more dangerous than ignorance."* – George Bernard Shaw (1856 – 1950).

FALSETTO – (fawl-*SET*-toh) An unnaturally or artificially high-pitched voice or register, especially in a man. Young prepubescent choirboys have falsetto voices. During the Middle Ages, great cathedrals would take in and raise orphan boys as monks. Often, they would be castrated in boyhood to maintain their sweet falsetto voices for the cathedral choir. Incidentally: In Detroit's famous Motown sound, singers like Smokey Robinson (b. 1940) skillfully employed falsetto in his popular recordings.

FAMILIAR – (*FAM*-mil-yur) (read: *FAMILY*-iliar) (Familiarity) Being well- acquainted, informal, personal, intimate, as in one's family. The familiar is comfortable, for like the family, the familiar feels safe. Familiarity is being in one's comfort zone.

FAMILIARS – (fam-*MIL*-yurs) In the witchcraft, and the occult, an animal that embodies a supernatural spirit and aids a witch in the performance of magik. Dogs, owls, rats, mice, bats, lizards, toads, and the familiar black cat have served as traditional familiars. Sometimes, the sorcerer may transform into a familiar, (shape shift) as with the vampire and bat. A familiar is an assistant in animal form. The creature is merely the carnal, material body of the guiding, cooperating spirit. This spirit will pass from one familiar animal to another. The spirit in the animal contributes energy to aid in the performance of the magick.

FAMILY – (*FAM*-lee) (Families, Familyhood) A simple term with complex connotations and interpretations. (Bear in mind that the terms family, familial, and familiar are cognates.) The traditional definition of the traditional family is a father and mother serving as parents to their children (sisters and brothers). If this grouping lives together, they comprise a household. Though the children will mature and depart the familial household, they still remain part of the parent's family. This basic unit (dad, mom, kids) constitute the *"nuclear family."* If other relatives are included in the household like grandparents, grandchildren, uncles, aunts, cousins, this extension creates *an "extended family."* So all families need not be traditional. Even extraordinary relationships can qualify as a family. Children may be adopted, and friends may be incorporated into the household. Too, the parents of the family may belong to the same sex. That's because a family is a malleable social organism. It is not dependent on gender, genetics, or social mores. The only glue that binds individuals together into a family is love. A loveless traditional nuclear household, strafed by strife, bitterness, rivalry, envy is hardly a family. Any social unit closely knit with love can qualify as a family. Incidentally: If you accept the Fatherhood of God, then you must accept the Brotherhood and Familyhood of Man. *"The problem with the world is that we draw the circle of our family too small."* – Mother Teresa (1910 – 1997). *"All happy families are alike; each unhappy family is unhappy in its own way."* – Leo Tolstoy (1828 – 1910).

FAMILY – (*FAM*-lee) The collective name for an assemblage of otters. *"The family of otters devoured every large fish in the pond."*

FAMILYHOOD – (*FAM*-lee-hood) (Family, Familial) The basic social unit of blood relatives, close kin. The immediate family is the *"nuclear family"* consisting of father, mother, brothers, and sisters. The *"extended family"* includes grandparents, uncles, aunts, cousins, nephews, and nieces. Family members are bound genetically and emotionally. That's why love and hatred is most intense within the family unit. Family members often adopt roles they subconsciously play on the family stage. They may include: the dictator, martyr, hero, clown, scholar, victim, outcast, or rebel. It's trite but true that *"We choose our friends, but our family we're stuck with."* Spiritual leader Ram Das (b. 1931) attested to this truth: *"If you think you are enlightened, spend two weeks with your parents."* Nevertheless, despite the tensions and rivalries within a family, *"Blood is still thicker than water."* In Analects 13: XVIII, *"The Duke of Sheh informed Confucius (551 – 479 BCE), saying, 'Among us here there are those who may be styled upright in their conduct. If their father have stolen a sheep, they will bear witness of the fact.' Confucius replied: 'Among us, in our part of the country, those who are upright are different from this. The father conceals the misconduct of the son, and the son conceals the misconduct of the father. Uprightness is to be found in this'."* Incidentally: A family member may be an adopted individual without a familial title. A friend may become so very dear, that she is emotionally incorporated into the family. Love knows no boundaries. Footnote: Human beings are joined in families, the families are joined in kinship groups, the kinship groups in clans, the clans in tribes, the tribes in nations. *"Family isn't defined by last names or by blood, it's defined by commitment and by love. It means showing up for each other when we need it most. It means having each other's backs."* – Dave Willis (b. 1970).

FAMILY ASSISTANCE PLAN – (*FAM*-lee ass-*SIS*-tans *PLAN*) A <u>Universal</u> <u>Basic</u> <u>Income</u> (UBI) proposal, made in 1969 by the unlikely politician, Republican President Richard Nixon (1913 – 1994). Though vague, the Family Assistance Plan would provide a cash payment to every American Family, Social Security for all. It would eliminate all other welfare programs. The conservative Republican Nixon, a former *"Friend,"* must have had a brief *"Quaker Moment."* His Republican colleagues thought he had lost his mind. After all, this was unadulterated Socialism. But Nixon soon recovered his stingy conservative bearings. The Family Assistance Plan was never discussed again.

FAMILY VALUES – (*FAM*-lee *VAL*-yous) The moral and ethical principles traditionally upheld and transmitted within a family. However families vary greatly and moral and ethical principles are culturally relative. Therefore, what is valuable to one family, may not be to another. Nevertheless, family values are a political talking point. Being a conservative concept, it is particularly associated with the conservative Republicans. Republican family values include *faith, patriotism, individualism, capitalism, loyalty,* and *discipline.* By *faith* Republicans refer to traditional Christian creeds that preach non-violence, acquiescence, and submission to authority. These values will assure the protection of property from those who need it. *Patriotism* to Republicans is blind obedience to the government controlled by the rich: *"My country, right or wrong,"* (even though I have no stake in it). *Individualism* translates to *"Every man for himself."* This absolves the Republicans from any responsibility to the needy. *Capitalism* legitimizes greed, and the gross disparity of wealth that the Republicans enjoy. It maintains the myth of the *"American Dream,"* that all can be rich. Republicans value *Loyalty* as unwavering support of the bossman and company. The loyal employee is submissive, and dedicated to increase corporate profits (even though he does not profit). Republicans expect the loyal worker to continue to toil, until the company moves to China, and he is relegated to the scrap bin. *Discipline* is a Republican family value that is transferred to the state. The police are to be regarded as the strict father, maintaining law and order, which is meant to preserve the hegemony of the rich. To Republicans, family values are the precepts valuable in maintaining their privileged position in society. Republican family values are designed to produce an authoritarian, if not dictatorial state.

FAMINE – (*FA*-min) Massive starvation, sometimes caused by natural calamities, but usually due to war and capitalist greed. A child dies somewhere on Earth of hunger every 5 seconds. Imperialist exploitation by the World Bank and I.M.F. (International <u>M</u>onetary <u>F</u>und) has sucked all the natural wealth out of underdeveloped countries, resulting in poverty, illness, hunger, starvation, and famine. Over 400 major famines have been recorded throughout human history. More times than not, famine will foment war. As Rabbi Benjamin Blech (b. 1933) so eloquently stated: *"People do not fight because they are wicked. War is waged primarily for the sake of what is central…bread. Help the needy. Feed the starving. Assuage the pain of those who are hungry. It is the means of preventing war and securing the great blessing of peace."* The great English writer and futurist, George Orwell (1903 – 1950) wrote: *"The greatest obscenity will be when half of the world's population watches the other half starve to death on television."* Incidentally: If all agriculture ceased, humanity would have a 60-day reserve of food.

FAN – (*FAN*) An enthusiastic devotee, follower, or admirer of a sport, pastime, or celebrity. Originally (c. 1895) the term *fan* had been taken from the term *fanatic.* Some fans move beyond boosterism to *fanaticism.* This is especially true of individuals who have so little to be proud about. *"I've never been number one is anything, but my team is #1. 'Go Jacksonburgh Jackasses!' We're number one!"* A fanatical fan will invest his emotion and ego into his team, which becomes his alterego. An athletic loss is a personal loss, a failure, and insult. Some fans will fight for the team they support, especially when en- couraged with alcohol. Fans have killed each other at sporting events throughout the world. Incidentally: On Friday, January 12, 2024, MSNBC News reporter Chris Jansing (b. 1957) proved that she is a dedicated Cleveland Browns football fan. The Browns made the NFL playoffs. Jansing actually asked the viewers to say a prayer for a Browns victory. Nothing wrong with asking for prayer, but on television to a national audience? What about the fans from the opposing team who are certainly watching? At any rate, the Browns lost. *"They didn't stand a prayer!"*

FANATIC – (fan-*NA*-tic) (Fanatical, Fanaticism) A zealot, true believer, a person of extreme dedication to an organization, institution, ideology, or leader. Fanaticism may be considered a neurosis. A sports fanatic is more than a fan, he is also an addict (fan-*atic*), addicted to the team. Sports fanatics can be dangerous when fortified in numbers and alcohol. Even more dangerous are political and religious fanatics. These groups have perpetrated some of the most heinous, horrendous atrocities in history, like the Inquisition and Holocaust. Fanatical leaders are obsessed with their cause. This is not always the case with fanatical followers. They are often people lacking learning, self- esteem, pride, and a sense of identity. They may have no deep convictions or core values at all. All they have is a sense of belonging to the team, the gang, the party, the movement. Their pride is invested in their Nazi uniform or their MAGA (<u>M</u>ake <u>A</u>merica <u>G</u>reat <u>A</u>gain) cap, which becomes their alterego. Today we see the silly fanatics cheering at the silly Trump pep-rallies. They may not even hear him, or understand what he is saying. They may be oblivious to Trump's lies, or just don't care. They may not even care that their support for Donald Trump (b. 1946) and the *Trumpified* Republican Party is economically injurious to them, personally. None of that matters. All they know is that they belong, they have comrades, and they have an identity. Trumpsters are indeed fanatics. *"A fanatic is one who can't change his mind and won't change the subject."* – Winston Churchill (1874 – 1965).

FANATICAL PREPPERS – (fan-*NAT*-ti-kuhl *PREP*-pers) Extreme survivalists. People obsessed with preparing for Armageddon. Fanatical Preppers are enthusiastic pessimists who anticipate and desire disaster to strike, because they have prepared for it. Unlike common prepers, the fanatics build elaborate shelters, saferooms, supplied with plenty of food, medicine, fuel, provisions, and an arsenal of ammunition. Their fortresses vary in sophistication and complexity according to their wealth and neurosis. Their bastions are usually in remote areas, in the deep woods, and sometimes underground. You won't find a *"Welcome"* sign at the site of their hideouts. Instead, beware of booby traps. That's because preppers are often anti-social, misanthropic, and sometimes psychotic. Fanatical preppers tend to be anti-government, right-wing, militia ideologues. Many are fascistic white supremacists, neo-Nazis. And they are gun nuts! The disaster that fanatical preppers anxiously prepare for can be natural or social, a pandemic, depression, earthquake, hurricane, whatever, accompanied by looting, anarchy, and a breakdown of law-and-order. That's why they are armed to the teeth. Two emotions motivate preppers: fear and hate. Incidentally: The 2020 COVID-19 Coronavirus catastrophe is the answer to the fanatical prepper's prayers. In a dark demonic way, fanatical preppers would love to put their plans, their preparations into practice. Fanatical preppers hope to see their investment pay off. Furthermore, fanatical preppers would enjoy using their weapons to protect their investment. Fanatical preppers would love to be sole survivors. They need to prove that they were right. Footnote: As *"rugged individualists,"* fanatical prepper's mantra is: *"I got mine, to hell with you!"* With the viral apocalypse, the mantra revises to: *"Don't touch mine, I'll shoot you!"*

FANATICAL PREPPER'S CREDO – (fan-*NAT*-ti-kuhl *PREP*-pers *CRAY*-doh) *"Don't touch mine, I'll shoot you!"*

FANBIKE – (*FAN*-byk) An *"elliptical"* exercise bicycle. A fanbike is a stationary bicycle with pumping handlebars. It therefore provides a great workout for both lower and upper body. A fanbike offers the best exercise next to swimming. Being seated prevents the pounding on the hips and knees caused by jogging. Being stationary enables the rider to close her eyes in reverie, without danger of accident. The rotating fan in the front wheel provides a cooling breeze. A fanbike workout is ideal for *"Naikan,"* a Buddhist exercise meditation session. The rotating fan wheel can be dedicated as a Buddhist Prayer Wheel that will project one's prayers through the Cosmos for their manifestation. Incidentally: With the serious exerciser, the fanbike will take a beating. It is therefore wise to invest in quality. The line of *"AirDynes"* by *Schwinn* are the best buy.

FANBOY – (*FAN*-boi) (Fanboying) A <u>fan</u>atic male fan. A fanboy is one obsessed with something – anything, like technology, electrical devices, science fiction, sports, music, video games, even some celebrity. Today, fanboys are often nerds, socially awkward individuals. Perhaps a big part of their problem is they invest all of their time, ambition, enthusiasm in their obsession. A fanboy does not live a balanced life. Incidentally: A few decades ago, a fanboy obsession was the pinball machine. This device has been replaced by the computerized video game.

FAN FUCKING – (*FAN FUK*-ing) (Fan Fucked, also Fucking the Fans) In the vulgar vernacular of street parlance, screwing sports enthusiasts. Taking advantage of citizen's loyal to a sports team by making them pay for the team's venue. Wealthy team owners fuck the fans that support their teams all the time. Every big league professional sports team is a family-owned, capitalistic enterprise. (The single exception is the Green Bay Packers football team, owned by 360,584 stockholders.) The team owners compete with each other to acquire the most spectacular (and expensive) stadiums and arenas. They alone own and profit from the teams, along with the stadiums and arenas, but the local tax payers must pay for these venues. It's like me saying: *"I'll move into your community, only if you buy me a nice house."* Ridiculous! But that is what the team owners do. So many fans become fanatical. They associate with the sports team as their alter-ego. They will fight to protect the team's reputation, like a family member. Team owners know this and they take advantage of it. Owners will demand an extravagant stadium to be built for them. If not, they threaten to move their team out of town. This is disgusting capitalist extortion. Fanatical fans panic, and vote the taxes to build the new stadium, to keep the team in town. For example, the citizens of poor Detroit had to buy rich Mrs. Martha Firestone Ford, *"Ford Field,"* at which her Lions football team plays. Headline: *FORD FUCKS FANS! "Mrs. Ford told the <u>Detroit News:</u> Vote to build and pay for that new stadium in Detroit, or you fans can kiss my football team goodbye! We'll move to San Antonio, or Portland, Oregon."* Really? Not really.

FANTABULOUS – (fan-*TAB*-yuh-luhs) (Fabtabulously) Excellent, marvelous, outstanding. A contrived term blending fantastic with fabulous. Fantabulous was a popular term in the youth culture of 1955 to 1960.

FARADIZATION – (fair-a-die-*ZAY*-shun) Original name for electroconvulsive shock therapy. The term was derived from the name of the scientist, Michael Faraday (1791 – 1867) a pioneer in electricity research. Electroshock is applied to the brain in cases of severe mental disorders. Electroshock of Faradization can subside *grand mal* epileptic seizures. However the treatment alters the personality, making the patient far more docile. Today, electroshock treatment is sparingly used, only when the patient's condition is infinitely worse than the bad side effects of the treatment.

FAR AGE REGRESSION – (*FAR AYJ* ree-*GRESH*-shun) Using hypnosis to go back in one's life to uncover answers. Far age regression can reveal the source of the stress for which present day neurotic defense mechanisms are being employed.

FAR FROM THE MADDING CROWD – (fahr fruhm thuh *MAD*-ing kroud) To escape to a peaceful, tranquil rural setting, away from the raging, furious tumultuous populous. The word *"madding"* is somewhat archaic today. It means frenzied, riotous, boisterous, gone mad. It is a Middle English term in popular use in the 1570s. The sentence, *"Far from the madding crowd"* was first used in 1751 by Thomas Gray (1716 – 1771) in his poem: *<u>Elegy Written in a</u> <u>Country Churchyard:</u> "Far from the madding crowd's ignoble strife, Their sober wishes never learn'd to stray; Along the cool sequester'd vale of life They kept the noiseless tenor of their way."* It is quite possible that Gray was influenced by earlier references as of William Drummond (1585 – 1649) who wrote in circa 1614: *"Farre from the madding Worlding's hoarse discords."* Even earlier, Edmund Spencer (1552 – 1599) wrote in 1599: *"But now from me hys madding mynd is starte, And woes the Widdowes daughter of the glenne."* No doubt, however, that Thomas Hardy (1840 – 1928) made the sentence famous as the title of his 1874 novel, <u>*Far from the Madding Crowd.*</u> *"Come away by yourself to a lonely place."* – Mark 6:31.

FARINA – (fa-*REE*-na) A starchy flour or meal made from various cereal grains, potato, or cassava root (yucca, manioc). Farina is cooked as a cereal mush, pudding, or a soup thickener. Incidentally: Tapioca is also a pudding mush made exclusively from cassava.

FARINACEOUS – (far-in-*AY*-she-us) Made of starch from flour. The flour can be made from grain like wheat, rye, barley, oats, or potatoes. Bread, macaroni, pancakes are farinaceous foods. Incidentally: One sees the term farina in <u>farina</u>ceous.

FARK – (*FARHK*) A Spanish acronym for the *"Revolutionary Armed Forces of Colombia,"* the *"People's Army."* Fark is a Marxist-Leninist guerrilla movement fighting the Colombian capitalists and American imperialists. Their primary goal is fair Socialistic agrarian reform. In the tradition of Che Guevara (1928 – 1967) these peasant partisans command the mountains and jungle. Fark is the military wing of the Colombian Communist Party. Fark is funded by the drug trade. They are responsible for 70% of the cocaine entering the USA, Fark's *"chemical warfare"* against America.

FARINACEOUS – (far-in-*AY*-she-us) Made of starch from flour. The flour can be made from grain like wheat, rye, barley, oats, or potatoes. Bread, macaroni, pancakes are farinaceous foods. Incidentally: One sees the term farina in <u>farina</u>ceous.

FARMERETTE – (far-mer-*ET*) A silly, archaic term for a female farmer.

FARRAGINOUS – (far-*RAJ*-jin-us) Mixed or heterogeneous. The term derives from the Latin *"farrago,"* meaning *"mixed grains,"* used to feed animals. *"Our league is comprised of gender farraginous soccer teams."* The term farraginous entered English in the first half of the 17th century (1630s perhaps).

FARRAGO – (fa-*RAY*-go) A confused hodgepodge. A farrago is often a contradictory mixture of ideas, emotions, or demands. *"Donald Trump's farrago of campaign promises and lies are ridiculously impossible to fulfill."* The term farrago is taken from Latin meaning *"mixed grain,"* with which to feed animals. The term entered English in the 1630s.

FART – (*FAHRT*) (Farting) Flatulence. A mildly vulgar appellation for passing gas, breaking wind. A fart is flatus (*methane gas,* CH4) emitted from the intestines, through the anus into the public domain. Being methane, farts have an unpleasant aroma (as does swamp gas). In both cases, the methane is brewed by decaying matter. Farts, like swamp gas are quite flammable. The vibration of the anus as the fart is expelled makes the procedure audible. This is usually considered impolite, a social *faux pas.* Nevertheless, many would find the incident quite amusing. Suppressing the release of a fart can be quite challenging and uncomfortable. It is considered insulting to refer to an individual as a fart, as in *"You old fart."* Though an essential physiological process, fart has been the *butt* of jokes. For instance: *"She lingers, like a fart in a phonebooth."* Or, *"Beer, Brats, and Kraut: as bad as an Oktober Fest Fart!"* Incidentally: Not everyone had been disgusted with farting. In Medieval Japan, public farting competitions were held. Lucrative prizes and honors were awarded to winners. Though the intense competition could take on a foul odor, the champion always came out *"smelling like a rose."* Incidentally: On August 23, 2019, Congressman John Yarmuth (b. 1947) from Kentucky referred to Donald Trump's (b. 1946) *"Brain-Fart Presidency."* It was reported that old Rudy Giuliani (b. 1944) suffered a *"fart attack"* with the Michigan delegation of fake electors during their coup conspiracy rehearsal. *"I think I would know Nora's fart anywhere. I think I could pick hers out in a roomful of farting women,"* – James Joyce (1882 – 1941).

FARTHING – (*FAR*-thing) A British coin, no longer in circulation, worth (1/4th d) a quarter of a penny. (A Caveat: Do not confuse farthing with *"farting."* One may assume farthing is the Medieval rendition of farting as in: *"Must thou persistith in this noxious farthing!?"*)

FARTLEK – (*FART*-lek) An aromatic unappetizing Swedish word for an exercise method meaning *"speed play."* It consists of alternating vigorous exertion with low-level activity, followed by more intense exercise. Fartlek jump-starts the heart and blood pressure, followed by brief slow pause, then repeating the procedure. The aerobic procedure of start-stop-start again makes fartlek very beneficial to the cardio-vascular system. For example: Sprint-walk-sprint.

FASCICULATION – (fas-sick-you-*LAY*-shun) (Fasciculate) The involuntary twitching of the muscles (contraction and relaxation). Muscles will fasciculate when resting after overwork.

FASCISM – (*FASH*-is-um) Right-wing dictatorship, capitalism metastasized to its maximum, ultimate climax. Unregulated capitalism will always degenerate into fascism, because: *"Fascism is capitalism in decay."* – Vladimir Lenin (1870 – 1924). The establishment of corpocracy (government by corporations) is the ultimate goal of capitalists. Corpocracy can be attained only in a fascist state. Therefore, fascism too is the ultimate goal of capitalism. In fact, *"Fascism should more appropriately be called corporatism,"* declared Benito Mussolini, *"because it is a merger of state and corporate power."* Fascism is always initiated by the rich capitalists, motivated by fear of loss and desire of glory. The rich fear the loss of their wealth, power, and privilege, especially to the masses through Socialism. Too, they long for aggrandizement in the return of some mythical golden age. The fascist rich win over the Socialistic masses with a false threat of some enemy – Jews, Communists, Blacks, Immigrants, Intellectuals, Democrats, any group, especially Socialists. Capitalist fascism is the polar opposite of Communism or Socialism. Where in fascism, the people live for the state, in Communism and Socialism, the state lives for the people. Hitler's Nazi Germany was the quintessential fascist state. Dr. Lawrence Britt, an expert on fascism warned: *"America will become fascist when big corporations have become our government."* I repeat, *"Fascism is capitalism in decay."* – Vladimir Lenin (1870 – 1924). Fearful people turn to fascism. Fear of internal and external enemies bring out the fascist impulse in some people. Misery stokes fascism. Capitalist economic depressions will entice the fearful and miserable to seek a fascist father figure, a fuhrer to solve the problems. The demand for national security will elicit a call for fascism. The murdered Socialist Senator Huey Long (1893 – 1935) warned: *"When fascism comes to America, it will come as anti-fascism, in the name of national security."* Socialist author Sinclair Lewis (1885 – 1951) concurred: *"When fascism comes to America, it will be wrapped in a flag and carrying a cross." "In its pure form, fascism is the sum total of all irrational reactions of the average human character."* – Psychiatrist Wilhelm Reich (1897 – 1957).

FASCISM SYNDROME – (*FASH*-is-um *SIN*-drome) The signs of creeping fascism. Vladimir Lenin (1870 – 1924) said that *"Fascism is capitalism in decay."* Corporate capitalism hoards wealth and power. Multinational corporations consolidate, grow bigger, swell like an infected boil. The boil ultimately erupts expelling its poisonous pus. At that point the nation is infected with fascism. Dr. Lawrence Britt is an expert on the fascism syndrome. He has drawn-up 14 signs of fascist infection. 1. Powerful and Continuing Nationalism; 2. Disdain for the Recognition of Human Rights; 3. Identification of Enemies/Scapegoats as a Unifying Cause; 4. Supremacy of the Military; 5. Rampant Sexism; 6. Controlled Mass Media; 7. Obsession with National Security; 8. Religion and Government Intertwined; 9. Corporate Power is Protected; 10. Labor Power is Suppressed; 11. Disdain for Intellectuals and the Arts; 12. Obsession with Crime and Punishment; 13. Rampant Cronyism and Corruption; 14. Fraudulent Elections. *"Fascism will come to America in the name of 'anti-fascism'… Fascism will come to America in the name of national security."* – Senator Huey Long, Socialist, (assassinated by capitalist fascists in 1935).

FASCISM VS. COMMUNISM – Polar opposite political ideologies. Fascism is extreme right-wing capitalism. Communism is extreme left-wing Socialism. Peter Ustinov (1921 – 2004) was a brilliant actor and intellectual, a British national of Russian heritage. Peter was neither a fascist nor a Communist. Nevertheless, in his impressive book, <u>My Russia</u> (1983), Peter provided a perspicacious explanation of the difference between fascism and Communism. *"Fascism is invariably simple-minded, based on the premise that discipline is the freedom of the ignorant* [Trumpsters]. *There are very few theories attached to it in its usual form,* [like the Trump Administration]. *It is basically flamboyant, grandiloquent, and the friend and ally of large financial interests* [capitalists], *who have as much to gain from discipline as the military leader with an eye for patters on the parade grounds. Fascism inspires confidence in the status quo because it 'works,'* [the lie], *and its aggressions stimulate the economy* [perpetual conflict]. *Communism is far more complicated, a religion for intellectuals. It is founded on universal, as opposed to particular, ideals. It is obsessed with morality. The Constitution of the Soviet Union is a fine document, with an understandably different emphasis from its American counterpart. The fundamental rights of the individual are related to duty towards the state* [read: citizenry] *and not as a protection from the state. In the U.S. Constitution, the state is, by implication, a necessary evil: in the Soviet Constitution, it is a necessary good* [Socialistic]. Incidentally: Despite its flaws, Communism is conscientious of the poor. Capitalism has no conscience. *"Fascism is capitalism in decay."* – Vladimir Lenin (1870 – 1924).

FASCIST AMERICANS – (*FASH*-ist am-*MER*-ri-kens) American Nazis. This is not a reference to the Nazi German-American Bund of the 1930s. This is reference to the 2024 Trumpist MAGA fascist Americans. They come from the rich and the poor, the cunningly educated, and the naively ignorant. The educated rich have everything to gain by fascism, while the ignorant poor have everything to lose. Fascism is always, everywhere funded by corporate capitalist wealth. These plutocrats, oligarchs live in perpetual fear that a woke citizenry will use democracy to tax away their privilege and wealth. They feel safest in a fascist state. But the educated rich, these corporate capitalists are few. They need the support of the proletariat masses. So they dupe the naïve poor with the culture war through propaganda outlets like FOX TV. They persuade the ignorant poor to vote against their own vested interests, for a manipulable demagogue like Donald J. Trump (b. 1946). The corporate fascists also win over the religious fascists with the notion of a

Christianized nation. Fascism is always racist, xenophobic, homophobic, and often anti-Semitic because it needs enemies for the ignorant naïvetés to vent their anger and hatred. These neo-Nazi fascists cannot take the government by storm, at least not in America. That would constitute a coup d'état. That would trigger a counter response of force by the democratic left – ergo civil war which the fascists may lose. They must therefore work within the democratic system to destroy the democratic system. They pack the state legislatures and the U.S. Congress with fellow fascists. Indeed, the constitutional Republican Party has been transformed into the fascist Trumpublican Party. More alarmingly, the fascist capitalists have hijacked the state and federal judiciary, including the United States Supreme Court. On July 1, 2024, the 6 fascists on the Supreme Court had declared Donald Trump above the law, *"immune"* from accountability for criminal activity while serving as President [read: dictator]. *The Heritage Foundation* (founded 1973) has mapped-out the plan for Trump to convert the U.S. Government and America into a fascist state. America and the world are approaching the crossroads. On election day, November 5, 2024, will the American people turn right or left? *"These are the times that try men's souls."* – Thomas Paine (1737 – 1809) in <u>*The American Crisis*</u> (December 19, 1776). *"When fascism comes to America, it will be wrapped in the flag and carrying a cross."* – Socialist Novelist Sinclair Lewis (1885 – 1951).

FASCIST FANTASIA – (*FASH*-ist fan-*TAY*-she-a) Dictatorial delusions, totalitarian mesmerism, Hitlerian hallucinations. All autocrats try to create an alternate universe in the realm they control. They demand absolute obedience, despite facts, proof, or truth. Therefore, dictators attempt to control the speech and the minds of their oppressants. Dictators are desperate despots, living in perpetual fear. Being paranoid, they hope to transfer their paranoia, and schizophrenia to the populous. They hope to convince the people that society, the nation, civilization will perish, collapse into chaos, without the Fuhrer's strong hand gripping the state. They attempt to create a grotesque hypnotic mindlessness among the citizenry. Tyrants transform reality into a mirage. *"Don't believe your lying eyes. Forget what you hear or see. It is all fake news. Just believe in me."* *"What seems to me white, I will believe black if the hierarchical Church do defines,"* declared mesmerized St. Ignatius of Loyola (1491 – 1556), (founder of the Jesuits, the *Storm Troops* of the Catholic Church). Dictators supplant logic with emotion through propaganda and pep-rallies. Totalitarians don't tolerate advice, debate, or discussion. They believe they possess *"unmatched wisdom."* They hope to infect the people with their fantasy. *"Rome has spoken, the case is closed,"* declared obedient St. Augustine of Hippo (354 – 430 CE). A familiar fascist fantasia is the cult of personality – conflating self with the nation. *"I am the state,"* declared French King Louis XIV (1638 – 1715). *"Hitler is Germany and Germany is Hitler,"* declared Rudolf Hess (1894 – 1987). *"Only I can save America. I am the Chosen One."* – Donald Trump (b. 1946). Like Hitler, when Trump goes down, he will attempt to take America down with him. The nation does not deserve to exist without him. That is quintessential to the Fascist Fantasia.

FASCIST FORD – (*FASH*-ist *FORD*) Henry Ford (1863 – 1947) was at heart a capitalistic fascist who held a mutual admiration with Adolf Hitler (1889 – 1945), and supported the German and American Nazi Parties. Ford was rabidly anti- Semitic. His prejudicial hatred was cultivated early in life. He hated "Jewish bankers," who denied him loans to finance his fledgling automotive business. Later, Ford wrote *"The International Jew,"* a 4 volume set of anti-Semitic booklets. Before the U.S. entered the war, fascist Ford had donated all the profit from his German auto plants to the Nazi Party. Too, he gave Hitler a $50,000 gift on each of his birthdays. Ford congratulated Hitler for destroying the German labor movement and imprisoning union members and Socialists in the Dachau concentration camp. Ford used Gestapo tactics to try to break-up the U.A.W. (United Auto Workers) in Detroit. Hitler praised Ford in *Mein Kampf* (1925, 1926), and kept a photo of Ford on the wall of his office. The bigoted fascist Ford would not allow Jewish-American doctors to practice at The Henry Ford Hospital in Detroit. In fact, Fritz Kuhn (1896 – 1951), leader of the Nazi German-American Bund had been employed as an X-ray technician in The Henry Ford Hospital. Kuhn, a disciple of Hitler, was the type of leader Ford desired. Fascist Ford would have certainly been delighted with the neo-Nazi Donald Trump (b. 1946) today. *"Fascism is capitalism in decay."* – Vladimir Lenin (1870 – 1924).

FASCIST NEXUS – (*FASH*-ist *NEX*-us) The obvious connection among fascism, capitalism, the Republicans, and Trump. That nexus is the Republican Party. All fascist hate-groups support the Republican Party. All corporate capitalists support the Republican Party. The link between fascism and capitalism is glaring. Today, the link between fascism and capitalism is the Republican Party. Fascism is capitalism metastasized to its most malignant mass. That's what Socialist Vladimir Lenin (1870 – 1924) saw when he said that *"Fascism is capitalism in decay."* The proponents of unregulated capitalism are the Republicans. NeoNazis, White Supremacists, Ku Klux Klansmen, racists of every stripe support Donald Trump's (b. 1946) Republican Party. Fascist leader David Duke (b. 1950) reminded Trump (August 2017) that *"It was White Supremacists who put you in the presidency."* Klansman Duke continued: *"We will take our country back. We will fulfill the promise of [Republican] Donald Trump. That's what we believe in. That's why we voted for [Republican] Donald Trump, because he said that he would take our country back, and that's what we've got to do."* All the pro-Republican hate-groups are rabidly anti-Socialist, dedicated capitalists. Socialist economist and political analyst Dr. Lawrence O'Donnell (b. 1951) remarked: *"All the hate-groups have one thing in common – they vote Republican – they voted for Trump."* The fascist-capitalist-Republican nexus could not be more clear.

FASCIST REPUBLICANS – (*FASH*-ist ree-*PUB*-lic-cans) The American conservative party, fanatically capitalist, representative of the rich. The rich fear democracy, which can result in the levelling of the nation's wealth. Therefore, the rich pay the Republican politicians to subvert democracy by suppressing the vote – the engine of democracy. The alternative to democracy is fascism. The Republican Party is an anti-democratic, fascist party. It recruits under-educated poor white people through right-wing propaganda media like Fox News. The Fascist Republicans use racial hatred, immigration fear, replacement anxiety, all the culture war lies to persuade poor whites to neglect their own economic interests and support the Republicans, who are supporting the rich. Interestingly, about 33% of Americans have fallen into the Fascist Republican trap. This is the same percentage that Adolf Hitler (1889 – 1945) and the Fascist Nazi Party received in Germany's last legitimate election before World War Two.

FASCIST THIRD – (*FASH*-ist *THERD*) The 1/3 of Americans (perhaps 32%) who are bigots, racists, and harbor fascist attitudes. They are mostly low-education, low-information voters from conservative Republican "red states." The fascist third resent the Civil Rights Movement, fear foreigners, hate immigrants, despise Liberals, and deplore diversity, distrust the educated. Hillary Clinton (b. 1947) accurately characterized them as *"deplorables."* The fascist third is terrified by the *"Browning of America."* These base people comprise Donald Trump's (b. 1946) base. They will excuse every Trump outrage and support him, come what may.

Trump's sexual lasciviousness, business corruption, political incompetence, tax evasion, lying, even treasonous relations with Russia are inconsequential, providing Trump shares their racism. That's why Trump's base percentage remains stable. Like Trump, the fascist third exhibit Nazi tendencies. Also like Trump, they get their indoctrination from Fox *News* Network. In fact, Fox was established in 1996 for the very purpose of cultivating, and nurturing the bigotry and racism of America's fascist third. *"If you cannot convince a Fascist, acquaint his head with the pavement."* – Leon Trotsky (1879 – 1940), Socialist Revolutionary.

FASHION – (*FA*-shun) Obsession with appearance over substance, especially in dress. Fashion is unduly concerned with upholding contemporary style. Playwright and philosopher George Bernard Shaw (1856 – 1950) viewed *"A fashion as nothing but an induced epidemic."* Fashion amounts to seeming rather than being. Modern fashion, as we know it, developed during the Renaissance (c. 16th century). In Italy, the rising middle class of merchants would emulate the aristocracy in dress. To distinguish themselves from these no-name upstarts, the aristocrats would change their styles. For a while, the fashion exposed a man's genitals. Single women at the court of Elizabeth the First wore garments that exposed their breasts. A clothier at the time said: *"A good tailor yesterday is of no use today."* Today, fashion generally percolates up from the bottom of society. Perhaps this is attributed to youthful defiance, a form of anti-authoritarianism. *"Fashion is the science of appearance, and it inspires one with the desire to seem, rather than to be."* – Rev. Edwin Hubbell Chapin (1814 – 1880). Incidentally: In *"The Gospel of Thomas,"* Jesus said: *"Do not worry from morning to evening and from evening to morning about what you will wear."* Furthermore, St. Teresa of Avila (1515 – 1582) said: *"After you die, you wear what you are."* Footnote: *"When a woman says, 'I have nothing to wear!' what she really means is, 'There's nothing here for who I'm supposed to be today'."* – Caitlin Morgan (b. 1975).

FAST FOODS – Simple meals like hamburgers, French fries, fried chicken, fish, pizza, or tacos prepared quickly, in quantity by a standardized method. The eateries are usually small, efficient food factories, at which the fare is mass- produced in assembly-line fashion. Fast food can be devoured in the modest restaurant, carried-out, or obtained at the drive-thru window. Fast food corporations are chain-stores, with hundreds or thousands of outlets. Some of the giants of the fast food industry are: McDonald's, Burger King, Kentucky Fried Chicken, Wendy's, and Taco Bell. The fast food business is a multi-trillion dollar enterprise, worldwide in scope, but originated in the U.S. for impatient Americans. Demands of capitalist employment have afforded Americans little time to enjoy a leisurely meal. The capitalist fast food industry is the beneficiary. Despite its unhealthy reputation, fast food is no less nutritious than Mom's food. What adds to fast food's favorability is its promptness and price. This cuisine is relatively cheap. But this is a double-edged sword. For what is good for the consumer, and great for the rich stockholder, is bad for the poor, under-paid worker. Fast food employees are the poorest paid laborers in America. (Of course, the industry is non-unionized.) Initially, *"flipping burgers"* at fast food jobs was reserved for teenagers, part-time, after school. But with the capitalist outsourcing of quality manufacturing jobs overseas (for non-union slave and child labor), fast food jobs have become primary employment. Though the average worker is now 28 years old, she or he still gets paid less than $8.00 dollars an hour. In fact, 1 in 4 (25%) Americans make less than $10.00 dollars an hour today. That's why over 146 million Americans, about half of the U.S. population do not have enough money to meet their basic needs. The penurious fast food industry has contributed to launching America down the fast track to *"Banana Republicanism."* Incidentally: It has been reported by the McDonald Corporation that indigent, desperate young ladies have been caught offering sex to customers at the restaurants for a *"Happy Meal!"*

FASTIDIOUS – (fas-*TID*-dee-us) Hard to please, excessively particular and critical. A fastidious individual would perpetually demand her own way.

FASTIGIATE – (fas-*TIJ*-ee-ate) (Fastidgiated, Fastigiating) To rise to a point. The Washington Monument is a fastigiated edifice.

FASTING – (*FAS*-ting) (Fast, Fasted) A sacrificial abstinence from food, an ancient form of prayer. Fasting is an exercise in commanding the flesh to serve the spirit. *"Fasting cleanses the soul, raises the mind, subjects one's flesh to the spirit, renders the heart contrite and humble, scatters the clouds of concupiscence, quenches the fire of lust, and kindles the true light of chastity."* – St. Augustine (354 – 430 CE). Fasting is spiritual, whereas dieting is medical or cosmetical in nature. Nevertheless, the spiritual practice of fasting has collateral physical benefits. *"Instead of using medicine, fast for a day,"* suggested Plutarch (c. 46 – 120 CE) the ancient Greek philosopher. For healthy or holy reasons, Confucius, Jesus, and Mohammed approved of fasting, while Buddha did not. Early in his career, Buddha almost killed himself by fasting into starvation. Fasting is a sacrifice, a form of prayer. Indeed, it is believed by religious/spiritualist scholars that while fasting, the power of our prayers are amplified, magnified, intensified, multiplied, fortified, and sanctified. In order to serve God, Jesus recommended we do 3 things: pray, give to the poor, and fast. Hundreds-of-millions of people are hungry in the world, and many millions are starving to death. When we feel the hunger pangs during a fast, we place ourselves in spiritual communion with those deprived of food. Though we can't help them physically, we can help them metaphysically – prayerfully. Fasting expands our compassion for the hungry poor. *"The fasting in which God delights must result in a higher ethical standard, in righteous living, liberality, unselfishness, and mercy."* From the Muslim <u>Notes on the Haftarah</u>, (p.314). Fasting is a challenge, a confrontation between the physical and the spiritual, the body and the will. Jesus knew this when he said: *"The spirit indeed is willing, but the flesh is weak."* – Matthew 26:41. Let's suppose that the body and the will are separate entities in one being. The will wants to fast, but the body is resistant. The body says: *"I need energy, but I don't was to withdraw it from my fat reserve. I must make the will break the fast and eat. Therefore, stomach, begin to ache so will gives in and feeds us."* But the will holds fast. It endures the discomfort and refuses to eat. After about 24 hours of fasting, the body gives up and begins to withdraw the energy from the fat reserve. The stomach no longer aches, the body is energized, and the will has maintained the fast. As the fat reserve was used the body lost weight. The triumph of the will over the body has benefited body, will, and soul. *"Fasting is an amazing thing. It gives people heart and soul."* – Rumi (1207 – 1273). *"Fasting is the greatest remedy – the physician within."* – Paracelsus (1493 – 1541). A Caveat: When fasting don't rest, keep occupied, be busy. Find chores, projects, hobbies to work on. Do not sit and watch TV. Enticing food commercials will make your stomach rebel with uncomfortable acid, tempting you to break the fast. Furthermore, postpone your grocery shopping for a non-fasting day. *"Every breath I take, every step I make is a prayer during a fast."* – Gary J. Pasieka (b. 1951).

FAST PITCHING – (*FAST PITCH*-ching) A simple rendition of baseball played in a limited space, with limited personnel. The primary requirement is a brick wall, barn door, or any solid structure to serve as a barrier. A box, representing the strike zone is chalked or painted on the structure. The batter stands aside the box. A pitcher's mound is stepped off. The pitcher launches a rubber baseball toward the box. After hitting the barrier, the ball, of course rebounds to the pitcher (an automatic catcher). If the ball hits within the box (strike zone), it's a called strike. Outside the box is a ball (leading to a base-on-balls or walk). Base running is optional, and rarely included in fast pitching. Depending on the amount of available space, flexible rules must be established as to what constitutes a single, double, triple, foul ball, and homerun. There is no limit to how many players comprise a team. Most importantly, a fast pitching game can be played by a few as two – the batter (the offense) and the pitcher (the entire defense). That is the brilliant part of fast pitching. It is baseball stripped down to its naked essentials. Of course, the pitcher, as infielder and outfielder as well, does a mighty amount of running shagging balls. That too is the brilliant part of fast pitching. The kids get apple exercise in the open air, rather than getting fatter at the computer, playing virtual baseball.

FAT – (*FAT*) An organic substance consisting of glycerol (OH), an odorless viscous liquid that coagulates as a spongy solid in animals as adipose tissue or body fat. Both animals and plants produce and accumulate fat. Fat is found as vegetable oil, butter, lard, and tallow. Fat is concentrated and stored energy. We acquire energy from the food we eat. Fat is an essential macronutrient along with carbohydrate and protein. Food energy is the fuel we burn to stay alive. If we take in more food than we need, that extra energy is stored as fat. A person who has stored too much fat is obese or overweight. This condition is socially unsightly and unhealthy. Being fat puts a strain on the body, especially the heart. This unhealthy condition compromises the immune system, putting fat people at risk from any number of diseases. For instance, 78% of the Americans who died of the COVID virus were too fat. The only way to eliminate excess body fat is to burn more while adding less fuel. In other words, eat less and exercise more. When exercising, the body will convert solid fat into liquid sugar that is burned away as energy. During starvation, the body is depleted of all body fat. Because no fuel is entering as food, the body begins to burn the protein in the muscles. You begin to cannibalize yourself and die. Moderate body fat is essential as an insulator from cold, and a cushion, a shock absorber protecting vital organs. Incidentally: A person who is very fat must not be criticized or mocked, but rather helped. She or he is indeed handicapped.

FATAL FIRE – (*FAT*-tal *FY*-yer) Lethal shooting of citizens by police. On average, 3 Americans are killed by police every day. Most of the victims are Black citizens. American police must be armed with guns, as long as American society is inundated with guns. But that does not give the police the authority to shoot to kill at whim. Deadly force must be a last resort. Only if the officer, and/or an innocent other are in mortal danger, should the cop have permission to shoot. Too, gun fire need not be fatal fire in every case. Fatal fire can be fearful fire, furious fire, or foolish fire. Fearful fatal fire is committed by frightened cops. These individuals do not have the nerve to serve as police officers in America. They are too quick at the draw. Furious fatal fire is committed by enraged cops, dying to blow someone away. They are bullies, often racists who displace their anger on poor people, whose families are powerless to fight back. Foolish fatal fire is committed by stupid cops who should not be on the force. These are low- information officers without imagination. They do not know how to de-escalate a volatile situation. So out of frustration, they use fatal fire. Fear, fury, and foolishness may overlap in some cops, creating true monsters.

FATALISM – (*FAY*-tal-is-um) Submission to fate. In philosophy, fatalism is the belief in fate, that all or some events are determined by some supernatural being or power. Fatalism maintains that certain events are decided upon as historical facts, inevitabilities, prior to their occurrence. Religion is fatalistic in the sense that God determines events, and man should surrender to God's good will. Islam is very fatalistic. In fact, the term Islam means *"surrender,"* and Muslim means *"one who surrenders"* to the will of Allah. *"Ensha Allah,"* God's will (shall prevail).

FATA MORGANA – (*FAH*-ta mor-*GON*-na) A super-mirage occurring almost always at sea. The illusion of ships, islands, mountains, forts, cities, and UFO's are perceived in the fata morgana. The term derives from the Italian translation of *"Morgan le Fay,"* a sorceress in Arthurian Legends. Fata morgana is an optical illusion when light rays are bent when passing through air layers of differing temperatures. The ghost ship, *"Flying Dutchman"* is certainly a fata morgana phenomenon.

FATE – (*Fait*) One's fortune, destiny, lot in life. If you are dissatisfied with your fate, don't blame the gods or planets, blame yourself. Fate is governed by the *Universal Principle of Karma*, in order to establish, re-establish, and maintain Cosmic balance and harmony. Philosophical parsing aside, God is good, all the time. Through Karma, God supports and sustains goodness throughout the universe. Good is destined to triumph over evil. Intelligent creatures possessing free will have the power to choose evil or good. That's when Karmic adjustments must be made. The fate of the evil is evil, while the fate of the good is good. *Karmic Justice* inevitably prevails. Therefore, fate is a form of *"determinism,"* but the determiner is man. Fate can be called *"predestination,"* but the destination is determined by man. Indeed, one's fate is inevitable. *"He who digs pits under others, will fall into them himself."* – Ecclesiastes 10:8. *"Do not be deceived, God is not mocked, for whatever one sows, that shall he also reap."* – Galatians 6:7. Incidentally: The word fate is derived from a 14th century Latin term *"fata,"* meaning *"a prophetic prediction, a guiding spirit ordained by God."*

FAT FARM – (*FAT* fahrm) (also Fat camp) A vernacular designation for a residential weight-loss institution located in the countryside. Overweight individuals may join the program for several weeks. The fitness regimen consists of physical and psychological training. Diet, exercise, athletics, games, and social activities are included. People with similar weight problems provide each other with positive reinforcement. The building of self-esteem and a fine self-image are paramount to the fat farm program. Participants learn coping techniques and new life skills to prevent future obesity. Room, specialized diet, professional counseling are not cheap. Only prosperous fat citizens can afford a stay at a fat farm. Low income or poor people must suffer with their handicap. This is another injustice of class-driven capitalism. Like the C̲ivilian C̲onservation C̲orps (CCC) which was part of President Franklin D. Roosevelt's (1882 – 1945) Socialistic *New Deal*, during the *Great Republican Depression*, government- operated fat farms should be a part of our *National Healthcare System*.

FATHERHOOD OF GOD – (*FOTH*-er-hood of *GOD*) The fact that all human beings are children of *"Our Father, Who art in heaven...."* Race, wealth, nationality, gender, or religion are inconsequential. All people are Sons and Daughters of God, as Jesus is the Son of God. That makes Jesus our Brother. By accepting the Fatherhood of God, you also accept the Brotherhood of Man. The Fatherhood of God and Brotherhood of Man insists that we are our Brother's keeper. In *The Effect of Humane Education on the Prevention of Crime* (1902), Metaphysician and Spiritualist Charles B. Patterson (1854 – 1917) wrote: *"So far as ethics and even the actual safety of society, government, and industry is concerned, Socialism is the only basis that can be acknowledged, and is certainly the only basis that can be deduced from an actual living belief in the great fact of the Fatherhood of God, and the Brotherhood of Man."* This is why every great religious avatar who walked the Earth has been a Socialist.

FATHOM – (*FATH*-um) A unit of measurement according to the Imperial or English System. A fathom is a measurement of depth, little over 2 yards or 6 feet. Depth of water at sea is measured in fathoms.

FATIMA PREDICTION – (*FA*-ti-ma *PRE*-dic-shun) On May 13, 1916, an apparition identified as the *"Angel of Peace"* appeared to 3 young children at Fatima, Portugal. It is said that the Angel prayed with the children and made a secret predication that was to be kept sealed for exactly 65 years. The sealed envelope was to be opened by the Pope on May 13, 1981. Sixty-five years later, to the day, Pope John Paul II opened the letter. It said that a holy man, dressed in white, will suffer greatly. Hours later, the Pope was shot. He was dressed in white.

FAT-PHOBIA – (fat *FOH*-bee-uh) (Fat-Phobic, Fat-Phobiac) Literally, fear of fat, meaning obese people. More accurately, fat-phobia is a dislike or hatred of obese people. Fat-phobiacs are nasty individuals. They derive ornery pleasure out of mocking overweight people. Those who are morosely obese are physical handicaps, which compounds the sin of fat-phobia. *"Father forgive them, for they know not what they do."* – Jesus in Luke 23:34.

FAT SHAMING – (*FAT SHAYM*-ing) Mean-spirited criticizing and humiliating people who are overweight. Fat shaming is the mocking of fat people. *"Fat ass," "fat pig," "fat bastard"* are old nasty insults. Why are fat people socially targeted, when in fact they are handicaps? Perhaps because fat people may be subconsciously equated with greedy gluttons, food hoarders, eating more than their share. This may account for the popular antagonism. Indeed, overeating will result in obesity. However, so is metabolic malfunctions, endocrinological disorders. Even compulsive overeaters suffer from psychological disturbances which rely on food as an anesthetic, a defense mechanism. Furthermore, poor people who must rely on empty calories from a cheap diet of cakes, chips, and soda pop will grow fat. Therefore, be kind, and *"Do unto others, as you would have others do unto you." "I find no sweeter fat than sticks to my own bones."* – Walt Whitman (1819 – 1892).

FATUITY – (fa-*TOO*-it-tee) Foolish, easily duped. One exhibiting fatuity is complacently stupid, as are Donald Trump's (b. 1946) base supporters.

FATWA – (*FAHT*-wah) An official religious decree issued by a Muslim Ulama, an Islamic holy man, religious leader. A fatwa usually involve some judgment on Islamic law. In the worst, albeit rare scenario, a fatwa can be a death sentence, an assassination order. It can be an oral wanted poster issued throughout the world to all Muslims, encouraging them to hunt down and kill some Islamic enemy. *"WANTED: Infidel. Dead not alive!"* Usually, the victim is an *"infidel,"* non-Muslim, who had committed a flagrant, public act of blasphemy (insulting the Prophet of Allah). The most notable example was the case of Ahmed Salman Rushdie (b. 1947), author of *The Satanic Verses* (1988). That publication brought a death fatwa on Rushdie's head in 1988, which resulted in an almost fatal stabbing attack in August 2022.

FAUCIAN DYSTOPIA – (*FOUW*-chee-in dys-*TOH*-pee-ah) A silly characterization by a silly but dangerous man, Florida Republican Governor Ron DeSantis (b. 1978). A *dystopia* is a perfectly awful, terrible society, the polar opposite of a *utopia*. Faucian is a reference to the eminent Dr. Anthony Fauci (b. 1940), renowned physician-scientist, immunologist. Dr. Fauci has served as the voice of reason, encouragement, and pandemic recovery in two Presidential administrations. In a speech to his Trumpistic, anti-mask and anti-vaccination supporters, DeSantis referred to the state of society as a *"Faucian dystopia,"* if Dr. Fauci and the CDC (<u>C</u>enter for <u>D</u>isease <u>C</u>ontrol) have their way. (It's doubtful that the Neanderthals in this segment of the population knows what dystopia means.) Business closures are indeed painful, awful, devastating in fact. But not as painful as a slow death, drowning in one's hospital bed. Wearing masks, social distancing, and avoiding crowded venues are tolerable sacrifices, in order to contain the contagion. DeSantis is a former naval officer, and Ivy League trained lawyer. He knows better. His deceitful appeal to the Trumpublicans is pure self- interest. DeSantis is as evil as Trump, but he is no buffoon, which makes him infinitely more dangerous. Furthermore, he has his eyes on the Republican nomination for the Presidency. If anyone in America today (August, 2021), qualifies as America's first Hitler (Mussolini anyway), it is Ron DeSantis. DeSantism or DeSantistan is the true dystopia.

FAUCIED – (*FOUW*-cheed) (Fauciing) To be upstaged by a competent authority figure, a trusted expert. This verb is an *eponym,* a word deriving from a proper name. It is taken from Dr. Anthony *Fauci* (b. 1940) renowned virologist/epidemiologist/immunologist, Director of the National Institute of Allergy and Infectious Diseases. To the consternation of President Donald Trump (b. 1946), Dr. Fauci had to be included on the Trump Administration's White House Coronavirus Task Force (January 2020). Trump hates experts. Trump despises education. Trump defies science. Trump resents challenge. Trump disrespects truth. This is why Trump despises Dr. Fauci. It is obviously apparent on Trump's miserable bloated face when Fauci is speaking. However, Trump is impotent, helpless, incapable of firing Fauci. This-drives-Trump-mad! In fact, Fauci is the only person who Trump cannot shoot on 5th Avenue, and get away with it. Like a bug trapped in a spider's web, Trump has been Faucied. Fauci has publicly taken Trump to school. Trump must stand there like an ignorant schoolboy and accept Fauci's corrections and contradictions to Trump's ignorance and lies. Trump and Fauci are working toward incompatible ends. Trump wants to bolster his reelection chances. Fauci wants to save lives. Unlike the worm Vice-President Mike Pence (b. 1959) and the snake Attorney General Bill Barr (b. 1950), Anthony Fauci is a man of integrity and courage. He cannot be threatened, bullied, or bribed to tote the Trump line. Trump has no authority or leverage over the Good Doctor. Trump can't do anything about him. Indeed, Trump has been thoroughly Faucied.

FAULT – (*FAWLT*) In geology, a fracture in the Earth's crust, due to tectonic forces deep beneath. A fault is a long fissure or crack in the Earth, along which the rock of either sides moves during earthquakes. If the fault is deep enough, magma may spew as lava to the surface.

FAUNOIPHILIA – (fawn-noy-*FEE*-lee-ah) (Faunoiphiliac) A neurotic paraphilial disorder in which one is sexually aroused by watching animals mate.

FAUSTIAN BARGAIN – (*FOW*-stee-an *BAR*-gin) To strike a Faustian bargain is to be willing to sacrifice anything to satisfy a limitless desire for knowledge and power. According to Johann Goethe's (1749 – 1832) novel *Faust* (1808), the German astrologer, alchemist and magician, Dr. Faust sold his soul the *Mephistopheles* (the devil) for power and knowledge. Making a Faustian bargain is a temptation that haunts most academicians and men of genius. Incidentally: Mephistopheles tried but failed to temp Jesus into a Faustian bargain, when Jesus was weakened, fasting in the desert for 40 days. *"Jesus said, 'You shall not put the Lord your God to the test.' Again, the devil took Jesus to a very high mountain and showed him all the kingdoms of the world and their glory. And he said to him, 'All these I will give you, if you will fall down and worship me.' Then Jesus said to him, 'Ne gone, Satan! For it is written, you shall worship the Lord your God and him only shall you serve'."* – Matthew 4:7- 10.

FAUX – (*FOH*) A French term for false, fake, phony, imitation, artificial. *"She wore a string of cheap, faux diamonds."*

FAUX-BAMA – (foh *BAH*-ma) Literally, *"fake-Bama,"* meaning imitation-Obama. Faux-Bama refers to a President Barack Obama (b. 1961) look-alike that Donald Trump (b. 1946) hired for a political attack in 2012. The objective was to humiliate President Obama. According to Trump's former lawyer/fixer, Michael Cohen (b. 1966), Trump had fake-Obama in a setting similar to Trump's TV show, *"The Apprentice."* The President sat humbly in front of Trump, who sat behind a great desk. On Trump's desk was a record file with Obama's name in large letters. Trump interrogated the faux-Bama like a big-shot boss. Faux- President Obama says: *"The private sector is doing fine."* Trump snaps back: *"The private sector is dying!"* Then Trump sarcastically gibes: *"Let's see what you've been up to."* He picks up Obama's file. *"This is your review. You promised hope and change. How did you do there?"* Crickets are heard in the background. Trump continued his scolding: *"You've run up almost as much debt as every other president combined. I know, I know, it wasn't your fault. You've inherited it, right?"* Trump concludes the beratement by rudely pointing a finger at the counterfeit-Obama. *"You're Fired!"* Trump bellows. This was Trump's ultimate fantasy, his wet dream in fact. Trump expected this insulting skit to be aired on the first night of the 2012 Republican National Convention. Trump was disappointed. The Republican rejected the production as unworthy. Trump was irate. Incidentally and ironically: The accusations Trump had made against Obama, fit Trump today like a glove. Karma can be a *"bitch."* Footnote: Indeed Trump is mocked by comedians, as on *"Saturday Night Live."* So was Obama. But President Obama never targeted Trump personally. Obama never even used Trump's name, until the last 6% (4 months) of Trump's tenure.

FAUX PAS – (foh-*PAH*) French for *"false step."* A faux pas is a slip or blunder in etiquette, manners, or conduct. A faux pas is an embarrassing social blunder, slip of the tongue, gaffe, or indiscretion. To fart at the dinner table qualifies as a faux pas.

FAVORITE SON – (*FAY*-ver-it *SUN*) A popular politician in his/her home state. Favorite sons are sought as Vice-Presidential running-mates, for it is expected that they will win their state for the Presidential ticket.

F-BOMB – (*EF BOM*) The middle-finger salute. It is generally considered an obscene gesture suggesting sexual violence (*"fuck-off"*). In the Hundred Years War (1337 – 1453) the French would amputate the middle finger of the English longbowmen, so they could no longer shoot. At the Battle of Agincourt (1415), English archers would flash the middle finger at the French in a gesture of defiance and insult. There's a very good chance that this was the genesis of the *"Fuck You"* gesture.

FCR = WPH – (ef see *AR = DUH*-ba-yoo pee *AYCH*) An initialistic formula for F̲ascism C̲apitalism R̲acism = W̲ar P̲overty H̲ate.

FEALTY – (*FEE*-al-tee) Loyalty, faithfulness, exhibiting fidelity. Historically, a Medieval vassal or knight was obliged to swear fealty to his lord.

FEAR – (*FEER*) Faith in the malevolent. Fear is generated by a threat of loss: the loss of life, love, property, prestige. Who or what is responsible for the fear of this loss is considered an enemy. The antidote for fear is to neutralize the enemy that is threatening the loss. Too, the fearful person can accept the loss as unpainful. After all, fear is merely an emotion, a feeling. We can change our feelings if we change our attitudes. It is natural to feel fearful in an unsafe environment. Dangerous conditions contribute to fear. What excites fear in one person or creature, may not in another. For instance the *"Cycle of Fear,"* proclaims that: *"A cockroach fears a mouse; a mouse fears a cat; a cat fears a dog; a dog fears a man; a man fears a woman; and a woman fears a cockroach." "Never be frightened! Be fearless! There is no room for fear. Fear is death, fear is sin, fear is hell, fear is adharma and fear is disloyalty. All delusions emanate from this evil called fear."* – Asaram (b. 1941).

FEARFUL LOVE – (*FEER*-ful *LUV*) An oxymoronic term with deep psychological implications. Fearful love is no love at all. On the contrary it is profound hate, fearfully masquerading as love. You will hate no one on Earth more than the one you fear. Because you must internalize that hate, and dare not express it, the hate incubates, intensifies. This is the case with most Republican politicians who publicly idolize President Donald Trump (b. 1946). They hate Trump for the humiliation of making them crawl. But they fear, not to publicly love Trump. Trump holds a cult-like Rasputin (1869 – 1916) command over these Republicans. But once the spell is broken, the hate will pour forth, and Trump will suffer a Rasputin fate. Republican politicians, professionals, mostly attorneys, hate having to adulate that ignorant nobody, who is Trump. They see themselves as humiliated sycophants, boot-lickers, ass-lickers. However, as with the Russian dictator Joseph Stalin (1878 – 1853), they fear being seen as the first one to cease the applause. Karma will prevail. Trump will fall. When Trump gets wounded, and his blood is in the water, the feeding frenzy will commence. The Republican piranha will tear Trump to shreds! Incidentally: There are parallels between Stalin and Trump. At the 22nd Communist Party Congress (October 1961) Russian President Nakita Khrushchev (1894 – 1971) denounced the deceased Stalin as a psychopath and butcher. At a later meeting, a Russian Congressman sent up a written question for President Khrushchev: *"Comrade Khrushchev, if Stalin was such a monster, why did you support him?"* Khrushchev read the question and replied: *"For the same reason that the comrade who sent up this question didn't sign it."* Further fearful love.

FEARFUL SOME – (*FEER*-ful *SUM*) Those Democrats that have *"some,"* are reluctant to share with those who have *"little"* or *"none"* for fear of losing their *"some."* This fear is exploited by the wealthy who have it *"all."* Actually, there is abundance for all. But those who have it *"all,"* frighten those who have *"some"* with the lie of lack. There's not enough to go around is the lie. Better hold on to yours. Don't share. Don't support bold Progressive programs to benefit the poor. You got yours, to hell with them. Rugged individualism, every man for himself. Share and you will lose your *"some."* This is the strategy, used by the rich, in order to protect their wealth and power. Divide and conquer. Wealthy capitalists call sharing Socialism, and compassion Communism. *"When I fed the poor, I was called a saint. When I asked why they were poor, I was called a Communist."* – Bishop and Saint Oscar Romero (1917 – 1980), murdered, martyred while saying Mass in San Salvador (by CIA supported death-squad), March 24, 1980. Fr. Romero is the Patron Saint of Socialists.

FEATHERBEDDING – (*FETH*-ther-bed-ding) A capitalist managerial slander that unions require superfluous workers, making unnecessary amount of work, in an inordinate amount of time, in order to assure maximum employment.

FEATHERS – (*FETH*-ther) The protective covering on birds which also enable flight. Feathers evolved on dinosaurs like raptors, long before they had adapted for flight. Feathers, like nails, hair, claws, hoofs, horns, and antlers are made of the protein keratin. Today, only birds on Earth bear feathers. However, millions of years ago, reptiles, some dinosaurs developed feathers in their transition to birds. Besides flight, birds use their downy breast feathers to quench their chicks in the nest. The feathers absorb water that is brought to the offspring in the nest. Incidentally: Feathers are associated with spirituality by the Amerindians. That may account for the feathers traditionally inserted in Indian headdresses.

FEBRIFUGE – (*FEB*-bri-fuj) Any medicine that will break a fever. FEBRILE – (*FEB*-brile) (also Afebrile) Pertaining to fever.

FECES – (*FEE*-sees) (Fecal matter) Solid or semi-solid remains of food that was not digested in the small intestines, and has been broken down by bacteria in the large intestines. Feces contains small amounts of metabolic chemical wastes, water, solid indigestibles (roughage), and dead epithelial cells from the lining of the gut. Skatole is a chemical compound that puts the stink in feces. (The term *"skatol"* is Greek for *"feces"*.) Feces, as well as urine are the manufactured products of the excretory system. Feces is distributed into the world through the anus. *"No shit!"*

FECKLESS – (*FEK*-less) Incompetent, ineffective, futile. A feckless individual is irresponsible, indifferent, careless, and lazy. It is impossible to read this definition, and not be reminded of Donald Trump (b. 1946) in the White House.

FECULENT – (*FEK*-yuh-lent) (Feculence) Foul, turbid, muddy. Feculent means full of dregs or fecal matter. An outhouse or shit-pit is feculent.

FECUND – (*FEE*-kund) (Fecundity = feh-*SUN*-di-tee) Fertile, potently, prolifically reproductive. Fruit, vegetation, animals and people can all prove to be fecund, or capable of producing many offspring.

FEDERAL AIR – (*FED*-er-al *AIR*) A fictitious albeit necessary National Government Airline. Federal Air would be a public option to the privately owned airline corporations. Federal Air would be the *"municipal bus service"* of air travel. It would charge a small fraction of what the corporate capitalist, for-profit airlines demand. As a government corporation, our public airline would be subsidized by our tax dollars. Too, it would be non-profit. It would have no greedy private owners, no stockholders. Most of the bloated cost of an airline ticket today is the profit, pocketed by the bloated stockholders. Federal Air would be strictly service (not profit) oriented. Federal Air would be Government operated, meaning publicly owned by all citizens. It would be administered by the Department of Transportation. Americans must not be held hostage by the corporate commercial airlines. Easily affordable air travel is the dividend that would be paid to the populous. As the multitude of fliers forswear Delta, United, American, and the lesser lights, let them specialize as opulence operators for the rich, providing champagne, caviar, and sexual favors if demanded. They will eventually go bankrupt and be absorbed into Federal Air. *"But Federal Air is Socialist!?" "You Bet!"* Incidentally: The great economist Dr. Karl Marx (1818 – 1883) warned that: *"Capitalism plants the seeds of its own destruction."* The thoroughly capitalistic airline industry is an example. By neglecting service, safety, maintenance, and personnel, inorder to increase profits, the airline industry is dreadfully failing. They are cancelling flights and losing luggage and customers. Now they want a government bailout, tax dollars from the people they left grounded. This is capitalist Socialism, or handouts to the rich. If the U.S. Government is going to pump money into the airline companies, it might as well be its own company, the public option – Federal Air.

FEDERAL AUTO – (*FED*-er-al *AW*-toh) A fictitious but ever so needful National Car Insurance Agency. The insurance industry, both auto and life, is the most voracious bloodsucker in the capitalist swamp. The auto insurance industry holds a gun to our heads – shut-up and pay-up – or walk. More depressingly, our government inadvertently conspires with the companies by making insurance mandatory inorder to drive. In fact, auto insurance is the only commercial product that the government makes you buy. This is outrageous! One buys insurance to guard against that day when something bad happens. Month after month, year after year, you pay the company for nothing. At last, when an accident does occur, you are punished like a bad boy or girl. Your premium payments are raised. But you paid, more than needed to cover this mishap. No matter. If the *"Insurance Lord"* feels magnanimous, you may be granted *"accident forgiveness!"* Forgiveness for what? Again, you already paid your dues. Only criminals beg forgiveness. The extortion scheme that is the insurance industry is criminal. That's why we need a public option. We need a nationwide, Government operated car insurance program to compete with the big auto insurance companies. *"Federal Auto"* would be a non-profit car insurance company in the newly established Department of Insurance. This cabinet-level Department would also include *"Federal Life,"* to compete with the private, for-profit life insurance corporations. The Department would be headed by the Secretary of Insurance, answerable to the President. Federal Auto would not be listed on Wall Street. Being a non-profit organization, it would not have any greedy stockholders. The billions of dollars in profits for investors, would translate into billions of dollars in savings for drivers. Federal Auto insurers would make one yearly payment, a fraction of what they used to pay. Being publicly owned and government controlled, Federal Auto would be subsidized by taxation. As motorists abandon private insurance, those companies will shrink until they shrivel. Eventually, they will be absorbed into Federal Auto, the Department of Insurance. As a bonus, we will no longer have those silly auto insurance commercials imposed on us through the television. Incidentally: In *Winning Through Intimidation* (1973) entrepreneur Robert J. Ringer (b. 1938) suggested that: *"The next time you pass one of those insurance company skyscrapers, look closely between the bricks. You probably thought they were held together by cement. Not so. The substance between the bricks is dried human blood. All those friendly insurance companies, the ones who run the ads on television showing their agents helping out some nice neighborhood family have built their building on human blood."*

FEDERALISM – (*FED*-der-ral-is-um) System in which power is divided between the national government and the several state jurisdictions. Federalism often makes the nation look like the *"Disunited States of America."*

FEDERAL RESERVE NOTE – (*FED*-er-al ree-*SERV NOTE*) Fiat currency. Our present day paper money created by the government. The Federal Reserve note is not redeemable in silver or gold any more. It has worth because the government says so, and the people trust it. Otherwise, it is just good quality paper. Incidentally: The average $1.00 Federal Reserve note will last, on average, 22 months in circulation.

FEDERAL RESERVE SYSTEM – (*FED*-er-al ree-*SERV SIS*-tem) There is nothing *"Federal"* about the Federal Reserve System. The term *"Federal"* is just a red herring to deflect attention from the fact that it is a private bank. In fact, it is the bank of banks, the banker's bank controlled by a few super-wealthy bankers and stockholders. When created by President Woodrow Wilson in 1913, the Federal Reserve Board was given exclusive control over the U.S. banking system. The Federal Reserve Board issues Federal Reserve Notes (money) to all the other banks. By controlling the monetary flow the Board controls the U.S. economy. In 1916, President Wilson (1856 – 1924) so regretted his mistake, saying that he *"Sold the country down the river."* *"Give me control of a nation's money, and I care not who makes the laws."* – banker Mayer Rothschild (1744 – 1812). More recently, industrialist Henry Ford (1863 – 1947) proclaimed that *"It is well enough that people of the nation do not understand our banking and money system, for if they did, I believe that there would be a revolution before tomorrow morning."*

FED-UP – (fed *UHP*) To be over-satiated with food. To have eaten more than is comfortably satisfying. The term originated in 19th century England where animals were forced-fed to fatten them up for market. The term had been expanded to mean more than enough of something or someone, to be bored or tired of them. Incidentally: In 1832, *"The Middlesex Courier"* was fed-up with the lazy, redundant aristocracy: *"Everything being done for them, they never learn to do anything; they are fed up, as it were, in a stall to exist and not act. It is rare to find a Prince who can walk decently across a room."* *"I'm fed up to the eyeballs,"* became a popular English expression.

FEEDBACK – (*FEED*-back) A reaction, comments, criticism or positive assessment. In education or any learning situation, feedback provides the practioner with direct, usable insights into current performance. Feedback is formative, helping the learned develop better habits.

FEEDING FRENZY – (*FEED*-ding *FREN*-zee) The convulsive tearing apart and consuming of a carcass, characteristic of a school of sharks or piranha. Feeding frenzies also occur in political waters, and in the media channels as well. Often a powerful,unpopular, but wounded politician who finds himself in hot water may excite a ruthless attack by political opponents. The sharks can smell blood. He's attacked from all sides, and the media too takes its pound of flesh. By the time the attack is over, only the bones of a political career remain of the feeding frenzy. Incidentally: The most horrendous feeding frenzy occurred during

World War Two in a Burma mangrove swamp. The British had pinned down about 1,000 Japanese soldiers in the swamp. At night, the crocodiles emerged and feasted. All but 20 men survived the feeding frenzy.

FEEL GOOD – (*FEE*-ill good) A sensation of total wellbeing, physically, emotionally, and spiritually. Feeling good entail a sense of security and contentment. One is comfortable in body, and free from pain, stress, anxiety, or worry. Spiritually, feeling good necessitates an atonement [read: *at-one- ment*] with God.

FEELING – (*FEE*-ling) (Feel) Sentience, sensating. Feeling is experiencing a sensation independent of the object or perception causing the feeling. One may feel physically or emotionally. *"I feel the warmth of the sun."* Feelings are purely objective emotional states that reveal aspects of the subject's subjective consciousness. *"I feel angry when confronted with injustice,"* or *"I feel depressed at the sight of homelessness"* speaks to one's core values.

FEH – (*"Feh!"* is an interjection that is pronounced like a "spitting" sound.) Feh is a Yiddishism, an expression of disgust, disapproval, displeasure.

FELCHING – (*FELL*-ching) (Felch, Felcher, Felched) A *"semen slurpee."* Felching is a sexual practice reserved for those with a strong stomach. It is the nauseating act of sucking out someone's anus after performing anal sex. Felching is eating out the creampie, then, with a sloppy kiss, transferring the cumcream into the mouth of the ass-fucked. Felching may prove to be a distasteful practice for most, even many exotic erotic connoisseurs. The term felching derived from the underground queer comics of the mid to late 1970s. Incidentally: Semen is pure protein. Though it smells like mushrooms, semen is quite tasteless, like raw albumen (egg white). Footnote: The popular band, *The Village People* were forced by their record label to remove a line about felching from their hit song, *"YMCA"* (1978). A Caveat: The author is merely the messenger; a reporter, not supporter. Like the <u>Urban Dictionary</u> or the <u>Freakypedia</u>, the <u>Liberal Lexicon</u> is a reference book.

FELICITATE – (fel-*LIS*-it-tate) (Felicitation) A congratulation. An expression of good wishes.

FELICITOUS – (fel-*LIS*-si-tus) Appropriate, well-chosen, apt. A felicitous statement or gesture is well-suited for the occasion.

FELICITY – (fe-*LIS*-si-tee) (Felicitous) A high degree of happiness, joy, or bliss.

FELLATIO – (fel-*LA*-she-oh) (also Fellation, Fellating, Fellatiolean) The practice of orally stimulating the male penis with the expectation of exciting orgasm. A crude, somewhat vulgar appellation for fellatio is *"blow job."* This is misleading for the procedure is more sucking and messaging the penis by the lips and tongue with an in-and-out motion. Orgasmic climax concludes with ejaculation. Fellation has proved successful as a traditional remedy for erectile dysfunction (ED). Incidentally: The wily former First Lady Barbara Bush (1925 - 2018) must have been skilled at the performance of fellatio. Barb had said: *"Clinton lied. A man might forget where he parks or where he lives, but he never forgets oral sex, no matter how bad it is."* *"The way to a man's hearth is through his penis."* – Chloe Thurlow. Footnote: God only blesses the uninhibited with sexual gratification.

FELLATIOLEAN – (fel-la-she-*OH*-lee-an) One who practices fellatio or oral sex on males. He/she excites their male sex partner by stimulating his penis in his/her mouth. A fellatiolean is called a *"cock sucker"* or a *"dick licker"* in the vulgar vernacular. Incidentally: Sex is perhaps the only occupation or procedure that is not enhanced by wealth.

FELLATION – (fel-*LAY*-shun) (Fellating) The act of fellatio. Fellation is oral sex is specifically performed on males. Fellation consists of sucking the erect penis, exciting the recipient, stimulating the organ with an in-and-out maneuver until orgasm is attained through ejaculation. The female counterpart to fellation is cunnilingus. A Caveat: The author is just the messenger.

FELLER – (*FEL*-ler) A woodcutter. From about 1400, feller meant one who fells trees, a lumberjack. If the feller is satisfied at his job, he qualifies as a *"happy feller,"* (*a conficta*).

FELLOWSHIP FOUNDATION – (*FEL*-lo-ship *FOWN*-day-shun) A crypto-Christo- capitalist cult of wealthy influence peddlers. Like the *Bilderberg Group,* the *Trilateral Commission,* and the *Bohemian Club,* the *Fellowship Foundation* is a secretive affiliation of the ultra-rich. They refer to their active members as *"The Family."* Their goal is to create a worldwide plutocracy. They lobby governmental leaders with a pseudo-Christian message in order to consolidate the wealth among an elite oligarchy. What sets the Fellowship Foundation apart from the aforementioned billionaire fraternities is the veneer of heretical, hypocritical Christianity with which they veil their mission. They evangelize a blasphemous mockery of Jesus' teachings. They believe that Jesus approved of the disparity of wealth. *"For you always have the poor with you, but you will not always have me,"* Jesus exclaimed in Matthew 26:11. Therefore, become rich in wealth, as Jesus was rich in grace. The Fellowship fellows interpret Jesus in Matthew 19:21 as meaning: *"If you would be perfect, go, and grasp all the wealth you can, and you will have treasure too in heaven, then come follow me."* Of course, the rich should be stewards over the poor, like a benevolent count, lording over his serfs. The organization contends that you help the poor by prospering the rich. The Fellowship Foundation advocates *"Trickle-down Christian largess."* God made the rich, and intends them to remain wealthy and in charge, they insist. This is a modern rendition of the Medieval *"Divine Right of Kings"* philosophy. Not only are the poor to be subservient to the aristocracy. Women are to serve men, (as in Biblical times), under the doctrine of *"Male Headship."* This esoteric cult attempts to recruit influential individuals into *"Prayer Cells."* *"I wish I can say more about it, but it's working precisely because it's private,"* declared President Ronald Reagan (1911 – 2004). The Fellowship Foundation was founded in 1935 by the Norwegian-born Methodist minister, Abraham Vereide (1886 – 1969). The organization was propelled to prominence by the charismatic preacher Douglas Coe (1928 – 2017). In 1953, Coe established the *National Prayer Breakfast* every February in Washington D.C. About 3,500 special guests are invited from over 100 nations. These are the power-brokers of government and big business. Every President since Dwight D. Eisenhower (1890 – 1969) has attended (including *"His Swineness,"* Donald Trump (b. 1946). The Fellowship has no problem embracing a godless hypocrite like Trump. For faith is the foil, power is the goal. *"We work with power when we can, we work with power where we can,"* – A Fellowship Official. Incidentally: One percent of the world's population controls about 84% of the world's wealth! Too, the 8 wealthiest people in the world, are richer than the poorer half of humanity all together (about 3,855,000,000 people)!

FELL SWOOP – (fel *SWOOP*) Suddenly, in a single action. The term is usually used in the sentence: *"At one fell swoop."* The word *"fell"* has many meanings today, none of which fit this context. Fell is an old, obsolete word that traces back to the 13th century. The old edition of the <u>Oxford English Dictionary</u> defines fell as: *"fierce, savage, cruel, ruthless, dreadful, terrible."* In fact, fell is the root for the word *"felon."* William Shakespeare (1564 – 1616) either coined or popularized the phrase *"one fell swoop"* in his play <u>MacBeth</u> (1605). On hearing that his family and servants were killed, MacDuff cried out: *"All my pretty ones? Did you say all? O hell-kite! All? What, all my pretty chickens and their dam at one fell swoop?"* In these lines, *"kite"* refers to the Red Kite, a bird of prey, that *"swoops"* down and kills its victims, chicken, or whatever. Therefore, MacDuff was referring to the murder of his entire household by MacBeth, in one fell swoop.

FELONY – (*FEL*-lon-nee) (Felons, Felonies, Felonious) A grievous crime punishable by extended imprisonment and loss of property. In some jurisdictions, some felonies like murder will demand the death sentence. A felony is far more serious than a misdemeanor, or minor crime.

FELONIOUS DISENFRANCISEMENT – (fuh-*LOH*-nee-uhs dis-en-*FRAN*-chyhz-ment) Not making it a felony to prevent voting, but making voting a felony by people who have committed a felony. This is shamefully un-American, because felons or former felons are still U.S. citizens. Over 4.6 million citizens are disenfranchised throughout the 50 states. Those who have gone wrong, but have paid their dues and have repented, must be welcomed back into society. This is the promise of rehabilitation. This is what decent people believe, except Republicans. Some states penalize former felons who had served their time with additional fines, fee, and stipulations, which prohibit them from voting. Imagine how those 4.6 million votes would change the political landscape. The Republicans have. That's why the voter suppressors are Republicans, of course. That's because most felons are poor people, and poor people vote Democratic in support of their vested interests. Too, felonious disenfranchisement is an exercise in racism. One in 19 African Americans of voting age is disenfranchised, a rate 3.5 times greater than that of non-African Americans. More than one in 10 African American adults is prevented from voting in 8 states: Alabama, Arizona, Florida, Kentucky, Mississippi, Tennessee, Virginia, and South Dakota (all Southern, one Western state). Furthermore, over 506,000 Latinx Americans or 1.7% of the voting population can't vote. About one million women are disenfranchised, comprising over 1/5 of the total disenfranchised population. Is it any wonder how a conservative minority party, the Republicans, can control so many political offices. This is a rendition of apartheid.

FELSIC LAVA – (*FEL*-sic *LA*-va) In volcanology, silica-rich lava. Volcanic lava impregnated with much sand. It will harden into a glossy glass.

FEMALE PERCEPTION – (*FEE*-mayl per-*SEP*-shun) A woman's sensory cognizance. Perception is apprehending by means of the senses as well as the extrasensory abilities. A woman's perception is demonstrably superior to a man's. Her recognition and recall of detail is far greater than her male counterpart. A woman will remember a face, the color of the curtains, and the style of her rival's dress. To the bane of husbands, a wife will remember every grievance or fault he has ever committed. Furthermore she will ruminate on it forever. All five senses in females surpasses that of males. Even in the supersensory parapsychological realm of intuition and clairvoyance, women generally surpass men. Why? The answer resides back to the time of the EEA (Environment of Evolutionary Adaptation). This was just before Homo sapien became fully sapien (the *"caveman"* days, vernacularly speaking). During the EEA, the final tweaks were being made on our brain to produce the creature we are today. Part of the fine-tuning differentiated the female brain from that of the male. This was done inorder that the two sexes complement each other in the struggle for survival. Males were endowed with physical superiority – strength, speed, endurance. Females were endowed with everything else. Men had to defend against wild beasts, as well as chase down and kill prey. Men were the hunters, but women were the gatherers. They had to remember the minute details of plants, roots, and berries, differentiate between shades of color, so as not to poison the family. They had to be able to smell and taste if food was turning dangerously rancid, spoiled. Mothers had to be able to see slight differences in infant's pallor, to determine if illness was coming on. Too, she had to fine-tune her hearing to distinguish the different cries her baby made and what they meant. The touch of baby's skin, its temperature gave our ancient mom vital clues. Women developed cleverness far beyond that of men, inorder to compete with, and compensate for man's strength. She evolved a cunning ability to manipulate men for her benefit. In many ways, the acute female perception is a natural defense mechanism. The human species may not have survived without it. Incidentally: The female's heightened sense of awareness was exemplified in 1917 by Jeannette Rankin (1880 – 1917) from Montana, the first women elected to the U.S. Congress. When entering the Capitol Building, Congresswoman Rankin's first comment was: *"The curtains need cleaning."* *"Why is it that a woman can see from a distance what a man cannot see close?"* – Thomas Hardy (1840 – 1828). *"Men who like women never notice what they wear."* – Anatole France (1844 – 1924).

FEMALE SUFFRAGE – (*FEE*-mayl *SUF*-rij) The right of women to vote. This right was granted nationwide in 1920, with the ratification of the 19th Amendment to the Constitution. By 1914 however, almost all Western states had granted female suffrage. That's because as pioneers, women were indispensable in the settlement and survival in the West. Eastern states continued to deny female suffrage. Corporate capitalists feared that women would vote to support unions, and anti-trust laws, and ban child labor. Incidentally: World War One persisted from 1914 to 1914. The United States did not get involved on the side of the Allies until April, 1917. President Woodrow Wilson (1856 – 1924) was being pressured by American bankers to help the allies (Britain and France) win the war, so the banks could be repaid their loans. But American women organized against U.S. involvement. Mothers, wives, and sisters did not want to send their men to war. So Wilson made a deal with the females. He would support female suffrage after the war, if women dropped their opposition to the war. The women agreed. The U.S. entered the war. The Allies won. The bankers got their money. Women got the right to vote.

FEMBOY – (*FEM*-boi) (also Femboi) A young man who identifies as a male who displays feminine characteristics. Femboys are often bisexual. They renounce the macho male masculine roles. A femboy may wear long beautiful hair and may apply makeup. Too, he may cross-dess. *"I am different. Let that not upset you."* – Alchemist Paracelsus (c. 1493 – 1541).

FEMDOM – (*FEM*-dom) An abbreviation for Female Dominance. In mainstream married life, a femdom relationship presents a commanding, dictatorial wife, lording over a weak, henpecked husband. In the culture of exotic erotica, femdom refers to a *"dominatrix,"* the female mistress in a master-slave relationship. Erotic femdom is part of BDSM, (Bondage, Discipline, SubMission) which is SadoMasochistic sexplay.

The femdom mistress will usually be scantily clad is black leather, armed with her whip. She is a sexy whipper-snapper, a professional punishment applicator. *"The only unnatural sex act is that which you cannot perform."* – Sexologist Alfred Kinsey (1894 – 1956).

FEMININE ENERGY – (*FEM*-in-nin *EN*-er-jee) Feminine energy in a magical or spiritual context refers to passive and yielding energy, versus masculine energy which is said to be active and penetrating. This is similar to the Eastern concept of *"Yin"* and *"Yang."* In magick, the feminine mind refers to the unconscious mind. This mind takes in everything and remembers everything, yet remains seemingly passive, though it exerts itself in the form of phobias. Deeply held faith, and instinctive wisdom, most intuitive. It is through this unconscious female mind that the collective unconscious can be reached and true magical knowledge and power accessed. The idea of masculine and feminine energy is often applied to plants, herbs, crystals, and other natural objects that may be used in spellwork. *"Revolutions are impossible without the feminine ferment."* – Dr. Karl Marx (1818 – 1883).

FEMININITY – (fem-in-*NIN*-ni-tee) (Feminine) The level of femininess, the degree of female or womanish qualities one exhibits. Femininity is ascribed to having a low measure of testosterone, the male sex hormone. Women with low testosterone levels are more dainty, pretty, submissive, curvy, nurturing, fertile, and more feminine. Low testosterone females are more home, family, and baby oriented. However they are not very sexual. They have a weak libido. Feminine women do not particularly enjoy sex. They prefer romantic foreplay and cuddling to genial sex. On the other hand, high testosterone women are not pretty, not shapely, nor very fertile. They are more masculine looking, competitive, athletic, and career oriented. However the more masculine females have a stronger libido. They are sexually aggressive, enjoy genital sex over foreplay, and are receptive to casual recreational sexual encounters.

FEMINAZIS – (fem-min-*NOT*-zees) A conservative opprobrium for activist, militant feminists. Feminazis are radical man-haters. They are certainly gay. *"A woman without a man is like a fish without a bicycle."* – Gloria Steinem (b. 1934).

FEMINISM – (*FEM*-min-is-um) The Progressive war against the forces of conservatism, to gain equal rights, justice, and dignity for women. Battles have been fought on the social, political, educational, economic, and reproductive fronts in the feminist war for equality. *"Equality Feminists"* seek justice. *"Gender Feminists"* seek revenge. These are the extremists, (Feminazis) radical man-haters. Lesbian by nature, gender feminists despise everything male. Gratefully, they are few. *"Despite being a feminist, wanting men to find me attractive is part of my DNA."* – Jane Fonda (b. 1937).

FEMME FATALE – (fem fa-*TELL*) An irresistibly attractive, seductive women who leads men into difficult, dangerous, or disastrous situations. The KGB uses professional temptresses, gorgeous agents as femme fatales in spy rings.

FEMTOSECOND – (*FEEM*-toh-sek-uhnd) (10-15) A measure of time, which is a super, sub-atomically brief timespan, one quadrillionth of a second, or one, one- millionth-billionth of a second. In other words, a femtosecond is to a second, what a second is to 31.71 million years. Such astronomical time frames are associated with cosmology, *Big Bang* occurrences, and are part of *"Plank Time."* (1/1,000,000,000,000,000 of a second.)

FENCING – (*FEN*-sing) Not athletic sword fighting, but the peddling of stolen goods. Anyone who participates in this activity, as seller or buyer, in engaged in a fencing operation. Hot merchandize is disposed of quickly, and very cheaply. Fencing is a criminal act for all involved. Obviously, it encourages more theft. But looking at it from another angle, fencing is a tax-free source of income for the forgotten poor. It is an integral part of the *"underground economy."* Quality products are *"expropriated"* from the quality suburbs, and sold at big bargain in the needy inner city. This amounts to a necessary redistribution of the wealth. Too, indigent residents are provided with merchandise they would never legitimately be able to afford. *"If anyone would take your tunic, let him have your cloak as well."* – Jesus in Matthew 5: 40.

FENDER BENDER – (*FEN*-der *BEN*-der) A fender is an automobile part that frames the wheel well. It prevents mud, rocks, and dirty spray from being thrown in the air by the rotating wheels. A fender bender is a minor accident in which the fender is slightly dented. Not anymore. What used to be a minor fender bender is today a major fender buster. That's because the fender is no longer made of steel, but of plastic or fiberglass. The front and back of the car was once protected by a chrome-plated steel bumper. As the name implies, this auto part served as a bump absorber. It was heavy-gaged steel. Not anymore. If you bump the bumper today, it will crack into a dozen pieces. That's because the bumper too is made of plastic or fiberglass. In fact, synthetic polymers have replaced metal throughout the vehicle. This makes the car cheaper to manufacture [read: *more profit*], and far more expensive to repair [read: *more profit*]. The auto industry gains at both ends. Today, what was once a minor bump or bender costs hundreds, or is a total loss. (You must buy another car.) Plastic cars are lighter, more fragile, and more dangerous, offering less protection in an accident. Imagine a collision between a 2021 auto, and a 1959 juggernaut. No contest! It would be as if the contemporary car was hit by a tank. This goes to show that all progress is not progressive, and all innovation is not improvement. It is inherent in capitalism to always put profit before people.

FEND OFF – (fend *AWF*) To resist, or keep someone or something away from you. The term *"fend"* is an archaic and obsolete word used only with the expressions: *"fend for yourself,"* or *"fend off."* There is no equivalent *"fend on,"* for example. The term fend traces back to the 14th century when it served as a back-formation of the word *"defend."* The English Sunday newspaper, <u>*The Examiner*</u>, recorded the following line in 1830: *"A committee is the fend-off to importunity, and the contrivance for obtaining time."* Today, to fend for yourself is the conservative, capitalist, Republican credo. *"Rugged individualism,"* [read: *"I got mine, to hell with you"* and *"Every man for himself"*] is the core value of capitalism. We must fend off the temptation to be selfish and share our abundant bounty Socialistically.

FENESTRATION – (fen-nes-*TRAY*-shun) Refers to the design and arrangement of the widows in a building.

FENTANYL – (*FEN*-tuh-nil) ($C_{22}H_{28}N_2O$) A powerful analgesic medicine, popularly abused as a deadly recreational drug. Fentanyl is a valuable anesthetic for traumatic physical injuries, as on the battlefield. As with all potent opiate drugs, fentanyl is a highly addictive narcotic. It is 100 times more powerful than morphine. That's wonderful, when confined to the hospital. But by the early 2000s, fentanyl had hit the American streets as a murderer. Over 70,000 overdoses were reported in 2021. The death toll is certainly higher today (April 2023). In fact, fentanyl is the leading cause of death among Americans between the ages of 18 and 45. There are any number of ways to introduce fentanyl into the body – by pill, injection, nasal spray, skin patches, or smoked. It is ever so dangerous, lethal, in untrained hands. In fact, handling powdered fentanyl being absorbed through the skin is dangerous. Fentanyl is a hallucinogenic drug that produces a state of euphoria. That accounts for its popular attraction. Only 2 milligrams of fentanyl will kill most people. (That amount can be concealed under a fingernail.) It kills by paralyzing the diaphragm, disabling breathing. What makes fentanyl exceedingly heinous is that it is cheap, and relatively simple to make. The chemicals come from China and India. They are exported to Central America and Mexico, where they are processed into the drug fentanyl. Ruthless Latin American drug cartels smuggle the poison to the USA, where it is sold at a tremendous profit. Fentanyl was first synthesized in 1959 by the Belgian physician Paul Janssen (1926 – 2003).

FERAL – (*FER*-rol) Wild plants or animals existing in a natural state, not domesticated or cultivated. Farm animals or pets that escape into the wilds, go wild. If they survive, they revert to their ancestral state. Feral animals will physically change over a few generations to resemble their original ancestors. Nature changed the creature to cope better in nature. This is going feral. Of course, feral animals are dangerous. Packs of feral dogs and pigs have killed people.

FERMENTATION – (fur-men-*TAY*-shun) (Ferment, Fermenting, Fermented, Fermentative) The chemo-biological process in which yeast enzymes turn fructose (fruit sugar juice) into ethyl alcohol. Fermentation is a natural process of decomposition. Fungus breaks down organic substances by consuming their nutrients. Yeast is a fungus. Yeast eats fruit sugar and urinates alcohol. That's how wine is made. Yes, wine is *"yeast piss"* (and it will make you *"piss drunk"*). Alcohol is made naturally when yeast invades fallen fruit and rots it on the ground. If the yeast is made to wallow in its own urine too long, it will turn the wine into vinegar. Through fermentation, the yeast breaks down the carbohydrate (sugar) in cereal grains, and turns it into beer (liquid bread). All the yeast needs is water. Furthermore, the yeast in the vinegar will turn cucumbers into pickles, and cabbage into sauerkraut. Yeast fermentation creates gas bubbles (flatulence) which causes raw dough to rise into bread. Indeed, yeast is our earliest and most precious domestic microbe. *"In the wine is a sea of organisms. By some it lives, by some it decays."* – Louis Pasteur (1802 – 1895). Incidentally: It was during his investigation of fermentation that was spoiling the wine, that Louis Pasteur discovered the *"Germ Theory,"* the greatest single accomplishment in the history of medicine (made by a chemist). *Holy hangover!*

FERMI PARADOX – (*FER*-mee *PAIR*-ra-dox) Contends that advanced extraterrestrial lifeforms could have easily made contact with us. They haven't, therefore, they don't exist.

FERMIUM – (*FER*-mee-um) (Fm) A transuranic element (#100) named after Enrico Fermi (1901 – 1954), the Italian physicist who produced the first controlled chain reaction. Fermium was discovered in 1952. The half-life or life span of fermium is 100.5 days before it decays. Fermium is used in nuclear experimentation.

FERN – (*FURN*) The oldest plant on Earth, the first plant on the planet. Ferns propagate through rhizomes, and spores rather than seeds. If all life on Earth was killed-off, ferns would be the first plant to return. Palms are advanced ferns that evolved into trees.

FERRET – (*FAIR*-ret) A mammal of the weasel family with blackish fur, small sharp teeth, and a feisty disposition. Ferrets range across Europe, Asia, and North Africa. Actually, a ferret is a semi-domesticated breed of European *"polecat."* For centuries, ferrets were used for driving rats and rabbits out of their burrows. Even the Romans were fond of rabbit hunting with ferrets. However polecats, even when domesticated as ferrets, are chicken hunters. In fact, the Middle English term *"polcat"* is derived from the Middle French *"poul"* (as in <u>poul</u>try) and the Middle English *"cat,"* ergo, *"chickencat."* Like all polecats, ferrets emit a strong pungent scent to mark-off territory. Though unpleasant, it is not a compelling deterrent like the spray of the skunk, the American polecat, and ferret's cousin.

FERROMAGNETISM – (fair-ro-*MAG*-net-is-um) (Ferromagnetic) Being paramagnetically attracted to a magnet. Ferromagnetic alloys contain iron.

FERRUGINOUS – (fer-*ROO*-jin-us) Means iron-bearing. Ferruginous soil like *laterite* is thick, red, and usually not very fertile.

FERTILE CRESCENT – (*FER*-till *CRES*-sent) A region in Southwestern Asia (Middle East) which served as the cultural hearth for some of the earliest civilizations in the world. The Fertile Crescent began in Mesopotamia and included the civilizations of Sumeria, Babylonia, Assyria, Akkadia, and Chaldea. From Mesopotamia between the Tigris and Euphrates Rivers the Fertile Crescent looped westward in an arch to include the Phoenician and Hebrew Civilizations on the Mediterranean Sea. It descended down the Nile to include Egypt. This crescent-shaped land formation had the best balance of climate, water, plants, and animals for civilization to emerge. The rivers enabled transportation, which encouraged communication and association which accelerated civilization. After Thought: Today, after millennia, the Fertile Crescent region is overwhelmingly Muslim. Coincidentally, the crescent is the symbol of Islam.

FERTILITY RATE – (fer-*TIL*-li-tee) The number of births that 1,000 women are expected to undergo in their lifetime. For sociological and biological reasons, the fertility rate is higher in high poverty regions, which are in the tropical/subtropical Southern Hemisphere. A high death rate must be compensated by a high birth rate, as a family insurance policy. Too, in the disease-ridden tropics, nature seems to have made the female more fertile to atone for the number of babies she will lose, due to poor living conditions. Finally, poor people have few entertainment options other than sex. Sex is the only human activity that is not enhanced by wealth.

FERVID – (*FER*-vid) Burning with enthusiasm, a vehement spirit. A fervid belief is essential for success.

FESTAL – (*FES*-tal) A festive holiday, gala occasion, befitting of a feast.

FETAL POSITION – (*FEE*-tal poe-*SISH*-un) The posture taken by the developing fetus as it grows in the uterus. The body is curled with head and limbs drawn in. Interestingly, psychotic patients in a state of fear or emotional withdrawal will assume the fetal position, usually backed into the corner of the room.

This may be a subconscious yearning to be back in the safety of mother's womb, implying that *"I wish I was never born!"* *"Why did I not die at birth, come out from the womb and expire? Why did the knees receive me?"* – Job 3:11-12.

FETICIDE – (*FEE*-tuh-syd) The aborting of a congregation of cells in the womb called the fetus. Potentially, those cells are evolving toward becoming a human being. *"Feticide"* is an emotionally loaded term designed to criminalize abortion. The suffix *"cide"* means *"to kill."* The term *"abort,"* as in <u>abort</u>ion, means to *"stop, end."* Abortion, which is stopping, ending a pregnancy is designated by abortion opponents as feticide, synonymous with homicide, killing of a human being. However, feticide is not, and cannot be <u>homi</u>cide because a fetus is not a <u>Homo</u> sapien or human being. Therefore, the very term *"feticide"* is problematically deceptive. Indeed, the cells that constitute the fetus are alive, as are the cells of any other bodily appendage, including blood cells. When blood is shed those cells die. But that is not considered killing (*hemocide?*), let alone murder. When a mangled finger, toe, arm, or leg is amputated, they are not being killed either. The cells that constitute the appendix are alive, as are the cells of a tumor. However, when the appendix or a tumor are surgically removed or aborted, they are not being murdered. Neither is the fetus. Therefore, the very term feticide is inaccurate, misleading, and wrong. Abortion is not killing. *"Let abortion be procured before sense and life have begun; what may or may not be lawfully done in these cases depends on the question of life and sensation."* – Aristotle (384 – 322 BCE).

FETISH – (*FET*-tish) (Fetishism, Fetishist) In anthropology, a sacred talisman or amulet. A fetish is an inanimate object believed to be the embodiment or habitat of a spirit. A fetish like a totem pole is believed to possess magical powers. Therefore, it is revered and even worshiped. In psychology, a fetish is an object or non-genital part of the body that elicits a habitual erotic response or fixation. One may develop a foot fetish, eyes, lips, or ears fetish, for example. Furthermore, totally unrelated objects may acquire the power of fetish over an individual. A car, a cake, a candle, anything under the sun can become one's fetish. The roots of a psychological fetish are embedded deep in the subconscious. *"A fetish is a story masquerading as an object."* – Psychiatrist Robert Stoller (1924 – 1991).

FETISH – (*FET*-tish) (Fetishism, Fetishist) Modern Paganism provides a more mystic description of fetishism. In this context, a fetish is an object designated to house a spirit-being. Traditionally, a fetish is the physical representation of an honored spirit, for example, an ancestor, deity, or spirit guide. It is a material and often portable object with which the bearer interacts, as if it were the spirit-being. They honor, present offerings, and pray to the fetish as the surrogate spirit. It is understood by the devotee that the interaction is not with an inanimate object, but with the spirit that resides within. In turn, the possessor of the fetish might receive blessings of good luck, protection, and perhaps fortified magical power and abilities. Fetishes may also be used to house other types of spirit-beings including *"servitors,"* whose purpose is to aid the possessor of the fetish, or to bring mischief or a curse upon an enemy. *"One will never worship well the idol, who knew it when it was a stump in the forest."* – African Proverb.

FETISHISM – (*FET*-tish-is-um) (Fetish, Fetishist) In psychology, a neurotic paraphilial disorder in which one is sexually aroused by non-sexual, non-living objects or parts of a person's body. Anything on Earth can serve as a fetish object.

FETISIST – (*FET*-tish-ist) One who enjoys (or is plagued) by some fetish. This is a fixation, obsession, compulsion that governs a part of his or her life. The fetish may be a person, thing, habit, activity, most anything.

FEUDALISM – (*FEW*-dal-is-um) The socio-political system of Medieval Europe. Feudalism prevailed from about the 9th to the 15th centuries. Kings allowed nobles use of the land in exchange for military service and protection of the realm. The common people labored the lord's land in semi-bondage as *serfs*. Feudalism was a static system with no social mobility. Feudalism was a pre- capitalist system of oppression and exploitation of the poor and powerless. Feudalism was ruralism. Urbanization and the development of a merchant middle class (bourgeoisie) helped to destroy feudalism. Incidentally: *"In democracy it's your vote that counts. In feudalism, it's your count that votes."*

FEVER – (*FEE*-ver) (Feverish) A generic term for the medical condition called *"pyrexia."* Fever is an abnormal rise in temperature, usually due to bacterial, viral, or parasitic disease. The pulse quickens, and the normal function of all the organs is disrupted. A pathogenic fever is to be distinguished from hyperthermia, the over-heating of the body due to external conditions, like extreme exercise in the sun. The normal body temperature is 98.6oF degrees (Fahrenheit). With some individuals, 99.0oF or up to 100.9oF may not be abnormal. But anything over this limit is fever, an indication of disease, illness. The presence of pathogenic organisms triggers the body to increase its temperature to fight the invaders. In the initial stage of illness, mild fever serves as a defense mechanism. Human pathogens replicate less well at a higher temperature. The immune system is more efficient in a slight fever. Too, antibiotics work more effectively when the temperature rises. On-setting fever produces a cold/hot reaction. When the body temperature first begins to rise, muscular contractions are triggered. This shivering causes a feeling of chills and cold. In reaction, the body produces more heat. Though the victim has chills, the body is getting hotter. Soon, the person begins to feel flushed, hot, and sweats. If the body temperature continues to rise, the person is in peril. Sometimes, the victim falls into febrile seizure, usually children. Delirium accompanies high fever as well. Fevers of 105.8oF to 107.6oF are life- threatening. Chemically, protein denaturation occurs at those temperatures. Human body cells are made of protein. The cells begin to die. Body organs malfunction. At 108oF the brain dies resulting in death. A plunge in a cold bath is an emergency measure to cool the body immediately.

FEVER – (*FEE*-ver) In this case, a fever is the collective name for an assemblage of stingrays. Incidentally: Stingrays are armed with a long, poisonous, dagger- tipped tail. It can administer a painful, dangerous sting that can be more of a fatal stab. In fact, in 2006, a stab in the heart by a stingray killed Australian zookeeper, conservationist, and wildlife expert Steve Irwin (1962 – 2006), *"The Crocodile Hunter." "Suddenly, the sand erupted with a fever of stingrays."*

FEXT – (*FEKST*) (Fexted) To mis-text. To send an unintentional text message, or to correspond via text to the wrong person. Fext is a neologism of the new digital age.

FEXTING – (*FEKS*-ting) (Fext, Fexted) In the vulgar vernacular, fexting has multiple meanings. According to the online *Urban Dictionary*, fexting can mean: *"Texting while fucking."* Apparently, some people are better at multitasking than others. Alternately, fexting can mean: *"Fake-Texting, the action of pretending to text message on your cell phone when someone you don't want to see or say hi to is walking right by you.*" Furthermore, fexting can refer to an insincere text message. The <u>Urban Dictionary</u> also defines fexting as: "*A text by a girl (usually to another girl) full of fakeness. Being fake includes pretending to like her when you really just want to punch her in the face, complimenting her when really you're just making fun of her, and/ or saying you need to hang out when really you'd rather stab yourself in the eye.*" One may resort to this form of fexting when you need something from the despised party. "*I hate that bitch but I need my stuff back. I'm fexting her.*" – <u>Urban Dictionary.</u> "*Hell hath no fury like a woman scorned.*" – William Congreve (1670 – 1729) in <u>The Mourning Bride</u> (1697). Incidentally: In the June-July edition of <u>Harper's Bazaar</u> (2022), First Lady Dr. Jill Biden (b. 1951) endowed fexting with still another meaning – arguing via text. In the interview, Mrs. Biden said that she argues with husband, President Joe (b. 1942) by "*fexting*" over text to avoid fighting in front of the Secret Service. I wonder if these correspondences are classified as official government property? On the other hand, do the Bidens text while they fuck in the White House?

FFM – (ef-ef-*EM*) (F2M) An initialism in the culture of exotic erotica for <u>F</u>emale, <u>F</u>emale, <u>M</u>ale. FFM is a sexual threesome, a menage a trois. F2M is an example od "*polyamory.*" According to the online sex encyclodictionary <u>Freakypedia</u>, an FFM enables: "*The girls to take care of him and make sure that his dick has plenty of holes to explore including mouths, pussies, and sometimes assholes.*" FFM is a universal, heterosexual fantasy of men to be in bed with two women – fucking one pussy, while eating the other. A Caveat: Don't blame the author who is serving as a journalist.

FFFM – (ef-ef-ef-*EM*) (F3M) An initialism in the culture of exotic erotica for <u>F</u>emale, <u>F</u>emale, <u>F</u>emale, <u>M</u>ale. F3M is an example of "*polyamory.*" Three chicks and a guy technically, officially qualifies as an orgy. This foursome can be a Neapolitan treat, for the guy with diverse taste. He can eat a blonde, brunette, and redhead, like eating vanilla, chocolate, and cherry icecream. Any number of sexual fetishes can be satisfied with this team of devas. A cosmopolitan gentleman would love to try a tri-racial fuck-o-thon. If lucky, he may be ravished by a White chick, a Black chick, and an exotic Oriental at the same time. A Caveat: Exotic erotica is indeed an exotic culture, foreign to most readers. Let the language of this reporting not upset you.

FFFFM – (ef-ef-ef-ef-*EM*) (F4M) An initialism in the culture of exotic erotica for <u>F</u>emale, <u>F</u>emale, <u>F</u>emale, <u>F</u>emale, <u>M</u>ale. FFFFM is a fivesome – quintessentially a quintuplet. F4M is an example of "*polyamory.*" It is a scene that one would imagine *cuming* down at the Playboy Mansion. This is a group sex orgy with all attention on one dick. Can one cock handle this ascension into vaginal Valhalla? Whatever transpires, this guy is one lucky fucker. With four pussies swarming over him, there is plenty of work for the dick and tongue. "*If you're going to be in an orgy, the middle is the best spot, isn't it.*" – Novelist Jim Butcher (b. 1971). It is interesting if a couple of the girls are bisexual. Nothing will rejuvenate a limberdick like a lesbian performance. Being overwhelmed by four females may turn the master into the slave. Imaginative S&M scenes can be played out. How could this bad boy resist a stinging spanking? They may further punish his ass by strapping on a dildo, and penetrate his rectum. "*One of the less well- advertised secrets of group sex was how often it came down to logistics.*" – Author Alex Hall. A Caveat: A <u>*LIBERAL LEXICON*</u> would not be very liberal if it self-censored, would it? "*The dirtiest book of all is the expurgated [censored] book.*" – Walt Whitman (1819 – 1892).

FIANCE – (fee-on-*SAY*) French for a male betrothed. A fiancé is a man about to be married.

FIANCEE – (fee-on-*SAY*) French for a female betrothed. A fiancée is a woman about to be married.

FIAT – (*FEE*-ot) Latin for *"let it be done."* Too, a fiat is a brief affirmation, shorter than a prayer like *"Angels protect us!"* or *"My prayer pack power!"*

FIAT – (*FEE*-ot) An official, authoritative decree, order, command. Fiats are usually associated with dictators. *"His Ludicroucy,"* President Donald Trump (b. 1946) in his ignorance, thought that he had the power to rule by fiat.

FIAT CURRENCY – (*FEE*-ot) In economics money made by government decree. Fiat currency is not backed by precious metals. (It is not an official I-O-U.) It has no alternative use. It can't be bartered or eaten. Fiat money has worth because the government says so, and the people believe it. Our Federal Reserve Note is fiat currency.

FICTIVE KIN – (*FIC*-tiv) Assumed family members. Fictive kin is the habit of treating non-family members as blood relatives. Close family friends may be called uncle, auntie, cousin, making up the fictive family or kin.

FIDEISM – (*FEE*-day-is-um) (Fideist = *FEE*-day-ist) The doctrine that religious truth is founded on faith alone, not on reason or empirical evidence. Fideists believe that faith is superior to philosophy or science as a source of knowledge. *"I do not seek to understand in order that I may believe, but I believe in order that I may understand. For this I also believe; that if I did not believe, I could not understand."* – <u>Proslogion</u> (Discourse, 1078) by St. Anselm of Canterbury (1033 – 1109).

FIDELISTAS – (fee-del-*LEES*-tahs) Supporters and admirers of President Fidel Castro (1926 - 2016) and the Socialist Revolution in Cuba that Castro fomented. Almost all of the people of Cuba are Fidelistas. They appreciate how this lawyer and Socialist hero expelled the corrupt dictator Fulgencio Batista (1901 – 1973), the American Mafia, and the U.S. corporate capitalists. Castro defied the C.I.A. Fidel had outlasted 10 American Presidents. Castro gave Cuba back to the Cuban people. The Fidelistas recognize that no leader of a small country had successfully stood up to the mighty United States except Fidel. Despite great hardships imposed by the United States, and multiple assassination attempts, Fidel and the Fidelistas have maintained their courage, independence, and dignity.

FIDO – (*FY*-doh) In police slang, an acronym meaning *"Fuck it."* The term *"fido"* is used when the cop does not feel like investigating a call. Fido translates into *"forget it," "drive on."*

FIDUCIARY – (fid-*DOO*-shee-air-ree) Not a professional douche administrator. A *"fi-DOCHE-shee-air-ree"* has nothing to do with female hygiene. In law it is a special relationship between individuals in which one person acts for another in a position of trust. Property or power of attorney is entrusted to someone acting as a fiduciary.

FIELD DEPENDENT – (FEELD dee-*PEN*-dent) A student having an external locus of control. He needs direction, praise, and external motivation and supervision.

FIELD INDEPENDENT – (FEEFD *IN*-dee-pen-dent) A student having an internal locus of control. She is an independent worker, self-motivated, needs little direction or supervision.

FIELD MARSHAL – (*FEELD MAHR*-shuhl) The ultimate military rank in many armies like Britain, Russia, and Germany. A field marshal is a general's general. The promotion is considered a high honor for some extraordinary military victory. British General Bernard Montgomery (1887 – 1976) was promoted to field marshal during World War Two. So was Russian General Georgy Zhukov (1896 – 1974). At the close of the Battle of Stalingrad (February 1943), German General Friedrich Paulus (1890 – 1957) was promoted to field marshal (*generalfeldmarschall*) by Adolf Hitler (1889 – 1945). The battle was all but lost. No field marshal in German/Prussian history had ever surrendered. Hitler hoped that this fact would prevent Paulus from surrendering to the Russians. At least, Hitler expected von Paulus to shoot himself. Hitler was wrong. Von Paulus said: *"I'm not going to shoot myself for that little corporal!"* Field Marshal Paulus surrendered the remnants of the German 6th Army and its foreign allies. Before World War Two, the United States was a non-military nation. The rank of field marshal was never awarded to an American general. However on December 14, 1944, Congress created the rank of *"General of the Army"* and awarded General George Marshall (1880 – 1959) the title along with a 5th star. Congress backed-off employing the title field marshal, because General Marshall would be called *"Marshal Marshall."* Incidentally: General Douglas MacArthur (1880 – 1964), *"The American Caesar,"* was awarded the title field marshal by the government of the Philippines. General Dwight D. Eisenhower (1890 – 1969) mockingly called General MacArthur *"The Field Marshal."*

FIELD-TO-TABLE – (*FEE*-ald too *TAY*-bul) Subsistence farming, living off one's garden. Field-to-table suggests no surplus. It is primitive existence without the luxury of trade or marketing. A field-to-table lifestyle is a step above hunting- and-gathering, and starvation.

FIFTH COLUMN – (*FIFTH COL*-lum) A group of people who act traitorously and subversively out of a secret sympathy with the enemy of their country. The term, fifth column is synonymous with a *"Trojan horse."* The term originated with the fascist General Emilio Mola (1887 – 1937) who served the dictator Francisco Franco (1892 – 1975) during the Spanish Civil War in 1936. Mola had declared that he had 4 columns of insurgents marching on Madrid, and a *"fifth column"* (*quinta columna*) already in the city.

FIG – (*FIG*) Looks like a fruit, but botanically is not. A fig is a sweet edible pod that contains the tree's flower and seeds. There is a vast variety of figs which are a staple for the creatures of the rainforest. In fact, the fig is the favorite food of the jungle. Luckily, fig trees are one of the few that fruit year around.

FIGGING – (*FIG*-ing) (Figged) A punitive anal condiment. Figging is a form of torture used in ancient Greece and Rome. It was applied particularly to female prisoners. A peeled finger of ginger would be inserted into the vagina or anus. The victim was restrained in order to restrict mobility while the burning sensation intensified. In 2 to 5 minutes the pain became excruciating. The burning persists for about 30 minutes. The ginger root, carved in the shape of a *"butt plug"* could be further skinned for a fresh application of agony. (*"Waste not want not?"*.) The sufferer instinctively tightens the anal muscles as the fiery sensation increases. For this reason, figging was often applied in conjunction with caning to stimulate clenching of the buttocks. This served to augment the damage of each blow. The term *"figging"* is a corruption of a 19th century word *"feaguing."* This meant to ginger the tail of a sluggish horse to make it livelier. The raw ginger root was inserted into the vulva or anus of the poor animal. Figging has been adopted by the sadomasochistic community as an erotically painful pleasure.

FIGMENT – (*FIG*-ment) A fantastic notion, a mere product of mental invention. *"A Trump Presidential Library is a figment of Donald's demented imagination. Paradoxically, Trump doesn't read!"* A *"Trump Presidential Cheeseburger Emporium"* would be more appropriate.

FILIBUSTER – (*FILL*-uh-bus-ter) (Filibustering) The purpose of the Senate is to make laws. The purpose of the filibuster is to prevent the making of laws. A filibuster is any obstructionist measure using delaying tactics to prevent the adoption of some plan, program or law. Therefore, a filibuster is an anti- democratic procedure in which a minority can cancel the will of the majority. Filibusters are mostly associated with the U.S. Senate. A zealous minority group may stall the proceedings with a series of long speeches, in order to *"talk a bill to death,"* by running-out the clock or the endurance of the Senators. Once a Senator is granted the floor, he can talk (about anything) until he drops to the floor. Truly ridiculous. This is particularly effective toward the close of a Senatorial session. Equally ridiculous is the *"Sixty Vote Rule,"* the super- majority. Any Senator can block a bill from reaching a final up-or-down vote by simply objecting. The objection can be overridden only by a three-fifths (3/5) Senate vote. This creates a de facto 60-vote threshold for legislation to pass – which in a partisanly divided Senate is almost impossible. This is how Republican Senate leader Mitch McConnell (b. 1942) has controlled the Senate and obstructed legislation. The obstructionist Sixty Vote Rule must be abolished in favor of a simple majority vote of 51 or more. This is called *"Reconciliation."* Incidentally: *"Filibuster,"* this odd word has an equally odd etymology. It probably originated with the Dutch *"vrijbuiter."* It was taken into French as *"flibustier."* The Spanish adopted the French term as *"filibustero."* That's when it entered English as *"filibuster."* The original meaning of the word was *fleebooter* or *freebooter*. It referred to rapacious American adventurers who, in the 19th century, infiltrated Central America and the Caribbean, intent on fomenting revolutions and gaining political power. The term entered the U.S. Senate in 1872. Vice President Schuyler Colfax (1823 – 1885) as President of the Senate declared that: *"Under the practice of the Senate the presiding officer could not restrain a Senator in remarks which the Senate considers pertinent to the pending issue."* The filibuster was thus established in the Senate. Senators employing the tactic were compared to the freebooters, the filibusterers who wreaked havoc south of the border. Footnote: President Barack Obama (b. 1961) called the filibuster *"A hangover from the Jim Crow era"* enabling racist Southern Senators to block passage of Civil Rights legislation. Footnote: In mid-March, 2021, serious discussion is underway to eliminate the filibuster in the Senate all together. This would re-establish simple majority rule, as democracy mandates. Too, it will turn the Senate into a law-making, rather than law-suppressing assembly. Up Date: Mid- February, 2024. Forget it! Futility again won over reform.

FILIGREE – (*FIL*-li-gree) Delicate ornamental work of twisted gold or silver wire.

FILLIP – (*FIL*-lip) To snap one's finger. One may fillip to the rhythm of music, or to get another's attention. Filliping or finger snapping can be a rude gesture, as ordering a subordinate to hurry up. *"Snapping a fillip, he demanded: 'Make it snappy, Pappy'."*

FILMOGRAPHY – (fil-*MOG*-gruh-fee) (Filmographer) The academic study, the history of motion pictures and its industry. Filmography includes the collection and investigation of movies, photos, essays, press releases, biographies, and interviews with actors, directors, producers, and movie critics. A filmograpgher is a movie expert, a professor of films.

FILTRATION CAMP – (fil-*TRAY*-shun *KAMP*) A precursor to a concentration camp. Filtration or filtering is to remove contaminants, impurities. A camp is a temporary, tentative lodging. A filtration camp is a prison where captive people are intensely investigated, interrogated, examined to determine their political, emotional allegiance. Various degrees of punishment are administered. A filtration camp is a sort of sorting pen, an intimidation, brainwashing reformatory. The Chinese have filtered as many as 2 million Uighurs (*WEE*- gurs), Muslim citizens through filtration and concentration camps so far. Since the commencement of the Russian invasion of the Ukraine (2022), over 45,000 Ukrainians have been kidnapped and confined in Russian filtration camps. The reason is *"de-Ukrainianization"* with the goal of *"Russofication"* – turning them into loyal Russian citizens. The Russians hope to identify those Ukrainians too *"contaminated"* with patriotism, who cannot become pure Russians. Their fate, of course, is sealed. The grand strategy of filtration camps is ethnic cleansing – nationality, identity termination, the eradication of a culture. The impromptu Russian filtration camps are in auditoriums, gymnasiums, any large, roofed enclosure. Permanent camps (a la China's) are in the making. There, the subjugated are photographed, finger-printed, cellphones confiscated, passwords coerced. Those scrutinized as *"salvageable"* are re-settled, scattered about huge Russia as thinly as possible. Incidentally: The Russian filtration camps awakens memories of the Nazi German *"Lebensborn"* program. One aspect of the program was to steal blond, blue-eyed infants and children from the occupied nations (especially Poland), and re-settle them in Germany as loyal fascists.

FINAL OPPORTUNITY – (*FY*-nahl op-er-*TOO*-ni-tee) The last chance; conclusive meeting; ultimate occasion; decisive visit; last reunion; terminal experience. Every who, what, when, where, and why in life has an end time. But the termination time is never revealed. When you kissed her good bye, you didn't know that would be the last kiss. The town you are departing you may never visit again. This may be the final fishing trip you have with him. You may never enjoy grandma's apple pie after today. There are not infinite sunsets to share. This may be your last sunrise. No, there isn't always tomorrow. So, appreciate, cherish today. Act now. Live fully in the here and now. Never delay a kindness or postpone love. Love unshared will result in tears. Therefore, treat people as if you knew a dark secret, that they would be dead tomorrow. Chances are, you may be right. So consider every occasion as the final opportunity. The epitaph of Brandon Bruce Lee (1965 – 1993) speaks poignantly on final opportunities. *"Because we don't know when we will die, we get to think of life as an inexhaustible well. Yet everything happens a certain number of times, and a very small number, really. How many more times will you remember a certain afternoon that's so deeply a part of your being that you can't even conceive of your life without it? Perhaps four or five times more. Perhaps not even that. How many more times will you watch the full moon rise? Perhaps twenty. And yet it all seems limitless."*

FINANCIER – (fee-nan-see-*ER*) A capitalist money man. A professional private profiteer. Financiers are intelligent, clever, devious, heartless, cut-throat who will destroy anyone to make a buck. Donald Trump

(b. 1946) is the quintessential poster-boy for all financiers. Financiers thrive in the noxious free-enterprise atmosphere, the freer the better. In fetid de-regulated air, financiers infectiously exploit the weak, ignorant, and helpless for personal enrichment.

FINANCIER'S CREDO – (fee-nan-see-*ERS CRAY*-dow) *"It takes money to make money."*

FIN DE SIECLE – (fon day *SAY*-kluh) French meaning the end of the 19th century. The end of the 1800's marked the fin de siècle. Therefore, technically, the last year of the fin de siècle was 1900, (as the last year of the 19th century).

FINDING – (*FINE*-ding) In law a conclusion of a court or jury regarding a question of fact.

FINGERING – (*FING*-ger-ing) (Fingered) A fundamental sexual technique in which one inserts at least one digit into a partner's orifice, vagina or anus. The index or middle fingers are employed. Fingering or finger fucking is usually performed on females by males or females. A proficient finger fucker will find the lady's sensitive G-spot, and bring her to orgasm. Of course, the anus is a welcomed location for a finger as well. It is the only option when pleasuring a male. Enter the ass with the finger curved upwards. In the proper depth, one will feel the sensitive prostate gland. Massaging the prostate with incite a profound orgasm with a profuse ejaculation. Fingering is a common and effective foreplay maneuver. A Caveat: Long sharp fingernails can be harmful during fingering. After Thought: Regard the author as a reporter, not necessarily a supporter of these entries.

FINE ARTS – (*FYN ARTS*) Those arts whose primary function is to produce an aesthetic experience of beauty, without regard to what economic or practical use they may be put. Some of the fine arts that may fall under this category are: architecture, poetry, literature, painting, music, dance, sculpture. The fine arts are often contrasted to the mechanical, vocational, or *"useful"* arts. Pedestrian philistines pejoratively regard the fine arts as *"occupations that do not bake bread."* Simple, tasteless people prefer arts-and-crafts to fine arts. A pot is more practical than a poem, a pan is more precious than a painting.

FINIS – (fin-*NEES*) Latin for *"The end."* One may still see the word FINIS at the end of old black-and-white movies from the early 1930's.

FIRE – (*FY*-er) The chemical reaction of oxidation (burning gas). It is a process of transformation and change, by which material elements are rejoined into new combinations. Fire is the only natural phenomenon that moves faster uphill, against gravity. That's because heat rises, so it gets hotter higher. Earth is the only planet we know of that can sustain fire. When the friction of rubbing sticks of wood reaches 300 degrees Fahrenheit, a flame will ignite. The first hominid to use fire was probably Homo erectus (*Peking Man*) in China over 800,000 years ago. The first use of fire was probably to ward-off dangerous predators. (Perhaps 6% of our earliest ancestors were killed by predators.) Fire is the gateway to technology, and therefore to civilization. With fire, mankind made the great leap forward. Fire provided warmth, light, and protection from more powerful animals. Fire cleared the forest, cooked the food, hardened the pot, and smelted the metals. Fire transformed Homo erectus, and Homo sapien into *"Homo technologica."* Incidentally: Fire remained an alchemical enigma, mystery, until the English theologian and chemist, Joseph Priestly (1733

– 1804) discovered the element oxygen (1774). This knowledge at last explained the nature of fire, and propelled chemistry forward, out of the Middle Ages. Footnote: At 1,000°F the fire flame turns white.

FIRE – (*FY*-er) Metaphysically speaking, fire is associated with the energy of life and in many traditions is considered the mouth of the Gods, as it is used to deliver burnt offerings. Fire is the soul driving force, it is energy! Fire is the passion behind creation, the obsession behind destruction. It is the necessary destructive force that brings about new life. Fire is creative and destructive, desirable, and terrible, essential and dangerous.

FIRE BASE – (*FY*-er *BASE*) An American artillery position during the Vietnam War (c. 1960 - 1973). The fire base was expected to command the area around it. They provided support for the infantry in their sector by directing fire along its periphery. The infantry would call-in artillery support when threatened. Fire bases were prime targets for night attacks by the Viet Cong and North Vietnamese Regulars.

FIREBRAND – (*FY*-er-brand) A torch, or stick of burning wood. A firebrand is also an incendiary personality who kindles strife, and agitator, a provocateur.

FIRED – (*FY*-yerd) To be discharged, dismissed, terminated from employment. The term originated in Northern England and Scotland. A fired individual is driven out, originally with fire. An unpopular person in the village would be burned-out. His home would be set aflame, forcing him to depart. That individual was fired by the village.

FIRE DRILL – (*FY*-er *DRILL*) A wooden stick that is drilled into a wooden hole by hand, which creates friction to generate heat and ultimately fire. The *fire bow* uses a string to more efficiently spin the dill. The motion is like playing a violin. A *fire plow* is a wooden board that is vigorously rubbed hot enough to ignite a fire. All of these fire-making techniques depend on friction. A temperature of 300 degrees Fahrenheit must be reached to initiate combustion. All of our ancient ancestors used these techniques as some point in their cultural development. It was also discovered that a fire can be kindled by striking a piece of flint against a piece of iron. The resultant spark is 5,500 degrees Fahrenheit, hotter than the sun.

FIRE LANCE – (*FY*-er lahns) Early Chinese weapon, ancestor of all firearms, which evolved into the gun. The fire lance first appeared in c. 950 CE in the battles among the Chinese warlords. It was simply a bamboo tube sealed on one end, attached to the head of a spear or lance. Gunpowder was poured into the tube and lit, making a short-range flamethrower. It served as an effective shock weapon. Later, pebbles and pellets were inserted into the tube with the gunpowder creating a primitive shotgun. When a larger round stone was used as the projectile, a rudimentary musket was devised. By the 13th century, metal replaces bamboo in the barrel manufacture. Enlarged and mounted on a wagon, the original fire lance became the first cannon. The fire lance as a projectile weapon terrified the invading Mongols in China. The Mongols brought this gun, descendent of the fire lance to Europe in the 13th century. Incidentally: No technological device had evolved and improved faster, in more places than firearms.

FIRE POINT – (*FY*-er *POYT*) The temperature at which burning materials will give off flammable gases that will sustain and feed a fire.

FIRE SALE – (*FY*-er *SAY*-ul) Literally, a special sell off of merchandise somewhat damaged by fire. The products are still usable, perhaps just smoke damaged. The items are sold very cheaply. The term *"fire sale"* is also applied to an emergency sale, to raise money quickly. Incidentally: In February, 2024, the courts of law had finally caught up with the cheat and fraud, Donald Trump (b. 1946). By the end of the month, Trump has been sued and fined to the tune of a half-a-billion-dollars. Trump will have to liquidate many of his properties in a huge fire sale.

FIRE SETTING – (*FY*-er *SET*-ting) Ancient technique to excavate rock or quarry stone. The rock face is heated with fire, then dowsed with cold water. Rock will crack along natural fault lines. For thousands of years before explosives, fire setting moved rock and mined minerals.

FIRESTORM – (*FY*-er *STORM*) A conflagration of such great magnitude that it noticeably creates its own wind conditions – fueling the fire further. A firestorm may be natural, accidental, or intentional. Natural forest fires ignited by lightning may result in a firestorm. Accidental explosions or plane crashes may trigger a firestorm. Aerial bombing with incendiary explosives will result in a firestorm, as happened in Hamburg and Dresden Germany, as well as Tokyo Japan during the Second World War. Tens-of-thousands are incinerated! Incidentally: 500 U.S. B-29 Superfortresses bombed Tokyo, with each plane igniting 1,000 fires. More people were killed than by the atomic bombings of Hiroshima and Nagasaki. Flying low, one bomber flyer said they could smell the burning human flesh. *Hideous!*

FIRESTORM – (*FY*-er *STORM*) A man-made conflagration by incendiary bombing, creating a *Hell on Earth*. Firestorms were intentionally created during World War Two in Hamburg and Dresden, Germany, and in Tokyo, Japan. In an urban setting, thousands of individual buildings are set alight. Explosive bombs were dropped first, followed by incendiary bombs which set the debris on fire. The flames coalesce into a single infernal. The temperature of the firestorm reaches 2,700 degrees Fahrenheit. The vortex or towering tornado of flame sucks-in oxygen, material, and people as fuel. Scorching hurricane winds 150 mph were produced. The heat explodes concrete. Asphalt melts into sticky lakes of blistering hot tar, which glues panicked people to ground to cook alive. Molten copper from rooftops dripped on panicked people below. The charred bodies of mothers and babies were found fused together. Those who sought refuge in basements were suffocated, as the oxygen was sucked-out of the premises by the heat outside. Cellars in Dresden were sometimes filled with melted fat, the people being reduced to lard. At Hamburg, the firestorm had ignited a half hour after the bombing raid. Over 42,600 perished in the flames in a single day. This was a greater death toll than in the entire London Blitz that lasted for 8 months, 1 week, and 2 days! Armaments Minister Albert Speer (1905 – 1981) whispered that 6 more raids like that and German morale would collapse. The firestorm that was ignited in Dresden ultimately consumed about 400,000 lives, for the population was swelled with refugees from the east, fleeing the advancing Russians. Over 170,000 tons of incendiary bombs were dropped on Japan. Over 120,000 died in the Tokyo firestorm, the greatest single day killing in the history of warfare. The interior walls of the houses were made of paper. The U.S. airmen claimed they could smell the cooking, burning flesh up in their planes. General Curtis LeMay (1906 – 1990) is charge of the firebombing told a young officer, Robert McNamara (1916 – 2009) that *"If we lost this war, we would all be tried as war criminals."*

FIRE TETRAHEDRON – (*FY*-er tet-tra-*HEE*-dron) A *"tetrahedron"* is a 4-sided object. The fire tetrahedron is based on the 4 components of igniting and extinguishing a fire. Each component represents a property necessary to sustain a fire: 1. Heat; 2. Fuel; 3. Oxygen; 4. A Chemical Reaction. Extinguishment is based upon removing or hindering any one of these 4 properties. The fire tetrahedron is an advancement of the traditional *"fire triangle"* consisting of only heat, fuel, and oxygen.

FIRE TRIANGLE – (*FY*-er *TRY*-ang-gul) An outdated model for understanding the major components necessary for a fire: heat, fuel, and oxygen. The fire triangle was supplanted by the *"fire tetrahedron"* which adds a 4th component, a chemical chain reaction.

FIREWALL – (*FY*-er-wall) A protective barrier against the spread of a dangerous fire. Firewall has also been applied to any event, thing, or person who serves as a barrier or protection against something undesirable. The term has entered the political lexicon. Politicians consider a firewall to be any type of assurance against a campaign or electoral disaster. For instance, *"This endorsement serves as her firewall against accusations of racism."*

FIRKIN – (*FER*-kin) A unit of measure equivalent to a quarter of a barrel (9 gallons). The term is usually applied in Britain. A firkin is also a small wooden barrel or tub used to store butter or lard.

FIRMAMENT – (*FUR*-ma-ment) The expanse of the sky, the vault of the heavens. This word is taken from the Latin *"firmamentum,"* which bore a dual meaning – both *"sky"* and *"a firm, strong support."* On the surface, the term firmament would seem to better represent the firm solid Earth, rather than the ethereal gaseous sky. The paradox is attributed to translations. In the Old Testament, the Hebrew term *"raqia"* meant both the *"vault of the sky"* and the *"floor of the Earth."* Because the floor of the Earth is solid, in the Syriac dialect of Hebrew, raqia meant *"to make firm"* or *"solid."* Therefore when raqia was translated into Greek as *"stereoma,"* it meant a *"firm"* or *"solid structure."* When stereoma was translated into the late Vulgate Latin as *"firmamentum,"* it came to mean both *"the expense of the sky, heavens,"* and *"a firm, strong support."* So, a firmament refers to <u>a</u> firm strong structure, while <u>the</u> firmament refers to the sky.

FIRST LADY – (*FURST LAY*-dee) (FLOTUS or <u>F</u>irst <u>L</u>ady <u>O</u>f <u>T</u>he <u>U</u>nited <u>S</u>tates) Title for the wife of the U.S. President. President James Buchannan (1791 – 1868) was a bachelor (perhaps gay). His niece, Harriet Lane (1830 – 1903) assumed the domestic duties in the White House. She couldn't be called the President's Wife. Not certain how to address her, James' sister came to be called the *"First Lady,"* (1853). So Harriet became the first First Lady.

FIRST NIGHT – (*FURST NITE*) A repulsive Medieval doctrine that the Lord of the estate had the right to sleep with his serf's brides on their wedding night. Serfs were semi-slaves. They were bound to the landlord's estate as mandatory labor, for a share of the crop. The Lord of the manner practically owned the serf, including his family and wife.

FIRST RESPONDERS – (firust res-*PON*-ders) The initial professional rescue personnel, on the scene of an emergency. Police, firefighters, paramedics, sometimes the National Guard qualify as first responders. They should be trained to react in a crisis, especially where injury is involved. Accidents, explosions, floods, earthquakes, hurricanes, tornados are some of the catastrophes requiring the assistance of first responders. The Covid-19 viral pandemic highlighted the critical importance of first responders.

FISCAL – (*FIS*-cal) Means related to the public treasury or revenues (taxes). Fiscal policy relates to the government's financial matters in general, and include monetary (money) policy, taxation, and spending.

FISCAL CONSERVATISM – (*FIS*-cal con-*SERV*-va-tis-um) Being cautious on spending, parsimonious with tax dollars. Fiscal conservatism is traditionally a Republican trait. But ironically, Republicans are only spendthrifts when the Democrats are in power. That's because conservative Republicans do not want to spend on Liberal Democratic programs and projects that benefit the poor and common folk. Republicans become concerned with the deficit, when spending on social entitlements like Social Security, Medicare, Medicaid, or welfare support. But when Republicans are in power, the deficit no longer matters. They forget fiscal conservatism, and spend lavishly on military build-up, law enforcement, corporate welfare, and taxcuts for the rich. Conservative capitalist Republicans are heartless hypocrites.

FISCAL RESPONSIBILITY – (*FIS*-cal res-pon-si-*BIL*-lit-tee) *"From each according to his ability, to each according to his need."* – Socialist Economist Dr. Karl Marx (1818 – 1883). Or as the American Philosopher John Dewey (1859 – 1952) put it: *"Voters must demand Congress tax wealth not want,"* (1933). Fiscal responsibility is wise taxation and the wise spending of public tax dollars. The health, safety, security, and advancement of the population is the responsibility of those who hold the purse strings. True fiscal responsibility strives for economic growth, starting at the bottom, up. A balanced budget is not as important as a balanced diet, for everyone. To capitalists, conservatives, and their Republican lackeys, fiscal responsibility does not include responsibility to the poor. It is deny the poor so the rich can have more. It is lowering the deficit by eliminating social programs for the needy. The only responsible way to get our fiscal house in order is to tax the rich and their wealthy corporations. Increase wages, reinforce all social welfare programs, eliminate poverty by redistributing the wealth. Find ways to put money in the hands of the poor. To those who cry *"Socialism!"* congratulate them for their insight. A fiscally responsible government distains opulence, and endeavors for modest prosperity for all. Democracy is dependent on distributive justice, which starts with fiscal responsibility. *"We can either have a great amount of wealth concentrated in the hands of a few [fascism], or democracy. We can't have both."* – Supreme Court Justice Lewis Brandies (1856 – 1941).

FISCAL YEAR – (*FIS*-cal *YEAR*) The budgetary year. It is the 12-month financial planning period that may coincide with the calendar year. The U.S. Federal Government's fiscal year runs from October 1st, to September 30th.

FISHING – (*FISH*-ing) (Fish, Fisher, Fishermen) The hunting of cold-blooded aquatic vertebrates with gills, fins, and scales (called fish). Fishing is conducted commercially by the thousands in great nets pulled by factory ships, and individually, by sportsmen with a pole, line, and hook. Fish serve as a primary human food, whether caught industrially or as sport. However, individual fisherman sometimes hook fish then toss them back into the water, a sort of game. No mind is paid to the fact that a fish, like a deer or duck is an animal, with a nervous system that feels pain. The hook tears up the animal's mouth and digestive tract, often causing death after release. We tend to treat fish differently from other animals because they are so alien to us, as is their watery environment. Fishing, like hunting, is primarily a male pursuit. Men go on fishing trips with friends to fraternize in the absence of women. Often, men go fishing alone, intentionally. Unlike females, males are solitary animals at heart. The philosopher Henry David Thoreau (1817 – 1862) realized that *"Some men fish all their lives without knowing it is not really the fish they are after."* Indeed, they are after the meditative peace that can only come from being alone. *"Gone Fish'en"* is the excuse. Most of the time fishing is devoted to doing nothing, sitting, waiting, relaxing, thinking, drifting into reverie. *"Sitting here doing nothing, spring comes, grass grows by itself."* – Zen Buddhist Proverb. Fishing and similar pursuits serve as a necessary mental health therapy for men.

FISHWIFE – (*FISH*-wyf) (Fishwives) A woman who is notoriously fluent in abusive, vulgar obscene language. Throughout the Middle Ages, Billingsgate, London on the Thames River was a fish market. The female fishmongers were an exceedingly rough, tough, ribald lot. The expression emerged and retains today that *"She swears like a fishwife."* Furthermore, the name Billingsgate came to mean abusive language.

FISSION – (*FISH*-shun) Splitting the nucleus of an atom into nuclei of lighter atoms, accompanied by the release of energy. Nuclear power plants and atomic bombs work on this principle. Complex atoms like uranium or plutonium are fissioned to yield more energy. That's because matter is congealed energy. Incidentally: Atomic fission is a 20th century discovery and implementation. However, back in the 9th century, a Turkish scholar had predicted: *"If the smallest particle of matter could be divided, it would release an amount of energy that could destroy a city like Baghdad."* The intuition is chilling.

FISSILE – (*FIS*-sul) Cleavable. Capable of being split or divided. In physics, fissile refers to fissionable, as in nuclear fission.

FISSURE – (*FISH*-shur) A narrow split or opening produced by cleavage or separation of parts. In geology and glaciology, a fissure is a long narrow split or crack in the Earth or ice. Earthquakes cause fissures as due creeping glaciers.

FISSURE ERUPTION – (*FISH*-shur ee-*RUP*-shun) A long low volcanic eruption, not forming a volcanic cone or mountain, but a long crack in the Earth, through which magma breaks the surface as lava. A fissure eruption can be 25 miles in length.

FIST BUMP – (FIST bump) A gesture of greeting or affirmation in which two people lightly tap each other's clenched fists. The fist bump originated in the boxing ring as the fighters symbolize sportsmanship by touching gloves together before the mayhem. A clench fist is a sign of aggression, which makes the first bump an ironic, oxymoronic gesture of friendship. (Incidentally, the handshake is an ancient traditional indication that I come in peace, bearing no weapon in hand.) The fist bump is an alternative to the *"elbow bump,"* which are both substitutes for the traditional handshake during a viral pandemic. The fist bump found popularity during the COVID-19 outbreak of 2020. On meeting, two people clash fists in what seems more like an aggressive gesture than a greeting. The open hand of the handshake is a sign of peace. The clenched fist of the fist bump is a sign of violence. Too, the hand is the germiest part of the body, and the fist is a closed hand. Though sillier, the elbow bump is safer. Incidentally, The warmest, most charming, sacred and safe greeting is the ancient Hindu *"Namaste"* (nam-*OS*-tee). It is the traditional Hindu expression on meeting or parting, used by the speaker, holding hands together in front of the bosom in a prayerful fashion. This Sanskrit word and gesture speaks volumes. It means *"I honor the truth, the light, the peace, the love in you. I salute your divine qualities. The God (ness) in me greets and honors the God (ness) in you. My soul bows to your soul. We are one in God."*

FISTING – (*FIST*-ing) (Fist, Fisted, Fister, Fistee) In the culture of exotic erotica, fisting is inserting the entire hand into one's orifice, either the vagina or rectum. Once the fingers than hand are worked in, the hand clenches into a fist. It is debatable among practitioners whether fisting qualifies as BDSM (Bondage, Dominance, SadoMasochism). But that's academic, especially as the ass and pussy are concerned. Anal sex can be uncomfortable before it feels pleasurable. But fisting is painful, even agonizing, and requires gradual practice, stretching both holes with increasingly larger dildos. Of course, plenty of lubricant is essential. Slop it into the orifice and all over the hand. The fistee must relax the muscles of the entrance. The vagina is a two-way tunnel. But the rectum is one-way only, and that's not in. The sphincter muscles of the rectum are designed for exit only. So entering the rectum through the anus is going against the grain, and therefore more painful. Of course, as with any painful experience, endorphins (natural morphine) will be released by the brain to enable the sufferer to cope better. Surprisingly, the rectum will stretch wider more easily than the vagina, except in childbirth. Prepare for the intrusion with greased fingers first. Then arrange the hand in the duckbill shape for easy entrance. Work it in and out slowly, progressing increasingly deeper. The most difficult part of the journey is the entrance of the knuckles. Once the whole hand has penetrated to the wrist, it clenches into a first. Fisting does not come without a risk. There is always the chance of tearing muscles or herniating the rectal or vaginal wall. The stretching of the sphincter muscle in the rectum diminish its elasticity. The ass hole will expand to a gaping size. The fisted victim may lose continence – the ability to control fecal discharge. Nevertheless, it is the spirit of human nature to want to go where no man or woman has gone before. So goes it with fisting. There is video evidence of fisting up to the elbow! Furthermore, there is a radical rendition of fisting called *"punching."* Unlike the slow, methodical technique of fisting, punching is a lubricated attack, a surge of the clenched fist into the vagina or rectum. Punching is a plunge rather than a violent punch. Nevertheless, punching qualifies as a BDSM activity. We beg the question: why would anyone desire to be fisted? Isn't a dick, finger, or tongue enough? Not for a few extraordinary people. The Philosopher Blaise Pascal (1623 – 1882) had reminded us that: *"The heart has its reasons that reason does not know."* Apparently, in some cases, so does the ass and pussy. *"The only unnatural sex act is that which you cannot perform."* – Sexologist Dr. Alfred Kinsey (1894 – 1956). *"I don't think there is that much difference between a photograph of a fist up someone's ass and a photograph of a carnation in a bowl."* – Photographer Robert Mapplethorpe (1946 – 1989). A Caveat: The author is usually speaking from research, not experience. Whether or not this topic or many others is disagreeable, nevertheless it occurs.

FITLY – (*FIT*-lee) The adverb of fit. Something done fitly is done in a suitable manner, at the proper time. It's fit for the job or occasion.

FITS AND STARTS – (fits and *STARTS*) To progress in short, interrupted, inconsistent intervals with much stopping and starting. *"He worked on the book for years in fits and starts."* Furthermore, *"fit"* refers to a paroxysm or seizure, while *"start"* refers to commencing or beginning. But when the phrase was coined in the 17th century, it simply meant sporadic activity. In *Albion's England* (1586), William Warner (c.

1558 – 1609) wrote: *"His seruants fear his solemn fittes."* Actually, the phrase *"fits and starts"* was originally tautological, (a redundancy) for both words bore the same meaning. In <u>Sermons</u> (1681), Robert Sanderson (1587 – 1663) wrote: *"If thou hast these things only by fits and starts."*

FIVE – (*FYV*) In spiritual numerology the appearance of 3 fives (555) refers to change, transition. It indicates that a major life-change is upon you. This change is the answer to your prayers. Therefore, stay hopeful and joyful.

FIVE EYES – (*FYV EYS*) Five closely allied nations: U.S., U.K., Canada, Australia, and New Zealand. The Five Eyes governments share secret intelligence information that no other nations can see. One nation (U.K.) is in Europe, two (U.S. and Canada) are in North America, two (Australia and New Zealand) are in the South Pacific. All five of these countries consist primarily of Caucasian, Christian populations. They are all English-speaking, and trace their historical origins to the Motherland England. All five had been English colonies. No Asian, African, or Latin American countries are included in the Five Eyes alliance. Incidentally: the <u>FIVE</u> <u>EYES</u> are usually written as *FVEY*.

FIVE FEARFUL D'S – (*FYV FEER*-ful *DEES*) Psychologists attest that the 5 fears that most haunt people are: <u>D</u>eath, <u>D</u>emons, <u>D</u>arkness, <u>D</u>ogs, and <u>D</u>entists.

FIVE LOVES – (*FYV LOAVS*) The five primary precepts that Chinese pre-school children are taught to cherish. The Five Loves are: 1. Love of Motherland; 2. Love of People; 3. Love of Physical Labor; 4. Love of Science; 5. Love of Public Property [read: *Socialism*]. Not bad! Sure beats the capitalist American Love of Money; Love of Competition; Love of Winning; Love of Leisure; and Love of Power.

FIVE MINUTES – (*FYV MIN*-nits) The subliminal benchmark in Western cultures separating the punctual from the tardy. Our patience begins to fray after the 5- minute mark. It is no accident that the analogue clock is divided into 5-minute intervals. The 5-minute limit applies only in *"monochronic"* societies where being on time is important. In Western societies, being late is a social faux pas, a discourtesy. Five minutes is not too early and more than 5 minutes means you're late. For a brief break, we *"take five."*

FIVE PILLARS – (*FYV PIL*-lers) (The 5 Pillars of Islam.) These are the basic acts in Islam, considered mandatory by believers and are the foundation of Muslim life. Islam is *orthopraxian,* meaning religion and social/civil lives are conflated. The 5 Pillars are: *Faith, Prayer, Charity, Fasting,* and *Pilgrimage.* Faith (*Shahada*) is summarized in the declaration: *"There is no god but God, and Muhammed is His messenger."* Prayer (*Salat*): Ritualized adoration with hands on knees 5 times a day. Charity (*Zakat*): Generous contributions must be made to the poor. Fasting (*Sawm*): Abstention from food and drink during daylight hours must be observed during the holy month of Ramadan. Pilgrimage (*Hajj*): At least one trip to Mecca (Saudi Arabia) must be made in a lifetime. After which, the pilgrim forever bears the honorable title of *"Hajji."* Incidentally: Islam is the most aggressive and militant of all the major religions, (contrasted to Buddhism which is the most pacific and tolerant).

FIVE PRECEPTS – (FYV *PREE*-septs) (The Five Precepts of Buddhism.) These are 5 promises to which a practicing Buddhist abides. 1. *"I vow to refrain from taking life."* 2. *"I vow to refrain from taking what is not given."* 3. *"I vow to refrain from sexual misconduct."* 4. *"I vow to refrain from false speech."* 5. *"I vow to refrain from intoxicants which lead to carelessness."* Incidentally: Buddhism is the most tolerant and genuinely pacific of all the major religions.

FIX – (*FIKS*) To repair, mend, put back into good order. The word *"fix"* is an Americanism, coined by our most intellectual, multifaceted President, Thomas Jefferson (1743 – 1826). Colonial America did not have an industrial base to manufacture replacement products. That was an ocean away in England. If something broke in America, it had to be *fixed.* Indeed, *"Necessity is the mother of invention."* This situation helped to nurture and sense of self-reliance and ingenuity in Americans.

FIXATION – (fiks-*SAY*-shun) (Fixate, Fixating, Fixated) A psycho-emotional obsession. An unreasonable preoccupation with one subject, issue, object, or person. A fixated person is fascinated, infatuated, spellbound by the subject of her compulsion. Stalkers are fixated on another individual. It's a mental addiction. The fixated victim is denied a normal life, being possessed by his attraction, obsession. The mind continuously circles on one track, thinking of nothing else. It is a debilitating way to live. A clinical fixation is a neurotic condition requiring professional help.

FIXED INCOME – (*FIKS'D IN*-cum) Income that does not increase, even though prices go up. Senior citizens dependent on Social Security survive on a fixed income. This accounts for tens-of-millions of our elderly and handicapped. Inflation, utility rate hikes, medical and drug costs, rent increases eat away at their disposable income. Millions live in poverty, on the mere substance level. They are considered a tax burden, *"takers"* on a fixed entitlement by conservative Republicans. On the other extreme are wealthy people whose income is fixed through inheritance or Wall Street dividends. *"I'm on a fixed income." "Yah! Fixed handsomely on Wall Street."*

FIXER – (*FIKS*-er) (Fix) One who repairs what's broken, usually used in a pejorative sense. In capitalist business/politics, a fixer is a consciousless, unscrupulous trouble-shooter who performs damage control for rich criminal clients. The fixer is usually a disreputable attorney who puts out the fire when his wealthy patron is boiling in hot water. The fixer acts as an attack dog. He bullies, bribes, and intimidates to cover his client's filthy tricks and tracks. A textbook example of a fixer was Meyer Lansky (1902 – 1983). This Jewish lawyer was Mafia boss Charles *"Lucky"* Luciano's (1897 – 1962) corrupt fixer. Donald Trump (b. 1946) had a quartet of notorious fixers, unscrupulous lawyers all. In his early career there was the godfather of depraved fixers, Roy Cohen (1927 – 1986). (Incidentally, gay Roy died of AIDS.) Later contemptable (albeit repentant) Michael Cohen (b. 1966) served the nasty role. Cohen helped create the illegal Trump financial empire, and concealed Trump's sexual indecencies. Michael was *"thrown under the bus"* by Trump, and went to prison. Next, *"mayor-cum-conniver"* Rudy Giuliani (b. 1944) filled the hole. Giuliani laundered Trump's money and sought dirt on Trump's political enemies. Finally, perfidious Attorney General William Barr (b. 1950) became Trump's *"ass-wiper."* Barr used his office to quash investigations into Trump's criminality and friends. Hopefully, Barr to be disbarred after Trump's demise. Fixers use and abuse the law to prevent vile, evil people the justice they deserve.

FJORD – (fee-*ORD*) A Norwegian geographic term for a long, narrow, deep inlet or gorge of the sea between steep mountain slopes. The fjords were carved by glaciers.

FLACCID – (*FLAS*-sid) Soft, limp, flabby, lacking any firmness. A flaccid penis, (<u>E</u>rectile <u>D</u>ysfunction) (ED) is a sexual challenge, handicap, (*"so they tell me"*).

FLAG – (*FLAG*) A piece of cloth varying in size, shape, color, and design, usually attached to the end of a pole or on a rope. A flag is a standard symbolizing a nation, state, or organization. Too often, undue and undeserved emotion is invested in the flag. People have died protecting the flag, a piece of cloth. The flag is not endowed with any spiritual or magical properties, like a totem pole. It is merely a form of address tag identifying from where a vessel, company, or group of people hail. A building, embassy, or territory's ownership or allegiance can be identified by its flag. Alfred Korzybski (1879 – 1950), the great Polish semanticist insisted the *"The map is not the territory."* Neither is the flag. Incidentally: Only 3 flags in the world do not include the colors of the American flag (red, white, and blue). Those countries are Libya, Mauritania, and Jamaica.

FLAGELLOMANIA – (fla-jell-o-*MAIN*-ee-a) A morbid obsession with whipping or flogging. Flagellomania is a sadomasochistic impulse, with psychosexual roots. It may be generated by guilt, shame, and the desire to be punished or administer punishment.

FLAGGING – (*FLAG*-ing) (Flagger) (also hanky code, handkerchief code, bandana code) Flagging is a system of color-coded cloth, worn on the body for non-verbal communication of one's sexual interests and fetishes. Flagging is reminiscent of semaphore communication, sending messages with different flags. Flagging is secret correspondence system. It is not used by people who are *"sexual outsiders."* It is utilized by people who wish to communicate only with others of similar sexual preferences, excluding all others. Closet gays, BDSM (<u>B</u>ondage, <u>D</u>ominance, <u>S</u>ado<u>M</u>asochism) enthusiasts, peculiar fetishists, others in the exotic erotic community may attempt to meet mates through flagging. The rules or code of flagging are complicated. For example, displaying a dark blue hanky indicates interest in anal sex. Worn in the left rear pocket identifies one as the insertive partner, while in the right rear pocket signifies one as the receptive partner. A black hanky identifies one as a sadomasochist connoisseur. A Dom (<u>D</u>ominator) will wear in kerchief on the left side, while the Sub (<u>S</u>ub<u>m</u>issive) will wear it on the right side. A light blue hanky says you love blowjobs, oral sex on the penis. A red kerchief says you are into fisting (inserting the fist up the ass). Again, the right side says I take it, while the left side says I give it. If the hanky is worn tied to the belt, in the middle rear, that means I will take it and dish it out. It would appear that being colorblind would be a dangerous handicap for a flagger. Incidentally: Flagging was very prominent in the 1970s, but it goes back to the 1849 gold rush and San Francisco. Gay prospectors sought gay prospects by signifying with bandanas. The Wild West suffered a shortage of females. So at barn dances, miners, cowboys, and railroad workers had to dance with each other. A code developed in which the men wearing blue bandanas preferred their male role, whereas the fellow who wore the red bandana submitted to play the female. Flagging was thus devised.

FLAGON – (*FLAY*-gon) A large bottle with a handle, narrow neck, and spout. Flagons were used to hold wine, cider, rum, liquors.

FLAGRANT – (*FLAY*-grant) (Flagrancy) Unabashedly open, glaringly noticeable. To throw a punch is a flagrant penalty in football.

FLAGRANTE BELLO – (flay-*GRAN*-tay *BEL*-lo) Latin for *"during war."*

FLAGRANTE DELICTO – (flay-*GRAN*-tay dee-*LIC*-tow) Latin for *"while the crime is going on," "in the very act."* Too, flagrante delicto also means *"while having illicit sex."*

FLAGS OF CONVENIENCE – (*FLAGS* of con-*VEEN*-yens) The corporate capitalist habit of registering merchant and cruise ships in a country other than the corporation's or owner's home nation. With foreign registry, the vessels fly the foreign flag. That's why dinky Panama and Liberia have such great armadas on the open seas. Registering in tiny or underdeveloped countries enables the ship owners to pay no corporate income tax. Too, them can skirt around crucial regulations concerning safety, labor, sanitation, everything. These countries, often poor, therefore corrupt, sell licenses to the ship owners, without any inspection or rules, not giving a damn about the crew, passengers, environment, or general security. The merchant or cruise lines can hire the cheapest crews, at the lowest wages, preserving the greatest profits. Without unions, the ship's crew is a polyglot of diverse foreigners, a babble of languages unable to communicate, minimally trained, and worthless in an emergency. *Carnival Cruise Lines* and her *"harmonized"* [read: *monopolized*] subsidiaries are the worst offenders. *Carnival* is the *Walmart* of cruise line industry. It is a greedy American company, flying the Panamanian flag, subject to Panamanian law. Very convenient and profitable for the fat-cat stockholders, berthed in Miami. Panama, Liberia, Marshall Islands, Bahamas, Malta, Singapore, Hong Kong, Cyprus, and many small counties sell flags of convenience. Incidentally: If a behemoth *Carnival* cruise ship is in trouble on the Caribbean, let it call the Panamanian, rather than the American Coast Guard or Navy. Post Script: On June 10, 2019, a Norwegian and Saudi Arabian oil tankers were attacked in the Persian Gulf. The Saudi ship flew the Panamanian flag, and the Norwegian ship flew the flag of the Marshall Islands. Nevertheless, the American taxpayers had to pay for the rescue by the U.S. Navy. Where's the proud Panamanian navy? Where's the naval forces of the mighty Marshall Islands? Will Norway, Saudi Arabia, Panama, or the Marshall Islands reimburse the U.S.? It's so convenient, to fly a flag of convenience, when you expect to be conveniently rescued by the Americans. Too, in a financial crash, let *Carnival Cruiselines* depend on the African Liberians bail them out, perhaps with bananas and coconuts.

FLAGSTONE – (*FLAG*-stohn) A flat, somewhat wide rock shaped for a pavement. Walkways, terraces, paths are paved with sandstone, usually shale or flagstone. Paving a garden path with flat but irregularly shaped flagstone creates a quaint natural appearance.

FLAMETHROWER – (*FLAYM*-throh-wer) A dreadful military weapon that pisses streams of burning napalm incinerating its target or victim. In politics, a flamethrower is a care-less arsonist. He or she has no agenda, no commitments, no scruples, and no conscience. They are evil-anarchists who want to burn- down the house. MAGA-Republicans or Trumpublicans in Congress are flamethrowers. They do not intend to legislate, but to annihilate. Pyromaniac MAGA Mike Johnson (b. 1972), this month's Republican Speaker of the House (October 2023) is a flamethrower.

FLAMMABILITY BARRIER – (flam-ma-*BIL*-lit-tee *BEAR*-ree-er) An elevation point up a mountain where forest fires normally could not ignite, because the environment is too damp. The slow, gradual melting of mountain snow normally keeps the upper reaches of the mountain quite wet. However global warming is interfering with this natural process. Mountain snowpacks are melting earlier, too early and quickly, leaving the brush and woods drier in the summer. Now, forest fires are surpassing the 8,000-foot mark on mountains. The burning of tree canopies exposes the forest floor to more warm sunlight, making the mountain drier and more susceptible to great conflagrations.

FLASHDRIVE – (*FLASH*-dryv) (Also Thumb Drive, Memory Stick or Drive, Cruise Glide, USB Drive.) A portable, thumb-size, solid-state hard drive that can be inserted into a computer (USB port) for storage and retrieval of data. The amount of information that can be stored on this 2-inch devise is astounding. Incidentally: The technical name for the thumb drive is UBS, an initialism for <u>U</u>niversal <u>S</u>erial <u>B</u>us.

FLASHFLOODS – (flash-*FLUDS*) A sudden, destructive rush of water, particularly down a narrow gully or over a sloping surface, caused by heavy rainfall. Dry, desert regions are especially susceptible to flash flooding. The parched, baked, hard ground cannot absorb the sudden torrent. Hilly Central Texas is the flashflood alley of the U.S.A.

FLASHING – (*FLASH*-ing) (Flasher, Flashed) The momentary display of bare female breasts. Flashing is a sexual tease technique in which a woman quickly lifts her shirt or bra up over her breasts, then back down. It is over in an instant or a *"flash."* A variant of flashing involves the rapid exposure of genitals (female or male). Ass-flashing is technically called *"mooning."* Female flashers are usually well lubricated with alcohol. Tipsy or not, flashing stimulates a degree of sexual arousal in the performer. Flashing is a harmless, amusing activity that should not be tainted with condemnation or shame. However, it can prove to be risky. Flashing may give aroused males the impression that the lady had issued an invitation. Too, if overly publicized, the flasher may be jeopardizing job or promotion opportunities, (or not, depending on the personality of the boss). Of course, flashing is illegal exposure, and can result in jail time, and being branded a *"sex offender"* for the rest of your life!

FLASHMOB – (*FLASH*-mob) A large gathering summonsed instantaneously via mass social media communications. In a flash, a social or political demonstration or protest can be organized. This ability is a dire threat to unpopular right-wing governments. That is why in fascistic sates, mass mediate is government controlled and carefully monitored. Besides censorship, the number of people with which one can correspond is limited in dictatorships. This is to prevent the ability to deploy a flashmob, which can become riotous, escalate into a revolt, and spawn a revolution.

FLASHOVER – (*FLASH*-oh-ver) The sudden simultaneous ignition of combustible materials in a closed space when the materials reach their fire point. This is the temperature at which the materials will burst into flames. With paper, for instance, the flashover point is Fahrenheit 451°.

FLAT BREAD – (*FLAT BRED*) The staff of life. Flat bread is an ancient and universal victual baked in multiple varieties in every culture on Earth. Flat bread is made from every type of grass-grain, seeds, and tubers. It can be leavened (includes yeast) or unleavened. What they all have in common is the flat, round, pancake shape. At least 39 varieties have been identified in Europe, 26 in the Middle East and Africa, 56 in Asia, and 12 in the Americas. Some familiar varieties are *pita* (wheat) from the Mediterranean, *matzo* (wheat) from Israel, *tortilla* (corn) from Mexico, *bammy* (cassava) from Jamaica, *oplatek* (o-*PWOT*- tek) (wheat) from Poland. In Jordan's Harrat ash Shaam (the Black Desert) in 2018, charred breadcrumbs were found at an ancient camp site dating back to 12,400 BCE (over 14,400 years ago). This was about 4,000 years before the discovery of agriculture. Analysis revealed that the hunters-and-gatherers picked wild barley, oats, einkorn wheat and tubers to make their flat bread.

FLATLANDER – (*FLAT*-land-ehr) A somewhat pejorative designation made by mountain folk toward all others. Flatlander is a clannish term of highlanders. There is more to this epithet than a geographical residency. The mountain dweller perceives the flatlander as an elitist, better educated, wealthier, and biased against *"Hillbillies."* In fact, *"Flatlander"* is a counter-pejorative to *"Hillbilly."*

FLATLINE – (*FLAT*-lyn) To flatline is to die. Flatline is a hospital term meaning all vital signs are gone. The medical machinery that monitors the brain, heart, lungs, blood pressure indicate no activity. There are no peaks and troughs being recorded – just a straight flat line of lifelessness.

FLAT TAX – (*FLAT TAKS*) A wealthy capitalist's fiscal *"wet dream."* The same percentage of tax levied across all incomes, from rich to poor. It is a deceptive ruse of the rich. If everyone paid 15% on their income, millionaires would still be obscenely rich, the middle class would be hurting, and the poor destroyed. That's because 15% wouldn't bother the rich, but will kill everyone else. Too, the poor will never clamor for higher taxes on the rich, for they would suffer all the more. The vulgar rich love to brag about how much they pay in taxes – thousands or millions. We don't care how much they pay. We want to know how much they have left – Millions? Billions? Trillions? That's too much! They flat-out must pay more taxes. A flat tax is a wolf in sheep clothing, and the wealthy know it. The only fair tax is a still progressive tax, free of all loopholes.

FLATTERY – (*FLAT*-ter-ree) Insincere praise, disingenuous adulation. Flattery is often a hypocritical attempt to manipulate an individual. Boastful people, rich or poor, concealing low self-esteem are most susceptible to flattery. One such individual is President Donald Trump (b. 1946). He is dangerously vulnerable to flattery from foreign leaders who manipulate him. Trump childishly believes he is being honored, when in fact, he is being naively played, on the world stage.

FLEA MARKET – (*FLEE MAR*-ket) A resale establishment, a market, often outdoors, consisting of a number of individual stalls selling old or used articles, curios, crafts, antiques, junk, treasures, cut-rate merchandize, you name it. Like a museum, a flea market is a fascinating place. There you can find great bargains on everything you never needed. Nevertheless, the excursion is an adventure. The term *"flea market"* entered English in 1910. It was named after the great Parisian flea market, the *"marche aux puces,"* meaning *"walk-through flea market."* Indeed, there is a connection between the flea market and insect infestation. Much of the used, marketed merchandize was flea infested. In a <u>New York Times</u> article entitled *"In Europe"* (February 8, 1922), Cardinal Dennis Dougherty (1865 – 1951) of Philadelphia wrote of the Paris flea market: *"Because there are so many second-hand articles sold of all kinds that they are believed to gather fleas."* *"Sleep tight. Don't let the bedbugs bite."*

FLEROVIUM – (fle-*ROW*-vee-um) (Fl) A transuranic element (#114) named after the Russian physicist Georgy Flyorov, founder of the Joint Institute for Nuclear Research in Russia. Flerovium was discovered in 1999. The half-life or life span of flerovium is 2.6 seconds before it decays. Flerovium's only use is in nuclear experimentation.

FLESH – (*FLESH*) Meat or animal tissue comprised of protein, as distinguished from plant tissue comprised of carbohydrate. Meat is an essential source of life- sustaining protein for carnivores, meat-eaters. But in the process, herbivores , plant eaters must sacrifice their lives.

FLESH-EATING DISEASE – (*FLESH EE*-ting dih-*ZEEZ*) Medically called *"Necrotizing fasciitis"* (*NEK*-ro-tyz-ing fas-see-*EYE*-tis) *"Necrotizing"* (necrosis) means dying, in this case, rotting away. Fascia is the internal connective tissue. *"Fasciitis"* is the inflammation of the fascia. A number of bacteria and fungi may trigger a necrotizing fasciitis, the eating away of the flesh. Flesh-eating disease is quite rare. People most at risk have pre-existing conditions like a compromised immune system from an illness, disease, or substance abuse. The infection enters the body through the smallest scratch, cut, burn, or puncture wound – any break in the skin. The infected area inflames, turns red and purple, and becomes very painful. Fever and vomiting ensues. The swollen skin ultimately breaks open as an ulcer that grows like a sinkhole on the body as the soft tissue putrefies. The most commonly affected areas are the legs, and the perineum, (the area between the anus and genitals). The decay (necrosis) spreads rapidly. Gangrene is one of the flesh-eating diseases. Endotoxins released by the bacteria accelerates the tissue decomposition. A cocktail of antibiotics is administered, but surgery is the only solution. Often infected muscles must be extracted and limbs amputated. Without treatment, death in inevitable from flesh-eating disease. *"Their flesh will rot while they are standing on their feet...."* – Zechariah 14:12 (The Good Book).

FLESHPOT – (*FLESH*-pot) A place providing luxurious and uninhibited sexual pleasure. A fleshpot is usually considered to be a house of prostitution.

FLESH TONE – (*FLESH* tohn) The shade of one's skin, depending on the amount of subcutaneous melanin present. Flesh tone corresponds to racial type, which was produced by environmental factors in the distant past. In the human family, flesh tone is a superficial factor, which provides welcomed diversity to the population. However, in a society where race spelled the difference between master and slave, acceptance and denial, skin color, flesh tone holds a prominent place in the collective psyche. The Caribbean is such a society. In 1955, *The Star* newspaper of Jamaica published an editorial entitled *"Ten Types One People."* A controversy arose around beauty contests, and what constituted a *"beautiful"* Jamaican woman. *The Star* delicately and with dignity found loveliness across the color spectrum of flesh tones: *"Ebony"* (black); *"Mahogany"* (colored); *"Satinwood"* (East Indian); *"Lotus"* (Chinese); *"Pomegranate"* (Mediterranean, Syrian-Jewish); *"Appleblossom"* (Caucasian).

FLETCHER – (*FLET*-cher) An artisan who manufactures arrows.

FLEXIBLE EXCHANGE – (FLEX-ib-bul ex-*CHAINJ*) A floating foreign exchange rate. It is a system that relies on supply and demand to determine the value of one currency in terms of another. The price of foreign currencies change from day to day, hour to hour. The flexible exchange rate is designed to provide maximum profit for the capitalist banks. Prior to 1971, the exchange rates were fixed in relations to each other and stable. Now the entire system is fixed to profit the capitalist bankers.

FLEXIBILITY – (flex-ib-BIL-li-tee) Being adaptable, able to adjust to change, to modify one's attitude and actions. The flexible are capable of bending without breaking. Flexible people do not get bent out of shape. "Bend like the willow, don't be rigid like the oak." – Zen Buddhist Proverb.

FLIES/FLYS – (*FLYS/FLYS*) The root word *"fly"* can be either a verb or a noun in a sentence. If *"fly"* is used as a noun, the plural form of that noun is *"flys."* For example: *"There were a lot of flys gathering around the trashcan." "The flys on their pants were open."* Notice that *"fly"* in these two examples are things, not actions. Now then, if *"fly"* is used as a verb, the plural in the third person singular is *"flies."* For example: *" The bird flies across the open ocean." "Everyone watches as the ball flies across the court."* In the above example, *"fly"* is performing the action of a singular subject. *"Time flies like an arrow. Fruit flys like a banana."*

FLIGHT – (*FLYT*) (Fly, Flying) The locomotion of the birds above. For a land- based creature like man, flight has become an underappreciated marvel of science, engineering, and technology. It is a miracle of physics. Flight has been a dream of mankind, as early as man was capable of dreaming. Every mythology and religion of every culture or civilization included human flight in some form. Flight entails leaving the ground, levitating, soaring, drifting, floating, maneuvering in the sky, in defiance of gravity. It is atmospheric travel. To our ancient ancestors the creation of a flying machine was comparable to the creation of a time machine today. Eventually, astonishingly, our ancestors succeeded. The attainment of flight had taken two routes – lighter-than-air, and heavier-than-air ships. A lighter-than-air ship is a hot air or hydrogen/helium filled balloon. It floated at the mercy of the wind. Adding an engine to the balloon made it a zeppelin, giving directional control to man. A heavier-than-air ship is a kite. It stays aloft due to air pressure on the wings – higher pressure below, lower pressure above the wings. Adding an engine to the kite created an aeroplane. Columbus (1451 – 1506) could have flown from Spain to America. Moses (c. 1391 – c. 1271 BCE) could have flown from Egypt to the Promised Land. The physics was the same, but the technology was missing. Flight revolutionized human life in wonderful and dreadful ways. It had shrunken the globe making all members of the human family neighbors. Today, the longest flights anywhere in the world are just over 17 hours, nonstop. (Longest flight today is the 18 hours, 50 minutes journey from Singapore to New York City.) This is amazing, wonderful. On the other hand, only a decade after the invention of the heavier-than-air ship, flight was weaponize in World War One (1914 – 1918). Cities were decimated in World War Two (1939 – 1945), bombed by airplanes, including the delivery of the first atomic bombs. With flight, no corner of this planet is safe from attack. This is distressing, dreadful. With intercontinental nuclear missile flight, civilization, humanity, life on Earth is in serious peril. *I have always felt it is my destiny to build a machine that will allow man to fly."* – Leonardo da Vinci (1452 – 1519). *"Thank God men cannot fly, and lay waste the sky as well as the earth."* – American Philosopher Ralph Waldo Emerson (1803 – 1882).

FLIGHT DISTANCE – (*FLYT DIS*-tans) The space or distance a wild animal will allow between itself and a human before it flees or attacks. Different animals have different fight-or-flight reactions. Taming a wild animal amounts to shortening the flight distance in incremental steps, lessening the fear and space until it amounts to zero. At that point, the animal allows man to approach, touch, handle or mount. Food is essential in the taming process. Taming or domesticating is altering the animal's natural inclinations or instincts and grafting onto the creature's psyche human mannerisms. Of course, this is unnatural. The goal of taming is to serve human needs. Tamed or domesticated animals are not totally submissive and dependent. They are not yet pets. Incidentally: Wild animals did not fear man until the invention of projectile weapons (throwing spear, sling, bow-and-arrow). These weapons put distance between man and beast, taking away the animal's advantage of tooth and claw.

FLIGHTMARE – (*FLYT*-mere) The horror that has become commercial flying. The airline industry has made flying a nightmare. That's because of their noxious capitalism. The airlines have put profit above safety, efficiency, fairness, convenience, comfort, courtesy, customer service, and common sense. Costs rise as comforts decline. Delays, cancellations, lost luggage have made flying a nerve-raking experience. Many people would rather go to the dentist than the airport. In today's world, people must fly. But the airlines are private, for profit industries. They don't care that people need to fly. They care about making money for their stockholders. Transportation, flying is too essential to be governed by the profit motive, which is intent on giving the consumer less and less for more and more. The capitalist airlines industry must be nationalized, taken over by the government. Flying is too important to be left in private hands. Again, the problem is capitalism, the solution is Socialism.

FLIGHT RISK – (*FLYT* risk) A criminal suspect who is not trusted to appear at his trial. As security that an indicted, arraigned suspect appears in court on her trial date, collateral is required in the form of bail money. Fail to show and you lose all the money. Too, you become a wanted fugitive, a criminal even before the original trial. Defendants judged to be flight risks must sit in jail until their trial. This may mean several months of imprisonment. What if the defendant is found not guilty? Too bad. They suffered imprisonment for nothing but a bad reputation. This is a moral, but not illegal miscarriage of justice. (Such cases should be compensated by the state.) Incidentally: Donald J. Trump (b. 1946) is accused of 91 felonies in three legal jurisdictions. Trump is presently free pending trials, out on a bail-less bail. The self-proclaimed billionaire did not have to fork-up a cent. Equal justice under the law? Trump is not considered to be a flight risk. Oh Yah? Better think twice – three times! Look at his prospects from Trump's perspective. Trump is saddled with 91 criminal counts, any one of which can land him in a cage for the rest of his life. Would Trump prefer living and dying in prison, unable to visit his properties or enjoy his tens-of-millions? Or live free in a foreign country, much more frugally with only a few millions? Indeed Trump is a flight risk, (if he is not elected President). He will attempt to escape, defect, seek sanctuary in a friendly foreign land, a country without an extradition treaty with the U.S. In his own words, Trump declared: *"Imagine, if I lose, I might have to leave the country."* Russia and China are out of the question as hostile nations. But Switzerland, Iceland, Bolivia, Ecuador, and Qatar are possibilities. However, any nation that friendly to Trump, will not be so friendly to America. Trump knows too much from his time as President and his stash of secret documents to be allowed to defect. Therefore, the FBI must be alert if Trump is making any large money transfers. Trump's passport will be seized, and he may be placed under house arrest at Mar-a-Lago until his imprisonment.

FLIMFLAM – (*FLIM*-flam) (Flimflammer) A trick or deception, especially a swindle or confidence game involving skillful persuasion or clever manipulation of a victim. The flimflam poster child has to be Donald J. Trump (b. 1946). The term flimflam entered English in the 1530s from Scandinavia. In Old Norse, the word *"flim"* meant a lampoon or ridicule. *"Mere flimflam stories, and nothing but shams and lies."* – Miguel de Cervantes (1547 – 1616).

FLINDERS – (*FLIN*-ders) Small fragments, splinters, slivers of anything.

FLIP – (*FLIP*) (Flipped, Flipping, Flipper)To turn over, to suddenly move over to the other side. Flip is also a legal vernacular for a frightened defendant who suddenly moves over to the side of the prosecution. In complicated cases, a minor defendant, found guilty, will flip as part of a plea bargain, to lighten his sentence. She will agree to cooperate with the prosecution, and turn over state's evidence. The goal of the state is to use the little fish, to get the big fish. The *"flippers"* will testify against their former criminal boss. By September, 2018, Federal Prosecutor Robert Mueller (b. 1945) succeeded in getting Trump co-conspirators Michael Flynn (b. 1958), George Papadopoulous (b. 1987), Michael Cohen (b. 1966), Rick Gates (b. 1972), Paul Manafort (b. 1949), and a host of other Trumpsters to flit. It is hoped that they will testify against the most perfidious racketeer and traitor, President Donald Trump (b. 1946). Incidentally: In his astounding ignorance, President Trump suggested legislation to outlaw flipping.

FLIP-FLOP – (*FLIP* flop) (Flip-Flopped, Flip-Flopping, Flip-Flopper) To flap in the wind, one way then the other. A sudden or unexpected reversal, as of direction, belief, attitude, or policy. Flip-flop has become a political term for a politician who contradicts himself. A flip-flopper will support one side of an issue one day, then move to the opposite side the next day. A flip-flopping politician is usually trying to be all things to all people, with no true convictions. Donald Trump (b. 1946), Republican Presidential candidate in 2016 flip-flopped more on the issues than any other candidate in U.S. History. He had officially changed his party affiliations 7 times. This indicates a total lack of any core values. A flip-flopper like Trump is motivated by pure expediency, what will benefit him in the moment. As President, Trump has reneged on every major campaign promise made to his *"low-information"* [read: *stupid*] supporters.

FLIRT – (*FLERT*) (Flirting, Flirted, Flirtation) Playful dalliance. To display an amorous or sexual interest in another. A flirtation is a lighthearted sexual foreplay, utilizing words, gestures, innuendo, and body language. The purpose of flirting is to transmit the message that I am romantically or just sexually interested in you. Flirtation is an essential communication device to convey attraction, a prelude to a romantic relationship. But flirtation comes with a risk, for one's esteem can be jeopardized. The person subjected to the flirtation may be flattered or affronted. Embarrassing rejection may be the outcome. Much depends on the personality of the person perused. Too, there exists an ethereal line, where flirting become sexual harassment.

FLOAT – (*FLOHT*) To be buoyant on water or lighter than air. To float is to drift, perhaps aimlessly. The verb, *"to float,"* has been adopted into the political lexicon. Politicians, always fearful of negative public opinion, like to float an idea out to the public in order to gage public response. It is a stealthy way to conduct an unofficial opinion poll, without committing oneself. Cagey politicians will float *"weather balloons"* bearing casual comments in order to test the direction of the political winds. President Donald Trump (b. 1946) was most proficient in this regard. Trump floated the idea of serving a third Presidential term, or becoming President for life. Trump floated the possibility of defecting if he had lost the election. Trump floated the idea of pardoning himself. Floating ideas as casual comments is the ploy of cowards.

FLOAT COPPER – (*FLOHT COP*-per) Nuggets of pure copper from Northern Michigan pushed south by glaciers, deposited at the glacial end point.

FLOATERS – (*FLOHT*-ters) In ophthalmology (eye medicine), floaters are microscopic dust particles that float in the fluid covering the eye. Floaters drift past our field of vision like ghosts, resembling blurry bacteria under the microscope.

FLOGGING – (*FLAWG*-ging) (Flog, Flogged) In this instance, not being punished by the lash, but by the test. Flogging is doctor's slang for ordering every imaginable test to diagnose an illness. The term flogging derives from the proverb: *"Flogging a dead horse."* In other words, a waste of time and money – the patient's money. Flogging may be another capitalist ploy to drive-up the cost of the treatment. Alternatively, the doctor may flog out of fear about being sued for not testing. *"I have to say I'm all for public flogging."* – Right-Wing Political Commentator Ann Coulter (b. 1961).

FLOOD – (*FLUD*) A destructive inundation. Floods kill more people than hurricanes, tornadoes, wind, lightning combined. Natural floods are caused by excessive rainfall which overflows rivers and lakes; storm surge from the sea, caused by a hurricane; or tsunamis caused by an earthquake. Floods are measured in *"acre feet."* That's the amount of water needed to cover one acre of land with 1 foot of water. Incidentally: About 18 inches of water will cause a car to float.

FLOOD BASALT – (*FLUD BAS*-salt) Runny liquid lava, that hardens into heavy, hard, black basalt rock. Basalt is the foundational rock for the Earth's crust. The ocean is in a depression because it is weighted-down by a heavy basalt floor.

FLOODPLAIN – (*FLUD*-playn) A landform of level, fertile ground built by sediment deposited by a river. A floodplain makes excellent farmland, provided the river does not flood. Eventually, it will, with devastating results. After all, the floodplain is a natural spillover for the river's excess.

FLOOR FISSURES – (*FLOOR FISH*-shurs) Great cracks in the ocean floor, over 45,000 miles around the globe. These are the boundaries of plates and ocean floor splitting that propels plate movement. Superheated mineral water vents erupt at floor fissures. These vents are called black smokers or dragon chimneys. This is a volcanic energy source. Crabs and giant tub worms over 10 feet long thrive in this scalding soup. They are the world's fastest growing invertebrates.

FLOP SWEAT – (*FLOP* swet) A sudden profuse outbreak of perspiration due to the stress of humiliation. People flop sweat when they are publicly embarrassed [read: em-*BARE-ASS*ed]. Watch Republican Congressman Kevin McCarthy (b. 1965) flop sweat when asked about his role in the January 6 attack on the Capitol Building and government.

FLORIMANIA – (flor-ri-*MAY*-nee-a) (Florimanic) One who is crazed over flowers.

FLORUIT – (*FLOR*-roo-it) Latin for *"he (or she) flourished."* Floruit is used to indicate when a person lived, when the exact birth and death dates are unknown. It is abbreviated *"fl."* or *"flor."* For example: Rev. E. Jack Yulate (fl. 1669).

FLOTSAM – (*FLOAT*-sum) The wreckage of a ship and its cargo found floating on the water, *involuntarily* lost at sea. Unlike jetsam, (voluntarily discarded), flotsam remains the legal property of the ship.

FLOTUS – (*FLO*-tus) An acronym for First Lady Of The United States, or the wife of the President. Ironically the 1st First Lady was not a wife. President James Buchanan (1791 – 1868) never married. (James was probably gay.) His niece, Harriet Lane (1839 – 1903) performed the White House social duties expected of the President's wife. Harriet called herself the *"First Lady."* There have been some notable First Ladies in American history: Dolly Madison (1768 – 1849), Mary Todd Lincoln (1818 – 1882), Edith Wilson (1872 – 1961), Eleanor Roosevelt (1884 – 1962), Jaqueline Kennedy (1929 – 1994), Hilary Clinton (b. 1947), and Michelle Obama (b. 1964), to name a few. All had championed some noble cause with which we associate them. Melania Trump (b. 1970 in Slovenia) assumed the position of FLOTUS in 2017. Melania is the first First Lady who will not reside in the White House. She will live with her son Barron Trump (b. 2006) in the ostentatious Trump Tower in New York City. Young Barron is autistic, a condition the Trumps refuse to publicly acknowledge. Perhaps President and dad Donald is ashamed? Barron must attend an elite special ed. school. That's fine. He's lucky. But the Trump's denial denies Melania a perfect cause to champion as the nation's FLOTUS. On the other hand, helping the handicapped is contrary to the Republican mission statement. So gorgeous Melania's hands may be cuffed.

FLOUNCE – (*FLOWNS*) To move about in an excited, exaggerated, convulsive manner. *"He flounced about like a burning Hercules."*

FLOW – (*FLOH*) A psychological/parapsychological state of perfect performance. Flow is an almost hypnotic sensation of total involvement, becoming one with the task. Everything magically falls into place in a state of flow. The popular psychologist, Dr. Joyce Brothers (1927 – 2013) maintained that *"Flow is a sensation present when we act with total involvement. During flow, action follows on action according to an internal logic that seems to need no conscious intervention on the part of the participant."* Flow is probably the result if *in- spiration* – the Holy Spirit performing within. Therefore *"Let God and let go, then go with the flow." "Grow within the flow."* – Dr. Timothy Leary (1920 – 1996).

FLOWER POWER – (*FLOUR POWER*) The philosophy or ideology of the Hippie Movement. It insisted on peace, *"make love not war."* It was anti-establishment, meaning anti-capitalist. The Hippies believed in distributive justice, sharing, communal living, environmentalism, Socialism, the entire Progressive platform. Flower Power advocated uninhibited free love, both sexually and universally.

FLOWERS – (*FLOU*-ers) Socially acceptable weeds. Flowers are angiosperms. Both *weed* and *flower* are generic, not botanical terms. Flowers produce precious fruit and seeds. The first flower evolved about 114 million years ago. Today, about 80% of plants bear flowers. Only 1% of the flowering plants on Earth have been tested for their medicinal benefits. Buddhists call flowers *"The enlightenment of plants."* Ralph Waldo Emerson (1803 – 1882) said the *"Earth laughs in flowers."* Emerson went on to assert that *"Flowers…are a proud assertion that a ray of beauty out-values all the utilities of the world."*

FLUFFER – (*FLUHF*-er) (Fluffering, Fluffery) In the adult film industry, a gay male seducer. A fluffer is a professional sexual arouser of male performers on the movie set. The fluffer is responsible for keeping all penises (or penes) erect and ready for hard work during filming. He is considered to be a member of the makeup department. (*"I can't make this up!"*) Fluffering requires an alluring, sexually skilled, enthusiastic practioner, a seductive personality. He must display excitement for the job in order to keep the actors excitement up. The fluffer must be a master of sexual psychology, gifted at non-penetrative sex, and proficient at fellatio. Today, fluffery may be giving way to technology. Drugs like Viagra help the performers to *"keep it up."* So does sexual prosthetics and medical implants. Nevertheless, there are specialized scenes like *"gangbanging,"* and *"bukkake"* (group ejaculation upon a person) which still require the services of an old fashion, hard-sucking fluffer. *"The only unnatural sex act is that which you cannot perform."* – Pioneer Sexologist, Dr. Alfred Kinsey (1894 – 1956). *"Don't shoot me, I'm just the messenger."* – The Author.

FLUFFY BUNNY – (*FLUHF-ee BUHN-ee*) A pejorative, dismissive term for a phony Wiccan, a fake witch. Fluffy bunny is a derogatory term used by genuine Wiccans and witches for imposters. There are those who think it is chic to be regarded as a witch. Their knowledge and practice of metaphysics is superficial. Fluffy bunnies are more like stage magicians than authentic practitioners of the esoteric arts. Fluffy bunnies make a mockery of true magick, and disgrace the reputation of Paganism. These *"cocktail party shamans"* are a curse to the mystic community. Incidentally: The term *"fluffy bunny"* gained popularity in the 1990s, largely due to the humiliating portrayal of Wiccans and Witches in the silly television series, *"Buffy the Vampire Slayer."*

FLUKE/TAIL – (*FLOOK TAYL*) The hindmost part of a fish or marine mammal, used for propulsion and maneuvering. Fish have tail fins. Marine mammals (dolphins, porpoises, whales) have flukes. Both of these triangular are analogous, they appendages serve the same purpose. The noticeable difference is that fish tails point up and down, while marine mammal flukes point side to side.

FLUMMOX – (*FLUM-uks*) (Flummoxed) To be confused, bewildered, perplexed, confounded. *"I'm in a flummox over these wedding plans."*

FLUORINE – (*FLOOR-reen*) (F) Named from the Latin *fluere* meaning *"to flow."* The 9 protons in its nucleus give fluorine its atomic number. Fluorine is a toxic, pungent, corrosive, pale-yellow gas, the most reactive nonmetallic element. Fluorine occurs combined with fluorite, cryolite, and phosphate rock. Fluorine is the most electronegative of all elements. Fluorine is used to make refrigerants and high-temperature plastics. As *fluoride,* fluorine is added to drinking water to prevent tooth decay.

FLUSTRATED – (*FLUSS-tray-ted*) A hybrid word, a cross between being flustered and frustrated. A flustrated person is at his wit's ends.

FLUX – (*FLUKS*) As a noun, flux means to flow, to change with movement. Being in a state of flux bears the connotation of chaos, being everywhere at once. As a verb, to flux is to melt, make fluid, to fuse by the use of a flux. This usage is utilized in metallurgy. The mineral cryolite is used as a flux to produce aluminum, for instance.

FLY-BY-NIGHT – (*FLY-by-nhyt*) To escape. To abscond under the cover of darkness to evade a responsibility, like a debt. Alternately, fly-by-night refers to any impermanent person or business of a poor *"here today, gone tomorrow"* reputation. When first coined in the 18th century, fly-by-night was a reference to a witch. In 1788, lexicographer Captain Francis Grose (1731 – 1791) wrote in the <u>*Classical Dictionary of the Vulgar Tongue*</u>: *"FLY-BY-NIGHT. You old fly-by- night; an ancient term of reproach to an old woman, signifying that she was a witch, and alluding to the nocturnal excursions attributed to witches, who were supposed to fly abroad to their meetings, mounted on brooms."* It is unclear how the meaning shifted from a witch, to an absconder or transitory wayfarer. Indeed, like a witch, the fly-by-night retreats into the shadowy darkness.

FLYING DUTCHMAN – (*FLY*-ing *DUHCH*-man) A ghost ship. The Flying Dutchman was a legendary cursed ship, devoid of crewmembers, condemned to sail forever, never making port. The myth originated during the 17th century Golden Age of the Dutch East India Company. Today, any abandoned ship or boat, set afloat, (a crime scene perhaps), is called a Flying Dutchman.

FLYING FUCK – (*FLY*-ing *FUCK*) Originally, sex, intercourse on horseback. Therefore, *"A fuck on the fly,"* so to speak. The term flying fuck first appeared about 1800 in a bawdy ballad entitled *"New Feats of Horsemanship."* From about 1929, the term meant *"I could care less,"* as in *"I don't give a flying fuck."* Alternately, a flying fuck has been recorded as a rare flightless African bird.

FLYOVER – (*FLY*-oh-ver) Literally, to soar or glide above something, someone, or somewhere. As an adjective, the term *"flyover"* is a pejorative, dismissive allusion to the interior of America, between the two coasts. It is unquestionable that the East and West Coasts are the Liberal, Progressive, sophisticated parts of the country. The interior *"heartland"* tends to be insulated, conservative, and intolerant. (Ironically, the Fundamentalist *heartland* is the most *heartless* concerning social welfare.) Coastal Liberals deride the interior as a nuisance, a flyover from New York to Los Angeles, or San Francisco to Boston for instance. The flyover region is depicted as being populated by hayseeds or country bumpkins. Of course, there are islands of Progressivism in the flyover region, usually urbane urban areas, and intellectual college towns. Though the disconfirming concept of flyover is indeed stereotypical, there is a kernel of truth in every stereotype. Incidentally: Over 88% of the wine consumed in the USA is on the two coasts, by about 11% of the population. The flyover region prefers beer and Jack Daniels.

FOAL – (*FOHL*) A young horse (pony), mule, or related animal especially one that is not yet one year of age.

FOAM – (*FOHM*) (Foaming) A thick frothy liquid almost cream-like. Foam is a collection of minute bubbles, packed so densely together that penetrating light produces a white appearance. Foam is created by agitating certain liquids and by the fermentation process. Gas is trapped in the microscopic bubbles creating thick suds. Foam is naturally produced by churning seawater alive with organic substances. Vigorously shake a half a bottle of milk to produce a full bottle of milky foam – a milkshake in fact. Let sit, and the foam bubbles will break and return to liquid. The lather in the shaving cream can is very thick foam. *"Trump's incendiary lies make me foam at the mouth!"*

FOEHN – (*FANE*) A warm, dry wind that flows down the north slopes of the Alps. It has long been said that the foehn induces bizarre behavior in people, similar to the mythology concerning the full moon <u>lunacy</u>.

FOG – (*FAWG*) (Fogging, Foggy) Clouds at ground level, reducing or impeding visibility. Fog consists of low lying water droplets or ice crystals. Ground fog is less than 200 feet high. An average glass of water can produce enough fog to rise 100 feet and cover over 7 city blocks.

FOG OF WAR – (fawg uhv *WAWR*) The confusing uncertainty during the terror of battle. The great Prussian German war strategist, General Carl von Clausewitz (1780 – 1831) coined the phrase *"Fog of*

War," (*"Nebel des Krieges"*) in his book, <u>On War</u> (<u>*Vom Kriege*</u>) published posthumously in 1832. General von Clausewitz participated in the Napoleonic Wars. In <u>On War</u> he wrote: *"War is the realm of uncertainty; three quarters of the factors on which action in war is based are wrapped in a fog of greater or lesser uncertainty. A sensitive and discriminating judgment is called for; a skilled intelligence to scent out the truth."* Military experts acknowledge that battle plans on paper are at best, optimistic intentions, vague hopeful aspirations that can be dashed in the first moments of battle. The enemy too has plans, and may thwart yours unexpectedly. The weather may change suddenly, altering the terrain. Communications may get garbled, or cut-off altogether. Reinforcements may not arrive, and the logistic supply-lines may break down. Confused, misunderstood orders may result in friendly fire casualties. Leadership may falter. Soldiers may simply lose their nerve. Few human encounters are more uncertain than the fog of war. *"We had to burn down the village to save it."* – An American Infantry Captain in Vietnam. *"Prepare for the unknown by studying how others in the past have coped with the unforeseeable and the unpredictable."* – U.S. General George S. Patton (1885 – 1944).

FOIBLE – (*FOY*-buhl) (Foibles) A slight fault, minor character flaw, personal weakness. Foibles can also refer to one's silly mistakes. *"I wince when I recall my youthful foibles."* The term entered English in the 1640s meaning *"a weak point of a sword blade."* Foible is a French word meaning *"a weak point, a weakness, failing."* It derived from the Old French *"feble,"* meaning *"feeble."*

FOILS – (*FOYLS*) (also Distractors) In educational assessment, incorrect answers added to a multiple-choice test. The test-maker must be certain that the foil is not an unfair entrapment, *"a got'ya"* answer. Foils must never be ambiguous.

FOLK ART – (*FOHK AHRT*) Usually vernacular crafts like handmade pottery, woodcarving, baskets, weavings, and traditional costumes. Folk art is created by rural people with traditional lifestyles, reflected in their work. It is sometimes designated in a pejorative manner as *"primitivism"* by professional artists (who cannot imitate their refreshing creative innocence). *"I spent my entire life trying to learn to draw like a child."* – Pablo Picasso (1881 – 1973).

FOLK ETYMOLOGY – (*FOHK* et-ti-*MOL*-lo-jee) (also Popular Etymology) Changing an unfamiliar word or phrase into a more familiar form. Often the strange- sounding word is of foreign origin. The contrived word often bears only a superficially sounding relationship with the original word. For example, the Greek word *"asparagus"* was changed to *"sparrow-grass."* Too, the Spanish word *"cucaracha"* was *"etymologized"* by the folks to *"cockroach."* Folk etymological alterations occur at the grass-root level. It comes from the common folk. Incidentally: The insect cockroach bears no resemblance to a cock (a rooster) or a roach (a fish).

FOLK MAGIC – (*FOHK MAJ*-ik) Common, everyday magical habits and techniques, used by common, uninitiated folk, unaware that they are practicing magic. *"God bless you!"* and *"Damn those Republicans!"* are a consecration and curse, form of spellwork. Superstitions, wearing an amulet, talisman, crucifix, holy medal qualify as folk magic. So is murmuring a prayer, or making the sign of the cross, especially with holy water. Sure this example is religious, but both religion and magic are spiritual.

FOLIO – (*FO*-lee-o) A sheet of paper folded in half to make two leaves (4 pages) for a book or manuscript. Folio also refers to a large book or manuscript constructed of folio sheets.

FOLIVORES – (*FOHL*-li-vors) Leaf-eating animals like giraffes, koalas, and pandas. Folivares are herbivores, of course.

FOLSOM – (*FOLE*-sum) (The Folsom Street Fair) (FSF) The best venue for displaying public performances of exotic erotic, including sexual humiliation is *"The Folsom Street Fair"* each September, in San Francisco's Market District. At Folsom, deviance is deified. The lascivious, licentious is licensed. What is normally considered to be indecent exposure is considered decently exposed. *"Folsom"* is a convention of BDSM (Bondage Dominance SadoMasochism) practioners and aficionados. This event is a carnival of uninhibited sexual fantasies, bizarre unrestrained libertinism, a walk on the wild side. It is Fundamentally *"Sodom and Gomorrah"* revisited. The Folsom Fair of Erotic Humiliation could only take place in libertarian San Francisco, California. One could not fathom the event occurring in repressed Muskogee, Oklahoma.

FONDUE – (fon-*DOO*) A Swiss sauce-like dish made with melted cheese and seasonings together with dry white wine, usually flavored with cherry kirsch. Fondue is served as a hot dip for pieces of bread.

FOOD – (*FOOD*) Nutritional sustenance vital for providing animals the energy to live. Food comes in plant and animal form, both of which must die in order to become food. Therefore, the act of eating is a sacrifice. Whatever is consumed, must sacrifice its life, so another may live. *"Take this and eat, this is my body...."* – Matthew 26:26. Consuming food should be considered a bodily function like breathing, sleeping, urinating, defecating, not a form of indulgence, recreation, amusement. Food is a means to an end, namely health, growth, and life. We should emulate the Buddhist monks who regard food as a medicine or fuel, rather than a treat, or indulgence. Incidentally: Avoid the declaration of the Yiddish proverb that states: *"I'm not hungry, my mouth is just bored."* Post Script: *"Waste not want not."* An estimated 1,300,000,000 (1.3 billion) tons of food is wasted, worldwide, every year.

FOOD BANK – (*FOOD BANGK*) A charity outlet where surplus, dated, expired, food is provided to the poor. A soup kitchen is a food bank that serves ready- to-eat meals. The blessed Salvation Army operates food banks nationwide. Supermarkets sometimes donate the dated excess food. Vegetables, canned and packaged foods are usually distributed. No charge, of course, is required. Food banks are increasing in capitalist America, as the disparity of wealth widens. Free food keeps many U.S. families alive. Food banks are not government financed, but private charitable organizations. To fund food banks with tax dollars would be too Socialistic, too compassionate for conservative, capitalist Republicans. It is appalling that food banks should be necessary in the richest country in the world. That's deceptive because the riches are all concentrated at the very top. Though charity is very righteous, poverty is not. Furthermore, *"Charity is no substitute for justice withheld."* – St. Augustine (354 – 430 CE).

FOOD CHAIN – (*FOOD CHAYN*) The hierarchy of animals, from the mightiest down to the simplest, that feed on each other for sustenance. This involves both carnivores and herbivores. Energy is passed up the food chain from the most rudimentary plants and animals to man. Of course, consumption involves extermination. What is eaten must be killed, be it plant or animal. Therefore, the food chain is a life chain, but also a death chain. *"The weak are meat; the strong eat."* – Japanese Proverb.

FOOD PUSHING – (*FOOD POOSH*-ing) (Food Pushers) Forcing victuals on a diner by persuasion, manipulation, or even guilt. An over solicitous mother or grandmother is the usual party guilty of food pushing. Food pushing is a form of forced-feeding through harassment. Children victimized by food pushers can develop bad eating habits, and become unhealthily obese. The child feels forced to eat more than she needs. In a sense, it is a form of abuse. Little does Mom know that she may be loving them to death. Food pushing can be a direct order, or a subtle dog-whistle. Following are some food pushing statements. *"Clear your plate." "Finish that little bit." "Don't make me throw that away." "No left-overs now." "There's no room in the fridge." "It's a sin to waste food." "I slaved all day at the hot stove." "I thought you liked my golabki?" "There are people starving in Africa!" "I cooked it with love." "Please have another helping." "I made so much!" "I love to see you eat." "You look so thin, have a little more." "You ate so little, don't you like it?" "I fried 4 because the eggs are so small."* To the baby boomers, especially those with grandmothers from Eastern Europe, food pushing was a way of life while growing up. Their grandmas survived wars, invasions, revolutions, pogroms, and famines. They insisted that their children and grandchildren fatten-up while times were good. So food pushing became a family tradition, passed through the generations.

FOOLED – (*FOOLD*) To be bamboozled, conned, played the fool. A fool is a person who does not learn from mistakes, who is duped time and again (a dupa). *"Fool me once, shame on me. Fool me twice –uh- shame on me again!" – His Fraudulency,* President George W. Bush (b. 1946).

FOOT – (*FOOT*) A unit of measurement originating as the length of English King Henry I's (c. 1068 – 1135) actual foot.

FOOTBALL – (*FOOT*-bawl) The geometrical shape of an American football is a *"prolate spheroid,"* a continuously curved three-dimensional object that is longer than it is around. The prolate spheroid shape allows the football to be thrown with less drag. Throwing it so that the ball spins around its short axis while in flight (a tight spiral), dramatically reduces drag further, allowing it to be thrown much farther than other ball designs. The football's nickname is *"pig skin,"* though it is made from cowhide. Old-time footballs required an inflated pig bladder inside, like a pneumatic tire, ergo the name. American footballs are used at the NCAA (college) and NFL (professional) levels. The immediate apparent difference between the two balls is the white stripe painted near the two ends of the college football. This is intended for better visibility. The pro football is all leather brown. However there are additional subtle differences in size. The pro football is a little longer and skinnier, while the college football is a little shorter and plumper. This makes it easier to throw the pro football, but easier to kick the college football. The pro ball is 11 inches from tip to tip, the college ball 10 inches. The plumper college ball holds more air (13.5 lbs. per square inch) than the pro ball (12.5 lbs. per square inch). Nevertheless, being a little larger, the pro football is a little heavier (15 ounces), compared to the 14- ounce college football. Incidentally: An experiment was conducted with a football inflated with helium. The results were unexpectedly counter- productive. The ball was too light to be thrown or kicked very far. Football Footnote: The oldest football in existence was discovered in the roof of Sterling Castle, Scotland, in 1981. It is made of deer leather with a pig's bladder within for inflation. The football dates back to about 1550. Post Script: On January 18, 2015, The New England Patriots had defeated the Indianapolis Colts, 45 to 7. It was discovered that Patriots quarterback Tom Brady (b. 1977) and head coach Bill Belichick (b. 1952) had connived to deflate the footballs to their team's advantage. The scandal came to be called *"Deflategate."* Tom Brady was suspended for 4 games. The team was fined $1 million dollars, and lost two future draft picks. It's worth noting that the cheating two footballers are dedicated supporters of another cheat, Donald Trump (b. 1946).

FOOTBALL – (*FOOT*-bawl) Most popular American team sport, because it serves as a vicarious aggressive blood-lust. American football is a sublimation for belligerence, and a subconscious imitation of warfare. That's why football has surpassed baseball as the national sport. Baseball is too slow and sedate – no violence. Football evolved or mutated from English rugby, which has its share of violence. In 1905, 19 college football players were killed and 137 seriously injured (many paralyzed). Progressive President Teddy Roosevelt (1858 – 1919) warned that he would abolish college football by executive order if it didn't reform. So the <u>N</u>ational <u>C</u>ollegiate <u>A</u>thletic <u>A</u>ssociation (NCAA) was established to clean-up and control the game. Incidentally: A football game is 60 minutes long. The average play lasts about 7 seconds, with about a two minute hiatus between plays. Therefore, out of those 60 minutes, there is only about 11 minutes of actual action in a football game (when the ball is moving). (About 17 minutes is devoted to replaying those 11 minutes.) So for 49 minutes the clock runs while nothing is happening. (The 2-minute warning in professional football can last a half-an-hour.) Furthermore, though the game is only 1 hour long, a televised professional football game drags on for 3 hours and 12 minutes. (The capitalists must get in their commercial advertisements.) Only less than 6% of that time on the couch involves watching actual action (11 out of 192 minutes). By the way, a college football game is a few minutes longer on average than a professional football game (3 hours & 15 minutes?). That's because the clock is stopped briefly after every firstdown in college ball. Incidentally: It was announced in November, 2019, that high school football participation is the lowest in history. The exception, however, is in the poor *"red"* states that supported Donald Trump (b. 1946), especially Alabama, Louisiana, and Oklahoma. Rednecks in the red states need their football fix. Nevertheless, participation is down overall because the game is too dangerous. However, badass Donald Trump (b. 1946) had criticized the new rules making football less risky. Trump said the sport is being *"sissified,"* (red meat for the red states). Ironically, Trump never played, and did not allow his sons to play high school football. More Trump hypocrisy. Footnote: Has football become sissified, or is football a virtual vestige of the gladiatorial games? On February 2, 2021, former professional football player Martellus Bennett (b. 1987) spoke out. *"Honestly, football made me such an angry person, everything bothered me. Football is interesting. Psychologically, it's some really dangerous shit. To really play the game of football you have to have some fucked up wiring in your head. It's chaotic. It takes years and years of brainwashing to go along with a lot of the shit. It starts at peewee. That's why you gotta watch who is coaching your kids and what they're teaching them beyond the game…. Most of your favorite players aren't good people."* Wow! And I thought football built character. Football Footnote: In the average football game the ball is snapped, on average, 63 times per team – 126 snaps per game.

FOOTBALL COACHES CREDO – (*FOOT*-bawl *CO*-ches *CRAY*-dow) *"End every series with a kick."* Translation: Either *kick* an extra point after a touchdown; or *kick* a field goal; afterwards *kick*-off; or *kick* a punt. But never turn the ball over without a *kick*.

FOOTBALLER – (*FOOT*-bawl-er) A soccer player, as distinguished from an American football player. Soccer, (called football everywhere in the world except the U.S. and Canada) is the ancient evolutionary ancestor of American football. Soccer is the real *"pedocentric,"* meaning *"foot-centered"* football game. So soccer players are indeed the real footballers.

FOOTBALL ODDS – (*FOOT*-bawl *ODS*) The *"prolate spheroid"* shape makes it practically impossible to calculate predictably which way a football will bounce. Don't try to bet on it. But you can bet on other aspects of the game, for which the odds of occurrence have been calculated from statistics. For example: 94.1% of extra points will be kicked successfully. Only 5.9% will be missed. A two point conversion will be successful 49.4% of the attempts. So 50.6% of the tries will fail. A *"Hail Mary"* pass will succeed 10% of the time. So when you throw-up the prayer, 90% will be unanswered. Turnovers are certain in a football game. There is a 94.7% chance of at least one interception in the game. There is even a greater chance (98.3%) that there will be at least one fumble. Too, fumbles are slightly more common on pass plays (blindsiding the quarterback). An onside-kick is almost miraculous, with a success rate of only 6%. So 94% of onside-kicks fail. It's even harder to earn a safety, with a 5.3% chance of occurrence. Just over 1 game in 100 (1.4%) will witness a runback on a kickoff for a touchdown. Most kickoffs sail into the end zone as a touchback. Of all kickoffs, only 0.27% are runback for a TD. Just over one-half of one percent (0.59%) of all punts are runback for touchdowns. Through the decades, field-goal kickers have been becoming increasingly stronger. Today, the chance of succeeding at a 50+ yard field-goal is at 39%. Blocking a field goal is a rare feat, which occurs only 3.5% of the attempts. However blocking a punt has proved to be nearly impossible. There is about a 0.55% success rate in punt blocking attempts. That's only a *one-half of one percent chance* of success (½%). You have a 7 times better chance of blocking a field goal, than blocking a punt. That's because with a field goal, 3 players handle the ball (center, holder, kicker). There's a better chance of making a mistake with a field goal try. With a punt, only 2 players handle the ball (center and kicker). Punts are quicker plays, and the trajectory of the ball is higher, (fly-ball), whereas the trajectory of a field goal is straighter (line-drive). Blocking a punt is a risky gamble, for the chance of a penalty (roughing or running into the kicker is high). Too, one sacrifices on run-back yardage when attempting a blocked punt. Nevertheless, for the intrepid, the team that blocks a punt wins the game 90% of the time. Incidentally: When attempting a field goal, the average time from hike to kick is 1.3 seconds. According to Baltimore Ravens field goal kicker, Justin Tucker (b. 1989): *"If the time is 1.4 seconds, chances are that the kick will be blocked."* Tucker holds the NFL recoded for the longest field goal, 66 yards, in Detroit (2021). The ball hit the crossbar and successfully dropped over. Footnote: The professional goalpost is 10 feet high and 18.5 feet wide.

FOOTPRINT – (*FOOT*-print) An impression in the soil or sand made by the step of one's foot, with or without shoes. A footprint is a sign of past presence, but nothing more. It is harmless, to be blown away by the wind, or washed away by the waves. That's why public parks advertised the injunction: *"Take only photos, leave only footprints."* You will hear the term 'footprint' more often in the media. The U.S. Army's communication division has adopted this term. As a footprint leaves an innocuous impression, the army wants to leave you with the impression that their presence in occupying a foreign country (ostensibly to protect corporate capitalist interests) is equally innocuous. This is a joke. The unobtrusive presence of U.S. forces is more of a crushing stomp on the society, than a gentle footprint. A military occupation is traumatic, never leaving a footprint, but a craterous scar, often a lunar landscape. Jackboots never leave mere footprints.

F.O.P. – (Fraternal Order of Police) Perhaps the only workers' union that works against the common man. The Fraternal Order protects police, good or bad. Right or wrong F.O.P. shields the cop. Sadistic, even psychopathic officers evade justice behind the Fraternal Order. The police are assigned to maintain law-and- order – translation: protect the property of the rich from those who need it. In doing so, the police brutalize the poor, minorities, anyone who poses a threat to the ruling plutocracy. The Fraternal Order of Police (F.O.P.) serves to exonerate police atrocities. *"The Myth: 'Only a few bad apples.' The truth, only a few good cops."* – Dr. Gary J. Pasieka (b. 1951).

FORAGE – (*FAWR*-ij) (Foraging, Foragers) The continual search for food by herbivorous animals. Foraging is the herbivore's counterpart to carnivore's hunting. Some plant-eaters graze on grass, others browse on leaves.

FORBEARANCE – (for-*BARE*-rans) (Forbear, Forbearing) To refrain, abstain, or desist from some action, especially something objectionable. Forbearance is patient endurance. The virtue of forbearance amounts to self-control, like having the forbearance to remain calm or sober. Forbearance is having the will power to abstain from evil.

FOR CAUSE – (for *KAWZ*) With justification. An action performed for a specific, legitimate reason. For example, the termination of a contract or a relationship of employment. The termination is based on a breach, misfeasance, or other inappropriate conduct of the terminated person.

FORCE – (*FORS*) Physical power or strength. In a competitive capitalist society, the strong (rich) use their force (wealth) to control, dominate, compel, and oppress the weak (poor). Bullies resort to force. Albert Einstein (1879 – 1955) recognized that *"Force always attracts men of low morality,"* such as the thug, Donald Trump (b. 1946). Force is often employed by low-brows without the intelligence to persuade. As wise Ben Franklin (1706 – 1790) put it: *"Force shits on reason's head."*

FORCED ORGASM – (forst *OR*-gaz-um) In the BDSM (Bondage, Dominance, SadoMasochism) culture of exotic erotica, forced orgasm is inducing a series of absolutely awesome orgasms in a captive female. The lady must be helplessly bound, legs spread on the bed. (Of course, she must volunteer for this erotic adventure and surrender all control.) According to the online encyclodictionary of sex, *Freakypedia: "A forced orgasm happens when you put a high-powered vibrator up to someone's pussy and then don't remove it even after they have cum, causing them to cum uncontrollably and even to the point of discomfort. You will notice that most girls get really sensitive after they cum – this causes multiple orgasm process to become unbearable after a while. But if a submissive girl is tied up with nowhere to go, there's nothing she can do about her master's will to make her cum over and over again."* The beneficiary/victim of the unremitting vaginal vibration treatment will scream, beg, and writhe with orgasm after orgasm. The line between ecstasy and agony is blurred. *"I think that I shall never see a poem as lovely as a hot-gushing, butt-cramping, gut hosing orgasm."* – Writer Chuck Palahniuk (b. 1962).

FORDITE – (*FORD*-dyt) A man-mad mineral produced serendipitously over many years in the paint department of the Ford Motor Plant. Fordite's alternate name is *"Detroit Agate,"* which it closely resembles.

Fordite is made accidentally by thousands of thin coatings of different colored paints that were used to paint cars. The baked paint encrusted on the painting machines. It is now chipped off and highly prized for making amazing jewelry. Incidentally: Fordite is produced in all old automotive paint departments.

FORE – (*FOR*) A prefix meaning be<u>fore</u>, or in front. On the silly golf course, fore is an interrogative warning that one is about to shoot, shouted loudly as *"Forrrrrrr!"* The expression is of military origin. Fore may be a truncation of *"beware before"* just prior to the cannon blast. Alternately, it may be a truncation or corruption of the command *"forward."* This was an order for the front (forward) row of musketeers to take a knee, enabling the row behind to fire (without blowing off any heads). The golf ball has replaced the musket ball with the exclamation *"Fore!"* The tradition has maintained since about 1881.

FORECASTING – (*FOR*-cas-ting) In meteorology, predicting the weather conditions. An 18-day forecast is computer generated. A 90-day forecast is statistically generated (based on past weather patterns). Nearly two weeks may be the ultimate limit of weather forecasting. Actually, no one can predict the detailed, day-by-day weather more than a week ahead. Forecasting skill generally drops off quickly after 3 or 4 days. This is due to the *"Chaos Factor."* It says that you will never know all the possibilities and their consequences. The infinite global causes and effects of the chaos factor make weather forecasting a tentative science, if not art. No technological breakthroughs will enable meteorologists to predict the weather 2 weeks in advance accurately – *NEVER!*

FORECLOSURE – (for-*CLOH*-zur) (Foreclose) In capitalist law, to deprive a mortgagor or pledgor the right to redeem her property, especially on failure to make payment on a mortgage when due. Ownership of property then passes to the mortgagee (usually a bank). The former property owner is evicted (usually from his home). Foreclosure is a victory of the rich and powerful over the poor and weak. It is a structural pillar in the sanguine edifice of capitalism. It is a means to assure the continued disparity of wealth. Foreclosure is the covert desire of capitalist lending institutions. They encourage *"predatory loans"* which they known cannot be paid back. The hope is that the borrower will default on the mortgage after making plenty of payments, so the bank can confiscate, seize the home as well through foreclosure. *"Banks are the biggest bloodsuckers in the capitalist swamp, second only to those leaches, the insurance companies."* – Gary J. Pasieka (b. 1951).

FOREGONE CONCLUSION – (*FOR*-gone con-*CLOO*-shun) An inevitable result, outcome, or settlement. A foregone conclusion is an opinion, or decision formed in advance of proper consideration of evidence.

FOREIGN ACCENT SYNDROME – (*FOR*-en *AK*-sent *SIN*-drohm) (FAS) A bizarre, idiosyncratic, spooky psycho-neurological condition in which a person unconsciously acquires a foreign accent in her speech. <u>F</u>oreign <u>A</u>ccent <u>S</u>yndrome (FAS) occurs (albeit rarely) when that part of the brain that governs speech rhythm and melody is damaged. The destruction can be on account of stroke, trauma, tumor, or multiple sclerosis. For example, an American may begin to speak English with an English accent, or like a German immigrant, or in whatever alien manner: *"YA Mon!"* The speech articulators (jaw, lips, tongue) begin to function differently. The vocabulary becomes awkward, using odd words in a clumsy manner – as would one who speaks English as a second language. Unusual syntax is employed like inverting sentences improperly. Of course, Foreign Accent Syndrome is not confined to English speakers. Too, one does not begin to speak a foreign language, but alters the sound of the language he knows. This condition requires much more study. Who knows, perhaps the brain damage had accidentally lifted a metaphysical veil that separated this life from a past existence. *"There are stranger things in heaven and earth, than are dreamt of in your philosophy."* – William Shakespeare (1564 – 1616) in <u>Hamlet</u>, Act I, Scene 5.

FOREIGN AID – (*FOR*-en *AYD*) Assistance, relief given to needy nations, but not from charitable compassion. U.S. foreign aid always comes with a quid pro quo. It is the *"carrot,"* in the American *"stick and carrot"* foreign policy. Socialist Michael Harrington (1928 – 1989) maintained that *"The foreign aid was assigned according to military and political priorities, rather than on the basis of the poor people's needs."* Foreign aid is often given to bribe foreign leaders to enable U.S. corporations to exploit their resources and people. Often, the recipient nation is obliged to purchase only American goods with the aid, even if they are more expensive, amounting to a subsidy to U.S. capitalists. America grants aid to nations to suppress or foment revolutions, in the U.S. interest. Crackdown on the Socialists will always elicit handsome aid from capitalist America. Accepting American foreign aid is a Mephistophelean bargain, a pact with the devil. Incidentally: No President has abused foreign aid as a weapon to advance his will than Donald Trump (b. 1946).

FORENSIC ACCOUNTANT – (for-*REN*-sik uh-*KOUNT*-tint) (Forensic Accounting) An accountant is a bookkeeper, one who records, maintains, inspects, and audits commercial accounts – financial operations of a corporation or business. Forensic, in this context, refers to legal anomalies. Therefore, a forensic accountant is a *"bookkeeper detective,"* an accounting inspector with the ability to uncover hidden irregularities and financial crimes. Forensic accountants are employed by prosecutors to find and provide criminal evidence in court proceedings. That's because they are experts at *"following the money."* These investigative accountants will recognize clever illegal transactions like money laundering, tax and securities fraud, bank and insurance fraud, illegal borrowing, inflating and deflating the worth of assets, secret shell companies, the entire panoply of criminal financial activity. Forensic accountants are the bane of corrupt capitalist businessmen. Incidentally: Neither the FBI, Federal nor State Prosecutors could touch gangster Al Capone (1899 – 1947). However, Frank J. Wilson (1887 – 1970), a bespectacled forensic accountant sent *"Scarface"* Al Capone to Alcatraz. The same fate will befall gangster Donald J. Trump (b. 1946). Cy Vance Jr. (b. 1954), District Attorney for New York County has hired forensic accountants to investigate, examine Trump's corrupt multifarious business empire. Who knows what will crawl out from under the slimy financial rocks the forensic accountants will turn over – and turn over to the court?

FORENSIC DISPUTATION – (for-*REN*-sic dis-pew-*TAY*-shun) (also Forensic Education) The practice of defending an issue you actually oppose. It is playing the *"devil's advocate."* Forensic disputation is a technique employed by lawyers all the time in court, where winning the case, not finding the truth, is the goal of the game. Forensic disputation or conditioning employs the inoculation effect. You discover and rehearse the arguments that your opponent will use against you.

FORENSICS – (for-*REN*-sics) Rhetoric. The art or study of argumentation and formal debate. Forensics is applied in public discussion or a court of law.

FOREPLAY – (*FOR*-play) Pre-sexual arousal techniques and activities. Foreplay includes any erotic exercise like kissing, feeling, licking, sucking, rubbing, stroking, and salacious talk, that will stimulate lustful desire prior to sexual penetration. Foreplay builds up sexual tension and excitation. Oral sex is the best form of foreplay, and a damn good form of aftplay. The online encyclodictionary of sex, *Freakypedia*, advises, encourages foreplay. *"Foreplay is something that should be a part of every sexual interaction. It is what happens when you tease and tantalize your partner before you have penetrative sex. Some people would argue that foreplay is more important than actual penetrative sex, if you believe that the journey is more important than the destination. Sex that just goes straight to the fucking isn't always so good. Sometimes is a pussy is involved the slit isn't lubed up quite enough and the cock isn't quite hard enough, but foreplay can help to get you there."* *"Conversation is the sexiest foreplay, the perfect prelude to sex, the fiery banter that gets you heated, the stimulation of the mind that transmits to the body."* – Actress Zara Barrie

FORESKIN – (*FOR*-skin) The loose fold of skin that covers the glans (head) of the penis. The foreskin is also called the prepuce. It is a long held religious tradition among Jews to circumcise the foreskin. This unnecessary operation on baby boys had become general practice in the medical field, for no good reason. If the foreskin did not serve a purpose, it would have degenerated. The foreskin enhances stimulation which results in erection.

FOREST – (*FOR*-rest) Woodland. A vast tract of land covered by trees. The world's greatest forest is the Siberian taiga holding a third of all the trees on Earth. The coniferous taiga stretches into Scandinavia and Northern Canada. The Amazon, primarily in Brazil, is the world's greatest tropical rainforest. It consists of deciduous broad-leaf trees. There are far more animals in the deciduous broad-leaf forests, than in the coniferous pine-needle forests. Many animals can digest broad leaves. Few, (except the moose) can digest pine needles. So there are far more herbivores, and therefore many more carnivores in the deciduous broad-leaf forests. Incidentally: About ¾ of Japan is forested, more than any other industrial nation. Forests are sacred to the Japanese Shinto. By contrast, only 2% of America's "virgin" forests still stand, mostly in the Northwest. Worldwide, forests and natural vegetation is being destroyed at a rate of over a hectare (2,471 acres) a second. Trees in the great forests absorb 55% of the carbon dioxide (CO_2) that we produce. This slows global warming. Dangerously, a swathe of forest the size of Scotland is destroyed worldwide annually.

FOREVER – (for-*EV*-ver) Endless, without conclusion. Forever is *"not ever."* What is forever will not stop. But anything that won't stop must have had a start. It must have had a beginning, to have no end. This begs the question: *"What is for-ever?"* It must exist as something real – a thing, place, person, or spirit. If it's a thing, its infinite. If it's a place, its eternal. If it's a person or spirit, it's immortal. Forever is timeless. Time is the engine of change. We measure time through change. Therefore, forever is changeless as well. Forever never ages, deteriorates, or dies. It is always. Is the universe forever? Unlikely. Because the universe responds to change in time. However, there may be an endless string of universes, experiencing deaths and rebirths – the reincarnation of the Cosmos. In this sense, the universe would be forever. Furthermore, the universe is matter, and matter is energy, and energy is light. The light can come from one source, and that is obviously God, which is forever. *"In the beginning, God created the heaven and the earth. The earth was without form and void, and darkness was over the face of the deep…. And God said, 'Let there be light,' and there was light. And God saw that the light was good."* Incidentally: The world's greatest physicists, past and present, admit, that the deeper we plunge into astrophysics, the farther we drift from traditional science toward theology.

FOREVER TRUMPSTERS – (for-*EV*-ver *TRUMP*-sters) Those perplexing individuals who support Donald Trump (b. 1946), despite his corruptibility, criminality, immorality, instability, dishonesty, barbarity, stupidity, infidelity, perfidy, and despicability. The Forever Trumpsters are not the corporate millionaires and billionaires who benefit from Trump's greed. They are the poor, low-educated Republicans (primarily rurals) who support Trump for his bigotry and racism. These are the indignant indigents, the angry people who need Trump in the White House to vent their rage at life. Forever Trumpsters are forever fed a diet of lies from Fox *"News"* Network, which is in fact *"The Trump Soundoff Station."* They dwell in an alternative universe of alternative facts, the truth being what *"Der Fuhrer, Herr Trump"* says is true. They are consumed by conspiracy theories. *"TV Trump's"* voters are his former viewers. Actual reality is *"fake news"* to the Forever Trumpsters. There are some who enjoy participating in the clown show. They are indeed circus-trained *"Trumpanzees."* The Forever Trumpsters are the *have littles,* who were convinced by the *haves muches,* to hate the *have nots,* and support the *haves muches,* so they can have more. The Forever Trumpsters are dupes, who vote against their personal economic interests by supporting Trump and the Republicans. The Forever Trumpsters constitute Trump's hardcore base, and base indeed they are.

FORGETTING – (for-*GET*-ting) A lapse in memory. Inability to retrieve information stored in the mind. Actually, forgetting is impossible. Every incident, fact, feeling, sensation is stored deep in the subconscious mind. The trick is to elevate that information into the conscious mind where it is again accessible.

FORGIVE – (*FOR*-giv) (Forgiveness) To release oneself of stress and resentment by releasing a guilty party of castigation and blame. For-giveness is for-giving oneself peace of mind. The best way to suppress resentment and express forgiveness is to acknowledge the fact that we all did the best we could, with who we were, and what we knew, at that point of time. In a very real sense, *"Forgiveness means letting go of the hope for a better past,"* – Lama Surya Das (b. 1950). *"Then Jesus cried out in a loud voice saying: 'Father forgive them, for they know not what they do'."* – Luke 23: 24. *"Love is an endless act of forgiveness. Forgiveness is me giving up the right to hurt you for hurting me."* – Beyoncé (b. 1981). Incidentally: Following is a heart-wrenching lesson about forgiveness. Jesus conducted a re-enactment of the Last Super in Heaven. The Apostles were congregated, the Passover meal was ready. But Jesus delayed. Much time passed, but the host, Jesus, would not give permission to dine. The Apostles were puzzled. Then the door slowly opened and in walked a man who Jesus embraced and kissed. *"Welcome Judas,"* Jesus said. *"Now we can eat."* *"Forgiveness is a form of the highest love."* – Ma Jaya (1940 – 2012).

FORGIVER'S CREDO – (for-*GIV*-vers *CRAY*-dow) *"He, she, I did the best we could, with who we were, and what we knew, at that point in time."*

FORLORN – (for-*LORN*) (Forlorned, Forlornly, Forlorness) Desolate, dreary, feeling sad, lonely, miserable. A forlorned individual is in despair, a state of hopelessness. Forlorn entered English in the mid-12th century as *"forloren,"* meaning *"disgraced, deprived."* It derived from the Old English (West Saxon) *"forleosan,"* meaning *"to lose, abandon, let go, destroy, ruin."* By the 1530s, forlorn came to mean *"forsaken, abandoned."* It was first recorded as meaning *"wretched, miserable"* in the 1580s.

FORMATIVE – (*FORM*-ma-tiv) Remedial evaluation, designed to form correct habits or understanding. Formative evaluation is performed during the learning, training program. It does not constitute pass-or-fail (summative evaluation).

FORNICATE – (*FOR*-ni-kate) (Fornication) Adultery. Voluntary sexual intercourse outside of marriage. To constitute fornication, the couple cannot be married to each other. Therefore, by definition, a married couple cannot fornicate.

FORTALICE – (*FORT*-a-liss) A small fort or outpost, extension of a larger fort.

FORTE – (*FORT*) or (for-*TAY*) A person's expertise, strong suit, most highly developed skill or talent. Actually the (for-*TAY*) pronunciation is correctly applied in a musical capacity, as in *"pianoforte."* Incidentally: the term piano- forte literally means soft-loud.

FORTHCOMING – (fawrth-*KUHM*-ing) Something about to happen, about to appear, about to come about. From another angle, a forthcoming person is thought to be candid, frank, cooperative, a no-nonsense person.

FORTHRIGHT – (*FAWRTH*-ryt) Proceeding on a direct course, not straying off line. On a personal level, a forthright person is frank, honest, truthful, one who conforms to the rules and provides the relative facts. In contract, Donald Trump (b. 1946) is not a forthright person.

FORTHWITH – (*FAWRTH*-with) Means immediately, at once, without delay. The term *"forthwith"* is often used in legal documents. The term *"forthwith"* entered English in about 1200. It evolved from the Old English (West Saxon) *"ford mid."*

FORTISSIMO – (for-*TEES*-see-mo) A musical term for very loud.

FORTNIGHT – (*FORT*-nyt) A time span covering 14 days and nights or 2 weeks. The use of the term fortnight is more common in Britain. The term fortnight derives from the Old English (Saxon) *"feowertyne niht,"* literally *"fourteen nights."* It preserves the ancient German custom of reckoning by nights, rather than days.

FORTRESS POLAND – (*FOR*-tres *POH*-land) The armed build-up of Poland as the strongest non-nuclear nation in Europe. Poland is the defensive bulwark of NATO (North Atlantic Treaty Organization) in Eastern Europe against Russian expansionism. Poland's geopolitical position has forced the nation to become NATO's arsenal. Poland borders war-torn Ukraine and hostile Belarus, a Russian puppet-state. The Baltic States (Lithuania, Estonia, Latvia) are north of Poland. These are former Russian-held territories, and potential targets for future Russian incursions. The heavily-armed Russian exclave of Kaliningrad lies north of Poland as well. Therefore, in 2022, with the Russo-Ukrainian War raging, Poland has consented to accept America's most sophisticated weapons. This will make Poland the strongest conventionally armed nation in Europe – a *"Fortress Poland."*

FORTUITOUSLY – (for-*TOO*-it-tus-lee) (Fortuitous) Luckily, fortunately, of good fortune.

FORTY – (*FOR*-tee) (40 or XL) Forty is a numerical symbol for a cardinal number, 10 x 4. Forty is a mystical number. Spiritually, 40 represents transition, change, renewal, a new beginning. The number 40 is believed to have the power to lift one up to a heightened spiritual level. The number 40 appears time and again throughout the Bible. It appears in situations where God intends to transform people. For example: For 40 days Noah, his family, and menagerie drifted in the Ark during the deluge. After departing Egypt, the Hebrews wandered in the desert for 40 years. Moses communed with God for 40 days on Mount Sinai. The Hebrew spies reconnoitered in the Promised Land for 40 days. Goliath challenged and taunted the Hebrews for 40 days before being slayed by David. God enabled the Prophet Elijah to survive for 40 days on a single meal. God allowed the people of Nineveh 40 days to change their evil ways. Jesus fasted in the wilderness for 40 days. In the Gospels, Jesus asks 40 questions, for every declarative statement he makes. Jesus communed with the Apostles for 40 days between his Resurrection and Ascension. Secular scholars maintain that the prevalence of 40 is coincidental. Others claim that the number 40 was symbolic, a euphemism for *"a long time."* These are weak assertions. Deists consider God *"The Cosmic Time Keeper."* If so, God has a penchant for the number 40.

FORTY-SEVEN PERCENT – (*FOR*-tee *SEV*-ven per-*SENT*) The bottom 47% of the American population castigated as *moochers, freeloaders, tax-consuming welfare recipients* by Republican presidential candidate Mitt Romney (b. 1947). Romney spoke what all Republicans believe. This statement was made to Romney's millionaire supporters and was surreptitiously recorded. Romney's arrogant elitist remark may have cost him the 2012 election. However, the same 47%er's bit the hand that fed them (the left hand) in the 2016 election. They forsook the more Progressive Democrats and voted for the Republican Donald Trump (b. 1946) in 2016. With this stupid move, the desperate and dispossessed voted against their own economic interests. There will be a painful price to pay for this stupidity.

FORWARD PARTY – (*FAWR*-werd *PAR*-tee) (Forwarder) A new U.S. political party announced on July 27, 2022. It is touted to be a coalition of disgruntled Democrats and Republicans, and an alternative to both parties. The Forward Party is professed to be neither left nor right, but forward looking into a vague future. Well, if the party is neither liberal nor conservative, it must be boringly moderate. Or is it? The *"Forward Party"* was the name of Andrew Yang's (b. 1975) campaign organization during his 2020 Presidential campaign. Yang is a lawyer, lobbyist, and apostate Democrat. He will co-chair the new Party along with former New Jersey Republican Governor Christine Todd Whitman (b. 1946). Three organizations merged to form the Forward Party: 1. Yang's supporters; 2. The right-wing *"Renew America Movement"*; 3. David Jolly's *"Serve America Party."* Reagan, Bush, and Trump supporters populate the Renew America Movement. David Jolly, a former Republican Congressman from Florida, is also a lawyer and lobbyist, like Andrew Yang. So by its very composition, the Forward Party is decidedly conservative, though it won't say so. In fact, the Forward Party boasts no specific policies, or no ideology. But your ideology represents your core values. Are they saying that the Party bears no specific convictions? That's remarkable! So far, Party representatives speak in glittering generalities of pluralism, diversity, Constitutional abstractions, and grass-roots support. David Jolly mentioned that people in Boston may have different priorities from people in Birmingham. How would Forward leaders decide priorities? Does the Party intend to conduct government by polling, survey, referendum? Who gets what and how much? What's its politics? Party officials stress the importance of shared values, but will not share with us what it deems valuable. Forward seems like a business-oriented institution. Where do the Progressives and Socialists fit in? It seems that the fledgling Party is afraid of alienating anyone. However, if you try to be everything to everyone, you will end up being nothing to anyone. Professional political analysts doubt the Forward Party's chances for survival. Update: It has not!

FORWARD PASS – (*FAWR*-werd *PAHS*) In American/Canadian gridiron football, throwing the ball in the direction in which the offensive team is trying to move, towards the defensive team's goal line. Football's ancient evolutionary ancestor is rugby. In an athletic sense, the forward pass served as another *American Revolution* against Britain. It was a *Declaration of Independence* of American gridiron football from British rugby football. American football was pretty much a variation of British rugby, which forbids the forward pass. But with the legalizing of the pass in 1906, American football became a new, independent sport. Till then, the football was not allowed to be advanced forward through the air. It had to be carried only. In 1905, a game was played in Wichita, Kansas between Washburn University and Fairmount College (today's Wichita State). Fairmount's Bill Davis threw the ball forward to Art Solter. Though not officially legal, many credit this as the first forward pass in football. The rule was changed in less than a year, making the pass legal. This exciting play opened-up the game and added an entirely new dimension. The first legal forward pass was thrown on September 5, 1906. Bradbury Robinson (1884 – 1949) of Saint Louis University threw an incomplete pass which was treated as a fumble, a turnover. Robinson later completed the first legal touchdown pass, a 20-yard strike to Jack Schneider (1883 – 1958). Saint Louis University Coach Eddie Cochems (1877 – 1953) is considered the *"Father of the Forward Pass."* Initially, an incomplete pass was treated as a fumble – a live ball. Imagine the chaos that caused! It is not easy to throw an egg-shaped rugby ball very far accurately. So the shape of the ball would have to change to accommodate the forward pass. The ball began to elongate in 1912. More changes came in the 1920s. Today the football (not a *"ball"* at all) is a *"prolate spheroid."* This enables the flight of tight spiral passes, like a bullet. Arguably, football would not have surpassed baseball as the most popular American sport, if not for the forward pass. Incidentally: Football violence encouraged the introduction of the forward pass. In 1905, 19 players were killed and 159 seriously injured playing football. President Theodore Roosevelt (1858 – 1919), himself a roughneck, threatened to ban football by executive order, unless the game was cleaned-up. So the NCAA (National Collegiate Athletic Association) was formed to enforce safety rules. One change was adopting the forward pass. It was reasoned that spreading the players out in a pass formation would eliminate some injuries caused by gang-tackling the ball carrier. In today's style of play, the forward pass has not eliminated injuries.

FOSSIL – (*FOS*-sil) A once living organism petrified in a sedimentary solution. A fossil is a stone cast of the former plant or animal. All the organic material has been *"disillusioned"* disintegrated. An estimated 10 million fossil species are preserved in sedimentary rock. Only about 100,00 or 1% are known to science. It takes at least 50,000 years for plant or animal tissue to fossilize. The skull offers 95% of the information of how the fossilized animal lived. The oldest known fossils are stromatolites (Blue-green algae) 3.7 to 3.8 billion years old, discovered in Greenland.

FOSSIL FUELS – (*FOS*-sil *FEWLS*) Fossilized sunlight, captured by ancient plants and animals. Fossil fuels are coal, oil, and gas, combustibles created from decayed organic matter over millions of years in the

Earth. It took nature 5 million years to produce the fossils fuels that mankind burn in 1 year. Burning fossil fuels produce greenhouse gases which enhance global warming which spells disaster for humanity. However, fossil fuels are profitable to industrial capitalists, so they will continue to pollute the planet.

FOSSILIFEROUS – (fos-sil-*LIF*-er-us) (Fossilization) Containing fossils, or being a fossilizing substance or medium. Only sedimentary rock is fossiliferous. Igneous and metamorphic rock is melted and crushed, not conducive to fossilization. A sedimentary slurry of fine mud, is a fine fossiliferous medium.

FOSSIL WATER – (*FOS*-sil *WAU*-ter) Ancient water pumped from subterranean aquifers. Fossil water may be the remains of ancient seas or lakes that have percolated underground, as in the Sahara. It is not replenished by rainfall.

FOSTER – (*FOS*-ter) To promote the growth or development of something. For instance, we must foster the establishment of a just, Socialist society.

FOUNDATION – (foun-*DAY*-shuhn) The natural or prepared ground or base on which a structure rests. A building, bridge, dam, any structure must be anchored to a solid foundation like bedrock. Otherwise, a calamitous collapse may occur. A disaster waiting to happen is at Montego Bay, Jamaica. Freeport is a spit of land that juts into the Caribbean Sea. It was artificially created by dumping crushed limestone and coral, connecting small islands. The water table is six, and in some places only three feet below the surface. Nevertheless, greedy capitalist entrepreneurs continue to build on this perilous foundation. Walls and walkways crack as buildings shift and sink, an ominous sign. High-rise hotels have been constructed in upscale Freeport. However, a moderate offshore earthquake will result in *liquefaction* of the foundation. The land on which the structures rest will turn to pudding. All will come tumbling down. The sea will reclaim Freeport. It has happened several times elsewhere. In Matthew 7: 24 – 27, Jesus warned: *"A wise man built his house on the rock. And the rain fell, and the floods came, and the winds blew and beat on that house, but it did not fall, because it had a foundation of rock…. A foolish man built his house on the sand. And the rain fell, and the floods came, and the winds blew and beat against that house, and it fell, and great was the fall of it."*

FOUNDING FATHERS – (*FOUND*-ing *FAH*-thers) The hundred or so men who forged the 13 British North American colonies into the United States of America. Through revolution and war, they gained independence from Britain (1775 – 1783). Through negotiation and compromise, they created a new nation, represented by the United States Constitution (1787). Fifty-six Founding Fathers signed the Declaration of Independence (1776). Thirty-seven crafted the Constitution, the U.S. Government on paper, the basic law of the land. In 1973, renowned historian Richard B. Morris (1904 – 1989) chose the 7 most influential members of the Founding Fathers: John Adams (1735 – 1826), Benjamin Franklin (1706 – 1790), Alexander Hamilton (1755 – 1804), John Jay (1745 – 1829), Thomas Jefferson (1743 – 1826), James Madison (1751 – 1836), and George Washington (1732 – 1826). The Founding Fathers were the aristocrats of colonial America. They were primarily wealthy merchants, lawyers, and plantation owners. They fomented and fought the War of Independence not for democracy, by for liberty. None of them supported the concept of democracy as we define it today – one adult one vote. Many were slave holders in fact. Their sons and grandsons would one day take up arms against the nation (Civil War) that the Southern Fathers had helped to create, in order to suppress universal democracy. Notice too that there were no *"Founding Mothers."* The Founders believed that females had no business meddling in politics. Like aristocrats everywhere, the Founding Fathers distrusted – nay, feared democracy. What did they fear about it? The equitable redistribution of their wealth and privilege – what today we call *"Socialism."* The naïve textbooks claim that the Founding Fathers intentionally made the U.S. Government slow, cumbersome, with numerous checks-and-balances. What needed to be checked? What needed to be balanced? The power of the common citizens to use the government to redistribute the Founder's wealth, and that of their descendants. Originally, it was planned that only white, propertied males had the right to vote. Originally, the U.S. Congress was unicameral, consisting only of the House of Representatives. Then the Founding Fathers realized that this put far too much democratic power in the hands of the voters. So they created an upper house, the Senate (an American version of the British House of Lords). This was meant to check-and-balance the power of the House Representing the People. Furthermore, the Senators were not elected by the people, but appointed by the wealthy aristocrats in each state. It wasn't until the 17th Amendment to the Constitution in 1913, that the people elected their Senators. Indeed, the Founding Fathers supported liberty, but not democracy. To them, liberty meant to be liberated from British royal and parliamentary restrictions and regulations, in order to maintain their social hegemony. They considered democracy to be mob rule. The Founding Fathers never supported government by the people. Incidentally: We can see a reflection of the Founder's fear of democracy in the Republican Party today. The suppressing of the vote, the censoring of history, the crippling limitations on democracy would be welcomed by our hallowed Founding Fathers. *"I am an aristocrat. I love liberty I hate equality."* – Founding Father John Randolph of Virginia (1773 – 1833), slave master.

FOUR – (*FOR*) (4) In spiritual numerology the appearance of 3 fours (444) refers to *angels*. It means that guardian angels surround and protect you. You need only call on them for help. You have a strong and clear connection with the spiritual realm. In fact, you may be an *"Earth Angel."* Too, the sequence 444 is the numerological designation for the name Jesus. *"Teleia agape"* or perfect love is associated with the number 444 as well. Meta-geophysically, 444 represents the ancient city of Damascus, Syria.

FOUR EVILS – (*FOR EE*-vils) there are 4 politico-economic evils that smother democracy and distributive justice. The 4 evils are: *privatizing, lobbying, gerrymandering,* and *voter suppressing*. These are capitalistic evils, supported and practiced by wealthy conservative capitalists, and the Republican politicians who represent them. Privatizing is *"hoarding."* What belonged to all is confiscated by the wealthy few. Lobbying is *"bribing."* The wealthy buy Republican politicians to do their bidding. Gerrymandering is *"cheating."* Republicans rig their Congressional Districts, making it impossible for opponents to compete. Voter suppressing is *"oppressing."* Republicans employ all nefarious means to keep the poor, especially minorities from voting. The four evils are employed to maintain capitalism, and its unjust distribution of the wealth. Conversely, the four evils are designed to suppress Socialism, the attainment of socio-economic justice.

FOUR FREEDOMS – (*FOR FREE*-dums) The war goals articulated by Progressive President Franklin D. Roosevelt (1882 – 1945) for the American people and *"Everywhere in the world."* The Four Freedoms were announced at America's entrance into World War Two (1941). FDR demanded that all humanity share these freedoms. 1. *"Freedom of Speech"*; 2. *"Freedom of Worship"*; 3. *"Freedom from Want"*; 4. *"Freedom from Fear."* The Four Freedoms Speech was delivered on January 6, 1941. *"Freedom from Want and Fear"* implies the fair distribution of wealth, a Socialistic economy.

FOUR F'S – (*FOR EFS*) (4 F's) The four essential requirements for every animal and man to survive as a species. The 4 F's of survival are: *"Feeding," "Fighting," "Fleeing,"* and, of course, *"Procreation."*

FOUR H – (*FOR AYHCH*) (4-H) An American agricultural youth organization whose mission is: *"Engaging youth to reach their fullest potential while advancing the field of youth development."* The letter H repeated four times represents *"Head," "Heart," "Hands,"* and *"Health."* These are noble aspirations that should not be confined only to the prosperous young. According to the LIBERAL LEXICON: *A Socialistic, Spiritualistic Encyclodictionary,* the other Four H's are the *"Hopeless," "Hapless," "Helpless,"* and the *"Homeless."* These are the 50 million Americans living in poverty, including 2 million homeless children. All suffer from various degrees of depression. Many are handicapped, physically and mentally. A large percentage are drug-addicted. They are ill with various diseases including terminal AIDS. All are desperate, hungry, and therefore angry, making them dangerous. Remedying our Four H problem is a moral imperative, and should be a national concern. But in competitive, dog-eat-dog capitalism, there will always be winners and losers. *"To the victors go the spoils."* As rugged individualists, capitalists justify their heartless acknowledgement: *"I got mine, to hell with you!"* Under capitalism, there will always be the hopeless, hapless, helpless, and homeless. That's because the problem is capitalism. The solution is Socialism.

FOUR L'S – (*FOR ELS*) (4 L's) The metaphysical nexus among "Light," "Life," "Lord," and "Love." Everything that is, is light. Every form of energy, matter, particle, or wave vibration in the universe is light. Therefore, all living things – life itself – is light. The universe is light, the light of the Lord. Every major religion refers to the Lord God as the *"Light of the world"* – all worlds. The omnipresent Lord is everywhere and in everything. The Lord is the light, which animates all sentient beings with life. Every major religion insists that the Lord God is love. When we are enLIGHTened, we love the Lord, the source of light, life, and love. Indeed, the Four L's together, (LIFE/LIGHT/ LOVE/LORD) forms the nexus of all spirituality.

FOUR NOBLE TRUTHS – (*FOR NOE*-bul *TRUTHS*) The Buddha's teaching that: 1. Existence involves inevitable suffering for all people; 2. This suffering springs from egocentrism; 3. Egocentrism can be rooted out; 4. This rooting out can come by following the Eightfold Path.

FOUR 0 ONE-K TRUMPSTERS – (for-oh-wun-*KAY TRUMP*-sters) (401-K Trumpsters) Selfish financial small fries. 401-K Trumpsters will support the vile insidious President Donald Trump (b. 1946), providing the economy is growing, and their retirement plan (401-K) in the stockmarket increases. Nothing else matters to them. Trump's criminality, corruptibility, perfidy, dishonesty, pomposity, insensitivity, impropriety, immorality, barbarity, despicability, infidelity, instability, and stupidity are inconsequential to the 401-K Trumpsters. (They're too narrow-minded to realize that the D.O.W. is in fact the Disparity Of Wealth index, between them and the plutocracy.) The Trumpsters have bought into the Republican credo: *"I got mine, to hell with you!"* They are oblivious to the fact that Trump and the Republicans are using them to further enrich the rich. They are but small chunks of meat to be ground-up when the Wall St. meat-market crashes again. However, without foresight (or conscience), the 401-K Trumpsters just live for today. As in 1929 and 2008, they are sitting on the rim of a volcano, and don't even know it. *Karmic Justice* comes to all, especially the greedily indifferent. Both Benjamin Franklin (1706 – 1790) and Thomas Jefferson (1743 – 1826) had independently warned: *"Those who would trade liberty for security, will have neither security nor liberty."*

FOUR SIGNS – (*FOR SYNS*) (also the Four Sights) In Buddhist tradition, an old man, a diseased man, a corpse, and a holy man. These signs influenced Prince Gautama Siddhartha (c. 563 – c. 483 BCE) to leave his luxurious home and go forth on the search for enlightenment that led him to Buddhahood.

FOURTEENTH AMENDMENT – (*FOR*-teenth a-*MEND*-ment) Constitutional alteration that made the freed slaves U.S. citizens (1868). Furthermore, the 14th Amendment was interpreted by the Supreme Court (*Santa Clara County v. Southern Pacific Railroad,* 1886) to mean that corporations too are U.S. citizens. That's how corporations became *people.*

FOURTH GRADE – (*FORTH GRAYD*) Pivotal year in the learning experience (age 9). Educational point where the student shifts from learning to read, to reading to learn. At this point, those students who have not learned the mechanics of reading begin to fall behind. This is called the *"4th Grade Slump."* In a cascade effect, the student finds each proceeding school year more difficult and frustrating. Inability to read by the 4th grade results in school failure and probable drop-out. As a matter of fact, reading at the 4th grade level (like a 9 years old) is considered minimally literate. Incidentally: Most Americans read at the 6th grade level, as are most U.S. newspapers.

FOWER – (*FOUW*-er) An archaic appellation for a street cleaner.

FOX – (*FOKS*) (Broadcasting) In this case, not the cagy animal, but the cagy, deceptive TV network that became the purveyor of fake news. Fox News is the Republican Party mouthpiece that uses the news to advance the conservative capitalist agenda, by duping the poor to vote against their economic interests. Fox News is more accurately *"Faux News."* Fox News is to the Trump White House, what *Russia Today* (RT TV) is to Putin's Kremlin. Fox News has become *"Trump News."* It is a de facto state-run medium in a media-run state. Fox News Network was specifically established to propagate the conservative corporate capitalist catechism and elect Republican politicians. The de facto credo of fallacious Fox News is: *"Turn the Have-Littles against the Have-Nots, so that the Have-Alls, can Have-More."* Fox Broadcasting was specifically designed and established (1996) to widen the rift between the *"Have-littles,"* and *"Have- nots."* Their grand strategy is to foment animosity, bigotry, and racism among the poor and lower middle-class, preventing them from developing a unified, Socialistic class consciousness. Solidarity would present a powerful united front (and big voting block) against the conservative, capitalist, Republicans, and rich. Fox News hate-mongers. It indoctrinates average, simple-minded Americans to hate the poor, minorities, Democrats, Liberals, Progressives, Socialists, intellectuals, and left-wing academicians. Fox has been successful in getting *"low-information"* poor people to vote against their own personal interests. The architect of the Russian Revolution, Vladimir Lenin (1870 – 1924) said that capitalism uses *"Falsehood and deception to hoodwink the masses of workers and peasants to stultify their minds."* According to *"Media Bias Fact Check"*: *"Overall, we rate Fox News right biased on editorial positions that align with the right and Questionable due to the promotion of propaganda, conspiracy theories, pseudoscience, the use of poor sources, and numerous false claims and failed fact checks. Straight news reporting from beat reporters is generally fact- based and accurate, which earns a Mixed factual rating."* In conclusion, Fox News is positioned on the extreme right with *"Low Credibility."* Incidentally: Donald J. Trump (b. 1946) now serves as the spokesman, the Press Secretary for *"President Fox N. Friends"* (b. 1996). Post Script: In November, 2019, Geraldo Rivera (b. 1943) reporter turned right-wing propagandist rightly declared that President Richard Nixon (1913 – 1994) would not have been found guilty of his crimes, and forced out of office, if he had Fox News to support [read: *lie*] for him. Update: Fox is about to go on trial for slander and liable. The Fox News Corporation had been highjacked by its own viewers. The deluder views dictate what they want to hear on Fox. In order to maintain viewership, Fox quit broadcasting news, and gave its audience the propaganda, lies, and fantasies it craves. As a matter of fact, former Australian Prime Minister, Malcomb Turnbull (b. 1954) referred to Fox News as *"angertainment."* This is entertaining an angry audience with the hate and anger they desire. *"Whoever controls the media, the images, controls the culture."* – Allen Ginsberg (1926 – 1997). Update: Fox News lost the slander suit for $787.5 million dollars. The second suit is pending.

FOX HUNTING – (*FOKS HUNT*-ing) A vile blood sport of the English landed gentry. Wealthy aristocrats on horseback with teams of hounds chase a fox across the countryside. The hounds corner the fox and tear it apart. Fox hunting is a hostile, contemptible activity. But not in every case. In power politics/economics, fox hunting can be an honorable, patriotic enterprise. That's if the victim hunted is contemptible FOX News Network (est. 1996). FOX hunting is the hostile takeover of that vile fake-news outlet by wealthy aristocratic Americans. Progressive billionaires like George Soros (b. 1930), Warren Buffett (b. 1930), Mike Bloomberg (b. 1942), Tom Seyer (b. 1957) and others can chase then purchase FOX News on Wall Street, then kill it. This would be an act of great loyalty to the Constitution, nation, and the truth. They would be transposed into beneficent billionaires, contrite capitalists, and patriotic patriarchs. As Lucius Cincinnatus (c. 519 – c. 430 BCE) saved ancient Rome, these plutocrats would become historic heroes. Rather than pursue politics, pursue the FOX. They can detoxify politics by exterminating the beast. That's because FOX News is a vile vector, a danger to democracy. It is a rabid animal, spreading an epidemic contagion. It is a diseased creature that is contaminating the minds of millions of Americans. Vicious FOX is a rabid animal, that has infected the brains of perhaps 40% of the U.S. population with lies, fear, and hatred. It has facilitated the rise of that fascist fox, Donald Trump (b. 1946). FOX has driven a large part of the American people crazy! FOX hunting and slaying would prove to be a turning point in American History. Exterminating this vicious vixen would unite our people and preserve our Progressive way of life.

FOX NEWS CREDO – (*FOKS NYOOZ CRAY*-doh) *"Turn the Have-Littles,"* against the *"Have-Nots,"* so that the *"Have-Alls,"* can have more."

FOYER – (*FOY*-yer) or (fwa-*YEY*) A vestibule or entrance hall. The lobby of a theater or hotel is a foyer.

FRACKING – (*FRAK*-ing) (Hydraulic fracturing) Fracking involves injecting high- pressured jets of chemicals deep into the Earth, fracturing rocks to release trapped natural gas. Toxic chemicals poison the water table and environment, but make the capitalist oil companies richer. Land has been contaminated, farms ruined, livestock and people killed by fracking. Rural people living near land that has undergone fracking have discolored, toxic water gushing forth from their pipes.

FRAGGED – (*FRAGD*) (Fragging) A Vietnam War vintage word (1960's – 1975) meaning to be killed by your own soldiers, usually with a FRAGmentation grenade. The victim's body is shredded. Unpopular, overzealous, or dangerously incompetent officers were the primary fragging victims. God only knows how many names on the *Black Wall of Vietnam War Dead* in Washington D.C., did not die in combat, but were fragged, murdered by their own subordinates. In 1969, there were 126 *"known"* murders of officers by fragging. In 2 years, the figure doubled. There were 200 confirmed fragging attempts against officers in 1970. The average U.S. soldier in World War Two was 26 years old, in Vietnam, 19 years old. In Vietnam, racial tension, drug addiction, despair, insubordination, and actual mutiny were destroying the army, which was on the verge of total collapse. Fragging was a symptom.

FRANC – (*FRANK*) Name of the currency formerly used in France and Belgium, having been withdrawn in favor of the Euro. The Franc is still used in Switzerland.

FRANCHISE – (*FRAN*-chyhz) A privilege of a public nature conferred on an individual, group, or company by the government. For example, to be issued a franchise to operate a bus system. A franchise is granted by private companies like Wendy's, McDonald's, or Kentucky Fried Chicken to manage one of their stores. They are granted a franchise to sell their French fries. The store, restaurant, business, or team is also referred to as a franchise.

FRANCISCA – (fran-*SIS*-ka) Ancient Frankish throwing-ax, judged as the best all- around weapon of antiquity. This weapon gave the Franks and later France their names. The Francisca was brought to America by French voyageurs, where it evolved into the tomahawk. If course, the Indians long had a tomahawk battle hatchet.

FRANCISCAN'S CREDO – (fran-*SIS*-can *CRAY*-doh) *"Pax et Bonum."* (Peace and Goodness.)

FRANCIUM – (*FRAN*-see-um) (Fr) The name derives from the Modern Latin *Francia* meaning "France." The 87 protons in its nucleus give francium its atomic number. Francium is an extremely scarce and reactive radioactive element of the alkali group. It is the most volatile of all the alkaline metals, and will violently explode even in moist atmosphere. Francium is very unstable and occurs in trace amounts in uranium ores. Francium is so rare that not more than 1 ounce is found in the Earth's crust at any time. Because it is so rare and hard to create, it may be the most expensive element, priced at over a billion dollars a gram. Francium is used for research in the field of chemistry.

FRANCOPHONE – (*FRANK*-o-fone) A Canadian of French ancestry, or has French as a first language. Francophone is contrasted with Anglophone, which are the English-speaking Canadians.

FRANKENSTEIN EFFECT – (*FRANK*-ken-styn ef-*FECT*) Accidentally creating monstrous animals, plants, bacteria, viruses, molds or fungus through bioengineering. Like Dr. Viktor Frankenstein's monster, these unnatural organisms may turn on their creators and their planet, wreaking biological havoc.

FRANKINCENSE – (*FRANK*-in-sens) (also Olibanum) an aromatic gum resin from a variety of Asian and African trees. The gum crystalizes and is burned as incense, particularly by the Roman and Orthodox

Catholic Churches. Frankincense has long been a trade product of Yemen. Tradition has it that the Magi (Three Kings) offered gifts of gold, myrrh, and frankincense, to the infant Jesus, indicative of its worth.

FRATERNAL ORDER OF POLICE – (fra-*TURN*-nal *OR*-der of *POE*-lees) (F.O.P.) Unlike every other union, this is a bad one. Its purpose is not to promote good, but to hide evil. All other labor unions protect workers from bad management. The F̲raternal O̲rder of P̲olice protects bad cops from the citizens they terrorized, even murdered – from justice. The union defends police brutality and thereby promotes the establishment of fascism – the police state. The job of the Fraternal Order of Police is to cover-up the most egregious acts of the most sadistic cops, especially murder. The credo of the fraternity is *"A cop can do no wrong."* *"The Myth: 'Only a few bad apples.' The truth, only a few good cops."* – Dr. Gary J. Pasieka (b. 1951).

FRATERNIZATION – (frat-turn-nys-*ZAY*-shun) (Fraternal, Fraternize, Fraternized, Fraternizing) The term derives from the Latin *"fraternus,"* meaning *"brotherly."* It entered English in the 1610s from the French *"fraternizer,"* meaning *"to sympathize as brothers."* Fraternization is to associate cordially, intimately, even with proclaimed enemies on the battlefield. Wars end when the foot soldiers, the *"cannon fodder"* refuses to fight their subjugated counterparts, but embraces them as brothers. Fraternization almost ended World War One (1914 – 1918) on the Western Front with the *"Christmas Truce of 1914."* Fraternization did end the War on the Eastern Front in 1917 with the *"Bolshevik Revolution."* Indeed, fraternization on the battlefield foments revolution among the warring nations at home. The capitalist military-industrial complex profits immensely from war. That's why fraternizers are court-marshaled and executed by career officers and capitalist politicians. Incidentally: Presently (November 2022) Russian citizens are being forced to fight their Slavonic brothers in the Ukraine. The invasion of the Ukraine is a naked land-grab to aggrandize the Russian Dictopresident Vladimir Putin (b. 1952). Rather than become murderers or be murdered, Russian soldiers are increasing fraternizing with the Ukrainians, as their great-grandfather did with the Germans in 1917.Prayerfully, another Russian Revolution will dethrone the fascist dictatorship and assure world peace. *"Workers [and soldiers] of the world unite, you have nothing to lose but your chains."* – Dr. Karl Marx (1818 – 1883), in the Communist Manifesto, 1848.

FRATRICIDE – (*FRAT*-ri-syd) (Fratricidal) The killing of one's brother. Literally fratricide is the murder of one's male sibling. Traditionally, the very first murder was a case of fratricide. According to the Biblical account, Adam's and Eve's first son, Cain, killed his younger brother Able. The vile crime of fratricide was not uncommon among medieval monarchies, in power struggles for the throne. Civil wars have been characterized as fratricidal, with countrymen killing each other. Poland suffered an appalling rendition of fratricide during World War One (1914 – 1918). Poland had been divided among Russia, Germany, and Austria since the 1770's. Therefore, when the Great War broke out, Poles in the German and Austrian armies were forced to kill Poles in the Russian army and otherwise, in fratricidal combat. So what qualifies as fratricide depends on one's definition of brotherhood. Police and even the army commits fratricide when they kill their brothers, by shooting their neighbors and family members in defense of capitalist property. When these armed forces of oppression refuse to execute fratricide, and turn their guns on the capitalist exploiters, we have revolution, as happened in Russia (1917). Yes, we are our brother's keeper, not our brother's killer.

FRAUDIFICATION – (frawd-di-fi-*CAY*-shun) (Fraudify) Purposeful falsification. To cleverly mislead in order to establish the *"Big Lie."* Fraudification turns fiction into fact. It is employed in dictatorships to falsely revise history. The propaganda machine alters documents and re-touches photos in this process. The Neo-Nazi campaign to deny the Holocaust is an example of fraudification. Incidentally: No Presidential administration had employed fraudification more lavishly than that of *"His Mendaciousness,"* Donald Trump (b. 1946).

FRAUDIT – (*FRAW*-dit) A <u>fraud</u>ulent aud<u>it</u>. A fake audit. A phony, deceptive, counterfeit examination and recount of the votes cast in an election. Unlike an honest, genuine audit, a fraudit is conducted by the angry losers, in a desperate hope of overturning the election results. Therefore, it is grossly biased, unprofessional, undemocratic, and illegal. Nevertheless, on March 31, 2021, the Arizona Senate *"Trumpublicans"* launched the nation's first fraudit in Maricopa County. In an *"auditorium-cum-frauditorium"* they began the hand-counting of over 2,100,000 ballots from the 2020 Presidential election. Though the results had been carefully counted, recounted, checked, rechecked, and certified as valid, the fascist Republicans still tried to overturn the legitimate victory of Joe Biden (b. 1942) over loser Donald Trump (b. 1946). These Republicans hired a bizarre alt-right Florida group, the *"Cyber Ninjas,"* to perpetrate the fraud. The fraudit was a clown show. However, the clowns who support Trump had faith in it. This farce was part of the *"Big Lie,"* that Trump was cheated out of the White House. The Ninjas were actually looking for shreds of bamboo fibers, said to prove that China miraculously stuffed 40,000 votes for Biden into the ballot boxes! Can you believe it? *"Trumpanzees"* do! But this comedy is no laughing matter. It is eroding popular trust in democracy. Too, Trumpublican politicians in other states (Pennsylvania, Wisconsin, Michigan) want to stage fraudits as well. Of course, the votes need not be recounted in districts where Trump and the Republicans had won, only where they had lost. These are the big cities with large minority populations, and Liberal college towns – Democratic strongholds. The Maricopa County charade was a stab in the heart of democracy. Incidentally: The term *"fraudit"* was coined by former FBI Assistant Director for Counterintelligence, Frank Figliuzzi (b. 1962). *"When injustice becomes the law, resistance becomes duty."* – Thomas Jefferson (1743 – 1826).

FRAUDULENT PRESIDENTS – (*FRAWD*-jew-lent *PRES*-si-dents) In our lifetime, (say the last 50 years), we have had five Presidents who had gained office through fraud. They were Republicans all: Richard Nixon (1913 – 1994); Ronald Reagan (1911 - 2004); George H. W. Bush (1924 - 2018); George H. Bush (b. 1946); and Donald Trump (b. 1946). The Vietnam War raged during the 1968 Presidential election. Democratic President Lyndon Johnson (1908 – 1973) was involved in Peace Talks to end the war. As a private citizen Richard Nixon illegally, secretly sabotaged the Peace Talks with the Vietnamese. His Republican operative, Henry Kissinger (1923 - 2023) persuaded the Vietnamese to: *"Wait! Don't make peace. You'll get a better deal from Nixon."* The war dragged on, many more died. Despite his treason, Republican Nixon was elected President (with the promise to end the war). In 1980, 52 American embassy personnel were being held hostage by radical Iranians. President Jimmy Carter (b. 1924) was locked in an election struggle with Republican candidate Ronald Reagan. Perfidious Reagan illegally contacted the Iranian leaders, as Nixon had contacted the North Vietnamese leaders. Regan told the Iranians not to release the American hostages until he was elected President. Reagan indeed won the election, largely due to Carter's hostage crisis. The Iranians released the hostages immediately after Reagan was sworn in as President. The captives had to suffer for 444 days. In 1988, the Democrats ran a strong candidate, Senator Gary Hart (b. 1936). Republican candidate George H. W. Bush was afraid to run against Hart. A nasty Republican operative, Lee Atwater (1951 – 1991) arranged for Hart to be stranded at a hotel in the Florida Keys overnight. The next morning, a gorgeous young woman, scantily clad flung herself at Hart and hugged the Senator. A photographer from the *"National Enquirer"* just happened to be on the spot. What luck for the Republicans! Gary Hart was branded a *"Womanizer,"* which destroyed his political career. (This was in pre-Trump America.) The result, Republican George H. W. Bush was elected President. In the 2000 Presidential election, the Democrats ran Vice- President Al Gore (b. 1948). The election between Gore and Republican George W. Bush was excruciatingly close. It all came down to Florida. The vote differential was a few hundred. But many votes in Democratic Broward and Miami-Dade Counties were not counted. A recount was ordered. If the recount took place, Gore would be elected President. However a perfidious Republican operative, Roger Stone (b. 1952) organized a boisterous pro-Bush demonstration (*"The Brooks Brothers Riot"*) at the Miami-Dade recount center. A gang of well-dressed middle-aged white Republican male rioters succeeded in halting the recount. The result, Republican George W. Bush was elected President. In the 2016 Presidential election it was slimy Roger Stone again who negotiated with the Russians and Wikileak to hack and steal emails, in order to dig up dirt on Democratic candidate Hillary Clinton (b. 1947). The ruse worked. As a result, Republican candidate Donald Trump won the election. (Incidentally, both Gore and Clinton won the popular votes.) Why is it that the Republicans are so toxically corrupt? *DESPERATION!* The Republicans represent the rich. There is nothing the rich won't do (lie, cheat, steal, betray, murder) to protect their wealth.

FRAUGHT – (*FRAWT*) Something full of or accompanied by something threatening, perilous, treacherous. *"The mission was fraught with danger." "We are living in fraught times."*

FRAZIL – (*FRAY*-zuhl) Ice crystals or granules sometimes resembling slush, that forms in rough seas, swift streams, and turbulent waters. The turbulence of the water prevents the formation of a solid ice sheet. Therefore, a slushy frazil forms, like partially melted snow. Frazil is a French Canadian word, taken from the French word *"fraisil,"* meaning *"cinders."* Perhaps frazil resembled water impregnated with cinders.

FREEDOM – (*FREE*-dum) Being in an unrestricted state of mind, contrasted with liberty which is having an unrestricted choice of movement. Freedom is internal, attitudinal, whereas liberty is external, environmental. A free-thinking prisoner in a dictatorship is freer that his servile jailer who is at liberty. Freedom is essential for mental health. *"Mental health is characterized by flexibility. The more choices you have, the freer you are."* – Psychologist John Bradshaw (1933 - 2016). In a laissez faire capitalist society, people are free to starve, with no governmental interference or intervention. Dr. Karl Marx (1818 – 1883) insisted that *"Rights* [read: *freedom*] *can never be higher than the economic level of society and the cultural development, which the economic level determines."*

FREEDOM CAUCUS – (*FREE*-dum *CAW*-cus) The ultra-right-wing conservative [nay: *"reactionary"*] Republican Congressmen, the residue of the Obama era Tea Party. They consist of 31 members of the House of Representatives in 2017 (30 men, 1 woman). The only freedom this caucus is interested in, is for wealthy conservative capitalists. There are no Democrats in this illiberal club. They are libertarian, militaristic, capitalistic, and fundamentalist. The Freedom Caucus hopes to free rich Americans from all taxation, regulation, or responsibility to the poor. They are free enterprise, free market capitalists who hope to be free to privatize everything for personal private profit. Many are Fundamentalist Christians unfamiliar with Christ's <u>Social</u>ist *Social Gospel* (Matthew 25: 35 – 40). The Freedom Caucus intends to turn back time by undoing 120 years of social progress. Deregulation, voter suppression, environmental indifference, corporate tax exemptions, welfare dismantlement, reproductive restrictions, immigration curtailment are all high on their list of priorities. Only the military deserves tax dollars, according to the Freedom Caucus. Certainly, the Freedom Caucus is owned by the rich corporate capitalists. The Freedom Caucus hopes to transform our constitutional democracy, into a fascist corpocracy. In order to realize their agenda, the Freedom Caucus must keep Donald Trump (b. 1946) in power. So they try to obstruct, obfuscate, and sabotage all investigations into Trump's treason, money laundering, racketeering, profiteering, treason, and general criminality.

FREE COLLEGE – (free *COL*-ledj) Complimentary public education through all levels of schooling. Free college is government paid, tax-funded higher education for everybody. It is cost-free university for all. There is no greater patriotic service, advantage, benefit that can be bestowed on a nation than universal education. It's the best long-term investment for the economy, the country. But corporate capitalists don't think long-term. They are only interested in the quick buck, the next quarter's earnings, and the market today. *"Show me the money!"* is a corporate capitalist mantra. Democracy requires, demands an educated electorate. This is precisely why Republicans oppose free college. As lackeys of corporate capitalism, Republicans covertly oppose democracy. Democracy is a levelling, equalizing force. Capitalist Republicans advocate fascism which hoards the wealth at the top. It is too difficult to suppress the vote of an educated citizenry. So why educated them? Wealthy capitalists have no incentive to pay for free college. Their banks would lose billions in student loans. Too, why should the moneyed-class desire to create competition for their rich kids, by educating the children of the poor? After all, education is the most potent *"Liberalizing"* transformative. The last thing the reactionary capitalists want is a Liberal, Progressive, (*God Forbid, Socialist!*) population. That may result in the nationalization of their corporate monopolies, and the just redistribution of their ill-gotten wealth. Finally, ignorant people are conveniently easy to manipulate. (Consider the red-capped Trump supporters.) A college-educated population could not be conned, duped, deceived by hucksters or cult figures like the Republican Donald Trump (b. 1946). Therefore, don't expect support for free college education from corporate capitalist Republicans.

FREE EDUCATION – (*FREE* ed-jew-*KAY*-shun) A Socialistic policy employed by advanced, Progressive nations. Cost-free education is the greatest investment in a society's or nation's future. Nothing advances a nation further faster than a learned populous. An educated electorate assures a corruption-free government. Economic prosperity depends on an educated citizenry. Businessman Charles Pillsbury (1842 – 1899) rightly stated that: *"Education is to business what fertilizer is to farming."* Advancing Socialistic countries have cost- free education from K. to Ph.D. Declining capitalist countries make education unaffordable for the vast majority of the people. College loans indebt the poor, enslaving them to the capitalist banksters. It is a capitalist belief that hoarding education will aid them in hoarding their wealth. They may be correct. Capitalists, represented politically by the Republican Party, fear an educated, but poor populous. They are indeed dangerous people. Educated people cannot be fooled about the cause of their poverty. Republicans cannot *"Out Fox"* (*Network*) the learned. A poor but educated people will demand distributive justice, [read: *"fair distribution of the wealth"*] or Socialism. The Republicans or capitalists cannot have that. Better keep the population uneducated, and therefore ignorant and poor, in order to maintain their privileged hegemony. *"To throw obstacles in the way of a complete education is like putting out the eyes."* – Elizabeth Cady Stanton (1815 – 1902).

FREE ENTERPRISE – (*FREE EN*-ter-prize) Private capitalist enterprise. The textbook definition of free enterprise is a market economy in which competition is allowed to flourish and privately owned businesses are free to operate for a profit with minimal government interference. Actually, competition is the bane of corporate capitalists in the free market. Their goal is to free themselves of competition by destroying all competitors, or illegally colluding with them to eliminate competition. Competition in the free enterprise is only found on the Mom-and-Pop level. With minimal governmental interference [read: *oversight, regulation*] enterprising capitalists are indeed free to exploit the consumer, hoard the wealth, and defile the environment.

FREE FIRE ZONE – (*FREE FY*-er ZONE) Areas in Vietnam that the American invaders declared as indiscriminate killing regions. Because the conflict was a Vietnamese civil war, friend could not be differentiated from foe. Therefore, the U.S. Army ordered that everybody, even animals were to be killed in Vietnam's free fire zones.

FREE MARKET – (*FREE MAR*-ket) The capitalist *"killing fields."* It is in the free market that the capitalists make their financial killings. The free market has nothing to do with freedom, except the freedom of the rich and powerful to exploit the poor and weak. The less regulated the market, the freer the market.

FREEMASONRY – (*FREE*-may-son-ree) (Freemasons, Masons, Masonry) Oldest, largest, most prestigious and charitable fraternity in history. During the early middle Ages, Masons were the intellectual aristocracy (like the watchmakes 500 years later). Masons were architects, engineers, builders, and geometers. Unlike serfs, they were not tied to the estate. Masons were free, and traveled about Europe freely, sure to find a job, and welcomed wherever they stayed. Their ability to build magnificent cathedrals and castles, gave them a mystic, magical, divine aura. The talents of the Masonic guilds were sworn to secrecy. This is where Freemasonry attained the reputation of a secret society. With the invention of printing, the dissemination of information through literacy, the democratization of education, Freemasonry lost its privileged status. By the 17th century, Freemason Lodges accepted members other than builders. (Today, the term *FREE*mason alludes to the fact that a Mason is free to pursue any occupation other than stone masonry.) Masonic tradition is renowned for its archaic, esoteric rituals, many of which are quasi-religious in character, and secrecy. There is much symbolism and allegory in modern Masonry. Masons today are still builders as their ancient forbearers. However, the temples they are building are temples within – the character and the soul. The 3 levels of Freemasonry are: 1st *Entered Apprentice*; 2nd *Fellow Craft* (Journeyman); 3rd *Master Mason*. (*Scottish* or *York Rite*, and the *Shriners* are auxiliary Masonic institutions.) Incidentally: About 200,000 Masons were murdered by the German Nazis in the concentration camps during the Holocaust (1933 – 1945). Foot Note: Freemasons are blamed for almost every conspiracy in the world. *"Our Masonic friends* *have it down very fine. I do not know where they got it so well. I have often wondered where they found out so many of the secrets of our High and Accepted Order of Masonry.*" – Pastor Charles Taze Russell (1852 – 1916).

FREEMASON'S CREDO – (*FREE*-may-sons *CRAY*-dow) "*Meet on the level; Act by the plumb; Part on the square.*"

FREE RANGE – (free *RAYNJ*) (also Cage Free) Allowing livestock to roam at liberty, enjoying their brief lives before being sacrifice as our food and leather. Socialists treat animals humanely, while capitalists treat animals like commodities (pork bellies). It is almost mystic, but happy animals provide meat that is healthier and tastes differently. Animals, like humans experience pain, fear, anxiety, and depression. These negative emotions and afflictions produce toxins in the body that are absorbed within the muscles, which becomes our meat. Free ranging animals do not develop these fearful detrimental chemicals. Naturally, free range animals feed on natural food. Cattle for instance eat grass as was intended, not grain (corn). Starchy gain gives cows gas, the damaging global-warming methane. But we are accustomed to the taste of cattle imprisoned in capitalist concentration camps (agra-factories), where they are being fattened for the slaughter. Their flesh is marbled with fat, and so is saturated with cholesterol. Nevertheless, it is moister, tenderer, and tastier than free range meat. Unhealthy fat tastes so good. True, free range meat is tougher, drier, and less tasty. This is because liberated animals get exercise, free to range where their heart desires, eating what is good for them. Prison- raised animals, treated like things will provide cheaper meat too. Nevertheless, insisting on free range meat is a moral imperative that the human animal must make. The blessed Church Father, St. Basil (330 – 379 CE) prayed: "*O God, enlarge within us the sense of fellowship with all living things, ever our brothers, the animals, to whom Thou gavest the earth as their home in common with us. We must remember with shame that in the past we have exercised the high dominion of man with ruthless cruelty so that the voice of the earth, which should have gone up to thee in song, has been a groan of pain. May we realize that they live not for us alone, but for themselves and for Thee and that they love the sweetness of life.*"

FREE RUSSIA LEGION – (free *RUSH*-uh *LEE*-jun) (FRL) Russian soldiers who had defected to the Ukraine, organized in the Ukrainian Army to fight the Russian invasion. The soldiers of the Free Russian Legion are not traitors but patriots, intent on freeing Russia from tyranny. They are not fighting against their country, but to rid their country of its dictator, Vladimir Putin (b. 1952). Too, they are fighting to defend the Ukraine from Putin's unprovoked and savage invasion. These young men are honorable conscientious objectors to an atrocious war. They have witnessed the plunder, rape, torture, and murder, and refuse to become monsters for Putin. Entrance into the FRL begins with a surrender on the battlefield. Once in Ukrainian custody, the Russians are not treated as prisoners. In fact, their conditions are far better than they were in the Russian Army. They are permitted to live in the Ukraine, for they certainly can't return to Russia. No defector is pressured to join the Free Russia Legion. But hundreds volunteer. In order to deter spies, the volunteers are intensely interrogated, and must pass a lie-detector test. If they pass, they undergo rigorous military training to become authentic soldiers. Once in the Free Russia Legion, they take on new identities, pseudonyms, and their faces disguised from cameras. Their banner is a white flag, with a thick, light blue stripe or band across the center. The Free Russia Legion is a direct affront to Vladimir Putin. Too, it represents a challenge to all Russian people to liberate themselves from fascist oppression. A

Caveat: Do not confuse the military unit, *Free Russia Legion* in the Ukraine, with the democratic partisan fighters, *Russian Liberation Army* in Russia.

FREE SOCIETY – (*FREE* so-*SY*-it-tee) An environment in which people are at liberty to do what the please, within the bounds of propriety – meaning, not hurting others. A culture governed by love deserves and can maintain its freedom. *"Love, and do as you please,"* advised St. Augustine (354 – 430 CE). Freedom of speech is at the core of a free society. All other freedoms are rooted in freedom of speech. Freedom of speech includes freedom after speech as well. The problem is that freedom cannot be too selective. A free society is open to the good, the bad, and the ugly. This has been demonstrated by the lies and fake news broadcasted by the Fox Network, The Trump Administration, and the *"Prince of Liars,"* President Donald Trump (b. 1946). A free society can be easily infiltrated, as the Russians had proved with their propaganda that elected Trump. A free society maintains a delicate balance between personal liberty, and the enemies of liberty, who will attempt to use freedom to destroy the fee society.

FREE STUFF – (*FREE* stuhf) Something, anything given as a gratuity, without cost, charge, or payment. In the political lexicon, *"free stuff"* is a Republican term of disparagement for entitlements, social benefits for the poor. Free stuff is a simplistic term designed to make the poor recipients simply look like freeloaders. Healthcare, childcare, college education, food stamps are some of the *"free stuff"* of which the Republicans object. Actually, the free stuff proposed by Democrats and Socialists should not be considered hand-outs, but as social entitlements, human rights, and investments in the nation. *"I got mine, to hell with you."* – Republican Ethos.

FREE TRADE – (*FREE TRAYD*) Open markets, no barriers on foreign trade. Free trade encourages a free flow of imports and exports. Too, industrialists are allowed to outsource, relocate abroad to take advantage of cheap, unregulated labor. Free trade creates sweatshop jobs in underdeveloped countries by eliminating union jobs in developed countries. The developed country is flooded with cheap goods. However, the jobless (victims of free trade), cannot afford to buy them. The opposite of free trade is protectionism. Free trade can only be effective if it is fair. Only nations with comparable pay scales and workers' benefits, as well as comparable corporate tax rates should participate in free trade. This will eliminate the incentive for greedy corporate capitalists (like the Trumps) from relocating, costing jobs.

FREE TRADER – (*FREE TRAYD*-der) A corporate capitalist or rich corporate shareholder. Workers dependent on industrial jobs are certainly not free traders. Free trade opens the door for cheap foreign imports that suppress the home manufacturing sector. Too, free trade leaves the door open for corporate capitalists to move plants abroad to take advantage of child and slave labor. Instead of elevating the foreign worker to American labor standards, free traders intend to lower the American worker to foreign peasant standers. In the process, the free traders becomes immensely rich. American workers become joblessly poor. And the stage is set for Socialist Revolution.

FREEWAY/EXPRESSWAY – (*FREE*-way eks-*PRES*-way) Two terms for high-speed thoroughfares that are usually used synonymously. Freeways or expressways are the highest form of highways (though highways are not freeways or expressways). Freeways/expressways are *"controlled access"* highways. Pedestrians, bicycles, horses, buggies are prohibited. That's because a freeway is expressly designed for maximum speed, an unimpeded express route. Traffic is unhindered by slow vehicles, traffic signals, intersections, railways, pedestrian paths or animals. Freeways/expressways are multi-lane roads. Opposite flow of traffic is divided by a median – a guardrail or grassy strip of land. Access ramps enable traffic to enter or exit by merging smoothly. Cross-roads make their way above or under the freeway/expressway through overpasses or underpasses. In congested urban areas, the freeway/expressway is descended, lowered below the city street level so to keep neighborhood disruption minimal. Unlike a highway, there are no buildings lining the freeway/expressway. Of course, there is a maximum and minimum speed limit on these roads. Freeways/expressways are very long interstate highways that traverse the entire nation. Interstate commerce is totally dependent on the interstate freeway/expressway system. Incidentally: Freeways/expressways are designed for speed, to save time, not for sightseeing. The drive is fast but boring. When constructed, the freeways/highways intentionally avoid bottlenecks like small towns. As a result, hundreds-of-thousands of small towns lost visitors as customers. So they shriveled like grapes on the vine. *"Thanks to the interstate highway system, one can drive from coast to coast and see nothing."* – Charles Kuralt (1934 – 1997).

FREE WILL – (free *WILL*) The ability to exercise the power of intention. A person with free will is not determined by others. Free will is the ability to choose our behavior. With free will, we can choose to become sinners or saints. Otherwise, there would be no right or wrong, and therefore no grounds for reward or punishment, good or bad. Though we have free will to choose between good or evil, God rewards and punishes [read: *teaches*] us about our choices through the *"Universal Law of Reciprocity"* known as *"Karma."* Indeed, we reap what we sow. Incidentally: The controversial debate over free will is ancient. It is illustrated in Genesis, the first book of the Bible. In the Garden of Eden with Adam and Eve were two special trees bearing forbidden fruit. The *"Tree of Life"* would bestow immortality from its fruit. The *"Tree of Knowledge of Good and Evil"* would provide wisdom. God warned Adam and Eve not to touch those two trees. This seemed to be a test, an excruciating test of their self-control. It seems that God used Satan as tempter, tester of Adam and Eve. They came to the *Tree of Knowledge of Good and Evil.* Satan said: *"God knows that when you eat of it your eyes will be opened, and you will be like God, knowing good and evil."* – (Genesis 3:5). Knowing good from evil enables one to choose the good or the evil – in other words, exercise free will. (However, did not Adam and Eve display free will when they willfully disobey God? Let us not complicate this story more than is necessary.) So Adam and Eve succumbed to their humanness and failed the test. They never got to the *Tree of Life.* Therefore, they would not be immortal. They were cast out of the Garden of Eden as punishment, and forced to live on the harsh Earth, needing to work for a living. *"By the sweat of your face you shall eat bread, till you return to the ground, for out of it you were taken; for you are dust, and to dust you shall return."* – (Genesis 3:19). So free will, the ability and necessity to choose between good and evil became our human inheritance, God's only animal to be so challenged. Interestingly, the *Tree of Life* was left alone. Mankind's collective parents choose free will over immortality for humanity.

FREEZE – (*FREEZ*) (Freezing, Frozen) To become hardened into ice or into a solid body. In the freezing process, a liquid is transformed into a solid. Water becomes ice, for instance. The result of freezing is becoming frozen. With the drop in temperature, the loss of heat energy, anything containing liquid will freeze. A temperature of 32o Fahrenheit or 0o Celsius/Centigrade are the freezing points on the thermometer. For living creatures, freezing results in death. This includes bacteria, which prevents putrefaction. So freezing preserves food. On the molecular level, atoms or molecules slow down their vibration with increased cold. When frozen, the molecules lock together, forming a solid.

FREEZER BURN – (*FREE*-zer *BERHN*) Not a burn caused by heat, but a dehydration scar. Freezer burn is a light-colored spot that appears on frozen food, caused by loss of surface moisture. The problem is caused by faulty packaging and improper freezing methods. Freezer burned food is still edible. It will be dried-out some, and may lose a little flavor.

FREEZE SPELL – (*FREEZ* spell) A simple but popular *"binding"* spell to stop someone from doing something. The freeze spell involves placing a taglock (lock of hair, nail clipping, body fluid, photo) of a person in the freezer. The intention is to freeze their malevolent, malicious behavior. As with every spell, the freeze must be performed with belief, concentration, and emotion.

FREEZING RAIN – (*FREEZ*-zing *RAYN*) Precipitation below the freezing point, that remains liquid through its fall. Freezing rain results when snowflakes melt into raindrops in the atmosphere. This raindrop does not possess a speck of dust (*microscopic nuclei*) around which to freeze. So it remains liquid, even though its temperature is below the freezing point. When the super-cooled raindrop hits any cold object on the ground, it freezes instantly, coating the object with a layer of heavy, clear ice. This is an ice storm. Incidentally: Geographical and meteorological conditions make Montreal the most vulnerable city for ice storms due to freezing rain.

FREI CORPS – (*FRY* kor) (Free Corps) Fascists German political street gangs early in the interwar period (particularly the 1920's). The Frei Corps were right-wing nationalist organizations consisting of embittered, disillusioned, vengeful ex- soldiers. These young toughs were humiliated by the defeat in World War One, and unemployed by the great depression. The most prominent Frei Corps leader was General Eric Ludendorff (1865 – 1937). Unable to admit defeat in the Great War, the Frei Corps subscribed to the *"stab-in-the-back"* delusion. The traitors at home who had caused the military and political disaster were the Socialists, Communists, Democrats, and Jews. The Frei Corps battled the Socialist *Spartacus League* throughout the streets of Germany. The Nazi Party was one of many Frei Corps groups. Adolf Hitler (1889 – 1945) was employed by the army to spy on the Nazis. He ultimately joined the Nazis (#555) and became their leader (fuhrer). The Nazis absorbed other Frei Corps groups and became the dominate fascist organization. Tragically, with support from the army, the Nazis defeated the Progressive Spartacus League. Its members died in Dachau. Instead of peace, prosperity, and brotherhood, the Nazis provided war, devastation, and genocide.

FRENCH – (*FRENCH*) The language spoken in France, southern Belgium, and throughout the world in present and former French colonies. A French speaker is called a *"Francophone."* French is classified as a *Gallo-Romance* language. Its bedrock is Celtic-Gaulic that was later Romanized by Vulgar (popular) Latin. This Gallo-Romance hybrid was topped-off by Old German contributed by the Germanic Franks (who also contributed the names France and French). Lastly, the Viking Normans added a Scandinavian flavor to the language. The hybrid language called French evolved unlike any of its neighbors. It does not sound Germanic like Dutch, Austrian, German, or English. Neither does it sound Roman or Latin like Italian, Spanish, or Portuguese. The Norman invasion of England (1066) infused French into English (about 29% of the vocabulary). This enriched English but complicated the language. Generally speaking, if you can't pronounce it, and you can't spell it, it is of French origin. Outside of Western Europe, dialects of French are spoken in Canada (Quebec), the Caribbean (Haiti, Lesser Antilles), and in French Guiana, in South America. Much of Northern and Western Africa is familiar with French, as well as French Indo-China (Vietnam, Laos, Cambodia). In the United States, a Creole French is spoken by the Cajuns of southern Louisiana. There are Francophones in northern Maine on the Canadian border, and in locations throughout upper New England. Incidentally: The French are stubbornly, fanatically protective of their language. They particularly fear the spread of *"Franklish,"* Anglo-American English words creeping into French. There is a government ministry that serves as the *"language police."* French newspapers are fined if they publish over 100 English words on a single page! New technical-scientific words cannot be adopted from English. French equivalents must be coined. International conferences of Francophone nations are held, in an attempt to keep the language pure. However, it is actually making French stale. Every language needs a constant transfusion of fresh blood to keep it vigorous. *"Language is a city to the building of which every human being brought a brick."* – Ralph Waldo Emerson (1803 – 1882). *"Last year's words belong to last year's language and next year's words await another voice."* – T. S. Eliot (1888 – 1965).

FRENCH ALGERIA – (*FRENCH* al-*JEER*-ree-ah) Algeria is a huge nation in North Africa, 36% larger than Alaska, though primarily Sahara Desert. During the 19th century period of neo-imperialism, France conquered Algeria in 1830. It was held as a French colony until 1962. After the French had lost Indochina in 1954, they repeated their mistakes in Algeria. Colonial Algeria was ruled in an apartheid manner by the French *"Colons."* These were French provincials who fled from Alsace-Lorraine in 1871, when the Germans took the province in the Franco-Prussian War. They migrated to Algeria and took total control of the colony. Though only 10% of the population, the Colons grabbed 90% of the useable land, the fertile Mediterranean coastline. Like the Scots-Irish migrants to Ulster, the Colons became fanatical nationalists. They practiced racism and distributive injustice toward the Arab majority. A ruling minority always lives in fear, and so is exceedingly brutal. Algerian Arabs rebelled. Riots escalated into civil war, the Algerian War of Independence (1954 – 1962). The war witnessed savage atrocities. The desperate Colons were fighting for their status, their wealth, and their survival. The French Government fell, and Charles DeGaulle (1890 – 1970) became Prime Minister in 1958. The Colons finally had their savior – or so they thought. They were bitterly disappointed. The wise general recognized the Algerian War as unwinnable. One Vietnam was enough! He called for an election in Algeria, which the Arabs were sure to win. Guerrilla warfare tore the colony asunder. To add fuel to the fire (quite literally) oil was discovered in Algeria. The stakes were raised even higher. The Colons failed at an assassination attempt against DeGaulle. French General Raoul Salan (1899 – 1984) staged a pro-Colon coup. He led the French Foreign Legion (mostly Germans) in rebellion against DeGaulle and France. Salan tried to get the entire army to mutiny. He failed and was arrested. To make this chaotic conflict more anguishing, the French had two atomic bombs at that time, both in Algeria, which was their testing ground. Just in time they detonated one far out in the desert, and destroyed the other. DeGaulle feared it might fall into the hands of mutinous Colon military forces. They could have blackmailed Paris. At long last, the referendum on independence was held on July 1, 1962. The Colons boycotted the election. Independence was won by 99.72% of the vote. The embittered Colons departed Algeria, but not peacefully. They conducted a miserably vindictive sabotage campaign, a scorch-earth retreat to France. The Colons destroyed every hospital, school, bank, building, wrecking the entire infrastructure of the newborn nation. Incidentally: The wise old President Charles DeGaulle had warned the novice young President John F. Kennedy (1917 – 1963) to get out of Vietnam, for that war was unwinnable. Kennedy listened. He told Democratic Senator Mike Mansfield (1903 – 2001) to work hard to get him re-elected President in 1964, so he could end the Vietnam War. This was one of the reasons why Kennedy was assassinated in 1963.

FRENCH FOREIGN LEGION – (*FRENCH FOR*-ten *LEE*-jun) A branch of the French Army established in 1831. It was initially organized to accommodate soldiers of the Polish Army, which was disbanded by the Russian Czar Nicolas I (1796 – 1855), after the Polish Revolt of 1831. Since then, the Legion has been opened to all foreigners. The commissioned officers are all French. The Legionnaires are a tough, highly-trained infantry division of about 8,900 fighting men. Their motto is *"The Legion is our Fatherland."* They are known for their *"esprit de corps."* Today, the Foreign Legion recruits from the French population as well, though 75% are from other nations. The Foreign Legion had traditionally been an escape route for fugitives who hoped to get lost and acquire a new identity. They became famous during their campaigns in North Africa, in the French wars of colonial conquests. The French Foreign Legion was bravely decimated at the siege of Dien Bien Fu in Vietnam (1954). Joining the French Foreign Legion is the fast-track to French citizenship.

FRENCH REVOLUTION – (*FRENCH* rev-vo-*LOO*-shun) The rising of the people and the overthrow of the monarchy in France, achieved with escalating bloodshed between 1789 and 1799. The French Revolution was the *"revenge of the poor and oppressed"* against the monarchy, aristocracy and clergy. The French Revolution was the first modern revolution, because it transformed the nature of society and introduced radically new political ideologies. The Revolution enabled France and Western Europe to amputate many medieval evils. The American Revolutionary declaration that *all men were created equal,* and *life, liberty,* and *happiness* was mere window dressing. The French Revolutionary *Liberty, Equality, and Fraternity* bore fruit for years to come.

FRENEMY – (*FREN*-na-mee) (Frenemies) A phony, false friend. Frenemy is a portmanteau word combining FRIEND and ENEMY. A frenemy is a person, group, or nation that acts friendly to another, because the relationship brings benefits, but actually harbors feelings of resentment or rivalry. A frenemy is a user, a fair-weather friend. One may be a frenemy to a person or nation to which you are dependent or beholding, but hate. Many nations are frenemy to Germany, particularly Poland and Russia (due, of course to World War Two, 1929 – 1945 atrocities).

FRENETIC – (fren-*NET*-tic) Frenzied, frantic, crazed activity. *"She ran about in a frenetic state."*

FREQUENTATIVE – (free-kwent-*TAY*-tiv) In grammar, an aspect or variation of a verb that expresses repeated or habitual action. A frequentative is a separate but not completely independent word. For example, *"wrestle"* is the frequentative of *wrest; "sparkle"* of *spark; "batter"* of *bat;* and *"crackle,"* the frequentative of *crack.*

FRESCO – (*FRES*-co) The difficult art of painting on a fresh moist plaster surface. The colors are ground-up in a limewater mixture and absorbed into the plaster. The fresco artist must work quickly, for an error requires chipping off dried plaster. The ceiling of the Sistine Chapel in Rome's Vatican is the most famous fresco. The artist was the incomparable Michelangelo (1475 – 1564).

FRESHENING – (*FRESH*-en-ing) Refers to the desalination of the Gulf Stream current by glacial melt, (global warming) which will trigger an ice age starting in Western Europe. This contradictory sounding phenomenon occurs when the salinity of the ocean is changed. The warm Gulf Stream would sink into the depths, below the cold fresh meltwater, no longer able to warm Western Europe. Cornwall England will trade its palm trees for icebergs, like Canada's Labrador.

FRESH MEAT – (fresh *MEET*) Not recently butchered produce in this instance, but prison slang for a batch of new inmates. Fresh implies that they are not seasoned to prison ways. Meat implies carnivorous consumption. Fresh meat is often eaten up in the big house. Fresh meat is flesh, to be devoured by the prison predators for the pleasures of the flesh.

FRESH/SALT WATER – (fresh sawlt *WAW*-ter) Two common varieties of the Earth's water (H_2O) supply. Most of the planet's water is salty, impregnated with sodium chloride (NaCL) dissolved from the rocks the oceans bathe. So the oceans, seas, and some lakes are saltwater to various degrees. The surface of the planet is 71% water, 97% of that water is salty. Except for saltwater sea creatures, fauna and flora, excessive saltwater is detrimental to all other plants and animals, including humans. The majority of aquatic creatures are fish. Some fish species (40%) dwell in freshwater, the majority of fish species (60%) dwell in saltwater. With very few exceptions (like salmon and the bull shark), fish cannot move freely from fresh to saltwater, and back again. Their body chemistry will not allow it. That's because nature insists on balance, harmony, homeostasis. A fish from fresh Lake Michigan placed in the salty Atlantic will desiccate, cells implode, shrivel up. The body fluid made salty by the ocean will burst the cell walls to enter into the fresh fluid of the cells. Conversely, a fish from the salty Pacific placed in fresh Lake Huron will waterlog, cells explode, bloat up. The body fluid made fresh by the lake will burst the cell walls to enter into the saltier fluid of the cells. This is the process of osmosis – biological equalization. In either case, either fish will die. The salt content of the cells, the body fluid, and the environment must be compatible. The same applies to plants. Salt water will kill almost all terrestrial plants. After a tsunami, for instance, the soil is contaminated with salt. Vegetation will dies until the soil has time to leach-out the salt. Animals and humans will die from drinking salt water, for the same physiological reasons as do the freshwater fish in saltwater. Survivors adrift after a shipwreck will not survive long if they fall to the temptation of drinking the ocean water. They will quickly dehydrate, go delirious and perish. *"Water, water everywhere, but not a drop to drink."* – Samuel Taylor Coleridge (1772 – 1834), *"The Rime of the Ancient Mariner"* (1797 – 1798).

FRETWORK – (*FRET*-work) An ornamental work of interlacing parts. Fretwork design is usually created with decorative perforations.

FREUD SQUAD – (*FROYD SKWOD*) British medical slang for psychiatrists.

FREUDIAN – (*FROY*-dee-an) The first school of psychoanalysis founded by Sigmund Freud (1856 – 1939). Freudianism stresses childhood trauma and the power of the sexual libido.

FREUDIAN SLIP – (*FROYD*-dee-an *SLIP*) An inadvertent mistake in speech or writing that is thought to reveal a person's unconscious motives, wishes, or attitudes. This type of miscommunication is attributed to the psychoanalytical theory of Sigmund Freud (1856 – 1939). The term *"Freudian slip"* became popular in the first half of the 1950s. For example, one may say: *"I gave at the orifice – I mean office!"* On May 19, 2022, the headline read: *"Freudian slip of the century: George W. Bush accidentally admits to 'brutal invasion' of Iraq in Ukraine speech."* Indeed, the former President made a historic, hysteric gaffe in a speech at Southern Methodist University in Dallas, Texas. Mr. Bush said: *"The result is an absence of checks and balances in Russia, and the decision of one man to launch a wholly unjustified and brutal invasion of Iraq – I MEAN OF UKRAINE!"* Guilty conscious? Karmic Justice? Or Freudian slip? The rest is up to the psycho-historians. *"The tongue never slips – remember this always. What goes on within the mind comes invariably on the tongue."* – Hindu Mystic Rajneesh (1931 – 1990).

FRICTION – (*FRIC*-shun) A resistance encountered when one body moves relative to another body with which it is in contact. Friction results when one item is rubbed against another. A persistent amount of friction produces heat, and can create a fire. For millennia, our ancient ancestors understood this principle. They had created fire by rubbing two sticks together. When the friction produces heat up to 300o degrees Fahrenheit, a flame bursts forth. Friction is detrimental to mechanical devices. Machines must be lubricated with grease or oil so its moving parts slide easily together with minimal friction. Otherwise, friction heat will burn-up the machine. Social friction, resulting in heated conflict, occurs when people rub each other the wrong way.

FRIEND – (*FREND*) A person who fulfills our physical, emotional, or material needs. There are degrees of friendship. A close friend is a faithful trusted companion in which one has invested affection and much emotion. He will accept you at your worst. She is your cheerleader, not competitor. He rejoices at your victories, and consoles you at your defeats. She would give you the last lick from her ice cream cone, so to speak. The most profound form of friendship is *"buddyship."* It is a rare, non-sexual closeness between two males. Buddyship often develops under the stress and mutual dependencies of combat.

FRIENDLY FIRE – (*FREND*-lee *FY*-er) Soldiers accidentally killing their comrades in the fog of war. Battles are chaotic. Strategy depends on tactics, and tactics often depend on luck – good and bad. Inevitably, troops will be killed by friendly fire. Incidentally: Towards the end of the Vietnam War (c. 1960 – 1973) American soldiers were intentionally killed by U.S. friendly fire, occasionally. The helicopters could rescue only 7 soldiers (8 if there was no co-pilot aboard). What of those soldiers left behind? With enemy forces converging on them, and capture inevitable, the helicopter would kill the unlucky stragglers with machinegun or rocket fire. It was considered merciful to kill your comrades, rather than allow them to be taken prisoner, and be fiendishly tortured to death. Such episodes will not be recorded in the history books. Footnote: American prisoners were sometimes found crucified to trees, penis sticking out of their mouths, with the *"Geneva Convention Card"* nailed to their foreheads. (America had never declared war on Vietnam. So technically, legally, the Geneva War Convention pertaining to prisoners did not apply. The Vietnamese considered the U.S. forces to be *"bandits,"* not soldiers. Unfortunately for all, they were legally right.)

FRIENEMY – (*FREN*-nem-mee) (Frienemies) Combining the words "friend" and "enemy." This oxymoronic term suggests an obligatory friendship. A powerful individual like a boss, who you hate, but must feign friendship is a frienemy. There is no one you will hate more than one you fear. That person is a true enemy. If you are dependent on that person in any way, he or she becomes a frienemy. No one has more frienemies that perfidious, despicable Donald Trump (b. 1946). As President, many people are dependent on Trump, despite his insults, bullying, and humiliation. Even Trump's friends are his enemies. It's a safe bet that in 2020, Donald Trump is the most hated man in America. *"There will be many a dry eye at his funeral."* – Irish Proverb.

FRIGOPHOBIA – (frij-o-*FOH*-bee-a) (Frigophobiac) Phobic fear of the cold.

FRINGE BENEFITS – (*FRINJ BEN*-ne-fits) Advantages received by employees in addition to wages or salaries. Fringe benefits include paid vacations, sick leave, retirement payments and health insurance. Fringe benefits were once a contractual right. With the destruction of the unions, and outsourcing of jobs overseas, that has all changed. Fringe benefits have disappeared, or have degenerated to an optional act of charity on behalf of the landlord-like employer. A Socialist economy would make fringe benefits a government entitlement.

FRINGE THEORY – (*FRINJ THEER*-ee) A theory is a plausible, albeit unproved proposition. A fringe is a border region, in this case an outlying, even outlandish area. So a fringe theory is an outlandish proposition. It is a viewpoint contrary to accepted scholarship, pseudo-scientific, laced with contradictions and false equivalencies – utter nonsense. Conspiracy theorists live on the lunatic fringe. The QAnon crazies and the MAGAmaniacal cultists subscribe to fringe theories.

FRIPPERY – (*FRIP*-per-ree) Fine, though gaudy, ostentatious dress.

FRISIAN – (*FRIZH*-uhn) (also Friese or Fryske) The Germanic language closest to English. The Frisians are a West German ethnic group indigenous to the coastal regions of the Netherlands and northwestern Germany. They inhabit an area known as *Frisia* and are concentrated in the Dutch province of Friesland and Groningen and, in Germany, East Frisia and North Frisia (which was a part of Denmark until 1864). The Frisian languages are still spoken by more than 500,000 people. West Frisian is officially recognized in the Netherlands (Dutch Friesland). North Frisian and Saterland Frisian are recognized as regional languages in Germany. The *Frisii,* ancestors of the Frisians invaded southern England in the 5th century CE from Holland, while the Angles, Saxons, and Jutes invaded other parts of England. Present day Frisian gives us the best clue as to the sound of early Anglo-Saxon English. Today in Frisian, cow is pronounced *"ko"*; lamb is *"lam"*; dung is *"dong"*; rain is *"rein"*; boat is *"boat"*. A cup of coffee is *"in kopke koffe."* Furthermore, it is said that *"Goede buter en tsiis is geode Ingelsk en Fryske."* (*"Good butter and good cheese is good English and Friese,"* in both languages.) According to Robert McCrum (b. 1953), William Cran, and Robert MacNeil (b. 1931) in <u>*The Story of English*</u> (1986): *"The evidence in a place like Friesland suggests that if the linguistic cataclysm, the Norman Conquest of 1066, had not occurred, the English today might speak a language not unlike modern Dutch."*

FRIVOLOUS – (*FRIV*-uh-luhs) (Frivolously, Frivolity) Senseless, silly, pointless, lacking seriousness. A frivolous argument carries no weight. Too, a frivolous person is silly, giddy, trivial, and superficial. *"Dozens of Donald Trump's (b. 1946) lawsuits against his election defeat were thrown out of court as frivolous."*

FROG – (*FRAWG*) A moist smooth-skinned amphibian with a great ability to leap. The webbed-footed frog must live in a semi-aquatic environment. The frog's gelatinous eggs must be laid in water. The frog's semi-terrestrial, drier-skinned cousin is the toad. Incidentally: Frog legs are a delicious delicacy in France, Quebec, and Michigan.

FROGTIE – (*FRAWG*-ty) (Frogtied, Frogtying) In the BDSM (<u>B</u>ondage, <u>D</u>ominance, <u>S</u>ado<u>M</u>asochism) subculture of exotic erotica, a bondage technique. When frogtying a submissive individual, lay them on their back, preferably on a bed. Tie their arms over their head, by the wrists to the bedposts. Bring their legs up in the air with knees bent. Then bind their ankles to their thighs. Their legs now resemble those of a frog. The legs can be spread open, fully exposing the genitals, giving wide range to any sexual desire. The frogtied person, though totally incapacitated, is not unduly uncomfortable. A Caveat: The author as messenger serves as a reporter, not necessarily a supporter.

FRONT – (*FRONT*) In meteorology, a zone where air masses of different densities clash (like a battle front). If warm air is advancing, it's a warm front. If cold air is advancing it's a cold front. Expect storms at the meeting of fronts.

FRONTAL STORM – (*FRONT*-tal *STORM*) What meteorologists call an *"extratropical cyclone?"* This is a Northern Hemisphere Temperate Zone storm caused by clashing warm and cold fronts. Frontal storms may cover a good part of the continent.

FRONTISPIECE – (*FRONT*-tis-pees) An illustrated leaf in a book, preceding the title page. This has been the case since 1607. The illustrations were originally columns, pediments, and other architectural details. In fact, in architecture, a frontispiece is an ornamented façade. The architectural usage (1597) preceded the literary application.

FROST – (*FRAWST*) Ice crystals formed when the dew point is below freezing (32o degrees Fahrenheit, or 0o degrees Celsius). At this point, water vapor directly enters the solid state. The ground is coated with a cold white *frost*ing.

FROSTBITE – (*FRAWST*-byt) A physical injury due to excessive exposure to extreme cold. Frostbite is bodily freezer burn. It affects the extremities of the body first: nose, toes, fingers, penis, hands, feet, face. These bodily extensions are the least protected body parts. The symptoms of frostbite are numbness, with the body part turning red, then white. This is caused by blood clots and ice crystals in the capillaries and small blood vessels. The affected body parts are blood-starved. *Necrosis* sets in. The tissue dies and turns black. Gangrene follows, rotting the flesh, requiring immediate amputation.

FROTTAGE – (fraw-*TAHZH*) An art rubbing. A technique in the visual arts of obtaining textural effects or images by rubbing lead, chalk, or charcoal over paper laid on a granular or relief-like surface. It is popular to make frottages of old tombstones, for example.

FROTTAGE – (fraw-*TAHZH*) (also Frotteurism) Erotic rubbing. The act of rubbing against another person for sexual gratification. One who engages in frottage is a *frotteur*. Frottage is the attainment of sexual stimulation and satisfaction by rubbing the erogenous body parts on another person. Alternately, masturbation can qualify as frottage as well. In this case, the genie is released by rubbing the magic lamp.

FRUGAL – (*FROO*-gul) Cheap, parsimonious, stingy, miserly. A frugal person hates to spend money. They have short arms and deep pockets, so to speak.

FRUGALMANIA – (froo-gul-*MAY*-nee-a) (Frugalmaniac) A manic or insane aversion to spending money. A frugalmaniac is a neurotic cheapskate. The term frugal means cheap, parsimonious, and miserly. A Caveat: To label this neurosis *"Frugalphobia"* (froo-gul-*FOH*-bee-a) would not be a misnomer, for the term literally means *"the fear of being cheap,"* the definitive opposite of frugalmania (*"fear of spending"*). At any rate, frugalmania is a mental illness that requires clinical attention.

FRUGIVORE – (*FRU*-gi-vor) (Frugivorous) A fruit eater. Animals like many monkeys are totally frugivorous, subsisting only on fruit.

FRUIT – (*FROOT*) The ripened ovary of a flowering plant that contains the reproductive seeds. A fruit is usually a sweet, fleshy, juicy organ, as reproductive organs should be. There are several thousands of fruits (and vegetables) on Earth, unknown to man. The Amazon rainforest is estimated to have over 3,000 undiscovered fruits hidden in its canopy. God knows what medicinal magic they may hold. At any rate, many fruits are deadly poisonous.

FRUMIOUS – (*FROO*-mee-uhs) Very angry, incensed, furious, fuming mad. In fact the term *"frumious"* is a blend of *fuming* and *furious*. It was coined by Lewis Carrol (1832 – 1898) in *Through the Looking Glass* (1871).

FUBAR – (*FOO*-bar) A military acronym for *"Fucked Up Beyond All Recognition."*

FUCK – (*FUHK*) (Fucked, Fucking, Fucker, Fucked Up) The F-word, the 4 letter F- bomb. Fuck is the vulgar, albeit popular vernacular for intercourse, coitus, fornication, copulation. The term *"fuck"* may have derived from the pseudo- Latin term *"fuccant."* This word appeared in a scurrilous 15th century poem (c. 1475) titled *"Flen flyys,"* meaning *"Fleas, Flies,"* [*and Friars*]. It was written in bastard Latin and Middle English. The relevant line reads: *"Non sunt in celi quia fuccant uuiuys of heli."* Translation: *"The monks are not in heaven because they fuck the wives of Ely Town."* So much for the frisky friars. Another etymological possibility is that *"fuck"* derives from the Norwegian *"fukka,"* meaning *"copulate."* Plausible. Alternately the term may be related to the Swedish *"focka,"* meaning *"penis"* and *"copulate."* At any rate, these Scandinavian terms made their way to Scotland by the Vikings where they evolved into *"fuck."* Whatever the fuck its origin, the term has served us well. In fact, the term fuck may actually be the most versatile word in the English language. The Hindu scholar, Guru Faqkuar explained it all marvelously. *"One of the most interesting words in the English language today is the word 'Fuck'. It is a magical word. Just by its sound it can describe pain, pleasure, hate, and love. In language, it falls into many grammatical categories. It can be used as a verb, both transitive: 'John fucked Mary,' and intransitive: 'Mary was fucked by John.' And as a noun: 'Mary is a fine fuck.' It can be used as an adjective: 'Mary is fucking beautiful.' As you can see, there are not many words with the versatility of fuck. Besides the sexual meaning, there are also the following uses. Ignorance: 'Fucked if I know.' Trouble: 'I guess I'm fucked now!' Fraud: 'I got fucked at the used car lot.' Aggression: 'Fuck you!' Displeasure: 'What the fuck is going on here?' Difficulty: 'I can't understand this fucking job!' Incompetence: 'He is a fuck-off!' Suspicion: 'What the fuck are you doing?' Enjoyment: 'I had a fucking good time!' Request: 'Get the fuck out of here!' Hostility: 'I'm going to knock your fucking head off!' Greetings: 'How the fuck are you?' Apathy: 'Who gives a fuck?' Innovation: 'Get a bigger fucking hammer!' Surprise: 'Fuck! You scared the shit out of me!' Anxiety: 'Today is really fucked.' And it is very healthy too! If every morning you do it as a transcendental meditation, just when you get up, first thing, repeat the mantra: 'Fuck you,' five times. It clears your throat too."*

FUCKABLE – (*FUHK-uh-bul*) (Fuckability) Literally, able to be fucked. In the vulgar vernacular, fuckable means being attractive and sexy enough to be a desirable intercourse partner. *"Fuckability,"* of course, is purely subjective, depending on personal tastes and degree of lustfulness (and drunkenness?). The *"fuckability test"* can be applied to either a male or female. However, almost always, it refers to males judging females. The concept of fuckability is exceedingly sexist, judgmental, and dehumanizing. It makes sex the only criterion of worth. It implies that only fuckable people [read: *woman*] are acceptable, lovable. Incidentally: It has been revealed that the racist, sexist, neo-Nazi Tucker Carlson (b. 1969) and his Fox *"News"* associates Judged women on their fuckability via emails. They freely used to denigrating term *"fuckable."*

FUCKING AUSTRIA – (*FUHK-ing AW-stree-uh*) Not a vulgar expletive against Austrians, but an actual village in western Upper Austria on the German border. No joke. Fucking is a tiny rural municipality of Tarsdorf, in the Innviertel region, with 106 citizens. The residents have been *"Fuckingers"* [not Fuckers] from 1303 to 2021, when the council voted to change their name to *"Fugging."* English tourists loved to be photographed next to the Fucking village sign. Many of those signs had been stolen. Everyone was not pleased with that Fucking change. The Fucking mayor for instance had this to say: *"Everyone here knows what it means in English, but for us, Fucking is Fucking – and it's going to stay Fucking. After all, we have been Fucking here for 800 years!"* So what the fuck, keep the original, historical name. It's even more interesting than Hell, Michigan, or Intercourse, Pennsylvania. A Consideration: *"Can you imagine going to Fucking High School, playing on the Fucking football team, and being a Fucking cheerleader?"*

FUCKIN' MORON – (*FUHK-in MORE-on*) A vulgar vernacular for a despicable incompetent, a contemptable simpleton. To be called a *"fuckin' moron"* is an obscene opprobrium, a scathing insult. Nevertheless, that's exactly what Secretary of State, Rex Tillerson (b. 1952) called President Donald Trump (b. 1946), in September, 2017. Trump, a clinically pathological liar insisted that Tillerson lie about mouthing the indignity. Tillerson refused. Unlike Trump, Rex Tillerson protected his integrity, which infuriated perfidious Trump. By the way, Tillerson is no longer Secretary of State. Incidentally: A variety of notables have publicly called Trump: *arrogant, egotistical, narcissistic, incompetent, ignorant, racist, idiot, daft twerp,* and an *asshole.*

FUCK'IT FACTOR – (*FUHK-it FAK-ter*) The term *"fuck'it"* is the epitome of disgusted renunciation, resignation. In the vulgar vernacular, fuck'it indicates abdication, abandonment. The fuck'it factor is a psycho-emotional dead-end. It says *"I had it!; I'm fed-up!; I'm finished!"* The fuck'it factor can apply anywhere, in business, in a relationship, or in politics. In the latter, a party supporter, and voter quits. He is so disappointed with the leadership of his political party and its direction, that she renounces participation. Many Democratic voters may lose enthusiasm and faith for the party. If President Joe Biden (b. 1942), the Democratic Congress, and Attorney General Merrick Garland (b. 1952) fail to bring mobster Donald Trump (b. 1946) to justice, supports may finally say *"fuck'it!"* and abandon politics altogether.

FUCK OFF – (fuhk *AWF*) A vulgar vernacular meaning *"forget it," "no way," "go away."* Incidentally: His secretary told him *"Fuck You!"* He replied, *"Your place or mine?"*

FUCKYOUISM – (fuhk-*YOO*-is-um) A portmanteau term, a vulgar explanation of why poor people support rich Trump (b. 1946), against their own economic interests. The term *"fuckyouism"* was coined by the distinguished Republican political strategist Steve Schmidt (b. 1970). Schmidt did not coin this word as a joke, but as an explanation, a philosophy. It is the fundamental reason why Trump and Trumpism appeals to so many lower-class Americans. In his incomparable manner, Schmidt explained: *"Trump is the philosopher of 'Fuckyouism.' Tens and tens of millions of Americans have lost faith, and believe the game is rigged. There is one set of rules for the people at the top, and another set of rules for everybody else. Among them, the millions and millions of Americans who lost homes after the financial collapse of 2008, while not a single Wall Street executive went to prison. Their only hope is that somebody, from somewhere, will deliver the only thing that they think they can count on. They just want someone to say 'Fuck You!' to the people they hold responsible for wrecking their American dream, and they feel utterly powerless against. How does Trump deliver for them? Again, they're not looking for policy results – they don't believe them. Even when something as grand as Biden's Infrastructure Act is passed, they're so poisoned by the billion-dollar propaganda machine that surrounds the empire of MAGA malice, that they don't believe a word of it. The only thing they see is the reaction by the people that they hate, by the people that they think condescend to them, that disrespects and ignores them. What they want to see is those people antagonized. What they hope to see and what they laugh about is how they react to Trump. Every day Trump delivers his 'Fuck You!' and the people cheer. Why? It's not in their interest. It's not in their country's interest. This is the cost of cynicism. The cost of disillusionment. When the only thing that millions and millions of people look for and count on from their political leadership in their country is to deliver a 'Fuck You!' When you reach that point, and we have, we're in a crisis. Trump is a part of the crisis. Trump is a threat and the greatest danger to American democracy. But politics in America is down-stream from American culture. A healthy society does not produce a President Trump. A sick, decaying, and rotten one does. These things happen in democracies, mistakes are made. But in the end, the next election is the one that matters. Because there is nothing new to learn about Trump. We know what he is. We know what he stands for. And we know that he means it when he talks about a platform of retribution and revenge. He does not have enough people in this country to support him to be elected. Unless, there are enough people who are apathetic enough to weigh-in with their indifference. And then maybe, just maybe he can achieve the small majority he needs to take power for the very last time. And then there will be chaos and there will be mayhem in American society."* And to all the democracy-loving Americans who object, Trump will say *"Fuck You!"* Over 60% of Americans live paycheck-to-paycheck. There are millions more with no paychecks. At the top, there are billionaires and multi- millionaires with no checks on their wealth and greed. This is not Trump's fault, but the fault of capitalism. Trump simply takes advantage of the misery and miserable people. The way to destroy Trump,

Trumpism, and future fascist Trumps is to say *"Fuck You!"* to capitalism. We must reestablish the American dream by instituting a fair Socialistic society, with prosperity for all.

FUCK YOU MONEY – (*FUHK YOO MON*-nee) A Wall Street insider phrase and aspiration. In corporate capitalist parlance, Wall Street brokers hope and strive to become so rich, that they could tell anyone *"FUCK YOU!"* with impunity, without any negative consequences. With *"Fuck You Money,"* you've Fucken arrived in capitalist circles. With such wealth, no one would be too powerful to castigate. After all, they would be in the elite capitalist club that is *"too big to fail, jail, or assail."* These are the people who control our capitalist economic system. They call the measure of wealth for which they strive *"Fuck you money."* Donald Trump (b. 1946) boasted that he loved to *"Grab women by the pussy."* Trump went on to explain that *"When you're rich, you can do anything!"* Trump controls *"Fuck You Money."* The resent poster-child of the *"Fuck You Wallstreeters"* has been hedge fund investor Anthony Scarmucci (b. 1964). Anthony *"The Mooch"* survived as Trump's Communications Director for a mere 10 days (July 2017). He was forced out of office by his shamefully obscene mouth. Mooches' Wall Street *"Fuck You Money"* did not protect him on Pennsylvania Avenue. Incidentally: Entrepreneur Malcolm S. Forbes (1919 – 1990) had observed that *"You can easily judge the character of others by how they treat those who can do nothing for them or to them."*

FUHRER – (*FUR*-rer) German for *"leader."* Title taken by Nazi dictator Adolf Hitler (1889 – 1945). This word has been so vilified by Hitler that it will never be used again in this context. Never!

FUHRER BRIDES – (*FUR*-rer *BRYDS*) Title ascribed to unmarried pregnant girls during the Nazi regime in Germany (1933 – 1945). The stigma of unwed pregnancy was changed to a badge of honor. After all, the girls were providing soldiers and breeders for the Nazi Reich.

FRUIT – (*FROOT*) (Fruity, Fruitful) The ovary of a plant that contains the reproductive seeds. The fruit need not be edible by people, and may even be poisonous to man. Nevertheless, it's still a fruit. But the plant intends its fruit to be eaten by some animals, birds, and insects, releasing and widely dispersing the seeds, its genetic offspring. In a narrower sense, fruit is considered people food. This would include what we consider vegetables as fruit as well. Fruit is an essential part of our diet. Our ancient evolutionary arboreal ancestors were fructivores (fruit eaters). Fruit contains sugar (fructose), vitamins, minerals, some protein, and fiber. The differentiation of fruit from vegetables is merely a social dining custom. Fruits tend to be sweet or sour and eaten more as a treat, snack, or dessert. Vegetables are considered to be more bland, basic fare, eaten as a side dish at the main meal. Fruits (including vegetables), along with grains and nuts are the subsistence of the vegetarian [read: *fruitetarian*] diet.

FUJITA SCALE – (foo-*JEE*-ta *SKAY*-al) The tornado severity scale introduced by meteorologist Tetsuta Fujita (1920 – 1998). The Fujita Scale ranks the twister's power from zero to five (F0, F1, F2, F3, F4, F5). An F0 tornado is merely a nuisance. An F5 tornado is devastating, turning towns to rubble.

FULL MOON – (fuhl *MOON*) When the entire splendid moon is fully visible from Earth, because it is on the opposite side of the Earth from the sun. This occurs every 29.53 days. If the moon passes through the Earth's shadow at this time, a lunar eclipse occurs. This happens every few months, though it is visible in any given location much less frequently. Much folklore and superstition surrounds the occasion of the full moon. The night of the full moon is an *"Esbats,"* (sacred night) in many witchcraft traditions. The werewolf legend is associated with the full moon. It is believed that people experience temporary *"lunacy"* or *"moon craziness"* during a full moon. Many police departments report higher crime rates during the full moon. This is hard to explain. Perhaps it's the influence of gravitational forces on the body fluids. Alternately, the additional light may make crime more inviting.

FULL NELSON – (full *NEL*-son) A joint-lock grappling hold in wrestling, introduced by the Canadian-American wrestler Bobby Nelson (1917 – 2002). The aggressor or holder is positioned on the back side of his opponent, with his arms extended upwards under the opponent's armpits, holding the back of the neck with interlaces fingers. By pushing his hands forward, pressure is exerted on the opponent's neck, pushing his head forward. A person caught in the grips of a full nelson is helpless. The full nelson is a dangerous maneuver in combat. Though painful in a fight, it can be most pleasurable in sex. Adult movie director and porn star Belladonna (Michelle Anne Sinclair) (b. 1981) is most laudatory about the full nelson as a love-making position. *"The 'full nelson' is my favorite, ever. It's a guy lying on his back. The girl is on top, on her back. The guy takes his arms and puts them ender her arms and behind her neck. She's holding her legs back behind her head, and he's pushing her face down to the action, making her watch [his penis thrust in and out of her vagina]. It's just a nasty position. It's funny because I recently discovered it a couple years ago and never knew it existed. I was like, 'Who came up with this, because it's the best position ever!'"* Apparently, Belladonna, a professional fucker, seems unfamiliar with the ancient Indian guide to making love, the *"Kama Sutra."* *"The only unnatural sex act is that which you cannot perform."* – Sexologist Alfred Kinsey (1894 – 1956).

FULL SCARAMUCCI – (full skar-ra-*MOO*-chee) A comical political cliché meaning 10 days. *"He did not last at that job for a full Scaramucci,"* means that he survived for less than 10 days. The phrase is an *eponym*, which is a proper name that has become a word. Investment banker and financier Anthony Scaramucci (b. 1964) served as President Donald Trump's (b. 1946) *Director of Communications* for only 10 days, (July 21 to July 31, 2017). Ironically, it was communications that got Scaramucci in trouble. During his brief tenure, Scaramucci blasted the airwaves with a tirade of obscene expletives. His vulgarity was too vulgar, even for the vulgar Trump administration. Scaramucci was axed. The hilarity of the fiasco gave rise to the phrase, *"not a full Scaramucci."*

FULL STOP – (*fuhl* STOP) A period. A full stop is a punctuation mark in grammar that resembles a dot. A full stop ends a sentence (a written full thought) or an abbreviation (a truncated word). Furthermore, the term *"full stop!"* followed by an exclamation point serves as an interjection abruptly stopping a discussion or argument quite forcefully. For Example: *"Trump is a buffoon, full stop!"*

FULL TILT – (fuhl *TILT*) At top speed with maximum force and momentum. Nothing held back. When performing at full tilt, one is expending ultimate energy. The term *"full"* fits this phrase, but what is meant by *"tilt"*? Tilt derives from an Old English (West Saxon) word *"titan"* meaning *"to be unsteady."* In the Middle Ages, the word *"tilt"* came to be synonymous with *"joust,"* and *"tilting"* meant *"jousting."* In fact, it is recorded by Miguel de Cervantes (1547 – 1616) in <u>Don Quixote</u> (1605) that his quixotic hero went *"tilting at windmills."* Whether steady or unsteady, the jousting knights charged at each other on horseback, armed with lances, at full tilt.

FULMINATE – (*FEW*-min-ate) (Fulmination) As a verb, to detonate. To explode with a violent noise. As a noun, a fulminate a a rapid combustible, like sulfur or gasoline.

FULSOME – (*FULL*-sum) Distasteful due to excess. Fulsome food may be over salted or too greasy. Fulsome praise may be sickening in the excess.

FUMERALS – (*FEW*-mer-als) Lava chimneys or vents on the ocean floor that spews-out hot water, gas, and an organic soup of minerals. The mineral substances from fumerals, together with minerals from comets and asteroids have contributed to the formation of life on Earth. Fumerals are sometimes called *"black smokers."* Fumerals are also land-based. They appear as cracks in the Earth's crust in volcanically active regions, releasing heat, gas, and magma (as lava). Incidentally: It is thought that the entire global ocean is absorbed into the Earth and spewed back every 10,000 years, enriched with minerals through the fumerals.

FUM-FUM – (*FOOM-FOOM*) Name for the braided cowhide whip, coined by Jamaican slaves and applied to them. The term fum-fum is an onomatopoeia, (on-no-mot-to-*PEE*-ah) meaning a word that imitates a sound. *"Fum"* was the sound the lash made as it whooshed through the air prior to ripping into the flesh, with a sickening crack. Doubling the term is characteristic of Pidgin English. Doubling tends to magnify, amplify the potency, the effect of the word, like *"good-good"* or *"bad-bad."* The fum-fum represents cruelty hard to imagine by most today. Nevertheless, the lash was considered essential to assure the capitalist supply-and-demand for sugar. English poet William Cowper (1731 – 1800) made the point: *"What I hear of the hardships their tortures and groans, is almost enough to draw pity from stones. I pity them greatly but I must mum, for how can we do without sugar and rum."*

FUMIGANT – (*FYOO*-mi-guhnt) (Fumigate, Fumigation) Any substance used to disinfect, to purify with fumes, and to serve as a pesticide. A fumigant may be a herb, resin, or chemical like sulfur which is burned for purification or aromatherapy. Fumigation with smoke has long been a religious rite of offering to the Gods. In this sense, incense may be regarded as a fumigant. The redolent aroma of incense still pervades Catholic Churches. Before modern medicine and the discovery of germs, locations were fumigated with smoke for medicinal health purposes.

FUN – (*FUHN*) Proceeding, performing with enjoyment. Fun occurs when the joy of what you're doing exceeds the labor required to do it. Fulfilling activities command great interest. Fun is doing what you want to do, as opposed to doing what you must do, which is work, and not always fun.

FUNCTIONAL ALCOHOLIC – (*FUNK*-shun-al al-co-*HALL*-lic) Successful people who are dependent on alcohol in order to maintain their success. An alcoholic is a distressed person addicted to drink (alcohol). Many alcoholics are devastated individuals, hapless, helpless, hopeless, and homeless. A functional alcoholic is different. She or he works, performs normally even successfully, and seems to be in control. They are not. Alcohol controls them. Their minds are always on the next drink. They have a few during lunch and head for the bar after work. A functional alcoholic wouldn't consider a restaurant that did not serve spirits. Functional alcoholics are in denial. They make light of their dependence. They joke about intoxication and *veisalgia* (hangovers). Functional alcoholics will not be able to function on alcohol indefinitely. Their appearance and their health will wane. As the tolerance level increases, so will the alcohol level. Memory will lapse. Social blunders will increase. Her alcoholism will become obvious to all. Incidentally: The Great Chinese sage Confucius (551 – 479 BCE) may have been a functional alcoholic. He insisted on moderation in everything except wine. Winston Churchill (1974 – 1965) was a notorious alcoholic who never seemed drunk or hungover. On the other hand, no one remembers him being quite sober. Therefore, his intoxication was his normal state. Actually, a perfectly sober Churchill would be unrecognizable. Remember: *"If you think you are an alcoholic, you are."*

FUNCTIONAL EXCLUSION – (*FUNK*-shun-al ex-*CLOO*-shun) In school law, a form of discrimination to disabled students. Though physically present in the regular classroom, functionally, the students are excluded from learning because special provisions which would enable them to learn have not been made. This may not be a case of neglect or care-less-ness. Poor funding of school systems results in poor schools. Special considerations for exceptional students on either end is prohibitive. *"You can't squeeze blood from a turnip."*

FUNCTIONAL FIXEDNESS – (*FUNK*-shun-al *FIX*-Ed-ness) A sociological term meaning being stuck in a paradigm, a single mindset. It is being unable to find fresh solutions, or innovation. A functionally fixed person is trapped in the old ways, as are all conservatives. They are unable to adjust to changing circumstances or times. A functionally fixed person would not be able to find new ways to use old tools to solve new problems. Being functionally fixed lacks imagination. It may also suggest a lack of intelligence. Because intelligence is the ability to adjust to changing circumstances.

FUNCTIONAL WHITES – (*FUNK*-shun-al *WITES*) Jamaican Whites. A racial designation applied in Jamaica and perhaps other Caribbean islands. Functional whites or whiteness would not be understood in the North Atlantic region. It applies to racial types that would pass for Caucasian. This includes those with light to tan skin-hues like Lebanese (called Syrians), Jews, or coffee-toned Colored. A narrow nose and straight hair, especially light also contributes to functional whiteness. Attitude too is a factor. Functional Whites, when not totally white have been derisively called *"Afrosaxons."* They forsake any African heritage. In a society where race spelled the difference between master and slave, acceptance and denial, skin color holds a prominent place in the psyche.

FUNDAMENTAL ATTRIBUTION ERROR – (fun-da-*MENT*-tal at-*TRISH*-shun *ER*-or) A favorite conservative, capitalist, Republican trick of blaming the people for what is actually the fault of the social environment. The error is the fundamental attribution of *"blaming the victim."* It is so much cheaper to blame the *"lazy poor"* for the slums, rather than the neglectful government. It is so much easier and cheaper to blame the character of the poor for criminality, rather than the poverty and lack of jobs. This is the fundamental attribution error.

FUNDAMENTAL FANATICISM – (fun-da-*MENT*-tal fan-*NAT*-ti-sis-um) The radical, intolerant beliefs of religious Fundamentalists. Fanaticism and Fundamentalism go hand-in-hand. It doesn't matter if the Fundamentalist is a Shiite Muslim or a Baptist Christian. Both regard archaic admonitions from ancient scriptures as applicable today. They refuse to admit that both the Koran and Bible are *"time contingent."* Both books were written long ago for different people living in different worlds, at different times. Certainly, the time-tested, edifying pronouncements should be gleaned from the Koran and Bible. However, to apply either text fundamentally, would result in savage injustice like stoning the adulteress and witch burning. Why are Fundamentalists concerned with other people's sexual preferences or reproductive liberty? Perhaps it's because they need conventional conformity to attain security. The Liberal philosopher and mathematician, Bertrand Russell (1872 – 1970) asserted that *"Conventional people* [read: *Fundamentalists*] *are roused to fury by departure from convention, largely because they regard such departure as a criticism of themselves."* *"Fundamentalist Christianity appeals to pre-civilized, prudish tribal people who are not ready for urban feudal pleasures."* – Dr. Timothy Leary (1920 – 1996).

FUNDAMENTALISM – (fun-da-*MENT*-tal-lis-um) (Fundamentalists) Religious extremists who profess to the letter of the law or word. They belong primarily to the Baptist/Methodist sects of Christian Protestantism. Christian Fundamentalists believe the Bible literally, fundamentally, word for word. Fundamentalist Muslims believe the Koran likewise. That includes the Taliban, al Qaeda, and ISIS. Intolerant Fundamentalists of all faiths profess ignorant and dangerous certainty. *"We are all capable of becoming fundamentalists because we get addicted to other people's wrongness."* – Pema Chodron (b. 1939), Buddhist Nun. Footnote: Much in the Old Testament (first 4/5ths of the Bible) is time contingent – meant for a particular people, in a particular place, for a specific reason, at a specific time. Furthermore, much is also ancient Hebrew mythology.

FUNDAMENTALIST PHONIES – (fun-da-*MEN*-tal-list *FOE*-nees) Fraudulent Christians, Evangelical hypocrites who support the corrupt, lascivious, deceitful politician, Donald Trump (b. 1946). They are indeed fundamentally phony. Many leaders of Protestant sects (Baptists, Methodists) have surrendered their integrity and morals in order to support the immoral Trump. Three of the headliners are Pastor Franklin Graham (b. 1952), Pastor Jonathon Falwell (b. 1966), administrator of the Christian Liberty University, Jerry Falwell Jr. (b. 1962), and Pastor Mike Huckabee (b. 1955). These Phony Fundamentalists comprise a large portion of Trump's base. By supporting the most un-Christian Trump, they are neglecting the fundamental teachings of the Christian Jesus. Seventeen times in the New Testament, Jesus condemned *"hypocrites."* How do Fundamentalists justify backing Trump, and being reconciled with Jesus? Through denial, by turning a blind eye, and a numbed conscience. They must at least admit that *"Trump is a flawed human being."* They justify their hypocrisy in temporal terms: *"We did not vote for, or support Trump's moral values, but for his conservative political policies."* However, no sin is too grievous to *"forgive,"* [read: *"ignore"*], providing Trump fulfills their Republican socio- political-economic agenda. Trump's crimes are dismissed as *"fake news."* In January 2018, former Republican Chairman, Michael Steele (b. 1958) railed at these duplicitous Evangelicals. *"After telling me how to live, who to love, what to believe, what not to believe, what to do and what not to do, and now you sit back and the prostitutes don't matter? The grabbing the you-know-what doesn't matter? The outright behavior and lies don't matter? Just shut the hell up!"* Indeed, these religious leaders deceive themselves and their congregations. But there will be a price to pay. *"Do not be deceived: God is not mocked, for whatever one sows that will he also reap."* – Galatians 6: 7.

FUNDAMENTALITY – (fun-da-men-*TAL*-li-tee) In school law, the legal right of all American children to a free public education on the elementary and secondary levels (grades 1 through 12). Fundamentality should be extended through college, as in France. After all, what better investment can a nation make, than in the education of its citizens? Question: What neighbors do you want? Would you rather live next door to educated people or uneducated people?

FUNDAMENTALITY – (fun-da-men-*TAL*-lit-tee) In constitutional law, a requirement to obtain redress under the equal protection clause regarding state constitutions through a claim that alleged discrimination affects a fundamental right.

FUNDING DISPERITY – (*FUN*-ding dis-*PAR*-it-tee) In school law, the unequal funding of schools based on tax distribution. Schools are primarily funded by local property taxation. As neighborhoods are neglected and allowed to deteriorate, the tax base drops. Empty lots and abandoned buildings don't pay taxes. The schools get less and deteriorate with the neighborhood. More affluent citizens move out (*white flight*), resulting in lower funding. *"Slumation,"* the creation of a slum, is well underway. The children left behind in the slum schools suffer. Funding disparity is contrary to equal protection under the law. How can this happen in the richest nation in the world? Don't be deceived. The riches are hoarded at the very top. Wall Street is not Nain Street.

FUNDOSHI – (fun-*DOH*-shee) Traditional Japanese under garment, for both males and females. A fundoshi is simply a loincloth. There are different varieties, some skimpier than others. Some resemble bikini bottoms. There is documentary film of Japanese soldiers surrendering toward the end of the war, wearing only fundoshi (to prove that they were not armed). After World War Two in 1945, Japan underwent a cultural Westernization, an Americanization. Underwear, both briefs and boxer shorts replaced the fundoshi. But traditions die hard. The fundoshi still can be seen on Japanese beaches as swimwear. It is still publicly worn in some ceremonies. Suma wrestlers still wear the fundoshi. *"Eight inches strong, it is my favorite thing. If I'm alone at night, I embrace it fully. A beautiful woman hasn't touched it for ages. Within my fundoshi there is an entire universe!"* – Japanese Zen Buddhist Monk Ikkyu (1394 – 1481).

FUNERAL – (*FEW*-ner-al) Mortuary or burial rites in remembrance and respect for the deceased. Actually, funerals serve as an opportunity for the survivors to grieve in sympathetic company. Many relatives who for years paid no attention to the deceased, pay their respects at the funeral. For show? This certainly makes the deceased most happy. *"The bitterest tears shed over graves are for words left unsaid and deeds left undone."* So said Harriet Beecher Stowe (1811 – 1896). A tradition persists among many of tossing a handful of soil on the coffin in the open grave. Why? This custom originated as a symbolic assurance that the spirit of the deceased remain buried, and does emerge to haunt the relatives. Incidentally: *"You got to go to people's funerals. Or when you die, they won't come to yours."* – Yogi Berra (1925 – 2015) baseball player and ballpark philosopher.

FUNGIBLE – (*FUN*-ja-buls) Exchangeable commodity. In barter or international commerce, fungibles can be substituted for each other. For example, in payment for debt, fungible commodities such as oil, wheat, or lumber may be traded for each other. Fungibles are a substitute for money.

FUNGICIDE – (*FUN*-ji-side) A substance prepared as a spray or dust used to kill fungi. *Mycota* or fungi is a primitive relative to plants. Fungi comes in various forms, as slimes, molds, even mushrooms. Athlete's foot is a fungal disease that invades humans. It is readily contracted in damp, steamy locker-room showers where the fungus incubates. It is thought that urinating in the shower contributes to athlete's foot. Wrong! On the contrary, urine contains ammonia which is a disinfectant. Masai mothers in Africa bathe their infants in cow urine as a sanitary precaution. Urine acts as a fungicide. If anything, urinating on the shower floor kills the athlete foot fungus.

FUNGUS – (*FUHNG*-guhs) (plural Fungi - *FUN*-jee or Funguses). (Fungal, Fungous) Fungus is a diverse group of eukaryotic single-celled or multinucleate organisms. Fungus was once classified in the Plantae Kingdom, with all other plants. They were considered to be a *"thallophyte,"* along with algae and lichens. That's because fungus could not be placed in the Animal Kingdom. Actually fungus is neither plant nor animal, though closer to plant. Today, all funguses are classified in the Fungi Kingdom. Fungus lives by decomposing and absorbing the organic nutrients from the substances on which it grows. Included in the Fungus Kingdom are mushrooms, molds, mildews, slims, smuts, biological rusts, and yeasts. Fungus helps to clean and renew the planet by decomposing the dead to make room for new life. In the forests, fungus as mushrooms breaks down dead wood creating fertile soil and space for new growth. Fungus like yeast devours sugar and excretes alcohol in the process of fermentation. It also provides the leavening for bread. There are many fungal diseases including black molds that can grow in the lungs causing death. Like all living organisms, fungus can be helpful or hurtful. Incidentally: The world's largest organism was discovered in Oregon's Blue Mountains in 1998. This was a single colony of *"Armillaria ostoyae,"* also known as honey mushroom. This humongous fungus is genetically one creature. Its mycelium or root system stretched to at least 2,385 acres (over 3.7 miles). Its roughly estimated weight is between 7,500 to 35,000 tons, the world's biggest living thing.

FURBISH – (*FUR*-bish) (Refurbish) Fix, renovate, polish, to put back into good condition. To furbish is to restore to its former fresh appearance. To refurbish is to furbish again (a second time), to furbish what had been previously furbished. Used items must be furbished.

FURLONG – (*FUR*-long) An archaic unit of distance according to the Imperial or English System of measurement. A furlong is equal to an eighth of a mile, 10 chains, 220 yards, or 660 feet.

FURRY FANDOM – (*FUR*-ee *FAN*-duhm) A subculture of animated cartoon enthusiasts. *"Furries"* are fans of anthropomorphic cartoon characters – animals with human characteristics. They display human-animal hybrid faces, walk erect, speak, wear clothes, and in every other way are human. These creatures even perform *"yiff,"* the furry term for having sex. There is even furry fandom pornography. Furry fandom has its origins in the 1970s underground commix movement. Gay males tend to be over-represented in furry fandom. *"One thing most furries agree on is this: they aren't sex freaks."* – Melissa Meinzer

FURTIVE – (*FUR*-tiv) Done in a sneaky, stealthy, shifty manner. Spies are secretively furtive. A furtive glance, for instance.

FUSILLADE – (*FYOO*-suh-layd) (Fusilladed, Fusillading) A massive rapid bombardment. A continuous discharge of firearms. The term fusillade has been generalized to mean any discharge or outpouring, as a sudden outburst of criticism.

FUSION – (*FEW*-shun) A thermonuclear reaction of forcing nuclei of lighter atoms together to form heavier atoms, accompanied by a release of energy. Fusion (H-Bomb) yields about 10 times more energy than fission (A-Bomb). Stars, the sun, work on the principle of fusion. That's how we get our heat and sunshine.

FUSION CRUST – (*FEW*-shun *KRUST*) Fusion in this case means melted together. Fusion crust is a thin layer of melted glass that coats the surface of meteorites. The intense heat caused by atmospheric friction melts the sandy quarts on the meteor creating the crust. Fusion crust will distinguish meteoric rocks from terrestrial rocks.

FUSSBUDGET – (*FUS*-bud-jet) A fussy fault-finding person. A fussbudget is a whining, critical annoyance.

FUTURITY – (fu-*CHUR*-ri-tee) In the future. For instance: *"Such questions should be left to futurity."*

FUTURES – (*FEW*-churs) In economics, contracts to buy or sell commodities or financial assets at a specific date, using a price agreed upon today. The futures market is a gamble, dependent on market forces of supply and demand. A futures investor will buy tons of wheat from next year's harvest, at today's price, not knowing if the price of the wheat will be higher or lower when it's in his possession. Of course, professional capitalist investors can manipulate the market to prevent loss.

FUTURISM – (*FEW*-chur-is-um) Literally, *"belief in the future,"* or belief in the ability to predict the future. In the 1950's and 1960's, history textbooks provided a final chapter as a look into the future. *"What Will Life Be Like In the Year 2000?"* At that time, this was a glance into a dream world. It was predicted that the big problem for workers would be what to do with all of their leisure time. Imagine that! Computers and computerized robots would be doing much of our work. The 4-hour workday would occupy the 4-day workweek. What went wrong? Corporate capitalists turned the tables on the workers. Instead of man working with the computer at man's pace, man was forced to worked by the computer at the computer's pace. In the year 2018, the worker is laboring longer, under more pressure than his dad and grandpa in the 1950's and 1960's, and for less real wages (spending power). Capitalists have turned technology into an oppressor, rather than a redeemer.

FYI – (ef-why-*EYE*) An initialism for *"<u>F</u>or <u>Y</u>our <u>I</u>nformation."* This usage had become popular with the abbreviated correspondences characteristic of emails and text messages.

G

G – (*JEE*) The 7th letter in the English alphabet, a consonant. G was an old slang term for <u>G</u>rand, meaning $1,000 dollars.

G – (*JEE*) The letter positioned in the middle of the square and compass of the Masonic Symbol. The letter G holds dual meaning. It stands for <u>G</u>eometry, the powerful science that helps unravel the mysteries and wonders of nature. Geometry enabled the original Masons to build the great cathedrals during the Middle Ages. Too, the letter G represents <u>G</u>od, the Master Geometer and builder of the universe.

GABBER – (*GAB*-ber) (Gab, Gabbing) An excessively loquacious individual. That's a polite way to describe an annoying chatterbox. A gabber is a garrulous talker who hardly takes time to come up for air. Most gabbers are women. It's part of the gregarious female nature. One cannot get a word in edgewise with a gabber present. Gabbers can drive a man crazy. They are often gossipers and rumor mongers, which provides them with fuel with which to gab. There's no retreat from a gabber's vocal barrage. A simple *"Goodbye"* to a gabber is a 20- minute soliloquy. A gang of gabbers in the house will drive a man to fish'en.

GABRIEL – (*GAY*-bree-al) One of the 7 Archangels, patron of guidance. Gabriel had served God as a messenger. It was Archangel St. Gabriel who informed the young girl Mary that she would give birth to Jesus. The name derives from Hebrew meaning *"God is my strength."* Only three Archangels are named in the Bible: Michael, Raphael, and Gabriel. All Archangels bear the honorable title of Saint (St.).

GAD – (*GAD*) (Gadding) To move restlessly or aimlessly from one place to another. To gad about with no purpose.

GADFLY – (*GAD*-fly) (also called Horsefly or Botfly) A large nasty fly the size of a bumblebee with a painful bite. Known in rural America as a horsefly, they torment horses, cows, all livestock, and people. The gadfly lays an egg under the skin of its victim which grows into a parasitic larva. As the maggot matures in the host's flesh, an agonizing boil erupts, from which an adult fly emerges. The gadfly is a vexatious pest, so persistent in its attack, that the term has been applied to exceedingly annoying people.

GADOLINIUM – (gad-o-*LIN*-ee-um) (Gd) Named after the Finnish chemist, physicist, and mineralogist, John Gadolin (1760 – 1852) its discoverer. The 64 protons in its nucleus give gadolinium its atomic number. Gadolinium is a ductile, malleable, silvery-white ferromagnetic rare-earth metallic element. Gadolinium is used to improve the heat and corrosion resistance of iron, chromium, and other metals. Gadolinium is used in the medical field as a radioisotope in bone mineral analysis.

GADZOOKS – (gad-*ZOOKS*) An archaic interjection, exclaimed as a mild oath. There was a time when one might exclaim, somewhat emphatically: *"Gadzooks! I saw him at the party!"* Gadzooks is a euphemism for *"God's hooks,"* the reference being to the nails that hooked Jesus to the cross. So gadzooks became a *"minced oath"* like saying *"I swear."* In 17th century England it was taboo to speak the name of God in vain, or otherwise. The euphemism *"gad"* emerged in the early 17th century. Robert Armin (c. 1568 – 1615) wrote in *A nest of ninnies* (1608): *"And, gad, she will."* Francis Beaumont (1584 – 1616) and John Fletcher (1579 – 1625) wrote in *The knight of the burning pestle* (1609): *"By gad, if any of them all blow wind in the tail on him, I'll be hanged."* So, the silly word gadzooks actually means: *"I swear on the nails that hooked Jesus to the cross."*

GAELIC – (*GAY*-lik) The ancient language of the Celts, derived from *Goidelic,* the original Celtic language. Gaelic is the oldest spoken language in Europe. It is spoken in the British West Country, Wales, Cornwall, West Scotland, the Scottish Islands, Ireland, and the Brittany Coast of France. A sample of Scottish Gaelic words incorporated into English are*: bog, galore, pet, plaid, trousers, bother, tantrum, whiskey, brogue,* and *shanty. Smithereens* is of Irish origin. The name Sean is Gaelic for John. Incidentally: Today, barely 1% of the Irish population speaks Gaelic.

GAFFE – (*GAF*) A social or political blunder, a *faux pas.* Among Washington politicians, a gaffe is an accidental blurting out of the truth. A historic case in point is Mitt Romney's (b. 1947) *"47%"* disclosure. The patrician was recorded saying that '47% of Americans are government moochers.'

GAGGLE – (*GAG*-guhl) The collective name for an assemblage of geese. *"A gaggle of geese overwhelmed the yard."*

GAIA HYPOTHESIS – (*GAY*-ya hy-*POTH*-thes-sis) The proposition that Nature, the entire planet is a self-regulating, self-healing, self-cleansing entity. Gaia or Mother Earth is a living organism. All organic and inorganic material, all plants and animals are symbiotically interdependent.

GALACTOPHILIA – (gal-lak-toh-*FEE*-lee-ah) (Galactophiliac) A neurotic paraphilial disorder in which one is sexually attracted to lactating, breast-feeding women, and the sight of breast milk. This paraphilia is not extraordinarily abnormal. There is a subliminal psycho-sexual, psycho-incestual quality to breasts. The average male is compelled to fondle and suck the female breasts. This is a mammalian instinct in man. Breasts bridge the female gap between mother and lover. *"Breasts are a scandal because they shatter the border between motherhood and sexuality."* – Iris Marion Young (1949 - 2006). *" woman without breasts is like a bed without pillows."* – Anatole France (1844 - 1924).

GALAXIES – (*GAL*-lex-ees) Great clusters of stars throughout the universe. The galaxies are on average, 20 light years apart. Galaxies are cosmic islands in the black sea called the void. Our galaxy is called the Milky Way. To date, over 2 trillion galaxies are estimated in the observable universe. Estimates for the entire universe swing from 400 billion to a trillion. This is speculation, more philosophy than cosmology. Incidentally: The term galaxy derives from the Greek *"galaxias,"* which is based on the Greek *"gala"* meaning *milk.* The galaxy containing our solar system is the Milky Way. The Greek myth has it that a goddess sprayed milk from her breasts through the dark cosmos, spotting the night sky with milk drops [read: *white stars*].

GALENICALS – (gal-*LEN*-ni-cals) Materia medica. The pharmacopeia of curative properties, healing agents in plants, applied by physicians, homoeopathists, and shamans. Over 80% of the world's population depends on plants as their medicine. Plants are chemical factories, medicine laboratories, and poison depositories. To date, over 80,000 plants with curative galenicals have been identified. Over 4,000 medical plants are in use in Africa alone. Amazonia is a treasure trove of curative flora. About 25% of our medicine providing plants grow in the Amazon. Nevertheless, less than 5% of plants, less than 1% of flowering plants on Earth have been tested for their medicinal qualities. God only knows what cures are hiding in the world's forests and jungles. *"All that man needs for health and healing has been provided by God in nature, the challenge of science is to find it."* – Paracelsus (1493 – 1541).

GALILEE – (*GAL*-li-lee) A rural region of northern Israel. Jesus was a Galilean born and raised in the town of Nazareth (not Bethlehem). Jesus exhibited the slurring speech of a Galilean which some sophisticated urbane Judeans found amusing. In a sense, Jesus was considered to be a *"hillbilly,"* which does not detract from his sacred Socialistic message.

GALIMATIAS – (gal-uh-*MAY*-shee-uhs) Gibberish, confused or unintelligible talk. For example: *"Donald Trump's (b. 1946) speech was galimatias as usual."* The term galimatias entered the English language from the French circa 1645. Its origin is obscure, but is first attested in the writing of the French essayist Michel de Montaigne (1533 – 1592), *"Jargon de galimathias."*

GALLICISM – (*GAL*-uh-siz-uhm) (Gallicize) A French idiom or expression used in another language, as *"C'est la vie,"* (say la *VEE*), *"That's life."* Gaul was the Iron Age name for the territory that became France. Incidentally: On October 14, 1066, William, Duke of Normandy (c. 1028 – 1087) began the Norman-French conquest of England with his victory at the Battle of Hastings. England now had a French king, whose knights became the French aristocracy. (Their French names still survive among the English gentry.) French became the language at the royal court and among the French lords of the realm – for less than 100 years. Within 3 generations, French became a second language, learned in school. However, the subconscious memory of the glorious conquest persisted. Till this day, upper-crust English snobs cannot resist throwing in a French phrase, a Gallicism, in every conversation. *"C'est la vie."*

GALLICIZE – (*GAL*-li-size) (Gallicized, Gallicization) To *"Frenchify."* To make or become French in language, attitude, character, and culture. The term Gallicize derives from the land of Gaul, the Iron Age region of Western Europe inhabited by the Celtic tribes, encompassing present day France.

GALLIUM – (*GAL*-lee-um) (Ga) The name derives from the Latin *Gallia* meaning "France." The 31 protons in its nucleus give gallium its atomic number. Gallium is a silvery metallic element that is liquid for a wide temperature range. It occurs in trace amounts in some ores. Gallium is a metal that will melt in the human hand. It was a joke at some university chemistry departments to fashion dining utensils of gallium that would melt in the hands of astonished guests. Gallium is used in high temperature thermometers because of its high boiling point, and in low-melting alloys.

GALLOPING INFLATION – (*GAL*-lup-ping in-*FLAY*-shun) An intense inflation rate, usually ranging from 100 to 300 percent annually. In a capitalist free-wheeling market, free of government control and regulation, galloping inflation is inevitable. A Socialist command economy has the power to hold the line on galloping inflation.

GALLOWS HUMOR – (*GAL*-lows *HEW*-mer) Dark or black humor. Humor that treats serious, frightening, or painful subject matter in a light, frivolous, or satirical way. Finding mirth in death, execution, war, disease, crime is gallows humor. Gallows humor, like *"whistling in a graveyard,"* is a defense mechanism to alleviate some of the stress generated by fear. During the last days of World War two doomed Berlins joked: *"Enjoy the war while it lasts, because the peace will be horrible!"* It was said among German women that: *"It is better to have a Russian on your belly [raped], than an American over your head [bombed]."* Perfect examples of dark gallows humor.

GAL PALS – (*GAL* pals) Girlfriends. A group of young ladies who are close companions. Gal pals socialize together, pal around, and confide with each other. Sometimes, a gal pal relationship may intensify beyond dear friendship. According to the online *Urban Dictionary*, gal pal is: *"The word straight people use when they don't want to acknowledge that lesbian relationships exist."*

GALVESTON HURRICANE – (*GAL*-ves-ton *HER*-ri-cane) (September 8, 1900) The greatest natural disaster in American History. The city of Galveston is a seaport on a low-lying island in southeast Texas, at the mouth of Galveston Bay in the Gulf of Mexico. In 1900, Galveston was a tourist town, and the richest city in Texas. Galveston Island was only 8 feet above sea level. The category 4 hurricane hit with 145 mph winds and a 15-foot storm surge. The island and city were swamped. About 8,000 people lost their lives. Today the island is presumably protected by a seawall, 10 miles long, 17 feet high, and 16 feet thick at its base.

GAM – (*GAM*) (also Pod) A gam is the collective name for an assemblage of whales. *"A great gam of whales emerged on the horizon."*

GAMBLER'S FALLACY – (*GAM*-blers *FEL*-la-see) (also Monte Carlo Fallacy) In statistics and games of chance, the belief that random events affect each other. The outcome of a particular event is more likely to occur because of what happened before. The gambler's fallacy is a false notion that an event (number, card, die) that has not occurred for a long time is *"over-due,"* and must turn up soon or next. For example, if no 7 has turned up with nine throws of the dice, the gambler's fallacy says that the tenth throw must be a seven. This is wrong.

GAMBLING – (*GAM*-bling) (Gamble, Gambled, Gambler) Testing fate. The act or practice of risking loss in order to realize gain. When one gambles he takes a chance with the unknown. The consequences of the gamble may be successful or disastrous. Gamblers often throw caution to the wind. The stakes may be petty or grave. The gamble may be a playful bet on a sporting event for a drink, for instance. Or one may seriously gamble with his life on a survival decision in an emergency. In either case, one is putting trust in one's fate. Unlike a sporting event, one's efforts play no part in the gamble. Though the gambler is quite helpless, she is not hopeless. Usually, gambling concerns a game of chance, where the prize to be won or lost is money. The outcome is based on luck. Will fortune smile or frown on one's efforts? Some find gambling exhilarating. To others, it is stressful. It depends on one's personality, or perhaps faith. In order to make a wise gamble, one should know and weigh the odds of success and failure. Perhaps gambling is governed by *Karma: The Universal Law of Reciprocity*. In other words, you reap what you sow. At any rate, it is said that the Gambler's Prayer is: *"Oh Lord, please enable me to break even!"* Incidentally: The great Church Father, St. Augustine (354 – 430 CE) said: *"The Devil invented gambling."*

GAME – (*GAYM*) Any organized playful activity for fun and recreation. A game must have some set of rules, or it is simple frolicking, merriment. Games often involve friendly competition between individuals or teams. Therefore, there must be some sort of scorekeeping. This will result in winners and losers. Most sports are games. Too bad they are often taken too seriously, losing their gamely spirit. Though a game is an amusing pastime, healthful exercise may be a collateral benefit. Winning or losing should not affect the joy of having participated. *"For when the One Great scorer comes to write against your name, He writes – not that you won or lost – but how you played the game."* – Sports Writer Grantland Rice (1880 – 1954).

GAME CHANGER – (*GAYM CHAIN*-jer) An idea, invention, innovation, or event with radically altering effect. The term is taken from the world of sports. In a football game for example, a late-game interception, fumble, or blocked kick may prove to be a game changer. A few game changers in human history have been: fire, farming, writing, iron, books, Christianity, Islam, gun, steam, train, microscope, electricity, oil, car, plane, antibiotics, computer. Often a game changer is a radical gamble that can turn a situation around. It can be an unorthodox concept, a creative process, and a totally unexpected move that may win a big game, win an election, or win a war. Game changers have altered the direction of human history.

GAMETES – (*GAM*-mates) The human sex cells: the male sperm (seed) and the female ovum (egg).

GAME THEORY – (*GAYM THEER*-ree) A mathematical application that deals with strategies for maximizing gains and minimizing losses within prescribed constraints, as the rules of a card game. However, game theory is not all fun- and-games. It is widely applied in the solution of various decision-making problems, as those of military strategy and business policy. Game theory is serious business involving statistical probability. Game theory was originally devised by two mathematicians: the American Merrill Flood (1901 – 1991) and the Polish-American Melvin Dresher (1911 – 1992) for the Rand Corporation in 1950.

GAME TRAIL – (*GAYM TRAY*-uhl) Path worn down by animals in the wild. Game trails will be created where animals will find natural resources like food, a water source, or saltlick. Hunters follow the game trails in search of animals. The trail is gradually well-defined by human traffic. The trail becomes a footpath that may eventually become a road. This explains why some modern roads display odd twists and turns. They originated as game trails.

GAME VERSUS SPORT – (*GAYM VER*-sus *SPORT*) Today the Olympic *Games* is cluttered with odd *athletic* events classified as *sports*. A few of the odder events are: croquet, roque, golf, shooting, trampoline, surfing, jet skiing, skateboarding, wall climbing, yachting. How did these recreational events, or games become classified as sports, worthy of Olympic competition? This question begs the question: What is the difference between a game and sport? This question is obfuscated by the fact that the two words are mistakenly used interchangeably. A football *game,* baseball *game,* basketball *game* are all *sports,* despite the wording. Both a game and a sport are governed by rules. Generally speaking, a game is an amusing pastime, a recreational activity. Many games are sedentary, (checkers), but sports are always active. Playing a video game is not a sport, but playing a rugby game certainly is. Game participants are called *players,* whereas sports participants are called *athletes*. A *"couch potato"* can play games on the computer, but not sports in the field. Games are casual events, played for fun. Sports are serious events, played to win. In a game, *"It's not whether you win or lose, but how you play the game."* So wrote sportswriter Grantland Rice (1880 – 1954). (Rice would never succeed in the capitalist sports world of today.) Games can be solitary amusement whereas sports require competition. It's not a sport without opposition. Team sports require cooperation. Most games do not. Sometimes, the border between a game and a sport is obscure. For example, billiards is a game that is often played competitively. But it can't be considered a sport when the players are smoking cigarettes and chugging down beers while competing. The same applies to bowling. These participants are not athletes. To excel at a sport requires dedication and work. One sweats at the sport. The same cannot be said about a game. Hunting is called a sport and the hunted the game. But the competition is so one-sided, and there are no rules governing predator and prey. Hunting, like fishing or farming, is neither a game nor a sport. Gambling is called *gaming*. An inebriated craps player is hardly an athlete. Incidentally: George Steinbrenner (1930 – 2010) was the volatile owner of the New York Yankees baseball team. On several occasions he chewed-out his players. *"You are prima donnas! You think you work? You don't work. Go out into New York City and drive a cab all day and night. That's work. You get paid millions to play a boys' game!"*

GAMMA RAY BURST – (*GAM*-ma *RAY BURST*) The greatest explosions since the Big Bang. A gamma ray burst is caused by an exploding supernova, or the explosive ejection of energy from a quasar, the backside of a black hole. The collision of twin neutron stars will also result in a cosmic-catastrophic gamma ray burst. A gamma ray burst will send a cataclysmic jet of energy across the entire universe. Galaxies in its path are doomed. A single gamma ray photon has a billion times more power, force, energy than a light photon.

GAMOOWA – (ga-*MOO*-wa) A Polish-American slang term for a dizzy, spaced- out individual. A gamoowa is clueless, unaware of his environment. She is the type of person who would typically sit on a freshly painted park bench, and not know it.

GANDHI'S PEACE PRAYER – (*GON*-dees *PEES PRAY*-yer) The "Mahatma," Mohandas Gandhi (1869 – 1948) was the liberator of India from British imperialist rule, non-violently. Gandhi was a pacifist saint, who would have been canonized as an official saint of the Church, had he been a Catholic. Gandhi's Prayer for Peace reads: *"I offer you peace. I offer you love. I offer you friendship. I see your beauty. I hear your need. I feel your feelings. My wisdom flows from the Highest Source. I salute that Source in you. Let us work together for unity and love."*

GANESHA – (gon-*NEE*-sha) The Hindu elephant-headed god, son of Shiva, another manifestation of Brahma. Ganesha is the god of wisdom, luck, and the patron of learning. Ganesha provides internal balance, eliminates doubt, and stills the rational mind. Hindus pray to Ganesha to remove obstacles and strengthen faith. Ganesha is represented as a short, pot-bellies man with 4 arms and an elephant head.

GANG – (*GANG*) (also Rafter) In this case a gang is the collective name for an assemblage of turkeys. *"The meadow was occupied by a gang of turkeys."*

GANG BANG – (*GANG BANG*) (Gang banged, Gang banger, Gang banging) To be group fucked. A gang bang may be a voluntary arrangement by a sexually needy lady, or a devastating rape. If the gang bang is a sexual assault, then it's the worst case of sexual violence, and major crime. It involves humiliation, aggression, and often physical injury or death. The psycho-emotional injury is immeasurable. The victim of a gang bang is usually female, though a male may be assaulted in a homosexual or homophobic, gang bang atrocity. The assailants are almost always men, due to the predatory nature of the male sexuality. No saying how many men may participate in the savagery, the more the deadlier. On the other hand, in the culture of exotic erotica, a gang banging session is a sexual banquet, an erotic smorgasbord. To be gang banged is the most common fantasy, and favorite role of sex-loving pornstars. It involves uninhibited vaginal, anal, and oral sex, often simultaneously. In the professional porn industry, a gang bang must consist of at least 4 M̲ales on 1 F̲emale. Therefore, it is labeled as MMMMF, (M4F). Four dicks are the minimum. Usually, there are several more guys, a group or gang, messaging their dicks to keep them hard for the camera, waiting their turn on the gal. The scene is reminiscent of a pack of male dogs on a bitch in heat – purely animalistic. That's why gang bang videos are so popular. The sex is carnal, wild, and beastly, back to nature. *"Sex is a part of nature. I go along with nature."* – Marilyn Monroe (1926 – 1962). All three female apertures are full-filled during the bang session. Indeed, a gang bang is a nymphomaniac's wet dream! Don't kid yourself. A gang bang is a nice girl's dark, secret fantasy. Repression of this subconscious wish, may be the root cause of all her other neuroses. Consult Dr. Sigmund Freud (1856 – 1939). *"The only unnatural sex act is that which you cannot perform."* – Sexologist Dr. Alfred Kinsey (1894 – 1956). A Caveat: The author serves as a reporter, not a supporter. The colorful language is representative of the culture of the subject.

GANGES RIVER – (*GAN*-jees *RIV*-ver) River of South Asia, originating as glacial melt water in the Himalayans. The river flows 1,500 miles through India, emptying into the Bay of Bengal. The Ganges is a sacred river to millions of Hindus. Incidentally: The Jamaican term *"ganja"* for marihuana was introduced by Hindu East Indians. It is a corruption of the name Ganges. Apparently, wild cannabis grows along its mighty banks. No wonder the river is sacred.

GANG OF EIGHT – (gang uhv *AYT*) A colloquial term in the political parlance for the 8 leaders in the U.S. Congress that must be briefed on classified intelligence matters by the President. This term strangely has a pejorative connotation reminiscent of Maoist politics. Nevertheless, these 8 Congressional leaders are power brokers in the co-equal branch of government with the executive branch. The Gang of 8 consists of the: *Speaker of the House; Senate Majority Leader; House Minority Leader; Senate Minority Leader; Senate Intelligence Committee Chair; House Intelligence Committee Chair; Senate Intelligence Committee Ranking Minority Member; House Intelligence Committee Ranking Minority Member.* In case of a national emergency, crisis, tragedy, the collective wisdom of all these elected representatives is imperative. Every President has availed himself of this asset, advantage except the self-proclaimed know-it-all, with a *"Big Good Brain,"* Donald Trump (b. 1946). Trump makes historic decisions whimsically. His primary concern is, *"Does it benefit Trump?"* Therefore Trump ignores counsel from the Gang of 8. Often it is not only imprudent, but illegal to disregard Congress. Trump confirms with no one. He makes world-shaking decisions on the golf course, influenced by the last person who had his ear.

GANG OF SIX – (gang uhv *SIX*) The dictatorial danger to befall the Supreme Court, if democratic judicial adjustments are not made. Perfidious President Donald Trump (b. 1946) has contaminated the Republican Congress, the Federal Judiciary, and the Supreme Court with a virulent ideological virus which is immune to justice. He has turned the Supreme Court into a biased Republican cabal which will rubberstamp his autocratic ukases. If justice cannot be attained in the Court, it will be attained in the street. The once hallowed Supreme Court has become a complicit *"Gang of 6."* This is because only 6 members out of 9 can scuttle, sabotage the will of the majority of the population. The Supreme Court has become a *"Sextyranny!"* *"If the judges are behind the times and if ever their integrity as honorable men is seriously questioned, then the Court and the country are in trouble. Believe me, it will be a bad day for Americans if ever the mass of them lose faith in this Court as their fair and final protector."* – British-American journalist and historian Allister Cooke (1908 – 2004) in his brilliant book *AMERICA* (1973).

GANGRENE – (gan-*GREEN*) Necrosis or death of soft tissue, due to obstructed circulation or infection. The gangrene bacteria release endotoxins that rot living tissue. The putrefying flesh gives off a sickening sweet smell. About ¾ of the operations during the American Civil War (1861 – 1865) were amputations, often due to gangrene. About 60,000 limbs were removed, more than any other war in history. The application of bromine helped to arrest the spread of gangrene.

GANGUE – (*GANG*) Rock or worthless waste materials in aggregate or mixed with valuable metallic ores that are mined. Quartz serves as a common gangue in mining.

GANJA – (*GON*-ja) Potent Jamaican marijuana. The Spanish first brought marijuana to the Caribbean. The term ganja is taken from Ganges, the sacred Hindu river. Indentured servants (workers) from India popularized marijuana in Jamaica, giving it the name ganja. Jamaican Rastafarians consider ganja the *"sacred weed,"* which is smoked sacramentally in religious services. It was the Rastas who courageously defied the law and challenged society's official view of ganja. They presented the narcotic as innocuous, harmless, and not deserving harsh punishment. Rastafari championed ganja use and normalized marijuana, like alcohol.

GANSA MEGILLA – (*GON*-sa meg-*GIL*-la) A Yiddishism for the entire story, *"the whole megilla."*

GARAGE BAND – (guh-*RAHJ BAND*) Typically, a group of young amateur musicians yet to find fame or fortune. Due to their humble modest middle-class status, they rehearse and record in a garage, or some similar non-professional venue. Guitars, drums, and electric keyboard usually comprise the garage band. All band members attempt at singing as well. Some garage bands became famous, and evolved into successful star performers. Others were *"one hit wonders."* Most grew grey in the garage. Those who remained together played gigs at the neighborhood tavern.

GARDEN OF EDEN – (*GAR*-den of *EE*-den) The Biblical paradise in which Adam and Eve, the first two angelic people blissfully dwelled, before becoming fully human. Actually, the Garden of Eden can be likened to the *"Womb of God."* The two *souls,* now called Adam and Eve existed in carefree euphoria. But there was trouble in paradise. Discontentment set in. The two souls wanted more. They wanted to know. They got their wish. Adam and Eve were punished by God for their dissatisfaction and ingratitude. They became incarnate assuming mortal bodies. Adam and Eve were born again as human beings. They were forced out of the Garden of Eden, to suffer all the travails of humankind, along with their progeny. But their souls longed for atonement (read: at-*ONE*-ment) with God. This they achieved, along with their descendants, when they surrender their bodies through death. In death, we return to the Garden of Eden, the *"Womb of God."*

GARDIAN ANGELS – (*GAR*-dee-an *AN*-jels) God's security guard agency. Celestial hosts assigned to each person as a personal bodyguard. Psalm 91: 11-12 assures us that *"God has given his angels charge of you, to guard you in all your ways. On their hands, they will bear you up, lest you dash your foot against a stone."* Many theological scholars content that every living creature – flora and fauna – has a guardian angel protecting them. *"Every blade of grass has its angel leaning over it whispering, 'Grow,' 'Grow'."* – The Talmud. The great Evangelist Rev. Billy Graham (1918- 2018) professed that *"Some Christian writers have speculated that UFO's could very well be a part of God's angelic host who preside over the physical affairs of the universe."*

GARISH – (*GAR*-rish) Crudely tastelessly colorful, showy, or elaborate as clothes or decoration. Garish is brightly colored, excessively ornate, and ornamental or elaborate as buildings. Too, over embellished writing can be garish.

GARLAN'D – (*GAHR*-lan'd) (also *GAHR*-lan-ded) A verb representing vile political perfidy. To be Garlan'd is to be denied a legitimate political appointment for purely political reasons. The term is an eponym alluding to U.S. Court of Appeals Judge Merrick B. Garland (b. 1952). Judge Garland was nominated by Democratic President Barack Obama (b. 1961) to fill a vacancy on the U.S. Supreme Court. The most perfidious politician, Republican Majority Leader of the Senate, *"Moscow"* Mitch McConnell (b. 1942) ignored the Constitution, and refused to bring Garland's nomination up to a vote for 293 days. On January 3, 2017, the nomination expired. McConnell and the defrauding Republicans won big. They prevented Garland's Liberal appointment to the Supreme Court. This enabled Republican President Donald Trump (b. 1946) to appoint a conservative. The term Garlan'd was coined by political pundit Ari Melber (b. 1980).

GARNER – (*GAHR*-ner) (Garnered) A verb meaning to gather, acquire, earn. As a noun, a garner is a grain bin. Therefore, to garner also means to gather grain into a storage bin, or to store, supply anything. *"Donald Trump quickly garnered a reputation as a buffoon."*

GARRULOUS – (*GAR*-yoo-lus) (Garrulity) Over-talkative, a rambling rattle- mouth. A garrulous person is prone to frivolous chatter.

GARVEYISM – (*GAR*-vee-is-um) The original *"Black Pride,"* *"Black Power"* Movement as promoted by Jamaican civil rights fighter and *"National Hero,"* Marcus Garvey (1887 – 1940). Marcus Garvey was born in St. Anne's Bay, Jamaica, descended from Maroons (escaped slaves). Racial injustice in British Colonial Jamaica turned Garvey to *"Black Nationalism."* He advocated economic independence of Blacks and organized the *"Universal Negro Improvement Association"* (UNIA) in 1914. Garvey travelled throughout the Caribbean, Latin America, England and the United States, attracting a huge following. Garvey became a *"Pan-Africanist,"* advocated the union of all Black people in one great African nation. His motto was: *"One God! One Aim! One Destiny!"* He organized the *"Black Star"* steam ship line to carry out his plans. American and British authorities viewed Garvey as a dangerous agitator. He was imprisoned in Atlanta,

U.S.A. for 2 years. Though his dreams failed to materialize, Marcus Garvey is considered the *"Father of Black Power,"* and is a *"National Hero"* of Jamaica.

GAS – (*GAS*) A vapor. A state of matter in which the molecular structure is very loosely packed, dispersed in fact, resulting in rapid, frenetic molecular motion. Natural gas is fossilized sunlight, captured by ancient marine creatures. They were converted in the Earth under heat and pressure into the fossil fuel gas. Incidentally: The inhalation of toxic gas, like the consumption of poisonous solids or liquids is fatal. Over 80,000 soldiers were intentionally killed in World War One (1914 – 1918) by poison gas. During World War Two (1939 – 1945), millions were killed by the German Nazis in genocidal gas chambers. This abominable atrocity forced the abandonment of the gas chamber as a means of execution in U.S. prisons.

GASCONADE – (gas-kun-*AID*) Extravagant boasting, boastful talk. *"Trump let loose a flatulent gasconade, highlighting his imaginary accomplishments."* The term gasconade entered English in the 17th century from the French *"gasconade,"* meaning *"bragging, boasting, a boastful story."* The French took the term from their province Gascony. This serves as a clue to how the Gascons were stereotypically perceived. Incidentally: There's a kernel of truth in every stereotype.

GAS GIANTS – (*GAS JY*-ants) The 4 outer planets from the sun: Uranus, Neptune, Saturn, and Jupiter which are not solid (but may have a rocky core). Gas giants are enormous planets with enormously powerful gravity. That's wht they can trap all the surrounding gas.

GASLIGHT – (*GAS*-lite) (Gaslighted, Gaslighting) To drive someone crazy by deluding their mind. To gaslight is to use psychological manipulation to cause a person to doubt their sanity. One who is gaslighted is convinced to doubt what they see. The term derives from the movie *"Gaslight,"* (1944). The storyline has an abusive husband attempting to drive his wife mad. He secretly, and repeatedly dims and brightens the gaslights in the house, while convincing the woman that she is imagining the flickering. In 2019, the term gaslight had entered the popular socio-political lexicon. It is used to describe FOX TV's propaganda campaign to manipulate the minds of Trump supports. FOX TV attempts to argue against logic, falsify the facts, construct conspiracy theories, present alternate realities over and over to drive their disciples crazy. *"Don't trust what you hear; don't believe what you see."* Gaslighting is an attempt to foment mild mass hysteria. FOX gaslights its viewers into denying their economic interests in support of Trump's Republican pro-wealth, fascist agenda. Incidentally: Gaslighting was the *Merriam-Webster Dictionary's* 2022 word of the year.

GASOHOL – (*GAS*-a-hol) A mixture of 90% unleaded gasoline and 10% grain alcohol. Gasohol can save 10% of the oil consumption in vehicles. This would make the U.S. 10% less dependent on Arab oil. Too, alcohol burns much cleaner than petroleum products. Of course, the capitalist oil companies view gasohol as a 10% reduction in profits. Nothing else matters. They are spending feverishly lobbying congressmen to discredit gasohol.

GASOLINE – (gas-o-*LEEN*) A volatile, highly flammable liquid mixture of hydrocarbons obtained from oil. Gasoline is the lightest constituent of petroleum. Natural gasoline was called naphtha by the ancients, and regarded as a dangerous waste product.

GASSER – (*GAS*-er) British medical slang for an anesthesiologist.

GASSING – (*GAS*-sing) A form of assault common in prisons. Prisoners splash guards with urine and excrement. Not only is gassing vile and humiliating, but dangerous as well. A witches brew of diseases can be transmitted in that filth including deadly HIV.

GASTROLITHS – (*GAS*-tro-liths) Fossilized stones found within the digestive system of a dinosaur or other reptile. Some creatures intentionally swallow small stones to aid with digestion by grinding the stomach contents. Chickens swallow gastroliths. Of course, chickens are birds that evolved from the reptilian dinosaurs. To a cricket, a chicken is still a Tyrannosaurus Rex.

GASTRONOME – (*GAS*-tro-nohm) (Gastronomy, Gastronomic) An epicure or gourmet, a professional eater [read: *"glutton"*]. An epicure, gourmet, gastronome is a connoisseur of fine food and drink. He has cultivated a discriminating palate for the enjoyment of the very best cuisine. A gastronome will always insist on the highest quality of exotic spices and ingredients. The dishes she consumes are meticulously prepared. All attention must go to detail, including presentation [read: *the art of food resting on a plate*]. Expense is never taken into consideration. It need not be. Only wealthy capitalists qualify as gastronomes. Eating is as pleasurable and important as sex for gastronomes, and often must serve as a sexual substitute for the gargantuan gaseous gastronomes.

GASTRONOMY – (gas-*TRON*-nom-mee) (Gastronomist, Gastronomic, Gastronome) Connoisseurism. The art or science of good eating – not necessarily healthy eating, but enjoyable, aesthetic eating. Too, gastronomy referrers to a cooking style of a particular region, as the gastronomy of Yorkshire or Poland.

GASTROPODS – (*GAS*-tro-pods) Snails of land or sea. Gastropods are shelled creatures like mollusks, snails, bivalves, and conchs with their magnificent shells. Land snails (gastropods) are slugs with shells. When snails slowly glide, leaving their slime trail, they are licking up lime from limestone and building their shells. They thrive on limestone to fortify their shells. Incidentally: The Queen Conch is the biggest gastropod (snail) in the world.

GASTROTOURISM – (gas-tro-*TUR*-is-um) To travel for the purpose of indulging in exotic cuisine. A major attraction in exploring foreign lands is foreign foods. The chef and traveler Anthony Bourdain (1956 – 2018) popularized gastrotourism in his TV show, *"Parts Unknown."*

GATE – (*GAYT*) When the term is used as a suffix, affixed to the end of a name or word, *"gate"* then refers to a political scandal. The term derived from the Water*gate* Hotel in Washington D.C. This was the site of the Democratic National Committee during the 1972 Presidential election. It was here that Republican President Richard Nixon (1913 - 2094) ordered former C.I.A. operatives to break into the Democratic Party's headquarters (1972). The break-in and cover-up resulting in the Water*gate* Scandal which brought down President Nixon (1974). Since then, all political scandals have adopted the suffix *"gate."* For example, Republican President Ronald Reagan's *"Iran-Contragate,"* (1985 – 1987). Today, Republican President Donald Trump is squirming through *"Trump-Russiagate,"* (2016 - present). Incidentally: The term *"gate,"* as a synonym for scandal has been adopted by the British. In January, 2022, Conservative Prime Minister Boris Johnson (b. 1964) is embroiled in a scandal called *"Partygate"* by the British press. With the pandemic raging in Britain, Johnson had laws passed restricting group gatherings throughout the nation. Nevertheless, being above the law, Johnson participated in 16 parties at 10 Downing Street. He claims he didn't know the law that he himself created! Johnson is being investigated by the police, and the conservative party. *"Every politician ends his career in failure."* – British Proverb.

GATED COMMUNITY – (*GAY*-ted com-*MUN*-ni-tee) Affluent suburban residential compounds under lockdown. The gated-community is a mentality as well as a security measure. These defensive quarantines represent the siege mentality of the rich. They fear the *"barbarians"* at the *GATE*. The wealthy must live in *"Fort Apaches"* to protect their surplus wealth from the poor outside the walls who need it.

GATEKEEPER SUBJECTS – (*GATE*-keep-per *SUB*-jects) Academic disciplines taught in secondary schools that open doors for future careers. The gatekeeper subjects are Mathematics, English, Science, Social Studies, and perhaps a foreign language. The gatekeeper subjects make up the core curriculum.

GATOR BAIT – (*GAY*-ter *BAYT*) (Alligator bait) Bait is food, commonly meat, uncommonly live creatures, used to lure dangerous animals, usually during hunting. Alligators have long been hunted. The University of Florida possesses the *"Gator"* as its athletic mascot. At sporting events, the students innocently chanted a *"Gator Bait"* cheer. Being oblivious of history, the fans were unaware that during the slavocracy, Black children were actually used as gator bait. University President W. Kent Fuchs (b. 1954) wrote: *"There is horrific racist imagery associated with the phrase [gator bait]. The Gator Band will discontinue the use of the cheer."* In Florida, Louisiana, and the swamps of the South, slave children, toddlers, and babies (*"pickaninnies"*) were forced to wade in shallow swamp water to lure the 400-pound bull alligators. The hunter safely hid with his rifle. Despicably depraved! However, the practice was sometimes maniacally satanic. It has been reported that diabolical gator hunters kidnapped Black slave babies. God forbid that this is true, because it is said they were skinned alive, their little writhing bodies strung from branches above the swamp. The dripping blood helped to lure the big bull gators that were shot. The gators died an infinitely more humane death than the precious babies. It is difficult for a human being with a conscience to conceive such inhumanity. If there is a Hell, it was for such creatures that it was created. A Caveat: Though this is written, the author refuses to grant this horror credence. *"Cruelty has a human heart."* – William Blake (1757 – 1827).

GAUCHE – (*GOWSH or GOESH*) A French term meaning lack of social grace, sensitivity, or acuteness. A gauche individual is awkward, tactless, and crude. Donald Trump (b. 1946) is a perfect example of a gauche guy. It is a humiliation to call him President.

GAUCHOS – (*GOW*-chohs) The cowboys of the Argentine Pampas (grasslands). The gauchos use the bola (3 balls secured to the end of a rope) to entangle the legs of running cattle, as the North American cowboys use the lasso.

GAULS – (*GAWLS*) The ancient Celtic tribe that lived in today's France. The Gauls were conquered by the Romans and by the Germanic Franks.

GAUNTER – (*GAWNT*-ter) An archaic appellation for a glovemaker, a craftsman who makes gloves.

GAUNTLET – (*GAWNT*-let) A medieval glove, as of chain mail or plate, worn by a knight in armor to protect the hand. To *"Throw down the gauntlet"* was a challenge to duel.

GAUNTLET – (*GAWNT*-let) A form of punishment once used by militaries and American Indian tribes, in which the offender or prisoner was forced to run between 2 rows of men who struck at him with whips, chubs, and weapons. The Indians used the gauntlet as a test of worthiness, whether the victim was to be adopted into the tribe, or burned alive. Those who endured and survived the gauntlet bravely were adopted, to replace a lost loved-one. The elderly women had the power to choose, adoption or death.

GAUR – (*GAU*-wer) The Indian, Asian buffalo. The gaur is a massive wild cattle of India, Southeast Asia, and the Malay Archipelago. It is the largest, strongest wild cattle in the world. It stands 6 feet tall at the shoulders, with some males even larger. The gaur is bigger than the water buffalo, Cape buffalo, and American buffalo. The gaur has been called a tiger killer. In death bouts with tigers, gaurs are more successful than not. Sadly, this great creature is now being reduced in numbers.

GAUSSIAN CURVE – (*GOW*-see-an *CURV*) On a graph of distribution, a bell- shaped curve. This is professed to be the normal curve. In school, the Gaussian curve is said to be the natural distribution of grades students will earn. According to the Gaussian curve, very few students will earn D's or F's, and very few students will earn A's and B's. The majority of students will earn C's. That's because the majority is always average. They will be plotted at the mid-point of mediocrity. The Gaussian curve presages a negative expectancy on the part of the teacher.

GAUTAMA – (gow-*TOM*-ma) The Buddha's family or surname, a patronymic handed down from his father. The name Gautama is Sanskrit meaning: *"Descendant of the great ox."* The Buddha's given or first name was Siddhartha. Traditionally the family name was pronounced first. Therefore, the Buddha was originally Prince Gautama Siddhartha.

GAVIAL – (*GAV*-vee-al) (also Gharial) A large Indian crocodilian with an elongated, gar-like jaw. It is the oldest crocodilian on Earth. The gavial, though fearsome looking, is a fish and frog eater. The gavial is an endangered species.

GAY – (*GAY*) In the realm of social-psychology, gay means homosexual. A gay individual displays a preference for members of one's own sex as love partners. Though both gay men, and lesbian women are homosexual, females are not usually referred to as gay. The term is more accurately reserved for males. In the 14th century, the term gay was borrowed from the Middle French *"gai,"* meaning merry, or happily excited. Its sexual connotation began to evolve in the 17th century. Gay came to mean *'given to unrestrained self-indulgence and the pursuit of pleasure'*. A gay individual exhibited a *"devil-may-care"* attitude. Terms like *"gay-blade,"* and *"gay-dog"* developed. Both were pejorative terms for licentious, heterosexual playboys. In 1703, English dramatist Nicholas Rowe (1674 – 1718) wrote <u>*The Fair Penitent.*</u> The main character in his story is an unscrupulous seducer of women named *Lothario.* Rowe introduced the term a *"Gay Lothario,"* who was thoroughly heterosexual. In the 1890's, the term gay began the shift toward homosexuality. It began in hobo culture. The term *"gaycat"* first appeared in print in 1897. It referred to a young hobo, or inexperienced homeless tramp. By the 1920's, gaycat was widely used among transients, drifters who resided in boxcars. A young gaycat would matchup with an older vagabond to gain survival skills. It was understood that the relationship between the youth and mature gentleman would eventually become a sexual liaisons. Together they would ride the rails, while the hobo would ride the gaycat. In a 1935 handbook of underworld and prison slang, *"Gaycat"* was defined as *"a homosexual boy."* However, *gay*, in its homosexual sense, is not known to have surfaced as an independent adjective until the 1950's. Sociologist Donald Webster Corey's (1913 – 1986) *The Homosexual in America* (1951) introduced the nation to a gay subculture. Outside the covert subculture, gays generally remained closeted. This changed in the 1960's with the Hippie Movement, Free Love Movement, Anti-Vietnam War Movement, Feminist Movement, and especially, the Civil Rights Movement. Gay Pride, Gay Activism, Gay Liberation emerged for good. The pivotal point was the historic *"Stonewall Rebellion"* of June 28, 1969. Beginning at the Stonewall Inn in Greenwich Village New York, gay citizens battled police and rioted, ending decades of humiliation, oppression, and abuse by cops. That was Gay America's *"Bastille Day."* *"We're here! We're queer! Get used to it!"* became the defiant gay battle cry. Despite the temporary aberration of *Trumpism*, our Gay Brothers and Lesbian Sisters now have their places at the table. Incidentally: The multisyllabic, clinical term *"homosexual"* is passé, and somewhat demeaning. *Gay* is the affectionate appellation.

GAYBLADE – (*GAY*-blade) (also Gaydog) An opprobrious 17th century English term for a world-wise playboy, licentious, uninhibited lady predator. A gayblade was thoroughly heterosexual, despite the homosexual connotation.

GAYCAT – (*GAY*-cat) A term that originated as American hobo slang in the 1890's. The term gaycat first appeared in print in 1897. A gaycat was a young, inexperienced boy, a runaway. Being vulnerable in the lawless world of the transients, the gaycat would befriend an adult vagabond in order to learn survival skills. By the 1920's, it was generally understood that the relationship between the young gaycat and his mature mentor would become a sexual liaisons. Together they would ride the rails while the hobo would ride the gaycat. In a 1935 handbook of underworld and prison slang, the entry *"Gaycat"* was defined as *"A homosexual boy."*

GAYDAR – (*GAY*-dahr) Having a keen ability to recognize a homosexual, even one who is still in the closet. Women seem to be intuitively adept at spotting a gay guy or gal by their subtle mannerisms. Too, gays or bisexuals have a strong sense of gaydar, for after all, it takes one to know one. Incidentally: The polar opposite of gaydar is being homoblivious – being naively unable to recognize even an obvious homosexual person.

GAY LOTHARIO – (*GAY* lo-*THAR*-ree-o) A notoriously depraved, debauched womanizer. Lothario was the licentious main character in Nicholas Rowe's (1674 – 1718) play, *The Fair Penitent* (1703). At that time, in this context, *gay* referred to an unrestrained self-indulgent pleasure-seeker. Lothario's pleasure was conquering ladies. Therefore, a Gay Lothario is thoroughly heterosexual, not in the least homosexually gay.

GAY MARRY – (gay *MER*-ree) (Gay Married, Gay Marrying, Gay Marriage) To legally wed a member of your own gender. To gay marry is presently (October 2023) legal throughout the USA, but not worldwide. Even in America, reactionary conservatives, Evangelical Christian Nationalists are working to undermine, rescind the civil right to marry whoever you wish.

GAY PANIC – (*GAY PAN*-nik) (also Trans Panic) A disingenuous, hypocritical homophobia defense, which amounts to blaming the victim. Gay panic is a ludicrous legal strategy to convince a jury that one had attacked and harmed a gay or trans individual, in a moment of temporary insanity. The defendant may allege that he was so shocked, offended, and frightened by a perceived sexual advance by a same-sex individual, that he lost his mind! The beating or murder was not his fault, for the *"sexual deviant"* had provoked him. It was a form of self-defense. Therefore, the assailant/defendant is not guilty. Of course, a bigoted jury will buy this defense. To date (Easter Sunday 2021), only 12 states have banned the astoundingly ridiculous *"Gay Panic Defense."* The only Southern state to do so is Virginia (in April, 2021). Incidentally: Anyone so emotionally traumatized by a proposition from a gay individual, is actually traumatized moreso by the realization of his own homosexual impulses.

GAY PRIESTS – (*GAY PREESTS*) Ordained Roman Catholic Priests who happen to be homosexual. Actually, the Church mandates that priests be *"asexual,"* without sexual yearnings, which is physiologically impossible. (Celibacy has been Church law since the year 1123.) Like the rest of us, the priest's sexuality is part of his humanity. Unlike us, his great sacrifice is not to act on it. In fact the number of priests who break their vow of Celibacy are very few and far between. There are sexual molesters, predators who are plumbers, lawyers, doctors, and presidents. But when it's a priest, it makes the headlines. Indeed, there is an incentive for pious gay men to become priests. The Sacrament of Holy Orders is a great substitute, or escape from the sacrament of Matrimony. A young man gets tired of hearing Auntie Wanda publicly asking at every wedding: *"And what's stopping a good looking boy like you from getting married?"* It's very convenient to hide one's homosexuality behind the white collar. Therefore, there may be a higher percentage of gays in the priesthood, than in other callings. That's just fine, provided they don't act on their impulses. There are far more heterosexual priests who molest married female parishioners, than homosexual priests, who molest altarboys. But it's the gay priest who encounters the full wrath of society, especially from Catholic bashers. Those who break moral and societal laws must face their consequences. But it's a travesty to paint all priests with the same brush, in gay colors.

GAZA STRIP – (*GA*-za *STRIP*) A territory along the Mediterranean Sea just northeast of the Sinai Peninsula. The Gaza Strip is 140 square miles total, 25 miles in length, 3.7 to 7.5 miles wide. That makes it a little larger than the City of Philadelphia. The land was Egyptian territory occupied by Israel during the Six Day War (1967). The Gaza Strip was part of the land set aside for Palestinians, and in 1994, put under Palestinian self-rule. Nevertheless Israel kept control the Gaza Strip. That was until 2005. Israel decided to turn the territory totally over to the Palestinians. Jewish settlements were forcibly closed by Israel, and the 9,000 Jewish settlers forced to abandon their homes. The Palestinians proceeded to elect their own leaders. The self-governing experiment seemed to succeed until 2007 when the Palestinian terrorist group Hamas usurped power in Gaza and subjugated the population. Hamas (supported by Iran, and Hezbollah in Lebanon) is dedicated to the destruction of Jewish Israel. Terrorist attacks and rockets fired at Israel from Hamas Gaza forced Israel to invade the territory in 2005 and 2006. In October, 2023, Hamas terrorists crossed into Israel, butchering Jewish citizens of all ages. Hamas has about 300 miles of defensive tunnels dug beneath Gaza City. Israel countered the Hamas incursion with a severe rocket bombardment and a land invasion which is in progress at the time of this writing. Update: (February 2024) The Israeli bombardment and invasion has killed about 30,000 Palestinians, with about 70,000 injured. It has cracked a rift between allies, the U.S. and Israel. It has damaged President Joe Bidens (b. 1942) re-election campaign. The Gaza War has cost Israelis and Jews the moral highground in world opinion.

GAZPACHO POLICE – (goz-*POCH*-oh poh-*LEES*) Gazpacho is a Spanish soup made of chopped tomatoes, cucumbers, onions, garlic, oil, and vinegar, and served cold. The soup has nothing to do with law enforcement. But Georgia Republican Congresswoman Marjorie Taylor Greene (b. 1974) didn't know that. On February 9, 2022, Greene aired an attack on the Democratic Speaker of the House, Nancy Pelosi (b. 1940). Greene accused the Speaker of employing *"Gazpacho"* Police, instead of *"Gestapo"* Police tactics. The Congresswoman's gaffe would be comical, coming from a comedian like Jerry Seinfeld (b. 1954). (The gaffe harkens back to Seinfeld's *"Soup Nazis"* comedy episode.) But Greene is an influential, consequential government Representative. In a democracy, people have the right to elect low-information, conspiracy theorist nut-jobs like Greene. It's not surprising that Marjorie Taylor Greene represents a district in the Southern State of Georgia. As democracy goes, if you elect a moron, you're well represented. *"It seems like when God made America, He shook it with a violent earthquake, and most of the nuts rolled down South."* – Philosopher Gary J. Pasieka (b. 1951).

GDP AND GNP – (*JEE DEE PEE* and *JEE EN PEE*) (*Gross Domestic Product* and *Gross National Product*) both describe the market value of all goods and services produced for final sale in an economy in 1 year. The difference is in the interpretation of *"economy."* GDP refers to the economy produced by Americans within America. The GDP only pertains to production within the nation. GNP refers to the economy produced by Americans globally. GNP pertains to production on the part of the nation's people anywhere in the world. Therefore, what is produced by U.S. corporations overseas in included in the GNP, but not in the GDP.

G.E.D. – (*GEE EE DEE*) (*General Education Development* Test) A second chance at a high school diploma for late bloomers. Such re-admittance is rare in class- obsessed Britain and Europe. In America, the G.E.D. is attained as adult education. It should be free. All education should be free, from G.E.D. to Ph.D. Nothing is a better investment in America.

GEDANKENEXPERIMENT – (ged-*DAN*-ken-ex-per-ri-ment) literally, *"Thought Experiment,"* Albert Einstein's (1879 – 1955) daydreaming sessions at which time his subconscious intuitive mind was unleashed.

GEEK – (*GEEK*) A digital-technology expert, a technonerd. Geeks are perceived, somewhat correctly, as being preoccupied with computers and robotic – high tech. They are therefore stereotypically considered to be social misfits. The term geek is applied both disparagingly, and as a term of self-referenced pride.

GEEZER – (*GEE*-zer) An old, cantankerous, and somewhat odd, eccentric man. To qualify as a geezer, one must be a grumpy, grouchy, old curmudgeon. Never do we find a young geezer, (though some youth display geezer tendencies like the *Young Republicans*). It takes a miserable lifetime to accumulate the volume of resentment to descend into geezerhood. Therefore, conservatism and advanced age are mandatory qualifications. Too, geezers are usually white, and always male. The term geezer has a convoluted etymology. It traces back to the 1885 Cockney term *"guiser."* A guiser was a *"masked pantomime,"* usually in odd costume as part of a performance. The term guiser derived from the Old French *"guise,"* meaning *"a style or fashion of attire"* (13th century). By about 1500, guise came to mean simply *"masked,"* as in *"disguise."* Therefore the original notion of *"one who went about in disguise,"* evolved into *"an odd fellow."* The Cockney came to conflate *"odd man"* with *"old man."* Before long, *"old guiser"* was corrupted into *"old geezer."* Incidentally: Today, elderly cantankerous white men, old geezers, comprise Donald Trump's (b. 1946) core supporters. Of course. Trump himself is an old geezer.

GELATA BABOONS – (je-*LA*-ta ba-*BOONS*) Unique apes of the Ethiopian Highlands. The red triangular marking on the breast had earned this creature the name, *"Bleeding-Heart Monkey."* The Gelata are mountain monkeys, the best climbers in the world. The exercise climbing had provided them with the strongest fingers of all primates. They are highly social creatures that live in large groups. The Gelata Baboon is the only monkey that eats exclusively grass.

GELATIN – (*JEL*-la-tin) (Gelatinous) Nearly transparent, tasteless, odorless glutinous substance derived from boiled animal bone and sinew. Gelatin is 99% protein, no fat, no carbohydrate, no sodium (salt). One tablespoon (10g) contains merely 35 calories. Commercially and in the kitchen, powdered or granulated gelatin is used as a thickener in jams, jellies, gravies, marshmallows, and desserts like Jell-O. *Aspic* is a natural gelatin that forms in the roastpan after the meat juices are chilled. Taken orally, gelatin repairs damaged cartilage in joints and restores collagen in sagging skin. This prevents wrinkles. Gristle on bone, and the flexible parts of our ears, nose, and spinal disk pads are solidified gelatin. Both cartilage and collagen are gelatinous. At age 18, the body ceases to produce natural gelatin (cartilage and collagen). It is therefore essential to take it orally to heal damaged joints, and drooping skin.

GELDING – (*GELL*-ding) A castrated stallion. A big, strong male horse made docile in order to be a more manageable draft animal.

GELOTOPHOBIA – (gel-o-tow-*FOH*-bee-a) Gelotophobiac) Phobic fear of being laughed at. No one except a comedian likes to be laughed at. But gelotophobiacs are obsessive in this fear.

GEMEINSCHAFT – (*GEM*-myn-shaft) A German sociological term for a warm, friendly, collegial community. This is a society which has eliminated class barriers. Poverty and racial animosity are absent in a gemeinschaft environment. Socialist dignity, cooperation, and distributive justice will produce a gemeinschaft society. This term had entered American sociology. *"Gemeinschaft Now!"* – Socialist Battlecry. Incidentally: The polar opposite of gemeinschaft is cold, selfish, capitalistic *"gesellschaft."*

GEMEINSHAFT NOW! – (*GEM*-myn-shaft *NOW*) The Socialist battlecry. Roughly translated from German as *"Brotherhood Now."*

GENDARME – (*ZHAHN*-dahrm) French for policeman.

GENDER – (*JEN*-der) A social sex role (female or male) that a society expects one to play. Gender is sociological (nurture) whereas sex is biological (nature). *"A gender-equal society would be one where the word 'gender' does not exist."* – Gloria Steinem (b. 1934).

GENDER DISPLEASURE – (*JEN*-der dis-*PLESH*-shur) What men and women most dislike. According to Dr. John Gray (b. 1951) in <u>Men Are from Mars, Women Are from Venus</u> (1992), of all things, what men hate the most is when women tell them what to do. *"You should keep your workroom tidier."* Conversely, what women hate the most is when men tell them how they should feel. *"You shouldn't get upset over a minor detail."*

GENDER DYSPHORIA – (*JEN*-der dys-*FOR*-ree-a) (Gender dysphoric) A state of deep depression and bewilderment when an individual is living in the body of the wrong gender. Poetically speaking, God intended the correct gender, but nature made a mistake. Of course, the individual has homosexual yearnings which she/he suppresses in youth. It's miserable to hate the body in which one is imprisoned. A transsexual metamorphosis is the only definitive solution to gender dysphoria. Only then will gender dysphoria be joyfully experienced as gender euphoria.

GENDER EUPHORIA – (*JEN*-der you-*FOR*-ree-a) (Gender euphoric) A psycho- sexual metamorphosis. Gender euphoria is a state of bliss experienced by trans- genders individuals when they begin to live the lives they are intended. Gender euphoria occurs when the transsexual persons are accepted and treated as the gender orientation that satisfies their souls. Gender euphoria is an emotional, spiritual awakening. In a sense, the soul and body has finally been united. The polar opposite of gender euphoria is *"gender dysphoria."* In this case, the transsexual is rejected in his or her transformation.

GENDER FLUID – (*JEN*-der *FLOO*-id) (Gender Fluidity) Individuals whose gender identity flows freely, fluidly. A Gender Fluid person may at any time identify as male, female, or neutrois, or any other non-binary identity, or some combination of identities. Their gender can vary at random, with mood swings, or in response to different circumstances. Gender Fluid people may feel more comfortable using gender neutral pronouns and display as androgynous gender expression.

GENDER NAIVETE – (*JEN*-der ny-*EV*-vi-tee) The cultural influence on gender behavior across social milieus. Different societies have different expectations in playing the gender roles. Misunderstanding of the gender expectations in a foreign culture is gender naiveté. For example, in Russia, men are not embarrassed to embrace, and kiss each other on the cheeks, even in official ceremonies. In France, women are flattered by a wink or whistle from an admiring stranger. In America, that women would feel compelled to act insulted (often deceptively).

GENDERQUEER – (*JEN*-der-kweer) Synonymous with non-binary gender identity (neither male nor female). Genderqueer is an umbrella term for all sexual orientations and gender identities beyond male and female.

GENE – (*JEEN*) A unit of heredity composed of DNA (<u>*Deoxyribo*</u><u>*Nucleic*</u> <u>*Acid*</u>) occupying a fixed position on a chromosome. A linear sequence of nucleotides (chemical molecules) are strung across the DNA *helix* (twisted ladder). This provides the coded instructions for synthesis of RNA (*ribonucleic acid*). RNA translates into proteins which advance the expression of hereditary characteristics. This all occurs in the genes. The human body holds 25,000 genes. It only takes 5% of them to clone a human being.

GENEALOGY – (jen-nee-*OL*-lo-jee) A record or account of the ancestry and descent of a person, family, or group. Genealogical research is the investigation of one's family tree. Genealogical research is a religious requirement of Mormons. In the Bible, *1 Corinthians 15* speaks of baptizing the dead. That's why the Mormons are obsessed with genealogy. They must find their ancestor's names in order to baptize them, in abstentia. Only then will they enter heaven. As a result, Salt Lake City, Utah, the Mormon capital, is also the genealogical capital of the world.

GENERAL – (*JEN*-ner-al) Highest rank in the U.S. army. A full general wears 4 silver stars, and is above a Lieutenant General. Rarely, a Full General may be given the honorary title of *"General of the Army,"* and awarded a 5th star. (After World War One, John J. Pershing (1860 – 1948) was awarded a 6th star, the only general in U.S. History to wear a half dozen.) One of America's most powerful generals was Douglas MacArthur (1880 – 1964). Nevertheless, he was relieved of duty in 1951 by the Commander-in Chief, President Harry Truman (1884 – 1972). As Truman had explained: *"I fired MacArthur because he disobeyed orders, he broke the law. I didn't fire him because he's a stupid son-of-a-bitch, though he is. That's not against the law. If it was, half, no three-quarters of the generals would be in jail. They are all stupid sons-of-bitches."*

GENERAL AMERICAN – (*JEN*-ner-al am-*MER*-ri-can) The flat-vowelled speech of the Midwestern U.S.A. most generally associated with Standard American speech. General American has a nasal quality and drawl in the voice. Americans tend to dwell on their words. Though considered boring, the Midwestern American dialect is the clearest variety of English spoken anywhere in the world. The University of Wisconsin at Madison is the mecca for language studies in the U.S.A.

GENERALIST – (*JEN*-ner-ral-ist) One knowledgeable of many things in many fields, though not an expert. A generalist knows something about everything, jack of all trades. However, she may not know everything about something – which is a specialist.

GENERAL STRIKE – (*JEN*-er-al *STRYK*) A nationwide shutdown of the economy. A general strike is a nuclear strike at the nation's political, economic leadership. A general strike is raw people power. All shops, industries, trades, corporations, schools, universities, banks close. Commerce ceases. Transportation halts. The country is paralyzed. Workers and students take to the streets. Wall Street hits the wall. Stocks stall. Profits dwindle. There is no better way to combat fascist capitalism than the general strike. The best way to hurt a corporate capitalist is to kick him in his moneybag. A general strike reveals the impotency of a dictatorial government. Security forces can sometimes clear the streets, but they cannot force people to go to work. In panic, the corporate capitalists and tyrannical government turn on each other. A general strike is a prelude to revolution. When the government's security forces (police, soldiers, spies) begin the join their families and neighbors in the street, the revolution has commenced. The oppressive government flees to some other fascist nation. The other exploiters, the capitalist oligarchs also try to escape with embezzled corporate wealth. The Socialist leaders of the general strike are ushered into power. The nation is blessed with distributive justice.

GENERATIONAL CURSE – (jen-ner-*RAY*-shun-al *KERS*) A malady passed down the family line for numerous generations. A generational curse is a heritable disorder, disability, or affliction. The curse may be a physical handicap or mental illness. Psychologically, emotionally, anger issues, depression, poverty, suicide, drug and alcohol addiction are typical generational curses. For example, if your dad was an alcoholic, you have a 10 times greater chance of befalling to alcoholism yourself. It runs in the family. But as Pastor Joel Osteen (b. 1963) reminds us, you can be the first in your family to break the generational curse. Even genetically inherited impairments can be overcome by environmental forces (prayer, willpower, therapy) as the study of epigenetics demonstrates.

GENERATION ALPHA – (jen-er-*RAY*-shun *AL*-fa) (also Gen Alpha) The demographic cohort born during the early 2010s to the mid-2020s. These are the contemporary children and pre-teens at the time of this writing (June, 2022). Alpha is the first generation born entirely within the 21st century. Gen Alpha succeeded Generation Z (1997 – 2012). That accounts for its name. There is no letter after Z, so one must revert back to A. The letter A in Greek is <u>A</u>lpha. This was the reasoning of Mark McCrindle who coined the name in his book, <u>*The ABC of XYZ*</u> (2009). To the Alphas, the smartphone is as common and familiar as the television was to the Baby boomers (1946 – 1964). In fact, the Alphas are forsaking the mighty TV for social networks, streaming services, portable smart technology. Generation Alpha faces an ominous future. They will have to combat pernicious, perilous fascism, racism, and capitalism. Democracy is bleeding the world over. Capitalism is hoarding more and more wealth in the hands of oligarchs. Bigotry, racism, hatred of diversity is becoming the new normal. Global warming is creating climatic chaos. The *"Damocles Sword"* of nuclear annihilation hangs over the Alpha's heads. This is the legacy bequeathed to Generation Alpha by all preceding Generations.

GENERATIONAL SPLIT – (jen-ner-*RAY*-shun-uhl *SPLIT*) A subliminal defense mechanism rooted in guilt. In generational split, the grandparents subconsciously try to atone for neglecting their children, by over-indulging their grandchildren. Now that the grandparents are retired, they can afford to devote the time. The grandkids get everything that the kids were disallowed. In generational split, the grandparents plaster the walls and refrigerator with pictures of the grandchildren. The grandchildren are pampered, indulged, spoiled like the children could not have been.

GENERATIONAL WEALTH – (jen-er *RAY*-shun-uhl *WELTH*) The gradual increase of wealth in a family, from parents to children to grandchildren to great- grandchildren down the generations. Generational wealth is the idealized expectation of progress. For example: an immigrant comes to America as a peddler. With dad's savings, the son opens a small market. His son graduates from Business College, and opens a supermarket, that grows into a chain of supermarkets. In America, the accumulation of generational wealth was part of the *"American Dream."* However, prosperity has proven to be only a dream. Covetous capitalism has hoarded the wealth at the very top. Good-paying manufacturing jobs have been outsourced abroad with the death of unions. Student loan debt has turned a college degree into a liability, an impediment. Opportunities have evaporated blocking social mobility. Generational wealth transfer has lessened for most American, except the obscenely wealthy. In many cases, generational wealth has metastasized into generation debt and poverty. Children today are worse-off than their parents, who, in turn, were not as prosperous as their parents. Capitalism is the problem. Socialism is the solution. Incidentally: In capitalist America, the American Dream has been reduced to winning the lottery.

GENERATION C – (jen-ner-*RAY*-shun *SEE*) The *"Content" Generation.* A designation for people who create and publish material (content) such as blogs, podcasts, videos, songs, documentaries on the internet. Incidentally: The C stands for Content.

GENERATION GAP – (jen-ner-*RAY*-shun *GAP*) A natural lack of understanding and communication between one generation and another, especially between young people and their parents. The gap is brought about by differences in values, outlook, attitude, tastes, and styles. The young are expected to be rebellious. It is a reasonable, essential *"changing of the guard."* About 6,000 years ago (c. 4,000 BCE) the Egyptian Vizier Ptahhotep (late 25th to early 24th century BCE) lamented: *"Our earth is degenerate these days. Children no longer obey their parents, nor their elders. Neither do they abide by the law, nor honor the gods. I fear that civilization will soon be extinguished."* More recently but long ago, the perspicacious English Philosopher John Locke (1632 – 1704) wrote: *"The ruling generation of every age believe that the youth were dragging civilization down to hell."* The generation gap is in fact a re-generation of civilization. I suspect that we shall survive.

GENERATION X – (jen-ner-*RAY*-shun *EKS*) Children of the Baby Boomers. Generation X members were born during the late 1960's to the early 1980's. Generally speaking, generation X is the post-Vietnam generation.

GENERATIONAL DESIGNATIONS – (jen-er-*RAY*-shun-al des-zig-*NAY*-shuns) The division of the population into 8 cohorts by sociological demographers over the past 130 years. These designations apply to people of Western culture, particularly Americans. The study begins with those born in 1883 and continues into the 2020s. The division are listed as: *Lost Generation* (1883 – 1900); *Greatest Generation* (1901 – 1927); *Silent Generation* (1928 – 1945); *Baby Boomers* (1946 – 1964); *Generation X* (1965 – 1980); *Millennials* (1981 – 1996); *Generation Z* (1997 – 2012); *Generation Alpha* (early 2010s to mid-2020s).

GENESIOLOGY – (jen-nes-see-*OL*-lo-jee) (Genesiologist) The scientific study of sexual reproduction. Genesiologists are medical personnel, rather than psychologists, as are sexologists.

GENII – (*JEE*-nee-eye) (also Geniuses) The actual plural of the word genius.

GENITAL CHASTISEMENT – (*JEN*-ni-tal chas-*TYZ*-ment) Corporal Punishment of the sex organs. In the BDSM (Bondage, Dominance, SadoMasochism) subculture of exotic erotica, genital chastisement is a popular performance of SadoMasochism. In legal, non-criminal genital chastisement, the participants are consenting adults, out for kinky fun. They are play-acting. The principal characters are the *"dom"* (dominator) and the *"sub"* (submissive). The dom plays the disciplinarian, while the sub plays the victim. If the victim is a female, the procedure is called *"pussy torture."* If the victim is a male, the punishment is called *CBT* (Cock and BALLS Torture). Although this is play acting, real pain is applied. (Consider boxing, also a game that depends on pain.) The sub is frogtied, with legs spread apart. He or she is rendered helpless, and may be suspended with ropes. Usually, the genitals are lashed with a small, thin-strand whip that will sting like a bee but cause no injury. It is popular to pinch this sensitive region with clamps or clips like clothespins. They are fastened to the labia and clitoris, the penis and scrotum. Small weights can be hung from these clips, enhancing the torment. Indeed the victims screams in pain, and beg for cessation of the torture. But this was anticipated. It was agreed that such pleas would be ignored. The show must go on! The script may call for the application of a burning cream made with capsaicin (hot red pepper) or a muscle rub like Deep Heat. The anguish is breath-taking, convulsive, but not damaging. It will wear-off in its own time. Plugs of freshly peeled ginger may be inserted into the vagina, and ginger slivers into the penis. Another plug may be jammed up the ass for good measure. This will burn like hell! In fact, the Romans (connoisseurs of torture) used ginger to spice up their punishment regimen in prisons, especially with women. Throughout this ordeal, the brain is sending pain-killing end<u>orphin</u>s (natural m<u>orphine</u>) to the genitals, encouraging the victim to cope. Screams of pain morph into moans of pleasure, as the agony becomes ecstasy. The sexual gratification of the exhausted victim begins to compensate for the discomfort. The genital chastisement may be performed before a live audience (a sex show), or a private production. Too, the ordeal may be videotaped. Genital chastisement is a popular porn subject. A Caveat: Genital chastisement should not be attempted by unexperienced novices. Serious injury can occur. The male genitalia is most vulnerable, being the most substantial and pronounced. The female genitalia is much tougher, and can sustain more stress. After all, look at the pounding it endures in intercourse, and the contortions is manages in child birth. *"The heart is capable of sacrifice. So is the vagina."* – Eve Ensler (b. 1953), <u>The Vagina Monologues</u> (1996). *"The only unnatural sex act is that which you cannot perform."* – *Sexologist Alfred Kinsey (1894 – 1956).* *"Judge not, that you may not be judged."* – Jesus, in Matthew 7:1-2. Incidentally: The author is a researcher, serving as a reporter, rather than supporter.

GENITALS – (*JEN*-ni-tals) External sex organs: the male penis and female vulva (inaccurately called vagina).

GENITAL STAGE – (*JEN*-ni-tal *STAYJ*) According the Freudian Psychoanalysis, the 3rd, mature stage of psychosexual evolution after the oral and anal stages. In the genital stage, interest shifts to one's own sex organs and to other's. Libidinal focus is no longer on the mouth or anus. Satisfaction from eating and bowel control is overtaken by sexual gratification. Masturbation is an early discovery of the genital stage. A mature "normal" *genital personality* is developed.

GENIUS – (*JEEN*-yus) A person of extraordinary intelligence, ingenuity, and capability in the arts, sciences, or technologies. The philosopher Arthur Schopenhauer (1788 – 1860) captured the essence of genius when he wrote: *"Talent hits a target that no one else can, while genius hits a target that no one else sees."* Genius comes in many forms. That's because: *"Genius is another word for magic, and the whole point of magic is that it is inexplicable."* – Ballerina Margot Fonteyn (1919 – 1991). *"Genius sees the answer before the question."* – Physicist J. Robert Oppenheimer (1904 – 1967). *"Genius gives birth, talent delivers."* – Jack Kerouac (1922 – 1969). All geniuses need not be intelligent. Some may be extraordinarily creative. *"Andy Warhol (1928 – 1987) is the only genius I've ever known with an I.Q. of 60."* – Gore Vidal (1925 – 2012), novelist, screenwriter.

GENOCIDE – (*JEN*-o-side) Extermination of an entire population of people. Genocide is employed as ethnic cleansing. History is littered with the bodies of genocidal victims. Native people had been exterminated on all continents. The Armenian genocide (1.5 million killed) at the hands of the Turks occurred during World War One (1915). Japan conducted a disorganized genocide in China (1937 – 1945) before and during World War Two. Germany conducted an organized genocide (Holocaust) during World War Two (1939 – 1945). In both cases, about 6 million people perished.

GENONTOPHILIA – (jen-on-toh-*FEEL*-lee-a) (Genontophiliac) Having a neurotic sexual attraction for the elderly.

GENOPHOBIA – (jen-o-*FO*-bee-a) (Genophobiac) Phobic fear of sexual intercourse. Genophobia is a specific aspect of the more generalized *"erotophobia,"* a neurotic fear of sex. Genophobia goes beyond asexuality, which is not having an interest or need for sex. Genophobia is a fear, like a phobic fear of fire, heights, or being on the water. Religious fanatics who were conditioned [read: *brainwashed*] to believe that sex is an evil sin, of the devil, warranting eternal punishment in hell, are genophobia candidates. Such people in the Middle Ages, especially crazed monks, castrated themselves. Genophobia is closely associated with another phobia, gymnophobia – a fear of nudity. All of these neurotic conditions require psychiatric intervention.

GENRE – (*ZHON*-rah) A category, class, style, especially in art or literature, sharing a common subject, content, form, or technique.

GENTILE – (*JEN*-tile) Anyone not an ethnic Jew, and professor of Judaism.

GENTLEMAN – (*JEN*-tul-man) A mature male, not necessarily educated but indeed wise, who puts other's needs before his own. A gentleman is kind, compassionate, generous, but strong. He is always a champion of the weak. A gentleman would never be a passive witness to another's pain. Most true male Socialists are gentlemen.

GENTLEMAN'S CLUB – (*JEN*-tul-man's *CLUB*) In class-crazed Britain, a private social club for upper-crust men in the 18th century. With industrialization, clever mechanics became rich, though without a family pedigree. Because of their wealth, the aristocratic landed gentry were force to accept them as peers. So gentlemen's clubs admitted upper-middle class men in the late 19th and early 20th centuries. The institution spread among the administrative class throughout the British Empire. The clubs were originally exclusively male. Ladies [read: *wives, mothers, sisters, daughters*] were not admitted. The females who were allowed into the clubs were far from *"Ladies."* The traditional British gentleman's club had dinning, bar, library, billiards, and smoking rooms. It was a place for moneyed-men to make deals. Few such private establishments remain today. Present day gentlemen's clubs are public establishments, drinking lounges. What constitutes them as clubs for gentlemen, are the ladies who bare it all on stage.

GENTLEMAN'S GENTLEMAN – (*JEN*-tul-man's *JEN*-tul-man) A somewhat silly English appellation for a valet, butler, or man-servant. The English more than most other people have been obsessed with rank, title, hierarchy, and class distinctions. It's apparent in their speech patterns and class accents. England had a Civil War (1642 – 1651) which merely substituted one upper class for the other. Too, England had a bloodless "Glorious Revolution" (1688) that merely switched kings. But unlike other European countries, England never had a bloody, leveling, social revolution. From the time of the Conquest (1066) by William of Normandy (1028 – 1087), the English aristocracy had remained intact. This accounts for their insufferable snobbish class consciousness. Well then, if an English valet rose to a social position of such prominence, that he too could have a valet, his servant might be designated a *"Gentleman's, Gentleman's, Gentleman"* (or perhaps *Gentleman cubed*, G3).

GENTRIFICATION – (jen-tri-fi-*KAY*-shun) (Gentrify) Eviction of the poor residents by the rich, from a neighborhood that has become chic and fashionable. To gentrify means to make appealing to affluent tastes. Old, inner-city areas are neglected for decades, allowing them to become derelict slums. Nevertheless, the neighborhoods are home for the poor, usually minorities. Inevitably, realestate capitalists will invest their capital, renovating the region, advertising it as the trendy, swank, stylish place to live for wealthy gentry. With gentrification, the poor residents are forced out of their homes which are demolished. Upscale apartments take their place. Gentrification often hides behind the euphemism of *"urban renewal."* It must be legislatively mandatory that the poor, indigenous residence of the gentrified neighborhood are resettled and compensated, when evicted. The cost must fall on the real estate developers, construction companies, prospective prorietors and the government. This compensation must be paid by those taking the property, and provided to the homeless. Only then should the neighborhood be turned over to the rich and famous.

GENTRY – (*JEN*-tree) The patricians. The well-born, well-bred, well-fed, well- wed, and well-read. The gentry are the landed aristocracy, just below the nobility. *"Because you are a great aristocrat [gentry], you think you are a great genius. You have taken effort to do nothing, but to be born!"* – Pierre-Augustin de Beaumarchais (1732 – 1799) in *The Marriage of Figaro* (1778).

GEOCHRONOLOGY – (jee-o-kron-*OL*-lo-jee) (Literally *"Earth Time."*) Geochronology is the scale of divisions of Earth's evolution. It is recorded as follows: *Eon* = 4 total, half a billion years or more; *Era* = 10 defined, several hundred million years; *Period* = 22 defined, tens to one hundred million years; *Epoch* = 34 defined, tens of millions of years; *Age* = 99 defined, millions of years; *Chronozone* = Subdivision of an Age, time between one event and another.

GEOFACT – (*JEE*-oh-fact) A nature-made object as distinguished from a man- made artifact. Often, a naturally fractured rock may closely resemble a man- made tool. This is a geofact.

GEOFICIAL – (jee-o-*FISH*-al) Made by nature, the opposite of *"artificial,"* which is made by man. Geoficial specimens are *"geofacts,"* as opposed to artificial specimens which are *"artifacts."*

GEOGLYPH – (*JEE*-o-gliff) An Earth drawing. A large design or motif, several feet or yards (perhaps hundreds) in length produced on the ground. The design is generally formed by clastic rock fragments or similar landscape durables like stones, gravel, or soil. A *positive geoglyph* is formed by arranging and aligning natural materials on the ground surface, in the manner of a *petroform*. A *negative geoglyph* is formed by removing surface material, scratching into the ground, exposing the unpatinated subsurface, in the manner of a *petroglyph*. Geoglyphs are found worldwide, though Nazca, Peru's spectacular petroglyphs are incomparable. Many geoglyphs are carved into the English chalk, including the enormous white horse near Birling Gap, East Sussex. Geoglyphs had gone unnoticed for millennia, until the age of flight. That's because they are only discernable at a height, from the air. The obvious question is who were the ancient engineers trying to impress, contact with these massive drawings? Ancient astronaut theorists insist it was extraterrestrials, teachers or forbearers.

GEOGRAPHY – (jee-*OG*-gra-fee) Literally means *"Earth drawing, recording or mapping."* There are two disciplines of geography, *physical* and *cultural.* Physical geography studies land formations, oceans, waterways, and climates, the environment. Cultural geography studies human distribution and how the environment effects their lives.

GEOLOGIAN – (jee-o-*LOH*-jee-an) A metaphysical Earth scholar, eco-spiritualist who subscribes to the *"Gaia Hypothesis."* Geologians are mystics in tune with the soul of the planet. Native people tend to have a geologian sense of their place in the scheme of life.

GEOLOGIC COLUMN – (jee-o-*LOJ*-jic *COL*-lum) An arrangement of rock layers based on the ages of the rocks. Geologists and paleontologists can read a geologic column like the pages of a book. A geologic column is an encyclopedia of the Earth's history and a catalogue of fossilized specimens.

GEOLOGIST'S CREDO – (jee-*OL*-luh-jists *KRAY*-doh) *"If it happened before, it will happen again."* This is concerning geological phenomena.

GEOLOGY – (jee-*OL*-luh-jee) (Geologist, Geological) Literally means "Earth study," or "Study of the Earth." Geology is the science that deals with the dynamics and physical history of the Earth. Geology is concerned with the rocks of which Earth is composed, and the physical and chemical changes that Earth has undergone and is undergoing.

GEOMETRICALLY – (jee-oh-*MET*-trik-lee) An increase in an exponential, geometrical fashion, vis. (2, 4, 8, 16, 32, 64, 128…), as opposed to a linear, arithmetical increase, vis. (1, 2, 3, 4, 5, 6…).

GEOMETRY – (jee-*OM*-met-tree) (Geometrical) Literally means *"Earth measuring."* Geometry is the mathematics of space and shapes. It is concerned with the position of points, lines, angles, shapes, and figures in space. Simply put, geometry is the mathematical study of space and shapes, in the same way as calculus is the study of change, and algebra is the study of operations and their application to solving problems. It was the great Greek mathematician and mystic, Pythagoras (c. 570 – c. 495 BCE) who linked geometry with numbers. Later, the Greek mathematician Euclid (Mid-4th century to mid-3rd century BCE) came to be considered the *"Father of Geometry."* Euclid's book, <u>*Elements of Geometry*</u> (c. 300 BCE) was translated and copied more than any other book except the Bible, right up to modern times. Incidentally: Geometry is vital to the practice of Freemasonry. Masonically speaking, Geometry comprehends all science, art, and philosophy, all skill and learning. All knowledge, can be defined as an understanding of the world, its laws and forces, and of the living beings which inhabit it. The great French scientist, Jean-Henri Fabre (1823 – 1915) maintained that: *"Geometry, that is to say, the science of harmony in space, presides over everything."* Geometry is particularly essential to Masons because a study of it leads to the conviction that behind universe there must be a Supreme Intelligence, an Architect who has planned and designed it, for under whom we work, and from whom we receive our wages. Post Script: The letter *"G"* in the Masonic symbol stands for *"God"* and *"Geometry."* *"Mighty is geometry; joined with art, resistless."* – Euripides (c. 480 – c. 406 BCE). *"Sire, there is no royal road to geometry."* – Euclid (435 – 365 BCE) to the king who wanted instant understanding of geometry. *"Geometry enlightens the intellect and sets one's mind right. All of its proofs are very clear and orderly. It is hardly possible for errors to enter into geometrical reasoning, because it is well arranged and orderly. Thus, the mind that constantly applies itself to geometry is not likely to fall into error. In this convenient way, the person who knows geometry acquires intelligence."* – Ibn Khaldun (1332 – 1406).

GEOPOLITICS – (jee-oh-*POL*-li-tics) The influence of geography on national power, foreign policy, politico-economic history. For example, the misfortune of Poland to be geopolitically nestled between Germany and Russia.

GEORGIA PEACH – (*JOR*-ja *PEECH*) Not the sweet Southern fruit in this case, but the sweetest baseball player of all time. *"The Georgia Peach"* was the nickname of Tyrus Raymond "Ty" Cobb (1886 – 1961), the greatest to play the game. Cobb was a center fielder for the Detroit Tigers from 1905 to 1926 (the last 6 years as player-manager). Cobb concluded his remarkable 23-year career with the Philadelphia Athletics (1927 – 1928). Ty Cobb was born in rural Narrows, but grew up in Royston, Georgia. In a field, Ty hung a tire from a tree and practiced throwing the ball through the tire from deep in center field. Being a Southern boy, Cobb met with prejudice from his bigoted teammates in Detroit. This made Ty very aggressive, gaining the reputation as a battler. Cobb disclosed that: *"I had to fight all my life to survive. They were all against me, but I beat the bastards and left them in the ditch."* His extraordinary talent and compulsive work ethic gained the admiration of his teammates and fans. Ty Cobb would do whatever it took to gain an edge. He always kicked the basebag forward, to gain a 2-inch advantage. In Detroit, Cobb ordered the grounds crew to flood the batter's box, making it muddy and slippery. This would slow the catcher in retrieving Cobb's bunts. *"When I played ball, I didn't play for fun,"* Ty admitted. *"I had to be first, all the time." "I may have been fierce, but never low or underhanded,"* Cobb declared. Opposing players might have taken issue with that statement. Many perceived Ty as a dirty player. *"When I played baseball it was a struggle for supremacy, survival of the fittest,"* he disclosed. *"Baseball was about as gentlemanly as a kick in the crotch."* Cobb felt that his vicious reputation gave him a psychological edge over other players. He was one of the fastest, quickest, smartest runners ever to round the diamond. Cobb stole 892 bases. It was said that watching Cobb get a walk, was more exciting than watching Babe Ruth (1895 – 1948) hit a home run. Cobb still holds the record for stealing home plate 54 times. Four times did he steal second base, third base, and home plate in succession, also a record. Ty insisted that: *"The base paths belonged to me, the runner. The rules gave me the right. I always went into the bag full speed, feet first. I had sharp spikes on my shoes. If the baseman stood where he had no business to be and got hurt, that was his fault."* Love him or hate him you had to respect him. Though a fighter with a short temper, Cobb was the first sports celebrity. He became the first baseball millionaire. Ty was exceedingly generous, a philanthropist. He was a non- drinker and an avid book reader. Through his career, Cobb had set 90 Major League baseball records, many of which still stand. He still holds the highest lifetime batting average, 366, over his 23-year career. At 34, he was the youngest player to reach 3,000 hits. Ty's 12 batting titles is the most ever. So is his 4,065 runs scored. Cobb hit 117 home runs and had 1,938 runs batted in. Ty Cobb was the most exciting player of all time. He was the first player to be inducted into the Baseball Hall of Fame (222 of 226 votes). On a personal note, a yellow journalistic rumor emerged that Ty was a racist. This is a dastardly lie. Cobb insisted that: *"The Negro should be accepted, and not grudgingly but wholeheartedly. They have the right to compete in sports, and who's to say that they do not?"* New York Yankee manager Casey Stengel (1890 – 1975) said that: *"I never saw anyone like Ty Cobb. No one ever. He was the greatest all-time ballplayer. That guy was superhuman. Amazing!"* Baseball Hall of

Famer George Sisler (1893 – 1973) said: *"The greatness of Ty Cobb was something that had to be seen. And to see him was to remember him forever."* Incidentally: Even the phenomenal Ty Cobb was human. Another record he holds is most errors (271) for an American League outfielder in a career.

GEOTHERMAL ENERGY – (jee-oh-*THER*-mal *EN*-ne-jee) Energy contained in and available from water heated by magma or gasses deep within the Earth. Super- hot steam turns turbines that generate electricity. Geothermal energy is natural, perpetual, clean, and free. Lucky are the nations blessed with this source of power: Iceland, New Zealand, Japan, and elsewhere. Of course, geothermal energy is associated with seismic activity and volcanism. Therefore, regions blessed with geothermal activity are also cursed with earthquakes and volcanic eruptions.

GEOTROPISM – (jee-o-*TROP*-is-um) (Geotaxis) The compulsion of some plants to turn toward the ground, the Earth.

GEPHYROPHOBIA – (jeh-fy-ro-*FO*-bee-a) (Gephyrophobiac) Phobic fear of bridges.

GER – (Also Gar) An Old Germanic term for spear. The ancient *GERmans* were spear-wielding warriors. Julius Caesar (100 – 44 BCE) referred to these forest folk as *"GERmani."* The Germans made very effective wooden weapons. In the woods, they did not shine in the moonlight, as did the Roman's metal weapons. The names Garret or Gary derive from the Germanic Ger or Gar, meaning *"spear bearer."*

GERIATRIC – (jer-ree-*AT*-rick) (Geriatrics) Pertaining or related to old age. A geriatric is an elderly person. Geriatrics is a branch of medicine dealing with the diseases, debilities, and care of aged persons. *"Watch the Republican Senators do the 'Geriatric Scuffle,' as they slither to lunch through the Hall of Shame."*

GERMAN DEFEAT – (*JER*-man dee-*FEET*) Reason behind the reasons why Germany lost the Second World War (1933 – 1945). At the outbreak of World War Two, Germany was the aggressor with all the momentum. The anti- German forces, east and west, were defensive, dispirited, even defeatist. Nevertheless, Germany lost the war. Tactics, strategies, statistics aside, Germany lost World War Two because of Adolf Hitler's (1889 – 1945) personal obsession. Hitler always put the needs of the Nazi Party above the German Army. Nazi ideology had priority over military possibility. Hitler hired and fired generals on their political loyalty – how Nazi they were – rather than their military skill. Therefore, Nazism, the cause of the war, was responsible for the loss of the war.

GERMANIUM – (ger-*MAN*-nee-a) (Ge) The name derives from *Germania,* Latin for "Germany." The 32 protons in its nucleus give Germanium its atomic number. Germanium is a rare crystalline gray element that is a semiconducting metalloid (having metallic and nonmetallic properties). Germanium occurs principally in zinc ores. Germanium is used to strengthen and harden alloys, as a catalyst, and in transistors.

GERMAN WAR AIMS – (*JER*-man *WAR AYMS*) Why the Germans started World War Two in Europe (1939 – 1945). In a sense, the Second World War was a continuation of the First World War (1914 – 1918). The German army had lost World War One, but Germany was not a defeated nation. The Peace Treaty of Versailles humiliated Germans who wanted revenge. The great inflation, followed by the great depression produced revolutionary misery. The emergence of the messianic Adolph Hitler (1889 – 1945) bolstered

German pride. Hitler (a la Trump), promised to make Germany *"Great Again."* As dictator, Hitler's war aims became Germany's war aims. Hitler flattered the Germans as a master race. Hitler exonerated the Germans by blaming all problems on the Jews, who he swore to exterminate. The Nazi fascists (extreme capitalists) hated Socialists, Unionists, Communists, and Progressives. They were *"concentrationalized"* in Dachau, the first prison camp. Hating, fearing Slavs, Socialists, and Communists, Hitler invaded Poland and Russia. His goals were *"ethnic cleansing"* and *"lebensraum"* (living room) for the new Germany. Unlike the First War, the German people thoroughly tasted their defeat in Second War, primarily at the hands of the Socialist, Slavonic Russians.

GERMOPHOBIA – (jur-moh-*FOH*-bee-ah) (Germophobe) (also Mysophobia, Verminophobia, Bacillophobia, Bacteriophobia) An irrational or disproportional fear of microbes and contamination. Germophobia is a pathological dread and horror of the unseen. It is a paranoia, a mental obsessive-compulsive disorder. A germophobe lives a miserable life. They are forever sanitizing, sterilizing, disinfecting, fighting a battle with an invisible enemy that is everywhere. There is never an indication of victory. Germophobe's lives are dominated by this ghostly enemy. Living in a pandemic, where there is a real threat from germs can drive these people, and their loved-ones mad.

GERM THEORY – (*JERM THEE*-ree) The monumental revelation that infectious diseases are caused by microorganisms (germs). The germ theory was the greatest discovery in the history of medicine. It was formulated not by a physician but by a chemist, the Frenchman Louis Pasteur (1822 – 1895). In 1856, Pasteur was commissioned to investigate why the wine was going sour? Using a microscope, Pasteur made a breath-taking observation: *"The wine is a sea of organisms. By some it lives, by some it decays."* From that day on, the quality of human life was immensely enhanced.

GERONTOPHILIA – (jer-ron-toh-*Fee*-lee-ah) (Gerontophobiac) A neurotic paraphilial disorder in which one is sexually attracted to old people. In the culture of exotic erotica, a *"GILF"* is an acronym or initialism for *"Grandma/Grandpa I'd Like to Fuck." "Some women wear a miniskirt to reveal their thighs; some wear one to conceal their age."* – Mokokoma Mokhonoana (b. 1985). It's common for a gold-digging bimbo to marry a rich old fart, as her sugar daddy. This is not gerontophilia. It is mutual exploitation. She finds him repulsive in fact. The blowjobs are her job. A gerontophiliac is turned on by the senior citizens. *"There she stood, half shadow half light. A sight to make an old man young."* – Alfred Lord Tennyson (1809 – 1892). A Caveat: As a researcher, the author must go where the investigation takes him. He is a reporter, not a supporter.

GERONTOPHOBIA – (jer-on-tow-*FO*-bee-a) (Gerontophobiac) Phobic fear of aging, growing old, or of old people.

GERRYMANDATE – (*JER*-ree-man dayt) (Gerrymandated) Combining the words gerrymander and mandate. This term expresses the fact that in Republican gerrymandered Congressional districts, the Congressman does not lead the people, the people lead the Congressman. Republican Congressmen are obliged, mandated to support, and pretend to believe whatever their ridiculous constituents demand, no matter how nonsensical or dangerous. They must lie to the camera to protect their voter's lies. Indeed, gerrymandering has backfired on the Republicans. Unethical Republicans created homogeneous congressional districts, devoid of diversity, populated by MAGAmaniacs that must be placated. All the level-headed citizens in their districts have been gerrymandered out. Only the crazies remain. Now Republican Congressmen have to act and vote just as crazily to keep their allegiance. Otherwise, the politician will be primaried by a crazier candidate. Incestuous relationships, even in politics, can produce freaks and monsters. Gerrymandering, which produced the gerrymandate, has robbed the Republicans in the House of Representatives of their authority, freedom, and dignity. So be careful what you wish and cheat for. Why aren't the Republican Senators gerrymandated? Because entire states cannot be gerrymandered. If they could, Republican Senators too would be slavishly full-MAGA lunatics.

GERRYMANDER – (*JER*-ree-man-der) (Gerrymandered, Gerrymandering) An example of apartheid, or minority rule. The unethical though legal political ploy of re-drawing congressional districts to the benefit of the party in power. In a gerrymandered political district, the voices of the minority or opposition is ignored. Gerrymandering apportions enough favorable votes in each district to assure electoral victory. In order to do this, the districts must be convoluted, contorted, deformed into ridiculous shapes, in order to include the desired voting population within. With gerrymandering, the politicians choose their voters, rather than the voters choosing their politicians. The result – you don't need a majority to win. Incidentally: The term Gerrymandering derives from the name, Elbridge Gerry (1744 – 1814) from Massachusetts. Gerry was a member of the revolutionary Committee of Correspondence, the Second Continental Congress, and a signer of the Declaration of Independence. Gerry was a patriot who became a dirty politician. In 1812, as governor of Massachusetts, Gerry redrew the Congressional District of Essex County grotesquely. Artist Gilbert Stuart (1755 – 1828) painted a dragon's head, wings, and claws on the district map. It was published. One politician said: *"That will do for a salamander."* Another quipped: *"No, a Gerrymander!"* The term was born. Today, the Republicans are the notorious gerrymanderers. That is why, though they are always in a minority, they still manage to control state legislatures and the U.S. House of Representatives. Ironically, Elbridge Gerry was a Democratic Republican, forerunners of the Democrats. Their opponents the Federalists, were the forerunners of the Republicans. Incidentally: A simple computer program can impartially, unbiasedly redraw the Congressional districts of every state. This is a *"Random Geometric Simplicity"* program. Every district would be shaped as closely as possible to box, squares or rectangles, some large, some small, but each including the same number of people. Let the votes fall where they may. This is blind justice, and open-eyed democracy. *"I think that the voters should choose the elected officials, not the elected officials choose the voters."* – Democratic Congressman Alan Grayson (b. 1958).

GESELLSCHAFT – (*GES*-cell-shaft) A German sociological term for a cold, suspicious, class-divided community. Capitalism produces a competitive, dog- eat-dog, gesellschaft society. It is characterized by the haves and have-nots, the servants and the served. Conflict between the rich and poor is just below the surface in a gesellschaft environment. The polar opposite is a *"gemeinschaft"* community which is warm, friendly, egalitarian, and Socialist.

GESHE – (*GESH*-shee) A Buddhist Doctor of Divinity. An exceptionally knowledgeable Tibetan guru.

GESTALT – (gesh-*TALT*) Holistic, synergistic, the big picture. Gestalt is a perceptual pattern or structure possessing qualities as a whole that cannot be described merely as a sum of its parts. Gestalt is a psychological tendency to make meaningful interpretations of physical patterns. In philosophy, gestalt means shape, form, the whole considered as more than the sum of its parts.

GESTAPO – (ges-*TOP*-poe) An abbreviation for the *Geheime Staatspolizei* (Nazi Secret State Police). The notorious Gestapo conducted a reign of terror in Germany and then in the conquered territories throughout Adolf Hitler's tenure, from 1933 to 1945. Every citizen of the Reich feared the chilling *"mid-night knock on the door."* Administered by the savage SS, the Gestapo claimed 32,000 members in 1944. They are remembered for their sadistic interrogation methods that included unimaginable tortures. Thousands were butchered or sent to their deaths in concentration camps by the bloody Gestapo.

GESTAPO COPS – (ges-*TOP*-poe *COPS*) Rogue police officers, lawless law- enforcement personnel. Gestapo cops, like those in Nazi Germany, perform as vile vigilantes. They believe that they are above the law, and their victims are below it. Gestapo cops feel entitled to take the law into their own hands. On the street they act like samurai – judge, jury, and executioner. Gestapo cops are bad cops, and bad people, angry men. They are sadistic, anarchistic, and ferociously cruel. They are bullies with badges. Most joined the police force in order to force their will on the weak. They sought a license to harass, oppress, molest, punish, beat, and even kill. Gestapo cops are racists who particularly hate minorities – Blacks, Hispanics, all people of color. Gestapo cops are neo- Nazi in character, and exhibit White-Supremacist attitudes. They represent a dangerous, divisive force in society. They must be stripped of all authority, and closely monitored by genuine law-enforcement officers. Incidentally: The Gestapo Cops network is the *Fraternal Order of Police.* This organization of brutality enablers must be broken. Supervisors up and down the chain of command must be held accountable for the actions of their subordinates. Going on duty without the bodycam functioning, should be like going on duty without a gun. The negligent, defiant cop must be immediately fired! Police investigate and collect evidence, even on fellow cops. Police lie, evidence is destroyed. So outside oversight must be present when cops are the criminal suspects. Armed men policing a city or neighborhood in which they do not live amounts to an occupying military force. They have no stake in the community, no regards for the residents. Cops must live in the neighborhoods they serve. Professionalize the police force. Insist on a bachelor's degree in Social- Psychology in order to qualify as a cop. Education is a liberalizing force. *"We must have a liberal mind behind the hand on the policeman's club and trigger."* – Educator, Philosopher John Dewey (1859 – 1852). Police records must be made public. Generous pay professionalizes an occupation. The new cops must be paid well, to attract good people. Federal laws across the states must govern police behavior. Criminally accused cops must be prosecuted by neutral Federal Officials. *"Just a few bad apples? Watch TV news. How man good cops can you count?"*

GESTATION – (jes-*TAY*-shun) The period from conception to birth when a mammal, including man, is developing in the womb. Also, to develop or gestate an idea or plan.

GESUNDHEIT – (gez-*ZOONT*-hite) A German-Yiddishism for good health, often spoken after a sneeze.

GET MEDIEVAL – (get med-*EE*-vuhl) (also Go Medieval) To apply such heinous torture worthy of the hellishly hideous persecution techniques of the Middle Ages or Medieval Period (5th to the late 15th centuries). The sadistic Medieval psychopaths devised pain-producing tools and machines beyond the warped imaginations of Hollywood horror-film producers. The term *"get Medieval"* is a rather recent American expression. It was brought to the public's attention in Quentin Tarantino's (b. 1963) and Roger Avary's (b. 1965) film, *"Pulp Fiction"* (1994). In the movie, the character Marsellus Wallace swears revenge on an attacker: *"I ain't through with you by a damn sight. I'm gonna git Medieval on your ass!"*

GETTYSBURG – (*GET*-tees-berg) Small town in southeastern Pennsylvania, site of the greatest battle in the American Civil War (July1-3, 1863). In fact, Gettysburg was the greatest battle ever fought in the entire Western Hemisphere. It was the only major battle of the Civil War fought in the North (barely North). Gettysburg marked the high-water mark for the South. General Robert E. Lee (1807 – 1870) fired 150 cannons, the greatest artillery barrage ever in the Western Hemisphere. The blasting noise was heard in Philadelphia, 150 miles away. General George A. Custer's (1839 – 1876) 400 Michigan cavalry troops attacked General "Jeb" Stuart's (1833 – 1864) 5,000 Virginia cavalry, with the cry: *"Charge Wolverines!"* Though they had over a 10 to 1 advantage, the Virginians fled. This denied the Confederates a crucial reinforcement. The result was the defeat of Confederate General George Pickett (1825 – 1875), who had broken through the Union lines at Cemetery Ridge. Victory was assured to the Union. The Battle of Gettysburg was the turning point in the war. Over 50 thousand Americans were killed in 3 days of fighting. The more than 25 thousand Confederate casualties could not be replaced. Therefore, Gettysburg marked the beginning of the end for the Confederacy. From that defeat in Pennsylvania, the rest of the war would be a defensive campaign for the Confederates, fought in the South. Incidentally: Almost a fourth of the soldiers in the American Union Army were immigrants, mostly from Ireland and Germany, but also from Poland.

GEYSER – (*GEY*-ser) A geothermal hot spring under pressure, that periodically erupts high into the air. Yellowstone National Park is renowned for its spectacular geysers. In fact, Yellowstone displays 2/3 of the geysers on Earth. This geologic phenomenon is associated with seismic activity and volcanism (earthquakes and volcanoes). Yellowstone is the world's greatest supervolcano, a time bomb getting ready to blow. The geysers are a warning sign.

GGG – (jee-jee-*JEE*) An initialism that stands for Good, Giving, Game. The GGG concept was devised by sexologist Dan Savage (b. 1964). Good, Giving, and Game describes the ideal way to share a sexy relationship. The online sex encyclodictionary *Freakypedia* describes GGG thusly: *"Good stands for essentially good in bed. Of course you have to work to find the partner that fills this quota since everyone has different things that they like. Giving means that each partner gets equal amount of time devoted to pleasure. Game means that you are down for a lot of different things and are open to trying things other people might not be."* GGG is an expectation of sexual compatibility, courtesy, and concern for each other's contentment. Nevertheless, each individual is responsible for their own orgasm. It almost always depends on one's frame of mind.

GHETTO – (*GET*-toh) An inner-city slum, where minority groups are concentrated because of joblessness, poverty, and social racial discrimination. About 53 million Americans are forced to live in ghettoes. These *"slumberhoods"* result from governmental neglect. They are unpleasant places because that is the nature of poverty. Ghettos are dangerous, high-crime areas because desperate people behave in a desperate manner. The illicit underground economy thrives in this environment. Capitalism shows little regard for the ghetto or its inhabitants. Only a Socialist solution can clear the slums through government spending, job creation, free healthcare and education, and distributive justice.

GHETTO TEACHER'S CREDO – (*GET*-toh *TEECH*-ers *KRAY*-doh) *"You haven't taught, until you've taught, those who do not want to be taught."* – Dr. Gary J. Pasieka (b. 1951).

GHOST BIKE – (*GOHST* byk) (also Ghostcycle or WhiteCycle) A roadside memorial of a white bicycle, placed at the site of an accident where a cyclist was killed, likely by a motorist. The white bikes are usually stripped of their rubber tires. The first ghost bike appeared in St. Louis, Missouri in 2003. Ghost bikes have become a new tradition in the U.S., Canada, and Europe (if the community allows).

GHOST CANDIDATE – (*GOHST CAN*-dih-dayt) A person paid to run in an election in order to siphon votes from a serious candidate and cause her defeat. This is a dirty and illegal trick, used primarily by the dirty, and often illegal Republicans. For example, in a congressional election in a Democratic minority district, the Republicans may pay an unknown Hispanic Democrat to run in order to split the Democratic vote. The result may be the defeat of the Black Democratic incumbent. In this example, the Hispanic candidate acted as a *"spoiler."* Is it any wonder that politician is the least respected, and most distrusted of all professions (worst than lawyers)?

GHOST DUST – (*GOHST* dust) (also Phantom Dirt) Invisible, actually non-existent dirt and dust swepted off the clean floor by an obsessive/compulsive *"clean freak,"* (a *katharismamaniac*) Though the dustpan is empty, the neurotic cleaner feels satisfied, fulfilled. Like all neuroses, obsessive/compulsive cleaning is a psychological defense mechanism that relieves the stress caused by some deep subconscious problem.

GHOST FOREST – (*GOHST FOR*-ist) An area of dead trees in formerly healthy woodlands. Ghost forests are typically in coastal regions where rising sea levels has introduced saltwater, poisoning the trees. Seawater flooding is due to global warming and sometimes to tectonic shifts. Earthquakes and tsunamis have also resulted in ghost forests. A ghost forest is an ecological disaster. All the creatures that depend on the forest perish as well, in a chain reaction. The green swaying giants give way to the haunted sight of dead, leafless trunks, anchored in a brown lifeless swamp.

GHOST GUNS – (*GOHST GUNS*) Homemade semi-automatic firearms, purchased online. Ghost guns are assembled from kits, and are therefore untraceable, like ghosts. Ghost guns elude the kind of background check required for traditional gun purchases. The legality of ghost guns is protected by cowardly Republican legislators beholding to the gun lobby, (National Rifle Association) and to gun- crazed constituents.

GHOSTING – (*GOHST*-ting) The sudden ending of all contact with a person, without explanation, especially a romantic relationship. This may apply to a social event or engagement as well. One suddenly leaves with no good reason, no goodbyes. One simply disappears, like a ghost. Ghosting is cruel and immature. Incidentally: Ghosting has been called both French goodbye and Irish goodbye.

GHOSTING – (*GOHST*-ting) (Vietnam Era) The custom of corrupt ARVN (South Vietnamese Army) officers to keep the names of dead soldiers on the roster in order to collect their pay. The Vietnam War (c. 1921 – 1975) was a Civil War. A major reason for the defeat of the South Vietnamese was their incredible corruption. It often happens that the side you support becomes increasingly dependent on you, and increasingly corrupt.

GHOST KITCHEN – (*GOHST KICH*-en) Also called a shadow kitchen, cloud kitchen, dark kitchen, or virtual kitchen. A ghost kitchen prepares food for delivery only. Some ghost kitchens may allow pick-up, and may even have drive-thru facilities. There is no customer seating, which differentiates a ghost kitchen from a restaurant. Furthermore, a ghost kitchen is not part of a commercial restaurant chain. Established restaurants may function as a ghost kitchen when they exclude sit-down customers, as during the Coronavirus pandemic. In this case, the facility is called a *"virtual restaurant."*

GHOST NETS – (*GOHST* nets) Man-made oceanic death traps. Ghost nets are fishing nets lost or left behind by fishermen at sea. Being nylon, ghost nets are not biodegradable, and will linger and kill indefinitely. Ghost nets are practically invisible in dim light. They drift in the open sea, or are washed ashore to be tangled on rocks and reefs. Ghost nets ensnare fish, sharks, dolphins, sea turtles, crocodiles, crabs, seabirds, and occasionally human divers. These nets are designed to entrap, restrict movement, and prevent escape. Captured marine creatures starve, suffocate, or drown in these nets. Those that do manage to escape are often lacerated, infected, and maimed for life. Other animals become ensnared, and must physically drag the burden of the net for the balance of their lives.

GHOST TOWN – (*GOHST TOWN*) A community that once flourished but is today deserted, usually because of the depletion of a nearby resource such as gold or silver. Many mining boomtowns are now ghost towns throughout the American West. Their spooky abandoned buildings bake and rot in the sun.

GHOST WORD – (*GOHST* werd) A legitimized mistake. A ghost word is a term that has come into existence by error rather than by normal linguistic transmission, as through a mistaken reading of a manuscript. It may be a scribal error, or misprint. A ghost word is meaningless, until it is endowed with validity by an authoritative publication like a dictionary, reference work, or *The Liberal Lexicon*. A Caveat: Although a ghost word is initially a new word, it does not qualify as a *"neologism."* That's because a neologism is intentional, while a ghost word is an accident, or mistake.

GHOST WRITER – (*GOHST RYT*-ter) A secret author who gives credit to some celebrity who allegedly writes a book. Unschooled celebrities, athletes, businessmen, and politicians who presumably author books, actually hire a ghost writer. The celebrity merely dictates facts, answers interview questions, and turns over documents. Like an invisible ghost, the ghost writer's name does not appear on the volume. Tony Schwartz (b. 1952) served as Donald Trump's (b. 1946) ghost writing of the *Art of the Deal* (1987). No way is Trump capable of writing an intelligible book. In fact, Schwartz questioned whether Trump can read.

G. I. – (*GEE EYE*) An initialism for Government Issue, (issued, provided, owned by the government). G. I. is also a designation for an American foot soldier. This is revealing. It indicates that when one is inducted into the armed services, he or she belongs to the government. They are no longer free citizens, but government property.

GIAC MY – (*ZOC*-me-*EE*) A North Vietnamese designation for American soldiers during the war. *Giac my* means *"bandits"* or *"pirates."* The U.S. had never declared *war* on Vietnam. They simply invaded, and imposed themselves into the civil war. Therefore, captured Americans were not afforded the legal courtesies of POW's, (Prisoners Of War). American prisoners were *"giac my,"* and therefore treated as bandits, pirates, criminals.

GIANT PANDA – (*JY*-ant *PAN*-da) (*Ailuropoda melanoleuca*) A large, black and white, bear-like mammal inhabiting the remote mountains of Western China. They dwell in the bamboo forests of Sichuan, Shaanxi, and Gansu Provinces. Panda bears can reach 6 feet in height, and an adult male can weigh 350 pounds. The name *"panda"* is a French corruption of the Nepali word *"ponya,"* originally applied to the raccoon-like red panda. For the most part, pandas are solitary creatures, coming together only to mate. Giant pandas are technically omnivorous. Though they will eat small animals and fish, almost 99% of their diet consists of bamboo shoots. Nevertheless, their large fangs indicate a carnivorous past. The panda paw is unique among animals. It has 5 fingers and 2 false thumbs on either side of the paw to facilitate the grasping of bamboo. Because of their poorly nutritious diet, giant pandas must devote 12 to 16 hours a day eating, as much as 44 pounds of bamboo daily. Powerful pandas have few predators. Youngsters are vulnerable to jackals, martens and snow leopards. Today, there are only about 1,000 giant pandas left in the wild. Incidentally: Cute, cuddly pandas can kill. In the wild, they will avoid approaching humans (their primary predators). But if confronted, their sharp claws, large fangs, and great strength will easily kill a man.

GIBBERISH – (*GIB*-ber-ish) (The verb form is Gibber.) Jabber. Meaningless, unintelligible speech or writing. Gibberish is talk in no known language – *"Double Dutch."* The term gibberish goes back to the 1550's. It was considered to be the language of rogues and Gypsies.

G. I. BILL – (*JEE EYE BILL*) Tax-financed education program for World War Two veterans. Thousands of former soldiers obtained free education and became professionals in all fields. The G. I. Bill stimulated the economy and helped (with the unions) to create the American middle class. The new professional middle class in turn created America's suburbia. This is attributed to the G. I. Bill and the unions.

GICHIGAMI – (gich-*EE*-gam-*EE*) Ojibwa Indian name for Lake Superior, meaning *"Big Water."* The Native Americans were right. This Great Lake is 31,700 square miles, larger than the states of Vermont, Massachusetts, Rhode Island, Connecticut, and New Hampshire combined. It is fed by 300 rivers. Superior is the world's largest fresh water lake. It holds 10% of Earth's fresh surface water. That amounts to 3 quadrillion gallons (3,000,000,000,000,000) enough water to flood the entire Western Hemisphere one foot deep. It is the cleanest, clearest of the Great Lakes. And it is cold, with an average year-around temperature of 40 degrees Fahrenheit. The storms on *Gichigami,* especially in November, are Biblical. Waves over 30 feet are common. Surprisingly, Lake Superior is the youngest great geological formation on Earth, only 10,000 years old. Incidentally: If the shoreline of Lake Superior was stretched-out, it would reach from Duluth, Minnesota to the Bahamas.

GIFTED – (*GIF*-ted) Used as an adjective, gifted is having been blessed with a talent or special ability. *"She is a gifted cellist."* That is a perfectly acceptable usage. However, it has become popular to use gifted as verb, which is awkward, terribly clumsy. *"He was gifted a new bicycle."* That is not acceptable, and hopefully will die out.

GIFTED-AND-TALENTED – (*GIF*-ted and *TAL*-lent-ted) In education, the highest ability group in a *"tracked"* school. The gifted-and-talented comprise the top 5th or 20% of the student population. Gifted students rank academically above talented students. Gifted students comprise the top 3% (98th to 100th percentile). Talented students comprise the next 17% (80th to 96th percentile) of the school population. Gifted-and-talented students are usually the advantaged, the affluent who had inherited the *cultural capital* to succeed.

GIGABYTE – (*GIG*-uh-byt) In computer technology and information theory, a gigabyte is a unit of storage space capacity in a memory bank. A single byte is a group or adjacent sequence of 8 bits (binary digits) of information. A gigabyte is 1,073,741,824 bytes of information. The prefix *"giga"* derives from the Greek *"gigas"* meaning *"giant."* A giga-number is indeed a giant, representing a billion. The term gigabyte was adopted into the scientific lexicon in 1947.

GIG ECONOMY – (gig ee-*CON*-nom-mee) A labor market characterized by the prevalence of short-term contracts or freelance work as opposed to permanent jobs. The term comes from the world of performing arts in which musicians, singers, comedians are paid for their individual appearances called *"gigs."* A handyman service is gig employment. Uber cab drivers, bicycle delivery personnel, some type of domestic work, even adjunct professors qualify as gig employment if their jobs are part-time or temporary. Capitalist employers, always on the alert to make an extra buck, are depending increasingly on the gig economy. This absolves them of responsibility for the worker. No benefits, insurance, healthcare are required. Incidentally: The perfidious businessman, Donald Trump (1946) exploits a gig system when he appoints *"acting"* heads of governmental agencies. An acting administrator is temporary and serves at Trump's will. The expectation is that the appointee will be absolutely loyal, servile to Lord Trump.

GIGGLE INCONTINENCE – (*GIG*-uhl in-*KON*-tin-ens) To pee in one's pants when laughing. The exertion of an extreme laughing attack will cause many to leak urine. This is not particularly abnormal. *"I laughed so hard I pissed in my pants!"*

GILA MONSTER – (*GEE*-la *MON*-ster) (Heloderma suspectum) Not an alien beast from the Planet Gila, but a large, fat, colorful lizard native to the desert of the American SouthWest and the Mexican Sonora desert. The gila monster is the largest U.S. lizard, and the only venomous species. The thick body of the gila monster will grow to two feet in length. The gila monster is slow and docile, but will give a painful poisonous bite (not usually fatal) if threatened. This lizard spends most of its life underground or in rock crevices. It feeds on bird eggs and any small animals. It's venom is not for hunting but for defense. The gila monster was named after the Gila River Basin of Arizona and New Mexico, where it was once plentiful. The most prominent feature of this animal is its colorful beaded skin. It is dappled in yellow, orange, and red on a black surface. It's a beautiful animal. This is an *"aposematic coloration,"* visually declaring: *"Look at me. Keep away. I am dangerous."* It is the polar opposite to camouflage. Incidentally: The gila monster's scientific name, *"Heloderm"* is Greek for *"studded skin."* *"Helos"* means *"the head of a nail or stud."* *"Derm"* means *"skin."* The hard beaded skin serves as a protective armor.

GILDED TRUMP – (*GIL*-did *TRUMP*) A hideous, cartoonish statue of Donald Trump (b. 1946) exhibited at the Conservative Political Action Conference (CPAC) in Orlando, Florida, on February 27, 2021. The

6-foot-tall effigy is the fault of California-based *"artist,"* Tommy Zegan (b. 1960). If Zegan had not testified otherwise, one would certainly consider the clownish object to be a joke. The bloated over-sized head with an Elvis Presley hairdo is glistening gold, (the monstrosity in made from fiberglass). It is more of a comic caricature than a likeness and reminds one of the Elias Brothers' *"Big Boy."* Gilded Trump took 6 months to construct and is a product of Mexico, (though the Mexicans did not pay for it). It weighs 200 pounds (about 50 lbs. less that the real Trump). Zegan explained his motives to CNN: *"Two years ago, when I saw all those statues of naked Trump and Trump on a toilet, I said, 'You know what? I can do better.'"* The proud papa of Gilded Trump boasted: *"It is museum-quality, and that's the one I'm eventually hoping to get in the Trump library."* (But Trump does not read.) *"It is literally priceless."* Not quite. For Zegan also appraised the grotesque hulk to be worth a million dollars! Zegan went on to interpret the symbolism: *The coat and the tie is the fact that he's a professional, he's a businessman. The red symbolizes he's a Republican. The red white and blue is that he's a patriot. The fact that he's wearing thongs and shorts is that he's at the age where he should be retired. He should be at the beach right now,"* Zegan concluded. Incidentally, Trump's shorts are made from the American flag, which adds to the hilarity. The only museum that Gilded Trump is eligible for is Barnum-and-Bailey's next to the bearded-lady. Indeed, Gilded Trump was worthy of the freak show that the Republican conference had become. However I challenge Zegan to ask Trump if he would give Gilded Trump pride-of-place in the lobby of gilded Trump Tower? I suspect Zegan would be disappointed.

GIN – (*JIN*) An alcoholic liquor distilled from grain mash and flavored with juniper berries. The word *"gin"* is a corrupted truncation of the word *"geneva,"* which derives from the Dutch word *"genevre,"* meaning juniper. (There is no connection with the Swiss city of Geneva.) Incidentally: English sailors first discovered gin in Holland, during the Anglo-Dutch Wars of the 18th century. The gin provided them with Dutch courage in battle.

GINGER – (*JIN*-jer) A reed-like plant native to the East Indies, now cultivated in the tropics world-wide. Ginger produces a thick, mangled-branched root which has long been prized as a spice and medicine. The ginger root has a spicy-hot pungent taste. It is a prominent flavoring agent in a broad variety of foods and drinks, including ginger ale. The medicinal qualities of ginger are multiple. It is used to relieve headaches and suppress coughs. Most importantly, ginger relieves stomach ailments and aids digestion. It was used to this effect by both the Native Americans of the Midwest, and the Chinese. The wise Chinese sage Confucius (551 – 479 BCE) ate a piece of ginger with every meal. Many claim that ginger ale was first produced in Jamaica, though this assertion is disputed. Incidentally: The Greeks and Romans had transferred this culinary condiment from the kitchen to the dungeon. A peeled plug of ginger would be inserted in a prisoner's anus, and in female prisoner's vagina. This was a tortuous punishment, for the burning pain was excruciating. This act of *"rehabilitation"* is called *"figging."*

GIN GIMLET – (*JIN GIM*-let) A cocktail made with gin, a spot of soda water and lime. A Caveat: A gin gimlet is not a gin-and-tonic. Soda water is not tonic water.

GINGIVAL – (*JIN*-ji-val) The medical term for gum tissue, the gums in the mouth that anchor the teeth.

GIRD – (*GERD*) (Girding, Girded or Girt) To bind, secure with a band, belt, or cloth. To gird is also to encircle, to make secure. For example, *"To gird your loins"* is keeping your *"boys"* secure, in place.

GITMO – (*GIT*-mo) America's *"Devil's Island."* Gitmo is an abbreviated nickname for "Guantanamo" Bay, the U.S. naval base on the southeastern coast of Cuba. Gitmo was built in 1898 as a war prize from the Spanish-American War. It occupies 45 square miles of Cuban territory. Gitmo is the oldest American overseas naval base, a vestigial remain of U.S. imperialism in the Caribbean. The U.S. still persecutes Cuba economically as an enemy, a vestigial remain from the Cold War. Gitmo serves as a constant humiliation to the Cubans, evidence of who is the bully and boss in the Western Hemisphere. Equally despicably, Gitmo serves as an American *"black site"* prison camp, though this is no secret. Muslim soldiers and sympathizers are held indefinitely, without trial at Gitmo as Islamic terrorists. They are tortured, interrogated, and locked-up out of sight, out of mind. Some prisoners may be war criminals, guilty and dangerous. Others are not. But none of them should not be treated like animals. That is not who we are, or should be. Gitmo stands contrary to every value democratic America had ever held dear. It is a dark stain on the American flag, and proof to the world that we are no better than the worst. The prisoners of Gitmo must be afforded the humane rights if International Law. The prison and base must be turned over to Cuba, as a token of rapprochement. Imagine if the Cubans, Russians, any foreign power occupied Key West, Florida. American *"gunboat"* diplomacy no longer serves U.S. interests. *"Abandon all hope, ye who enter here."* – Dante Alighieri (c. 1265 – 1321), <u>*Divine Comedy*</u> (1320).

GIULIANISM – (jew-lee-*ON*-is-um) (Giulianied = jew-lee-*ON*-need) To deceive the citizenry in defense of a guilty public official. To *Giuliani* is to torture the truth. It is to intentionally distort, obfuscate, and falsify the facts, twisting a story to the point of incomprehensibility. The term is an eponym taken from the name Rudy Giuliani (b. 1944), former Mayor of New York City. The once respected mayor of the 9/11 drama has become a clownish cad, an apologist for President Donald Trump's (b. 1946) obscenities, illegalities, and criminalities. Giuliani is Trump's public propagandist, TV *"lie-meister."* In an August 2018 interview, Giuliani shamelessly declared that *"Truth isn't Truth."* Adolf Hitler (1889 – 1945) had his Joseph Goebbels (1897 – 1945), Donald Trump has his Rudy Giuliani.

GIVEN NAME – (*GIV*-ven *NAYM*) One's first name, as distinguished from one's shared family or surname. The given name has been called one's Christian name. Ironically, the most common *"Christian"* name in the world is *Mohammed.* Given names are trendy. They come and go like the fashions. Biblical names were most common in the 19th century. Hollywood influenced the names of the Baby Boomers, as did soap operas later. Incidentally: Rock star Frank Zappa (1940 – 1993) named his daughter *"Moon Unit"* (b. 1967).

GIVING – (*GIV*-ving) Bestowment, an act of charity. Giving is to voluntarily and cheerfully contribute money, food, clothing, and property to the needy. Charitable giving is an act of compassion demanded by all the great religions. A giver expects no quid pro quo. Giving is at the heart of Jesus' *"Social Gospel"* (Matthew 25: 35 – 40), as well as benevolent Socialism. The great Church Father St. Augustine of Hippo (354 – 430 CE) admonished us to *"Find out how much God has given you and from it take what you need; the remainder is needed by others."* *"The habit of giving only enhances the desire to give."* – Walt Whitman (1819 – 1892). *"The giver gives, but really he is sowing the seed for later, the gift of a rich harvest."* – Sathya sai Baba (1926 – 2011).

GIVING TUESDAY – (*GIV*-ving *TOOS*-day) A movement of charitable altruism designed to exploit the holiday spirit of gratitude. Giving Tuesday falls 5 days after Thanksgiving Thursday. Too, it is also hoped to capitalize on the guilty feeling of self-indulgence provoked by Black Friday and Cyber Monday. The first Giving Tuesday was initiated by theater producer Carlos Lorenzo Garcia in 2011. Though a noble act of philanthropy, giving Tuesday should be unnecessary in the world's richest nation. Capitalism makes charitable giving essential every day of the year. Distributive injustice enriches the wealthy and impoverishes the rest. Charity is a bandaid for a hemorrhage, an anesthetic for a fatal injury, the deadly disease of capitalism. *"Charity is no substitute for justice withheld."* – St. Augustine (354 – 430 CE).

GIZA – (*GEE*-za) A city in northeast Egypt on the West Bank of the Nile. Giza is site of the Great Pyramid of Giza or Cheops (also Khufu). It is the oldest of the 7 wonders of the ancient world, completed in 2560 BCE. This colossal structure weighs over 6 million tons. At 481 feet, the Great Pyramid of Giza remained the tallest man-made structure in the world for 3,800 years until the Eifel Tower was constructed in 1889. The structure consists of about 2,300,000 limestone blocks (*numulite,* fossilized seashells), weighing from 2 to 30 tons. Some blocks weigh 50 tons. The pyramid is a tomb for the Pharaoh Khufu (or Cheops in Greek). It had to be completed in 22 years of Khufu's life, supposedly ready for his death. That meant emplacing an average of 12 blocks into place each hour, day and night for all that time. About 800 tons of stone a day was moved. The entire structure weighs about 5,955,000 tons. It was not stepped as today, but smoothly finished with a layer of glaring white limestone. The apex was capped in gold. To date, 97 pyramids have been discovered in Egypt. Incidentally: Historically, the pyramids were acknowledged as tombs for the pharaohs. But no pharaoh mummies have ever been found in any of the pyramids, not even Khufu. Therefore, the purpose of the pyramids is still unknown.

GIZADA – (giz-*ZAD*-da) A sweet round coconut pie, introduced by Lebanese immigrants to Jamaica, locally called *"pinch-me-round"* for its bordering crust.

GIZMO – (*GIZ*-moh) A popular term for a gadget, device, widget, doodad, doohickey. A tool or any item for which you don't know the technical name can become a gizmo. The term *"gizmo"* is an Americanism of unknown origin. We know that it first appeared as naval slang for anything that you can't put a name to.

GLABROUS – (*GLA*-brus) Means hairless, bald.

GLACIAL DRIFT – (*GLAY*-shul *DRIFT*) Sediments deposited by a glacier. The weight of the mighty glacier pulverizes the rock it creeps upon. Glacial drift, produces fine rich soil. The pulverized rock is fertilized with every sort of minerals crushed with the rocks.

GLACIAL ICE – (*GLAY*-shul *EYS*) (Glaciers) Blue ice compressed by excruciating pressure, squeezing out the air bubbles, altering the molecular structure, making the ice incredibly hard. At almost 100 feet in depth, the pressure of weight sets the glacier in motion, like the planchette on an Ouija board. This occurs when the ice crystals slip over each other, a process called *internal plastic flow.* Continental glaciers move, on average, 1 foot per year. But mountainous alpine glaciers may race 3 feet a day, being pulled down-mountain by gravity. If all the glacial ice on Earth melted, 7% of the land would be inundated.

GLACIAL MILK – (*GLAY*-shul *MILK*) Milky white water flowing down mountains, impregnated with healthful minerals from crushed rocks by alpine glaciers. Montane longevity sites are watered with glacial milk. Longevity sites the worldwide tend to be high in mountains. What do these diverse people share in common? They live high in elevation, is thinner air. The topography, terrain demands more exertion (exercise), just to get around daily. They drink and irrigate their produce with glacial milk.

GLACIATION – (glay-she-*AY*-shun) An ice age. A glaciation can be triggered by an 8 to 10 (some say 15) degree decrease in the world temperature. Cooler summers, not colder winters, at 65 degrees north latitude will trigger a glaciation. It is thought that changes in the Earth's orbit around the sun results in warm and cold periods. A more circular orbit results in a warm period (the last 10,000 years to the present). A more elliptical orbit will result is a cold period, triggering a glaciation. It is believed that we are at the end of our warm period. It takes about 90,000 years for an ice age to develop, and about 10,000 years for it to melt away. There have been several ice ages (glaciations) in the history of Earth. The last glaciation which ended about 12,000 years ago covered over 17 million square miles at its height. Over 69,000 trillion tons of ice covered the continent. The average temperature in North America dropped by 26 degrees Fahrenheit. The glaciers moved south at a speed of 3 feet a day. The sheet of ice was over 12,000 feet thick in places. With so much water locked-up in ice, the level of the oceans dropped by 440 feet. Glaciations may have several triggers. They may have been caused by an asteroid collision (*impact winter*), supervolcanic eruptions (*volcanic winter*), or some anomaly in the rotation, or revolution of the planet. During glaciations the tropics that were not icebound were inundated by torrential rains. Incidentally: With the emergence of the ice, and the decline in vegetation, humans were forced to eat more meat than plants. The additional protein resulted in greater brain growth and heightened intelligence.

GLACIERS – (*GLAY*-shers) Great moving mountains of ice. Glaciers are created by prolonged global chilling. Snow fall year after year fails to melt. It accumulates, its weight compressing the snow into super-hard glacial ice. Continental glaciers move about a foot a year on average. The physics of the glacier's excruciating weight makes it move somewhat like a planchette on an Ouija Board. This occurs when the ice crystals slip over each other, a process called *internal plastic flow*. Alpine glaciers in mountains may race about 3 feet a day. The glacier levels mountains, crushes rock, moves boulders, cuts valleys, and gouges-out lakes. They deposit mineral-rich nutrients into the soil and the sea, which increases fish yields. Two-thirds of the world's fresh water is locked- up as glacial ice. Today, about 10% of the land on Earth is ice-covered. The greatest are the *continental glaciers,* 90% covering Antarctica, and 10% hovering in Greenland. The Antarctic ice sheet is 7 times larger than the Greenland ice sheet. *Alpine glaciers* are found in high mountain valleys. The global advancement of glaciers is known as a glaciation or ice age. There have been several in Earth's history. Incidentally: It takes about 10 trillion tons of glacial ice melt to raise the ocean level 1 inch. Since 1992, ice sheets at the poles have lost 5 trillion tons, raising the ocean level ½ inch. In the 1990's, Greenland's glacier was melting at a rate of 55 billion tons a year. Today, it is melting at over 290 billion tons yearly. Furthermore, if all the glacial ice melted, it would inundate 7% of the land on Earth, coastal regions, some of the most populated parts of the planet.

GLAD-HAND – (*GLAD* hand) (Glad-handing) To greet in an insincerely effusive manner, with feigned enthusiasm and warmth. Glad-handing is a common ploy of duplicitous diplomats and politicians. A glad-handed diplomat is a patriot who goes abroad to lie for his country.

GLADIATORS – (*GLAD*-dee-ay-tors) Individuals who fought to the death as public entertainment in ancient Rome. Gladiatorial combat was introduced to the Romans by the Etruscans. Most of the gladiators were slaves and prisoners of war who were compelled to fight. But others were sadistic thrill-seekers, psychopathic megalomaniacs who gained an adrenaline-rush by butchering others in public. These professional killers signed-up for 5-years, and could become very wealthy. Gladiatorial training lasted 3 grueling months. About 20% of the combats resulted in a death. Of course, those who enjoyed it were those who succeeded. The professional gladiators lived. The compelled gladiators died, most by the age of 23. They were trained as specialists with different weapons. They fought each other and wild animals. At its height, gladiatorial games were held on 170 days of the year. The gladiators were made addicted to opium, a pain killer. The gladiator surgeon, Galen (129 – c. 200 or 216 CE) warned of opium's dangers. Victorious gladiators became the rock stars of their day, along with an entourage of female groupies. They prostituted themselves to horny, rich widows. They sold vials of their sweat to wealthy ladies as an aphrodisiac. A successful professional gladiator could make $200,000 for a popular victory. Some did retire as rich men. The vile gladiatorial *games* continued for 400 years in the Roman Colosseum, costing the lives of over a half-a-million people. Furthermore, there were over 400 arenas in the Roman Empire. Incidentally: During the siege and sack of Rome (410 CE) by Alaric (c. 370 – 410 CE), the city was gripped in famine. Cannibalism broke out. *"Gladiator meat"* was sold in the markets.

GLAMPING – (*GLAM*-ping) Glamorous Camping. Glamping is the opposite of roughing it, but rather easing it. It is camping with all the amenities of a comfortable hotel. Glamping is enjoying the *"great indoors,"* albeit in the outdoors, even wilderness. A luxury cabin (toilet, shower, stove, refrigerator, central heating, air conditioning, TV, internet) in the woods is glamping. So is a fully equipped travel van or bus.

GLARING – (*GLAIR*-ing) (also Clowder) The collective name for an assemblage of cats. *"A glaring of cats crept about the old lay's house."*

GLASNOST – (*GLAS*-nos) Russian for frank and open discussion. Glasnost was the policy initiated by Soviet leader Mikhail Gorbachev (1931 - 2022) in 1985. It eased the restrictions maintained by the Communist Party. The economic weaknesses of the Soviet Union were publicly examined. Next, Gorbachev introduced economic and political reforms (*perestroika*). Gorbachev had unwittingly let the capitalist genie out of the bottle. Gorbachev believed in Socialism and hoped to humanize Communism. But under his successor, the alcoholic Boris Yeltsin (1931 – 2007) the Soviet Union imploded, the Communist Party was banned, and Socialist security evaporated (1993). Socialism was replaced by poverty, gross economic inequality, homelessness, and crime – all the blessings of capitalism. Mikhail Gorbachev died in regret. *"Jesus was the first Socialist, who wanted to create a better life for all people."* – Mikhail Gorbachev. *"The road to hell is paved with good intentions."* – St. Bernard of Clairvaux (1090 – 1153).

GLASS – (*GLAS*) A translucent, often transparent substance made from molten silica quartz (sand). Glass is neither a solid nor a liquid, but a hard wax, a liquid crystal. Fast cooling glass produces small crystals which are clear. Slow cooling glass produces large crystals which are frosty or opaque. Glass unperceptively flows with gravity like any other wax, in the process called *"creep."* That's why an old mirror will reflect a distorted image. Glass will eventually return to the sand from which it came. Incidentally: One great modern skyscraper holds more glass than the Roman Empire produced in its entire history. Archeologists have found small piles of sand like ant hills in Egyptian pyramids millennia old. They were glass vials that time had reduced to their natural, original state. Due to the phenomenon of creep, ancient stained-glass windows in Medieval cathedrals and castles are in danger. As the glass flows downward, the tops of the windows are growing thin and weak.

GLASS CEILING – (*GLAS SEE*-ling) A series of invisible, unspoken barriers intended to block women from climbing the corporate capitalist ladder. Though illegal, the chauvinistic attitudes of the *"old boys club"* die hard. A glass ceiling on advancement has been known to hinder minority members as well. Incidentally: Only 27 out of 200 world leaders are women (June, 2023).

GLASSED – (*GLAST*) To be assaulted by having a glass bottle busted over one's head.

GLAZE – (*GLAYZ*) In meteorology, when super-cooled rain spreads out before freezing, producing a dangerous, smooth icy surface. Super-cooled raindrops are snowflakes that liquify on the way down. Snowflakes do not have microscopic nuclei within. So the raindrop cannot freeze hard. It remains liquid even below freezing temperature. But when the super-cold rain hits the ground or any object, it instantly freezes producing a coating of ice. This is the making of an ice storm. Water covered glaze (ice) is the slipperiest substance known to man.

GLIB – (Glibber, Glibly, Glibness) Thoughtlessly talkative, superficially gabby, an insincere chatterbox.

GLIOBLASTOMA – (gly-o-blas-*TOH*-mah) (Glioblastoma Multiforme) The most heinous, wicked form of cancer. One-third of brain tumors are malignant. Glioblastoma is the most aggressive cancer which begins within the brain. The chance of contracting the disease is said to be one in half-a-million. Signs and symptoms of glioblastoma are initially non-specific. They include headaches, nausea, personality changes, and symptoms similar to those of a stroke. Bizarre behavior is common. Worsening of symptoms is rapid. Blindness occurs. The pain is excruciating, requiring the strongest narcotics. The victim descends to unconsciousness. Glioblastoma is a death sentence, claiming 17,000 American lives yearly. Victims often die 6 months after discovery. In 1965, this hideous brain cancer took singer Nat King Cole (1919 – 1965). In 2009, glioblastoma claimed the life of Senator Ted Kennedy (1932 – 2009), and political columnist Robert Novak (1931 – 2009). Beau Biden (1969 – 2015), son of Vice-President Joe Biden (b. 1942) succumbed to the cancer in 2015. Randy A. Pasieka (1954 – 2017) construction worker and my dear brother had fallen victim to the tumor in January, 2017. In that same year, opera star Dmitri Hvorostovsky (1962 – 2017) fell victim. Republican Senator John McCain (1936 - 2018) was diagnosed with glioblastoma in July 2017, and died the next year. Like all Republicans, McCain was anxious to repeal *"Obamacare,"* depriving millions of Americans health insurance. But once confronted with his mortality, McCain experienced an epiphany. He could not vote to take medical care from millions, when he was receiving the best that wealth and privilege could buy. He gave the dramatic thumb-down to Trump's Republican bill to kill healthcare. Too, being faced with eternity, McCain finally discovered Jesus' *"Social Gospel"* (Matthew 25:

35 – 40), which includes the admonition: *"When I was ill, you healed me."* Incidentally: It's curious that of 90 notables from all fields, who perished from brain cancer, 38 succumbed to glioblastoma. That's a shocking 42%! Furthermore, the average year of those 38 deaths was 2006. Some resent environmental factor must be responsible for the tremendous increase of this form of brain cancer. Can the suspected murderer be microwave radiation, from ovens, towers, and the ubiquitous cellphones? This frequency of light has permeated and penetrated our atmosphere, communities, homes, bodies, and brains. Perhaps microwave radiation from cellphones are killing us. But the phones are far, far too capitalistically profitable to be held accountable. Incidentally: Don't expect the cellphone telecommunications CEOs to admit to Congress, on television, that their phones can cause cancer, like the cigarette companies CEOs had done.

GLITCH – (*GLICH*) A Yiddishism for a minor problem. A glitch is a hiccup in the program.

GLITTERING GENERALITY – (*GLIT*-ter-ring jen-ner-*RAL*-li-tee) Pointless platitudes. A deceptive propaganda technique that utilizes grandiose assertions, pontifical proposals to make imperious impressions. Glittering generalities are empty, emotional boasts that are meaningless. Generally speaking, all that glitters is not gold. *"I will make America great again!"* – Donald Trump (2016). So what? A mere glittering generality.

GLOBALIZATION – (glo-bol-li-*ZAY*-shun) The internationalization of gargantuan corporations in order to exploit on a world-wide level. Globalization is a natural capitalist process. Globalized multinational corporations are beyond the control of any single nation. They hold allegiance to no single country. Their only patriotism is profits. A global economy makes capitalist exploitation of underdeveloped countries all the more efficient. Globalization serves the capitalists by emasculating labor unions. American workers are expected to compete with foreign workers from underdeveloped countries. Like commodities, American wages are expected to compete with the low wage scales in primitive regions. Therefore, American workers' wages should drop to world market levels (say 99 cents an hour?), rather than lift world wages to U.S. unionized standards. That's the capitalist interpretation of globalization.

GLOBAL EDUCATION – (*GLO*-bal ed-jew-*KAY*-shun) An aim of multicultural programs that helps students to understand that all peoples living on earth have interconnected fates. The underlying goal of global education is to create the Brotherhood of Man.

GLOBAL EMPIRE – (*GLO*-bal *EM*-py-yer) The United States, the New Rome, maintains a global empire of over 737 military bases in over 150 countries, manned by 2.5 million military and mercenary personnel. The estimated cost to maintain this military empire is about a trillion dollars annually. This expense exceeds the military budget into several other funding sources, like CIA secret *"black sites."* The rest of the world combined spends about 59 trillion dollars on the military. Therefore, 1 out of every 60 dollars spent on the military in the world, is spent by the United States. What is the U.S. protecting? Certainly not the homeland. This obscene expenditure protects corporate capitalist interests abroad. That's where the taxes go – to protect the profits of the rich, while exploiting poor peasants overseas.

GLOBAL WARMING – (*GLO*-bal *WRAM*-ing) A man-made disaster now in progress. It is fueled by greed in the form of fossil fuels, particularly coal. Coal is carbon which becomes carbon dioxide, a global warming greenhouse gas, but it is cheap to burn. Industrial capitalists profit immensely by burning cheap coal, care-less of the planetary consequences. In the last century, the temperature of the ocean has risen by 1.2 degrees Fahrenheit. A warmer ocean will result in climactic chaos. Hurricanes will escalate into hypercanes. Polar meltdown will raise the ocean level. If all the glacial ice melted, 7% of the Earth's land, housing most of the population would be inundated. Some regions will be drowned. Other regions will experience drought that will trigger desertification. Global warming results in more water being evaporated into the atmosphere, resulting in more powerful storms – hypercanes and super- tornadoes. In fact, research at Florida State University revealed that tornadoes are becoming 5% stronger each year. Global warming will alter civilization and threaten mankind's very existence. *"We must reduce all emissions that are destroying the planet. However, that requires a change in lifestyle, a change in the economic model. We must go from capitalism to Socialism." "If the climate were a bank, the capitalists would already have saved it!"* – Venezuelan Socialist President Hugo Chavez (1954 – 2013).

GLOBESITY – (glo-*BEES*-sit-tee) Global obesity or transnational *trans-fat*. The swelling profits of the bloated multinational corporations. Globesity is the gross capitalist consumption of world market shares.

GLOBULAR CLUSTERS – (*GLOB*-bu-lar *CLUS*-ters) In cosmology (astronomy) a (comparatively older, spherically symmetrical, compact group of millions of old stars, held together by mutual gravitation, located in a gaseous halo. Globular clusters move in great, highly eccentric orbits around a galactic center. Globular clusters appear as concentrated sources of light in the night sky.

GLORIOUS REVOLUTION – (*GLOR*-ree-us rev-vo-*LOO*-shun) The replacement on the English throne, in 1689, of a Catholic monarch James II by his Protestant daughter Mary and her Dutch husband, William of Orange. This bloodless coup marked the end of absolutism and the beginning of constitutional government in England. Actually, the Glorious Revolution was not very revolutionary for the common man. Like the Magna Charta (1215), the Glorious Revolution benefited the landed gentry, and wealthy capitalist industrialists. It did little for the poor peasants or wretched slum dwellers.

GLORYHOLE – (*GLOR*-ree-hohl) (Glory holing, Glory holer) A prop used in an erotic sexual fantasy game. A glory hole is an opening, aperture, or hole in a wall or partition through which sex is performed. An erect penis is projected into the hole, protruding through the partition into the next room. The person in the next room is invited to perform fellation, or anal, vaginal sex with the unidentified, penis. The individuals remain anonymous to each other, which intensifies the mystery, excitement, and eroticism. Gloryholes originated in the lavatories of gay bars, and sex arcades. The concept was adopted by the adult film industry, and came to be applied to both sexes. An advanced rendition of the gloryhole is a large opening in the wall resembling a *"doggie door."* A naked person (of either sex) lays either on the back or front, with the lower part of the body exposed for intercourse through the gloryhole. Only the legs, ass, and genitals are visible, making for anonymity. The legs are tethered, spread open for quick, convenient coition. The sex host is penetrated vaginally or anally, anonymously. Similar to the *"masked singer,"* the gloryhole furnishes a *"masked fucker."* Advanced age, homeliness, or even ugliness will not disqualify a gloryhole participant from experiencing fanaticized sexual ecstasy. Any number of individuals may participate (gang bang). The *"glory holer"* hosting the orgy, being in bondage, experiences a sadomasochistic satisfaction. A caveat: It's possible that the anonymity may result in unintended, accidental incest. Nevertheless, gloryhole has been introduced to fraternity houses at some institutions of high learning, as a form of entertainment and recreation, relief from the rigors of academic pursuits. A Caveat: Exotic erotica is an alternated lifestyle, foreign to most, albeit very real. The author serves as a reporter, not supporter, in the service of informative research. Thank you.

GLOSS – An explanatory note or comment accompanying a text. In the transmission of Biblical documents, marginal comments made by a scribe were sometimes incorporated into the text by later copyists.

GLOSSOPHOBIA – (glos-o-*FO*-bee-a) (Glossophobiac) Phobic fear of public speaking. Glossophobia is a form of performance anxiety. It is a very common neurosis. Many people panic when they must express themselves before a crowd. The cure for Glossophobia is practice, in incremental steps. Nothing succeeds like success, even little ones. The only way out is through. One must abandon self-consciousness, and concentrate on the message. A beta-blocker, a mild blood pressure pill will help to get the fearful Glossophobiac through the imaginary crisis. Quick Fix: If you feel that you are about to panic, tell the audience how you feel. Instantly, you will be relived.

GLOTTAL STOP – (*GLOT*-tal *STOP*) The accent of London's East End, home of the Cockney. It displays a halting quality whereas the T's in a word like bottle are dropped becoming *"bo-ul,"* as well as the H's in a word like hedgehog, which becomes *"edge-og."* Cockney was the standard speech at court in Elizabethan times.

GLUCOSAMINE CHONDROITIN – (gloo-*CO*-say-meen con-*DROY*-tin) Glucosamine chondroitin is actually just gelatin, as is cartilage, collagen, and Jell-O. Then why not call it plain gelatin? Because a 7 syllable, medically sounding name is required to impress and dupe the consumer. Glucosamine chondroitin is a sophisticated scientific-sounding synonym for cartilage (gristle) between the joints, connecting the ribs, shaping the nose and ears – a hardened gelatin. Cook any meat product, let cool, and you'll produce aspic or gelatin. You'll chew it off the ends of chicken bones too. So glucosamine chondroitin is simply gelatin intended to impress. It sells for an average of $44.44 a jar as a "dietary supplement" for rebuilding damaged cartilage in joints. If the capitalist drug companies can lobby [read: *bribe*] the capitalist Congress to declare glucosamine chondroitin a "drug," this common gelatin could sell for over $144.44 a jar. Pure gelatin can be purchased by the pound from a brewery store.

GLUTEN – (*GLOO*-ten) A tough, viscid substance remaining when the flour of wheat, rye, spelt, barley, and other grain is washed to remove the starch. The term gluten is taken directly from Latin meaning *"glue."* The term applies to the glue-like property of wet dough. This glue-like property of gluten makes the dough elastic and gives bread the ability to rise during baking. It also contributes the chewy texture. The 2 main nitrogenous proteins in gluten are *glutenin* and *gliadin*. Gliaden is responsible for most of the adverse health effects of gluten. Most people have no issue with gluten. However, it can cause problems for people with wheat allergy, gluten sensitivity, and *celiac disease.* About 1% of the population is severely gluten intolerant due to celiac disease. This is an autoimmune disorder in which the body treats gluten as a foreign invader. As the immune system attacks the gluten, collateral damage is done to the gastrointestinal tract causing painful inflammation. On the other hand, gluten sensitivity is not an autoimmune condition, but can have similar symptoms like diarrhea and abdominal pain.

GLUTTONY – (*GLUHT*-ton-nee) (Glutton) Excessive eating and drinking. A glutton doesn't eat to live, but lives to eat. Gluttony is an eating disorder, often a defense mechanism, that requires professional psychological help. Gluttony is one of the *"Seven Deadly Sins."* The term can be expanded to represent obscene overindulgence in general, as in a *"gluttony of wealth."* A glutton is a selfish pig, usually a wealthy pig. *"Tonight, Lucullus is host to Lucullus"* – Epicurean Philosopher and Glutton Titus Lucretius Carus (c. 99 BCE – c. 55 CE).

GLUTTONY TAX – (*GLUHT*-ton-nee *TAKS*) An overabundance tax. A duty or levy on the piggishly rich. It is unconscionable, preposterous, and immoral that certain individuals should control more wealth than entire nations. No matter how they got it, they don't deserve it, as long as so many others without it, desperately need it. There are at least 735 billionaires in America;495 in China; 169 in India; 126 in German; 105 in Russia – at least 2,640 billionaires in the world. The richest 1% of the world population controls over 83% of the wealth on Earth. So 7,000 people in the world control practically everything. Jeff Bezos (b. 1961), Bill Gates (b. 1955), and Elon Musk (b. 1971) together, are richer than the bottom 50% of the U.S. population. The wealth controlled by these people can eliminate want, need, and misery on Earth. But they won't do it. So make them do it. Tax the swine, a gluttony tax. Jesus said: *"Where your treasure is, there your heart is too."* – Matthew 6:21. *"Go, sell all you own and give it to the poor. Then come follow me,"* Jesus challenged all of us (Mark 10:21). For those who will not follow Jesus, make them follow in admonition of Socialist Senator Bernie Sanders (b. 1941). *"Make billionaires illegal!"* The gluttony tax could do it.

GLYPTICS – (*GLIP*-tics) The art of engraving on gemstones. Glyptography is the study of such artwork.

GNASH – (*NASH*) (Gnashing) To grind, grip, or clinched the teeth together, especially in rage, grief, or pain. *"Cast the worthless servants into the outer darkness. In that place there will be weeping and gnashing of teeth."* – Jesus in Matthew 25:30. This should be a dire warning to the capitalists on Wall Street.

GNOME – (*NOHM*) The word comes from the Greek *"genomus,"* meaning *"earth dweller."* Gnomes were described by Paracelsus (1493 – 1541) in the 16th century as earth elementals, small humanoid creatures who could move through solid earth as easily as humans can move through air.

GNOSIS – (*NOH*-sis) (Gnostics, Gnosistic) Mystical knowledge, paranormal intelligence, inherent awareness of spiritual matters beyond the natural, in the realm of the supernatural. Gnosis is Divine wisdom, spiritual truths. What God reveals to her prophets is gnosis. There term gnosis enter English from the Greek in 1703.

GNOSTICISM – (*NOS*-ti-sis-um) A religious and philosophical movement that attempted, during the 1st centuries of the Christian era, to unite diverse elements of Greek and Oriental mysticism with Christianity. Its name derives from its emphasis on esoteric knowledge (*gnosis*) as a way to salvation.

GNP – (gee en *PEE*) (Gross National Product) The total monetary value of all final goods and services produced in a country in one year. The GNP is a vague estimate of how rich is a country. It is a vague estimate, because the riches, like the richness of cream, always floats up to the top.

GOAL – (*GOLE*) An aim or object towards which an endeavor is directed. The goal is the result of achievement. A goal is a dream with a deadline.

GO A-MAYING – (*GO* a *MAY*-ing) An ancient pagan [read: *pre-Christian*] custom practiced on May 1st, *May Day*. The death of winter meant the spring of new life. Young people danced around the May Pole, an obvious phallic symbol. Young couples would spend the night frolicking in the forest. The girls often emerged pregnant when they'd *"go a-maying."* After all, May 1st was the Wiccan holiday of fecundity, fertility, and sex. Many traditions and rituals are being revived by the neopagan Wiccans.

G.O.A.T. – (*GOHT*) An acronym for <u>G</u>reatest <u>O</u>f <u>A</u>ll <u>T</u>ime. This declaration contends that the recipient had no equal in his/her field, athletics, art, music, literature, whatever. The original GOAT was the boxer Muhammad Ali (1942 - 2016). He proclaimed himself *"The Greatest."* In 1992, Ali's wife Yolanda "Lonnie" Williams (b. 1940) add that Muhammad was *"The <u>G</u>reatest <u>O</u>f <u>A</u>ll <u>T</u>ime,"* or *"G.O.A.T."* Furthermore, she copyrighted G.O.A.T. in this context. In 2000, rapper LL Cool J (b. 1986) released an album entitled *"G.O.A.T."* Since then, the term caught on to mean anyone who is at the pinnacle of their profession. *"It is popularly agreed that Tom Brady is the GOAT quarterback."*

GOAT MEAT – (*GOHT* meet) (also Goat's Meat) *"Chevon,"* the edible flesh from the hollow-horned ruminant, related to the sheep, called a goat. The domestic goat is the *Capra aegagrus hircus*, in zoological parlance. There was no specific name for goat's meat in English (as there was *"mutton"* for sheep's meat), until 1922. In that year the French, connoisseurs of cuisine combined the words *"<u>chevre</u>"* meaning goat, and *"mou<u>ton</u>"* meaning sheep, to create the term *"chevon,"* meaning goat's meat. So today, in some restaurants, you can impress your dinner guests by ordering chevon. However, unless you're in France, the waiter won't understand you, (which will make you look all the smarter). In Portuguese and Spanish, goat's meat is called *"cabrito"*; in Italian, *"capretto."* Goat is one of the earliest domesticated animals. Its meat has therefore been cooked for thousands of years. Goat is eaten worldwide, but particularly, in underdeveloped countries. In Europe, it is usually a Mediterranean dish. In the U.S. and Canada, goat's meat is available only in certain ethnic neighborhoods. Incidentally: In the English-speaking Caribbean Islands, both sheep and goat's meat are referred to as mutton among the Black residents. As slaves on the sugar plantations, they learned to speak English from poor, uneducated Irish overseers. These unschooled White lads never differentiated between a sheep and a goat. It all became mutton and remains so today. In Jamaica, the rich East Indian heritage has contributed the delicacy, *"curry goat"* a national dish. Furthermore: Goat's head soup is a Middle Eastern delicacy, readily available in greater Detroit, (Hamtramck and Dearborn).

GOBBLEDYGOOK – (*GOB*-bull-dee-gook) An Americanism for nonsensical speech or correspondence. Gobbledygook is language characterized by circumlocution and jargon, almost impossible to understand. It is particularly characteristic of pompous talk of government officialdom. The term *"gobbledygook"* was coined by Texas Congressman Maury Maverick (1895 – 1954) who was chairman of the *U.S. Smaller War Plant Corporation* during World War Two (1941 – 1945). On March 30, 1944, Maverick wrote a memo in which he forbade all governmental *"gobbledygook language."* He jokingly threatened that: *"Anyone using the words <u>activation</u> or <u>implementation</u> will be shot!"* Maury Maverick created the word gobbledygook in imitation of a turkey's gaggle (a gobbler). Incidentally: Representative Maury Maverick was somewhat of a Congressional *maverick.* So was his grandfather, Samuel A. Maverick (1803 – 1870). In fact, Samuel Maverick inspired the term *"maverick,"* as a rebellious nonconformist. Samuel was a rancher, some would say a cattle rustler. He would confiscate all non- branded cattle as his own. Samuel Maverick was indeed a maverick rancher.

GOBI DESERT – (*GO*-bee *DES*-sert) *"Gobi"* is a Mongol word meaning *"very large and dry."* Asia's largest desert, the Gobi is located in northern China and southeast Mongolia. The Gobi is the world's most northerly desert. Too, being centered, landlocked in the middle of the biggest continent, no place on Earth is farther from the sea than the Gobi. It is about 3 times the size of California, with only 500 miles of road. The Gobi region is on the leeward side of the torrential monsoons. The rain-saturated winds cannot get over the high Himalayas, resulting in the desert. This desert is the home of the two-humped Bactrian camel, though only about 500 survive in the wild. The Gobi Desert is a prime location for the discovery of dinosaur fossils.

GOBLIN MODE – (*GOB*-lin *MOHD*) Being in goblin mode is exhibiting a type of behavior which is unapologetically self-indulgent, lazy, slovenly, or greedy, typically in a way that rejects social norms or expectations. Incidentally: Goblin mode was chosen by the <u>*Oxford Dictionary*</u> as the 2022 word of the year.

GOD – (*GOD*) The universal creator, the first cause, the prime mover, the cosmic mind. God is the soul of all life. God is the perpetual singularity. *"You may call God love, you may call God goodness, but the best name for God is compassion."* – Meister Eckhart (c. 1260 – c. 1328). God has been called the *"Light of the World."* Light is energy. Matter is reducible to energy. Energy is light. Matter is light. So all is light. God is light. God is all. All is light. So I am light. I am God. We all are God. God is indeed a mystery. Roman philosopher Lucius Seneca (c. 4 BCE – 65 CE) asked: *"What is God? The Mind of the Universe. What is He? All that you see, and all that you do not see."* The scholarly Church Father, St. Augustine (354 – 430 CE) insisted that*: "God is not what you imagine, or what you think you understand. If you understand, you have failed." "God? He is the breath inside the breath."* – Kabir (1440 – 1518). *"God is just a name to refer to something that is beyond all limitations."* – Jaggi Vasudev (b. 1957).

GOD BELIEVER – (*GOD* bee-*LEEV*-ver) The official governmental designation in atheist Nazi Germany for a religious citizen. No differentiation of creed or sect was recognized. It is not an exaggeration to say that the state god was Adolf Hitler (1889 – 1945), the religion, Nazism. The Nazis tolerated the concept of God, grudgingly. God Believers were not accepted enthusiastically during Hitler's reign. It could be an impediment to Party membership and an obstacle to advancement and promotion. Popularly outspoken God Believers were persecuted as subversives.

GODDAMMIT – (god-*DAM*-it) (also Goddamnit) A portmanteau blend of the words *God, dam,* and *it.* Goddammit is an interjection, spontaneously used at the moment of anger, disgust, perplexity, or amazement. Goddammit is an offensive term. Actually, this term is a curse. It is beseeching God to damn, condemn, or destroy something or someone. Sometimes the initial letter in <u>G</u>od is capitalized. *"Goddammit everybody in the world wants an explanation for your acts for your very being."* – Jack Kerouac (1922 – 1969).

GOD FEARERS – (*GOD FEER*-er) Originally, Gentiles who sympathized with Judaism. The first to be designated as God-fearers were semi-converts to Judaism. They were a Gentile/Jewish hybrid. Circumcision was the great inhibition to becoming a Jew. Christianity did not demand this condition. So many early Christians were recruited from the God-fearers. The name God-fearer was also applied to the nascent Christian/Jewish hybrid. The God Fearers were disciples of St. Peter in the Jerusalem Church. God Fearers were also Jewish converts to Christianity. They kept their Jewish traditions and religion, on which they layered a veneer of Christianity. Incidentally: The Jews, the believers of the Old Testament, would choose the term God-*FEARERS*. The Christians, the believers of the New Testament would choose the term God-*LOVERS*. That indicates the difference in conception that God acquired after Jesus.

GOD'S ACRE – (gods *AY*-ker) An English translation and adaptation of the German *"Gottesacker,"* meaning *"Field of God,"* an ancient reference to a burial ground. Therefore, God's Acre is a cemetery, a graveyard. The dimension need not be confined to one acre. The term acre was a convenient substitute that sounded similar to the German *"sacker,"* meaning *"field."* Every churchyard served as a burial ground, consecrated earth dedicated to God. The term God's Acre has become a traditional designation of the Moravian Church of German origin. Henry Wadsworth Longfellow (1807 – 1882) memorialized the term in his poem, <u>God's Acre!</u> (1866). Longfellow wrote: *"I like that ancient Saxon phrase, which calls the burial-ground God's Acre! It is just; It consecrates each grave within its walls and breathes a benison o'er the sleeping dust...."*

GOD SHYNESS – (*GOD SHY*-ness) A fear of faith. A term coined by psychiatrist and Holocaust survivor Viktor Frankl (1905 – 1997). God shyness is being afraid to surrender. It is the fear of letting go and letting God.

GOD VERSUS JESUS – (*GOD VER*-ses *JEE*-sus) God is Spirit, whereas Jesus was a man. God is an innate, inherent feeling in all human beings, everywhere. Jesus was a historical figure that must be taught to human beings. Therefore, I've always known God, I learned about Jesus. Jesus, like you and I, was natural.

God is Supernatural. The worship of God is spiritual. The worship of Jesus is cultural. Everyone worships God, but only informed Christians worship Jesus. Jesus was created by God, as were we. God was not created. God does not need a religion, church, priests, and gospels to be understood, as does Jesus. People don't need to be converted to God by missionaries, as they do in order to understand Jesus. The worship of God is inspirational. The worship of Jesus is instructional, institutional. No one was ever martyred for not believing in God. Atrocious atrocities were committed for accepting or not accepting Jesus. Was Jesus the Son of God? Of course! But so are you and me. The Church made Jesus, but God made us all. *"If God and Christ were equal then Christ should be called God's brother, not God's Son."* – Theologian Arius (256 – 336 CE). *"There was a time when Jesus was not."* – Arius. *"What is God? – The Mind of the Universe. What is God? – All that you see, and all that you don't see."* – Seneca (c. 4 BCE – 65 CE) Roman Philosopher.

GOETHE'S NYN REQUIREMENTS – (*GUR*-tuh's nyn re-*KWY*-yer-ments) Johann Wolfgang von Goethe (1749 – 1832), philosopher, writer, and diplomat devised 9 imperatives necessary for a good life. *Health*: Enough to make work a pleasure. *Wealth*: Enough to support your needs. *Strength*: Enough to battle with difficulties and forsake them. *Grace*: Enough to confess your sins and overcome them. *Patience*: Enough to toil until some good is accomplished. *Charity*: Enough to see some good in your neighbor.

Love: Enough to move you to be useful and helpful to others. *Faith*: Enough to make real the things of God. *Hope*: Enough to remove all anxious fears concerning the future.

GOETHE'S REQUIREMENTS – (*GER*-tahs re-*KWY*-er-ments) the great German Philosopher Johann Wolfgang von Goethe (1749 – 1832) devised 9 requirements which are perfectly applicable for our time. The master had said*: "There are 9 requirements for contented living: HEALTH enough to make work a pleasure; WEALTH enough to support your needs; STREGTH enough to battle with difficulties and forsake them; GRACE enough to confess tour sins and overcome them; PATIENCE enough to toil until some good is accomplished; CHARITY enough to see some good in your neighbor; LOVE enough to move you to be useful and helpful to others; FAITH enough to make real the things of God; HOPE enough to remove all anxious fears concerning the future."* God bless Lutheran Saint Goethe.

GO FULL MAGA – (goh full *MA*-guh) MAGA is an acronym for Make America Great Again, Donald Trump's (b. 1946) phony campaign slogan. The term MAGA has become associated with Trump and all the nonsense he represents. MAGAmaniacs are Trump's cult devotees. Their devotion to Trump has traumatized and mesmerized Republican politicians. Trump has hijacked the Republican Party. Any Republican politician who wants to remain at his or her job must become Trumpublicans. This is Going Full MAGA. They must adopt Trump's lies, conspiracies, hatreds, and absurdities. They must declare fealty to Lord Trump like a feudal serf. They must surrender their integrity, pride, and self-respect to placate the Trump. To Go Full MAGA is to submit to Trump as to a Medieval Pope. History will not look kindly of the Republican Trump ass- kissers. *"Politicians in Washington would sell their own mothers to stay in power."* – Republican Senator Lindsey Graham (b. 1955). Takes one to know one.

GOFUNDME – (GoFundMe) (goh-FUHND-mee) An American social crowdfunding platform that collects charitable contributions for victims of accidents, tragedies, illnesses, any challenging circumstances, as well as celebrations. Whatever the circumstances, GoFundMe helps to help the helpless. GoFundMe was founded by Brad Damphousse (born c. 1982) and Andrew Ballester in Redwood, California its headquarters in 2010. The company has offices in San Diego, and Dublin Ireland, with operations in France, Spain, Italy, Germany, and the United Kingdom. Initially, GoFundMe was a for profit organization. It gleaned 5% from each donation. But with success and stability, GoFundMe dropped the donation fee. Like all companies, GoFundMe has employees and overhead bills to pay. Therefore, it must charge a 2.9% processing fee plus 30 cents ($0.30) per donation. GoFundMe will accept gratuities or *"tips"* as well. GoFundMe makes charity more convenient. From 2010 to 2020, GoFundMe has collected over $9 billion dollars from over 120 million donors for worthy causes. *"Charity is no substitute for justice withheld."* – St. Augustine (354 – 430 CE).

GOIDELIC – (goy-*DELL*-lick) The ancient language of the Gaulic Celts (in France). Goidelic was a proto-Gaelic tongue.

GOING POSTAL – (*GO*-ing *POST*-tal) To go violently insane in a fit of rage. The term originated from a series of shooting at the U.S. Postal Service (in post offices) by overworked employees who had become unglued.

GOITER – (*GOY*-ter) An enlargement of the thyroid gland at the front and sides of the neck, usually symptomatic of abnormal thyroid secretion, especially *hypothyroidism* due to a lack of iodine in the diet. The thyroid gland produces the hormone *thyroxin,* essential for the regulation of metabolic rate and protein synthesis. The thyroid needs iodine to produce thyroxin. Iodine is a dietary mineral. If iodine is lacking in the diet, the thyroid gland will swell greatly, in an attempt to absorb more iodine. This is the goiter. Some regions have iodine- poor soil. This is true of some mountainous regions, as in parts of the Alps. It is critical to ingest *iodized* salt.

GOLAN HEIGHTS – (*GO*-lan *HYTS*) (also Al Jawlan) A hilly plateau located in Syria that overlooks the Jordan River and the Sea of Galilee. This strategic location has been occupied by Israel and is a lightning rod for conflict.

GOLABKI – (go-*WUMP*-kee: In Polish, the diacritical slash across the letter L, gives it a W sound.) Polish Stuffed cabbage rolls. Boiled cabbage leaves stuffed with minced-meat (beef and pork) and rice, with diced onion added, topped with stewed tomatoes, cooked in a roastpan. The term actually means *"pigeon,"* referring to the fist-sized cabbage rolls. Golabki is sometimes popularly called *"pig-in-a-blanket."* Incidentally: The champion Golabki cook of Hamtramck – Detroit, Michigan was Mrs. Dolores M. Pasieka (1928 – 2018).

GOLD – (*GOHLD*) (Au) The name gold is an Old Saxon term, the Latin being *aurum,* which provides its chemical symbol. The 79 protons in its nucleus give gold its atomic number. Gold is a rare precious metal with a yellow luster, long used as currency. Most of Earth's gold was deposited billions of years ago during meteor bombardments. Nature gold is not 100% pure. It is mixed with other metals. Most of the gold mined in American is about 85% pure, right out of the rock. Lustrous gold is malleable, ductile and inert (incorrodible) which makes for fine jewelry. The oldest gold jewelry was fashioned about 6,000 years ago. The oldest stash of gold jewelry was discovered in Bulgaria, about 6,000 years ago. Perhaps only sex has generated more lust throughout history than has gold. Gold is 14 million times scarcer than iron. The rarity of gold adds to its preciousness. All the gold ever mined would only fill 3 Olympic-sized swimming pools, or will cover a tennis court, 30 feet high. Gold is almost indestructible. There is nothing in nature that can dissolve gold. It is inert, and will not naturally react with other elements. The gold that was in Cleopatra's neckless, Mansa Musa's staff, or Montezuma's crown may be in your wedding band. Today, perhaps 2/3 of the world's accessible gold is deposited in the Niger River region of West Africa. Incidentally: Most of the planet's gold is beyond man's greedy reach, in the Earth's molten core. Only one percent of the iron/nickel core is gold. Nevertheless, that is enough gold to cover all the land on Earth, knee deep! By the way, the ancient Inca believed that gold way the solidified sweat of their sun-god.

GOLD COAST – (*GOHLD COHST*) The European colonial name for Ghana. The Gold Coast was the great Kingdom of Asante, a rich source of gold and slaves [read: *"Black Gold"*]. When the slave trade was abolished, the Asante economy collapsed. The British attacked the Asante Kingdom, capturing a strip of territory along the sea, calling in Gold Coast (1867). The Asante Kingdom was landlocked. Six years later the British incorporated all of the Asante lands into the Gold Coast colony.

GOLD DIGGER – (*GOHLD DIG*-ger) A women who pursues a man for his money. The willing victim is usually a rich elderly male (sugar daddy), while the assailant (gold digger) is sometimes a gum-snapping bimbo half his age, with a buxom body. Both the gold digger and sugar daddy are fulfilling a need, using each other. As writer Warren Farrell (b. 1943) wrote in <u>*The Liberated Man*</u> (1993): *"Men use women as sex objects; women use men as security objects."*

GOLDEN EGGS – (*GOHL*-den *AYGS*) This reference is taken from *"The Goose that Laid the Golden Eggs,"* by the great Greek fabulist (and slave) Aesop (c. 620 – 564 BCE). Long ago and far away, a poor farmer luckily acquired a magic goose that laid eggs of gold, one at a time. The farmer became wealthy, and as wealthy people tend to do, became greedy. In fact, the impatient farmer was overcome with greed. So he impulsively cut the goose open to get all the golden eggs at once. But alas, there were no golden eggs, and now no more goose. Greedy capitalists should take note, and learn from this ancient wisdom. Their workers are the producers of their gold. Their customers are the providers of their gold. Pay your workers a pittance, move their jobs to China, and your workers will not be able to buy your products. Raise prices greedily, and none of the consumers will be able to purchase what you manufacture. You'll be killing the goose that laid your golden eggs. Most greedy corporate capitalists learn this lesson after their goose is cooked.

GOLDEN CALF – (*GOHL*-den *CAFF*) A symbol of idolatry, or any form of false worship, like the worship of money. In the story of the Ten Commandments, Moses ascended Mount Sinai and remained for 40 days. The people believed that the old man had perished in the wilderness. They demanded that his older brother Aaron fashion the golden calf. *"And Aaron received the gold from their hand and fashioned it with a graving tool and made a golden calf. And they said, these are your gods, O Israel, who brought you up out of the land of Egypt!"* – Exodus 32:4. Could this have been a great misunderstanding? Perhaps the Hebrew were following an Egyptian custom and creating a monument to their fallen leader and deliverer Moses. Therefore, the golden calf did not represent a god, but symbolized Moses. The incident became a tragic misunderstanding when the priestly Tribe of Levi executed 3,000 Hebrew *"calf worshippers."* But Aaron was the Chief Priest, the leader of the Tribe of Levi. He was not executed, and he built the golden calf. Indeed, God works in mysterious ways.

GOLDEN HORSESHOE – (*GOHL*-den *HORS*-shoo) The region between Oshua and Windsor, Ontario, Canada's auto industry area. Windsor is conveniently across the Detroit River from the Motor City. Of course, the auto companies, Ford, Chrysler, and General Motors are all American owned corporations.

GOLDEN HOUR – (*GOHL*-den *OUW*-er) In medical parlance, the crucial 60 minutes or so after a severe physical trauma, when life can be saved. After a serious accident, a victim may be in shock, hemorrhaging blood, depriving the body, especially the brain of oxygen. Under such life-threatening conditions, medical professionals may have but one vital hour to save the victim's life, the golden hour.

GOLDEN PARACHUTE – (*GOHL*-den *PAR*-ra-shoot) A corporate bail-out bribe. The multi-million dollar severance packages given to capitalist CEO's to force them to leave without trouble. They cannot be allowed to leave angry, for they know too many corporate secrets. Only in capitalism, can a leader ruin a company and get rewarded for doing it. Corporate capitalist CEO's are *"Too big to fail, too big to assail."*

GOLDEN RULE – (*GOHL*-den *ROOL*) The law of compassionate reciprocity. The most recognized and simplistically profound moral imperative in the world. The great Pastor Harry Emerson Fosdick (1878 – 1969) had written that *"To keep the Golden Rule we must put ourselves in other people's places, but to do that consists in and depends upon picturing ourselves in their places."* The Golden Rule, like everything righteous, is inherently, Spiritually Socialistic. In the positive, the Golden Rule exhorts one to *"Do to others what you would want others to do to you."* In the negative it entreats one *"Not to do to others what you would not want done to you."* The Golden Rule has been the admonishment of every avatar and appears in every holy book on Earth. In Luke 6:31, Jesus declared: *"As you wish that would do to you, do so to them."* *"What you do not want done to yourself, do not do to others."* – Confucius (551 – 479 BCE) in Analects 15: XXIII. Philosopher Immanuel Kant (1724 – 1804) referred to the Golden Rule as the *"Categorical Imperative."* Kant's rendition advised us to *"Act only according to that maxim whereby you can, at the same time, will that it should become a universal law."* In simpler words, *"Act the way you would want everyone in the world to act."* Incidentally: The most efficient way to assure compliance with the Golden Rule is to fantasies that everyone can read your mind.

GOLDEN RULE – (*GOHL*-den *ROOL*) This moral imperative of human interaction appears in every religion past, present, and future. An ancient Egyptian proverb admonished: *"That which you hate to be done to you, do not do to another."* The following are examples from some of the world's major faiths. <u>Hinduism</u>: *"This is the sum of duty; do naught onto others what you would not have them do into you."* – Mahabharata 5, 1517. <u>Zoroastrianism</u>: *"That nature alone is good which refrains from doing another whatsoever is not good for itself."* – Dadisten-I-dinik, 94, 5. <u>Taoism</u>: *"Regard your neighbor's gain as your gain, and your neighbor's loss as your loss."* – Tai Shang Kan Yin P'ien. <u>Jainism</u>: *"One should treat all creatures in the world as one would like to be treated."* – Mahavira Sutrakritanga. <u>Judaism</u>: *"What is hateful to you, do not do to your fellowman. This is the entire Law; all the rest is commentary."* – Talmud, Shabbat 3id. <u>Buddhism</u>: *"Hurt no others in ways that you yourself would find hurtful."* – Udana – Varga 5, 1. <u>Confucianism</u>: *"Do not do to others what you would not like yourself. Then there will be no resentment against you, either in the family or in the state."* – Analects 12: II. <u>Greek Philosophy</u>: *"Do not do to others what would anger you if done to you by others."* – Isocrates (436 – 338 BCE). <u>Christianity</u>: *"All things whatsoever ye would that men should do to you, do you so to them; for this is the law of the prophets."* – Jesus in Matthew 7:1. <u>Islam</u>: *"No one of you is a believer until he desires for his brother that which he desires for himself."* – Sunnah. Post Script: Karmic Corollary to Golden Rule: *"Do unto others as you would have others do unto you. For eventually, others will do unto you, as you have done unto others."*

GOLDEN SHOWER – (*GOHL*-den *SHAUW*-wer) A sexual *"water sport."* A golden shower is a rather eccentric sexual practice in which one stands naked above another naked individual and urinates. A tinge of sadomasochism can be read into this exotic erotic ritual. Nevertheless, according to sexologist Alfred Kinsey (1894 – 1956): *"The only unnatural sex act is that which you cannot perform."* Is a golden shower sanitary, safe? According to the online encyclodictionary of sex, *Freakypedia: "There's not much difference in drinking someone's pee than eating their pussy."* Therefore, being sprayed by urine is certainly harmless. In fact, Masai mothers in Africa use cow urine, and Mongol mothers in Mongolia use horse urine to wash their babies. The ammonia in urine, which provides the pungent odor, also provides the antiseptic. One famous case of golden shower was discovered by Harvard Professor William L. Langer (1896 – 1877). Langer was commissioned by the Office of Strategic Services (now CIA) to produce a psychological profile of Adolf Hitler (1889 – 1945) during the war. The love of Adolf's life was his niece Angela *"Geli"* Raubal (1908 – 1931). Dr. Langer discovered that Hitler would demand that Geli stand nude over his naked body. After examining her genitalia and becoming sexually aroused, she was ordered to urinate on the Fuhrer, (a golden shower), at which time Adolf would masturbate. This practice is perfectly acceptable between consenting adults. But Geli was compelled and repulsed, calling the ritual *"The Performance."* In 1931, Geli shot herself in the heart, so it was reported. Incidentally: According to the <u>*Trump – Russia Dossier*</u> (*"Steele Dossier"*) by MI6 Officer Christopher Steele (b. 1964) and the book, <u>*Russian Roulette: The Inside Story of Putin's War* *on America and the Election of Donald Trump*</u> (2018), by investigative reporters Michael Isikoff (b. 1952) and David Corn (b. 1959), Donald Trump participated in golden showers with several Russian prostitutes during the Miss Universe Pageant in Moscow (2013). This fact was verified by former FBI Director James Comey (b. 1960) in his book, <u>*A Higher Loyalty*</u> (2018). Comey stated that Trump and prostitutes peed on each other and the escapade was secretly videoed by the Russians. This porn flick that Vladimir Putin (b. 1952) is holding over Trump's head is called the *"Pee Tape."* This may account for Trump's slavish public admiration for Putin. The dictator is blackmailing the potential-dictator. This should not be shocking considering Donald Trump, *"President Pig."* Post Script: *"This is the end of my Presidency. I'm fucked!"* – Donald Trump.

GOLDEN WINDOW – (*GOHL*-den *WIN*-doh) A medical term for that 72-hour period when life hangs in the balance. This applies to a person who had been seriously injured and desperately needs medical attention. The initial 60 minute period is called the golden hour. The term *"golden window"* most often applies to people trapped under rubble, as after an earthquake, or similar disaster. It is nothing short of a miracle that a human being can survive 3 days, crushed under debris with no water. But miracles do happen, even to babies.

GOLDFISH – (*GOHLD*-fish) (Carassius auratus) A freshwater fish native to China, a member of the carp family along with the koi. *"Little Goldie"* in the fishbowl seems harmless. Don't be fooled. Goldfish can be troublesome, even dangerous. Goldfish were first selectively bred by the Imperial Chinese Court well over a thousand years ago, during the Jin Dynasty (266 – 420 CE). Today, they are becoming an ecological problem in North America and Australia. Goldfish have invaded the Great Lakes. Starting in 2013, it was noticed that the invasive carp had declined, but their cousin the goldfish have increased. Pet owners have released the goldfish into the natural environment. They had made their way into the Great Lakes. Feral fish lose their gold and turn silvery- gray. To be bright gold in the wild with no great defense mechanisms is not advantageous. In a large body of water with plenty of food, they can grow very large. So far, the biggest caught weighed 9 pounds. Too, they can live and procreate for 40 years. There are tens-of-millions of goldfish in the Great Lakes alone. Veracious goldfish are dangerous, in that they compete with native species for food. Too, they are muddying the clear water. Goldfish are not the cleanest fish. They are bottom feeders. So they disturb the substrate or sediment, mixing it up making the water turbid and murky. This stops the growing of vegetation, upsetting the entire foodchain. Furthermore, these wild goldfish are dangerous to people. They ingest a lot of harmful contaminants like fertilizers, industrial chemicals, and heavy metals. When the goldfish become prey, consumed by larger game fish, the toxins are passed up the foodchain to humans. Goldfish present the most challenging problem of all Great Lakes invasive species.

GOLDILOCKS EFFECT – (*GOHL*-dee-locks ef-*FECT*) The many astounding ways in which the Earth has been serendipitously or providentially blessed in scores of ways to make the plant livable for plants and animals. Like Goldilocks' porridge, Earth is "*not too hot, not too cold but just right.*" So is our planets position in the solar system, the distance from the sun and moon, the tilt of the axis, the time of rotation and revolution, the ozone layer, the magnetic field, the amount of water, the chemical composition of the air, the ability to control fire. Everywhere we are comfortably between extremes, making Earth a miracle planet.

GOLDILOCKS ZONE – (*GOHL*-dee-locks *ZONE*) The habitable zone. The placement and position of planet Earth in the solar system in relations to the Sun. Being just over 93 million miles from our star, Earth is not too hot, and not too cold, but just right (like Goldilocks' porridge). Every living organism needs water. If the Earth was too close to the Sun, our water would boil into steam. If the Earth was too far from the Sun, our water would freeze into ice. In fact, the first planets that exobiologists examine for extraterrestrial life are planets in the goldilocks zone.

GOLD MINING – (*GOHLD MINE*-ning) The activity of seeking and extracting the rare precious metal gold. The 2 methods are alluvial prospecting, and hard-rock burrowing. Alluvial prospecting consists of panning for small nuggets and gold dust, washed down into a stream from the motherload, deep in the mountain. This is a simple, solitary, small-time means of gold mining. Sand and gravel is scooped from the creek and swirled in the pan. Gold being 8 times heavier than sand will sink to the bottom of the pan, as the sand and water are flushed out. As the debris is extracted, the heavier gold will settle at the bottom of the pan. One tends to find alluvial gold on the inside bend of running rivers, usually mixed in heavy black sand. Hard-rock gold mining is an industrial procedure. Heavy equipment must drill into the mountain, blast and tunnel to the site of the motherload. Geologically, hot liquid quartz cools and hardens into crystals. The liquid quartz is impregnated with gold. The hot fluid concentrates the gold in veins of quartz. Gold deposits are a geological rarity. The biggest concentrations are in Australia, China, South Africa, Peru, and the Western U.S.

GOLD STAR – (*GOHLD* stahr) Refers to mothers, fathers, wives, and husbands who have lost a loved one while serving in the military. This especially pertains to the loss of a loved one in combat. One may tragically become a Gold Star mother, Gold Star father, Gold Star wife, or Gold Star husband. If the family member had not been killed, a Blue Star is displayed in the window. Incidentally: In September, 2020, it was disclosed that President Donald Trump (b. 1946) had disparaged all military personnel, living or dead. He had referred to them as "*suckers!*" and "*losers!*" This was the "*Commander-in-Chief*" of the military speaking, no less!

GOLDWATERED-DOWN MAGA – (*GOLD*-waw-ter'd down *MA*-ga) Bring down MAGA with the terrible truth of a Trump Presidency. The Democratic Party must blitz the airwaves with the dire threat of Donald Trump (b. 1946), as they did about Barry Goldwater (1909 – 1998) in 1964. Republican Senator Barry Goldwater was a warmonger. He was reckless concerning relations with the Soviet Union. He put America in danger. Trump is infinitely more dangerous, particularly to democracy and liberty. President Joe

Biden (b. 1942) must attack Trump the way President Lyndon Johnson (1908 – 1973) successfully attacked Goldwater. Trump's *"Project 2025"* must be revealed as his *"Mein Kampf."* The MAGA Nazification plan for America must be spelled out, simply, in all its horror. In 1964, the Democrats scared Americans into voting for Johnson. As a result, LBJ won 44 states, with over 61% of the vote. That's what the Democrats have to do to MAGA Trump in 2024. To hell with Biden's age! It doesn't matter who the Democrats run, because the election is between Trump and Democracy. This election is about beating Trump and saving America. *"Now, I'm going home, have six or seven drinks, and go to bed."* – Senator Barry Goldwater on election night, November 3, 1964.

GOLDWATER RULE – (*GOHLD*-waut-ter *ROOL*) An order in the American Psychiatric Association's code of ethics. The Goldwater Rule states that it is unethical for psychiatrists to give a professional opinion about a public figure they have not examined in person. They must obtained consent from the individual to discuss their mental health in public statements. The rule is named after 1964 Republican presidential candidate Barry Goldwater (1909 – 1998). The issue arose when *FACT* published the article *"The Unconscious of a Conservative: A Special Issue on the Mind of Barry Goldwater."* The magazine polled psychiatrists about Senator Barry Goldwater and whether he was mentally fit to serve as president. Goldwater sued for libel and was awarded $75,000. Thus emerged the Goldwater Rule.

GOLF – (*GAULF*) (Golfer, Golfing) A silly game in which clubs with wooden or metal heads are used to hit a small hard, white ball into a number of holes, usually 9 or 18, in succession. The holes in the ground are situated at various distances over a grassy course having natural and artificial obstacles. The object of the game is to get the ball into each hole in as few strokes as possible. The term *"golf"* entered the English language from the Scottish *"gouf,"* which was first recorded in 1457. The term "gouf" derived from the Middle Dutch word *"colf"* meaning a *"bat, stick, or club."* Golf is a patrician pastime indulged by the affluent. It is especially favored by the retired rich. Many a fat, wealthy shareholder had dropped dead on the golf course. Hilariously, this child's game of hitting a small ball into a hole with a stick has been made into a science, with coaches, instructors, lessons, exercises, books, videos, techniques, high-tech sticks, and workshops. Golf is the most selfish, wasteful use of the finest real estate yet contrived by capitalism. This prime private property should be nationalized, socialized as public parks, playgrounds, picnic areas, and nature walks. All the U.S. golf courses combined would be larger than the State of Delaware. By the way, in case of nuclear war or pandemic plague, golf courses have been secretly slated by the government to serve as mass graveyards. (You won't even need to hold membership anymore – egalitarian eligibility at last.) Incidentally: Palm Springs, California, the playground of the stars, has more golf courses per square mile than anyplace else in America. Too, the oldest golf course in the Caribbean is in Mandeville, Manchester Parish, Jamaica (1865). Footnote: By the end of *July, 2019,* President Donald Trump had spent 123 days golfing, 20% of his term in office. His travel and security to his golf courses had cost the taxpayer $72,181,957 to date. It probably doubled today. *"They have been playing golf for over 800 years and nobody has a satisfactorily said why."* – British-American Journalist Alistair Cooke (1908 – 2004).

G.O.L.F. – (*GAULF*) The popular myth for the etymology of the word *"golf."* The story goes that G.O.L.F. is an acronym for <u>G</u>entlemen <u>O</u>nly <u>L</u>adies <u>F</u>orbidden. Apparently, this is not true. But this story is repeated so often, and is so intriguing, that if it isn't true, at least it ought to be! The legend has it that when golf was first invented in the early 15th century Scotland, ladies [read: *wives, daughters, sisters, mothers*] where not allowed on the premises. Prostitutes were welcomed, but they were not considered to be proper *"ladies."* (This is why the gentlemen forbad their ladies from attending.) Of course, golf enabled the gentlemen to intercourse at the course, a safe place to *"tee-off."* (Why is Donald Trump (b. 1946) so obsessed with golf courses?) The 18 holes was not a vulgar reference to group orgies. There happens to be 18 shots in one bottle of Scotch whiskey. The Scottish gentlemen would take a shot, after each shot. When the bottle ended, so did the silly game. Golf is still a silly and expensive pastime of the rich. In fact, golf is to the patricians what bowling is to the plebeians. Incidentally: The real etymology of the word *"golf"* derived from the 15th century Scottish word *"gouf,"* which was taken from the Middle Dutch *"colf,"* meaning *"stick, bat, club."* The British-American Journalist, Alistair Cooke (1908 – 2004) perspicaciously analyzed the game of golf: *"To get an elementary grasp of the game of golf, a human must learn, by endless practice, a continuous and subtle series of highly unnatural movements, involving about sixty-four muscles, that result in a seemingly natural swing, taking two seconds to begin and end."* A Conficta: *"Mr. Smith shot a birdie; Mr. Brown shot par; Mr. Jones shot a bogey; in the clubhouse bar."*

GOLLIWOG – (*GOl*-ee-wog) A demeaning Black fictional character created by the American-born English cartoonist, Florence Kate Upton (1873 – 1922). Golliwog was a racists degrading depiction of a Negro that Ms. Upton created for a series of late 19th century children's stories. Golliwog was later represented as a grotesque rag doll. The doll was black with huge white eyes and big red lips. It sported a clownish frizzy hairdo. Golliwog was a creature of an insensitive time of imperialism and Eurocentric White supremacy, especially in arrogant Great Britain, and toward colonials.

GOMCHENS – (*GOM*-chens) Buddhist lamas known for their extreme mysticism. The mystic Gomchens of Tibet are contrasted with the practical Zen Buddhist monks of Japan.

GONADS – (*GO*-nads) Internal sex organs: the female ovaries and the male testes (testicles). Gonads are glands, to be confused with genitals (penis and vagina) which are external sex organs.

GO NATIVE – (*GO NAY*-tiv) To live *au naturel*. More specifically, *"going native"* refers to women defying the trend to shave their legs, armpits, or pubic hair. It has become stylish for ladies to denude their genitalia, appearing like pre-pubescent girls. Skimpy bikinis may have prompted the habit. Noticeable pubic hair seems strangely embarrassing. Perhaps it's a subliminal pedophilia among some men that encouraged women to shave. Whatever the reason, the unnatural shaving is considered to be sexy. Ironically, pubic and armpit hair exists to waft sex pheromones which heighten passionate excitement. It is therefore biologically sexier to simply go native. Incidentally: According to the Koran, the Queen of Sheba had gone native. *"Queen Sheba's legs and feet were hairy like the legs of an ass. Solomon desired to marry her, but he disliked the hair upon her legs. So the devils made for him the depilatory of quicklime, wherewith Sheba removed the hair, and Solomon married her."*

GONDWANALAND – (gond-*WA*-na-land) A great southern landmass that broke away from the global continent *Pangaea* about 200 million years ago. Gondwanaland consisted of present day Africa, India, Australia, Antarctica, and South America. Its northern counterpart was *Laurasia* (North America and Eurasia). Gondwanaland was created by perpetual continental drift, driven by tectonic forces in the Earth.

GONE FISH'EN – (gawn *FISH*-en) The manifest, prosaic meaning of gone fish'en is to go angling, to catch by hook aquatic animals for food, sport, or recreation. But latently, gone fish'en is a euphemism for getting away on one's own. In bygone days, a sign on the shop door reading: *"Gone Fish'en"* meant *"closed for the day."* (The implication was: *"I had enough for one day."*) It pertains almost exclusively to males. Men are basically solitary by nature. Unlike women, men have few friends – many acquaintances – but few friends. For example, the husband's friends are usually arrived at by way of the wife. Periodically, men need to be alone, a respite from the wife. If a man can't get away, he may go silent for a spell, withdraw within himself. This is natural. Dr. John Gray (b. 1951) highlighted this point in his perspicacious popular study: *"Men are from Mars, Women are from Venus,"* (1992). Gray explained that when women are depressed or troubled, they seek companionship with their coterie of friends to talk, to vent, to talk and talk. Men, on the other hand, need to go out into the wilderness, so to speak, in order to brood and think, alone. The difference between the genders is hardwired in the female and male brain. Therapy for men is *"going fishing."* Philosopher Henry David Thoreau (1817 – 1862) understood this truth. Thoreau wrote: *"Many men go fishing all of their lives without knowing that it is not fish they are after."*

GONE SOUTH – (gawn *SOUWTH*) (also, Go South, Heading South) An expression to indicate that something had went wrong and is heading for failure. *"After he quit, the entire business had gone south."* What has gone south has depreciated in value. Alternately, gone south means to disappear, escape, vanish. As early as 18th century Colonial America, it was recorded that Indians believed that their souls went south after death. Perhaps this can be the genesis of the term.

GONE WEST – (gawn *WEST*) A euphemism for death. The far West has been considered the abode of the dead in several cultures from time immemorial. After all the sun sets or *"dies"* in the west daily. In the Ancient Greek epic the *Odyssey* (Book XI), Odysseus needed to seek advice from a seer in the land of the dead. To do this, he sailed to the far west. To the ancients of the Mediterranean, Europe, and Africa, the Atlantic, the great unknown to the west was the place of no return. In colonial and early America, to have gone west was a life-or-death gamble. Wild terrain, wild animals, and wild Indians were encountered by the pioneers. That's why, in the cultivated East, as well as in Europe, the term *"Gone West"* meant death, through the period of World War One (1914 – 1918), according to historian Alistair Cooke (1908 – 2004).

GONNA, GOTTA, WANNA – (*GUN*-na, *GOT*-uh, WONN-na) These three terms are contractions, or informal reductions. Despite their awkward sound in a spoken sentence, they are not said to be pronunciational corruptions. Gonna is a contraction for *"going to,"* gotta for *"got to,"* wanna for *"want to."* One might hear: *"We're gonna finish the job."* Or: *"I gotta get going."* Or: *"I wanna surf."* Neither usage is Standard English. Outside of literary dialogue, one will not read these words in formal print. They are mere speech affectations, primarily American. A linguist from Detroit's Wayne State University commented: *"Linguists would not consider these forms to be corrupted – not at all. Instead, the term often used for "gonna," "gotta," and "wanna" is "contracted" forms, in the sense of contracting two words into one, and there are some interestingsyntactic rules and restrictions that apply to such contractions, which are of interest to theoretical syntax."*

GONORRHEA – (gon-nor-*REE*-a) A sexually transmitted disease caused by the bacterium *Neisseria gonorrhoeae.* Gonorrhea is characterized by inflammation of the mucous membranes of the genital and urinary tracts, an acute discharge of pus, and painful urination, especially in men. Women often have no symptoms, making the infection more insidious. Being a bacterial disease, gonorrhea can be eradicated with antibiotics.

GONZO – (*GON*-zoh) Weird, crazy, eccentric. The term *"gonzo"* entered American English in 1971, first as *"gonzo journalism,"* which was popularized by investigative reporter and author Hunter S. Thompson (1937 – 2005). In gonzo journalism, the reporter becomes part of the story, interacting with the principals, often under-cover. (Thompson risked his life by infiltrating and exposing the *Hell's Angels*.) *"The only way to write honestly about the scene is to be part of it."* – Hunter S. Thompson. In 1972, Thompson said he borrowed the term gonzo journalism from <u>The Boston Globe</u> editor, Bill Cardossa (1937 – 2006). Thompson said that gonzo is *"some Boston word for weird, bizarre."* Actually, *"gonzo"* is a Neapolitan Italian word meaning *"rude,"* as a rude sot or drunk. At any rate, the term gonzo has expanded to be applied to fields outside of journalism. In the adult film industry, *"gonzo pornography"* is an attempt to draw the viewer into the scene. It tries to create the illusion that the spectator is a participant in the orgy. You are being inserted into the drama, along with the male member. The viewer is literally becoming a *"fucking partner."* This genre of adult film was pioneered by Jamie Gillis (1943 – 2010) in his *"On the Prowl"* series of the late 1980s and early 1990s. With this technique, the camera is positioned above, below, and even inside the copulating couple when possible. The picture angle favors close-up, tight shots of the genitalia engaging, rather than broad body shots. Again, the attempt is to share the orgasm with the audience. You are being inserted into the drama, along with male member. You are literally become a *"fucking partner."* Gonzo porn caters to the hardcore virtual voyeur, the Triple XXX connoisseur. *"The only unnatural sex act is that which you cannot perform."* – Sexologist Alfred Kinsey (1894 – 1956). Incidentally: Serious research was conducted on salesmen who overnighted in hotels. Thousands who purchased pornographic movies were polled. It was discovered that the average guy watched they skin-flick for only 7 minutes after which he masturbated and fell asleep. *"Crazy man, Crazy,"* as the beatniks would say.

GOOCH – (*GOOCH*) The perineum or crotch region. The area between the scrotum and anus in males, and the vulva and anus in females. The gooch is a highly sensitive erogenous zone. It serves as the midpoint between the ass and genitals. Another slang term for gooch is *"taint."* Taint is a folksy rendition of *"ain't."* That's because this fleshy region ain't the ass and ain't the genitals. The gooch is erotically responsive to a good licking.

GOOD/BAD – (*GOOD BAD*) The basic diametrically opposed states of consciousness. Being good or bad is a personal characterological state of being. Some, particularly conservative philosophers will try to blur the borders between good and bad by referring to those terms as merely subjective adjectives. They are wrong. There are more – much, much more to being good or bad. Beneath the semantics and sophistry is the bedrock of fact and truth. Given examples, people of all cultures will agree on what is good and what is bad. The good are righteous, the bad are evil. The good are forgiving, the bad or vengeful. The good are honest, the bad are deceitful. The good are generous, the bad are covetous. The good will agree to: *"Treat others as I wish to be treated."* The bad will ask: *"What's in it for me."* The good will agree that: *"I am my brother's keeper."* The bad will argue that: *"I got mine, to hell with you."* The religiously oriented would insist that the good are or the side of God, while the bad are on the side of Satan. So *good* and *bad* correspond to what is *right* and *wrong*. Freedom is good, and bondage is bad. That's why democracy is paramount over fascism. Sharing is good and hoarding is bad. That's why Socialism is paramount over capitalism. However, with the advent of amoral Donald Trump (b. 1946) the definitions of good and bad have been blurred, adulterated. Among Trump supporters, including Republicans, *good* means *win,* and *bad* means *lose.* Therefore anything goes. Lying, cheating, bribing, stealing, law breaking are all good, if they lead to winning. To be honest is bad if it results in loss. Even the destruction of democracy, and the establishment of fascism is good if it guarantees winning. According to this philosophy of morality, the ends always justify the means. In fact, the means are meaningless. Of course, the end result of winning is holding power. The main reason to hold power is to hoard wealth. This is bad. *"We penetrated deeper and deeper into the heart of darkness."* – Joseph Conrad (1857 – 1924). *"My means are sane, my motives and my object mad."* – Herman Melville (1819 – 1891). Incidentally: In the post-Trump era, the ultra-MAGA Trumpublicans have substituted *"losing"* for bad, and *"winning"* for good.

GOOD/BAD COP – (good bad *KOP*) (actually Good Cop, Bad Cop) A cop is a police officer. This is not a reference to ethical or corrupt police officers. "Good cop, bad cop" is an interrogation technique or ploy used to wrench information or confessions from criminal suspects. One officer, the bad cop acts the part of an intimidating bully. He upsets the suspect by screaming in his face, pounding the table, and kicking over the chair, threatening the victim. It's all a violent act. The point is to scare and wear down the victim. The bad cop departs the room, and the good cop takes over. This officer speaks softly, playing the part of a friend. The good cop offers coffee and a cigarette. He gently asks the same questions as the bad cop. The good cop tries to win the suspect over emotionally. Too he warns the suspect that the bad cop will soon return, in a worse mood. Often, the suspect relents, cooperates out of relief and gratitude, providing the sought after information. The *"good cop, bad cop"* treatment works with young, inexperienced criminals. Veteran offenders will not fall for this trick.

GOODBYE – (good-*BY*) Farewell, a conventional expression used at a friendly parting. In Spanish it is *"adios,"* in French it is *"adieu."* Both *"dios"* and *"dieu"* mean God. In other words, *"Go in the care of God."* In English, goodbye evolved from the phrase: *"God be with you."* The phrase gradually eroded over time to *"God be wy you,"* in the 16th century, to *"God b'y you"* in the 17th century. By the 18th century, people were bidding each other *"God bye."* Alas, in the 19th century, we recognized God's goodness, but substituted good for God, with the departing salutation, *"goodbye."* Therefore, when you bid a person goodbye, you are blessing them as well – sort of. *"It's the emptiest and yet fullest of all messages: 'Good-bye'."* – Kurt Vonnegut (1922 – 2007).

GOOD HURT – (*GOOD* herht) Not a reference to the exotic eroticism of *BDSM* (Bondage Discipline SadoMasacism) in this case. The term *"good hurt"* is in itself, oxymoronic. Can hurt ever feel good? Yes. It happens all the time to all of us. It is a physiological defense mechanism controlled by the brain. The brain has its own pain-killers called endorphins. When we are injured, the brain will immediately send these chemical anesthetics to the point of pain. Certainly, the pain won't go away, but it will ease to the point to maintain consciousness, so we can get help. Of course, if the intensity of the pain is great enough to kill, the brain will terminate consciousness. End*orphin* is natural m*orphine*. When you have an itch, scratching makes it feel better because of the endorphin sent to the scratched area. Case in Point: You've strained or pulled a muscle in your back. You are undergoing a message. The therapy hurts. *"Oh, oh, oh, that hurts!" No, No, No, don't stop. It hurts but it's a good hurt. It's feeling better in fact!"* That's because the endorphins have reached the painful region.

GOOD NAZI – (*GOOD NAHT*-zee) It is oxymoronic to speak of any fascist Hitlerite as *"good."* Nevertheless, there was one – John Heinrich Detlef Rabe (1882 – 1950), (pronounced *ROB*-eh in German). John Robe was a nondescript, inconspicuous middle manager, a bureaucrat in a German industrial company in China. Historical events put Rabe in circumstances that made him a hero, if not a saint. John Rabe is virtually unknown, even in Germany, but not in China. In fact, he has been called the *"Oskar Schindler of China."* He saved the lives of over 200,000 Chinese during the Japanese *"Rape of Nanking,"* early in World War Two (1937). Rabe was a patriotic German Nazi who idolized Adolf Hitler (1889 – 1945). Away from Germany, he had served his German company in China for decades. If *"ignorance is bliss,"* than no one was more blissfully ignorant than John Rabe. He was privy only to positive propaganda from Nazi newspapers. He was oblivious of the Nazi atrocities, the concentration camps and Holocaust. Rabe was a proud, loyal, good Nazi. As the dark clouds of war gathered, Germany allied with Japan. In 1937, Japan was invading China. They intended to take the Chinese capital, Nanking. The invasion didn't go well. Thousands of Japanese soldier were killed. When they did take the city on December 13, 1937, the Japanese army was spoiling for revenge. They went on the greatest military rampage in history. For six weeks, the Japanese soldiers were free to loot, rape, torture, plunder, and murder. Men, women, and children were bayonetted, beheaded, burned or buried alive, and raped to death, over 300,000 in all. Almost all foreigners in Nanking fled. Not John Rabe. Something snapped within this simple man that made him a messiah. Rabe took command of a handful of stranded foreigners, missionaries, including some Americans. He organized the *"International Protection Committee."* The terrified Chinese civilians obeyed Rabe's every word, and called him *"Master."* The Chinese government abandoned Nanking to Rabe, leaving him only $40,000 dollars and wishing him good luck. Rabe cordoned-off a few square miles of Nanking, declaring it the *"Protection Zone."* He flew the Nazi Swastika flags throughout the zone and warned the Japanese army and government to keep out, in the name of The Fuhrer, Adolf Hitler and the German Government. Rabe was bluffing of course. But the Japanese thought that Rabe was receiving orders from Berlin. Japan was afraid to alienate their German ally. Thousands of Chinese flooded into the Protection Zone. It was crushingly crowded like the Warsaw Ghetto would be 7 years later. Rabe was an experienced supervisor, manager. He organized for tons of rice to be brought in from the countryside. He even shared his food and personal living quarters with strangers, refugees. If drunken Japanese soldiers scaled the wall into the safe zone, Rabe confronted them wearing his Nazi armband. The intruders would immediately leave. What a striking irony. The Nazi Swastika was a symbol of humanity and compassion in Nanking, China. After 6 hellish weeks, the Japanese army had moved out and on. Over 200,000 Chinese lives were saved in the Protection Zone. These Holocaust survivors considered John Rabe to be a living Buddha. (*"Look within. Thou art the Buddha."* – Buddha.) John Rabe made his way back to Germany. The war still raged in Europe. With film and an enormous diary, Rabe contacted influential Nazis, and even wrote to Hitler. He began to give lectures on the savage Japanese atrocities, not knowing that the Germans were committing atrocities too. It wasn't long before Rabe got a visit from the Gestapo. He was arrested. After 3 days of interrogation, Rabe was released. He never spoke of his Nanking experience again. John Rabe sank into oblivion – except in China. Today, a monument stands in Nanking, China honoring him. The inscription reads: *"John Rabe, The Good Person of Nanking."* Indeed, John Rabe, the *"Good Nazi,"* was *"Righteous Among the Nations."* *"Some are born great, some achieve greatness, and some have greatness thrust upon them."* – William Shakespeare (1564 – 1616) in <u>Twelfth Night</u>, Act II, Scene 5; (c. 1601-02).

GOOD NICK – (good *NIK*) Being in splendid form, condition, or health; being in good shape. Being in good nick is primarily a British usage. The definitive origin of the term escapes us. The word *"nick"* is cognitive to the terms *"notch"* and *"niche."* We are familiar with the phrase: *"in the nick of time,"* meaning just made it, which would put us in good nick. *"Though a late-model vehicle, it is still in good nick."*

GOOD OLE DAYS – (*GOOD* olh days) Ah! Those were the good ole days! Oh? Were they really? The good ole days is a romantic albeit fanciful notion of a happy, carefree past. They are imbued with nostalgia, and a longing to go back. However, the good ole day's phenomenon is a psychological illusion and delusion. It is the result of a psychological defense mechanism called *"repression."* Unlike suppression, which is intentional forgetting, repression works on the subconscious level. It defends or protects us from going mad. If we remembered every guilt, shame, and sorrow, with regret, remorse, and resentment, we would be dysfunctional emotional wrecks. Therefore, the sting of the bad, painful events of the past gradually fade with time. That produces the illusion that the past wasn't so bad, in fact, it was much better than the present. Furthermore, we long for those good ole days that really never were. In fact, even back in the good ole days, we longed for the good ole days. Incidentally: Some old-timers even regarded the Great Depression and World War Two as the good ole days. You would hear them say: *"Life was very hard, but we were happy."* Oh? It will be interesting to see if the 4 years of *"Trump Trauma Drama,"* will be regarded by anyone as the good ole days.

GOOD SAMARITAN – (*GOOD* sa-*MARE*-ri-tan) A person who exhibits compassionate aid to the afflicted. A Good Samaritan will provide help to the distressed, endangered, or needy, and kindness to strangers. Good Samaritanism is a core value of Socialism. The credo of the Good Samaritan [read: *Socialists*] is: *"Never be a passive witness to another's pain."* Rugged Individualism is a core value of capitalism. The credo of the rugged individualist [read: *capitalist*] is: *"What's in it for me?"* The original Good Samaritan came from Samaria, the capital of the ancient Northern Kingdom of the Jews. Samaritans were Jews who did not acknowledge the Jerusalem Temple because they considered their own sanctuary on Mount Gerizim to be more sacred. This was sacrilegious to orthodox Jews. Therefore, Samaritans and their Jewish cousins from the Southern Kingdom were not on good terms (somewhat like Sunnis and Shiites, or Catholics and Protestants). That set the stage for a profound parable by Jesus. In Luke 10: 30-37, Jesus admonished a crowd to *"Love thy neighbor as thyself."* A bystander responded with, *"Who is my neighbor?"* Jesus replied with a story: *"A certain man [a Jew] was going down from Jerusalem to Jericho, and he fell among robbers, who both stripped him and beat him, and departed, leaving him half dead. By chance a certain priest was going down that way. When he saw him, he passed by on the other side. In the same way a Levite [Holy Man] also, when he came to the place, and saw him, passed by on the other side. But a certain Samaritan, as he travelled, came where he was. When he saw him, he was moved with compassion, came to him, and bound up his wounds, pouring on oil and wine. He set him on his own animal, and brought him to an inn, and took care of him. On the next day, when he departed, he took out two denarii, gave them to the host, and said to him, 'Take care of him. Whatever you spend beyond that, I will repay you when I return.' Now which of these three do you think seemed to be a neighbor to him who fell among the robbers?" Jesus asked. The man said, "He who showed mercy on him." Then Jesus said to him, "Go and do likewise."* – Luke 10: 30-37.

GOOD SAMARITAN LAW – (*GOOD* sa-*MARE*-ri-tan *LAW*) A law that states that one cannot be sued for trying to help a stranger in a crisis. For example, one cannot be held liable for breaking an accident victim's arm, while puller her out of a burning car. Not all states provide protection to heroes in this manner.

GOOD TROUBLE – (*GOOD TRUH*-bull) (also Necessary trouble) Causing disorder, disturbance for a noble, worthy cause. *"Good trouble"* is a term coined by the Civil Rights icon, Congressman John Lewis (1940 – 2020). Though an advocate of passive resistance, Lewis understood the benefit of making racists as miserable as possible. John Lewis was a trouble maker against illegal laws and fascist leaders. This is good trouble. *"Do not get lost in a sea of despair. Be hopeful, be optimistic. Our struggle is not the struggle of a day, a week, a month, or a year, it is the strength of a lifetime. Never, ever be afraid to make some noise and get in good trouble, necessary trouble."* – John Lewis.

GOOGLE – (*GOO*-gul) The largest number with a name. A google is 10, followed by 100 zeros. Incidentally: The term google is associated with a homey story. The word was coined in 1940. In that year, two American mathematicians, James R. Newman (1907 – 1966) and Edward Kasner (1878 – 1955) wrote *Mathematics and the Imagination*. Dr. Kasner asked his 11 year old nephew, Milton Sirotta (c. 1929 – c. 1981) to think of a name for an enormous number. The lad suggested *"google,"* perhaps influenced by the comic strip character *"Barney Google."* The term appeared in the book, and caught on in the mathematical jargon. Today, google is a legitimate number (10 to the 100th power). Dr. Kasner related that Milton provided a name for an unimaginably huge number, ten to tenth power, to the hundredth power, a *"googolplex."*

GOOMBAY – (*GOOM*-bay) A Caribbean musical rhythm related to calypso, associated with the Bahama Islands.

GOONS – (*GOONS*) Private police employed by corporate capitalists to break-up strikes and dissident workers. Goons use terror tactics to intimidate workers. Henry Ford (1863 – 1947) was known to maintain a goon squad in his failed attempt to prevent unionization.

GOOSE STEP – (*GOOS* step) (Goose Stepping) A military parade march performance in which the troops swing their legs in unison off the ground while keeping each leg rigidly straight. To all but fascists, goose stepping looks silly, like a performance of the girls in the *"Radio City Rockettes."* The goose step was introduced by the German Field Marshall Leopold I of Anhalt-Dessau (1676 – 1747) who became drillmaster of the Prussian army. The goose step was called *"Stechschritt,"* (piercing step). It was an exercise to keep troops in formation on the battlefield while advancing toward the enemy (an archaic tactic). Czar Paul I (1754 – 1801) adopted the goose step in the Russian army. The goose step was made famous by German Nazi soldiers (1930s – 1940s). Since then, scores of governments have adopted the goose step in their militaries as a symbol of authoritarian window-dressing. It is precision marching that is precisely silly. The leg-kick ascends to varying degrees. It Russia, Cuba, and elsewhere, the color-guard kick up to

45o at a right angle. This is not an exercise for old soldiers. Incidentally: The proud goose step was indeed named after the silly walk of a silly goose.

G.O.P. – (gee oh *PEE*) "*Grand Old Party,*" namely the Republicans. G.O.P. should stand for "*Guard Our Property!*" No political party in history had deviated further from its foundational origin than the Republican Party. How did the "*Free*" Party become the "*Tea*" Party? How did the "*Emancipation*" Party become the "*Corporation*" Party? How did the "*Radical*" Republicans, became the "*Reactionary*" Republicans? How did the "*Federal Union*" Party, become the "*States' Rights*" Party? How did the "*Equality*" Party, become the "*Racist*" party? How did the Party of "*Lincoln,*" become the Party of "*Trump?*" Before his death, arch-conservative and Republican leader Willian F. Buckley, Jr. (1925 – 2008) said: "*We should lose this election. Then wander out into the wilderness and get cleansed.*" Those who call themselves Republicans, have a great deal of soul-searching. Incidentally: In early January 2021, The G.O.P. had come to be called by normal citizens the G.Q.P. for the Grand QAnon Party. This is because the Republicans had adopted the lunacy of the QAnon conspirators. Footnote: The G.O.P. or Republicans have metastasized into the Trumpublicans and has become totally MAGAmaniacal.

GORDIE HOWE BRIDGE – (*GOR*-dee *HOW BRIJ*) A new cable-stayed span for motor vehicle traffic over the Detroit River. The Gordie Howe International Bridge will connect Detroit, Michigan U.S.A. with Windsor, Ontario Canada. It is being built down-river from the good old Ambassador Bridge (1929). The bridge is appropriately named after the Canadian hockey great Gordie Howe (1928 – 2016) who starred for the Detroit Red Wings for 25 years! The bridge will stretch 1.6 miles over the river. It will be 123 feet wide, 722 feet high. It will span 138 feet above the water. The bridge will cost $5.7 billion dollars and will be opened in 2025. The Gordie Howe International Bridge will be the primary thoroughfare between the U.S. and Canada on the continent.

GOREE ISLAND – (*GOR*-ree *EYE*-land) An island off the coast of Senegal that served as a major departure point for slaves during the African slave trade. Goree Island was the last glimpse of Africa that the kidnapped slaves, and their descendants would see in perpetuity.

GORGET – (*GOR*-jit) An armor throat protector during the middle Ages. Also a crescent-shaped ornament worn on a chain around the neck. Gorgets are ancient artifacts, initially fashioned from stone. "*Gorge*" is an archaic name for throat.

GORMAND – (*GOR*-mand) (Gormandize) A greedy ravenous glutton. Gormandization is symptomatic of capitalism. Distributive injustice results in a superfluity of abundance in the hands, and mouths of a few.

GORNISHT – (*GOR*-nisht) A Yiddishism for less than nothing, ridiculously small.

GO ROGUE – (*GO ROAG*) To take an independent, unpredictable, uncontrollable stance or path. One who has gone rogue is no longer governed by the conventional dictates of authority. A renegade politician who does not tote the party line has gone rogue. The term "*go rogue*" was popularized by celebrity politician Sarah Palin (b. 1964).

GOSH – (*GOSH*) An interjection denoting an exclamation of mild surprise or wonder. One might say: *"Gosh, you got big tits!"* The term *"golly"* is sometimes used in the same manner. Incidentally: Both gosh and golly are euphemisms for God.

GOSPELS – (*GOS*-puls) The *"Good News"* about Jesus. The 4 canonical books included in the New Testament (Matthew, Mark, Luke, and John) that relate the ministry of Jesus. After the death of Jesus (c. 33 CE) there were 80 to 100 Gospels 50 of which were major works. The early Church initially approved 27 Gospels. Later Church Fathers did not deem them worthy for inclusion in the religion. They were reduced, edited, homogenized down to four. Church leaders had created an image of Jesus, a perception that the 4 accepted Gospels did not challenge. Incidentally: Sts. Matthew, Mark, Luke, and John did not write the Gospels that bear their names. They were given credit for the authorship, in order to lend the stories credence and authority. *"Where would Jesus be if no one had written the gospels?"* – Chuck Palahniuk (b. 1962).

GOTCH YA – (*GOCH-YA*) (A corruption of *"Got You"*.) A gotch ya question is a verbal trap, set to catch a crooked politician in a lie. It is intended to corner a corrupt politician, forcing him to involuntarily tell the truth. Nasty politicians will avoid clever reporters and TV shows that employ gotch ya questions. A great example of a gotch ya moment occurred in February, 2019, on the *Morning Joe* discussion show. Co-host Mika Brzezinski (b. 1967) asked billionaire Presidential candidate Howard Schultz (b. 1953) *"How much does a box of Cheerios [cereal] cost?"* Big money-man Schultz was oblivious. He hadn't a clue. Of course not. Billionaires are totally out of touch with the daily lives of common folk. That's why they cannot serve as President. Incidentally: On a TV show, billionaire Schultz insisted that billionaires not be called billionaires, but rather, euphemistically *"men of means."*

GOTHAM – (*GOTH*-am) Nickname for New York City (pop. 8,622,698). The name was taken from the English village of Gotham, Nottinghamshire (pop. 1,563). In 1807, author Washington Irving (1783 – 1859) with brother and friend published a humor periodical entitled *Salmagundi.* In it he lampooned the politics, fashion, theater, manners, everything about of his beloved New York City. Irving called NYC *"Gotham,"* which was known as a proverbial *"Land of the Crazies."* The name stuck. Ironically, it was the *"Wise Men of Gotham"* in the Middle Ages who convinced the King they were crazy. As the story goes, King John of England (1166 – 1216) intended to build a Royal Highway that would run through the village of Gotham, Nottinghamshire in the East Midlands. The residents would be expected to maintain their segment of the route with taxes and labor. Therefore, the villagers devised a plan to act insane. Madness was considered to be contagious in medieval times. King John's knights quickly retreated from Gotham, and the Highway was re-routed. Therefore, Gotham City is a satirical, if not crazy nickname for New York. Then again, considering NYC, perhaps madness is contagious. Incidentally: New York City is 5,517 times larger than Gotham, England today.

GOTHIC – (*GOTH*-ic) An architectural style originating in France in the middle of the 12th century and persisting in Northern, Western Europe into the middle of the 16th century. During the Middle Ages, architecture was exemplified in the great cathedrals. Gothic churches symbolize and characterize the cultural divide between Northern and Southern Europe, Teutonic and Romanic Europe, Germanic and

Latin Europe. The tall, slender, light spires of Gothic churches were influenced by the great coniferous forests of the north. The spires taper toward the top, just like a pine tree, and like the trees, rise up to heaven. Quintessential Gothic churches have survived the wars at Cologne, Chartres, and Amiens. (Though the Franks of France were Romanized, they were a Germanic tribe.) The light Gothic architecture of the north stands in contrast to the heavy masonry of the Romanesque churches (9th – 12th centuries) in the southern part of Europe. The huge basilicas of Latinized regions (Rome, Constantinople, Jerusalem), are fortress-like, to be expected from the Romans. They utilized great domes (which are revolving arches) invented by the Romans. The Germanic cathedrals were first mocked as Gothic, an insult. They were said to be barbaric, like the ancient Goths. Interestingly, the humble Protestant churches in America, simple white wood, all have a spire, imitating the Gothic. After all, the Protestants came from Northern Europe, seat of the Reformation and Gothic.

GO-TO-GUY – (goh *TOO* gahy) A leader's top lieutenant. The fixer, enforcer, trouble-shooter, problem-solver. A go-to-guy gets things done – legally or illegally, one way or another. SS Officer Otto Skorzeny (1908 – 1975) was Adolf Hitler's (1889 – 1945) go-to-guy to perform impossible missions. Attorney Michael Cohen (b. 1966) was Donald Trump's (b. 1946) go-to-guy, until perfidious Trump got into trouble, and through Cohen under the bus, so to speak.

GOTTA – (*GOT*-uh) A slang rendition for *got to* or *have got to*. For example: *"I gotta go to the toilet."* The term *gotta* is used imperceptivity, when one speaks quickly, informally. Gotta is also used to mean *got a*, as in: *"Hey man, gotta match?"*

GOTTERDAMMERUNG – (got-ter-*DOM*-mer-rung) German word for *"twilight."* It was the title of Richard Wagner's (1813 – 1883) last cycle *"Twilight of the Gods,"* in his 1876 opera, *"The Ring of the Nibelung."* The term gotterdammerung has since come to mean a catastrophic downfall, as depicted in the play. The collapse of a society or regime marked by disastrous violence and disorder. Nazi Germany ultimately suffered a gotterdammerung, particularly at the hands of the Russians (1945).

GOTT MIT UNS – (got *MIT* oons) German for *"God is with us."* The so-called *"Godless Germans"* wore the fiat: *"Gott Mit Uns"* on their belt buckles during the insane First World War (1914 – 1918). Imagine the irony of two Christian people, praying to the same God, for deliverance from each other.

GOUGE – (*GOWJ*) An ancient woodworking tool which is a chisel with a curved, spoon-like blade-head for *"gouging-out"* wood. Gouges were first fashioned from stone, later in metal.

GOULASH – (*GOO*-lahsh) A thick soup or stew of beef or veal, with a variety of vegetables, seasonings, including paprika, which provides the dish its rusty-red color. Goulash originated in the 9th century with Hungarian shepherds. Today, it is the national dish of Hungary. It is prepared throughout Central Europe. The term goulash is a corruption of *"gulyashus,"* Hungarian for *"herdsman's meat"* (c. 1865).

GOURMET – (goor-*MAY*) An epicure, a connoisseur of fine food and drink. A gourmet does not eat to live, but rather lives to eat. This is unnatural in the animal world, including human beings. Food is sustenance, energy to keep us moving, and nutrition to keep us well. Taste is simply a fringe benefit. To gourmets, eating becomes dining, their hobby, an artform. Not only must food be delectable, but decorative as well. It's not good enough for a dish to be savory, it must also be elegant. Gourmets use the most exotic ingredients in the most meticulous preparation – an obscene, opulent waste of money and time. Gourmets must be wealthy, and often unhealthy. Professional eaters grow fat. Gourmet, along with its contradictory, hunger, famine, starvation are the natural outcome of capitalism: *"I got mine, to hell with you." "The greatest obscenity will be when half the world's population watches the other half starve to death on television."* – George Orwell (1903 – 1950). Incidentally: Different classes of people regard eating and food differently. The concern of the poor is: *"Did you get enough?"* The concern of the middle class is: *"Did it taste good?"* The concern of the rich gourmets is: *"How's the presentation?"*

GOUT – (*GOWT*) An acute recurrent disease characterized by painful inflammation of the joints, chiefly the hands and feet, particularly the great toe. Gout is caused by uric acid, (sodium urate), that forms crystals around the joints. The hands, and especially the feet swell, deform, crack forming open lesions, sores that can infect and become gangrenous. The condition at this advanced stage requires amputation. Gout is most prevalent in alcoholics. It is caused by the consumption of heavy (sweet) wines and excessive beer. Gout is an ancient ailment that plagued the ancient Egyptians. It usually attacks men, who are usually the heavy drinkers. Gout has been called the *"Disease of Kings,"* and the *"Rich man's disease."* This is because royalty and wealth had the money and leisure time to eat rich foods and drink alcohol excessively. English King Henry VIII (1491 – 1547) died in excruciating pain with the gout. He was addicted to the newly produced port wine from Portugal. The term gout derives from the French *"goutte,"* which was taken from the Latin *"gutta,"* meaning *"a drop of fluid."* The Romans believed that drops of viscous humors (it was uric acid) seeped from the blood to the joints. In a sense, the Romans were right.

GOVERNMENT – (*GOV*-vern-ment) Organized control over a large group of people which constitutes a nation. Government bears a different meaning to conservative capitalists, than it does to Liberal Socialists. Wealthy capitalists expect government to maintain law and order [read: *the status quo*]. This protects their privileged position and wealth. Otherwise, conservative capitalists want government to fade into the background, and let business run the nation. Business unshackled by any regulations or rules is the capitalist ideal. In a totally free market, capitalists would be totally free to exploit the populous with impunity. That to conservatives defines liberty. An active government is alien to corporate capitalists, an enemy in fact, as President Ronald Reagan (1911 – 2004) designated it. Conservative capitalists cannot regard government as the will of the people, the majority. The majority of the people are poor, and don't want to be. They must never control government, but rather be controlled by government. In their hearts, wealthy conservative capitalists fear Democracy. So in the final analysis, they prefer a fascist government that will protect their wealth. Liberal Socialists abhor fascism, the imposition of control by a ruling elite. They agree with Count Leo Tolstoy (1828 – 1910) that conservative fascist *"Government is a union of property owners for the protection of their property from those who need it."* Liberal Socialists do not see government as alien, for they are the government. Their purpose is to regulate, control business for the benefit of all. Government is not an enemy but a protector of civil liberties, economic parity, and the environment from the conservative corporate capitalist attempt to impose fascism [read: *Trumpism*]. In conclusion, conservative capitalists expect government to protect their wealth and power from the poor. Liberal Socialists expect government to protect the poor from the wealthy and powerful. The best way to do that is to distribute wealth as equally as possible. *"We can either have a great amount of wealth concentrated in the hands of a few, or democracy. We can't have both."* – Supreme Court Justice Lewis Brandies (1856 – 1941).

GOVERNMENTAL DUTY – (gov-vern-*MEN*-tal *DOO*-tee) The paternal responsibility of those chosen by the people to rule. In a word, the overall duty of the government is public safety. The citizens of the nation must be protected from foreign and domestic harm. That is the responsibility of the people's military and police forces. But bodily harm comes in many forms in many ways. Governmental duty involves protection from social, environmental harm, as well as physical harm. This is the harm from lack, neglect, and want. Keeping citizens safe also entails protecting them from disease, injury, illness, hunger, starvation, exposure, homelessness, and unemployment. This fulfillment of governmental duty will only occur in a Socialist society. In a capitalist society [read: *"every man for himself"*] the military's duty is to protect corporate capitalist investments abroad, while the duty of the police is to protect capitalist wealth at home (from those who need it). That's where capitalist governmental duty ends. As always, the problem is capitalism, the solution is Socialism. *"Capitalism is the cause of all evil."* – Pope Francis (b. 1936) February 2014.

GOVERNMENTAL FUNCTION – (gov-vern-*MEN*-tal *FUNK*-shun) The purported and expected function of government agencies to protect the welfare of the general public. Under capitalism, governmental function has come to be the protection of wealth, from those who need it.

GOY – (*GOI*) (plural Goyim) A Yiddishism for a Gentile, one not Jewish.

G.P.A. – (gee ay *PEE*) (Grade Point Average) A measure of academic attainment computed by dividing the total number of grade points earned, by the total number of classes taken. Conventionally, an A = 4.0, B = 3.0, C = 2.0, D = 1.0, F = 0. The G.P.A. was first used at Yale College in 1813.

G.Q.P. – (jee kew *PEE*) A derisive, deprecatory initialism, a designation for the debased G.O.P. or Republican Party. G.O.P. stood for Grand Old Party. But the Republicans had adopted the Trumpist lunacy of the QAnon movement, along with all of its crazy conspiracy theories. So by early January, 2021, The G.O.P. was being called the G.Q.P.

GRACE – (*GRAYS*) Metaphysically, grace is Divine favor, providential power, enthusiasm, and creativity. By the grace of God, one is endowed with the opportunity to serve as an Angel Agent, attending to the poor. *"What is grace? I knew until you ask me; when you ask me, I do not know."* – St. Augustine (354 – 430 CE).

GRACIOUS LOSING – (*GRAY*-shuhs *LOO*-sing) (Gracious Loser) To be gracious is to be kind, cordial, dignified in all circumstances. It is easy to be gracious when one wins. The test to one's graciousness is in defeat. Nowhere is this more evident than in sports and in democratic elections. Democracy depends on gracious losers. Denying the efficacy of an election because one had lost is the death of the democratic system. The most ungracious loser in American history has been Donald Trump (b. 1946). By sowing the seeds of election denial, Trump has introduced a virus, a cancer into democracy. As the football, baseball, and basketball teams must graciously accept the numbers on the scoreboard, so must the people in a democracy accept the election results, win or lose.

GRADE – (*GRAYD*) An evaluation, or placing *VALUE* on an item, project, or person. In most schools, a grade is a symbolic representation (A, B, C, D, and F) of what the student had learned. A grade is an educated guess on the part of the teacher, based on data from tests, quizzes, papers, observation, and attendance record. Nevertheless, only you (student) really know how much you have learned. Many know more than they can show. Exams, tests, grades are merely necessary nuisances in our test-driven, credential-crazed, measurementally-mad, accountability-obsessed society. *"He got all A's but flunked life."* – Author Walker Percy (1916 – 1990).

GRADE INFLATION – (*GRADE* in-*FLAY*-shun) Marking a student higher than her performance warrants. During the Vietnam War (1960 – 1973), when the government began to draft poorly performing college men, compassionate professors inflated grades in order to save lives. Slowly but surely, the grading system inflated. Standards fell. It never quite regained its efficacy. Today, some educators inflate grades in order to avoid conflict with students and parents.

GRADUATE ASSISTANT – (*GRAD*-jew-wit ass-*SIS*-tant) An academic serf. A servile student striving for an advanced degree, usually the Ph.D. A graduate assistant is at the beck and call of his advising professor, to whom he must kowtow. The grad assistant runs errands, corrects papers, performs research, and teaches low-level courses when the senior professor would rather not bother. Being a graduate assistant is a rite of passage in the stratified world of the academe.

GRADUATION – (grad-joo-*AY*-shun) (Graduate, Graduating, Graduated) The term derives from the Latin *"gradus,"* meaning *"a step,"* figuratively, *"a step higher, rising."* In common usage, graduation, to graduate, is to advance academically, after a long period of study and service, to a higher status. Graduation can be applied in a metaphysical sense as well. Death, the transformative passing from this life to the next is a graduation. After a life of opportunities to learn to serve God by serving our less blessed mortals, we graduate to a higher life. Whether we graduate with honors, distinctions, or demerits, depends on our life on this level, at *"University Earth."* Perhaps we had come short of credits, have not made the grade, or have failed the course. In this case, we will be required to go back to school to learn the lessons we've missed, perhaps through a more challenging, rigorous, stressful course, even a boot-camp. Some have designated this re-education as *Reincarnation,* and the individual lessons *Karma.* Our lives are a curricula, a course of study. Like the law exam, one may be forced to take the course over and over until we pass the test. Then we will have been fully, honorably graduated, to dwell in the Ivory Tower, among the Saintly scholars and Angels. Therefore, never say a loved-one had died. Rather, say she had passed or graduated.

GRAFFITI – (gra-*FEE*-tee) (plural, Graffito) Street art, or perhaps vandalism. The difference depends on one one's level of intelligence, sophistication, and aesthetic proclivity. Portraits, drawings, symbols, slogans, initials are usually spray-painted on walls, buildings, bridges, sidewalks, both public and private buildings. Like all art, some graffito is sublime, others are subpar, or just junk. Graffiti becomes vandalism when it is applied without permission. High-grade graffiti lends color and life to a dreary, depressed area. Graffiti has been an urban phenomenon in ancient Egypt, Greece, and Rome. It is a good way for the voiceless to be heard. It can serve as a socio-political barometer, especially in poor ghettoes and barrios. Some graffiti is spectacular. It serves as an emotional outlet for nameless geniuses. Graffiti can serve as a socio-political barometer, especially in poor ghettoes and barrios. *"You feel like a prisoner if you don't create. You're jailed up inside yourself."* –Singer Edie Brickell (b. 1966).

GRAMMAR – (GRAM-mer) Grammatical, Grammaticality) Correct sentence construction. Grammar is a branch of linguistics that provides rules of morphology (word formation) and syntax (word positioning in a sentence). Grammar keeps a language coherent. *"Grammar is the analysis of language."* – Edgar Allan Poe (1819 – 1849). *"I hate commas in the wrong places."* – Walt Whitman (1819 – 1892). *"If you want to break the rules of grammar, first learn the rules of grammar."* – Kurt Vonnegut (1922 – 2007). *"Remove literary, grammatical and syntactical inhibitions."* – Jack Kerouac (1922 – 1969). *"When your last breath arrives, grammar can do nothing."* – Adi Shankara (788 – 820 CE). *"There ain't no grammatical errors in a non-literate society."* – Marshall McLuhan (1911 – 1980).

GRAND CANYON – (*GRAND CAN*-yon) The Colorado River gorge in northern Arizona, one of the most spectacular geological wonders on Earth. The gorge is a gargantuan, multi-colored strata topped by a high plateau. About a billion tons of rock had been gouged-out to from the canyon. It covers about 1,008 square miles, 280 miles long, 4 to 18 miles wide, and over a mile deep. The Grand Canyon is the longest canyon system in the world. It can hold all the world's river water, and still be only half filled! It would take 6 months for Niagara Falls to fill the Grand Canyon. The Colorado River is carving the gorge, but it could not do it alone. Geological uplift due to earthquakes have contributed to its magnificence. Too, in the distant past, a natural dam-burst created a tremendous flood of Biblical proportions. This also gouged-out the gorge as well. To the wonderment of geologists, the Grand Canyon is only 5.5 million years old.

GRANDFAMILY – (*GRAND*-fam-lee) A family in which the children are raised by the grandparents. In a grandfamily, the grandparents become the functional parents, again. The tragic death of the parents may bring to pass a grandfamily. It had happened that single moms had become drug addicted forcing her aging parents to take care of her children. Though the term grandfamily entered the dictionary in 2023, it was first recorded in the early 1960s.

GRAND GUIGNOL – (gran gee-*NOL*) A horror show of the slasher genre. A gruesome movie or play depicting grisly murders, horrendous tortures, and rapacious rape, hellish displays of inhumanity. This strange sounding French term was the name of a strange theater in Paris from 1897 to 1962. The name literally means *"The Theatre of the Great Puppet."* The atrocious mayhem entertained a distinguished audience of celebrities, dignitaries and European royalty. The Grand Guignol appealed to the vicarious sadomasochistic yearnings in many individuals. *"Cruelty has a human heart."* – William Blake (1757 – 1827).

GRANDILOQUENT – (gran-*DILL*-o-kwint) (Grandiloquence) Magniloquent. Speaking in a pompous, bombastic, exaggerated lofty style.

GRANDSIRE – (*GRAND*-sy-er) An archaic appellation for grandfather.

GRANDSTANDING – (*GRAN*-stand-ing) (Grandstander) A grandstand is the main and choice seating area of a stadium, racetrack, parade route, wherever people congregate to see a performance or hear a speaker (1761). Grandstanding is putting on a show or performance to impress the audience in or out of the grandstand. It is an exaggerated performance. The term *"grandstanding"* emerged in 1895 from *"grandstand player"* (1888), a show-off baseball player. Today, grandstanding is applied to show-off politicians.

GRANITE – (*GRAN*-nit) A hard igneous rock formed deep in the Earth when basaltic lava mixed with super-heated water. The lighter granite rose to the surface forming the foundations for the continents. The watery Earth had land. The roots of mountains are often made of granite. These roots are called *plutons.* That's why granite is called *"basement rock."* Granite is one of the hardest, most durable rocks on Earth. It will weather erode at the rate of 1 inch, per 10,000 years. Granite monuments like presidents carved into Mt. Rushmore (South Dakota), and the Confederate generals carved into Stone Mountain (Georgia) may be the last reminders of human existence left on planet Earth. The Mt. Rushmore sculptures will take well over 50,000 years to erode away. Stone Mountain is the largest exposed piece of granite in the world. It is 5 miles in circumference and 825 feet high. Its *pluton* (subterranean root) plunges 9 miles into the Earth.

GRANOLA – (gran-*NO*-la) A breakfast food consisting of rolled oats, brown sugar, nuts, and dried fruit, eaten in a bowl of milk. Granola is highly nutritious and packed with energy. Being dried, granola never spoils. That's why it is also an essential ingredient in scroggin or trail mix for hikers. Incidentally: The term "granola" derives from the Italian *"grano,"* meaning grain. The suffix *"ola"* was applied in 1886 by Will Keith Kellogg (1860 – 1951) of cornflakes fame.

GRAPEFRUIT – (*GRAYP*-froot) A large, round, yellow-skinned citrus fruit, having a bitter, juicy, acidic pulp. The grapefruit grows on a tropical or semitropical tree. The grapefruit is a cross between the Polynesian citrus fruit called the *Shaddock,* and a *sweet orange.* Both Barbados and Jamaica take credit for the hybridization of the plant. The softball-size yellow fruit was first recorded in Barbados in 1750 as the *"Forbidden Fruit."* The name was first recorded as *"grapefruit"* in Jamaica (1814). The grapefruit was first commercially cultivated in the U.S.A. The large fruit grows in clusters like grapes, ergo the name.

GRAPHIC – (*GRAF*-fik) (Graphically) Explicit, descriptive, realistic. A graphic photo is uncensored, realistic. For example, TV may warn that a war documentary contains graphic battle scenes, not appropriate for immature audiences.

GRAPHITE – (*GRAF*-hyt) Crystalized carbon. Also called *plumbago,* graphite is a common mineral, a soft native carbon, occurring in black to dark-gray foliated masses (thin, layers). Graphite has a metallic luster and greasy texture. Called black lead, graphite is familiar as the lead in pencils. Powdered graphite like soot, serves as a good lubricant. Being a good conductor of heat and electricity, graphite is used to manufacture crucibles, heat-resistant bricks, solar panels, electrodes, and batteries. Incidentally: Under extreme pressure, a hunk of graphite can be converted into a diamond (which are chemically identical).

GRAPHOMANIA – (graff-o-*MAY*-nee-a) (Graphomaniac, Graphomaniacal) Obsession with writing. Graphomania, like any obsession, is a neurotic condition. Nevertheless, all great writers must show signs of graphomania.

GRASPING REFLEX – (*GRAS*-ping *REE*-fleks) (Also the Palmer Reflex.) One of the few vestigial instincts retained in infant Homo sapiens. The grasping reflex is demonstrated by stroking a sleeping infant's palms.

It will lock-on to the fingers tight enough to be lifted off the bed, without awakening. Our ancient arboreal mothers needed free hands to climb trees. Baby needed to hold-on without falling, even when asleep.

GRASS – (*GRAHS*) Most important plant on the planet, covering 1/4 of the land on Earth, with over 10,000 varieties. Grass covers more land and feeds more wildlife than any other plant. Herbivores eat grass and carnivores (including man) eat herbivores. Man also eats the grasses in the form of wheat, corn, rice, oats, barley, rye, sugar and others. Nevertheless, the greatest consumer of grass is insects, devouring 1/3 of the grass on Earth. The tallest grass leafy grass (not cane) is the elephant grass of Northern India. Grass is almost indestructible. It can be flooded, burned, baked, dried, stampled, eaten and it will grow back. Actually, sugarcane and bamboo are both grass. Bamboo is the toughest, strongest, hardest, fastest growing grass in the world (about a foot a day). On a quiet, wet, tropical night, you can hear the groaning of the bamboo growing. Incidentally: Humble grass played a vital role in the evolution of man. Universally, the great grasslands appeared at about the same time. In Africa, the grass choked much of the forest. Our arboreal ancestors had far fewer trees in which to dwell. Less space and food forced some out of the trees, onto the grassland. There, they were forced to become bipedal to see over the tall grass. This freed the hands to manipulate tools and weapons, which provided more food. Evolution was accelerated, all thanks to grass.

GRASSLANDS – (*GRHAS*-lands) The Earth's geographical regions dominated by grasses, covering about 25% of the land. Grasslands are mostly broad flatlands. *Prairie* is a drier locale, heavier, taller, hardier grass, but too dry for trees. The upper roots of the grass soaks-up what little rain that falls, before the moisture can reach the lower tree roots. *Plains* accommodate shorter grass, though less hardy. Though plains receive a little more rain than prairies, still trees are unable to take hold. Trees spring up along moist riverbanks. A *steppe* is real dry terrain with short grass often far between. The treeless steppe is always in danger of desertification. A *savannah* has very tall grass, with wet and dry seasons. Scattered trees dot the savannah. Incidentally: The great expanse of the Eurasian Steppe is the world's largest grassland.

GRASS ROOTS – (grhas *ROOTS*) A political movement that starts on the local level. A grass roots movement begins with the common people. As it gains momentum and popularity, the politicians will jump in, and try to get to the head of the parade. Later, big business with big money will join the movement to see what's in it for them. Black Lives Matter (BLM) was a grass roots protest, demonstration that reacted to the killing of Black men by police in 2013. BLM expanded into a nation, then international movement with grass roots.

GRATITUDE – (*GRAT*-ti-tood) A feeling of thankfulness or appreciation, as for gifts, favors, or love. Expressing gratitude is the essence of graciousness. One who fails to display proper gratitude is an *"ingrate."* Ingratitude is an indication of poor manners and perhaps poor upbringing. *"Gratitude bestows reverence, allowing us to encounter everyday epiphanies, those transcendent moments of awe that change forever how we experience life and the world."* – John Milton (1608 – 1674). Gratitude is a magical emotion. *"Gratitude unlocks the fullness of life. It turns what we have into enough, and more. It turns denial into acceptance, chaos into order, and confusion to clarity. It can turn a meal into a feast, a house into a home, a stranger into a friend. Gratitude makes sense of our past, brings peace for today, and creates a vision for tomorrow."* – Melody Beattie (b. 1948). It is most painful when a family member or loved-one shows ingratitude. As William Shakespeare

(1564 – 1616) had written in *"King Lear"* (1605): *"How sharper than a serpent's tooth it is to have a thankless child!"* Gratitude is the gateway to gain. You won't be blessed with more, until you are grateful with what you have. *"Gratitude is what opens the spiritual doors to all the blessings. Everything becomes clear, you see, you feel, you live."* – Omraam Mikhael Aivanhov (1900 – 1986). Incidentally: In the most astounding display of hubris, Louis XVI (1638 – 1715), the arrogant French *"Sun King,"* accused God of ingratitude! *"Has God forgotten all I had done for Him?"* Louis lamented.

GRAVAMEN – (*GRA*-va-men) In law, the most damaging evidence. Gravamen is that part of the accusation weighing most heavily against the accused.

GRAVE WAX – (*GRAYV* waks) An epithet for Adipocere (*AD*-uh-poh-seer). Grave wax is a fatty, waxy substance produced by the decomposition of dead animal bodies (including humans) in moist ground or under water. Grave wax is a soapy organic substance formed by the anaerobic bacterial hydrolysis of fat in tissue. In its formation, putrefaction is replaced by a permanent firm cast of fatty tissues, internal organs, and the face.

GRAVEYARD SHIFT – (*GRAYV*-yard *SHIFT*) Working at a job that usually starts at midnight, and continues until at least 8:00 a.m. But the origin of the term is far more interesting. Before modern times, the English were running out of cemetery space. Very old graves were dug up and reused, (the old bones deposited in a bonehouse). This was the time before embalming. When the old coffins were opened, 1 out of 25 (4%) of the coffins were found to have scratch marks on the inside. The people had been mistaken for dead and buried alive. So a thin rope would be tied on the wrist of the corpse, running from the coffin, up through the ground, to a bell mounted on a pole over the grave. Someone would have to sit out in the graveyard all night in case the bell rang, the *"graveyard shift."* People indeed had been *"saved by the bell."* Those equipped with the bell precaution who still expired were considered to be *"dead ringers."*

GRAVITAS – (*GRAV*-vi-tas) With solemnity, sobriety, in a grave manner. A speech given in gravitas is very important and serious.

GRAVITY – (*GRAV*-vi-tee) A fundamental, universal force, the most pervasive force in the universe. Gravity is the attractive force among all matter in existence. Its influence is exerted on the microcosmic (sub-atomic) and massive macrocosmic planetary (galactic) levels. The larger, more massive the body, the greater its gravitational force. Gravity keeps the heavenly bodies in their familiar orbits. Gravity is responsible for objects falling down to the ground. Gravity keeps our feet planted firmly to the Earth, literally. Without gravity, the Earth would literally explode. It is the magnetic force of gravity that attracts space debris, making a celestial body grow. When an object in space grows to one-half mile across, it attains gravitational force that will rapidly attract smaller bodies (meteors) accelerating its growth. As it grows to about 6 miles across, its internal gravitational force will be strong enough to start rounding it out, into the shape of a sphere. When a rocky body (asteroid) reaches 373 miles (600 km) in size (mass) its internal gravity will become a sphere. If the body is made of ice (comet), it will have to reach 249 miles (400 km) in size for its gravity to make it a sphere. Gravity produces an attraction of all matter to matter. With gravity, size matters. So does density. The larger or denser the object, the greater its gravitational force or attraction. A *black hole* (collapsed supernova) is the densest object in the universe. It therefore displays the greatest gravitational force, stronger than the escape speed of light. Planets, stars and light pulled into this hyper-gravitational mass cannot escape, making the black hole black. The gravity of a black hole is unimaginably dense. For example, if the Earth was to become a black hole, it would have to be squeezed to the size of a golf ball!

GRAY – (Spelled *GREY* in Britain.) Color produced by mixing white (*all color*) with black (*no color*). Gray is a neutral color, being between all and nothing. It has been associated with gloom, as in a gray sky or gray spirits. Gray is a dignified dress color, somewhat formal and business-like. Being so neutral, gray will match with every other color. Incidentally: If you mix every can of paint in the paint store, the color you will produce will be grey – neutral.

GRAYS – (or GREYS in Britain.) Designated name for the extraterrestrial aliens, believed to have visited Earth. The name derives from the gray corpulence of the corpses, said to have been recovered at the Roswell, New Mexico UFO crash of 1947. The Grays have been encountered and described multiple times since the historic crash at Roswell. They are reported to be petit beings, 3.5 to 4 feet tall, with thin bodies, long arms and fingers, large heads, with huge almond- shaped eyes. Obviously, they are far superior intellectually and technologically than human beings, (otherwise, we would be visiting them). Their skin, of course, is said to be gray. No one was more closely, seriously associated with the Grays that Lieutenant Colonel Philip James Corso (1915 – 1998). In 1961, Corso became the Chief of the Pentagon's Foreign Technology desk in Army Research and Development. [*Foreign* here actually means *Alien*.] Corso testified that they reverse engineered artifacts from UFO crashes, (including Roswell's). As a result, he said, we learned of: particle beams, fiber optics, lasers, Kevlar, night vision technology, super-tenacity, integrated circuit chips, and stealth technology. Far beyond the technology, Col. Corso saw the corpses, the actual Grays. Corso described their anatomy: *"First I thought it was a child, because it was small. The head was different. The head was not really that big, but looked big in relations to their tiny bodies. The arms were spindly. It had no mouth, no ears, no nose and no sex organs. Its skin was gray in color and atomically aligned to repel radiation and harmful effects. It must not have been able to breathe air, because it wore a space helmet. There was more than one. Autopsies were performed. They were cut open. They could not speak because they had no vocal chords. The brain was different. There was no digestive system. They must have been humanoid clones."* Another UFO insider was Benjamin Robert Rich (1925 – 1995), the *"Father of Stealth Technology."* Rich was an Aeronautical Engineer, Director of Lockheed's *"Skunk Works"* – the secret military research and development division. Ben Rich once told the press: *"There are UFOs that we make, and there are UFOs that they* [extraterrestrials] *make."* Incidentally: If extraterrestrial Grays visit Earth, they will obviously be far more advanced than us. Hopefully, they will serve us, and not for dinner! The great theoretical physicist and cosmologist, Stephen Hawking (1942 – 2018) warned us about alien encounters: *"If aliens came to visit us, the outcome may be just like when Christopher Columbus came to America – which didn't turn out too well for the Native Americans."*

GRAZE – (*GRAYZ*) To forage on grass, in contrast to browse which is to forage on leaves. Herbivorous grazers have shorter necks than browsers.

GREASE FIRE – (*GREES FY*-er) Not all fires are alike. The characteristic of the fire depends on what it consumes as fuel. A grease fire is a common, but dangerous kitchen accident. A grease fire is burning lard, oil, fat in a frying pan or deep fryer. It is a particularly hot fire with high flames. The burning grease has the potential of spilling, splashing, spreading flaming hot liquid everywhere and on everyone. Grease fires occur when the cooking oil gets far too hot and emits flammable gases that ignite, setting fire to the grease. The panic reaction is to douse the hot pan with water. *No! Don't! Never!* The result will be an explosive flashover. The entire kitchen will be set alight. The oxygen in the water adds fuel to the fire. Too, the water instantly vaporizes, blasting the flaming hot grease out of the pan in all directions. Grease fires must be smothered with a cover or lid, depriving the flames of oxygen. Towels will merely spread the oil and fire. Stay cool, calm, and smother the fire. Incidentally: Never drop a wet or frozen chicken or turkey into a hot vat of oil in order to deepfry. It will explode! This is a common Thanksgiving Day tragedy.

GREASE MONKEY – (*GREES MUHNG*-kee) A pejorative slang name for an auto mechanic. In a stereotypical sense, a grease monkey is a young, high school dropout, probably a hillbilly. Let's call him *"Skeeter."* His fingernail are perpetually caked with black grease. Skeeter is a fairly accomplished mechanic, but that's all he knows. He pumps gas and works in the garage at the corner gas station. In his spare time, Skeeter monkeys about on his hotrod, or shares his Jack Daniels with his friends (Bubba, JimBob, Homer, and Selma) in the junkyard. He smokes Luck Strikes. Skeeter the grease monkey listens to the country/western radio station. He sports tattoos, including a confederate flag, and the mournful declaration: *"Born to Lose."* Skeeter has friends and family in prison, and has had a few brushes with the law himself. Skeeter's fantasy is to be a racecar driver. His realistic dream is to manage the gas station – to become the *"alpha-monkey of grease."* Skeeter is a rabid racist, though he knows not why. He has almost no contact with people of color. But it outrages him to see a successful non-white person, for if there is no group below him, than Skeeter is at the very bottom. Skeeter is blindly, fanatically patriotic. However, he cannot explain the contradiction of flying the confederate flag – the symbol of rebellious anti-American treason. History is not Skeeter's strong suit. Skeeter the grease monkey idolizes President Donald Trump (b. 1946). If asked why, he will direct you to Fox TV. If the Liberals (Skeeter calls them *Hippies*) hate Trump, he must be right. Trump speaks Skeeter's language. Trump, like Skeeter, is a man of few words – [read: *poor vocabulary*]. Indeed, Skeeter doesn't say much. But when he does – he doesn't say much. Too, Skeeter loves guns and Trump doesn't care. Skeeter the grease monkey is a lost soul, a waste of humanity. With a generous emersion in Liberal education, Skeeter can be rescued from his futile existence. Incidentally: The day of the grease monkey has already passed Skeeter by. Technology had altered the auto engine from mechanics to electronics. Much of the grease has been replaced by silicon chips. To fix a car today, Skeeter needs 2 years of community college and an Associate's Degree. Grease monkeys must now be technicians.

GREASY – (*GREE*-see) (Grease) Being smeared, covered, or soiled with a slimy, slippery, oily substance generally called grease. The word grease is an umbrella term for a variety of semisolid viscous substances. Grease may be of organic or inorganic origin. It may be a petroleum constituent like Vaseline or axle grease, and animal fat constituent like lard, a dairy constituent like butter, or a vegetable constituent like oleomargarine. Being a thickened oil, grease has a lubricating quality. Salves and face creams are greasy. What makes a substance greasy? As with all else, it is its molecular structure. The molecules of a greasy substance have the ability to seep into the pores of a surface and stick where it makes contact. So greasy is semi-sticky. Unlike a truly sticky substance that will hold fast, grease will slide on the surface. It will smear. That's the difference between grease and glue. A greasy item is slippery, greatly reducing friction. Both mechanical parts and human parts move with greater ease when greased.

GREAT BARRIER REEF – (*GRAYT BER*-ree-er *REEF*) The world's oldest ecosystem, going back over 600 million years. The Great Barrier Reef is called the largest living organism on Earth (if taken as a single organism, and not a community of organisms). It is half the size of Texas, and visible from space. About 400 species of coral comprise the reef. Australia's Great Barrier Reef in the Pacific is the only living organism visible from space (over 1,400 miles long). Coral reefs are one of the most prolific biomes on the planet. There is a greater biodiversity in the Great Barrier Reef, than in all the rest of the open Pacific Ocean.

GREAT DEMISE – (*GRAYT* dee-*MISE*) Term for Buddha's death at age 80 in c. 483 BCE.

GREAT DEPRESSION – (*GRAYT* dee-*PRESH*-shun) (More accurately, the Great *Republican* Depression.) It was the most devastating period of economic decline in American History, lasting from 1929 to 1941. Greedy capitalist speculation; the heavy reliance on credit; the unregulated gambling casino that was the stock market; resulted in a crash on Wall Street that reverberated around the world. Corporate stocks became worthless, factories closed, jobs evaporated. One out of four U.S. families had nothing coming in, no income. It was the greatest disaster to befall America, second only to the Civil War. Over 5,000 banks had failed. Some states did not have a single functioning bank. Over 9 million savings accounts were wiped out. It took the bombing of Pearl Harbor and World War Two to jar the nation out of the Depression. (Depression was converted into revenge.) Massive federal spending on armaments put the people back to work. The same results can be realized by spending on construction, as on destruction. Any depression or recession can be alleviated by Socialistic government spending – creating jobs and putting money into poor people's packets.

GREAT DISTRACTION – (*GRAYT* dis-*TRAK*-shun) A distraction is a diversion, a deviation from what's really happening. A distraction can be a scheme to draw away attention from one's true intention. This is what the Republican *"Culture War"* actually is – *"The Great Distraction."* The Republicans are the lackeys of the rich – the corporate capitalist oligarchy. The Republicans have to cajole the poor, middle class, common Americans to vote against their economic interests, in favor of the oligarch's interests [read: vote Republican]. They do this by diverting attention away from economic issues, to culture war issues. Abortion, racial strife, immigration invasion, Socialism, mask/vaccination mandates, school curriculum, gun control, Confederate statues are some of the contrived controversies the Republicans have initiated in order to find a cause, greater than the common voter's economic interests. They use right-wing fascist media, especially FOX TV to disseminate their culture war propaganda. In fact, FOX TV was established in October 1996 just for this purpose, to distract common Americans away from their economic interests. They have been astoundingly successful, as the emergence of Donald Trump (b. 1946) testifies. Simply put, FOX TV is the great Republican, capitalist distractor. Its grand strategy is to use racism and the culture war to keep Blacks and Whites from uniting and demanding economic justice, which would spell Socialism.

GREATER ANTILLES – (*GRAY*-ter an-*TIL*-lees) A group of the larger islands in the Caribbean Sea including Cuba, Jamaica, Hispaniola, and Puerto Rico.

GREATEST GENERATION – (*GRAY*-test jen-er-*RAY*-shun) *"Never in the field of human conflict was so much owed by so many to so few."* – Prime Minister Winston Churchill (1874 – 1965). The Greatest Generation is a celebratory designation given to the population born between 1901 and 1927. They met their prime when the world was convulsed in history's greatest war. The Greatest Generation worked, sacrificed, fought, suffered, died, and survived to rid the world of fascism, and preserve democracy – *albeit temporarily.* They were preceded by the *Lost Generation* (1883 – 1900) and succeeded by the *Silent Generation* (1928 – 1945). The Greatest Generation was toughened by the Great Depression. Very many were the sons and daughters of immigrants. Through their collective strength and will, they won World War Two (1939 – 1945), not only on the battlefields, but in the factories and research labs. The honorary title was given to this segment of the population by journalist Tom Brokaw (b. 1940) in his book: *The Greatest Generation* (1998). Many of the soldiers who survived the war took advantage of the G.I. Bill which democratized higher education. They became doctors, lawyers, teachers, professors, and engineers. Together with the labor unions, they creating the American middle class. The American middle class, in turn, created suburbia. Incidentally: The first U.S. President of the Greatest Generation was Dwight D. Eisenhower (1917 – 1969). He was succeeded by John F. Kennedy (1917 – 1963); Lynden B. Johnson (1908 – 1973); Richard Nixon (1913 – 1994); Gerald Ford (1913 – 2006); Jimmy Carter (b. 1924); Ronald Reagan (1911 – 2004); George H. W. Bush (1924 – 2018). *"There is a mysterious cycle in human events. To some generations much is given. Of other generations much is expected. This generation of Americans has a rendezvous with destiny."* – President Franklin D. Roosevelt (1882 – 1945).

GREAT LAKES – (*GRAYT LAYKS*) (Lakes Superior, Huron, Michigan, Erie, and Ontario) The Great Lake present the greatest accumulation of fresh water anywhere on Earth. Altogether, the Great Lakes are the size of the state of Utah. They hold 100 times more water than all the rivers in the world. The lakes were carved by glaciers and initially filled by glacial melt. The ice followed the paths of existing rivers to form Lakes Michigan, Huron, and Erie. Glaciers also carved-out Lakes Superior and Ontario, but tectonic earth splitting also contributed in these two cases. That's why Superior is the deepest, Ontario second. In fact, half of Lake Superior is below sea level. Too, the floor of Lake Superior is the lowest point in North America. Over 1,000 trillion tons of earth and rock was gouged-out of the Great Lakes Basin. The State of Michigan is in the center of the Great Lakes Basin. If the Great Lakes overflowed their basin, the 48 contiguous states would be inundated by 10 feet of water. Commercially, the Great Lakes constitute one of the busiest, most important sea-lanes in the world. Through the centuries, over 6,000 ships, with about 30,000 casualties have gone down in the Great Lakes. Today, over 34 million people live along the Great Lakes. A few of the Great Lakes cities are Chicago, Milwaukee, Detroit, Cleveland, Buffalo, Toronto, Hamilton, and Montreal (on the St. Lawrence Seaway created by the Great Lakes. *"Erie, and Ontario, and Huron, and Superior, and Michigan possess an ocean-like expansiveness, with many of the ocean's noblest traits...they are swept by Borean and dismasting blasts as direful as any that lash the salted waves; they know what shipwrecks are, for out of sight of land, however inland, they have drowned full many a midnight ship with all its shrieking crew."* – Herman Melville (1819 – 1891). Incidentally: It takes 204 years for a drop of water entering Lake Superior to join the Atlantic Ocean. It takes 191 years for that drop to enter the St, Mary's River between Sault Ste. Marie Michigan and Ontario. The drop will take 13 years to flow through Lake Huron, into the St. Clair River, into Lake St. Clair, into the Detroit River, into Lake Erie, into the Niagara River, over Niagara Falls, into Lake Ontario. The drop of water proceeds through the St. Lawrence Seaway into the Atlantic Ocean in Canada. *"We are America's Great Lakes people, her freshwater people, not an oceanic but a continental people. Whenever I swim in the ocean, I feel as though I am swimming in chicken soup."* – Kurt Vonnegut (1922 – 2007).

GREAT LEAP FORWARD – (*GRAYT LEEP FOR*-werd) A hasty, impractical attempt by Mao Zedong (1893 – 1976) to instantly transform China from an agrarian to an industrial society (1958 – 1961). In the mid-20th century, steel production was the yardstick of economic virility. Mao expected to surpass Britain, Russia, and America in steel production in 15 years. Everyone was expected to make steel in pre-industrial, backyard furnaces. Farms, shops, and schools were neglected to meet the steel quotas. The nation practically stopped working. Everything made of iron was melted down. Everything made of wood was used as fuel – tools, furniture, picture frames, and even old coffins. The people were ignorant of scientific, metallurgical principles. A great amount of useless steel was produced. In the frantic race to create steel, agriculture was neglected. The government requisitioned the surplus grain. Starvation set in. The Great Leap Forward was followed by the Great Famine, in which about 30 million people died. Indeed, Maoism was *NOT* Communism or Socialism.

GREATNESS – (*GRAYT*-ness) Being exceptionally outstanding. Primary greatness refers to who you are, the type of person you are. Secondary greatness refers to what you had accomplished. A person's greatness is revealed in how she treats those not considered great, the needy and helpless. *Some men are born great, some achieve greatness, some have greatness thrust upon them."* – William Shakespeare (1564 - 1616) in <u>Twelfth Night</u>, Act II, Scene 5, (c. 1601 - 02).

GREAT PATRIOTIC WAR – (*GRAYT* pay-tree-*OT*-tic *WAR*) The Russian designation for the European Theater (Eastern Front) in the Second World War. No nation contributed and lost more to defeat the German Nazis than Russia. The invasion of Russia commenced on June 22, 1941, and continued for 1,418 days. About 90% of the German army was thrown at the Russians. Over 80% of the German casualties were suffered on the Eastern Front. Much of the war was fought on Russian soil. Over a quarter of the country was occupied. The carnage was absorbed by the Russian people. Somewhere between 27 and 40 million soldiers and civilians perished. Not a single Russian family had not lost at least one relative, loved-one. Over 5 million Russian soldiers were taken prisoner. Over 3/5 of them would not return. No nation or empire in history had ever absorbed such losses and survived. The Great Patriotic War stimulated a 2nd Industrial Revolution (this time in Russia). Over 1,500 factories with a million workers had to be moved on 18,000 trains eastward, deep into Russia. Unlike the war in Western Europe, the Eastern conflict was a war of annihilation. It was a racist war in which the Germans considered the Slavonic Russians to be *"untermenschen,"* [read: *subhuman* or *animals*]. All told, over 1,710 Russian cities and towns were destroyed; 70,000 villages; 32,000 factories. Russia suffered over $485 billion dollars in damages. In today's dollars, that would be over 6 trillion, 364 billion dollars ($6,364,000,000,000). In the West, it was capitalist Germans versus capitalist British and Americans. In the East, it was capitalist Germans versus Socialist Russians. No doubt, Communist zeal helped win the Great Patriotic War.

GREAT PLAINS – (*GRAYT PLAYNS*) The vast treeless grasslands of central North America (c. 501,933 square miles) that is largely treeless and ascends to 4,000 feet above sea level. The Great Plains include the states of: Kansas, Nebraska, North Dakota, South Dakota, parts of Colorado, Montana, Minnesota, Iowa, New Mexico, Oklahoma, Texas, and the southern parts of Canadian Alberta, Manitoba, and Saskatchewan. The Great Plains is a world food basket.

GREAT QUESTION – (*GRAYT KWES*-chun) Prosaically, this means an insightful enquiry. However, the term has become a trite, almost unconscious response when answering any question. Introducing the answer with the phrase, *"Great question,"* provides a momentary pause, allowing the responder time to think of "a great answer." This is especially true of politicians. The *great question* response has become a speech affectation, sometimes used as an interjection. *"Is Trump a fascist?" "Great question!..."*

GREAT REPUBLICAN DEPRESSION – (*GRAYT* ree-*PUB*-li-can dee-*PRESH*-shun) (1929 – c. 1941) The stock market crash that plunged the nation and world into economic calamity. There were no rules governing the stock market or banks in the Roaring 20's. The nation's economic structure was totally deregulated. Anyone could open a bank. Wall Street was like a gambling casino. The economy was run on credit. *"Buy now, pay later"* was introduced to consumers. Everyone tried to get-rich-quick by playing the stock market. People bought stocks *"on margin,"* [read: *credit*]. A dollar stock could be purchased with 10 cents. Corporations and investors did get rich *"on paper."* But there wasn't enough money to back-up all the stock certificates. The economy was a mountain of credit, on a molehill of actual cash. The Republicans had controlled the White House throughout the 1920's. President Herbert Hoover (1874 – 1964) was oblivious to all the rumblings in the economy. Hoover was sitting on a volcano and never knew it. On *"Black Thursday,"* October 24, 1929, an unknown shopkeeper from the Bronx saw a discouraging newspaper article about *The Bank of the United States.* He went to the bank to cash-in, to sell his bank stocks. The management was reluctant. The shopkeeper spread the rumor that the bank would not pay out. There was a rush on the bank. People panicked. Other banks were stampeded. The banks did not have the cash on hand to pay-off all their depositors. Banks closed. People rioted. The Great Republican Depression was on. People lost their life's savings. Their stock certificates became worthless. Corporations went under. Factories closed. Unemployment soared. In 28 states not a single bank remained open. American loans to Europe ceased. European banks crashed. The depression spread to all industrialized capitalist countries. The misery generated was the direct cause of the rise of Nazism and World War Two.

GREAT WAR – (*GRAYT WAR*) (1914 – 1918) World War One, the greatest war in history, until World War Two (1939 – 1945). The butcher's bill amounted to over 12 million soldiers and 9 million civilians killed. Over 9 million prisoners were taken. The Great War was a family feud among cousins: Kaiser Wilhelm II Hohenzollern of Germany (1859 – 1941), King George V Windsor of England (1865 – 1936), and Czar Nicholas II Romanov of Russia (1868 – 1918). All were the grandsons of Queen Victoria (1918 – 1901) of England. The main combatants were the Allies: Britain, France, and Russia, versus the Central Powers: Germany Austria-Hungry, Turkey. (The Allies were joined by Italy in 1915, and America in 1917, but lost Russia in 1917). The Great War was indeed a World War. It was fought in Western and Eastern Europe, Africa, the Middle East, the Atlantic and South Pacific. The Great War was a 20th century conflict fought with 19th century tactics. On the Western Front, barbed-wire and trenches stretch from the North Sea to the Alps. On the prototypical level, all the weapons of World War Two were introduced in the Great War: warplanes, submarines, tanks, machinegun, and flame throwers, all except the atomic bomb. The machinegun fired 30 times faster than a rifleman. The firepower of the defense defeated the offense 4 to 1 in this conflict. Artillery accounted for 60% to 70% of the deaths. The next most fatal weapon was the machinegun. The armies of all the belligerents were wiped-out and replaced, wiped-out and replaced, and wiped-out and replaced a third time! On both the Western and Eastern Fronts, the war was one long continuous battle. Poison gas was used in the Great War, but not in the Second World War. This was the first war in history in which disease was not the greatest killer. Though participating for only 200 days (1917 – 1918), the American entrance on the side of the Allies assured their victory. World War One was the most transformative war in history. Four dynasties and empires crashed in the Great War: The Hohenzollerns of Germany; the Hapsburgs of Austria-Hungary; the Romanovs of Russia, and the Ottomans of Turkey. Nevertheless, the conflict resumed in 1939, after a 21 year armistice (World War Two). Incidentally: The greatest tragedy of the Great War was the victory of nationalism and capitalism over internationalism and Socialism.

GREAT WHITE – (*GRAYT WITE*) The largest shark and *"predatory"* fish in the world. The Great White is a magnificent monster fish. A male can grow to 20 feet in length, weighing up to 4,300 pounds. They can live for 70 years. The Great White is one of 4 true man-eaters, along with the Bull shark, Tiger shark, and Oceanic White Tip Shark. Nevertheless, about 96% of the time, the Great White's bite is exploratory, just one bite, for the taste. Still the bite can be fatal. Great Whites prefer the colder temperate waters near the roaring 40's in latitude. This region supports great schools of fish and marine mammals like seals, ample food for the shark. California Great Whites are larger than their Australian and South African cousins, but less aggressive than the latter two. Great Whites can never stop swimming, or they will suffocate. Even when asleep they move forward, forcing oxygenated water into their gills. Incidentally: Sharks, including Great Whites seemed repelled by the odor of dead sharks in the water. This scent is being researched as a shark repellant. Sharks have no bones, just cartilage. Killer Whales (Orcas) have learned to ram Great Whites, rupturing internal organs which result in death. Sharks like the Great White experience a physiological phenomenon called *"tonic immobility."* When turned on their backs, they enter a helpless hypnotic state. Intelligent mammalian Orcas have learn to flip Great Whites on their backs, killing and eating them.

GREED – (*GREED*) (Greedy) Lust for more, generated by the false capitalist scarcity mentality. Greed is economic gluttony, never satisfied with enough. Whereas the miserly are motivated by fear, the greedy are motivated by lust. The competitive private property, private profit nature of capitalism naturally generates greed. President Herbert Hoover (1874 – 1964), a staunch capitalist lamented that *"The only problem with capitalism is capitalists. They are too damn greedy."* The capitalist scarcity mentality is a myth. *"There is plenty on Earth to satisfy man's need, but not man's greed."* – Mohandas Gandhi (1869 – 1948). Capitalist greed was the only vice that provoked the saintly Jesus to lose his temper. He violently cast the money-changers out of the Holy Temple Plaza. *"My who life I've been greedy, greedy, greedy for money. I grabbed all the money I could get, I'm so greedy."* – Donald J. Trump (b. 1946).

GREED AND FEAR – (*GREED* and *FEER*) Avarice plus dread. These are the two motivating factors of capitalism, the driving force of *"The Wall Street Casino."* The New York Stock Exchange, the epicenter of capitalism, is a gambling house. Like every game of chance, it is based on bets that are inspired by greed and fear – greed for more, fear of losing all. Such raw emotions like fear and greed squeeze out any room for love. Wall Street is an unlovable place. That's because a capitalist economy is a win/lose proposition. There must be victors and vanquished, no room for love. In this cut-throat competitive system, only the strong [read: *ruthless*] survive. A gambling casino is no way to run a national economy. Greed and fear provokes the sentiments: *"What's in it for me?"* and *"I got mine, to hell with you!"* Are these the values you hope to nurture in your children? Are these the values you hope to see in your neighbors? Do you really prefer living among capitalists? Capitalism excites the worst instincts in people – *"Keep out! No Trespassing! Intruders will be shot!"* Wall Street has no concern for Main Street, unless it benefits Wall Street [read: *the rich*]. Compassion is foreign to capitalism. It is considered a sign of weakness. When profit becomes the motivation, as in capitalism, people become raw material, the means to an end. Capitalism generates greed and fear. Socialism generates sharing and love.

GREEDITIS – (greed-*EYE*-tis) Enlargement and inflammation of the greed gland, an ailment of the capitalist system. Greeditis is cured by the removal of the capitalist system by Socialist surgery.

GREEDY VERSUS MISERLY – (*GREE*-dee *VER*-sus *MY*-zer-lee) Being greedy is being avaricious, rapaciously desirous of profit, wealth, more. Being miserly is being penurious, excessively stingy, and cheap. Both the greedy and miserly suffer from a similar character flaw, social disorder, and neurotic condition called "capitalism." Both are insecure individuals lashed by fear. The greedy fear they will not get their share. The miserly fear losing their share. Both believe in lack, the false concept that there is not enough to go around. They have not accepted the spiritual, Socialistic concept of abundance, that there is plenty for everyone. The greedy and miserly are unhappy, tortured souls. Both greediness and miserliness are capitalist generated ailments. Their common refrain is: *"I got mine, to hell with you!"* The remedy or cure for both greediness and miserliness is charity, sharing, giving to those in need. Jesus said: *"Give, and it will be given to you. Good measure, pressed down, shaken together, running over, will be put into your lap. For with the measure you use it will be measured back to you."* – Luke 6:38.

GREEK FIRE – (*GREEK FY*-er) An ancient flamethrower. Greek fire was a Byzantine naval weapon (c. 670 CE). It pumped an incendiary fluid from a tube onto enemy ships. The formula for the concoction was a carefully kept state secret. There has been much speculation as to what were the ingredients. Greek fire is thought to have consisted of naphtha (natural gasoline), pine resin (turpentine), potassium nitrate (saltpeter), calcium phosphide, quick lime, and sulfur. This flammable mixture burned on water. The story has it that a Syrian alchemist invented an oily substance that was flammable, even in water. He tried to sell it to the Syrian Caliph of Damascus, who was disinterested. So he approached the Emperor of Byzantium who bought it. The emperor successfully used the incendiary against the Caliph's navy, with devastating effect. Therefore, due to a lack of imagination, the flamethrower came to be known as Greek fire, rather that Syrian fire.

GREEN CARD – (*GREEN* kahrd) Officially, the *"Permanent Resident Card."* The green card is a document issued by the U.S. Government permitting a foreigner to live and work in the U.S.A. Obtaining the green card is a major step in the arduous process for an immigrant seeking American citizenship. This was not always the case. Racist, xenophobic President Donald Trump (b. 1946) and his fascist henchman, Stephen Miller (b. 1985) have thrown every possible obstacle in the path of prospective new citizens. Never has it been so difficult to obtain a green card. Nevertheless, many persist and succeed. By the way, the green card is no longer green. It resembles an official state I.D. card or driver's license. Presently, there are about 13.2 million green card holders in the United States awaiting citizenship. Incidentally: Republicans Trump and Miller have slapped a moratorium on the swearing-in of all eligible green card holders. Trump rightly fears that the new citizens will vote against him.

GREEN CORN – (*GREEN* kawrn) Corn-on-the-cob, which is yellow, not green in color. The term green means fresh, nor dried hard for preservation. Fresh, soft, sweet maize for human consumption. Green corn could be roasted, boiled, canned, or eaten raw right off the stalk. Only about 10% of the maize grown in the U.S.A. is green corn for dinner. Most American corn if fed to animals as fodder, in order to produce meat.

GREENHOUSE – (*GREEN*-hows) an indoor garden, a nursery structure for cultivating plants. Constructed of framed glass, the greenhouse allows solar heat to penetrate, but not to dissipate. Therefore, greenhouses are hot and humid (due to transpiration of oxygen by the plants). Greenhouses enable even tropical plants to be cultivated in cold, temperate climate regions. "This is the *greenhouse effect.*" Incidentally: Wrought-iron and glass greenhouses were the first prefabricated structures manufactured and sold, in 19th century England.

GREENHOUSE EFFECT – (*GREEN*-hows ef-*FECT*) The layer of atmospheric gasses released by the burning of coal and petroleum that traps infrared solar energy, causing global temperatures to increase. The global warming opens a *Pandora's Box* of climatic and human disasters. Capitalist industrialist's insistence on burning dirty but cheap coal is the major contributor to the greenhouse effect. President tycoon, Donald Trump (b. 1946) has deregulated every protection afforded the environment in order to profit himself and his corporate capitalist supporters. By doing so, Trump has greatly exacerbated the global greenhouse crisis to an emergency pitch.

GREENIES – (*GREEN*-neez) A mockingly pejorative designation for members of Liberal environmentally conscious political parties. Conservative capitalists tend to call Green Party members Greenies. Green Parties play a political role in European parliamentary governments. Greenies are ecologically concerned, environmentally protective. They fight for regulatory legislation that will nurture nature. These environmental safeguards cost money. They cut into corporate capitalist profits. That's why conservative capitalists despise the Green Parties and call their members Greenies (among other names).

GREENLAND SHARK – (*GREEN-land SHAHRK*) (also Gurry or Grey Shark) A rare member of the Somniosidae family of fish. They dwell in the cold northern water of the Atlantic and Arctic Oceans, as around Greenland. The Greenland shark has the longest known lifespan of all vertebrates (backboned) species (estimated to be 250 to 500 years). This deep water, slow moving fish has a slow moving metabolism which contributes to its longevity. They will feed on any bite-sized creature they come upon, as well as hunting seal. They are huge fish over 21 feet long, weighing over 2,200 pounds. The shark has a high concentration of *trimethylamine N-oxide* in its tissues, which makes its flesh toxic to eat – a defense mechanism. This too contributes to its long life – no serious predators. Incidentally: After careful treatment of its meat,

Greenland shark is made edible. It is an Icelandic delicacy called *"kaestur hakarl,"* which is fermented, dried fish. It has an ammonia aroma (as does all shark flesh).

GREEN POWDER – (green *POU*-der) A health additive made from dried pulverized green vegetables, berries, leafy greens, and green tea. Green powder is often mixed with powdered protein and probiotics (good bacteria). It serves as a healthy antioxidant (boosts immune system and inhibits signs of aging).

GREEN ROOM – (*GREEN* room) A show business term for a space in a theater or television station that functions as a waiting room and lounge for performers or guests before and after their appearance on stage or on the air. Green rooms are furnished with comfortable with sofas and refreshments. Green rooms are not necessarily painted green. This designation is just a theatrical tradition. Some English theatres contain several green rooms, each ranked according to the status, fame, and salary of the actor. Furthermore, one could be fined for using a green room above one's status. How very typically British! The definitive origin of the term *"green room"* is lost to history. London's old Blackfriars Theatre (1599) included a room behind the scenes, where the actors waited to go on stage which was painted green, and called *"the green room."* Later (1662), London's Cockpit-in-Court theatre included a green baize dressing room. These may have provided the origin of the term.

GREENWASHING – (*GREEN*-wawsh-ing) (Greenwashed, Greenwasher) A new term added to the dictionary in 2023. Greenwashing is another form of corporate capitalist deception. It is the practice of promoting or affiliating a product, company, or industry with environmentalism (green) as a ploy to divert attention from its policies and practices which are anti-environmentalist. The oil companies are the most flagrant greenwashers, as is exemplified in their deceptive TV commercials.

GREEN WITCH – (*GREEN WICH*) A nature oriented witch. A Green Witch focuses his/her practice on the natural environment, materials, and energies. Green Witches are skilled herbalists. They are gardeners, horticulturalists, and proficient in *"wildcraft,"* (collecting medicinal plants and mushrooms). Green Witches are acutely attuned to the cycles of nature. They are dedicated environmentalists. To a Green Witch, all natural places are sacred. Protecting God's holy nature is a sacred duty.

GREGARIOUS – (greg-*GAR*-ree-us) (Gregarity) Needing human company, hungering for human companionship. Man is a social animal, thus longing to be among others. This is gregarity. This is why solitary confinement is a punishment in prisons. French poet and dramatist Paul Claudel (1868 – 1955) expressed the need exquisitely. *"There is no one of my brothers I can do without. In the heart of the meanest miser, the most squalid prostitute, the most miserable drunkard, there is an immortal soul with holy aspirations which deprived of daylight, worships in the night. I hear them speaking when I speak, and weeping when I go down on my knees. There is no one of them I can do without. Just as there are many stars in the heaven and their power of calculation is beyond my reckoning, so also there are many living beings. I need them all in my praise of God. There are many living souls but there's not one of them that I'm not in communion in the sacred apex when we utter together the Our Father."*

GREGORIAN CALENDAR – (greg-*GOR*-ree-an *CAL*-len-der) The 1582 revision of the Julian calendar made by Pope Gregory XIII (1502 – 1585). The Gregorian calendar is currently used in most of the world.

GRENADINE – (gren-na-*DEEN*) Pomegranate juice syrup. Grenadine is a favorite mixer in cocktails.

GRIDIRON – (*GRID*-eye-ern) A utensil made of parallel metal bars, used to grill meat. A barbeque grill, if squared (not round) qualifies as a gridiron. Actually, any framework of lateral bars, usually iron, like the gate or window of a prison cell or the grillwork on a sewer opening can be called a gridiron. Incidentally: During the cruel Middle Ages, gridirons were used as a common instrument of torture. A victim would be chained to a gridiron which was slowly heated through convection, until the device was red hot, and the victim roasted alive. That's going Medieval.

GRIDIRON FOOTBALL – (*GRID*-eye-ern *FOOT*-bawl) An alternate, though seldomly used name for North American (U.S./Canadian) football, as opposed to British Rugby (Union or League) football. The 100-yard football field in America is marked out with chalk into twenty 5-yard intervals. The 110-yard Canadian field is divided into twenty-two 5-yard intervals. Though the Canadian field is 10 yards longer, both create the image of a gridiron, ergo, the name.

GRIDLOCK – (*GRID*-lock) A monumental traffic jam. The stoppage of free-flow vehicular traffic in an urban area at major intersections. A *"grid"* is a series of intersecting horizontal and vertical lines. In this case, its streets or roads forming junctions. Gridlock is the blockage in the movement of vehicles locked up the grid. The cause of gridlock could be construction, an accident, bad weather, or just too many cars. The term *"gridlock"* was coined by Sam *"Gridlock"* Schwartz, a transit engineer for the New York City Traffic Department. Sam, along with fellow engineer Roy Cottam were on duty in April 1980, during a strike by city transit workers. In 2001, Schwartz declared that: *"One day, Roy spoke of his fears if we closed the streets in the Theater District, the grid system would 'lock-up' and all traffic would grind to a halt. Soon we simply juxtaposed the word, and the term gridlock was born."* Gridlock is more than a massive pain-in-the-ass. It is deadly. Police, Fire Department, and Ambulance cannot penetrate the gridlock, any more than you can. Incidentally: Eliminate gridlock by eliminating privately-owned cars. Government-owned mass transit is the inevitable future solution.

GRIEF – (*GREEF*) (Grieve) The pain of dealing with profound loss. A death is a prime generator of grief, especially the death of a child (son or daughter). We are most vulnerable in times of grief. *"You cannot grieve alone. You need somebody who legitimizes and validates your pain."* – Psychologist John Bradshaw (1933 - 2016).

GRIEF SPIRAL – (*GREEF SPY*-roll) The centrifugal movement of emotional pain, due to a tragedy like death. The pain of grief drifts outward in concentric circles from an epicenter of hurt, where the misery is most intense. The agony, weakens as it drifts outwardly, nevertheless, it is still felt. A good analogy is the ripples a pebbles makes when tossed in a still pond. It has been estimated on average that at least 20 people are affected in the grief spiral.

GRIEVANCE POLITICS – (*GREE*-vansz *POL*-li-tics) A grievance is a resentment, a complaint for some hurt, wrong, or injustice. Grievance politics is playing the victim role. A grieved politician is seeking sympathy support, a pity vote. She tries to convince the electorate that she is being treated unfairly. Donald Trump (b. 1946) is accomplished at grievance politics. Despite his overt criminality, illegality, corruptibility, immorality, Trump is able to convince his stupids that he is the mistreated martyr. In his grievance politics, Trump claims to be persecuted by the Liberal elite, because he is a champion of the common man. Actually, Trump is the benefactor of the rich. Grievance politics first became apparent during the President Barack Obama (b. 1961) Administrations (2009 – 2017). It made its debut with the *"Tea Party Movement,"* and their slogan: *"Give me my country back!"* Grievance politics propels the culture war. It depicts the common man as persecuted by the Liberal elite. It utilizes mass paranoia of barbarians at the gate, immigrants and colored people intending to dispossess and replace middle-class white America. In the post-Trump era, Republicans-cum-Trumpublicans have nothing substantial, beneficial to offer the common man but fear and hate. This is grievance politics. The emphasis of the culture war's grievance politics is *"what you are against,"* for it has nothing it stands for. Grievance politics is tailor made for the *"Party of NO!"*

GRIFT – (*GRIFT*) (Grifting, Grifter) Swindling, cheating, obtaining money or property through fraudulent means. A grifter is a conman, a crook like corrupt Donald Trump (b. 1946). A grifter may be a big-time embezzler and defrauder like Trump, or a petty thief, scammer, pickpocket. The term grift is a corruption of the term *"graft."* It was contrived in 1906 as an American underworld slang.

GRIMACE – (*GRIM*-uhs) (Grimaced, Grimacing) An ugly, contorted facial expression, an emotional reaction that indicates disapproval, disgust, or pain. *"He grimaced when she asked if he's voting for Trump."*

GRIMOIRE – (greem-*WAHR*) A manual of magic and witchcraft used by sorcerers and witches. The term made its way into English by 1849. A grimoire contained esoteric incantations to invoke the devil.

GRIM REAPER – (grim *REEP*-er) A universal symbol, depiction of death. The adjective grim means sinister, ghastly. A reaper is one who cuts down grain with a blade like a sickle or scythe. The Grim Reaper is the ghostly figure of a skeleton shrouded in a dark, hooded robe, carrying a scythe. The Grim Reaper first appeared in 14th century European art. This was during the world's worst pandemic, the Bubonic Plague or *"Black Death"* of 1347 – 1351. One third of Europe's population perished in the plague. The Reaper is a skeleton representing death in a decomposed human body. Its garb represents the clergy that presided over funerals. The scythe it carries symbolizes the cutting down of lives. The Grim Reaper is a hellish, frightening figure. It bereaves life of faith and hope of life after death.

GRINDADRAP – (*GRIN*-dah-drap) A yearly festival of slaughter that takes place in the Faroe Islands. The victims are whales and dolphins. The Faroe Islands are an isolated group of small treeless islands in the cold North Atlantic Ocean. The Faroes lie north of Scotland between Norway to the east, and Iceland to the west. The Faroe Islands are a self-governing dependency of Denmark. The term *"grindadrap"* derives from the Faroese word *"grindhvalur"* meaning *"pilot whales,"* and *"drap"* meaning *"killing."* Each year, an average of 700 whales and dolphins are herded and trapped in a small shallow bay by fishing boats. The panicked mammals beach themselves where they are hacked to death. Once beached, the pitiful creatures are killed by severing their spinal cords, in view of the mass of residents and tourists. The grindadrap tradition dates back to the Vikings in the 9th century. The beach and bay runs red with blood, like beet juice. Then the animals are butchered. The meat is consumed and marketed. Whale blubber oil still has some commercial uses, but no longer a necessity for heating or lighting. Incidentally: Like bull fighting, grindadrap is a long standing cultural tradition. So was witch-burning. That doesn't make it right.

GRINDING – (*GRINE*-ding) (also Junking or Freaking Wining) A salacious dance maneuver in which the partners rub and bump each other's genital regions. The female usually presents her buttocks, being slightly bent over, while the male makes contact with his crotch. He holds her hips, and fondles her breasts and buttocks. Grinding emulates intercourse. Interestingly, the term grinding had for millennia held a risqué double entendre. The dual meaning traces back at least to the Biblical story of Samson (c. 835 BCE), about 3,000 years ago. The strongman Samson was enslaved by the Philistines and *"put to grind,"* (Judges 16:21). It has been assumed that Samson was grinding grain. But grinding also meant copulating. Some scholars suggest that he may have been grinding slave girls, as a stud, a sex slave. Because of his great strength, the Philistines may have hoped to breed a slave army of giant warriors. After all, the giant Goliath was a Philistine.

GRINGO – (*GRING*-goh) A pejorative Mexican term for Americans. Often a simple term has an ancient and convoluted etymology. Such is the case with *"Gringo."* A Medieval Latin proverb read: *"Graecum est; non potest legi."* ("It is Greek; it cannot be read.") That proverb is the ancestor to the popular saying: *"It's Greek to me."* In Spanish, *"hablar en griego"* (literally "to talk in Greek") is to speak unintelligibly. In time, *"Griego"* altered slightly to *"gringo."* According to the <u>*Diccionario Castellano*</u> (published in 1787) written by Esteban de Terreros y Pando (1707 – 1782*), "In Malaga, they call <u>Gringos</u> those foreigners who have a certain type of accent which keeps them from speaking Spanish easily…."* [English translation]. By the 1840's, Spanish-Mexicans were applying the term gringo to Anglo-American foreigners whose speech they could not understand. By the time of the Mexican-American War (1846 – 1848), the term gringo took on an opprobrious connotation. The first English record of gringo in print comes from the 1849 diary of John Woodward Audubon (1812 – 1862), called the <u>*Western Journal*</u>. It reads: *"We were hooted and shouted at as we passed* through and called 'Gringoes'."* "Once you label me, you negate me." – Philosopher Soren Kierkegaard (1813 – 1855).

GRINGOLANDIA – (gring-goh-*LAN*-dee-ah) A Latin American ethnic slur for the United States of America.

GRIOTS – (*GREE*-ots or *GREE*-ohs) Professional cultural/historical memorizers in parts of preliterate Africa. Griots utilize the mnemotechnical system of committing information to memory for posterity. They are living tribal encyclopedias.

GRIPE – (*GRYP*) (Griped, Griping, Griper) Gripe is colic, pain in the bowels or intestines. Gripe is a gastrointestinal ailment, usually caused by indigestion and gas. It is an uncomfortable or mildly painful condition, albeit temporary. Nevertheless, gripe will put a person in a foul mood. He's likely to become irritable and begin to complain or gripe. Having become impatient with the griping, a companion might chide: *"Stop your griping"* or *"bellyaching."*

GRISTLE – (*GRIS*-sul) Semi-solidified gelatin. Gristle is a firm, elastic cartilaginous connective tissue, translucent white in color. It is found in joints where bone attaches to bone as in the shoulders, knees, ribs, and spine. Gristle serves as a padding to prevent friction and as a shock absorber. Being cartilage, the spinal discs are made of gristle, as well as the ears and the tip of the nose. The rubbery substance at the end of chicken bones is gristle. In order to keep gristle (cartilage) healthy, consume gelatin.

GROATS – (*GROTES*) Specifically buckwheat. Groats more generally refers to a hulled grain as oats, wheat, barley or others, cracked into a cereal.

GROG – (*GROG*) (Groggy, Gorged) An alcoholic drink, a mixture of rum and water. As a cocktail today sugar, lemon, and spices are often added to the drink. Grog is sometimes served hot as a toddy. The term *"grog"* came from a coarse fabric called *"grogram,"* which was used to make naval coats. British Admiral Edward Vernon (1684 – 1757) wore a grogram coat. The British sailors at Port Royal, Jamaica came to call Admiral Vernon *"Old Grog."* At the time, British sailors were given a ration of half-a-pint of rum a day. That's a lot of intoxicant. In 1740, Admiral Edward *"Old Grog"* Vernon ordered the rum ration cut with a quart of water. This mixture came to be named grog after him. The sailors were displeased. The Royal Navy continued Vernon's grog ration until 1970 (*"the tot"*). Indeed, grog was much weaker than straight rum. The British military also mixed rum with laudanum (opium Juice), used as an potent anesthetic in surgery. This too came to be called grog. It was more tolerable to have one's arm or leg sawed off when groggy. Footnote: One of Admiral Edward Vernon's junior officers was Lawrence Washington (1684 – 1757), George Washington's (1732 – 1799) big brother. Lawrence idolized his commander, Admiral Vernon, so much so that he renamed the family plantation in Virginia. *"Little hunting Creek"* plantation was re-chastened *"Mount Vernon."*

GROOMER – (*GROO*-mer) (Grooming) A pedophile. *"Groomer"* is a conspiratorial term used by anti-gay slanderers. It is applied to Liberals usually in a position of stewardship and authority, over children, primarily teachers. Homophobic individuals, like Florida's fascist Governor Ron DeSantis (b. 1974) suggest that Liberal or gay teachers indoctrinate young children in school to be tolerant toward homosexuality. They *"groom"* the kids to accept a gay lifestyle, it is claimed. Ergo, they have been maliciously branded as *"groomers."* The nasty implication is that the teacher is a covert pedophile. Of course, this is all right-wing nonsense, a salvo in the culture war to rile-up ignorant people for political support. The only real groomers are the fascist politicians who are grooming the public to reject democracy. DeSantis attacked groomers in the *"Don't Say Gay"* Act (H.B. 1557) of April 2022. DeSantis' Press Secretary Christine Pushaw (born c. 1992) called the sexist act the *"Anti-Grooming Law."* It makes education in sexual diversity impossible, if illegal. Incidentally: Ron DeSantis is the most dangerous politician in America today. Unlike Donald Trump (b. 1946) whose sun is setting, DeSantis' sun is rising. DeSantis is as nasty and as Nazi as Trump, but unlike *"The Donald,"* *"The Ronald"* is no buffoon, which makes him infinitely more dangerous to democracy. It is perfectly possible to vote away your freedom, as the Germans did in 1933. *"When fascism comes to America, it will be called 'anti-fascism,' and it will come in the name of national security."* – Socialist Senator Huey Long (1893 – 1935). *"When fascism comes to America, it will be wrapped in the flag and carrying a cross."* – Socialist Novelist Sinclair Lewis (1885 – 1951).

GROOVING – (*GROOV*-ving) Learning, adopting a routine, *"getting into the groove."* In education, grooving consists of conditioning students to cooperate with classroom regulations, procedures, and expectations, without being told.

GROPE – (*GROAP*) (Groping, Groped) In the vulgar vernacular, *"To cop a feel."* To grope is to grabble, manipulate, and fondle another's body for sexual pleasure. To be groped without permission constitutes an assault. It is the most common sexual abuse maneuver employed by men over women. *"His Piggishness,"* President Donald Trump (b. 1946) was caught on tape boasting: *"I love to grab [grope] women by the pussy. When you're rich, you can do anything."*

GROTESQUE – (grow-*TESK*) (Grotesquely, Grotesqueness) An abomination. Monstrously ugly in shape, appearance, or personality. What is grotesque is a distorted aberration from the normal.

GROTTO – (GROT-*toh*) A shallow depression like an alcove or small cave in a rock wall. In doors, a grotto in a wall accommodates a bookshelf or a religious shrine.

GROUND MORAINE – (*GROUND* mor-*RAYN*) In geology, unsorted material, rock, gravel, shingle, soil, left beneath a glacier when the ice melts.

GROUNDHOG DAY – (*GROUND*-hog *DAY*) February 2, a minor folk holiday in the U.S. and Canada. A groundhog, also called a woodchuck, is a large ground squirrel that burrows in the ground. Early in American History, a weather lore was established among the Pennsylvania Dutch [read: *"Deutch,"* or Germans] called *"Grundsaudaag."* They believed that if the groundhog emerged from its burrow on a sunny February 2 and saw its shadow, winter would continue for 6 more harsh weeks. If the day is cloudy, and the creature could not see its shadow, spring would come early. There is no scientific validity supporting the Groundhog Day proposal whatsoever. Meteorologically speaking, if the rodent sees his shadow, it's a sunny winter day, governed by a high-pressure ridge, bringing clear, dry, crisp, cold weather. If she does not see her shadow, it's a cloudy winter day, governed by a low-pressure trough, bringing overcast, damp, snowy weather. In either case, the groundhog doesn't care. This superstition was brought to America from Germany, where the badger (not groundhog) served as the weather forecaster. The groundhog observation ceremony still occurs on February 2, at the town of Punxsutawney in Western Pennsylvania. The term *"Groundhog Day"* has entered the popular parlance meaning a perpetually repeating occurrence. This was attributed to the 1993 comedy film entitled *"Groundhog Day,"* staring Bill Murray (b. 1950). In the movie, Murray plays a cynical television weatherman covering the annual Groundhog Day ceremony in Pennsylvania. He becomes trapped in a time-loop, forcing him to relive the day repeatedly. His life became a *"Déjà vu all over again,"* to quote Yogi Berra (1925 – 2015). *"It was Groundhog Day in the Capitol as the House Republicans unsuccessfully voted over, and over, and over to try to make Kevin McCarthy (b. 1965) Speaker of the House."*

GROUPIES – (*GROOP*-pees) Young persons, usually teenage girls who are ardent admirers of rock musicians, and accompany them on tour. Star struck groupies make themselves available to the celebrities in any way they desire.

GROUP PARALYSIS – (*GROOP* pa-*RAL*-li-sis) A psycho-sociological phenomenon that often occurs to individuals in a crowd during a crisis. Normally responsible, dependable, courageous people who would jump into action in an emergency, may freeze when part of the crowd. An emotional paralysis sets in. Personal responsibility fades because the person is subconsciously subsumed by the crowd. The individual fails to respond or give aid. It seems that a group mind commandeers the personal mind. Intervention becomes the group's responsibility, not the individual's. Every person waits for someone else to react first.

You may even hear the pitiful cry: "*Won't somebody do something!?*" However, if someone takes charge and does commit to action, group paralysis can quickly be transformed into group impulsiveness, in a frenzy of united action. Incidentally: In Uvalde, Texas, at Robb Elementary School, 376 heavily armed, militarized police officers failed to confront one 18 year old boy with a gun. This was while little children were being executed, slaughtered! Nineteen children and two adults were murdered. The battalion of "*good guys with guns*" froze, did nothing. Certainly, several of these police officers had performed heroically, alone, in the past. What happened at Robb Elementary School? "*Group Paralysis*" has to be a partial explanation, though not an excuse. The brave Texans exhibited "*testicular constriction*" – big hats but small balls.

GROUPTHINK – (*GROOP*-think) Homogenized thought, uniformity of opinion, coordination of cognition. Groupthink is a sociological term referring to the tendency of organizations to promote the party line, and suppress individualist thought. The greatest practitioner of groupthink is the military. The command structure of the military makes for simplistic attitudes. You are either an ally or enemy, with us or against us. Soldiers are not expected to think, but to react in conditioned response. Diversity or difference of opinion is unpatriotic. All ideas are filtered (even censored) through the organizational sieve. As Alfred Lord Tennyson (1809 – 1892) wrote: "*Theirs' is not to reason why; Theirs' is not to make reply; Theirs' is just to do and die….*"

GROVEL – (*GROV*-uhl) (Groveled, Groveling, Groveler) To behave in an abject humiliating manner, out of fear or utter servility. A groveler abases oneself, surrendering all dignity, pride, honor, and humanity. To grovel is to shamelessly crawl, so to speak, by supporting one's master implicitly. Slaves are obliged to grovel. It is an act of extreme "em-*BARR-ASS*-ment." Never in American History have politicians, legislators groveled to a President as the Republicans have slithered and squirmed at the feet of bloated Donald Trump (b. 1946). No amount of propriety, patriotism or pride can prevent the Republican groveling. They are terrified of a reproach or insult from Trump that would enrage their simple-minded constituents against them. The Republicans in the states and federal Houses and Senates are anilingus all [read: *ass lickers*]. As with all slaves, they have a secret, visceral hatred for Trump, their humiliator. But like most in bondage, they can't muster the courage to liberate themselves from the Trump. The Republicans will pay a price for serving as "*Trump's Punks.*"

GRU – (jee-are-*YOU*) A Russian initialism for "G̲lavoye R̲azvedyvatel'noye U̲pravleniye," meaning "*Chief Intelligence Headquarters.*" The GRU is Russia's primary foreign intelligence or spy agency. With the disintegration of the Soviet Union (1991), the GRU was established in 1992 as successor to the KGB ("K̲omitet G̲osudarstvennoy B̲ezopasnosti," meaning "*Committee of State Security*)." The GRU is the Russian counterpart to the American CIA.

GRUBSTAKE – (*GRUHB*-stayk) Money, supplies, or other assistance furnished at a time of need, or when starting a new enterprise. Grubstake is not a reference to beefsteak, though it could include food (grub). The term derives from American Western miner's slang, (c. 1876). Grubstake was a deal made with the storeowner to provide the needed supplies as an investment. The lender had a *stake* in the enterprise. Mining involved some sort of digging. The term "*grub*" derived from Old English (West Saxon) (c. 13th century) meaning "*to dig in the ground.*"

GRUEL – (*GROOL*) Thinned-out porridge, eaten by the poor. Gruel is a light, thin, cooked cereal made by boiling meal, especially oatmeal, in water or milk. Gruel was a staple of the indigent of Victorian England. It is a low nutritional food, a cereal soup or broth.

GRUNT – (*GRUNT*) Self-imposed name for an American soldier in the Vietnam War (1960's – 1975). The grunt was usually an unwilling draftee who could not afford college or maintain his deferment [read: *good grades*]. The grunt's personal mission in Vietnam was to stay alive, serve his time, and get the hell out in one piece.

G-SPOT – (*JEE*-spot) (<u>G</u>rafenberg <u>*Spot*</u>) A patch of tissue in the front wall of the vulva, claimed to be erectile, highly erogenous, and sensitive to orgasmic stimulation. The G-spot is probably an extension of the 8,000 clitoral nerve endings (more than anyplace else on the body). To find and stimulate this *"sweet spot,"* will excite an explosive orgasm. Tickling the G-spot with the finger, tongue, dick, or toy will make many women gush or squirt. *"My God, a moment of bliss!"* – Fyodor Dostoyevsky (1821 – 1881).

G-STRING – (*JEE*-string) A small patch of cloth that barely covers the vagina. The cloth is fastened to a string that passes between the buttock cheeks and is attached to a skimpy waistband around the hips. Although the G-string conceals the genitals, it exposes the entire ass. The G-string is designed for the unabashedly uninhibited. It will not suit those easily *"emBARE-ASSed."* It is a seductive *"garment"* worn by professional strippers, flirtatious bathers, and newly wed wives. The G-string may be the minimal amount of apparel one can wear, and not be considered totally nude. The concept of the G-string may have been inspired by the loincloth worn by American Indians. The term is an Americanism that dates back to about 1878. It may have derived from the lowest and thickest violin chord, the *G-string* (1831).

GUADALCANAL – (Gwa-dal-*CAN*-nal) A mountainous Tropical Island in the southwest Pacific, the largest in the Solomon Group. It is a populated island of 2,500 square miles. During World War Two, Guadalcanal marked the southernmost point of the Japanese defensive perimeter. Guadalcanal was the first offensive action taken by the U.S. against the Japanese in the Pacific War, August, 1942. The mission was to take the strategic airstrip on the island, Henderson Field. The battle became a bloody 6-month campaign, which included vicious naval and air engagements. The U.S. lost 31 ships, the Japanese 38. About 615 U.S. aircraft were lost, the Japanese losing as many as 880. The elite Japanese naval aviation corps was decimated at Guadalcanal. On February 9, 1943, hostilities ceased on the island with an American victory. The Japanese lost 31,000 troops. The Americans lost about 2,000 of the 60,000 deployed. An additional 5,100 British, Australian, New Zealander, and Islanders troops were killed as well. Guadalcanal was the Japanese Army's counterpart, to their Navy's defeat at Midway. They never fully recovered. The momentum in the Pacific War from then on was with the Americans.

GUANACO – (goo-an-*NA*-co) The American camel. The South American camel- like llama.

GUANO – (goo-*AN*-o) High-nitrate bird and bat droppings consisting of urates, oxalates, calcium, phosphates of ammonium and mineral salts. Guano produces a very valuable fertilizer and an important ingredient in high explosives. So valuable is guano that wars have been fought among South American nations for control of guano islands on the Pacific Coast. When mixed with rain water, guano becomes a corrosive solution that eats through concrete and metal. In time, this destroys buildings, roads and bridges. Corrosion due to guano from pigeon waste solution contributed to the tragic collapse of the I-35 Mississippi River Bridge in Minneapolis (2007), with 13 fatalities.

GUARDIAN AD LITEM – (*GAHR*-dee-an ad *LEE*-tem) In law, a guardian appointed by a court to represent a minor unable to represent her or himself.

GUARDIAN ANGELS – (*GAHR*-dee-an *AYN*-jel) Celestial protectors assigned to each person and perhaps animal. That incredible act of good luck that saved us from harm or death may have been the work of our Guardian Angel. Psalm 91:11 assures us that *"God orders His angels to protect you wherever you go."* Furthermore, according to the Talmud, *"Every blade of grass has its angel bending over it whispering, 'Grow!' 'Grow!'"*

GUARDRAIL – (*GAHRD*-rayl) A protective barrier or railing along a roadway or stairway. A guardrail along a dangerous curve in the road may prevent one from going off the deep end. This term has entered the political lexicon by being applied to government. A level-headed, mature advisor or assistant may serve as a guardrail for an erratic, impulsive leader. He may be the only emotional *"adult,"* in the room. She may keep the leader on the right track, and not go off the deep end with rash, ill-conceived decisions. Several advisors had hoped to serve as President Donald Trump's (b. 1946) guardrail. To no avail. They were all caught off guard. Trump had them all run out on a rail. A Caveat: If, *God Forbid,* Trump is re-elected in 2024, there will be no guard rail to keep him on the democratic road.

GUAVA – (goo-*AV*-a) A sweet, roundish fruit, native to the Caribbean basin (Mexico, Central America, northern South America). Guava has been naturalized throughout the tropical/semitropical world. Varieties of guava appear in greenish-yellow and red rinds with pink or cream-colored pulp. It has a gritty texture like pears. This versatile fruit provides a deliciously sweet juice. It is used to flavor ice cream and many other desserts. In bush medicine, the leaves from the guava tree are brewed into a tea to treat diarrhea, dysentery, ring worm, and eczema.

GUACAMOLE – (gwau-kuh-*MOH*-lee) In Mexican cuisine a green dip made of mashed avocado mixed with tomato, onions, and seasonings. The term guacamole was first recorded in about 1915. It is derived from *"ahuacamolli"* in the Nahuatl language of the Aztec Indians meaning *"avocado sauce."*

GUARANA – (*GWAHR*-uhn-nah) Paullinia cupana, a woody, climbing shrub of the soapberry family, native to the Amazon, particularly in Brazil. Guarana seeds contain caffeine, which is used as a stimulant in various drinks. The Guarana fruit is eerie to look at because it is looking back at you. It looks so much like an eyeball, the dark brown seed embedded in the white fruit surrounded by the bright red shell. In fact, the word *"guara-na"* in the native Guarani language means *"eyes of the people,"* or *"eyes of the gods."* The stimulant substance extracted from Guarana has an apple/berry flavor. It is an additive in energy drinks like *"Red Bull,"* and *"Monster."* *"Smirnov"* has a vodka drink favored with Guarana. Amazonian Natives have used guarana as a health tonic. It revitalizes the skin with increased blood flow, making the skin firmer and more refreshed.

GUARD RAILS – (*GARD RAY*-uhls) Safety barriers along the sides of the road, particularly at dangerous locations, like curves. In around 2022, the term guard rails had been adopted into the political lexicon. The reason was Donald Trump's (b. 1946) 3rd run for the U.S. Presidency. The refrain has rung out from all sensible politicians and political commentators that a second Trump Presidency would have no checks-and-balances, no restraints, no guard rails. The fascist Trumpublican Supreme Court has already granted Trump monarchical immunity for all crimes he may commit as President. Too, there will be no patriotic professional advisors around Trump this time. They will all be ass-licking yes-men, chosen for their degree of loyalty to the Fuhrer Trump. The nation will be transformed into a fascist dictatorship as Trump applies *"Project 2025,"* his "*Mein Kampf.*" This time, there will be no guard rail to prevent America from plunging over the abyss.

GUBERNATORIAL – (goo-ber-nuh-*TAWR*-ree-uhl) (Gubernator, Gubernation) Not relating to a goober or peanut, but of or relating to a state governor or the office of a state governor. Then why not state *"gubernor?"* After all, the Latin word for governor is *"gubernator."* In fact, the term gubernator was used in English from the 1520s. Likewise, the term *"gubernation"* was used from the mid-15th century. Both words are rarely used today. The adjective *"gubernatorial"* is primarily an Americanism from 1734. The term was popularized and perpetuated by U.S. newspapers. Nevertheless, the state's chief executive is still called the governor. In about 1300, the term *"gouernour"* appeared in English. It meant a *"protector, guide, personal keeper."* This term was taken from the Old French *"governeor,"* meaning *"prince, ruler, administrator."* Governeor derived from the Latin gubernator.

GUCCIFER 2.0 – (*GOO*-si-fer 2.0) The pseudonym for a team of Russian military- intelligence agents determined to sabotage American democracy. The enigmatic name, *"Guccifer 2.0,"* was first used by a Romanian computer hacker, Marcel Lazar Lehel (b. 1971) in 2016. The name was usurped by the Russian intelligent agents. The Russian agents are also computer hacking experts. Their goals are to sow chaos in America; turn the American people against each other; disrupt and influence the 2020 election; aid Republican politicians; and assure the re-election of President Donald Trump (b. 1946). Guccifer's interference helped elect Donald Trump in the 2016 Presidential election. They hacked into the Democratic National Committee computer (a la Watergate) and leaked confidential documents which proved detrimental to Democratic candidate Hillary Clinton's (b. 1947) election chance. This was the intention of Guccifer 2.0. Dictator Vladimir Putin (b. 1952) and the Russians refer to Trump as: *"Our man in the White House."* Prior to the November 2020 Presidential election, Guccifer 2.0 continues to hack, burglarize, and divulge political information damaging to Democratic politicians in order to aid their Republican rivals. The Republicans are grateful for the unfair, unethical, and illegal help. That's why they refuse to take measures to curtail it. This perfidy has won Republican Senate Majority Leader Mitch McConnell (b. 1942) the epithet *"Moscow Mitch."* The overall grand strategy of Putin, Russia, and Guccifer 2.0 is the subversion of the American Constitution, and the destruction of the United States, hopefully by fomenting a civil war. Incidentally: The FBI has identified all the members of Guccifer 2.0. Though they continue to meddle in U.S. politics safely from Russia, they are officially wanted by the FBI and Interpol. Incidentally: Champagne corks popped in the Russian Congress on the day Trump was elected in November, 2916.

GUERNICA – (gwair-*NEE*-kah) A Basque town in the province of Biscay, in northern Spain. During the Spanish Civil War (1936 – 1939), the Spanish Fascist leader Francisco Franco (1892 – 1975) was aided by the German Fascist leader Adolf Hitler (1889 – 1945), and the Italian Fascist leader Benito Mussolini (1883 – 1945). The town of Guernica was an anti-Fascist, Republican stronghold. On April 26, 1937, bombers from the German Condor Legion and the Italian Aviazione Legionaria carpet-bombed Guernica. The Fascist airforces were testing their destructive capability in practice for the future World War. Guernica was the first city in history to be thoroughly demolished by indiscriminate aerial bombing. An estimated 1,654 civilians were killed. This was an atrocity for its time. Guernica was the prelude to the destruction of Warsaw, Rotterdam, London, Coventry, Hamburg, Dresden, Berlin, Tokyo, Hiroshima, and Nagasaki. In 1937, Spanish artist Pablo Picasso (1881 – 1973) painted his *Guernica*, a commemoration to the sacrificed city. Incidentally: During World War Two, a German office visited Picasso in occupied Paris. He happened to see the painting of *Guernica*. The German officer was shocked by the modernist *"chaos"* of the painting. He asked Picasso: *"Did you do this?"* Picasso calmly replied: *"No, you did this."*

GUERRILLAS – (ger-*RIL*-las) Irregular freedom fighters, usually Socialist peasants challenging capitalist oppressors. Guerrillas are partisans employing bush tactics, war in the shadows. Their means include sabotage, hit-and-run raids, war of attrition. Their goal is usually liberation from capitalist imperialist exploitation, oppression, and persecution. Guerrillas conduct war in the shadows. It has been suggested that a guerrilla cannot be killed by a bomb, but by a knife. *"Guerilla warfare is used by the side which is supported by a majority but which possesses a much smaller number of arms for use in defense against oppression."* – Che Guevara (1928 – 1967) Socialist Revolutionary. *"The conventional army loses if it does not win. The guerrilla wins if it does not lose."* – Henry Kissinger (b. 1923).

GUESTIMATION – (ges-ti-*MAY*-shun) (Guess, Guestimate, Guestimated) An estimation which is based on intuition. A guestimation is an informative guess, as opposed to an arbitrary hunch or gamble. Knowledge and experience backs a guestimation.

GUILLOTINE – (*GILL*-o-teen) Beheading machine of the French Revolution. The guillotine was invented in 1789 as a quick, humane means of execution by physician and Freemason Joseph-Ignance Guillotin (1738 - 1814). It was not the first decapitation machine invented. The guillotine was a simple pillory with a heavy suspended blade that fell onto the victim's neck. In the French Revolution (1789 - 1799) it served as a retribution for the poor against their oppressors, the rich. The guillotine decapitated a good part of the French aristocracy.

GUILDER – (*GIL*-der) Name for the currency formerly used in the Netherlands, replaced by the Euro.

GUILE – (*GYHL*-uhl) Duplicitousness, dishonestly crafty, artfully deceptive. A cunning conman like Donald Trump (b. 1946) is imbued with guile.

GUILELESS – (*GAHY*-uhl-lis) Without guile. In other words, honest, sincere, frank, straight forward.

GUILT – (*GILT*) (Guilty) The feeling generated when the conscience passes moral judgment on itself. Feeling guilty is judging past behavior by one's present revised moral condition. You've changed. The guilty person is denouncing an individual who no longer exists. To the point, the great comedian and scholar

Steve Allen (1921 – 2000) once remarked: *"Everyone one meet today was once someone else."* It is said that we spend the first part of our lives being outrageous, and the last part regretting it. Guilt is *"I did something wrong,"* in contrast to shame which is *"I am something wrong."* However, guilt can metastasize into shame. Reasonable guilt can serve positively whereas shame cannot. Reasonable guilt is a product of conscience. In either case, a great deal of remorse is generated. Guilt often provokes a desire for self-punishment. *"Lay me on an anvil, Oh God. Beat me and hammer me into a crowbar!"* – Poet Carl Sandburg (1878 – 1967). Therefore, be kind to yourself. Remember: You did the best you could, with who you were, and what you knew, in those points in time, space, and life. *"I was blind but now I see."* – John 9:25. *"I played the fool, and have errored greatly."* – King Saul (c. 1050 – 1010 BCE) in I Samuel 26:21.

GUINEA – (*GIN*-nee) A region along the west coast of Africa extending from the Gambia River to the Gabon estuary. Guinea is also an independent nation in that region, with its capital at Conakry. The term *"guinea"* probably derives from the Tuareg, Berber Muslims of the Sahara. The Tuareg used the term *"aginaw,"* meaning *"black people."* This is likely to be the origin of the name Guinea. By the 1740's the term *"Guinea Negro"* was applied derogatorily for black people or those of mixed ancestry. In 1546, Spanish explorer Inigo Ortiz de Retes named the great Indonesian island New Guinea because of the dark skin natives. Incidentally: The curative herb Guinea Hen was imported from New Guinea.

GUINEA CORN – (*GIN*-nee *KORN*) New World name for millet or sorghum, grains brought from Africa to the Americas to feed the plantation slaves cheaply. In this case, the term corn refers to grain in general, not maize. Today, Guinea corn is used as a fodder crop or birdseed.

GUINEA GRASS – (*GIN*-nee *GRASS*) Not marijuana from Guinea, but *Panicum maximum,* a heavy tall grass native to Africa, as well as Israel and Yemen. Guinea grass serves as excellent fodder silage for grazing, foraging animals. That's why it has been exported throughout the tropical/subtropical world. Different varieties of Guinea grass will grow from 1.5 to 11.5 feet tall. Its leaves or blades are rich in protein, from 6% to 25%. Guinea grass was imported into Australia in 1865 and 1869. Under good conditions, the grass will spread uncontrollably. In some areas like Sri Lanka, Hawaii, and Texas, Guinea grass has become an invasive nuisance. Guinea grass is an important fodder for animals in Jamaica (cattle and goat). It was introduced to the island accidentally in 1744. George Ellis had served as the Chief Justice of Jamaica. A slave ship captain gave Mr. Ellis a bag of Guinea grass seeds from West Africa to feed his exotic birds. After the birds died, Mr. Ellis scattered the seeds in the field at Greencastle, St. Mary. They germinated and propagated. Guinea grass spread throughout the island. It is here to stay.

GUINEA HEN WEED – (*GIN*-nee *HEN WEED*) (*Petiveria alliaces*) A flowering plant in the pigeonberry family, indigenous to tropical/semi-tropical America. Guinea Hen Weed is found in the Amazon, Caribbean, Central America, Mexico, South Texas, and Florida. It has been introduced to Benin and Nigeria, Africa. It grows into a 3-foot shrub. Known as *Anamu,* Guinea Hen Weed is used as an abortifacients by Amazonian natives. Guinea Hen Weed kills several strains of cancer, differentiating malignant cells from the healthy. Too, it serves as an immunostimulant by inducing the body to produce more lymphocytes, our disease-destroying cells. Galenicals in Guinea Hen Weed fights all kinds of infections, relieves pain, and lowers blood sugar levels. It is a little known miracle medicine. Incidentally: Guinea Hen Weed will produce a garlic-like taste and aroma in the user. Animals that eat Guinea Hen Weed will provide garlic-flavored meat. In fact, the plant is sometimes called *"Garlic Weed"* in Jamaica.

GUINEA MAN – (*Gin*-nee *MAN*) A slave fresh from Africa, also called *"saltwater Negro."* Guinea Men were often former warriors, dangerous prisoners of war. It was reasoned that they had to be seasoned, which meant tamed, hopes dashed, spirit broken. The most threatening Guinea Men were the *"Coromantee,"* who were shipped from the slave fort of Koromantine in present day Ghana. These proud and courageous Africans were strong, great for labor, but rebellious and threatening. The Coromantee led several revolts, in that many plantation owners were afraid to purchase them. One reason why Jamaica had so many slave revolts is because of the large population of Coromantee. A Guinea Man was matched-up with an acclimated slave from the same region as a teacher. Seasoning took anywhere from 1 to 3 years.

GUINEP – (*JIN*-ep) (also *Genip* or *Honeyberry*.) A tropical American tree that bears an ovoid green fruit that grows in bunches like grapes. The large marble- sized fruit is related to *"lychee."* It has a thin crispy skin that readily breaks with a bite. Inside is the tart, tangy, or sweet pulp of the fruit encasing a large seed. The pulp is juicy, usually a creamy orange color. Guinep was relished by the Taino Indians in Jamaica. The juice from the guinep seed yields an indelible blue-black stain when exposed to air.

GULAG – (*GOO*-lag) A Russian acronym for *"Main Camp Administration."* Originally, the system of forced-labor camps throughout the Soviet Union. Today, gulag applies to any prison especially for political dissidents. Guantanamo Bay, Cuba may qualify as an American gulag.

GULFCOAST EXCEPTION – (*GUHLF*-coast ex-*SEP*-shun) Coastal America (Atlantic and Pacific) tend to be the Progressive, well-educated, and Liberal parts of the nation. Coastal populations with a *"window on the world"* tend to be outward- looking, opened-minded, and tolerant of diversity. This is in contrast to the insulated, isolated interior conservatives. The coastal exception in America is the Gulfcoast residents. The coastal Southern States are conservative, closed- minded, reactionary rather than Progressive because they are Southern States. These states are confined along the Gulf of Mexico, not the broad Atlantic and Pacific. Despite their window on the Caribbean and Latin America, Gulfcoasters are intolerant and bigoted as are most Southern citizens. It's part of their historical heritage. Their voting pattern reveals that they will sacrifice their own economic interests and support Republicans, in order to maintain their bigoted (even racist) society. Gulfcoast Southerners supported the buffoon Donald Trump (b. 1946) in the 2016 election. Conservative Southerners (even on the coast) have the lowest educational level in the nation. The exceptions are the urbane big cities and educated college towns.

GULF STATES – (*GUHLF* stayts) (United States) The American states that border the Gulf of Mexico: Florida, Alabama, Mississippi, Louisiana, and Texas.

GULF STATES – (*GUHLF* stayts) (Middle East) The oil-rich Islamic nations that border the Persian Gulf: Bahrain, Iran, Iraq, Kuwait, Oman, Qatar, Saudi Arabia, and the United Arab Emirates. Incidentally: If the export of the Gulf States was olive oil instead of petroleum oil, we would not be able to locate them on a map. The billionaire sheiks would be milking camels and living in desert tents, as did their ancestors.

GULF STREAM – (*GUHLF* streem) A powerful warm current generated in the sub- tropical Gulf of Mexico. It is the world's strongest current. It flows at almost six-and-a half miles per hour. The force of the Gulf Stream is almost 100 times the flow of the mighty Amazon River, and 5 times more powerful than all the rivers of the world combined. Twenty million cubic meters of water per second surges through the Gulf Stream like a giant conveyor belt. The current is known as the Gulf Stream while it hugs the North American coast. But when it turns eastward at Labrador, and enters the broad Atlantic Ocean, it becomes known as the North Atlantic Drift. The Gulf Stream keeps the climate of Western Europe mild and prosperous. That's why they can grow food. Incidentally: Because of the Gulf Stream, Cornwall England has palm trees, while Labrador Canada (at the same latitude to the west) has icebergs. Incidentally: The technical, scientific name for the Gulf Stream is the *"Atlantic Meridional Overturning Circulation"* (AMOC).

GULLAH – (*GUL*-la) an archaic slave-ship pidgin variety of English, still spoken by a few poor, isolated Afro-Americans on the Sea Islands off the Carolina coast. Gullah is an English/West African hybrid dialect. Actually, Gullah was a refinement of West African Pigeon. Gullah refined into Plantation Creole, which evolved into Ebonics (Black Inner-City Dialect).

GULLIBLE – (*GUL*-li-bul) (Gullibility) Easily fooled, deceived or cheated. Gullible people are naively simple-minded, credulous, and can be readily tricked or taken to advantage. Conservative Fox *News* Network preys on people's gullibility. They induce poor and working-class citizens to vote against their own economic interests for capitalist Republicans. Gullibility reached a level of mass hysteria in 2016, with the election of Donald Trump (b. 1946) as president. Former Republican president, George W. Bush (b. 1946) exhibited shameless gullibility when he admitted: *"Fool me once, shame on me. Fool me twice – uh – shame on me again!"*

GUN – (*GUHN*) A firearm, great or small. A gun (pistol, rifle, and canon) uses an explosive powder to propel a projectile (ball, bullet, shell) in order to damage or kill. As a tool, the gun is used to hunt game for food. As a weapon, the gun is used to kill human beings in warfare or in crime. The gun was invented in China, after the discovery of gunpowder. The very first gun was a bamboo pole that fired a spear (c. 1000 CE). Later, metal tubes shooting stones were devised. It's a fact that no invention in history had spread throughout the world faster than the gun. By the 12th century, the technology was spreading through the rest of Asia, and into Europe by the 13th century. Only 40 years after the Chinese had invented the gun, it was in Europe undergoing improvements, the greatest being the trigger. Incidentally: The word gun derives from an Old Norse term *"gunnr"* meaning battle. Norse legend speaks of many fierce female warriors. It became traditional to name weapons after women, using Norse names. For example, the ballista (large missile-throwing crossbow) that protected Windsor Castle in the 14th century was named *"Lady Gunilda."*

GUNBOAT DIPLOMACY – (*GUHN*-boat dip-*PLO*-ma-see) The American policy to *"Speak softly, but carry a big stick"* everywhere South of the border. The U.S. has been eager to beat the brown people of Latin America and the Caribbean with that stick, whenever they threatened American corporate capitalist interests. It is ironic that the U.S. is appalled at Russian intervention (with propaganda) in the 2016 election, (helping to install Trump). Since World War Two, the C.I.A. has overthrown at least 35 governments, and bombed at least 65 nations. Since 1890, American forces had invaded Latin America and the Caribbean at least 57 times. The victims had been Argentina, Venezuela, Bolivia, Uruguay, Chile, Mexico, Honduras, Nicaragua, Guatemala, Costa Rica, Panama, El Salvador, Puerto Rico, Dominican Republic, Cuba, Haiti, and Grenada. To corporate capitalists, and the politicians they had bought, *"Democracy"* is a façade, a joke. They use the military to install the most vicious, sadistic fascist dictators, who promise to protect corporate profits. Socialists who intend to nationalize the countries' natural resources for the poor are slaughtered by C.I.A. *"death squads."* Marine Corps General Smedley Butler (1881 – 1940) spoke of his participation in gunboat diplomacy. *"I spent 33 years and 4 months in active military service and during that period I spent most of my time as a high class muscle man for Big Business, for Wall Street and the bankers. In short, I was a racketeer, a gangster for capitalism. I helped make Mexico and especially Tampico safe for American oil interests in 1914. I helped to make Haiti and Cuba a decent place for the National City Bank boys to collect revenues in. I helped in the raping of half a dozen Central American republics for the benefit of Wall Street. I helped purify Nicaragua for the International Banking House of Brown Brothers in 1902 – 1912. I brought light to the Dominican Republic for the American sugar interests in 1916. I helped make Honduras right for the American fruit companies in 1903. In China in 1927 I helped to see to it that Standard Oil went on its way unmolested. Looking back on it, I might have given Al Capone a few hints. The best he could do was to operate his racket in 3 districts. I operated on 3 continents."* Here is another answer to the naïve question: *"Why do they hate us?"*

GUN CONTROL – (*GUHN* kon-*TROHL*) An appeal for reasonable gun safety laws, in order to prevent mass murder. There are more guns in America than there are people. The United States is only 4% of the world's population possessing 42% of the world's guns. There are over 340 million guns in the USA. Over 65 millions of them are in Texas. Interestingly, 78% of Americans do not own a single gun. Conversely, only 3% of the population owns over half of those guns. Therefore, only about 9 million people own over 170 million guns (amounting to 19 guns per person). These are right wingers, the fascist leaning type of the Alt- Right, Survivalist, White Supremacist population. They tend to be bigoted, racist, pro-Trump Republicans. Many are armed-up for some futuristic race-war or to fight a Socialist take-over (a conflict for which they dream). Over 30,000 Americans are shot yearly. Over 10,000 of them are killed. (That dwarfs Afghanistan.) Gun control would take dangerous firearms out of the hands of criminals, the mentally unstable, and dangerous fascists. Assault weapons designed for battlefield carnage would be banned. However, conservatives led by the National Rifle Association (NRA) twist the intent of gun control to mean universal gun seizure. This scares gun owners from supporting reasonable regulation. Incidentally: By 2018, guns killed more Americans than cars. More Americans died from gun fire than from auto accidents. Gun deaths rose dramatically: older white men by suicide, Black Americans by homicide. In 2022, more American children were killed by guns than by car accidents – thanks to the Republicans. The Republicans want American mass-murderers to be the best armed in the world. Footnote: 34 states (68%) require permits of licenses to own a gun. So 16 states (32%) do not.

GUN CONTROL – (*GUHN* kon-*TROHL*) Specifically, *"Republican Gun Control."* What would it take to get the Republicans, conservatives, the National Rifle Association (NRA) to support gun control? Arm the poor. Distribute guns freely to the have-nots in the ghettoes, barrios, and trailer camps. Foment a Socialist Revolution. Threaten the capitalist's wealth, and the Republicans, conservatives, NRA will squeal like pricked pigs for immediate gun control. A cry would ring out from Republicans to abolish the 2nd

Amendment. If armies of armed indigents demanded distributive justice, their fair share of the wealth, the conservative forces of capitalism would urgently demand the banishment of all firearms. It happened before in the tumultuous 1960's. When the Black Panthers seemed like a real threat to law-and-order [read: *capitalist wealth*] the NRA lobbied for gun control! The NRA saw the elimination of guns as the safest way to preserve the status quo and protect capitalist wealth from those who need it. The problem is always capitalism. The only solution is Socialism.

GUN CULTURE – (*GUHN KUHL*-cher) A unique American attraction, in some cases obsession with firearms. A culture is a shared societal philosophy, ideology which arises from what a population cherishes. A great many Americans cherish guns. A nation's culture reflects its collective personality. The culture is rooted in the nation's historic experience. Multiple components comprise a culture. In America, one of the major cultural components is guns. Guns are older than America. Ancient societies, European cultures were founded with swords. American culture was founded with guns. When the earliest Europeans settled America, they did so with guns. Guns put meat on the table. This was untamed, primal land, populated by wild animals and *"wild Indians."* Guns protected the homestead from justifiably hostile, vengeful natives who were being dispossessed. A revolution fought with guns helped Americans win independence from Britain. Post-war fear prompted the Founding Fathers to amend the Constitution with a much misunderstood *"Right to bear arms."* Indeed, guns helped win the West for the young United States. The fear of guns helped to maintain the Southern Slavocracy. Simultaneously, guns helped allay the Southerner's fear of justifiably hostile, vengeful slaves. Guns initiated the Civil War splitting the nation, and concluded the conflict, reuniting the nation. An infinite supply of guns helped the USA (the *"Arsenal of Democracy"*) to arm its military and allies to win world wars and gain worldwide hegemony. Indeed, guns have played an integral part in American history. Today, there is not a baby boomer who did not have a toy gun as a child. The boy's gun was the counterpart to the girl's doll. Americans own nearly half the guns in the world. There are about 466 million guns in this country. About 98% of those firearms are owned by civilians. What is feeding the gun obsession, the American gun culture today? Simply stated, fear and hate. These related negative emotions are two sides of the same coin. The people who own the most guns are the people who fear the most. They hate the fact that they fear, and their hate has many sources. First and foremost is racism and bigotry. The changing of American demographics, the browning of America, the arrival of non-white immigrants, the rise of minority groups terrifies many white Americans. You will not find a racist who does not own guns. Fear of crime, lawlessness, anarchy caused by pandemics, fear of war, or natural disasters empowers the gun culture. Conspiracy theories of an oppressive government intent on banning guns increase gun sales. Gun profiteers have spread propaganda and fear to accelerate gun distribution. At the same time they had bought-off politicians (Republicans) to do their bidding in government. The gun culture will subside when fear subsides, and hate diminishes. This will take place as the American population and culture changes. Young, educated people in power will be our salvation. *"God made some men tall, God made some men small. But Samuel Colt made all men equal."* – American Proverb. A epitaph at Boothill Graveyard, Tombstone, Cochise County, Arizona reads: *"Here below Lies Lester Moore, He took Four Slugs from a 44. No Les, No More."*

GUNG HO – (guhng *HO*) Chinese for cooperation, working together. Gung ho is popularly used to mean enthusiastically, wholeheartedly, eagerly, in a successful manner. The term is taken from a Chinese Communist organization, *"Chung-kuo kung-yey ho-tso she"* meaning *"The Chinese Industrial Cooperative Society,"* founded in 1938. During World War Two (1942) American Lt. Col. Evans Carlson (1886 – 1947) was assigned to China to organize the Second Raider Battalion to fight the Japanese. Carlson was impressed by the zeal, determination, and enthusiasm of the Chinese Communists. He barrowed the abbreviated term from the Communist Cooperative, as *"gung ho"* to inspire his troops. The term survived.

GUN INSURANCE – (*GUN* in-*SHUR*-ranz) Mandatory insurance serves as a form of indirect permission granted by the government. In order to drive a car, a person must have a license and insurance. The same requirement must be demanded for gun ownership. Thirty-four states (68%) require a permit or license to own a gun. (Indeed, it should be all 50.) All gun owners must also be required to have gun insurance. Any law that makes it harder to own a gun is a positive. If Republicans can make it harder to vote with all kinds of restrictions, they can make it harder to own a gun as well. There are many people who do not drive because they can't afford the insurance. It would be good if these people could not afford a gun as well. Too, the Government *"Police Powers"* would enable it to confiscate guns from those without insurance. If the U.S. Government granted the insurance, this would be another source of income. If commercial companies issued the insurance, this powerful industry would have a vested interest, an economic stake in gun safety. They would be a mighty counterbalance to the NRA (National Rifle Association). How do we know? We have an example. It was the insurance industry that demanded that the government force the auto industry to install seatbelts. The insurance industry was hemorrhaging too much money by people being killed in car crashes. The government mandated that the people use seatbelts. The insurance industry would do everything in its power to be sure people did not misuse guns. They would not want to hemorrhage money by people being killed by guns. *"Everything is impossible, until it's not."* – *"Star Trek's"* Captain Jean-Luc Picard.

GUNNA – (*GUN*-nah) An American corruption if the phrase *"going to."* For instance: *"I'm gunna consult Congress."* Gunna is a run-on word that occurs because we think infinitely faster than we speak. The term gunna is used by many, perhaps most Americans, of all socio-economic, educational levels.

GUN POWDER – (*GUHN POW*-der) The most revolutionary military advancement since metal. The original black powder was accidentally invented by a Chinese alchemist monk in the 9th century (Tang Dynasty). He was searching for the elixir of life and produced a recipe for death. Basic gunpowder consists of 3 parts sulfur, 3 parts charcoal, 8 parts saltpeter (potash or potassium nitrate). The soil around Beijing is impregnated with saltpeter, which proved fortuitous for him. For some time the Chinese used gunpowder for fireworks only. Then it was discovered that an arrow or a small stone could be propelled at great velocity from a bamboo pipe with explosive black powder. The gun appeared. The Ming Dynasty was established by defeating the Mongol Yuan Dynasty with gunpowder. Black gunpowder obscured the battlefield in a cloud of white smoke. In Europe, alder wood charcoal was discovered to produce the best gun powder. Gunpowder absorbs water and is destabilized. After wet gunpowder dries, it becomes more volatile and dangerous. The powder clings together, burning less evenly and sometimes explodes more powerfully.

GUN SHY – (*GUHN*-shahy) (Gun shyness) Fear of firearms. More precisely, the fear of the sound of firearms. The term gun shy is usually applied to dogs that fear the loud blast of a gunshot. Gun shyness is usually learned in puppyhood. This makes for a useless hunting dog. Humans can become gun shy, a symptom of <u>Post</u>-<u>Traumatic</u> <u>Stress</u> <u>Disorder</u> (PTSD) suffered during combat. During the World Wars, this neurosis was called *"shell shock."* Stereotypically, a gun-shy person may instinctively dive under a table at the sound of a loud blast.

GUNS OR BUTTER – (*GUHNS* or *BUT*-ter) A cliché to express national priorities. On what do we spend our limited tax dollars, the bloated military, or the starving social programs? Republicans support the funding of the military (guns) over the needy (butter). The Democrats place the need people (butter), before the greedy military (guns). Why it is when we bomb people, there is no discussion about how much it costs. But when we feed people, the cost is always a great debate and limiting factor? Wealthy capitalists and their Republican representatives do not benefit by distributing butter, but do get richer by manufacturing more guns. *"Guns will make us great. Butter will make us fat."* – Nazi Air Marshal Hermann Goering (1893 – 1946). Ironically, Goering grew very fat.

GURU – (*GOO*-roo) Hindu holy man, Swami, Yogi, spiritual teacher and sage. *"If anyone steps on your ego, instantly, he becomes your enemy. But the Guru is a friend who constantly tramples your ego."* *"A Guru is not someone who holds a torch for you. He is the torch."* – *"A Guru is not a crutch, he is a bridge."* – Jaggi Vasudev (b. 1957).

GUSHER – (*GUSH*-sher) (Gush, Gushing) (also Squirt, Squirter, Squirting) Female ejaculation. A woman who discharges a gush of watery liquid from the vagina at the climax of orgasm. This forceful flow or jet of fluid is usually clear and odorless. The vaginal gush is like a reverse douche. The liquid is not urine. Research suggests that the fluid comes partly from the *"Skene's Glands,"* (the *"gusher's geysers"*) also known as the *"female prostate."* Additional research is required. The Skene's fluid is a milky-watery ultrafiltrate of blood plasma. This is the watery constituent of blood plasma with a concentration of glucose and fructose (sugars). (It's not sweet.) The definite function of this ejectate is not known, though it does serve as a lubricant for the urethral opening, and probably has some antibacterial property. Not all females gush or squirt. Those who do, gush as a result of clitoral stimulation, and/or G-spot (Grafenberg spot) stimulation of the sensitive front wall of the vagina. A gusher presents a rude splash in the face to a cunnilingus participator. Incidentally: In Rwanda-Rundi of East Africa, gushing is called *"kunyaza."* In that culture, a woman is not considered to be a successful lover if she doesn't gush. *"Gosh!"*

GUSTATION – (gus-*TAY*-shun) The act of tasting, as when enjoying food.

GUSTFRONT – (*GUST*-front) In meteorology, the blast of cool, damp air from an approaching thunderstorm. The gustfront is created by a storm in the distance. You feel the air cooled by blowing through a distant rainstorm. This is an indication that the rain is headed your way soon.

GUSTLOFF TRAGEDY – (*GUST*-lof *TRAJ*-je-dee) The greatest maritime disaster in world history. On January 30, 1945, a Russian submarine sank the German hospital ship, MV Wilhelm Gustloff on the

Baltic Sea. Over 9,400 people perished, German refugees fleeing Eastern Germany from the Red Army. The Russians sank 23 German ships packed with refugees on the Baltic during that cruel war.

GUY – (*GEYE*) Synonymous with fellow, an informal appellation for a man. One might say, *"He's a good guy."* Actually, Guy is a proper male name in French (pronounced *"gee"*), related to the Italian Guido (*"GEE*-doe"). The most famous guy in English history is Guy Fawkes (1570 – 1606). He was an English Catholic who conspired with Spain to assassinate the Protestant King James I. The goal was to restore a Catholic monarch on the English throne. Guy Fawkes and other English Catholics devised a plan to blow-up Parliament and ignite a revolution. They planted 20 barrels of gunpowder in the basement of Parliament. The *"Gunpowder Plot"* was discovered on November 5, 1605. Fawkes was arrested. After a period of interrogation in the torture chamber, Guy's public execution was scheduled for January 31, 1606. He was to be *"partially"* hanged, then drawn and quartered alive. However, to the bitter dismay and disappointment of the vast audience, Guy Fawkes fell off the scaffold, breaking his neck to death, depriving the revelers of the gruesome mayhem. Nevertheless, The Gunpowder Plot is still celebrated in England on November 5, the English counterpart to the American Thanksgiving Day. Bonfires [read: *bonefires*] are lit throughout the country and effigies of Guy Fawkes are burned. The gala festivity is accompanied by fireworks (alluding to the big bang that almost took out Parliament). English children can be seen on Guy Fawkes Day soliciting in the street, asking *"a penny for the guy,"* in order to buy fireworks. This is comparable to Halloween's *"trick-or-treaty."* By 1806, the term guy came to mean the straw-stuffed effigies of Guy Fawkes. By 1836, guy came to refer to any poorly, shabbily dressed Englishman, like Guy's effigy. But in America by 1847, guy took on its present meaning as just a fellow. (Parenthetically: Guy Fawkes had used the alias Guido Fawkes at times. The Fifth of November could have been celebrated as *"Guido Fawkes Day"* in England.) Incidentally: It is illegal for a Catholic to serve as monarch of the United Kingdom.

GUYOT – (gee-*OH*) A flat-topped, submerged seamount. A guyot is a sub- oceanic plateau.

GYMNASIUM – (jim-*NAY*-zee-um) The ancient Greeks were a most cultured people. They insisted on the balance between physical and intellectual fitness. Every Greek polis (city) had a public area for exercise, sports, as well as training in music, literature, and philosophy. This was the Greek gymnasium. Living in a warm climate, it was unreasonable to be encumbered by clothing. So the lads exercised in the nude. The Greek term *"gymnasion"* literally means *"school for naked exercise,"* from the verb *"gymnazein,"* meaning *"to exercise naked."* Both terms derive from the adjective *"gymnos,"* which means *"naked"* in Greek. The more inhibited Romans adopted the *"gymnasium"* but in two distinct senses: an exercise ground, and a public school. The term gymnasium first appeared in English at the end of the 16th century. It had entirely lost its original connotation to nakedness. Today an American gymnasium is a large auditorium equipped with exercise machines, athletic equipment, basketball rims and volleyball nets. Don't expect your American gym coach or teacher to instruct music, literature, or philosophy. However in Germanic nations, the *gymnasium* is still a secondary school preparing students for the university. Incidentally: One wonders if the ancient Greek gymnasiums had cheerleaders or did that present too much of a distraction.

GYMNOSPERMS – (*JIM*-no-sperms) Cone-bearing plants, like coniferous pine trees.

GYMNOPHOBIA – (jim-no-*FO*-bee-a) (Gymnophobiac) Phobic fear of nudity. Certainly, it is abnormal to fear nakedness in all situations. A desire to avoid public nakedness is understandably normal, according to our shared Western cultural mores. But gymnophobia is neurotic, unreasonable, a defense mechanism as are all neuroses. A gymnophobiac requires professional psychological help.

GYMPIE-GYMPIE – (*JIM*-pee *JIM*-pee or *GIM*-pee *GIM*-pee) (*Dendrocnide moroides*, also Stinging Bush). Gympie-gympie is the most pain-provoking plant yet known. It is native to the rainforests of Malaysia, Indonesia, Australia, and the Molucca Islands. The name *"gympie-gympie"* is from the Gubbi Gubbi Aborigines of south-eastern Queensland. Its scientific binominal is taken from the Greek *"dendron"* meaning *"tree,"* and *"knidos"* meaning *"stinging needle."* Gympie-gympie is an attractive flowering, fruit-bearing plant, usually less then 10 feet tall. It has large, heart-shaped leaves up to 8.5 inches long, 7 inches wide. *Beware of the leaves!* Actually, the entire plant is covered tiny white filaments, fine brittle hairs called *"trichomes"* that embed into the skin. They are hollow like a hypodermic needle and inject a toxic cocktail that was identified in 2020 as *"gympietides."* To the touch, the pain is said to feel like being burned with hot acid and electrocuted at the same time. No amount of morphine or other anesthetic grants relief. In 1963, a Queensland Parks and Wildlife Service Officer, Ernie Rider was slapped in the face and torso with a branch of the foliage. He recounted that: *"For two or three days the pain was almost unbearable. I couldn't work or sleep. I remember it feeling like there were giant hands trying to squash my chest. Then it was pretty bad pain for another fortnight or so. The stinging persisted for two years and recurred every time I had a cold shower. There's nothing to rival it. It's ten times worse than anything else."* The miniscule needles cannot be pulled out with tweezers. They are too tiny, thin, tight, and numerous. The only way to extract them is with a hot-wax treatment, as when removing hair. If only one of the hundreds of needles remain or breaks-off, the pain will persist for years. Horses that stumbled into a gympie-gympie bush had to be shot. The agony inflicted by the plant killed a man in New Guinea in 1922. The story is told of Cyril Bromley, an Australian soldier in World War Two who had used a bright green gympie- gympie leaf as toilet paper. The torturous torment drove him mad. He was strapped to a hospital bed. Eventually, Bromley shot himself. Plants can't run, nor can they bite or fight. But they can defend themselves with needles, stings, and toxins.

GYNAECOMANIA – (gy-na-co-*MAYN*-ee-a) (Gynaecomaniac) Having an abnormal sexual obsession with women. Gynaecomania is a life-debilitating condition. A victim of this neurosis is quite crazed. Their condition is a sexual addiction. Like any other addict, they need immediate help.

GYNECOMASTIA – (gy-neh-koh-*MAS*-tee-ah) *"Man boobs."* Masculine chest turned to feminine breast. Obesity will result in womanish man boobs, which is fair enough. But so will the normal process of aging. That's not fair. In late middle-age, the tone of the chest muscles weakens, causing them to droop and drop. This is the result of *"andropause,"* which is male menopause, with the natural reduction in the *testosterone* level. This is the hormone that keeps males masculine. Despite desperate exercise, this embarrassing natural process will continue, unabated. Manly *pecs* will become womanly *tits*. Ironically, men who built large, powerful chest muscles in youth will have more chest muscle to sag in old age [read: *"bigger tits"*]. So bodybuilders ultimately have the largest man boobs. Vladimir Putin (b. 1952) is a tough little guy in great condition for his age (72 in 2024). He holds a black belt in karate. Putin is often photographed bare-chested. Despite his machismo, 72-year-old Vlad too has developed man boobs (albeit, *"tiny-boppers"*). Therefore, don't agonize over your man boobs fellas. *"Tits"* not worth it. Incidentally: The term gynecomastia has been in use in English since 1881. *"Gyneco"* derives from Latin meaning female, woman. *"Mastos"* also derives from Latin meaning breasts. Furthermore, it has long been recognized that with age, men begin to look like *little old ladies,* and women begin to look like *little old men.* This is not merely a myth. This is due to the drop in male testosterone, and female estrogen levels. Life is cruel.

GYNOPHOBIA – (gy-no-*FO*-bee-a) (Gynopobiac) Phobic fear of women. This is a debilitating condition that requires intense psychotherapy. A gynophobia victim is a virtual recluse. Society, life itself is closed to them. They might as well be in solitary confinement. The subconscious cause of this emotional malady must be uncovered. The only way out is through.

GYP – (*JIP*) (also Gip) (Gypped, Gypping, Gypper, Gypster) The term gyp is used as both a verb and a noun. As a verb it means to defraud or rob by some sharp practice. As a noun it means a swindler who cheats an unwary customer. So a gyp is a conman who will rip you off. The term gyp entered English in 1840. It is a disparaging abbreviation of the name <u>Gypsy</u>. So gyp actually means, *"I was Gypsied"* [read: *cheated*]. Gypsies, called *"Travelers"* had a reputation for cheating and stealing. They were considered to be traveling swindlers. (There is a kernel of truth in every stereotype.) By 1889, the term gyp, meaning to cheat or swindle was well established in American English.

GYPSUM – (*JIP*-sum) (Hydrated calcium sulfate.) Gypsum is a compound of limestone (calcium carbonate) and sulfuric acid which forms calcium sulfate ($C_A SO_4.2H_2O$). Gypsum is a natural mineral compound that is mined. When mixed with water, calcium sulfate becomes gypsum. Gypsum crystalizes in water. This mineral used in the production of cement, plaster and drywall, is made from limestone. The magnificent crystals in Mexico's *Cave of the Giant Crystals* are chemically gypsum. Incidentally: The term *"gypsum"* is Latin, taken from the Greek *"gypsos"* meaning *"chalk."*

GYPSY – (*JIP*-see) (Plural, Gypsies) The *"Romani"* people. Gypsies are a nomadic Caucasian people, generally of swarthy complexion, who migrated into Asia and Europe from Northwestern India from the 9th century onward. They had later come to North America. Gypsies speak an ancient Indic language called *"Romany."* They acquired the name Gypsy c. 1600, because many believed that these mysterious people came from mysterious Egypt, ergo *"Egyptsies,"* or Gypsies. The ancient Gypsies lived in India. Legend has it that they first migrated to Europe with Alexander the Great's (356 – 323 BCE) army as camp- followers (327 BCE). Early in the 16th century, Gypsy forces were used to try to fight back the Islamic Mogul invaders in India. After the Mogul victory, the Gypsies began to migrate westward. Gypsies traditionally travel in colorful horse-drawn wagons, which provided their English appellation, *"Travelers."* They often try to live off the land. This sometimes led to squatting, poaching, and theft for survival. This vagabond lifestyle has resulted in a bad reputation for the entire population. Gypsies are extremely resourceful survivors. They have gained the reputation as mystics, fortunetellers, and con artists. They are therefore often unwelcomed guests. The eccentric Gypsies had been persecuted throughout history, especially by the German Nazis. Incidentally: About 500,000 Gypsies were murdered by the German Nazis during the Holocaust (1933 – 1045). Today about 11 million Gypsies roam the Earth.

GYRE – (*JY*-er) A ring, circle, circular course or motion. An oceanic gyre is one of several ring-like systems of ocean currents, rotating clockwise in the Northern Hemisphere, and counterclockwise in the Southern Hemisphere. They are the result of wind belts and the rotation of the Earth (*Coriolis Effect*). The great Northern Pacific Gyre, between America and Hawaii is the world's greatest trash dump the size of Mexico. It contains over four-and-a-half million tons of plastic waste from Asia and America. Plastic in the sea takes a very long time to biodegrade. Incidentally: In 30 years, by 2020, it is estimated that there will be more pieces of plastic in the ocean than fish! News Flash: By mid-February, 2024, a great part of the Pacific trash gyre has been collected.

GYRO – (*YEER*-roh) In Greek cuisine, a huge rack of lamb, roasted on a vertical spit. The outer portion of the meat roasts first, and is cut away in thin slices. The lamb is served on pita bread with onions. This style of cooking dates back to 1970. In Modern Greek, *"gyros"* means to *"turn"* or *"revolve,"* as does the lamb on the spit.

H

H – (*AYCH*) The 8th letter in the English alphabet, a consonant. H is the chemical symbol for the element Hydrogen, as indicated on the Periodic Table of Chemical Elements.

HABERDASHER – (*HAB*-er-dash-er) (Haberdashery) A retail dealer in men's clothing, such as suits, shirts, ties, socks, gloves, and hats. The etymology of the term is obscure. Haberdasher entered the English language in the 14th century. *"Habredache"* is an Anglo-French term. *"Hapertas"* may have been a kind of cloth. Haberdasher may have been a family surname in the 13th century and earlier. For instance, *"Haberdasher & Sons"* may have sold men's clothing. The name may have become applied to all clothiers.

HABILE – (*HA*-bile) Being dexterous. Having the ability to manipulate (*manually*) with the hands. Being habile is being *handy*, literally. The hand drove the subsequent evolution of the brain. The hand is the cutting edge of the human mind. That's why the term habile was chosen in its Latin original to designate *"Homo habilis,"* (*hand-y* man). This proto human was our ancestral tool maker.

HABILIMENT – (ha-*BIL*-li-ment) The accoutrements, trappings, the standard, characteristic garb. Habiliment especially refers to the clothing worn in a particular profession, or way of life. *"He was festooned with the habiliment of a high-ranking naval officer."*

HABIT – (*HA*-bit) (Habitual, Habitude) An acquired behavior pattern regularly followed until it has become almost involuntary. Habits are classed as positive or negative which are merely social dictates. Research has discovered that it takes 21 to 30 days of concentrated effort to break or make a habit. Habitual behavior is called routine. *"Habit has a kind of poetry."* – Simone de Beauvoir (1908 – 1986). *"Life is habit. Or rather life is a succession of habits."* – Samuel Beckett (1906 – 1989).

HABITATION FOG – (ha-bit-*TAY*-shun *FOG*) Smog. A fog caused by fumes and smoke from cities. In ultra-cold Siberia, even the vapor from human breath contributes to the habitation fog. It is phenomenal. A line of exhaled breath will linger in the air, and slowly sink to the ground where a perpetual fog lingers in the winter on calm days.

HABITUDE – (*HAB*-bit-tood) A habit, tendency, or custom. Habitude refers to the customary condition of character as: *"A poor emotional habitude."*

HABOOB – (*HAH*-boob) An Arabic word meaning *"blast"* or *"drifting."* A haboob is a tremendous sandstorm. It is a great wall of sand blown by the wind into the atmosphere. A haboob is a tsunami of sand in the desert. It will suffocate people and animals and bury entire villages.

HACKING – (*HAK*-king) (Hacker, Hacktivist, Hacktivism) In cyber-security to circumvent security and break into a computer, network, or file, usually with malicious intent. Hacking is cyber-trespassing, cyber-vandalism, and cyber- theft. Computer technology has made society so vulnerable to hacking, creating the potential for *technoterrorism*. During the 2016 presidential election, Russian hackers in support of the Republican candidate Donald Trump (b. 1946) hacked information from the Democratic Party leadership. This information was used to discredit the Democratic candidate, Hilary Clinton (b. 1947) and tip the victory to Trump.

HACKING – (*HAK*-king) In amateur engineering, hacking is imaginative improvising of devices and materials in novel, extraordinary ways, to solve immediate problems, especially in an emergency. In the popular parlance, hacking is finding *"half-ass solutions."* Taking parts from unrelated tools, devices, and machines to create a unique, useful device in hacking. A successful hacker is displaying a high level of intelligence. Function fixedness (single- minded usage) gives way to functional imaginativeness (multiple usages).

HADAL ZONE – (*HAD*-dal *ZONE*) The benthic (oceanic) environment of the sea deeper than 19,685 feet. The hadal zone descends to the ocean floor.

HADITH – (*HA*-dith) Islamic tradition and commentary outside the actual Quran (Koran). The Hadith is comparable to the Jewish Talmud or Catholic Canon Law.

HAFNIUM – (*HAFF*-nee-um) (Hf) Named after *Hafnia,* the Modern Latin name for "Copenhagen." The 72 protons in its nucleus give hafnium its atomic number. Hafnium is a bright-gray metallic, toxic element found in zirconium ores. Hafnium has a high melting point, over 3632 degrees Fahrenheit. It is used in tungsten filaments (electric strove burners and toaster coils). Hafnium is also used as a neutron absorber in nuclear reactors.

HAGIOMANIA – (ha-gee-o-*MAY*-nee-a) Manic obsession with Saints.

HAGANAH – (hag-gon-*NAH*) (Also Irgun and Stern) Jewish defense and terrorist organization established by Menachem Begin (1913 – 1992) during the civil war that created the State of Israel (1948). The Haganah declared guerrilla warfare on their Palestinian rivals, and the occupying British mediators. Their subsidiary, *Irgun,* blew-up the King David Hotel in 1946, killing 91, injuring 46. As a terrorist organization, the Haganah was responsible for atrocities against the Palestinian people. It had evolved into the Israeli army.

HAG STONE – (*HAG* stohn) Hag is an Old English (West Saxon) reference to witchery. A hag stone is a smoothly eroded rock with a naturally occurring hole through it. Hag stones are often found near water (which was responsible for eroding the hole). Many magical powers are attributed to hag stones, including healing and protection. Hag stones go by many other names as: *holey, holed, fairy, adder,* or *Odin stones,* as well as *spindle whorl.*

HAIL – (*HALE*) A meteorological phenomenon of ice pellets or balls showering from a storm cloud. A hail stone forms when a raindrop freezes, falls, and is projected back skyward by an updraft. Layers of water freeze on the hailstone, like the layers of an onion. Most hail falls in swathe of 5 to 10 miles, but 100- mile areas have occurred. These swaths are 10 miles long as well. A hailstone weighing a pound, falling at 90 mph can kill.

HAIL MARY – (*HALE MER*-ree) The *"Ave Maria"* prayer (in Latin). It is the traditional Roman Catholic intercession to the Blessed Virgin, Mother of Jesus. The pray is traced back to about 1050. A similar devotion is said in Eastern Orthodox and Oriental Orthodox Churches. Anglican and Independent Catholic Churches pray the Hail Mary as well. It's pronounced: *"Hail Mary, full of grace, the Lord is with thee. Blessed art thou amongst women, and blessed is the fruit of thy womb, Jesus. Holy Mary Mother of God, pray for us sinner, now, and at the hour of our death. Amen."*

HAIL MARY – (*HALE MER*-ree) (American football) It must first be understood that the *"Hail Mary"* is an important Catholic prayer of supplication to Mary, the Mother of Jesus. With the Hail Mary, the supplicant is begging Mary to intercede with Jesus for a miracle. The term Hail Mary has become a football cliché for a miracle. A *Hail Mary* is a desperation pass, an *"alley-opp"* thrown up-for-grabs in the end zone at closing seconds of a game. Because a Hail Mary pass is a free-for-all, with several players packed together, like under a basketball rim, the pass interference penalty is called-off – not officially, but actually. It is a losing team's last *prayer.* (It reminds me of the half-intoxicated woman, fighting for the wedding bouquet.) Actually, the Hail Mary pass is successful 1 out of 10 times (10%), better than many prayers. The expression *"Hail Mary"* dates back to the 1930s when it was used publicly by Elmer Layden (1903 – 1973) and Jim Crowley (1902 – 1986), two Notre Dame football players, members of the famous *"Four Horsemen."* The term was confined to Notre Dame and other Catholic universities for over 40 years until December 28, 1975. In a game between the Dallas Cowboys and the Minnesota Vikings, Cowboys quarterback Roger Staubach (b. 1942) said about his game-winning touchdown pass to wide receiver Drew Pearson (b. 1951): *"I closed my eyes and said a Hail Mary."* The term became a part of American football lexicon. Incidentally: The term has been expanded and is now used as a political cliché referring to a drastic, desperate gamble. For example, Senator John McCain (b. 1964) threw a Hail Mary pass when he chose vivacious Sarah Palin (b. 1964) as his vice- presidential running-mate in the 2008 election. Unfortunately for McCain, Palin proved to be an air head.

HAIL TO THE CHIEF – (*HALE* to the *CHEEF*) The official Presidential anthem of the United States. The tune is played at public appearances of the President. It is preceded by 4 *Ruffles and Flourishes* (drum and bugle rolls). The title is taken from a verse in Sir Walter Scott's (1771 – 1832) <u>*The Lady of the Lake*</u> (1810): *"Hail to the Chief who in triumph advances!"* The music was written by an English violinist, James Sanderson (c. 1769 – c. 1841). In 1849, First Lady Sarah Childress Polk (1803 – 1891) ordered *Hail to the Chief* to be played whenever her husband, President James Polk (1795 – 1849) entered a crowded room. James was short. Sarah wanted to be sure that James was noticed. Hail to the Chief became the official anthem during President Harry Truman's (1884 – 1972) administration (1945 – 1953). Incidentally: To patriotic, decent Americans, especially those with a sense of history, its gut-wrenching, nauseating, to hear that hallowed refrain played for that corrupt, ignorant, nasty pig, Donald Trump (b. 1946).

HAIMISH – (*HAY*-mish) (also Heimish) A Yiddishism meaning homey, cozy, and unpretentious. Haimish derives from the Middle German *"heimisch,"* for *"heim"* means home. Haimish entered English in the mid-1950s.

HAIR – (*HAIR*) (Hairy) (also called *pilus*) A threadlike pigmented filament that grows from follicles beneath the skin of mammals. Non-human hair is called fur. Hair consists of dead keratin cells, the same substance that produces nails, claws, feathers, and beaks. Human hair comes in a spectrum of colors and textures. Perfectly straight hair, as with Orientals has rounded hair shafts, like spaghetti. Kinky hair, as with Negroes is ribbon-like. Curly hair is somewhere in-between. The entire human body, male and female is hair-covered, except the palms of the hands and soles of the feet. Much of the hair is too fine to notice. The male sex hormone, testosterone, makes for heavier hair in both genders. When human ancestors lost their heavy body hair, they acquired sweat glands to keep cool. No longer did they have to pant. This accelerated the development of vocal articulators, speech and language. The hairiest part of the body is the head, and for good reason. Hair helps protect the brain from heat and cold. Other conspicuous hairy regions are the armpits and groin. Hair amplifies scent. Armpit and pubic hair wafts sex pheromones that stimulates erotic excitation on both conscious and subconscious levels. It is said that hair continues to grow after death, along with nails. Some men had to be shaved 11 days after death, it is reported. (This information is spurious.) For scientists, forensic anthropologists, hair serves as a chemical diary. Diet can be determined, as well as medications, drugs, poisons, chemicals of all sorts, can be detected in ancient corpses' and mummies' hair. The longer the hair, the further back in time the data can be traced. Hair has been a symbol of vanity for as long as we have been human. This was and is especially true about women. There are over 86,000 hair dressing solons in the U.S., generating $57 billion dollars in revenue. The Bible has much to say about hair. *"If a woman has long hair, it is her glory."* – 1 Corinthians 11:15. Proverbs 16:31 declares: *"Gray hair is a crown of glory, it is gained in a righteous life."* Hair has been a sign of hubris. That's why monks shave the crown of their heads bald, (the tonsure) as a sign of humility. For a woman, losing her hair is a tragedy, and humiliation. That's why after World War Two (1939 – 1945) French woman who entertained and collaborated with the Nazis were publicly shorn bald.

HAIR ART – (*HAIR AHRT*) Transforming a head of hair into an esthetic spectacle. Hair styles, cuts and dressings trace back for millennia. But today, it has risen to an astonishing level. A few extraordinary barbers have become extraordinary artists – hair portrait masters and sculptors. Long hair has been raised high above the head in astounding shapes. It may be weaved into images of the Eiffel tower, a famous bridge, building or sculpture. Other hair artists are designers and portrait painters. The hair is first shaved close to the scalp. Then the barber-artist shaves a message, a face, a landscape or a famous painting onto the back of the head in magnificent, excruciating detail. They may use paints to highlight, accentuate their masterpiece. A tattoo artists could hardly produce a more detailed artwork. It is nothing short of amazing!

HAIR DOWN – (*HAIR DOUN*) *"Let your hair down."* The expression means, let loose, or relax, have fun. The expression originated during the industrial revolution. The hard-worked ladies in the East Lancastershire cotton mills had to pin their hair up, so not to have it entangled in the machinery. They had to be highly vigilant in their dangerous surroundings. But after work, they were able to *"let their hair down."*

HAIR HYGROMETER – (*HAIR* hi-*GROM*-met-ter) A meteorological instrument used to measure relative humidity, based on the fact that human hair stretches as humidity increases. A human or animal hair is used measure the changing humidity by its shrinking and lengthening.

HAIR ONFIRE – (*HAIR* on-*FAH*-uhr) Literally, a burning head, an agonizing crisis, emergency. When one is accused of having their hair onfire, the statement is meant figuratively. It means being frantically excited, unreasonably furious, frenzied about some issue, proposition or program. A politician who becomes apoplexic during an interview has his hair onfire. Reactionary cultists like the Trumpublicans, MAGAmaniacs, and QAnonnuts always have their hair onfire.

HAITI – (*HAY*-tee) Nation that occupies the western 1/3 of the island of Hispaniola in the Caribbean. The capital city is Port-au-Prince. The people speak French and Haitian Creole. Haiti is populated by black descendants of African slaves. Under the leadership of Toussaint L'Ouverture (1743 – 1803), the Haitians gained their independence from Napoleon and the French, through violent Revolution (1793). The Haitians engineered the only mass successful slave revolt in history. Too, they were the first nation in the Western Hemisphere to abolish slavery. Today, Haiti is the poorest nation in the Western Hemisphere, and 19th poorest on Earth. A history of brutal dictatorship, crippling corruption, and natural disasters has strangled Haiti's economy. Natural disasters like hurricanes, earthquakes, and tsunamis have added to the misery. Incidentally: Though a Catholic country, Haiti is the home of voodoo, a hybrid of African, Christian, and Indian beliefs and rituals.

HAJJ – (*HOJ*) One of the 5 Pillars or duties of Islam. A Hajj is a pilgrimage to Mecca (*Makka*) in Saudi Arabia. It is an intense and demanding religious obligation required of all Muslims, at least once in a lifetime. A successful pilgrimage entitles the pilgrim to forever bear the title *"Hajji,"* (one who made the pilgrimage). About 2 million pilgrims perform the Hajj annually. Half of them come from overseas.

HALAL – (ha-*LOL*) The Muslim counterpart to Jewish Kosher. Halal refers to the Islamic dietary rules and food preparation. Halal is also a prescribed manner in which to slaughter an animal and butcher the meat, according to Islamic law. The animal must be killed cleanly, quickly, painlessly, with dignity.

HALCYON – (*HELL*-see-on) (Halcyonic) A peaceful, calm, tranquil period, the *"halcyon days."* The Obama Period (2009 – 2016) were halcyon times compared to the four terrible Trump years (2017 – 2020).

HALCYON DAYS – (*HELL*-see-on *DAYS*) A period of peace and calm. Traditionally, 14 days of calm weather around the winter solstice, which is December 21st. The halcyon period is said to begin on December 14th. According to Greek legend, this is the time when the European Kingfisher is brooding her eggs. In fact, *"Halcyon"* is the Greek name for the European Kingfisher bird. The ancients believed that the birds constructed floating nests in the Aegean Sea. In order to keep their chicks safe, the Halcyons had the power to calm the sea, it was said. This belief came about from Greek mythology. According to the Roman poet Ovid (43 BCE – 18 CE) Aeolus, the ruler of the wind, had a daughter named Alcyone, who was married to Ceyx, the King of Thessaly. Ceyx was drowned at sea and Alcyone threw herself into the waves in a fit of grief. Instead of drowning, she was transformed into a bird (the Halcyon) and carried to her husband by the wind. This myth came to the English-speaking world in the 14th century when in 1398, John Trevisa (fl. 1342 – 1402) translated Bartholomew de Glanville's (1265 – 1345) *De proprietatibus rerum* (1247) (*"On the Property of Things"*) into Middle English: *"In the cliffe of a ponde of occean, Alcion, a see foule, in wynter maketh her neste and layeth egges in vii days and sittyth on brood…seuen dayes."*

HALF-ASS – (*HAF ASS*) Any job done carelessly, haphazardly. *"If you can do a half- assed job of anything, you're a one-eyed man in the kingdom of the blind."* – Kurt Vonnegut (1922 – 2007).

HALF-ASS SOLUTIONS – (*HAF ASS* so-*LOO*-shuns) (Half-Assing) A mocking, negative attitude toward a practical, positive outcome. Finding *"half-ass"* solutions is thinking out of the box. It is inventing simple, cheap, innovative ways to solve complex and perplexing problems. This involves improvisation, hacking parts from different tools, devices, and machines to create a novel, ad hoc device to solve an immediate problem. Poor peasants in underdeveloped counties are masters of the half-ass solution. Tape, wire, glue, junk are half-ass essentials. The innovative half-ass solution is concerned solely for utility, not aesthetics. Half-ass solutions may not be professional or pretty, but they work. Utility, not aesthetics governs half-ass solutions. Half-ass solutions can extend the utility of a tool, machine, appliance, whatever, far beyond its expected lifespan. Incidentally: Half-ass solutions reveals high intelligence. It is imaginative, pragmatic thinking. It is not being functionally fix to a required way to fix a problem. It shows real ingenuity [read: ingeniousness]. It was half- ass solutions, in the form of makeshift repairs that saved the astronauts' lives in Apollo 13 (1970). Mission Statement for half-ass solutions: *"When we can't do as we will, we will do as we can."*— Dr. Gary J. Pasieka

HALF-LIFE – (*HAF LYF*) The time it takes for half the mass of a radioactive element to decay into its daughter elements. A radioactive element like uranium is so complex and unstable that it is constantly falling apart, decaying, shedding beta particles. This is radiation. The rate of decay and transmutation is known and used as a measuring rod. This is the significance of half-life.

HALIBUT TREATY – (*HAL*-li-but *TREE*-tee) (1923) Called Canada's *"Declaration of Independence."* It was an agreement negotiated by Prime Minister William MacKenzie-King (1874 – 1950) with the U.S. It was the first time Canada concluded a treaty independent of Britain. The Halibut Treaty was a giant step toward Canadian autonomy and sovereignty.

HALIFAX – (*HAL*-li-fax) Atlantic seaport and capital city of the Canadian Province of Nova Scotia. In the 18th century, New England fishermen and merchants were attack by French pirates based at Louisburg, on Cape Breton Island in Canada. So the New Englanders persuaded the British to build the seaport/ naval base of Halifax in 1749. Later, it was the British fleet stationed at Halifax that prevented Nova Scotia (which included New Brunswick) from joining the 13 American colonies that rebelled against Britain. This is significant, because if Nova Scotia had joined the anti-British revolution, The U.S. and Canada might have been one nation today.

HALITOPHOBIA – (hal-lit-to-*FO*-bee-a) (Halitophobiac) Phobic fear of bad breath. A Halitophobiac may be a *"germophobe."*

HALLELUJAH – (hal-le-*LOO*-ya) Praise the Lord. Hallelujah is an interjection, an exclamation of joy, praise, and gratitude to God. The term comes from the Hebrew *"hallalu-yay,"* meaning *"praise you Jehovah."*

HALLMARK DISILLUSIONMENT – (*HAWL*-mahrk dis-i-*LOO*-zhuhn-ment) A psycho- emotional disorder afflicting bored, unfulfilled, unhappy housewives. Many women escape reality into the fantasy world of Hallmark Romance novels or movies. Hallmark features exciting, fun-filled romances in idyllic settings, usually some winter wonderland. Hallmark episodes are presented with extraordinarily beautiful people, plentifully prosperous, of cheerful disposition. In their unrealistically stress-free lives, their only concern is who is going to be laid by whom. Too, the cozy, quaint, safe, *"Hallmarkvilles"* stand in bleak contrast to many housewives' hometowns. This all makes the already disappointed housewife more disenchanted with her life. Soon *"Hallmark discontent"* sets in. She unfairly begins to blame her innocent husband for her unhappiness. He is accused of being responsible for her dissatisfaction. In her mind, husband does not match-up well against the Hallmark Romeos and Don Juans. Before long, everything about him is unsatisfactory. Prince Charming he is not. She begins to resent him. Husband becomes her target for sarcasm and criticism. She longs for a white knight to sweep her off her feet and transport her to some enchanted Never-Never Land hallmarked by romance. In this stealthy way, Hallmark TV, as well as Harlequin Romance Novels can sour a good relationship, and can destroy a marriage. Pastor Joel Osteen advised: *"Wives, know that there are plenty of women out there who would love to have your husband, just the way he is."* A wise caveat.

HALLOWEEN – (hal-uh-*WEEN*) Originally from the Scottish, *"Halwemesse Day,"* from ancient times to the late 13th century. This was the last night of October, which was the last night of the year in the old Celtic calendar. Halwemesse Day was known as *"Old Year's Night,"* which was the night of witches. This pagan holiday was dedicated to ritualistic baptism. With conversion to Christianity, the holiday converted into *"Allhallow-even"* (1550s), the *"The Eve of Holy All Saints Day"*. (All Saints Day is November 1.) By 1781, the name evolved into *"Hallow-e'en."* Incidentally, the Scots Irish (Protestants) and Catholic Irish brought the custom of Halloween to America in the 1840s. Halloween never lost its pagan religious association, its relationship to the occult and witchcraft. It is a strange, dualistic holiday that indirectly or subconsciously pays homage to evil. Too, unlike Shintoism, which honors our deceased ancestors, Halloween converts them into evil ghouls! Footnote: If there's a chance to make a buck, the capitalists will find it. Halloween has been ghoulishly converted into a multi-billion-dollar retail holiday, selling candy, costumes, and parties.

HALO – (*HAY*-lo) In Medieval art, rings of light circling the head of a holy personage, to indicate a degree of divinity. In meteorology, any of the rings or arcs of light around the sun or moon caused by ice crystal clouds.

HALOCLINE REACTION – (*HAL*-lo-cline re-*ACT*-shun) Refers to the salinity of the oceans and the fact that denser heavier saltwater sinks below lighter fresh water. The Halocline Reaction effects the warm and cold *Thermohaline Circulation* of ocean currents which effects our weather. *Thermo* means heat and *haline* means saltiness. Freshening the ocean by glacial melt and excessive rain (global warming) will disrupt the Halocline Reaction, which will change the Thermohaline Circulation, causing climatic chaos. Normally, dense salty cold water between Canada and Greenland sinks as it flows south. This allows the dense salty warm Caribbean water to rise to the surface, creating the Gulf Stream Current. The Gulf Stream drifts across the Atlantic, warming Western Europe. But freshening the cold water from the north will make it less salty and lighter. It will not sink. The cold lighter fresh water will float atop the warm denser salty Caribbean water, extinguishing the Gulf Stream. Western Europe would freeze. Cornwall, England would trade its palm trees for icebergs like Labrador, Canada, at the same latitude.

HALO EFFECT – (*HAY*-lo ef-*FECT*) A curious psychological phenomenon that when a student or any other person is first judged as good, it becomes difficult to find fault with her. Even when the person is dead wrong, the halo effect meliorates the infraction.

HALOPHYTE – (*HAL*-oh-fyht) The term "halo" comes from the Greek *"halos,"* meaning *"a lump of salt." "Phyte"* derives from the Greek *"phyton,"* meaning *"that which has grown."* So a halophyte is a plant that grows in a salty environment – soil or water. Excessive salt will kill most plants. Halophytes have organs that can filter-out the salt from the water it takes in. Mangroves that grow in ocean lagoons are typical halophytes.

HALTING TIME – (*HALL*-ting *TYM*) In education, a teacher's pause in talking in order to give students time to think about presented materials or directions. Students can be overwhelmed by an avalanche of information. It may all become garbled, if time is not given to allow students to digest the information.

HAM – (*HAM*) In butchery (meatcutting) ham refers to the cut of meat from the heavy-muscled section of the hog's rear quarter, between the hip and hock. In other words, the ham-cut is the hog's hind leg. Being hog or pig-meat, the ham is pork. If cooked after butchering, without smoking or curing, the ham would taste like a porkroast. In familiar cuisine, the ham must be smoked and cured to be recognized as ham.

HAMAS – (hah-*MAHS*) The name is an Arabic acronym for *"Harakat al- Muqwamah al-Islamiyyah"* (*Islamic Resistance Movement*). Hamas is a militant Palestinian political party consisting of Sunni Islamic Fundamentalists. Hamas is a client of militant Iran. Hama was founded in 1987 with headquarters in the Gaza Strip, a self-governing Palestinian enclave in Israel. Hamas is anti-Zionist, anti-Israeli, and antisemitic (and increasingly anti-American). They had broken away from the PLO (Palestine Liberation Organization). Hamas consists of Palestinian nationalists who wish to reinstate the nation of Palestine where Israel exists today. That would require the eradication of the State of Israel. Hamas is also opposed to all the Western capitalist nations that prop-up Israel, especially the United States. Hamas is supported by anti-Israeli nation, including Russia, Turkey, and China. Hamas has participated in wars against Israel. They incite protests, riots, and violence against Israel. Hamas is considered to be a terrorist organization. However, a terrorist to one man is a patriot to another. A Caveat: Do not confuse Sunni Palestinian Hamas, with Shiite Lebanese Hezbollah, another Islamic militant group. Both groups are supported by Iran and are rabidly anti-Semitic, anti-Israel. Parenthetically: Those who are considered terrorists to one population are considered patriots to another population. Often, oppressed people must employ terrorism as a form of guerrilla warfare. Footnote: Hamas has proven to be a Palestinian rendition of ISIS, just as inhumanely savage.

HAMBURGER – (*HAM*-ber-ger) (also Burger) A foodstuff more American than apple pie. However, like most Americans, like apple pie, hamburger is an immigrant. In fact, the term *"Hamburger"* is a *"demonym,"* the name of a population from a certain location. Hamburgers are residents of Germany's second largest city, Hamburg. Nevertheless, on May 18, 2021, the *National Geographic Society* had officially declared the hamburger to be the national food of the United States. The American hamburger is a patty of ground beef which has been fried, grilled, or flame broiled, and placed inside a sliced bread roll or bun. It is usually garnished with cheese, onion, lettuce, tomato, pickles, even bacon, with condiments such as ketchup, mustard, mayonnaise, whatever. English cook and author Hannah Glasse (1708 – 1770) wrote: *The Art of*

Cookery <u>*Made Plain and Easy*</u> (1747). In the 1758 edition, Glasse included a recipe for *"Hamburgh sausage."* This beef (not ham) patty was served on toasted bread. The reference is clearly to the City of Hamburg. Back in Hamburg, the city burghers ate *"Frikadeller,"* a hamburger steak on bread. Having become fed-up with Hamburg, many of these Germans immigrated to America. They ate hamburger steak on buns during their passage on the *Hamburg American Line,* when they sailed to America. In 1884, the <u>*Boston Journal*</u> referred to the *"Hamburger steak."* On July 5, 1896, the <u>*Chicago Daily Tribune*</u> made a highly specific claim regarding a *"hamburger sandwich"* in an article about a railroad *"Sandwich Car"*: *"A distinguished favorite, for only 5 cents, is Hamburger steak sandwich, the meat for which is kept ready in small patties and 'cooked while you wait' on the gasoline range."* [It seems uninviting to wait on a hot grill, but we'll grant the reporter journalistic license.] Today, hamburgers are sold and eaten by the billions the worldwide, especially in America. The hamburger is indeed American cuisine in fastfood outlets, diners, and high-end restaurants.

HAMMERSCALE – (*HAM*-mer-skay-uhl) Flaky crud or hollow spheroids, byproducts of iron forging. Hammerscale is comprised of black or dark gray iron oxide of magnetite. These waste minerals are pounded out of white or red hot iron as the glowing metal oxidizes in the air. Ancient heaps of Hammerscale indicate early ironworking.

HAMTRAMCK – (ham-*TRAM*-mik) A city in the heart of Detroit Michigan (2 sq. mi. /pop. 22,500). A traditionally Polish enclave, Hamtramck is now increasingly cosmopolitan, becoming a haven for artists and intellectuals. Today, the small city is 90% Islamic. In fact, after the election of November 2015, Hamtramck, Michigan became the first city in the United States to be ruled by Muslims (Mayor and City Council). The city is named in honor of John Francis Hamtramck, French-Canadian-American (1756 – 1803) Indian fighter, Revolutionary War hero, and commander of Fort Detroit. Incidentally: Hamtramck Township was once the largest in America (1798). Hamtramck was the most populated village in America (1901), before it incorporated as a city (1922). At that point, Hamtramck became the 6th largest city in Michigan. Update: In 1970, Hamtramck was 90% Polish. Today, the city is 90% Muslim, Bengali, and Yemenis, primarily. Actually, over 40 languages are spoken in Hamtramck today. Over 45% of the citizens are foreign born. Droves of Bengali Muslims from New York City are moving to Hamtramck Michigan for the cheaper cost of living. Where Detroit's population is still shrinking, Hamtramck's population is growing. Hamtramck is the only overwhelmingly Muslim city in America. Incidentally: Hamtramck is the original hometown of the author of this book.

HAND – (*HAND*) The terminal, prehensile part of the upper limb in humans and other primates, consisting of the wrist, metacarpal area, fingers, and thumb. The human hand is a highly sophisticated organ with a very complex nervous system. The opposable thumb (opposite the fingers), enables <u>man</u> to <u>mani</u>pulate his world. In fact, the verb *"<u>mani</u>pulate"* means *"to <u>handle</u> skillfully by <u>hand</u>."* About 2.31 million years ago, our ancestors in East and South Africa were the first proto humans to make rudimentary tools with their own <u>hands</u>. That's why they had been named *"Homo habilis,"* meaning *"<u>handy</u> man."* Simple stone and wood tools become more complex and eventually advanced into machines that encouraged technology that resulted in civilization. The hand enabled man to create <u>arti</u>facts, everything, anything <u>arti</u>ficial, including <u>art</u>. Man is the only animal to produce art. And it all started with the hand. *"The hand is the visible part of the brain,"* declared philosopher Immanuel Kant (1724 – 1804). Indeed, neurobiologists believe that brain and hand complement, stimulate each other's abilities. The hand made the brain smarter, while the brain made the hand more skillful. The hand helped the human species to dominate the animal kingdom. A Conficta: *"Anthropologists now believe that man began to walk erect in order to free his hands so he could masturbate."* – Comedian Lily Tomlin (b. 1939) from Wayne State University, Detroit.

HAND AX – (*HAND AKS*) The celt. Proto-mankind's first and longest used stone tool. The hand ax goes back 1.5 million years to our hominid ancestor, Homo habilis, the first tool maker. The hand ax is an oval stone which is knapped creating a sharp cutting edge. The blunt end is held in the palm of the hand in the power grip. (The ancestors of man had a short thumb, and therefore could not manipulate very delicately, but could use the power grip.) Unlike its later, more sophisticated descendant, the hand ax is not hafted (it has no held or handle). The handle was attached to the hand ax about 50,000 years ago. Therefore, it took our ancestors 1,450,000 years to learn to add a handle to the ax head. Progress marches forward, albeit slowly.

HANDFASTING – (*HAND*-fahst-ting) (also Handbinding) A ritual in modern Paganism that binds two people together for a specified period of time. The couple may be ordained as partners for a day, month, year, till love lasts, till death, for eternity. Handfasting was and still is performed as a wedding ceremony.

HANDLE – (*HAN*-dul) A respectful title, a reference of deference like Mr., Mrs., Dr., Rev., Sir, and so on.

HANDJOB – (*HAND*-job) The act of being masturbated by another. A handjob is the manual counterpart of the oral *"blowjob."* The erect penis is manually massaged to climactic, orgasmic ejaculation. The executor of the handjob can be a female or male. The beneficiary is obviously a male. The handjob is another technique in the toybox of sexual gratification. *"We have reason to believe that man first walked erect to free his hands for masturbation."* – Comedian Lily Tomlin (b. 1939), Wayne State University grad. Incidentally: God only blesses the uninhibited with sexual gratification. *"Love, then do as you wish."* – St. Augustine (354 – 430 CE).

HAND-ME-DOWNS – (*HAND MEE DOWN*) Used clothing bequeathed to a younger sibling after the older had outgrown them. Hand-me-downs may also come from relatives or friends. Obviously, this clothing is worn and sometimes shabby looking. This custom is an emergency measure employed by families in poverty. Hand-me-downs, along with resale shops and food banks are characteristics of a capitalist society where distributive injustice prevails. The dog-eat-dog capitalist economy produces few winners, and multitudes of losers. The losers become the *"Have-Nots"* who wear hand-me-downs.

HAND-OVER-FIST – (hand *OH*-ver-*FIST*) Performed quickly, continuously. To create or manufacture at a tremendously rapid pace. The origin of this phrase is ambivalent. It has been suggested that this is a nautical term referring to the climbing and pulling on ropes by hand. However, these references read *"hand over hand,"* not *"hand-over-fist."* The legendary Captain James Cooke (1728 – 1779) wrote in the Royal Society's *Philosophical Transactions* for 1736: *"A lusty young Man attempted to go down (hand over hand, as the Workmen call it) by means of a Rope."* In 1769, William Falconer (1732 – 1770) wrote in *An Universal Dictionary of the Marine*: *"Main avant, the order to pull on a rope hand-over-hand."* In 1825, William Glascock (fl. 1825) wrote in *The naval sketchbook: "The French…weathered our wake, coming up with us, 'hand over fist,' in three divisions."* Though this is also a naval topic, it does not concern ropes, but rather speed and rapidity. In <u>*The life and writings of Major Jack Downing,*</u> the American writer Seba Smith (1792 – 1868) recorded: *"They…clawed the money off the table, hand over fist."* This reference is closer to the present day meaning of obtaining money quickly, rapidly, hand-over-fist. This leads to another possible etymological origin of the phrase. Before money can be earned, it first has to be made – literally. When all money was coinage, the blank pieces of silver and gold had to be stamped by a hammer on a die. The craftsman held the die in one hand, while gripping the hammer, in the fist of the other hand. The die would be struck, imprinting the coin. The money was made hand-over-fist. To the author, this is a more plausible explanation for this term.

HANDS – (*HANDZ*) A pen-and-ink drawing (c. 1508) by German artist and printmaker Albrecht Durer (1471 – 1528). The work is popularly known the world over as *"The Praying Hands."* The story is told of two brothers Albert and Albrecht, part of a poor family of 18 children in 16th century Nuremberg, Germany. Both talented brothers dreamt of attending art school. There were no funds. So they agreed to flip a coin. The winner would go to the academy, the loser would go to the mine, to pay the tuition. On graduating, the artist would pay for his brother to attend art school by selling his works. Albrecht won and went to school. Albert lost and went to the mine. After only 4 years, Albrecht had become an artistic sensation. A great feast was organized for his graduation. Albrecht had lifted his glass to toast his beloved brother. *"Now Albert, it's your turn. You go to the academy, and I'll provide for you."* All that time Albert's face was buried in his gnarled hands moaning *"No! No! Dear brother,"* Albert lamented, *"it's too late for me. See what four years in the mine had done to my hands? I have broken every finger at least once. I have arthritis so badly that I cannot even hold this glass to return your beautiful toast. How can I hold a pen or brush? It's too late for me."* In tribute to his brother, Albrecht drew Albert's crippled hands. For over 500 years people have been inspired by *"The Praying Hands,"* and perhaps more so now. The original print is in the Albertina Museum, Vienna, Austria.

HANDSEL – (*HAND*-suhl) A token or gift for good luck or as an expression of good wishes, as at the beginning of a new year or when entering upon a new situation or enterprise. A handsel is often given at graduation, when starting a new business, or as a house-warming gift when entering a new home. This term is used primarily in Scotland, Ireland, and Northern England. Handsel is an ancient word that dates back to about 1000 CE. It derives from the Old English (West Saxon) *"handselen,"* meaning *"hand-gift."* The Old English noun *"selen,"* meant *"gift,"* and is akin to the verb *"sell."* Too, handsel is related to the Old Norse *"handsal,"* meaning *"handshake."*

HANDSHAKE – (*HAND*-shayk) (Hand Shaking, Shook Hands) The common *"dexiosis,"* which is Greek for *"greeting." "Dexios"* is Greek for *"right hand."* The handshake is conducted with the right hand only. That is because 89% of humanity is right-handed. The handshake is a global tradition in which two people clasp each other's right hand, accompanied by a brief up-and-down movement of the hands. A handshake is a greeting and parting custom, as well as a sign of reconciliation, congratulations, and a symbol that an agreement has been concluded in good faith. Anthropologists believe that the handshake dates back before written history. It served as an indication of peace, for the open handheld no weapon. The oldest depiction of the handshake is an Assyrian relief of the 9th century BCE. It shows Assyrian

King Shalmaneser III (859 – 824 BCE) shaking hands with Babylonian King Marduk-zakir-shumi I (d. 819 BCE) to seal an alliance. Until the Coronavirus pandemic of 2020, people shook hands unthinkingly, as a common courtesy. The contagion had reminded us that the hands are the germiest part of the body. So almost universally the elbow and fist bump, even the silly *"footsie brush"* displaced the handshake as a safety precaution. Actually, the most dignified, charming, sacred, and safe substitute for the handshake is the ancient Hindu *"Namaste"* (nam-*OS*-tee). This is the traditional Hindu expression on meeting or parting, used by the speaker, holding hands together in front of the bosom in a prayerful fashion. This Sanskrit word and gesture speaks volumes. It means *"I honor the truth, the light, the peace, the love in you. I salute your divine qualities. The God (ness) in me greets and honors the God (ness) in you. My soul bows to your soul. We are one in God."*

HAND-TO-MOUTH – (hand too *MAWTH*) Barely existing, as do the lumpenproletarians – the poorest of the poor. The emaciated street people, the homeless live hand-to-mouth. They escape death by begging. As the term suggests, those who live hand-to-mouth must immediately consume what they are given. They never enjoy the luxury of a surplus [read: *save some for later*]. Rather than a pleasurable activity, eating is a medical emergency, more like an immediate transfusion than a leisurely dessert. Being national citizens, the poor are the nation's responsibility. Being human beings, they are our personal responsibility as well. Many people fall between the cracks in capitalist societies. Capitalism is predicated on competition. The hand-to-mouth survivors are the losers in this win/lose economic game. Actually, society produces abundance, more than enough for all. But in a society dominated by capitalists, the abundance is hoarded by a few, creating scarcity for the rest. That's why in an affluent society, so many desperate people live hand-to- mouth. The problem is capitalism. The solution is Socialism.

HANGDOG – (*HANG* dawg) Wearing a sad-sack look, a browbeaten, defeated appearance. A hangdog face has drooping eyes, the look of hopelessness. A person plagued with prolonged misfortune, illness, anxiety will eventually develop a hangdog face. The term *"hangdog"* traces back to the 1670s. The phrase *"befitting a hangdog"* was popular, depicting a despicable, degraded fellow. A hangdog was a lowly person fit only for hanging, like a dog. Incidentally: A perfect example of a hangdog face is worn by that vile, vicious Russian mercenary leader, Yevgeny Prigozhin (1961 - 2023). The former restaurateur began his career as *"Putin's Chef."* He now heads the savage criminal mercenary organization called the *"Wagner Group."* Update: Yevgeny Prigozhin was killed by his dictator-cum-rival Vladimir Putin (b. 1952) in August, 2023. Putin had Prigozhin blown-up in a plane crash. Dictators have no rivals. *"Nature gives you the face you have at twenty; it is up to you to merit the face you have at fifty."* – Coco Chanel (1883 – 1971).

HANG/HUNG – (*HANG HUNG*) (Hanged, Hanging,) To hang is to fasten or attach so that it is supported only from above, or suspended from a point near the top. One can *hang* a picture or *hang* a man. Too, a picture is *hung* on the wall, but a man is *hanged* on the gallows. A man is never *hung* (at least not in this sense). In fact, past, present or future, a man was *hanged,* is being *hanged,* or shall be *hanged,* are the correct usages. Incidentally: A gentleman generously genitaled is said to be *"well hung." "Sweet Jesus, he's hung like a horse!"*

HANGING CHADS – (*HANG*-ging *CHADS*) Defective punchcards. Fragments of paper that have failed to detach from a computer punched card, leaving a clean hole as intended. This leaves questions as to the operator's intention. Hanging chads on the Florida voting ballots in the 2000 presidential election gave the state and election to the Republican, George W. Bush (b. 1946) over the Democratic candidate Al Gore (b. 1948), making Mr. Bush *"His Fraudulency, the President of the United States."*

HANGOVER – (*HANG*-oh-ver) The flu-like symptoms suffered after over- indulging in alcohol. Consumable alcohol is ethanol (CH_3CH_2OH). However, ethanal (CH_3CHO), acetaldehyde a toxin, is produced in the gut when ethanol is exposed to oxygen. Ethanal is a hangover chemical. The hangover includes a pounding headache, nausea, sweats, dry-mouth, dehydration, dizziness, blurry vision, a nervous feeling of angst (*hangxiety*). Hangovers are the bane of party animals. The medical term for this illness is *veisalgia*. It is an ancient ailment. Like intoxication, the hangover sneaks up on its prey like a snake: *"In the end it bites like a serpent or like a poisonous adder."* – Proverbs 23:32.

HANGRY – (*HANG*-gree) Feeling irritable or irrationally angry as a result of being hungry. In fact, hangry is a portmanteau term which attaches the letter H from <u>h</u>ungry to the word <u>a</u>ngry, creating <u>h</u>angry. Hunger is a discomfort that escalates into pain. This makes animals more aggressive. All animals, including man, are more dangerous when hungry. When hangry, people are less tolerant, and lose patience quickly. Try to avoid stressful situations when hungry, or you may become hangry.

HANGXIETY – (hang-*ZY*-et-tee) The vague feeling of dread, apprehension, angst that accompanies a hangover (veisalgia). Hangxiety involves worries about real or imagined faux pas from the previous evening. One feels a sense of guilt, without knowing why. Neuropsychopharmacologists inform us that chemical imbalances in the brain, due to alcohol is responsible for hangxiety.

HANKER – (*HANG*-ker) (Hankering, Hankered) To have a restless or incessant longing for something. One may say: *"I hanker for…,"* or *"I'm hankering after…,"* anything. Hanker and hankering (or *hanker'en*) is usually associated with American Southern or *"Hillbilly"* dialect. The term hanker entered English in the 1640s. It meant *"linger in expectation."* Hanker probably was adopted from the Flemish term *"hankeren,"* meaning *"to long for."* *"I'm a-hanker'en for some Southern fried chicken and cornbread."*

HANKY PANKY – (*HANG*-kee *PANG*-kee) This is one of those nonsense terms that was made up and persisted because of its attractive alliteration and rhyme – like *"bee's knees,"* or *"mutt's nuts."* Hanky panky originally meant *"deceitful, unethical behavior, trickery"* (1841). The term may have evolved from the British slang term *"hoky-poky,"* meaning *"fraud, deception."* Both terms may be traced back to the magician's term *"hocus-pocus."* The term is first recorded in relation to its original *"trickery"* meaning in the first edition of <u>*"Punch, or the London Charivari,"*</u> Vol. 1, September 1941: *"Only a little hanky-panky, my lud. The people like it; they love to be cheated before their faces. One, two, three – presto – begone. I'll show your ludship as pretty a trick of putting a piece of money in your eye and taking it out of your elbow, as you ever beheld."* The later meaning of *"hanky panky"* concerns *"sexual activity or dalliance, especially of a surreptitious nature."* In his play <u>Geneva</u> (1939), George Bernard Shaw (1856 – 1950) wrote: *"She: No hanky panky. I am respectable; and I mean to keep respectable. He: I pledge you my word that my intentions are completely honorable."*

329

HAPHAZARD – (hap-*HAZ*-erd) (Haphazardly, Haphazardness, Haphazardry) Performed aimlessly, lacking order or planning. What's done haphazardly is a half-ass job. Haphazardness is dependent on chance, luck, *and "I hope it works out."* The term haphazard is recorded in the 1670's. Its origin dates back to the 1570's with the union of *"hap,"* (chance, luck) and *"hazard"* (risk, danger). Indeed, one is taking a risky chance by constructing a structure haphazardly.

HAPLESS – (*HAP*-lis) (Haplessness, Haplessly) Being without hap? Yes, originally. The term *"hap"* derived from the Old Norse *"happ,"* meaning *"chance, good luck."* The term hap entered English in c. 1200, meaning "chance, fate, fortune, good luck." The term evolved to hapless by c. 1400. Today, hapless means *"luckless, unlucky, unfortunate."* A hapless person is perpetually plagued by bad luck. He becomes hopeless, then helpless. Hapless people need compassionate encouragement and substantial aid in the form of money and physical, emotional support. Often, just one break of good luck can turn a hapless person's life around. *"Good luck should bring happiness."*

HAPHEPHOBIA – (hap-uh-*FO*-bee-a) (Haphephobiac) Phobic fear of being touched. A haphephobiac may be a *"germophobe"* as well. Haphephobia is a neurosis, and therefore serves as a defense mechanism hiding a more serious psycho-emotional problem eating away in the victim's subconscious.

HAPLOGROUP – (*HAP*-lo-groop) A group sharing the same *"haplotype."* In genetics, a haplogroup is a set of similar DNA sequences on one chromosome (a haplotype), inherited together. Furthermore, a haplogroup is a population sharing a set of similar DNA sequences (haplotypes). For instance, Celts, Vikings, Slavs, Mongols are all haplogroups. Haplogrouping is used to understand genetic lineages.

HAPPENSTANCE – (*HAP*-pen-stans) A chance occurrence, a random event. A happenstance is related to fate, luck, a chance happening.

HAPPINESS – (*HAP*-pee-nis) (Happy) A euphoric feeling of blissful contentment. Happiness is dependent on peace of mind, being satisfied with the present situation. Peace of mind is brought about by physical and economic security. It's a valid cliché that *"Money can't buy happiness."* However, a lack of money can produce misery, the polar opposite of happiness. Those who are happy with the least, are happy the most. According to the ancient Taoist book, <u>Zhuangzi</u>, *"Happiness is the absence of striving for happiness."* Incidentally: On being shown Coney Island amusement park in New York, the Russian writer Maxim Gorky (1868 – 1936) responded: *"This must be a very sad people to need a place like this to make them happy." "Happiness wishes everybody happy."* – Victor Hugo (1802 – 1885). Incidentally: Happy is one of those relative terms that cannot be fully understood without knowing its opposite, sadness. *"The only reason why you are unhappy is because you are trying to be happy."* – *Jaggi Vasudev (b. 1957).*

HAPPINESS – (*HAP*-pee-nis) (Happy) Happiness is more than a personal sensation. It is also a democratic imperative. Happiness is contentment, satisfaction, a secure sense of good fortune and wellbeing. In the Declaration of Independence, our Founding Fathers agreed on the gravitas of *"Life, Liberty, and the pursuit of <u>Happiness.</u>"* Not *"Liberty, Equality, and Fraternity"* as in the French Revolutionary declaration. Nor *"Life, Liberty and Justice"* – but *"Happiness."* The Republican political strategist, Steve Schmidt (b. 1970) explained that: *"Our Founding Fathers talked about happiness. They believed that happiness was deeply linked* *to the concept of freedom."* And so it is. A Stoic proverb states: *"You can't be happy on the rack."* Likewise, you can't be happy if racked by poverty. If a person has to choose between liberty and bread, she'll always choose bread. Indeed, democracy cannot function in a poor, unhappy society. Nothing results in more unhappiness than poverty. Unhappy citizens of a democracy will elect a fascist demagogue who promises deliverance and happiness. The unhappiness of the Great Capitalist Depression ushered Adolf Hitler (1889 – 1945) to power in 1933. As Steve Schmidt warned: *"A healthy society does not produce a President Trump. A sick, decaying, and rotten one does."* Capitalism is rotting our society by increasing unhappiness. Capitalism is predicated on unfair competition, consolidation, acquisition, accumulation, hoarding and greed. Socialism is predicated on cooperation, dissemination, distribution, sharing and need. The capitalist says: *"I got mine, to hell with you!"* The Socialist says: *"There's plenty for everyone."* Indeed, capitalism is smothering democracy in America. The oligarchic triumvirate of Bazos-Gates-Musk together is richer than the lower half (50%) of the U.S. population! That's over 167,000,000 people! This is the unhappy monster that capitalism has produced. If we truly hope to establish and preserve *"Life"* and *"Liberty,"* we must create genuine *"Happiness"* through Socialism. Incidentally: Research reveals that the happiest countries in the world are all Democratic Socialist, or heavily Socialistic. This includes all the Scandinavian Nations. *"Fascism is capitalism in decay."* – Vladimir Lenin (1870 – 1924). *"It is the inalienable right of all to be happy."* – Elizabeth Cady Stanton (1815 – 1902).

HAPPY HOUR – (*HAP*-pee *OW*-er) A promotional ploy in bars, taverns, and pubs to drum-up business. During *"happy hour,"* alcoholic drinks are half price or two for the price of one. Hopefully, the customers will stay beyond happy hour, and will return as regular patrons.

HAPPY MARRIAGE – (*HAP*-pee *MER*-ij) Living Lovingly with one's life mate. The following *Rules for a Happy Marriage* are from *"Fratelli Bonella,"* an Italian Catholic publishing house. 1. Never both be angry at the same time. 2. Never yell at each other unless the house is on fire. 3. If one of you has to win an argument, let it be your mate. 4. If you have to criticize, do it lovingly. 5. Never bring up mistakes of the past. 6. Neglect the whole world rather than each other. 7. Never go to sleep with an argument unsettled. 8. At least once every day try to say one kind or complimentary thing to your life's partner. 9. When you have done something wrong, be ready to admit it and ask for forgiveness. 10. It takes two to make a quarrel, and the one in the wrong is the one who does the most talking.

HAPPY TALK – (*HAP*-pee *TAWK*) Overconfident, hyper-optimistic speech, intended to persuade an audience that a bad situation is really good. Happy talk is cheerful propaganda in the face of a calamity. It is hoped to minimize the negative fallout from a personal catastrophe. Happy talk is an indirect, deceptional cover-up of incompetence and fault. The term *"happy talk,"* emerged during the early days of the Coronavirus pandemic in the U.S., from January to May 2020. President Donald Trump (b. 1946) did nothing, too little, or the wrong thing in dealing with the lethal outbreak. Trump's plan is having no plan. Trumps only concern was the illusion of economic recovery that Trump falsely thought would bolster his re-election chances. In order to divert justifiable blame, Trump downplayed the carnage, despite the warnings of specialists, and the tens-of-thousands of deaths. On April 10, 2020, CNN reporter Jim Acosta (b. 1971) accused Trump and his White House Briefings as *"Happy talk,"* amid the wildfire pandemic. Acosta admonished the President: *"We hear a lot of people who see these briefings as sort of 'happy talk' briefings.*

And you [Trump] *and some of these officials paint a rosy picture of what is happening around the country. If you look at some of these questions, do we have enough masks? 'NO.' Do we have enough tests? 'No.' Do we have enough PPE?* [Personal Protection Equipment]? *'No.'" "At a point, optimism becomes naiveté, and naiveté becomes stupidity."* – Dr. Gary J. Pasieka (b. 1951).

HARBINGER – (*HAR*-bin-jer) An omen. A forerunner or a herald. A harbinger is a messenger sent ahead with an announcement of news or information. Too, a harbinger may be a sign or omen that foreshadows the future. For instance, sight of a comet was once considered a harbinger of misfortune or disaster. Incidentally: Try not to be the harbinger of bad news, sad news. Try to put the best, brightest positive spin on negative narratives. You will put people at ease and be more popular.

HARDCOPY – (*HARD*-cop-pee) Information printed on paper, as opposed to information electronically displayed on a computer screen (soft copy). Often a hard copy is printed from a computer's soft copy.

HARDLINERS – (*HARD*-line-ers) Rigid, dogmatic, uncompromising individuals, usually the reactionary right-wing of a party. Though there may be examples of Liberal hardliners dedicated to Progressivism, conservatism by its very nature is ossified, hard, hardliner. The compulsion to conserve hardens the heart, and the line of action, with no options from which to choose.

HARDNESS – (*HARD*-ness) The opposite condition to softness. Hardness is the result of minimal molecular motion. Stable molecules make for hard material. The molecular motion of a solid is slower than in a liquid, and the molecular motion of a liquid is slower than in a gas. Therefore, a solid is harder than a liquid, and a liquid (so to speak) is harder than a gas. With solid materials, hardness is the measure of the ability of a mineral to resist scratching. Substances like metals that will not shatter are made harder when wrought (hammered). Hammering crushes the molecular matrix of the metal, preventing the molecules from sliding or moving. The metal is therefore harder (work- harden). Similar results are attained when an alloy (mixing metals) is produced. The atoms of the added metal wedge between the molecular matrixes preventing the sliding motion resulting in more hardness.

HARDSHIP COMMAND – (*HARD*-ship com-*MAND*) The most brutal, conscienceless German soldiers in Russia during World War Two, dedicated Nazis. Hardship commandos volunteered to slaughter the orphaned children, something normal soldiers could not do. They were honored and promptly promoted for their *"Mission of Hardship."* Most members of the Hardship Command were young SS troopers. The SS were the fanatical Nazi ideologues. Too, young soldiers had years of indoctrination in Nazi schools, and the Hitler Youth which warped their minds and concealed their conscience. Normal German soldiers, who had maintained a conscience fell into despair, often committed suicide. Others went mad and were institutionalized. Those who suffered the most by witnessing the atrocities were those with young children of their own.

HARD DRIVE – (abbreviated UD or HDD) In computer technology the hard drive is a non-volatile memory hardware device that permanently stores and retrieves data on a computer. A hard drive is a secondary storage device that consists of one or more platters to which data is written using a magnetic head, all inside an air-sealed casing. Internet hard disks reside in a drive bay, connected to the motherboard using special cables, and are powered by a connection to the power supply unit. All computers have a hard drive installed in them, which is used to store files for the operating system, software programs, and a user's personal files. A computer cannot function without a hard drive.

HARD POLYTHEISM – (*HAHRD* pol-lee-*THEE*-iz-uhm). Polytheism is the belief in many Gods. Hard polytheism is a rendition of this belief. The many Gods in hard polytheism exist separately, independent of each other. Each God has her or his own unique personality. This is in contrast to the belief that the many Gods are aspects of a singular God. The Greek and Roman pantheons represented of hard polytheism.

HARD/SOFT POWER – (*HAHRD SAWFT POU*-wer) In international relations, hard/soft power are the opposite options with which a nation may gain its goals. Hard power is Machiavellian, the method of bullies. It includes threats, intimidation, troop movements, and attack – invasion and war. Soft power takes the diplomatic route. It involves negotiation, persuasion, granting aid packages. Where hard power is the *"stick,"* soft power is the *"carrot."* Russian Dictopresident Vladimir Putin's (b. 1952) savage invasion of the Ukraine (March 2022) exemplifies hard power. American Democratic President Joe Biden's (b. 1942) organization of opposition against Putin exemplifies strong soft power.

HARDWARE – (*HARD*-where) (abbreviated HW) In computer technology hardware is best described as any physical component of a computer system that contains a circuit board, integrated circuit, or other electronics. A perfect example of hardware is the computer screen. Whether it be a computer monitor, tablet, or smartphone, it's hardware. Without any hardware your computer would not exist and software could not be used.

HARD WATER – (*HARD WAUT*-ter) Water that contains relatively large amounts of dissolved minerals, particularly magnesium, iron, or lime (calcium) from limestone. Lakes and rivers with hard water are good for bass and perch fishing. Mineral-free lakes and rivers (soft water) are good for trout fishing. In hard water, soap, shampoo, detergent will not lather. Washing in mineral-rich hard water is hard. So water softening agents are added to neutralize the effect of the minerals that make the water hard. This chemically changes the properties of the magnesium, iron, or calcium ions. Water softeners enable hard water to work-up a lather and suds for efficient washing.

HARDWIRED – (*HARD*-wy-erd) Innate, inherent, originally and permanently implanted into a system or organism. Hardwired information, knowledge, or behaviors are pre-programmed. In organisms, it is instinctive, genetic, not learned knowledge. In a mechanical brain (computer), hardwired information or abilities are built into the hardware of the machine, not added later as is software. Hardwired information cannot be altered or changed. *"Bees cannot customize or change the design of their hive, because that design is hardwired into their DNA."*

HAREDIM EXEMPTION – (har-*REE*-deem eks-*EMP*-shuhn) (plural Haredi) The Haredim are the ultraorthodox Jewish religionists in Israel. (The Haredim are known as Hasidic Jews in America.) Israel is confronted with an identity crisis. Is it a Western Democracy, or a Middle Eastern Theocracy? That's because like the little Vatican, Israel is both a sovereign nation and a religious capital. Israel is the homeland of the Jews, and a practicing Jew is a religious citizen. But the Jewish citizens of Israel are religious to various degrees.

The Haredim have carved out a powerful subculture in Israeli society, that presents a divisive force. In 1948, Israel's first Prime Minister, David Ben Gurion (1886 - 1973) exempted 400 Haredim Yeshiva (religious school) students from military service. In 2023, there were over 66,000 such students. Every other young Israeli, male or female, at 18 years of age are subject to military service. The Haredim are given a generous government stiped for studying. In 1977, the Haredim Exemption was expanded to include the entire religious sect. These ultraorthodox citizens procreate at a 4.2% annual increase, twice the national average. The average Haredim family produces 7 children. Of the 9.2 millions Israeli citizens, 1.1 million (12%) are Haredim ultraorthodox Jews today. At this rate, by 2050 (in 1 generation) the Haredim will comprise 1/3 of the national population. That's a mighty heavy load for the other 2/3 to carry. Knesset member Yohanan Plesner (b. 1972) lamented that: *"This is a controversy that can bring down the government. This is one of the biggest open wounds in Israeli society."* Ultraorthodox Chief Sephardic Rabbi, Yitzhak Yosef (b. 1952) warned: *"If they force us to go to the army, we'll all move abroad. All these secular people don't understand that without [religious scholars], the army would not be successful.... The soldiers only succeed thanks to those learning the Torah."* The Haredim are not Gandhiesque pacifists. They just don't want to do the fighting. The Rabbi perceives the Haredim as *"Prayer Warriors,"* as vital to the war effort as arms manufacturers and weapons researchers behind the line. Haredim are aligned with the Shas Party. David Menahem (b. 1980) one of the leaders said: *"We understand that we are part of a bigger picture, and that we should contribute too because we are also benefiting from it. But the army is a red line. The army would like men and women to serve together. But we think a married man and a married woman serving in a tank together for 12 hours – it's not correct. It's forbidden according to the Torah."* So the Haredim are unpatriotic cowards, right? Not so fast. Ordained clergy are exempt from the military in the United Sates. So are the pacific Amish, and other legally recognized conscientious objectors. But they are a tiny fraction of the population. Too, unlike Israel, The U.S. is not in a perpetual siege emergency. The Haredim and the Israeli nation have some hard decisions to make. Incidentally: Religious missionaries are illegal in Israel. It's against the law to try to convert any Jew to any other religion, publicly or privately. Democracy or Theocracy? Addendum: The radical right, headed by the Haredim presently (March 2024) rules Israel under the leadership of Benjamin Netanyahu (b. 1949). Netanyahu is not a Haredim but both are using each other. Netanyahu is using the Haredim to stay out of prison for corruption. The Haredim is using Netanyahu to implement their agenda: *"ethnic cleansing."* The theocratic Haredim wants to cleanse Israel of all non-Jews and non-Judaism. The Haredim wants to banish all Palestinians, first by making Gaza unlivable. If the entire Muslim population starves to death, so be it. The Haredim will certainly justify their abomination with quotes or prophesy in the Bible. The Haredim believes itself to be the conscience, the soul of Israel. The United States must not aid and abet this travesty with American weapons. The Haredim must be exposed and deposed, and Netanyahu must be imprisoned. Update: The pressure had become too excruciating. On March 27, 2024. The Israeli High Court, (the very court that the Haredim and Netanyahu tried to suppress), ruled that the ultraorthodox religionists will no longer get preferential treatment. Their government grant for studying the Torah is revoked. They are subject to the draft, to protect Israel, like every other citizen. The High Court of Israel chose Democracy over Theocracy.

HAREM – (*HAIR*-um) Means *"Forbidden"* in Arabic. The Turkish Ottoman Sultan's assortment of female Christian sex-slaves. They were gifts or war booty. The girls were converted to Islam and schooled in the sexual arts. At its height, the harem housed over 1,000 ladies who lived in luxurious bondage. Few actually slept with the Sultan. Only the most ravishing were ravished, chosen for sex, which happened only once. The boss never slept with the same woman twice. There was nothing like marriage. Each concubine was allowed but one son, who was a prince. So a slave girl could become the lucky mother of the next Sultan. The harem system guaranteed plenty of heirs to assure succession.

HARES – (*HAIRS*) Long-eared rabbits. Hares, like rabbits are rodents.

HARLEQUIN – (*HAR*-le-kwin) A buffoon. A clown in ridiculous dress.

HARLEQUINADE – (har-le-kwin-*AID*) A farce, buffoonery. A comic play or pantomime performed by a harlequin clown.

HARLOTRY – (*HAR*-lot-tree) (Harlot) A harlot is a prostitute. Harlotry is the art of prostitution.

HARMONIZATION – (har-mon-nize-*ZAY*-shun) To coordinate, homogenize, bring into agreement. Harmonization is a deceptive euphemism employed by *Carnival Cruiselines* to exploit the people in their ports of call. Carnival controls a virtual monopoly of the industry. Despite anti-trust laws, Carnival had lobbied [read: *bribed*] Congress to allow them to buy-up their competitors. Carnival is the *"Walmart"* of the cruiseline industry. Their clientele primarily consists of *"Wahoos,"* the *"Trump Rally"* types. The other cruiselines that Carnival had swallowed are upscale, catering to a wealthier, more educated, sophisticated individuals. They expect better service and they pay for it. The Carnival crowd is interested in bars, beer, beach, and bikinis. These cheaper people pay cheaper fares. The tour operators at the ports of call must work harder and spend more resources accommodating the guests from the non-Carnival vessels (owned by Carnival). Naturally the tour operators must charge more when servicing these more demanding clients. But capitalist Carnival doesn't see it that way. Though they charge more per ticket to the non-Carnival passengers, Carnival expects the tour operators to *"harmonize"* the price for all Carnival Corporation clientele. Carnival wouldn't think of harmonizing the ticket prices for all ships. After all, you cannot expect caviar for the cost of hardboiled eggs. Nevertheless, Carnival expects penthouse service at bargain-basement prices from the tour operators, and the people dependent on them. This defies basic economic logic. Carnival expects tour operators, guides, and bus drivers to work for nickels and pennies per customer, while Carnival pockets hundreds of dollars. Harmonization is pure capitalist greed, putting profit before people. Capitalist Carnival is an American mega-corporation that treats foreign associates like bugs, to be squashed. Carnival's *Harmonization Scheme* is another answer to the naïve question: *"Why do they hate us?"*

HARPAXOPHILIA – (har-paks-oh-*FEE*-lee-ah) (Harpaxophiliac) A neurotic paraphilial disorder in which one is sexually aroused from being the victim of a burglary or robbery.

HARPAXOPHOBIA – (har-paks-oh-*FO*-bee-a) (Harpaxophobiac) Phobic fear of being robbed. Though it is prudent to be wary of seedy environments were robbery may be a possibility, a harpaxpphobiac's fear is unreasonable, exaggerated, and neurotic.

HARPOONING THE WHALE – (*HAR*-poon-ing thuh *WAY'L*) A doctor's term for attempting to give an epidural anesthetic injection to an obese woman in labor. If the patience's only knew what transpired behind their backs.

HARPSICHORD – (*HARP*-si-cord) Keyboard percussion instrument, half harp, half piano. The harpsichord was the precursor to the piano.

HARROWING OF HELL – (*HAR*-oh-ing uhv *HEL*) The archaic meaning of the verb *"harrow"* is to *"violate, despoil."* In theology, the *"Harrowing of Hell"* refers to Jesus violating, despoiling Satan's plans to imprison the righteous, including Jesus himself in hell. In the Catholic Apostles' Creed, the perplexing line appears: *"He [Jesus] descended into hell...."* This Jesus purportedly did after his death on the cross. *"And on the third day, he arose <u>again</u> from the dead...."* This infers that Jesus went to hell during his weekend (3 days) in the tomb. (The term *"again"* is puzzling and significant.) It suggests that immediately after being entombed, Jesus rose from the dead to descend into hell. After confronting Satan, Jesus returned to his Earthly tomb, *"And on the third day, he rose <u>again</u> from the dead."* Therefore, Jesus experienced two resurrections. The line, *"He descended into hell,"* is official Catholic Church dogma, which baffles most contemporary Christians who tend to ignore it. But to early Christians, it was significant. Before the New Testament was canonized in final form (393 CE), there were scores of Gospels. One popular rendition was the *"Gospel of Nicodemus."* This was the text that informed the early Church Fathers of Jesus' descent into hell. This Gospel relates Satan's plan to imprison Jesus in hell. (Be aware that at that time, hell was an obscure, vague concept, conflated with esoteric *"Limbo,"* both a sort of *"Purgatory".*) At any rate, the story goes that rather than a captive, Jesus served as the liberator of hell. Jesus freed the pre-Christian saints, patriarchs, prophets, the righteous of the Old Testament (Abraham, Isaac, Jacob, Moses, Isaiah, et al., back to and including Adam and Eve). All were escorted out of hell, and ushered into heaven, thanks to Jesus. Satan was infuriated, having been harrowed in hell by Jesus. Therefore, as is alluded to in the Apostles' Creed, Jesus defied death twice; entered and escaped from hell; freed Satan's Biblical hostages; and defeated Satan in the *"Harrowing of Hell."* Incidentally: Some modern, revised renditions of the Apostle's Creed substitute the word *"dead"* for *"hell."* Hell implies the realm of evil, of the condemned. *"He [Jesus] descended to the dead,..."* suggests that he liberated the pre-Christian souls, enabling them to enter heaven.

HARVEST – (*HAR*-vest) (Harvesting, Harvester) The gathering of ripened crops in season. Only plants are harvested, not animals. Farmers cut down or reap grain. Hunters, acting as *"Grim Reapers"* cut down animals. Harvesting has become a deceptive hunting euphemism for killing. Harvesting was not meant to be a bloody endeavor. In order to protect profits, the capitalist hunting industry tries to sanitize killing, in order to sound politically correct. Killing becomes collecting, like picking fruit. Hunting is called harvesting. So is trapping and fishing. Nevertheless, you don't harvest a fish, you hook it. You don't harvest a beaver, you trap it. You don't harvest a deer, you shoot it. Therefore, a perfect *harvest* would entail a *reap* directly into the animal's heart, with minimal chase, mess and suffering. According to this twisted verbiage, would a manhunt for an escaped prisoner be a *"personnel harvest?"* Too, were 3 U.S. soldiers *"harvested"* in an ambush by the Taliban in Afghanistan yesterday? Ridiculous!

HARVEST MOON – (*HAR*-vest *MOON*) The full moon closest to the Autumnal equinox. In the Northern Hemisphere this happens in September, though the harvest moon may appear in October on occasion. In the Southern Hemisphere, the harvest moon appears in March or April.

HARVEY WALLBANGER – (*HAR*-vee *WAL*-bang-ger) A cocktail made with vodka, Galliano (a sweet herbal liqueur), and orange juice. It is a variation of the screwdriver. The cocktail was invented in 1969. Marketing executive George Bednar (1942 - 2007) created the character Harvey Wallbanger, a surfer, as the tagline for the drink.

HASH – (*HASH*) (Hashed) A variety of substances or edibles chopped, diced into small pieces, minced and mixed together. Meats, vegetables, cooked grains, any leftovers can be hashed together and sautéed in the frying pan for a quick, cheap meal. Cooked rice, barley, pasta, even mashed potatoes can be hashed and fried with hamburger and diced onions to make a filling and gratifying meal. One can feed a small army with hash.

HASH – (*HASH*) A truncated rendition of <u>hash</u>ish. Hash or hashish is the flowering crown, buds, and young top leaves of the Indian hemp plant (cannabis or marijuana). Hash is chewed, eaten, drunk as tea but primarily smoked. Hash has the highest concentration of THC (<u>T</u>etra<u>H</u>ydro<u>C</u>annabinol), the psychoactive component in the hash. The hashish crown of the plant is sticky with THC. This is the substance that will make you high.

HASHSHASHINS – (hash-*SHASH*-ins) Cult of Muslim hashish breathers during the bloody Crusades (1090 - 1275 CE). A secret sect of Islamic jihadists who would inhale cannabis before murder sprees. Hashshashin gave us the names *"hashish"* and *"assassins."*

HASHTAG – (*HASH*-tag) (Also called Hash Mark represented as the symbol #). Not a minced meat dish. On social media websites, hashtag is a word or phrase is sometimes preceded by a hashtag or mark (#). The mark is used within a message to identify a keyword or topic of interest, to facilitate a search perhaps. (In other words, for further information on this topic, consult the hashtag.) So a hashtag is a research convenience indicator.

HASIDIM – (ha-*SEE*-deem) (Hasidism = ha-*SEE*-dis-um) The Hasidic Jews. The most conservative, traditional Jewish denomination, recognizable by their beards, hair locks, black suits and hats. These Jewish Fundamentalists follow the letter of the law. In the latter 18th century, the environment for poor Polish Jewry grew increasingly hostile. There were massacres perpetrated by Cossacks and Russians. The Jesuits and Polish Commonwealth became less tolerant of Jews. It was during these hard times that Hasidism was born. It was founded in Podolia, Poland by Rabbi Izrael ben Eliezaer (1698 – 1760), who was also known as Baal Shem Tov. The Hasidim was a mystical ecstatic cult, rejecting painful realities and offering a spiritual palliative that attracted vast numbers of the poorest Jews in the teeming provincial shtetls of Poland. Izrael ben Eliezaer was a charismatic who preached that since God was everywhere He should be worshipped in everything and every action, even in eating, drinking and dancing. The joyful ceremonies he promoted appealed to the poorest Jews but drew the ire of the orthodox rabbis.

HASSIUM – (*HASS*-see-um) (Hs) A transuranic element (#108) named for the Latin form of the name Hessen, the German state where the work was performed. Hassium was discovered in 1984.

HASSOCK – (*HAS*-sok) An ottoman. A low padded seat, usually armless, sometimes also serving as a chest. Originally, hassocks were thickly cushioned footstools or kneelers. The term hassock derived from the Old English (West Saxon) *"hassuc,"* meaning a *"clump of grass."* By the 1510s, hassock was considered a thick cushion. The clump of grass reference probably related to the stuffing that provided the cushioning. Hassocks as kneelers were used in prayer. The adjective *"hassocky"* meant *"softly cushioned."*

HATE – (*HAYT*) An intense fear of loss in the present. Hate is a passionate emotion of hostility and fear – primarily fear. For hate is generated by fear, because hate and fear are the two faces of the same coin. We hate people who present a threat of loss to us. The loss can be in the form of security, liberty, love, property, prestige, life, whatever. It is popularly considered that the polar opposite of hate is love. False! The opposite of hate is indifference. Hate is a powerful negative or evil energy force. Indifference is dull, inert care-less-ness. (For Example: The Nazi SS Extermination Units did not hate their victims, they felt total indifference, like squashing a bug. That made the Holocaust all the more vile, heinous, demonic.) The only antidote for hate is to disarm the fear. You fear and therefore hate the enemy on the battlefield. But if the same person becomes your next-door neighbor, you will no longer fear nor hate him. The Holy Buddha (c. 563 – c. 483 BCE) advised us how to live and love in a hate- filled world. *"Live in this sinful world as the spotless leaf of the lotus, unsoiled by the mud in which it grows. As the lotus will grow full of sweet perfume and delight upon a heap of rubbish, thus the disciple of the truly enlightened Buddha shines forth by his wisdom among those who are like rubbish, among the people that walk in darkness. Let us live happy then, not hating those who hate us!* Among men who hate us let us dwell free from hatred! Let us live happily then, free from all ailments among the ailing! Among men who are ailing let us dwell free from ailments! Let us live happily, then, free from greed among the greedy! Among men who are greedy let us dwell free from greed."

HATE CRIME – (*HAYT* krahym) A felony, usually violent, motivated by prejudice or intolerance toward an individual's national origin, ethnicity, color, religion, gender identity, sexual orientation, or disability. In other words, a hate crime is an attack on anyone not like oneself. Throughout President Donald Trump's (b. 1946) four-year administration (2017 – 2020), hate crimes in America skyrocketed, as did racism. This was due to Trump's personal hatreds and poisonous public pronouncements. Trump targeted Muslims, Blacks, Latinos, Gays, Immigrants, and Orientals. Even after his defeat, violent attacks continued, especially against all East Asians into 2021, because of Trump's vile rhetoric. He referred to the deadly Coronavirus as the *"China Virus"* and *"Kung Flu."* This turned the wrath of racists against Chinese, Japanese, and Korean Americans. A hate crime is a federal crime which rightfully carries a harsh punishment.

HATE RADIO – (*HAYT RAY*-dee-o) Nasty politico-social broadcasting intended to incite the meanest passions of the populous. Hate radio is always right-wing, conservative, reactionary, and fascist. Its message appeals to lowly-educated skinheads, Klansmen, and neo-Nazis. Hate radio feeds on racism, bigotry, militarism, xenophobia, and supra-nationalism. Hate radio elevates obnoxious demigods to political prominence. Hate radio created the atmosphere for the rise of fascist Donald Trump (b. 1946).

HATHA YOGA – (*HATH*-tha *YO*-ga) Physical yoga, as opposed to raja yoga which is a mental discipline. Though all yoga involves the yoking together of the body, mind, and soul, hatha concentrates on gaining mental mastery over the body. It is a path of release through union of the mind with the body.

HAUNTED BLUE – (*HAWN*-ted *BLOO*) A sky-blue shade that was painted on the ceilings of 19th century mansions. It was reasoned that wasps would be deceived in thinking the ceiling was the sky, and therefore not attempt to build a nest on the ceiling. This anecdotal theory has not been tested scientifically.

HAUNTING HURTS – (*HAWN*-ting *HERTS*) Painful memories of past pain from sins that still gnaw at our conscience. Many of us had spent the first part of our lives being outrageous, and the second part regretting it. As boxer-cum- philosopher, Mike Tyson (b. 1966) said: *"We get old too soon, we get smart too late."* However, there is redemption. If we repent, and live in forgiveness, we too will be forgiven, and experience God's peace of mind. Karmic regret, remorse, resentment, and revenge will evaporate. Like the blind man healed by Jesus, we too will say: *"I was blind but now I see."* – John 9:25.

HAUTE – (*OHT*) French for high-class, high-toned, very fancy and expensive.

HAUTE BOURGEOISIE – (*OHT* booshz-wa-*ZEE*) A member of the high-middle class. The prosperous, though not filthy rich bourgeoisie or capitalists. The haute bourgeoisie employ workers, with the family members often serving as the business managers. Haute capitalists are at the mercy of the great corporate capitalists. Competition is a factor at this middle level of capitalism.

HAUTE COUTURE – (oht koo-*TOOR*) French for high-fashion, the most stylish and influential designing and dressmaking. The leading dressmaking establishments in the world are considered haute couture collectively. It's no accident or coincident that these are French terms. Paris, France has long been the mecca of high fashion. So is Italy, to a lesser degree, as is New York City. The cost of this apparel is ridiculously, extravagantly exaggerated. One pays for the name on the tag on the dress. Haute couture appeals to the obscene ostentation of the filthy rich.

HAUTE CUISINE – (oht kwi-*ZEEN*) French for fine gourmet cooking. Haute cuisine is high-class cooking, feeding the aristocracy, oligarchy, plutocracy. Haute cuisine is prohibitively expensive for most. It is self-indulgent dining. It rises far above mere sustenance. Haute cuisine must serve as a work of art. Appearance is as important as taste. It is obscene that haute cuisine should be indulged in a world with starving people.

HAVANA SYNDROME – (huh-*VAN*-uh *SIN*-drohm) *Anomalous Health Syndrome,* according to the U.S. Government. A mysterious, debilitating neurological condition, still under investigation. The Havana Syndrome is a brain disorder caused by Pulsed RadioFrequency/MicroWave (RF/MW) or UltaSound (RF/US) radiation. Victims suffer migraine headaches, dizziness, sleeplessness, forgetfulness, tinnitus, nausea, exhaustion, depression, loss of coordination, inability to concentrate, general cognitive disruption. In extreme cases, victim's entire bodies seem to pulsate. Some have been crippled, or gone deaf or blind. When being attacked, computers turn off-and-on, and the battery in one victim's phone swelled. Havana Syndrome dates back to late 2016 as an enigmatic brain disorder suffered by U.S. and Canadian diplomats in Guangzhou China, and *Havana* Cuba, ergo the name *"Havana Syndrome."* It was later discovered that the symptoms were noticed two years earlier in Germany (2014). The expression *"Havana Syndrome"* was coined by Dr. Ludwig DeBraeckeleer in *Intel Today*, October 3, 2017. It is thought that the microwave/ultrasound radiation effects the fluid in the brain and inner ear, resulting in misery and brain damage. The diplomats reported hearing a low humming sound, followed by the dreadful symptoms. Entire families: wives, children, and pets were affected in China, Vietnam, Germany, Russia, Cuba, the U.S, in many parts of the world. People are not injured by microwave accidently. The Havana Syndrome victims were assaulted in their host countries. The buildings which they occupied were bombarded by a heinous microwave/ultrasound weapon. The targets have been CIA and FBI agents who were working on Russian related projects. A Russian spy was caught in Miami, Florida with enigmatic electrical equipment. Since then, there is undeniable proof that the Russians are responsible for the Havana Syndrome. It is perfectly acceptable to spy on diplomats with cameras and microphones. But to injure diplomats and intelligence officers is an act of war. The U.S. Government is in a quandary. How do we defend our citizens from these attacks? How do we retaliate? To what degree do we punch back? That's why the Government will not publicly recognize the threat and attacks, despite all the evidence. How does the Government recruit for the Intelligence Service, when it cannot protect its personnel? The Havana Syndrome has the potential of being an explosive diplomatic crisis.

HAVE-LITTLES – (*HAV LIT*-tuls) The poor, underemployed, just scraping by, a step above the Have-nots. The Have-littles are usually employed at menial, non- union, low-paying jobs. They often must work more than one job. They were once classified as poor, but by today's standards, are categorized as the lower- middle class. The Have-littles were once homeowners, before the corporate capitalists outsourced their jobs abroad for more profit. They now dwell in trailers. It's a bizarre phenomenon that the Have-littles always side with the Haves against the Have-nots. This may be a case of denial. Though the Have- littles are poor, they are envious of the Have-nots who are destitute. They resent the government assistance awarded to the Have-nots. Fox Broadcasting exploits the rift between the Have-littles and Have-nots by widening it. Their grand strategy is to foment animosity, bigotry, and racism among the poor and middle class, preventing them from developing a unified, Socialistic class consciousness. This would present a united front (and huge voting block) against the conservatives, capitalists, Republicans, and rich. Fox has succeeded in getting poor people to vote Republican, against their own economic interests. *"The test of our progress is not whether we add more to the abundance of those who have much. It is whether we provide enough for those who have little."* – Democratic President Franklin D. Roosevelt (1882 – 1945).

HAVE MORES – (*HAV MORS*) The obscenely rich. There are at least 735 billionaires in the U.S.A. today, the corporate capitalist aristocracy. Worldwide, there are at least 2,640 billionaires. That means pro-capitalist America has 30% of the world's billionaires. This is money made on other people's money and labor, in the form of dividends, interest, investments, bonuses, rents, while paying no taxes. *"The rich's paradise was created by the poor's hell."* – Victor Hugo (1802 – 1885).

HAVE NOTS – (*HAV NOTS*) The poor omega class. The indigent, exploited, oppressed class under capitalism. If the Haves are the alphas, then the Have nots are the omegas. The Have nots are underprivileged, dispossessed, and disenfranchised. They are the less fortunate, not born into wealth and privilege. The Have nots are the neglected in the struggle for survival. The great Chinese sage Confucius distinguished the Haves from the Have nots. *"The people who live extravagantly are apt to be snobbish and conceded. And the people who live simply are apt to be vulgar. I prefer the vulgar people to the snobs."*

HAVES – (*HAVS*) The wealthy alpha class under capitalism, the rich and famous who are well fed, well bred, well read, and well wed. The Haves are the capitalistic apex predators, the winners in the struggle for survival, in the capitalist jungle, red in tooth and claw. It's natural that the Haves would fear the Have-nots. As the Haves say: *"We are rich, they are poor. We want peace, they want change."* The Haves glorify *"law and order,"* in order to maintain their hegemonic status quo. The Haves are conservative, obsessed with conserving their wealth. They are also reactionary, reacting against any legislation that would curtail their wealth. *"I do intend to see that the rich man is held to the same accountability as the poor man."* – Progressive President Theodore Roosevelt (1858 – 1919). The resentment generated by the overindulgence of the Haves has festered for millennia. *"In a rich man's house there is no place to spit but his face."* – Greek Philosopher Diogenes of Sinope (c. 412 – 323 BCE).

HAVES/HAVE NOTS – (*HAVS HAV NOTS*) The Haves are the endowed, the Have Nots are the deprived. A haughty Have was Alexander Hamilton (c. 1755 – 1804). Hamilton declared it natural that *"All communities divide themselves into the few and many. The first are the rich and well-born, the other are the mass of turbulent people."* Could the *"well-born,"* be born well because they are rich? Could the *"turbulent"* be so because of their poverty? Haves: *"We are rich."* Have Nots: *"We are poor."* Haves: *"We want peace."* Have Nots: *"We want change."* It is incumbent on the Haves to convince the Have Nots to vote against their own economic interests and support the conservative, capitalist, Republican agenda. This is done through propaganda issued from Fox News Network, right-wing hate radio, and demagogues like Donald Trump (b. 1946). *"My grandmother used to tell me that there are only two families in the world, the Haves and the Have nots."* – Miguel de Cervantes (1547 – 1616). *"The world is split between those who do not sleep because they are hungry and those who do not sleep because they are afraid of those who are hungry."* – Philosopher Paulo Freire (1926 – 2002). Incidentally: A rich lady once came up to the blessed St. Vincent de Paul (1581 - 1660) and confessed: *"Fr. Vincent, the poor frighten me."* *"Yes,"* replied St. Vincent. *"The poor are frightening. As frightening as God's justice."*

HAWAII – (ha-*WHY*-yee) Last (50th) state to join the United States (1959). Hawaii is a string of volcanic islands in the middle of the Pacific Ocean. It is actually the location of a hotspot under the Earth's crust. The crust moves over the hotspot, spewing magma, forming the string of volcanic islands. The crust is moving 30 mile every million years. Hawaii is part of the vast geologic composition of 25 or 30 thousand islands called *Oceania.* The subdivision of Oceania that includes Hawaii is *Polynesia.* Hawaii is the most isolated *thoroughly populated* location on Earth. Hawaii is the southernmost U.S. state with a tropical climate. It is the only state where the sun is ever exactly overhead. Too, Hawaii is the most diverse, racially harmonious state in the union. That's because Hawaii is the only state where minority Americans (Polynesians and Japanese) outnumber the majority Euro-Americans. Incidentally: Hawaii is the most tsunami threatened and battered landform on Earth. Hawaii is in the middle of the Pacific Ocean. The Pacific is enclosed by the *"Ring of Fire."* This is the most tectonically, volcanically active region in the world. These forces produce earthquakes which produce tsunamis. Hawaii is in the bullseye.

HAWK – (*HAWK*) Ornithologically, a large bird of prey with keen vision (hawk- eyed) sharp talons and beak. Unlike its cousin the falcon, hawks spend much more time on the ground. They sight their prey from a height and attack it on the ground. The falcon hunts on the wing.

HAWK – (*HAWK*) Politically, a person, usually a general or politician who is eager to conduct war. The counterpart to the hawk (a bird of prey) is the dove (a symbol of peace and love). Doves consider hawks to be war mongers. Hawks are quick on the trigger finger. Their solution to any crisis is military force. They tend to be impulsive. Hawks believe in shooting first, asking questions later. Conservatives (Republicans) tend to be hawkish. Perhaps the most dangerous American hawk of recent time has been U.S. Air Force General Curtis LeMay (1906 – 1990). *"The only difference between peace and war is where we place our bombs."* – General Curtis LeMay. Another hawkish American was General George S. Patton (1885 - 1944). *"God have mercy on my enemies, because I won't."* – General Patton.

HAY/STRAW – (*HAY STRAW*) Both hay and straw are cut and dried grass. Both are pale yellow in color. Hay is from short grasses like field grass (lawn) clover, alfalfa, etc. Hay is softer, finer, more tender than straw. So hay is used for forage or fodder for cattle and horses. Straw consists of the long-ridged stalks from tall grain grasses like wheat, oats, rye, and barley. A straw shaft is hollow, creating a natural straw. Straw is coarser, tougher material than hay. Straw is better suited for animal bedding, basket weaving, and for thatching roofs. Incidentally: The story has it that during the Civil War (1861 – 1865) some farm boys in the Union Army didn't know their left from their right. So in order to teach them to march in formation, their sergeants would put hay in one boot, and straw in the other. Then the command would be barked out: *"Hay foot, straw foot! Hay foot, straw foot!* The story is specious.

HAYWIRE – (HAY-whyuhr) In disorder, not functioning properly, out of control, erratic, even crazy, gone haywire. Actually, hay wire is soft, thin steel strand used to bind bales of dried grass or hay 1891. By 1905, the term *"haywire"* came to mean *"makeshift,"* *"poorly equipped,"* *"half-ass."* This meaning evolved in the New England lumber camps. There, hay wire came to be used as a universal fix-it remedy. It was the duct tape of its era. A *"hay wire outfit"* became the contemptuous term for a poorly trained logger crew with inferior equipment. The term *"gone haywire"* took on its present meaning by 1915.

HAZARD PAY – (*HAZ*-zerd *PAY*) (also Hero pay) Extra remuneration, as stipulated by the contract, for working on risky or dangerous jobs. Hazard pay must be granted to workers who volunteer for the perilous assignment. Hazard pay is a union inspired obligation. No union, no contract, no hazard pay. In this case, the worker has no more rights than a combat soldier. Incidentally: The 2020 Coronavirus pandemic open people eyes to the unappreciated essential workers on whom we so depend. Healthcare personnel, transport workers, food distributors, sanitation workers in some cases had been granted additional hazard pay during the emergency. However, capitalism, being profit-motivated, cut back the gratuity as soon as possible. The supermarket giant, Kroger, rescinded the $2.00 an hour hazard pay to their employees in mid-May, 2020, when they deemed the pandemic emergency was over.

HAZMAT – (*HAZ*-mat) A blend word formed from the term, <u>Haz</u>ardous <u>Mat</u>erials. Hazmat includes dangerous solids, liquids, gasses, or radiation that may cause injury, death, or damage if released or triggered.

Hazmat professionals are specially trained to deal with such dangerous chemical emergencies. They are aided by special protective suits and safety equipment.

H-BOMB – (*AYCH BOM*) (<u>H</u>ydrogen <u>Bomb</u>) A thermonuclear reaction that employs fusion of atoms rather than fission, or splitting of atoms (the atomic bomb). With an H-bomb, hydrogen atoms are squeezed or fused together forming a helium atom, and a scintilla of energy (H+H+H+H = He + E). A mere 2% of the matter in a fusion reaction is converted into energy. Nevertheless, a fusion reaction (H-bomb), on average releases 10 times more energy that a fission reaction (A-bomb). In fact, fission is required to produce the heat to ignite the fusion reaction. In other words, a small atomic bomb must be exploded to trigger the hydrogen bomb. The first hydrogen bomb was detonated by the U.S. at Bikini Island in the South Pacific (1954). The bomb weighted 65 tons and sat in an airplane hangar. This 15 megaton H-bomb was 1,000 times more powerful than the Hiroshima A-bomb. The fireball rose 3 miles up into the sky. The island was vaporized. In 1961, the Russians detonated the *"Czar Bomba,"* a 57 megaton H-bomb in the Siberian Arctic. The Russia bomb was dropped from a plane. The blast shattered windows 50 miles away. Fusion is the same reaction the fuels the sun, all stars in fact. Detonating an H-bomb is actually exploding a tiny star on Earth. Every element the universe had ever created is re-created in an H-bomb blast.

HEADCHEESE – (*HED*-chees) A seasoned meatloaf made of the flesh from the head, sometimes including the tongue and brains of a calf or pig. Headcheese is molded in the natural aspic (gelatin) of the boiled head meat. This gives it a chewy, rubbery consistency. Headcheese is flavored with garlic and vinegar. In Britain, headcheese is called *"brawn."*

HEADLINE – (*HED*-lyn) A concise title of a newspaper story, relating the gist of the following report. A headline should not serve as bait, but as instant information. Great care must be taken by journalists in writing headlines so as not to make them confusing, ambiguous, or ridiculous. The following are actual examples of ridiculously worded headlines. *"Man Kills Self Before Shooting Wife And Daughter"*; *"Hospitals Are Sued By 7 Foot Doctors"*; *"Something Went Wrong In Jet Crash, Experts Say"*; *"Police Begin Campaign To Run Down Jaywalkers"*; *"Panda Mating Fails, Veterinarian Takes Over"*; *"Miners Refuse To Work After Death"*; *"Juvenile Court To Try Shooting Defendant"*; *"War Dims Hope For Peace"*; *"If Strike Isn't Settled Quickly, It May Last Awhile"*; *"Cold Wave Linked To Temperatures"*; *"Enfield Couple Slain, Police Suspect Homicide"*; *"Red Tape Holds Up New Bridges; "Man Struck By Lightning Faces Battery Charges"*; *New Study Of Obesity Looks For Larger Test Group"*; *"Astronaut Takes Blame For Gas In Spacecraft"*; *"Kids Make Nutritious Snacks"*; *"Local High School Dropouts Cut In Half."*

HEAD SHOT – (*HED* shot) Literally going for the kill. A shot in the head is certain death. Figuratively speaking, a head shot means going all the way, no half- measures. In politics, a head shot means no holding back. It is throwing everything you have at your opponent. Nice guys avoid head shots, and in politics, nice guys usually lose. *"That's the difference between us Republicans and you Democrats: we always go for the head shot, while you always go for the pillow fight."* – Donald Trump (b. 1946) advisor and friend, Steve Bannon (b. 1953).

HEADWATERS – (*HED*-wat-ters) The origin of a stream. The headwaters is usually at a height in the mountains. Snow and glacial melt provide the first trickles and flows downstream gaining volume and momentum. The stream graduates to a river as it rushes toward a greater river, lake, or the sea.

HEARKEN BACK – (*HAR*-ken *BAK*) (sometimes Hark Back) Hark or hearken means to heed, to hear. They also mean to pay attention or listen attentively. *"Hark, the herald angels singing...."* Hearken back or hark back refers to a return to a previous point, position, or subject in speech or thought. Furthermore, to hearken back is to think or dream of a long gone past, some former historic time. *"So let us hearken back to the days of old when knights were bold...."* This expression originally alluded to the hunt. Hounds would hearken back or retrace their course when they had lost the quarry's scent.

HEALING – (*HEE*-ling) (Heal, Healed, Healer) To cure. Healing is to make whole, healthy, free of ailment, restored to health. The healed are absolved from illness, from dis-ease. They are placed back at ease, physically and emotionally, but primarily spiritually. The New Thought Christianity Minister and Pastor of the Church of the Healing Christ (N.Y.C.) Dr. Emmet Fox (1886 - 1951) wrote: *"God is here. God is Love. God is love now, and you know it. God desires only your good. He never sends ill. He wants you to be well. He is healing you now and you know it."* Thomas Troward (1847 – 1916), English mystic and New Thought Christianity leader wrote: *"When the aid of a healer or practitioner is sought, the function of the healer is to find entrance to the subconscious mind of the patient and to impress upon it the suggestion of pure health. This he is able to do by submitting his own objective or conscious mentality, which he describes as will joined to intellect, for that of the patient. As soon as the healer realizes that the barriers of personality between himself and his patient have been removed, it is possible for him to speak to the subconscious mind of the patient as though it were his own, for both being pure spirit, the thought of their identity makes them identical."* We think of physicians as healers. But are they really? Nobel Prize winning biologist and surgeon, Dr. Alexis Carrel (1873 – 1944) witnessed the spiritual side of healing. *"Our present conception of the influence of prayer upon pathological lesions is based upon the observation of patients who have been cured almost instantly of various affections... The process of healing changes little from one individual to another. Often, an acute pain. Then a sudden sensation of being cured. In a few seconds, a few minutes, at the most a few hours, wounds are cicatrized, pathological symptoms disappear, appetite returns.... The only condition indispensable to the occurrence of the phenomenon is prayer. But there is no need for a patient himself to pray, or even to have religious faith. It is sufficient that someone around him be in a state of prayer."* Neurologist Dr. Titus Bull (1871 – 1946) reminded us that: *"Matter is spirit at a lower rate of vibration. When a patient is cured, it is spirit in the cell doing the healing, according to its own inherent pattern. No doctor ever yet cured a patient. All he can do is to make it possible for the patient to heal himself."*

HEALTH – (*HELTH*) A state of overall wellness, physically, emotionally, and spiritually. According to the United Nation's World Health Organization: *"Health is a state of complete physical, mental, and social well-being, and not merely the absence of disease and infirmity"* (1948). To assure this condition of health would require worldwide distributive justice. That means no more corporate capitalist exploitation. It's little wonder why conservative capitalists hate the UN. At any rate, the key to personal wellness was recognized by the Buddha (c. 563 – c. 483 BCE) about 26 centuries ago. *"The secret of health for both mind and body is not to mourn for the past, not to worry about the future, not to anticipate troubles, but to live the present moment wisely and earnestly."* According to the founder of the Church of Christian Science: *"Health is not a condition of matter, but of mind."* – Mary Baker Eddy (1821 – 1910). *"Health is my expected heaven."* – John Keats (1795 – 1821).

HEALTHCARE – (*HELTH*-cair) Freedom from illness, a human right, though not a political, constitutional right in America. Free speech, free press, free assembly, free anything are worthless without free healthcare. America is the only modern nation in the world without free universal healthcare. Shamefully, America is the only developed country on Earth that does not recognized the health of its people as a civil and human right. The Republicans representing the capitalist insurance industry hope to keep it that way. In the healthcare debate, the Democrats are interested in saving lives, while the Republicans are interested in saving money. The Democrats believe that healthcare is a human right, while the Republicans believe that healthcare is an exclusive privilege. Human health is not a commodity like pork bellies, from which to profit. Private, for-profit, capitalist corporations have no business administering human healthcare. Under the free market, capitalistic healthcare system, Americans pay the most and get the least of any modern nation. Presently, more than 1 out of 5 Americans (20%) cannot afford the medicine their doctors prescribe. Over 18,000 American die each year due to lack of adequate healthcare. Incidentally: It is estimated that 75 cents out of every healthcare dollar is spent during the last 6 months of a dying person's life to extend that life by 2 weeks. Nevertheless, healthcare must be nationalized, medicine Socialized. The so-called healthcare industry must be illegal. Health should not be sold to those who could afford it. Healthcare must be single-payer, that being the government. Only then will we enjoy universal coverage for all. *"You are a human being. You have rights inherent in that reality. You have dignity and worth that exists prior to law."* – Lyn Beth Neylon. *"If you get sick, America, the Republican health care plan is this: Die Quickly."* – Democratic Congressman Alan Grayson (b. 1958).

HEALTHCARE PROVIDER – (*HELTH*-kair pro-*VY*-der) A clumsy, calculating euphemism for a doctor (of sorts). The term *"healthcare provider"* was introduced by the insurance industry when it moved to usurp authority from the medical profession. Insurance agents cannot legally call themselves doctors or physicians. But they can imply, hoping to be associated in people's minds with the actual healers. Insurance agents did not attend medical school, but they dictate to doctors on medical tests, procedures, and care, based on cost. To legitimize their authority, they try to blur the border between themselves and your doctor by lumping everyone together as healthcare providers. Healthcare providing involves the entire business. And like all capitalist businesses, this means making them money, not making you well. As a matter of fact, the Department of Health and Human Services supports this interpretation. The Department defines a healthcare provider as: *"Any person or organization who <u>furnishes, bills, or is paid</u> for health care in the normal course of business."* So the insurance agent, the girl who mails you your co-pay bill, the entire insurance company are recognized by the government as your doctor too. It was inevitable that in our capitalist society, the emphasis on healthcare providing would fall not on healing, curing, or saving lives, but rather saving money. Incidentally: In <u>*Winning through Intimidation*</u> (1973) entrepreneur Robert J. Ringer (b. 1938) suggested that: *"The next time you pass one of those insurance company skyscrapers, look closely between the bricks. You probably thought they were held together by cement. Not so. The substance between the bricks is dried human blood. All those friendly insurance companies, the ones who run the ads on television showing* *their agents helping out some nice neighborhood family have built their building on human blood." "If you get sick, America, the Republican healthcare plan is this: 'Die Quickly'."* – Democratic Congressman Alan Grayson (b. 1958).

HEARING – (*HEAR*-ring) In law an examination of a legal or factual issue by a court. A hearing is an oral proceeding before a court or quasi-judicial tribunal. Hearings that describe a process to ascertain facts and provide evidence are labeled *trials*. Hearings that relate to a presentation of ideas as distinguished from facts and evidence are known as *arguments*. Trials occur in trial courts and arguments occur in appellate courts.

HEARING AID – (*HEER*-ring ayd) A compact electronic amplifier worn to improve one's hearing, placed in and behind the ear. The hearing aid is powered by a tiny disc-shaped battery, or may be re-chargeable. The device is designed to be as inconspicuous as possible. People tend to hide the fact that they depend on an aid to hear. There seems to be a sense of embarrassment attached to it. That's silly. After all, people are not ashamed to rely on eyeglasses as visual aids. Perhaps it's because people of all ages depend on eye glasses, whereas hearing aids are usually consigned to the elderly. The stigma is getting old. Like a cane – a walking aid – the hearing aid symbolizes old age. Old age is associated with mental and physical feebleness.

HEARSAY – (*HEAR*-say) In law, secondhand evidence. Hearsay is facts not in the personal knowledge of the witness, but a repetition of what others said. Hearsay is rumors. Hearsay is generally not allowed as evidence at a trial, although there are many exceptions. *"I hear say that he cheated on his wife."*

HEARTBURN – (*HART*-burn) A medical gastric/digestive disorder that closely mimics a heart attack. Heartburn is a distressing condition of burning in the stomach, up the esophagus (chest) sometimes burning the throat with stomach acid. This can trigger a sore throat. In severe cases, gas in the stomach can cause it to jolt, impacting the heart above. The chest pain can fool a physician into diagnosing heart attack for heartburn.

HEART CHAKRA – (*CHAK*-ra) One of 7 major interconnected energy centers throughout the body. The Heart Chakra governs our ability to love. It is located in the center of the chest just above the heart. It is attuned with love, joy, inner peace.

HEAT – (*HEET*) Ecologically, the increase of planetary temperature due to global warming. Unregulated burning of fossil fuels is responsible for the rise in temperatures. Carbon dioxide and other pollutants produce the *"greenhouse effect."* Solar heat is trapped at the Earth's surface and cannot escape into space. Heatwaves kill more people than all other natural disasters combined. Incidentally: At 140 degrees Fahrenheit, the Earth's water will begin to evaporate.

HEAT – (*HEET*) In the physics of thermodynamics, heat is the rapid random motion of atoms. Therefore, heat is the energy of motion. The application of energy causes a substance to heat-up, setting the molecules in motion. As a substance heats, its temperature rises.

HEATHEN – (*HEE*-then) (Heathenism, Heathenistic) In historical context a heathen is person who does not acknowledge God of the Bible. So a heathen is one who does not practice one of the Abrahamic faiths: Judaism, Christianity, or Islam. The term *"heathen"* entered English from the Old English (West

Saxon) *"haeden,"* meaning *"Not Christian or Jewish."* (This predated Islam.) Originally, *haeden* (heathen) meant *"dweller on the heath, inhabiting uncultivated land."* So heathen were uncultivated folk, nomads, living in the wilds. They had not settled down or settled in to Christianity or Judaism. Like the Latin *"paganus,"* meaning *"country folk,"* the heathens held on to their *"Old Religion."* Many refused to convert. For this they were mocked and persecuted by the Christians. Heathens and pagans became heretics, and also bonfire tinder. Nevertheless, heathen traditions and knowledge has survived in modern day Paganism: practitioners of the Old Religion.

HEATHENRY – (*HEE*-then-ree) Modern Paganism. Heathenry is the modern observance of the *"Old Religion."* Heathenry is a polytheistic reconstruction of Pre-Christian Germanic religious traditions. It is animistic and nature oriented. The rites, rituals, customs, ceremonies, and holy days of *Odinism, Asatru, Forn Sior,* and *Druidry* make up modern Heathenry. These religious traditions come from ancient Celtic, Teutonic, and Norse sources from Northern and Western Europe (Germany, Scandinavia, the British Isles).

HEAT INDEX – (*HEET IN*-deks) A scale determined by multiplying the temperature times the humidity. The heat index provides the sensual temperature or how hot you feel. Evaporation of sweat carries away body heat with the moisture. When the humidity is high, the air cannot hold any more moisture. The sweat remains on your body along with the heat. The heat index is also called the apparent temperature.

HEAT LIGHTNING – (*HEET LITE*-ning) A glowing flash in the clouds, not related to heat. Heat lightning is so far away that the sound of the thunderclap had evaporated before reaching the viewer.

HEAVEN – (*HEV*-ven) Traditionally, the abode of God. Heaven has historically, customarily been characterized as a celestial paradise, an eternal reward for living a righteous life. And perhaps it is an Elysium, Nirvana, or Valhalla for the deserving. Heaven may be a state of blessed bliss in the life after Earthly life. Jesus said, *"The Kingdom of Heaven is within you."* This seems to mean that we can find Heaven on Earth by attaining atonement [read: *at-ONE-ment*] with God. The great Chinese sage Confucius (551 – 479 BCE) maintained that *"Heaven means to be one with God." "Heaven is such that all who have lived well, of whatever religion, have a place there."* – Emanuel Swedenborg (1688 – 1772).

HEAVILY INVESTED – (*HEV*-vi-lee in-*VEST*-ted) A conservative euphemism for being filthy rich. Capitalist fatcats are heavily invested and heavily infested with greed. Fear of distributive justice induced the rich to play down their wealth with these disguising euphemisms. Heavily invested is designed to suggest that the rich carry such are tough burden. Remember: a euphemism is a word you use, when you are embarrassed to use the word you need. Heavily invested simply means *"rich bitch."*

HEBDOMADAL – (heb-*DOM*-uh-dul) Weekly or once a week. What is hebdomadal occurs once every 7 days, like a TV show or publication. The term derives from the Latin *"hebdomas,"* meaning *"seven, the seventh day, a week."*

HEBETUDE – (*HEB*-bi-tood) Being in a dull, lethargic condition. A person displaying hebetude is indifferent, apathetic, disinterested. A person struck with hebetude is bored with the situation at hand. President Donald Trump (b. 1946) showed hebetude toward the Coronavirus that was killing Americans.

HEBRAIC CHRISTIANS – (hee-*BRAY*-ic *KRIS*-chins) (*Judaisers*) Early Jewish Christians, who follower St. Peter (the fisherman). They were centered in Jerusalem. The Hebraics believed that one should adopt Judaism, as a prerequisite to becoming a Christian, including circumcision, and the dietary restrictions. They were opposed by St. Paul (the rabbi) and the Hellenic Christians (Gentiles). The Hebraic Christians believed that Jesus was the *"Son of Man,"* (primarily a prophet). The Hellenic Christians (mostly Greek) turned the *"Son of Man"* into the *"Son of God."* Incidentally: In the Gospels, Jesus called himself *"Son of God"* 5 times, *"Son of Man"* 86 times.

HEBREW BIBLE – (*HEE*-brew *BY*-bul) The Jewish Bible or Old Testament. It consists of the first 4/5 (80%) of the Bible, minus the late Christian addition, the New Testament. The ancient Hebrew Bible was organized, compiled by Rabbi Johanan ben Zakkai (c. 1 – c. 90 CE). The Hebrew Bible replaced the destroyed Temple as the Jewish center of worship.

HECKLER'S VETO – (*HEK*-lers *VEE*-to) To drown-out a speaker with loud, rude taunts. Heckler's veto is a form of mob censorship depriving freedom of speech. It was widely applied by the Tea Party, the Republican lunatic fringe.

HEDGE BETS – (hej *BETS*) To take an action in order to offset a potential future loss. When you hedge your bets, you try to have it both ways. One tries to create a win/win situation. For example, donating money to all political candidates is hedging your bets. Too, betting on both teams is a hedge. Incidentally: President Donald Trump (b. 1946) tried to hedge his bets on the re-opening of the economy during the Coronavirus outbreak. On the one hand, Trump declared that he was in charge. His White House had set Federal Guidelines to be met in order to re-open society. On the other hand, Trump delegated responsibility to the state governors to re-open at will, despite the guidelines. Actually, Trump desperately wanted the economy to revive, for political benefit. So Trump contradicted his own guidelines, encouraging the governors to ignore them as well. If the re-openings succeeded, Trump would take credit, due to his guidelines. If the re-openings failed, Trump would shirk responsibility, and blame the governors for not following his guidelines. Trump tried to hedge his bets.

HEDGE FUNDS – (*HEJ FUNDS*) According to economist Kimberley Amadeo (b. 1955) *"Hedge funds are privately-owned companies that pool investors' dollars and reinvest them into complicated financial instruments. The goal is to outperform the market, by a lot. They are expected to be smart enough to create high returns regardless of how the market does."* A hedge fund is often an offshore investment fund, typically formed as a private limited partnership, which engages in speculation using credit or borrowed capital. However, according to *The Economist, "There is no simple definition of a hedge fund (few of them actually hedge)."* First, to hedge is to reduce your overall risk. Hedging involves deliberately taking on a new risk that offsets an existing risk. You *"hedge your bets"* at the gambling casino on Wall Street. In hedging, you may play the exchange rate against the interest rate, or commodity price against both. The hedge funds are considered the villains of the financial markets, responsible for wreaking instability. Hedge funds seek to maximize their absolute returns rather than relative returns. They concentrate on making as much money as possible, not simply on outperforming an index (like mutual funds). Hedge funds often bet against the herd of investors and disrupt financial markets by their speculation. They are another economic dis-ease of for-profit capitalism.

Confusing? Of course! It's meant to be. Big league capitalist economics is intentionally esoteric so only a chosen few can play the game or market. The participants are few (1%er's) because their wheeling-and- dealing is unethical and often illegal. Wall Street obfuscates its money-making schemes so they can manipulate the economy with impunity, and become obscenely rich. Capitalism must be regulated – right out of business. *"It is well enough that people of the nation do not understand our banking and money system, for if they did, I believe there would be a revolution before tomorrow morning."* – Henry Ford (1863 – 1947).

HEDGEWITCH – (*HEJ*-wich) A mystic practitioner of the esoteric arts. A Hedgewitch is knowledgeable is *"wortcunning,"* (gathering medicinal herbs and mushrooms), and in *"hedge jumping"* (astral projection). A Hedgewitch is a shaman, medicineman, witch doctor. She or he is adept in healing with natural medicines and nature spirits. They are masters of divination. In Old English (West Saxon), the word hedge referred to a border or boundary of any kind. This included the border between the garden and the wilderness, the boundary between life and death, the physical and spiritual, between the natural and supernatural worlds. Hedgewitches have the power to cross hedges into alternate realms, as with astral projection.

HEDONISM – (*HEE*-don-is-um) (Hedonists, Hedonistic) The doctrine that pleasure or happiness is the highest good. Therefore life should be dedicated to the search for pleasure. However, in philosophy, there are two strata or degrees of hedonism. Aristippus of Cyrene (c. 435 – c. 356 BCE) professed the self-indulgent theory. He maintained that the aim of life should be the pursuit by any means whatever of as much physical pleasure for each moment as possible, without taking heed of the consequences that might follow. Another Greek philosopher Epicurus (341 – 270 BCE) processed a more contemplative theory of hedonism. He maintained that the highest good in life is the absence of pain and vexing pleasures that cause pain or discomfort as their consequences. Epicurus insisted that the aim of life should be tranquility, imperturbability of body, mind and spirit. In Greek this is called *"Ataraxia."*

HEDONISTIC PARADOX – (hee-don-*NIS*-tic *PAR*-ra-dox) In philosophy, the apparent contradiction in the hedonist's claim that pleasure is the only good, for the person constantly seeking pleasure will not find it. However, if a person helps others to find pleasure, he will in the process find pleasure for himself. The hedonistic paradox maintains that pleasure is not something to be sought after directly. It is not to be thought of as an end in itself separate from an activity or an experience. Therefore pleasure is attainable only as an attitude or feeling accompanying other things.

HEGEMONY – (hej-*JEM*-mo-nee) (Hegemonic, Hegemons) Control of the weak by the powerful. To predominate, lord-over is hegemony. Hegemonic power is exercised by the rich over the poor. That is how they got rich. The wealthy who direct the economy and the security forces are the national hegemons.

HEIL – (*HY*-el) German for "salvation." *Heilen* means "heal" in German. Therefore, the Nazi salute, *"Heil Hitler,"* literally meant *"Hitler save or heal us."* This speaks volumes about the state of the collective German psyche in those crazy inter-war years and through World War Two (1918 – 1945). Incidentally: Heil Hitler is called the *"Hitlergrus"* meaning Hitler greeting.

HEISENBERG'S UNCERTAINTY – (*HIGH*-sen-bergs un-*SER*-tan-tee) A principle of quantum physics discovered by German physicist Werner Heisenberg (1901 – 1976) in 1927. The Heisenberg uncertainty maintains both the exact position and the exact momentum (motion, velocity) of subatomic particles cannot be known at the same time. If the position is known, then a determination of its motion will be uncertain. Conversely, when the motion of the subatomic particle is known, the determination of its position will be uncertain. Furthermore Heisenberg maintained that the very process of investigating subatomic phenomena affects what is being investigated. Therefore, the phenomena as observed do not depict true reality. In other words, merely looking at, and working with subatomic particles effects the nature of the particles. This phenomenon has an explanation. Our most powerful tool for peering into the infinitesimally small is the electron microscope. But the light energy emitted by that microscope scatters the quarks instead of displaying them. Incidentally: It is in the extreme ends of physics, microcosmic quantum mechanics, and macrocosmic cosmology (black holes), that physics and metaphysics, science and theology converge. The Heisenberg Uncertainty Principle applies beyond quantum physics, universally. It maintains that no event, not even atomic events, can be described with certainty, that is, with zero tolerance for doubt.

HELD – (*HELD*) An ax handle or haft. This innovation is 50,000 years old. The held is not a trivial commonality. It took our ancestors 1.5 million years to think of putting a handle on the hand-ax. The held (handle) is an extension of the arm that greatly multiplies the force of the ax head.

HELICICULTURE – (hel-*LIS*-see-cul-cher) (also Heliculture = *HELL*-lee-cul-cher) Snail farming. Heliciculture is the commercial raising of snails primarily for consumption. Food snails are called escargot. Snail eggs are also eaten as a type of caviar. Snail slime is used in medicines and cosmetics. The best ediblesnail is the African snail, also called the Roman or Burgundy snail. They populate much of Europe.

HELICOPTER PARENT – (*HEL*-i-kop-ter *PAIR*-uhnt) (also Cosseter or Cosseting Parent) A parent who is excessively, intrusively involved in their child's life. A father or mother who is overly-protective and meddling, particularly at the child's school. Psychologist Haim G. Ginott (1922 – 1973) in his book, <u>Parent & Teenager</u> (1969) coined the term: *"Mother hovers over me like a helicopter."* Helicopter parents are the bane of teachers and school administrators. In extreme cases, the child may be victimized by the smothering parents even into college. For example, Kyle McCord (b. 2002) was the 21-year-old quarterback on the Ohio State Buckeyes football team. In November 2023, Kyle led his team down in defeat to the rival University of Michigan Wolverines. His position as starting quarterback looked shaky. On *"The OHIO Podcast,"* Eric Boggs reported that Kyles dad, Derek McCord confronted head football coach Brian Day (b. 1979), demanding that his son Kyle be declared the starting quarterback for next year. Coach Day said Kyle must compete for the position, like everyone else. On the air, Eric Boggs referred to dad Derek McCord as Kyle's *"helicopter parent."* Incidentally: Kyle has entered the transfer portal and will be leaving Ohio State to play elsewhere. Question: Was this Kyle's decision or Derek's decision?

HELICOPTER RIDE – (*HEL*-i-kop-ter *RYD*) A modern mob-like death threat. The implication of helicopter ride is dropping a victim from a great height to his death. Unlike a car, a helicopter is not a common vehicle possessed by everyone. A helicopter is more associated with the government, as in *"black helicopters"* of the secret police. So a helicopter ride alludes to a dictatorial government executing state enemies by helicopter drops. Incidentally: After the seizure of stolen secret government documents from Donald Trump's (b. 1946) residence by the FBI, Trump cultists insisted on treating FBI agents to a helicopter ride.

HELIOGRAPH – (*HEL*-lee-o-graf) Literally, *"sun writing."* A heliograph is an archaic sunlight telegraph. Morse Code was sent with sunlight by a mirror device on which the message was tapped like a telegraph.

HELIOPHOBIA – (hel-lee-o-*FO*-bee-a) (Heliophobiac) Phobic fear of sunlight, sunshine.

HELIOTROPISM – (hel-lee-o-*TROPE* is-um) (Heliotaxis) The compulsion of most plants to turn toward the sun light. Plants deprived of sunlight will perish. Plants supplied with their adequate amount of sunlight will flourish. Sunlight is as important to plants as air is to animals. Through the process of photosynthesis, plants use sunlight to create chlorophyl, which is the plants counterpart to animal's blood. No sunlight, no plant life. That's why many plants are heliotropic.

HELIUM – (*HEE*-lee-um) (He) Helium's atomic number is 2, representing the 2 protons in its nucleus. Its name is from the Greek *helios* meaning *"sun."* An inert gaseous element present in the sun's atmosphere and in natural gas. Helium is the second simplest element after hydrogen. It is colorless, odorless, tasteless, and nonflammable. Being inert, helium does not react with any other element. Helium is used as a substitute for flammable gases in dirigible balloons. Helium has the lowest boiling and melting points of all the elements. It is the only element that will never freeze solid under any conditions. Therefore, helium is valuable in *cryogenic* (deep freezing) research. Incidentally: In a star like our sun, hydrogen atoms weld together to produce helium at 18 million degrees Fahrenheit. This is the start of the thermal nuclear reaction.

HELL – (*HEL*) In religious tradition a place of vengeful eternal pain, incompatible with the concept of a compassionate, all-merciful God. The great anthropologist, Margaret Mead (1901 – 1978) had reservations about (*not in*) hell. *"It is an open question whether any behavior based on fear of eternal punishment [hell], can be regarded as ethical or should be regarded as merely cowardly."* Nevertheless, if there is a hell, certainly there is a special place reserved for greedy capitalists, banksters, brokers, and insurance company CEO's responsible for so much misery. According to the censored *Gospel of Nicodemus,* Hell is not a place of eternal torment as depicted. It is more of a holding-pen, a limbo for souls. In the *Apostle's Creed,* Jesus *"Descended into Hell"* to forgive and release the souls secluded there, including Old Testament prophets and patriarchs. In the censored *Apocalypse of Peter,* Jesus tells Peter a secret, not to tell anyone else. Those in the prison of Hell will be forgiven and released. Jesus wanted this to remain a secret so people would not become complacent, casual toward sinning. Incidentally: In a controversial interview with Eugenio Scalfari (b. 1924) of the Italian newspaper <u>La Repubblica</u> (March 30, 2018), our Socialistic Pope Francis I (b. 1936) declared that: *"There is no hell; there is the disappearance of sinful souls."* *"Hell is not punishment, its training."* – Shuryu Suzuki (1904 – 1971). A Consideration: Jesus did not curse his tormentors and killers with: *"May you all burn in hell!"* Instead, Jesus pardoned his murderers, saying: *"Father* [God], *forgive them, for they know not what they do."* – Luke 23:34. Doesn't it stand to reason that Jesus seek the same compassion for all murderers and sinners condemned to the fires of hell? It is said that the coming of Jesus marked the beginning of a New Testament, or a New Covenant. Perhaps, with the coming of Jesus, hell, like all sin, would be forgiven and forgotten. *"There is no murky pit of hell awaiting anyone."* – Lucretius (99 – 55 BCE).

HELLACIOUS – (hel-*LAY*-she-us) (Hellaciously) Remarkable, astonishing, usually in a bad way. Hellacious can be horrifying, hellish, unbelievably bad. *"Donald Trump is hellaciously corrupt!"*

HELLBENT – (*HELL*-bent) Stubbornly, rashly, recklessly determined. Proceeding at an alarmingly dangerous speed. To advance in a hellbent manner with all abandon. *"He was hellbent to go full speed ahead, right for the rocks!"*

HELLENIC – (hel-*LEN*-nik) (Hellenistic, Hellenism) Related to, or characteristic of ancient Greece and the Greeks. Hellenic refers to the Greek history, culture, mythology, philosophy, religion, and language.

HELLENIC CHRISTIANS – (hel-*LEN*-ik *KRIS*-chins) (*Hellenizers*) The Gentile Christians (initially Greeks) who followed St. Paul. The Hellenics did not believe that only Jewish converts could become Christians. They were opposed by the followers of St. Peter, the Hebraists (Jewish Christians). The Hebraist Christians believed that Jesus was the *"Son of Man,"* (primarily a prophet). The Hellenic Christians turned the *"Son of Man"* into the *"Son of God."* Incidentally: In the four Gospels Jesus called himself *"Son of God"* 5 times, *"Son of Man"* 86 times.

HELLHOUND – (*HEL*-hownd) Devil dog. Every culture has myths and legends about evil dog/wolf spirits that kills people. In Greek mythology, Cerberus was the vicious hound that guarded the gates of Hades. In other cultures, devil dogs have left their abode in hell to torment mankind. One of the most famous and documented hellhound attack occurred in Blythburgh, Suffolk England. On August 4, 1577, a terrible storm rocked the old Holy Trinity Church with thunder and rain. As the worshippers prayed, a huge black shaggy dog or wolf rushed into the stone church. The beast was reported to be the size of a calf or horse. It had fiery red eyes. The monster sank its canines into a man and boy killing both. The hellhound left its claw marks on the oak church door, clearly visible today. Traditionally, the English called this devil dog the *"Black Shuck."* The term *"shuck"* derives from Old English (West Saxon). It is a corruption of the terms *"succa,"* meaning *"devil,"* and *"skuh,"* meaning *"terrify."* *The poetic lines were recorded: "All down the church in midst of fire, the hellish monster flew. And, passing onward to the quire, he many people slew."*

HELLO – (huh-*LOH*) An interjection, the most common English salutation of greetings. We usually say hello when we meet someone in person, hail someone on the phone, or contact someone via email. Early reference to the greeting hello goes back to 1848 in the American Western frontier. Habitations were isolated, few and far between. The threat of attack by bandits and Indians was real. So it was dangerous to approach a homestead unannounced. One may be greeted with a shotgun blast. So visitors would make themselves known with a hardy yell: *"Hello the house!"* This eliminated the surprise and served as an assurance of good intentions. However to holler a hello as a shout of attention goes back to Middle English of the 14th century. Hello is a corruption of *"hallo,"* which was an alteration of *"holla,"* which derived from *"halouen"* and *"hallouing,"* which meant *"shouting, hollering in the chase."* The use of the greeting hello acquired ubiquity with the emergence of the telephone in the 1880's. Telephonic etiquette required a salutation when answering the phone. The inventor, Alexander Graham Bell (1847 – 1922) suggested the interjection *"Hoya!"* or *"Ahoy!"* the maritime call from ship to ship. However the public preferred hello. The ladies who worked at the Central Telephone Exchange (operators) came to be called *"Hello girls."* Chances are that a day doesn't pass, in which an English speaker anywhere doesn't use the greetings hello.

HELLSCAPE – (*HEL*-skayp) A <u>hell</u>ish land<u>scape</u>. An absolutely horrible, terrifying scene. A hellscape is a diabolically destructive environment, provoking imaginary perceptions of hell. *"No man's land,"* the lunar landscape between enemy trenches during World War One (1914 – 1918) qualifies as a hellscape. So does the carnage that was the city of Hiroshima after the atomic bombing.

HELP – (*HELP*) Aid, assistance, relief, support, succor, cure, rescue. The term is both a verb and noun. Help is an Old English (West Saxon) word. It derives from the Proto-Germanic *"helpo,"* the source of the Old Dutch Frisian *"helpe,"* from which came the English help. In America's New England of the 1640's the term help expanded to include *"servant,"* as in *"the help."*

HE-MAN – (*HEE*-man) A macho man. A strong, muscular, tough, virile man. Many actors had gained fame by acting-out the he-man role. The quintessential American he-man was actor John Wayne (1907 – 1979). He died of cancer, shriveled up, having smoked himself to death.

HEM AND HAW – (hem and *HAW*) (Hemming and Hawing, Hemmed and Hawed) To speak indistinctly, indecisively with frequent nervous pauses. More generally, hemming and hawing is acting hesitantly, doubtfully, tentatively, in a wishy-washy manner. Hemming and hawing is an indication of disinterest. The two-word construct, *"hem and haw"* is, like numerous English phrases, made from two terms of similar meaning which are put together for the sake of emphasis. (Other examples of this are *"beck and call," "aid and abet.")* The <u>Oxford English Dictionary</u> defines *"hem"* as: *"To give a short sharp cough as a signal; to clear the throat; to stammer or hesitate in speech; to express disapproval of a speaker by factitious coughing."* *"Haw"* is defined as: *"An utterance marking hesitation."* *"The way she hemmed and hawed made obvious her lack of interest."*

HEMATITE – (*HEM*-ma-tite) Iron oxide, the principal ore of iron. The rusty red pigment from hematite has been called ochre, and has been used for art and war paint for thousands of years. The red planet, Mars, is red due to hematite.

HEMATOPHILIA – (hee-mat-toh-*FEE*-lee-ah) (also Hematolagnia = hee-mat-toh- *LAHG*-nee-ah) (Hematophiliac) A neurotic paraphilial disorder in which one is sexually attracted and aroused by the sight of blood. Whatever the subconscious cause of hematophilia, it is terrifyingly dangerous disorder. It stands to reason that those who are sexually stimulated by the sight of blood are ideal candidates to become serial killers. A Caveat: This term should not be confused with Hemophilia, which is a genetic bleeding disease.

HEMICRANIA – (hem-mee-*KRAY*-nee-ah) Severe pain confined to one side of the head, as in a migraine attack. The enigmatic migraine is not the only cause od hemicrania. A glioblastoma or brain tumor will bring sever pain in the area of the brain in which it grows.

HEMISPHERE – (*HEM*-mis-fear) (Hemispheric) Literally means *"half-a-sphere."* Cut an orange in half, and you'll have two hemispheres. Geographically, hemisphere refers to the halving of the globe into north/south and east /west. The equator is the dividing line between the Northern and Southern Hemispheres. The "New World" of North and South America comprise the Western Hemisphere. The rest of the continents are in the Eastern Hemisphere. So the United States is both in the Northern and Western Hemispheres.

HEMOGLOBIN – (*HEE*-mo-glo-bin) (Hb) The iron-rich, oxygen-carrying pigment of red blood cells (erythrocytes). The iron-oxide in hemoglobin gives blood its red color and rusty taste. Hemoglobin carries oxygen to all the bodily tissues, which sustains life.

HEMOPHOBIA – (he-mo-*FO*-bee-a) (Hemophobiac) Phobic fear of blood. It is common to feel light-headed, a bit ill at the sight of blood. Many medical students get sick, early in their training program. But as with all phobias, hemophobiacs react in an unreasonable, exaggerated manner. Usually they faint. Psychological intervention is in order with hemphobia. A Caveat: Do not confuse hemophobia with hemophilia, the medical disorder that results in uncontrollable bleeding.

HEMOSTATIC – (hee-mo-*STAT*-ic) A medicinal agent that arrests the flow of blood within the vessels. A hemostatic is a styptic that stops hemorrhaging.

HEMOTOXIN – (*HEE*-mo-tox-in) Blood poisoning. Snake venom that causes internal bleeding. The brain can bleed to death with the introduction of a hemotoxin.

HENCEFORTH – (*HENS*-forth) From now on, from this point forward.

HENOTHEISM – (hen-o-*THEE*-is-um) A form of polytheism (many gods) in which the minor gods must express their loyalty and obedience to the Supreme Being. The Greek pantheon with Zeus as king of the gods was henotheistic. The minor gods had to express homage to King Zeus.

HENTAI – (*HEN*-teye) Highly sexual Japanese animation. Hentai refers to realistic pornographic cartoons. One's sexual imagination can go wild with hentai.

HEPTARCHY – (*HEP*-tark-kee) Literally, a government of seven. Historically, the Heptarchy were the 7 principal Anglo-Saxon kingdoms in 7th and 8th centuries England. They were: Kent, Mercia, Northumbria, East Anglia, Sussex, Essex, and Wessex.

HERB – (*HERB*) (Herbaceous plants) A flowering plant that does not have a woody stem or trunk like a bush or tree. Many herbs are valued for their scent, and as spices or medicines. A herb can reach the size of a small tree, as do banana and papaya. Incidentally: In the culture of modern Witchcraft, all plants that are harvested for any reason are called herbs.

HERBALISM – (*HER*-bal-is-um) The study and application of the medical properties (*galenicals*) of plants. Over 80% of the world's population depends on herbalism, plants for their medicine. Plants are chemical factories producing poisons and medicines. All of our present-day medicine comes directly from plants or indirectly (synthesized plant formulas). Over 80,000 health plants have been identified. Shamans across the globe know of countless more.

HERBISAURS – (*HER*-bi-sors) The plant-eating dinosaurs. Actually, 19 out of 20 (95%) were herbivores. The balance were the *carnisaurs*.

HERBIVORE – (*HER*-bi-vor) A plant eater, therefore forager, grazer, browser, like a cow, deer, horse, giraffe. Herbivorous animals feed on grasses, leaves, fruits, seaweeds, vegetation rather than meat (carnivores).

The world's largest land creatures are herbivores: elephants, hippos, rhinos, giraffes, buffalo, cows, horses. That's because plants are far less nutritious than meat. Therefore, herbivores must eat a great deal more, eat constantly, in fact. To accommodate this great volume of food, herbivores need enormous stomachs, or more than one. It takes a big animal to carry a big stomach. That's why herbivores are so large. Carnivores, on the other hand, feed sparingly but efficiently, on the protein in the nutritious herbivore's flesh.

HERD – (*HURD*) A somewhat unexpected collective name for an assemblage of rabbits. *"A herd of rabbits invaded the pasture."* We usually imagine herds of large, four-footed animals like bison, horses, or elk, not little rabbits.

HERD IMMUNITY – (*HURD* im-*YOO*-ni-tee) In virology/immunology, a biological defense mechanism, the natural rise-and-fall of a pandemic disease, as it runs its course. Herd immunity is attained when 70% of the herd (population) has survived and acquired immunity to the infection. This is how great herds of animals on the savannah, steppes, plains withstand outbreaks. The old, weak, sickly, vulnerable perish, eliminating an easy incubation host for the contagion. The strong will survive, acquiring immunities, and pass them on through procreation. It's cold natural selection, survival of the fittest in fact. The herd is culled, pruned, thinned-out through natural selection. The population is fortified for the future. When herd immunity, as a rendition of survival of the fittest is applied to human population, it becomes *"Social Darwinism."* A human herd immunity policy is laissez faire, do nothing, let *"nature red in tooth and claw"* take her course. Today, the Coronavirus, left to *"burn-out,"* would kill 2.1 to 3 million Americans. This is reminiscent of the Nazi eugenics program. Of course, human intervention can override natural selection. With universal testing, vaccination, and medical care, we can attain the herd immunity level without the natural sacrifice of human life.

HERD MENTALITY – (*hurd* men-*TELL*-li-tee) President Donald Trump's (b. 1946) notorious malapropism of September 15, 2020. Instead of *"mentality,"* Trump should have said *"immunity."* Trump was alluding to the Coronavirus contagion. Actually, an *"immunity mentality"* is the Trump Administration's pandemic program. It translates into no program, oblivious of options. Herd mentality is the mentality of the Trump herd of sheep. More accurately, Trump and his cult members suffer from *"mentality immunity."*

HERESY – (*HAIR*-uh-see) (Heretic, Heretical) Belief contrary to the official orthodoxy of an institution, particularly the church. A heretic is one who holds those dissentient, nonconformist beliefs. The word heretic evolved with the status of the Catholic Church. In the original Greek, *"Hairetikos,"* (heretic) simply meant *"One being able to choose."* A heretic was one free to choose her spiritual path and not obliged to accept any religious dogma. As the Church grew in confidence and power, heresy and heretic came to mean *"One who is mistaken."* A heretic was one who held the wrong religious beliefs and required correction. When the Church became the preeminent authority in Europe, heresy and heretic evolved into *"One sinfully condemned."* The heretic held a demonic, abominable belief because it did not conform to the official party line. Only 73 years after the last Christian [read: Roman heretic] was murdered in the Roman arena, the Catholic Church murdered its first heretic in 385 CE. Heresy is a crime against religious orthodoxy. In other words, heresy is free thought. *"Oppressed minorities, on becoming majorities, oppress minorities."*

HERETOFORE – (*HEER*-too-for) Until this time; from now on; starting now.

HERITABLE – (*HAIR*-it-ta-bul) Inheritable or capable of being inherited. Genetic traits are heritable. Physical characteristics like height, skin, hair, eye color are transmitted heritable factors.

HERMAPHRODITE – (her-*MAFF*-ro-dite) An androgen, being androgynous. A hermaphrodite is unisexual, appearing to be both female and male. A rare genetic anomaly occurs when a person is born with both male and female genitalia. This is hermaphroditism. In Greek mythology, Hermaphroditus was a normal, handsome young man. His beauty attracted the passionate attentions of a water nymph. Her amorous advances were unrequited. Hermaphroditus made the mistake of bathing in her pool, whereupon she rapturously embraced him and pulled him down into the lower depths. The nymph prayed to the gods that he and she might forever be joined. Her prayer was answered for their bodies became one. Hermaphroditus emerged with a female figure, breasts, and male genitals. Incidentally: In *"The Gospel of Thomas"* Jesus Said: *"When you make the two into one, and when you make the inside like the outside and the outside like the inside and the above like below – that is, to make the male and the female into a single one, so that the male will not be male and the female will not be female,…then you will enter the Kingdom."* *"In all things, there is neither male nor female."* – Buddha (c. 563 – c. 483 BCE).

HERMENEUTICS – (her-men-*NU*-tic) A term that means different things in different contexts. Hermeneutics means the science of interpretation of human behavior, social institutions, or religious scriptures. In existential philosophy, hermeneutics is the discussion of life's purpose. In theology, hermeneutics refers to the principles of Biblical interpretation.

HERMETICISM – (her-*MET*-ti-siz-um) (Hermetic) Belief in the body of secret, esoteric writings and knowledge relating to occult science, particularly alchemy. Hermeticism is the purview of the select initiates.

HERO – (*HERE*-ro) (Heroism) One who has risked or sacrificed her life or well- being in the service or salvation of another. *"A man can be a hero in any profession."* – Walt Whitman (1819 – 1892). Heroism involves self-sacrifice. Heroes tend to put others before themselves.

HEROIN – (*HAIR*-ro-in) A white, crystalline powder, a powerful narcotic drug. The euphoric effect of heroin on the brain makes it extremely addictive. An overdose of heroin is fatal. Heroin is an opioid derived from morphine which is manufactured from opium. The technical names for heroin are *diamorphine* or *diacetylmorphine* ($C21\ H23\ NO5$). Heroin is illegal, a Federally controlled substance in the U.S.A. Heroin was first synthesized by an English pharmacist in 1874 as a cure for his morphine addiction. (Ironically, the body converts heroin to morphine.) In 1898, the Baer (Aspirin) Company marketed heroin in a cough medicine.

HERO'S CREDO – (*HERE*-os *CRAY*-dow) *"Never be a passive witness to another's pain."*

HERON – (*HAIR*-on) Ancient Hebrew custom to take no loot, take no prisoners from a conquered city, however, destroy everything and everyone. God had supposedly instructed the Hebrews to kill every man, woman, child, and animal. Take none of the food, for all is considered polluted. Heron was a cleansing process. This is how the Hebrews (God's Chosen People) captured village after village from the Canaanites, and established their kingdom. (Gaza 2024?) It was far worse than a Muslim Jihad. The *"Good Book"* (Bible) reads: *"Oh daughter of Babylon, doomed to be destroyed, blessed shall he be who repays you with what you have done to us! Blessed shall be he who takes your little ones and dashes them against the rocks!"* – Psalm 137: 8-9. Gratefully, intelligent Jews and Christians understand that the Bible is a time contingent book, much of which was written for a specific people, at a specific time, for a specific reason.

HERZEGOVINA – (hair-ze-go-*VEE*-na) A Slavonic province on the Balkan Peninsula, traditionally allied to Bosnia. Herzegovina is presently united with Bosnia as one nation. Herzegovina makes up the southern part of the united nation. At 4,409 square miles, (smaller than Delaware), Herzegovina is much larger than Bosnia, but the population stands at only 466,300. About 48% are Croatian (Catholic), 26% are Bosniacs (Muslims), and 21% are Serbian (Orthodox). Another volatile mixture. Herzegovinians speak Serbo-Croatian. Herzegovina had been ruled by the Ottoman Turks, the Austro-Hungarians, and the Serbian-dominated Yugoslavia (South Slavia). With the disintegration of the Yugoslav Union in the 1990's, Herzegovina was embroiled in the Bosnian War. In that convoluted conflict, rape and mass murder proved pandemic. The line between victim and villain was blurred. Herzegovina is presently experiencing a warless truce with her sister state, Bosnia, and her hostile neighbors.

HE SAID SHE SAID – (*HEE* sed *SHEE* sed) A verbal disagreement between a male and a female. A *"he said she said"* dispute usually involves conflicting testimony. Both arguments are plausible but cannot be both true. Facts are spun in a he said she said to match the opposing arguments. Women usually have an advantage in a he said she said, for they are more proficient is recalling minute detail. Only a third-party testimony of a witness can corroborate what he said or what she said to be true. A classic, historic example of a he said she said was the Congressional hearing of September 27, 2018. Dr. Christine Blasey Ford (b. 1968) swore that she was sexually molested by Judge Brett Kavanaugh (b. 1965), while both were in high school. Kavanaugh denied the entire allegation. The he said she said was not resolved because the Republican Congress refused to investigate the evidence. They feared that Dr. Ford was telling the truth, and their Supreme Court candidate, Judge Kavanaugh was lying (under oath).

HETAERISM – (het-*TEER*-is-um) Concubinage. Hetaerism is also a social system in which the women are considered common property. His may be the case in some extraordinary cult communes.

HETERODOX – (*HET*-ter-ro-dox) (Heterodoxical) Unorthodox, heretical. Doctrine incompatible with the theology and dogma of the dominant religion or church.

HETEROINSEMINATION – (het-er-o-in-sem-in-*NAY*-shun) Being artificially impregnated without sexual congress. In human heteroinsemination, the semen need not be from a husband. Incidentally: Dr. Cecil Byran Jacobson (1936 - 2021) had impregnated several patients with his own sperm at his reproductive clinic in Fairfax County, Virginia. Furthermore, Dr. Jacobson reported that he had impregnated a baboon with his own sperm in the 1960s, while at George Washington University Medical School. He aborted the pregnancy after 4 months. *The Island of Doctor Moreau* (1896), by H. G. Wells (1866 - 1946).

HETERONOMY – (het-ter-*ON*-o-mee) The condition of being under the domination of an outside authority, either human or divine.

HETERONORMAL – (het-er-o-*NOR*-mal) (Heteronormative) Being absolutely straight, without any homosexual tendencies, fantasies, or curiosities. (Not likely!) It is highly doubtful that anyone on Earth is 100% heteronormative. After all, we all came from both a man and a woman. Simplistically put, the average man is 60% male, 40% female. Conversely, the average woman is 60% female, and 40% male, endocrinologically (hormonically).

HETERONORMATIVE – (het-er-oh-*NOR*-ma-tiv) (Heteronormativity) The assumption of heterosexuality as the social norm. Heteronormative individuals abide by the traditional male/female gender roles. Being heteronormative is not necessarily homophobic. A heterosexual, straight person need not be intolerant and mean-spirited.

HETERONYM – (*HET*-ter-ron-nim) A word that is spelled in the same way as another, but has a different sound and meaning. For example: *"lead"* (to conduct), and *"lead"* (a metal). Also *"bow"* (for arrow) and *"bow"* (of a ship).

HETEROTROPES – (*HET*-er-o-tropes) (Heterotropic) Lifeforms that eat other lifeforms. Animals are heterotropes. Carnivores eat other animals while herbivores eat living plants. The first animal was a plant that turned cannibal.

HETMAN – (*HET*-mon) An ataman. A title granted to a chief in post-Medieval, pre-modern Poland, Czechoslovakia, the Ukraine, and other Slavonic regions of Eastern Europe. The term may be of Czech origin. The hetman was a governor, leader, general, sometimes appointed, other times elected. The office of hetman was most prominently associated with the Ukrainian Cassocks.

HEURISTIC – (hur-*RIS*-tic) (Heuristical, Heuristics) A problem solving method by incremental exploration, using models and working hypotheses (the Heuristical Method). A heuristic approach is a more informal, intuitive technique than scientific experimentation. It tends to stimulate interest, encourages further investigation and learning.

HEURISTICS – (hur-*RIS*-tics) (Heuristical) The name for the discipline that studies the methods by which facts, ideas, truth are discovered and sometimes communicated.

HEURISTIC LEARNING – (hur-*RIS*-tic *LERN*-ning) The discovery approach that employs projects, field trips, and hands-on manipulation of materials. Heuristic teaching and learning is Progressive. It conforms to the Liberal philosophies of Pragmatism and Existentialism. The opposite of heuristic learning is traditional didactic learning, which employs lecturing.

HEX – (*HEKS*) In popular parlance a hex is a curse, jinx, an evil spell meant to bring misfortune and mischief. The word *"hex"* is German for *"witch."* In modern German, *"hexen"* means to cast a spell.

HEXAKOSIOIHEXEKONTAHEXAPHOBIA – (hex-a-ko-see-oy-hex-e-kon-ta-hex-a *FO*-bee-ah) Fear of the number 666. This is the number or sign of the anti- Christ, the Beast, as described in the Biblical Book of Revelations. With 29 letters, this may be the longest non-hyphenated word that appears in English usage. *"You must borrow me Gargantua's mouth first before I can utter so long a word; 'tis a word too great for any mouth of this age's size."* – William Shakespeare (1564 – 1616) in *As You like It*, (1599).

HEYDAY – (*HAY*-day) A time in the prime. The stage or period of greatest vigor, strength, or success. *"In its heyday, transoceanic luxury liners were the grandest form of travel."* The late 16th century term *"heyday"* is an alteration of the exclamation *"heyda"* (1520s), which served as the present day term *"hurrah."* The modern sense of the word *"heyday"* was first recorded in 1751, meaning *"stage of greatest vigor."*

HEZBOLLAH – (hez-bal-*LAH*) The term is Arabic for *"Party of Allah,"* or *"Party of God."* Hezbollah is a militant Lebanese political party consisting of Shia Islamists. It was founded in 1985 with headquarters in Beirut, Lebanon. Hezbollah is anti-Zionist, anti-Israeli, antisemitic. Too, Hezbollah campaigns against the Western capitalist powers (U.S.A.) that prop-up Israel. Hezbollah is supported by Lebanon, Iran, Iraq, Syria, Cuba, North Korea, Venezuela, and Russia. Hezbollah incites anti-Israeli protests, riots, and violence. They are often referred to as a terrorist organization. However, a terrorist to one man is a patriot to another. A Caveat: Do not confuse Shiite Lebanese Hezbollah, with Sunni Palestinian Hamas, another Islamic militant group. Both groups are supported by Iran and are rabidly anti-Semitic, anti-Israel. Parenthetically: Those who are considered terrorists to one population are considered patriots to another population. Often, oppressed people must employ terrorism as a form of guerrilla warfare.

HIATUS – (hi-*AY*-tus) A break in the work. A hiatus is an interruption in the action. A restful, uneventful period. The halftime of a football game is a hiatus.

HIBERNO-ENGLISH – (hy-*BER*-no *ENG*-lish) (Literally, the *Irish-English*) The Hiberno-English are the Ulsterites, the Protestant Orange men of Northern Ireland. Actually, they were Anglicized Lowland Scotts sent to occupy Northern Ireland. So they are also known as the Scotts-Irish. Many Hiberno-English migrated to America, populating the Appalachia Mountains. They became the pathfinders, the Indian fighters, with the coon-skin caps and Kentucky long rifles. Today, they are pejoratively referred to as the hillbillies.

HIBISCUS – (hy-*BIS*-cus) The *"China Rose."* A vast variety of woody shrubs with large, spectacular flowers that bloom in a great variety of colors. Hibiscus is native to the highlands of western China. Universally cultivated, it serves as the national flower of Malaysia and South Korea, as well as the state flower of Hawaii. Hibiscus flowers are dried and made into a tea called *"bissap"* in West Africa, *"sorrel"* in Trinidad and Jamaica, and *"agua de jamaica"* in Honduras and Mexico. The flowers are used as a garnish and vegetable in Mexico and the Philippines. Hibiscus is one of several candidates considered to have been the mysterious *"Rose of Sharon"* in the Old Testament.

HICKEY – (*HICK*-kee) (Hickied) In the popular parlance, a *"love bite."* A hickey is a very minor injury. It is a contusion or bruise caused by a sucking-kiss. Though the skin does not break, subcutaneous blood vessels do. The wound bleeds beneath the skin, causing the red mark to turn purple (as the blood deoxygenates). It takes about 2 weeks to lighten, fade to yellow, then disappear. Hickeys are displayed, usually on the neck, by adolescents. It would be juvenile, comical, to see a hickey on an older person. For youngsters, it is a symbol that they are sexually active, and attractive enough, worthy to have a boyfriend or girlfriend. Incidentally: The application of witchhazel will speed the fading of the hickey or any other bruise.

HIDDEN CURRICULUM – (*HID*-den ker-*RICK*-you-lum) In education, instructional norms and values not openly acknowledged by teachers or school officials, nevertheless transmitted to students. The hidden curriculum consists of all the collateral, latent, incidental learning that inadvertently takes place in the classroom. The teachers' attitudes, the learning environment, the décor, the disciplinary and reward systems shout volumes to the impressionable youngsters. Messages in the hidden curriculum concern issues and attitudes about race, gender, class, authority, justice, school, knowledge, and much more. All contribute to the children's hidden curriculum and education.

HIDDEN COST – (*HID*-den *CAWST*) Sneaky price hike performed by family restaurants. Places like *Bob Evans, Cracker Barrel, IHOP* (International <u>H</u>ouse of <u>P</u>an<u>C</u>akes) display very low prices for entrées, lower than is profitable. But these are cagy capitalists. They make up for their low food prices, on very high drink prices – milk, tea, coffee, juice. A glass of milk may cost $3.50. That may be 25% the cost of the meal. But the customer looks at the low meal prices. The cost of drinks may not even be listed. Therefore, never feel sorry for a capitalist. Do take pity on the poor waiters and waitresses who serve you and must depend on your generous tips for most of their wages.

HIDEOUS – (HID-ee-uhs) (Hideously, Hideousness) Horribly frightening, ridiculously repulsive, monstrously grotesque. What is hideous hits the heights of horribleness. *"Donald Trump's plans for the future America are heinously hideous."*

HIERARCHICALISM – (hi-er-*AR*-kick-cal-is-um) Belief in a stringent class or caste system in which power resides in a small group of aristocrats of birth or wealth.

HIERARCHY OF NEEDS – (*HY*-er-are-kee of *NEEDS*) Introduced in 1943 by Humanist Psychologist Abraham Maslow (1908 – 1970). The four lower-order deficiency needs provide for physical, biological, and psychological well-being. They are: 1. *Physiological/Biological Needs*; 2. *Safety*; 3. *Love/Belongingness*; 4. *Esteem*. The two higher-order fulfillment needs are: 1. *Understanding/Aesthetic Needs*; 2. *Self-Actualization*, (realizing your maximum potential). Years later, just before his death, Maslow added the ultimate, highest-order need: *Spiritual Atonement* (at-*ONE*-ment) or Oneness with God.

HIEROGAMY – (hy-er-*ROG*-gam-mee) A marriage made in heaven. A divine marriage, literally. Hierogamy is a marriage between two gods, as that of Zeus and Hera in Greek mythology.

HIEROGLYPHICS – (hi-ro-*GLIF*-ics) An advanced form of pictographic writing characteristic of the ancient Egyptians. Actually, hieroglyphs are a transition from pictographic writing (pictures) to ideographic writing (ideas).

HIEROGRAM – (*HY*-er-uh-gram) Any sacred symbol, as an emblem, or a holy picture.

HIEROMANIA – (hi-ro-*MAY*-nee-a) Pathological visions or delusions of a religious nature.

HIGGLER – (*HIG*-ler) A street vender, peddler, somewhat of a huckster. Higglers tend to be hagglers from whence they get the name. Though sometimes pushy and annoying, at least they are not mugging people for a living.

HIGH – (*HY*) Psychologically, getting high is transforming one's mood, shifting one's frame of mind, altering one's state of consciousness. This can be achieved through alcohol, drugs, hypnosis, meditation, or prayer. Getting high can involve being *"hopped-up"* or *"mellowed-down."* It is a universal pursuit of man from time immemorial. Even children attempt to get high. At play they will spin like Whirling Dervishes in order to attain dizziness (get high).

HIGHBALL – (*HY*-ball) The simplest of cocktails, consisting of an alcoholic spirit and a mixer. Popular highballs are whiskey and ginger ale, rum and coke, vodka and orange or tomato juice.

HIGH BROWN – (*HY BROWN*) A Jamaican racial designation for a light complected Negro or Black person.

HIGHFALUTIN – (hy-fal-*LOOT*-tin) An Americanism circa 1839 meaning *"high- flying."* It came to be associated with anything pompous, fancy, pretentious. A highfalutin remark or speech is expressed in, or marked by language that is overly elaborate, haughty, and bombastic. Highfalutin Americanisms were liberally employed by author Mark Twain (1835 – 1910).

HIGHLIGHTING – (*HY*-lyt-ing) (Highlight, Highlighter) To emphasize, focus-on, make prominent with a colored marker. Highlighting a book is an essential study technique. Profound passages in a literary work are highlighted with a florescent yellow, green, or pink marker so the information is outstanding and easy to locate. You highlight that information you deem worthy of remembering. Highlighting takes time, and it is an interference in the read. However, it is well worth the effort. In the future, one may re-read the highlights in the book, reviewing the gist in a fraction of the time. A highlighted book, also annotated with notes, is exponentially more valuable to you. *"Marking a book is literally an experience of your differences or agreements with the author. It is the highest respect you can pay him."* – Edgar Allan Poe (1809 – 1849).

HIGH MAINTENANCE – (*HY MAIN*-ten-ans) Any person, place, animal, or thing that requires constant attention. In a relationship, the high maintenance partner or spouse is usually female. She has a fragile ego and finds offense in innocent episodes. A high maintenance lady is difficult to please, almost never quite satisfied. She is perpetually complaining about something or other. The table at the restaurant is never good enough. She will always have to send a meal back, because something is wrong. Favors and gifts must be supplied in abundance as pacification. A high maintenance wife or girlfriend easily falls victim to envy (*"I want what's yours"*), and jealousy (*"You want what's mine"*). To make matters worse, high maintenance women usually have anger issues. They are prone to temper tantrums. It takes the patience of Job, and the wisdom of Solomon to maintain a relationship with a high maintenance woman. *"The lady doth protest too much me thinks."* – William Shakespeare (1564 – 1616) in *Hamlet* (c. 1599 to 1602).

HIGH MAGICK – (hy *MAJ*-ik) Employing the esoteric arts in self-improvement. The goal of high magick is transformation on the spiritual level. The practitioner of high magick seeks enlightenment through atonement [read: *at-one-ment*] with *"The All,"* which is God. The *"high"* in high magick is a reference to the gentry, the upper or high class who had the leisure time to pursue self- improvement. They didn't have to sweat at labor all day for their bread. Therefore, high magick was the reserve of the high brows, the aristocracy and clergy. This is no longer the case, if it ever was. Every mundane task, any menial chore can be dedicated as a pray, sacrifice, offering to God. Atonement is not for sale to the highest bidder. *"I draw water. I cut wood. That is my miracle."* – Zen Buddhist Proverb.

HIGH MASSA – (*HY MA*-sa) (sometimes Big Massa) A slave name for God in Jamaica and other English-speaking slave plantation colonies.

HIGH PRESSURE – (*HY PRESH*-sher) In meteorology, high barometric pressure (H). A high pressure system is an anticyclone. The uneven heating and cooling of the ground produces air pressure differences. With high pressure, the air weighs more heavily on the Earth. This air does not rise, so clouds do not form. A high pressure ridge produces clear, bright, dry, sunny weather. The cloudless sky reflects solar heat making for cool or very cold temperatures.

HIGH SCHOOL – (*HY SKOOL*) America's secondary educational institution with a student age range from 14 to 18 years. The evolution of this institution has been from the Latin Grammar School, to the Academy, to the Elite High School, to the Comprehensive High School. The Kalamazoo Case (1874) created the *"elite"* public high school supported by taxation. The NEA's (<u>N</u>ational <u>E</u>ducation <u>A</u>ssociation) Cardinal Principles (1918) created the *"comprehensive"* high school for all. The Progressive Cardinal Principles made the *Public* School, the *Public's* School. High school is one of the most important social institutions in America. It is the temple of transition and transformation of American youth. Adolescent boys and girls enter high school as children, and depart 4 years later as young men and women. We make close friends and discover our first loves in high school. Some meet their life-long spouses in those classrooms. Some of life's greatest joys and most crushing disappointments are experienced in high school. Some of our most lasting memories are forged in high school. High school is one of the very few experiences shared by every American. *"High school is closer to the core of the American experience than anything else I can think of."* – Kurt Vonnegut (1922 – 2007).

HIGHWAY – (*HY*-way) The main public road linking towns and cities. Since antiquity, highways were the connecting routes of civilization. The Romans maintained their empire for so long, because if their marvelous highway system. The highway was the fastest way, often the only way to travel long distances inland until the creation of freeways/expressways in the mid-20th century. Today, the highway is not the fastest, but is indeed the most important road in the community. Highways are heavily trafficked roads with high speeds between the urban areas, where the traffic lights are few. Within the town or city, the highway shares the way with many intersecting roads. The community's business, commercial enterprises line the highways. High Street is that part of the highway that bisects the downtown area. Residential streets branch off the highways. In different locations, highways are referred to as avenues and boulevards.

HIJAB – (*HEE*-job) The traditional veil that covers Muslim woman's hair, neck, and sometimes face. (The face veil is specifically called a *niqab*.) Hijab also refers to the dress code prescribed for Muslim women. In August, 2023, Molvi Mohammad Sadiq Akif, Spokesman for the Afghan Taliban Ministry of Vice and Virtue said: *"It is very bad to see women without the hijab. Women's faces should be hidden. It's not that her face will be harmed or damaged. A woman has her own value and that value decreases by men looking at her. Allah gives respect to females in hijab and there is value in this."* Therefore, it seems that according to this

Sharia law, seeing a woman's face, is like driving a new car out of the showroom. It instantly loses 10% of its value. In the Taliban case, the woman would be analogous to a camel or ass.

HILLBILLY – (*HIL*-bil-lee) A facetious though sometimes pejorative designation for a white Southern Appalachian backwoodsman. The hillbillies originated with the Scotts-Irish pioneers with names like Boone, Jackson, and Crockett. They broke into the Eastern Mountains, cleared the forest and Indians. These homesteaders were later swindled and dispossessed by the great cotton barons, then by the great coal companies. They became impoverished Appalachians or hillbillies. The name hillbilly has come to be applied to all low-educated, unsophisticated, conservative Americans with a Southern accent. Though the connotations behind hillbilly are stereotypical, there is a kernel of truth in every stereotype. There is a good chance that a fellow named Bubba, in a beat-up pick-up, with a Confederate flag and a Trump bumper-sticker is most likely a hillbilly. Too, you can identify a hillbilly's abode by the junked cars up on blocks, monuments to hillbilly ineptitude.

HIMALAYAS – (him-a-LAY-yas) *Roof of the world*, greatest, highest mountain range on Earth. The Himalayas are twice the size of the Rocky Mountains. The Indian sub-continent broke-off from Antarctica and drifted north toward Asia. In only 30 million years, India raced 4,000 miles north, moving at 10 to 12 inches a year. India slammed into Asia and subducted under the continent, pushing 2 inches a year. The uplift created the Himalayas. They host 14 of the world's tallest mountains, including Mt. Everest, the tallest, at 5.5 miles high. The range is still growing 1.35 inches a year. However, they are eroding 1.1 inches a year, for a net growth rate of .25 (1/4) inch a year. The Himalayas occupy 1/10 of the Earth's surface. The mountain range traverses 5 countries: India, Nepal, Bhutan, China (*Tibet*) and Pakistan. Many of the world's greatest rivers have their source in the Himalayas: Indus, Ganges, Irrawaddy, Brahmaputra, Mekong, Yangtze, Huang Ho, and others. These rivers provide water for about 45% of humanity. The mighty Himalayas alter the weather and geography. To the south, monsoon rains create rainforests. To the north, the mountains produce the arid Gobi Desert.

HIMARS – (*HY*-mars) An acronym for the M142 HIgh Mobility Artillery Rocket System. A HIMARS is a 5-ton truck that carries a rocket launcher of 6 GPS guided, tactical ballistic missiles. It is manufactured by the American Lockheed Martin Corporation, first in 2010. Each missile cost over $168,000, the entire system over $4 million dollars. The HIMARS vehicle can fire its 6 missiles up to 50 miles, far over the battle line, within 33 feet of the target, then quickly change position to escape counterattack. So far, the HIMARS has been an essential weapon that has deprived the Russian juggernaut from rolling over the Ukraine. *"If the Javelin [anti-tank missile] was the iconic weapon of the early phase of the war, HIMARS is the iconic weapon of the later phase,"* according to Mark Cancian, from the Center for Strategic and International Studies. Russian reporter Roman Sapenkov witnessed a HIMARS missile strike on a Russian airbase in Kherson. *"I was struck by the fact that the whole packet five or six rockets, landed practically on a penny,"* he wrote. According to Professor Yagil Henkin of the Israel Defense Forces Command and Staff College, the HIMARS have forced *"the Russians to move their ammunition depots farther to the rear, thereby reducing the available fire power of Russian artillery near the front lines and making logistical support more difficult."* The HIMARS enable the Ukrainians to hit bridges and disrupt Russian supply efforts. High-tech weaponry from America and NATO allies has kept the much smaller Ukrainian forces in the fight against the mighty Russian invader.

HINAYANA – (hin-a-*YAN*-a) Southern Buddhism (Southeast Asia). Hinayana is conservative, fundamentalist Buddhism. Hinayana does not deviate from the old time religion, the original rites.

HINDU-ARABIC NUMBERS – (*HIN*-doo *AIR*-ra-bic *NUM*-bers) The universal numerical symbol system in use today. The Romans had a clever though cumbersome numeral system. They were prohibited from performing high mathematics because they did not have the zero (0). Around the 3rd century BCE, Hindu scholars had devised the *Brahmi* numeral system in India. This was the predecessor of the Hindu-Arabic Number System we use today. The Arabs were the great merchants of antiquity. Among the treasures that Arab middlemen brought to Europe from Asia was the new numbering system. In 825 CE, the great Persian (Iranian) mathematician Mohammed al-Khwarizmi (780 – 850 CE) wrote <u>On the Calculation with Hindu Numerals</u>. By 976 CE the number system had made its way to Europe. The greatest European mathematician of the Middle Ages was the Italian Leonardo Fibonacci (c. 1175 – c. 1250). His book, <u>Libar Abaci</u> (1202) (<u>The Book of Calculations</u>) went far to popularize the Hindu-Arabic Number System with European scholars. The Hindu-Arabic Numerals are designed for positional notation in a decimal system (or sets of ten), for example, 1, 2, 3, 4, 5, 6, 7, 8, 9, 10. There are only ten symbols in our Hindu-Arabic Number System, certainly because we have ten digits or fingers with both <u>hands</u> which were <u>handy</u> in calculation. It is the place in which each symbol stands that announces whether it represents thousands, hundreds, tens, or units, not the symbol itself, (as in the Roman system). Using the zero (0), we merely repeat the set with the next higher tenth, 11, 12, 13, 14, 15, 16, 17, 18, 19, 20, and so on. Zero (0) is the key.

HINDUISM – (*HIN*-doo-is-um) (Hindu) World's oldest religion, polytheistic in nature, dominant in India. Buddhism and Jainism are offshoot religions of Hinduism. The name Hindu came into use when the Persian Muslims invaded India. The Islamic Persians attempted to label all non-Muslim people living behind the Sindhu River. They mispronounced Sindhu as Hindu, ergo the name. Hinduism was not founded by one individual. Rather, it is the result of a coming together of many religious beliefs and philosophical schools. Primarily, the merging of the beliefs and practices of two groups, the people of the Indus Valley in India, and the Aryans of Persia resulted in Hinduism. With over a billion practitioners, Hinduism is the 3rd largest religion on Earth. It is centered on the Indian Subcontinent, Southeast Asia, the Island of Bali, and scattered pockets throughout the world. There are thousands of major and minor Hindu gods. They all are manifestations of the Ultimate Reality, Brahman. In this sense, Hinduism is a polytheistic monotheosis. Incidentally: Traditionally, a non-Hindu cannot convert to Hinduism. Hindus believe that one can only be a Hindu if one is born into a Hindu family. *"Many faiths are but different paths leading to one reality, God."* – Sri Ramakrishna (1836 – 1886), <u>Vedanta</u>. *"Hindu is a geographical identity, or at the most a cultural one – not a religion. There is no set of beliefs that everyone has to adhere to."* – Jaggi Vasudev (b. 1957).

HINDU CREDO – (*HIN*-doo *CRAY*-dow) *"Om Nama Shivaya."* (Salutations to Lord Shiva.) This most popular Hindu mantra is associated with qualities of prayer, divine-love, grace, truth, and blissfulness.

HINGLISH – (*HIN*-glish) Hindi flavored English. Hinglish is the variety of English spoken in India. Hinglish is the most populously spoken variety of English on Earth.

HIP HOP – (*HIP* hop) A socio-cultural movement created by American youth of African, Latino, and Caribbean decent in the South and West Bronx of New York City. Hip Hop includes rap music, break dancing, and graffiti art. The hip hop scene emerged in the mid-1970s at block parties in the Bronx. The terms *"hip"* and *"hop"* have long been part of the musical lexicon. They had borne different meanings at different times. In 1982, the term hip hop was assigned to this new socio-cultural art movement. Hip hop has permeated mainstream American and world youth culture.

HIPPIE CREDO – (*HIP*-pee *CRAY*-dow) *"Make love not war,"* and *"Turn on, tune in, drop out."* – Dr. Timothy Leary (1920 - 1996).

HIPPIES – (*HIP*-pees) The *"flower children"* of the 1960's and early 1970's. The hippies were courageous members of a movement that coalesced against the War in Vietnam. Hippies were anti-establishment [read: *anti-capitalist*]. They characteristically wore long hair, beads, flowers, and old clothes. Hippies may have been influenced by Jamaican *Rastafarians,* who they resembled. They smoked marijuana and were sexually uninhibited. They often lived Communistically in communes. The hippies represented peace, love, sharing, and communalism [read: *Socialism*].

HIPPOCRATIC HYPOCRITES – (hip-po-*KRAT*-tic *HIP*-po-krits) Republican physicians opposed to healthcare for all. These are doctors against *"Socialized Medicine."* They support *"Capitalist Medicine"* that puts profits before patients. There are presently (March 2020) 16 physicians in the U.S. Congress (only 2 are Democrats). Therefore, there are 14 Republican doctors, *Hippocratic Hypocrites* in the United States Congress. In the Senate there is Dr. John Boozman (b. 1950), Dr. John Barrasso (b. 1952), Dr. Bill Cassidy (b. 1957), and Dr. Rand Paul (b. 1963). The House of Representatives is represented by Dr. Phil Roe (b. 1945), Dr. Mike Simpson (b. 1950), Dr. Michael C. Burgess (b. 1950), Dr. Neal Dunn (b. 1953), Dr. Ralph Abraham (b. 1954), Dr. Tom Price (b. 1954), Dr. Andrew P. Harris (b. 1957), Dr. Brad Wenstrup (b. 1958), Dr. Roger Marshall (b. 1960), Dr. Larry Bucshon (b. 1962), Dr. Scott DesJarlais (b. 1964), And Dr. Raul Ruiz (b. 1972). The Hippocratic Oath is a sacred vow, established by Hippocrates of Kos (c. 460 – c. 370 BCE), *"The Father of Medicine,"* in ancient Greece. It is traditionally considered the credo of the Medical Community. Many physicians have a copy of the oath displayed in their office. Though it had been somewhat modernized the gist of the oath declares: *"I swear that I will use treatment to help the sick according to my ability and judgment, but never with a view to injury and wrong-doing.... I will remember that I do not treat a fever chart, a cancerous growth, but a sick human being, whose illness may affect the person's family and economic stability. My responsibility includes these related problems, if I am to care adequately for the sick."* How can any doctor who takes this oath be against universal healthcare? If healthcare is not for all, who would these doctors-cum-legislators exclude? To deny any person medical care because they are poor and uninsured is vile, despicable. How is this sin of omission not *"injury and wrong-doing?"* Nothing affects a *"person's family and economic stability"* more than illness, injury, lack of healthcare coverage. There has to be a special place in Dante's Hell for doctors opposed to universal healthcare – those *Hippocratic Hypocrites.* Incidentally: It was announced on May 20, 2020, that the Trump Administration is looking for disreputable doctors who will lie to the public on the health dangers of the Coronavirus. Trump hopes these phony physicians will convince the public to seek employment and commerce, despite the contamination. Perhaps they may also endorse Trump's lethal hydroxychloroquine as well. Any self-seeking doctors who would doctor the truth for Trump are indeed *"Hippocratic Hypocrites."*

HIPPOCRATIC OATH – (hip-po-K*RAT*-tic *OATH*) The sacred vow put forth by Hippocrates of Kos (c. 460 – c. 370 BCE) in ancient Greece, *"The Father of Medicine."* It has become a traditional obligation for all physicians to abide by this Oath. The gist of Hippocrates' Oath is: *"I swear that I will use treatment to help the sick according to my ability and judgment, but never with a view to injury and wrong-doing."* In 1948, the World Medical Associate amended the Oath vowing that: *"I will remember that I do not treat a fever chart, a cancerous growth, but a sick human being, whose <u>illness may affect the person's</u> family and <u>economic stability</u>. My responsibility include these related problems, if I am to care adequately for the sick."* In too many cases, though the patient may be cured, the trauma of the economic cost of the treatment may debilitate him and his family. The medical cost, the debt may kill him. This is often due to greedy doctors and insurance companies who put profit before patients. Withholding medical care from those who cannot pay the price, is tantamount to blackmail, extortion, or ransom, *"pay-up or die!"* It turns the *Hippocratic Oath* into the *Hypocritic Oath.* Money-hungry doctors better abide by Jesus' "Social *Gospel*" (Matthew 25: 35 – 40) or face a dire Karma. *"He who saves one life, saves the world entire."* – (Talmudic quote that inspired Oskar Schindler (1908 – 1974) to become a Messiah.)

HIPPOPHAGY – (hip-*POF*-uh-jee) (Hippophagism) The term *"hippo"* means horse, and *"phagy"* means eat in Greek. Hippophagy is the eating of horseflesh. Horse in French is *"cheval."* Therefore, cheval or chevaline has come to mean horse meat. Hippophagy is as feasible as eating beef, and safer than eating pork. However throughout the millennia, hippophagy had acquired a taboo, tantamount to cannibalism. That's because the horse, like the dog, has become our companion. The horse plowed our fields, transported us about, fought in our wars, and in America, helped to win the West. So under normal conditions, the horse became too valuable to kill and eat. Only in a dire emergency, a war, disaster, triggering famine will hippophagy become acceptable.

HIRSUTE – (*HUR*-soot) Hairy, shaggy. *"The werewolf was a hirsute beast with fangs and claws."*

HIRUDIN – (*HEAR*-u-din) Leach saliva, (or its synthetic equivalent), a potent anticoagulant drug used to dissolve bloodclots. Leaches are enabled to feed on animal bold because the hirudin in their saliva prevents coagulation and scabbing of blood at a wound. This chemical is used medicinally with heart attack patients.

HISPANIC/LATINO – (his-*PAN*-ik la-*TEE*-noh) The terms Hispanic and Latino are not synonymous. Too, the difference is complicated and confusing. When you hear H<u>ispanic</u>, think of Spain and Spanish. When you hear <u>Latino</u>, think of Latin Americans. Hispanics are Spanish-speaking people. So Hispanic is a cultural designation and linguistic group. Latinos are people from Latin America, or their descendants. Latinos are a racial blend of Latin American populations. Most Latinos speak Spanish, so most culturally qualify as Hispanic. But Latino is an ethnic designation as well. So a Hispanic from Madrid is not a Latino. Conversely, a Latino who cannot speak Spanish is hardly Hispanic. For example, the American-born grandson of Mexican immigrants living in Phoenix, who cannot speak Spanish, is indeed a Latino ethnically, but culturally not very Hispanic. Similarly, a German immigrant to Argentina will never be a Latino, and will become Hispanic when she learns Spanish. Still a little confused? Actually, this is all academic, and should stay that way. We get into trouble when we take these differences and designations socially and politically too seriously.

HISPANIOLA – (his-pan-nee-*OH*-la) The second largest Caribbean island (after Cuba), located in the Greater Antilles. Hispaniola is a little larger than the state of South Dakota. The eastern 2/3 of the island in occupied by the prosperous Spanish-speaking Dominican Republic. The western 1/3 of the island is occupied by the devastated French-speaking Haiti. Some of the earliest European settlements in the New World were planted on Hispaniola.

HISSY FIT – (*HISS*-see *FIT*) A hysterical temper tantrum. Stereotypically, the term is traditionally ascribed to women. (There is a kernel of truth in every stereotype.) The term hissy fit gained popularity around 1983. However the notion of hysterical temper tantrums by females goes back to antiquity. The term *"hystera"* is Greek for *"womb," "uterus."* The word *"hissy"* may be related to hystera. Hysteria [read: *hissy fits*] was considered to be a neurotic condition peculiar to women and thought to be caused by a dysfunction of the uterus. Political correctness aside, things are what they are.

HISTAMINE – (*HIS*-ta-meen) An irritating chemical compound released by specialized cells when tissue is injured or in allergic and inflammatory reactions. The release of histamine causes dilation of small blood vessels, and contraction of smooth muscles. Histamine is a chemical defense mechanism. But in some people, its affects are counter-productive, even injurious. Autoimmune allergies may erupt. Therefore, antihistamine medications are applied.

HISTORIAN – (his-*TOR*-ree-an) A chronicler of past events. A historian records what happened, and may interpret the cause and effect. He may be an actual witness or she may be a documentary scholar, a student of the events. The more factual, accurate, and neutral the writer, the more professional he/she is as a historian. One may be formally trained as a historian in college, but that is not essential. All human beings hold sentiments, perspectives, emotions. These attitudinal predilections will be detected in his writing of history. It is important to curtail one's biases when writing history. It is helpful to discover the historian's background before reading her works. Historians and propagandists are antithetical, mutually exclusive. *"Anybody can make history; only a great man can write it."* – Oscar Wilde (1854 – 1900). *"The men who make history have not time to write it."* – Austrian Chancellor Klemens Von Metternich (1773 – 1859). *"Historians ought to be precise, faithful, and unprejudiced; and neither interest nor fear, hatred nor affection, should make them swerve from the way of truth."* – Miguel de Cervantes (1547 – 1616).

HISTORIAN'S CREDO – (his-*TOR*-ree-ans *CRAY*-dow) *"All that is past is prelude."* This is the inscription on the National Archives Building in Washington D.C.

HISTORICAL INTERPRETATION – (his-*TOR*-ri-cal in-ter-pret-*TAY*-shun) Different ways to study, perceive, and understand the past (history). Though the facts remain the same, interpreting the meaning of those facts may be quite different, depending on one's perspective. Conservatives take a celebrationist, traditionalist view of history. This glorifies the unjust status quo. Liberals take a revisionist, and postmodernist view of history which demands change and social justice. *"Historians ought to be precise, faithful, and unprejudiced; and neither interest nor fear, hatred nor affection, should make them swerve from the way of truth."* – Miguel de Cervantes (1547 – 1616).

HISTORICISM – (his-*TOR*-ri-siz-um) (Historicistic, Historicistically) The theory that history is determined by immutable laws and not human agency. Man does not make history. Historicism maintains that man is carried by a tide of great inevitable events that will determine historical outcomes. The world is the way it is because of unavoidable historical determinants. Historicism insists that historians must seek and study historical laws in order to understand the past, and help predict the future. The idea that history repeats itself is historicistic. *"Those who forget their history are condemned to relive it."* – George Santayana (1863 – 1952).

HISTORIOGRAPHY – (his-tor-ree-*OG*-ra-fee) The history of history. The body of techniques, theories, and principles of historical research and preservation. Historiography entails the methods of historical scholarship. Historiography compares how different historians had interpreted history. Lancelot de La Popeliniere's (1541 – 1608) *L'Histoire des Histoires* (1599) was the first historiographic work in history.

HISTORY – (*HIS*-tor-ree) The term is taken from both the Greek and Latin word *"historia,"* meaning *"to inquire into, examine, relate."* History is the written record of mankind's experience. Because formal history must be written, all the time before writing is pre-history (prehistoric). It's a common cliché that history repeats itself. It doesn't. But human nature does. As philosopher George Santayana (1863 - 1952) admonished: *"Those who forget their history are condemned to relive it."* Too, those who fail to forgive their history are also condemned to relive it. The sad Balkans stand as an example to the world. *"History is the depository of great actions, the witness of what is past, the example and instructor of the present, and monitor to the future."* – Miguel de Cervantes (1547 – 1616). *"If we don't know our history, we are deemed to live it."* – Philosopher Hannah Arendt (1906 – 1975). *"A different history is being taught in different parts of the country. This can't be good. There are certain things that are common to us all."* – Richard N. Haass (b. 1951). *"History is Philosophy teaching by example."* – Thucydides (c. 460 – c. 400 BCE).

HISTORY TEACHER – (*HIS*-tor-ree *TEECH*-er) A professional storyteller, a culture preserver and transmitter, a conservation manager of the past, a torch passer. A history teacher may serve on several levels, in schools, universities, museums, tour busses, TV, or video. Students consult the history teacher in order to learn of our heritage. After all, we can't know where we're going, and we won't know where we are, if we don't know where we've been. The academic history teacher explains the story of the past to students who must relate the story back. Then the history teacher must evaluate the students on the accuracy of their stories. This assures that the story, the history, remains alive in our culture. It is said that *"We stand on the shoulders of giants."* The history teacher knows those giants' names. Too, she may be preparing future giants. Incidentally: The racist Governor of Florida, Ron DeSantis (b. 1978) began his carrier as a high school history teacher. He taught a twisted version of the Civil War in which slavery was a positive good! Now, as governor, DeSantis is scheming to censor and alter history in favor of white, Christian supremacy.

HISTRIONIC – (his-tree-*ON*-ic) Relating to acting as actors. Therefore, when one deliberately acts overly dramatic, she is behaving histrionically– over acting.

HITHER AND YON – (*HITH*-er and *YON*) Hither means *"to or toward a place."* Yon is a truncation of *"beyond"* or *"yonder."* Therefore, hither and yon means *"here and there"*; *"to and fro"*; *"to this place and that place."* In <u>*A Provincial Glossary: with a collection of local proverbs and popular superstitions*</u> (1787), lexicographer Francis Grose (1731 – 1791) wrote: *"Hither and yon, here and there, backwards and forwards."* Hither and yon is an old English expression that has lost steam in the middle of the 20th century.

HITHERTO – (*HITH*-ther-too) An adverb meaning until now, up to this time, up to here, here now. Hither derives from the Old English (West Saxon) *"hinder,"* which was taken from the Proto-Germanic *"hithra,"* which stems from the Gothic *"hidre."* In all cases it means *"here."* In this application, *"to"* means *"now."* Therefore, hitherto means here now, from thos point on. *"Hitherto, we shall pray grace before every meal."*

HITLERGRUS – (*HIT*-ler-groos) Literally, *"Hitler greeting"* was the stiff-armed, straight-hand, Nazi salute. It was also called the *"Deutscher Grus,"* or *"German greeting."* The salute was often accompanied by the laudation *"Seig Heil,"* (Hail victory) or *"Heil Hitler"* (Hail Hitler). The Hitlergrus was originally Mussolini's salute. Early on, Adolf Hitler (1889 – 1945) admired and emulated Benito Mussolini (1883 – 1945) and his Fascist Party. In fact, Hitler stole the stiff-armed salute (Hitlergrus) from Mussolini's Fascists. (Incidentally, the salute was never a part of ancient Roman culture, as Italian fascists claimed.) Nazism is demonic and in many places illegal today. The Hitlergrus is forbidden by law in Germany, Poland, and Slovakia. The salute is illegal in Italy if made in association with the Fascist Party. Canada, France, Switzerland, Sweden, Netherlands, Russia, and the Czech Republic consider the Hitlergrus a form of *"hate speech."* Incidentally: According to former Secretary of State Madeleine Albright (b. 1937) in her book, <u>*Fascism: A Warning*</u> (2018): *"American schoolchildren performed the stiff-armed salute while reciting the 'Pledge of Allegiance' (1890s). Once World War II began, that form of salute was phased out, and civilians were instead encouraged to place the right hand over the heart."*

HITLERIAN BANALITY – (*HIT*-ler-ree-an ban-*NAL*-li-tee) Banal or banality means common place, ordinary, nothing special. Today, Adolf Hitler (1889 –1945) is regarded as evil personified, incarnate. Actually, in many respects he was a pedestrian figure with common prosaic tastes and habits. British Prime Minister Neville Chamberlain (1869 – 1940) observed that: *"Hitler looked entirely undistinguished. You would never notice him in a crowd….He is the commonest little dog I had ever seen."* Austrian by birth, Hitler's ethnic background was probably Moravian (meaning Czech), so he was actually Slavonic (like the Poles and Russians he so hated). Furthermore, evidence indicates that his paternal grandfather was a Jew. As a youngster, Hitler had served as an altarboy and choirboy at his Catholic monastery school. In his youth, Adolf sported a long droopy mustache because of his long triangular nose. He was ordered to trim it during the First World War in order to better accommodate a gas mask. The signature toothbrush mustache thus came into being (under banal circumstances). Hitler was a vegetarian, non-drinker, non-smoker. He feared developing a pot-belie. His suits had padded shoulders and he wore elevated shoes. Hitler wore glasses, but never in public. No one was ever allowed to see Hitler in his underwear, not even his butler. He took speech and acting lessons. He practiced for hours in front of the mirror. He was a decently talented artist. Hitler was afraid of water, the sea. He carried a photo of his mother till the day he died. Hitler's 2 favorite Englishmen were Henry VIII (1491 – 1547), and Oliver Cromwell (1599 – 1658). Hitler's favorite movies: *"Snow White,"* *"King Kong,"* and *"Life of a Bengal Lancer."* His favorite actors: Marlena Dietrich

(1901 – 1992) and Shirley Temple (1928 – 2014). He loved Mickey Mouse cartoons. His favorite song: *"Whose Afraid of the Big, Bad, Wolf."* His favorite books: <u>*Don Quixote,*</u> <u>*Gulliver's Travels,*</u> <u>*Uncle Tom's Cabin.*</u> He loved cowboy novels of the American Wild West. He believed that the Russians fought like Indians. Hitler was <u>Time Magazine's</u> *"Man of the Year"* in 1938. Incidentally: Over half of the Germans who voted for Hitler were women. Women testified that *"As a man he was not attractive. His attraction was his power."* (A typically female reaction.)

HITLERITE – (*HIT*-ler-yt) Idolizer of the fascist dictator Adolf Hitler (1889 – 1945). Adolf Hitler may be the most reviled man in history. This Austrian-born German tyrant plunged the world into World War Two (1939 – 1945). Chances are that the Japanese would not have launched their invasions in Asia, if the world was not also threatened by Hitler's war in Europe. Though there is no evidence that Hitler's hand ever took a life, he was responsible for the deaths of tens-of- millions. A Hitlerite is a confused, angry individual who admires and supports the evil policies of this vile man. In order to qualify as a Hitlerite, one must be a racist, homophobe, xenophobe, anti-Democratic and anti-Socialist. Hitlerites, like Hitler's Nazis are bullies. They seek personal power under a demagogic leader. They dream of authority and fame in an elite, exclusive group. They seek a radical ideology to religiously worship. A member of a white supremacist militia, or an outlaw motorcycle gang presents a good example of a typical Hitlerite.

HITLER'S AMNESTY – (*HIT*-lers *AM*-nes-tee) The fateful day during World War One when Adolf Hitler's (1889 – 1945) life was spared by a compassionate British soldier. *"The Wolf,"* as his comrades called him was on a dangerous message-run, and he was wounded. It was September 28, 1918, in the woods of Marcoing, France. As 29 year old Corporal Hitler turned, a rifle barrel was pointed at his chest. He stared into the eyes of 27 year old British Private Henry Tandy (1891 – 1977) from Coventry. Seconds of indecision passed before Private Tandy lowered his rifle. Corporal Hitler nodded in a gesture of gratitude, then disappeared in the woods. At that moment, World History took a tragic radical turn. As Nazi dictator, Hitler related the story to British Prime Minister Neville Chamberlain (1869 – 1940) at the Munich Conference (1938). Hitler showed Chamberlain a painting by an Italian artist entitled *"The Menin Crossroads."* It depicted British soldiers evacuating their wounded. Hitler claimed that he recognized one of the British soldiers in the painting as the man who saved his life. *"That man came so close to killing me,"* Hitler said, *"I thought I should never see Germany again. Providence saved me from such devilishly accurate fire as those English boys were aiming at us."* Incidentally: Henry Tandy survived as the most decorated British Private of the World War One. After Though: If Tandy would have pulled the trigger, we would never had heard of Adolf Hitler. Scholars agree that without Hitler, there would not have been a Second World War. The Japanese would not have attacked Pearl Harbor is the U.S. was not distracted by events in Europe. There would have been a European war though, with the capitalist West attacking Communist Russia. We can only speculate.

HITLER'S CONCESSION – (*HIT*-lers con-*SESH*-shun) Towards the end of the World War Two, when Germany and Nazism were obviously doomed, Adolph Hitler (1889 – 1945) made a desperate peace offer to the Allies. He would end all hostilities and agree to peace on the following conditions: Germany would not be invaded. No German territory would be surrendered. Germany would evacuate all conquered nations except Denmark and Norway. Denmark and Norway would be incorporated into Germany. World War Two would end. Hitler was ignored.

HITLER'S MISCALCULATION – (*HIT*-lers mis-cal-kew-*LAY*-shun) Adolf Hitler (1889 – 1945) had made several false assumptions. He assumed that Russia would collapse and Britain would sue for peace. Another great miscalculation was declaring war on the U.S.A. after the Pearl Harbor attack by the Japanese (December 7, 1941). Germany's Tripartite Pact with Italy and Japan stated that each nation would come to each other's aid *if attacked.* But America did not attack Japan. Japan attacked America. So Germany was not obliged to declare war against the U.S.A. to help Japan. So why did Hitler declare war on America (December 11, 1941)? Hitler saw America as soft, pleasure-seeking and decadent. The population was mongrelized with Negros, Slavs, and Jews. The U.S. Army was 16th in size, smaller than Belgium's. Hitler thought the U.S. would take years to re-tool and mobilize for war (as during World War One). But there was a more strategic reason for this monumental gamble. Hitler hope Japan would be grateful. If Germany fought Japan's enemy, America, Japan would fight Germany's enemy, Russia. Japan would attack Russia in Siberia, a resumption of the 1938 hostilities. This would force Russia into a 2 front war. It would tie-down millions of Russian troops in Asia that would not be used against Germany in Europe. In fact, Japan made indications to Hitler that they would declare war of Russia, if Germany declared war on America. Hitler, the great deceiver, was deceived by the Japanese. Japan had no desire to resume hostilities with the Russian Red Army. Too, Hitler did not believe that America would initiate hostilities against Germany in Europe, with the Japanese war raging in the Pacific. Having been attacked, America would turn on the Japanese first, Hitler insisted. But Hitler miscalculated. The Americans rapidly mobilized and gave the German war priority over the Japanese conflict (in order to save Britain). Hitler's miscalculation doomed Germany.

HITLER'S PERFORMANCE – (*HIT*-lers per-*FOR*-mans) *"The Performance"* was the euphemistic name given by Geli Raubal (1908 – 1931) to a sexual routine that she was compelled to play with her older uncle Adolf Hitler (1889 – 1945). Since 1925 when Geli was only 17, she lived with Uncle Adolf. They became lovers, or perhaps more accurately, sex partners. Hitler was 19 years her senior. In the *Performance,* both would strip naked. Hitler would lie on the floor, with Geli standing, legs spread, over him. Adolf would examine and manipulate her genitals. As Hitler masturbated, Geli was expected to urinate on him. *"My uncle is a monster,"* Geli once reported to a friend. *"No one can imagine what he expects of me."* After 6 years, Geli grew disgusted with the *Performance* and with Uncle Adolf. But Hitler was obsessed with her. Geli virtually became his prisoner, a sex slave. In 1931, Geli apparently shot herself in the heart. Suicide was the official conclusion, but rumors that Hitler had killed Geli Raubal were never quelled.

HITLER'S SUICIDE – (*HIT*-lers *SOO*-i-syd) As do megamaniacal dictators, Adolf Hitler (1889 – 1945) had conflated his ego with Germany. In his malignantly narcissistic mind he was Germany. Germany was being put to death by the Russians. So it was time for Hitler to meet his death. Hitler had received cyanide tablets from his closest lieutenant Heinrich Himmler (1900 – 1945). But Himmler had attempted to negotiate with the Western Allies behind Hitler's back. Himmler proposed to release a million or more concentration camp prisoners for an armistice with Britain and America. They ignored him, but Hitler did not. Hitler ordered Himmler's arrest on treason. Now Hitler's paranoia flared-up. Perhaps Himmler's cyanide pills were merely sleeping pills, Hitler pondered. Himmler may want to keep Hitler alive, and sell him to the Russians. The Russians would display Hitler naked in a cage, he thought. So Hitler tested the poison pills on his beloved dog blonde. They worked. The dog died. He gave the cyanide to his wife of one day, Eva Braun (1912 – 1945) and took them himself. For good measure, Hitler immediately shot himself in the head with his Walther pistol.

HIV – (aych eye *VEE*) (<u>H</u>uman <u>I</u>mmunodeficiency <u>V</u>irus.) HIV is the virus that caused the disease AIDS (<u>A</u>cquired Immune <u>D</u>eficiency <u>S</u>yndrome.) With AIDS, lymphocytes (white blood cells) are destroyed disabling the body to defend itself against diseases like pneumonias and cancers. HIV is a retrovirus (one that commandeers DNA replication). It is transmitted chiefly through contaminated blood entering the body's bloodstream. This usually occurs through sexual contact, by way of the mother's placenta, or from infected hypodermic needles. HIV is a *"zoontologic virus."* It originated in African monkeys. Perhaps in the Cameroon, a chimpanzee ate a small monkey infected by HIV. The virus was transmitted to humans by bites, or eating infected chimp meat. Once in the human, the virus mutated into HIV.

HIWIS – (*HEE*-wees) An abbreviation of the German term "<u>Hilfs</u><u>W</u>illinger." It means *voluntary assistant*, or *willing to help*. Hiwis were foreigners who served the Nazis as collaborationists, auxiliary police, or actual soldiers. Entire Hiwi SS divisions were recruited from several occupied countries. Ironically, even Slavs, who the Germans considered to be subhuman, served as Hiwis. The Ukrainians and Croatians were the most enthusiastic. Thousands of Russians (prisoners of war) served as well. Little mercy was shown to the Hiwi traitors after Germany's utter defeat.

HNWI – (aych en dub'l-yoo *EYE*) An initialism for <u>H</u>igh <u>N</u>et <u>W</u>orth Individuals. HNWI is another clumsy euphemism for rich people. An euphemism is a word you use, when you can't say the word you mean. Why won't the rich just call themselves rich. Their political sponsor, Donald Trump (b. 1946) has no trouble doing so. Trump boasts of his wealth. Perhaps some wealthy people still have a fragment of conscience and are embarrassed of their over-abundance. At any rate, there is no technical definition of High Net Worth Individuals. HNWIs are generally considered to be people with access to at least a million dollars in cash. The term HNWI is used primarily in high-end retail sales. *"Our aircraft company caters to the HNWI class."*

HOA – (aych oh *AY*) An initialism for <u>H</u>ome <u>O</u>wner's <u>A</u>ssociation. This is an organization in a subdivision, planned community, or condominium building that makes and enforces rules for the properties and residents. HOAs are run by a board of directors who are elected by the residents. The association collects monthly or annual fees to pay for common area maintenance and the upkeep of facilities. Those who purchase property within an HOA's jurisdiction are contractually obliged to abide by the ordinances. Some homeowners association boards can be very restrictive about what members can do with their property. Others give residents much leeway. Those who break the HOA rules will be legally fined, as stipulated in the contract. The HOA constitution governs behavior concerning guests, sanitation, noise, parking, recreation, decoration, whatever affects the community as a whole. The HOA concept leans toward Socialistic <u>Community</u> (<u>Commun</u>ist) living, as compared with capitalistic *"rugged individualism."* Rules are necessary to insure considerate courtesy. After all: *"If men were virtuous, there would be no need for laws at all."* – James Madison (1751 – 1836). Nevertheless, HOA regulations must be as unintrusive as possible. They must respect individual freedom, and not strive for conformity. The HOA board must not become the *"CondoGestapo."*

HOARD – (HORD) (Hoarder, Hoarding, Hoarded) As a noun, a hoard is a stash or cache of hidden, protected money, valuables, precious materials, anything. As a verb, to hoard is to selfishly, greedily accumulate treasure or valuable material with no intention to share. Hoarding resides in the very soul of capitalism. The hoarder's credo is: *"What's in it for me?"* and *"I got mine, to hell with you!"* Hoarders are obsessed with accumulation, and abhor dissemination. Most wealthy people are hoarders. They support the Republican Party so they can escape paying taxes. The vulgar rich hoarders fear nothing more than Socialism, which is government mandated distribution, dissemination, sharing of the wealth. *"Do not hold grain waiting for higher prices when people are hungry."* – Zoroaster (d. 583 BCE). *"And Jesus answered them: 'Whoever has two tunics is to share with him who has none, and whoever has food is to do likewise'."* – Luke 3:11. *"The paradise of the rich is made out of the hell of the poor."* – Victor Hugo (1802 – 1885).

HOARY – (*HOR*-ree) Having grey or white hair due to advanced age. *"His hoary head indicated years of wisdom."*

HOAX – (*HOHKS*) (Hoaxed, Hoaxing, Hoaxster) A canard. Anything intended to deceive or defraud. A practical joke qualifies as a hoax. As a verb, to hoax is to hoodwink. The term *"hoax"* is perhaps a contraction of *"hocus pocus,"* a magical conjuration from the 1630's. In a sense, a hoax is legerdemain, stage magic, smoke-and-mirrors. By 1796, hoax came to mean *"ridicule, deceive with a fabrication."* Therefore, by 1808, *"a cheat or imposter"* came to be called a hoax. Incidentally: Hoax is a favorite word in President Donald Trump's (b. 1946) limited vocabulary. Every Trump illegality, crime, indecency, absurdity that comes to light is branded a hoax by Trump. The Russian electoral interference on his behalf was called a hoax. Trump even called the Coronavirus pandemic a *"Democratic hoax,"* which cost America hundreds-of-thousands of lives. The great Speaker of the House Nancy Pelosi (b. 1940) said: *"Donald Trump is a hoax!"* Indeed, Trump is a cheat and imposter, a hoaxster.

HOBBY – (*HOB*-bee) An activity of interest pursued for pleasure or relaxation and not (usually) as a main occupation. If work is anything you do, when you'd rather be doing something else. Your hobby qualifies as that something else. A hobby is a fun activity, a true pursuit of happiness. Cursed are those who have no hobby. Life for them is a drudgery and bore. The truly blessed are those who can make their hobby into an occupation – a means of making a living. These lucky few never work a day in their lives. That's because a hobby is a labor of love. Most hobbies are creative, aesthetic, crafty, athletic, or accumulative, as in collecting. Reading and learning quality as hobbies. So does charitable service to others – whatever appeals to the heart. In fact, a hobby is a great health regimen for the heart, and for the blood pressure and nerves. A hobby is a natural tranquilizer. The interest [read: *inter-rest*] invested in a hobby is literally *"intering"* or *"entering"* rest – very enter-resting. Indeed, a hobby can be the therapy that preserves one's sanity.

HOBSON'S CHOICE – (*HOB*-sons *CHOYS*) Having to choose between what is offered or nothing. Therefore, a Hobson's choice is no choice at all. That was the choice offered by Thomas Hobson (c. 1544 – 1631) of Cambridge, England. Hobson ran a courier service transporting passengers, letters, and parcels between London and Cambridge. Too, he rented his horses to students. Of course, they always wanted the fastest horses. To prevent his best mounts from becoming overworked, Hobson gave his customers the choice of taking the next horse rested for rental, or no horse at all. In other words, no choice. His rule came to be known as *"Hobson's choice."*

HOBNOB – (*HOB*-nob) To associate on very friendly terms. One may hear, *"He likes to hobnob with celebrities."* Back in 18th century England, hobnob meant *"To drink alternately to each other's health."* Before long, the term came to mean *"sociable drinking"* in general. Though drinking is not mandatory in present day hobnobbing, a little spirits serves as a successful social lubricant.

HO CHI MINH CITY – (hoe chee *MIN SIT*-tee) Vietnamese seaport, largest city in Vietnam (population 8,500,000). Ho Chi Minh City was the capital city of independent South Vietnam. At that time, it was called Saigon. As Saigon, the city served as the American headquarters in the Vietnamese Civil War (1960 – 1975). The enormous black market, fed by unlimited American loot, made Saigon rich, and the most corrupt city in the world. With the departure of the U.S. military in 1973, Saigon lived on borrowed time. With the final victory of Communist North Vietnam (1975), Saigon was renamed Ho Chi Minh City (1976), after the great Vietnamese nationalist leader, Ho Chi Minh (1890 – 1969).

HOCKEY MOM – (*HOK*-ee *MOM*) A right-wing stereotype of an antagonistic young White woman, but bearing a kernel of truth. A hockey mom is a tough conservative Republican-voting lady. She is commonly depicted as driving a SUV (Sports Utility Vehicle), constantly carting her children to hockey practice and games. Observe that hockey is almost an exclusively White sport, far more so than basketball is a Black sport. The dog-whistle is audible. Being overwhelmingly White, hockey is predominantly a suburban activity, the suburbs being predominantly White as well. This parent could have been a *"baseball mom,"* *"football mom,"* or *"basketball mom,"* but she intentionally wasn't. *"Soccer moms"* too are thoroughly White and suburban, but they are not necessarily conservative Republican, or *"Karenesque"* enough to qualify with the alt-right. Hockey is the most aggressive sport, in that fighting has become an accepted, expected part of the game. Hockey mom is a fighter for Republican causes, and a devotee to Trumpism. *"What the difference between a hockey mom and a pit bull? Lipstick."* – Republican Sarah Palin (b. 1964) hockey mom promoter, high school cheerleader, and Vice-Presidential Candidate.

HOCUS-POCUS – (*HOE*-cus *POE*-cus) Trickery or chicanery. The term hocus-pocus is a mystifying jargon used by stage magicians when performing. Hocus-pocus serves as an incantation in conjuration. Actually, hocus-pocus is a sham invocation of Latin that first appeared in the 1620's. The term may have originated in black magic rituals. The English prelate, John Tillotson (1630 – 1694) suggested that hocus-pocus was probably based on a perversion of the sacramental blessing from the Mass: *"Hoc est corpus meum,"* ("This is my body").

HODONYM – (*HOD*-don-nim) (also Odonym) A name for a road or street. *"M-1 that divides Detroit into Eastside - Westside bears the hodonym Woodward Avenue."*

HODGEPODGE – (*HOJ*-poj) A jumbled heterogeneous mixture. A hodgepodge is a muddled miscellany, a conglomeration of odds-and-ends. There is no system, no rhyme-or-reason in a hodgepodge. The term has a culinary origin. It traces back to the early 13th century Old French *"hotchpotch,"* being *"a kind of stew made with goose, wine, herbs and spices."* By the early 15th century, the term was established in English as hodge podge, a generalized mixture.

HOE – (alternately *"Ho."*) In street slang a vulgar, actually obscene appellation for females. *"Hoe"* is a corruption of *"hole,"* alluding to the female orifices (vaginal, anal, oral). This opprobrium originated in the Black ghetto, and was popularized by the nastier, aggressive hip-hop music culture. Hoe is a most demeaning, debasing, degrading indignity because it is dehumanizing, making a woman into a mere aperture in which to ejaculate. To be considered a hoe is worse than being considered a slave, for a hoe is a thing (and a hole is actually a *no thing* or nothing). Anyone inclined to use this vile term should first consider his mother or sister. It would be futile to consider his wife, for she is probably designated as *"his hoe."*

HOE CHECK – Not an inventory of garden tools but prison slang for a gang beating of a new inmate. The attack is a test to see if he is a man or a hoe (pussy, female). Will he stand up for himself or whimper like a bitch? The hoe check will determine the new prisoner's status in the dystopic community.

HOGGING – (*HAWG*-ing) (Hogged) A hog is a fat pig – literally. In order to qualify as a hog, a pig must weigh over 120 pounds. Pigs, especially hogs have a bad reputation of being gluttonous, sloppy, grossly fat pigs. This is unfair, for it is their innate, animalistic nature. It's infinitely more unfair, nasty and cruel to ascribe these traits and mannerism to people. Hogging is a vile, vulgar, vicious indignity practiced by heartless, hateful, inhumane young men against overweight girls. It is a form of sexual abuse. Hogging consists of shaming a fat girl during sex. It involves insulting her body making her feel like a pig. Hogging is common on college campuses, among the pernicious fraternities and sororities. It is often part of the detrimental hazing tradition. For example, a group of frat boys will fuck a fat girl. They will take bets on who can persuade the woman to perform outrageous, disgusting, humiliating sex acts. Because over-weight females display low self-esteem, they often comply, and cooperate in their humiliation. The girl may suffer permanent psychological damage from being hogged, which can result in suicide. This vomitus activity should be illegal, categorized under rape. Likewise, fraternities and sororities should be banned from university campuses. They are detrimental to academia. *"It's okay to be fat. So you're fat. Just be fat and shut up about it."* – Roseanne Barr (b. 1952).

HOG AND HOMONEY – (*HAWG* and *HOM*-mon-nee) An early American pioneer mainstay, consisting of pork boiled with corn. Pork was America's primary domesticated meat before the Civil War (1860's). The river port of Cincinnati was originally called *"Porkopolis."* Cincy was Port Pork. After the Civil War (1861 - 1865), with the westward movement, cowboys, and the great cattle drives, beef had replaced pork as America's meat of choice.

HOGSHEAD – (*HAWGS*-hed) Not a pig's cephalous but a barrel. A hogshead is a large cask holding 63 to 140 gallons of substance.

HOGTIE – (*HAWG*-ty) (Hogtied, Hogtying) A bondage technique that totally incapacitates an individual. Lay the person on their stomach with their legs extended behind them. Tie their ankles together, then tie their wrists together behind their buttocks. Then loop another rope around to tie their ankles and wrists together at a single point. The victim is helpless. Hogtying was an efficient way to gain control of a pig. Too, it was used on cattle for branding.

HOI POLLOI – (*HOY* pol-*LOY*) The masses, the common people. The term hoi polloi is usually preceded by *"the."* This is technically inaccurate, for hoi polloi literally means *"the many"* in Greek. The term is used to suggest what the commonality of people think.

HOLARCHY – (*HOL*-lar-kee) The term suggests *"ruled by the whole."* A holarchy is a nested hierarchy. It is a series of levels of organization, with smaller units functioning within larger units, and even smaller units comprising the small units, all working holistically. A good example is a gear within a gear, within a gear. We can think of the universe holistically, organized in a series of levels of organization in a nested hierarchy or holarchy. At each level, things are both wholes and parts. Atoms are wholes consisting of subatomic parts, themselves wholes at a lower level. Molecules are wholes made up of molecular parts. Likewise cells within tissues, tissues within organs, organs within organisms, organisms within societies, societies within ecosystems, ecosystems within Gaia, Gaia within the solar system, the solar system in the galaxy, and so on – everywhere levels within levels of organization. Furthermore, it has been suggested that at each level of the organization, morphic *energy* fields animate the organisms, providing them their habits and their capacity to organize themselves. In this sense, molecules, stars, galaxies are alive, as are microbes, plants, and animals. Then can we conclude that they are conscious? Do they possess an intelligence?

HOLDING – (*HOL*-ding) The ruling of law in a court case. That part of the judges written opinion that applies the law to the facts of the case and about which can be said *"the case means no more and no less than this."* A holding is the opposite of a *dictum* (judge's opinion).

HOLD MY BEER – (hohld mahy *BEER*) An idiomatic cliché in plebeian parlance that became popular on the internet in the 2010s. The phrase *"hold my beer,"* is pronounced by someone who is about to perform some action, or attempt a stupidly dangerous stunt. On the internet, *"hold my beer"* is used to mock a bad decision, especially one made by a public figure or company: *"Elon Musk and Twitter did what? Hold my beer!"* The *"hold my beer"* cliché is particularly popular among American Southerners when making *"hillbilly"* or *"redneck"* jokes. For instance: *"What is a redneck's last words? 'Hold my beer and watch this'."* Incidentally: *"If your buddy says, 'Hold my beer and watch this,' go ahead and drink it. You probably won't be seeing him the rest of the night."* – Redneck Comedian Jeff Foxworthy (b. 1958).

HOLIDAY – (*HOL*-li-day) A special 24 hour period or day fixed by law or custom in commemoration of some event or in honor of some person. Usual business and labor are suspended on an official holiday. (In very capitalistic England, such a day is called a *"bank holiday"*.) Some holidays may have originated as religious holydays, and are multinational like Easter and Christmas. Other holidays are confined to specific nations like Independence Day on the 4th of July, Thanksgiving Day on the last Thursday in November, or Martin Luther King's (1929 – 1968) birthday on January 15th in the U.S.A. Materialistic, profit-hungry Americans do not observe holidays as seriously as do other nations and cultures. Large capitalist American stores are open on holidays for *"Holiday Sales."* Many covetous Americans spend holidays shopping for *"Holiday Bargains."* Unionized workers will choose to labor on holidays for double-time wages (even on Labor Day). This is not the case the world over. Jamaica for instance has 13 public holidays: *Labor May*

Day; Emancipation Day; Independence Sunday; Independence Monday; National Heroes' Day; Christmas Day; Boxing Day; New Year's Eve; New Year's Day; Ash Wednesday; Good Friday; Easter Sunday; Easter Monday. These days are held sacred. You cannot make a Jamaican work on any of these days, even domestic workers. What accounts for this holiday fervor? *Slavery.* African slaves worked every day from sun-up, to sun-down in the sugarcane fields. They got 3 days off a year: 2 days for Easter, I day for Christmas (then called *"Little Easter"*). The appreciation of holidays for celebration and rest has been passed on through the generation, as it should be.

HOLISTIC – (ho-*LIS*-tic) (Holism) The thesis of wholeness. The whole is greater than the sum of its parts. A holistic approach considers a broad spectrum of options, methods, or cures. The holistic approach concerns the whole issue. The term holistic derives from the Greek *"Holos,"* meaning whole, complete. The "W" was a late 14th century attachment to the word.

HOLISTIC APPROACH – (ho-*LIS*-tic a-*PROACH*) A Progressive educational design that takes into consideration the *"wHOLe"* child, intellectually, but physically and emotionally as well. For example, providing free breakfast for poor children is part of the holistic approach. After all, hungry kids can't learn.

HOLISTIC GRADING – (ho-*LIS*-tic *GRAY*-ding) An aspect of Whole Language instruction which disregards incorrect spelling and grammar for the amount of text written. Holistic grading elevates quantity over quality, mediocrity over accuracy.

HOLLANDAISE SAUCE – (*HOL*-an-days *SAWS*) A thick, creamy yellow gravy-like liquid relish consisting of egg yolks, butter, lemon juice, and seasoning.

HOLLYWOOD CODE – (*HOL*-lee-wood *COHD*) A doctor's term for a *"pretend resuscitation."* In other words, the medical staff is going through the motions of saving a patient who is beyond saving. The Hollywood code is usually performed for the benefit of the patient's loved ones.

HOLLYWOOD SIGNBOARD – (*HOL*-lee-wood *SYN*-bord) The most grotesque, monotonous landmark in the world. It is a series of 9 giant white letters, 45 feet tall, 350 feet long, that spell out "HOLLYWOOD." This monumental monstrosity is erected on Mount Lee, in the Santa Monica Mountains, overlooking Hollywood/Los Angeles, California. This trashy monument was initially 31% uglier, for it originally read: HOLLYWOODLAND, when constructed in 1923. It was created as a temporary advertising stunt for a local realestate development. Unfortunately, the unimaginative billboard remained. The Hollywood signboard is a cringe-worthy example of vulgar capitalist tastelessness. It has all the charm of a junkyard. It is a blasphemous defilement of the natural environment. Pedestrian plebeians see it as a cultural icon, whereas aesthetes see it as a cultural eyesore. The Hollywood signboard is a fitting symbol for a shallow community. This tinsel landmark accurately reflects *"Tinsel Town."* Incidentally: Hollywood is a magnet for beautiful young people aspiring to stardom. Conversely, Hollywood has the most handsome bartenders, and the most gorgeous waitresses in the world.

HOLMIUM – (*HOL*-mee-um) (Ho) The name derives from the Modern Latin *Holmia,* the name for Stockholm. The 67 protons in its nucleus give holmium its atomic number. Holmium is a malleable silver-white metallic element of the rare-earth group. Holmium's compounds are highly magnetic. Holmium is used to make electrical devices and in scientific research.

HOLOCAUST – (*HOL*-lo-caust) Literally a cataclysm by fire. Specifically the Nazi German extermination of millions in death camps, particularly the Jews (*Judaicide*). The Holocaust was a program of ethnic cleansing on an industrial scale. Nothing in history closely compares to the bureaucratic murder of the Nazi/German Holocaust. The concentration camps were designed with maximal efficiency to exterminate human beings, to commit homicide as if performing insecticide. It is difficult for sane people to come to terms with the fact that human beings did this to other human beings. The closest resemblance we have today of the Holocaust is the slaughterhouses of Chicago's Southside. The gruesome sight of cows and pigs hooked on conveyor belts, hanging upside down, carcasses slit open, may provide the emotional jolt. William Blake (1757 – 1827) had written: *"Cruelty has a human heart."* Humans other than Germans have hearts that can turn cruel – hellishly, demonically cruel. *"Well, there are six million of us [Jews] in Germany. What is Hitler going to do? Kill us all?"* From the movie *"Ship of Fools,"* (1965).

HOLOCAUST COST – (*HOL*-lo-caust *CAUST*) The incalculable price that humanity and civilization paid for the genocidal Nazi German exterminations (1933 – 1945). Military deaths are not counted as holocaust victims. The high-side of the death count stands at: 6 million Jews; 5.7 million Soviet citizens; 3.3 million Poles; 600,000 Serbs; 500,000 Romani (Gypsies); 25,000 Slovenes; and an assortment of other victims. Think of the millions and millions of years of education, study, learning, talent, practice, and experience that died with these people. How many potential Albert Einsteins (1879 – 1955); Mohandas Gandhis (1869 – 1948), Jonas Salks (1914 – 1995), Ernest Hemingways (1899 -1961) perished in muddy pits or gas chambers. How many Nobel Laureates were incinerated in the ovens? It's a waste that's seldom considered when we calculate the cost of the Second World War (1939 – 1945). The concentration camps practiced murder on an industrial scale, like Henry Ford's (1863 – 1947) assembly line, that Adolf Hitler (1889 – 1945) admired so much. Most of the extermination factories were built in Poland. The Nazi Germans sought to kill every educated Pole. As *"untermenschen"* (sub-humans) the surviving Slavs were to be worked-to-death, as beasts of burden. Consider where we might be today if those millions of minds, and those thousands of geniuses had not perished. Perhaps cancer, like smallpox, would merely be a historic nightmare. New energy sources might have arrested global warming and violent climate change. Agricultural breakthroughs in food production might have provided abundance for all. Scientific, artistic, musical, architectural, and literary contributions might have ignited a Neo-Renaissance. We can only fanaticize on our loss. *"Of all sad words of tongue and pen the saddest are these, what might have been."* – John Greenleaf Whittier (1807 – 1892).

HOLODOMOR – (ho-lo-*DOE*-mor) Ukrainian for *"Death by hunger."* The Holodomor was the Ukrainian Holocaust, the genocidal famine of 1932 – 1933. The death count is uncertain, but about 7,500,000 Ukrainians may have perished. The starvation campaign was intentionally orchestrated by Russian Dictator Joseph Stalin (1878 – 1953). Many Ukrainians did not support the Bolshevik Revolution of 1917. A strong nationalist independence movement had swept through the Ukraine. Collectivization of private farms did not appeal to the Ukrainians. They resisted and failed to cooperate. So Stalin punished the region with the Holodomor. Grain, vegetables, livestock, all food was confiscated by the Russian government. Those who hid food were executed. Many who cooperated starved to death. Incidents of cannibalism occurred. The Holodomor was a man-made cataclysm. Ukrainian bitterness toward Russia led some Ukrainians to join the German army during World War Two, (even though Nazism was anti-Slavic). We can expect more conflict between Russia and Ukrainia in the future. The present day dictator of Russia, Vladimir Putin (b. 1952) intends to re-incorporate the Ukraine into Russia. *"The death of a single person is pathos. The death of a million persons is statistics."* – Joseph Stalin. Update: Under Dictator Vladimir Putin (b. 1952), Russia invaded the Ukraine in February, 2022. In February 2024, the wars still rages.

HOLOPHRASE – (*HO*-lo-frays) A single word that functions as a complete sentence. For example: *"Go"* or *"Stop!"* *"Yes"* or *"No!"*

HOLOPHYTIC – (ho-lo-*FY*-tic) (Holophytes) Sentient organisms like plants that do not eat other sentient organisms. Holophytes synthesize their nutrition from inorganic molecules like water and minerals in the soil. Too, holophytic organisms photosynthesize sunlight into sugar (plants). Holophytes are not cannibalistic. Holophytes are not killers.

HOLY – (*HO*-lee) Sacred, Sacrosanct, Divine, Heavenly. Holy has the same root in English as *"whole"* or *"holistic."* Both mean united. So to be holy or whole is to be one with the Divine, in atonement or *"at-one-ment"* with God.

HOLY FOOLS – (*HO*-lee *FOOLS*) Mystics, religious men in Czarist Russia who had healing and psychic powers. They were not fools at all! They were honored, feared, and consulted. Holy fools were fortune tellers. They had license to speak their minds, even to the Czars. The renowned Able, and famous Grigori Rasputin (1869 – 1916) would fall into this category.

HOLY GRAIL – (*HO*-lee *GRAYL*) The cup from which Jesus drank at the Last Supper. It had to have been a humble piece of pottery, rather than a precious bejeweled chalice. After all, Jesus was poor. The Holy Grail is thought to be endowed with supernatural powers. It has become the subject of legend and a lifelong quest of adventurers. Alternately, it has been suggested that the Holy Grail is a euphemism for the womb of Mary Magdalene, that carried the love- child of Jesus.

HOLY INJUSTICE – (*HO*-lee in-*JUS*-tis) Actually, holy injustice is justifiable retributive justice. It is judging those who commit the same crime differently, on the basis of their character and history. A greedy capitalist is judged differently than a generous Socialist. In a court of law, this is called mitigating, extenuating circumstances. According to Dante Alighieri (1265 – 1321) in <u>The Inferno</u> (c. 1300) *"Divine Justice weights the sins of the warm-hearted, and the sins of the cold-blooded in different scales."*

HOLY SITES – (*HOH*-lee *SYTS*) Hallowed locations; divine destinations; sacred sanctuaries. A holy site is a spiritually powerful place conducive to devotion. Churches, Temples, Mosques, Pagodas, and Synagogues are considered to be holy sites. Actually, God, the creator of all is omnipresent. So everyplace is holy. It is naïve to believe that God can only be found and encountered in a specified man-made building. Prayers can be answered and miracles can occur anywhere, everywhere. Jesus said: *"Where two or three are gathered in my name, there I am among them"* (Matthew 18:20). Therefore, being in church is a state of mind, an emotion of the heart. In fact, Jesus said: *"The Kingdom of God is within you"* (Luke 17:21). He did not say it is in the church. Certainly, those who struggle with faith, or are weak in imagination may need a special place in order to feel divinely engaged. Those more spiritually enlightened can commune with the Supreme outside the church. Indeed, God gave us holy sites of worship, but also the discernment how and when to use them. *"I like the silent church before the service begins, better than any preaching."* – Ralph Waldo Emerson (1803 – 1882), Transcendental Philosopher. *"Some people observe the Sabbath by going to church. I observe the Sabbath by staying at home."* – Emily Dickenson (1830 - 1886).

HOLY SPIRIT – (*HO*-lee *SPEER*-rit) According to Catholic dogma, the third manifestation of God in the Holy Trinity. The Holy Spirit (or Ghost) is that part of God that dwells in us all. It is the still small voice that intuitively guides us in the holy direction, even when we choose not to listen. Perhaps the Holy Spirit is the eternal soul, that provides the life-force to all sentient creatures. In *"The Gospel of Thomas,"* Jesus said: *"Whoever blasphemes against the Father, it will be forgiven him. And whoever blasphemes against the Son, it will be forgiven him. But whoever blasphemes against the Holy Spirit, it will not be forgiven him, neither on earth nor in heaven."*

HOLY SPIRITS – (*HO*-lee *SPEER*-rits) Blessed alcoholic spirits, namely vodka. In both Russian and Polish, vodka is pronounced *"VOOD*-ka,"* and means *"little water."* If ever there was a holy water, it has to be vodka. That's because vodka saved Russia and Eastern Europe for Christianity. In 987 CE, Grand Prince Vladimir the Great (c. 958 – 1015) of Russia was searching for a religion to unite the people of his fledgling country. Vladimir was initially impressed with Islam. However he was informed that the Russians would have to forsake pork (sausages) and vodka. *"Drinking [vodka] is the joy of all Rus,"* Vladimir declared. Instead, Vladimir forsook Islam and adopted the Eastern Orthodox rendition of Christianity. Imagine the turmoil today if Russia, Ukraine, Bulgaria, Belarus, Serbia, and the Balkan States were Muslim! Vodka should be as prominent in the Christian ritual as wine.

HOME – (*HOHM*) The place where we anchor our roots. Home is both a location and an emotion. It is a state of mind. Home offers a sense of belonging. It is (or was) the abode of our loved-ones. Home is where our children grow up. Affectionate memories and ghosts reside at home. At home, we feel the security of the familiar [read: *family-iliar*]. Poet Robert Frost (1874 – 1963) said: *"Home is the place where, when you have to go there, they have to take you in."* At home, we can be our true selves, and not have to play our adopted roles. Rarely at home do we have to ask permission. Home is a place where we are allowed to make mistakes, without retaliation. Be it ever so humble, home offers peace, security, comfort. Poet Maya Angelou (1928 – 2014) had written that *"The ache for home in all of us, the safe place where we go as we are and not be questioned."* *"Home is the dearest spot on earth, and it should be the center, but not the boundary, of the affection."* – Founder of the Christian Science Religion, Mary Baker Eddy (1821 – 1910).

HOMEFIELD ADVANTAGE – (*HOHM*-feeld ad-*VANT*-tidj) Having the benefit of a familiar environment. After all, *"There is no place like home,"* (1823) – John Howard Payne (1791 – 1852). The homefield advantage was apparent on the battlefield of the American Civil War (1961 – 1865). For almost all of the war, the Confederates or Southerners defended their homeland. They knew every hill, mountain, valley, forest, swamp, creek, and river. That's a major reason why the war lasted four long years. But the term, *"homefield advantage,"* is most commonly applied to sports. Gamblers know that even the worst teams are allotted a few extra points just for playing before a friendly, hopeful audience. Most upsets occur when the underdog team is playing at home. Why is this so? Legally, all fields and courts, home or away, are the same length. The goalposts and nets are the same width, the baskets are the same height. There is very little difference among sporting venues. So what is the homefield advantage? It is spiritual. Spiritualists, mystics, priests, and increasingly, scientists are saying that there is power in wishful thinking [read: *prayer*]. When thousands of people, together, in one confined space are wishing, hoping, praying for a specific outcome, tremendous positive psychic energy, vibration is released. The spiritual holds command over the material, because the material is merely coagulated spirit. The fan's spiritual power is physically manifested as crowd noise. Indeed, there is a homefield advantage, but it's not the stadium or arena. *"Block that kick!"*

HOMELESSNESS – (*HOHM*-less-ness) Being without shelter, at the mercy of the elements – both natural and human. Homelessness is a tragedy, atrocity, obscenity of capitalist greed and indifference. It is the result of joblessness and carelessness. Homelessness is the extreme end of poverty. Over 41 million Americans live in poverty in 2018, 18.5 million in dire conditions. The ultimate losers in the capitalist competition, those rendered to the gutter are the over 550,000 homeless. (That's 15,000 more people than reside in Tucson, Arizona.) These are the residents of dumpsters, cardboard boxes, water conduits, and under bridges. Many are addicted, many are retarded, and many are just children. This alone is damning evidence of the failure of capitalism. In *The Gospel of Thomas,* Jesus said: *"I marvel how this great wealth has taken residence in this poverty."* Under Socialism, unemployment, poverty, homelessness, and great wealth are illegal. Jesus further stated in *The Gospel of Thomas*: *"Foxes have their holes and birds their nests. But the Son of Man has no place to lay his head down and to rest."* Incidentally: Five days before Christmas, 2019, the Department of Housing and Urban Development (HUD) announced that homelessness in the U.S.A. had increased by 2.7% to 567,715 victims nationally. Therefore, 14,885 more people are shelterless than in 2018. That's as if the population of Albuquerque, or Milwaukee, or Wyoming were cast into the street.

HOMEOPATHY – (hohm-ee-*OP*-path-thee) The science of natural remedies, using the pharmacopeia of galenicals or healing plants. Holistic remedies, natural drugs in minute doses are administered in homeopathy.

HOMEOSTASIS – (hoh-mee-oh-*STAY*-sis) (Homeostatic) Balance, equilibrium, symmetry, harmony. Homeostasis is the tendency of a system, especially the physiological system of higher animals, owing to the coordinated response of its parts to any situation or stimulus that would tend to disturb its normal condition or function. Nature is predicated on homeostasis. Weather conditions are governed by the need to find balance. Dis-ease illness and wellness are forms of homeostasis.

HOME RUN – (hohm *RUN*) The easiest was to score in the game of baseball, by hitting the ball into the stands in fair territory. A home run is an athletic success. Therefore, the term was adopted out of the baseball lexicon, into general parlance. If someone does anything great, particularly in a competitive context, it is said that he hit a *"home run."* An alternative way of stating this is that: *"He hit it out of the park."* *"Vice-President Kamala Harris hit a home run in the September 10 Presidential Debate."* *"We hoped he'd just survive, but he surprised us all by hitting it out of the park."*

HOME SCHOOLING – (*HOHM SKOOL*-ling) The movement to educate children outside the public or formal school setting. Home schoolers object to the public schools as too Liberal or too atheistic. It is farcical to think that parents can provide the same quality education as a professional team of scholars. If this was the case, schools would not have been invented. Nevertheless, home schooling is fundamental to many Fundamentalists. The Father of Fundamentalism, Fr. Martin Luther (1483 – 1546) preached: *"If the government can compel such citizens as are fit for military service…how much more has it a right to compel the people to send their children to school."* Home schooling should be illegal. Education is the most vital responsibility of society, the bulwark of civilization. Over 2,500 years ago, Greek Philosopher Aristotle (384 – 322 BCE) insisted that: *"There should be legislation about education and that it should be conducted on a public system."* *"My father was an angry and impatient teacher and flung the reading book at my head."* – William Butler Yeats (1865 – 1939).

HOME SECURITY – (*HOHM* sec-*CURE*-ri-tee) A frantic, sometimes paranoid attempt to keep one's dwelling safe from intruders. The home security industry cleared over $47 billion dollars of profit in 2020. The devices it installs include doors, locks, alarms, lights, cameras, and motion detectors, in order to burglarproof your home. There are no guarantees. Professional burglars become more sophisticated along with the technology. It's a cat and mouse game. Like the insurance industry, the home security industry preys on people's fears. They try to convince you that eventually you'll be robber, raped, kidnapped, tortured, or murdered if you don't do business with them. If fear doesn't work, perhaps guilt will. Your wife and children will be raped and murdered. The home security industry manipulates emotion to the point of extortion. The phenomenal growth in the home security industry reflects the fear of a society suffering from distributive injustice. The cause of the disparity of wealth is capitalism. As the army of the poor and desperate grows larger, so does its strength and threat. The prosperous fear the *"barbarians at the gate."* They naively depend on home security to protect them. Under capitalism, the situation will not improve, but rather exacerbate. Fear will turn to terror. The only real security is economic equity through Socialism. The poor cannot sleep because they are hungry. The rich cannot sleep because they fear those who are hungry.

HOMEWORK – (*HOHM*-werk) Schoolwork expected to be performed at home, rather than at school where it belongs. Neither children, teachers, nor parents appreciate homework, or any unnecessary work. Homework is mandated by administrators as a sign of scholastic rigor, and a symbol of accomplishment. Mandatory homework is a counterproductive waste of time. Students hate to do homework. Parents hate to have to help with homework. Teachers hate to have to check homework, which becomes their homework. If adults object to bringing their work home, why should children? If school children were unionized, homework would be abolished.

HOMEY – (*HOH*-mee) As an adjective, homey means cozy, homelike, comfortably familiar [read: *"family-iliar"*], friendly. As a noun, homey refers to a friendly, brotherly figure. Homey is a slang appellation of the ghetto or hood (neighbor<u>hood</u>). The term derives from the Afro-American argot. Homey is the new designation for a *"soul brother."* A homey is a *"hoodmate."*

HOMINIDS – (*HOM*-mi-nids) (Hominoids) Proto-humans. Hominids were our ancient man-like progenitors, far down the evolutionary scale, in the distant past. Hominids are our Neanderthal and Denisovan ancestors, and all the man- like creatures down the evolutionary line.

HOMME D' AFFAIRES – (awm da *FER*) French for a businessman.

HOMME DE LETTRES – (awm day let-*RAY*) French for a writer, a man of letters. HOMME D' ESPIRIT – (awm de es-*SPREET*) French for an intellectual.

HOMME DU MONDE – (awm do *MUND*) French for a man of the world, a cosmopolitan fellow.

HOMOBLIVIOUS – (hoh-moh-*BLIV*-vee-uhs) One who is unable to recognize a homosexual when one is encountered. He or she is oblivious or unaware. Genuinely gay individuals usually transmit signals, either consciously or unconsciously that they are psycho-emotionally associated with the same sex. Gay guys come across as feminine (girly), whereas gay gals come across as masculine (butch). This is natural. Furthermore, fewer gay individuals today hide their gender preference status. Therefore, it would take a parochial, provincial, naïve person to be homoblivious today. Incidentally: The opposite oh homoblivious is *"gaydar,"* being keen to recognize a homosexual, even one in the closet.

HOMO ERECTUS – (*HO*-mo er-*REC*-tus) (*"Upright man"*) An early human ancestor of the Pleistocene epoch (c. 1.9 to 250,000 years ago). Homo erectus succeeded his ancestor, Homo Habilis. Homo erectus walked erect, freeing his hands to manipulate his environment. She had a well-evolved postcranial skeleton, but with a small brain, low forehead, and protruding face. Homo erectus was a scavenger, hunter and gatherer. He had mastered the art of making primitive stone tools, like the hand ax. Stone tools became increasing sophisticated. Homo erectus was able to chop wood, kill and butcher animals for food. In a revolutionary evolutionary leap forward, Homo erectus was our first hominid ancestor to use fire. She therefore cooked their food. These ancestors contributed to our present day existence.

HOMO FLORESIENSIS – (*HO*-mo flor-res-see-*EN*-sis) A new human ancestor, Flores Man, nicknamed the *"Hobbit."* The fossilized bones, including the skull of this new humanoid species was found on the Indonesian Island of Flores in 2014. It lived from 60,000 to 100,000 years ago during the Pleistocene era. Primitive stone tools were found with the skeletal remains. Except for its diminutive stature, Homo floresiensis would be recognized as an *"unattractive"* human today. It stood only 3 feet, 7 inches, which accounts for the nickname, *"Hobbit."*

HOMOGRAPH – (*HO*-mo-graff) A word spelled the same but etymologically unrelated. A homograph is a word of the same written form as another but of different meaning and usually origin. Homographs may or may not be pronounced the same way. For example: *bare* (naked), and *bear* (the animal); *lead* (to conduct), and *lead* (the metal); *sow* (female pig), and *sow* (plant seeds). A Caveat: Don't confuse a *homograph* with a *homonym* like *pitcher* (of water), and *pitcher* (in baseball). Too, don't confuse a *homograph* with a *homophone* like *flower* and *flour.*

HOMO HABILIS – (*HO*-mo *HA*-ba-lees) (*"Handy man"*) An early human ancestor. Homo habilis is an extinct species of upright East African hominid having some advanced human-like characteristics (c. 2.4 to 1.5 million years ago). Homo habilis was the first hominid to make stone tools, which explains his handiness. It was the hand of Homo habilis that drove the subsequent evolution of the brain. *"Handy Man's"* hand became the cutting edge of the human mind.

HOMOIOTHERMIC – (ho-moy-yo-*THERM*-al) (Homoiothermic, Homeotherm) A warm-blooded creature like mammals, including man. A warm-blooded homeotherm must maintain a constant body temperature, despite the environment. All mammals generate their own body heat, and are not dependent on the sun's warmth, as are coldblooded reptiles. Homo sapiens are homoiothermic. Having to regulate the metabolism internally, warm-blooded creatures require 10 times the food energy as do coldblooded reptiles. Warm- blooded does not necessarily translate into warmhearted. There are pitiless, coldblooded individuals, lacking empathy and compassion. They will certainly meet their Karmic Justice. *"For God weighs the sins of the coldblooded and the sins of the warm-hearted in different scales."* – Dante Alighieri (c. 1265 – 1321) *Inferno* (c. 1314).

HOMOLOGICAL – (ho-mo-*LOJ*-ji-cal) (Homologic) Sometimes called autological. Refers to words whose meaning characterizes or applies to itself. For example, the word *polysyllabic* is itself a polysyllabic word. A contradiction in terms is an oxymoron. *Oxy* means sharp, *moron* means stupid. So the word oxymoron is homological.

HOMO LUZONENSIS – (*HO*-mo loo-zon-*NEN*-sis) A new human ancestor. The fossilized bones of a new humanoid species was found in a cave on the Philippine Island of Luzon (April, 2019). This *"apeman"* was more man than ape. The bones and teeth of 3 individuals date back to the late Pleistocene era, as recent as 50,000 years ago. This was the time when Homo sapiens were migrating to Europe. Homo luzonensis had curved fingers and toes, indicating that it still climbed trees. This species of hominin didn't make the evolutionary cut. It had gone extinct.

HOMONOIA – (ho-mo-*NOY*-ah) The concept of order, unity, being together of one mind, a union of hearts. Homonoia was the spirit, the ideology behind the conquests of Alexander the Great (356 – 323 BCE) which would, however, require the imposition of Hellenic culture on Asians. Today Homonoia embraces agape (a-*GOP*-pay), universal love, an idealistic state of the brotherhood of man. It is a state of goodness for which to strive.

HOMONYMS – (HOM-mo-nims) Words that are spelled the same, pronounced the same, but have different meanings. For example, a *pitcher* of water, and a baseball *pitcher*. Also *right* (being correct), and *right,* (opposite of left). A Caveat: Don't confuse homonym with homograph like *sow* (female pig), and *sow* (plant seeds). Too, don't confuse a homonym with a homophone like *flower,* and *flour.*

HOMOPHOBIA – (ho-mo-*FO*-bee-a) (Homophobiac) Literally the conscious fear of gays, accompanied by the subconscious fear of exposing one's own latent homosexual tendencies. Indeed, blatant homophobia is a clumsy overcompensation to masquerade one's own homosexual feelings. Religion has exacerbated homophobia by declaring homosexuality a sin [read: *evil in the eyes of God*]. *"Thou shalt not be gay,"* does not appear in the Ten Commandments. Furthermore, the gentle Jesus never made reference to homosexuality. Jesus castigated the hypocritical Pharisees, the greedy money changers [read: *capitalists*], the selfish rich, but never mentioned homosexuals. But the *"Vicar of Christ"* did. It was disclosed in May, 2018, that the compassionate Socialist Pope Francis I (b. 1936) said to Juan Carlos Cruz, a gay man: *"God made you like this. God made you gay and your sexuality doesn't matter. God loves you like this. The Pope loves you like this, and you should love yourself, and not worry about what people say."* God does not sin. God does not make sin. God made some people gay, but not sinful, therefore being gay is not a sin, according to Pope Francis,

"The Vicar of Christ." "There was nothing abnormal about it when homosexuality was the norm." – Marcel Proust (1871 – 1922).

HOMOPHONES – (*HO*-mo-fones) Words that sound alike but are different in meaning, and spelling. Examples of homophones are *male* and *mail, tale* and *tail, discreet* and *discrete, flower* and *flour, wright* and *right*. A Caveat: Don't confuse a <u>homophone</u> with a <u>homonym</u> like *pitcher* (of water), and *pitcher* (in baseball). Too, don't confuse a <u>homophone</u> with a <u>homograph</u> like *sow* (female pig) and *sow* (plant seeds).

HOMO SAPIEN – (*HO*-mo *SAY*-pee-en) Literally *"wise man"* in Latin, with *homo* meaning *man,* and *sapien* meaning *wise*. Homo sapiens are human beings, present day humankind. On the ever changing line of evolution, Homo sapien are where we are at this time. As animals, we are sometimes depicted according to the Linnaean classification system as Homo sapiens. Homo sapiens evolved from more primitive primate hominids in Africa circa 300,000 years ago. Our primal ancestors migrated out of Africa to populate the planet. The closest living animal to Homo sapien today is the chimpanzee. Perhaps 96% to 98% of genes are common to man and chimp. (*"Well I'll be a monkey's uncle!"*) Homo sapiens are bipedal primates with a large brain capacity averaging 1400 cubic centimeters. This provides us with high intelligence, though at times, questionable wisdom and judgement. Homo sapiens depend on language and writing to communicate, fire for technology, and have mastered the manufacture of sophisticated tools. Homo sapiens are divided into racial groups which are merely superficial differences precipitated by environmental diversity. Homo sapiens occupy the apex of the food chain, masters of Planet Earth. It is our moral imperative to serve as stewards of all creatures, great and small, animals and plants dependent on us, and at our mercy.

HOMOSEXUALITY – (ho-mo-sex-you-*AL*-it-tee) (Homosexual) Being gay. Sexual desire for members of one's own sex. For long, homosexuality was regarded as an aberration and abomination. Today it is regarded as an alternative to heterosexuality. Being gay is not a choice. It is a biologically inherited disposition, like blue or brown eyes. In any case, one's sexual preference, like one's spiritual beliefs, is nobody's business, especially the government's. *"The most vital right is the right to love and be loved."* – Anarchist Emma Goldman (1869 – 1940). Ms. Goldman went on to say: *"It is a tragedy, I feel, that people of a different sexual type are caught in a world which shows so little understanding for homosexuals and is so crassly indifferent to the various gradations and variations of gender and their great significance in life."* Metaphysically speaking, perhaps homosexual impulses or a gay preference can be attributed to Karmic residue – leftover emotions from a past life. Perhaps an individual actually was a member of the opposite sex in a former existence, with several gratifying love affairs. Perhaps this may contribute or accounts for one's homosexuality today. Fundamentalist Christians and Muslims still consider homosexuality to be a sin, an offense against God. In some Islamic societies, homosexuality is punishable by death. This is a time contingent law in the Koran and Bible. After all, homosexuality does not produce soldiers. This is perilous in nomadic cultures that are perpetually trespassing and at war. Of course, all sacred books are statically time contingent. In truth, *"Heaven is large and affords space for all modes of love and fortitude."* – Transcendental Philosopher Ralph Waldo Emerson (1802 – 1882). Incidentally: Special attention and appreciation must be granted to Democratic Presidential Candidate (2020) Mayor Pete Buttigieg (b. 1982). His personal intelligence, experience, and dignity has done much to dispel and disarm homophobia. Mayor Pete is responsible for eliminating much of the fear, stereotypes, bewilderment, and embarrassment of being gay. A better representative for the gay community could not be found. *"It doesn't matter who you love or how you love but that you love."* – Rod McKuen (1933 – 2015). *"Choose to love whomsoever thou wilt: all else will follow."* – St Augustine (354 – 430 CE).

HONCHO – (*HON*-choh) An assertive leader, an authoritarian chief, "a head honcho." The term honcho, like Poncho sounds Mexican. It's not. Honcho, like Honshu is of Japanese origin. It derives from *"hancho"* meaning *"group leader"* in Japanese. *"Han"* means a *"squad"* or *"corps."* *"Cho"* means *"chief"* or *"head."* The term honcho entered AmerEnglish in 1947, from American soldiers in occupation of Japan (like the author's dad, Joseph E. Pasieka, Jr.).

HONE – (*HOHN*) A whetstone of fine grit and compact texture, for sharpening knives, swords, razors, all blades and cutting tools. As a verb, to hone is to sharpen, literally and figuratively. One may hone a sickle, or hone one's writing skills. The term hone derives from the Old English (West Saxon) *"han,"* meaning *"stone, rock."* A hone as a whetstone for sharpening blades and tools emerged in Middle English, in the early 14th century. According to the <u>Century Dictionary</u>: *"A hone differs from a whetstone in being of finer grit and more compact texture."*

HONEY – (*HUN*-nee) Sweet viscid fluid produced by bees, the only food in the world that never spoils. Honey is the only food consumed by humans that is made by insects. The ancient Egyptians were first to domesticate the honeybee. In fact, an edible jar of honey over 6,000 years old was discovered in Egypt. Amazingly, honey will last for a million years in a hermetically sealed jar, but the jar won't. Honey has elixir qualities yet to be discovered. Honey is one of the best cough medicines. It will readily break up mucus and phlegm. When pure honey is applied to burns, it will prevent infection and stop bleeding. Depending on the flowers the bees service, some honey can be poisonous or hallucinogenic. Bees are busy and must work hard for their honey. Bees must work 2 million flowers to produce 1 pound of honey. On average, a typical honeybee produces about 1/12 of a teaspoon of honey in a lifetime. In other words, it takes about 12 bees to produce 1 teaspoon of honey. (Depending on the species, a honeybee may live from 8 weeks to 5 years.) Incidentally: Honeybees kill more people in the Western World than any other venomous creature. Many people are allergic to bee venom.

HONEY HOLE – (*HUN*-nee *HOHL*) The reference is to a fortuitous discovery of a beehive, often encased in the hollow of a tree, or some other hole. The hole, of course, is ladened with sweet honey. It is a honey hole. The term has been expanded to refer to any lucky find, such as a great fishing spot, a source of valuable resources, some other treasure. Furthermore, the term honey hole is applied in the vulgar vernacular to refer to a vagina. Securing this honey hole may also qualify as a sweet find.

HONEYMOON – (*HUN*-nee-moon) The initial days of blissful harmony (perhaps 30?) after the wedding. A time for romance and exploration, especially if the courtship was brief, and the couple had not cohabited. Often, the newlyweds get away to some romantic location to enjoy each other in privacy. The term *"honeymoon"* entered English least 480 years ago in the 1540s as *"hony moone,"* but may be even older. Honey refers to the sweetness of the new relationship. Moon, referring to month, also refers to the estimation of how long the sweetness will last. It takes the moon one month to change its aspects. Likewise, it was predicted that the bliss and harmony too would phase out. Actually, it takes about a month for the couple to discover *"other sides"* of each other, *"the dark side of the moon"* that was hidden during courtship. The honeymoon is over when the mundane and stressful aspects of life intrude. The task of organizing a household, and making a living begins to overshadow the romance. Fantasy gives way to reality. Adjustments toward compromise and toleration must take place. The sexy negligee is traded in for the stodgy pajamas. The relationship becomes like a pair of old shoes: with time, some luster has worn off, but they became more comfortable. A Caveat: Young couples need not despair. It is normal for the honeymoon to end. The phases of the marriage like the phases of the moon will forever be changing, waxing and waning.

HONEYPOT – (*HUN*-nee-pot) Any type of bribe, a sweet temptation. A honeypot can be a person or thing that acts as a lure, bait, decoy in a trap to seduce or scam. A honeypot may be money, property, gifts, a job, or sex – most anything that will move a person to some action. In the vulgar vernacular, honeypot refers to the vagina. That's because it is common to used prostitutes as honeypots to frame or blackmail unsuspecting gentlemen. Intelligent Services, especially the Russian KGB has been successful using female and male agents as prostitutes (honeypots) to turn foreigners into spies. A lurid honeypot scheme was devised by Charles Kushner (b. 1954), father of Jared Kushner (b. 1981), Donald Trump's (b. 1946) corrupt son-in-law. The entire Kushner family is corrupt money gluttons. Millionaire Charles Kushner was being investigated by the FBI for tax fraud. His brother Murray Kushner (b. 1951) and wife were cooperating with the FBI. So Charles hired a honeypot prostitute to seduce his brother and have the sex video-taped. The porn flick was sent to Charles' sister- in-law, Murray's wife. Unimaginable perfidy! Charles went to prison. That's Jared Kushner's debauched dad. Well, the fruit does not fall far from the tree. Incidentally: The equally filthy President Donald Trump (b. 1946) had pardoned Charles Kushner.

HONKY – (*HON*-key) (also Hunky or Hunkey) Originally, a contemptuous, insulting slur used to refer to a person of Hungarian descent. The pejorative term was expanded to include all East European immigrants of Slavic ethnicity. A honky was typically an unskilled or semi-skilled manual laborer. By 1967, honky was adopted by the African-American vernacular to refer to all white people.

HONORED TRAITORS – (*HON*-nerd *TRAY*-ters) Confederate rebels, turncoats, secessionists celebrated and esteemed in bronze and stone. Honored traitors were treasonous politicians, generals, soldiers, planters, and treacherous Southern businessmen who rebelled against their country, made war against the United States killing Americans. Nevertheless, they have been memorialized with statues and monuments. Simply outrageous! Where is our statue to General Santa Anna; Field Marshal von Hindenburg; General Rommel; or Admiral Yamamoto? Oh, they were enemies? So were General Lee; General Pickett; and General Stonewall Jackson. Worse than the foreigners, the Confederates were fellow countrymen, brothers. Their crime was vile fratricide. Rather than honored, the Confederates could have been hanged. They should have been hanged, according to all the European leaders. These seditious separatists and insurrectionists tried to dis-unite the United States, just so they could maintain their profitable slavocracy. They committed treason, a capital crime. They provoked a rebellion that cost about 700,000 American lives and maimed tens-of-thousands more. An entire generation of young men was wiped out, at their command. The honored traitors have blood on their hands. They were the ultimate terrorists. Rather than be eulogized, they must be criticized. Rather than be dignified, they must be denounced. Statues of Confederate insurrectionists and slave-drivers appeared after Reconstruction, during the early Jim Crow Era (after 1880's). The horror of the war was fading, and mythological nostalgia setting in among Southern whites. The shock and shame was giving way to myth and hate. Monuments to Confederate slavocrats served as a warning to uppity blacks, who forgot their place. Finally, in 2020, a *"New Reconstruction"* movement had dawned. The intimidating, demeaning statues that honored traitors are tumbling down. Incidentally: European leaders were astonished that the Confederate traitors were not hanged. If the Civil War would have occurred in Britain, Robert E. Lee's (1807 - 1870), Jefferson Davis' (1808 - 1889), Stonewall Jackson's (1824 - 1863) statues would have been their own heads-on-a-pike, *"proudly"* displayed on London Bridge!

HONOR KILLING – (*ON*-nor *KIL*-ling) The execution of female relatives who have shamed the family. The main reason for this horrendous custom is fornication before marriage or adultery. The murderers are usually the husband, or father and brothers. This primitive tradition is condoned in primitive parts of the world. About 5,000 women (mostly Muslims) are sacrificed annually in honor killings.

HOOD – (*HOOD*) A Black slang truncation of the term *neighborhood.* The hood refers to the ghetto, the neglected, poverty stricken inner city, populated primarily by jobless African-American citizens. The hood is not the safest location in the city. Capitalist carelessness, parsimony, and racism has embittered many of the residents. The underground economy [read: *"illegal enterprises"* or *"crime"*] flourishes in the hood. Denial of gainful unemployment has robbed the residents of any other choices. The hood can be transformed into a livable, lovely neighbor-hood, with a transformation from capitalism to Socialism.

HOODOO – (*HOO*-doo) African-American voodoo. A form of magic practiced by the descendants of African slaves in the United States. Hoodoo is a melding of West and Central African religious beliefs with animism, shamanism, and European Christianity, particularly Catholicism. The center of hoodoo in America is New Orleans, Louisiana. A person who is hexed through hoodoo is said to have been *"hoodooed."*

HOOKEM AND BOOKEM – (*HOOK*-em and *BOOK*-em) Police slang for handcuffing a suspect and transferring him to the police station for incarceration processing.

HOOK OR CROOK – (*HOOK* or *KROOK*) *"By hook or by crook"* is an old English phrase meaning *"by any means necessary"* today. The phrase first appeared in John Wyclif's (c. 1328 – 1384) <u>Controversial Tracts</u> (1380). The definitive origin of the phrase is obscure. A plausible explanation concerns the gleaning of firewood. Custom had it that peasants were allowed to collect firewood from the common land. They were forbidden to chop down the trees, but they were allowed to pull down branches they could reach from the ground with a "bill<u>hook</u>" (pruning tool) or "shepherd's <u>crook</u>." So they were allowed to take what they could *"hook or crook."*

HOOK-UP – (*HOOK* up) A one-night stand. A daring sexual encounter with a virtual stranger. The hook-up has become a fad on American college campuses. Fueled with alcohol, a young couple retreat from the bar to the bed for an adventurous engagement in recreational sex. They may know no more than each other's names. There is no expectation of a follow-up meeting. Incidentally: For decades, sexual license had been denied in China by Maoist oppression. But today, Chinese youth are discovering sex stores and nightclubs. The hook-up in China is called a "419." 4 = For, 1 = One, 9 = Night, *"For one night."*

HOOP – (*HOOP*) (Hooped, Hooping) Not a reference to a basketball rim, but to an anal rim. Hoop is prison slang for hiding contraband in one's body cavity, more specifically up one's ass. Weapons like sharp shanks, or drugs are transported and carried in prison up the ass.

HOOSEGOW – (*HOOS*-gow) An Americanism for jail. Hoosegow is a Western U.S. term dating back to 1911. It is a mispronunciation of the Mexican Spanish *"juzgao,"* meaning a court or tribunal, which is related to *"juzgar,"* meaning to judge.

HOOSIERS – (*HOO*-shurs) Indianans or citizens of the State of Indiana. The etymology of the term is shrouded in mystery. Hoosier originated in the 1820's. It may have derived from the English Cumberland term *"hoozer,"* meaning unusually large. That term was in use by Ohio River boatmen. Alternately, *"hoosier!"* may have been a greeting like *"howdy!"* used by Kentucky homesteaders as they moved into Indiana. The word Hoosier first appeared in print on January 1, 1833 in the <u>Indianapolis Journal</u>. It was used in a poem, *"The Hoosiers Nest,"* by John Finely. The author had penned the poem back in 1830. The term Hoosier also denoted a country bumpkin. Although Indiana is primarily rural, and covered with corn, the pejorative connotation does not accurately apply today.

HOOVER – (*WHO*-ver) (Hoovered, Hoovering) To sweep clean with a vacuum cleaner. To suck-up the dirt, grime, any filth that may be corrupting the house. A Hoover is used to clean house. The stock market on Wall Street, specifically the D.O.W. (<u>D</u>isparity <u>O</u>f <u>W</u>ealth index) needs to be hoovered. That's what was needed in 1929. The Republicans controlled the government with Herbert Hoover as President. They presided over the stock market crash, the Wall Street collapse, the economic crumble. The Great Republican Depression commenced. In the next election, the American people cleaned house. Hoover and the Republicans were swept from power. It took an economic calamity to rid us of the Republicans. We need another good Hoovering today, on Wall Street and in Washington. A collapse of the economy is an acceptable and worthy price to pay to save the U.S. Government, Democracy, and the Soul of America. Like Hoover, Trump must be Hoovered out of the White House. Update: In 2020, Trump was evicted, hoovered out.

HOOVER DAM – (*WHO*-ver *DAM*) (Originally Boulder Dam.) An enormous concreate gravity-arch dam located on the Colorado River, between Arizona and Nevada, one of the engineering marvels of the modern world. Hoover Dam is 727 feet high and 1,180 feet wide. It creates America's largest reservoir, Lake Mead. Construction began during the Great Republican Depression in 1931, commencing operations in 1936. Cavernous diversion tunnels had to be drilled into the mountain side to divert the flow of the Colorado River before construction of the dam. Over 1,500,000 cubic yards of material had to be excavated and transported. Over 3,250,000 cubic yards of concrete was poured into the dam. As the concrete cured, it generated heat. It would have taken 120 years to dry and harden. So 582 miles of cooling pipes were laid into the concrete. 112 men died constructing the dam, mostly in the diversion tunnels from carbon monoxide (CO) poisoning, due to vehicles and poor ventilation. The dam cost $49 million (1931) dollars, which would amount to $995 million today (2024). Incidentally: Hoover Dam is a Socialist Project, in that it was funded by the Federal Government, and is owned and operated by the Government, for the good of the people. It has not been privatized. Thousands were employed on the dam in those depression years. Water, electricity, and a recreational lake were provided to the people. Hoover Dam made Las Vegas livable. Incidentally: According to the documentary, *"America: The Story of Us,"* *"Hoover Dam was the 1930s equivalent of putting a man on the moon."* If people vanished from the planet, after about 2,000 years, Hoover Dam would be the last engineered structure on Earth to collapse.

HOPE – (HOHP) (Hopeful, Hopeless) Confident expectancy and bearing an optimistic attitude based in faith. Hope is trusting God to act in His good timing for your greater good. However, hope is faith, with a tinge of doubt. That's why hope is for gamblers, but faith is for believers. Nevertheless, faithful believers do hope. Hope is being confident in a better future, a favorable outcome. Hope comes in a strong and weak rendition. Strong hope is courageous confidence in a victorious outcome. Weak hope is a gambler's wish as in: *"I hope I win this time."* Weak hope is impregnated with uncertainty. *"I may not win, again."* Strong hope is spiritually-based, predicated on God's love. Strong hope is expressed in patient prayer and faith in God's good timing. Positive visualization, expectation, and intentionality will set in motion the *Law of Attraction* to bring one's dreams to pass. Indeed, the self-fulfilling prophecy is predicated on hope. Psychiatrist Erik H. Erikson (1902 – 1994) maintained that: *"Hope is both the earliest and most indispensable virtue inherent in the state of being alive.... If life is to be sustained hope must remain, even where confidence is wounded, trust impaired."*

HOPLOPHOBIA – (hop-lo-*FO*-be-a) (Hoplophobiac) Phobic fear of guns, firearms. It is not unreasonable to have a normal, healthy fear of guns. But hoplophobia is neurotically extraordinary beyond reasonability. A hoplophobiac will panic in the presence of firearms. Such a person requires professional psychological help.

HOPS – (*HOPS*) (Hopped) (*Humulus lupulus*) Not a rock-n-roll dance party from the 1950s but a herbaceous perennial flowering plant that grows as a vine. Hops is a member of the *"Cannabaceae"* family which includes cannabis, the marijuana plant. Hops have been used medicinally as an anti-bacteriostat. However, hops is most useful in the brewing of beer. Only the flowers of the female plant are used to flavor beer. It provides a bitterness which favorably balances the sweetness of the malt. Furthermore, the anti-bacterial quality of hops prevents early spoilage of beer. Hops gives beer its distinctive taste. Eliminate the hops, and you would not recognize the beverage as being beer. Hopless beer can be traced back to the ancient Egyptians and Babylonians. Back then, beer was favored with honey, dates, various fruits, berries, and spices. Today, we would not consider these drinks to be beer. The hops plant is indigenous to Northern Europe. Before the introduction of hops, a herbal mixture called *"gruit,"* (dandelion, marigold, horehound, burdock root, and ground ivy) was used to bitter beer. The first documented hop cultivation was in 736 CE, in the Hallertau region of Germany. The first documented account of hops being used in brewing beer was by St. Hildegard (c. 1098 – 1179) of Bingen, Germany. Hopped beer was introduced late into England, about 1400 from Holland. Today, you'll see the tall pillars of hop vines climbing up heavy string in Kent, Sussex, and southeastern England. *"The hop for his profit I thus do exalt, It strengtheneth drink and it flavored malt; And being well-brewed long kept it will last, and drawing abide, if ye draw not too fast."* – Thomas Tusser (c. 1524 – 1580) in *Five Hundred Points of Good Husbandry* (1557).

HORIZONTAL EQUITY – (hor-ri-*ZON*-tal *EK*-kwit-tee) Actual equality. Horizontal equity is treating equal people equally. This is fair only if all the people are in fact equal. Horizontal equity is sameness.

It is unfair if the people are unequal. For example, horizontal equity would match a high school with a professional baseball team. They both play baseball, after all. Both would be treated equally, but the game would be far from fair.

HORIZONTAL MERGER – (hor-ri-*ZON*-tal *MER*-jer) A combination of two or more companies producing the same product. Such mergers eliminate competition and deprive the consumer of choice. Horizontal mergers result in mega- corporations that corner the market. They are monopolistic and illegal, and should not be allowed to combine. But well-funded lobbyists in Congress manage to magically skirt the law. In capitalism, money merges.

HORN/ANTLER – (*HORN ANT*-ler) Defensive headgear worn by quadrupedal ruminates, ungulates. Horns and antlers (along with hoofs, hair, nails, claws, feathers and bills) are made of the protein keratin. But the horn and the antler are not identical. A horn is one of the bony, *permanent, hollow* paired growths, often curved and pointed, projecting from the upper part of the head, on cattle, sheep, goats, buffalo, or antelopes. An antler, on the other hand, is a *solid,* deciduous (*temporary*) horn, branching from both sides of the head, of mammals in the deer family. Deer, moose, caribou, and elk shed their antlers annually, and re-grow a fresh pair. The rhinoceros horn and narwhal's tusk (horn) are made of tightly matted hair.

HORNBOOK – (*HORN*-book) A single printed page containing the alphabet, syllables, a prayer, and other simple words, tacked to a wooden paddle and covered with a thin transparent layer of cow's horn (the laminate of its day). The hornbook was durable and used in colonial times as the beginner's first book or preprimer in school.

HORNET/WASP – (HOR-net *WOSP*) Flying insects of the Vespidae (wasp) family. There are over 100,000 known species of wasps. Hornets are the largest sub- species of wasps. Wasps are long and thin with dangling legs. They are brightly colored. Hornets are a larger, more rounded and robust than wasps. Hornets are black and white with dashes of color. Hornets are social creatures living in huge nests. Wasps can be social or solitary. Both feed on sweet fruit but can be predatory, hunting small insects. Hornets lay eggs in their nests. Wasps lay eggs parasitically, in the bodies of captive insects. Both wasps and hornets will sting, several times. The hornet is more aggressive and possesses a venom in the sting that can kill a human. The *"Murder Hornet"* or *Giant Asian Hornet* is over 2.8 inches long, the world's biggest wasp. It is very dangerous.

HORNSWOGGLE – (*HOWRN*-swog-uhl) An early Americanism (1829) meaning to swindle, cheat, hoodwink, and a hoax.

HORNY – (*HAWR*-nee) (Horniness) Lustful, randy, sexually excited, hot-to-trot. Originally, in the 14th century, horny simply meant *"made of horn."* The colloquial meaning, sexually aroused, perhaps traces back to 1863. It derives from the 18th century slang expression, *"to have the horn,"* meaning to display an erection. However, horny came to be applied to lascivious ladies as well. *"Men have only two emotions: hungry and horny. So if you see him without an erection, make him a sandwich."* – Adi Da (1939 – 2008).

HOROSCOPE – (*HOR*-ruhs-skohp) An ancient diagram of the heavens, showing the relative position of planets and the signs of the zodiac, for use in calculating births, and foretelling events in a person's life. The study and interpretation of horoscopes is astrology. Horoscope interpreters are called astrologers. *"A child is born on that day, and at that hour when the celestial rays are in mathematical harmony with his individual Karma. His horoscope is a challenging portrait, revealing his unalterable past and its probable future result. But the natal chart can be rightly interpreted only by men of intuitive wisdom. These are few."* – Sri Yukteswar Giri (1855 – 1936).

HORRENDOMA – (hor-ren-*DOH*-ma) A doctor's term for an especially bad or complicated medical condition. Horrendoma is a contrived term, a blend of *"horrendous"* and *"oma,"* the suffix for tumors.

HORRIPILATION – (hor-rip-pi-*LAY*-shun) Goose bumps. A temporary roughness of the skin caused by the erection of the papillae (hair roots), induced by cold or fear. Under those two conditions our hair bristles producing the bumps at the roots of the hair follicle. Goose bumps or horripilation is a vestigial remain of our pre-human fury past. In cold, the puffed-up fur trapped heat. In fear, the puffed-up fur provided a defensive coat against laceration. We still say: *"He made my hair bristle."* The fur will stand up on the back of a dog's or wolf's neck when in attack mode. Incidentally: The Latin name for horripilation is *"cutis anserine"* meaning goose flesh.

HORSE – (*HORS*) A large mammal, solid-hoofed, herbivorous quadruped, domesticated since prehistoric times. Today, horses are bred for carrying and pulling loads, plowing fields, riding and racing. Horses evolved in North America, but died-out in the late Pleistocene Era (c. 11,000 years ago). Luckily, enough crossed the Bering Land Bridge into Siberia, where they flourished on the Eurasian Steppe. Mongol nomads introduced the horse to the Arabs. Arabic Moors from North Africa brought their smaller, fast horses to Spain. The Spanish brought the horse back to North America. Spanish horses broke free and proliferated in the American West as the mustang. These were the animals the Plains Indians trained in their *"Horse Culture."* The horse tripled the distance a man could travel in a day. No animal has served man more laboriously than the horse.

HORSE CULTURE – (*HORS CUL*-cher) The semi-nomadic Indian tribes of the Great Plains: the Sioux, Cheyenne, Kiowa, Navaho, Arapaho, Comanche, Apache, Shoshone. Like the Mongols of Asia, and the Cossack tribes of the Eurasian Steppe, the Plains Indians mastered the horse, around which they built their culture. They lived in portable teepees and hunted the buffalo in horseback, following the herd. The dividing line between the Plains Indian Territory and White Civilization was the 95th meridian that began at Fort Snelling in Minnesota. The Comanche were considered the best horsemen. They were so belligerent that they prevented much Mexican colonization of Texas, saving the territory for the Americans. The Navaho were the first Plains Tribe to attack white settlers on horseback. This was the start of 60 years of warfare with the mobile Plains Indians. About 15,000 Indians and 12,000 Americans were killed through the 6 decades. The Comanche killed the most Americans and were perhaps the most vicious. The Cheyenne probably suffered more than any other tribe. The Horse Culture kept the Plains Indians free and free-wheeling longer than any other Amerindian tribes.

HORSE MEAT– (*HORS* meet) Cheval is French for horse. *"Chevaline"* is horse meat. The flesh of the horse is perfectly edible. It is red meat like beef but darker, with coarser grain and yellow fat. It is a healthy form of protein. Chevaline provides almost as much omega-3 fatty acids as farmed-raised salmon and twice as much iron as beef streak. Unlike the pig, the horse is a very clean animal. Chevaline is much safer to eat than pork. *"Hippophagy"* (hip-*POF*-fuh-jee) is the ancient practice of eating horses. (*"Hippo"* means horse and *"phagy"* means eat in Greek.) Early on, Jewish religious scholars had prohibited the eating of horse meat. In 732 C.E., Pope Gregory III (d. 741) declared the consumption of horse flesh as an *"impure and detestable pagan practice."* During the Middle Ages, the horse became a symbol of royalty, aristocracy, and power. Where would the armored knight be without his horse? At that time, butcher's guilds discontinued the sale of horse meat. They wanted to highlight the distinction between professional meat cutters and the *"knackers"* who broke-down old horses as cheap food for the poor. By the 16th century, hippophagy became a capital offense in France. This changed with the Enlightenment. The Age of Reason found no reason for not eating horses. As urban population swelled, so did the demand for cheap meat. Eating old horses became more common throughout Europe. It was a different story in America. The forests provided plentiful game. There was no shortage of fresh meat. Too, horses were too valuable to be sacrificed for food. Americans had developed a special emotional relationship with the horse. As elsewhere, the horse plowed our fields, transported us about, fought in our wars, but also helped us win the West. The horse became our companion, like the dog. Horses served as last resort food in emergencies like famine, wars, and natural disasters. At the conclusion of the Battle of Stalingrad (August 1942 – February 1943) the defeated German army ate their frozen horses raw. In America, during the rationing of World War Two (1941 – 1945), many citizens are convinced that they were sold horse meat for beef. Horse or chevaline can be ground and sneaked into sausages. The only prohibition against eating chevaline is traditional. Incidentally: President Donald Trump (b. 1946) wanted to cut the budget of the Bureau of Land Management. Trump insisted that instead of feeding wild horses, why don't we feed on wild horses? Trump tried but failed to sell the wild mustang herds to Canadian and Mexican slaughterhouses. *"I'm so hungry I can eat a horse!"*

HORSEPOWER – (*HORS*-pa-wer) (hp) A unit of measurement of power, or the rate at which work is done. There are many different types of horsepower relating to many different applications. The term was coined by Scottish mechanical engineer James Watt (1736 – 1819), who improved the steam engine. Horses were the primary beasts of burden before steam. They were essential in mills and coalmines. Watt determined that a horse in a mill could turn a 12 foot radius mill wheel 144 times in one hour. Watt knew that a *foot-pound* is a unit of work or energy equal to the work done by a force of one pound moving a distance of one foot. Watt made an arbitrary estimation that horsepower is 33,000 foot-pounds of work in one minute. In a coalmine, one horse, exerting 1 horsepower can raise 330 pounds of coal 100 feet in one minute; or 33 pounds of coal 1,000 feet in one minute; or 1,000 pounds of coal 33 feet in one minute. To Watt, any combination of feet and pounds applied, as long as the product is 33,000 foot-pounds per minute to have a measurement of horsepower. Today a horsepower is considered to be equivalent to 550 foot- pounds per second. Too, the average mid-sized car has about 170 to 190 horsepower.

HORSESHOE SEATING – (*HORS*-shoo *SEE*-ting) An efficient, intelligent method of classroom management. Arrange students' desks in a horseshoe, open end facing the instructor. When lecturing, stand outside the horseshoe. This position subliminally endows the speaker with authority. Step within the horseshoe to create rapport, becoming part of the audience. This encourages questions and discussion. Place a chair within the horseshoe to become one with the audience, an equal. Step back out again for authoritative control. The instructor can control the audience and direct the lesson by stepping in and out of the horseshoe.

HORS D' OEUVRE – (or-*DERVS*) French for appetizing bite-sized munchies of spicy meat, spreads, cheese, fish, creams, or caviar on crackers, served at cocktail parties.

HORTATORY – (*HOR*-ta-tor-ree) Tending to exhort, encourage, urging some course of action. A hortatory person is always trying to do something. *"He gave a hortatory speech to the crew before the project commenced."*

HORTICULTURE – (*HAWR*-tee-kuhl-cher) (Horticultural, Horticulturalist) The science and art of cultivating plants. Horticulture includes the raising of a garden, orchard, or plant nursery. Fruits, flowers, vegetables, and house plants are produced by horticulturalists. Horticulture is below the scale of agriculture. Whereas farming is a large scale commercial enterprise, horticulture is usually a modest endeavor, often a hobby. The term horticulture derives from the Latin *"hortus,"* meaning *"garden."* It entered English in the 1670s.

HOSANNA – (hoh-*ZAN*-uh) An interjection, an exclamation, originally an appeal to God for deliverance. Later, the term was used in praise of God or Christ. *"So they took branches of palm trees and went out to meet him [Jesus], crying 'Hosanna! Blessed is he who comes in the name of the Lord, even the King of Israel!'"* – John 12:13. The term hosanna entered Old English (West Saxon) via the Bible as *"osanna."* It derived from Latin, which took it from Greek, which took it from the Hebrew *"hoshi'ah-nna,"* meaning *"save, we pray."*

HOSPITALITY – (hos-pit-*TEL*-lit-tee) (Hospitable, Hospitably) The warm, friendly reception and treatment of guests and strangers. Hospitality is the application of the Golden Rule: *"Do unto others, as you would have others do unto you."* The term hospitality derives from the Latin word *"hospitalitem,"* meaning *"friendliness to guests."* Some cultures take hospitality more seriously than others. The mountain tribes of Albania consider hospitality a code of honor. They are known for their deadly blood feuds. However, if an enemy is in their house, he is treated as a prince. The moment he leaves the host's property, he can be killed. On February 23, 2022, Russia invaded the Ukraine in a naked land-grab. The Ukrainian's cousins, the Polish displayed remarkable hospitality by welcoming over 2 million refugees into their country. *"Do not neglect to show hospitality to strangers, for thereby some have entertained angels unawares."* – Hebrews 13:2.

HOSPITALITY WORKERS – (hos-pit-*TEL*-lit-tee *WER*-kers) The 8 million people who labor in the service industries. Hospitality workers are employed in hotels, bars, restaurants, casinos, sports venues, ski lodges, vacation sites, camps, recreation parks, theme parks, and transportation. Hospitality workers feed, lodge, and help to keep us entertained. They are usually low-paid, un- benefited, and unprotected for they are often not unionized. They often earn minimal wage or lower, depending on tips to supplement their pay. Tips are a capitalist ploy, gratuities – nay, charity – which enables the employer to pay peasant or slave wages. Hospitality workers may be the most exploited, oppressed workers in America. The problem is capitalism. The solution is Socialism.

HOSTAGE – (*HOS*-tij) An innocent person taken prisoner and held as human collateral for the fulfillment of demanded conditions, promises, material, or money. Hostage taking is a cowardly, desperate, immoral activity. Criminals and terrorists take hostages as negotiation chips. Hostage taking is effective only if the opposing side cares about the wellbeing of those taken captive.

HOSTAGED WEALTH – (*HOS*-tij'd *WELTH*) Abundant money and property belonging to criminal nations or governments, frozen in the banks of foreign nations. The outlaw leaders abroad cannot access this wealth. It is mostly locked away in foreign banks. Today, (February 2024) the U.S. Biden Government is caught on the horns of a dilemma. Our Ukrainian ally desperately needs more American weapons to defend itself from the invading Russians. But Speaker of the House, Republican Mike Johnson (b. 1972) refuses (on Donald Trump's (b. 1946) orders) to bring the aid bill to the floor for a vote. Like Trump and the MAGAmaniacals, Johnson is pro-Putin, pro-Russian (because Trump demands it). But there is a solution. Through Executive Order, President Joe Biden (b. 1942) can ship all the frozen wealth belonging to Putin and his oligarchs to the Ukrainians. Too, he can demand, persuade, or bribe other nations to do likewise. With that wealth, the Ukrainians can obtain weapons. Simple? Yes! But *"Sleepy Joe"* won't do it. That would be un-capitalistic! To non-Socialist Democrats like Biden, capitalism is as sacred as democracy. This sets a dangerous precedent. Perhaps in the future, some nation might freeze and appropriate the wealth of our corporations abroad. Too, Biden does not want to fight with Wall Street (the banks), that want to keep holding the Russian money, and make money on that money. So there you have it. The fascist Trumpublicans, and the capitalist Democrats will be responsible for the Ukraine's demise. All the gains of the Soviet Cold War Period (1945 - 1991) lay in the balance.

HOSTILE ARCHITECTURE – (*HOS*-ty-ul *AHR*-ki-tek-cher) *"Hideous"* architecture is age old. But *"Hostile"* architecture is something shamefully new. The term hostile architecture entered the dictionary in 2023. To be hostile is to be aggressive, inhospitable, mean-spirited. A hostile building, public station or park is targeting the homeless poor. With hostile architecture *civil engineering* gives way to *social engineering*. These places have built-in impediments, obstacles, obstructions to make the painful lives of the homeless more agonizing. Hostile architecture is designed to keep out people with no place else to go. It involves a variety of construction deterrents to trespassing. Benches have measured armrests and low walls are dotted with spikes to prevent sitting, resting, sleeping. Roofed floor area is jammed with huge flowerpots and art works to occupy potential sleeping space. Dark corners are fitted with angular concrete surfaces that would redirect urine back on the urinator. Security cameras, gates, fences, sprinklers, even loud music is used to make public and private spaces *"homeless proof."* This war against the homeless is blaming the victim. We do not solve the homeless problem with nasty capitalism – *"I got mine, to hell with you!"* Poverty is a <u>social</u> problem that will be solved only through <u>Socialism</u>. Like it or not, *"You are your brother's keeper."* – Genesis 4:9. *"Truly I say to you, as you did it to one of the least of these my brothers, you did it unto me."* – Jesus in Matthew 25:40.

HOSTILE TAKEOVER – (*HOS*-ty-ul *TAYK*-oh-ver) The seizure of a business, company, corporation that is not approved or welcomed by the management, stockholders, or proprietors. This is accomplished through secret stock purchases and other nefarious maneuvers. Hostile takeovers are common practice in the *"dog-eat-dog"* world of capitalist covetousness.

HOSTLER – (*HOS*-tler) One who tends to the horses, especially at an inn. Later, hostler came to apply to one who services buses, cabs, trains, or other vehicles after their regular service. The vehicle had replaced the horse.

HOT – (*HOT*) (Hotter, Hottest, Hotly) Anything high in temperature, having and giving-off heat. Hot substances are highly energetic – heat energy. The molecules in their structures are vibrating in a hot solid, dancing as it melts into a liquid, and bouncing frantically as it heats into a vapor or gas (like steam). However, what is hot cannot remain hot forever. As energy dissipates through natural entropy (decay), hot material gradually cools until it goes cold. This includes the stars as our sun.

HOT – (*HOT*) An adjective attributed to curvaceous, sexy ladies. *"Damn, you're hot!"* is a compliment that every woman desires, though many pretend to resent. Such a statement does not represent a lack of respect, or etiquette in this present generation. The term *"hot"* used to indicate *"a lustful sexual desire for an attractive woman"* goes back 600 years! Your great-great-grandfather, at least 20 generations past, thought that the chick in the next village, or in the other hut was hot. That's because research indicates that *"hot"* in a sexual context goes back to the 15th century. Incidentally: The actress Mary Anderson (1918 – 2014) was hot. She once asked the director Alfred Hitchcock (1899 – 1980): *"What is my best side, Mr. Hitchcock?"* Alfred replied: *"You're sitting on it, my dear."*

HOTEI – (ho-*TY*) (c. 915 CE) (also Budai) The popularly depicted rotund Buddha, sometimes called the *"Laughing Buddha."* Actually the Buddha Hotei was a Chinese saint who provided for poor children, reminiscent of Santa Clause. The Buddha Hotei appeared about 1,444 years after the Buddha Prince Gautama Siddhartha (c. 563 – c. 483 BCE). Buddha Hotei walked the streets of China during the T'ang Dynasty. He carried a huge bag filled with sweets and treats for poor children. Hotei solicited 1 penny from the merchants to buy his wares. Incidentally: There have been many Buddhas (*Enlightened Ones*) throughout history. His physique, bag of goodies, and love for children makes Hotei the Chinese Santa Claus. Furthermore, if he were a Roman Catholic, he would have been canonized a saint.

HOT MIC – (hot MYHK) Not a horny Irishman, but to be unknowingly caught on microphone. A hot mic is a microphone that is actively recording or broadcasting, especially if it captures a controversial comment or conversation that the speaker intended to be private. Politicians are particularly susceptible to being burned by a hot mic. In an unguarded moment, thinking they are off the air, they may say what they really believe, not what they tell the citizenry. On May 23, 2010, at the passage of the *"Obama Care"* healthcare Reform Bill, Vice-President Joe Biden (b. 1942) said to President Obama (b. 1961): *"This is a big fucking deal!"* It was caught on a hot mic. On September 18, 2012, Republican Presidential candidate Mitt Romney (b. 1947) was addressing a private group of millionaire donors. Romney was caught on a hot mic castigating the poor. *"All right, there are 47% who are with him [Barack Obama], who are dependent on the government, who believe that they are victims, who believe that the government has a responsibility to care for them, who believe that they are entitled to healthcare, to food, to housing, to you- name-it. And these are people who pay no taxes."* This hot mic gaff did not help Romney's electoral fortune. On October 7, 2016, Republican Presidential candidate Donald Trump (b. 1946) spoke of his lust to grab, fondle, and kiss women on a hot mic. Trump bragged about grabbing ladies by the pussy. His mocking conversation was with the *"Access Hollywood"* TV host Billy Bush (b. 1971). In 2021, Israeli President Benjamin Netanyahu (b. 1949) didn't know that the mic was hot when he joked: *"America is easy to turn"* [meaning to manipulate]. America gives Israel $4 billion dollars in cash annually, with no strings attached. In 2023, brash Republican Presidential candidate Vivek Ramaswamy (b. 1985) didn't know that he entered the men's room wearing a hot mic. The people attending the meeting could hear Vivek taking a pee. He's luck that he did not need to take a dump.

HOT PEPPERS – (hot *PEP*-pers) A large variety of small fruit grown on a bushy plant, native to the semi-tropical and tropical regions of the Western Hemisphere. Hot peppers were first cultivated thousands of years ago in Central America and Mexico. Hot peppers are also called chili peppers. They are red, orange, yellow, and green. Hot peppers burn the mouth to various degrees, from discomfort to 911. They are essential in a variety of food dishes. The chemical ingredient *capsaicin* puts the fire in hot peppers. The more capsaicin the hotter the pepper. Hot, rainy environments produce the hottest pepper. Being a fruit, the mother plant intends the peppers to be eaten by animals in order to disperse the seeds. But the stomach acids of mammals will damage the pepper seeds. Birds do not have this damaging stomach acid. So the plant developed capsaicin in the fruit to make the peppers hot. This deters the mammals from eating the peppers. The peppers do not burn the birds, so they do eat the fruit and disperse the seeds. Too, the capsaicin serves as an insect repellent for the plant. So the peppers became hot as a defense mechanism. The peppers can burn humans as well, but people are not deterred. There is no thermal heat in a pepper. The hot pepper tricks the brain into thinking your mouth is on fire. It's all about that chemical compound capsaicin. Capsaicin binds to the pain receptors on our nerves called TRPV1. These are the heat receptors that, when burned, send warning signals to the brain. Capsaicin causes TRPV1 to send the same emergency signals. So you react like your mouth is burning. The brain puts the body into cooling mode, to put out the fire. The face turns red and you start to sweat. Eyes tear up and nose runs. The burning runs down the esophagus into the stomach. The brain may order the development of water-filled blisters to the perceived burn areas. This is to begin the healing of damaged tissue. The vomit reaction may be triggered. A pepper-burn victim may fall into anaphylactic shock. Consider that the hottest pepper like the *Carolina Reaper* is 200 times hotter than a fiery *Jalapeno*! The capsaicin of the hottest peppers will melt through rubber gloves and blister the hands. Too, they will make the air chokingly unbreathable! A bite of this fruit can knock a grown man to his knees. And it can kill, as from a heart attack. Why do people put themselves through this torture? In response to the pain, in compensation for the suffering, the brain releases endorphins and dopamine – the feel good neurotransmitters. This produces a euphoric high feeling. Research reveals that people who tend to be daredevils, adrenaline junkies also tend to enjoy very hot chili peppers, because risky activities also produce the euphoric high. Incidentally: The TRPV1 heat receptors on the nerves in the mouth can become increasingly desensitized as one eats more pepper. A tolerance can be built up. Furthermore, milk, cream, all dairy products contain the substance *casein* which attracts capsaicin molecules, pulling them off the pain receptors and dissolving them. So in a hot pepper crisis, drink milk. Footnote: To demonstrate how chemically hot some peppers can be, consider that farmers in India plant pepper bushes as hedges to keep out wild elephants. Too, the Indian army stocks capsaicin hand grenades. *"But God said, 'You shall not eat of the fruit…in the midst of the garden, neither shall you touch it, lest you die.'"* – Genesis 3:3.

HOTROCKS COOKING – (*HOT-rocks KOOK*-king) Hotrocks in this case is not a reference to testicles, burning with lust. It is an ingenious technique of cooking by Neolithic (New Stoneage) people. It is still used by primitive (technologically simple) people today. These people did not or do not have metal implements like cooking pots. Their unfired clay pots and waterproof baskets could not be placed directly on the fire. Therefore, the pot or basket are filled with water. Meat and vegetables are added. Stones or rocks are heated in a fire. Then the very hot rocks are dropped into the container. The water instantly, vigorously boils, cooking the food. The containers are not damaged. The pre-contact Native Americans employed the hotrock technique. On the Great Plains, the stomach of the buffalo was used as the cooking appliance. Likewise, on the great Asian steppe, Mongolian nomads boil horsemeat in this fashion, in horsehide bags.

HOTSPOTS – (*HOT*-spots) Places on Earth where the crust is very thin, enabling hot magma from the mantle to ooze or explode to the surface as a volcano. Where you see volcanism, there are hotspots. Famous hotspots are Yellowstone, Iceland, New Zealand, Japan, Indonesia, The Aleutians, and Hawaii. The hotspot created the chain of the Hawaiian Islands. As the Earth's crust drifts over the stationary hotspot, new volcanoes burst forth from the sea creating new islands.

HOT TODDY – (*HOT TOD*-dee) A type of julep drink. A hot toddy is made with whiskey or bourbon or Scotch mixed in hot water. Honey, spices, and herbs (such as in tea) are added. A cinnamon stick and twist of lemon might be included. A hot toddy is a traditional medicinal elixir for colds.

HOTWIFE – (*HOT*-wyf) (Hotwifing) A women who has sexual relations outside of her marriage, with the consent and encouragement of her husband, who does not have extramarital affairs. A further variation of hotwifing involves the husband witnessing the fornication and perhaps masturbating during the affair. This paraphilial affair is rooted in the neurotic disposition of the husband, and sometimes wife as well. They solicit lovers to fornicate with the wife. "*I am different. Let this not upset you.* " – Medieval Alchemist Paracelsus (c. 1493 - 1541).

HOT ZONE – (*HOT*-zohn) A contaminated area of a hazmat accident. The hot zone must be cordoned-off, isolated. Hazmat professionals with protective suits and equipment must enter and decontaminate the hot zone. According to the United Nations Emergency Response Guidebook, the minimum hot zone distance from unknown material with unknown release is 330 feet. The hot zone is surrounded by the *"warm zone"* where decontamination efforts commence. The contaminants of a hot zone may be toxic liquid or gas, or radioactive material.

HOUR PRAYER – (*OUW*-er *PRAY*-er) A brief worshipful invocation uttered on the hour, of every waking hour. Hour prayers require extreme piousness, dedication, and conscientiousness. Benedictine monks perform hour prayers at the tone of chimes, every 60 minutes. It is easier to participate in an hour prayer program in a controlled environment like a monastery. But in normal life, on the job, this would present a challenge. Nevertheless, credit must be given to Sunni Muslims who take time to pray on their knees 5 times a day, no matter where they may be.

HOUSEHOLD NONSENSICALS – (*HOWS*-hohld non-*SEN*-si-kuhls) Unnecessary, nonessential, annoying articles that intrude into a living space. Household nonsensicals serve no purpose. They take up room and get in the way. The following are some common nonsensical household items. *Decorative pillows*: A half-a-dozen may clutter the couch and bed, but they're never intended to comfort a head. They are meant for show. Decorative pillows get in the way of sitting or laying. Fat *ornamental candles* that one does not burn. Even during a blackout, the ornamental candles provide no light. Big bushy *plastic plants*, leafy dust-collectors certainly qualify as a household nonsensical. *Exotic cookbooks* occupy the kitchen, but never have been opened. They serve as a ruse deceiving visitors that the cook is a chef. A dusty *bookshelf* that is dusty from lack of use. The books are meant to give the impression of scholarship. A *bed skirt* is a kind of curtain that drapes from the mattress to the floor. It serves no purpose other than hiding the dust kittens under the bed. A *complicated corkscrew* designed by M.I.T. engineers. The screw is an ancient tool that can't be improved. With a little muscle, a corkscrew will open a bottle of wine. But nonsensical corkscrews are a complex piece of machinery with several moving parts. They are expected to impress the gadget nut. *Souvenir towels* that hang for show. They are never to get wet. Extraneous, superfluous *kitchen utensils* that are meant to give the impression of exotic cuisine preparation. A *china* cabinet displaying dishes that are too old to eat off. They are too fragile and precious to use. A *classical music* collection that is never played. Like the Great Books collection, the classical music is meant to lend an air of sophistication. The *exercise room* belonging to the couch potato. All household nonsensicals have one thing in common: they put *form* before *function,* seeming before being.

HOUSE/HOME – (*HOWS HOME*) Trite but true, *"a house is not a home."* This proverb is far more profound than at first glance. Indeed, both are places, but a house is a building whereas a home is an emotion. With time, a house can become a home. The magic ingredient responsible for the transition is beautiful memories. Home houses a happy family, or perhaps their spirits. Wealth cannot make a house into a home. A palatial palace of cold white marble, stuffed with antiques may qualify as a museum or mausoleum but not a home. On the other hand, a modest, even meager apartment, eclectically furnished with Salvation Army odds-and-ends may serve as a home. Home is the safe harbor from the storm. The very word *home,* elicits feelings of comfort, warmth, security, peace, and love. *"Be it ever so humble, there's no place like home."*– John Howard Payne (1791 - 1852) from the song, *"Home! Sweet Home!"*. *"Home is the place where, when you have to go there, they have to take you in."* – Robert Frost (1874 - 1963). *"Home is the dearest spot on earth, and it should be the center, but not the boundary, of the affection."* – Mary Baker Eddy (1821 - 1910). *"The ache for home in all of us, the safe place where we go as we are and not be questioned."* – Maya Angelou (1928 – 2014). *"Houses are like the human beings that inhabit them."* – Victor Hugo (1802 – 1885).

HOUSE MOUSE – (*HOWS* mows) In police slang, a desk clerk officer. A house mouse is a cop who does not go out on patrol. It is a pejorative term. The cop that does the paper work is as vital as any officer on the force. He may be approaching retirement. He may be a hero who was wounded in action and cannot perform on the street as before.

HOUSE OF REPRESENTATIVES – (*HOWS* of rep-ree-*SENT*-ta-tivs) The lower larger chamber of Congress. The House, along with the Senate, comprises the legislative branch of government. The House has always been elected directly by the people for 2 year terms from Congressional Districts in each state. Today, each Congressional District contains about 750,000 citizens, to assure equal representation. The 50 states are divided into 435 Congressional Districts. The more people in the state, the more Congressional Districts, and the more Representatives it sends to the House of Congress. The 435 House members are called either Representatives or Congressmen. The House ratifies laws but it also *"holds the purse strings."* This means the House controls how Federal taxes are spent. All laws requiring funding must originate in the House of Representatives. Two issues make the House of Representatives unrepresentative: *gerrymandering* and *lobbying.* Congressional districts throughout the South, West, and rural America are intentionally drawn and re- drawn so that the Republicans cannot mathematically lose. This is gerrymandering, and this is anti-democratic. Too, corporate capitalist lobbyists have contaminated, corrupted the House as badly as they have the Senate. Add voter suppression and you learn that America is a democracy in name only.

HOUSEWIFE – (*HOWS*-wyf) (Housewifery = hows-*WIF*-fer-ree) A stay-at-home mom who devotes all her worktime to homemaking for husband and children. Housewifery has become a lost occupation. The change occurred in 1980 with the election of the Republican President Ronald Reagan (1911 – 2004) and the *"Revenge of the Rich."* Wealth has been trickling, then gushing upwards with each Republican administration. It takes 2 incomes to maintain the middle class lifestyle that required one before the *Reagan Revolution.* Today, mom goes to work outside the house. She can't afford to serve as housewife. Capitalist distributive injustice made mom change her first allegiance, from the home to the company. The Republicans, the self-professed party of family values have destroyed the family through capitalist greed. *"I have too many fantasies to be a housewife. I guess I am a fantasy."* – Marilyn Monroe (1926 – 1962). *"A good wife is one who serves her husband in the morning like a mother does, loves him in the day like a sister does and pleases him like a prostitute in the night."* – Chanakya (370 – 283 B.C.E.). *"Woman has been the great unpaid laborer of the world."* – Elizabeth Cady Stanton (1815 – 1902).

HOUSEWIFERY – (hows-*WIF*-fer-ree) (Housewife) The occupation of a stay-at- home wife and mom. Housewifery is the occupation of a housewife or homemaker. It has been a denigrated job from all sides, including feminists. Nevertheless, housewifery is the glue that holds the family together, and by extension, society. Depending on the size of the household, a housewife may work upwards of 98 hours a week. Too, she is on emergency call, 24/7. So what is housewifery worth in dollars? According to 2019 data from *Salary.com*, a housewife's median annual salary would amount to $178,201 dollars. That's because her duties include: housecleaner, cook/chef, nanny, nurse, tutor, chauffeur, launderer, grocery shopper, often bookkeeper and secretary, as well as live-in-lover. Using minimum wage per hour for its calculations, an analysis by *Oxfam* in 2020 reported that housewifery, as an occupation, would be worth $1.5 trillion dollars in the U.S.A. It is dearly hoped that the wife is happy in her house. Nothing will make a husband more unhappy than an unhappy wife. *"Much contention and strife will arise in that house where the wife shall get up dissatisfied with her husband."* – Persian Philosopher Saadi (1210 – 1292).

HOUSEWORK – (*HOWS*-werk) The necessity of maintaining the living quarters. Housework is traditionally the purview of women, even after they themselves find outside employment. That's because the house is the woman's nest. To men, the house is a camp. Housework to men is a job. Housework to women is primming the nest. Men reduce housework to its basic essentials and eliminate all the niceties that women consider important. That's why a woman will never be satisfied or pleased with the man's rendition of housework. *"Excuse the mess, we live here."* – Roseanne Barr (b. 1952).

HOWEVER – (hou-*EV*-er) A handy adverb meaning yet, nevertheless, in spite of that, or on the other hand. However is a blend of 2 words: how and ever. *"Trump is an ex-President, however a criminal as well."*

HOW I ROLL – (hou eye *ROHL*) *"That's just the way I am."* A justification for how and why someone behaves a certain way. *"How I roll"* evades responsibility and accountability, insinuating that my actions are part of my nature, not choice. *"Why do you eat so fast?" "Because that's how I roll." "I'm not perfect, but I'm enough"* – Carl Rogers (1902 - 1987). *"I ain't much baby, but I'm all I got."* – Jess Lair (1917 - 2000). "If God had wanted me otherwise, He would have made me otherwise." *"I am what I am, so take me as I am."* – Johann von Goethe (1749 - 1832).

HOWITZER – (*HOW*-wit-zer) Invented by the Dutch, the howitzer is half-way between a canon and a mortar. It is a short gun for high-angle firing of shells at low velocities.

HOYDEN – (*HOI*-den) A tomboy. A bold, brash, boisterous girl. The term hoyden is of Dutch origin.

HUBBLE'S LAW – (*HUB*-buls *LAW*) The universe is expanding, spreading out. The farthest galaxies are accelerating the fastest. Hubble's Law was the first indication of a Big Bang. This observation was set forth by the great astronomer Edwin N. Hubble (1889 – 1953).

HUBRIS – (*HEW*-brees) Excessive pride, arrogance, self-confidence, ambition. Hubris proverbially leads to the transgressor's fall and ruin. *"Pride, hubris precedes destruction; an arrogant spirit before a fall."* – Proverbs 16:18. Sometimes those freshly endowed with a little authority exhibit the most hubris. For instance, during World War One, General John Pershing (1860 – 1948) was walking through the dark American trenches one night when a sergeant yelled at him: *"Put that cigarette out you fool!"* Then the mortified sergeant realized it was General Pershing, and profusely apologized. Pershing laughed and said, *"That's alright sergeant. You're just lucky I wasn't a lieutenant."* Nowhere will you find more hubris than in the stratified, ranked community of the military. Incidentally: In the most astounding display of hubris, Louis XIV (1638 – 1715), the arrogant French *"Sun King"* accused God of ingratitude. *"Has God forgotten all I had done for Him?"* Louis lamented. Finally, the Surrealist Artist Salvador Dali (1904 – 1989) broadcasted his hubris when he declared: *"There comes a moment in every person's life when they realize they adore me."* Hubris will get you in trouble. *"When you think you are the smartest man in the room, that is when you start failing."* – Jack Barsky (b. 1946), ex-KGB agent.

HUDUD – (*HOO*-dood) I Arabic, *"boundaries"* or *"limits."* According to Shari'a Law, a capital crime against God warranting death. Included in Hudud is blasphemy, adultery, homosexuality, and religious conversion out of Islam.

HUEGELKULTUR – (*HYOO*-guhl-cul-chur) German for *"mound bed."* Huegelkultur is a technique of organic horticulture. The base of the plant bed is a pile of dried tree branches, decaying wood. Compostable biomass of any kind (grass clippings, kitchen refuse, garden vegetation) is piled atop the wood. The mound is topped with soil. Seeds or young plant shoots are embedded into the soil. The decaying wood and compost holds moisture, provides warmth, and fertilizes the mound. A huegelkultur mound remains fertile for 5 to 6 years.

HUG – (*HUHG*) (Hugger, Hugging, Hugged) The term is taken from the Old Norse *"hugga,"* meaning *"to comfort."* It can be engaged by both genders, non- homophobically. A hug is the most intimate non-sexual touch in which people can publicly engage. A hug has miraculous therapeutic powers, especially in combating depression. The loveable Leo Buscaglia (1924 – 1998) was the famous *"Doctor Hug,"* whose health regimen still heals through his many books. Incidentally: The miraculous healing power of the hug was demonstrated on October 17, 1995, at the University of Massachusetts Memorial Hospital. Twin girls, Brielle and Kyrie Jackson were born, 12 weeks premature. Kyrie, weighting only 2 lbs. 3 oz. was in peril. She took on a bluish-gray corpulence. Her breathing and heartrate weakened, and her blood-oxygen level declined. Kyrie was expected to die. There was nothing more medically that could be done for her. Then, perhaps by divine intuition, a nurse suggested to place the two tiny infants in the same incubator. Though against hospital procedure, there was nothing to lose. Astonishingly, baby Brielle immediately wrapped her tiny left arm over her sick sister Kyrie in a loving hug. Instantly, all of Kyrie's vital signs improved, and were soon perfectly normal. The miracle was memorialized in a now famous photograph. It is called the *"Rescuing Hug."* (The photo is still available online.) Today, Brielle and Kyrie are beautiful young ladies. Indeed, *"Hugs Heal."* Footnote: Research reveals that hugs lasting over 20 seconds release a chemical in your body called oxytocin, a feel-good neurotransmitter. This substance heightens one's sense of wellbeing and trust.

HUMAN BEING – (*HYOO*-muhn *BEE*-ing) Homo sapien, mankind. Actually human is form, while being is formless. Human is matter, being is spirit. Human being or being human is spirit inhabiting matter, soul, or God in man.

HUMAN CAPITAL – (*HYOO*-muhn *CAP*-pit-tal) In capitalist economics, the worker considered as a means of production. The human machine must be in good working order in order to realized maximum profits. That's why his skills and abilities must be honed, her motivation must be encouraged, and his health must be adequate, enough to get the job done, according to the capitalist manager. The most valuable element in the capitalist manufacturing process is the worker – human capital.

HUMAN COMPOSTING – (*HYOO*-muhn *KOM*-post-ing) (Human Compost) Facilitate the decomposition of a corpse into fertile soil, a burial alternative. Human composting is being proposed in the bellwether state of California, as well as in progressive Washington, Oregon, Colorado, and Vermont. This is a government regulated process of natural organic reduction of human remains into nutrient-rich earth. *"Man, you shall return to the ground, for out of it you were taken; for you are dust, and to dust you shall return."* – Genesis 3:19. The Bible seems to confirm human composting. In fact, the name *"Adam,"* the Biblical first man, derives from the Hebrew *"adamah,"* meaning *"one formed from the ground."* Furthermore, the Latin word for earth or soil is *"humus,"* which is a cognate with *"human."* The human body is perfectly biodegradable. It can be converted into compost, a fertile mixture of decayed organic soil. It takes about 100 years for an embalmed corpse to thoroughly break down in a buried coffin. With human composting, it takes from 30 to 45 days. The body is placed in a steel vessel and buried in wood chips, alfalfa, and other biodegradable-inducing material. The fertile soil that is produced is donated to conservation land or returned to the family to be used in their garden. It will produce beautiful flowers, delicious tomatoes, or potent marijuana, in honor of the deceased. (You can still enjoy the fruits of your loved-one's labor.) To the squeamish, bear in mind that bringing home human compost is no different than bringing home human ashes, placed in an urn next to his bowling trophy. Human composting is less costly than a traditional funeral, but more expensive than cremation, on average. It saves precious land, wasted as cemeteries. *"I request that my body, in death be buried not cremated so that the energy content contained within it gets returned to the earth so that flora and fauna can dine upon it just as I dined upon the flora and fauna throughout my life."* – Dr. Neil DeGrasse Tyson, (b. 1958) Astronomer, Astrophysicist, Teacher.

HUMAN CONSTITUENTS – (*HYOO*-muhn kuhn-*STICH*-oo-uhnts) The combination of elements that create the human body, and everything else in the universe. Man consists of 60 elemental chemicals. The most plentiful are: Oxygen (65%), Carbon (18.5%), Hydrogen (9.5%), Nitrogen (2.6%), Calcium (1.3%), Phosphorus (0.6%), as well as a very little amount of Sulfur, Sodium, Chlorine, Magnesium, and 50 trace elements. Of course, these same elements also create all the animals, plants, mountains, soil, everything else. Consider these chemical elements to be like the letters of the alphabet. Those 26 symbols create every word in the language. The words differ because the letters are arranged differently. The same applies to the chemical elements of the Periodic Table.

HUMANE JURISPRUDENCE – (*HUE*-mayn *JUR*-ris-pru-dens) Merciful justice in our courts of law. Humane jurisprudence operates by the *"spirit of the law,"* not the *"letter of the law."* A humane judge realizes that the law was made for man, not man for the law. There is no place for mandatory sentences or zero tolerance policies in humane justice. Mitigating, extenuating circumstances always apply, because every court case is unique. Revenge is never a consideration in sentencing. *"Then Jesus stood up and said: 'Let him among you who is without sin cast the first stone'."* – John 8:7.

HUMAN ENDOWMENTS – (*HYOO*-muhn en-*DOW*-ments) Four qualities that raise us above other animals. They are: 1. *Self-Awareness* – I know that I exist as a unique, independent creature, physically and spiritually. 2. *Conscience* – I have an inherent innate sense of what is right and wrong. 3. *Independent Will* – I am free to make choices, and am accountable for the choices I make. 4. *Creative Imagination* – My vision of the world is unlike that of any others. I have the power to alter my environment to suit my emotions. These are the Human Endowments.

HUMANISM – (*HYOO*-muhn-is-um) An existential school of psychology (*phenomenological*) that promotes man's personal freedom, individuality, responsibility, and self-actualization. Fundamentalists disparage the term, incorrectly associating it with atheism (secular humanism). Historically, Humanism was a product of the Renaissance (14th to 17th centuries). With the revival of classical learning, obsession with religion was lessened, and emphasis was put on man, in the here and now. This new attitude came to be called humanism.

HUMANIST CREDO – (*HYOO*-muhn-ist *CRAY*-dow) *"Man is the measure of all things."*

HUMANISTIC EXISTENTIALISM – (hyoo-muhn-*NIS*-tic ex-is-*TEN*-chee-al-is-um) The philosophical belief that the universe is not itself intelligible. Humans make it intelligible. The universe does not conform to any rational, logical order or process. It is not created, supported, or designed by an omnipotent, benevolent God. All things are contingent. There is no objective moral realm. Moral values do not exist outside of consciousness.

HUMANITY'S PROBLEMS/SOLUTIONS – (hyoo-MAHN-ni-tees *PROB*-lems so-*LOO*-shuns) Mankind has troubles, problems. But there are answers, solutions. <u>Problems:</u> Nationalism, Racialism, Militarism, Materialism, Ethnocentrism, Sectarianism, Capitalism. <u>Solutions:</u> Pacifism, Altruism, Internationalism, Fraternalism, Compassionism, Socialism.

HUMANMETRICS – (hyoo-mahn-*MET*-rics) Personality typology testing. Humanmetrics will determine dominate personality characteristics. For example, the degree that one is introverted or extroverted, tolerant or rigid. The research will determine whether one is more intuitive or logical; introspective or rational; insightful or reasonable. This measure will reveal whether one tends to be more Liberal or conservative, compassionate or indifferent. The test will make career recommendations and report famous comparable, compatible personality types. The *Jung-Keirsey Typology Personality Test* is one such Humanmetrics assessment.

HUMANOCENTRISM – (hyoo-mahn-o-*SENT*-tris-um) (Humanocentric) (also Anthropocentrism) Literally, *"human in the center."* Humanocentrism is the ethical belief that man, being at the pinnacle of life on Earth, has dominion over the planet, and all its creatures. All lifeforms are here to serve man. It is right for man to have life or death authority over all simpler beings, great and small. Only God reigns above mankind. Humanocentrism views man as more than the stewards of the planet, but its dictator. Proponents of anthropocentrism or humanocentrism refer to Biblical evidence of man's dominance. *"Let man have dominion over the fish of the sea and over the birds of the heavens and over the livestock and over all the earth and over every creeping thing that creeps on the earth."* – Genesis 1:26. Therefore humanocentrism is divinely ordained. This is a naïve, simplistic, and self-serving view. The polar opposite of humanocentrism is *biocentrism* (or *ecocentrism*). This ethical belief maintains that man is a link in the chain of life, and all lifeforms hold sacred value.

HUMAN RIGHTS – (*HYOO*-muhn *RITES*) Natural endowments, entitlements to all people due to their humanity. Human rights go beyond civil rights which are privileges of citizenry. Human rights are privileges of humanity. They are inalienable and inviolable. Human rights do not distinguish between rich and poor, and does not recognize cultural and racial difference. Human rights revolve around dignity. They include the basic freedoms of speech, religion, assembly, information, and mobility. Human rights also include protection from foreign and domestic harm, decent healthcare, employment, housing, nutrition, and education. To endow a nation and planet with human rights requires unselfish sharing. This is antithetical to capitalism. (*"I got mine, to hell with you!"* – capitalist credo). Only in a Socialist society can real human rights be realized.

HUMAN TRAFFICKING – (*HYOO*-muhn *TRAF*-fic-ing) (Trafficker) *"The flesh trade."* Labor or sex slavery. Human trafficking is the abduction, incarceration, and exploitation of people for forced labor or sexual prostitution. The United Nation's International Labor Organization estimates that about 21 million people worldwide have been trafficked into bondage. About 16.4 are work slaves, and about 4.5 are sex slaves. It is a lucrative capitalist enterprise. Labor captivity is worth over $150 billion dollars a year while sex servitude brings in over $99 billion annually. Poor people in poor, therefore corrupt nations are mostly targeted. But any young, attractive, naïve girl on spring break can be kidnaped anywhere. Sometimes they are sold into forced marriages, or as an addition to an oil sheik's harem. Many are simply raw material, destined to work the streets as prostitutes until used up and discarded. Incidentally: In July, 2019, billionaire American investment banker Jeffery Epstein (1953 - 2019) (friend of Presidents Bill Clinton (b. 1946) and Donald Trump (b. 1946), awaits trial on charges of human trafficking of adolescent girls for sexual favors. Epstein's *"pimpress"* was Ghislaine Maxwell (b. 1961). Tender *"nymphets"* would be flown on Epstein's plane, *"The Lolita Express,"* to his *"Orgy Island"* (aka: *"Pedophile Isle"*) in the Caribbean. Update: It is February 2024. Epstein is dead. He was assassinated (hanger himself?) in prison on August 10, 2019. His pimpress lover Ms. Maxwell is in prison.

HUMAN ZOO – (*HYOO*-muhn *ZOO*) Homo sapiens displayed as beasts. Human zoos cage people for public amusement and profit. Throughout history and the world, human beings had been imprisoned in communal exhibitions. Usually they were racially diverse war captives from exotic cultures. This was not an ancient atrocity, abomination alone. Human zoos flourished during the 19th and early 20th centuries. During the 19th century, European neo-imperialists carved-up the *"primitive"* parts of the globe as colonies. The indigenous populations were non-Christian, non-White. They were considered to be *"untermenschen,"* sub-humans, to use a Nazi German term. Many natives were bought and brought to Germany, Britain, France, Belgium, and elsewhere, to be displayed in human zoos. Impresario entrepreneurs profited capitalistically from the humiliation and suffering of caged people. The Belgians were especially savage. Their contemptable King Leopold II (1835 – 1909) truly had <u>*"A Heart of Darkness,"*</u> to quote Joseph Conrad (1857 – 1924). He owned the Belgian Congo and its rubber plantations and populations. Leopold brought specimens from his human collection to be exhibited in zoos. The Christian Belgian citizens would throw peanuts at the caged Negroes. In London, insane British citizens were displayed to voyeuristic Victorian ladies and gentlemen in asylums. It became a tradition to gawk at the naked madmen and women in the madhouses on Sunday outings, after church, in these human zoos. During World War Two (1941 – 1945) the Japanese put captured American airmen in cages, naked, for public mockery. This boosted the morale of the prurient Japanese citizens who were being bombed. Times have changed but human nature has not. There are still blotches of darkness in the human heart. Human zoos, like fascism and death camps can be revived. *"Cruelty has a human heart."* – William Blake (1757 – 1827).

HUMBLE PIE – (*HUM*-bul *PY*) To be taught a lesson in humility. It is said that we *"eat humble pie"* when we are embarrassingly stripped of our lordly arrogance, and compelled to be humble. Humble pie was originally *"umble pie."* It was made of the offal, guts, umbles of the animal, historically a deer. After the hunt, the best venison meat was the lord's. The peasants got what was left. The umbles were often ground into sausages. Traditionally in England, it was stewed and backed into a pie – umble pie or humble pie. Humble pie was the cuisine of the inferior class.

HUMBOLDT SQUID – (*HUM*-bolt *SKWID*) A huge, dangerous predatory squid that lives in the water of the Humboldt Current in the eastern Pacific. From Tierra del Fuego to Alaska, the squids are normally found at depths of 660 to 2,300 feet. It may grow to 5 feet in length, and weigh about 100 pounds. They are fished commercially in Mexico and Peru. The fishermen call the Giant Humboldt Squid the *"red devil."* The Humboldt squid has 3 hearts, blue blood, and the biggest gills of all sea creatures. Too, its enormous, human-like eyes are the largest of all animals. With its gigantic sharp parrot-like beak, the squid has killed divers. This colossal calamari will eat anything, including people. Its natural predator, the sperm whale, will hunt and devour the giant squid. Incidentally: The sperm whale is the largest carnivorous, predatory mammal on Earth, land or sea.

HUMBUG – (*HUHM*-buhg) (Humbugged, Humbugging, Humbugger, Humbuggery) As a verb, the quality of falseness or deception. Humbug is something intended to delude or deceive. As an interjection, humbug is used as an expletive to express rejection of something as being completely false, untrue, nonsensical. Footnote: The exclamation *"Bah humbug!"* conveys curmudgeonly displeasure. The phrase was popularized by *Ebenezer Scrooge* in Charles Dickens' (1812 – 1870) novel, <u>*A Christmas Carol*</u> (1843).

HUMIDITY – (hu-*MID*-di-tee) The amount of water vapor in the atmosphere. The relative humidity is the percentage of water vapor in the atmosphere as it approaches the saturation point of 100%. At that point the air can hold any more water, so it must rain. When humidity is high, and the air cannot hold much more moisture, sweat will not evaporate off the skin, taking body heat with it. You are uncomfortably wet clammy, and hot. A Caveat: To clear up a confusion, know that a wet body loses heat 25 time quicker than a dry body. That's providing the air is dry enough to evaporate that wetness and heat. If the relative humidity is approaching 100%, the wet and heat clings to the body.

HUMILIATION – (hu-mil-lee-*AY*-shun) A feeling of uttermost pain at the loss of pride, self-respect, or dignity. One may be humiliated by word or action. Humiliation is a mortifying emotion. Nevertheless, it is still an emotion, a feeling. If we can control our feelings, we can refuse the humiliation. It is a Karmic virtue to never put another in a humiliating position. Mohandas Gandhi (1869 – 1948) said: *"It has always been a mystery to me how men can feel themselves honored by the humiliation of their fellow beings."* *"What you think of me is none of my business."* – Terry Cole-Whittaker (b. 1939). There is something liberating about public humiliation." – Joaquin Phoenix (b. 1974).

HUMILITY – (hu-*MIL*-li-tee) Virtuous humbleness, meekness of spirit. *The Song of Prayer* exalts that: *"Humility brings peace for it does not claim that you must rule the universe, nor judge all things as you would have them be."* The humble are devoid of hubris, excessive pride, without arrogance. Humility is showing restraint from a position of strength. It is not being a doormat, but rather a foundation stone. Humility is not thinking less of yourself, but thinking of yourself less. Hindu Yogi Swami Sivananda (1887 – 1963) assured us that *"Humility is not cowardice. Meekness is not weakness. Humility and meekness are indeed spiritual powers."* Incidentally: Winston Churchill (1874 – 1965) was a most *un-humble* man. When his Liberal rival, Clement Attlee (1883 – 1967) was praised for being humble, Churchill agreed: *"Yes, he has much to be humble about."*

HUMILITY TEST – (hu-*MIL*-li-tee *TEST*) A public confession of one's flaws, defects, shortcomings. Young Japanese executive candidates for big corporations must pass a humiliating humility test. They must stand in public on a soapbox, in a busy area like a bus or train station, and yell-out their faults and weaknesses. With tears streaming down their cheeks, they endure this ordeal for the coveted position, a rung on the corporate ladder. The humility test seems more like a fraternity hazing stunt.

HUMMINGBIRD – (*HUM*-ming-bird) Western Hemispheric bird, the world's smallest with the fastest wing fluctuations. The smallest is the size of a bee and native to Cuba and Jamaica. This Bee Hummingbird (2 inches, 0.056 ounces) is the smallest bird in the world. Hummingbirds do not hum. The humming or buzzing sound is produced by the super-fast fluctuations of their wings (100 flaps per second in some species). It is the only bird that can fly backwards. The hummingbird has the highest metabolism of all animals. Its heart beats 1,000 times a minute. While awake, the hummingbird burns so much energy, it must eat every 2 hours or starve to death. It must consume its body weight in nectar daily. Hummingbirds are partially carnivorous. They pluck tiny insects to feed their teeny young in the nest. When asleep, they enter into a hibernation to lower their metabolism and conserve energy and heat. Nevertheless, they still risk the chance of starving or dying of hypothermia while asleep. Hummingbirds are necessary to pollinate pineapple plants, and many other varieties of flowers. One bird can pollinate over 1,000 flowers a day. Even with hundreds of blossoms on a bush or tree, the bird somehow remembers which ones he had serviced. Hummingbirds are attracted to colors, not fragrance. They are very territorial. A male hummingbird will protect a patch of flower he had claimed to the death. Hummingbirds supplement their diet of nectar and pollen with tiny flying insects for protein. They feed the bugs to their chicks, who suffer a high mortality rate.

HUMOR – (*HYOO*-mer) (Humorous, Humorless, Humored, Humoring) The expression of the amusing or comical. What is said or done humorously is funny – literally done for fun. Employing humor is an act of playfulness, which is the opposite of seriousness. Displaying a sense of humor is a universal, trans-cultural human trait. Humor makes humans happy. The response of all normal human beings to humor is a smile or laughter – both signs of joy. The wit of a comedian or the buffoonery of a clown, if amusing, quality as humor. Experiencing humor is essential for mental and physical health. Humor, in the form of elation, is the polar opposite of depression. *"If it wasn't for a sense of humor, I'd be a lunatic years ago."* – Mohandas Gandhi (1869 – 1948).

HUMP DAY – (*HUMP* day) A designation for Wednesday, the day in the middle of the work week. If the week was a bell-shaped curve, Wednesday would be at the peak. So after Wednesday, one is over the hump of the week. Hump day holds a disparaging allusion. It connotes the drudgery of the capitalist work week. When one lives to work with little return, one looks forward for the week to end. For most, capitalism, working to enrich others, produces a depressing existence.

HUMPTY TRUMPTY – (*HUM*-tee *TRUMP*-tee) A poem: *"Humpty Trumpty cried for a Wall; Humpty Trumpty had a presidential fall; All of Putin's money and KGB men; Couldn't put Trumpty in the White House again."* – Gary J. Pasieka (b. 1951), January 29, 2018.

HUMUHUMUNUKUNUKUAPUAA – (hoo-moo-hoo-moo-noo-koo-noo-koo-ah- poo-*AH*-ah) This is not baby babble, or the gabble of a stroke victim. This is a legitimate native Hawaiian-American word for two species of Indo-Pacific triggerfish that inhabit coral reefs. This amazing word consists of 12 syllables of 21 letters. The *humuhumu* element means *"triggerfish,"* while *nukunuku* translates as *"short, blunt"* and *"small snout,"* and means *"like,"* and *pua'a* means *"pig."* So Humuhumunukunukuapuaa literally means *"triggerfish with small, short blunt shout like a pig."* The word was first recorded in English in the 1860s.

HUMUS – (*HU*-mus) Organic compost. The dark rich organic paste in soils produced by the decomposition of vegetable or animal matter, essential to the fertility of the Earth.

HUNCHBACK – (*HUNCH*-back) (*Kyphoscoliosis* or *Kyphosis*) A physical deformation in which a person's back is humped in a convex position because of abnormal spinal curvature. During the Middle Ages, it was considered good luck to rub a hunchback's hump. This act was thought to result in some *lucky "hunch." "I got a hunch the Lions will win the game."*

HUNDRED FLOWERS CAMPAIGN – (*HUN*-dred *FLOU*-wers cam-*PAYN*) The great deception of 1956. Chinese dictator Mao Zedong (1893 – 1976) again proved that Maoism was not Communism or Socialism. He encouraged the people to criticize the government, schools, every societal institution. Mao convinced the populous that a diversity of views and solutions were welcomed. He said: *"The policy of letting a 'hundred flowers' bloom and a hundred schools of thought contend is designed to promote the flourishing of the arts and the progress of science."* The government installed suggestion boxes (like mailboxes) throughout the country. People were encouraged to lodge their criticisms and drop them in the box. Liberals, Progressives were delighted! Just when it looked like true Socialism was about to come alive in China, Mao's paranoia flared-up. All the people who had criticized the regime and society were arrested as traitors to the state and disappeared. *"Where have all the flowers gone?"*

HUNGER PANGS – (*HUHNG*-ger *PANGS*) A pang is a sharp, sudden pain. A hunger pang is an agonizing ache, a gnawing sensation in the stomach when deprived of food for some time. The hunger pang is accompanied by abdominal spasms and stomach growling. Hunger pangs serve as a defense mechanism – the body alerting the person that it needs nutrition to maintain health. Hunger pangs are the initial warning signal that the body needs food. Though uncomfortable, the body is not yet in danger. Fasting for instance will produce hunger pangs, as exercise can produce muscle pangs. However, both are health regimens. (*"No pain, no gain."* – Weightlifters credo.) An interesting phenomenon concerning hunger pangs occurs when one fasts. Let's consider what happens during a 3 day fast – simplistically. Day #1 – Stomach rebels. First discomfort followed by hunger pangs. *"I want food!"* the stomach demands. *"I will force you to feed me!"* Day one is tough. Day #2 – even tougher. *"I will punish, to torture you!"* the stomach threatens. Indeed, the stomachache is at its apex, it pangs with pain. Day #3 – still no food forthcoming. Exhausted, the stomach surrenders, quits the fight. It comes to the physiological realization that there will be no food forthcoming. *"I'll find my own food, from within my own body,"* the stomach laments. *"I'll start to burn the emergency food supply, the fat tissue."* When this occurs, the entire body is nourished, and the hunger pangs lessen. One may still feel hungry, but not in agony. You will survive as long as the fat supply exists. This too is a defense mechanism. As you burn your fat, you begin to lose weight and slim down. Incidentally: A fast is not a diet. A fast is a spiritual sacrifice, a form of worship. The spiritual element of the fast also eases the hunger pangs. *"Every breath I take, every step I make is a prayer during a fast."*

HUNGER STRIKE – (*HUHNG*-ger *STRYK*) (Hunger Striker) A form of non-violent resistance in which participants fast, indefinitely, even to death, as an act of political protest. The hope is to provoke the feelings of guilt and shame in others, with the objective of achieving a goal, such as a change in policy. Hunger strikers are not masochistic or suicidal, but deeply dedicated to a cause. A hunger strike is a drastic and dangerous demonstration of protest, usually employed by prisoners, detainees, political dissidents, and the oppressed. Imprisoned Socialists often employ hunger strikes against fascist capitalist tyrants. A hunger strike is a battle of wills, between the protestor and the authority figure, between the oppressed and the oppressor. Though the hunger striker refuses to eat, he does take liquids. Death by dehydration is too quick, a few days. Death by starvation may take two-and-a-half months, plenty of time to elicit publicity, sympathy and drum-up support. Hopefully, public outrage will force the authority figure to relent, and meet the emaciated protestor's demands. However, hunger strikes are only effective if the oppressor, the authority figure cares about public opinion. For example, a hunger strike in a Nazi concentration camp would prove futile, ludicrous in fact. If the powers of authority care (or fear) about their public image, they may attempt to force- feed the starving striker, so he doesn't look so pitifully mistreated, and gain public pity and support. Mohandas Gandhi (1869 – 1948) skillfully employed hunger strikes in his campaign for India's independence from Britain. Many revolutionary captives have resorted to hunger strikes. Recently, (2021) the democratic Russian political candidate, Alexei Navalny (b. 1976) staged a well- publicized, albeit unsuccessful, hunger strike in prison. Navalny opposes the Vladimir Putin (b. 1952) dictatorship in Russia. Incidentally: In order to magnify Navalny's misery and tempt him off his hunger strike, the Russian prison guards allowed inmates to roast chicken in the cells near Navalny's. And it smelled *"fuck'en' finger-lick'en good!"* Update: On February 16, 2014, Alexei Navalny was killed in a Siberian gulag. He was 48 years old.

HUNG JURY – (huhg *JER*-ree) In this case, hung means suspended, not on solid ground, neither here nor there. In a court of law, when a jury is hung, that means the 12 jurors could not unanimously agree on a verdict. In a criminal case, if one juror out of 12 cannot find a defendant guilty, the jury is hung and the case is over. Though the defendant goes free, he is not officially pronounced innocent. She can be tried again when new evidence emerges, or when the government takes a different approach to the prosecution.

HUNKER-DOWN – (*HUHNK*-ker *DOWN*) To hide-out or take shelter. Hunker- down is a folksy expression referring to riding-out a natural emergency like a blizzard or hurricane. Hunker down is a Southern American phrase from 1902, that became popularized around 1965, due to the hurricanes that batter the Southern USA. People never *"hunker-down"* for a funeral or wedding, only during a natural disaster. So to hunker is to *"batten down the hatches."* The term hunker entered English in 1720 from Scotland. It meant *"to squat or crouch."* Hunker was probably a nasalized borrowing of the Old Norse word *"huka,"* meaning *"to crouch."* When you cower in the bathtub or under the bed, you are hunkering down. Therefore, hunkering is a somewhat cowardly act. [Incidentally: As I write these words, I am hunkered-down in Tampa, Florida, awaiting the wrath of *Hurricane IRMA,* (September 8, 2017). *"I hanker to hunker with you."*

HUNKY – (*HUHNG*-kee) A bigoted, contemptuous name for an unskilled immigrant worker of Slavonic ethnicity. The pejorative hunky was especially applied to Hung(arian) immigrants, (who are not Slavonic). The term hunky emerged as an Americanism circa 1895. Incidentally: Beginning in the 1960's, radical, bigoted African-Americans were applying the term hunky to all white Americans.

HUNKY-DORY – (*HUHNG*-kee *DOHR*-ee) Satisfactory, fine, okay. Hunky-dory means as well as could be expected. Hunky-dory is an Americanism from about 1866. The term was popularized in 1870 by a

Christy Minstrel song. However, a theory from 1876 traces the term to *"Honcho Dori,"* a street in Yokohama, Japan's red light district where American sailors found satisfaction.

HUNTER-GATHERER – (*HUHN*-ter *GATH*-er-ers) A wondering nomad preoccupied with his daily search for food. For about 90% of human existence, our ancestors survived as hunters-gatherers. The men tracked game, the women dug roots, picked berries, and plucked wild grain. People lived in small wandering bands. Little time was devoted to any other pursuit, other than food procurement. The caloric cost of hunting-gathering is high. If you take-in fewer calories than you burn searching for them, you will slowly starve to death. The accidental discovery of farming changed everything. Now we had a surplus. Where a hunter-gather family needed 10 square miles to survive, the farmer needed only 1/10 of a square mile. Survival was pretty much assured.

HUNTING – (*HUHNT*-ing) (Hunt, Hunted, Hunter) The pursuit and chase of wild game for the purpose of catching or killing. Hunting is a predatory survival activity essential to all carnivores. It is the counterpart to herbivore's grazing and browse on leaves. Hunting is killing in order to eat. The victims of the hunt are usually herbivores. That's why nature had seen to it that herbivores outnumber carnivores by at least 10 to 1. All carnivores below man hunt only for food. Only man hunts also for sport. The victims of man's hunting are both herbivores and carnivores. Sport-hunters try to sanitize their bloodlust by calling their killing *"harvesting."* This is a sloppy euphemism. A skilled hunter should be able to *"harvest"* a buck right through the heart with a single shot. In this case, the *"harvest"* would not prove too painful. Incidentally: Islam prohibits sport-hunting. Muslims are forbidden from killing animals just for the fun of it. Incidentally: A gruesome form of cruelty is fox hunting, enjoyed by the English aristocracy. Patricians on horseback ride the countryside, along with packs of dogs that tear the fox apart, alive. Great fun! The public didn't think so. In June, 2017, Conservative Prime Minister Theresa May (b. 1956) promised to re-instate the bloodsport fox hunting. In the election, the Conservatives lost their majority. *"You can't teach a hunter it's wrong to kill."* – Baba Hari Dass (b. 1923).

HURONIA – (hur-*RONE*-nee-a) Land of the Huron (or Wyandotte) Indians. The epicenter of Huronia was Georgian Bay region of Lake Huron in Ontario, Canada. The Huron were an Iroquoian nation originally from the Lake Ontario region. They speak an Iroquoian dialect. Though cousins, the Iroquois and Huron were long-time enemies. Jacques Cartier (1491 – 1557) sailed up the St. Lawrence River in 1535 -1536 and met some Huron natives. Cartier asked them where they lived. The Huron replied *"Kanata"* meaning *"The Village."* Cartier assumed the region was called Kanata, which evolved into Canada (The Village). Initially, the French in Canada presented a greater threat than the English, because the French settled in permanently, as families. Therefore, the Iroquois allied with the English against the French. Therefore, the Huron allied with the French against their traditional enemy, the Iroquois. The combatants were positioned for the French and Indian War (1754 – 1763). The French were defeated by the British, and the Iroquois finally decimated the Huron. Huronia vanished as the Hurons scattered about among other tribes and the French settlements.

HURRICANE – (*HER*-ri-cayn) Earth's most violent storm, a phenomenon of the hot tropics. The name is taken from a Taino Indian word *"huracan,"* meaning *"great violent wind."* The average hurricane packs the *energy* of 4,000 average hydrogen bombs. A hurricane may be 300 miles across with winds exceeding 156 mph. The most powerful part of the storm is the eye-wall. The torrential rain and sea rise (*storm surge*) causes catastrophic flooding. Actually, a hurricane is a planetary air conditioner, converting excessive heat energy in tropical water into wind and wave energy. In this way, the planet sweats and the Earth's heat budget is balanced. About 80 hurricanes form over Earth's tropical oceans annually. About 12% enter the Caribbean. About 30 % slam into East Asia and the North Pacific.

HURRICANE BELT – (*HER*-ri-cayn belt) The region in North America where *"tropical cyclones"* are most prevalent. Historically, the Caribbean has been the Atlantic hurricane belt. That has been changed by global warming. Nature loves diversity and harmony [read: balance] – not too cold, not too hot. That's why warm air and water drifts toward cool regions, and cool air and water drifts toward warm regions. With man-made climate change, the Earth is warming. Naturally cool regions are getting warmer. Therefore, warm hurricanes must travel farther north to find cool air. So warm hurricanes are skipping the Caribbean and hitting farther north – the American Atlantic and Gulf Coasts. The planet's hurricane belt has moved to America.

HURRICANE FATIGUE – (*HER*-ri-cayn fa-*TEEG*) A case of *"vigilance exhaustion."* Becoming enervated by being in a prolonged, tense, state of siege by an impending hurricane. One can maintain a condition of alert for just so long, before complacency sets in. This is what occurs in hurricane fatigue. Warnings of disasters that are averted breeds distrust. It's the old story of the boy crying *"Wolf!"* People take lightly future warnings. They choose to hunker-down, and ride-out the next storm. Sometimes the consequences are dire, deadly. The best advice is to combat hurricane fatigue, until the hurricane is fatigued.

HURRICANE PARTY – (*HER*-ri-cayn *PAR*-tee) An involuntary Socialistic exigency brought about by the impending disaster of a hurricane. Hurricane parties are familiar in Jamaica and other Caribbean islands battered by great storms. On a small island, there is no place safe to which to retreat. One must batten-down the hatches and hunker-down in place. An apocalyptic attitude seems to take hold. In the emergency, electrical power will certainly be lost, resulting in no refrigeration for many days. Frozen food will spoil. Rather than waste the food, it is generously distributed, or cooked en mass and shared with whoever is available for the feast. (*"Eat, drink, and be merry, for tomorrow we may die."* – Ecclesiastes 8:15.) This is the *"hurricane party."* It is an act of communal charity, compelled by the emergency, the desperation precipitated by the hurricane. It is enlightening how people become cooperative, collaborative, codependent, communal [read: *Communistic*], and generous in a critical crisis. All catastrophes force us to re-evaluate our core values and priorities. (Your money and jewels are worthless, when all you want, need is water and bread.) Perhaps a universal cataclysm would convince humanity that we need each other. The desperation of mutual dependence would force the rich to acknowledge that *"We are our brother's keepers,* and that *"No man is an island onto himself."* A world-wide calamity may convince humanity that Earth is a Brotherhood of Man. This is exemplified, in a small way, in a small place, at a Caribbean Hurricane Party. *"Then Jesus said: 'When you give a feast, invite the poor, the maimed, the lame, the blind. And you will be blessed, because they cannot repay you'."* – Luke 14: 13-14.

HURRY – (*HER*-ree) (Hurried, Hurrying) To rush, to move, proceed, or act with haste. Hurry raises blood pressure, generates tension, stress, which will result in anxiety. St. Francis de Sales (1567 – 1622) warned us to *"Never be in a hurry; do everything quietly and in a calm spirit. Do not lose your inner peace for anything whatsoever, even if your whole world seems upset."* Projects performed in a hurry usually lack quality. This is particularly true when forced to hurry against one's will. To be made to hurry is insulting and degrading. *"'Hurry up', ranks up there with 'You need to', as a destroyer of our humanity."* – Jonathan Lockwood Huie (b. 1945). Buddhist Dr. Jon Kabat-Zinn (b. 1944) insists that *"This doesn't mean you can't hurry when you have to. It is possible even to hurry patiently mindfully, moving fast because you have chosen to."* Though people can be hurried, nature cannot. *"Rivers know this: there is no hurry. We shall get there some day."* – Author Alan A. Milne (1882 – 1956).

HURTERS – (*HER*-ters) People who are hurting, not physically but emotionally. Their hurt is usually generated by guilt, (*"I DID something wrong"*). The feeling of guilt often metastasizes into shame (*"I AM something wrong"*). This feeling of self-loathing generates great hurt. Carrying the pain can become so unbearable, that the sufferer must transfer some of the weight to others, in order to ease their load. That's why hurters are often time bombs. A minor dispute or misunderstanding provides them with an outlet to project, displace their guilt, shame, and hurt onto others. Hurters need to hurt others, in order to relieve their pain (hurt). Therefore, they explode in rage, venting the most vile vituperations. Their reactions are never measured. They go for the jugular immediately. Hurters need to come to terms with past guilt and shame. They must embrace their humanity, believing that they did the best they could, with who they were, and what they knew and felt, at that point in time, space, and life. Too, God forgives, and can heal all hurts.

HUTIA – (hoo-*TEE*-a) A rare Caribbean guinea pig, also called a *Coney*. Jamaica was once a *"coney island."* But the tasty rodent was hunted and eaten almost to extinction. The hutia is a rare protected animal in Jamaica today.

HYBRID – (*HY*-brid) The offspring of two animals or plants of different breeds, varieties, species, or genera, especially as produced through human manipulation for specific genetic characteristics. Hybrids in nature is rare. Creatures that are close but of different species may mate and sometime produce offspring (like a lion and tiger). But the offspring is usually infertile, the end of the line. Dogs and wolves are close enough to mate and produce viable young. The term "hybrid" is also used outside the purview of biology. This book, THE LIBERAL LEXICON: *A Socialistic, Spiritualistic Encyclodictionary* is a hybrid of encyclopedia and dictionary.

HYBRID VIGOR – (*Hy*-brid *VIG*-gor) The genetic phenomenon in which a superior offspring results from the mating of animals from different parts of the world. Nature loves variety. A large gene pool for any creature (including man) will produce stronger offspring. However, stronger to one species, is dangerous to other species. Hybrid vigor may result in animal and plants that may prove detrimental (the *Frankenstein Effect*). Charles Darwin (1809 – 1882) recognized early on the damage invasive species can cause. *"What havoc does the introduction of a foreign species wreak before the indigenous creatures learn to adjust to the invader?"*

HYBRID WARFARE – (*HY*-brid *WAWR*-fair) A hybrid is a crossbreed. Warfare is a violent military struggle. Hybrid warfare is a military struggle or strategy that avoids direct violence. The struggle consists of a crossbreed of attacks with espionage, propaganda, disingenuous diplomacy, disinformation, cyber incursions, bribery, and malicious electoral intervention. Therefore, hybrid warfare is irregular, non-conventional, political warfare. The term was introduced by Frank Hoffman (fl. 2007) in *Conflict in the 21st Century: The Rise of Hybrid Wars* (2007). The goal of hybrid warfare is to destroy a rival or enemy nation without firing a shot. The strategy is to destabilize the nation's society. It seeks to plant the *"Apple of Discord."* It hopes to disrupt the economy, sow distrust in the political system, delegitimize election results, instigate cultural disputes, bigotry, racism, and turn citizen against citizen. Patriotism is eroded, and citizens lose faith is the future of the nation. In a sense, hybrid warfare is a germ warfare. Its intention is to infect the social/psychological health of the population, so the nation self-destructs. Does this sound familiar? *"We have met the enemy, and they are us."* – Comic Strip Character *Pogo*.

HYBRISTOPHILIA – (hy-bris-toh-*FEE*-lee-ah) (Hybristophiliac) A sexual attraction to criminals and criminality. Hybristophilia is a neurotic paraphilial disorder in which one is sexually aroused and attracted to people who have committed cruel, outrageous crimes. It is the *"Bonnie and Clyde"* syndrome. This is an anti-social fetish that can get a gal in trouble. Girls or ladies who submit to serve as groupies for the *Hell's Angels,* for instance, can be characterized as hybristophiliacs. *"A bad boy can be very good for a girl."* – Author Melissa De La Crux (b.1971).

HYDRAGYRUM – (hy-*DRAJ*-jee-rum) The ancient Greek term for the element mercury. In Greek, *"hydro"* means *"water,"* and *"argyos"* means *"silver."* Mercury or quick silver is indeed a silvery liquid.

HYDRATION – (hy-*DRAY*-shun) To water, saturate a dry area. A thirsty plant, animal, or person hydrates, when it drinks in water. A human being, like the Planet Earth, is over 70% water. To be dehydrated will reduce physical and intellectual capacity, and impede the reflexes. In an emergency situation, eating snow or ice for hydration can be fatal. Too much body heat is sacrificed in the process of eating cold ice. Too, too much air is ingested in the process of eating snow. In both cases, the solidified water must be first melted.

HYDROELECTRIC ENERGY – (hy-dro-el-*LEC*-tric *EN*-er-jee) Energy produced by running water. Natural waterfalls or man-made dams provide the force of water falling onto turbines that generates electricity. Not many regions are fortunate to have the benefit of a natural water source for hydroelectric energy generation. Nevertheless it is a clean safe means of making electricity.

HYDROGEN – (*HY*-dro-jen) (H) The name derives from the Greek *hydro* and *gen,* meaning *"water-forming."* On Earth, hydrogen combines with oxygen to provide life sustaining water. Hydrogen is the simplest, most plentiful element in the universe. It is the mother of all elements. Its atomic number is 1, indicating only 1 proton in its nucleus. Everything directly or indirectly was created from hydrogen. In the sun and other stars, at 18 million degrees Fahrenheit, hydrogen atoms collide and fuse to form helium atoms. The collisions and fusions continue to form all the elements. About 90% of the universe is made of hydrogen, the elemental element. A hydrogen fire is invisible, because a hydrogen burn produces no carbon soot, resulting in no flame or smoke. Commercially, hydrogen is used in the production of ammonia and other chemicals, in the hydrogenation of fats and oils, and in welding.

HYDROGEN BOMB – (*HY*-dro-jen *BOM*) (H-Bomb) The most destructive weapon devised by man. The H-Bomb is a fusion weapon. It imitates the physics of the stars by fusing hydrogen atoms to become helium atoms. A by-product of this reaction is energy. Detonating a hydrogen bomb is like releasing a tiny bit of the sun on Earth, with catastrophic consequences. The simpler atomic bomb is a fission weapon. It splits atoms like uranium and plutonium with a release of energy. Only 1/10 of 1% of the uranium in an A-Bomb is fissioned. In an H- Bomb, ½ of 1% of the hydrogen is fussed. On average, the hydrogen bomb is 10 times more powerful than an atomic bomb. In fact, a small atomic bomb must be detonated as the triggering device, to get the hydrogen bomb to explode. Incidentally: In 1960, the Russians detonated *"Czar Bomba,"* the *"Emperor Bomb"* in the Siberian Arctic. This 57 megaton H-Bomb was the greatest man- made explosion in history. It was 2,500 times more destructive than the Hiroshima atomic bomb. Czar Bomba was equivalent to 50,000,000 tons of TNT. That is like a train with a million boxcars full of high explosives. The blast shattered windows in Sweden, 1,000 miles away, and knocked people off their feet 50 miles away. Indeed, hydrogen bombs can shatter the planet.

HYDROGEN PEROXIDE – (*HY*-dro-jen per-*OX*-ide) (H2O2) A colorless liquid compound of 2 hydrogen and 2 oxygen atoms. Hydrogen peroxide is used as a bleaching agent, and an antiseptic. Many bacteria is *"anaerobic,"* meaning it cannot live in the presence of oxygen. That's why hydrogen peroxide kills these germs in open wounds. It oxygenates the germs to death.

HYDROLOGIC CYCLE – (hy-dro-*LOJ*-jic *SY*-cal) The continuous circulation of water among the atmosphere, the ocean, and the Earth. Sea water evaporates into clouds. The clouds rain upon the land. The rainwater flows back into the sea to be re-evaporated.

HYDROLOGY – (hy-*DROL*-uh-jee) (Hydrologist) (also Geohydrology) Literally, the study of water. Hydrology is the science dealing with the occurrence, circulation, distribution, and properties of the waters of the earth and its atmosphere.

HYDROMETEORS – (*HY*-dro-meet-tee-ors) In meteorology, liquid or solid water in the atmosphere such as snow, rain, hail.

HYDROMETER – (hy-*DROM*-met-er) An instrument for determining the specific gravity of a liquid, commonly consisting of a graduated tube weighted to float upright in the liquid whose specific gravity is being measured.

HYDROMETHANE – (hy-dro-*METH*-thane) (CH4-5.7H2O) or (4CH4-23H2O) Methane hydrate or methane clathrate is methane gas trapped within a crystal structure of water, forming a solid ice. It was previously thought that Hydromethane existed only deep out in space. However great deposits of Hydromethane has been found on the ocean floor, and in Russia's deep Lake Baikal. Terrestrial deposits have been discovered in Siberian and Alaskan sedimentary rocks. Hydromethane is very flammable, and is therefore called *"burning ice."* It yields a clean, pollution-free flame that is considered a fuel of the future. Incidentally: Evaporating gas bubbles from oceanic hydromethane can create such turbulence capable of sinking ships. It is theorized that this is the cause of some mysterious maritime disasters in the *"Bermuda Triangle."*

HYDRONYM – (*HY*-dro-nim) Name for a body of water: pond, creek, river, lake, sea. For example, the Missouri River is called the *"Big Muddy."*

HYDROSPHERE – (*HY*-dro-sfear) A meteorological term referring to the watery portion of our planet. As the atmosphere refers to air, the hydrosphere refers to water. Hydrosphere includes the oceans, seas, lakes, rivers, and the vapor (clouds) in the atmosphere.

HYDROTHERMAL VENTS – (hy-dro-*THERM*-mal *VENTS*) Tall oceanic chimneys that spew-out super-heated water impregnated with minerals. Hydrothermal vents are called *"black smokers."* The hot water comes from beneath the oceanic crust, where tectonic plates converge. The water temperature is about 455 degrees Fahrenheit, on average. Nevertheless, life upon a hydrothermal vent flourishes. Extremophiles like small crabs, fish, and giant tubeworms thrive in the scalding water that would cook most other creatures. Incidentally: The entire content of the global ocean is circulated, recycled through subduction faults into the Earth, and spewed back up through hydrothermal vents on the ocean floor every 10 million years.

HYDROTROPISM – (hy-dro-*TROP*-is-um) (Hydrotaxis) The compulsion of some plants to turn toward a source of water.

HYDROXYCHLOROQUINE – (hy-drox-ee-*CLOR*-ro-kwyn) An orally administered medication sold under the brand name *"Plaquenil,"* used to treat malaria, lupus, and rheumatoid arthritis. In 2019, hydroxychloroquine had been studied as a possible treatment for COVID-19 Coronavirus. Results have been inconclusive. Nevertheless, President Donald Trump (b. 1946) enthusiastically, shamelessly promotes the unproven drug as a cure. Why is Trump so eager to sell this dubious medication? Obviously, he stands to gain. Trump and family have invested in the product, hoping to make a killing. If not formally invested, the Trumps were certain offered a secret kickback from the drug company. Trump is driven by pure capitalistic greed. Unregulated self-administration of hydroxychloroquine has killed people with heart conditions throughout the world. But like a snake-oil peddler, Trump still hawks his *"elixir"* on his White House Coronavirus TV rallies. Doctors and scientists warn about using this untested remedy. Trump publicly contradicts them. Trump relies on his intuition, hunches, and *"big good brain."* Furthermore: *"He who serves as his own doctor has a fool for a patient."* Nevertheless, on May 18, 2020, President Trump announced that he takes unapproved hydroxychloroquine. Being a coward, Trump is probably lying, again. Speaker of the House Nancy Pelosi (b. 1940) said: *"He's our President and I would rather he not be taking something that has not been approved by the scientists, especially in his age group and in his, shall we say, weight group, morbidly obese, they say."* Trump's assertion is a lethal message to the stupids who still believe in him.

HYENA – (hy-*YEE*-na) Dog-like African-Asian predator/scavenger, pack animal with several cat-like characteristics. When the ancient Greeks first saw hyenas, the animal's bristly mane resembled that of a hog to them. The Greek name for hog is *"hys."* The beast was christened hyena. Disparaged as scavengers, hyenas hunt down 90% of their food. They are highly intelligent team hunters. In fact, having been on Earth for over 8 million years makes the hyena perhaps the oldest predator in the world. They will resort to cannibalism, though they are not partial to the taste of hyena. So they allow the carcass to amply putrefy before dining. Hyenas are the only mammal born with a full complement of functional teeth. Their rear teeth are pyramidal-shaped, perfect for crushing hard bone. Hyenas administer the strongest bite of all mammals, of all land creatures, about 2,000 pounds per square inch, as strong as an alligator. They can chomp through bone, skull, hoofs or horns. They are able to eat skin, hide, sinew that other predators like lions cannot. Furthermore, hyenas are the fastest eaters of all mammals. The larger females dominate the pack. They have enlarged genitals that resemble the males. Hyenas are known for their frightful laughing-like cries. They communicate with a variety of vocalizations.

HYGROSCOPIC – (hy-gro-*SCOP*-pic) Substances and materials having the ability to attract moisture from the air. Alcohol, paper, cotton, caramel, honey, glycerol, salt are all hygroscopic substances that absorb water molecules in the air.

HYKSOS – (*HYK*-sose) A nomadic Semitic tribe that migrated from Asia to Egypt in ancient times. The Hyksos conquered and ruled Egypt from about 1700 to 1580 BCE (between the 13th and 18th dynasties). It was a Semitic Hyksos pharaoh who welcomed his Semitic Hebrew cousins, (Joseph, Jacob, and the brothers) to Egypt during the famine. When the Hyksos were overthrown and the Egyptians restored to power, the Semitic Hebrews were regarded as a *"fifth column,"* a danger to the state. The Hebrews were stripped of liberties and they were eventually enslaved. They remained so until liberated by Moses (c. 1273 BCE).

HYLOZOISM – (hy-lo-*ZO*-is-um) In philosophy, the belief that all matter is living substance. All matter possesses some degree of life qualities and all life possesses a material basis. Hylozoism maintains that matter and life are inseparable. In this sense, hylozoism maintains that everything is sentient. The universe is everywhere alive. This belief is similar to animism which endows everything with a soul. After all, there is no good definition of life, no good differentiation between the living and non-living. Too, everything is made up of the same few simple elements: hydrogen, oxygen, nitrogen, carbon, iron, silicon. Therefore, perhaps there is no difference between the organic and inorganic, as hylozoism claims.

HYMEN – (*HY*-men) A fold of mucous membrane that partly covers the entrance of the vagina. The hymen is ruptured when sexual intercourse takes place for the first time. Therefore, an intact hymen can be considered proof of virginity. Incidentally: *Hymen* was the ancient Greek god of marriage.

HYPERBOLE – (hi-*PER*-bol-lee) A Hyperbolic (hi-per-*BOL*-lick) statement is an intentional exaggeration for effect. For example, *"I said a thousand times…,"* or *"I must have walked a thousand miles."* Hyperbolic language is not spoken, or intended to be taken literally (by a stable person). *"His Ignorancy,"* President Donald Trump (b. 1946) recklessly engages in hyperbolic language.

HYPERCANE – (*HY*-per-kain) Meteorological Armageddon. A mega-storm, a monstrous super hurricane the likes of which man has never seen. Global warming due to industrial burning of fossil fuels will release the energy into the atmosphere to ignite catastrophic hypercanes. A hypercane far surpasses a category 5 hurricane, which has sustained wind speeds of over 157 mph. A hypercane is off the scale (category 6 perhaps?), with sustained winds of over 250 mph, with gusts of 325 mph or more. (The entire hurricane would have the force of a compacted category 5 tornado or greater, but of super-hurricane size.) It would be as large as a medium size state. The storm surge would be tsunamic. Such a storm would scour the landscape clean of all manmade structures and artifacts. Incidentally: Meteorologists have suggested adding a Category 6 to the hurricane scale.

HYPERGAMY – (Hy-*PER*-gam-mee) (Hypergamous) The term *"gamy"* comes from the Greek *"gamia"* meaning marriage. The prefix *"hyper"* is Greek meaning *"over."* Hypergamy is marrying over or above your station, to one of higher social class and status. Some culture take this very seriously. In India, Hindu women are forbidden to marry below their caste or class.

HYPERINFLATION – (hy-per-in-*FLAY*-shin) Runaway inflation in excess of 500% per year. Hyperinflation is capitalism in its death throes. It marks the last stage of a monetary collapse.

HYPER-LIBIDINAL – (*Hy*-per li-*BID*-din-al) (Hyper- libidinous) A dignified, euphemistic way of saying over-sexed, lustful, lascivious, horny.

HYPERNESIA – (hy-per-*NEE*-shee-a) Hypernesia is a rare state of hysteria, the polar opposite of amnesia. In hypernesia, a trauma victim recalls every excruciating detail of her ordeal, reliving the horror.

HYPERNOVA – (*HY*-per-no-va) A mega-supernova. The death and destruction of a hypernova will produce the greatest explosion in the universe since the Big Bang, and will discharge a *gamma ray burst*, a radiation beam that can kill across the cosmos. The collapsed hypernova will become a massive black hole.

HYPERPHAGIA – (hy-per-*FAY*-jee-a) (also Polyphagia) Literally, *"super-eating."* Ravenous, being constantly, unnaturally hungry. Hyperphagia is having an insatiable appetite. In the natural world, hyperphagia is the period of voracious feeding in late summer and early autumn in preparation for hibernation. These mammals overload with calories in order to gain fat for the winter denning and hibernation.

HYPER REALISM – (*HY*-per *REE*-uhl-is-um) (Hyper realistic) Illusionary art, so realistic that it cannot be distinguished when set aside actual items. The drawing/painting serves as a 3-dimensional deception. A master hyper realist artist is like a magician, an illusionist. For example, a hyper realistic artist can paint a sinkhole on the street that will halt traffic.

HYPERSEXUALITY – (hy-per-seks-yoo-*AL*-li-tee) (Hypersexual) The prefix *"hyper"* mean *"over, more"* it's opposite *"hypo,"* means *"under, less."* Hypersexuality is being over sexed. It is a subjective term that must be defined or measured in degrees. One may be clinically diagnosed as hypersexual, having a neurotic compulsion, obsession to fuck. When sex dominates and interferes with normal life, a male is said to be afflicted with *"satyrism,"* a female with *"lesbianism."*

HYPERSONIC – (hy-per-*SON*-nic) A velocity 5 times the speed of sound (Mach 5) 3,806 mph.

HYPERTEXT – (*HY*-per-text) Interconnected, multi-referenced information. Hypertext is a hyperterm associated with computer technology. Hypertext is a computer software system that links topics on the screen to related information and graphics, which are typically accessed by a point-and-click method. Uncovering hypertext information is analogous to peeling an onion, increasing the discovery of information.

HYPERTHERMIA – (hy-per-*THUR*-mee-ay) Overheating – when the body gains more heat than it loses. Hyperthermia must be distinguished from fever, which is an abnormal rise in body temperature due to disease. Hyperthermia usually results from over-exertion in hot weather. The amount of heat a body can tolerate varies with individuals and their level of conditioning. However, on average, hyperthermia kicks in at 100.9oF body temperature and above. When hyperthermia reaches 104oF heat stroke occurs. The physical symptoms include slurring speech, reddening of the skin, excessive sweating, dehydration, dizziness, disorientation, headache, nausea, vomiting. In a heat stroke, the heart rate races, blood pressure rapidly increases, rapid breathing occurs, consciousness is ultimately lost. These physiological abnormalities may result in the damage of muscles, kidneys, heart, and brain. Vital organs cook. Ultimately, hyperthermal heat stroke kills. Of course, the elderly, with weaker overall constitutions are at greater risk. Too much exercise in the hot sun, wearing too much clothing and drinking too little water will certainly result in heat stroke.

HYPHEN – (*HY*-fehn) (Hyphenate, Hyphenated) A short line (-) used to connect parts of a compound word or the parts of a word divided for any purpose. For example: *"mother-in-law"; "anti-Putin"; "pro-Democratic."* A hyphen is shorter than a dash, half the size.

HYPNOGENIC STATE – (Hip-no-*JEN*-nic *STAYT*) Also called the alpha state, being between waking and sleep, in the twilight zone. Daydreaming, indulging in reverie is a hypnogenic condition. Hypnosis puts one in a hypnogenic state, making her open to hypnotic suggestion.

HYPNOSIS – (hip-*NO*-sis) (Hypnotism) The term is taken from the Greek god of sleep, *Hypnos.* Hypnosis is *"Meditation on steroids."* It is a sleep-like condition or trance related to dreaming, reverie, and meditation. Hypnosis was introduced by the Scottish surgeon James Braid (1795 – 1860) in a treatise entitled: *Neurypnology, or the rationale of nervous sleep,* in 1843. Through much of the 19th century, hypnosis was known as *"Braidism."* Reality is perception. Hypnosis commandeers perception in order to alter or control one's reality. Some people are more susceptible to suggestion, and are more easily hypnotized than others. Hypnotism is most successful under voluntary, cooperative conditions. Hypnosis can tap into the limitless potential of the subconscious mind. Through hypnosis, unconscious wounds may be located and healed. Too, positive subliminal suggestions can be implanted in the mind. Conversely, negative, dangerous, lethal suggestions can be implanted in the mind as well. Hypnotism can be manipulated into mind control, as with the C.I.A.'s *"Manchurian Candidate"* Program.

HYPOCHONDRIAC'S EPITAPH – (hy-po-*CON*-dree-acs *EP*-pi-taf) *"SEE!"*

HYPOCHONDRIAC – (hy-po-*KON*-dree-ak) A valetudinarian. A person neurotically obsessed with sickness, germs, disease, and ill health. Incidentally: The Coronavirus pandemic of 2020 is a hypochondriac's pipe dream. It feeds and validates every one of her exaggerated fears. It brings the entire population into her anxious orbit. The pandemic empowers her to vent her anxiety. With the pandemic, the hypochondriac hopes to recruit everyone into the realm of hypochondria. *"One cannot live with one's finger everlastingly on one's pulse."* – Joseph Conrad (1857 – 1924).

HYPOCHONDRIASIS – (hy-po-kon-dree-*AYS*-sis) (Hypochondria) Health/illness anxiety. An excessive fear of illness or belief that one is perpetually unwell. The *Law of Attraction* can actually bring on the illness the person dreads. That's because the subconscious mind cannot tell fantasy from reality. Incidentally: The epitaph on the tombstone of the hypochondriac read: *"SEE."*

HYPOCRACY – (hip-*POC*-cra-see) (Hypocrite) Being duplicitous. Hypocrisy is insincerity, dishonesty, a pretense of virtue. A hypocrite is a liar, phony. In fact, the term means *"actor"* in Greek. Jesus condemned the Pharisaical hypocrites 17 times in the New Testament. At one incident, Jesus railed at the Pharisees: *"You hypocrites! First take the plank out of your eye, and then you will see clearly to remove the speck from your brother's eye."* – Matthew 7:5. In the Gospel of Mark 12:40, Jesus condemned the hypocrites who *"Devour widow's houses and for a show make lengthy prayers. Such men will be punished most seriously."* This applies to capitalist banksters today. Perhaps Andre Gide (1869 – 1951) premeditated Donald Trump (b. 1946) when he wrote: *"The true hypocrite is the one who ceases to perceive his deception, the one who lies with sincerity."* *"Only the hypocrite is really rotten to the core."* – Philosopher Hannah Arendt (1906 – 1975).

HYPOCRITICAL CHRISTIANS – (hip-po-*CRIT*-ti-cal *KRIS*-chins) Jesus hated hypocrites. Jesus castigated rich Pharisees who made great show of their Temple donations, but despised the poor. Jesus condemned them 17 times in the New Testament. He compared these holy hypocrites with tombs that appeared white and clean on the outside, but concealed rot on the inside. Wealthy capitalists and their Republican representatives who destroy labor unions, and deny minimum wage to workers are hypocritical Christians. Those who lobby to cut welfare for the poor and Social Security for the elderly are the nastiest hypocrites whom Jesus would rebuke. Jesus' greatest Earthly concern was the plight of the poor, as enunciated in his Social Gospel. Catholics consider the Pope the representative of Jesus on Earth. Pope Francis I (b. 1936) said in February, 2017, *"It is better to be an atheist than a hypocritical Catholic [Christian], living a double life. It is not Christian to fail to pay your employees proper salaries, exploit people, do dirty business and launder money."* *"It's better to be an outspoken atheist than a hypocrite."* – Swami Prabhupada (1896 – 1977).

HYPOGEUM – (hy-poh-*JEE*-uhm) (Hypogean) An ancient subterranean vault, usually a burial chamber. The adjective hypogean means underground.

HYPOSEXUALITY – (hy-poh-seks-yoo-AL-li-tee) (Hyposexual) The prefix *"hypo"* means *"under, less,"* its opposite *"hyper"* means *"over, more."* Hyposexuality is suffering a lack of sexual satisfaction or relief. Hyposexuals are often frustrated, irritable people, especially males. Sex is a vital psycho-emotional need. Those who are denied this need develop neurotic maladies in other areas. Serial killers, murderous misogynists overwhelmingly suffered from hyposexuality.

HYPOTHERMIA – (hy-poh-*THUR*-mee-uh) Abnormally low body temperature, caused by prolonged exposure to cold. With hypothermia, the metabolic functions of the body are disrupted and will fail, resulting in death by freezing. The normal body temperature is 98.6oF, with a minimum normal at 96oF. If the body temperature drops by 10%, to 88.7oF, one becomes disoriented and may lose consciousness. The 4 levels of hypothermia are: Mild = 95oF to 89.6oF; Moderate = 89.5oF to 82.4oF; Severe = 82.3oF to 68oF; Profound = 67oF and lower. With the onset of hypothermia, all mechanisms that generate heat kick into action to regulate the body temperature. Muscles begin to shiver, blood pressure and heart rate increase, breathing becomes rapid, peripheral blood vessels constrict to preserve and generate heat. The liver releases glucose, raising the blood sugar level. Insulin secretion falls. If hypothermia advances to the moderate stage, shivering become violent, mental confusion ensues, body movements slow, a bluish pallor develops, one may lose consciousness. In the severe stage of hypothermia, heart rate and blood pressure drop dramatically, speech slurs, amnesia occurs if the victim is still conscious, organs fail resulting in death.

A Caveat: A wet body loses heat 25 times – (not percent but times) – faster than a dry body. Therefore, if one gets drenched in the extreme cold, it is safer to strip naked, than to wear the wet clothing.

HYPOTHETICO-DEDUCTIVE – (hy-po-*THET*-ti-co dee-*DUC*-tiv) A hypothesis that is not empirical (has not been witnessed). The event has never happened, so the theory is uncertain. A hypothetico-deductive is a method in which a hypothetical model based on observations is proposed and is then tested by deduction of consequences from the model. For example: there has not been a nuclear war because nuclear weapons have served as the deterrence. This deductive hypothesis cannot be proven unless we have a nuclear war. Likewise, alien visitation, abduction, instruction, or construction is a hypothetical- deductive because there is not proof of aliens, dead or alive.

HYPOTHESIS – (hy-*POTH*-thes-sis) A hypothesis is a proposition, or set of propositions, set forth as an explanation for the occurrence of some specific group of phenomena. It is a tentative proposal for the explanation of phenomena that has some degree of empirical substantiation or probability. A *working hypothesis* is asserted as a provisional conjecture to guide investigation. A hypothesis may be accepted as a highly probable explanation of a problem that is based on facts. In science, a hypothesis describes what will or would occur under certain conditions. If its predictive and/or explanatory power is high, a hypothesis may be elevated to the status of a theory or law.

HYPOTHESIS/THEORY – (hy-*POTH*-thes-sis THEER-ee) (Hypothetical/Theoretical) Two term used interchangeably, but with a nuance of difference. Both theory and hypothesis are assumptions of truth at different levels of validity. Neither a hypothesis nor a theory is a fact. A fact is an ironclad truth that will never change. For example: the Earth rotates on its axis and revolves around the sun. This fact cannot be argued. But both a hypothesis and theory fall below the factual threshold, a hypothesis lower than a theory. Both the hypothesis and theory can be testable and falsifiable. Too, a theory is not factually based at all time. So let's compare the differences. A hypothesis is considered as an unproven statement which is being tested. A theory is a scientifically tested and proven description or fact. A hypothesis depends upon suggestions, predictions, or possibilities. A theory is carried out by evidence, hence, it is verified. A hypothesis can or cannot be proved true, so its result is not verified. A theory can be *"assumed"* to be true, so its results can be considered verified. A hypothesis is based on a limited amount of data. A theory is based on a wide set of data. A hypothesis is usually based on accurate research and is limited to that instance only. A theory is the verification of common principals through experiments and multiple tests. A theoretical system may be applied to different types of situations. So a theory comes into existence when several ideas are made and accepted by the wider community. When a hypothesis is proved to be reasonably true by passing all tests and critical analysis, it is upgraded to a theory. A theory should have the capability to forecast future events.

HYPOXIA – (Hy-*POKS*-ee-ah) (Hypoxic) Low or lack of oxygen. Living organisms cannot survive in a hypoxic environment. In pathology, hypoxia is oxygen starvation of the brain. Strangulation, suffocation, drowning all result in death from hypoxia.

I

I – (*EYE*) The 9th letter in the English alphabet, a vowel. I is the chemical symbol for the element Iodine, as indicated on the Periodic Table of Chemical Elements. Too, I serves as the Roman numeral for 1, (one).

I – (*EYE*) The ego. I is the nominative singular pronoun, used by a speaker in referring to herself or himself. I is used as the subject (before the verb). When used as the direct or indirect object (after the verb), I becomes *me*. In either case, I (or me) represents the physical, material, mortal body that houses the spiritual, ethereal, immortal soul. *"When I say 'I,' I mean a thing absolutely unique, not to be confused with any other."* – Philosopher Ugo Betti (1892 – 1953). *"Of all the thoughts that rise in the mind, the thought 'I' is the first thought."* – Ramana Maharshi (1879 – 1950). *"All the evil in the world, and all the unhappiness, comes from the I-concept."* – Wei Wu Wei (1895 – 1986). *"When you know yourself, your 'I'ness vanishes and you know that you and Allah are one and the same."* – Ibn Arabi (1165 – 1240). *"I know that I exist; the question is, what is this 'I' that 'I' know."* – Rene Descartes (1596 – 1650).

I AM – (eye *AM*) The shortest but most profound sentence in the English language. In the *Torah*, God as *Yahweh* identified Himself to the prophet Moses from the burning bush as *"I AM, WHO AM,"* or *"I AM THAT I AM."* I do not need to *"Think, therefore I am,"* as the philosopher Rene Descartes (1596 – 1650) suggested, because God said, *"I AM."* If God is, then *I AM*, for *I AM* a part of that Holy Spirit which is God. The *I AM* represents the God Spirit in me and in you. <u>A COURSE in MIRACLES</u> (1976) associated with the Unity Church says, *"I AM as God made me."* Furthermore, *"God is love and so 'AM I'."* Every time I utter *"I AM," I AM* saying *"God is,"* and within me. The *"I"* alone represents the ego, the temporal, carnal carcass that houses the immortal spirit while the body performs its duties on this plane of existence. In <u>Prayer Changes Things</u> (1951), Unity Spiritual author Dana Gatlin (1884 – 1940) had written: *"I am is an ancient name for God, the All-Creator, and in us it is the divine presence by which we identify ourselves individually with the eternal creative power by which we love. 'I am!' It is our assertion of individual expression and our experience of life: 'I am' protected! 'I am' guided! 'I am' quickened, inspired! 'I am' alive, uplifted, strong! 'I am.' I have no troubles – 'I am' identified with God, with good! with life, love, intelligence, harmonious activity, success!"* *"'I Am' is the name of God, God is none other than the Self."* – Ramana Maharshi (1879 – 1950). *"I am not this body. I am in this body, and this is part of my incarnation and I honor it but that isn't who I am."* – Ram Dass (b. 1931).

I AND I – (eye and *EYE*) A Rastafarian religious concept comparable to the Judeo- Christian *"I AM."* I and I represents *"Jah's"* (God's) life-force or energy within all people and living creatures. The first I represents God, the second I represents oneself. The primary goal in Rastafarian meditation is maintaining awareness of I and I. This is *"Livity,"* or living a righteous life.

IATROPHOBIA – (eye-a-tro-*FO*-bee-a) (Iatrophobiacs) Phobic fear of doctors. Fear of doctors, as a fear of dentists develops in early childhood from painful, frightening experiences that proved to be traumatic. This is a common phobia, and a reasonable one. Iatrophobia can be eradicated through psychological counseling and many successful, pleasant trips to the doctor. The only way out is through.

IBERIAN PENINSULA – (eye-*BEER*-ree-an pen-*NIN*-su-la) A southwestern peninsula of Europe bound by France, the Mediterranean Sea, and the Atlantic Ocean and occupied by Spain and Portugal.

IBID. – (Ibid. = *"ibidem"*) Latin, meaning in the same book, chapter, page, etc.

ICE – (*IHYS*) Solid frozen water. Ice is one of the 3 states of water, along with liquid and vapor. Liquid water solidifies into ice when the temperature reaches and drops below 32oF or 0oC,(extracting the heat energy). When cooled, the water molecules in ice (H-O-H) become locked in a hexagonal crystal, and are vibrating very slowly. Though the molecules vibrate, they do not have enough heat energy to move freely (flow like a liquid). That's what makes ice a solid. Ice put under excruciating pressure will change its molecular structure, becoming light blue and very hard. This is glacial ice. Incidentally: There is over 12 million square miles of ice on Earth, twice the size of the USA. Antarctica holds 70% of the planet's fresh water locked-up in 90% of the planet's ice. It is easier for ice to form on land than on water. Land cools faster than water. Too, ice exists throughout the universe.

I.C.E. – (*IHYS*) Acronym for the "Immigration and Customs Enforcement" Agency. I.C.E. is President Donald Trump's (b. 1946) Republican Gestapos. They are operated by the Department of Homeland Security (a covert, anti- democratic organization with extra-constitutional powers). I.C.E. therefore fits- in perfectly at Homeland Security. I.C.E. is responsible for studying threats to the U.S. borders (Homeland Security Investigations), and arresting/deporting undocumented residents (Enforcement and Removal Operations). Most of the undocumented victims of I.C.E are Latin Americans. Many thousands had arrived in America as children or infants. They have established families and homes, and must work at the most menial jobs to avoid detection. Undocumented residents live in terror of the *"Gestapo-like knock on the door,"* by I.C.E. Yes, they are technically called illegal aliens. But human beings are neither *"technicalities,"* nor *"aliens."* They do not pose a safety threat to America. *Safety,* the *"Spirit of the Law,"* has given way to *Enforcement,* the *"Letter of the law."* The Immigration and Customs Enforcement Agency breaks up families, derails lives, and generates unspeakable fear and misery. Under President Donald Trump (b. 1946) I.C.E. has torn children and infants from parents, perhaps never to be reunited again. Republicans support I.C.E. enthusiastically. Rather than award wholesale citizenship, they hope to deport the undocumented, especially Latin Americans. Why not just document them? Because they will attain the right to vote. They will assuredly not vote Republican. Red states in the Southwest particularly will turn purple than blue (Democratic). Too, the *"Browning of America"* is not a Republican aspiration. Today, I.C.E. targets the undocumented. But the precedent is established for anyone to receive that *"Midnight knock on the door."* The Immigration and Customs Enforcement Agency is openly fascist in its activities. The assassinated Socialist Senator Huey Long (1893 – 1935) warned us that *"When fascism comes to America, it will come as national security."* Incidentally: The motto of I.C.E. is: *"Protecting National Security and Upholding Public Safety."*

ICEBERG – (*IHYS*-berg) The term literally means *"city of ice."* Icebergs are drifting mountains of ice in the polar oceans. Icebergs begin as compacted snow on a glacier. Icebergs break-off or *"calve"* from the great Antarctic glacier at the South Pole, or off the great Greenland glacier in the northern polar region. About 40,000 icebergs of various sizes adrift in the world's oceans. Actually, icebergs indicate the slow death of the glacier. There are 3 categories of icebergs, determined by their shape: *Dome, Wedge,* and *Block Icebergs.* (The Titanic hit a Dome Iceberg.) Only about 10% of the iceberg is visible, floating above the ocean surface. An iceberg the size of Rhode Island once calved off of Antarctica (1,545 square miles). The Greenland icebergs are more dangerous because of the busy sealane they enter. About 400 icebergs drift south from Greenland past Labrador, Canada yearly. The most tragic iceberg disaster was the 1912 sinking of the Titanic. Since then, no ship has been sunk by an iceberg, due to safety measures. Incidentally: In July 2017, an iceberg almost twice as big as Delaware (3,604 square miles), broke off the Antarctic ice shelf. Further evidence of global warming.

ICE BOMBS – (*IHYS BOMS*) (Megacryo Masses) Giant chunks of ice or hail falling from the sky, a meteorological mystery. A vaguely plausible explanation is that the ice bombs were expelled from jetliners.

ICEHOUSE EFFECT – (*IHYS*-hows ef-*FECT*) A natural counter-balance to the greenhouse effect. Where the greenhouse effect heats the planet, the icehouse effect helps cool the planet. All rain is slightly acidic. Acid rain takes carbon dioxide (a greenhouse gas) out of the atmosphere and deposits it into rocks, especially limestone. As the acid eats the rocks, the carbon dioxide is infused into the rocks, out of the atmosphere. A loss of carbon dioxide results in global cooling. The icehouse effect competes with the greenhouse effect.

ICE STORM – (*IHYS STORM*) Climatic condition between a rain and snowstorm. The condition that produces an ice storm is a stationary temperature inversion. An upper layer of warm air acts as a lid to a layer of cold air below. The raindrop must fall through the cold air near the ground. Super-cooled raindrops instantly freeze on contact with the ground, coating everything with a hard, heavy layer of ice. An ice storm is caused by freezing rain. A snowflake can melt into a raindrop. The drop does not possess the speck of dust (*condensation nuclei*) to freeze around. Therefore, the raindrop remains liquid, though its temperature is below the freezing point. When the rain hits any cold object on the ground, it instantly freezes, coating the object with heavy, clear icing. Montreal is geologically and climatologically most vulnerable cit for ice storms.

ICE WEDGING – (*IHYS WEJ*-jing) The mechanical weathering caused by the freezing and thawing of water that seeps into cracks in rocks. Ice wedging also creeps into pavements creating damaging potholes at northern latitudes.

ICEWORMS – (*IHYS* werms) (Enchytraeid annelids) Any of 77 known species of small worms that live in glacial ice. Iceworms are one of the few creatures that live their entire life cycle in temperatures below freezing (32°F or 0°C). Iceworms burrow through solid ice like earthworms burrow through soft soil. Iceworms feed on snow algae and bacteria. Iceworms are included in the group of extraordinary animals called *extremophiles* – living in extreme environments.

ICH DIEN – (eek *DEEN*) German for *"I serve."* Ich Dien is the motto of the British Prince of Wales, heir to the throne of the United Kingdom.

I CHING – (eye *CHING*) An ancient Chinese book of divination in which 64 pairs of trigrams (3 adjacent letters) are shown with various interpretations.

ICHOR – (*EYE*-core) (Ichorous) In classical mythology, ichor was divine blood. It was the ethereal fluid flowing in the veins of the gods. Today in pathology, ichor is not so heavenly. It is the acrid, watery discharge, as from an ulcer or wound.

ICHTHYOLOGY – (ich-thee-*OL*-lo-jee) (Ichthyologist) Ichthyology is not the study of itches, but rather fishes. Ichthyology is the branch of zoology dealing with fish. An ichthyologist is a marine biologist or zoologist, a fish scientist.

ICHTHYOPHOBIA – (ich-thee-o-*FO*-bee-a) (Ichthyophobiac) Phobic fear of fish. A phobic reaction to any animal must result from frightening, painful, traumatic experiences with those animals.

ICHTHYS – (*ICH*-thees) Greek for fish. Ichthys is also the Greek acronym for *"Jesus Christ Son of God Savior."* When Christianity was illegal and dangerous in the Roman Empire, the fish (ichthys) was the secret Christian symbol. It remained so until supplanted by the crucifix when the cult was accepted as a religion. Today the ichthys has been resurrected as the *"Jesus Fish"* on the back of automobiles. ></))))*>

ICON – (*EYE*-kon) (Iconic, Iconology) A religious picture of God, Jesus, Mary, some Saint or Angel. Icons are traditional in the Eastern Orthodox Church. Icons are two-dimensional paintings on wood. In Eastern Orthodox Christianity, three-dimensional statues are forbidden. Dogmatically, it is considered idolatrist to pray to a three-dimensional statue, but not a flat icon. Pagan cultures worshiped anthropomorphic statute as gods. Nevertheless the icons are venerated and believed to possess divine, supernatural power. Ironically, one famous Russian Orthodox icon depicts Jesus armed with a sword – which is thoroughly counter-Christian. Incidentally: The term icon has drifted out of the realm of religion, to be applied to the *"adoration"* of entertainment and sports heroes, as if they were gods.

ICONIC – (eye-*KON*-nic) Originally, relating to the sacred art of the Eastern Orthodox Church. The term has evolved to mean a person or item that is revered or idolized. An iconic monument is representative of a location, as the Eiffel Tower to Paris, or the Statue of Liberty to New York.

ICONOCLASTS – (eye-*KON*-o-clasts) (Iconoclastic, Iconoclastism) Originally, fundamentalist fanatics in Russia who destroyed the precious religious art (icons) in the Eastern Orthodox Church. Wanton vandalism (Iconoclastism) is an ancient plague on civilization and humanity. The fabulous Library of Alexandria was burned by the Romans, Christians, and Muslins successively. The British Puritans defiled Catholic and Anglican churches throughout the island. Ancient art and artifacts were massively destroyed by the ISIS zealots. What almost all iconoclast have in common is religious fanaticism. The term iconoclast has been broadened. Today an iconoclast is a debunker. He is one who attacks cherished beliefs, traditions, institutions, and personalities (iconic figures) as false and unworthy of praise.

ICONOLAGY – (eye-kon-no-*LAG*-nee) A sexual fetish for statues of naked people. The sight of realistic genitals carved in stone will prompt the person to masturbate. *"No nude, however abstract, should fail to arouse in the spectator some vestige of erotic feeling, even if it be only the faintest shadow – and if it does not do so it is bad art and false morals."* – Art Historian Kenneth Clark (1903 – 1983).

IDEA – (eye-*DEE*-a) A specialized thought, directed toward some action, plan, or solution. An idea is a concentrated thought, more purposeful than a reverie. An idea in goal-oriented. *"I got a good idea."* Ideas are the result of laborious directed thinking.

IDEALISM – (eye-*DEE*-al-is-um) Oldest philosophy, maintains that there are universal, absolute, God-given truths. Idealists think in terms of good and evil, right and wrong. Idealists will punctuate their discourse with *"God said…"* or *"It is written…."* Classical idealism would be better served by the name *"idea-ism."* For it maintained that only the mind, spirit, ideas are real. Reality is dependent for its existence upon a mind and its activities. The entire universe, in fact, is the embodiment of a mind, the idealists contend. All religion, everything metaphysical, spiritual, mystic, divine, transcendental, other-worldly falls under the rubric of idealism.

IDENTITARIANISM – (eye-den-ti-*TARE*-ree-an-is-um) (Identitarians) A collection of ultra-alt-right white supremacist parties in several primarily white nations. Of French origin (*Bloc Identitaire*), Identitarianism has spread throughout Europe and North America. They are all fascistically nationalistic and racist. Identitarians seek a pure white homeland. They are anti-immigration from non- white nations. Identitarianism is neo-Nazi and anti-Semitic to various degree in different nations. The most visible American Identitarians are the members of Identity Europa. Being fascist, Identitarianism is a grave threat to democracy.

IDENTITY – (eye-*DEN*-ti-tee) The authentic self, the real you. Identity is one's personality, individuality, distinctiveness. One's identity must be integrated, meaning being the same person under all circumstances, which indicates integrity.

IDENTITY EUROPA – (eye-*DEN*-ti-tee *YOUR*-ro-pa) An American neo-Nazi white supremacist, nationalist organization founded in 2016 (year of the Trump), by Nathan Damigo. They were modeled after French fascist groups. As its name implies, Identity Europa identifies with European Americans [read: *whites*] excluding Jews. Identity Europa is an ultra-alt-right hate group. They intend to unite all fascist hate groups. Their goal is the Nazification of America. They recognize a hero in Donald Trump (b. 1946). Identity Europa is striving to infiltrate and gain control of the Republican Party. Republican Congressmen refuse to condemn or comment on the group, in fear of alienating their vile followers. Identity Europa protests for the immediate exclusion of all non-white immigration to America. They are anti-Semitic, anti-Hispanic, anti-Black, anti- Oriental, and anti-Muslim. This hate group also hates Liberals and Progressives, the voices of diversity, inclusion, and toleration. The Jewish Anti-Defamation League and the Southern Poverty Law Center both designate Identity Europa as potentially dangerous. Consider them as a vigorous virus, a single cancer cell attempting to metastasize. Perhaps the next American Civil War will not be North versus South, but Left versus Right. Incidentally: Identity Europa is perplexedly anti-capitalist. All fascists, including the Nazis are fanatical capitalists. Their economic identification does not identify Identity Europa as Socialist in any way. Socialism is universal, all-inclusive, racially tolerant, as well as anti-capitalist.

IDENTITY MARKERS – (eye-*DEN*-ti-tee *MAHRK*-ers) Personal characteristics, qualities, attributes, that collectively define a person as a unique individual. Our identity markers determine who we believe we are, and how others view us. Biology and sociology (nature and nurture) determine identity markers. Gender, race, ethnicity, body type, facial features, personality type, emotional qualities are genetic identity markers. Cultural identity markers include: Class, religion, political affiliation, group membership, educational level, job choice, lifestyle, sexual preference. The overriding psychological identity marker is one's attitude – how one feels about the biological and sociological identity markers. *"If God had wanted me otherwise, He would have created me otherwise."* – Johann von Goethe (1749 – 1832).

IDENTITY POLITICS – (eye-*DEN*-ti-tee *POL*-li-tiks) Political activity or movement based on or catering to the cultural, ethnic, gender, racial, religious, or social interests that characterize a group identity. It is particularism in the place of pluralism. Identity politics is tribalistic. It emphasizes the first name in the hyphenated-American: for instance *"African"*-American, *"Mexican"*-American, *"Polish"*-American. By doing so, identity politics highlights differences, rather than commonalities. Identity politics tends to become exclusive, clannish – *"us and them."* Extreme identity politics can develop into bigotry and racism. Fascist hate groups like *"Identity Europa"* are spawned in identity politics. Indeed be proud to be a Mexican, Polish, or Korean-American. Just keep the emphasis on American.

IDEOGRAPHS – (*ID*-dee-o-grafs) (also Ideograms) Literally means *"idea writing."* An ideograph is an early form of writing in which a symbol represents an entire idea. An ideograph is a stylized rendition of a pictograph (hieroglyph). Ideographic writing is an advancement over pictographic writing, but is still very cumbersome compared to alphabetic writing. Modern Chinese is still ideographic. That's why a Chinese keyboard needs 6,000 keys. Incidentally: The Chinese ideograph for *trouble*, is *"2 women under 1 roof."*

IDEOLOGY – (id-dee-*OL*-lo-jee) A deeply held belief or doctrine that guides one's life, rooted in one's philosophy. One's ideology is a coherent set of ideas and beliefs that forms the basis of a political or economic theory, and which provides a distinctive explanation of the way the world works. Ideology is part of one's core values. The ideology of this text is Socialistic and Spiritualistic.

IDES – (*EYEDS*) In the old Roman calendar, the 15th day of May, July, October, and March, as well as the 13th day of the remaining months.

IDES OF MARCH – (*EYEDS* of *MARCH*) (*Idus Martii* in Latin.) March 15th, 44 BCE, the day the Roman general-cum-tyrant, Julius Caesar (100 – 44 BCE) was assassinated by members of the Senate. Caesar held executive power in Rome, and began to usurp legislative power as well, becoming a dictator. Caesar's sycophants in the Senate named him *"Dictator Perpetuo,"* (Dictator Forever). This was too much for the more Liberal Senators who respected the Republic, wanted to retain some semblance of democracy, and the safe division of authority. The only form of impeachment was the dagger. So a delegation from the Senate stabbed Caesar 23 times to death. In William Shakespeare's (1564 – 1616) play, *"The Tragedy of Julius Caesar"* (1599), at a victory party, a soothsayer warned jubilant Caesar, *"Beware of the Ides of March."* Since then, March 15th (*The Ides*), like Friday the 13th, has been considered to be a day of bad luck. Too, it's a lesson and warning to all prospective tyrants. *"Trump, are you listening?"*

IDIOCRACY – (id-dee-*OC*-ruh-see) (Idiot, Idiocy, Idiotic, Ideocracies) A crazy suggestion, performance, project, or person. Donald Trump (b. 1946) is a walking, talking ideocracy.

IDIOM – (*ID*-dee-um) (Idiomatic, Idiomatocity) A figure of speech that makes no sense in any other language. Idioms provide problems for translators. An idiomatic statement is often culturally connected. Therefore, to one outside the culture, the statement is misinterpreted or totally nonsensical. Incidentally: *Idiomaticity* presented extraordinary challenges for missionaries in far-off parts of the world. When translating the Bible, they insisted on keeping the meaning as authentic as possible. In the South Pacific, the very concept of snow was alien. Therefore, the passage Isaiah 1:18, *"Though your sins be scarlet, they shall be made white as snow,"* had to be adjusted to: *"Though your sins be scarlet, they shall be made white as coconut meat."* Now there is an idiomatic challenge.

IDIOPATHIC – (id-dee-oh-*PATH*-ik) (Idiopathically) A medical mystery. A medical term referring to a disease or ailment that arises spontaneously or from an obscure, unknown cause. The prefix *"ideo"* derives from the Greek *"idios"* meaning *"private,"* or *"one's own." "Pathic"* derives from the Greek *"pathikos"* meaning *"to suffer"* the effects of disease. So an idiopathic disease can be one uniquely peculiar to an individual. Also, an idiopathic disease may have an unknown cause like primary idiopathic epilepsy. Therefore, the term idiopathic applies to one of a kind, or a onetime event. When the doctors don't know, they will call it idiopathic.

IDIOSYNCRACY – (id-dee-o-*SINK*-cra-see) (Ideosyncratic) A unique characteristic, eccentricity, odd mannerism, or unusual habit peculiar to an individual. In fact, the prefix *"idio"* derives from the Greek *"idios,"* meaning *"private"* or *"one's own."* An idiosyncrasy may actually be a neurotic defense mechanism. Incidentally: Geniuses, very talented people, in the arts or science tend to be eccentrically idiosyncratic. Normalcy, or normality is mediocrity. "I *am different. Don't let that upset you."* – Medieval Alchemist Paracelsus (c. 1493 - 1541).

IDIOT – (*ID*-dee-it) Once a legitimate psychological term for the lowest grade of mental defective. An idiot was classed below both the *"moron,"* and the *"imbecile."* An idiot was considered totally helpless, in need of constant care. The terms idiot, imbecile, and moron are no longer used in psychological circles, for they have become popular insults. Incidentally: Idiot is the most prevalent characterization secretly attributed to Donald Trump (b. 1946) by his subordinates. Notable figures had publicly referred to President Trump as an idiot. They include H. R. McMaster (b. 1962), Trump's former National Security Adviser, who confidentially referred to Trump as a *"dope"* with a *"kindergarten mentality,"* and an *"idiot."* Former White House Chief of Staff Reince Priebus (b. 1972) called Trump an *"Idiot."* Present White House Chief of Staff John Kelly (b. 1950) called Trump an *"idiot."* Treasury Secretary Steven Mnuchin (b. 1962) called Trump an *"idiot."* Former FBI Director Michael Hayden (b. 1945) called Trump an *"idiot."* More so, Hayden depicted Trump as *"Vladimir Putin's* (b. 1952) *useful idiot,"* as well as *"a congenital liar."* Former Secretary of State Rex Tillerson (b. 1952) upgraded Trump to a *"moron."* Former economic adviser Gary Cohn (b. 1960) promoted Donald Trump even high as being merely *"dumb"* – *"dumb as shit."* This speaks volumes about Trump's supporters. After all, as they say, *"It takes one to know one."*

IDITAROD – (eye-*DIT*-ter-rod) A 325 mile long-river in southwestern Alaska. The name *"Iditarod"* is a corruption of *"Haiditirod,"* a Shageluk Indian word meaning *"clear water."* The river's name has been given to a torturous sporting event called *"The Last Great Race."* (Thank God!) The Iditarod is a long-distance sled- dog race in early March from Anchorage to Nome Alaska. The competition first started in 1973. The racer called a *"musher"* rides a sled pulled by 14 dogs. The race runs on snow through the frozen Alaskan wilderness for at least 938 punishing miles in wind chill temperatures that can drop to -100OF. The teams mush on through white-out blizzards. It may take anywhere from 8 to 15 days or more depending on weather conditions to complete this survival test. In order to be considered a finisher, at least 5 of the 14 dogs must survive the ordeal and be on the tow line at the finish line. (Animal cruelty you think?) The Iditarod is perhaps the most grueling, dangerous sporting competition in the world. Incidentally: PETA (People for the Ethical Treatment of Animals) have applied every means to put an end to the Iditarod. Since 1973, over 160 dogs have been killed in the competition. Scores of dogs die later from health complications or must be put down. Many, many more are maimed or crippled for life. Disabled dogs are discarded. But mushing and the Iditarod are profit generators, therefore the game will go on. There are 48 teams competing in 2021 consisting of 672 dogs. To date, just over 700 mushers have managed to cross the finish line. *"We Must Mush On!"*

IDOLATRY – (eye-*DOLL*-la-tree) Extreme adulation. The worshiping of idols as divinities. Idolatry pays homage and adoration to material objects of wood and stone, like statues. It takes overwhelming faith to be an idolatrist and worship a static material object, no matter how artfully created. *"It is hard for one to worship the idol, who knew it when it was a tree stump in the forest."* – Polish Proverb. According to the Jewish Midrash, Abraham's father was an idols maker. He manufactured idols of stone. One day, Abraham smashed all the idols. Abraham told dad that the idols fought and destroyed each other. Impossible, dad angrily replied. The idols are powerless. They are made of stone. Then why do you worship them? Abraham asked. Incidentally: The following inscription was found in Rome. *"Marcus the physician made an offering to the marble Zeus today. Though marble, and though Zeus, the funeral is tomorrow."* *"Hitler is simply pure reason incarnate."* – Nazi Party Secretary Rudolf Hess (1894 – 1987).

IDOLATER'S LAMENT – (eye-*DOLL*-la-tors la-*MENT*) *"It's hard to worship the idol, who knew it when it was a tree stump in the forest."* – Polish Proverb.

I.E. – (i. e. = *"id est"*) Latin for *that is. "A second Trump Presidency would be catastrophic, i.e. kill democracy."*

I.E.D. – (eye ee *DEE*) (Improvised Explosive Device) A homemade poor man's bomb, a landmine planted at the roadside to destroy moving vehicles or rigged- up in a building. The terrorist's I.E.D. today, is what the partisan's booby-trap was in the 20th century and the anarchist's Orsini Bomb was in the 19th century. Being improvised, this explosive device can be made from anything that will explode. Often captured enemy shells are used against them. The I.E.D. was successfully employed by anti-American forces in Iraq. It added the element of terror to the combat. One never knew where the I.E.D. was planted.

I.E.P. – (eye ee *PEE*) (Individualized Educational Plan), Special accommodations, considerations made in school for handicapped students. I.E.P.'s are federally mandated and contractually binding. Regulations for the helpless, (as the I.E.P.) are being eliminated by imbecilic President Donald Trump (b. 1946) and his clueless Education Secretary Betsy DeVos (b. 1958). Update: The Democratic Presidency of Joe Biden has saved the Individualized <u>E</u>ducational <u>P</u>lan for America's handicapped students.

IF – (*IF*) (Iffy) A tiny word packing enormous power. The conjunction if means in case that; on condition that; granting or supposing that something will happen. All ifs are based on contingencies. *"If pigs had wings they'd fly." "If you can keep your head when all about you are losing theirs and blaming it on you…."* The poem *"IF,"* (c. 1895) by Rudyard Kipling (1865 – 1936). Iffy is an adjective meaning full of unresolved points or questions. *"It's an interesting, albeit iffy proposal."* So what is iffy is uncertain, doubtful. The term *"if"* derived from the Old English (West Saxon) *"gif"* (pronounced *"yif"*).

IF ONLY – (if *OHN*-lee) A mournful phrase which indicates regret. If only is a lament for a second chance, usually to right a wrong. Everybody lives with the pang of *"if only's."* It's a sad condition of being human. *If only* pertains to our personal behavior, as in: *"If only I had been more patient, understanding, tolerant, loving."* Or: *"If only I had been less stubborn; if only I had taken that job."* The most painful rendition of *if only* relates to our relations with loved ones, especially those who have passed. Most people are haunted by regrets which are stated in terms of: *"I should've…I wish I would've…."* This concerns acts of commission and omission that we presently bemoan. *"Things I wish I hadn't said; deeds I did that now I dread. Now it seems like such a crime, that I hadn't taken the time."* To avoid the anguish and despair of *If only* regrets, pray to those you have offended for forgiveness. They will *"Forgive us our trespasses, as we forgive those who trespassed against us."* This is how you halt the hurt. Furthermore, avoid putting yourself in new *If only* situations and positions. Simply follow the Golden Rule: *"Do onto others, as you would have others do onto you."* Too, practice this exercise suggested by the inspirational author and speaker Og Mandino (1923 – 1996). Pretend you know a deep dark secret about the other person. Pretend you know that that person will be dead in 24 hours. How would you treat that person? Certainly not in a manner that would engender future *If only* regrets. Trite but true, life is short. Time is running out. Don't save your love for the tomorrow which may never come. *"We get old too soon, we get smart too late."* – Boxer Mike Tyson (b. 1966).

IGEN – Actually "iGen" (*EYE*-jen), The iPhone Generation. The generation captivated, mesmerized by the iPhone. These are the young adults and teenagers from 2007 to the present. Much of a generation has become addicted to the multi-functional smartphone. This is the *"Swiss army knife"* of high-tech telephony. It provides the functions of a phone, camera, computer, television, and more. But research indicates that this multi-touch device has put the iGeneration out-of-touch. Alarming warning signs had been noticed by 2012. Isolation among teenagers is growing precariously. Socialization decreases as depression increases. The iGen is dating less and has fewer friends. Ever more teenagers suffer from lack of sleep, due to the smartphone. The suicide rate among youngsters is at an all-time high. Human contact is sorely lacking. High-tech will never substitute for high-touch. The perspicacious Albert Einstein (1879 – 1955) lamented: *"I fear the day that technology will surpass our human interaction. The world will have a generation of idiots."* Can this be the iGen?

IGLOO – (*IG*-gloo) An ingenious dome-shaped dwelling constructed from blocks of compressed snow, by the Inuits (Eskimos). Air bubbles in the snow blocks serve as an insulator. Human body heat is trapped in the air bubbles. The temperature in an igloo can rise to a tolerable 61 degrees Fahrenheit. The Inuit, inured to the cold, would often remove a block from the ceiling, to let out some heat. Igloo construction has become a lost art, like the teepee or wigwam, an anthropological curiosity.

IGNEOUS – (*IG*-nee-us) Rock of fiery volcanic origin. Igneous rock was crystalized from molten magma in the Earth's mantle. The heavy basalt is the igneous rock that sank as the ocean floor. Some igneous basalt sank into the Earth, melted and mixed with water. It metamorphosized into lighter granite. The granite rose as a platform for the continents.

IGNORAMUS – (ig-nor-*RAY*-mus) Latin for *"We do not know."* Today, in popular usage, an ignoramus is a clueless fool, a know-nothing, an exceedingly ignorant person. The word has an interesting history. <u>*Ignoramus*</u> is the title of a Cambridge University farce written in 1615, by English playwright George Ruggle (1575 – 1622). The title character is the Magistrate of the Town of Cambridge, (or Recorder of the Borough) Francis Brackyn, whom Ruggle named *"Ignoramus."* This fact was lost on no one, which made the play wildly popular and controversial, especially among the students at that time. Mr. Ignoramus was arrogant and authoritarian, though remarkably stupid. He got embroiled in a town-and-gown feud with the university personnel. In the play, Ignoramus was perpetually being duped and humiliated. Eventually, he was judged to be possessed by demons, subjected to exorcism, and locked up in a monastery. Incidentally: *"Ignoramus"* is actually a legal term, a verdict by a Grand Jury. In law it means: *"<u>We do not know</u> of any reason why this person should be indicted on these charges."* Certainly, George Ruggle intended his play to serve as a satire of the judiciary too. As Town Magistrate, the real Francis Brackyn must have brought frivolous charges against many Cambridge students that were thrown out of court. So many of his charges proved to be ignoramus. This accounts for Ruggle's choice of this legal term for Magistrate Brackyn's name. (Parenthetically: Donald Trump (b. 1946) is a *de facto* ignominious ignoramus. But *de jure,* he is not. A Grand Jury will indeed find Trump guilty of a variety of *High Crimes and Misdemeanors,* and felonies.)

IGNORANCE – (*IG*-nor-rens) (Ignorance) A term used as a pejorative, even insult, and shouldn't be. One who is ignorant (in the state of ignorance) simply lacks knowledge, information, facts, due to a lack of learning, communication, or schooling. Therefore, ignorance is not a personal character flaw, but rather the result of educational deprivation. Poverty, circumstances, bad luck may prevent one from gaining education and remaining ignorant. Many ignorant people have high I.Q.s, are highly intelligent. But ignorance often suppresses their intelligence, forcing it to lie dormant. *"The smartest kids are on the streets."* – Rapper Cindy Campbell (b. 1961). Ignorance is not synonymous with stupidity. A stupid person may be apply intelligent yet follow an ignorant path. People trapped in ignorance are gullible, easily persuaded, and the prey of demagogues. This is why poor people will forsake their own socio-economic interests and support a fascist like Donald Trump (b. 1946) and his wealthy backers. The American oligarchs are manipulating the ignorance of many poor to join the *MAGA, QAnon* army, in defense of the rich. Only learning, the eradication of ignorance, will defeat fascism. An honest, educated person is naturally Liberal, Progressive, Compassionate, and Socialistic. Awaken to the truth, they stand woke, eyes fully open. *"I was blind but now I see."* – John 9:25.

IGNORANT – (*IG*-nor-rant) (Ignorance) Lacking knowledge, learning, training, information. An ignorant person may be stupid too, but not necessarily so. An ignorant person is stupid if he does not want to learn.

She is stupid if she is pleased to stew in her ignorance. This is the case with those Trumpsters addicted to FOX News Network. Ignorant people are gullible. Wealthy conservative Republicans exploit the ignorance of the poor to their selfish benefit – perpetuation of personal power and privilege. *"The poor do not know the source of their miseries. Ignorance, the daughter of bondage, makes them docile instruments of privileged."* – Socialist Louis Blanqui (1805 – 1881). Corporate capitalists dupe the ignorant into voting against their own economic interests. *"There is a cult of ignorance in the United States and there always has been. The strain of anti-intellectualism has been a constant thread winding its way through our political and cultural life, nurtured by the false notion that democracy means that my ignorance is just as good as your knowledge."* – Scientist Isaac Asimov (1920 – 1992). Furthermore, Asimov reminded us that: *"Uncertainty that comes from knowledge (knowing what you don't know) is different from uncertainty coming from ignorance."* Gratefully, teaching cures ignorance. An ignorant person can be educated out of their ignorance.

IHS – (eye aych *ES*) An ancient Latin Christogram devised as a partial transliteration of the first three letters of the name Jesus in Greek: *"Iesus Hominum Salvator,"* ("Jesus Savior of Mankind"). *IHS* has been the dominant Christogram in the Church from the 15th century to the present. It frequently appear in religious art, and on the large ceremonial Eucharist host.

IL DUCE – (ill *DOO*-chay) Italian for *"The Leader,"* the title adopted by the fascist Italian dictator, Benito Mussolini (1883 – 1945) in 1923. *"Ducem"* means to lead in Latin. Mussolini and his Italian fascists drew the blueprint for Adolf Hitler's (1889 - 1945) more extreme Nazi fascists. In the early days, Hitler admired and emulated Mussolini.

ILK – (*ILK*) Means of the same family, class, or kind. For example, *"People of that ilk should not be admitted."*

ILLEGALLIES – (ill-*LEE*-gal-lys) A neologism for *"illegal lies."* Lying, intentionally telling falsehoods is a character flaw – not a crime. But it should be when it involves national security, and social-political stability. Dangerous conspiracy theories, flagrant political lies as disseminated by fascist organizations, the hate mongers should be prosecuted. An independent, non-partisan Federal *"Veracity Court"* in the Justice Department should have the power to investigate and indict gross illegal liars. After all, if it's illegal to lie under oath in court, as well as to slander and liable, lying to the public while running or serving in public office should be prosecutable too. Our democracy weighs in the balance. All the institutions of a democratic society are based on trust. Illegal liars intend to erode that trust and destroy democracy. That is treasonous. That is grounds for prosecution. Incidentally: The terms politician and liar have become synonymous. We must change that. Government is too important to be a den of deception. Therefore, every person who registers to run for any office on any level should swear an oath, to: *"Tell the truth, the whole truth, and nothing but the truth."* To break this oath should be the prosecutable crime of perjury, just like in court. Let the dishonest politician go through the trouble and expense to defend his lies, publicly in court. Politicians will think twice before they lie to us.

ILLEGITIMATE – (ill-leh-*JIT*-tih-mat) (Illegitimacy) Literally, means not legal. In a sociological contexed, illegitimacy is a *"bastardy"* condition. It is having a child out of wedlock. Such a child is illegitimate. The crazy inference is that there is a legal and an illegal way to be born. The very concept of illegitimacy is mean-spirited. It is an archaic vestigial remain of a theocratically dominated society. No longer is a person born of unmarried parents braded a bastard.

ILLEGITIMATE PRESIDENT – (ill-leh-*JIT*-tih-mat *PRES*-si-dent) An illegal President. A person who had gained the Presidency under false pretenses. In 2016, Donald Trump (b. 1946) received 3,000,000 less votes that his Democratic opponent, Hillary Clinton (b. 1947). But that does not make Trump illegitimate. The archaic, undemocratic Electoral College put Trump in the White House. Trump is an illegal President because of illegal Russian help in the election. Russian money, propaganda, intelligence, vote tampering, electoral interference made their man, Trump, the President. On June 28, 2019, former President Jimmy Carter (b. 1924) was asked about Russian electoral interference and Trump's illegitimacy. Carter exclaimed: *"The president himself should condemn it, admit that it happened, which I think 16 intelligence agencies have already agreed to say. And there's no doubt that the Russians did interfere in the election, and I think the interference although not yet qualified, if fully investigated would show that Trump didn't actually win the election in 2016. He [Trump] lost the election, and he was put into office because the Russians interfered on his behalf.… Based on what I just said, which I can't retract, I would say tes. Trump is an illegitimate president."*

ILL-FATED – (*IHL FAY*-ted) Bringing bad fortune. Destined, as though by fate, to an unhappy or unfortunate end. *"The ill-fated Trump Presidency will have lasting poisonous results."*

ILLIBERAL – (ihl-*LIB*-ruhl) (Illiberalism, Illiberality) Not liberal, contra-liberal, anti- liberal [read: *conservative*]. An illiberal individual is narrowminded, bigoted, often racist. The illiberal are anti-progressive, therefore regressive or reactionary. They hope to go back to the *"bad ole days,"* perhaps to racial segregation, the white supremacists even to slavery. All *"Trumpanzees"* are illiberal. An illiberal person would endorse fascism, for democracy is inherently liberal. So liberalism is liberating, while illiberalism is ill-fated fascism. The Republican ethos is illiberal, the Democratic ethos more liberal, the Socialist ethos most liberal and liberating of all.

ILLICIT INDIGENCY – (ill-*LIS*-set *IN*-di-jen-see) Making poverty illegal. A government sponsored insurance and re-assurance program that avows that no one will be poor. It will be unlawful to be impoverished. Not the needy citizen, but the negligent government would be held culpable as the lawbreaker, if someone was judged poor. It's the government's responsibility to guarantee that nobody is destitute. Jobs, welfare, food, lodging and education – the entire social arsenal would be employed by the government to eradicate poverty. The legal minimum wage will be more than merely *"livable,"* it will assure *"prosperity."* Universal income will fortify the standard of living for all citizens. Under illicit indigency, poverty is regarded as a disease. Illicit indigency is part of the Socialistic *"War on Poverty."* To attain this degree of decency requires the redistribution of the wealth. That is done by equitable taxation. *"Voters must demand Congress to tax wealth, not want."* – Philosopher Dr. John Dewey (1859 – 1952). *"From each according to their ability, to each according to his need."* – Dr. Karl Marx (1818 – 1883).

ILLITERATE – (il-*LIT*-ter-rit) (Illiteracy) Unable to read or write. Illiterate is distinct from *alliterate* which means not having reading or writing, and perhaps not knowing what they are. An American citizen in Toledo, Ohio who cannot read is illiterate. An Amazonian Indian in the rainforest who cannot read or write is aliterate.

ILLOGICALITY – (il-loj-ji-*CAL*-lit-tee) (Illogical) An example of the nonsensical. An illogicality disregards the rules of logic. It is thoughtless thinking. It's an exhibition of unreasonable reasoning. Many examples of illogicality are displayed in President Donald Trump's (b. 1946) silly daily tweets.

ILLUSION/DELUSION – (*ILL*-loo-shun *DEE*-loo-shun) Both refer to being deceived by a false or misleading impression of reality. The difference is that an illusion is a real environmental deception, where as a delusion is an unreal mental deception. A magician produces a real illusion. A psychosis produces an unreal delusion. An illusion is a mistaken vision produced by an intended or actual trick. A natural illusion is a mirage in the desert. Though the pond of water was not really there, it was actually seen to be. Sane people see mirages. A delusion is a mental fantasy, seen only in the mind's eye. One susceptible to illusions may be merely gullible or naïve. One susceptible to delusions may be mentally ill. *"All spiritual practices are illusions created by illusionists to escape illusions."* – Ram Dass (1931 – 2019).

ILLUSORY TRUTH EFFECT – (il-*LOO*-sor-ree *TROOTH* ef-*FEKT*) (also the Validity or Reiteration Effect) An illusion is a false, misleading impression. The illusory truth effect is a social psychological phenomenon in which people tend to believe false information if it is repeated often enough. This phenomenon was formally identified in 1977 in studies at Villanova and Temple Universities. However, one need not be a social psychologist to know that if you tell a lie often enough, it will begin to ring true in the minds of weak-minded people. Back in the 1930s, Nazi Minister of Propaganda, Dr. Joseph Goebbels (1897 – 1945) declared: *"If you tell a lie big enough and keep repeating it, people will eventually come to believe it."* True. The headliners on FOX *"FAKE"* NEWS – Tucker Carlson (b. 1969), Sean Hannity (b. 1961), Laura Ingraham (b. 1963) – all know the power of repeating lies as well. It was eerily premonitory that the Nazi Goebbels coined the Trumpist term, *"Big Lie."*

IMAM – (im-*MOM*) A Muslim prayer leader, who sings the prayers high up in the minaret. The Imam is not necessarily a religious scholar like a Mullah or an Ulama. Too, an Imam does not have the political power of a Mullah or Ulama in Islam, where theocracy is the norm.

IMBECILE – (*IM*-bi-sill) Once a legitimate psychological term for an intermediate grade mental defective. An *"imbecile"* was classed above an *"idiot"* but below a *"moron."* An imbecile must live in a supervised setting at all times. His intelligence level makes him semi-independent.

IMBROGLIO – (im-*BROG*-lee-yo) A bitter, complicated disagreement, misunderstanding between persons or nations. An imbroglio is a convoluted, perplexing state of affairs, as in a diplomatic dispute. To be embroiled in an imbroglio can result in conflict and war. *"The diplomatic imbroglio between Russia and the Ukraine seems unsolvable. So too is the Israeli-Palestinian dilemma."*

IMDB – (written IMDb) (eye em dee *BEE*) An initialism for Internet <u>M</u>ovie <u>Da</u>ta<u>B</u>ase, (imdb.com). This is an online database, owned by *Amazon*, of information related to films, television programs, home videos, video games, and streaming content online. The information includes cast, production crew and personal biographies, plot summaries, trivia, ratings, and fan and critical reviews. As of January 2020, IMDb has approximately 6.5 million titles (including episodes) and 10.4 million personalities in its database. There are about 83 million registered users.

I/ME – (*EYE/MEE*) Both words are in reference to oneself, the personal ego. *"I"* is the nominative singular pronoun, used by a speaker in reference to herself/himself. *"Me"* is the objective case of I, used as a direct or indirect object. When used as the subject (before the verb), use I. Example: *"You and I are going."* When used as the direct object (after the verb), use me. Example: *"You are going with me."*

I-MESSAGE – (*EYE MESS*-saj) A conflict resolution strategy that informs an offensive party of the effect their behavior is having on you. In education, the I- message sends a clear message telling a student how the teacher feels about a problem situation and implicitly asks for corrected behavior. For example: *"Chris, I get upset when you litter, because I have to pick up the trash, and I don't think that is fair."* The I-message never lays blame on the offender.

I.M.F. – (eye em *EFF*) (International <u>M</u>onetary <u>F</u>und) Like the World Bank, the

I.M.F. is an economic arm of the U.S. State Department, established (1944) to quash Socialism, and promote corporate capitalism in underdeveloped countries. The I.M.F. drains the poor countries of their meager wealth through deceptive predatory loans. They then gain control of the nation's economy and rob them blind. *"We have to keep an iron grip on the third-world countries because they are poor. They want riches, and the riches will have to come from us."* – General Maxwell Taylor (1901 – 1987), U.S. Commander in Vietnam War. The I.M.F. is another answer to the naïve question: *"Why do they hate us?"* *"The interests of the IMF represent the big international interests that today seem to be established and concentrated in Wall Street."* – Che Guevara (1928 – 1967), Socialist Revolutionary. *"I do wish that the IMF and the World Bank would disappear soon."* – Hugo Chavez (1954 – 2013) Socialist Revolutionary President of Venezuela. Footnote: Thanks to the capitalist I.M.F. and World Bank, over 3.3 billion people live in countries that spend more on debt interest than education and healthcare. That's one-third of humanity.

IMINTATION – (im-mi-*TAY*-shun) LAW OF IMITATION. The psychological phenomenon that we become like those we admire. We emulate the life, follow the examples, and mimic the mannerisms of people we revere. This is especially so if our transformation is intentional. To be Christlike, Buddhistic, Lincolnian, or Gandhian, study the lives and teachings of these great avatars and heroes. Copy whom you'd like to be, and you'll soon be like whom you copy. Of course, the Law of Imitation is a double-edged sword. One can become a monster, as well as a saint.

IMMACULATE CONCEPTION – (im-*MAC*-kew-lit con-*SEP*-shun) *Feast of the Immaculate Conception* is a Catholic Holyday that concerns the birth of Mary, not Jesus. It is commonly mistaken to as referring to Mary's sexless, divine pregnancy. Actually, the Immaculate Conception celebrates Mary's birth without Original Sin, (the curse of Adam and Eve). The Feast of the Immaculate Conception falls on December 8, in the Catholic Church calendar.

IMMANENT – (*IM*-man-nent) In philosophy, being within, indwelling, inherent. The opposite of immanent is transcendent.

IMMIGRATION – (im-i-*GRAY*-shuhn) Immigrant, Immigrate, Immigrating, Immigrated) Immigration is the legal relocation of people for permanent residency and citizenship in a foreign country. The Earth is natural. Nation States are artificial. People are natural residents of Earth. It is therefore natural for people to migrate and immigrate throughout the Earth. After all, animals, fish and fowl, even insects are allowed to freely migrate over national borders, but human beings cannot. However, nations have limited and suspended immigration for economic, ethnic, racial, security, and spatial reasons. People migrate and immigrate in search of a better life. The land that became the United States of America has been the primary immigration destination for mankind for over 400 years. The USA is <u>*A Nation of Immigrants*</u> (1958), as President John F. Kennedy (1917 – 1963) had written. *"We call England the Mother Country because most of us come from Poland and Italy."* – Comedian Robert Benchley (1885 – 1945). It is said that immigrants built America, when actually immigrants are America. One would be hard pressed to identify a typical American name. That's because we Americans are not a tribe, but an amalgamation, assimilation of every human tribe. Indeed, our strength is in our diversity. Unfortunately, racist Caucasian Christian Nationalist Americans deny our true make up. They fear the voting power of immigrants. Republicans-cum- Trumpublicans would close the boarders or even deport our new neighbors. Their fear is rooted in the loss of their privilege. American has long symbolized a refuge from tyranny, poverty, a beacon of hope. May our doors be forever open. *"If we ever close the doors to new Americans, our leadership of the world will be gone."* – President Ronald Reagan (1911 – 2004). *"Give me your tired, your poor, Your huddled masses yearning to breathe free, The wretched refuse of your teeming shore. Send these, the homeless, tempest-tost to me, I lift my lamp besides the golden door."* – *"The New Colossus,"* (1883), by Jewish- American Emma Lazarus (1849 – 1887). The poem is cast in bronze on the *Statue of Liberty* (1903).

IMMISERATE / IMMISERIZE – (im-*MIS*-er-rate im-*MIS*-er-rize) To cause agony, anguish, grief, misery. To immiserate or immiserize is to make miserable.

IMMOLATION – (im-mo-*LAY*-shun) To be burned alive as a horrific execution or sacrifice. Witches were burned at the stake in a *"bonefire"* (later corrupted to <u>bon</u>fire). So were religious heretics. Perverse executioners would sometimes pull away the burning tinder after the victim's clothing was burned away, in order to get a better view of the naked blistered body. Sadistic executioners would choose to use slower-burning green wood, so the victim cooked, prolonging the agony. However fumes from the green wood often made the sufferer faint or mercifully choke to death. Native Americans burned prisoners alive with torches, red-hot irons, or in bonfires. Pain was a test of courage. The screams of the victims were welcomed. The Indians believed that as the screams dissipated, the strength and courage of the sufferer was absorbed by the tribe observing the immolation.

IMMORTALITY – (im-mor-*TAL*-lit-tee) (Immortal) Eternal life; living forever; never dying. Immortal means not mortal, which means not human. Immortality is one of the qualities that distinguishes a human from a god. In Genesis, the first book of the Bible, it is written that in the Garden of Eden, mankind's original home (as represented by Adam and Eve), grew the *"Tree of Life"* which would endow immortality. God forbade Adam and Eve from eating the fruit of the tree and attaining God-like immortality. Ever since, Magi, alchemists, scientists have sought an elixir of life, the magic formula that would grant immortality, (the fruit of the Tree of Life). But is immortality a *"Faustian Bargain,"* a curse rather than a blessing? The testimony of supercentarians reveals that extraordinarily long life is remorseful. It's no pleasure out-living your children and having to attend their funerals. It's a lonely world without relatives and friends who are agemates, with whom to share memories. Death is part of the contract we signed when we agreed to be born. Immortality was not in the deal.

IMMUNOCOMPROMISED – (im-you-no-*COMP*-pro-myzd) To have weakened or lost one's natural immune system, the body's defenses against disease. Many viral diseases like HIV compromise the immune system, making the body vulnerable to any number of lethal ailments.

IMMUNOL – (im-*MUN*-nol) In immunology, an inherited tendency to be hypersensitive to certain allergens.

IMMUNOLOGICAL MEMORY – (im-you-no-*LOJ*-ic-al *MEM*-or-ree) The ability of the body's defense cells to quickly and specifically recognize a pathogen that the body had previously encountered and initiate a defensive counter-attack. The immune system remembers old enemies, how they fought, and how to fight back. The immune system is fighting a constant war throughout the body with foreign invaders – viruses, bacteria, infections. Once a war has been won (the body recovers health), future invasions will be successfully repulsed. The body has acquired an immunity.

IMPACT PLAY – (*IM*-pakt *PLAY*) Impact is collision, forceful contact, striking one thing against another. In the BDSM culture (Bondage Discipline SadoMasochism) impact play is a form of rough sex, tough love. Impact Play is sadomasochistic recreation, a sexuoerotic fetish. It involves striking a sex partner for mutual erotic gratification. This may consist of spanking, paddling, caning, cropping, or whipping. The severity of the punishment will vary. Ordinarily, the fatty, fleshy parts of the body are subjected – the buttocks and thighs. With extreme impact, the back, shoulders, abdomen, breasts/chest, even genitals are targeted. Incidentally: Remember that *"What's sauce for the goose is soup for the gander." "The only unnatural sex act is that which you cannot perform."* – Sexologist Dr. Alfred Kinsey (1894 – 1956). Furthermore, God reserves sexual satisfaction for the uninhibited.

IMPACT STATEMENT – (*IM*-pakt *STAYT*-ment) A written or oral statement as part of a judicial process. The impact statement allows crime victims to vent their feelings in court during the sentencing of a convicted person or at a parole hearing. Impact statement sessions are usually deeply emotional, sometimes hysterical. The purpose is to convince the judge or parole board to show no leniency. An environmental impact statement is data produced from an impact study of how a corporate capitalist resource exploitation will impact, or *"Affect the quality of the human environment."* An environmental impact statement is mandated by the *National Environmental Policy Act* of 1969.

IMPACT WINTER – (*IM*-pakt *WIN*-ter) The calamitous, life-terminating result of a gargantuan asteroid collision. Smoke and debris would cloud the sky, blocking the sun, dropping the temperature, killing the vegetation, igniting mass extinction. This would be the result of an impact winter. It has happened before. Incidentally: Geologist's Credo: *"If it happened before, it will happen again."*

IMPASSE – (*IM*-pass) French for a blockage, barrier, deadlock. At an impasse in negotiations, for instance, there is no prospect for movement toward agreement.

IMPASTO – (im-*POS*-tow) Paint so heavily applied that it stands out in relief, in lumps or swirls on the canvass. With impasto, the artist applies the paint with pallet-knife.

IMPEACHMENT – (im-*PEECH*-ment) The Constitutional process (Section 4, Article II) for removing a public official from office for *"high crimes and misdemeanors,"* (whatever that means). Actually, impeachment is the first step in the removal process that takes place in the House of Representatives of Congress. An impeachment is an official accusation by at least 50% +1 of the House members. Once officially accused (impeached) the officer must stand trial before the entire Senate of Congress. A 2/3 vote is needed for conviction. Two American Presidents had been impeached before the 21st century: Andrew Johnson (1808 – 1875) in 1868, and Bill Clinton (b. 1946) in 1999. The Senate failed to convict Johnson by 1 vote. The Senate did not take up the Clinton case. Richard Nixon (1913 – 1994) would have been impeached in 1974, but he resigned the Presidency before the vote took place. Incidentally: Andrew Johnson's impeachment was spurious, resulting from the aftershock of Civil War. The impeachment of Bill Clinton was unfounded, based on personal infidelity, and Republican animus. But Donald Trump's (b. 1946) two impeachments were imperative. Trump met every constitutional mandate for impeachment. The Founding Fathers had a Trump in mind, when they framed the Impeachment Clause of the Constitution. Trump invited Russia, Ukraine, and China to interfere in American elections on his behalf. He withheld congressionally allocated defense funds ($391 million dollars) from the Ukraine, in return for a denunciation of his political rival, Joe Biden (b. 1942). Trump stood in contempt of Congress by withholding information, documentation, and ordering subordinates to ignore Congress. He profited on the Presidency in violation of emolument laws. He practiced overt, public nepotism by installing family members in the government. Trump certainly took millions from foreign governments (Russia, Saudi Arabia, Turkey, at least). Trump had been recorded making over 14,000 lies at the time of his first impeachment. Trump has been the most corrupt politician in U.S. History. Trump was impeached on December 18, 2019. Incidentally: The preposterous presidential pretender, Donald Trump (b. 1946) said that he's just peachy: *"I don't feel impeached,"* the buffoon blurted. Trump got a second chance to *"feel impeached"* on January 13, 2021. One week before the end of his Presidential term, Trump was again impeached. Trump was formally accused by the House of Representatives for inciting an insurrection against the United States. Indeed, Trump had organized and orchestrated the riotous attack on the U.S. Capitol Building on January 6, 2021. Trump had planned to prevent the legal transfer of power to President-elect, Joe Biden (b. 1942). By so doing, Trump intended to install himself as the dictator of the United States. Astoundingly, the cowardly Republicans in the Senate were too frightened of Trump to convict him.

IMPERATIVE – (im-*PAIR*-uh-tiv) (Imperatively) Absolutely necessary, required, unavoidable. *"It is imperative that you vote for President Biden in this upcoming election!"* In some cases, an imperative is an order, a command. The philosopher Immanuel Kant (1724 – 1804) pronounced his *"Categorical Imperative,"* which stated that it is absolutely necessary to act the way you wished every human acted. This, of course, is a rendition of the *Golden Rule.*

IMPERATIVE – (im-*PAIR*-uh-tiv) (Imperatively) In grammar, an imperative is an adjective denoting the mood of verbs used in giving orders or making requests. For example: *"Listen!" "Go!" "Please leave."* Too, a polite request that does not require a question mark is also a grammatical imperative. For example: *"Could you sign here, please." "Will the audience sit down now."*

IMPERFECT COMPETITION – (im-PER-fect com-pet-*TISH*-shun) A sanitized euphemism for a monopoly. The term imperfect competition is embarrassingly used by capitalist economists to describe a mega-corporation like Walmart. Gargantuan companies become behemoths by crushing the competition. That is the ultimate goal of capitalism – eliminate all competitors and corner the market, as Walmart has done. The object is to turn the *"Free Market,"* into the *"Me Market."* Competition in capitalism is to be used as steppingstones, and competitors are to be stepped on. Imperfect competition results in imperfect liberty [read: *fascism*].

IMPERIAL CAPITAL – (im-*PEER*-ree-al *CAP*-pit-al) Washington District of Columbia, the seat of government for the United States of America. Never had a capital city been more ill-conceived architecturally, so incongruous in representing the history, environment, and ideals of a nation. Washington D.C. has been satirically called *"a city of wedding cakes."* The cold white marble of neo-classical buildings is representative of ancient Rome, rather than contemporary America. Washington exemplified the Old World, rather than the New World. How does Pennsylvania Avenue in Washington D.C. reflect Washington Avenue in Wilkes-Barre, Pennsylvania? A Greek Pantheon, Roman Dome, and Egyptian Obelisk does not fit well anywhere in North America. Winston Churchill (1874 – 1965) reminded us that: *"We shape our buildings and afterwards, our buildings shape us."* Indeed, our architecture influences our character. Our bellicose-appearing imperial capital sends the wrong message to the world. A democratic people, dedicated to the pursuit of liberty, should not wish to emulate belligerent, dictatorial Rome. Ancient Italy had exhausted its trees by the time Rome built its edifices of stone. America had about 90 billion trees when the capital city was being built. Our governing city should have been constructed of wood, as was most of America. *"Rome-on-the-Potomac"* was an odd setting for buckskin tunics and coonskin caps. The mausoleum-like Lincoln Memorial belongs on the Palatine Hill in Rome, not on the Capitol Hill in Washington. Abe Lincoln was born in a log cabin, not a Roman temple. Lincoln in a toga is unimaginable. Actually, it would be historically more appropriate to construct our government buildings to resemble Native American teepees and wigwams. Too, the Statue of Freedom, which stands atop the imperious Capitol Rotunda is another architectural historical incongruity. A woman in a classical toga, wearing a feathered helmet, bearing a sword. Very fitting! A statue of a Native American in headdress would have been more appropriate.

IMPERIALISM – (im-*PEER*-ree-al-is-um) (Imperial, Imperialistic) Enforcing rule over weaker foreign regions, exerting oppression to enable economic exploitation. Imperialism has enriched capitalist corporations and nations, while condemning native people to poverty. The age of naked colonial imperialism may have passed. Today, capitalist economic imperialism has taken its place. Through predatory loans, the avaricious World Bank and I.M.F. (International Monetary Fund) have conquered poor nations' economies. They have captured the natural resources and sucked-out the tax revenue, leaving underdeveloped nations dependent and impoverished. This neo-economic imperialism requires no responsibility on the part of the exploiting nation, like colonial administration or military enforcement. *"Imperialism was born when the ruling class in capitalist production came up against national limits to its economic expansion."* – Philosopher Hannah

Arendt (1906 – 1975). *"I have often before now been convinced that a democracy is incapable of empire."* – Thucydides (c. 460 – c. 400 BCE).

IMPERIAL UNITS – (im-*PEER*-ree-al) The traditional English system of weights and measures, revised and instituted in 1825. Imperial Units is also called the Exchequer Standards. The Imperial System provides was with units such as the inch, foot, yard, chain, furlong, mile, league, fathom, link, rod, pint, quart, and gallon. The substitution for the Imperial System is the Metric System, first initiated during the Napoleonic Era (1804 – 1814). The metric system is based on 10. The Imperial system evolved arbitrarily.

IMPERMEABLE – (im-*PER*-me-a-bul) Not passable. In chemistry and geology, impermeable means not allowing a fluid like water to pass through a substance or rock. Impermeable rock holds water. Impermeable soil like clay results in wetlands.

IMPERSONATION – (im-per-son-*NAY*-shun) (Impersonate, Impersonator, Impersonating) The prefix *"im"* is a Latin variation of *"in,"* meaning *"not."* So to impersonate is to act like the individual or person you are not. Actors are professional impersonators, who admit their fraud. (Indeed, the word actor in Greek is *hypocrite*.) We appreciate actors, but we do not appreciate conmen, swindlers, criminals, who usurp a false identity to deceive us for ill-gotten gain. Sexual predators have committed atrocities by impersonating police. Politicians, particularly Republicans, have enriched themselves from corporate capitalists by impersonating to be champions of the common man. The biggest fraud is Donald Trump (b. 1947) who impersonated being a President.

IMPERVIOUS – (im-*PER*-vee-us) Impenetrable. Impermeable. Not permitting penetration or passage, as of water or light. To be impervious to pain is to be exempt from painful injury or impairment. An impervious personality is stubborn and cannot be influenced or persuaded. Do not expect her to see your point or change her mind.

IMPINGE – (im-*PINJ*) (Impinging, Impingement) To make an impression, to have an effect or impact. To impinge is also to encroach, as to impinge on another's rights. To deny freedom of speech is an impingement of the 1st Amendment.

IMPLACABLE – (im-*PLAK*-ka-buhl) Inexorable. Cannot be appeased, mollified, or pacified. No negotiations with an implacable enemy. An implacable person cannot be moved or swayed by reason. *"MAGAmaniacs are as implacable as they come!"*

IMPLICIT – (im-*PLIS*-it) (Implicitly) Anything implied, rather than expressly stated. For example, an implicit affirmation may be a nod of the head, rather than a spoken permission. Too, implicit refers to anything that is unquestioned, unreserved, and unconditional. For example: implicit trust; implicit obedience; implicit confidence.

IMPLICIT BIAS – (im-*PLIS*-it *BY*-uhs) A milder, unconscious form of racism exhibited through subtle preferences for or against a person or group of color. A practitioner of implicit bias is unaware of her prejudices. Nevertheless, they are revealed in actions, comments, and assumptions.

IMPLIED POWERS – (im-*PLIED POW*-wers) Congressional powers not listed in the Constitution but *implied* through the *"Elastic"* or *"Necessary and Proper"* clause. Article I, Section 8, Clause 18 reads: *"Congress shall have the power to make all laws necessary and proper...."* This provision legally enables Congress to pass laws to meet unexpected contingencies that are not mentioned in the Constitution but are implied by the clause. With implied powers, Liberals as *loose constructionists* can stretch the Constitution, to pass Progressive legislation. Conservatives as *strict constructionists* oppose reading into the Constitution what is not there. Rich conservatives fear that implied powers will someday day result in the re-distribution of their wealth.

IMPLOSION – (im-*PLOH*-shun) (Implode, Implosive) Bursting inward, the opposite physical force of an <u>ex</u>plosion. Unlike an explosion where the pressure within bursts out, an implosion is where the pressure without bursts inward. An implosion is an exterior force pushing, crushing an object from all sides. An imploded object is compressed, reduced in size but increased in density, crushed. Creating a vacuum within a hollow object will induce an implosion, as the atmosphere pressures all sides, striving to enter. The excruciating pressure of the water in the deep sea will cause a tin can, or a submarine to implode.

IMPOLITIC – (im-*POL*-li-tik) (Impolicy) The act or instance of being injudicious, lacking judgment, being unwise.

IMPORTANT – (im-*POR*-tant) Mattering much, of great significance or consequence. What's important to one, may not be important to another. Too, what is important is not necessarily urgent. Importance is internal, urgency is external. Importance is personal, what's most meaningful to you. Urgency is environmental, what is most meaningful to others. My urgency is not necessarily your urgency. Too, what's important to you won't be important to me unless you are important to me – a family member, friend, loved-one, or boss.

IMPOSSIBLE – (im-*POS*-si-bul) (Impossibly) Not possible, it cannot happen. In statistics, beyond calculable probability. If the probability falls to only 1 in 10 to the 50th power, it is officially considered statistically impossible. (Ten to the fiftieth power is called *one hundred quindecillion*.) That is such an astronomical number that almost anything is possible. Consider that the estimated number of atoms in the visible universe is 10 to the 80th power! For instance, it is statistically possible to calculate the probability that a pot of water placed on a hot stove will freeze. It takes a miracle for the impossible to occur. However, what is impossible in the natural, is possible in the *SUPER*natural. *"I never said it was possible, I only said it was true."* – Sir William Crookes, (1832 - 1919), physicist commenting of spiritualism. Incidentally: Researchers have discovered that the use of the word *"impossible"* has dropped by 50% over the last 100 years. *"Things are only impossible until they're not."* – Captain Jean-Luc Picard, fictional character in the TV show *"Star Trek."*

IMPOUNDING RULE – (im-*POWN*-ding *ROOL*) (also Impounding Power) To impound, in this case, means to seize and hold property or money by legal right. In many instances, the government has the power to impound funds. But the Impounding Rule, as applied to the U.S. Presidency, is not legal – yet. Congress, The House of Representatives *"holds the purse string."* Only they can allocate tax dollars for governmental programs. When Congress votes to pass a bill to award money for a program, the President cannot impound that money, refuse to pay it out. This would disrupt the checks-and-balances inherent in the government. Congress would be emasculated, made impotent. This is what the Impounding Power in the hands of the President would do. President Richard Nixon (1913 – 1994) was very authoritarian, and fought hard, unsuccessfully, to acquire the Impounding Power. Incidentally: Donald Trump (b. 1946) and the fascist intellectuals of the *Heritage Foundation* include the Impounding Rule in their Project 25 – the plan to turn America into a fascist Nazi state.

IMPRECATE – (*IM*-pre-kayt) (Imprecation, Imprecated, Imprecatory) To swear, curse, or blame. To imprecate is to invoke or call down evil upon someone. *"May God strike you blind! He imprecated."*

IMPRESARIO – (im-pre-*SAR*-ree-o) A showman. An impresario is a producer or manager of public entertainments, especially concerts, operas, or ballets. *"Donald Trump (b. 1946) is the impresario of grift."*

IMPRESSIONISM – (im-*PRESH*-shun-is-um) Artistic style (late 19th, early 20th centuries) characterized by fleeting vague impressions of faded light and soft shadow. Impressionism induces a dreamy impression: haunting music, foggy landscapes leaving much to the imagination. Impressionism conveyed the *"cult of clouds."*

IMPRESSMENT – (im-*PRESS*-ment) Historically, the British kidnapping of U.S. sailors on the high seas, in order to fight in the British navy against Napoleon. Over 6,000 American seamen were impressed into the British service during the Napoleonic Wars. Impressment was a major cause of the War of 1812 (1812 – 1814) between the US and Britain.

IMPRIMIS – (*IM*-prim-is) Latin for *"in the first place."*

IMPRINTING – (*IM*-print-ting) A conditioning phenomenon first discovered by Austrian zoologist, Konrad Lorenz (1903 – 1989). Imprinting is a very rapid learning process by which a newborn or very young animal establishes a behavior pattern of recognition, attraction, and imitation towards other animals of its own kind, or surrogate creatures. Imprinting occurs soon after birth or hatching. Ducklings, for example, will imprint upon and follow the first creature or large moving object they observe. In the natural order, this will be its mother. However, the surrogate can be a dog, raccoon, person, or soccer ball. Obviously, unnatural imprinting can establish in life-long behavioral abnormalities.

IMPROVEMENT – (im-*PROOV*-ment) (Improved) Betterment. The conscious, purposeful increase in the value or desirable condition of something, anything – land, possessions, art or self. Concerning personal skills, persistent laborious practice results in improvement. The great Socialist cellist Pablo Casals (1876 – 1973), at age 95 got up early and practiced for 5 hours. When asked why he pushed himself so, Casals replied: *"I think I'm getting better."*

IMPROVIDENT – (im-*PROV*-vi-dent) (Improvidence) Lacking foresight, careless, shiftless, thriftless. An improvident person would neglect to save or provide for the future.

IMPRUDENT – (*IM*-proo-dent) (Imprudence) Lacking discretion, indiscreet, rash, incautious, heedless. *"His Imprudency,"* President Donald Trump (b. 1946) was most imprudent when he declared that *"Trade wars are good,"* (March, 2018). Update: In February 2024, Trump admitted that he is running for the

Presidency to be a dictator. He promised to cancel the Constitution, abandon NARO, and welcomed Russia to invade NATO nations. Trump promised revenge on all this enemies. Isn't that beyond imprudence?

IMPUDENT – (*IM*-proo-dent) (Impudence) Rude, insulting, disrespectful. *"The imprudent pack of boys mocked the crippled old man."*

IMPUGN – (im-*PYOON*) To cast doubt. To challenge the truth or veracity of one's statement or motives. *"It is wise to impugn everything a Republican-cum- Trumpublican politician says."*

IMPULSE BUYING – (*IM*-puls *BY*-ing) Whimsical shopping. Making rash purchases with little consideration. Impulse buying is irrational, emotional, rather than logical. It is the mission of capitalist advertisers to gain control of consumer's impulses, and therefore their grocery money. Impulse buying turns luxuries, superfluities into necessities, essentials. Impulse buying was once considered to be carelessness, recklessness. You couldn't buy more than the cash in your pocket allowed. But the credit card has legitimized and encouraged impulse buying. Debt is no longer a calamity, but a way of life. Impulse buying is highly responsible. To eliminate impulse buying, avoid the need to keep up with the Joneses, and don't go food shopping when hungry.

IMPULSIVENESS – (im-*PUL*-siv-ness) Being impetuous, tactless, unable to control one's emotions. Impulsive people do not think-out their actions. They just act and react on raw feelings. Such people lack discernment. Impulsive people justify rudeness with the rationalization, *"I tell it like it is."* Impulsiveness is most dangerous in a powerful leader. *"His Impetuousness,"* President Donald Trump (b. 1946) will react on a whim, a gut feeling. His impulsive policies can often be traced to the last person who had spoken to him.

IMPUTATION – (im-pew-*TAY*-shun) An attribution or accusation of a fault or crime. Evil imputations fall onto capitalism. In February, 2014, the Socialist Pope Francis lamented: *"Capitalism is the root of all evil."*

IMPUTE – (im-*PUTE*) (Imputing) To attribute or ascribe, especially a dishonesty, disgrace, or criminal offense to a person or ideology. For example, one must impute poverty to capitalism.

IN – (*IN*) The opposite or alternative of out. It is impossible to define this simple word without avoiding improper *"circular delineation,"* which is defining a word by that same word. For example: *In is being inside. In is being within. In is what is internal.* In is part of the spiritual concepts of inspiration and intuition. Inspiration is being in the Spirit. When you're inspired, the power of the Spirit is within you. Intuition is knowledge from within. Your intuition is Spiritual correspondence. When the answer or solution spontaneously dawns on you, you are in touch with your Spiritual intuition. *"When the solution is simple, God is answering."* – Albert Einstein (1879 - 1955). Einstein, one of the greatest scientists understood intuitive inspiration.

IN ABSENTIA – (in ab-*STEN*-cha) Latin for *"in the absence."* It refers to a person who is not present. To be convicted by a court in absentia for instance, means the person found guilty was not at the proceedings.

INALIENABLE SOCIALISM – (in-*AY*-lee-un-buhl *SO*-shul-is-um) (also Unalienable Socialism) Constitutionalized Socialism. Guaranteed prosperity for all. Comprehensive well-being by the sharing of our natural abundance provided by Socialistic economic policies from a Socialistic Government. Socialism and Democracy are compatible. Capitalism and fascism are inevitable. Therefore a genuinely Democratic nation cannot be capitalistic. History has taught that Socialist nations have not lasted long. That's because they immediately come under attack from fascist capitalist enemies within and without. In order to succeed, a Democratic Socialist nation must protect its Socialism from counter- revolutionary capitalist saboteurs. Fascist capitalist provocateurs will used Democratic freedom to undermine both Democracy and Socialism. So Socialist policies and rights must be chiseled in stone, in the Constitution. Only Inalienable Socialism will survive to succeed. It must be considered a categorical imperative, beyond any legislatures, executives or courts to alter. Democratic Socialist *Life, Liberty,* and *Happiness* must supplant fascist capitalist *death, oppression,* and *depression.* If *"All men are created equal,"* why do most languish while others prosper? Because we are not at Liberty to pursue a *Life* of *Happiness* under capitalism. *"We hold these truths to be self-evident, that all men are created equal, that they are endowed by their Creator with certain unalienable Rights, that among these are Life, Liberty and the pursuit of Happiness – That to secure these rights, Governments are instituted among Men...."* – American Declaration of Independence (July 4, 1776). *"You must list your liberties and put them down on paper!"* – Thomas Jefferson (1743 – 1826) debating the Bill of Rights.

INAMORATA – (in-am-or-*RA*-ta) A sweetheart. A girl or woman with whom one is in love.

INANE – (in-*AYN*) (Inanity) Silly, silliness. The inane lack sense, ideas, or significance.

INASMUCH – (*IN*-as-much) (Often appearing as "inasmuch as....") Inasmuch means because; insofar as; in the degree that; or in view of the fact that.... It is a conjunction used to introduce an explanation or reason. It is also used to introduce a comment that limits the extent of something. *"Inasmuch as you have done it unto one of the least of these my brethren, you have done it unto me."* – Jesus in Matthew 25: 35-40.

INAUSPICIOUS – (in-aws-*SPISH*-us) Ominous, ill boding, unfavorable, unlucky. *"She considered the black cat an inauspicious omen."*

IN CAMERA – (ca-*MER*-a) (*"In chambers"*) In law, proceedings in a judge's private office. A hearing in court with all spectators excluded.

INCARNATION – (in-car-*NAY*-shun) (Incarnate) Literally, made into flesh, given a body. Incarnation is the core doctrine that God become man in the body of Jesus Christ (c. 7-2 BCE – c. 30-33 CE). Incarnation is the basic foundation of Christianity and Catholicism. God could have become any man – a rich merchant, a powerful prince, a prestigious pope. But God chose to embody a poor peasant, a humble worker with no prestige, power, capital, or wealth. What was God's hidden message? What does this infer about God's attitude concerning wealth, ostentation, greed, and capitalism? At any rate, the Son of God became the Son of Man in the body of Jesus. This was essential in order for Jesus to teach, be crucified, and resurrect from the dead.

INCAS – (*INK*-kas) The great Indian civilization of South America, the *"Romans of the New World."* The Inca Empire was established in the Andes Mountains. They have been called the *"Romans of the New World,"* because their empire included present day Peru, Ecuador, Bolivia, Chile, parts of Argentina, and Columbia. This amounted to over 3,000 mile of coastline between the Andes and the Pacific. Like the Romans, the Inca were masterful engineers, builders, with an extensive road system. Their empire reached its height from 1438 to 1533. They terraced the mountain sides to enable agriculture. There primary staple crop was the precious potato, which they bequeathed to the rest of the world. They developed a civilization built around irrigation for food production. The Inca capital city was Cusco, and another magnificent location was Machu Picchu. The Inca worked with stone, wood, cane, copper, and bronze. They had no iron or steel, no wheeled vehicles, no plow, and no form of writing. Enigmatically, unlike primitive rainforest tribes, the Inca had not developed the bow-and-arrow. Too, these incredible masons did not utilize the arch. The Inca ultimately succumbed to superior Spanish weaponry and European diseases. In 1532, the illiterate Spanish conquistador Francisco Pizarro (c. 1471 – 1541) rode into Peru with no more than 62 cavalry troops (on the beastly-looking horses) and 106 foot soldiers. After pillaging all the Inca gold, Pizarro broke his word and murdered the captive Inca Chief Atahualpa (c. 1502 – 1533). This was the death knell for the mighty Inca Empire and civilization. Incidentally: Coca bushes are indigenous to the Andes Mountains, and there grow wild. When processed, the coca leaves yield cocaine. Chewing raw coca leaves acts as a mild stimulant (not narcotic). Only the royal family of the Emperor was allowed to enjoy the boost. Eventually, everyone in that rigorous terrain and low oxygen region of the Andes chew coca leave, as Americans drink strong coffee. Footnote: None of the great American civilizations (Aztec, Maya, Inca) had developed the wheel or plow. Both required big strong draught animals to pull wagons and plows. The Americas had no such creatures that could be domesticated. The Incan llama was far too weak for the job. Furthermore, while the Aztec and Maya had the bow-and- arrow, the Inca did not.

INCEL – (*IN*-sel) A blend word from *"INvoluntary CELibate."* An incel is a bitterly frustrated and neurotic (sometimes psychotic) male who suffers from the lack of female affection. The sexual deprivation and frustration can drive them insane. Incels become misogynous women-hater, hateful enough to kill them. In fact, an incel is a candidate for a serial killer. You can be assured that and incel had never had a woman who loved him – not even his mother. Those who become serial women killers are subconsciously, repeatedly murdering their mothers. According to the *Urban Dictionary, "An incel, aka 'involuntary celibate,' is a person (usually male) who has a horrible personality and treats women like sexual objects and thinks his lack of a sex life comes from being 'ugly' when it is really just his blatant sexism and terrible attitude. Incels have little to no self- awareness; even when they see other 'ugly' men with girlfriends, they consider these men to be tricksters who have somehow beat the system and can get women despite being cursed with unattractiveness (in other words, they're respectful to women and women are attracted to their personalities, but incels can't comprehend such a phenomenon). They believe that women owe them sex, and many of the more extreme incels like to spend time in incel communities on the internet coming up with ways to make women have sex with them) often involving genocide of people of color, genocide of 'Chads' (men who have sex), taking rights away from women, raping them, having sex with women's dead bodies, and other horrid, disgusting things. They can't understand that this is PRECISELY why women want nothing to do with them)."* Obviously, true incels need psychiatric help.

INCENSE – (*IN*-sens) Perfumed smoke. Incense is an aromatic biotic (organic) material that releases fragrant smoke when burned. Incense is composed of compressed plant matter or resins containing perfumed essential oils. Incense is usually fashioned in sticks or small cones. Ancient cultures in Asia, Africa, the Middle East, and the Americas have used incense in religious ceremonies. Incense serves as a burnt offering, the smoke curling up to heaven. Incense smoke has been used to placate the gods and to ward-off evil spirits. Hinduism and Buddhism particularly rely on incense, and Catholicism to a lesser degree. The Catholic Church still uses incense in religious rites, as at funerals. Incense is used in aromatherapy, meditation, and to help produce a romantic ambience. In a more utilitarian sense, incense serve as a deodorant and as insect repellent.

INCENTIVE – (in-*SEN*-tiv) A positive stimulus that encourages or incites action or greater effort. An incentive can be offered as a reward, bonus, grant, or benefit. To capitalists, incentive is a euphemism for *greed.* The opportunity to make more money is incentive to the rich. But capitalists believe that incentive applies only to the rich. Inexplicably, money doesn't incite the poor to greater effort, capitalists contend. Transfer payments or money given by the government to the poor makes them lose incentive. Tax breaks for the rich boosts incentive, but tax breaks for the poor (welfare) stifles incentive. Capitalist ideology maintains that money mysteriously increases incentive for the rich but decreases incentive for the poor. That's why capitalists are pro-tax breaks and anti-welfare. Too, that's why capitalists abhor Socialism. Capitalists insist that Socialism stifles incentive. Indeed, it stifles and curtails the opportunity to hoard. There is no incentive to making money on other people's labor and money through dividends, interest, bonuses, and rent under Socialism. Greed in a socialist society is anti-social and illegal. People lose the incentive to be greedy. *"A good many of the people in the stock market, far from being the nation's most productive citizens, are functionless parasites."* – Socialist Leader Michael Harrington (1928 – 1989).

INCEPTION – (in-*SEP*-shun) Commencement, beginning, start of something new. *"The inception of American Socialism was the 2021 Coronavirus Recovery Act, enacted solely by the Democrats."*

INCESSANT – (in-SES-sant) (Incessantly) Non-stop, unending, ceaseless, continuing uninterruptedly. *"Would you stop that incessant noise!"*

INCEST – (*IN*-sest) (Incestually) Sexual relations with immediate family members: father-daughter, mother-son, brother-sister. Incest is a powerful taboo in most cultures and illegal as well. Incest has been the topic of tragedies like Sophocles' (c. 497 – 405 BCE) <u>Oedipus Rex.</u> (429 BCE). White slavemasters would impregnate their mulatto daughters, then their granddaughters in the process of *"washing my blackamoors white,"* (bleaching the black out of the female sex slaves). Incest leaves lasting traumatic scars on its victims. Incidentally: The Book of Deuteronomy 27:22 admonishes: *"Cursed is the one who lies with his sister, the daughter of his father or the daughter of his mother."* The Koran proscribes much concerning the incest taboo. *"Marry not those women whom your father have married, but what is past is past; surely such marrying is an indecency and a heinous affair; and an evil way. Forbidden to you are – your mothers, and your daughters, and your sisters, and your paternal aunts, and your maternal aunts, and the daughters of your brother, and the daughters of your sister, and the mother who have given you suck, and your foster-sisters, and the mothers of your wives, and your step-daughters, who are being brought up under your care, from wives from whom you had intercourse, but if you have not had intercourse with them, then there is no harm for you, and the wives of your sons who are from your own loins, and it is forbidden to you to have two sisters as wives together."* Incidentally: The patriarch of the Jewish and Arabic people, Abraham, had married his (half) sister Sarah. In Genesis 20:12 Abraham admitted that Sarah was *"The daughter of my father, but not the daughter of my mother; she became my wife."* God works in mysterious ways.

INCH – (*INCH*) A unit of measurement originating in medieval Scotland and England consisting of 3 dry kernels of barley placed side by side lengthwise. Inch, like the foot and yard, are part of the traditional, albeit arbitrary Imperial Measurement system.

INCHOATE – (in-*CO*-ate) Undeveloped, immature, rudimentary, not yet complete or ready. *"Inchoate embryos are not children, no matter what cross- carrying, fascist, Christian Nationalist Republicans insist."*

INCIDENTAL LEARNING – (in-sid-*DEN*-tal *LERN*-ning) Collateral learning, which is acquired latently, covertly, accidentally. Incidental learning results from the *hidden curriculum* in schools. These are all the informal messages that are not a part of the classroom lessons. Incidentally: Research at U.C.L.A. revealed that if you drive 12,000 miles a year, (3.5 miles a day) and listen to educational C.D.'s in the car, in 3 years, you would have gained the equivalent of 2 years of college (an Associate Degree). That is incidental learning too.

INCIDENTALLY – (in-sid-*DEN*-tal-lee) (Incidental) Apart or aside from the main subject of attention, discussion, or entry. Incidentally is an after-thought. It is information presented parenthetically (*"oh, by the way...."*). An incidentally is an addendum to a story. This encyclodictionary presents incidental facts at the conclusion of many of the entries. This information may be tangentially related to the topic but is oh so interesting.

INCIPIENT – (in-*SIP*-ee-ent) Nascent, in an initial stage, just starting or beginning. *"It appears that fascism is in its incipient stage in America."*

INCISION – (in-*SISZ*-shun) Means cutting into, as opposed to *excision* which is cutting out. A surgeon makes an incision, in order to make an excision of a tumor.

INCISIVE – (in-*SISE*-siv) (Incisively, Incisiveness) Penetrating, cutting, biting as in a sarcastic remark. On the other hand, a sharp, incisive presentation would be remarkably clear, direct, cutting to the heart of the issue.

INCLUSION – (in-*CLOO*-shun) Mainstreaming disabled students into the regular school program for their entire educational experience. The problem with inclusion is that many handicapped children are not inclusionable, (despite their parents heart-felt wishes). Some challenged children can only be served by highly professional, special education (in a specialized setting). However, some parents in denial retard their child's progress, by forcibly including them into a mainstreamed classroom.

INCLUSIONISTAS – (in-cloosh-on-*EES*-tas) Radical full-inclusionists, determined to eliminate all special education programs, and mainstream all challenged children, despite the severity of their handicap. Inclusionistas are in denial and motivated by emotion, rather than logic. This is highly detrimental to the disabled children and the regular classroom. The inclusionistas are desperate parents unable to face reality. Incidentally: The term *"inclusionistas"* is a Hispanic rendition, mimicking the radical Hispanic revolutionaries in many Latin American nations.

INCOGNEGRO – (in-cog-*NEE*-grow) A demeaning racist slur for an African American who supposedly is trying to *"act white."* An incognegro is an incognito Black person. They are also referred to as *Oreos,*

Afrosaxons, and *Uncle Toms*. Normal Black people consider them to be *"race traitors."* The quintessential incognegro is rap singer and celebrity Kayne West (b. 1977). His subconscious hatred of his *"Blackness"* had turned Kayne into a racist, pro- Trump anti-Semite.

INCOME TAX – (*IN*-cum *TAKS*) A fair tax provided it is *"A heavily progressive or graduated income tax,"* as Dr. Karl Marx (1818 – 1883) demanded. This means that the more you make the more you pay, with no loopholes or exemptions. Period. Incidentally, Dr. Marx first suggested the income tax. Jesus would approve of a fair income tax, for he said: *"To whom much is given, much is expected."* – Luke 12:48. (Jesus would approve of Karl Marx too, for that matter.) At any rate, during the Cold War paranoia in the 1950's the richest Americans paid 91% of their income in taxes. This paid for World War Two, the Korean War, the arms race, space race, and built our interstate highway system. And the rich were still rich. Republican *Reagan's "revenge of the rich,"* and the two Bush presidencies along with Trump's *"welfare for the rich"* have practically exempted the rich from paying taxes. Stripped of the preferences for the rich, a graduated income tax is a marvelous way to redistribute the wealth. The great German educational innovator Friedrich Froebel (1782 – 1852) declared that *"According to the measure of how much he receives, so much must he be able to give away."* This was the original expectation for the income tax. Tragically, criminally, the system was rigged. Billionaires and multi-millionaires don't pay income tax, because they technically have no income. That's right! It is Wall Street legerdemain. Taxable income is generated by work. The filthy rich capitalists don't work. They sit in their mansions, yachts, and private jets and collect hundreds-of-millions of dollars in dividends from stocks. That money in not taxed. It is interest on investments. The wealthy don't work to produce it. Millions of workers work to produce that wealth for the rich. So it's the workers, not the rich, who must pay the income tax. If you see something wrong with this picture, you are not a capitalist, but rather a Socialist. *"The rich don't pay taxes, only little people pay taxes."* – Wealthy Heiress Leona Helmsley (1920 – 2007).

INCOMMENSURABLE – (in-com-*MEN*-sur-a-bul) Immeasurable, not comparable, like apples and oranges, so to speak. Theories with no basis, measure, or standard of comparison are incommensurable. These theories are mutually exclusive, for example, Genesis *vs.* evolution, meteorology *vs.* rain dancing, capitalism *vs.* Socialism.

INCOMMUNICADO – (in-com-mu-ni-*COD*-doh) Out of communication or not communicating. A prisoner held in isolation is held in incommunicado. A hiker high up in the mountains, out of correspondence range is incommunicado. A person who simply refuses to talk is also considered incommunicado. Once one is corresponding again, she is *"communicado."*

INCOMPATIBLE – (in-com-*PAT*-ti-bul) (Incompatibility) Discordant. Not capable of coexisting in harmony. In logic, incompatibility is mutual inconsistency. This refers to statements that cannot be consistently related logically and/or conceptually.

INCONGRUITY – (in-con-*GREW*-it-tee) (Incongruent, Incongruence) Inappropriate, inconsistent, disharmonious, out of sorts. To be in incongruity is living a life at variance with the truth.

INCONTINENCE – (in *KON*-tin-ens) The inability to restrain or control the natural discharges or evacuation of urine or feces. The Excretory System manages the discharge of these bodily wastes. There are many causes of incontinence including physical malfunctions and environmental stresses. Loss of strength, weakness due to old age will bring on incontinence. Stress due to great excitement, startle, fear, extreme laughter will also make one pee in their pants. A dangerously frightening experience may result in shitting one's pants.

INCONTROVERTIBLE – (in-con-tro-*VER*-ti-bul) Unquestionable, undeniable, uncontestable, indisputable, cannot be contradicted. *"We have incontrovertible proof that Donald Trump is a Russian fellow traveler."*

INCREDULITY – (in-cred-*DUL*-li-tee) (Incredible, Incredulous) Unbelievable. Inability or unwillingness to believe.

INCRIMINATE – (in-*CRIM*-in-ate) (Incriminating, Incriminated) In law, to involve in a crime. To cause one to appear guilty. When the police plant false evidence on a victim or suspect, they are incriminating.

INCUBUS – (*IN*-que-bus) A demonic male spirit that seduces women in their sleep. Many a pregnant nun was said to be the victim of an incubus. The female counterpart to the satyristic incubus is the ever erotic *succubus,* (said to be responsible for nocturnal discharge).

INCULCATE – (*IN*-cul-kate) (Inculcation, Inculcated) To instill, to drill into the mind with persistent repetition. One may inculcate the multiplication tables to memory. *"I had inculcated several prayers to memory."*

INCULPATE – (*IN*-cul-pate) (Inculpatory) To declare culpable, incriminate, accuse, blame, fault, to charge with a crime.

INCUMBENT – (in-*KUM*-bent) As an adjective, the term incumbent means obligatory, compelling, urgently necessary. It is incumbent that government helps those who cannot help themselves.

INCUMBENT – (in-*KUM*-bent) (Incumbency) As a noun, the term incumbent means an elected office holder whose term is expiring, up for re-election. Being an incumbent politician has advantages and disadvantages. The advantage is name recognition, and a political machine already intact. An incumbent may have accumulated debtors who owe him favors. On the other hand, an incumbent may have made enemies as well. She has a record to run on, but that record may also be a source of criticism.

INCURVATE – (*IN*-cur-vate) (Incurvation) To curve, especially inward.

INDECOROUS – (in-*DECK*-cor-us) (Indecorum) Unseemly, exhibiting bad behavior or character. An indecorous individual violates the generally accepted standards of good taste or propriety. *"His Indecorousness,"* President Donald Trump (b. 1946) is the epitome of indecorum.

INDEED – (in-*DEED*) In fact, with certainty, for sure, truly, not merely talk, but with deed. Indeed is a useful adverb that indicates emphasis, confirms and amplifies a previous statement, indicates a concession or admission, or interrogatively obtains information. For example: *"Indeed, Trump is a liar."* *"Did you indeed resign?"* Also, as an interjection, indeed is used to express surprise, irony, incredulity. *"Indeed! I can't believe that Trump is in jail!"* Etymologically, indeed is a contraction of the prepositional phrase *"in dede,"* meaning *"in fact, in truth, in reality,"* (c. 1600). It derived from the Old English (Saxon) *"daed"* (early 14th century) meaning *"an act, action, event, a doing."*

INDEMNITY – (in-*DEM*-ni-fy) (Indemnify) Monetary compensation for loss or damage. An insurance policy should provide indemnity in an emergency. That's not always the case. Capitalist insurance companies are in the money making – not money distributing – business. They will try everything in their legal power to avoid indemnifying a client justly.

INDENTUTRED SERVITUDE – (in-*DEN*-churd *SER*-vi-tood) (Indentureship or Indenturesure) A form of neo-serfdom, semi-slavery established in the 17th and 18th centuries throughout the Americas. An indentured servant would sell himself to a plantation master as labor for a specified number of years, usually seven. The master provided transportation, lodging and sustenance. The servant paid with his labor and liberty. The indentured worker was a prisoner on the plantation. He was not allowed to marry and could be flogged for violating the contract. If the servant survived his tenure, the master was obliged to provide him with land of his own. It therefore behooved the master that servants not survive. This made for a rough life on the plantation. Indentured servitude was called *"white slavery."*

INDEPENDENT – (in-dee-*PEN*-dent) Being free, at liberty. In U.S. politics an Independent is a politician who is free, not aligned with either the Republican or Democratic Parties. An Independent is somewhat of a lone wolf that does not run with the pack (exclusively). They do not necessarily subscribe to a party platform. If the Independent is Liberal, he will caucus (meet) with the Democrats. If she is conservative, she will caucus with the Republicans. The two political parties may or may not contribute to the Independent's campaign. The two Independent Senators in 2022 are Angus King (b. 1944) from Maine, and Bernie Sanders (b. 1941) from Vermont. Senator King is a Progressive, Senator Sanders is a Progressive Socialist. Both caucus with the Democrats.

INDEPENDENT PRACTICE – (in-dee-*PEN*-dent *PRAC*-tis) In education, tasks a student completes alone, as seatwork or homework.

INDETERMINATE GROWTH – (in-de-*TUR*-min-nant *GROHTH*) Indeterminate means uncertain, not predictable. Growth, in this case, refers to an increase in size. In botany and zoology, indeterminate growth refers to an organism's unlimited ability to increase in size, until it dies. Under ideal environmental conditions, plants and some animals can spread or grow to immense, extraordinary size, checked only by death. These ideal conditions include perfect climate, environment, fertility, prey, space, and lack of competitors and predators. Now then, all living creatures (flora and fauna) are subject to entropy, meaning aging and physical breakdown that ultimately results in death. But with indeterminate growth, that process is slowed, resulting in enormous growth. Indeterminate growth is far more common in plants than in animals. Genetics holds a tighter grip on mammals than on other animals. Fish, mollusks, amphibians, and reptiles are more common indeterminate growth candidates. A good example is the Burmese python, and African rock python and their vicious hybrids in South Florida. The Everglades is the ideal environment, a paradise for these invasive species. It seems that they will breed and grow, and grow and grow, until killed by their only rival, the giant alligator that has also grown indeterminately. The two titans prey on each other, and the victor grows.

INDETERMINISM – (in-dee-*TUR*-min-is-um) The inability to distinguish validity with certainty. Indeterminism is uncertainty. It is the acceptance of contradiction. In mathematics for instance, a proposition may be *true, false* or *undetermined.* In quantum mechanics, the *"Heisenberg's Indeterminacy Principle"* of Mathematics asserts that there is a fundamental limit to the precision with which physical properties of particles can be known. In fact, the very nature of light reflects the concept of indeterminism. The wave/particle duality principle submits that light sometimes behaves as a wave, and other times as a particle. This is known as the *"Complementary Principle."* The very nature of light, (which is everything), in indeterminate. The *"Chaos Theory"* asserts that a multiplicity of indetermined unforeseen factors will make some predictions impossible to determine. This is the case with global weather forecasting. Never will an accurate weather forecast be made close to 2 weeks in advance. This too will remain in the realm of indeterminism.

INDEX FOSSIL – (*IN*-dex *FOS*-sil) A guide fossil. An index fossil is one found in a rock layer of only one geologic age and is used to establish the relative age of the rock layer.

INDIAN CORN – (*IN*-dee-an *KORN*) American maize with attractive mottled coloration, used as a decoration, but can be ground into corn meal.

INDICATIVE – (in-*DIK*-uh-tive) (Indicatively) To indicate, showing, signifying, or pointing out something. In a sentence, the word indicative is usually followed by the preposition *of.* For example: *"The 'no' vote on the food aid bill is indicative of Republican heartlessness."* In grammar an indicative word pertains to the mood of the verb used for ordinary objective statements or questions. For example, the verb *"plays"* in *"Emile plays softball."*

INDICTMENT – (in-*DYHT*-ment) (Indict, Indicted) In law, to bring a formal accusation by a grand jury against someone, requiring the accused to stand trial. An indictment is based on evidence presented to the grand jury by a prosecuting attorney. After an indictment, a suspect officially becomes a defendant. A Caveat: Don't confuse *arraignment* with indictment. An arraignment does not involve a grand jury. It is simply bringing a suspect to court before a judge, to be official charged with a crime. *"Donald Trump will certainly be indicted in Georgia for election corruption, and in New York for business corruption, and in Washington D.C. for insurrection."*

INDICTMENT/ARRAIGNMEMENT – (in-*DYHT*-ment uh-RAYN-ment) (Indicted/Arraigned) Both an arraignment and indictment are legal accusations of a crime by a court of law. The difference involves the type of crime and the legal procedures employed. Both court proceedings involve felonies (serious crimes). Actually, an indictment is a complex, extended form of arraignment. An arraignment is a pretrial procedure. The defendant appears in court before the judge. The defendant is informed of his rights, including the right to be represented by an attorney. The defendant is given the option to plead not guilty, guilty, or no contest (accepting the sentence without accepting guilt). A guilty or no contest plea will result in a sentence from the judge. If the defendant pleads not guilty, the judge considers the option of bail. Too, the judge announces the trial date. This ends the arraignment. The vast majority of crimes are processed in court through arraignments. An indictment is a formal charge by a district attorney that a person had committed a crime and must stand trial. This decision, the charge, is determined by a grand jury – a group of 12 to 23 citizens chosen to consider the evidence in the matter. The grand jury meets in private, and votes on whether the evidence warrants a trial – not guilt or innocence. That will be determined by a trial jury. Once the person is formally indicted by the district attorney, he is arraigned in court before a judge. Serious, albeit simple crimes can be processed through the simpler arraignment. Serious, albeit complex crimes are better handled through a grand jury indictment. For example, conspiracies, and crimes involving government officials (like Donald Trump b. 1946) are grand jury indicted.

INDIFFERENCE – (in-*DIF*-fer-ens) (Indifferent) A don't-give-a-damn attitude. Indifference is disinterest, apathy, emotionlessess. It is the degree of remorse most feel when they squash a bug. It cannot even generate anger or hatred. The opposite of love, in fact, is indifference. Indifference is often misread as tolerance. Much of American *tolerance* of religious differences is actually religious *indifference.* This applies more toward the multitude of Christian sects, as opposed to an entirely foreign religion (like Islam). Nevertheless, *"The worst sin toward our fellow creatures is not to hate them, but to be indifferent to them: that's the essence of inhumanity."* – George Bernard Shaw (1856 – 1950). *"Do not sit with indifferent people whose breath comes cold out of their mouths."* – Rumi (1207 – 1273). Indifference is a Nazi-level of empathy and compassion. It was with indifference that the Nazis murdered millions in the industrial-scaled death camps. Joseph Stalin (1878 – 1953) once said: *"The death of a single person is pathos. The death of a million persons is statistics."* That's indifference.

INDIGNANT – (in-*DIG*-nant) (Indigance) Feeling, characterized by, or expressing strong displeasure at something considered unjust, unfair, offensive or base. Capitalist greed, resulting in the unjust distribution of wealth that produces poverty generates indigance. It is indignant that half of the American population would not be able to find $400 dollars in case of an emergency today.

INDIGNANT – (in-*DIG*-nant) (Indignation, Indignantly) Righteous anger. Expressing strong animosity at something considered unjust, unfair, offensive, or insulting. Jesus was indignant when he drove the money changers (capitalists) out of the Temple.

INDIGNANT IMMIGRANTS – (in-*DIG*-nant *IM*-mi-grants) Displaced super- patriots. Indignant immigrants are ignorant aliens who migrate to a foreign nation, then slam the door on new arrivals. (*"I got in, to hell with you!"*) The level of selfishness exhibited by indignant immigrants is astounding. So is the level of stupidity. Time does not fade the fact that one is a foreign migrant. All immigrants should be thankful and grateful to the native citizens who welcomed them. To deny the same hospitality to newcomers is deplorable, worthy of deportation. Of all citizens, immigrants should support an open-door immigration policy. But remarkably, that's not always the case. Some misguided immigrants foolishly adopt the *"nativist"* philosophy of neo-Nazis, white nationalists or supremacists. They are ignorant of the fact that they too are thoroughly hated by the neo-Nazis, who support Donald Trump (b. 1946). *"Go back where you came from"* pertains to all immigrants, today's and yesterday's. This particularly pertains to immigrants from black and brown regions like Africa, Latin America, and the Caribbean. Why would past immigrants deny access to present immigrants? It's a strange socio- psychological phenomenon that converts often over-compensate as fanatics, super-patriots. Consider: Napoleon was Corsican, not French; Hitler was Austrian, not German; Stalin was Georgian, not Russian. All three dictators were immigrants. Too, egocentric indignant immigrants express the selfish Republican attitude: *"I got mine, to hell with you!"* Indignant immigrants better beware of what they wish for. If, (a very BIG IF), a Trump-like neo-Nazi gained totalitarian power, all immigrants, decent and indignant will be arrested by Immigration and Customs Enforcement (I.C.E.) dispossessed, and deported.

INDIGENOUS – (in-*DIJ*-en-us) The original home of some flora or fauna. An indigenous creature is a native, natural species of plant or animal not introduced from elsewhere. Unlike endemic creatures, the indigenous can be successfully transplanted elsewhere.

INDIGO – (*IN*-di-go) A deep blue/violet-blue dye extracted from the indigo plant. Indigo was cultivated by slaves on New World plantations, along with sugar, tobacco, and cotton. It is still raised commercially, as the plantation gave way to the agribusiness.

INDISCERNIBLE – (in-dis-*SER*-na-bul) Being exactly alike. Not recognized in any way as being different. Identical twins appear indiscernible.

INDITE – (in-*DITE*) (Inditer, Inditement) To write or compose as an essay or poem. Therefore, an iditer is a writer, and an inditement is a written composition or literary work.

INDIUM – (*IN*-dee-um) (In) The name derives from the dark violet-blue color "indigo." The 49 protons in its nucleus give indium its atomic number. Indium is a rare soft silvery-white metallic element associated with zinc ores. Indium is used in alloys, electronics, and electroplating.

INDIVIDUALISM – (in-div-*VIJ*-jew-al-is-um) Going one's own way, concerned only with oneself, being care-less of others. Self-centered individualism is considered *"rugged"* in America. It is inherent in the ethos of capitalism. *"Every man for himself"* is the individualist's credo. *Rugged* individualism [read: *selfish-sufficiency*] is contrary to gregarious human nature. Interdependence is the Socialist Credo. *"Interdependence is and ought to be as much the ideal of man as self-sufficiency. Man is a social being."* – Mohandas Gandhi (1869 – 1948).

INDIVIDUALISTIC GOAL STRUCTURE – (in-div-vij-jew-*WAL*-lis-tic *GOLE STRUC*-chur) In education, a class management structure in which rewards are given on the basis of an individual's performance, unaffected by the performance of other students. With the individualistic goal structure, the student competes with herself. This relieves students from the pressure of competition and comparison. For example: Jenny's A works would warrant a C if done by Heather. Jenny is doing the best that she can. Heather is more gifted, but does not work to her potential.

INDIVIDUALIZED INSTRUCTION – (in-div-*VIJ*-jew-wal-lyzd in-*STRUC*-shun) The lofty goal of customizing lessons to accommodate each student's unique needs. In actual school settings, individualized instruction is more rhetoric than reality, for it is impossible to engineer. Individualized instruction occurs in private tutorials, not a conventional classroom. Simply put, a class of 30 students would require 30 teachers to initiate real individualized instruction. A Caveat: Don't believe a principal who claims his school employs individualized instruction. She is making a false boast.

INDIVIDUATION – (in-di-vid-jew-*AY*-shun) Becoming an authentically unique person, an individual. Individuation is the necessary separation of children from parents. This occurs at about age 11 or 12, in the 7th grade of Middle School. Tension mounts as children individuate. They tend to adopt an *"oppositional identity."* They question rules, authority, form cliques, and adopt contra- cultural styles in dress, music and speech. Though not always pleasant, individuation is a crucial part of the gradual transition from child to adult.

INDOCHINA – (in-do-*CHY*-na) Geographically an East Asian peninsula located south of China which includes Myanmar (Burma), Thailand, Laos, Cambodia, Vietnam, and Malaysia. Politically, *"French"* Indochina was a colony of France comprised of Cambodia, Laos, and Vietnam. These 3 nations gained their independence from France in 1954.

INDOCILE – (in-*DOS*-sill) Unruly, fractious, unwilling to accept discipline, training, or instruction. An indocile pupil will not learn because he refuses to be taught.

INDOCTRINATION – (in-doc-trin-*NAY*-shun) Instruction through propaganda. Indoctrination insists on accepting the official party line unquestionably. Indoctrination leaves no room for uncertainty or debate. It is therefore not education, but rather miseducation. Indoctrination occurs in the schools of dictatorships. Incidentally: The argument can be made that catechetical teaching and learning is a form of propaganda. Catechisms are used in religious instruction to teach the tenants of the Church. It consists of question- and- answer memorization, devoid of debate.

INDO-EUROPEAN – (*IN*-dow-your-o-*PEE*-an) The language family from India to Ireland, which includes English and all the other European languages. Sanskrit of India is the parent tongue of the Indo-European group.

INDOLENT – (*IN*-doe-lent) (Indolence) Lazy, slothful, sluggish, torpid. An indolent individual lacks ambition, enthusiasm, and pep. A *"couch potato"* exhibits indolence. Incidentally: Donald Trump (b. 1946) was the most indolent U.S. President of modern times.

INDOLOGY – (in-*DOL*-la-jee) The academic study of ancient India. A scholar of Indology is an Indologist, an India specialist. Indologists have a place in the university and in the government State Department.

INDOMITABLE – (in-*DOM*-mit-ta-bul) Unconquerable, cannot be dominated, subdued, or defeated. Such a person exhibits an indomitable will.

INDONESIA – (in-do-*NEESH*-shee-a) A republic in the Malay Archipelago consisting of over 13,677 islands covering over 741,098 square miles. Indonesia in the most *"islandesque"* nation on the globe, the largest cluster of islands on Earth. Sumatra, Java, Sulawesi, Bali, Madura, the Moluccas, South Borneo, and West New Guinea are parts of Indonesia. The fractured country was geologically formed when the Australian plate subducted under the Pacific plate. Tectonic plates collide faster in Indonesia, than in any other place on Earth. This results in seismic and volcanic catastrophes like no place else on the planet.

Indonesia has more volcanoes than anyplace else in the world, 150 of the planet's 500 active volcanoes (33%). This is a grave danger for the 259 million citizens, the 4th most populated country in the world. The Indonesian waters host a greater variety of fish than anyplace else on Earth. That's because of its wealth in coral reefs. These are the oldest ecosystems in the world, and richest in marine life. Over one-fourth of all oceanic life inhabits coral reefs. Indonesia is blessed with 80% of the planet's coral reefs, containing over 600 varieties of coral. The reefs provide the habitat for the richest, most diverse marine environment on Earth. Too, Indonesia's location at the juncture of the Pacific and Indian Oceans adds to the diversity. Over 17% of the planet's bird species, and one-fifth of the world's reptiles are found in the islands. That includes the monstrous Komodo Dragon, the world's biggest lizard. Incidentally: Non-Arabic Indonesia has the greatest Muslim population of all nations. Only the exotic island of Bali is predominately Hindu.

IN DUBIO – (in *DOO*-bee-o) Latin for "*in doubt.*"

INDUBITABLE – (in-*DOO*-bit-ta-bul) (Indubitably) Unquestionable, without doubt, self-evident. If it's indubitable, it's unquestionably true, absolutely certain. "*Trump is a Nazi fascist indubitably.*"

INDUCE – (in-*DOOS*) To lead or move by persuasion or influence as to some action or belief. In philosophy, to induce is to take bits of evidence, then draw a general truth from them. This is an *a posteriori* logic and the basis for science (induction). The opposite of induce is deduce.

INDUCTION – (in-*DUC*-shun) An *a posteriori* statement or concept. Start with evidence to arrive at absolute truths. Science is inductive. With induction, one must "*see it to believe it,*" which is contrary to deduction (faith), in which one must "*believe it to see it.*" Galileo Galilei's (1564 – 1642) revolution consisted of elevating induction above deduction as the logical method of science. Instead of building conclusions in an assumed set of generalizations (deductions of the Greeks), the inductive method starts with observations and derives generalizations (deduced axioms) from them. Induction relies on experimentation, not faith, as deduction does. However, the inductive (scientific) method cannot make generalizations about what it cannot observe or measure. Faith-based metaphysical phenomena are therefore beyond the realm of induction. Since God, or the soul are not observable by any direct means yet known, these spiritual subjects lie outside inductive investigation. Induction cannot explain miracles.

INDUCTIVE REASONING – (in-*DUC*-tiv *REE*-son-ing) A problem-solving methodology in which generalizations are based upon observation and experience. Conclusions are summative but do not exceed the limits of observable data. Inductive reasoning is *a posteriori*. Knowledge is gained through direct human experience. A posteriori, inductive reasoning begins with experience and infers conclusions. This experience may derive from scientific experimentation. The scientific method is a posteriori, inductive reasoning. Its opposite is *a priori deductive reasoning.*

INDULGENCES – (in-*DULL*-jens-es) In the Roman Catholic Church, a partial remission of purgatorial punishment for sins after absolution. Indulgences are inextricably tied to the concept of Purgatory. The Catholic Church cautiously embraced the notion that the prayers and other actions of the living could shorten the time the decreased spent in Purgatory. As a merciful intercessor, the Virgin Mary was named the "*Queen of Purgatory,*" to whom prayers for the deceased were addressed. In the 16th and 17th centuries, the Popes sold indulgences to ignorant peasants in order to collect money to build Saint Peter's Cathedral in Rome. Indulgences were hawked as *"out of jail cards"* for souls suffering in Purgatory, and *"pre-paid passports to heaven."* It was this abuse of indulgences that incensed Fr. Martin Luther (1483 – 1546) and precipitated the Protestant Reformation (Revolution). In the words of the jingo that so offended Martin Luther: *"As soon as the money in the coffer rings, the soul from Purgatory springs."*

INDURATE – (*IN*-dur-rate) (Induration) To harden like rock, or to make callous. An indurate person is hardheaded and may be hard hearted. She is stubborn and perhaps unfeeling.

INDUSTRIALIZATION – (in-dus-tree-al-ize-*ZAY*-shun) The socio-economic changeover from an agricultural, to a manufacturing society. Industrialization in many respects is modernization. But as with all change, it can come with great social upheaval and emotional trauma. Capitalist promoted industrialization has brought hardship. When profit is the motif, people are merely tools. Socialist industrialization takes the emphasis off profit, and places it on people. The machine serves the man, in Socialist industrialization. The man becomes a part of the machine, in capitalist industrialization.

INDUSTRIAL REVOLUTION – (in-*DUS*-tree-al rev-vo-*LOO*-shun) The social and economic transformation of agrarian societies into industrial, urbanized [read: *slum*] societies. Beginning in 18th century Britain, the process was driven successively by the development of steam power, coal fuel, the advent of factory production, and the construction of railroads. The other indispensable ingredient was the blood, sweat, and tears of the countless laborers who languished in the squalid factories to make the capitalist industrialists and investors filthy rich. The worker became factory fodder, to be used and used up.

INDUSTRIAL UNION – (in-*DUS*-tree-al *YOON*-yun) The united workforce of an entire industry. The members of the union perform a variety of jobs, unlike a trade union.

INEBRIAC – (in-*NEE*-bree-ac) An alcoholic. A compulsive intoxicator. One victimized by alcohol addiction. An inebriac uses alcohol to become consciously obliterated.

INEDIA – (in-*NEE*-dee-a) (Inedians) Literally Latin for "fasting." This phenomenon is also called Breatharianism (breth-*AIR*-ree-in-is-um), literally, the ability to live on air. Inedians or Breatharians believe that a person can live without consuming food, and in some cases, from also abstaining from water or any liquids. In the natural world, abstaining from food and drink is suicidal. But Breatharianism or Inedia are thought to be supernatural. It is said to be practiced by mystics, spiritualists, alchemists, yogis, and Ascended Masters. Practioners claim that enlightened humans can be sustained by *"Prana,"* the vital life force in Hinduism. The Hindu god *Ayurveda* established the ancient homeopathic medicinal system *"Ayurveda."* It claims that sunlight is a primary source of Prana. Therefore, initiated practioners of Inedia or Breatharians can miraculously subsist on sunlight alone. What's impossible with man in the natural, is possible with God in the supernatural.

INEFFABLE – (in-*EFF*-a-bul) Unutterable. Incapable of being expressed, indescribable, beyond words. Ineffable is often used to mean unspeakably divine, heavenly or ethereal.

INEPTITUDE – (in-*EP*-tit-tood) (Inept) Haplessly incompetent. Lacking skill or aptitude for a particular task or assignment. No president is American History was less prepared and more inept than Republican Donald Trump (b. 1946).

INERRANT – (in-*ER*-rant) Infallible, free from error. *"His Erroneousness,"* President Donald Trump (b. 1946) is a self-declared inerrant. That's why he refuses to ever admit a mistake or apologize.

INERTIA – (in-*NER*-sha) In a scientific sense, inertia is the natural expenditure and dissipation of energy over time. Inertia is a form of resistance, slowdown, breakdown, decay. All inorganic and organic matter is subject to inertial. All material will disintegrate, and creatures will die. Inertia results in the recycling of the atomic structure of matter. The stars will fall, the sun will die, and so will you and me. Incidentally: Today, the average, worldwide life span is 83 years. By 83, all the forces of inertia usually gain a critical mass that results in shutdown or death.

INERTIA – (in-*NER*-sha) Concerning people, inertia is a lack of ambition. Inertia is a state of inactivity, immobility, apathy, especially in regard to exerting effort. Depression results in inertia. The depressant feels listless and lethargic. Procrastination is a form of inertia associated with the avoidance of distasteful tasks.

IN EXTENSO – (in ex-*TEN*-so) Latin for *at full length.*

INEXORABLE – (in-ex-*OR*-a-bul) (Inexorably) Unyielding, unalterable, unable to be persuaded. The connotation of inexorable is somewhat negative. An inexorable person would be stubborn, relentless, severe, pitiless, merciless, even cruel. Prayers or entreaties (begging) would not move an inexorable individual. A tyrannical king or dictator would be inexorable. Incidentally: From 2008 to 2016, the Republicans were inexorably opposed to President Barack Obama (b. 1961). As the party of *"NO!"* the Republicans inexorably attempted to block any proposal made by the President.

INEXPIABLE – (in-*EX*-pee-a-bul) Unforgivable, unpardonable, unatonable. Not allowing for amends or rectitude.

INEXPLICIT – (in-ex-*PLIS*-it) Not clear or clearly stated. An inexplicit explanation is not understandable.

INEXPUGNABLE – (in-ex-*PUG*-na-bull) Unconquerable, impregnable, cannot be taken by force.

IN EXTREMIS – (in ex-*TREE*-mees) Latin for *"In the last extreme."* In extremis refers to being at the point of death.

INEXTRICABLE – (in-ex-*trick*-a-bul) (Inextricably) Beyond extrication. Any item or situation that is so muddled, entangled, perplexing, or hopelessly ensnared, that one cannot disengage or escape.

INFANTILISM – (in-*FANT*-til-is-um) (Infantile, Infantilist, Infantilistic) A neurotic paraphilial disorder in which one derives sexual pleasure by dressing, acting, and being treated like a baby.

INFANTRY – (*IN*-fan-tree) The heart or guts of the army. The infantry consists of the foot soldiers, the *"grunts,"* the boots on the ground. In order to be victorious in battle and win wars, territory has to be taken, neutralized, and held. That takes numbers. That takes the infantry. The infantry fights with small arms, but supported by artillery, heavy mechanized weaponry, and air power. At first it seems ironic that the term infantry derives from the Latin *"infans"* meaning *"incapable of speech."* The reference is to young babies. In Medieval France, a young soldier from a prominent family who had not acquired knighthood was called an *"enfant."* Similarly, in Italy one of the soldiers who followed a mounted knight on foot was an *"infante."* Soon foot soldiers collectively became *"infanteria,"* which was borrowed into French as *"infanterie,* and adopted by the English as *"infantry."* Incidentally: As Latin infans were incapable of speech, so are infantry troops. As Alfred Lord Tennyson (1809 – 1892) wrote in <u>Charge of the Light Brigade</u> (1854): *"Their's is not to reason why. Their's is not to make reply. Their's is just to do and die."* (Parenthetically: Infantry soldier are considered dispensable, to be used and used up.)

INFELICITY – (in-fel-*LIS*-si-tee) (Infelicitous) Being in a state of unhappiness or suffering perpetual misfortune.

INFERENCE – (*IN*-fer-ensz) (Infer, Inferring) To arrive at a conclusion through logical reasoning, utilizing evidence or premises. An inference may be deductive or inductive. A deductive inference arrives at a conclusion from premises that are accepted as true. An inductive inference arrives at a conclusion from factual statements taken as evidence for the conclusion. Theological, Spiritual, metaphysical inferences are deductive. Scientific, material, physical inferences are inductive. A deductive inference: *"God is omnipotent. I therefore infer that God performs miracles."* An inductive inference: *"Man is a mammal. I therefore infer that man is warm-blooded."*

INFERIORITY COMPLEX – (in-fear-ree-*OR*-rit-tee *COM*-plex) A neurotic disorder from the conflict between the desire to be noticed and the fear of being humiliated. Inferiority complex was identified by psychiatrist Alfred Adler (1870 – 1937). It is characterized by either extreme reticence (shyness) or, as a result of overcompensation, by extreme aggression. A person suffering from inferiority feels a persistent sense of inadequacy and a tendency to diminish oneself. He is constantly haunted by the feeling that he is not good enough, that he does not belong. What is required to combat the inferiority complex is self-confidence. This can be acquired through a series of small successes, building on each other, until the person feels competent and self-assured. Its trite but true, nothing succeeds like success.

INFERIOR SCRIPT – (in-*FEER*-ree-or *SKRIPT*) Written or printed low on a line of text. For Example: the small numbers or letters in a chemical formula are written in inferior script: H_2O, CO_2, N_ACL. Both number *twos* and the letter *a* are written in inferior script.

INFIBULATION – (in-fib-yu-*LAY*-shun) The stitching or wiring of the female vulva or male prepuce (foreskin) in order to prevent the *"sin"* of masturbation. Infibulation was a common practice into the prudish Victorian Era. This is an outrageous form of humiliation and torture. To perform infibulation today would be a felonious act of abuse.

INFIDELITY – (in-fid-*DAL*-lit-tee) Adultery. Being unfaithful, especially to the matrimonial vows. Infidelity is the primary killer of marriages. It is condemned in the Mosaic Ten Commandments as adultery. Incidentally: In *"a conficta,"* it has been said that when Moses descended from Mt. Sinai with the

Decalogue, he told the Hebrews: *"I have good news and I have bad news. The good news – I got Him down to ten. The bad news – adultery is still in."*

IN FIERI – (in fee-*AIR*-ree) Latin for *"in the process of becoming."* An in fieri project is not yet complete but is a work in progress. It is still being created or developed.

INFINITESIMAL – (in-fin-it-*TES*-si-mal) Infinitely, indefinitely, immeasurably, incalculably small.

INFINITY – (in-*FIN*-nit-tee) (Infinite, Infinitely) Forever, eternal, everlasting, endless, timeless. The term infinity was taken from the French *"infinite,"* which derives from the Latin *"Infinitus,"* meaning *"boundlessness, endlessness."* Don't expect what's infinite to end any time soon. It won't. It is speculated by some that the universe is infinite. Perhaps, however if it had a genesis, a beginning (*"The Big Bang"*), it's reasonable to believe that it will have an end (perhaps a *"Big Crunch"*). Whatever is material, made of matter, cannot be infinite. Entropy will always set in, and to dust, then light energy it will transform. The human soul is spirit, not matter. It therefore is infinite or eternal as is God, the Cosmic Soul.

INFLATED PRICE – (in-*FLAY*-ted *PRYS*) Another capitalist scheme to deceive and cheat the consumer. A phony and outrageously high price is tagged onto an item. Then a much lower sales price is also tagged on. It is hoped to deceive the customer into thinking she is getting a great bargain on an expensive item. Like so much in capitalism, this is unethical, but not illegal. Take for example, a lady's purse. It may be priced at $144.95. Another tag will read: *"Sale price, $88.95."* This is the price the retailer hoped to get for the purse in the first place. (Actually, the purse cost the manufacturer $12.44 to be made by non- union workers in Indonesia.) Capitalism is a win/lose system. Inorder for the capitalists to prosper, the consumers must be bilked.

INFLATION – (in *FLAY*-shun) A capitalist economic sickness in which money loses its worth. Consumer prices skyrocket as money loses its value. It takes more and more to buy less and less. The people become poorer. In economics as in any other facet of life, the more you have of something, the less it is worth. When this applies to money, we call it inflation. Too much money in circulation results in inflation. With more money, people spend more. Greedy capitalist take advantage of this demand by hiking prices. This is inflation. To combat inflation, the government will raise interest rates to make barrowing more expensive, slowing down spending. This should lower inflation. People will buy less so cagy capitalists will lower prices. But take care, because too little spending will result in recession. This will result in layoffs. Incidentally: In poor underdeveloped countries, the I.M.F. (International Monetary Fund) introduces deceptive predatory loans, then devalues the currency (igniting inflation) which benefits foreign capitalist corporations and banks that the I.M.F. represents.

INFLECTION – (in-*FLEK*-shun) Voice modulation. A variation in the pitch and tone of voice which communicates subtle emotional implications. The degree of voice inflection is both a cultural and personal matter. The British inflect far more than Americans, particularly the Midwesterners. *"There are tones of voice that mean more than words."* – Poet Robert Frost (1874 – 1963).

INFLECTION POINT – (in-*FLEK*-shun poyt) In this context, inflection refers to a bend or an angle. In mathematics, the inflection point is the spot on the graph where the line bends or changes direction from concave (downward) to convex (upward) or vice versa. In Sociology, the inflection point is the point of no return. It is some incident or event that altered a relationship. Physical abuse, infidelity, any humiliating disgusting episode may serve as an inflection point, where a relationship concaves or caves-in. Incidentally: On January 6, 2021, as the last days of the *Trump Travesty* sank into history, the rats began to jump ship. For many, the treasonous atrocity of the Trump-inspired invasion of the Capitol Building by an army of thugs was the last abomination. One of the *Johnnie-come-lately* rebels included the incompetent Secretary of Education Betsy DeVos (b. 1958). *"Billionaire"* Betsy exclaimed: *"[Trump]," there is no mistaking the impact your rhetoric had on the situation [the riot], and it is the inflection point for me."* Prayerfully, all Trumpsters will reflect, and inflect on their devotion to Herr Trump.

INFLORESCENCE – (in-floor-*RES*-sens) (Inflorescent) A type of flower cluster. An inflorescence occurs in plants that produce groups of small or tiny flowers, rather than a single flower on each stem. Elderberry and dill are great examples. An inflorescence can be called a spike, panicle, raceme, or umbel, depending on the shape it creates.

INFLUENCER – (*IN*-floo-en-ser) (Influence, Influencing, Influenced, Influential) A powerful person with the ability to sway people's opinions and actions. An influencer is often a popular celebrity, politician, religious, or sports figure. She or he has a wide media platform through which to propagate information. Influencers exert great influence on society – not always for the better. Undoubtedly, the most toxic, dangerous influencer in American History is Donald Trump (b. 1946). If the American experiment in democracy fails, it will be due to the venomous influence of Trump.

INFODEMIC – (in-foh-*DEM*-mik) (Infodemical) A massive amount of widely and rapidly circulating information about a particular crisis or controversial issue, consisting of a confusing combination of fact, falsehood, rumor, opinion, and conspiratorial nonsense. Social media is custom-made for infodemics. Donald Trump (b. 1946) and his enablers have used infodemics as smokescreens to camouflage their crimes.

INFOMANIA – (in-fo-*MAY*-nee-a) (Infomaniac) Excessive neurotic devotion to accumulating facts. An infomaniac would do well on a quiz show like *Jeopardy*. A Caveat: Memorizing facts is not having wisdom. It is being knowledgeable in a sense, by uselessly so. Infomania is like collecting bricks, with no knowledge of have to build a house.

INFOMERCIAL – (*IN*-foe-mer-shals) (also Info<u>com</u><u>mer</u>cial) An annoying corporate capitalist advertising fit on the television. An infomercial is a long (program- length) commercial that informs and instructs, especially in an original and [presumed] entertaining manner. The purpose is to sell. The underlying purpose is to profit. Knives, glues, detergents, juicers, music, anything, everything is imposed on the TV audience in infomercials. It always includes some amazing demonstration. Infomercials attempt to turn novelties into necessities. They blast the viewing audience away with *"sound compression."* The entire presentation is broadcasted at the maximum level of loudness allowed by the FCC (<u>F</u>ederal <u>C</u>ommunications <u>C</u>ommission). There is no modulation of sound or voice. The entire production is loud, which is most disturbing. Incidentally: Congress considered banning sound compression in TV commercials, but Republicans (big business lackeys) scuttled the legislation. Foot Note: It has been testified that Donald Trump (b. 1946) never expected to win the Presidential election. His candidacy was a lark, a publicity stunt to elevate the prestige and value of the Trump product name. Trump had said that his election campaign *"Would be the greatest infomercial in history!"* nothing more.

INFORMATION – (in-fer-*MAY*-shun) In its basic form, information is facts and data. Information is not synonymous with knowledge. Knowledge is information processed in a useable, practical, form. Knowledge, on the other hand, is not wisdom. Wisdom is knowing when and how to apply knowledge in the wisest way. For example if information represents bricks, then knowledge is the building the bricks created. Wisdom is converting the building to a hospital, school, or library.

INFORMATION POLLUTION – (in-fer-*MAY*-shuhn puh-*LOO*-shuhn) (Information Polluters) A new term introduced into the dictionary in 2023. Information pollution is to intentionally adulterate the truth. *"Flood the media with shit!"* advised Trump's advisor Steve Bannon (b. 1953). Pollution is filth, toxins, contaminants. Information pollution is the introduction of falsehood, irrelevance, bias, and sensationalism into a source of news, contaminating its validity. The intended result is to dilute or outright suppress the essential facts. The Republican Party, particularly the Trumpublican wing are notorious information polluters. They are masters at obfuscating the facts, introducing red herrings, submitting false equivalencies to escape the truth. *"Sure Trump is indicted in four jurisdictions with 91 felony counts – but what about Hunter Biden's laptop, or lapdog, or lap-dance, whatever!"*

INFORMED CONSENT – (in-*FORMD* con-*SENT*) In law, a person's agreement to allow something to happen (such as being the subject of a research study) that is based on a full disclosure of facts needed to make the decision intelligently.

INFOWAR – (*IN*-foh-wawr) (Information Warfare) The propaganda campaign to win peoples' minds and allegiance. The infowar is fought on the battlefield of broadcast and social media. The enemies in the present day American infowar are Progressives versus Conservatives; Democracy versus Fascism; Socialism versus Capitalism; the rich versus the rest. The ammunition used in information warfare are culture-war issues – abortion, immigration, vaccination, racism, replacement theory, electoral legitimacy, authentic history, police powers, partisan judiciary, wealth disparity, Trumpism, and many others. The conservative Republican right, the lackeys of the rich, are so hysterical to preserve their wealth through governmental power, that they have forsaken all rules of fair, decent combat. They have renounced Democracy for an apartheid rendition of fascism. On their great battleships like FOX TV, anything goes. Truth is not a requirement and lying is not an inhibition. The infowar, as fought from the right, is tearing America apart. One person, Donald Trump (b. 1946), is mostly responsible. (Satan could not have found a more proficient saboteur to punish America, than Trump.) The historic, democratic America may not survive the culture war as fought through the infowar. Too many *"low-information"* – nay – stupid, uneducated bigots – are now brainwashed POWs of the right-wing infowarriors. *"The difference between us Republicans and you Democrats is that we go for the head-shot, while you go for the pillow-fight."* – Steven Bannon (b. 1953). *"How stupid can a nation get and still survive?"* – Journalist Eugene Robinson (b. 1954).

INFRASTRUCTURE – (*IN*-fra-struk-tur) The basic, underlying framework or features of a system or organization. Infrastructure is the engine of civilization. In a nation, the infrastructure includes roads, bridges, canals, sewage, water supply, communication systems, power plants, public schools, post offices, hospitals, libraries, and parks – all that facilities that make civilization possible. The infrastructure is the basic support system needed to keep the economy moving and people alive. That's why our national infrastructure must be government owned and operated, for public benefit, not private profit. It is a dangerous travesty that about 80% of our water and electrical power grid are privately owned. Privatization, overspending on the military, and lack of spending on domestic essentials have left America's aging infrastructure in shambles. According to the Association of American Engineers, it would cost over $2.5 trillion dollars over a 5 year period to upgrade the nation's neglected infrastructure to only an adequate level. With capitalist Republican privatization, 70% to 80% of the U.S. infrastructure (water supply, electricity, power grid) is now privately owned. Though they charge top dollar to cornered consumers, these capitalists expect tax-payer's dollars to shore up their private enterprises. Welfare for the rich! That's why all utilities essential to the public must be owned by the public. Incidentally: Nine out of 10 infrastructure projects, on average, go 25% over budget.

INFUSION – (in-*FEW*-shun) A liquid extract, as tea, prepared by steeping or soaking. Essential oils are extracted from plants by boiling or soaking them in hot water. A pharmacy of precious medicinal curse and health elixirs can be produced through knowledgeable infusion.

IN FUTURO – (in few-*CHUR*-ro) Latin for *in the future.*

INGRESS – (*IN*-gress) Entering or the entranceway. Ingress is the act of going in. Egress is the opposite of ingress, exiting, going out.

INHIBITION – (in-hi-*BISH*-shun) (Inhibit) A restraint, hindrance, prohibition, or check on some action, deed, impulse, or desire. Often inhibitions are personal, psychological blockages to attaining what we want. Lack of self-confidence, embarrassment, shame, fear of ridicule, sin or punishment can inhibit an individual. The inhibition may concern asking for a dance, a date, or sex. In Matthew 7:7, Jesus encouraged us to: *"Ask, and it will be given to you; seek, and you shall find; knock, and it will be opened to you."* Sex is riddled with inhibitions. The inhibited lover is being cheated of much physical, emotional satisfaction.

INHUMATION – (in-hum-*MAY*-shun) To inter or bury. Inhumation is committing a corpse to the Earth, as in a graveyard or cemetery.

INIMICAL – (im-*NIM*-mi-cal) Hostile, adverse in tendency and effect. An inimical person is aggressive and threatening.

INIMITABLE – (in-*IM*-it-ta-bul) Unique, matchless. An inimitable person cannot be copied or imitated.

INITIALISM – (in-*NISH*-al-is-um) A special type of acronym. A set of letters (initials) representing a name, organization, or the like, with each letter pronounced separately. FBI, CIA, IRA, IQ, UAW, ACLU, ESP, or G.I. for example, are initialisms. The series of letters do not comprise a word, as do *acronyms*. An initialism is distinguished from an acronym which creates and sounds-out a new word – like NATO, for North Atlantic Treaty Organization, or OPEC, for Organization of Petroleum Exporting Cartel.

INITIATED – (in-*NISH*-shee-ay-ted) (Initiate) To be introduced and instructed in some secret, esoteric knowledge, subject, or organization. On the metaphysical level, the initiated are the elite enlightened elect, the chosen people made privy to Divine Spiritual information. An initiate is a mystic, saint, prophet, healer, miracle worker in atonement [read: *at-one-ment*] with God. An initiate is often tested for worthiness with a descent into a Divine Karmic Purgatory for cleansing, a *"Dark Night of the Soul."* This is the Holy Initiation. Not many are initiated. As Jesus said: *"Many are called, but few are chosen."* – Matthew 22:14. Furthermore, in *The Gospel of Thomas* Jesus said: *"I tell my mysteries to those who are worthy of my mysteries."*

INITIATIVE – (in-*NISH*-shee-a-tiv) To initiate or take leadership. An initiative is an introductory act or step leading to action. Initiative is one's personal readiness and ability to take action, to set events in motion. *"Initiative is doing the right thing without being told."* – Victor Hugo (1802 – 1885).

INITIATIVE – (in-*NISH*-shee-a-tiv) (Political Science) A *"people"* generated proposal put to the voters. This is contrasted with a referendum which is *"politician"* generated proposal put to the voters.

INJUNCTION – (in-*JUNK*-shun) In law, a court order prohibiting a person from committing an act that threatens or may result in injury to another. In labor relations an injunction is a court order to prevent a company or union from taking action during a labor dispute.

IN LOCO PARENTIS – (in *LO*-co par-*RENT*-tees) Latin for *"In the place of the parents."* The ancient educational doctrine that the school personnel take the place of the parents while the children are in their care.

INMATE TRUMP – (*IN*-mayt *TRUMP*) Convict Donald J. Trump (b. 1946) incarcerated most likely in federal prison, for his multifarious crimes. If equal justice under the law is a reality in the United States of America, Trump's bloated carcass will be incarcerated. Never before had an American been sent to prison with his personal, government-provided bodyguards. That's because as an ex-president, Trump has at least 4 Secret Service Agents protecting him at all times. He is awarded this privilege by the generous government he tried to destroy. Nevertheless, what becomes of Trump's guardians when Trump goes to prison? Congress could rescind the guardian privilege with the cooperation of the Supreme Court. Not likely. Some prisoners are relegated to solitary confinement for their own protection. This can be Trump's fate, according to attorney Katie Phang (b. 1975). Too punitive perhaps? Then the Secret Service Agents would have to accompany Trump to prison. Not a sweetheart assignment. There is no *"Presidential Suite"* in the big house. Trump's bodyguards would have to occupy the same or adjacent cells. Prison space in expensive. Trump would have to be forced to pay the agent's room-and-board himself. Alternatively, Trump's 4 bodyguards can share the time, working 6- hour shifts. Trump may have to supplement their wages as hazard pay. This too should come at Trump's expense, not paid for with tax dollars. Whatever the solution, Trump's Secret Service protection should not be an *"out-of-jail-pass."* House arrest at his luxury resort at *Mar-a-Lago* is not accountability or justice. *"Where are the Proud Boy when you need them?"* Breaking News: (August 5, 2023) A few hours after writing this article, the Federal Bureau of Prisons announced that they would have no problem accommodating a prisoner and his Secret Service entourage. This was tantamount to hanging a *"WELCOME TRUMP!"* sign on the prison gate.

IN MEMORIAM – (in mem-*MOR*-ree-um) Latin for *"In memory"* of, or to the memory of. In memorium is used as a memorial, and is often written on tombs, gravestones, and in obituaries. It is abbreviated: *in mem.*

INNATISM – (in-*NAYT*-is-um) The term *innate* means inborn, existing in one from birth. Innatism is an *epistemological* (knowledge-related) concept that we are born with a priori knowledge in the mind. Classical Idealism [read: *Idea-ism*] insists that knowledge is within us. We must find ways to release it into consciousness. The Eastern concept of Karma contends that knowledge within from former lives influence our present, and account for coincidences, serendipities, deja vu, and love-at-first-sight experiences. This too can be considered a form of innatism.

INNER-BITCH – (*IN*-ner *BICH*) Inherent bitchery, an attitudinal trait shared by all women. A deep seeded propensity or ability of females to be malignantly malicious, and viciously vindictive. This is not a sexist, misogynous slur, but a cerebral hard-wiring that occurred during the *"Environment of Evolutionary Adaptation"* (EEA) when male and female sex differences were being established for survival purposes. Men are on average 20% to 25% stronger than women. Women must therefore use their wits, emotions, sexuality, stealth, speech, memory, and manipulation, psychological warfare as a defense mechanism to compete and defeat men. This is their inner-bitch. Additionally, every woman is in conscious or subconscious competition with every other woman. This rivalry over attractiveness, sex appeal breads envy and jealousy which fortifies the inner bitch. For instance, the comment: *"She looks so good, I hate her!"* has become a cliché. The inner-bitch is exercised through *"rumination,"* never forgetting or forgiving. Females can be relentless, ruthless, and punitive like a man cannot. *Chivalry* is a male trait and counter-intuitive to the inner-bitch. Nowhere is inner-bitchery more ferociously evident than a *cat- fight* between women. The fangs and claws come out, because each knows that she knows. (Incidentally, research reveals that women would overwhelmingly prefer working for a man (who they can man-ipulate) than for a woman.) Some women find the *"menopause card"* most convenient to justify the expressing, venting of their inner bitch. English poet William Congreve (1670 – 1729) hit the mark when he wrote: *"Hell hath no fury like a woman scorned!"* <u>The Mourning Bride</u> (1703).

INNOCUOUS – (in-*NOCK*-yu-us) Harmless, not risky, dangerous, or injurious. Anything innocuous is inoffensive, not likely to irritate. It is non-controversial like a standard answer to an innocuous question.

INNOVATOR'S CREDO – (*IN*-no-vay-tors *CRAY*-dow) *"Improve, Adapt, and Overcome."*

INNUENDO – (in-yoo-*WEN*-doh) Deceptive indirect use of derogatory, disparaging intimation, always maintaining a degree of deniability. A *"dog- whistle"* remark, to be understood by the initiated, falls in the category of innuendo. Innuendo is subtlely suggested without outright saying it. However, the message gets across. Sarcasm is innuendo. Innuendo provides deniability. If criticized for the comment, the guilty party can insist, *"I didn't mean it that way!"*

INNOXIOUS – (in-*NOK*-shuhs) (Innoxiously, Innoxiousness) Innocuous, harmless, not noxious.

INOCULATION EFFECT – (in-noc-kew-*LAY*-shun ef-*FECT*) To make one immune or resistant to a disease. In disputation, to strengthen one's convictions and argument by studying the arguments of one's opponent. The inoculation effect imbues the person with the power to resist the compelling points of the opponent's argument. Politicians employ inoculation effect exercises in preparation for public debates.

INORGANIC – (in-or-*GAN*-nic) Any substance not made up of living organisms or the remains of living organisms. Chemically speaking, inorganic compounds are not hydrocarbons or their derivatives. Take a hammer, for instance. The iron hammer head is inorganic. It was never alive. But the handle is organic, for the wood was once alive as a branch on a tree. Furthermore, a fossil is inorganic, for the organic material was turned to stone. But a bone is organic, for it was part of a living body.

IN PERPETUUM – (in per-*PET*-chew-um) Latin meaning *"Forever."*

IN PRAESENTI – (in pray-*SEN*-tee) Latin for in the *"present time."*

IN PURIS NATURALIBUS – (in *PUR*-ees na-chur-al-*LEE*-boos) Latin for *"stark naked."*

INQUIETUDE – (in-*KWAY*-it-tood) Uneasy, restless, laced with anxiety. Disquieting thoughts results in inquietude.

INQUISITION – (in-kwis-*SISH*-shun) The generic term inquisition simply mean to inquire. But historically, the Inquisition was the judicial institution of the Roman Catholic Church (1232 – 1820) founded to discover and suppress heresy. The *"Holy Roman and Universal Inquisition"* was created by *"His Holiness,"* Pope Paul III (1468 - 1549) in 1542 to suppress the spread of Reformation (Protestant) doctrines. However, as early as 385 CE, the Catholic Church had executed its first heretic. (This was only 73 years after the last Christian was killed in the Roman Colosseum.) Savage tortures were applied to force confessions. Wiccans (witches) and Jews were common victims. The Roman Inquisition was theologically motivated, whereas the Spanish Inquisition was also politically motivated. Both were economically motivated as the property of the condemned was expropriated by the Church and state. The most gruesome tortures usually ended in immolation in the bonfire [read: *"bone fire"*]. Dying on the cross, Jesus yelled out in a loud voice: *"Father forgive them, for they know not what they do!"* – Luke 23:34. That leads us to wonder, what would be Jesus' reaction to the Inquisition, executed in his name? Incidentally: St. Augustine (354 – 430) urged a policy of physical coercion in the hope of suppressing heresy. Thus he sanctioned the use of physical force against Christians by Christians. Centuries later, Augustine's support of such *"corrective measures"* would be used to justify the use of torture by the Inquisition.

IN RE. – (in *RAY*) (*In the matter of.*) In law, a method of entitling a judicial proceeding in which there are no adversaries. In re. Is a prefix to the name of a case, often used when a child is involved? For example, *"In re. Wanda Wojciechowski"* might be the title of a child neglect proceedings though it is really against the parents.

INSANITY – (in-*SAN*-nit-tee) To be legally determined *non compos mentis*, out of one's mind. An insane individual cannot be legally held responsible for her actions. On the other hand, to be considered crazy affords one great latitude of behavior. Insanity is used in a court of law as a defense against ghastly crimes. Philosophically, we may argue that murder is always an insane act. But that does not make one legally insane. To be legally insane, one must be judged so medically. But the defense attorney must still convince the jury to believe the medical diagnosis. If the insanity plea succeeds, the defendant is judged not guilty, but still dangerous. So he may spend the rest of his life in a mental institution.

INSECTICIDE – (in-*SEK*-ti-syd) Literally, *"killing bugs."* This is a verb. As a noun, insecticide is a chemical poison to massacre, annihilate, exterminate insects. In fact, professional bug killers are called *"exterminators,"* which literally means *"killers."* It's hard to get emotional over the massive deaths of these *"low lives."* During World War Two in Europe and Asia, millions of human beings were massacred, annihilated, exterminated by chemical poisons too. They were discompassionately *"squashed like bugs."* It was an abhorrent, abominable extinction of life. So is insecticide, albeit a lower level of life, but life just the same. It is still killing. Life at any level is a miracle. Man can extinguish life, but not create life. Life is so divinely mysterious in fact, that we don't even know what it is. (Incidentally, we also kill about 12 billion higher animals for food annually.) Man tops the food chain. Indeed, it is regrettable, lamentable that life must depend on death for survival. But so it is. We commit wholesale insecticide for our protection and comfort. It protects us from disease and saves much of our food supply. Nevertheless, respect, revere life at all levels, as do the Jains, and as did the saintly Dr. Albert Schweitzer (1875 – 1965). Never squash a bug, just because it's there. That's unnecessary insecticide. When you must swat a mosquito, whisper in your heart, *"Forgive me,"* for you have destroyed a miracle. You will evolve into a more edified human being. *"I can do no other than be reverent before everything that is called life. I can do no other than have compassion for all that is called life. That is the beginning and foundation of all ethics. Any religion or philosophy which is not based on a respect for life is not a true religion or philosophy.... We must fight against the spirit of unconscious cruelty with which we treat the animals.... Until we extend our circle of compassion to all living things, humanity will not find peace."* – Dr. Albert Schweitzer, Physician, Missionary, Humanitarian. *"Summer will have its flies. And if you want to take a walk in the woods, you must feed the mosquitoes."* – Ralph Waldo Emerson (1903 – 1882). *"All the time I pray to Buddha I keep on killing mosquitoes."* – Zen Proverb. *"Don't worry spider, I keep house casually."* *"Don't kill! The fly is asking you to save his life by rubbing his hands together."* – Kobayishi Issa (1763 – 1828).

INSENSATE – (in-*SENS*-sate) Not sensitive, without sensation, therefore inanimate. Too, an insensate is one without human sensitivity or feeling. So an insensate is cold, may be cruel, even brutal.

INSIDIOUS – (in-*SID*-dee-us) Deceitful, stealthily treacherous. An insidious plan, intention, or person is one intended to entrap or beguile. President Donald Trump (b. 1946), his family, appointees, supporters, and sycophantic Republican enablers are all insidious creatures.

INSIGHT – (*IN*-syt) (Insightful, Insightfulness) Literally, looking within to see the solution. Insight is a metaphysical phenomenon related to intuition and inspiration. It is spiritual in origin. Insight resides in our subconscious, which is the dead-drop area for Divine messages. God communicates with us by way of insight. Insight does not require investigation, experimentation, research, nor thinking – no work or effort of any kind. It is gratuitive knowledge. Answers dawn on us unexpectedly, in a *"Eureka!"* moment, like a bolt from the blue. One must pray for insight. Prayer is talking to God. But insight comes through meditation. Meditation is God talking to us. Indeed, it is necessary to empty one's mind in a meditative state in order to be blessed with an insight. Insight solves insoluble problems. *"If you have insight, you can use your inner eye, your inner ear, to pierce to the heart of things, and have no need of intellectual knowledge."* – Zhuangzi (369 – 286 BCE).

INSIPID – (in-*SIP*-pid) Bland, tasteless, dull, vapid, boring. An insipid person lacks spirit. He is a dead-beat.

IN SITU – (in *SIT*-too) Latin for in its natural place. In situ has been adopted by anthropologists and archeologists referring to fossils and artifacts that have not been moved by wind, water or scavengers. They are in their original position, where they fell thousands or millions of years ago.

INSOUCIANT – (in-*SOW*-see-ent) (Insouciance) Carefree, unconcerned, nonchalant. An insouciant soul is absolved of worry, anxiety, and therefore stress. It is a valuable virtue to display a degree of insouciance. *"Naked did she dance, with insouciance."*

INSPIRATION – (in-spur-*RAY*-shun) (Inspire, Inspired) literally, *"To breathe-in the Spirit."* When inspired, one is *"in the Spirit,"* or the *"Spirit is in you."* Inspiration is the *power,* whereas intuition is the *knowledge* which is inspired. To be inspired is to be divinely motivated, encouraged, and energized. Inspiration is a Holy Blessing from God. Prophetic revelation is providential inspiration. It is a heavenly connection. Inhuman ambition, unbelievable coincidence, impossible innovation, fantastic creativity, tremendous talent, even good luck [read: *Karmic reciprocity*] are Godly inspired. So is enthusiasm [read*: "en Theos,"* or *God in you*]. Pray for help, then listen for that *"still, small voice within"* for inspiration. If karmicly deserving, you shall be inspired. The great scientist Albert Einstein (1879 – 1955) declared that: *"When the solution is simple, God is answering." "We talk to God – that is prayer; God talks to us – that is inspiration."* – Religious Mystic H. Emilie Cady (1848 – 1941).

INSTINCT – (*IN*-stinct) Inborn or genetic knowledge or behavior, as opposed to thinking, which is cerebral or learned knowledge or behavior. Instinct is knowledge on the cellular level that has evolved over time. Unlike thinking, instinct is unalterable. Instinct is pre-programed knowledge or intelligence. The software is the DNA. Behavior governed by instinct cannot be changed. An instinctual animal is a slave to its behavior. It cannot be creative. The bee or the spider cannot say: *"After so many hundreds-of-millions of years, why don't we try a different design?"* They are lock-in by their genetic instinct. Incidentally: Human beings traded the large cerebrum for instinct. Human beings reason.

INSTITUTIONALISM – (in-sti-*TOO*-shun-al-is-um) (Institute, Institutionalist) An institution is instituted, or a man-made entity. It is an organization, establishment, foundation, society, or the like, devoted to the promotion of a particular cause or program, especially one of a public, educational, or charitable character. The church, public school, military, baseball club are all examples of institutions. Institutionalism is a deep attachment to some institution. People become emotionally devoted to their institutions. Fanatical devotees are called *"institutionalists."* They are ultra-conservatives, intent to conserve their institutions, defend them from change. Institutionalists block innovation and stand in the way of progress. The institutions become sclerotic when under the command of the institutionalists. *"If you want to see what an institution is about, try to change it."* – Psychologist Kurt Lewin (1890 – 1947).

INSTITUTIONAL POVERTY – (in-sti-*TOO*-shun-al *POV*-ver-tee) Societal distributive injustice. Destitution that is hard-wired into the system. Poverty is inherently calculated in the institution of capitalism. This is meant to create a great army of poor, serving a tiny cadre of rich. Institutional poverty is unnatural, according to the naturalist Charles Darwin (1809 – 1882). *"If the misery of the poor be caused not by the laws of nature, but by our institutions, great is our sin."* Institutional poverty is contrived by the noble aristocracy, the landed gentry, the corporate capitalists, in connivance with conservative politicians.

It is maintained by unfair taxation benefiting the rich, inheritance laws bequeathing wealth, legislation profiting big business, privatization of public utilities and institutions, lobbying [read: *"bribing"*] legislators, outsourcing jobs abroad, destruction of labor unions, purchasing elections, and voter suppression. Capitalists create scarcity to maximize profits which also exacerbates poverty. Under capitalism, democracy is window dressing, reinforcing institutional poverty. Only under Socialism will we achieve *"Institutional Prosperity."* *"The test of our progress is not whether we add more to the abundance of those who have much. It is whether we provide enough for those who have little."* – Progressive President Franklin D. Roosevelt (1882 – 1945).

INSTITUTIONAL RACISM – (in-sti-*TOO*-shun-al *RAYS*-is-um) Racist policies and practices built into organizations and institutions, such as schools, corporations, the legal system, and law enforcement. Schools were once institutionally segregated, as well as the military and pro sports. A Black corporate CEO was once unthinkable, due to institutional racism. Stereotypical depictions of Blacks in motion pictures fell under the rubric of institutional racism. Banks and realestate companies were egregiously institutionally racist. Though it may not be as blatant, institutional racism still infects society.

INSTRUCTION – (in-*STRUC*-shun) Teaching methodology. A formal, systematic method of imparting information. Instruction is the *"how"* of teaching, how will the information be transferred from teacher to student.

INSUBORDINATION – (in-sub-bor-din-*NAY*-shun) Disobedience to one's lawful superiors, a subordinate. Refusal to carry-out a legal, reasonable order or duty is insubordunation. Insubordination is grounds for disciplinary action and dismissal. If the order is illegal, immoral, or unreasonable, insubordination for non-compliance does not apply.

INSUFFERABLE – (in-*SUF*-fer-a-bul) Intolerable, unbearable, not to be endured. *"This insufferable heat will drive me mad!"*

INSULT – (*IN*-salt) A profound, contemptuous indignity of disrespect. An insult is a great assault on one's self-esteem, if the insulted party allows it. After all, in most cases, an insult is only words. To be egregiously insulted in an incomprehensible foreign language, for instance, would have no humiliating affect at all. That's because you were unable to understand the words. So why allow words to command so much power over you? This is a human frailty. *"Sticks and stones can break my bones, but words can break my heart!"* *"What you think of me is none of my business."* – Terry Cole-Whittaker (b. 1939).

INSUPERABLE – (in-*SUP*-er-a-bul) Incapable of being surmounted, overcome, passed over. An insuperable mountain, river, swamp, gorge is an impossible barrier. *"This river will provide an insuperable defensive line."*

INSURANCE INDUSTRY– (in-*SHUR*-rans *IN*-dus-tree) Pessimism mongers, prophets of doom, who scare people into paying for security, but reluctant to pay back when calamity occurs. Big insurance is a vulgar, obscene, 3 trillion dollar a year industry! The insurance industry profits by encouraging fear of disaster, while calculating and betting that all will be well. Like the banks and brokerage houses, the insurance industry is a capitalist bottom feeder. In fact, the insurance industry is the most heinous, voracious bloodsuckers in the putrid capitalist quagmire. The health insurance is the vilest, for it sells health to those who could afford it. All others are condemned to perish. Abolish private insurance, for public assurance for all. In

Winning Through Intimidation (1973) entrepreneur Robert J. Ringer (b. 1938) suggested that: *"The next time you pass one of those insurance company skyscrapers, look closely between the bricks. You probably thought they were held together by cement. Not so. The substance between the bricks is dried human blood. All those friendly insurance companies, the ones who run the ads on television showing their agents helping out some nice neighborhood family have built their building on human blood."* Incidentally: 90% of life insurance policies never pay off anything. Incidentally: During the Republican Nixon Administration (1969 - 1974) the insurance industry was enabled to hijack the medical profession. That put Wall Street profits before patient health. America has the lowest life expectancy of all advanced nations. America has the highest death rate from preventable causes of all advanced nations. America spends over twice the amount on healthcare of all advanced nation. So why are Americans so unhealthy? Where is the money going? To insurance company stockholders, CEOs and lobbyists.

INSURRECTIONIST CAUCUS – (in-sur-*REK*-shun-ist *KAW*-kus) An insurrectionist is one who rises in revolt, rebellion against the established government. A caucus is a meeting of party members within a legislative assembly. In this case, the Insurrectionist Caucus refers to the perfidious group of seditious Republican Congressmen who supported the January 6, 2020 coup or insurrection against the U.S. Government. Feeding on Donald Trump's (b. 1946) *"BIG LIE"* that the 2020 presidential election was stolen from him and the Republicans, the Insurrectionist Caucus bought into the plan to prevent the Democratic winner, Joe Biden (b. 1942) from being officially installed as President. They tried to overturn the results of the 2020 Presidential Election. What they did was unconstitutional, anti-constitutional, and un-American. These Republican politicians were dissatisfied with the democratic process and results. They wanted to re-establish their losing candidate, Donald Trump in the White House. This is contra-democratic, and therefore fascist. But that's no great revelation. The Republicans, as lackeys of the rich, fear democracy. Democracy, fueled by the vote, is people power. People power can override financial power. Through democracy, the people can redistribute the wealth. That's why corporate capitalism through the Republicans suppress the vote to weaken democracy. Their alternative is fascism, in the form of oligarchic rule, government by the plutocracy. (A *"Putinic"* Russia is their ideal.) They failed in 2020, so they staged an insurrection to overthrow the government. That too failed – barely, this time. Thirty-five Republican Senators, and 175 Republican House members directly or indirectly supported the anti-American coup. The insurrectionist leaders were: Senators Josh Hawley (b. 1979) Missouri; Ron Johnson (b. 1955) Wisconsin; Lindsey Graham (b. 1955) South Carolina; Rand Paul (b. 1963) Kentucky; James Lankford (b. 1968) Oklahoma; Cynthia Lummis (b. 1954) Wyoming; Mike Braun (b. 1954) Indiana; John Kennedy (b. 1951) Louisiana; Steve Daines (b. 1962) Montana; Tommy Tuberville (b. 1954) Alabama; Marsha Blackburn (b. 1952) Tennessee; Bill Hagerty (b. 1959) Tennessee; Ted Cruz (b. 1970) Texas. The insurrectionist leaders in the House of Representatives includes the following Republicans: Kevin McCarthy (b. 1965) California; Mo Brooks (b. 1954) Alabama; Scott Perry (b. 1962) Pennsylvania; Jim Jordan (b. 1964) Ohio; Lauren Boebert (b. 1986) Colorado; Matt Gaetz (b. 1982) Florida; Elise Stefanik (b. 1984) New York; Steve Scalise (b. 1965) Louisiana; Glenn Grothman (b. 1955) Wisconsin; Thomas (b. 1971) Kentucky; Chip Roy (b. 1972) Texas; Marjorie Taylor Greene (b. 1974) Georgia; Andy Biggs (b. 1958) Arizona; Paul Gosar (b. 1958) Arizona; Dan Bishop (b. 1964) North Carolina; Madison Cawthorn (b. 1995) North Carolina. American Constitutional Democracy is in dire danger from the Fascistic Republican-cum-Trumpublican Party.

INTEGRAL – (in-*TEG*-ral) A constituent part or component of a whole apparatus or project. An integral part is absolutely essential, indispensable. An employee may be an integral part of the business. Likewise, the pedals are an integral part of the bicycle.

INTEGRITY – (in-*TEG*-grit-tee) Being physically, psychologically, and spiritually integrated, or on the same moral page. Integrity is consistently walking your talk. With integrity, the public and private you are the same person. A person with integrity is fully integrated. *"Happiness is when what you think, what you say, and what you do are in harmony,"* said Mohandas Gandhi (1869 – 1948). Without integrity, a person has no credibility or respectability. That is the case with the unscrupulous Donald Trump (b. 1946). Senator Alan K. Simpson (b. 1931) rightly concluded that: *"If you have integrity, nothing else matters. If you don't have integrity, nothing else matters."*

INTEGRATION – (in-teg-*GRAY*-shun) (Education) A Progressive methodology of collaboration of teachers in interdisciplinary teams.

INTEGRATION – (in-teg-*GRAY*-shun) (Sociology) Social inclusion breaking down racist walls. Integration is counteracting segregation.

INTEGUMENT – (in-*TEG*-yu-ment) A natural covering as skin, shell, or rind.

INTEGUMENTARY SYSTEM – (in-*TEG*-yu-men-ter-ee *SIS*-tum) The skin, along with hair, nails, hoofs, claws, scales, and feathers that cover animals' bodies. The integumentary system protects the body from damage, such as water loss, and abrasion from exterior sources. This organ serves to waterproof the body, safeguards vital organs and tissues, excretes wastes, and regulates temperature. The sensory receptors to detect pain, pressure, and temperature are located in the integumentary system. The integumentary system is the largest of animal organs. In humans, it covers about 13 feet of the body surface and comprises 12% to 15% of the total body weight. Incidentally: We shed about 1,500,000 skin cells a day.

INTELLECTUAL INCEST – (in-tel-*LEK*-chew-al *IN*-sest) In academia, the bad habit of schools hiring their former students as teachers. This results in lack of diverse thought, academic ennui. An institutional staleness sets in, a hardening of the attitudes. This is particularly true on the college level, especially small instutions. All organizations can be susceptible to intellectual incest, not only schools. Corporations, even legislative bodies are vulnerable. An incestual relationship between the U.S. and Israel was perpetuated in Congress. That was until the 2018 election of two Muslim Congresswomen, Ilhan Omar (b. 1981) from Minnesota and Rashida Tlaib (b. 1976) from Michigan. Both Representatives are Democrats.

INTELLECTUAL INCEST – (in-tel-*LEK*-chew-al *IN*-sest) In social-psychology, being absorbed in biased, prejudiced news, misinformation and propaganda. An incestual intellect is a closed mind. It is a form of brain-washing. Watching only Fox *"Fascist Fake"* News or Alt-Right podcasts and social media reinforces this mental interbreeding. Autocrats, dictators employ intellectual incest to control people. This is precisely how Russian Dictopresident Vladimir Putin (b. 1952) forces the Russian people to fight and die in Putin's war in the Ukraine. Control the news and control the national intellect. There is no opposition news. All information is incestual.

INTELLECTUALIZATION – (in-tel-lec-chew-al-eyes-*ZAY*-shun) Psychological defense mechanism in which a person tries to think a problem away: *"Let's analyze this further."*

INTELLECTUAL PROPERTY – (in-tah-*LEK*-chew-al *PROP*-er-tee) The capitalist compulsion to hoard knowledge and ideas, in order to profit from them. Private property is the very core of capitalism. Private property refers to personal possession. In other words: *"I got mine, to hell with you!"* The concept of intellectual property is selfish and careless. It is care-less of public need, care- full of private greed. Technology, drug, and medical corporations will hoard, holdback life-saving ideas, medications, cures, devices, and research so they can monetarily benefit from their discoveries. Conversely, the modest genius Jonas Salk (1914 – 1995) refused to patent and profit from his polio vaccine discovery. Preventing the crippling of children was more important to Dr. Salk than his bank account. Not so with the heartless, consciousless capitalist corporations. To expect a capitalist corporation to bypass profit for humanitarian benefit is simply counterintuitive. They must be forced to share by the government. Only a Socialist government has the courage, conscience, and compassion to do so. *"The capitalists will sell you the rope to hang them."* – Vladimir Lenin (1870 – 1924).

INTELLIGENCE – (in-*TEL*-leh-jens) In psychology, the capacity to learn, reason, understand, and communicate. An intelligent person can process information into a useful form. Intelligence is the mental capacity to know what to do, when you don't know what to do. In other words, an intelligent person can *"think out of the box."* This means, apply old ideas in new way, to novel situations. The great and intelligent astral-physicist, Stephen Hawking (1942 – 2018) insisted that *"Intelligence is the ability to adapt to change."* Though it requires intelligence to acquire a good education, intelligence and education are not necessarily synonymous. A homeless, illiterate, street-smart survivor is likely to be highly intelligent. *"Knowledge is not intelligence."* – Heraclitus (535 – 475 BCE). Incidentally: Intelligence is not confined to people. Animals possess a degree of intelligence too. The smartest animals in order are: chimpanzees, dolphins, orangutans, elephants, pigs, and dogs. The crow is considered to be the most intelligent bird.

INTELLIGENCE – (in-*TEL*-leh-jens) In espionage, information collected, and projects performed, that benefits the government in taking action. Intelligence is essential in formulating foreign policy. There are at least 17 Intelligence Agencies in America. The world of intelligence is the *cloak-and-dagger* world of the spy. It is a dirty world that involves by its very nature deception, lies, betrayal, intimidation, sex, bribery, pain, and murder. There are two aspects to intelligence, defensive and offensive. Defensive espionage involves information gathering, stealing documents, bugging apartments, taking photographs, encouraging defections. Offensive espionage or intelligence is much more aggressive (to put it mildly). It involves disseminating disinformation, rigging elections, kidnapping, overthrowing governments, training terrorist death squads, applying torture, assassinations, installing sadistic puppet dictators. The primary U.S. intelligence service, the C.I.A., (Central Intelligence Agency) claims to work abroad to protect *"American interests."* Actually, their primary purpose is to protect *"corporate capitalist property."* This answers the naïve question: *"Why do they hate us?"* Incidentally: The job of Intelligence Agencies is to *"speak truth to power,"* good or bad news. President Donald Trump (b. 1946) has been at war with his Intelligence Agencies. Intelligence Agencies have warned Trump of Russian interference in American elections. However, because Trump is a Russian operative or agent, he approves of helpful Russian interference. Trump therefore resents the Intelligence

Agencies. Footnote: In Ancient Rome, the intelligence agents were the postal workers, the mailmen. This was logical, for they were everywhere, in every neighborhood. The mailmen knew all the neighbors, every address, and learned all the gossip. So they served as perfect spies for the government.

INTELLIGENT DESIGN – (in-*TELL*-li-jent dee-*SINE*) A Fundamentalist ruse for teaching Creationism in the secular public schools. Intelligent design is meant to contradict scientific, biological evolution. It is the illegal encroachment of church on the state. Intelligent design is Biblical religiosity masquerading as historical and scientific fact. In defending the concept of evolution, English biologist Thomas Huxley (1825 – 1895) referred to Creationism as *"A beautiful theory killed by a nasty, ugly little fact."*

INTENSIFIER – (in-*TEN*-si-fy-er) In grammar, a word, especially an adverb, that emphasizes, dramatizes, elevates the force of the next word being modified. For example, the intensifier *"damn"* makes good, *"damn good."* Other intensifiers are *plumb* loco, and *fucken'* aye.

INTENSIVE AGRICULTURE – (in-*TEN*-siv *AG*-ri-cul-chur) Non-automated farming. Agriculture that requires much human labor. No machines on intensively farmed land. Underdeveloped nations must practice intensive agriculture. The very most is squeezed out of every foot of soil. It is subsistence farming with very little wastage.

INTENTION – (in-*TEN*-chun) (Intent, Intentional, Intetionality) One's intent or intention is one's purpose, goal, aim, objective, motive. The intention is the real reason why one performed some activity, and the outcome one expected. We express the goodness of an intention when we say: *"She meant well."* One may do good things with bad intentions, or bad things with good intentions. In fact: *"The road to hell is paved with good intentions."* – St. Bernard of Clairvaux (1090 – 1153). Whatever the ultimate outcome, the intention was the impulse of the heart. All great religious Avatars recognized the gravity of intention. In fact, they claim that in the eyes of God, our intentions weigh more than the results. The great Church Father St. Augustine (354 – 430 CE) insisted that: *"God bestows more consideration on the purity of the intention with which our actions are performed than on the actions themselves."* Later, the mystic Maximus the Confessor (c. 580 – 662) declared: *"In all our actions, God considers the intention: whether we act for Him or for some other motive."*

INTENTIONAL DREAMING – (in-*TEN*-shuhn-ahl *DREE*-ming) To dream with intent or purpose. Intentional dreaming is using this sleep-time to serve beneficial purposes. Before sleeping, state out loud or write down the intentions you hope to play out in your dreams. You may wish your dreams to be lucid, with easy recall. You may hope to communicate with spirits during dreaming. You may request answers, solutions to problems during your dreams. One may desire to fulfill sexual fantasies, realistically, in the dream space. Most of our wish-fulfillments are possible with intentional dreaming.

INTENTIONALITY – (in-ten-shuhn-*AL*-it-tee) (Intent, Intention, Intentional) The capacity of the mind to will into existence desires or wishes. Intentionality is the power of faithful expectancy, purpose, intention to manifest miracles like casting spells, directing the future, getting what you need. Intentionality is the crucial component of prayer and meditation. One must visualize the successful outcome, and express gratitude in advance. *"Ask and it will be given to you; seek and you will find; knock and the door will be opened to you,"* – Jesus in Matthew 7:7, Luke 11:9. In the metaphysical, esoteric arts, intentionality or intent is crucial to the performance of magick. In fact, magical intent is the purpose of magickal work – the true purpose, with all the unnecessary frills stripped away. Your intent is the foundation of the magical work. It is your goal, what you truly wish to accomplish. Successful spellwork, magick begins with intent and surrounds it with actions, ceremonies, props, ambience in order to produce the emotion that will enable you to achieve your will. Incidentally: The 3 ingredients essential to cast a spell are: *Belief, Concentration*, and *Emotion.*

INTER ALIA – (*IN*-ter *AL*-lee-a) A legal term (Latin) meaning *"among other things."*

INTERCALATE – (in-*TER*-ca-late) To interpolate or interpose. To insert extra words in a quote or passage. The Bible, especially the Gospels have been thoroughly intercalated by Church Father, to render the correct image of Jesus.

INTERCESSION – (in-ter-*SESH*-shun) (Intercede) To petition the angels, saints, and heavenly spirits, including deceased relatives (ancestor worship) to appeal to God for help.

INTERCOURSE – (IN-ter-kawrs) In sexual terms, coitus, coition, copulation between a man and a woman. Intercourse is the clinical designation for the popular parlance of the vulgar vernacular – fucking. Genital intercourse is not technically possible between two males or two females. The plumbing parts are not available. The prefix *"inter"* means *"between,"* but it also means to *"enter."* The only genital intercourse possible is the entrance of the penis into the vagina (the genitals). By 1798, the word *"sexual"* was added to intercourse. By 1771, the term intercourse no longer required the qualifier, sexual, to mean copulation. Through intercourse, human beings get back to nature, in the most basic, uninhibited way. It is a celebration of our animalism. During intercourse, social, class, ethnic, racial, all boundaries are breached. Wealth cannot enhance, nor poverty diminish the euphoria of intercourse, whether performed on silk sheets or a bed of straw. The couple engaged in intercourse are mutually dependent, totally equal, becoming almost one living organism. Intercourse is purely biological. There must be no rules or qualifications. The most rewarding intercourse consists of raw, thoughtless fucking. *"Sexual intercourse is a slight attack of apoplexy"* – Democritus (c. 460 – c. 370 BCE).

INTERDEPENDENT KARMA – (in-ter-dee-*PEN*-dent *CAR*-ma) To be interdependent is to be mutually reliant. Karma is the spiritual, cosmic law of reciprocity – retribution or remuneration. Interdependent Karma insists that what happens to us depends to a large degree on what happens to those close to us. Our Karma is related to the Karma of our close associates. For example, you may deserve the good fortune of winning the lottery. But your husband does not. Both of you would share the good fortune. So his bad Karma cancelled-out your good Karma. Result – no lottery win. Like clouds, spirits interlace, influencing each other. Karma is spiritual. So what affects us, effects other spirits. As brothers and sisters share much of the same genetics, we also share much of the same Karma. In Genesis 4:9, God asked Cain where is his brother Able. With the first question mankind (represented by Cain) asked God, Cain replied: *"Am I my brother's keeper?"* The answer is definitely *"YES!"* Our interdependent Karma is proof. Like actors in a performance, we all play roles throughout or lives. Our roles depend on the roles played by others. Sometimes we are casted as protagonists, other times we are casted an antagonists. God, of course, is the director of the performance. God uses us to act on, to affect other's Karma, positively or negatively, for good or for bad. Indeed, we may sometimes say: *"I don't know why I behaved that way?"* Well, God knows. We may have been employed by God to affect another's Karma, for their just deserts. This is possible because of our interdependent Karma.

INTERDICT – (*IN*-ter-dict) (Interdiction) A form of Ecclesiastical blackmail, a group excommunication. By interdiction, a Pope cuts-off all the subjects of an excommunicated prince from communion with the Church. All loyal supporters of the Pope's enemy are condemned to hell. The Pope's expectation is that panicked subjects will rebel and overthrow the excommunicated prince. In this way, the Pope is rid of an enemy. In the early Middle Ages, the very threat of an interdiction made kings submit to the Pope's dictates.

INTERDISCIPLINARY – (in-ter-*DIS*-sip-plin-air-ree) Collaboration of teachers from different subject areas teaching a common group through integrated units of study. Interdisciplinary teaching take very much cooperation. It robs teachers of personal independence, for the success of the team. Scholarly teachers are independent by nature. Interdisciplinary teaching is very challenging for them.

INTEREST – (*IN*-trest) In economics, sweatless profit. Making money on working people's debt. Interest was once the sin of *usury*. According to the Quran (Koran), *"That which you put aside in interest (riba), to grow by using the property of other people will have no increase with Allah."* – Sura 30. 39. Interest is the tainted blood of the capitalist beast. Private banksters get obscenely rich on interest. They give a pitiful .01% or less interest to small depositors, while demanding 16% or over 20% interest on creditcard debt. Banksters only charge 3% or less interest when lending to fellow banksters. The problem is capitalism, the solution is Socialism. Nationalize the banks. Private Banks must be made illegal. Incidentally: Jesus was not interested in interest, or debt collecting for that matter. In *The Gospel of Thomas* Jesus said: *"If you have money, do not lend it out at interest. Rather, give it to the one from whom you will not get it back."* Jesus would make a poor capitalist.

INTEREST – (*IN*-trest) In psychology, the *"inter-rest,"* or place between the rests. In other words, interest is the difference between where you are, and were you want to be (rest). Therefore, what *inter-rests* you, tells you what you want and where you want to be. That's why it is interesting. Interest is tied into reward and pleasure. If one stands to gain by some matter, it will be of interest. The gain may be simply pleasure. Closed-minded people have few interests, whereas open-minded people have many. Education opens the mind. Travel, as a form of education does the same. Liberally educated people usually have more interests and are therefore more interesting. *"There is not a sprig of grass that does not interest me,"* reported the erudite Thomas Jefferson (1743 – 1826), our most intellectual President to date.

INTERFACE – (*IN*-ter-fase) To bring together, to enmesh. Interfaced entities are compatible. The point of interaction or communication between a computer and another entity, such as a printer or a human operator is an interface.

INTERGENERATIONAL DRAG – (in-ter-jen-ner-*RAY*-shun-al *DRAG*) A sociological term for the cultivation of hopelessness, generated by years of poverty. Intergenerational drag results from lack of opportunity, being relegated to the social bottom. Contra-cultural survival techniques are passed down from father to son, mother to daughter. For example, 90% of the people in U.S. prisons had or have relatives in prison. This is the case in the neglected, poverty-racked ghettoes and barrios. Very often, the only opportunities reside in the illegal underground economy. This drags generations of poor people into lives of crime and prison. Racism and the unjust distribution of wealth, power, and opportunities perpetuates intergenerational drag. This accounts for the disproportionately high percentage of crime committed by minorities and the poor. Ultimately, capitalism is the cause. Socialism is the solution.

INTERIOR CONSERVATIVES – (in-*TEAR*-ree-er con-*SER*-va-tivs) The insulated, isolated, landlocked and mindlocked residents of the nation's midsection, the interior heartland. Heartlanders (interior conservatives) tend to be provincial, closed-in and closed-minded. They are not cosmopolitan like the residents of the East and West Coasts with their *"windows on the world."* Interior conservatives look inward, rather than outward. They distrust diversity, and Progressivism. Most interior conservatives are intolerant, bigoted, and rural. The so-called heartland is not the smartland. Interior conservatives are easily duped by wealthy Republicans to vote against their own economic interests. They elected the bozo Donald Trump (b. 1946) in 2016, for instance. The islands of Progressivism in the American interior are the urbane urban centers and educated college towns.

INTERJECTIONS – (in-ter-*JEK*-shuns) To interject is to insert between other things, to interpose abruptly or sharply. In speech, an interjection is a word representing an emotional outburst resulting from surprise, fear, upset, elation, any emotional shock. It is interjected between the sentences. Expletives are interjections. In writing, an interjection is accompanied by an exclamation point. Some interjections are: *"Duh!" "Hi!" "Wow!" "Great!" "Damn!" "Ouch!" "Shit!" "Oh Fuck!"*

INTERLARD – (in-ter-*LAHRD*) To diversify by adding or interjecting something unique, striking, or contrasting. Initially, this was a cooking term. Interlard derives from the Old French *"entrelarde,"* meaning *"to cook with lard or bacon fat."* The term entered Middle English in the mid-15th century as *"interlarden."* As the term evolved to interlard, it expanded to mean adding anything, not only lard.

INTERLOCUTOR – (in-ter-lo-*QUE*-tor) A person participating in a conversation or dialogue. So when you are talking to someone, you and he/her are interlocutors.

INTERLOPER – (*IN*-ter-lo-per) An intruder. A person who encroaches into a region, field, or trade without authority or license. An interloper interferes or meddles in other people's affairs. He may introduce himself into a profession or social circle where he does not belong.

INTERMARIUM – (in-ter-*MAR*-ree-um) The expanded re-establishment of the powerful Polish-Lithuanian Commonwealth as in the 16th and 17th centuries. At that time, Poland-Lithuania was the strongest nation in Europe, stronger than Russia. Today, the Intermarium would be a united, Pan-Slavic Federation of East European nations and the Baltic countries to stand against Russian imperialism. The term *"Intermarium"* means *"between seas,"* namely the Baltic, Black, and Adriatic Seas. In Polish, Intermarium is *"Miedzymorze,"* (from *"miedzy"* meaning between, and *"morze"* meaning sea). Intermarium was a plan conceived by Polish Marshal Jozef Pilsudski (1867 – 1935) after World War One (1914 – 1818). Actually, a Russian controlled Intermarium of sorts existed during the Cold War as the *Warsaw Pact.* The revived Intermarium (which would include former Russian Ukraine and Belarus) would be a federation, an alliance (within NATO), a bulwark against Russian expansionism. With American aid, Poland has become the most powerful military force in Eastern Europe. It is natural that the Intermarium would be led by Poland. Incidentally: *"Never Again!"* The vow of the Polish Military. Never again will Poland be dominated by Russia, Germany, or any other nation.

INTERMEDIATE SCHOOLS – (in-ter-*MEED*-dee-at *SKOOLS*) The educational institutions between Elementary and High Schools. The original model (1930's) was the Junior High School (grades 7, 8, 9). The Junior High School is articulated to the High School. The newer model is the Middle School (grades 6, 7, 8). The Middle School is articulated to the Elementary School. About 25% of today's Intermediate Schools are still Junior High Schools. The majority of the present day Intermediate Schools (75%) are Middle Schools. Middle Schools are more progressive, affective, nurturing than are Junior High Schools. Look for all Junior Highs to be phased out in favor of the Middle Schools.

INTERMENT – (in-*TUR*-ment) (Inter, Interred, Interring) The act of ceremonial burial of the dead. The deceased are interred in the earth. A Caveat: Do not confuse interment with *"internment"* (with an *N*), which means confinement.

INTER-MILITARY RIVALRY – (*IN*-ter *MIL*-li-tair-ree *RYE*-val-ree) Envious, jealous competition among branches of the military. Inter-military rivalry goes beyond the playing field to the battle field. The military branches vie for resources, weapons, and jurisdiction, like greedy capitalist corporations. The waste in duplicated programs and projects is astounding. Every militarized nation suffers from this wasteful competition. Prior to World War Two, the Japanese army and navy were in turmoil due to inter-military rivalry. Japan had defeated Russia in the Russo-Japanese War (1904 – 1905). Hostilities resumed in the summer of 1938 on the Russian-Manchurian border. This time, the Russian Red Army pounded the Japanese Army into submission in 2 weeks. Humiliated, the Japanese again attacked in 10 months. Again, General Georgy Zhukov (1896 – 1974) soundly thrashed the Japanese Army. The Japanese Army wanted revenge, a show-down with Russia in the north. But the Japanese Navy wanted a show-down with the Americans and British in the south. That's where the natural resources, especially the oil was located, in the Dutch East Indies (Indonesia). First, the Japanese had to expel the Americans from the Philippines, and the British from their colonies (Hong Kong and Singapore). In this inter-military rivalry, the Navy won out. The Japanese invasion would be to the south. But first and foremost, the U.S. fleet at Pearl Harbor, Hawaii had to be neutralized. The Japanese never fought the Russians, except in the last week of the war when Russia attack the Japanese in Manchuria and Korea.

INTERNALIZED HETERONOMY – (in-*TER*-nal-lyzd het-ter-*RON*-nom-mee) When young children first develop a sense of subordination to authority, and submission to rules. This first occurs in kindergarten or pre-school when children congregate in groups, under the authority of a teacher. The teacher becomes the sovereign, the rules become the divine law. The children internalize this heteronomous arrangement with absolute zero tolerance. Woe to the classmate who dares to break the rule!

INTERNAL PLASTIC FLOW – (in-*TER*-nal *PLAS*-tic *FLOW*) The slow movement of a glacier in which ice crystals slip over each other. Continental glacial speed is about a foot a day. Alpine glaciers, aided by gravity move much faster.

INTERNAL SECURITY – (in-*TER*-nal sec-*CUR*-ri-tee) This term in Latin America is a euphemism for *"Make war on your own people."* Internal security is the concern of American corporate capitalists, fearful about keeping and protecting their property from the poor peasants who need it. The C.I.A. trains right wing terrorist groups, *"death squads,"* like the *"Contras"* in Nicaragua to provide internal security against popular Socialist movements. Pro-American, pro- capitalist, fascist dictators are installed to brutalize their people. The dictator is merely head of the American corporation's security guards. Internal security means a steady flow of exploited, corporate profits. Internal security is another answer to the naïve question: *"Why do they hate us?"*

INTERNECINE – (in-ter-*NES*-seen) Refers to conflict or struggle within a group. It is an organizational civil war. Internecine disputes are mutually ruinous, destructive, and suicidal to the feuding group. The Trump White House has witnessed internecine conflict beyond anything in American History.

INTERNET – (*IN*-ter-net) The system established to enable computers to communicate with each other. The internet is an absolute revolution in communications, but not the first. Language, writing, printing were communication internets that preceded the computerized version. Today (2022) 5 people out of 8, or 62.5% of humanity are online with the internet. In 1969, four computers talked to each other over the phone line. The internet was born and the first email was sent. Incidentally: The electrical impulses (electrons) that comprise internet communication is light. Light is energy, and energy is a condition of matter. Matter has weight. In 2011 Harvard University's Russell Seitz (b. 1947) wondered: How much does the internet weigh? Seitz calculated that all the electrical impulses that comprised the world-wide internet weighted about 50 grams, as much as a fat strawberry. Perhaps today, 13 years later, all the internet communication together must weigh at least as much as 2 fat strawberries, or one plum.

INTERNMENT – (in-*TURN*-ment) (Intern, Interned, Interning) Confinement. Being imprisoned. People suffer internment in prison camps. A Caveat: Do not confuse internment (with an *N*), with *"interment"* meaning burial.

INTER NOS – (*IN*-ter *NOS*) Latin for *"between ourselves."*

INTERPERSONAL RACISM – (in-ter-*PER*-sun-nal *RAYS*-is-um) One-on-one racial animus and bigotry. The dominant form of interpersonal racism is hating your Black, Indigenous, Oriental, Asian neighbor, just because of his race. Of course racism can and does proceed from a minority group to the dominant population too. Indeed, systemic and institutional racism feeds interpersonal racism. Personal racism runs in families. It is passed on through the generations. It is nurtured in neighborhoods. Also, the personal variety may also have originated with some bad personal racial incident, like a confrontation. Too, low SES (Social Economic Status) individuals may feel the need to be racist, in order to salvage a morsel of self-esteem. As low as they are on the socio-economic scale, it's gratifying to believe that they are not at rock bottom – that there is an identifiable group below them. They are racist for personal reasons.

INTERPOLATION – (in-ter-po-*LAY*-shun) The introduction of something additional or extraneous between original parts, especially in a text. Interpolation is to interject, interpose, intercalate, which serves to contaminate the original text. The Scriptures (Bible) have been badly interpolated through the ages. Muslims boast that The Quran (Koran) in interpolation-less.

INTERPOSE – (*IN*-ter-pose) To place between or among other things. Furthermore, to interpose is to interject a remark, comment, or question in a running speech or conversation. Usually, to interpose requires an interruption.

INTERPRESIDIUM – (in-ter-pres-*SID*-ee-um) Literally, *"The period between presidents."* The term was inspired from the *"Interregnum,"* (*the period between kings*) in England from 1649 to 1660. The ruthless Oliver Cromwell (1599 – 1658) ruled as Lord Protector [read: *Dictator*]. Likewise, America has embarked on an *"Interpresidium,"* in 2017, scheduled to run until 2020. That's because another ruthless dictator, the unqualified, uncouth buffoon, Donald Trump (b. 1946) has gained power. Trump does not deserve the title *"President."* Therefore, for the period of his tenure, America will not have had a president. This time span in American History will be the period between presidents, the Interpresidium.

INTERSCHOLASTIC – (in-ter-sko-*LAS*-tic) Between opposing schools. Formal competitive activities, especially sports played between schools. The competition generated by interscholastic activates produces a mean-spirited win/lose condition.

INTERSECTIONALITY – (in-ter-sek-shuhn-*NAL*-it-tee) (Intersectionally) (also Intersectional Theory) The theory that overlapping identity markers, as race, ethnicity, gender, class, education, sexuality, body type, contribute to the specific type of systemic discrimination and oppression one experiences. For example, a poor, black, overweight, uneducated, female is most intersectionally at risk. She has several social handicaps working against her. This framework conceptualizes the multiplier effect of bias, prejudice, and stereotyping – all disadvantages experiences by people's overlapping identities. The point of understanding intersectionality is to realize the variety of oppression that one may experience simultaneously at any given time.

INTERSEX – (*IN*-ter-seks) (Intersexual, Intersexuality) A hermaphrodite. Being androgynous. The prefix *"inter"* means between. An intersexual is between male and female, or both. Intersex refers to a person, animal, or plant having male and female reproductive organs, or in which the chromosomal patterns do not fall under typical definitions of male and female. Intersexuals possess the gonads and genitals of both genders. This condition is very rare, only 0.02% to 0.05% of births. *"Love isn't a choice. You fall for the person, not their chromosomes."* – I. W. Gregorio, *None of the Above*, (2015).

INTERSTATE – (*IN*-ter-stayt) (Among the states.) The marvelous American expressway system, the biggest engineering project in U.S. history. As a young officer, Dwight Eisenhower (1890 – 1969) was ordered to report to his new post. The cross-country drive took him 62 days. During the war, Ike was impressed by Germany's autobahn. As president, Ike began the *"Eisenhower U.S. Interstate Highway System."* Over 42 billion cubic yards of earth was moved during the Interstate project. It cost $129 billion dollars, and was sold to congress as a cold war necessity. It was designed to move the U.S. urban population out of the cities in a nuclear attack, and to facilitate troop movements in case of invasion. Too, 1 in every 5 miles had to be perfectly straight, to serve as military landing strips. The interstate made suburbia feasible. Today, there are over 50,000 miles of road in the Interstate system. The downside of the Interstate is that it bypassed thousands of small towns dependent on traffic for a livelihood. So many small communities withered on the vine. *"Thanks to the Interstate Highway System, it is now possible to travel from coast to coast without seeing a thing."* – Charles Kuralt (1934 – 1997). Incidentally: Hitler's autobahn was not the first super highway. The original was built by Benito Mussolini (1883 – 1945) from Milan in the north to southern Italy. In the early days, Hitler admired Mussolini and copied much of Mussolini's accomplishments.

INTERSTICE – (*IN*-ter-stys) (Interstitial) a small intervening space, a minute gap or crevice between items, usually lined in a series.

INTERTIDAL ZONE – (in-ter-*TY*-dal *ZONE*) First of the 5 benthic (oceanic) zones. The benthic environment that lies between the low-tide and high-tide lines.

INTERVENTION – (in-ter-*VEN*-chun) The act of involvement. In therapeutics, intervention is a group *"carefrontation."* An intervention is a conspiracy of family and friends, on behalf of a loved-one in trouble. Usually, the person confronted is suffering from some addiction that is life-threatening. An intervention is an ambush. The afflicted individual is corralled and must hear the testimony of all the people dear to him. She must learn how her behavior is hurting many, beyond herself. Most importantly, the impaired person must agree to professional help, if the intervention is to be proved successful.

INTERVENTION DUTY – (in-ter-*VEN*-chun *DOO*-tee) (Actually, "Duty to Intervene.") Intervention Duty is a policy to prevent police brutality. This is an imperative policy that municipalities, states, and the federal government must apply. It is simply counterintuitive that we should need such a law. It is nearly inconceivable that a law enforcement officer would passively stand by as a law enforcement officer breaks the law – especially murder! But it happens, all too often. Intervention Duty makes it obligatory, mandatory, compulsory for cops to prevent other cops from beating, raping, or murdering helpless or innocent civilians. Those who don't comply with the law are guilty of complicity. This policy is beyond Good Samaritan to Good Humanitarian. Dallas Texas was the first city to impose an Intervention Duty on its police force (June 5, 2020). The police atrocities during the protests that followed the police killing of George Floyd (1974 – 2020) on May 25, 2020, will induce other governmental agencies to adopt the Duty to Intervene policy as well. *"Never be a passive witness to another's pain."* – Dr. Gary J. Pasieka (b. 1951).

INTESTATE – (in-*TES*-tate) Refers to a person who has not made out a will. Too, a property with no prospective owners is intestate.

INTIFADA – (in-ti-*FAH*-da) A violent uprising by oppressed Palestinian Arabs in Israel, first initiated in 1987. Literally, intifada means *"to jump up,"* or *"shake oneself"* to action. Since then, every Palestinian uprising against Israeli injustice has been called an intifada.

IN TOTO – (in-*TOW*-tow) Latin for in *the whole,* entirely, in general.

INTOXICATION – (in-tox-i-*KAY*-shun) (Intoxicated) literally, to *"intake poison or toxins."* Intoxication is inebriation, or drunkenness on alcohol. Ethyl alcohol is the intoxicating chemical found in alcoholic beverages. It is related to ether. Like ether, ethyl alcohol will anesthetize or numb the brain, resulting in bizarre behavior, and eventually blackout. Extreme intoxication is lethal. Nothing has caused more domestic turmoil in human history than alcohol. The literary sage, William Shakespeare (1564 – 1616) lamented the curse of intoxication when he wrote: *"Oh God, that man should put an enemy in his mouth to steal away their brains! That we should with joy, pleasure, revel and applause transform ourselves into beasts."*

INTRACTABLE – (in-*TRAC*-ta-bul) Exceedingly stubborn, obstinate. An intractable person is unmanageable, unteachable.

INTRAMURAL – (in-tra-*MUR*-al) Within the same school. Informal activities, especially sports, played for fun. Intramural activities are participational, rather than competitive. They are played for recreation in a win/win atmosphere. Most importantly, everybody gets to play.

INTRANET – (*IN*-truh-net) A private Internet. The prefix *"inter"* means without, between, among. The prefix *"intra"* means within. The Internet is accessible globally, while the Intranet is an internal website, a private network for a corporation or organization. Intranet access is limited to those insiders, with permission, and secret access.

INTRANSIGENT – (in-*TRAN*-si-jent) (Intransigence) Unmovable in the sense that the person refuses to agree or compromise. An intransigent individual is inflexible, stubborn, and closed-minded. Sounds like the MAGAmaniacals.

INTRINSIC – (in-*TRIN*-sic) From within. Not needing external influences to motive behavior. The opposite of intrinsic is extrinsic.

INTRINSIC EDUCATION – (in-*TRIN*-sic ed-jew-*KAY*-shun) Learning for learning's sake. Education for self-improvement, edification, fun. Intrinsic education may not guarantee any extrinsic, material gain. As an old Professor once put it: *"Taking my economics course may not keep you off the breadline, but at least you'll know why you are there."* In other words, intrinsic education does not teach how to make a good living, but how to live a good life.

INTRINSIC MOTIVATION – (in-*TRIN*-sic mo-tiv-*VAY*-shun) When learners work on tasks for internal reasons, such as pleasure in the activity or love of learning. Intrinsic motivation is greatest asset a person can display. Nothing will produce better results than intrinsic motivation – the internal desire to succeed.

INTROVERT – (*IN*-trov-vert) Generally, a shy person. Psychologically, an introvert is one primarily concerned with his own thoughts and feelings. An introvert is inward directed. Her social relations are minimal. He is pensive, contemplative and meditative. Introversion is not a neurotic condition but a personality type. The opposite of introversion is extroversion (outwardliness). Both were identified by psychiatrist Carl Gustav Jung (1875 – 1961).

INTRUSIVE – (in-*TROO*-siv) Barging in. Coming without invitation, or unwelcomed. Intrusive species are invasive foreign plants or animals that enter a new biome and wreak ecological, environmental havoc.

INTRUSIVE SOUNDS – (in-*TROO*-siv *SOUNDS*) Hesitation or pause markers, a form of speech disfluency. An intrusive sound is an unpleasant speech affectation that provides a pause in the flow of conversation. This gives the speaker an instantaneous moment to think about what to say next. Some familiar intrusive sounds are *"uhhh," "errr," "aye," "you-know."*

INTUIT – (in-*TOO*-it) (Intuited, Intuition) To know, by obtaining direct knowledge. Intuit, as related to intuition refers to direct perception of truth, independent of reasoning. Intuited knowledge is not thought-out but endowed from a Higher Power.

INTUITION – (in-too-*WISH*-sun) (Intuitive) Literally, internal knowledge, in- spired from within, spiritually. Intuition is angel murmurs, the still small voice within that endows spiritual knowledge. Inspiration is the divine ambition that encourages our intuition. In philosophy, intuition is the faculty of knowing by mental inspection and without recourse to reason. Intuition is direct knowing or awareness which is neither deductive nor inductive but revelatory. The great Dr. Jonas Salk (1914 – 1995), conqueror of polio insisted that: *"Intuition will tell the thinking mind where to look next." "Intuition transcends reason but does not contradict it."* – Sivananda (1887 – 1963). *"Intuitive knowledge is an illumination of the soul, whereby it beholds in the light of God those things which it pleases Him to reveal to us by a direct impression of divine clearness."* – Rene Descartes (1596 – 1650).

INTUITIVE ARTIST – (in-*TOO*-a-tiv *ARE*-tist) A self-taught, natural artistic talent. An intuitive artist is not formally trained, and cannot be assigned to any particular school of art. They have been labeled *"nativists"* or *"primitivists."* Their style is eclectic, their genre is folksy. Outside the Western World, intuitive artists tend to rebel against Eurocentric art conventions.

INUIT – (*IN*-yoo-it) The Native Americans of the frozen north. The named Eskimos is a pejorative name given these people by the Cree Indians (*askimowew*), which disparagingly means *"raw meat eaters."* The Inuits and their Aleut cousins are culturally closer to their Siberian relatives than to the other North American Indians. The Inuit came late to America, by boat. Ice melt had inundated the Bering Land Bridge by then. The Inuit traveled back and forth between America and Siberia. To the Inuit, there was no Cold War, just the cold sea.

INUNCTION – (in-*UNC*-shun) Anointing. The rubbing in of an oil, grease, ointment or unguent.

INURNMENT – (in-*URN*-ment) An urn is a large decorative sealed vase. The ashes of cremated deceased are entered into urns. The funerary right of burying or interring the urn in the ground, or in a sarcophagus is inurnment.

INVARIABLE – (in-*VAR*-ree-a-bul) (Invariably) Not varying, constant, unchanging, not subject to alteration, incapable of being amended.

INVARIANT BE – (in-*VAR*-ree-ant *BEE*) A non-standardized use of the verb *"be"* in English. The invariant be is prevalent in *"Ebonics,"* the Afro-American English dialect. This usage of the verb refers to action that takes place habitually over time. For example: *"He always be saying that."* Used in this way, there is no exact Standard English equivalent.

INVASIVES – (in-*VAY*-sivs) (Invasive species) Unwelcomed fauna and flora immigrants. Invasive means thrusting in, taking over, occupying or invading. Invasive species are intrusive foreign plants and animals, aliens that invade a new biome and wreak environmental, ecological havoc. Hawaii has lost much of its rare flora and fauna to invasive species. So has Florida. These two tropical/semitropical states have the most unique and fragile ecosystems of all the 50 states. About 400 destructive invasive species have been allowed to invade Florida. The most dangerous is the Burmese Python (perhaps over 75,000 to date) which has taken control of the Everglades. In all, over 4,000 invasives have been introduced into America, beginning in colonial times. Most have naturalized, and seem natural to us today, like the sparrow, starling, and dandelion. Many species of flora and fauna have perished in the struggle with aggressive invasive species. They have gone extinct. The most bizarre and biggest invasive species is the hippopotamuses in the Columbian rivers. They were part of drug lord Pablo Escobar's (1949 – 1993) menagerie and released into the wild at his demise. Charles Darwin (1809 – 1882) early on recognized the danger. *"What havoc does the introduction of a foreign species wreak, before the indigenous creatures learn to adjust to the invader?"*

INVECTIVE – (in-*VEC*-tiv) A vehement or violent denunciation, accusation, or censure. An invective is a scathing reproach, an abusive insult.

INVEIGH – (in-*VAY*) To protest strongly or attack vehemently with words. To inveigh is to attack verbally, to rail against, as to inveigh against capitalist greed.

INVEIGLE – (in-*VAY*-gul) To entice, lure, ensnare, manipulate with flattery. The naïve are susceptible to inveigling. No American President is or has been *"played"* more, by more people than *"His Worship,"* President Donald Trump (b. 1946).

INVENTORY – (*IN*-ven-tor-ree) In business, a complete listing of merchandise or stock held in reserve. Inventory includes finished goods waiting to be sold and raw materials to be used in production. Keeping inventor is expensive, requiring space and care.

INVERSE – (*IN*-vers) Reversed in position, order, direction, or tendency.

INVERSION – (in-*VER*-shun) A stagnant atmospheric condition with a layer of warm air above a layer of cold air. The warm air creates a lid, trapping the stale, polluted, smoggy cold air at ground level. Inversions can kill those with respiratory illnesses. Too, temperature inversions can stall a storm weaking meteorological havoc.

INVERTEBRATES – (in-*VER*-ti-brayts) Simple animals without backbones, represented by worms, slugs, snails, mollusks, and jellyfish.

INVETERATE – (in-*VET*-ter-at) Long established, deep-rooted or ingrained within one's character. For example: *"Donald Trump is an inveterate liar."*

INVESTIGATORY COMMISSION – (in-*VES*-ti-ga-tor-ree com-*MISH*-shun) A formal committee of experts assembled by the government to determine *"what went wrong."* A catastrophe, assassination, or monumental failure will warrant the summonsing of an investigatory commission. In too many cases, the message from the investigatory commission is: *"The horse is out of the barn, let's close the gate."* Investigatory commissions have been misused to whitewash a tragedy or crime, protecting those *"Too big to jail, too big to assail."*

INVEST – (in-*VEST*) To devote time, effort, resources for a purpose or achievement. We invest for future security and wellbeing. The best investment is not financial but charitable and spiritual. Invest in the needy, infirm, helpless, homeless, and hopeless. Provide compassionate charity and joy. God will co- sign what you invest. Karmic dividends will be returned to you.

INVESTITURE – (in-*VES*-ti-chur) In Feudal society, the formal bestowal of the possessory right to a fief or other benefices. Those being so rewarded became wealthy landlords counts and dukes). They were presented with a title, vestments, and insignia of office or rank. Investiture was granted to Church officials by kings, and by the Church to royal officials. Investiture embroiled the Church in greedy temporal real estate and politics. Investiture contributed to corrupting the Church, which led to the Protestant revolt called the Reformation in the 16th and 17th centuries.

INVESTMENT – (in-*VEST*-ment) In capitalism, to infuse capital (money) into a corporation in order to gain profitable returns in the form of dividend payments. In capitalism the economy, the government are controlled by rich investors. Investors greedily hope to buy cheaply and sell dearly. They intend to sell their shares in the business when they reach maximum worth. Investment is like a bubble. Wealthy investors want to own the bubble while it is growing but sell the bubble before it bursts. Hopefully, the greedy invest will not wait too long, and have the bubble burst in his portfolio. So investment is a gamble, as is capitalism in general.

INVETERATE – (in-*VET*-er-rit) Long established. Inveterate describes anything that has become chronic, habitual, firmly established. One may have an inveterate love of justice, and therefore an inveterate disdain of capitalism.

INVIDIOUS – (in-*VID*-dee-us) Hateful, giving offense, and generating ill will. One may make invidious racial remarks or make invidious comparisons. *"Donald Trump (b. 1946) is an invidious creature, full stop!"*

IN VINO VERITAS – (in-*VEE*-no *VER*-ree-tas) Latin for *"truth in wine,"* meaning an inebriated person will speak what's really on his mind. Yes, he may, but it may not be true or sincere. The wine eliminates inhibitions. It encourages the drunk to vent, what he does not really mean.

INVIOLATE – (in-*VY*-o-late) (Inviolable) Undisturbed, uninjured, free from injury or violation.

INVITEE – (in-vy-*TEE*) In law, a person who is on the property of another by expressed invitation. A welcomed guest.

IN VITRO – (in *VEE*-troh) Latin for *"in glass,"* in this case meaning in a glass test tube in a laboratory. Whatever is produced in a lab, particularly biological specimens are created in vitro. Probiotics (beneficial bacteria), anti-viral agents, biological food supplements created in a lab are created in vitro. In vitro fertilization involves impregnating an egg cell with a sperm cell in a glass test tub, then transplanting it into a woman or female animal. *"She couldn't conceive until fertilized in vitro."* Incidentally: The theocratic

Alabama Supreme Court had declared frozen fetuses to be children. That's right. Your heard well. *"Stupid is as stupid does."* – Alabamian Forest Gump (fl. 1994).

INVOKE – (in-*VOHK*) (Invocation) Literally to *"call in,"* in contrast to evoke which is to *"call out"* or *"call forth."* In the practice of magick, to invoke a spirit is to summon or draw a spirit being into your own body. So to invoke is an invitation of possession. This is usually done to facilitate communication between the spirit world and the material world. Invocation is an important part of many magico-religious practices. *"To 'invoke' is to 'call in,' just as to 'evoke' is to 'call forth'. This is the essential difference between the two branches of Magick. In invocation, the macrocosm floods the consciousness. In evocation, the magician, having become the macrocosm, creates a microcosm."* – Magician, Occult Practitioner Aleister Crowley (1875 – 1947).

IODINE – (*EYE*-o-dyn) (I) The name derives from the French *iode,* which was taken from the Greek *ioeides* meaning *"violet."* The 53 protons in its nucleus give iodine its atomic number. A bluish-black, nonmetallic element occurring as a crystalline solid, that sublimes into a dense, irritating violet vapor when heated. Iodine is used in medicine as an antiseptic. It is also useful in photography and producing dyes. The radioisotope iodine-131 (radioiodine) is valuable in the diagnosis and treatment of thyroid diseases.

ION – (*EYE*-on) An electrically charged atom that has lost or gained one or more electron. So an ion is a variation of the original element.

IOSEB JUGHASHVILI – (eye-*OH*-seb joog-hash-*VEE*-lee) Joseph Stalin's (1878 – 1953) actual Georgian birth name. Perhaps he wouldn't have been taken too seriously if Stalin would have kept his real name.

IOTA – (eye-*OH*-ta) The 9th letter of the Greek alphabet, (I, i). The iota is the smallest, simplest symbol in the Greek alphabet. Iota therefore came to symbolize something tiny, a small amount. In the Bible's Matthew 5: 18, it is written: *"Until heaven and earth pass way, not an iota, not a dot will pass from the Law until all is accomplished."* Still today, *"not one iota"* means not even a little bit, not the slightest amount.

IPSE DIXIT – (*IP*-see *DIX*-it) Latin for *"He himself has said."* In other words, hearsay. So ipse dixit is an assertion without proof, an arbitrary and unsupported statement. Ipse dixit testimony is useless in court.

IPSO FACTO – (*IP*-so-*FAK*-tow) Latin for *"in and of itself."* In law, Ipso facto means by the mere fact that, as a necessary consequence.

I.Q. – (eye *KEW*) Intelligence Quotient. An aptitude test purported to reveal one's mental capacity. The I. Q. Test formula is: Mental age divided by chronological age times 100 = I. Q. score. *"Andy Warhol is the only genius I've ever known with an I.Q. of 60."* – Gore Vidal (1925 – 2012), novelist, screenwriter. I.Q. is a weak measuring rod of how smart an individual really is. I.Q. does not take into account one's emotional condition. *"He got all A's but failed life."* – Walker Percy (1916 - 1990).

IRA – (eye are *AY*) (Irish Republican Army) In this case, not the tax man, but the independence fighter. The IRA is an underground Irish nationalist organization founded in 1917 to work [read: *fight*] for Irish independence from Great Britain. The kernel of the IRA was Irish Volunteers who refused to serve in the British army during World War One. The British had oppressed the Irish for nearly 700 years. The Irish agitation for independence would have culminated with an all-out British invasion of the island, had the war in Europe not intervened. The Irish Republican Army fought British occupation while the British fought the Germans in France. The Irish were encouraged by the Germans. The IRA used guerrilla tactic they had learned from the Dutch Boers who had successfully fought the British in the South African War (1899 – 1902). After World War One, Britain was exhausted. But the IRA continued to fight war-weary Britain winning Irish independence in 1921. Now the Irish Republican Army turned its attention to Ulster, the 6 counties of Northern Ireland, still controlled by Britain. *"One Island, One Ireland,"* is the IRA unification credo. In the 1960's the Irish Republican Army widened its theater of operations to include British cities, including London. Migrating from the countryside to the city, guerrilla warfare takes on the guise of terrorism. Theaters and pubs were bombed, government officials were assassinated. Whether the IRA are terrorists or patriots depends on one's allegiance. In every kind of war, innocent people are killed. The Irish Republican Army has paused its military operation, but not its zeal for a united Ireland. Much of its activities have been over-shadowed by radical Islamic terrorism.

IRA CREDO – (eye are *AY KRAY*-doh) *"One island, one Ireland."* The commitment of the Irish Republican Army.

IRAN – (ir-*RON*) Islamic nation in the Middle East, historically called Persia. Iranians are not Arabs, but Caucasian Aryans. In fact, the term Iran derived from Aryan. Iranians are Muslims though. Iranians speak Persian but write in Arabic. In fact, Iran is the fulcrum of Shi'ism (Shiite Islam), the minority sect (20% of all Muslims). This puts it at odds with the majority of other Muslims who are Sunnis. Iran would be only of archeological interest if it wasn't awash in oil. Incidentally: A bilateral agreement of 1907 between capitalist/imperialist Britain and Russia divided Iran (Persia) into a Russian north, British south, and a neutral middle sphere. So why do we naively wonder: *"Why do they hate us?"*

IRAN-CONTRA SCANDAL – (ir-*RON KON*-truh *SKAN*-duhl) An illegal, convoluted conspiracy in the Reagan Administration which involved selling illegal arms to Iran, the enemy, in order to illegally finance a fascist coup in Nicaragua, (August 20, 1985 to March 4, 1987). Ronald Reagan (1911 – 2004) was the corporate capitalist's President. He supported capitalist exploitation around the world. The *"Reagan Doctrine"* involved training and funding fascist terrorist groups to overthrow Socialist governments and establish pro-American capitalist dictators. Nicaragua had been liberated from capitalist oppression by the Socialist Sandinistas. Reagan wanted the fascist dictator back in power. So he had the CIA train the Contras to foment a fascist coup. The Contras were savage killers, torturers, and cocaine smugglers. (They raped and murdered nuns.) Reagan called them: *"The moral equivalent of the Founding Fathers."* But the Democratic Congress passed the Boland Amendment which prevented the CIA from training and funding terrorist militias. Reagan needed secret money for the Contras. At the same time, the Muslim Hezbollah was holding 7 American hostages in Lebanon. Reagan needed to liberate them for political reasons. Iran held influence over Hezbollah. But Iran was our enemy for storming the U.S. Embassy and holding 52 Americans hostage for 444 days (November 4, 1979 to January 20, 1981). Too, an arms embargo was in effect for Iran. But Iran was fighting a war with Iraq and needed weapons, and Reagan needed money. So Reagan illegally sold 1,500 missile to Iran for $30 million dollars. (Reagan double-crossed Iraq which was an American ally at that time.) It was discovered by the Justice Department that Lieutenant Colonel Oliver North (b. 1943) had illegally diverted $18 million from that dirty money to the Nicaraguan Contras.

Reagan denied the entire affair than later, under pressure confessed the truth. North and Reagan Administration officials lied. The *Iran-Contra Hearings* were held in Congress. But nothing came of the scandal. Ronald Reagan should have been impeached, convicted, deposed, and jailed. He wasn't. Republican Senator Howard Baker (1925 – 2014) later confessed that Reagan could have been impeached and ousted. However Baker negotiated with Democratic Senators and all came to the conclusion that America could not stomach another *"Nixon-Watergate Trauma."* Ronald Reagan gained the sobriquet, *"Teflon Ron."*

IRAN-HOSTAGE CRISIS – (ir-*RON HOS*-taj *CRY*-sis) The storming of the U.S. Embassy in Tehran, Iran, and the capturing of 52 American diplomats on November 4, 1979. The Americans were held prisoners for 444 days, until January 20, 1981. Since the discovery of oil in the early 20th century, America and Britain had been intrusively involved in Iranian affairs. To maintain the corporate capitalist grip on the oil, the C.I.A. bombed buildings, and fomented riots overthrowing the Democratically elected Socialist Prime Minister Mohammad Mosaddegh (1882 – 1967) [*MO*-sa-day], in 1953. The U.S. installed the corrupt, right-wing Shah Mohammad Rezi Pahlavi (1919 – 1980), trained his secret police (SAVAK) in Nazi torture techniques. In 1979 the Iranian Islamic Revolution broke forth. The Shah was deposed. The hostage crisis was a reaction to American interference and exploitation that had taken place for years. The hostage crisis dominated American politics and much of Jimmy Carter's (b. 1924) Presidency. Operation Eagle Claw, the failed attempt to rescue the hostages resulted in 8 Americans and 1 Iranian dead. The C.I.A. wanted to write-off the hostages, tell the American people that they were dead, and invade Iran. The result would have been a Niagara of bloodshed! To spite Carter, the hostages were released the moment Ronald Reagan (1911 – 2004) was sworn-in as President (January 20, 1981). However the C.I.A. had negotiated a quid pro quo with the Iranians beforehand. Panamanian dictator Manual Noriega (b. 1934) was the C.I.A.'s drug-runner. The C.I.A. used Noriega's drug money to buy Israeli arms for the Iranian Islamists in order to free the American hostages. Defending capitalism is a dirty game.

IRAQ – (ir-*RACK*) (Region of the Middle East, once known as *Mesopotamia,* the site of several ancient civilizations. Modern day Iraq was created by 3 people: imperialist Winston Churchill (1874 – 1965); soldier/spy T.E. Lawrence of Arabia (1888 – 1935); and anthropologist Gertrude Bell (1868 – 1926). The trio forced together 3 hostile provinces: *Mosul, Basra,* and *Baghdad.* They knew that these people would be preoccupied fighting each other, and therefore would not be able to fight the British. Meanwhile, the *Anglo-Persian Oil Company* (now BP or <u>B</u>ritish <u>P</u>etroleum) would be free to suck out the oil for Britain. In modern history, Iraq had been exploited, oppressed, laid-low by Western powers. However in ancient times, Iraq was Mesopotamia, the land between the Tigris and Euphrates Rivers, a birthplace of civilization. The first mighty empires like Sumeria, Babylonia, Assyria, Akkadia, and Chaldea all emerged in the forlorn land that is today Iraq.

IRIDIUM – (ir-*RID*-dee-um) (Ir) A rare silver-white metallic element resembling platinum. It was named after *Iris,* the Greek goddess of the rainbow. Iridium bears the atomic number 77, for that's the number of protons in its nucleus. Iridium is used in platinum alloys for the points of gold pens. It is one of the 9 rarest stable elements in the world. But it is not so rare out of this world. Iridium is fairly common in asteroids and meteorites. Therefore a terrestrial location rich in iridium is a sure indication of some ancient meteor strike.

IRIE – (*EYE*-ree) A popular Jamaican salutation in *"patwa"* or Jamaican dialect meaning *"alright!"* or *"all is well!"* The connotation of the term is satisfaction, excellence. Irie had been taken from the Jamaican Rastafarian tradition.

IRISH BLESSING – (*EYE*-rish *BLES*-sing) *"May the road rise up to meet you, May the wind be ever at your back. May the sun shine warm upon your face and the rain fall softly on your field. And until we meet again, may God hold you in the hollow of His hand."*

IRISH COFFEE – (*EYE*-rish *CAW*-fee) (*"Caife Gaelach"* in Irish.) A cocktail consisting of hot coffee, Irish whiskey, and sugar, stirred and topped with thick cream.

IRISH LOGIC – (*EYE*-rish *LOJ*-jek) Alternative thinking pattern as exhibited is some rural parts of Ireland. For example, an American found himself in a small train station outside of Killarney, Ireland. While waiting for the train, he noticed that there were two clocks on the wall that told two different times. The Yank asked the elderly station manager why they had <u>two</u> clocks that told <u>two</u> different times. The logical Irish response was: *"And what would we be wanting with <u>two</u> clocks, if they both told the <u>same</u> time?"* Indeed, there is a kernel of truth in that Irish logic.

IRON – (*EYE*-ern) (Fe) The name derives from the Old English (West Saxon) term *Iren* meaning iron tool or weapon. The Latin name for iron is *"ferrum,"* which accounts for its elemental symbol. The 26 protons in its nucleus, provides iron with its atomic number. World's most useful and plentiful *natural* metal, iron makes up 5% of the Earth. It is 500 times more plentiful than copper. Iron forms in rock when minerals are superheated in the presence of air. As the rock ages, its iron gets redder. Iron is hard and brittle. But the strong, malleable, and flexible alloy steel is made when the molten iron is *carbonized*. First, carbon is added to the iron oxide burning-off the oxygen atoms, leaving only iron. The carbon content of iron is 10 times more than purified steel. That's why iron is harder, more brittle, less flexible, and flakes. This excess carbon must be burned out of the iron at about 2,500 degrees Fahrenheit. Then a carefully measured amount of carbon is re-added to turn the iron into steel. About 95% to 98% of steel is iron. The center of the Earth is a molten iron core larger than the moon. Its magnetic influence wards-off dangerous solar radiation and keeps our atmosphere in place. Otherwise, our life-supporting atmosphere would drift into space. The Earth would become like the moon or Mars. Incidentally: When a star reaches the age when it begins to create iron, its death is imminent. The iron absorbs all the energy in the star's nuclear fusion. Once this happens, the star's gravity will crush it and the star will implode, a prelude to an explode as a supernova.

IRON CURTAIN – (*EYE*-ern *KUR*-tin) The armed border between Communist East and capitalist West Europe during the Cold War period (1945 – 1991). The nations of Western Europe were united in N.A.T.O. (<u>N</u>orth <u>A</u>tlantic <u>T</u>reaty <u>O</u>rganization) dominated by the U.S.A. The nations of Eastern Europe were united in the Warsaw Pact dominated by Russia. The term *"iron curtain"* was coined by Dr. Joseph Goebbels (1897 – 1945) Nazi Propaganda Minister. Goebbels had hope that the capitalist West and capitalist Nazi Germany would unite, presenting an *"iron curtain"* against Socialist Russia. Winston Churchill (1874 – 1965) picked up the term and used it in his famous Westminster College speech in Fulton, Missouri (March 5, 1946). *"From Stettin in the Baltic to Trieste in the Adriatic an iron curtain has descended across the continent."*

IRON DOME – (*EYE*-ern *DOHM*) The Israeli mobile, all-weather air defense system, consisting of C-RAMs (Counter Rocket, Artillery, Mortar systems). The Israeli system was developed by *Rafael Advanced Defense Systems* and *Israel Aerospace Industries* with generous American funding (billions). The Iron Dome was first installed in 2011. One C-RAM launcher loads 25 missiles and is quickly re-loadable. Its sensitive radar will detect incoming rockets and artillery shells fired from 2.5 to 43 miles away, predict its trajectory and point of impact. At least 90% of these weapons fired at Israel are intercepted and destroyed in mid- air. Israel has at least 15 mobile C-RAM batteries with 3 or 4 launchers each that can be quickly transported where needed. Each battery is capable of defending 60 square miles of territory. Each launcher cost over $50 million dollars. Each missile costs over $50 thousand dollars. (Aggression is expensive!) Israel's C-RAM system needed a popular name. The project leader of the *Administration for the Development of Weapons and Technology Infrastructure,* simply identified as Colonel S., devised the name of the defense system with the help of his wife. They came up with the name, *"Golden Dome."* Later, they agreed that it sounded too ostentatious. So they cheapened the metal to *"Iron Dome."* This is an appropriately imaginative name for an aerial defense system. *"Then the Lord rained on Sodom and Gomorrah sulfur and fire from out of heaven."* – Genesis 19:24.

IRON TRIANGLE – (*EYE*-ern *TRY*-ang-guhl) An alliance of groups with an interest in a policy area. The 3 corners of the iron triangle are bureaucrats from the relevant agency, legislators from appropriate committees, and interest groups affected by the issue. The great governmental concern of iron triangle members is: *"What's in it for me?"* The term iron triangle can be applied to ant number alliances.

IRONY – (*EYE*-ron-nee) (Ironic, Ironical) An irony or ironic meaning conveys an opposite message from the one intended. An ironic assertion is often amusing, surprising, and sometimes a mockery. Irony makes for stinging insults. Actor Jack Nicholson (b. 1937) stated that*: "I always found it ironic when my mom would call me a son-of-a-bitch."*

IROQUOIS – (*EAR*-ra-kwoy) A powerful confederation of 5 Amerindian Tribes: the Mohawk, Oneida, Onondaga, Cayuga, and Seneca (joined later by the Tuscarora). The Iroquois occupied upper New York and across into Canada. They were the fiercest of the Eastern Woodland Tribes, called the *"Romans of the East."* The Iroquois were in constant conflict with all the Algonquin Tribes, and their Huron cousins, whom they ultimately destroyed. The Iroquois were always the aggressors. In the 17th century, an Algonquin Federation led by the Miami halted the Iroquois incursion into the Midwest. The Iroquois sided with the British against the French and Algonquin in the French and Indian war (1754 – 1763). Later, the Iroquois aided the British against the Americans in the Revolution (1775 – 1783). The Iroquois were exceedingly cruel to prisoners, inflicting unspeakable tortures, including making captives eat themselves alive!

IROQUOIS THANKSGIVING – (*EAR*-ra-kwoy thanks-*GIV*-ving) *"We return thanks to our mother, the earth, which sustains us. We return thanks to the rivers and streams, which supply us with water. We return thanks to all herbs, which furnish medicines for the cure of our diseases. We return thanks to the moon and stars, which give us their light when the sun is gone. We return thanks to the sun that has looked upon the earth with a beneficent eye. Lastly, we return thanks to the Great Spirit, in whom is embodied all goodness, and who directs all things for the good of her children."*

IRRADIATION – (ear-ray-dee-*AY*-shun) In psychology, irradiation is a subconscious defense mechanism to deal with stress. It is a form of projection, more accurately displacement. However with irradiation, the sufferer displaces on everyone and everything. It is a shotgun approach in which the entire world is at fault.

IRRATIONAL – (ir-*RASH*-shun-al) (Irrationally) Absurd, nonsensical, not in accordance with reason or rational powers. The Trump White House is philosophically, logically irrational.

IRREDENTISM – (ear-ri-*DENT*-is-um) (Irredentists) A political and popular nationalist movement in which citizens seek to occupy territory held by another nation. Often, the disputed territory was lost is a war. This land is usually populated by ethnic kin of the irredentists. Irredentists feel patriotically duty-bound to redeem their homeland by reincorporating these territories. Therefore, irredentism is a lightening-rod ideology which can easily ignite a war. The term *"irredentism"* derives from the Italian *"irredento,"* meaning *"unredeemed."* With Italian unification during the second half of the 19th century, the battle cry was *"Italia Irredenta!"* or *"Unredeemed Italy!"* Italians sought to annex lands in the Austro-Hungarian Empire inhabited by ethnic Italians. Irredentism pushed Italy into World War One (1915 – 1918) on the Allied side against Austria-Hungary and Germany. Irredentist movements have had momentum is scores of countries. Officially, governmental irredentist claims are presently active in: Argentina, Bolivia, China, Comoros, Guatemala, India, Philippines, Japan, Spain, Venezuela, Russia, Sri Lanka, Israel and Palestine.

IRREFRAGABLE – (ir-*REF*-fra-ga-bul) Undeniable. Not to be disputed or contested is irrefragable.

IRREGARDLESS – (ir-ri-GAHRD-lis) Notwithstanding, despite of, showing no regard, regardless. *"Some MAGA Republicans will vote for Trump, irregardless of his criminality."*

IRRELIGIOUS – (ir-ri-*LIJ*-uhs) Literally not religious or subscribing to any religious belief, doctrine, or organization. An irreligious individual is not necessarily hostile to religions, just disinterested and unneedful. An irreligious person may be very spiritual, even sanctified. It is for that reason that they do not need religion as a roadmap to enlightenment or salvation.

IRRESOLUTE – (ir-*RES*-o-loot) Doubtful, wavering, hesitating, vacillating, infirm in purpose, lacking resolution. *"Trump and the Trumpublicans have turned America's commitment to NATO irresolute."*

IRRESPECTIVE – (ear-ri-*SPEK*-tiv) Regardless, discounting, ignoring. What is irrespective is without regard to something else, especially something specified. *"Our votes will be counted irrespective of Republican suppression laws."*

IRREVOCABLE – (ir-*REV*-o-ca-bul) Unalterable. Cannot be changed, revoked, recalled, or undone. *"The right to vote is irrevocable, despite Republican suppression laws."*

IRRITABLE MALE SYNDROME – (*IR*-rit-ta-bul *MALE SIN*-drome) (I.M.S.) Masculine menopause, the male counterpart to the female *"change of life."* Irritable Male Syndrome is a condition encountered by some aging men as their testosterone level begins to drop. They may become moody, lethargic, depressed, and irritable. Like the ladies, some guys become bitchy. Exercise counters irritable male syndrome somewhat, by increasing the testosterone level. Have patience with the Old Man.

IRS – (eye are *ESS*) An initialism for the Internal Revenue Service. The tax man. Branch of the Treasury Department that collects taxes. Republican politicians deplore the IRS because their vulgarly rich sponsors deplore the IRS.

ISAAC – (*EYE*-sac) According to Biblical tradition, the son of the patriarch Abraham and wife Sarah. Isaac became the Father of the Jews. Isaac was half- brother to Ishmael, Father of the Arabs. Therefore, hostile Arabs and Jews claim the same ancestor.

ISANDLWANA – (is-ond-*LWAN*-na) British battle against the Zulus in South Africa, January 22, 1879. The Zulus lost 1,000 warriors. The modernly equipped British lost 1,300 out of 1,700 soldiers. This was only 11 days after the 6 month war commenced. Isandlwana was the greatest military defeat of the British throughout the long Victorian Era. The Zulus won the battle but lost the Anglo- Zulu War January 11 – July 4, 1879).

ISBN – (eye ess-bee *EN*) An initialism for International Standard Book Number. ISBN is a unique, internationally utilized number code assigned to books for the purpose of identification and inventory control. The ISBN makes location and purchase of books much easier.

ISHMAEL – (*ISH*-may-el) According to Biblical tradition, the son of the patriarch Abraham (Ibrahim) and servant girl Hagar. Ishmael became the Father of the Arabs. Ishmael was half-brother to Isaac, Father of the Jews. So both the Jews and Arabs claim Abraham as their Patriarch, ancestor. The two hostile people are half-brothers.

ISIS – (eye-*SIS*) An acronym for Islamic State of Iraq and Syria. (Alternate names for this organization are ISIL [Islamic State of Iraq and the Levant] and DAESH, [*DASH*] an Arabic acronym for [Islamic State of Iraq and Syria].) Whatever it's called, ISIS is a barbaric, savage terrorist community. It consists of Sunni Muslims. It is an organized crime syndicate operatizing under the guise of religious fervor. Isis is the creation of American capitalist greed in the oil-rich Middle East. Isis is an apocalyptic group that seeks the utter destruction of all religions and cultures other than their skewed interpretation of Islam. In 2015, ISIS was the richest and best organized terrorist group in history. They had taken control of much of Iraq and Syria, and obliterated ancient archeological treasures. ISIS cells had spread terror worldwide. They are social media savvy and recruit disaffected youth from around the globe. ISIS is the anti-Christ in- aggregate.

ISLAM – (*IS*-lom) Arabic for *"self-surrender"* to the Will of God (Allah). *"Salm"* means peace, and *"silm"* means submitting one's will to God. Islam is the religious faith of Muslims, which also serves as a political ideology and a mark of group identity. It is the youngest great religion, and most militant, founded by the Prophet Mohammad (c. 570 – 632 CE). According to scholar Jacob Bronowski (1908 – 1974) in *The Ascent of Man* (1973) *"Mahomet had been firm that Islam was not to be a religion of miracles; it became in intellectual content a pattern of contemplation and analysis. Mohammedan writers depersonalized and formalized the godhead: the mysticism of Islam is not blood and wine, flesh and bread, but am unearthly ecstasy."* There is no hiding the fact that Islam was the first religion to instruct its faithful to fight disbelievers of other religions. Monotheistic Islam is descended, in great part, from Judaism and Christianity. Its holy book, The Quran

(Koran) makes many Biblical references. Islam's sacred religious capital is Mecca in Saudi Arabia, however the religion dominates 32 countries. The two great denominations of Islam are the Sunnis (80%) and the Shia (20%). About 20% of the world is Islamic. Islam is the fastest growing religion today. Incidentally: Western and southeaster China has Muslim minorities being persecuted by the government. Islam is the only religion that the Communist Chinese were unable to suppress. *"Mohammed is the messenger of Allah and the seal of the Prophets." –* <u>The Koran</u>, Surah 33:40.

ISLAMIC CREDO – (is-*LOM*-mic *CRAY*-dow) The Muslim or Islamic credo is *"La ilaaha illa allah,"* meaning *"There is no God but Allah."*

ISLAMIC HEAVEN – (is-*LOM*-mic *HEV*-ven) Life after death for deserving Muslims (men) in the Eternal Paradise. Allah has provided a garden of carnal, sensual delights for those who had faithfully followed His strictures, as were recorded by His Prophet, Muhammed. Islamic Heaven is actually an exclusive *"Gentlemen's Club."* Leisure, sex, delicacies, alcohol, and eternal youth are promised to faithful Muslims (particularly men) in Heaven by the Koran. The holy text reads that they will: *"Upon inwrought couches, reclining thereon face to face. Youths ever young shall go unto them roundabout with goblets and ewers and a cup of flowing wine – their heads shall not ache with it, neither shall they be confused; and the fruits of their choice, and flesh of birds to their desire; and damsels with bright eyes like hidden pearls.... Wives exalted – verily we produced them specially and made them virgins, amorous, of equal age.... Therein the best and comeliest maids, bright-eyed, kept in tents. Man hath not touched them before, nor Jinn; reclining on green cushions and fine carpets."* So, in Islamic Heaven, the green couches are comfortable, (a reference to oases perhaps?), and the finest Halal foods are free. Your wives are always happy and horny. The old ladies regain their youth and beauty, and never age or lose their virginity, to your delight. They are forever delighted to serve. Too, for variety, you have all the pearl-eyed virgin mistresses your loins can manage – (of no age limit). The alcohol that was denied to you on Earth, is copiously offered in Heaven – without drunkenness or hangovers. (Apparently, Islamic Heaven has an *"open bar."*) There is a Spiritual element that is lacking in Islamic Heaven. To Christians, especially Americans, it sounds more like a college fraternity house.

ISLAMIC INEQUALITY – (is-LOM-mic in-ee-*KWAL*-li-tee) Religiously sanctioned injustice, distributive disparity accepted by Muslims as the will of God (*"Ensha Allah"*). Islam maintains that man is blessed with talents, potentials, and abilities required for life. These blessings are physical, mental, and moral. But God in His wisdom had not distributed these talents equally. Their equal distribution would have made men totally independent of one another. This would impair the possibility of mutual care, cooperation, and the opportunity for compassion. There would be no need for charity, if all men were equal.

ISLAMISM – (is-*LOM*-is-um) Islam politicized. Islamic theology merged with political ideology. Islamism sets the stage for the formation of a Muslim theocracy, governed by *Shari'a Law.* It produces *patrimonialism,* the confusion or melding of private and public realms. Islamism melds *orthodoxy* (religious conformity) with *orthopraxy* (behavioral conformity). The Taliban and ISIS are prime examples of Islamism at work. *"Islam is under obligation to gain power over all nations." –* Ibn Khaldun (1332 – 1406).

ISLAMIZATION – (is-lom-eye-*ZAY*-shun) The conversion of a person or community to Islam, becoming Muslims. Islamization has occurred voluntarily and forcibly, by book and by sword.

ISLAMOPHOBIA – (is-lom-o-*FO*-bee-a) (Islamophobiacs) Literally, fear of Islam or Muslims. Islamophobia is generated by radical Islamism. Barbaric, savage terror groups like ISIS and al-Qaeda breed suspicion and resentment toward the entire religious culture. Though unreasonable, a phobia is an unreasonable fear. The terrorists are a minute fraction of the Muslim population. By far, the greatest victims of Islamism are virtuous Muslims. They have the greatest reason to be Islamophobic.

ISLAM'S ARTICLES – (*IS*-loms *AR*-ti-kuhls) Actually Islam's Five Articles of Faith. The Prophet Muhammad (c. 570 – 632 CE) admonished all Muslims to: 1. Believe in One God who has absolutely no association with Him in His Divinity. 2. Believe in God's Angels. 3. Believe in God's books, and in the Qur'an (Koran) as His last book. 4. Believe in God's prophets, and in Mohammad as His final messenger. 5. Believe in life after death.

ISM – (*IS*-um) Ism is a suffix. A suffix is a bit of a word that is affixed to the end of a word to alter its meaning. Ism means *"belief in,"* or *"devotion to"* a theory, ideology, doctrine, principle. Examples of *"isms"* are fascism, capitalism, Socialism, Catholicism. The suffix ism was selected as the Merriam-Webster Dictionary 2015 word of the year.

ISLAND – (*EYE*-land) A body of land completely surrounded by water that is not large enough to qualify as a continent. There are over 670,000 islands dotting the planet. Islands are miniature worlds to the plants and creatures who inhabit them. Islands may develop in salt or fresh water – rivers, lakes, seas, or the oceans. Islands form in different ways. *"Continental islands"* had been cut off from the mainland by tectonic forces (earthquakes) and by flooding. Britain, Greenland, Sicily, and Madagascar are examples. Continental islands rest on the continental shelves. *"Oceanic islands"* do not. They are formed from volcanism. Magma breaks through thin parts of the Earth's crust (hot spots), spewing lava that builds up as islands. Hawaii, Iceland, the Aleutians are oceanic islands. Oceanic islands may be isolated in the middle of the ocean. Coral islands are created by the calcareous skeletons or shells of minute sea creatures, coral. Over millions of years the chalky deposits are laid forming reefs that erode into white sandy islands. The islands are small, and the topography is low, just above sealevel. Coral islands form is shallow tropical seas throughout the world. The Bahamas are coral islands. Islands can form from silt deposits, sandbars in rivers. The largest island in the world is Greenland, followed New Guinea, Borneo (Indonesia), Madagascar, Baffin (Canada), Sumatra (Indonesia), Honshu (Japan), Victoria (Canada), and Great Britain. Incidentally: Canada's Manitoulin Island in Lake Huron, is the largest fresh water island in the world (1,068 square miles).

ISOKINETIC – (eye-so-kin-*NET*-tic) (also Isometric) Static exercise that pits muscle against muscle (as opposed to muscle against dead weight). Theoretically, isometric or isokinetic exercise should give you twice the benefit for the same investment of work and time.

ISOLATIONISM – (eye-so-*LAY*-shuhn-is-um) (Isolate, Isolationist, Isolationistic) The term *"isolationism"* is an Americanism of the early 1920s. It is a policy or doctrine of insulating, isolating one's country from the affairs of other nations by declining to enter alliances, foreign economic commitments, or international agreements. Isolationists seek to devote the entire efforts of one's country to its own advancement and remain at peace by avoiding foreign entanglements and responsibilities. In his 1797 farewell address, President George Washington (1732 - 1799) warned American posterity to: *"Avoid foreign entanglements."*

President John Adams (1735 - 1826) likewise warned that: *"If we hope to keep our democracy at home, we cannot go looking for monsters to kill overseas."* Both leaders were 18th and 19th century men, and they were right – for 18th and 19th century America. This self-centered rendition of isolationism applied to a novice nation protected by two oceans. As war clouds gathered over Europe and Asia in the 1930s, the U.S. regretted involvement in the Great War (1914 - 1918) in 1917. Isolationism griped the citizenry with the *"America First Movement."* This would all change with the German bombing of London (1940) and the Japanese bombing of Pearl Harbor (1941). U.S. entrance into World War Two (1939 - 1945) assured the righteous victory. America emerged on the world stage as the premier superpower. Leadership was thrust upon America, and the free world depended on the United States for security. That's where America stands today – the captain of a global economy on an interdependent planet. There is no going back to isolationism. Nevertheless, naïve simpletons like Donald Trump (b. 1946) and his MAGA (Make America Great Again) cultists hope to forsake the world. *"Why should we spend our money rebuilding Iraq, the Ukraine, and Latin America? Let's rebuild Detroit, Cleveland, and Appalachia."* This is an alluring argument. Indeed: *"For every subtle and complicated question, there is a perfect, simple, and straightforward answer, which is wrong."* – H. L. Mencken (1880 - 1956). Our security and prosperity, even in Detroit, Cleveland, and Appalachia depends on global security and prosperity. We cannot exist on this planet alone. Furthermore, there is the righteous humanitarian issue. *"The greatest obscenity will be when half of the world's population watches the other half starve to death on television."* – George Orwell (1903 - 1950). Today, it is the imperative duty of the United States to *"kill"* John Adam's *"monsters overseas"* because morality demands it.

ISOLATIONIST'S CREDO – (eye-so-*LAY*-shuhn-ists *CRAY*-dow) *"If we hope to keep our democracy at home, we cannot go looking for monsters to kill overseas."* – John Adams (1735 – 1826).

ISOMETRIC EXERCISE – (eye-soh-*MET*-rik *EKS*-er-syz) – A resistance workout. Physical exercise exerting the body in a healthful manner. Aerobic exercise entails raid movement like running, dancing, and swimming. This conditions the body. Weightlifting bulks-up muscle mass. This sculptures the body, presenting a powerful looking physique. Isometrics pits muscle against muscle or muscle against an immoveable object like a heavy table or wall. This is motionless resistance exercise. It induces positive stress and strain on the muscles and tendons that connect the muscles. Isometric exercise increases strength. The tendons are the strong elastic tissues that bind muscle to muscle, and muscle to bones. (Ligaments connect bone to bone.) It has been suggested that real strength is attributed to strong tendons, as well as muscles. Legendary Lithuanian strongman, Alexander Zass (1888 – 1962) insisted that: *"Without tendons, we would turn to jelly. Tendons must be trained. In my experience, a mam of large composition is not necessarily strong, just as a man of modest composition is not always weak. I do not believe in big muscles if there is no real strength in the tendons. You can see many physical culture enthusiasts who have very large muscles. However what is the point in having muscles if there is no rudimentary strength in the tendons? They can not fully use the strength of their muscles during the moments that truly test their strength. This is why their strength is a sheer illusion. One gets best increase in the tendon strength when their power is applied to a motionless object. They become stronger from resistance, and not from the movement."* In other words, Alexander Zass was an advocate of isometric exercise, muscle against muscle, or muscle against thing. Incidentally: Mr. Zass seems to have been describing the popular *YouTube* strongman Vladimir Shmondenko (b. 1999) perfectly.

This Ukrainian celebrity is popularly known as *"Anatoly the Gym Janitor."* In his baggy overalls and mop, Anatoly looks like a skinny comedian. That's until he out-lifts the muscle-bound giants who are left in speechless awe. Anatoly has a fine sculpted physique, but is not bulging like a freak. Still, he is amazingly strong. Perhaps it's his tendons?

ISOPODS – (*EYE*-so-pods) Any sea crustacean of the order Isopoda, including *sowbugs* and *slanters.* Isipods have flattened bodies with several legs. They are parasitic. Isopods resemble giant marine wood lice.

ISOTOPE – (*EYE*-so-tope) Any of two or more forms of a chemical element, having the same number of protons in the nucleus, (the same atomic number), but having different numbers of neutrons in the nucleus, (different atomic weight).

ISRAELI/JEW – (is-*RAY*-lee *JOO*) The terms Israeli and Jew are not synonymous. Israeli is a nationality, Jew (or Jewish) is a religio-cultural ethnic designation. Israel is called the *"Homeland of the Jews."* That is only partially correct. Indeed, Israel is the historic homeland of Jews and Judaism. Most Israelis are Jews, but not all. Of 9.05 million people in Israel, 6.5 million, or 72% are Jews. There are about 15 million Jews in the world, and at least as many Jews in America, as in Israel. So about 28% of Israelis do not practice Judaism, and are therefore not Jews. To be a Jew, one must practice Judaism. To be an Israeli, one must hold an Israeli passport (citizenship). One can be of any ethnic origin, and be an Israeli. Jews are an ethnic group culturally, but not racially. There is no typical Jew, as there is no typical American. Jews, like Americans, trace their ancestry to many nations. Sometimes the facts cloud and complicate the simplistic stereotypes. This topic is primarily academic. It should remain that way. We get into trouble when we take these nationality, ethnic, religious designations too seriously.

ISRAELPHILIA – (is-ray-ol-*FEE*-lee-ah) (Israelphiles = is-*RAY*-ol-fy-als) An unwarranted allegiance and affection for the nation of Israel. Israelphilia is not patriotism, for the Israelphiles are not Israeli citizens. Israelphiles are both Jews and Gentiles who conflate the Nation of Israel with International Jewry and the religion of Judaism. Therefore, to oppose policies of the Israeli Government is being anti-Semitic. That's a mistake, that's a deception, and that's intentional. To object to Israel's treatment of their Palestinian minority is considered anti- Semitism. Israel can do no wrong in the eyes of the Israelphiles. Anyone who refuses to give Israel a blank-check of support is slandered as a *"Jew Hater."* To oppose the tyrannical government of Saudi Arabia does not brand one as a *"Muslim Hater"* or *"Arab Hater."* To disagree with the right-wing British Brexit Movement, does not make one anti-English. Furthermore, to despise the corrupt war-monger, Israeli President Benjamin Netanyahu (b. 1949) is not to despise your Jewish-American neighbor. But that is the covert objective of Israelphilia. It is rooted in subliminal sorrow and guilt from the Holocaust. These emotions are disingenuously manipulated and exploited by extreme Israelphiles. (The children should not be blamed for the sins of the parents, too the children should not be exonerated for the suffering of their parents.) The pro-Israeli fanatics create an artificial dualism: One is either an *Israelphile* or an *Israelphobe* [read: *Jew Hater*]. Israel is not America's 51st state and should not be treated as such. Jewish-Americans should have no stronger allegiance to Israel, than Russian-Americans have to Russia, or Italian-Americans have to Italy. American Israelphilia is reminiscent of Irish-American support for the I.R.A. (Irish <u>R</u>epublican <u>A</u>rmy). Israelphilia tarnishes America's reputation as an honest broker in international affairs. Let's at least try to maintain the image of fair impartiality. Holding Israel accountable does not make one anti-Semitic. Incidentally: A fanatical group of Israelphiles are Fundamentalist Christians. They have devised some mystic, cultish doctrines concerning prophecy, Israel, and the Second Coming of Christ. This is an invalid bases on which to formulate foreign policy. Foot Note: *"Oppressed minorities, on becoming majorities, oppress minorities."*

ISTANBUL – (*IS*-tan-bul) Old Constantinople, the capital of Byzantium (Eastern Roman Empire). It was the capital of the Ottoman Empire until 1923. Istanbul is located on both sides of the Bosporus, the strategic waterway connecting the Black Sea with the Mediterranean. Istanbul is the only great city in the world on 2 continents, Asia (Turkey) and Europe (Thrace).

ISTANBUL CANAL – (*IS*-tan-bul can-*NEL*) (also Kanal Istanbul) A controversial construction project begun by Turkey in March, 2021, as an alternative sealane to the Bosporus Straights. The $15 billion dollar project is being dug 18.5 miles west of the Bosporus through European Istanbul. Though only 25 miles from end-to-end, the canal will long be an international hotspot. This canal has become a dangerously contentious issue, a possible source of crisis with the Russian invasion of the Ukraine in March 2022. The story is convoluted and complex. The Bosporus Straights separates European from Asian Turkey and connects the Aegean and Mediterranean Seas with the Black Sea. Black Sea nations like Bulgaria, Romania, Ukraine, and Russia must pass through the Turkish Bosporus in order ship cargo to and from the world. So the Bosporus is one of the busiest and most strategic sealanes on Earth. During World War One, Turkey held the Bosporus in a choke hold. But Turkey was defeated in the war. After the revolution, the Turkish Republic signed the Lausanne Treaty in 1923, which demilitarized the Straights and opened it up to unrestricted maritime traffic. But with the belligerent rise of fascism in Italy, Turkey sought to revise the treaty for her protection. The result was the Montreaux Convention of 1936. This agreement enabled Turkey to re-militarize the Bosporus. Too, it restricted non-Black Sea nations from sailing warships through the waterway. Montreaux also reinstated the free passage of all civilian merchant ships. This arrangement kept Turkey neutral during World War Two. Too, it prevented Axis warships access to the Black Sea to attack Russia. However, Turkey could not profit from international traffic through her waterway. After the war, Russia demanded joint control with Turkey over the Straights, and a permanent Russian military presents in the region. Turkey said *"NO!"* to this preposterous proposal. But the wily Russians devised a ruse. Montreaux stipulated that no more than 9 foreign warships with a total tonnage of 15,000 tons may pass through the Bosporus at any single time. So the Russians positioned their largest warship in the Straights permanently. This prevented any other nations besides Turkey from ever being able to pass any warships through the Straights. Russia hoped to make the Black Sea a Russian lake. Turkey knew that she could not resist Russian pressure alone. Therefore, in 1952, Turkey joined NATO (North Atlantic Treaty Organization). Now Turkey was Russia's Cold War opponent. However, the Montreaux Convention was still in effect. This restricted non-Black Sea nations from entering the Bosporus with large warships. This meant that NATO (except Turkey) and the U.S. could not enter the Black Sea with ships armed with guns larger than 8 inches in caliber. So in the 1960's the Americans sent their limited quota of *"missile"* ships through the Bosporus into the Black Sea. The Russians protested. They always expect other nations to abide by the rules. Turkey legalistically argued that the missiles were not guns, plus since missiles did not exist in 1936 when the Convention was signed, they are not part of the restrictions. But the Montreaux Treaty is still a hindrance to U.S. naval build-up in the Black Sea. This proved to be particularly critical with the Russian invasion of the Ukraine in March 2022. American and NATO naval power (aircraft carriers and submarines) are prevented from aiding the Ukrainians from the Black Sea, via the Bosporus. The Black Sea is the only strategic waterway on Earth where the U.S. does not have a strong naval presence. And it is needed now more than ever. Furthermore, Turkey is handcuffed by the Montreaux Convention from controlling its own waterway. Which brings us all the way back to the Istanbul Canal Project. The Bosporus and Montreaux restrictions would be made moot with an alternative entrance into the Black Sea. It's questionable if the canal will prove helpful to the Ukrainians in their freedom fight. But it will flood the Black Sea with U.S. and NATO naval power. Furthermore, the Russians will be livid! But as the Ukrainian defenders of Snake Island told the (now sunk) Russian cruise *"Moskva"*: *"Go Fuck Yourself!"*

ISTHMUS – (*ISTH*-mus) A geographical land formation in which a narrow neck of land acts as a bridge to connect two larger bodies of land. The Isthmus of Panama is the prime example. It connects Central America to South America.

ITAL – (*EYE*-tal) The religious dietary restrictions of Rastafari. As kosher is to Judaism, and halal is to Islam, ital is to Rastafarianism. Many Rastas are strict vegetarians. Other abstain only from pork (as done in Judaism and Islam). The different Rasta mansions (sects) observe different degrees of adherence to ital. All foods must be pure and natural, without additives or preservatives. Foods produced with chemical fertilizers or insecticides are not ital. Some Rastafarian will eat only what comes from the Earth. That prohibits them from eating what comes from the sea, for fish too are living creatures. Eggs and dairy products are forbidden by some. Rastas avoid salt, unless its sea salt or kosher. Metal cooking utensils cannot be used. Pottery and wood cooking pots, wooden cutlery, and dried calabash shells are used as bowls. Moderate alcohol, sugar, coffee, and chocolate is permitted by the less orthodox Rastafarians. Marijuana, on the other hand, is a sacred plant, the smoking of which is a sacramental duty. The purpose of ital dietary regulations is to increase *"Livity,"* the life-force of God within you. Incidentally: The term Ital is taken from the English word Vital, minus the letter V. The emphasis on the letter I is found throughout Rastafari vocabulary to signify the unity of the person with nature.

ITALIAN ELECTION – (it-*TAL*-lee-an el-*LEC*-shun) (1948) The C.I.A.'s first victory. The intervention in the Italian election of 1948 was the first political covert action by American Intelligence in history. The Italian Communist Party was poised to win a great democratic victory. The capitalist, anti-Socialist forces intended to use any and all means to thwart a Communist victory. The C.I.A. distributed bags of Marshal Plan money to bribe all to vote against the Communists. The agency persuaded Italian-American to write over 10 million letters to family and friends in Italy, persuading them not to vote Communist. Outrageous scare tales were told. The Vatican, under the pro-fascist Pope Pius XII lied to the people about the nature of Communism. He promised to excommunicate any Catholic who voted Communist. The Pope called the Italian Communists anti-Christ. The Vatican and the C.I.A. supported the conservative, right-wing, capitalist Christian Democrats in the election. In a crushing upset, the Communists lost the election. Incidentally: It's ironical that in 2016, the Americans were up in arms because of Russian meddling in the

Presidential election. The C.I.A. wrote the book on election fraud, tampering, interference and overthrowing governments. The Italian election of 1948 is another answer to the naïve question: *"Why do they hate us?"*

ITCH – (*ICH*) (Itching) Medically called *"Pruritus"* (pru-*RITE*-tus). An itch is an annoying feeling of tickle or tingle of the skin that causes a desire to scratch the affected area. Itching like hurting has resisted adequate attempts at classification as one type of sensory experience. One man's itch is another man's pain. Itch has many similarities to pain. However, where pain elicits a withdrawal reflex, itch elicits a scratch reflex. Both sensations use the same nerve bundles. Itching may be caused by any number of abnormalities. Infection, allergens, medications, irritants, healing wound, parasites, skin diseases, insect bites, nervous conditions, hairy back, wooly cloths and many more conditions may trigger itching. Scratching triggers mild pain receptors at the point of the itch. The message is sent to the brain which triggers serotonin, the feel-good brain chemical to the location. The scratching in satisfying, for a little while anyway. Soon the serotonin may trigger those same itch receptors again, even more intensely. So the itch-scratch-itch cycle may be interminable. Incidentally: Rubbing lightly or slapping the itching area has the same satisfying effect as scratching, without the possibility of irritating and damaging the skin. A Caveat: A persistent intolerable itching may be caused by an abnormally high white blood cell count. This indicates an infection, like cancer. *"Oh I'm itching, and I don't know where to scratch. Come here baby, scratch my back. I know you can do it, so baby get to it."* – Slim Harpo (1924 – 1970) *"Baby Scratch My Back."* (1966).

ITERATION – (it-er-*RAY*-shun) (Iterate, Iterating) A repetition, the act of repeating. Therefore, to <u>re</u>-iterate is to repeat a repetition.

ITERATIVE – (it-*TER*-ra-tiv or *IT*-ter-ray-tiv) (Iteration, Iteratively, Iterativeness) Repetitious, repeating, occurring again. *"Her iterative suggestions were unsolicited and unappreciated."*

ITERATIVE EVOLUTION – (it-*TER*-ra-tiv ev-vo-*LOO*-shun) A rare process in which repeated evolution of a new species from the same ancestor at different times. Iterative evolution proves that similar evolutionary pressures result in the same evolutionary path for organisms. A startling example of iterative evolution occurred in the Aldabra Islands, Indian Ocean, in May 2019. The flightless white-throated rail was thought to be extinct for 136,000 years. It had been wiped-out long ago by great floods. But it had reemerged on another island, the result of iterative evolution. Incidentally: The white-throated rail is called a *"Lazarus creature,"* (the Lazarus effect), for though thought extinct, it had come back from the dead, so to speak.

ITHYPHALLICISM – (ith-ee-*FAL*-li-sis-um) (Ithyphallic, Ithyphallicist) Worship of the erect penis or phallus. Ithyphallicism was practiced as a fecundity rite, a reproductive or fertility ritual by primitive cultures. So an ithyphallicist is a dick worshiper.

ITINERARY – (eye-*TIN*-ner-air-ree) A plan of travel. An itinerary is a detailed plan for a journey. It is a list of places to visit, times to be there. A Caveat: Do not confuse the itinerary with the agenda, which is the topics and order of discussion.

IT IS WHAT IT IS – (it *IZ* hwuht it *IZ*) A mundane, albeit peculiarly profound phrase that had become increasingly popular after 2020. It purports to define a situation by the situation, (which is a cardinal sin of lexicography). It is what it is conveys a sense of resignation, acquiescence, futility in the possibility of changing a bad outcome. For instance: *"What do you think about the election loss?"* *"Well, it is what it is."* In other words, we indeed lost. There's nothing we can do about it now. We must live with the consequences without excuses and make the best of it. After all, it is what it is. In the metaphysical or spiritual realm, it is what it is applies to surrender to the forces of the universe, or to God. Don't try to force your will on a hopeless situation. That can drive you mad. Just let God and let go. Indeed, it is what it is, and furthermore, it will take as long as it takes. Incidentally: *MAGA* election deniers would do well to accept the fact that *"It is what it is."*

IVORY – (*EYE*-vree) A hard whitish, beige, or yellowish coating of dentine on teeth and tusks. Ivory has been carved into fine figurines, statuettes, knives, utensils and pistol handles, piano keys, curios of all sorts. This has endangered many animals (elephants and walruses) that bear ivory on their bodies. Ivory is also obtained from hippopotamus, boars, wart hogs, and some whales. The best ivory is robbed from slain walruses. Ivory from African elephants is softer and easier to carve than ivory from Indian elephants. Incidentally: General George S. Patton (1885 – 1945) wore his two famous six shooters with ivory handles. He hated when they were called pearly.

IVORY TOWER – (*EYE*-vree *TAU*-wer) A derisive reference to academia, the university, the professoriate. Ivory tower implies an attitude of aloofness or disdain from the real world of practical affairs. Hawksmoor Towers of Oxford University's All Souls' College were originally ivory in color when constructed in 1716. That edifice may have inspired the ivory tower reference. In 1911, English writers Frederick Rothwell, Henry Brereton, and Cloudesley Shovell wrote in <u>H.L. Bergson's Laughter</u>: *"Each member [of society] must be ever attentive to his special surroundings – he must avoid shutting himself up in his own peculiar character as a philosopher in his ivory tower."* Philosopher John Dewey (1859 – 1952) an *"ivory tower"* resident himself, albeit activist once lamented: *"Brawny bullies rule the world, while saints introspect in their ivory towers."*

IVY ILLUSION – (*EYE*-vee il-*LOO*-shun) The false assumption that the elite, North Eastern Ivy League schools provide a superior education. The Ivy League schools are some of the nation's oldest, therefore most prestigious. But that does not automatically mean that a student will learn more at Harvard, than at Ball State. The Ivy league Schools include: Harvard, Yale, Princeton, Dartmouth, Brown, Columbia, Cornell, and Pennsylvania. Age alone does not constitute competency. Tradition can calcify into stagnation. But that's not why an Ivy League education is not necessarily superior and may actually be inferior. Ivy League exceptionality is a myth, an illusion, perception hoping to translate into reality. The faculty roster of Harvard, Yale, and Princeton is indeed stellar. Famously published professors, Nobel Prize winners, television news consultants may be on the list, but not often on the campus. You'll never see them because they are always on television. The faculty roster is a fraud – just for show. Famous professors are far too busy doing research and writing books to bother with underling undergraduates. A stipulation in their recruitment contract is that they will not have to waste their time teaching! Indeed, the courses are under their names, but taught by their graduate assistants – students, working on Ph.D.'s. So at famous Ivy League schools, you may not be taught by fully qualified professors, but rather by professor *"wannabes."* By contrast, at state universities like Michigan State, Montana State, or Wayne State, you are taught by experienced, fully qualified professors, genuine scholars. So where do you think you will get a better education? The question begs the answer. The name of an Ivy League school on a diploma is hoped to impress. But a name, or even a diploma, is not a guarantee of competence. *"You can tell a Harvard man, but you can't tell him much."*

IVY LEAGUE – (*EYE*-vee *LEEG*) America's oldest and most prestigious universities, dating back to colonial days. They are located in New England and the Upper Atlantic states. Ivy League schools include Harvard, Yale, Princeton, Dartmouth, Cornell, Columbia, Brown, and the University of Pennsylvania. The *"Ivy"* is a reference to their ivy-covered walls, indicating age. A diploma from an Ivy League college may open doors, merely by the power of reputation. (Perception becomes reality.) Actually, a college education from one of these snob schools, is no better than an education from a standard state university. In fact, a far better education is attained from a small, personal college. The real advantage of an Ivy League education, is the opportunity to network with the rich and powerful.

I, WE/ME, US – (*EYE WEE MEE UHS*) Personal pronouns, singular and plural. This is a clarification of a grammatical confusion. *I* and *we* are noun-pronouns. *Me* and *us* are object-pronouns. *We* is the plural of *I*. *Us* is the plural of *me*. *I* and *we* are the subject form of the pronoun. *Me* and *us* are the object form of the pronoun. For example: *I* or *we* do things, whereas things get done by *me* and *us*. *I* or *we* can look after others, while others look after *me* or *us*. As the subjects, you'll tend to use *I* and *we* at the beginning of the sentence, but *me* and *us* toward the end of the sentence.

I, WE/ME, US – (*EYE WEE MEE UHS*) Personal pronouns, singular and plural. The use of *I, we/me, us* is profoundly significant, sociologically, economically, politically, and spiritually. I and me are capitalistic pronouns, whereas we and us are Socialistic pronouns. I and me are selfish, we and us are generous. I and me suggests hoarding: *"What's in it for me?"* We and us suggests sharing: *"There's plenty for all of us."* I and me are ruggedly individualistic: *"Every man for himself."* We and us are lovingly generous: *"May we prosper together."* I and me represent the philosophy of the Republicans: *"I got mine, to hell with you."* We and us represent the philosophy of the Democrats: *"Come, join us at the table."* How one uses the pronouns *I, we/ me, us* speaks volumes of the complexion and health of one's soul. *"Illness begins with 'I', wellness begins with 'we'."* – Sivananda (1887 – 1963). *"The root of all evil is 'I', 'Me', 'Mine'."* – St. Padre Pio of Pietrelcina (1887 – 1968).

IWO JIMA – (*EE*-woh *JEE*-ma) A small uninhabited Japanese island 750 miles south of Tokyo. The 8 square mile island is dominated by Mount Suribachi, a 554 foot smoldering volcano, mother of the island. Iwo Jima is a hellish place with steamy hot black sand, a sulfuric atmosphere, and no vegetation or fresh water. In fact, the name Iwo Jima means *"Sulfur Island."* Amazingly, in February and March, 1944, The U.S. Navy landed 110,000 Marines on the island to arrest this chunk of wasteland from over 21,000 entrenched Japanese defenders. Why the urgency? To capture the 3 air strips needed as an emergency landing location for disabled B-29 bombers that were attacking Japan. (About 2,500 planes with 20,000 U.S. Airmen survived because they were able to land their damaged bombers on Iwo Jima.) The Japanese were dug into 11 miles of defensive tunnels. The desperate enemy fought with suicidal ferocity. They had to be burned out of their tunnels and caves with flamethrowers. The battle raged for 5 anguished weeks. It was the toughest combat in U.S. Marine Corps history. Though a total U.S. victory, Iwo Jima was the only Pacific battle in which American casualties outnumbered Japanese casualties. The casualties were proportionally worse than on D-Day, the invasion of France. The Marines suffered 19,217 wounded and 6,821 killed. Over 18,375 Japanese were killed, 216 taken prisoner, and about 3,000 were lost in the tunnels and caves. Iwo Jima's Mount Suribachi was the site of the marine's flag raising, which became the iconic American photo of World War Two. Incidentally: The Marines were unable to take cover in foxholes on that demonic island. The volcanic sand was too hot on which to lay. Many slept on cardboard. Incredibly, cans of food were heated in holes in the ground.

J

J – (*JAY*) The 10th letter in the English alphabet, a consonant.

J6 – (*JAY*-siks) (J Six) An abbreviation of *January 6* (2021), the day of the failed Trump insurrection. Donald J. Trump (b. 1946) hoped to lead, but instead incited a riotous mob of thousands to attack the Capitol Building, in order to prevent the transfer of the Presidency from himself to Joe Biden (b. 1942). J6 will forever stand as an infamous date in American History. It represents an attack on our Constitutional Democracy, like the rebel attack on Fort Sumpter. However, the Confederate Rebels were never able to make it to the capital. Trump, the perpetrator of the failed coup will be recorded in America's rogue gallery. Political commentator Rachel Maddow (b. 1973) rightly said: *"Future Americans will not ask why Trump wasn't held accountable for this crimes; they will asked how could the American people have elected Trump in the first place?"*

JACKAL – (*JACK*-kal) Not the crafty dog-like animal, but an intelligence agency animal. A jackal is a person who performs nefarious or despicable deeds often as an accomplice. C.I.A. jackal is an assassin who kills honest foreign leaders who cannot be bribed. In most cases, the C.I.A. jackal is working on behalf of corporate capitalists to protect their interests abroad. The victims of jackals are usually honest Socialist leaders, intent on expelling the multinational capitalists, for the good of his exploited people. A C.I.A. jackal will confront a Socialistic foreign president in his office. He may ask: *"Is that a photo of your wife and children? Lovely family. It would be too bad if something ever happened to them."* Alternatively, the jackal may present the president with two clenched fists. In one is a bank order for a great amount of money. In the other is a bullet. The jackal asks him to choose. The message is understood.

JACKASS – (*JACK*-ass) A male donkey (the female being a Jennyass). The term jackass is used as a common opprobrium for a contemptibly stupid, stubborn person, exhibiting donkey-like characteristics. It is an insult that hits home, without the use of vulgarity or obscenity. The premiere political jackass is Donald Trump (b. 1946).

JACKASSISM – (jack-*ASS*-is-um) (Jackass) Being in a most foolish, absurd, ridiculous condition. One cursed with jackassism is a perpetual clown, the court jester by design or destiny. Blunders and buffoonery accompany jackassism. Indeed, jackassism fits the role that Donald Trump (b. 1946) plays in the White House.

JACKASS ROPE – (*JACK*-ass *ROPE*) A long braided cord of tobacco coiled in a large ball and sold in measured segments. The cord resembled the rope used to secure donkeys or jackasses. Jackass rope was available in Jamaican markets and elsewhere in days gone by.

JACKED-IN – (jakt *IN*) A traditional initiation of a new gang member by obliging him (or her) to commit a crime. Theft or robbery are the usual prescribed felonies, and in rare cases murder. Criminal activity is recognized as daring by street gangs.

JACKED UP – (jakt *UP*) Originally (1860) to be jacked up meant to be hoisted, raised, lifted with a jack. This definition still applies. Today, the term *"jacked up"* also means to be hoisted, raised, lifted physiologically by drugs. It means to be energized, perhaps frantically by caffeine or amphetamines. A Caveat: Don't confuse *"jacked up"* with *"jacked off"* which has meant to masturbate since 1916.

JACKFRUIT – (*JAK*-froot) The world's largest tree-borne fruit, indigenous to southeast India and Sri Lanka. Jackfruit can weigh up to 110 pounds and grow to a 3 foot oblong oval-shape. It has a pale green *"lizard skin."* Much of the fruit is starchy and fibrous. The sweet juice is very sticky. The fruit-flesh separates into yellow kernels in which a seed is embedded. The seeds too are edible after roasting or boiling. Jackfruit is called *"vegetable meat,"* because when canned, it has the texture of meat. It can be shredded like pulled pork or chicken. The ripe jackfruit is eaten raw as a laxative. Jackfruit is the national fruit of Bangladesh and is now found throughout tropical America. Jackfruit looks like an alien pod in a science fiction movie. Incidentally: Jackfruit was brought to Jamaica by British Captain William Bligh (1754 – 1817) of *"Mutiny on the Bounty"* fames.

JACK GAGGER – (*JAK GAG*-er) In the parlance of exotic erotica, a husband who prostitutes his wife (or guy, his girlfriend). The jack gagger will solicit men to pay him for ravishing his woman. Profit is not the primary motif, for Jack is a voyeur, who must watch the copulating couple, masturbating during the steamy performance. *"The only unnatural sex act is that which you cannot perform."* – Sexologist Alfred Kinsey (1894 – 1956). *"I am different. Let that not upset you."* – Medieval Alchemist Paracelsus (c. 1493 - 1541).

JACK JUMPER – (*JAK JUM*-per) (Hopping ant) A large venomous ant of southeast Australia and Tasmania with great leaping ability. Its bite can kill, sending the victim into anaphylactic shock. Australia has more venomous creatures that can kill you, than anyplace else on Earth.

JACOBEANS – (ja-co-*BE*-ans) Members of the Stuart dynasty begun by James I Stuart (1566 – 1625). Jacobean derives from *Jacobus* which is Latin for James. King James I was the son of Mary, Queen of Scots (1542 – 1587). He succeeded Elizabeth I Tudor (1533 – 1603) to the English/Scottish thrown, who was childless. Jacobeans is not to be confused with *Jacobins* or *Jacobites*.

JACOBINS – (*JA*-co-bins) A member of a radical society or club during the French Revolution. The Jacobins promoted the Reign of Terror (revenge for centuries of oppression) and other extreme measures, against the monarchy, aristocracy, and clergy. They were chiefly active from 1789 to 1794. Their name derived from the Dominican convent in Paris where they originally met. Jacobins is not to be confused with *Jacobeans* or *Jacobites*.

JACOBITES – (*JA*-co-bites) Scottish supporters of Charles Stuart (1720 – 1788), the *"Bonnie Prince Charlie,"* called the Stuart Pretender to the Scottish throne. Incidentally: Charles was half Polish, his mother being a Polish Princess, granddaughter of Polish King John Sobieski (1629 – 1696). Jacobites is not to be confused with *Jacobeans* or *Jacobins*.

JACUZZI – (juh-*KOO*-zee) Not a cannibalistic Amazonian tribe, but the trade name of a company that manufactures hottubs, whirlpool baths, and pools. The Jacuzzi Company began as a family business founded in 1915 by the seven brothers Jacuzzi – Giacondo, Frank, Rachele, Candido, Joseph, Gelindo, and Valeriano. The company headquarters is in Irvine, California. With 8 factories in Italy, Jacuzzi is the largest hydrotherapy manufacturer in Europe. By 1979, 257 Jacuzzi family members had stakes in the business, which inevitably led to disputes. So the company was sold for $70 million dollars. The family name remains. Incidentally: The family name, *"Jacuzzi,"* is an accident. The actual sur name was *"Iacuzi."* But when brothers Giacondo and Frank first came to America in 1907 from Italy, a spelling mistake by an immigration officer changed the family name forevermore. Furthermore, as often happens, the proper name Jacuzzi has been popularly applied to the product, the hottub. This is called an *"eponym,"* (a name that becomes a thing).

JADED – (*JAY*-did) (Jadedness) Dulled or satiated by overindulgence. To feel jaded is to be bored, weary, tired of *"the same ole same ole."*

JAGUAR – (*JAG*-gwar) World's 3rd biggest cat after the tiger and lion. Jaguar is bigger than a cougar (#4) and a leopard (#5). The jaguar is the New World's biggest cat, living primarily in the Amazon rainforest, but also in Central America. Like the tiger, the Jaguar loves water, unusual for most cats. It is the best swimmer of the big cats. The jaguar is the only cat that kills with a bite to the skull, not the throat. It has the most powerful bit of all the great cats.

JAIL BAIT – (*JAY'L* bayt) According to the <u>Urban Dictionary</u>: *"Jail Bait is a female who is under the age of consent but who dresses, acts and appears as if she is over the age of consent and who does nothing to correct that impression when she is bedded."* Jail bait is a nymphet or Lolita who deceives and seduces older males with her sexuality (bait). If the men succumb to her tantalizing charm, they are liable for imprisonment (jail). The danger of copulating with an under-aged girl is the charge of *"statutory rape."* This is not *de facto* rape (actual), but *de jure* rape (legal). It is rape according to the law, not according to the girl. Even if the jail bait defends the accused man, he is still going to jail.

JAIL/PRISON – (*JAY'L, PRIS*-son) Both are governmental institutions of incarceration. But there are differences. A jail is a small lockup compared to a large prison. Jails are operated by local governments, like towns, cities, or counties. Prisons are huge institutions operated by the state or federal government. Miscreant citizens are jailed for short periods like a night, a few days, weeks, or perhaps a few months while awaiting trial. On the other hand, people are imprisoned if found guilty at trial for long periods, years, or for life. Too, in some states, capital felons are executed for heinous crimes in prisons, never in jails. Both jails and prisons are intended for social segregation, punishment, rehabilitation, and deterrence. A Caveat: The trend among conservative capitalist entrepreneurs and their Republican lackeys is to privatize jails and prisons. They would be administered by private enterprise, but funded with tax dollars. This is disastrous. When profit is the motif, service always suffers. Private jails and prisons cut-corners to save money. Guards are fewer, food is cheaper, medical care is denied. This makes these institutions far more dangerous and miserable. Why don't we privatize for profit the police and fire departments, or the U.S. Military, as far as that goes?

JAINISM – (*JANE*-is-um) (Jains) An ascetic religious offshoot of Hinduism, older than Buddhism, practiced in India. Jains practice extreme austerity, self-denial, pacifism, self-mortification, and public humiliation through nudity. Vegetarian Jains are also forbidden from eating any food grown underground. Uprooting tuber vegetables disturbs and kills insects in the soil, a Jainistic sacrilege. Devout Jains will sweep the street before every step, so not to accidentally step on an insect. After all, that insect may be a former human or relative, transmigrated through Karma. Incidentally: Jainism is the first religion that has made vegetarianism a fundamental necessity for transforming consciousness.

JAMAICA – (jam-*MAY*-ka) The 3rd largest of the 51 major Caribbean islands. The name Jamaica derives from the Taino Indian word *"Xaymaca"* (xam-*MAY*-ca) from the Arawakan language meaning *"The Island of springs."* The population stands at under 3 million, one-third of those people live in the capital Kingston. Almost the entire population is of African descent, whose ancestors were brought to the island as slaves. Jamaica is the largest English-speaking island in the Caribbean West Indies. Jamaicans speak a variety of Standard English and Jamaican *"Patwa."* Of all English dialects, Jamaican patwa is the furthest afield from the mother tongue. It was implanted on the island by uneducated Irish overseers. Perhaps 30% of the vocabulary consists of West African words. Jamaica was the first English colony acquired by conquest, taken from the Spanish in 1655. It was the first British Caribbean colony to gain independence in 1962. At the height of sugar plantation era (and slavocracy), Jamaica was one of Britain's most lucrative possessions. In 1773, Jamaica's exports to Great Britain were 10 times those from New England. From 1714 to 1773, Jamaica's exports were one-fifth greater than those of Virginia and Maryland combined. Incidentally: Jamaica was the first British colony with a postal service, 1688. Jamaica's Manchester Golf Course is the oldest in the Caribbean, 1868. Jamaica was the first Caribbean island to produce rum commercially, and the first in the Western Hemisphere to produce bananas for commerce. There are more churches, *per capita,* in Jamaica, than in any other nation on Earth. It was the first country to impose economic sanctions on the apartheid regime of South Africa. Jamaica has won more Olympic medals, *per capita,* than any other nation in the world (track). It was the only tropical country ever to qualify for a Winter Olympics event (bobsledding, Calgary Olympics, 1988). Libya, Mauritania, and Jamaica are the only nations in the world with a flag that does not include the colors red, white, and blue. Jamaica has the only national anthem that's a prayer. Footnote: The Jamaica in New York is probably a Delaware Indian word from the Algonquian language meaning *"beaver pond."*

JAMAICANESE – (jam-may-kan-*NEES*) Patwa (patois) or Dialect. Jamaicanese is Jamaican Creole. Perhaps 70% of the vocabulary is English, with 30% derived from West African languages, particularly the *Twi* dialect. The syntax does not quite conform to Standard English. From all the varieties of English worldwide, Jamaican Patwa is perhaps the farthest afield from the mother tongue. Educated middle class Jamaicans may not be able to communicate with their poor, Patwa-speaking countrymen speaking Jamaicanese.

JAMAICAN INCURSION – (jam-*MAY*-kan in-*CUR*-shun) The aborted invasion of Jamaica, 1980. Another U.S. Caribbean invasion that was averted through C.I.A. perfidy (1980). It is ironic that the U.S. is appalled at Russian intervention (with propaganda) in the 2016 election, (helping to install Trump). Since World War Two, the C.I.A. has overthrown at least 35 governments, and bombed at least 55 nations. Since 1890, American forces had invaded Latin America and the Caribbean at least 57 times. Few people know that the U.S. was poised to invade Jamaica in 1980. Michael Manley (1924 – 1997) served as Jamaican Prime Minister from 1972 – 1980, and 1989 – 1992. The Manleys were to Jamaica, what the Kennedys were to America – the political first family. Michael's father Norman Manley (1893 – 1969) had founded the left-leaning *"Peoples' National Party."* After independence (1962) the standard of living dropped for most Jamaicans. The wealthy prospered as always, but life became hard for the common folk. The American capitalist I.M.F. (International <u>M</u>onetary <u>F</u>und) sucked all the wealth it could out of the island. Michael Manley recognized that the problem was capitalism, the solution was Socialism. Manley befriended Cuba's Fidel Castro (1926 – 2016) and formulated a Socialist agenda for Jamaica. Wealthy capitalists squealed like pricked pigs. Manley reminded them that *"Five planes leave Kingston for Miami daily."* Many scurried-off (*so much for patriotism*). Manley was up for re-election in 1980. His opponent was the *"Slimy Syrian,"* Edward Seaga (1930 - 2019) of the right- leaning *"Jamaican Labor Party."* (Incidentally, the *"Labor"* Party is actually the *"Business"* Party, another euphemistic, corporate capitalist misnomer.) The C.I.A. was not about to let Jamaica become another Cuba. The C.I.A. had supported the capitalist Seaga with money and guns. Like Noriega in Panama, and Hussein in Iraq, Seaga became *"our man in Jamaica."* Seaga was an American lackey and traitor to his people. The Tivoli (*TIV*-oh-lee) ghetto of Kingston became an armed fortress for Seaga's thugs, an arsenal for C.I.A. American weapons. The campaign was violent, and the election was bloody with 899 deaths, and many more wounded as the C.I.A. had planned. Violence is always a prelude, a justification for American military intervention. If Seaga had lost, the U.S. would have invaded to end the bloodshed they had caused. On election night, C.I.A. guns were trained on the homes of every Peoples Party politician. A Manley victory would have brought in the U.S. Marines. But he didn't. American manipulation of the election threw the victory to Seaga. Suddenly Michael Manley became mysteriously silent, absent. Though he won another election for the *Peoples' Party* in 1989, serving till 1992, he was no longer a Socialist. The American wouldn't allow it. That had all the markings of a lethal C.I.A. ultimatum. No doubt, his life and those of his family were threatened by the C.I.A. to keep him *"capitalist-friendly"* and pro-American. The Manley family sank into obscurity. Jamaica was saved by the U.S. for future capitalist exploitation. The nation continued to spiral downward into poverty. Jamaica had gained political independence from Britain in 1962. Only 18 years later, Jamaica lost its economic independence to America in 1980. Here is another answer to the naïve question: *"Why do they hate us?"*

JAMAICAN PATOIS – (jam-*MAY*-kan pat-*WA*) The 3 versions of Jamaican English. *Acrolect* is very close to Standard English, with the cello-like tones of the Caribbean. Acrolect is the speech of the educated class. *Mesolect* is the intermediate speech between Standard English and street dialect. *Basilect* is the most distant variety of English from the mother tongue. Basilect is the common dialect of the uneducated, street talk or country. It is infused with much traditional African speech and a great deal of slang. With time, Basilect words and usages become legitimized, and work their way up to Mesolect and even Acrolect speech. The acrolect -> mesolect -> basilect dialect pattern applies to many patois other than Jamaican. Incidentally: In Jamaican Mesolect, patois is spelled *"patwa."*

JAMAICAN PATTY – (jam-*MAY*-kan *PAT*-tee) A popular lunch consisting of a crescent pastry, folded over, and filled with a spicy beef or chicken paste. The patty pastry is orangey-yellow and flaky. The Jamaican patty resembles the Cornish pasty, but there is no relationship. The patty was introduced by

French- Haitian refugees in the 18th century. In fact, the word patty is a corruption of the French *"pate"* (pa-*TAY)* meaning *"little pie."*

JAMAICAN SOLICITY – (jam-*MAY*-kan suh-*LIS*-si-tee) To solicit is to entreat, beseech, implore, beg. Jamaican solicity is an embarrassing bad habit of too many common Jamaicans. They will readily beg for money, materials, treats, gifts, anything. It is uncertain if this shameful behavior is characteristic of all Black Caribbeans, English-speaking West Indians only, or just Jamaicans. They will trade their honor, trade their pride to get anything for nothing. This cultural character flaw is certainly a vestigial remain of slavery, that has been passed down the generations. Under slavery, survivors learn to swallow their pride. They learn that when all goods are controlled by the master, to gain anything good, one must not be too proud to submissively beg. To gain is to win, whatever the price. For instance, strangers will come to your picnic table and plead: *"Can I have some of that cake?"* Others may be more forceful and declare: *"What do you got for me?"* If you return from overseas, you're sure to be asked: *"Did you bring me anything?"* Like a child, a Jamaican will inform you out of the blue: *"Today is my birthday,"* with the implication to give her something. As in the bad ole slave days, White people are particularly targeted. Jamaican solicity particularly shocks tourists. Do not be put on the defensive. Do not feel intimidated or guilty. Stand firm and firmly reply, *"NO!"* They may plead, but don't give in. Again rely, *"I said NO!"* They may mumble in imperceptible Jamaican *"patwa,"* or they may laugh and leave you for some weaker target. The master-slave relationship subconsciously resurrects in Jamaican solicity.

JAMBALAYA – (juhm-buh-*LY*-uh) A Creole dish consisting of rice cooked with ham, sausage, chicken, shrimp, shellfish, herbs, spices, and vegetables, especially tomatoes, onions, okra, and hot peppers. Jambalaya is a pot luck stew concoction into which any available edible is welcomed. Jambalaya is quintessentially Creole – a cultural mixture of West African, French, Spanish, and Native American cookery. Jambalaya is a Creole rendition of Spanish Paella (py-*AY*-yah).

JAMERICAN – (jam-*MER*-ri-can) A Jamaican ex-patriot in America. A Jamerican is an American citizen who is also a Jamaican immigrant. Furthermore, Jamerican is Jamaican English spoken with a contrived American accent. Jamerican is a peculiar sounding speech pattern.

JAMES BOND – (jayms *BOND*) Fictitious British secret agent *007* from the literary imagination of Ian Fleming (1908 – 1964). Fleming served in British Intelligence during World War Two. He helped to supply aid to the Yugoslav Communist hero Josip Broz Tito (1892 – 1980) and his partisans who fought the Nazis. In his adventures, Fleming had met a Serbian playboy prince, Dusko Popov (1912 - 1981) sympathetic and popular with the Nazis, (but actually a British double- agent). The prince was Fleming's model for James Bond. In retirement, Ian Fleming wrote his James Bond novels at his estate, *"Goldeneye"* in St. Mary, Jamaica. The name *"James Bond"* was discovered on Fleming's bookshelf. The real James Bond (1900 – 1989) was an American ornithologist who had written *Birds of the West Indies* (1936). In his own words, Fleming recounted the christening: *"I was looking for a name for my hero – nothing like Peregrine Carruthers or 'Steadfast' Maltravers – and I found it, on the cover of one of my Jamaican bibles: Birds of the West Indies by James Bond, an ornithological classic…. Would these books have been born if I had not been living in the gorgeous vacuum of a Jamaican holiday? I doubt it."* Incidentally: Much of the first James Bond movie, *"Dr. No"* (1962) was filmed in Kingston, Ocho Rios, Falmouth, and Crab Island, Jamaica. Scenes from the 1973 movie *"Live and Let Die"* were shot at the Green Grotto Caves and Rose Hall in Jamaica. In 2019, another 007 thriller *"No Time To Die,"* was filmed in Portland, Jamaica. (This was Daniel Craig's (b. 1968) last James Bond portrayal.) Footnote: The British actor and playwright Noel Coward (1899 – 1973) purchased Ian Fleming's estate and renamed it *"Firefly."* Coward is buried on the grounds, in St. Mary, Jamaica. Post Script: Ian Fleming (MI6) was influential in the formation of the OSS (O̲ffice of S̲trategic S̲ervices), the precursor to the CIA (C̲entral Intelligence A̲gency). By the way, President John F. Kennedy (1917 – 1963) was a big James Bond fan.

JANE SOCCERMOM – (*JANE SOCK*-er-mom) A generic, stereotypical, somewhat disparaging name for a typical suburban housewife. Jane is usually unfulfilled, trapped in a routinized life which revolves around her children and pets. She lives vicariously through her children. Jane is perpetually driving her brood to athletic practices, particularly soccer, (a mildly elitist suburban sport). In her ranch-style house with the manicured lawn, Mrs. Soccermom is bored to death. Politically, Jane Soccermom is a low-information voter. She parrots conservative talking points because suburbanites are expected to. After all, they fled the Liberal city for the conservative suburb to escape from the Blacks. So Jane is mildly bigoted out of fear. She votes Republican against her economic interests because her husband does. Jane Soccermom's prosaic existence mimics her prosaic environment.

JANGGA – (*YON*-ga) A West African word (Ashanti/Akan) for a freshwater crayfish (crawdad). The jangga resembles a little grey lobster. It lives in creeks and rivers under rocks. Jamaicans call jangga *"river shrimp."* When boiled, jangga turn bright red, and are spiced, becoming *"pepper shrimp."*

JANISSARIES – (*JAN*-ni-sar-rees) The elite military unit of the Turkish army first organized in the 14th century. The Janissaries began as Christian boys abducted in the Balkans as part of the *"Blood Tax."* They were converted to Islam and trained as fanatical fighters. The Janissaries were like the French Foreign Legion of Ottoman Turkey. Janissaries served as royal bodyguards and shock troops, special forces. Some Janissaries were sent back to their original homelands as Muslim governors. The Janissaries were corrupted with the rest of the Ottomans and were purged in 1826.

JANUS WORD – (*JAN*-us werd) An *"auto-antonym"* or *"autantonym"* (aw-*TAN*- ton-nim). A Janus word is also called a *"contronym"* (*CON*-tron-nim). It is a word with two or more meanings of which one is the opposite, reverse, a contradiction of the other. To complicate this explanation further, this linguistic idiosyncrasy is called *"enantionymy"* (en-an-ty-*ON*-ni-mee) (*"enantio"* means opposite) or *"antilogy"* (an *"anti-word"* or *"word against itself"*). At any rate, Janus was the two-faced Roman god, patron of opposites, dualities, beginnings- and-ends, entrance-and-exit. A list of autantonym, contronym, or Janus words follows. *Cleave* can mean *"to cling"* or *"to split off."* *Clip* can mean *"attach"* or *"cut off."* *Sanction* can mean *"approve"* or *"penalize."* *Oversight* can mean *"accidental omission,"* *"error,"* or *"close scrutiny and control."* *Peruse* can to *"consider with attention and in detail,"* or *"look over or through in a casual or cursory manner."* *Dust* can mean *"to remove dust* (as in house cleaning) or *"to add dust,"* (as dust for fingerprints). Janus words testify to the care we must take in accurately communicating.

JAPAN INVASION – (ja-*PAN* in-*VAY*-shuhn) Sometimes called *"X-DAY."* The anticipated and dreaded attack on the Japanese home islands that did not happen. The 2 year campaign would have been the most horrendous and fatal battle in American History. The two invasions would each be close to 3 times the magnitude of the D-Day landing. It was cancelled by the dropping of the 2 atomic bombs. *Operation Olympic,* planned for November I, 1945 would be the initial landing on the southernmost island of Kyushu by 33 Marine divisions (perhaps 495,000 troops). They would be spearheaded by the 2nd Marine Division. (Incidentally, no mention of the 2nd Division is mentioned after the first 5 days. It was assumed that they would all be annihilated.) In fact about 100,000 men were expected to be lost in the initial invasion. This would provide a staging base for *Operation Coronet* (March, 1946) the invasion on Honshu, the main island, and the drive to Tokyo. In comparison, the Japan invasion would have made the Normandy invasion seem uneventful. About 6 million U.S. and allied troops would encounter about 4 million Japanese soldiers. Too, over 30 million Japanese conscripts were pledged to defend their home to the death. The Americans expected to suffer over 1.7 million casualties. Well over 10 million Japanese were expected to be killed. The Japanese intentionally made the Battle of Okinawa (April 1 – June 22, 1945) exceptionally gruesome as a forewarning and preview of what to expect in the Japan invasion. The Japanese intended to transfer their million-man *Kwangtung Army* home from China to fight the Americans in the south, and the Russians invading Hokkaido Island in the north. (No telling how many Japanese would be killed by the Red Army.) Over 1,500 kamikaze planes were held in reserve to launch against the U.S. invasion fleet, especially targeting troop transports, hospital ships, and blood bank vessels. Three U.S. freighters would carry only whole blood. It would be a blood bath. The entire Japanese population was mobilized, *"kamikaze-ized."* Citizens pledged to serve as suicide bombers. Terrorism, sniping, guerrilla, and urban warfare were expected and feared. The government distributed millions of pamphlets on *"How To Kill Americans,"* with common kitchen and garden implements. Schoolchildren were issued wooden spears and drilled on school playgrounds in how to kill Americans. The Japanese believed that if enough Americans were killed, the U.S. would sue for peace. (Another Japanese miscalculation.) Japan had chemical and biological weapons that they had used against the Chinese. Indeed, fanaticism would surely have been met with fanaticism. The U.S. planned to gas 26 Japanese cities, killing over 5 million residents, 15 days before the invasion. The Japan invasion and pacification would have been hellishly atrocious. Too, Japan, like Korea, would have been divided into Communist North, and capitalist South, the North possibly falling under Russian control, as did North Korea. This is what the demonic atomic bombs prevented: a ghastly tradeoff.

JAPANESE SURRENDER – (jap-pan-*NEES* sur-*REN*-der) The Japanese surrender on the deck of the U.S.S. Missouri, September 2, 1945 formally ended World War Two. The capitulation is attributed to the dropping of the atomic bombs on Hiroshima (August 6) and Nagasaki (August 9). What's omitted is that Russia declared war on Japan on August 8, 1945. It was the fear of a Russian invasion, not the atomic bombings that convinced the Japanese to end the war. The Japanese wanted to surrender to the Americans before the Russians had a chance to invade. Japan had humiliated Russia in the Russo-Japanese War (1904-1905). Russian territory on the Pacific was seized by Japan. Russia yearned for revenge. In 1939, the Japanese were badly mauled by the Russians led by General Georgy Zhukov (1896 – 1974) in Siberia. Since then, the Japanese had been paranoid, terrified of the Russians. On August 9, 1945, The Russians smashed the Japanese in Manchuria, Mongolia, and invaded North Korea. The Russian invasion force was

1,600,000 tough veterans who had destroyed the Nazis in Europe. The Red Army attacked South Sakhalin and the Kuril Islands north of Japan. The Russians recovered territory lost in 1905. Now they were poised to invade Hokkaido, the northernmost Japanese home Island. Next in line was Honshu, the main island. So on August 15, Emperor Hirohito (1901 – 1989) announced the secession of hostilities, in order to avert a Russianinvasion. If the Russians had invaded, Japan would be two nations today, as are the two Koreas. It must be noted that the American atomic bombs dissuaded the Russians from challenging the Americans by invading Japan. Ironically, the same atomic bombs that initially ravaged Japan, ultimately rescued Japan from Russia.

JAPANESE WAR AIMS – (jap-pan-*NEES WAR AMES*) Why Japan started World War Two in Asia. America brokered the peace in the Russo-Japanese War (1904-1905). Japan felt cheated by the Americans. Arrogance: The Japanese felt superior, a master race over other human beings. In the 1930's, war- mongering militarists gained control of the Japanese government. America had gained the Philippine Islands in the Spanish-American War (1898). Japan desired this territory just south of their nation. Japan was a modern industrialized country with no natural resources. Japan wanted China's coal and iron, Indonesia's oil, tin, and rubber. Japan resented European colonies in East Asia. Japan wanted to seize control of East Asia, then all of Asia. The U.S. fleet stationed at Pearl Harbor, Hawaii, blocked Japan from realizing her war aims. At its height, the Japanese had conquered 17 million square miles of Asia and the Pacific, about 20% of the globe. Japan was responsible for over 50 million deaths in World War Two.

JAPLISH – (*JAP*-lish) The English-infused Japanese language. Over 25,000 English words are in everyday use in Japan.

JAVELIN – (*JAV*-uh-lin) A throwing spear, an ancient, primal weapon. The first javelin was prehistoric, a simple wooden shaft with a sharpened point. Unlike the trusting spear the javelin left the hand, being hurled threw the air at game or an enemy. It was the first manufactures missile, predated only by the rock. Javelins have been in use for about 400,000 years. Charring the wooden point of the javelin hardened it. Later, a sharpened stone or metal point was attached to the javelin. The Roman javelin was called a *"pilum."* Its point was at the end of a soft metal rod that bent on impact. This javelin would pierce the enemy's shield and become locked-in, forcing the foe to discard the shield, becoming most vulnerable. The Javelin has again become a crucial weapon in warfare, as is being witnessed in the Russo-Ukrainian War (February 2022 to present). Today's Javelin is a sophisticated, albeit simple guided missile, manufactured first in 1996 by the American Lockheed Martin and Raytheon corporations. At $178,000 a piece, it is a rather cheap weapon that gives a lot of bang for the buck. The Javelin is a shoulder-fired, guided anti-tank missile that can be deployed by a single soldier. Ironically, this high-tech Javelin requires less effort to deploy than its predecessor thousands of year ago. Today's Javelin is a *"fire-and-forget"* weapon. On a video screen, the gunner places the cursor over the selected target. The Javelin command launch unit then sends a lock- on-before-launch signal to the missile. The operator shoots and takes cover. No aiming required. The missile is programmed to find its way to the target. A Javelin will blow the turret right off a Russian tank. The Javelin missile is one of many reasons why the Goliath Russia has been unable to vanquish the Ukrainian David. So popular and successful has this weapon been, that the Ukrainian soldiers had christened it *"Saint Javelin."*

JAZZ – The word originated as a musical slang term meaning *"speed up."* Jazz is an American contribution to the world of music. Jazz was born in New Orleans around the beginning of the 20th century. It was primarily conceived by African- American musicians. Jazz subsequently developed through various increasingly complex styles. All variations are marked by intricate, propulsive rhythms, polyphonic ensemble playing, improvisation, virtuosic solos, and melodic freedom. The harmonic idiom of jazz ranges from simple diatonicism through chromaticism to atonality. Of all classes of music, jazz in unique. It is totally aleatoric, meaning improvised. No two renditions of a jazz piece, even by the same musician, will ever be played identically. *"Anyone who understands jazz knows that you can't understand it. It's too complicated. That's what's so simple about it."* – Yogi Berra (1925 – 1015).

J'CANS – (*JAY*-cans) A truncated, abbreviated reference to Jamaicans.

JEALOUSY – (*JEL*-lus-see) The fearful feeling that *"You want what's mine."* Science fiction writer Robert A. Heinlein (1907 – 1988) wrote that: *"A competent and self-confident person is incapable of jealousy in anything. Jealousy is invariably a symptom of neurotic insecurity."* Incidentally: Jealousy is always confused with envy, which is the covetous feeling that *"I want what's yours."* According to Mary Baker Eddy (1821 – 1910), the founder of the Christian Science Religion: *"Jealousy is the grave of affection."* *"Jealousy is not contemptible, real love has a beak and claws."* – Simone de Beauvoir (1908 – 1986).

JEEPERS – (*JEE*-pers) An interjection denoting an exclamation of mild surprise or wonder. One might hear: *"Jeepers, what an ass!"* Incidentally: Jeepers is a euphemism for Jesus. Likewise, *"Jeepers creepers"* is a euphemism for Jesus Christ. *"Jeepers creepers, where'd you get thos peepers? Jeepers creepers, where'd you get those eyes?"* – Song from the movie, *"Going Places"* (1938), sung by Louis Armstrong (1901 - 1971).

JEEZ – (also Geez) An interjection denoting surprise, disappointment, or astonishment. One might say: *"Jeez, stop whining!"* Incidentally: Jeez is a euphemism for Jesus.

JEHOVAH'S WITNESSES – (ja-*HOE*-va *WIT*-nes-ses) An American-bred cult-cum- religion. Jehovah means God. To witness means to proselytize or to missionary. There are over 8.4 million Jehovah's Witnesses in the United States and around the world. The founder of this religious cult was Minister Charles Taze Russell (1852 – 1916) in Allegheny, Pennsylvania in 1884. *The New World Translation* is the Witnesses' version of the Bible. Their ubiquitous publication is *The Watchtower.* It is the most widely circulated magazine in the world. Over 62 million copies are published every 2 months in 303 languages. As conscientious objectors, over 3,500 Witnesses were arrested and jailed during World War Two. They refuse to pledge allegiance to the flag, for their only allegiance is to Jehovah (God). The Jehovah's Witnesses is an ambitiously proselytizing religion. They are noted for their doorbell ringing campaigns in order to win salvation. Though they do not believe in hell, they do believe that they must work their way to salvation. The Witnesses believe in one God but no Holy Trinity. Jesus is not God, but God's first creation. When in heaven, Jesus is transformed into the Archangel Michael. He died on the cross, but only his soul ascended to heaven. Jehovah's Witnesses accepts predestination. God has pre-chosen certain people to join Him and Jesus (St. Michael) in Heaven. These chosen people are the *"The Little Flock,"* consisting of only 144,000 individuals. The anointed (the church leadership) have a reserved place in heaven. This number derives from verses in Revelations 7: 4-8, which actually refers to the 12 Tribes of Israel. *"An angel...put a seal on the foreheads of the servants of our God. Then I heard the number of those who were sealed: 144,000 from all the tribes of Israel."* All the rest of the Jehovah's Witnesses, *"The Other Sheep,"* are called *"Jonadabs."* They are the drones, the worker bees who must serve as missionaries in order to win salvation. But even all this effort will not get them to heaven. The best that the Jonadabs can hope for is eternal life on an Eden-like Earth. Jehovah's Witnesses are rabidly anti-Christian. The witnesses believe in an upcoming atomic holocaust, the *"Battle of Armageddon,"* in which all the Christians will perish. After the battle, there will be a 1,000 year period before the Last Judgement. All the great Biblical personalities will be resurrected. Those survivors who had not a chance to accept the teachings of Jehovah's Witnesses can convert during the millennium. After this period, the 144,000 anointed will go to heaven, while the worthy Jonadabs will enjoy Eden-on-Earth. The rest of humanity will be annihilated, body and soul. Obviously, it is incorrect to include the Jehovah's Witnesses as a Christian sect. Incidentally: About 5,000 Jehovah's Witnesses were murdered by the German Nazis in concentration camps during the Holocaust of 1933 – 1945. *"Christ came to the Kingdom in 1914, but unseen by men."* – <u>*The Truth Shall Make You Free.*</u>

JEJUNE – (je-*JOON*) Dull, insipid. Being jejune is being without interest or significance. The juvenile, immature, childish are jejune.

JEN – In Chinese philosophy, virtue, true manhood, the moral principles of masculinity.

JENKEM – (*JEN*-kem) The stench of the gas released by fermented human feces. It has been discovered that the foul stinking gas when inhaled, acts as an intoxicant, actually a hallucinogen. One must be most desperate to get high, to take the time to inhale the jenkem. It must reek to *high* heaven, but high is high.

JENNY ASS – (*JEN*-nee *ASS*) Not a reference to Jennifer's derriere. A jenny ass is a female donkey, the female counterpart to the male jackass. A jenny ass is a beast of burden. One may mount a jenny ass and take her for a ride.

JERK – (*JERK*) The popular Jamaican-style barbecue. The Taino Indians and Buccaneers [read: *Barbecuers*] contributed to this delicious rustic cuisine. The meat (usually pork or chicken) is seasoned with hot pepper and roasted on a grill of pimento logs. The spicy wood imparts its flavorful essence into the meat. Incidentally: Jerk Bar-BQ is older than Jamaica. But this cooking technique was popularized at Boston Beach, in Portland Jamaica, in the northeast of the island.

JEREMIAD – (jer-ra-*MY*-ad) A long, mournful speech. A prolonged lamentation. Jeremiad is a reference to the Old Testament Prophet Jeremiah (c. 650 – c. 570 BCE). Jeremiah begged and warned his Hebrew people to quit their evil ways. He railed against idolatry, greed, distributive injustice. Jeremiah is credited for writing the Biblical Book of Lamentations, a collection of Jeremiads.

JERRY-BUILT – (*JER*-ree *BILT*) Constructed haphazardly with cheap materials, in order to save money. A jerry-built structure is flimsy, shoddy, and unsafe. Jerry-building appeals to corporate capitalists, motivated by profits, rather than safety, workmanship, or customer satisfaction.

JESUIT'S CREDO – (*JEZ*-soo-wits *CRAY*-dow) *"Omnia ad majorem gloriam Dei."* (All for the greater glory of God.)

JESUITICAL – (jez-soo-*WIT*-ti-cal) Intriguing, sly, crafty, being of a *"cloak-and- dagger"* nature. Jesuitical refers to the Jesuit Order (*The Society of Jesus*). They were founded by Ignatius Loyola (c. 1491 – 1556), a Spanish soldier turned priest. The Jesuits were organized in a para-military fashion. They were the shock-troops of the Church. Jesuits were used by the Catholic Church during the Reformation and Counter-Reformation as the spies, saboteurs, assassins, partisans of the Vatican. This is how jesuitical came to be associated with espionage, connivance and conspiracy. Catholic Jesuits won Poland away from the Protestants, to the detriment of the Jews and the Polish Kingdom. Too, it was the Jesuits who inspired the Catholic Mary Queen of Scots (1542 – 1587) to conspire against her cousin Queen Elizabeth I (1533 – 1603) that cost Mary her head.

JESUS – (*JEE*-zus) (c. 7-2 BCE – c. 30-33 CE) The name is the Greek rendition of the Hebrew *Yeshua.* In English it's *Joshua.* In Latin, Jesus is *Jason,* and in Arabic, *Issa.* The name means *"salvation,"* or *"savior."* Jesus was the greatest avatar to grace this planet, truly the Son of God, *as are you and me.* The difference was that Jesus believed it. Indeed, Jesus was the most enlightened individual of all time. No one was ever in greater atonement [read: *at-one- ment*] with God than was Jesus. Actually, he was a rabbi of the common folk, a radical left-wing Pharisee in the tradition of the Prophet Isaiah. Jesus was mesmerizing, literally. He was a hypnotist, a hypnotic healer. Of his 24 miracles, 33 (73%) entailed healings. Jesus healed by manipulating, controlling then changing the sufferer's mind. Jesus insisted that his patients have faith that they believe in him, in order for the cure to take hold. Therefore, Jesus the *Christ* was the first *Christian Scientist.* This is the ancient *Gnostic Christian* view of Jesus. It maintains that Jesus was a man, who became a *"Christ"* when God's power was increased in him, above other human beings. Of course, this God power is within us all to a greater or lesser degree. We are all *Christs.* Jesus said: *"Whoever believes in me, the things I do* [miracles], *you shall do, and greater things shall you do."* – John 14:12. Personally, Jesus exhibited the slurring speech, characteristic of a Galilean (comparable to a *"hillbilly"*). This would prompt some sophisticated Judeans to laugh (until they heard his message). In the Scriptures, Jesus referred to himself as the *"Son of God"* 5 times, and the *"Son of Man"* 86 times. It is the divinity of Jesus that presents problems for Jews, and his humanity that presents problems for Christians. Jesus was a great miracle worker, edifying teacher, and a dedicated Socialist. Jesus' *"Social Gospel"* is a Socialist admonition. *"I was hungry and you fed me. I was thirsty and you quenched me. I was naked and you clothed me. I was ill and you healed me. I was homeless and you sheltered me. I was imprisoned and you visited me. Truly I say to you. What you have done to the least of my children, you have done unto me."* – Matthew 25: 35 – 40. *"Jesus was the first Socialist, the first to seek a better life for mankind."* – Russian Communist/Socialist leader Mikhail Gorbachev (1931 - 2022).

JESUSCARE – (*JEE*-sus-care) Healthcare as Jesus would have had it. Anyone who knows the Scriptures understands Jesus' *"Social Gospel."* They would know that Jesus spoke of economic disparity more than any other topic. Twenty-four of the thirty-three (73%) miracles that Jesus performed concerned healings. Jesus never charged a cent in premiums or deductibles. He was never concerned about people's pre-existing conditions. Social status was meaningless to Jesus. He cared for all, especially the unhealthy, who could not care for themselves. His Apostolate was a non-profit organization. Jesuscare extended beyond healing and health. He was speaking to all of us when he said: *"Peter, If you love me, feed my lambs, feed my sheep,"* (John 21:15). In the Social Gospel Jesus said: *"I was hungry and you fed me. I was thirsty and you quenched me. I was naked and you clothed me. I was ill and you healed me. I was imprisoned and you visited me. Truly I say to you, what you have done for the least of my children, you have done unto me,"* (Matthew 25: 35 – 40). Jesus multiplied the loaves and fishes and distributed the food free of charge. Jesus' *Social* Gospel expressed his *Social*-ism, which is the essence of Jesuscare. Anyone who supports legislation that would deny healthcare or take food out of the mouths of poor people are repudiating Jesus, and all he stood for. The Socialistic Pope Francis I (b. 1936) calls such people *"Fake Christians,"* (Republicans Paul Ryan (b. 1970) and Ted Cruz (b. 1970). *"Jesus preached more and taught more about helping the poor and the sick and the hungry than he did about heaven and hell. Shouldn't that tell us something?"* – Writer John Grisham (b. 1955).

JESUSISM – (*JEE*-sus-is-um) Taking the Social Gospel of Jesus (c. 7-2 BCE – c. 30- 33 CE) seriously, literally. Feed the poor, clothe the naked, house the homeless, simply eradicate poverty through distributive justice was the Social Gospel. According to attorney and author, John Grisham (b. 1955) *"Jesus preached more and taught more about helping the poor and the sick and the hungry than he did about heaven and hell. Shouldn't that tell us something?"* Jesusism entails the acknowledgement that Jesus was a Socialist. *"Come ye blessed of my Father, inherit the Kingdom prepared for you from the foundation of the world. For I was hungry and you fed me. I was thirsty and you gave me drink. I was a stranger and you took me in. I was naked and you clothed me. I was sick and you visited me. I was in prison, and you came on to me. Verily I say unto you, in as much as you have done it to one of the least of my brethren, you've done it to me."* – Jesus (Matthew 25: 34–40). Incidentally: The great Church Father St. Jerome (c. 345 – c. 420) admonished: *"Our walls glitter with gold, yet Christ is dying at our doors in the person of his poor, naked, and hungry." "Capitalism is the way of the devil and exploitation. If you really want to look at things through the eyes of Jesus Christ – who I think was the first Socialist – only Socialism can really create a genuine society."* – Hugo Chavez (1954 – 2013) Socialist Revolutionary President of Venezuela. *"Jesus was an anarchist savior. That's what the Gospels tell us."* – Priest and Philosopher Ivan Illich (1926 – 2002). *"Jesus was the first Socialist, the first to try to create a better life for the people."* – Mikhail Gorbachev (b. 1931), Last Russian Communist Leader.

JESUS JUSTICE – (*JEE*-sus *JUS*-tiss) The socio-economic behavior, conduct, and compassion exemplified by the avatar Jesus of Nazareth (c. 7-2 BCE – c. 30-33 CE). Jesus Justice is Socialistic. *"Whoever has two shirts is to share with him who has none, and whoever has food should do likewise."* – Luke 3:11. And Jesus Justice is merciful. *"If anyone would take your shirt, give him your coat as well."* – Matthew 5:40. Jesus Justice is fair. *"Let him who is without sin throw the first stone."* – John 8:7. Jesus Justice eschews violence. *"Put away your sword, for he who lives by the sword shall perish by the sword."* – Matthew 26:52. Jesus Justice is generous. *"If you would be perfect, go, sell what you possess and give to the poor…and come follow me."* – Matthew 19:21. Jesus Justice is helpful. *"If anyone forces you to go one mile, go with him two miles."* – Matthew 5:41. Jesus Justice is honest. *"Woe to you hypocrites! For you are like whitewashed tombs, which outwardly appear beautiful, but within are full of dead people's bones and all uncleanness."* – Matthew 23:27. Jesus Justice is pacifistic. *"You have heard it said, 'An eye for an eye and a tooth for a tooth.' But I say to you, Do not resist the one who is evil. But if anyone slaps you on the right cheek, turn to him the other also."* – Matthew 5: 38-39. Jesus Justice is forgiving. *"Father forgive them, for they know not what they do.* – Luke 23:34. Jesus may have been the most perfect human being to have walked the Earth. And indeed, *"Jesus was the first Socialist, the first to want a better life for mankind."* – Russian Socialist Leader Mikhail Gorbachev (b. 1931).

JESUS' SIBLINGS – (*JEE*-zus-es *SIB*-lings) The brothers and sisters of Jesus of Nazareth (c. 7-2 BCE – c. 30-33 CE), the Galilean carpenter/prophet/avatar. Jesus had at least 6 or 7 siblings. It would be socially disgraceful at that time for a Jewish couple, Joseph and Mary to be childless, or confine their family to one child. Furthermore, it would be contrary to God's Will: *"Be fruitful, increase and multiply and fill the earth."* – Genesis 9:1. So Jesus indeed came from a large family, which was an average family, at that time and place. The Book of Matthew 13:55, and Mark 6:3 mentions four of Jesus' brothers: James, Joseph (Joses), Judas (Jude) and Simon. According to John 7:5, James and his brothers disbelieved and disapproved of Jesus' ministry initially, but were eventually converted into disciples. (Jesus said: *"A prophet is not accepted by his own relatives in his own household."* – Mark 6:40.) John 7:5 also eludes to two un- named sisters. (Chances are they were Martha and Mary, with brother-in-law Lazarus.) James the Just was the oldest brother of Jesus. Jesus was somewhere in the middle of the birth order. The youngest brother (perhaps 17 during the crucifixion) was John, *"The disciple who Jesus loved the most."* John was the only brother to stand beneath the cross. In the Book of John 19:25 – 27, Jesus said to his mother Mary from the cross: *"Woman, behold your son [John]!"* Then he said to John: *"Behold your mother [Mary]!"* The Church felt it necessary to strip Jesus of his siblings, his family, in order to postulate the divine virginity myth of Mary.

JESUS WEPT – (*JEE*-zus *WEPT*) The shortest verse in the Bible, from the New Testament Book of John 11:35.

JET – (*JET*) A stream of liquid or gas forcefully shot out of a small nozzle. A jet produces propulsion, as in a jet engine. A jet engine in an aircraft creates a simpler and faster flying machine than a piston-driven aircraft with propellers. Air is taken into the jet engine which explosively burns an alcohol-based fuel, providing the jet with thrust. The key is the oxygen intake. Jets must remain in the oxygenated atmosphere in order to burn fuel and fly. Jet engines perform most efficiently in the thin air of the stratosphere. Jets cannot venture into airless space. Rockets, which work on the same jet-thrust principle can, because rockets carry their own oxygen supply in liquid or solid form. Rockets are not dependent on atmospheric oxygen.

JET LAG – (*JET* lag) Physical malaise due to long-distance flight travel. Rapidly crossing several time zones disturbs one's circadian rhythm (biological clock, sleep schedule). Normal sleep patterns are disturbed which result in an exhausted hang-over sensation. The lack of rest and ill feeling can depress the immune system, which can result in more serious illness. Usually, jet lag symptoms are tiredness, lethargy, irritability, and suppressed intellectual ability. Globe-trotting diplomats better take jet lag into consideration. Incidentally: *Emporiatrics* is a new branch of medicine concerned with the health of travelers.

JETSAM – (*JET*-sum) Jettisoned goods, *intentionally* cast overboard in an emergency and washed ashore. Unlike flotsam, jetsam is the legal property of the finder. So beach combers can legally keep jetsam finds, but not flotsam finds.

JETSTREAM – (*JET*-streem) Rapidly flowing river of air in the high atmosphere, with winds greater than 57 mph. The Jetstream is a westerly ribbon of wind blowing at about 100 to 300 mph. A plane with the Jetstream at its back will travel faster, arrive quicker, and save fuel. Conversely, to be flying into the teeth of the Jetstream with slow down the aircraft, requiring the burning of more fuel (in really bad cases, all the fuel). The Jetstream was discovered by long distance bomber pilots during World War Two (1939 - 1945).

JETTISON – (*JET*-ti-sin) (Jettisoned, Jettisoning) To cast goods overboard in order to lighten a vessel or aircraft or to improve its stability in an emergency. To jettison is to discard or throw-off any burden or obstacle. The items or material jettisoned is called jetsam. Jettisoning is an intentional act and loss. So the jetsam that is jettisoned belongs to the finder (finders keepers). Flotsam is accidentally lost overboard, not jettisoned. So flotsam still belongs to the owner who lost it.

JEWISH BRIGADE – (*JOO*-ish *BRIG*-gayd) (1944 – 1946) A military formation of the British Army composed of 5,000 Jewish volunteers from Yeshuv, Palestine during World War Two. The Brigade, formed in 1944, was commanded by Jewish-British officers. They fought the Germans in the Italian campaign. The Jewish Brigade took it upon itself to hunt-down obscure Nazi war criminals, too lowly to make it to Nuremberg for trial. They held quick courts in the woods. The Nazis judged guilty were strangled to death. After the war, Jewish Brigade veterans helped Holocaust survivors to immigrate to Palestine. What the Jews learned in the British Army during World War Two would serve them well in organizing the Israeli Army, and the fight for nationhood against the Palestinians and their allies.

JEWISH NAZIS – (*JOO*-ish *NAZ*-sees) Right-wing, even fascist Jews. Jewish Nazis are racist ultra-nationalists content to use anti-democratic, dictatorial methods of governance. European History, culminating in the Holocaust (1933 – 1945) has inspired most Jews to be Liberal, tolerant, even Socialistic. (*"Live and let live"* is a Yiddish Jewish proverb.) A democratic dissemination of power proved to be the safest environment for the Jews everywhere. Nazi Jews are a rare aberration. They are usually in positions of governmental power. Nazi Jews are white supremacists, forgetting or ignoring that true Nazis consider Jews (and Slavs) to be *"sub-human."* Nevertheless, they tend to serve as advisors to neo- Nazi leaders like Donald Trump (b. 1946). Trump's most Nazi Jew is the viciously racist, cold-blooded Stephen Miller (b. 1985). Miller is responsible for blocking legal immigration, breaking-up families, ripping children away from parents, and putting kids in cages. The concentration camps for Mexican migrants are a Millerian manifestation. Miller provides the terror in the deterrent of the Trump immigrant policy. Miller is a ghastly ghoul. His very appearance is demonic. Miller's fiendishness is etched in his gaunt face. Disney could not create a more Mephisphelean looking figure on the drawing board than Steven Miller. Hollywood's central casting would put him in a Nazi SS uniform on sight. Miller looks the part because he is the part. His satanic heart of darkness reflects in his face. Jew or no Jew, Stephen Miller would be promoted to the highest echelons of Adolf Hitler's (1889 – 1945) *Death's Head Division.*

JEWITCH – (*JOO*-wich) (also Jewwitch, Jew Witch) (Jewitchery) A Jewish witch. Someone who identifies as both Jewish and as a witch. The nature of both Judaism and Witchcraft can vary greatly among individual Jewitches. The mystic Kabbalah is a treasure trove of Jewitchery.

JEWISH SUPREMACISTS – (*JOO*-ish suhp-*PREM*-uh-sists) (Jewish Supremacy) The extreme right-wing, militant Israelis, who intend to make Israel into an exclusive, Judeo-Theocracy. In Conservative Judaism (like Islamism), the borders among religion, nationality, and ethnicity are blurred. In this respect, the Jewish Supremacists are similar to the American Christian Nationalist White Supremacists. Both groups are fascistically oriented. Jewish supremacists are ultra-nationalists as well as Eretz Israel expansionists. Their grand strategy is to drive out all Palestinians, and eradicate all Arabic, Islamic influence in Israel.

Almost all Israeli Jews are European immigrants, or *"Sabra,"* the Israeli-born descendants of European immigrants. The Jewish supremacists among them want to make Israel into a European nation in the Middle East (albeit illiberal). The Jewish supremacists are not democratic, but rather authoritarian. There will be no peace for Israel as long as the Jewish supremacists wield any influence. *"Oppressed minorities, on becoming majorities, oppress minorities."*

JEWITCHERY – (joo-*WICH*-er-ree) (Jewitch) The practice of Judeo-Witchcraft. Jewitchery is the practice of magick by a Jewish witch. Jewitchery melds the mystic aspects of both traditions. The Jewish Kabbalah is a treasure trove of esoteric arts.

JEW PLUM – (*JOO PLUM*) (Also known by its corrupted name, June Plum.) A tropical fruit native to the South Pacific, brought to Jamaica in 1882 by British Captain William Bligh (1754 - 1817). Jew plum grows on a large tree up to 99 feet tall. The greenish-yellow fruit is the size and shape of a large egg. The plum had a thick, leathery skin and dendritic (fibrous or spiny) seeds. While unripe, the flesh is crisp and firm with a tart acidic taste. As it ripens, it turns yellow and becomes soft and develops a sweet taste and fragrant aroma. Both ripe and unripe fruits are eaten raw. Jew plum is also prepared by juicing, stewing with ginger and sugar, pickled with peppers and spices.

JEWS – (*JOOS*) A small but incredibly influential ethic group who practice the religion of Judaism. Jews were originally a Middle Eastern people, many of whom were scattered among European counties, especially in Slavic Eastern Europe. Jews had aggressively won a homeland in the Middle East called Israel. Jewish populations are found all over the world, particularly in the U.S.A. where they are the most successful Americans. Jews have been the most persecuted people in history. Nevertheless they have been influential far beyond their numbers. This influence is the result of Jesus of Nazareth (c. 4 BCE – 30-33 CE), who was born a Jew. The Jewish people have given us the Bible, as well as Spinoza, Marx, Freud, Einstein, and countless other professors, scientists, physicians, and philosophers.

JFK ASSASSINATION – (jay-ef-*KAY* ass-sas-sin-*NAY*-shun) The murder of President John F. Kennedy (1917 – 1963) in Dallas Texas on November 23, 1963. Many people had many reasons to see Kennedy killed. The C.I.A. hated JFK for purging the agency and firing its head, Allen Dulles (1893 – 1969) in 1961. This was after the Bay of Pigs fiasco to invade Cuba. The Mafia hated John Kennedy and his brother Robert for their vigorous war on organized crime. Too, JFK had an affair with the mistress of a Mafia Don. Corporate capitalists hated Kennedy for his intension to end the lucrative War in Vietnam. It has been suggested that the Mafia planned the killing of the President, in order to get rid of his brother, the Attorney General. Robert Kennedy (1925 – 1968) had declared war on the Mafia and had put Teamster President Jimmy Hoffa (1913 – 1975?) in prison. Killing RFK would result in his replacement by a more fanatical crime buster by JFK. But kill the President, and the Attorney General is replaced as well. You're rid of both Kennedys. In May, 1963, Hoffa went to prison. John Kennedy was dead in 8 months. New Orleans Mafia boss Carlos Marcello (1910 – 1993) initially order the murder of President Kennedy. In 2014, a former C.I.A. and Mafia associate, James Files (b. 1942) admitted being President Kennedy's assassin. James Files (alias Jimmy Sutton) worked under Chicago Mafia boss Sam Giancana (1908 – 1975), as did Jacob Rubenstein (alias Jack Ruby 1911 - 1967). Assassination plots against John Kennedy failed in Chicago and Tampa but succeed in Dallas. Lee Harvey Oswald (1939 – 1963) was innocent, used as a patsy, as he had claimed. Oswald was hung-out as a red herring. But before he could talk, Oswald was killed by Jack Ruby (1963), James Files' associate. James Files (if still alive) is serving a 50 year murder sentence at the Stateville Correctional Center near Chicago, for an unrelated murder.

JFK'S CURSE – (jay-ef-*KAYS KURS*) President John F. Kennedy (1917 – 1963) suffered from *"Addison's disease"* or primary adrenal insufficiency. This is a genetically initiated endocrine disorder in which the adrenal glands do not produce a sufficient amount of the hormones *cortisol* and *aldosterone.* The disease was discovered by the English physician Thomas Addison (1795 – 1860) in 1855. Perhaps 12 out of 100,000 people are plagued with Addison's disease. The physical symptoms include: darkening of the skin in areas, fatigue, weakness, lowered blood pressure, nausea and vomiting, weight loss, extreme abdominal and lower back pain. The mental symptoms of the disease are: anxiety, irritability, depression, poor concentration, loss of consciousness, and possibly death. JFK was known to suffer from severe back pain, attributed to his military injury in World War Two (1941 – 1945). This was a lie. The Kennedys and JFK's staff covered-up his Addison's disease. JFK fainted on many occasions and had been rushed to the hospital. His entourage was able to keep this secret. He once lamented that he would give up all of his fame and political success, just to be pain free. Once in the upper private residence of the White House, John Kennedy's brother, Robert Kennedy (1925 – 1968) was snooping in the medicine cabinet. Bobby was astounded at what he discovered – opioid drugs and cocaine. He confronted his brother: *"Jack, what are you taking? These are illegal and dangerous!"* John bellowed back: *"I don't care if its horse piss! It makes me feel good!"* Of course, President John F. Kennedy was put out of his Addison's disease misery in Dallas, Texas, on November 22, 1963. He was 46 years old. Some doctors believed that he didn't have long to live. They doubt if President Kennedy would have survived an entire second term.

JIHAD – (*JEE*-hod) Arabic word meaning *"struggle."* The term appears in the Quran (Koran) 164 times. A jihad may be activist or quietist. There may be jihad of the heart, tongue, hand, or sword. In most references jihad applies to a personal war of the individual against sin, temptation, and human frailty. The most common jihad is that of the heart. It consists of a spiritual transformation toward enlightenment and godliness. Jihad also refers to the *"defense"* of Islam from non-believers (*infidels*). The *Mujahedin* who perish in defense of Islam are awarded a fast pass to Paradise. Therefore, proper jihad as a holy war is purely *defensive.* Radical Islamists who go on the *offensive* abroad are not practicing jihad, but naked terrorism, contrary to the Quran. *"Declare your jihad on thirteen enemies you cannot see – Egoism, Arrogance, Conceit, Selfishness, Greed, Lust, Intolerance, Anger, Lying, Cheating, Gossiping, and Slander. If you can master and destroy them, then will you be ready to fight the enemy you can see."* – Persian Philosopher Al-Ghazali (1058 – 1111).

JINGOISM – (*JING*-go-is-um) (Jingoistic) Extreme, aggressive nationalism, a prelude to war. Jingoism is belligerent chauvinism, *"patriotism on steroids."* *"America: Love it or leave it"* is jingoistic.

JINRICKSHAW – (jin-*RICK*-shaw) (also Jinrikisha or Rickshaw) A small, two- wheeled buggy with a fold-down top, accommodating a passenger, pulled by a runner. Jinrickshaws were widely used in pre-modern Japan and China. One can hardly imagine a more menial and servile occupation than a jinrickshaw runner.

Human muscle power substituted for animal muscle power. The runner served as a human animal. But jinrickshaws were replaced by horse power, in the form of the taxicab.

JITNEY – (*JIT*-nee) A small bus that transports passengers short distances on regular circuitous routes. For example, a jitney may make the round from the hotel to the shopping district and back all day.

JOB – (*JOB*) A piece of work, whereas labor or work implies steady, long term employment. Job is technically differentiated from work. Work may consist of several jobs. One may have a multiple job description at work. At work, one may have the occasion to say, *"That's not my job."* So a job is a specific task, assignment, project done as part of one's occupation or for an agreed wage. If you work as a mason, your job today could be to build a fireplace, tomorrow, a wall.

JOBBING GANG – (*JOB*-bing *GANG*) Slaves owned by an urban master, in contrast to a plantation slavocrat. Jobbing gang or slaves were vocationally skilled laborers. They could be carpenters, masons, plumbers, house painters, who were hired-out by their master. The jobbing gang would leave to perform a project, then remit back to the master with the wages they had earned.

JOB CREATORS – (*JOB* cree-ATE-tors) A deceitful title that millionaire C.E.O.'s assigned to themselves. It is designed to dupe the workers into believing that the corporate capitalists deserve their astronomical wages because they create jobs for the poor. In reality, through outsourcing, corporate capitalists are *"job destroyers."* In every case, everywhere, the workers' sweat makes the capitalist boss rich. *"As self-made man is about as likely as a self-laid egg."* – Mark Twain (1835 - 1910).

JOBIAN TEST – (*JOH*-bee-an *TEST*) The belief that God may put on trial a pious person's faith and devotion with hardships. The term *"Jobian"* is taken from the name Job (*JOBE*), the central figure in the Biblical Book of Job (6th century BCE). Job was a healthy, wealthy, happy man, blessed with good luck. Too, he was deeply devoted to God. The story goes that Satan made a bet with God. Satan insisted that Job would lose his faith if plagued with bad luck. So God put Job to the test. Everything Job had and loved he lost – wealth, property, children, health. Job's friends, and even his wife turned against him. Though Job fell into deep despair, he never blamed or cursed God. Instead, he lamented: *"Naked did I come into this world and naked shall I return. The Lord giveth, the Lord taketh away. Blessed be the name of the Lord."* – Book of Job 1:21. Satan lost the bet. *"Why do bad things happen to good people?"* This question has been asked through the ages. Perhaps it's a Divine Jobian Test? Anyone can be faithful in the good times. But genuine faith will withstand the drought and flood. Why would an all-powerful God want to test a humble man? Perhaps so man can contemplate the results. Or, perhaps to see if the man is worthy of power. Many believe that the hardships, if suffered patiently, are a prelude to greatness. Too, a victorious believer serves as an example to all others.

JOB-LOCK – (*JOHB* lok) A corporate capitalist servitude trap. The job-lock phenomenon is a form of employment captivity, worker bondage, involuntary servitude in the sense that the employee does not have the option to leave the job she hates. What locks a worker into a miserable job is the need of healthcare and a pension. Involuntary servitude is a sophisticated term for slavery. Job-lock is a corporate capitalist connivance to maintain a captive workforce, a corps of indentured servants. No matter how low the pay, or how bad the working conditions, the employee is bound by the shackles of healthcare and pension. Capitalist management wants to keep it that way. They want a submissive, servile, powerless workforce, devoid of options. That's why they have paid their Republican lackeys to oppose government supplied universal healthcare, and a livable Social Security as pension. The worker would tell the boss to *"stick his job up your ass!"* Corporate capitalists fear an empowered workforce with leverage over wages and working conditions. They fear what has been called *"The Great Resignation,"* if white, blue, and no collar workers were guaranteed government healthcare and a pension. A recent poll indicates that one-third, (33%) of American workers would quit their jobs today if they were not constrained by pension and healthcare. If the workers were assured a Socialistic pension and healthcare, they would have employment options, which is freedom. Corporate employers would be forced to hike wages and improve working conditions to compete for workers. That is anathema to capitalists. But as this day dawns, American workers are still held in bondage. That is why you see elderly gentlemen, approaching 80, packing groceries in your supermarket.

JOB SECURITY – (*JOHB* sek-*KUR*-rit-tee) Feeling assured that one's remunerated employment will continue. Job security is peace of mind that one will be able to make a living in support of family and self. Employment breeds self-respect and confidence that one is a contributing member of society. This is a powerful psychological need. Job security is guaranteed when there is plenty of work to complete. Therefore, never complain about too much work – that is your job security. Outsourcing of manufacturing abroad is a great threat to job security. In a capitalist economy of sellers and buyers, workers are needed to manufacture what is sold. Workers are paid by the employers so they can buy what they manufacture. This is a delicate balance. But capitalist employers are greedy. They move production overseas for cheaper labor [read: *more profit*]. By eliminating domestic employment, they are eliminating the buyers. Short term gain results in long term loss – for the entire economy. Automation too robs workers of jobs. Machines may be easier to control than people. But robots do not buy what they manufacture. If the capitalists automate the entire economy, they better pay the laid-off workers for not working, if they hope to sell what their machines made. People will buy if they are secure in the fact that they will have a job. Job security produces national prosperity. As always, the wealthier the lower classes, the more prosperous the entire nation.

JOB SHAMING – (*JOHB SHAY*-ming) To belittle or embarrass someone for the nature of her work or job. There is a prestige hierarchy in the minds of people concerning labor. Highly trained and compensated professional jobs are at the apex, with low-skilled, under-paid menial jobs at the base. However, in order for a society to function, every division of labor must be respected and fairly rewarded. The physician must assure that the trash collector is in good health, or the physician will wallow is unhealthy trash. One cannot survive without the other. Both jobs are vital. Society is based on mutual dependance. Attorney Mohandas Gandhi (1869 – 1948) insisted that: *"Each man's labor is as important as another's. In fact, while you are doing it, cleaning the toilet is far more important than [practicing] the law."* All honest work bears dignity. *"Let us not be ashamed or slow to do humble work,"* admonished Mother Teresa (1910 – 1997). The dichotomy of labor between prestige and shameful work is a competitive capitalist concept. The Biblical Prophet Joshua (1355 – 1245 BCE) certainly misunderstood the Divine Nature when he decreed: *"Now therefore you are cursed, and some of you shall never be anything but servants, drawers of water and hewers of wood for the house of my God."* – Joshua 9:21. The Socialist Buddhists were more in touch with the Divine in declaring: *"I draw water, I hew wood. That's my miracle."* – Zen Proverb. Therefore, never shame any job. Instead pray with the Hindu Guru Paramahansa (1893 – 1952): *"O Infinite Creator… I know that all work is Thy work, and that no task is too difficult or menial when offered to Thee in loving service."* *"If a man is called to be a street sweeper, ne should sweep streets as a Michelangelo painted or Beethoven composed music or Shakespeare wrote poetry. He should sweep streets so well that all the hosts of heaven and earth will pause to say, 'Here lived a great street sweeper who did his job well'."* – Martin Luther King (1929 - 1868).

JOBS' RULES – (*JOHBS ROOLS*) Steve Jobs (1955 – 2011) for a time ruled the computer industry. Jobs was co-founder and CEO of Apple Computer Inc. The following are three profound rules by which Steve Jobs lived. 1. *"Your time is limited, so don't waste it living someone else's life."* 2. *"Don't be trapped by dogma – which is living with the results of other people's thinking. Don't let the noise of others' opinions drown out your own inner voice."* 3. *"Have the courage to follow your heart and intuition – they somehow already know what you truly want to become."*

JOCKISM – (*JOK*-is um) A moniker or nickname for motor elite. Jockism is the worship of talented athletes. The athletic elites, the super-jocks are the big men on campus. Jockism is especially egregious on college campuses. They need not worry about class, tests, or grades, as long as they are scoring touchdowns. Jockism puts the great athletes above the rules and laws. They are never held accountable for their actions. The multi-million dollar athletic department always covers for them, even in criminal matters like rape. With jockism, the college or university confuses its priorities, forgets its purpose.

JOCK ITCH – (*JOK ICH*) (also Jock Rot or Crotch Itch) The dermatological term for jock itch is *"tinea cruris."* Jock itch is a contagious, though superficial fungal infection of the genitals, groin, thighs, and buttocks regions. Jock itch is most prevalent in male athletes. It is associated with athletes' feet and nail fungus. Its symptoms are a red raised rash with a scaly, well-defined border. The disease tends to conform and confine to the area in contact with the athletic jockstrap. That's because a contaminated jockstrap is where the fungus breeds. A hot, sweat-wet, unwashed jockstrap, rubbing against the sweaty flesh will generate jock itch. And good-God does it itch! – excruciatingly! – in places that can't be scratched in public! Of course, scratching a fungal infection only worsens and spreads it. Like athletes' feet, jock itch fungus is readily transmitted in steamy, unsanitary showers and locker rooms. Gratefully, jock itch is remedied with anti-fungal medication. A Caveat: Sexual intercourse is not advisable for one suffering with jock itch.

JOCKSTRAP – (*JOK*-strap) A male genital brace. A jockstrap is an elasticized belt with a pouch that envelopes the penis and testicles, the way a brazier embraces the female breasts. Straps attached to the pouch connect it with a belt around the waist from between the legs. Jockstraps are designed for protection, rather than comfort. The device prevents the genitals from bouncing about during athletic competitions. A jockstrap may be fitted with a hard plastic cup for additional protection. A Caveat: It's critically important to wash jockstraps after every application to prevent the maddening *"jock itch"* fungus.

JOCOSE – (jok-*COSE*) Being jocular, of a humorous, jesting, joking character.

JOCULAR – (*JOK*-kew-lar) (Jocularity) Being jocose, of a joking nature, of good humor.

JOE SIXPACK – (*JOE SIKS*-pak) A generic, stereotypical, disparaging name for the common White, middle-aged, working bloke. The sixpack is not a reference to his *rectus abdominis* muscles (abs). They are well concealed behind an extruding beer belly, the result of quaffing multiple sixpacks. Joe is the quintessential angry Caucasian Trump supporter. Down in Dixie, he often goes by Bubba. Up north, he may be called Buck. Joe is minimally educated, culturally deficient, a low-information voter. He is unimaginably unimaginative. Although a slow learner, Joe can parrot the conservative talking points he had learned from Fox News Network. He votes Republican, against his own economic interests, simply because Liberals vote Democratic. Mr. Sixpack's prosaic life generates bigotry and racism. He always blames minorities for his lack of success. Joe would wall-out all immigrants, and wall-in all Blacks, in prison, if he had his way. Joe Sixpack's gullibility and repressed rage makes him the target of demagogues like Donald Trump (b. 1946). Indeed, Joe is a Trumpublican, a MAGAmaniac.

JOGGING – (*JOG*-ging) Most popular form of exercise. Jogging is trotting at a leisurely pace, a moderate run. A proficient jogger can maintain a speed of 7 mph. Although a jogger runs, there is a distinction between a jogger and a runner. A runner is competitive, performing for speed. Jogging is leisurely compared to running. Nevertheless, jogging and running provides the same therapeutic benefits. *"The moment I fell in love with running, I started forgetting my grief and traumas….Running has made my life worthwhile. I used to be more dead than alive after the personal tragedy in my life….Running makes you more spiritually aware and in tune with your inner-self."* – Fauja Singh (1911 - 1970).

JOHN BULL – (jon *BULL*) The national personification of the United Kingdom in general, and England in particular. John Bull is the British counterpart to America's Uncle Sam. However, whereas Uncle Sam is an *ectomorph* (tall and skinny), John Bull is an *endomorph* (big and fat). John Bull originated as a satirical character created by Scottish physician John Arbuthnot (1667 – 1735) in his pamphlet *Law is a Bottomless Pit* (1712). John Bull is therefore an 18th century gentleman, a country squire. He sports a black top hat and boots, white tights, with a blue overcoat and tails. His shirt is the Union Jack (British flag), which clings to his bulbous belly. To call John Bull portly is kind. He is obese. Incidentally: Whereas lanky Abraham Lincoln (1809 – 1865) perfectly fits the caricature of Uncle Sam, stout Winston Churchill (1874 – 1965) fits that of John Bull.

JOHNSON AMENDMENT – (*JON*-son a-*MEND*-ment) A 1954 adjustment to the U.S. tax code making it illegal for churches and other tax-exempt organizations to back or oppose a political candidate. Indeed, the separation of church and state is a crucial tenet in the preservation of liberty. Some of the worst governments that ever existed have been theocracies. However, it is the moral duty of religion to speak-out and fight social, economic, and political injustice and oppression, as is the case with *"Liberation Theology."* Therefore, the age-old controversy concerning the religion and the church persists: Is its purpose merely to save souls, or to save people and their souls? Incidentally: the Evangelical, Fundamentalist community (Baptists and Methodists) comprise part of President Donald Trump's (b. 1946) loyal base. This is despite the fact that Trump is a liar, a lecher, a cheat, a fraud, and a traitor. As long as their agenda is satisfied, Protestant Churchmen will support Trump.

JOHN THE APOSTLE – (*JON* the a-*POS*-sul) (c. 15 – 96 CE) It is startling how quickly Christianity solidified into a bureaucratic, hierarchical corporation: The Catholic Church, Inc. John the Apostle was the youngest of Jesus' entourage. He was the Apostle that Jesus was said to love the most. John was the only Apostle to stand below the cross through Jesus' agony and death. He stood there and consoled Mary, Mother of Jesus. John was said to have cared for Mary to her last day. Of course, after all, Mary was John's mother too. John was Jesus' kid brother (about 17 years old). *"When Jesus saw his mother [Mary] and the disciple [John] whom he loved so much, standing by the cross, Jesus said to his mother, 'Woman, behold your son [John]!' Then he said to the disciple [John, his brother], 'Behold your mother!' And from that hour the disciple [John] took [Mary] into his house."* – John 19: 25-27. Now then, the Gospel of Luke tries to hide this fact by eluding a nameless woman as the mother of James and John (brothers). Why was this mention necessary? To imply that Mary was not John's mother and maintain the belief that Jesus was Mary's only child. After all, if Jesus had siblings, the Virgin Mary could not have been very virginal. It is unlikely that John wrote the Gospel attributed to him. It is foreign to the 3 synoptic Gospels (Matthew, Mark, and Luke). The mystical Gospel of John reads as if it had been written in the east, perhaps by a Greek. John was the only Apostle not martyred, and the last to die (in 96 CE). John was the last person to have known Jesus personally. Though he had lived with Jesus, John was regarded as no more than a respected celebrity in the nascent Church. He held no authority. Power resided in the C.E.O., Pope Clement I (c. 35 – 99 CE) in Rome, the 4th Pope. As the creators of a corporation are often ousted by the CEO and corporate board, John was left out of the governance of the new Church.

JONAH – (*JOH*-nuh) (sometimes Jonas). The name Jonah has come to represent a person (or thing) that brings bad luck, especially aboard ship at sea. The term is taken from Jonah (late 9th to early 8th century BCE) a Hebrew Prophet who was commanded by God to go preach to the people of Nineveh (northern Iraq). Instead, Jonah boarded a ship for Tarshish (Lebanon). Jonah's disobedience ignited God's wrath, who caused a great storm on the sea (Mediterranean). Confessing to the crew that he was the cause of the violent storm, Jonah was cast overboard. He was miraculously swallowed by a great fish and remained alive for 3 days in the creature's stomach, after which he was spit-out on the shore. Having learned his lesson, Jonah proceeded to Nineveh to fulfill God's wish. Incidentally: Though this story is hyperbolic, the message is listen to your intuition. It may be a command from God.

JOPHIEL – (*JO*-fee-al) One of the 7 Archangels, patron of illumination. The name derives from Hebrew meaning *"Beauty of God."* All Archangels bear the honorable title of Saint (St.).

JOT OR TITTLE – (*JOT* or *TIT*-tal) Both jot and tittle mean a tiny bit, a small mark. Together as a phrase, *"jot or tittle"* means not a bit, not at all. The phrase entered English via Willian Tyndale's (c. 1494 – 1536) translation of the New Testament in 1526. Matthew 5:18 reads: *"One iott or one tytle of the lawe shall not scape."* Tyndale's use of *"iott"* is a reference to *"iota,"* the smallest letter in the Greek alphabet. In the 1611 King James Version, *"iott"* was translated as *"jot,"* and *"tytle"* was changed to *"tittle."* Tittle is a combination of <u>ti</u>ny and <u>little.</u> (Substitute the t in tiny, for the l in little.) King James Version reads: *"For verily I say unto you, Till heaven and earth pass, one jot or one tittle shall in no wise pass from the law, till all be fulfilled."* – Matthew 5:18.

JOURNEY – (*JUR*-nee) A long travel. A journey may also be a psycho-spiritual passage. In psychology, a journey is an exploration to discover oneself. In religion and metaphysics, a journey is a truth-seeking mission. Through prayer and meditation, one perceives deeper truths about the self and connects with multiple aspects of the self. This self-examination is an inward journey. The outward journey may be facilitated through astral projection (teleportation) through time and space. On the outward journey, one may meet individuals from the past or future. We may be introduced to our cosmic cousins dispersed throughout the universe, in whatever form God has assigned to them. A thoroughly enlightened avatar may journey to heaven, finding herself in the presence of God.

JOURNEYMAN – (*JUR*-nee-man) (Journeymen) A person who has served an apprenticeship at a trade or handicraft and is certified to work at it assisting or under a master performer. A journeyman is competent, experienced, and ususaly dependable, although a routine worker or performer. In sports, a journeyman is a back-up, a second-stringer. Journeymen provide depth to the roster. A journeyman becomes a hero when the star player gets hurt. *"I wasn't a star, but I did participate and contributed."*

JOVIAN PLANETS – (*JO*-vee-an *PLAN*-nets) The 4 outer gas giants with properties like Jupiter. The Jovial planets are Saturn, Uranus, Neptune, and Jupiter. (Pluto, the outermost *"planet,"* has been demoted to a planetesimal or comet.)

JOYCEAN – (*JOY*-see-an) Reminiscent of James Joyce's (1882 – 1941) novels. It often includes sordid scatological subject matter, with much symbolism and stream of consciousness. Verbal inventiveness, applying puns, and the use of the English language beyond the limits of readability is characteristically Joycean.

JUBILEE YEAR – (jew-bil-*LEE YEAR*) *"And ye shall hallow the fiftieth year, and proclaim liberty throughout all the land unto all the inhabitants thereof: it shall be a jubilee unto you."* – Leviticus 25:10. A Jubilee Year was an ancient Hebrew law established every 50th year as a year of emancipation and restoration. All Hebrew slaves were freed, all debts cancelled, lands were restored to their former owners, fields were left uncultivated. The mercies of God would be made manifest each Jubilee Year. In jubilation was distributive justice applied. The social deck was re-shuffled. Wealth was redistributed. Generational lag due to poverty was prevented. Such Divine Socialism held the Hebrew people together, even under captivity. As Jesus said centuries later: *"And behold, those who are first shall be last, and the last first."* – Matthew 19:30, Luke 13:30.

JUDAISERS – (*JOO*-day-eye-sers) Jewish Christians who wanted gentile Christians to become Jews, as a condition to becoming Christians. Judaisers wanted all new Christians to undergo circumcision and abide by Jewish law. Peter was initially a Judaiser. He had heated battles with Paul on the issue. It was agreed that Peter and John would preach to the Jewish Christians, and Paul would preach to the gentile Christians. Later, Paul won out over Peter. Peter submitting to accepting gentiles as Christians, without becoming Jews first. *"Roses are red and violets are bluish, if it wasn't for Paul, we'd all be Jewish."*

JUDAISM – (*JOO*-day-is-um) The monotheistic religion of the Jews, having its ethical, ceremonial, and legal foundation in the precepts of the Old Testament and in the teachings of the Talmud. Only 0.5% of the world population practice Judaism. But Judaism influences over 50% of the world's people. That's because both Christianity and Islam have their roots in Judaism. Familiar Judaism did not begin with Abraham or Moses, but during the Babylonian Captivity (597 – 539 BCE) when the Scriptures were recorded on paper. The core value, the primary tenant of Judaism is justice. It is therefore a monumental irony that the modern Judaic State of Israel should spawn so must injustice concerning the native Palestinian population. *"Hear, O Israel the Lord our God, the Lord is one." –* <u>*The Shema.*</u>

JUDAS – (*JOO*-das) A betrayer. The word Judas is an eponym, taken from the name Judas Iscariot (died c. April, 29 – 33 CE). Judas was one of Jesus' original 12 Apostles. The name Judas is the Greek form of Judah (the Latin Judea). Judas must have been from the Kingdom of Judah, perhaps Jerusalem. Therefore, Judas was the only *true Jew,* the other Apostles and Jesus being Galileans from the Kingdom of Israel (Israelites). So Judas was the only street- smart city boy. (Jesus and the other Apostles were considered to be provincials, *"hillbillies,"* so to speak.) His urbanity probably accounted for Judas being chosen the bursar of the entourage. His surname Iscariot may identify Judas as a *"Sicarii,"* a revolutionary who assassinated Romans with a dagger. In fact, Iscariot can be translated into *"dagger man."* Perhaps Judas expected Jesus to lead an anti-Roman revolution. He may have felt bitterly conned to learn that *"My Kingdom is not of this world," –* John 18:36. Perhaps that's why Judas betrayed Jesus to the Jewish authorities. However, if Jesus came to die for mankind's sins, he would need many accomplices, including Judas. Then Judas was not a villainous betrayer, but Jesus' ally. Furthermore, everyone associated with the crucifixion was in league with Jesus, whether they knew it or not. Jesus knew that Judas was about to betray him. *"What you must do, do quickly" –* (John 13:27) Jesus told Judas at the Last Supper. This suggests that the betrayal was staged, planned together by Jesus and Judas. It may be that Judas is the most unfairly maligned personage in history. Incidentally: Today it is illegal in Germany to name your son Judas. *"If I were Jesus Christ, I would save Judas." –* Victor Hugo (1802 – 1885).

JUDDER – (*JUHD*-er) (Juddered, Juddering) To shake and vibrate violently, usually with a rattling noise. A judder is a sign of a loose or broken mechanical part. The term judder first appeared in 1926, about the time when the first automobiles appeared in greater numbers. With the bad and unpaved roads, the early cars juddered along the best they could. There is no precise etymology for the word. One may surmise it is a combination of the words *"jolt," "jerk,"* and *"shudder."*

JUDGE – (*JUHJ*) (Judges, Judging, Judged, Judgment) A public magistrate authorized to hear and decide cases in a court of law. Judges are either elected or appointed by elected officials. Judges resolve disputes and help to determine guilt or innocence. Of all governmental officials, it is most crucial that judges be honest, impartial, knowledgeable, and virtuous public servants. If the judiciary is corrupt and rotten, the entire government is decayed. The judiciary is the non-political branch of government. If it becomes politicized, all is lost! That's because the terms *judge* and *justice* are cognates – you cannot have one without the other. A judge must know and rely on the *word* of the law. But she must also consider the *spirit* of the law – not just what the law reads, but what it intends, for words are not always reliable symbols. Therefore, a judge must always consult his conscience. A judge is the most consequential officeholder in the government. She has the power over life or death, freedom or bondage, right or wrong. This requires the ideal judge to have Solomonic wisdom. Incidentally: The worst, the most unjust judge in recent times has been Aileen Cannon (b. 1981), U.S. District Court for the Southern District of Florida. Cannon was appointed by President Donald Trump (b. 1946) in 2020. Corrupt Trump was able to recognize a corrupt judge. Trump intended to use Cannon as an insurance policy, for favorable decisions, for extra-legal preferential treatment. In the Stolen Documents Affair, Cannon reacted more as Trump's defense attorney, than as a fair impartial judge. She was so outrageously biased for Trump that the Three-panel Circuit Court had to slap her down, in a humiliating rebuke. Aileen Cannon demonstrates what a judge is not. *"You're no judge because you're not judging – rather you're dictating your personal prejudices."*

JUDGE SHOPPING – (*JUHJ SHOP*-ing) The legal albeit unethical practice of filing a federal judicial action in a district with a favorable judge. No judge on any level should be politically partial in any way. But all federal judges are appointed by the President. Presidents intend to appoint judges in harmony with their political ideology. That's normal. Nevertheless, after appointment, no judge is legally beholding to any President. However, weaker characters may retain an emotional allegiance to that President and his political agenda. This is dangerously troublesome. Furthermore, an unethical President or his acolytes may search out such a favorable judge, and file a case in her district, hoping to take advantage of skewed justice. This is judge shopping. Of course, this dishonest maneuver is reserved for the rich and powerful with political clout, which makes it even more unjust. A bad example of judge shopping occurred in August and September, 2022, when Donald Trump (b. 1946) filed his objection to the Justice Department's seizure of Trump's stolen secret documents at his golf-club residence at Mar-a-lago, Florida. Trump's lawyers drove 70 miles to file in the Southern Florida District Court of Judge Aileen Cannon, (b. 1981), his appointee just two years prior. Trump obviously expected and got a ridiculously biased and favorable ruling by Judge Cannon, prohibiting the Justice Department from further examination of Trump's stolen secret documents. Judge Cannon is shamelessly performing like a defense attorney for Trump. Every reputable legal mind from both political parties condemned Cannon's reasoning as outlandish. Hopefully, her career is ruined. Nevertheless, Trump's judge shopping has paid off. At least it has served to delay, prolong his inevitable day of reckoning. *"The mills of the gods grind slowly, but they grind exceedingly fine."* – Greek Philosopher Sextus Empiricus (2nd century CE). Judge shopping is a symptom of the politicization of the judiciary. This is a fatal blow to justice and democracy. In his brilliant book, <u>America</u> (1973), British-American journalist and historian, Allister Cooke (1908 – 2004) forewarned that: *"If the judges are behind the times and if ever their integrity as honorable men is seriously questioned, then the Court and country are in trouble… Believe me, it will be a bad day for Americans if ever the mass of them lose faith in this Court as their fair and final protector."* That bad day has dawned. Footnote: One must be woefully naïve to believe that Trump did not bribe court authorizes to place Judge Aileen Cannon (b. 1981), a Trump appointed sycophant to preside over his stolen secret documents case. *"Don't tell me what the law is. Tell me what the judge is."* – Attorney Roy Cohen (1927 – 1986), disbarred Mafia lawyer and Donald Trump's favorite lawyer. *"Where is my Roy Cohen?"* – Donald Trump (b. 1946).

JUDGMENT – (*JUHJ*-ment) (Judge) To determine, to differentiate, to discriminate between right and wrong. A judgment is an estimate of the goodness or badness, worthiness or unworthiness of an individual. Judgments are usually laced with emotion. All major religions admonish against judgment, claiming it the exclusive province of God. The Buddha (c. 563 – c. 483 BCE) said: *"Do not be the judge of people; do not make assumptions about others. A person is destroyed by holding judgments about others."* Over 500 years later, Jesus (c. 7-2 BCE – c. 30-33 CE) said: *"Judge not, that you may not be judged."* By this, Jesus did not mean that we should absolve from calling-out evil oppression or capitalist exploitation. Jesus had admonished us not to be fault- finders.

JUDGMENT – (*JUHJ*-ment) In law, an adjudication or arbitration. A conclusion or determination in a dispute, made by an authority figure (a judge). In jurisprudence, a judgment is a decision rendered by a court.

JUDICATURE – (*JOO*-di-cay-cher) The administration of justice, as by a legal court or judges.

JUDICIAL ACTIVISM – (joo-*DISH*-shal *ACT*-ti-vis-um) Creation of law by the courts through their legal decisions. Ideally, the legislature creates the laws; the executive branch enforces the laws; and the judiciary (courts) interprets the laws. But government is not that neat or simple. Every court case presents the law from a different perspective. So judicial activism is quite unavoidable. However, some judges with a political agenda may attempt to expand or constrict the law to conform to their socio-political (or religious) convictions. These are *"activist judges"* who intentionally initiate judicial activism (law making). Generally speaking, conservative judges try to constrict the law in favor of the wealthy. Liberal judges try to expand the law in favor of the poor.

JUDICIAL DEMOCRACY – (joo-*DISH*-shal dem-*MOC*-cra-see) Assuring that the judiciary reflects the will of the people. Judicial democracy demands judicial adjustments to changing times. This involves the judges and the law. Biased federal judges appointed for life, by a vindictive President with a political agenda is contra-democratical and are often in opposition to popular will. Donald Trump (b. 1946) proved that our democracy is too fragile to withstand lifetime judges appointed as political hatchet men. (A politically immune justice requires an individual with a level of integrity that no longer exists in American governance.) Consider that a Federal Judge may reign for 40 years, almost 2 generations! In his brilliant book, <u>*America*</u> (1973), British-American journalist and historian, Allister Cooke (1908 – 2004) forewarned that: *"If the judges are behind the times and if ever their integrity as honorable men is seriously questioned, then the Court and country are in trouble… Believe me, it will be a bad day for Americans if ever the mass of them lose faith in this Court as their fair and final protector."* That bad day has dawned. The Supreme Court is about to become an ideological cabal, an autocratic *"Gang of Nine,"* (six anyway). Therefore, all federal judges, even the Supreme Court, must be elected by the people, in a nonpartisan manner. They must not run as a Democrat or Republican, but on their reputation, their record. They may be identified as Liberal, Moderate or Conservative on the Judiciary Slate. Endorsement by a political party or politician is forbidden. They must be judged at the polls on their judicial laurels. Like Senators, federal judges must be elected for 6 year terms. Also like Senators, one-third should be up for re- election every two years. In the case of the Supreme Court, three justices would be up for re-election every two years. It is indeed ironic, that putting judges up for election would *de-politicize* the judiciary. After all, the courts, especially the Supreme Court, should be the peoples' court.

JUDICIAL EPIPHANY – (joo-*DISH*-shal ep-*PIF*-fan-nee) A miraculous transformation of a Supreme Court Justice from a cold-blooded conservative to a warm-hearted Progressive. The Supreme Being works in mysterious ways, even with the Supreme Court. Earl Warren (1891 – 1974) was a staunch conservative Republican. Attorney General Warren of California orchestrated the cold-hearted internment of Japanese-Americans during World War Two. In 1953, Republican President Dwight Eisenhower (1890 – 1969) appointed Warren to the U.S. Supreme Court. Ike assumed that he had appointed a stiff conservative. Surprise! A Divine Epiphany! In his brilliant book, *America* (1973), British-American journalist and historian Allister Cooke (1908 – 2004) wrote: *"I've noticed that an odd and impressive thing happens, can happen, when a man is appointed to the Court. The president may think that he has installed a ventriloquist's doll, but suddenly the man is paid for life and can become himself, a quite different character from the one the president ordered up."* So it was with Chief Justice Earl Warren. He had become perhaps the most Progressive, Liberal Justice in American History. Incidentally: When Eisenhower was asked what was the biggest mistake of his Presidency, Ike replied: *"Appointing Earl Warren to the Supreme Court."* Pray for an epiphany!

JUDICIAL FIAT – (joo-*DISH*-shal *FEE*-ot) Judicial refers to law, court, judges. A fiat is an authoritative dictate, order, command. So a judicial fiat is a major determination by a judge that interprets, changes, or makes a law, that effects the lives of the nation. Unlike a legislative statute or popular referendum, the people have no say with a judicial fiat. Like a royal edict from a king, a judicial fiat is the opinion, desire of one person. Nothing can be more undemocratic, unconstitutional, anti-American and monarchical. Federal judges are appointed, not elected. This includes the nine who supremely sit on their Supreme Court thrones. Like a king, they are empowered for life, and are not beholding to the people by way of the ballot. They may act as tyrannically as they wish without consequences. In fact, many more corrupt kings have been removed throughout history than Supreme Court Justices – which is none. Judicial fiat results in fascism. Any federal judge may arbitrarily impose their biases, prejudices, even religious convictions on the entire populous through judicial fiat. This is what happened on June 24, 2022, when the *Row versus Wade* decision that gave American women the right to choose their reproductive destiny was cancelled by fiat of 5 Supreme Court monarchs. This contradicted the will of the vast majority of the American people. A judgment by a Justice is almost always unjust, when it subverts the will of the people. This arrogant Republican/Trumpublican quintet on the Supreme Court is another pistol pointed at the heart of our democracy.

JUDICIAL RECALL – (joo-*DISH*-shal *REE*-call) A Progressive proposal that citizens have the right to override, by popular vote, a Supreme Court decision on the constitutionality of an issue or law. The judicial branch, headed by the Supreme Court, had long attempted to remain above the fray of politics. This is no longer the case. Appointing partisan Federal Judges has become the spoils of political warfare. Therefore, court decisions are made on the bases of political allegiance. A perfect example is the Republican *Citizens United Case* (2010), which defines money as *"free speech,"* and enables billionaire to *"buy elections."* The remedy such judicial abuses, the people should be able to cancel bad decisions through judicial recall.

JUDICIAL REVIEW – (joo-*DISH*-shal rev-*VUW*) The power of the court to interpret the law. Also, the power of the court to declare a statute unconstitutional. The courts sit in judgment. That's why their officers are called judges. It is hoped that the judge will be a just and impartial evaluator, dedicated to serve the people, not the party or special interest. The Supreme Court's power of judicial review, to determine if any law or action is constitutional, was established in 1803, is the case, Marbury v. Madison.

JUDICIAL TRUTH – (joo-*DISH*-shal *TROOTH*) Accurate honest justice in a court of law, where the innocent are exonerated and the guilty convicted. This is the idealistic desire that the truth will prevail in court. This is not always the case because attorneys or lawyers are committed to their clients, not the truth. The attorney can be working for the defense or prosecution. In either case, the lawyer's job is to win the case, even if the lawyer must become liar, and justice miscarries. For example, an attorney who knows his client is guilty, will twist the facts to convince the court otherwise. He lies! She's expected to lie for her client, either the suspect or the state. He's a professionally trained liar. After all, Law School is also Lie School. There she's taught the art of persuasive lying. Lawyers are not sworn-in to tell the truth in court. Anyone else who lies in court is accused of perjury. Not attorneys. Our judicial system is a game, dedicated to procedure, due process, not truth, and therefore not justice. Footnote: A defendant cannot be forced to act as a witness against himself. A defendant cannot be compelled to self-incriminate. The attorney is an extension of the defendant, her alter-ego in court. The same right against self- incrimination therefore extends to the lawyer. Perhaps this doctrine affords the lawyer the right to lie for the client.

JUDICIOUS – (joo-*DISH*-us) Discreet, prudent, using good judgment. A judicious use of power is measured and tempered, for instance.

JUDICIUM DEI – (joo-*DISH*-ee-um *DAY*-ee) Latin for the *"judgment of God."*

JUDO – (*JOO*-dow) The term means *"the soft way."* Judo is a martial art which reflects the sense of moderation as practiced in Zen Buddhism. It is a weaponless defense based on jujitsu. However, unlike jujitsu, judo bans dangerous blows, stressing the athletic element. It is more of a sport than a fight.

JUDOKA – (joo-*DOE*-ka) A judo practioner or contestant.

JUGGERNAUT – (*JUG*-ger-nawt) An overpowering, destructive force that will flatten anything in its path. Juggernaut is often applied to a gigantic vehicle or vessel on the move. It may be a huge truck, tank, or battleship for instance. The term juggernaut has also been associated with a mighty storm, and unstoppable football team, anything exhibiting tremendous momentum. The term made its way into English by Odoric of Pordenone (1286 – 1331), an Italian Franciscan missionary. In the early 14th century Odoric traveled to the Far East. In India, he witnessed a procession to *Jagannath,* an avatar of the god Vishnu. The spectacle included a gargantuan vehicle or carriage. The crushing of the crowd resulted in accidental crushings under the colossal wheels of the vehicle. Too, some hysterics threw themselves under the unceasing wheels in sacrifice. Odoric's story spread throughout Europe. By the 19th century, Jagannath became juggernaut in English. It came to mean a massive inexorable force or object that crushes everything in its path. Incidentally: the *Automobile Review* of April 15, 1903 criticized the car as *"The rich man's juggernaut."*

JUGGING – (*JUHG*-ing) (Jugger) In plebeian parlance a form of theft committed by a perpetrator who waits at a bank, near an ATM, or outside an expensive store, watches for customers who might be carrying a large amount of cash or goods. The jugger follows the targeted victim to steal the money or goods from the person or vehicle. If the valuables are taken directly from the person, the crime is robbery, which would include a mugging or assault. If the jugger breaks into the car, the crime is burglary. The term jugging was first recorded in 2010 and was entered into the dictionary in 2023. The etymology of this strange word *"jugging"* is uncertain. Indeed, a *juggernaut* is a large, overpowering force. Too, juggernaut is considered anything requiring blind devotion (submission?) or cruel sacrifice, as a jugging victim may be. Actually, the term is shrouded in the slang of the criminal underground economy.

JUG WINE – Inexpensive, low-grade wine sold in huge bottles.

JUJITSU – (joo-*JIT*-soo) The term is taken from the Japanese words *"ju"* meaning softness, gentleness, and *"jutsu"* meaning art or science. The first martial art, of Japanese origin. It was devised by Buddhist monks (1700's) who were inspired by snowflakes collecting on tree branches. The stiff resistant branches broke. The flexible nonresistant branches prevailed. Jujitsu is a means to defend oneself without weapons by using the adversary's strength and weight against him. The basic premise of jujitsu is surprise and balance. The jujitsu credo could be: *"Bend like the willow, don't resist like the oak."*

JULEP – (*JOO*-lip) A variety of sweet drinks, often alcoholic (cocktails) that are sometimes medicated for some ailment. The mint julep (bourbon, sugar, a sprig of mint) is traditional in the American South.

JULIENNE – (*JOO*-lee-en) A method of cutting vegetables into thin strips or small pieces, like matchsticks.

JUMPED-IN – (juhmpt *IN*) Membership by ordeal. A traditional initiation into a street gang in which the prospective member is *"jumped"* by the other gangsters. He is beaten often senseless by the other members. Girls too are jumped-in by female gangsters. The beating is a trial by ordeal, testing the toughness of the initiate. Individuals have been maimed and murdered in these jumped-in rituals.

JUMP THE GUN – (juhmp thuh *GUHN*) To start prematurely, before preparations are complete. The phrase *"jump the gun"* derives from American track and field races. This phrase was preceded by *"beat the pistol"* or *"beat the gun."* It is traditional that such competitions begin with a shot from a starting pistol. In <u>*Rowing and Track Athletics*</u> (1905), Samuel Crowther (1880 – 1947) and Arthur Brown Ruhl (1876 – 1935) wrote: *"False starts were rarely penalized, the pistol generally followed immediately on the signal 'Get set!' and so shiftless were starters and officials that 'beat the pistol' was one of the tricks less sportsmanlike runners constantly practiced."* The phrase *"jump the gun"* had escaped its athletic origins and had filtered into the popular parlance. The term appeared in a November 1921 edition of <u>*The Iowa Homestead*</u>: *"Give the pigs a start; jump the gun, so to speak, and get them in a grain ration before weaning time."* Incidentally: The use of the term *"jump"* in both phrases refers to *"making a sudden, unexpected movement."* This usage is apparent in earlier phrases like *"jump someone's claim,"* *"jump ship,"* and in the mid-20th century, *"jump the queue."*

JUNCTURE – (*JUNK*-cher) A crucially important point of time, made so by circumstances. For instance, *"At this critical juncture in the battle...."* Too, juncture is a point of articulation, where two points or bodies meet.

JUNE BUG – (*JOON* buhg) Not a summer insect but prison slang for an inmate who serves as a slave for others. June bugs are timid creatures hiding in the shadows. They are exploited and oppressed by powerful tyrannical inmates. June bugs are in double bondage – prisoners of the prisoners in prison. To magnify their wretched existence, they may be forced to serve as sex-slaves as well.

JUNETEENTH – (joon-*TEENTH*) (A portmanteau of *"June"* and *"nineteenth"*.) *Emancipation Day in America.* June 19, celebrated by historically minded African-Americans as the anniversary of emancipation of slaves in Texas on June 19, 1865. On that date, Union General Gordon Granger (1821 – 1876) read the federal order at Galveston, Texas. This was 2 full years after legal emancipation was declared throughout all the United States. Finally, formal, de jure slavery was abolished in America. On June 19th, 2021, President Joe Biden (b. 1942) made June 19th an official federal holiday. Well, you'd never know it was a federal holiday is most of the red [read: *red neck*] states. Only 23% (3 states, Texas, Georgia, and Virginia) of the 13 states of the old slavocracy recognizes Juneteenth as a paid state holiday. This is a racist demonstration of disrespect through disregard – rotten resentment of losing the Civil War (1861 – 1865). Too, only 30% of private employers approach Juneteenth as a paid holiday. Juneteenth is a paid state holiday in: Colorado, Connecticut, Delaware, Georgia, Illinois, Louisiana, Maine, Massachusetts, Maryland, Nebraska, New Jersey, New York, Ohio, Oregon, South Dakota, Texas, Virginia, Washington. Incidentally: Slavery was abolished in the British Empire in 1833. So America suffered slavery for 32 years after the evil was condemned in places like Jamaica. In fact, the vulgar rich sugar barons and slavocrats of Jamaica conspired to join the United States (the South), in order to maintain their slavery.

JUNGIAN – (*YOUNG*-gee-an) Refers to the psychoanalytical theories of Karl Gustav Jung (1875 – 1961). Jungianism rejects Freud's sexual libido theories. It introduces the unconscious, the collective unconscious, and personality types to psychoanalysis.

JUNIOR COLLEGE – (*JOON*-yur *COL*-lej) Community college. A tertiary school that provides the first 2 years of college. The junior college was intended to be a vocational training school for the working class. It was hoped to keep the masses out of the universities, so those institutions remained socially elite. (Monopolize education and you monopolize the wealth.) The plan backfired big time. Working class students have used the junior college as a stepping stone to enter the major universities.

JUNIOR HIGH – (*JOON*-yur *HY*) America's first intermediate school established in 1918. The junior high consists of grades 7, 8, and 9 which includes students in the 12 to 15 years age range. The junior high is articulated with the senior high, meaning a lower extension of that upper institution. It is patterned after the high school organization, with departmentalized class periods. The purpose of the junior high was to separate the younger children from those approaching adulthood. Junior highs are being supplanted by middle schools.

JUNGLE – (*JUNG*-gal) Tropical wilderness of impenetrable foliage, entangled vines and thick groundcover. A jungle should not be mistaken for a rainforest with its high tree canopy. You may walk through a rainforest but must chop your way through a jungle. Jungles line the riverbeds on the sides of the rainforest. Ordinarily, jungles are more bush than woods. About 80% of the world's insect species live in jungles and rainforests.

JUNK – (*JUHNGK*) (Junky, Junked) Any old, discarded objects or material that is regarded as useless and worthless. As a verb, to junk is to relegate some broken item to the trash heap. That's a mistake. Junk can be a precious commodity to the innovative and imaginative. Much valuable wood, pieces of metal and plastic, hinges, magnets, glass, screws, nuts-and bolts, whatever can be salvages from junk. This material can be used in an infinite number of projects and art works. Junk inspires ingenious *"half-ass solutions"* to problems. It's an age-old adage that: *"One man's junk is another man's treasure."* The universal problem that junk presents is lack of storage space. Nevertheless, find a safe place for your junk, guard it, despite her complaining. Incidentally: The definition of junk expanded over the centuries. In the mid-14th century, junk was confined to *"old rope and scrap cable."* The word entered English by way of the Old French term *"junc,"* meaning *"reeds, plant stems, dead branches." "One man's junk is another man's treasure."* – Hector Urquhart (1829 – 1880) in <u>Popular Tales of the West Highlands</u> (1860).

JUNK – (*JUHNGK*) In the vulgar vernacular, junk refers to the genitals, sex organs, especially the male dick and balls.

JUNKET – (*JUHNK*-ket) A holiday or vacation disguised as a fact-finding study by a government official at public expense. Junkets have come to be considered *perks* by elected officials. A Congressman on a junket may go to the French Riviera to study poverty.

JUNK FEES – (*JUHNGK* fees) A covetous capitalist trick as old as capitalism. Junk is worthless, useless, meaningless material. So are junk fees. They are hidden costs in the small print to pad the bill that the customer must pay. This is pure capitalist greed. Hotels, resorts, airlines, banks are notorious for charging junk fees. Junk fees are a deceptive scheme targeted at the consumer. The advertised cost is very cheap, somewhat like bait. The money is made up by the hidden junk fees. *Frontier Airlines* offers flights under $100 dollars (which is financially impossible). But a passenger must pay and equal amount or more for luggage, baggage, a drink of water, perhaps a seat, everything. The hotel room is unreasonably cheap. But all the expected necessities are outrageously expensive. You must pay to use a beach chair, and umbrella. Room service is an extra fee. You have a parking fee to pay as well. Burying a mandatory tip in the bill is a way that capitalist businessmen transfer the cost of employees' wages to the customer. Bankers are the slimiest leeches in the capitalist swamp – second only to insurance CEOs. Banks will charge junk fees to writing a check, casing a check, opening an account, closing an account, making a deposit, making a withdrawal, transferring funds, everything. What was once customer service, is now corporate self-serving. Disguised junk fees are illegal is many advanced nations. Not in the United States – until now. In June, 2023, Democratic President Joe Biden (b. 1942) is proposing legislation to outlaw junk fees. It's extraordinary for the government to dictate prices to a private business in a capitalist economy. But the government can demand that all junk fees be included in the advertised cost. Fees cannot not be hidden. That is false advertising. Parenthetically: A family staged an anniversary party at a hotel. A custom-made cake was brought by the family to the party. The hotel demanded a $3.00 dollar fee for each serving of the cake, that wasn't even theirs! How do you figure?

JUNK FOOD – (*JUHNGK FOOD*) Snacks like potato chips, cookies, cakes, candies, and soda pop. Such edibles are called junk food because of their nutritional worthlessness – like junk. Junk foods are high in fat, sugar, and salt, all very unhealthy in excess. Junk foods are responsible for diabetes and many other health hazards. Junk foods provide empty calories, low in nutrition and relatively cheap. That's why junk food is popular with the poor. Too, that's why so many poor people are obese. The ignorant affluent may consider obesity among the poor as a sign of prosperity rather than poverty. In truth, it is due to poor diet, cheap junk food, and poor health.

JUNKYARD – (*JUHGK*-yahrd) An enclosed area where old, crashed, rusting, disassembled vehicle parts are collected, stored, and offered for resale. A junkyard is a dirty business, not morally, or legally, but literally. It is the most depressing looking location in the city. A deep sadness permeates the junkyard. It is an automobile graveyard. The chaos of car body parts resembles the aftermath of a battle. (I often wonder how many people drew their last breath in those mangled vehicles.) But there is method to this apparent madness. The junkyard man knows the location of every part. Junkyards are ugly places, the antithesis of a flower garden. Trees and shrubs give way to twisted, rusting metal. Green grassy turf gives way to black greasy ground. Nothing natural will grow in a junkyard, not hardly any weeds. The earth has been contaminated by gasoline, motor oil, antifreeze/coolant, brake and transmission fluids – a toxic witches brew. It's an ecological disaster zone between those four walls. Nature shuns the junkyard. Birds and squirrels have no place to rest, nest, and nothing to eat there. You will encounter rats though, plenty of rats. The debris provides perfect shelter for rodents. And then there's the junkyard dog – perhaps the meanest creature in the city. There may be more than one. They are a vicious guard-dog breed, conditioned to attack. Their job is to tear apart thieves in the night. They will be chained-up during business hours but be ever so vigilant! The grimy dilapidated shack that serves as the junk man's office is appropriately furnished with a junky desk and three rickety chairs. The obligatory calendar (2 years old) with the naked girl serves as décor. The junkyard man is a rough, tough, grizzled character, somewhat like a pirate. He always has a third of a smoldering cigarette stuck to his lower lip. He is stereotypically reminiscent of *Captain Quint,* the shark hunter from the 1975 movie *"JAWS."* Indeed, a junkyard is an unpleasant place, but it may provide you with a rare old car part, cheaply. *"One man's junk is another man's treasure."*

JUNTA – (*HOON*-tah) (sometimes Anglicized as *JUN*-tah) A junta is a Spanish term for dictatorship, a government ruled by generals after a military takeover (coup). Juntas tend to be right-wing, fascist regimes. Ordinarily, a cabal of perfidious generals are bribed by the C.I.A. to overthrow a Socialist government, for the benefit of capitalist multinational corporations. They must employ terror (torture, rape, prison, murder) to maintain their rule. The United States government supports pro-capitalist juntas everywhere. This is another answer to the naïve question: *"Why do they hate us?"*

JUPITER – (*JOO*-pit-ter) The 5th planet from the sun, a gas giant two-and-a-half times more massive than all the other planets in the solar system combined. In fact if Jupiter had grown a little larger, thermal nuclear reactions in its core may have ignited, and the planet may have become a *"Red Dwarf,"* tiny star. Its mass is that of 318 Earths. Jupiter is the 4th brightest body in the solar system. Its surface temperature is -162.4 degrees Fahrenheit. Jupiter has 4 thin rings. It takes Jupiter 11.8 years to orbit the sun. A day on this planet is 9 hours and 55 minutes. The Jovian atmosphere is primarily hydrogen, with upper layers of ammonia and sulfur crystals. The planet consists of compressed hydrogen gas, liquid metallic hydrogen, and a core of ice, rock, and metals. The Great Red Spot is a titanic storm that has raged for at least 350 years. It could swallow 3 planet Earths. Jupiter has 67 moons, the largest, Ganymede is bigger than the planet Mercury. Jupiter's tremendous gravitational force deflects asteroids that would have bombarded Earth. Incidentally: Jupiter's extraterrestrial atmosphere sometimes rains diamonds.

JURE DIVINUM – (*JUR*-ray dee-*VEE*-noom) Latin for *"divine law."*

JURISDICTION – (jur-ris-*DIC*-shun) In law, a court's authority to hear a case. Also the geographical area within which a court has the right and power to operate. Original jurisdiction means that the court will be the first to hear the case. Appellate jurisdiction means that the court reviews cases on appeal from lower court rulings.

JURISPRUDENCE – (*JER-* ris-proo-dentz) (Jurisprudent, Jurisprudential) Basically, the philosophy of law. Ideally, laws are made to promote justice – to protect the weak from the powerful, to protect the good from the bad. Jurisprudence seeks to answer the question: What is the law, and who should it serve? Jurisprudence is a French word that entered English in the 1620s. The French derived it from the Latin *"iurisprudential,"* meaning *"philosophy of law."* (The Roman Latin alphabet did not have the letter "J".) In Latin, *"iuris"* means *"law,"* and *"prudential"* means *"a knowledge to foresee."* Lawmakers must be able to foresee the consequences of the laws they make. But alas, they don't, and all laws are not prudent or jurisprudential. At the American Constitutional Convention (1787), representative James Madison (1751 – 1836) admonished the nation-makers: *"If all men were virtuous, there would be no need for laws at all."* But alas, they're not. So men record laws on paper using words. Words are imprecise symbols. That's why the spirit of the law is often lost in the language of the law. Furthermore, the legalese language is hardly decipherable by the common man. Words are intentionally chosen to provide loopholes, exceptions, exemptions, technicalities, escape clauses to benefit the rich and powerful, to the detriment of the poor and weak. What ends up on the books is often the furthest from the lawmaker's conscience and intention. But there it is, in writing, in the law, so it is legal and sacred, so must be obeyed. Prudence means wise, just, good judgment. Where is the prudence in jurisprudence? The juris or law is often far from prudent. Enabling multi-billionaires to skip paying taxes is not jurisprudential. Neither is suppressing the democratic vote. Consider: killing with a weapon on the street is imprudent. But allowing killing to proceed due to want and lack are not. The government punishes those who cause death by murder. But the government is not punished when it causes death by neglect, malnutrition, starvation, exposure, or illness due to lack of food, shelter, or medical care. Is this nation jurisprudential? Hardly! *"The law, in its majestic equality, forbids the rich as well as the poor to sleep under bridges, to beg in the streets, and to steal bread."* – Anatole France (1844 – 1924), *The Red Lily* (1894).

JURY NULLIFICATION – (*JUR*-ree nul-li-fi-*KAY*-shun) A deplorable situation when a trial jury discounts the law, ignores evidence, disregards obvious facts and decides or judges on their emotions or prejudices. The O. J. Simpson (b. 1947) acquittal (1994), or the failures to convict the murderers of civil rights workers in the 1950's and 1960's are miscarriages of justice due to jury nullification. Police officers often benefit from the phenomenon of jury nullification. Many naïve citizens find it difficult to convict a cop. (So do prosecuting attorneys who are allied to the police.) Cops therefore often get away with murder.

JUS GENTIUM – (*JOOS* jen-*TEE*-oom) Latin for *"international law."*

JUS SANGUINIS – (joos sang-*GWIN*-nees) Latin for *"right of blood."* Jus sanguinis is the legal principle that the country of nationality of a child is that of the country of nationality of the parents. Therefore, if your parents are French citizens, and you are born in America, you too are a French citizen.

JUS SOLI – (joos *SOH*-lee) Latin for *"right of soil"* (meaning land). Jus soli is the legal principle that a person's nationality at birth is determined by the territory within which he/she was born. If one is born on American soil, she is an American citizen – even if his parents are not. *"If the first breath you inhale is American air, you are heir to American citizenship."*

JUST DESERT – (*JUST* dee-*SERT*) Karmic Justice; reaping what one had sown; getting what you earned; experiencing one's comeuppance. A just desert can be positive or negative, a reward or punishment. In this instance, the term desert is not related to the sweet treat known as dessert (dee-*SERT*). One's just desert may justifiably be very bitter. (A common error is to spell the term as "just *dessert*." Desert and dessert are *"homophones"* – words with the same sound, but different spellings and meanings.) The term desert in the usage under discussion derives from the Old French verb *"deservir,"* meaning *"to deserve."* Just desert, meaning reward or punishment has existed in English since the late 1200's. To further complicate this verbal issue, the noun desert (*DEZ*-sert) represents a dry region. Too, the verb desert (dee-*SERT*) means to abandon someone. (In this case, the 3 deserts are *"homographs"* – words that are spelled the same but have different sounds and meanings.) Actually, this is all academic anyway, (albeit interesting to *"word-nerds"*).

JUSTICE – (*JUS*-tis) *"Comforting the afflicted and afflicting the comfortable,"* as the Quakers say. Justice is right over might. It is people-power over money- power. It is law over influence. It is equality over privilege. It is people before money. It is Socialism over capitalism. *"There is no such thing as justice in the abstract; it is merely a compact between men in their various relations with each other, in whatever circumstances they may be, that they will neither injure nor be injures."* – Epicurus (341 – 270 BCE). *"Justice without force is powerless; force without justice is tyrannical."* – Blaise Pascal (1623 – 1662).

JUSTICE (DISTRIBUTIVE) – (*JUS*-tis dis-*TRIB*-bu-tiv) The soul of Socialism. Distributive justice is to parcel-out the bounty of the Earth equitably. Through distributive justice, Socialists seek to eliminate the rich class and the poor class and create one comfortable class living abundantly. But distributive justice is antithetical to capitalism, the economy of greed. Distributive justice can only be achieved through Socialism.

JUSTICE (JURISPRUDENTIAL) – (*JUS*-tis jur-eis-proo-*DEN*-chal) Justice under the law. Jurisprudential justice is blind justice, meaning one's wealth, color, sex, religion, or social status must have no influence in the judication of a case at law. But the law has always been skewed in favor of the rich, for the protection of their wealth. After all, the rich and powerful make the laws. In <u>Le Lys Rouge</u> (1894), (<u>The Red Lily</u>), Anatole France (1844 – 1924) wrote: *"The majestic equality of the law…forbids the rich as well as the poor to sleep under bridges, to beg in the streets, and to steal bread."*

JUSTICE (RETRIBUTIVE) – (*JUS*-tis ret-*TRIB*-bu-tiv) (also Retaliative or Retaliatory Justice) Punishment, punitive justice whose principal aim is revenge, as indicated in the verse *"An eye for an eye, a tooth for a tooth, a hand for a hand, a foot for a foot."* – Exodus 21:24. Retributive justice seeks to get even. It is a most unjust, discompassionate justice of the lynch mob. You'll hear proponents of retributive justice yelling: *"Crucify him!" "Hang 'em high!" "Lock her up!"* Incidentally: Candidate Donald Trump (b. 1946) promised revenge, retribution, if elected President (2024). *"I will be your retribution,"* he promised his MAGA lunch mob. What Trump means is vindication over his political enemies, a *"Night of the Long knives."*

JUSTICE FOR ALL – (*JUS*-tis for *AWL*) A silly, schmaltzy recording made by former President Donald Trump (b. 1946) and the *"J6 Prison Choir,"* a gang of about 20 imprisoned felons, thugs who participated in the riotous January <u>6</u> attack on the United States Capitol. The recording is 2:20 minutes in length and was released on March 3, 2023. The song consists of Trump reciting the *"Pledge of Allegiance to the United States,"* interspersed with the J6 Prison Choir singing *"The Star- Spangled Banner."* The song concludes with a puerile, plebeian chant of *"U-S- A!"* six times. Trump's contribution was recorded at his Mar-a-Lago resort. The jailbirds sang and were recorded over a prison phone. Royalties from the recording is supposed to go to the families of the imprisoned insurrectionists. Astoundingly, only their heroes who had injured police officers are eligible for the reward money. However, prudence requires careful monitoring of Trump, when money is concerned. Trump declared: *"I call them the J6 hostages. Not prisoners. I call them hostages."* Trump is trying to plant the seed in the public's mind that if he is incarcerated, he too would be a hostage, a political prisoner. Trump went on to say: *"When the song came out, it went to No. 1 song. It was beating everybody. It beat Taylor Swift. It beat Miley Cyrus."* Indeed, there are a number of *"Trump Davidians,"* in Steve Bannon's (b. 1953) words, who will venerate any crap that Trump dishes out to them. Incidentally: *"Justice for All"* is a justified title, for the insurrectionists are getting their just deserts in prison.

JUSTIFIABLE HOMICIDE – (jus-ti-*FY*-uh-bul *HOM*-mih-syd) Excusable murder. Killing another person in self-defense or to prevent a forcible felony. To take a life in the protection yourself, loved ones, innocent potential victims or the protection of property from robbery would be considered justifiable homicide. Such a clear-cut case would not even make it to trial. Tragically, because of unjust regulations, biased prosecutors and judges, corrupt police union, and a complacent public, almost all homicides by police officers are deemed justifiable. This is particularly true when the victim is a minority citizen. For too many cops, *"Black Lives Don't Matter."* Incidentally: In Texas, it is legal to kill a man who is in bed with your wife, but not the wife. *"Texas law – I. Adultery: Article 1220 of the Texas Penal Code provides: Homicide is justifiable when committed by the husband upon one taken in the act of adultery with the wife, provided the killing takes place before the parties to the act have separated."* The statute uses the phrase *"before the parties have separated."* This has been interpreted to mean only that the adulterous couple are still in each other's company, not that they are still united in the act of copulation. Furthermore, *"The wife is not justified in taking the life of her husband's mistress, nor the life of her husband."* The Wild West is still wild. Footnote: The fact that a man can legally kill his wife's lover (in bed), but a woman cannot legally kill her husband's lover (in bed) speaks volumes. It implies that the wife is the property of the husband, but the husband is not the property of the wife. By killing the wife's lover, the husband is killing a thief, a robber. The murder is in defense of his property.

JUST-IN-TIME – (just-in-*TYM*) Provided when needed without a moment to spare. Medication may be administered just-in-time to save a life. In the capitalist world of manufacturing and commerce, just-in-time is a cost-cutting efficiency method. Almost all manufacturing industries depend on supplies of parts to complete assembly. A surplus inventory of parts is prudent, if not essential. But storing parts in a warehouse costs money. In its ever compulsive desire to make an extra buck, capitalists came up with the idea of foregoing the inventory of spare parts. Rather, they depend on their suppliers to provide the components when requested, expeditiously. This is just-in-time. This is fine in a perfect world. But in reality, it is a major gamble. Any delay from the supplier can trigger a domino effect that will freeze production.

A storm, a strike, an accident at a plant can cut the supply chain. All production ceases. It a time of crisis like war or pandemic, just-in-time can result in a tragic time for the nation.

JUS UBIQUE DOCENTI – (*JOOS* oo-beek-*WAY* doe-*SEN*-tee) Latin for *"The right to teach anywhere."*

JUTLAND – (*JUT*-land) A Northern European peninsula that consists of Denmark and northern Germany.

JUTLAND – (*JUT*-land) (The Battle, May 31 to June 1, 1916.) History's greatest naval battle up to that date, occurring during World War One. Jutland was the last naval battle in history between great capital surface vessels, toe-to-toe. The combatants were the Royal British Navy and the Imperial German Navy. The engagement took place in the North Sea west of Denmark's Jutland Peninsula. The British naval blockade was starving out Germany. The German Naval Commander Alfred von Tirpitz (1849 – 1930) intended to break the British blockade. The powerful, though inferior German fleet sailed out of their base at Kiel, and ran into the superior British fleet. The British battleships opened the greatest salvo of fire power in naval history. From miles away, the huge guns battered each other. The British lost 3 battlecruisers, 3 armored cruisers, and 8 destroyers. The Germans lost 1 outdated battleship, 1 battlecruiser, 4 light cruisers, and 5 torpedo-boats. A total of 6,094 British seamen were killed, 674 wounded. The Germans lost 2,551 dead, 507 wounded. The Battle of Jutland was a tactical victory for Germany, but a strategic victory for Britain. Though the German fleet wreaked more damage on the British, they were forced to retreat back to Kiel. They had failed to break the British naval blockade.

JUXTAPOSITION – (jux-ta-po-*SISH*-un) Anything placed close together, usually side-by-side, especially for comparison of contrast. To be juxtasupposed is being in juxtaposition.

K

K – (*KAY*) The 11th letter in the English alphabet, a consonant. K is the chemical symbol for the element Potassium, as indicated on the Periodic Table of Chemical Elements. Incidentally: The ancient Roman educator and scholar Quintilian (c. 35 0 c. 100 CE) did not favor the letter K. Quintilian said: *"So K, I think shouldn't be used at all.... The letter C keeps its strength before all the vowels."*

K – (*KAY*) The letter K was the symbol used as a message by downed pilots in the Vietnam War (1960 – 1973/75). It meant *"I'm on the run."* The evanescent airman would form the letter K in a clearing with rocks, logs, foliage, or scratches in the soil, to be seen from the air. Hopefully, he would be located and rescued before being captured. The U.S. military was far more ambitious in rescuing pilots than *"grunts"* (foot soldiers). Pilots are highly trained and therefore more valuable. Too, they had knowledge about aircraft and tactics that the government did not want the enemy to learn.

KA'ABAH – (ka-*BAH*) (also KA'BAH, KAABA) The Muslim House of God, located at the Great Mosque at Makka (Mecca). It is said to be the site of a small house that Ibrahim (Abraham) had built for the worship of God. The Ka'abah is holiest shrine in Islam, a cube-shaped structure housing the sacred black stone (meteorite). Tradition also has it that Abraham (Ibrahim) rested on the holy black stone. The Ka'abah is comparable to the Jewish Arch of the Covenant.

KABAB – (ka-*BOB*) Small pieces of meat and/or seafood seasoned or marinated and broiled on a grill, with tomatoes, green peppers, onions, and other vegetables, usually on a skewer.

KABBALA – (ka-*BAL*-la) (Also Kabala, Cabala, or Kabbalah) Sacred, secret Jewish book of magic. The term means *"deceive"* in Hebrew. The Kabbala is a system of esoteric *theosophy* (divine intuition) and *theurgy* (miracles) developed by rabbis, reaching its peak about the 12th and 13th centuries. The Kabbala had influenced metaphysicians, alchemists, and Christian theologians throughout the Medieval and Renaissance Periods. The Kabbala is based on a mystical method of interpreting Scriptures by which initiates claimed to penetrate sacred mysteries. Among its central doctrines are that all creation is God's handiwork, and that all souls exist from eternity.

KABUKI THEATER – (ka-*BOO*-kee *THEE*-ter) A Japanese cultural tradition that has come to represent posturing. It refers to a performance in which nothing substantial is done. Kabuki Theater means going through the motions.

KAFKAESQUE – (kaf-ka-*ESK*) Reminiscent of Franz Kafka's (1883 – 1924) novels. To be Kafkaesque is to be nightmarish, with loss of identity, helplessness against evil bureaucracies which are insanely logical, though bewildered and bewildering. Kafka's imaginary world is a totalitarian spider's web, in which citizens are ensnared bugs. Law and justice are a *"Catch 22,"* and quite arbitrary. When dealing with the government, you are damned if you do, and damned if you don't. In a Kafkaesque society, one can be arrested without rhyme, reason, or cause, without explanation. The midnight knock-on-the-door by men-in-black is a dire fear. Incidentally: In mid-July, 2020, the Fascist Trump regime displayed its Kafkaesque impulses by sending unidentified federal agents to arbitrarily arrest protesters in Portland, Oregon. *"Black Lives Matter"* demonstrators were randomly apprehended, kidnapped, and hauled away in black unmarked vans. This is the way of dictators, as Kafka had warned.

KAHLENBERG MOUNTAIN – (*KA*-len-berg *MAWN*-tan) (also, Battle of Vienna) One of the pivotal battles of European and World History, September 12, 1683. Polish King Jan Sobieski (1629 – 1696) defeated the Ottoman Turkish Muslims under Pasha Kara Mustafa (1634 – 1683) at the Gates of Vienna. Sobieski hauled cannon atop Mt. Kahlenberg and for several hours fired tens-of thousands of shells upon the Turks below. When the Turks were reduces to chaos, 20,000 Polish heavy riders attacked, including 3,000 elite *"Winged- Hussars."* In this, the greatest cavalry charge in history, Furthermore, this was the greatest congregation of horses ever seen in one place at one time. Over 40,000 elite Turkish *"Janissaries"* were slaughtered. Thousands more drowned in the Danube River trying to escape. The Muslim Turks were totally defeated and retreated. As a result of the Battle of Kahlenberg, Austria was saved and Hungary liberated from the Turks. Christianity in Europe was preserved.

KAKISTOCRACY – (ka-kis-*TOC*-ra-see) A government by the worst leader possible. A kakistocracy is the polar opposite of a meritocracy. Obviously, the Donald Trump (b. 1946) regime is America's first authentic kakistocracy.

KALASHNIKOV – (ka-*LASH*-ni-kov) An *AK-47* Russian-made assault rifle, most ubiquitous gun on Earth. It is simple, reliable, never jams, the terrorists' and guerrilla fighters' weapon of choice. The AK-47 kills more people than any other gun in the world. Over 50 million used models are in circulations for as little as $50 dollars each. Incidentally: The Kalashnikov is Russia's top export, followed by caviar and vodka.

KALININGRAD – (kul-*LEE*-nin-grad) An exclave (detached) part of Russia sandwiched between Lithuania and Poland, on the Baltic Sea Coast. Kaliningrad Oblast (province), (like the Crimea in the Ukraine), is not a contiguous part of the Russian mainland. Geopolitically, it may be considered the most precarious location in the world. At 5,800 square miles, Kaliningrad is a little larger that Connecticut. Its provincial capital is the city of Kaliningrad (formerly German Konigsberg) on the Gdansk Bay of the Baltic Sea. Almost a million Russian citizens populate the province, though it is 230 miles from Russia. So Kaliningrad is a Russian island in the middle of the European Union and NATO (North Atlantic Treaty Organization). For 684 years, Kaliningrad was a part of German East Prussia, founded by the Teutonic Knights in the 13th century. In World War Two, 1945, the Russian Red Army captured East Prussia. The largest part to the south was annexed to Poland. A small part of northern East Prussia was ceded to Lithuania. The central section of East Prussia, including the capital city of Konigsberg became Russian Kaliningrad Oblast. Dictator Joseph Stalin (1878 – 1953) recognized the strategic military value of the territory. It was named after the Russian military hero, General Nikolai Kalinin (1937 – 2008). At the time of the partition of East Prussia, the 3 Baltic States (Lithuania, Latvia, Estonia) were part of Russia. Poland was a Russian satellite state. The geopolitical balance of power has radically changed. Today, the Baltic States and Poland are free nations, part of the European Union and NATO. Since the Russian invasions of the Ukraine in 2014 and again in 2022, Poland and the Baltic States are hostile to Russia. The city of Kaliningrad is Russia's only ice- free port on the Baltic Sea. It is the home of the Russian Baltic fleet. Kaliningrad Oblast is heavily armed with Russian naval and air power. This includes nuclear missiles that could strike Warsaw, Stockholm, Copenhagen, and Berlin, NATO capitals. Furthermore, Kaliningrad is only 40 miles from Belarus, a dictatorship and staunch Russian ally. The *Suvalki Corridor*, consisting of Lithuanian and Polish territory separates Kaliningrad from hostile Belarus. In a conflict with NATO, Russian dictator Vladimir Putin (b. 1952) plans to invade and capture the Suvalki Gap, uniting Kaliningrad to Belarus, blocking the 3 Baltic States from Poland. Then he intends to attack Lithuania, Latvia, and Estonia from Belarus and Russia. But the overwhelming might of the United States and all the NATO Allies will be hurled at Kaliningrad, Belarus, and Russia. NATO will surely win, a Pyric Victory at that. There will be no victors if the conflict escalated into a nuclear world war. Back in the Cold War days of the Russian Soviet Union, Nakita Khrushchev (1894 – 1971) admitted: *"After a nuclear war, it will be impossible to distinguish the capitalist ashes from the socialist ashes."* Update: The Russian population of Kaliningrad is tired of being Russian. Over 72.1% want to secede from Russia and become an independent Baltic State. They say that they are Western Europeans, not Eurasian Russians. Kaliningraders oppose Vladimir Putin's invasion of the Ukraine and the subsequent war. They do not want to fight the Ukrainians. Most of the citizens refer to their capital city by the old German name, Konigsberg. It is certain, that when Russia collapses from the weight and strain of Putin's Ukrainian War, Kaliningrad will break away. It is perfectly plausible to see Kaliningrad in the EU and a member of NATO too. Footnote: Kaliningrad is in the heart of amber country, on the Baltic Sea. This is a precious economic asset. Footnote: In late February, 2024, Sweden had been admitted to NATO, as the 32nd member. That turns the Baltic Sea into a NATO Lake. Kaliningrad is really isolated, cut off from Russia now.

KAMAKAZE – (ka-ma-*KAZ*-zee) Japanese for *"divine wind."* A human suicide/smart bomb. The renowned Japanese suicide pilots who, in desperation, crashed into American warships toward the end of World War Two, (Battle of Okinawa, 1945). About 19% of the kamikazes succeeded in hitting US ships. In the 82-day battle, they sank 30 U.S. ships and damaged 200 others. On average, 30 American sailors a day were killed by kamikazes during the Battle of Okinawa. This was the greatest American naval death loss in history, after the Pearl Harbor attack. The kamikaze attacks accounted for about 20% of the total naval loses in the Second World War. About 5,000 U.S. sailors and 4,000 fanatical Japanese were killed. Therefore, each kamikaze killed, took 1.25 Americans with him. About 5,000 kamikaze planes were poised for the American invasion of Japan, with an additional 5,500 in reserve. The invasion of the southern Japanese home islands would be a bloodbath, of *Stalingrad standard.* The entire population was *"kamakazefied,"* with weapons and explosives. Even school children were issued spears. A Russian invasion of the northern islands would be required for victory. But all was settled with the atomic bombings. Incidentally: Admiral Chester Nimitz (1885 – 1966) kept the U.S. fleet within kamikaze range intentionally. If the fleet was moved to safety out to sea, out of kamikaze range, the Japanese planes would be used against the U.S. ground forces fighting on the island of Okinawa.

KAMALA – (ka-*MAL*-la) In this entry, a mispronouncement of the female name Kamala (*KAM*-ma-la). Kamala is a Hindi name, taken from ancient Sanskrit meaning *"lotus"* or *"pale red,"* as are some lotuses. (The lotus is the symbol of Buddhism.) Starting in the early 2020s, Donald Trump (b. 1946) and the Trumpublican cultists have intentionally mispronounced Vice-President Kamala Harris' first name as Ka-*MA*-la, (purposely putting the accent on the penultimate syllable). Ms. Harris is ethnically East Indian and Jamaican, a lady of color. The name alteration is a dog-whistle attempt to make her name sound foreign, associate her with Africa, an outlander, a darkie, the other. This is how low the Republicans-turned-Trumpublicans must crawl in a hope to win elections. Hopefully, in November 2024, Kamala Harris will become the first female American President, and a woman of color at that.

KAMALANOMENON – (ka-ma-la-*NOM*-men-on) Combining the female name <u>Kamala</u>, with the truncated rendition of the word ph<u>enomenon</u>. Kamalanomenon refers to the phenomenal popular appeal of the Democratic Presidential Candidate, Vice-President Kamala Harris (b. 1964). Her celebrity status is a great political surprise. That's because she had been ignored by the press through the 4 years of the Joe Biden (b. 1942) Presidency. Kamala's youthful, energetic, exciting personality has captivated much of the American public, including the electorate. That's bad news for Republican Candite Donald Trump (b. 1946) and his fascist MAGA cultists. Kamala Harris is attracting 15,000 to 20,000 supporters to her political rallies, to the chagrin and grief of bitter old Donald Trump. Kamala is approaching rock star status, which translates into Kamalanomenon and votes. Never before in American political history had an election been turned on its head in so short of time. This is indeed a Kamalanomenon.

KAMA SUTRA – (*KA*-ma *SOO*-tra) An ancient Hindu sex manual written in the 2nd century CE by the Indian sage Vatsyayanna (lived 2nd century CE). The Kama Sutra is a detailed instruction book in the art and techniques of coitus. Many of the erotic sexual positions were designed for young, acrobatic, sexual Olympians, *"professional copulators."* Footnote: In Sanskrit, *"Kama"* means text. *"Sutra"* means pleasure, desire, love, sex. Therefore Kama sutra can be translated into *"Sex Manual."*

KAMIDANA – (kam-me-*DA*-na) Literally *"God shelf."* A kamidana is a Japanese Shinto house shrine. It is an altar with a statue of Buddha, candles, flowers, and memorabilia of ancestors, relatives who had passed. Incenses are burned on the kamidana.

KANGAROO COURT – (kang-guh-*ROO KAWHT*) The word kangaroo is from the *Guugu Yimidhirr* language of the Endeavour River-area Aborigines of northeast Queensland Australia. It is the name for the iconic hopping marsupial of Australia. The term kangaroo entered the English language in 1770, introduced by explorer Captain James Cook (1728 – 1779) and botanist Joseph Banks (1743 – 1820). A kangaroo court is a sham legal proceeding conducted by vigilantes. It is designed to provide instant justice, often just revenge. Kangaroo courts have been employed by prisoners, soldiers on the battlefield, or settles in the wilds, regions devoid of law-and-order. The origin of the term *"kangaroo court"* is unknown. It is tempting to place its beginning in Australia, even without any evidence. However it's plausible that the term actually originated during the California Gold Rush of the 1850s. Of course, kangaroos are phenomenal jumpers. Too jumping to conclusions judicially may have been meted out to claim jumpers by vigilantes in the prospecting fields. After all, the term kangaroo was known in America of the early 1800s.

KAOLIN – (*KAY*-o-lin) A fine white clay used in the manufacture of porcelain.

KAPOK – (*KAY*-pock) Cotton fiber derived from the Cotton Silk, Cotton Wood, or Kapok Tree. Kapok is a silky down that invests the plant's seeds. The tree grows in the East Indies, Africa, and tropical America. The kapok flaws was used in pre-Columbian times to make cotton textile goods. The Taino Indians using kapok made Jamaica the cotton trade center of the Caribbean.

KAPOS – (*COP*-pohs) Jewish prisoners, often gangsters, who received better treatment for serving as brutal policemen and guards for the Nazis in the ghettos and concentration camps. The kapos, with their clubs and whips were usually sadistic thugs, comparable to the vicious Jews of the Detroit Purple Gang during the Prohibition Era. But not always. The story is told of a prisoner saying about a particularly brutal kapo: *"Look at that big important man, how far he has come. And to think that I knew him when he was just a bank president."* (Banker -> Bankster -> Gangster -> Kapo.)

KAPUT – (kuh-*POOT*) The German word *"kaput,"* was barrowed into English in 1895. In German, kaput means *"finished, worn out, dead."* Today, kaput means pretty much the same in English, including *"ruined, done for, demolished."* *"By August, 2023, Ron DeSantis' presidential campaign was kaput!"*

KARAITES – (*CAR*-ra-ites) A Jewish sect founded in Persia in the 8th century C.E. by the religious reformer Anan ben David (c. 715 – c. 795). The Karaites rejected the Talmud and all the teachings of the rabbis in favor of strict adherence to the Bible as the only source of Jewish law and practice. The Karaites were a Jewish Protestant, back-to-basics movement. As such, they too were persecuted by the orthodox authorities. Many Karaites settled in tolerant Eastern Poland in the 16th and 17th centuries C.E. In Troki, Poland, (now Traki, Lithuania) a Karaite catechism was written by Isaac ben Abraham (c. 1533 – c. 1594) called *The Fortress of Faith.* It was published in several countries. Voltaire (1694 – 1778) considered this Karaite catechism the greatest refutation of the divinity of Jesus ever written.

KARAOKE – (kar-ee-*OH*-kee) A popular form of interactive entertainment in some clubs and bars. Patrons are encouraged to sing-along, on stage, with recorded music, using a microphone. The music is from some well-known song, minus the lyrics. The words are displayed on a screen to aid the performer. Karaoke originated in Japan in the late 1960s. The term is a clipped compound of two Japanese words: *"kara,"* meaning *"empty"* and *"okesutora"* meaning *"orchestra."* Indeed, the karaoke orchestration is empty of lyrics.

KARAT – (*CARE*-rat) A measure of the purity of gold. One karat is 1/24th part pure gold. So 24 karat (24K) gold is 99.9% pure. 18 karat (18K) gold contains 18 parts gold to 6 parts alloy. 14 karat (14K) gold contains 14 parts gold to 10 parts alloy.

KARATE – (ka-*ROT*-tay) The term *"kara"* means empty in Japanese. Karate is a martial art using the empty hand. It is a weaponless defense that can kill. Hands, elbows, knees, or feet are used to strike sensitive areas of the aggressor's body. Courts of law have considered a master's hands, feet, arms and legs deadly weapons. Incidentally: Karate, the early martial arts were devised by the peaceful Japanese Buddhist monks. The samurai knights had disarmed the population. So Zen Buddhist monks devised fighting techniques using common farm implements and their hands and feet.

KARATE CHOP – (ka-*ROT*-tay *CHOP*) In martial arts, a sharp blow delivered by a slanting stroke with the side of the hand. Great blocks of concrete and wood can be split with the bare hand with a karate chop. The hand must hit the target at least 200 mph and withdrawn just as fast. The hand must not make contact with the surface struck for more than 5 to 10 one-thousandth of a second (*5/1,000* or *10/1,000*). At this speed, the entire shock wave is transferred to the target and not the hand. The target, not the hand is shattered. A professional karate chop can shatter a skull as well. Incidentally: This principle of physics is also demonstrated in a headbutt. The aggressor applying the blow is not injured. But the butt victim will require stitches or surgery.

KARDASHEV SCALE – (kar-*DOSH*-ev *SKAYL*) A method of measuring a civilization's level of technological advancement based on the amount and type of energy they are able to use. This measure was proposed by Russian Cosmologist Nikolai Kardashev (1932 – 2019) in 1964. The Kardashev Scale has 3 designated categories: Type I Civilization, also called a *"planetary civilization"* is what we experience on Earth. We use and store fossil fuel energy available on our planet, like coal, oil, and gas. Type II Civilization, also called a *"stellar civilization,"* is sophisticated enough to use and control energy throughout its own solar system. A stellar civilization can mine neighbor planets. Type III Civilization, also called a *"galactic civilization,"* can control energy at a scale of its entire host galaxy. A galactic civilization may be over a thousand years more advanced than Earthlings. This civilization will harness energy sources of which we have not yet dreamed.

KAREN – (*CARE*-ren) (Karenesque) A proper female name, in popular parlance, a pejorative slur for an obnoxious, angry, bitchy white woman. A Karen is typically middle-aged, moderately affluent, thoroughly suburban lady who flaunts her social entitlement. Karen exploits her privileged status to get her way. She is usually depicted wearing a blonde bob hairstyle. Stereotypically, Karen is constantly policing other people's behaviors. She is the *"Queen of Chutzpa."* Karen is combative, audacious, conservative, and bigoted, if not racist. She is forever arrogantly demanding to speak to your manager or supervisor. Insufferably litigious, Karen is always threatening to sue. The term and concept of Karen became widely popular in 2020. Viral videos on social media captured Karen-figures engaged in tantrums and confrontations, often of a racist nature. The origin of the Karen-character is unclear. It may have originated among African-American women. Historically, prior to Karen, *"Miss Ann,"* then *"Becky"* were used in a similar manner. Furthermore, the Karen- concept may have been reinforced in the popular culture by a *"Saturday Night Live"* comedy skit (April 18, 2018) on national television. Then, actor/comedian Chadwick Boseman (1976 - 2020) introduced Karen to the public. Incidentally: The male counterpart to Karen is Kevin.

KARMA – (*CAR*-ma) Restoration of Cosmic harmony through the Divine Law of Reciprocity. Karma is the causal and moral law of the universe. Karma is neither reward nor punishment but rectification, restored balance. It is a spiritual accountability debt or payment. People create their own Karma. As Jesus said: *"The Kingdom of Heaven is within you."* Therefore, by extension, so is the Kingdom of Hell. On the personal level, Karma is the reaping of what one had sowed. Karma is applied to this life, and to successive lifetimes. If life is a classroom, Karma is the lessons. *"Fate is nothing but the seeds committed in a prior state of existence,"* the Hindu Proverb proclaims. A perfect example of Karma follows. A couple were rabid racists. As a result, their daughter and first child married a Black man, of dark complexion. Their grandchildren are mulattoes. A punishment? Of course not. A Karmic lesson. *"That which ye sow, ye reap, reaper of the things he sowed."* – Buddha (c. 563 – c. 483 BCE). The Buddha also explained that: *"All creatures are what they are through the Karma of their deeds done in former and present existences."* A thousand years later, the Prophet Muhammad (c. 570 – 632 CE) warned: *"Verily your deeds will be brought back to you, as if you yourself were the creator of your own punishment."* Though life may not be fair, God, through Karma is. *"Karma means ultimate responsibility. You even take responsibility for your genetics."* – Jaggi Vasudev (b. 1957).

KARMA YOGA – (C*AR*-ma *YO*-ga) In Buddhism, devoting mundane daily chores as prayers. Karma yoga is the path that leads to release through selfless activity. It is finding holiness in every banal task: *"All I do I do in Zen."* Karma Yoga is action meditation, also called *"Naikan." "Kinhin"* for instance is walking meditation, a form of Karma Yoga. *"I draw water; I carry wood. That is my miracle."* – Zen Proverb.

KARMIC CLEANSING – (C*AR*-mik *KLEN*-sing) An act of contrition, a form of spiritual penance for past sins. Karmic cleansing is absolution when one is absolutely sorrowful and begs for Divine Forgiveness. However, one must serve her sentence in his personal Karmic Purgatory. This Purgatory is the prison of one's conscience. There, one re-lives, in painful detail, all the misdeeds of one's life. Every crime, dishonest, hurtful evil deed is relived with remorse, regret, shame, guilt, and humiliation. The mental anguish is excruciating but cleansing. However, this agonizing Karmic Cleansing is essential in order to attain grace and enlightenment. Though Karmic Cleansing is a *Dark Night of the Soul,* it rescues the soul from darkness. One must petition God to provide a Karmic Cleansing. It is open to everyone. Jesus said: *"Many are call, but few are chosen"* – Matthew 22:14. More accurately: *"All are called, but few choose to listen."*

KARMIC CURRICULUM – (C*AR*-mik ker-*RIK*-que-lum) Divine lessons each individual is obliged to learn as we pass through life on the road to enlightenment. Nothing that happens is an accident, and there are no coincidences. Every experience, all of our choices – good and bad – serves as lessons in the Karmic Curriculum. The most painful lessons were the most necessary. No two people share the exact same syllabus. Every victory and defeat, every success and failure, every disappointment and blessing is intended to teach. This educational process lasts a lifetime – several lifetimes if necessary. The goal of the curriculum is perfection, sanctity, enlightenment. Successful, satisfactory accomplishment of the Karmic Curriculum results in atonement (*at-ONE-ment*) with God.

KARMIC INSTRUMENT – (C*AR*-mik *IN*-struh-ment) A Divinely recruited agent, a heavenly appointed assistant. One selected by God to settle a Karmic score. Many Old Testament Prophets are said to have served as Karmic instruments. One may be chosen to serve as an instrument in God's hand. It is possible that a wrong inflicted on another, is righting a past wrong committed by that other. God simply used an individual to mete out his Karmic judgement. Indeed, God works in mysterious ways. Nevertheless, this is a controversial and risky precept. The Karmic instrument concept can serve as a justification for capital punishment. An executioner can be considered an angel of retribution or death. Or maybe not. This is a dangerous proposition, open to atrocious abuse. Any sadist or psychopath can justify any act of savagery by declaring: *"God made me do it. He had it coming."* Perhaps the concept of Karmic instrument is better left as a theoretical, philosophical theory.

KARMIC INTERRELATEDNESS – (C*AR*-mik in-ter-ree-*LAY*-ted-nes) (Interrelated Karma) Karma is a spiritual accountability debt or payment. It is justice for past sins, crimes, offenses, or for kindness, generosity, righteousness. The purpose of Karma is to teach the individual, and to restore cosmic balance and harmony. To be interrelated is to be connected, associated, reciprocal with others. All souls are interrelated. This is even more so among soul mates or loved ones. Married couples, families share interrelated Karmas to some degree. What happens to one member will affect all others in some way. Our Karmas function complementarily. For example, it may be in my Karmic account to win the lottery. After all, in the past or in some past life, I was generously charitable. This *"good luck"* would make my wife and children instantly wealthy. But in their Karmas, they may not deserve the good fortune. Therefore I fail to win the lottery, due to Karmic interrelatedness. This may be an explanation why bad things sometimes happen to good people.

KARMIC JUSTICE – (*CAR*-mik *JUS*-tis) Divine reciprocity. Karmic Justice is a Spiritual righting of wrongs, a readjustment to cosmic balance and harmony. Whether he knows it or not, Pastor Joel Osteen (b. 1963) is citing Karmic justice when he advises us to *"Let God be your vindicator."* Karmic Justice is the reason why some metaphysicians believe that Donald Trump (b. 1946) was elevated to the Presidency. Trump is the perfect representative of *"American Exceptionalism"* [read: *"hubris"*]. Karmic Justice will bring the bully down, along with the bully nation he commands. *"Make America Great,"* will manifest as *"Humiliate America,"* for flirting with fascism. Too, Donald Trump had criminally hurt and destroyed so many people in his life. New York City is too small a stage for his Karmic humiliation. Divine reciprocity had elevated Trump to the pinnacle of power and visibility, so his fall is from the greatest height before a global audience. That will be Trump's Karmic justice. Never cast or pray a curse on another. Simply pray for God's Karmic Justice. Only the righteous, compassionate, guiltless pray God's Karmic Justice on themselves. The guilty, immoral, contemptable wouldn't dare. *"For as the heavens are higher than the earth, so are My ways higher than your ways and My thoughts higher than your thoughts, declares the Lord."* – Isaiah 55:9.

KARMIC PROXY – (*CAR*-mik *PROK*-see) Karma is Divine Justice, the re- establishment of cosmic harmony. A proxy is an agent, deputized to perform a service. To understand the karmic proxy concept, understand that all souls, as spirit, are united. Individual spirits are parts of the whole. So in this sense, we are all one spiritual organism. When one part of the organism goes wrong, the others must react to promote correction. That's why people are recruited to serve as karmic proxies. We are deputized as angel agents, to set our brothers and sisters straight. We will not be aware of the mission assigned to us. We may use cruelty to advance another's karmic justice, which is all part of a Divine Plan. God had used Satan as a karmic proxy in the Book of Job (1:9-11). In fact, the name *"Satan"* is Hebrew for *"adversary."* Satan was used to lash Job with misfortune in order to test his faith. We too may act satanically toward others, not knowing that we are serving as God's karmic proxy. Perhaps that was in Jesus' mind when he said: *"Father forgive them, for they know not what they do."* – (Luke 23:34).

KARMIC PURGATORY – (*CAR*-mik *PUR*-ga-tor-ree) A Divine opportunity to redress past transgressions for future bliss. Serving time in a state of Karmic Purgatory is paying a spiritual debt in order to reestablish the Cosmic balance. It should not be seen as Providential punishment. It is comparable to a spiritual bankruptcy, which clears the way for a new and better life. Indeed, Karmic Purgatory will entail suffering, misfortune, grief, a *"Dark Night of the Soul."* But this is all part of the Spiritual purgative (cleaning) which is the purpose of Purgatory. Successfully serving a sentence in Karmic Purgatory is an epiphanal experience, which will result in a better human being. One learns empathy, sympathy, compassion, forgiveness, and love. Karmic Purgatory is the portal to spiritual Enlightenment. *"Beings with un-redeemed earthly Karma are not permitted after astral death to go to the high causal sphere of cosmic ideas but must shuttle to and fro from the physical and astral worlds."* – Sri Yukteswar Giri (1855 – 1936).

KARMIC REACTION – (*CAR*-mik ree-*AK*-shun) The balancing of the *Akashic Books*. (Akashic Record has been defined as *"God's memory"*.) Many mystics believe that this is neither punishment nor reward, but harmonizing the Cosmos, the *Law of Universal Reciprocity* at work. There are no victims or persecutors in a Karmic Reaction, only Karmic performers. Each are playing a preordained role. This is a difficult concept to accept on the egocentric level. For example, an apparently innocent child suffering from disease, starvation, or persecution may seem like cruel injustice. However, the soul of the child may have inhabited a vile tyrant who murdered children in a former life. That is a Karmic Reaction.

KARMIC RECYCLING – (*CAR*-mik ree-*SY*-cuhl-ling) (Karmicly Recycled) Expedited reincarnation. To be reincarnated or born again in the flesh or recycled. Of course, one must first die. To expedite death is to be killed. This expedites the reincarnation which is Karmic Recycling. Karma is one's just deserts. If one lives an evil life, he (or she) will be reincarnated or recycled for another go at life. Hopefully she (or he) will get it right this time. The most evil people are sometimes the most powerful. These are dictators. They are responsible for mass killings, genocide, ethnic cleansing, torture, horror, misery on a massive scale. With such evil people, Karmic Justice demands Karmic Recycling – or assassination. This is not a call for general capital punishment. In fact, reincarnation is not an act of punishment or reward. Their Karma determines if they warrant immediate recycling. It is giving a vile person another chance at life, free of evil ways. Evil dictators should be Karmicly Recycled.

KARMIC RESIDUE – (*CAR*-mik *RES*-si-doo) Debits from a former existence. Unpaid debts or assets that weren't squared then, must now be adjusted. The *Akashic Books* must be balanced. Karmic residue may account for bouts of good and bad luck. Some mystics maintain that enigmatic pains may also result from past-lives traumas. Love at first sight may be the Karmic Residue from a relationship in a former life. An instant dislike of a stranger may be residual emotions from an earlier existence. Perhaps homosexual impulses or a gay preference is due to actually being a member of the opposite sex in a former life, with several gratifying love affairs.

KARMIC VOMITIVE – (*CAR*-mik *VOM*-mit-tiv) A national regurgitation of social- political-economic toxins, accumulated over decades, culminating with the disgusting Trump Presidency (2017). A collective catharsis will sweep across American, as the people recover from their flirtation with fascism, embodied by Donald Trump (b. 1946). Trump, his co-conspirators, corporate capitalists, Republican and Evangelical supporters, along with his racist and stupid admirers have *"Sowed the wind, and now will reap the whirlwind,"*– Hosea 8:7. They will face their Karmic justice. (In February, 2018, Arizona Congressman Ruben Gallego (b. 1979) warned: *"You* [Trump] *are a psychopath…. America will regret the day you were ever born!"*. The social debacle, political fiasco, economic catastrophe, and spiritual abasement brought about by Donald Trump will have served as America's *"Dark Night of the Soul."* Like a punitive Biblical plague, America will be scared straight. The nation will initially stagger with illness, hungover from her anti-democratic debauchery. The neo-Nazi orgy will require a collective catharsis by the American people.

After the Trumpistic fascism has been vomited, a Karmic relief will overcome the country. We had stood at the brink of the abyss, but managed to step back in time, toward sanity. Never again will the right-wing be allowed to take us off the right-track. The Liberal, Progressive reaction will come swiftly. The reign of the rich will be ended. Nationalization will overtake privatization. Corporatism will give way to collectivism. Socialism will replace capitalism. Cooperation will supersede competition. Need will supplant greed. Just taxation will redistribute the wealth. Distributive justice will have been accomplished. In a manner Trump could never have imagined, totally contrary to his intentions, Trump's tenure would serendipitously *"Make America Great Again."*

KARP – (*CARP*) (Karping) A peevish complaint. Karping is finding fault or complaining querulously. *"Stop your karping already."*

KARST – (*CARST*) A rugged limestone terrain of jagged rock, caves, sinkholes, subterranean rivers. Unearthly landscapes are carved out when karst deposits dissolve in acidic rain. Central Jamaica's mountainous *"cockpit country"* serves as a good example of karst topography, a hideaway for escaped slaves (Maroons).

KARUNA – (car-*ROON*-na) The Mahayana Buddhist term for compassion, a Bodhisattvas trait.

KASBAH – (Or Casbah, pronounced cash-*BAH*.) (also Casbah) A fortified Berber house in North Africa, during the days of the great camel caravans. They were especially prominent in Algeria. The merchants lived in their Kasbah and stored their valuable merchandise. The Kasbah had to be fortress-like to repel marauding bandits. *"Come with me to ze Casbah."* Pepe le Moko (Charles Boyer, 1899 - 1978) to Gaby (Hedy Lamarr, 1914 - 2000) in the movie *"Algiers,"* (1937).

KASHA – (*KA*-sha) A Polish/Russian word for porridge or gruel but most likely oatmeal. A breakfast (or staple for the very poor) made of buckwheat or oats (any grain actually), boiled in milky water (if milk can be afforded).

KASHMIR – (*CASH*-meer) A state in the Indian sub-continent adjacent to India, Pakistan, Sinkiang, and Tibet. Though today a part of India, Kashmir has been a bloody bone of contention between Muslim Pakistan and Hindu India (both nuclear powers). Incidentally: The Kashmir goat provides the fine soft wool called cashmere.

KASHUBIANS – (ka-*SHOO*-bee-ans) (Kashubs) A West Slavic, Polish minority group with a high degree of Germanic and Danish blood and ethnicity. Though Polish citizens, the Kashubian dialect is distinguishable with difficulty from mainstream Polish. The original homeland of the Kashubs is in Pomerania (Northern Poland) at the mouth of the Vistula River on the Baltic Sea. The Major city with a Kashubian population is Gdansk (Danzig in German).

KATABATIC WIND – (ka-ta-*BA*-tic *WIND*) A rapid flow of dense cold air rushing down the slopes of high ice-caped mountains or glaciers.

KATANA – (ka-*TON*-na) Traditional Japanese Samurai sword, most remarkable metallurgical artifact known to man. It was perfected in the 13th century to repel the Mongol invasion of Kublai Khan (1215 – 1294). The katana is about 23 to 28 inches in length, sharpened on one edge. It is forged from 32,000 layers of steel, each only a hundred-thousandth-of-an-inch thick (1/100,000). It will take a traditional craftsman 8 to 10 months to create one sword. The manufacturing process is a mystic Zen procedure. Tests have shown that a perfected katana is able to slice through 3 to 5 corpses in one great swipe. Incidentally: The katana was the primary weapon of the Samurai. They depended on the peasants for their keep, even for their katanas. In return, the Samurai protected and robbed the villagers.

KATHARISMA – (cath-ar-RIS-ma) Greek for cleaning. Katharisma means sweeping, mopping the floors, vacuuming the rugs, dusting the furniture, general housekeeping, washing-up, cleaning, in the Greek language.

KATHARISMAMANIA – (cath-ar-ris-ma-*MAY*-nee-ah) (Katharismamaniac) (also Purusomania) The neurotic condition of obsessive/compulsive cleaning. A katharismamaniac is driven to clean the house, sweep and wash the floors whether they need it or not.

KATHARISMAMANIAC – (cath-ar-ris-ma-*MAY*-nee-ak) (also Purusomaniac) A neurotic condition in which a person is an obsessive/compulsive cleaner. Almost always a woman, the katharismamaniac is addicted to house cleaning. She can drive the other members of the household crazy. The house becomes more a museum than a home, a living quarters.

KATHARISMAPHOBIA – (cath-ar-ris-ma-*FOH*-bee-ah) (Katharismaphobiac) (also Purusophobia) A neurotic distaste, even fear of house cleaning. Most no one enjoys cleaning house. But a katharismaphobiac has a psychological dread, that requires professional attention.

KATHARISMAPHOBIAC – (cath-ar-ris-ma-*FOH*-bee-ak) (Katharismaphobia) (also Purusophobiac) One suffering from a neurotic dislike or fear of house cleaning. House cleaning is work, a necessary chore. Few people find it to be fun. But a katharismaphobiac would rather go to the dentist, than clean the house. It goes without saying that the house is a sight! *"Excuse the mess, we live here."* – Comedian Roseanne Barr (b. 1952).

KATHENOTHEISM – (ka-then-no-*THEE*-is-um) A form of polytheism (many gods) in which each God is worshiped as supreme at a designated time of the year. Each God represents some divine quality or power and is recognized and revered at His/Her special feast-time. In kathenotheism, the gods take turns as chairman of the heavenly department.

KATOPTRONOPHILIA – (cat-top-tro-no-*FEE*-lee-ah) (Katoptronophiliac) A sexual fetish in which one is aroused by having sex before mirrors. A katoptronophiliac becomes extremely excited when he or she can watch themselves undress, masturbate, or participate in intercourse. This is accomplished by lining the bedroom with mirrors – walls and ceiling. If mirrors serve as an aphrodisiactic agent, how is it different from dim candle light, wine, romantic music or stimulating drugs? It's not. *"The only unnatural sex act is that which you cannot perform."* – Sexologist Dr. Alfred Kinsey (1894 – 1956).

KATRINA – (ka-*TREE*-na) The category 5 hurricane that divested New Orleans and surrounding area on August 29, 2005. Katrina wreaked over $100 billion dollars of damage and killed almost 2,000 people. It also killed George W. Bush's (b. 1946) Presidency. The incompetence of his government, and mismanagement of his administration doomed Bush's legacy. Since then, the name Katrina had been added to the political lexicon to indicate a monumental failure, by which the leader will be defined. There is a strong possibility that the vile, despicable child separation policy applied to Hispanic immigrants will serve as Donald Trump's (b. 1946) Katrina. We can only hope.

KAYFABE – (*KEE*-fayb) (Kayfabing) Faking a performance. Kayfabe is a slang term in the parlance of the WWE (<u>W</u>orld <u>W</u>restling <u>E</u>ntertainment). Kaybabe means maintaining the illusion, the parts and personas assumed by the wrestlers as actors. In a movie, a professional actor strives to create an image of a fictitious character. So do professional wrestlers, and this is their kayfabe. Wrestlers assume roles. Some play the hero, others the villain. They take on fake personalities and wear costumes, create rivalries that's portrayed as genuine hatred. It is all showboating, contrived, rehearsed. However, unlike movie actors whose characters die when the actor is off the set, the kayfabe does not end out of the ring but must be played out through their daily lives. World Wresting is indeed Entertainment. That's not to say that the wrestlers are not great athletes. They certainly are. Unlike movie actors, wresting actors serve as their own stuntmen and women. Often do they get hurt. Some have died young soon after retirement. But that's not to say that there isn't the occasional *"chicken blood"* applied to reinforce the kayfabe. Incidentally: The term *"kayfabe"* has been used in pro wrestling since the 1980s. The origin of this term is uncertain. It may have originated in the carnival world as a code word for *"fake."*

KATYN – (ka-*TEEN*) A forest in Russia near Smolensk where in 1940, Russian secret police executed over 22,000 Polish POW's. They especially targeted the Polish officer corps. They were shot in the back of the head, after digging their own graves. The Poles were captured after the dual-invasion of Poland by Germany and Russia in 1939, commencing World War Two. Joseph Stalin (1878 – 1953) blamed the mass murder on the Nazis. Actually, he had hoped to decapitate the military/intellectual leadership of Poland, in order to make the country more manageable to govern and exploit. The Katyn Forest Massacre was the greatest atrocity of its type in history. This atrocity was committed by *"Stalinists,"* not by *Communists* or *Socialists*. In 1992, Russian President Boris Yeltsin (1931 – 1007) presented the Polish President, Lech Walesa (b. 1943) (pronounced *Vawesa*) with the original order of execution, signed by the vile Stalin.

KATYUSHA ROCKETS – (kat-tee-*YU*-sha *ROC*-kets) Katyusha is a Russian diminutive of the name *Kathy*. Katyusha was the Russian M-13 rocket launcher first introduced during World War Two. Several rockets are mounted on a truck, making the weapon very mobile. This self-propelled artillery weapon was inaccurate (like a shotgun) but terrifying and effective. It scattered explosive charges on the enemy's position. The Katyusha Rocket had a distinctive sound, a blood-curdling wail or whine like a pipe organ. That won it the nickname, *"Stalin's Organ."* The Katyusha Rocket launcher is still in use by the Russians, having undergone at least 9 upgrades.

KAZAKHSTAN – (kah-zahk-*STAHN*) A huge Central Asian nation (1,052,100 square miles) with its western region reaching into Eastern Europe (10%). Kazakhstan is almost as large as Alaska, Texas, and New Mexico combined. The name translates into the *"Land of the Wanderers."* The Kazakhstanis were historically a nomadic people. With a population of 19,398,331, Kazakhstan has fewer people than New York State. Most of its citizens are Muslims. In 1990, Kazakhstan gained its independence from Russia with the disintegration of the Soviet Union. Today, its 4,254 miles border with Russia is the second longest in the world, (surpassed only by the U.S. – Canada border, 5,525 miles). With Russia's bellicose and expansionist government (2022), Kazakhstan is in a precarious geopolitical position. Geography has been challenging to Kazakhstan. It is the largest landlocked nation in the world, a great disadvantage. This means that it must be dependent on neighboring nations for access to the sea, which jeopardizes its international trade. Kazakhstan borders China on the east; Uzbekistan, Kyrgyzstan, and Turkmenistan on the south; Russia on the north and west; with the landlocked Caspian Sea also on the eastern border. Kazakhstan's geography presents an economic handicap but positions it with great strategic importance. Kazakhstan is certain to become more prominent in international affairs and in the news, if it petitions to join the EU (European Union) and NATO (North Atlantic Treaty Organization).

KEA – (*KEE*-ya) Vampire Bird. A large New Zealand parrot with olive-green plumage and bright orange under the wings. It inhabits the forest and mountain regions of the South Island. The kea is the world's only alpine parrot. It nests in crevices among the tree roots. The kea is thought to be the world's most intelligent bird (though the jay or crow family is said to be the smartest group). It has a large, sharp, curved beak. The kea is omnivorous, consuming leaves, berries, insects, and carrion. The kea is called the *"vampire bird."* It will bite animals like sheep on the back, and feast on its fat.

KEBAB – (kuh-BOB) (also Kabob) A simple culinary delight consisting of various meats, seafood, and vegetables (tomatoes, green peppers, onions, most anything), skewered on a stick. The kebabs are usually the size of a single meal. The kebab is roasted or barbequed.

KEISTER – (*KEES*-ter) One's buttocks or ass. In prison slang, keister is a verb meaning to hide contraband in one's rectum.

KELLOGG – (*KEL*-log) A hog breeder and butcher. The names derives from the 13th century term *"kill hog."* The kellogg provided the village with pork. The term bears no present day relationship to *"Kill Hog Cornflakes."*

KEMALISM – (kem-*MAUL*-is-um) The socio-political philosophy, ideology of Mustafa Kemal (c. 1881 – 1938), historically known as *Ataturk, "Father of the Turks."* Kemal as Ataturk was the founder of modern Turkey. After Turkey's defeat in World War One (1914 – 1918), Mustafa Kemal, a military officer led the revolution that ended the ancient Ottoman dynasty. Ataturk intended to transform Turkey into a stable Western, European-like nation, rather than a shaky Islamic, Middle Eastern entity. This is Kemalism – Progressivism. Ataturk struggled to liberalize Turkey. Primarily, he divorced religion from government. The Islamic caliphate was abolished, Sharia Law forbidden. The mosques were stripped of their political power, and their services monitored. Turkish women were fully liberated, as are European women. The Arabic Turkish language, script was Latinized. Schools were secularized. Only non-religious political parties were tolerated. Ataturk appealed to Europe for guidance: Switzerland for civil law; Germany for commercial regulations; France for administrative practices; and, for a criminal code, to Italy. Like all great men, Ataturk was thoroughly loved and thoroughly hated. Conservative, reactionary Islamists, anti-revolutionaries detested him. Despite them, Ataturk knew what was best for his people, and for the future of Turkey. In fact, Ataturk's motto was: *"For the People, In Spite of the People."* Ataturk forced a resistant Turkey down the Liberal, Progressive path. Like heroic Josep Tito (1892 – 1980) of old Yugoslavia, Ataturk was a benevolent despot of sorts. Former Secretary of State Madeleine Albright (1937 - 2022) characterized Kemalism as *"Parliamentary democracy, but one that is operated within a secular cage."* America and other nations must learn from Ataturk's example. A Socialistic Kemalism can be introduced, or imposed on a resistant America, *"For the People, In Spite of the People."* Like Islamism in Turkey, oppressive, reactionary capitalism can be abolished. Democracy can flourish in a free America, within a Socialist cage. Like Democracy, Socialism would be untouchable, constitutionally protected. Counter-revolutionaries would not be tolerated. When President Thomas Jefferson (1743 – 1826) purchased the Louisiana Territory, he never consulted Congress. Jefferson explained: *"The Executive, which so much advances the good of his country, has done an act beyond the Constitution....It is the case of the guardian to his ward saying, 'I did this for your good!'"* So too was Kemalism. Incidentally: Presently (July 2021), the fascistic Turkish President, Recep Erdogan (b. 1954) is chipping away Kemalism, as fascistic Donald Trump (b. 1946) had chipped-away at Democracy. Footnote: On every November 10, at precisely 9:05 a.m., the entire nation of Turkey pauses for one full minute. Every flag is lowered half-mast; all labor and commerce ceases; all TV, radio, internet, music, noise is silenced; all traffic stops and motorists exit their vehicles, and stand at attention, as do all pedestrians. Nobody speaks for one full minute. This is the moment that Mustafa Kemal Ataturk died in 1938. This is the greatest tribute to any leader anywhere in the world.

KENDO – (*KEN*-dow) The ancient Japanese art of swordsmanship.

KENSHO – (*KEN*-show) In Buddhism, seeing into one's nature, or the first experience of *satori, "awakening."*

KEPT MAN – (kept MAN) A gigolo, or boy-toy. A kept man is provided money and lodging, usually by a wealthy older lady, in exchange for sexual favors. A kept man need not work, except on his romantic and sexual skills. He is the counterpart to the female *"gold-digger."* A Caveat: Do not confuse a kept man with a retired man, especially one with a younger wife that still works. A retired man collects Social Security for the decades of his labor. Too, he may have bonds, inheritances, stocks, pensions or may write and sell books. Therefore, a retired man has independent income, though he does not depart each morning to a workplace anymore. In fact, the *"kept-man"* may be keeping his wife above water, economically. Incidentally: In August 2023, corrupt Supreme Court Justice Clarence Thomas (b. 1948) has been called a *"kept man"* by political pundits. Thomas is *"kept"* (as was his enslaved ancestors) by powerful rich white men. Thomas has sold his influence to these capitalist billionaires for many millions of dollars-worth of gifts, favors, vacations, and money. Thomas's greed and perfidy is absolutely shameless. Any other American, other than a Supreme Court Justice would be behind bars long ago.

KERATIN – (*KER*-ra-tin) A protein found in the dead outer skin layer. Horns, antlers, hoofs, hair, nails, claws, feathers and bills are made of keratin. All of these accoutrements are insensitive to pain. That's why the surgery called a haircut does not hurt (unless it's a terrible job).

KERFUFFLE – (ker-*FUFF*-fill) A big commotion, confusion, dispute, a huge fuss. Kerfuffle is primarily an American usage, a variant of the English *"carfuffle,"* also used in Scotland and Canada. The term probably derives from the dialectical Scottish verb *"fuffle,"* (1530's) meaning *"to throw into disorder."*

KEROSINE – (ker-o-*SEEN*) (also Kerosene) A mixture of liquid hydrocarbons obtained by distilling petroleum or bituminous shale. Kerosine is sometimes called paraffin. It ignites slowly, unlike explosive gasoline. Therefore kerosene is used in domestic heaters, lamps, and to light barbecues. Never put dangerous gasoline in a can marked kerosine, or a tragedy may occur. Kerosine is also used as an aircraft fuel, solvent, and cleanser. Incidentally: A few ounces of kerosine in the soapy wash bucket will give the floor a fresh scent, shiny gleam, and repel bugs.

KETCHUP – (*KECH*-up) A condiment sauce consisting of pureed tomatoes, onions, vinegar, sugar, and spices. Ketchup is the most popular condiment flavoring in the world. The term originated from the Chinese *"kechiap,* meaning *"brine of fish."* The sauce and term migrated to Malaysia where it modified to *"kichap."* Arriving in England the condiment became recognized as *"catchup"* (1680's). We would not recognize catchup as our *"ketchup,"* because it did not include tomato paste. Food additives were essential before refrigeration, for meat often came to the table rancid. Condiments were necessary to disguise the putrid taste. That's why in Pittsburgh, Pennsylvania, Henry J. Heinz (1844 – 1919) sought the perfect sauce. After exhaustive experimentation, Heinz developed our ketchup in 1869. He packaged his tomato sauce in clear bottles, to see its rich red purity. Heinz used the railroads to distribute the product nationally. Heinz became a multi-millionaire. Competitors copied Heinz recipe and undercut his price with cheaper inferior and dangerous additives. Heinz protested and lobbied Congress which contributed to the enactment of the Food and Drug Act in 1906. Incidentally: The small plastic packets of Heinz ketchup distributed by fastfood outlets, if lined-up, would stretch to the moon.

KETOSIS – (kee-*TOH*-sis) A metabolic defense mechanism in which the liver releases *"ketone bodies"* into the bloodstream when glucose or sugar level is too low. Ketone bodies or ketones are water-soluble molecules (CH_3COCH_3) that break down body fat and converts it to glucose or sugar. Therefore, ketosis is a physiological term for losing weight. Every organ, every cell in the body must be fed. The brain and live will consume only sugar or glucose. When one diets, fasts, or starves, glucose in the body is depleted. You feel painful hunger pangs and a headache. The body, especially the brain is hungry. That's when the brain orders the liver to release the ketones. The ketones burn the body fat into sugar (glucose). Suddenly, the hunger and headache are gone. This is why the initial hours of a diet or fast are uncomfortable or painful. But when the ketones convert your body fat to sugar, you feel fine. As long as you have body fat to burn (turn to sugar) all is well. In fact, the diet or fast becomes easier and you continue to lose weight. But beware of extremes. Once all your body fat (glucose reserve) is gone, you enter starvation. The ketone bodies can find no more fat, so they start to digest your muscles. This dangerous advanced ketosis is self-cannibalism. You can see the result of this process in famines, as in concentration camp victims.

KETTLE LAKES – (*KET*-tal *LAYKS*) Glacial lakes or lakes created by glaciers. Glaciers had gouged-out great depressions and had embedded themselves into the ground like colossal ice cubes. When they melted, a kettle lake was formed. Northern latitudes are rich in kettle lakes. Incidentally: Canada has more lakes that the rest of the world combined, most being kettle lakes.

KEVIN – (*KEV*-in) The male counterpart to the loudmouth busybody Karen. Kevin, like Karen, is a butt-in. He too makes everyone's business his concern. Whether he is on the left or right, Kevin is the self-appointed gendarme of the community. He is opinionated, argumentative, dictatorial, and confrontational. Kevin will stubbornly try to impose his bias on others. Of course, he's a know-it- all. Kevin styles himself as an attorney. A Kevin next door will lower the value of your home.

KEVORK – (ker-*VORK*) (Kevorked, Kevorking) Mercy killing. To kevork is to fulfil one's wish to hasten one's death by some form of assisted suicide. The assistant is a physician and death is induced by lethal injection. The term *"kevork"* is an abbreviated eponym taken from the name of Dr. Jack Kevorkian (1928 – 2011), a pioneer advocate of voluntary euthanasia. Dr. Kevorkian, an *"Angel of Mercy,"* was branded *"Doctor Death."* He served time in prison upholding his conviction that a person living in agony has the right to die if they wish. Too, it should be a dignified, peaceful, painless death, not blowing out one's brains. After all, we put animals, pets out of their misery, but not our loved-ones. As with abortion, kevorking or mercy killing is an example of the law lagging behind the social need. *"Thank Heaven! The crisis, the danger is past, and the lingering illness, is over at last, and the fever called 'Living' is conquered at last."* – Edgar Allan Poe (1809 – 1849). *"Death is not the greatest of evils. It is worst to want to die, and not be able to."* – Sophocles (c. 497 – 406 BCE).

KEYNESIANISM – (*CAIN*-see-in-is-um) The Liberal logical economic prescriptions of John Maynard Keynes (1883 – 1946). Keyes maintained that it is the duty of government to direct the economy and assure full employment by massive public spending on social programs. Put money in the hands of the poor for an overall healthy economy. This is done by taxing the rich and corporations.

KFC – (*kay-ef-SEE*) An abbreviation (initialism) for Kentucky *FRIED* Chicken. The corporate capitalists of KFC quit using the original full name to downplay the word *FRIED*. As America became health conscious and aware of the risks of fat and cholesterol, KFC profits dropped. So in order to distract and deceive the consumer about consuming more fat, the word *FRIED* was censored. Actually, Kentucky *FRIED* Chicken is pressure cooked, which is deep *FRIED* in grease. A case of capitalist deception. Incidentally: Its questionable how many pieces of *KFC* is actually *KFR* – *"Kentucky Fried Rooster."* *"Seek midday nourishment. Visit memorial acclaimed war hero Colonel Sanders."* – Chuck Palahniuk (b. 1969).

KGB – (kay-jee-*BEE*) A Russian initialism for "Komitet Gosudarstvennoy Bezopasnosti," meaning *"Committee of State Security."* The KGB was the Russian secret police and chief foreign intelligence, spy organization. With the disintegration of the Soviet Union in 1991, the KGB was supplanted by the GRU "Glavoye Razvedyvatel'noye Upravleniye" (*"Chief Intelligence Headquarters"*) in 1992. Vladimir Putin (b. 1952), Dictopresident of Russia, is a firmer KGB Officer.

KHADIJA – (ka-*DEE*-jah) Khadija (c. 555 – 620) was a rich Arab merchant woman who became Mohammad's first wife. She was much older than Mohammad and supported him. Khadija is regarded as the first Muslim. She was the first person to accept the prophecy of Mohammad. British-American scholar, Thomas C. Pasieka (b. 1996) declared: *"The irony that many Muslim women are kept in virtual bondage today (Purdah). After all, the first Muslim was a woman, Khadija, who was Mohammed's wife. Too, Khadija supported the Prophet, enabling the birth of Islam."*

KHAKI – (*CA*-kee) A tough, durable, twilled cotton cloth, dull yellowish-brown, perhaps beige in color, used especially for military uniforms. *"Khaki"* is a Persian (Iranian) word for *"dust."* It originally meant *"dust-colored,"* but was soon applied to the color of that fabric. Having khaki or dust-colored uniforms was a camouflaged advantage in the Middle East. The fabric khaki is still associated with the color beige. However, all khaki uniforms are not beige today. Nevertheless, green uniforms made of khaki material are not called khaki.

KHASHOGGI MURDER – (ka-*SHOW*-gee *MUR*-der) The kidnapping, torture, murder, and dismemberment of American resident and Washington Post journalist Jamal Khashoggi (1958 – 2018) by the Saudis at their consulate in Turkey (October 2018). The assassination was ordered by the de facto dictator of Saudi Arabia, Crowned Prince Mohammad bin Salman (b. 1985). The Saudis are the slimiest Arab allies of America. They buy U.S. weapons and protection, while funding anti-American terrorists. Almost all of the terrorists who attacked America on 9/11 were Saudis. They are vilely perfidious! President Donald Trump was right once when he declared that *"Saudi Arabia would not last two weeks without American military protection."* Jamal Khashoggi was accosted by 15 Saudi hitmen in the consulate. His fingers were sliced-off during the interrogation. Khashoggi was then beheaded. His body was dissected by a coroner with a bone saw. The remains were carted away in a trunk. Savagely, medievally gruesome! But there was no outrage on the part of the U.S. Government. In fact, President Trump and his Republican lackeys tried to excuse the atrocity. Trump and his son-in-law, Jared Kushner (b. 1981) are heavily invested in the Saudi royal family. Trump boasted: *"The Saudis pay me millions, hundred-of-millions. They buy my toys and make me rich. What am I supposed to do, dislike them?"* Trump and Jared are as slimy as the Saudis, a match made in hell. Incidentally: Since then, the Saudis had given Trump's son-in-law, Jared, 2 billion dollars. That is yet to be investigated and adjudicated.

KHAT – (pronounced *COT*) (also Kat, Qat) *Catha edulis* is a flowering bush native to the Arabian Peninsula and the Horn of Africa. Like coca leaves in the Andes, Khat leaves have been chewed by native people for thousands of years. It is a stimulant, appetite suppressor, and euphoriate. Khat is widely partaken in Djibouti, Kenya, Ethiopia, Somalia and Yemen. About 80% of the Yemenis men chew Khat regularly. The drug produces a mild dependence and is a controlled substance in America. If khat is illegal, cigarettes should be as well.

KHE SANH – (kay *SAHN*) The longest battle of the Vietnam War (77 days) from January 21 to July 9, 1968. Khe Sanh was a fire base on a plateau in Quang Tri Province, Vietnam. About 6,000 U.S. Marines were trapped by 24,000 NVA (Northern Vietnam Army) regulars around their fire-base on a flat hilltop. The siege resembled the French defeat at Dien Bien Phu in 1954. To avoid the same result, the Americans dropped over 100,000 tons of bombs (5 tons for each invading Vietnamese) costing over a billion dollars. The marines were supplied by air with great peril to the flyers. The U.S. Marines withstood the siege and withdrew from Khe Sanh, allowing the base to fall to the NVA. About 274 Americans were killed. The Vietnamese lost about 20 times that number. Therefore, the Battle of Khe Sanh was a tactical U.S. victory, but a strategic defeat, as was the entire war. The overall U.S. commander, General William Westmoreland (1914 – 2005) asked to use tactical nuclear weapons against the Vietnamese at Khe Sanh. He was denied. Never trust the military!

KIBITZ – (*KIB*-bitz) A Yiddishism for banter, joking around, good-natured raillery. To kibitz is to exchange light, playful teasing remarks.

KIBITZER – (*KIB*-bit-zer) A Yiddishism for a wisecracker, especially in a serious situation. A kibitzer tends to offer unsolicited advice readily.

KIBBUTZ – (*KIB*-bootz) (Kibbutzim) Socialistic Jewish Israeli collective communes, reminiscent of the *Commun-ist* farms in Russia, which inspired them. The Israeli kibbutz is our best example of a successful, harmonious Socialist community. Kibbutzim are practically synonymous with cooperation. The positive effects of communal living are evident in the fact that the average I.Q. of the communards in the kibbutz is 115, which is 15 points above the national average. Because of the success of the collective, Socialistic, Communistic Kibbutzim, the U.S. and Britain were initially reluctant to support and recognize the new state of Israel. Russia did.

KICKBACK – (*KICK*-back) A nefarious capitalist transaction to impede free trade by favoring big business. This unethical and often illegal rebate is given by suppliers (of raw materials, for instance) to manufacturers as a gratuity for the business. Smaller suppliers cannot afford to offer kickbacks [read: *bribes*], so they are out of business. Kickbacks stifle competition (which big capitalists loaths) and makes the big business bigger.

KID – (*KID*) (Kidder, Kidding) Originally, a young goat. This ancient word is of Scandinavian origin, taken directly from the Old Norse *"kid."* The term entered English with the arrival of the Vikings in the 12th century. The meaning of kid was transferred from young goat to young child in the 1590s. This was probably due to the playful nature of both creatures. By 1811, *"kid"* came to mean *"to coax, hoax,"* or *"wheedle"* in thieves' slang. This usage is probably related to the notion of *"treating one as a child."* or *"makes a kid of someone."* By 1888, a *"playful teaser"* came to be called *"a kidder."* The interjection, *"no kidding!"* meaning *"that's the truth,"* dates back to 1914. I kid you not. *"Here's looking at you, kid."* – Humphrey Bogart (1899 – 1957) in the movies, *"Casablanca"* (1942).

KIDNAP – (*KID*-nap) (Kidnaped, Kidnaping, Kidnaper, also spelled Kidnapper.) To seize and carry off a person by force, to be held as a hostage or for ransom money. Kidnaping is an ancient tradition and military tactic. Chances are better than good that our ancient great grandmothers may have been kidnaped from another tribe in prehistoric times, by our ancient great grandfathers. This was common practice among American Indians. The kidnaping of the Spartan Queen Helen by the Trojan Prince Paris ignited the Trojan War (c. 1260 – 1180 BCE). Throughout history, millions have been kidnaped to toil as slave laborers. Kidnaping for ransom is not new. But as a fund raising activity, it has increased exponentially. With the vastly disproportionate disparity of wealth, kidnaping is overtaking bank robbery. Kidnaping is quicker, easier, and safer than robbing an alarmed and armed bank. Abducting a millionaire or his offspring is not too difficult. Hopefully, the project will playout without violence or death (as of a bodyguard). The difficult part is collecting the ransom without detection. Millions can be exacted from a billionaire for the safe return of his child or grandchild. Though kidnaping is difficult to condone, it is equally difficult to condemn – especially in the face of savage economic injustice. In poor regions of the world, kidnaping has become an industry, as has kidnap prevention. A successful kidnaping is like winning the lottery. Capitalism creates distributive injustice, which forces the desperate to capitalize on kidnaping. Perhaps the outbreak of kidnaping is the wakeup call that the American plutocracy, corporations and government needs to redistribute the wealth fairly. Kidnaping is criminal, but so is capitalism. Comedian, philosopher Bill Mahr (b. 1956) warned: *"If you're rich, you should be begging the government to redistribute your wealth. Because do you know what happens in countries where there's a huge disparity between the rich and the poor? The rich get kidnaped.... Do you really think your trophy wife is going to empty out the Swiss bank account to save your sorry ass? I'm talking to you, Donald Trump!"* Well, if kidnaping seems like too cruel a remedy, consider this: If you posed a threat to the rich capitalist's financial empire, do you think that he would hesitate to have you and your family and friends all murdered? Don't be naïve! Incidentally: Seventy-two people, on average, are kidnaped daily in Mexico for ransom. Footnote: Multi-billionaire Mark Zuckerberg (b. 1984) dished-out $2,500,000 dollars in 2018 for security, primarily against kidnaping.

KIDS – (*KIDS*) Children. The progeny of a mother and father. Kids are sons and daughters. The term *"kids"* and its synonym *"children"* implies youth, youngsters. That's linguistically problematic. Sons and daughters grow up and grow old. Nevertheless they are still *"the kids,"* and are referred to as such. There is not a single appropriate word in the English language for adult children or kids. For example: Ivanka, Eric, and Donald Trump Jr. are the *"legitimate"* children (kids) of lecherous Donald J. Trump (b. 1946). We have no vocabularial choice but to refer to these adult rascals as the *"Trump children."* Now then, if justice is rightly served, the Trump kids (children) will join dad in prison. But we don't put children (kids) in prison. But in the end, it's all academic, literally. Incidentally: A plausible neologism for <u>adult</u> chil<u>dren</u> is *"adultdrens."* Adultdrens is a clipped compound of <u>adult</u> and chil<u>dren</u>. This term was coined by engineer Carl Ballou (1961 - 2023) from Detroit, Michigan.

KIELBASA – (kill-*BA*-sa) The delicious Polish sausage, made in a wide variety from beef, pork, or other meats, smoked or fresh, with plenty of garlic. The term may originate from the Turkic *kol basa* meaning *"hand pressed,"* or more likely from the Hebrew *kol basar* meaning *"all kinds of meat."* Kielbasa is the most famous, cosmopolitan Polish cuisine of choice. Incidentally: In the Ukraine it is called *"kowbasa,"* in Canada it is called *"kubasa."*

K.I.G. – (kay eye *JEE*) (<u>K</u>ingston <u>I</u>ndustrial <u>G</u>arage) The Oldest Ford Motor Car dealership in the world (1907), and the first outside the U.S.A., located in Kingston, Jamaica. The Kingston Industrial Garage was established by the Henriques Brothers. Henry Ford (1863 – 1947) had written to the brothers inquiring: *"Please advise if I should enlarge my factory [in Detroit] to take care of your requirements."* Today, K.I.G. (<u>K</u>ingston <u>I</u>ndustrial <u>G</u>arage) is part of the Lascelles Group of Companies.

KILLBOT – (*KILL*-bot) (<u>Kill</u>er <u>Rob</u>ot) Automatonical Assassin or Autoassassin. Killbots are machines programmed to select and attack targets, destroying and killing, using artificial intelligence, without human control. Killbots exemplify life imitating art in that science fiction becomes science fact. It is a terrifying prospect, mechanical bounty hunters. Machines often go haywire. Like a horror movie, one can imagine a computerized Frankenstein's Monster turning on its masters, murdering indiscriminately. Presently, the U.S., U.K., China, Russia, Israel, and South Korea are developing Killbots. In fact, the Russian arms manufacturer Kalashnikov announced that it had developed an automated weapon able to *"Identify targets and make decisions [to kill]."* On September 12, 2018, the European Union (EU) took a strong stand against

Killbots. Its parliament passed a resolution calling for an international ban on the development, production, and use of weapons that kill without a human deciding to fire. Killbot is technology run amuck. Our *Brave New World* doesn't need more efficient ways to kill people. Bodil Valero, EU Parliamentary Spokesperson declared that: *"Autonomous weapons systems must be banned internationally. The power to decide over life or death should never be taken out of human hands and given to machines."*

KILLER BEES – (*KIL*-ler bees) (Africanized bees) A fatally dangerous cross between African and European honeybees (*Frankenstein Effect*). Killer bees were bred in Brazil in the hope of producing a hybrid that produced more honey. Some escaped the lab, propagated and migrated throughout the tropical and semi-tropical Americas. The bees crossed into the U.S.A. at Arizona in 1990. They attack perceived threats unrelentingly, to death. About 40 Americans die annually from bee attacks. African bees are inherently more aggressive because their African environment hosts many more predators. Killer bees will pursue a victim for over a mile. They will hover over the water, waiting for a submerged person to surface. If a European honey bee hive is threatened, 10 to 20 defenders will initially be sent out to attack. The aggressive Africanized bees will *"go nuclear,"* so to speak, sending out 60% of the colony. Each hive houses about 60,000 bees, so that translates to 36,000 attackers! About 1,300 stings is fatal to an adult. That amounts to 5 to 10 stings per pound of body weight. The toxin from bees is similar to that of the rattlesnake. This makes the Africanized bees killers. Furthermore, bees detect carbon dioxide in breath and go for the mouth. Incidentally: The Romans, who were most innovative in their execution techniques would tie a victim in a basket and hoist him up a tree against a bee hive to be stung to death.

KILLING – (*KIL*-ling) To take a life (animal or plant). Killing needlessly is murder, the ultimate crime. When the victim is a human being, the killing is called homicide (killing a Homo sapien). About 3 times as many people have been killed in the 20th century, than in all of earlier history combined. In fact, about every 20 seconds, one human being kills another somewhere on Earth. Nevertheless, killing preserves life, for all animals must kill to live. Eating entails killing, even for herbivores or vegetarians, because plants too are living organisms. We must kill a tree for lumber. All animals hunt and eat other animals or plants. In fact, the first animal was a plant that turned cannibal. *"What says the law? You will not kill. How does it say it? By killing?"* – Victor Hugo (1802 – 1885). *"Dear Buddha, I sit here praying for all living creatures, and all the while killing mosquitoes."* – Gary J. Pasieka (b. 1951).

KILLING/MURDER – (*KIL*-ling *MUR*-der) Both terms refer to the extinguishment of life. But there's a difference. Killing may be justifiable (hunting, self-defense) or unjustifiable (murder). Wanton killing is murder – unjustifiable killing – a crime and a sin. This presents the question whether killing in war is murder? Again, it depends if the killing is justified [read: *"if the war is justified"*]. World War Two presents a glaring example. The Nazi SS soldiers killed helpless men, women, children, babies and elderly. Was that justifiable? No! So was that murder? Of course! The Allied soldiers killed Nazi SS soldiers. Was that justifiable? Yes! So was that murder? Of course not! The admonition in the Ten Commandments is not, *"Thou Shalt Not Kill,"* but rather *"Thou Shalt Not Murder,"* in the original Hebrew. Rabbi Reuven Laffer (b. 1964) explained it thusly: *"There is no commandment not to kill – the commandment is not to murder. This does not include commandments from God, Himself, and it does not refer to situations of war or times of danger, it is referring to times of peace. The Torah is teaching us that, under normal circumstances, human life is sacrosanct."*

KILLOLOGY – (kil-*LOL*-lo-jee) The study of homicide, or why and how people turn to murder. Killology includes the effect of media violence, particularly virtual mass massacre games, and their effect on the psyche. The military are avid students of killology. Basic training is a psycho-emotional exercise to turn normal young men (and now women) into professional killers. The military turns morality on its head. *"Though Shalt Not Kill"* become a treasonable offense. Warfare, the business of the military, is government sanctioned, encouraged, and rewarded killing. In the last 6,000 years, over 3,500,000,000 (3.5 billion) people have been killed in over 14,000 wars. That is about 60% of all the people alive today!

KILOANNUM – (kee-lo-*AN*-um) (Ka) A time measurement designation meaning one-thousand years. Therefore 5 Ka denotes five-thousand years, (5,000) or years ago.

KIMBERLITE PIPES – (*KIM*-ber-lite *PYPS*) Volcanic vents descending deep into the Earth that spew-up diamonds. The diamonds are carbon crystals created by chemical reactions under great heat and pressure in the bowls of the planet. The kimberlite pipes act as pneumatic vacuum tubes that blow the diamonds to the surface, from as far down as 100 miles into the Earth's mantle. Diamonds, like gold, copper, rubies, all minerals, are accidents of geology. With the break- up of the last supercontinent Pangea (175 million years ago), great kimberlite pipes were formed that spewed showers of diamonds from deep in the Earth. Kimberlite pipes are a geological serendipity. South Africa is rich in kimberlite pipes.

KIMCHI – (*KIM*-chee) A Korean salad dish consisting of spicy pickled or fermented mixture of cabbage, onions, and sometimes fish, variously seasoned with garlic, horseradish, red peppers, and ginger. The word *"kimchi"* derives from the Middle Korean and means *"submerge vegetables."* Kimchi is relished in South Korea and in North Korea (if they can afford it).

KINDERGARTEN – (*KIN*-der-gar-ten) German for *"a garden of/for children."* A kindergarten is a pre-school invented by the German educator Friedrich Froebel (1782 – 1852). Kindergarten should be an exercise in socialization for the children. Five-year-olds should learn to share, cooperate, be courteous, and wait their turn. Self-esteem should be nurtured in kindergarten. Kindergarten should not be an academical school, but a grooming for academic school.

KINDLE – (*KIN*-dl) (Kindled, Kindling) As a verb, kindle is to start a small fire. As a noun, kindle or kindling is the small twigs and flammable material used to start a fire. *"Trump kindled the flames of racial animus among his cultists."*

KINDLE – (*KIN*-dl) (also Litter) The collective name for an assemblage of kittens. *"A kindle of kittens squirmed in the basket."*

KINDNESS – (*KYND*-ness) Being good to people, especially those who least deserve it. Kindness is exhibiting a caring feeling and helpful attitude toward others, especially those in need. The Taoist avatar Lao Tzu (c. 604 – c. 531 BCE) taught that *"Kindness in words creates confidence. Kindness in thinking creates profoundness. Kindness in giving creates love."* The difference between mere politeness and profound kindness is in depth and expression of goodness performed. *KIN*dness is *KIN*ness or treating others as family or *KIN*. Those who had never experienced kindness mistake it for weakness. They need kindness the most. *"Kindness is the light that dissolves all walls between souls, families, and nations."* – Paramahansa Yogananda (1893 – 1952).

KINDNESS REVENGE – (*KYND*-ness ree-*VENJ*) A spiritually superb way to attain retribution, while avoiding wickedness. Someone who hurt you expects you to retaliate in kind – not in kindness. Being good to a bad person is a good way to make them feel bad. In the vulgar vernacular, it will *"make them feel like shit."* After all, that's the goal of revenge. The formerly nasty person will feel shame and guilt, and a degree of remorse. You turned the table on her. But don't leave him that way to suffer. The spiritually superb response must be forgiveness and reconciliation. *"But I say to you, Love your enemies and pray for those who persecute you."* – Jesus in Matthew 5:44.

KINESICS – (kin-*NEE*-siks) (Kinesiology = kin-nee-see-*OL*-lo-jee) The study of body movements, gestures, facial expressions, as a means of communication. Kinesiology is a relatively new discipline in university physical education departments. It studies the body movements of athletes in performance. There is a semi-scientific quality to the subject. The discipline has been abused by college athletic coaches as a phony major for athletes who are actually majoring in football or basketball. Kinesics provides college athletes, unaccustomed to study, with an easy, albeit legitimate sounding major, which will not demand time or effort off the field or court.

KINETIC – (kin-*NET*-tik) Pertaining to, causing, or characterized by motion. Kinetic energy makes things move. The term derives from the Greek *"kinetikos"* meaning moving or putting in motion.

KINETIC WEAPONS – (kin-*NET*-tik *WEP*-uhn) Kinetic means motion or movement. A weapon is a tool used to harm or kill. Weapons are the equipment of war. A kinetic weapon is one that wreaks damage simply by the force if its motion. A thrown rock or a stone slung from a sling are the simplest kinetic weapons. A kinetic weapon need not penetrate like a spear, arrow or bullet, though they often do. Too, it does not bear an exploding warhead. Its lethality is in its weight (mass) and speed (velocity) alone, creating blunt trauma, or collision shock (a crater). Young David (c. 1010 – 979 BCE) killed the giant warrior Goliath with a stone flung from his sling, a kinetic weapon. Legally, the hands of a martial arts master may be registered as kinetic weapons. The kinetic weapon concept is not new, but as old as aerial warfare. During World War One (1914 – 1918) solid darts were dropped from aeroplanes that simulated machine-gun fire. During World War Two (1939 – 1945), the Russians dropped heavy sand-fill oil drums on targets. In the Korean and Vietnam conflicts, the U.S. Air Force dropped small solid bombs that reached a speed of 500 mph. On impact, they penetrated 9 inches of concrete. During the late 1950s, Boeing researcher Jerry Pournelle (1933 – 2017) invented the *"Rods from God,"* in *"Operation Thor."* This kinetic weapon was a 9-ton tungston missile, the size of a telephone pole. During the Cold War (1945 – 1991) nuclear, chemical, and biological weapons were forbidden in space by treaty. Laser and kinetic weapons were not. Today, the U.S. Space Force is experimenting with kinetic weapons in space. The military aerospace industry calls them *"Hit-and- Kill"* weapons. Such weapons do not carry explosives. They don't need to. The heavy solid missiles disintegrate their targets on impact in space or on Earth with astronomic force.

Fired to Earth from a satellite, this gravity powered missile will travel 5 miles per second in orbit, and reach a fall velocity of Mach 10, ten times the speed of sound (7,610 mph). At that speed, atmospheric friction from air molecules will make the rod flame like a meteor. It will hit the Earth with the force of a tactical nuclear weapon, or more accurately, a small asteroid, for there is no radioactive nuclear fallout. It would penetrate hundreds of feet into the ground, and release all its kinetic energy, equivalent to 11.5 tons of TNT. In order to compete in a kinetic weapons arms race, a nation must have a space program. Too they need a great deal of money, for putting heavy objects in space is very expensive.

KING DONALD – (*KING DON*-old) Donald Trump's (b. 1946) autocratic, dictatorial, fascist tendencies are glaringly apparent. His lust for absolute power is a primary reason why he is in constant conflict with other branches of government. The world leaders that Trump admires the most are all totalitarian tyrants. In March 2018, Xi Jinping (b. 1953), China's authoritarian leader became China's dictatorial leader. Trump's envious reaction was revealing. Trump said: *"Now some people might call him the king of China. But he's called president.... He's now president for life. And look, he was able to do that. I think it's great! Maybe we'll have to give that a shot someday."* Trump was planting a subconscious seed. Astonishing sentiments from the President of the United States, Leader of the Democratic World! Try to imagine, from jester to king, *"His Jackassness,"* Donald The First, the pisspot despot. Incidentally: When the Founding Father were constructing our government, it was seriously considered making Washington (1732 – 1799) King George The First. This was soon after we had deposed England's King George III (1738 – 1820). General Washington's reaction: *"This is a proposition I must repudiate and condemn with severity!"* Would that have been Trump's reaction? Good God, how did America degenerate from Washington to Trump?

KING MAKER – (*KING MAY*-ker) The power behind the throne. King maker is a political term for a very powerful, influential person who can make or break a political career. A king maker's power may reside in tremendous wealth, or in public opinion. He may have a captivating sway over the population, especially over voters. A king maker's endorsement or condemnation may propel a politician to office or deny him a chance to get on the ballot. Political bosses, and centibillionaire donors have served as king makers. The most powerful and absolute king maker of the 21st century has been the twice impeached, one- term defeated former President, Donald J. Trump (b. 1946). Trump's anger, racism, and general ignorance resonated with the lowest third of the electorate who are like him, and therefore like him. They have permitted Trump to do their thinking for them. Therefore, they have enabled Trump to choose which politicians are worthy of governance. Trump's king making power is confined to the Republican Party. That's why politicians in the Republican Party must pledge fealty to Trump as his vassals. Trump is their lord, maker, and king – king maker.

KING PHILLIP'S WAR – (*KING FIL*-lips *WAR*) (June 20, 1675 – April 12, 1678) A bloody conflict between New England Colonists and a confederation of Indians led by the Wampanoag. There had been several disputes between the dissimilar cultures. Generally speaking, the Native Americans attempted to drive the English intruders out of their land. The Natives were commanded by a Pokunoket Chief Metacomet, who had adopted the name, *"King Phillip."* Several battles were fought in Massachusetts, Connecticut, Rhode Island, and Maine. Twelve frontier villages had been destroyed. King Phillip's War was marked by savage atrocities, as were all the Indian conflicts. With the capture and beheading of King Phillip, the

Native aggression withered. Many Indians fled to Canada. Others were captured and sold into slavery. The Indians suffered over 3,000 killed, while the colonists lost over a thousand. The colonial population was still small at that time. Therefore, the losses loomed large. As a matter of fact, a greater percentage of the American population was killed in King Phillip's War, than in any other war in American History.

KING'S KILLING – (*KINGS KIL*-ling) The assassination of the Reverend Dr. Martin Luther King Jr. (1925 – 1968) in Memphis Tennessee, April 4, 1968. All great people are thoroughly loved and thoroughly hated. Every racist and bigot in the country hated Dr. King, the great civil rights leader. FBI Director J. Edgar Hoover (1895 – 1972) particularly hated Rev. King. Hoover tried to blackmail Dr. King with FBI prostitutes and cameras in motel rooms. Hoover sent King a letter suggesting that he commit suicide. Corporate capitalists had multiple reasons for wanting Rev. King killed. He was a vocal opponent of the lucrative war in Vietnam. He advocated the unionization of all workers. In fact, he was in Memphis supporting a sanitation worker's strike when he was assassinated. But what sealed Dr. King's fate was his call for distributive justice, the redistribution of the wealth. Days before his murder, King appeared on television. He said that Black people and poor people would never attain political equality without economic equality. Corporate capitalism could not tolerate such a powerful Socialist voice. A patsy was found in James Earl Ray (1928 – 1998). Like Lee Harvey Oswald (1939 – 1963) and Sirhan Sirhan (b. 1944), Ray was falsely blamed for the murder. The police protection for Rev. King had been mysteriously called off. After the assassination misinformation was radioed by police concerning Ray's whereabouts. The conspiracy was protected. The next Progressive victim in 1968 would be Senator Robert F. Kennedy (1925 – 1968).

KINGSTON – (*KING*-stun) Capital city of Jamaica, located on the southeast Caribbean Coast of the island. The metropolis is 190 square miles with a population of 680,000 (larger than Detroit, smaller than Boston). About a third of the population of the nation lives in Kingston. It is the largest English- speaking city south of Miami, Florida. Kingston is the governmental and commercial center of the country. It has the 7th largest natural harbor in the world. After the great earthquake of 1692 that destroyed the pirate capital, Port Royal, construction of Kingston began across the harbor. Kingston is the administrative center of the University of the West Indies. Incidentally: In the 18th century when sugar was king, Kingston was the richest, most sophisticated English city in the Western Hemisphere. Boston, New York, Philadelphia, Charleston could not match Kingston. In fact, Broadway plays were advertised as being *"A Great Hit in Kingston!"*

KINHIN – (*KIN*-hin) The Zen Buddhist *"Sutra Walk."* Kinhin is the walking meditation or prayer. Some Japanese Zen Masters maintain that: *"Meditation in movement has a thousand times more value than meditation in sitting."* The Indian Guru and Spiritual teacher Osho (1931 – 1990) said: *"Walking is Zen, sitting is Zen. Then what will be the quality? Watchfully alert, joyously unmotivated, centered, loving, flowing, one walks."* The most mundane, menial task can become a prayer if dedicated as such. This is known as *"Naikan"* in Buddhism. Kinhin is converting a walk or jog, any physical activity into a prayer. *"I draw water, I carry wood. This is my magic."* – Zen Proverb. *"Solvitur ambulando,"* It is solved by walking." – St. Augustine (354 – 430 CE). *"Meditation in the midst of activity is a thousand times superior to meditation in stillness."* – Hakuin Ekaku (1686 – 1769).

KINKEEPER – (*KIN*-kee-per) (Kinkeeping) A protector of family cohesion. A kinkeeper works to maintain and enhance family ties. He or she organizes social events, reunions, remembers birthdays and anniversaries, works the phone and email, sends cards and gifts, and reminds other family members of special occasions. A kinkeeper is a peacemaker, an apologist, a mediator, a reconciliatory. Kinkeepers tend to be selfless. They serve as the glue that binds families together. The term kinkeeper was entered into the dictionary in 2023, though it had been first recorded as early as 1975.

KINK KULTURE – (*KEENK CALL*-chur) (Kink) All the participants, devotees to extraordinary, unconventional, even bizarre sexual practices. The Kink community subscribes to sadomasochistic roleplaying. Kinks come in a variety of orientations. They are totally tolerant, lavishly libertine, and absolutely non-judgmental. Homosexuality is commonplace in Kink Kulture. Their recreational sex revolves around BDSM (<u>B</u>ondage, <u>D</u>iscipline/<u>D</u>ominance, <u>S</u>ubmission, <u>S</u>ado<u>M</u>asochism). Fantasies and fetishes are given full vent. One cannot be an inhibited or bashful Kink. Collars, whips, chains, sex toys are equipment for the games. Public nudity is sometime required. Voluntary humiliation is popular as well as harmless hurt. Pleasurable pain is inflicted, but injury is avoided in Kink Kulture. Kinks consider strait-laced sexualists as performing boring *"vanilla sex."* The uninitiated will consider Kink Kulture deviant, perverse, even insane. Nevertheless: *"There are nine and sixty ways of constructing tribal lays, and every single one of them is right!"* – Rudyard Kipling (1865 – 1936) <u>*In the Neolithic Age.*</u>

KINKY – (*KEENK*-key) (Kink) Displaying unusual, uncommon, even bizarre sexual preferences. Fetishism like bondage, cross dressing, or sadomasochism qualify as kinky. However, *"What is soup to the goose is sauce to the gander."* Kinky sex is offered for a fee, for example, by *"Frau Hilga,"* at *"Das Schpanken Hausen."*

KINNIKINNICK – (kin-ni-*KIN*-nik) (A variety of spellings.) A Chippewa Indian word for *"hand mix."* Kinnikinnick was a mixture of tobacco with leaves and bark from willows, sumac, dogwood trees, and white sage and cedar shavings. It was smoked in pipes by the natives of the Ohio Valley.

KIOSK – (*KEE*-osk) A small hut-like structure with one or more open sides, used as a newsstand, bandstand, refreshment stand, or sales outlet for cheap jewelry, cellphones, or trinkets. The term derives from the Turkish *"kioshk,"* meaning open pavilion.

KIPA – (*KEE*-pa) (also Kippah) Often called a yarmulka (yar-*MULE*-ka.) A kipa is a skull cap worn especially during prayer and religious study by Jewish males, particularly those adhering to Orthodox or Conservative tradition. The kipa expresses devotion to God. Worn in public, the kipa identifies one as a Jew.

KIRSCH – (*KEERSH*) A fragrant, colorless, unaged brandy distilled from a fermented mash of cherries. Kirsch is popular in Switzerland, Germany, and Alsace, France. It is customary to pour kirsch on ice cream.

KISH – (*KISH*) A dross mixture of graphite and slag separated from and floating on the surface of molten pig iron or cast iron as it cools. A film of kish develops as a skin in molten lead and other melted metals. Kish is a waster product, and impurity that must be skimmed off.

KISMET – (*KIS*-met) Fate or destiny. Kismet is a Muslim term for the *"Will of Allah,"* in Islamic, *"Ensha Allah."* Kismet is not doleful resignation, but rather faithful surrender that God's way will be good.

KISSING – (*KIS*-sing) *"Feeding affection."* Usually a mouth-to-mouth contact, the universal representation of love (or lust). Anthropologists maintain that kissing originated in pre-human times. Mothers pre-masticated (chewed-up) tough uncooked food and transferred the soft moistened mash into their baby's mouth. This was the ultimate expression of love that evolved into kissing. Therefore, kissing is a form of feeding each other affection.

KISS-N-TELL – (*KIS* en *TEL*) (Kiss-n-telling, Kiss-n-teller) The puerile, untrustworthy habit of some males to brag about their sexual conquests. It seems that men who engage in intercourse the least, are most apt to boast about it, in exaggerated terms. To these gentlemen, getting laid is a victory, and the female partner a trophy. But to the lady, publicizing her sex life is humiliating, even devastating. Kiss-n-tell is a hurtful, nasty practice. Incidentally: A joke has it that *"Australian men engage in intercourse so quickly, because they can't wait to get to the pub to tell the blokes."* – Robert Benchley (1889 - 1945).

KISZKA – (*KEESH*-ka) A Polish blood sausage or black pudding that is popular throughout Eastern Europe and the American Midwest. The name means *"gut"* or *"intestine."* Kiszka is made from buckwheat, pig or beef blood, and pig meat (pork) – cuts that could not be used in any other manner, as the flesh off the hog's head and face. The minced mash is stuffed in a casing of pig intestine. A Caveat: Do not confuse the Kiszka sausage with kasha (oatmeal) or keesh (quiche) the custard pie. Incidentally: The sausage gained fame from the 1950's polka hit, *"Who Stole the Kiszka?"*

KITCHEN – (*KICH*-chen) A room equipped for cooking. Stove, oven, sink, toaster, refrigerator, tables, counters, blender, mixer, knives, utensils are all included in the kitchen. Like a carpentry shop, a kitchen is a workplace where raw food is prepared for consumption. Like all workshops, kitchens are messy places. Food, grease, water will be splashed about. It's all part of the job of cooking. The goal is the production of a good meal. The clean-up is an afterthought. Therefore, keep unnecessary, especially precious artifacts out of the kitchen. You wouldn't put a rare Ming vase in a blacksmith's shop. Do not drape the kitchen with valuable, flammable tablecloths, and decorative placemats, and rugs. Save those for the dining room. Incidentally: *"If you can't take the mess, stay out of the kitchen."*

KITCHEN BITCH – (*KICH*-chen *BICH*) Not a nasty female cook. A kitchen bitch is an old, traditional Jamaican oil lamp, most handily used in the kitchen.

KITCHEN MIDDEN – (*KICH*-chen *MID*-den) An archeological deposit of ancient refuse. Wherever there was a camp there was a garbage dump. The kitchen midden consists of bones, shells, husks, seed, and charcoal from cooking fires. They provide valuable information about the diets and lifestyles of our ancient ancestors.

KITCHEN TABLE ISSUES – (*KIT*-chen *TAY*-bul *ISH*-yoos) Critical concerns that trouble ordinary families. Kitchen table issues are anxieties often discussed by the family, during meals at the kitchen table. These are survival apprehensions and trepidations. They primarily involve economic and security forebodings. This translates into the cost of living and the fear of dying. Healthcare is a major concern. The price of medical procedures, hospital bills, the cost of drugs and medicines haunts families. Food prices, fuel costs, clothing expense, rent payments, mortgage, creditcard, and bank debts generate constant anguish. Employment anxiety, whether one's job will go to China is a dreaded kitchen table issue. Can we afford the cost of college? Too, is the quality of the kids' school good enough to enable them to succeed in college? Security issues include fear of crime, gun violence. Are we safe in our home in this neighborhood? Are the kids safe at school? Will we be able to retire in dignity, with adequate social security? Kitchen table issues are tangible, not philosophical. They hit home hard. They are not the concern of Wall Street, but of Main Street. They are divorced from the D.O.W. which is the <u>D</u>isparity <u>O</u>f <u>W</u>ealth index. It is to serve and solve kitchen table issues that we pay taxes and maintain government. Incidentally: Kitchen table issues form the compelling imperative of a Socialist economy. *"It's the economy, stupid."* – A phrase coined by political strategist James Carville (b. 1944) in Bill Clinton's (b. 1946) successful Presidential campaign of 1992. This phrase is the credo of kitchen table issues.

KITH AND KIN – (kith and *KIN*) An archaic appellation for one's relatives and homeland, used since at least the 9th century. *Kith* is an old term for *"familiar country,"* or a *"place that one knows well."* (The opposite of *"kith"* was the term *"uncouth,"* which originally meant *"unfamiliar, not understood or accepted".*) *Kin* refers to *"kinfolk"* or *"family."* Among kith and kin implies unpretentious relaxation among family. The earliest use of 'kith and kin' in print is found in William Langland's (c. 1332 – c. 1386) Middle English narrative poem, <u>*The Vision of William Concerning Piers Plowman,*</u> (1370). *"Fer fro kitth and fro kynne yeal yclothed wedwn."* (Far from kith and from kin they evil- clothed went.) In modern English, Robert Burns (1759 – 1796) used the phrase in <u>*Poems & Songs*</u> (c. 1796). *"My Lady's white, my Lady's red, And kith and kin o'Cassillis' blude."*

KITTY KITTY – (*Kit*-tee *Kit*-tee) Not a fluffy pet pussy but prison slang for a female correctional officer. It takes women with *"balls"* to work as prison guards in a male institution.

KIWIFRUIT – (*KEE*-wee-froot) (*Actinidia chinensis*) Kiwifruit was formerly known as *"Chinese gooseberry,"* (though not related to the gooseberry). It is native to China where it is called *"yang tao."* It is an oval fruit, grown on a bush, little smaller than a tennis ball. Kiwifruit has a fuzzy brown skin, with pale green flesh embedded with small edible seeds. It has a unique, strawberry/lime-like taste. Kiwifruit was brought to New Zealand from China in 1906. Hayward Wright (1873 – 1959), a New Zealand nurseryman developed a hybrid variety of kiwifruit which became very popular. In 1953, New Zealand began to export the product. The Kiwi is the flightless bird native in New Zealand, a national symbol. Too, Kiwi is an informal nickname for New Zealanders. So the fruit was renamed kiwifruit. With the change of name and its association with New Zealand, the product became popular worldwide. Today, kiwifruit is grown primarily in New Zealand and California. Research has shown the fruit to be very beneficial for a healthy heart and arteries.

KKK – (kay-kay-*KAY*) An initialism for the <u>*Ku Klux Klan*</u>. KKK is the American counterpart to the NAZIS ideologically. It is a violent, hateful organization formed after the slavocracy was defeated in the Civil War (1865). Their initial, primary goal was to keep Black Americans powerless and subservient. The KKK targets the helpless. Its primary enemy is African Americans, but also Jews, Catholics, Gays, Liberals, Intellectuals, pretty much the same enemy's list as had the Nazis. They too preach a white supremacy doctrine. From the Civil War (1860's) to Civil Rights (1960's), the KKK served as the *"ISIS of the South."* The Ku Klux Klan is strongest in unsophisticated rural regions of the South and West, conservative country. KKK members are low-educated and mean-spirited individuals. They were readily identified by their white ghostly sheets. Many Southern politicians had been secret members of the Ku Klux Klan. Today, the KKK has traded its sheets for microphones on conservative talk radio. They gravitate to the Republican Party, and are open supporters of the racist, fascist Donald Trump (b. 1946). *"We are determined to take our county back. We are going to fulfill the promise of Donald Trump. That's what we believe in. That's why we voted for Donald Trump, because he said he's going to take our country back."* – KKK Leader David Duke (b. 1950). *"As a matter of social class Ku Klux Klan would have been regarded as white trash."* – Kurt Vonnegut (1922 – 2007).

KLATSCH – (*CLATSH*) A drinking social. A klatsch is a casual gathering of people for alcoholic refreshments and informal conversation. The term *"klatsch"* is German for *"gossip."* The term entered English in 1953.

KLEPTOCAPITALISM – (clep-tow-*CAP*-pit-tal-is-um) The creation of an oligarchy by a capitalist plutocracy. Kleptocapitalism is the degeneration of capitalism jettisoning democracy, adopting fascism. Kleptocapitalism is robbing the economy of all fairness, honesty, and freedom. The economy is controlled by a handful of powerful plutocrats, a few oligarchical families. These patrician families serve as a board of directors with a fascist dictator as the CEO. The kleptocapitalists steal, arrest control of all industries, utilities, natural resources, the stock market, entire economic superstructure of the nation. They run the government and rule the economy for their own self-aggrandizement. They are rich beyond comprehension, while over 99% of the nation struggles to survive. The kleptocapitalistic aristocrats are like Medieval Feudal Lords, with the rest of the population being their serfs. But there is nothing noble about these aristocrats. They are mobsters, gangsters, and banksters. They have no royal blood, though they spill blood royally. The nation is headed by a right-wing strongman. Vladimir Putin's (b. 1952) Russia is the best example of a fascist kleptocapitalist kleptocracy. (Controlling at least 200 billion dollars, Putin is one of the richest men in the world.) A kleptocapitalist dictatorship is what Putin's protégé Donald Trump (b. 1946) strives to create for America and his family. *"Fascism is capitalism in decay."* – Vladimir Lenin, (1870 - 1924) Socialist.

KLEPTOCRACY – (klep-*TOC*-ra-see) A government run by thieves. Dictatorships are always kleptocracies. Dictators have absolute power to raid the public coffers. Capitalist kleptocracy is a little more subtle, covert, and discreet. The theft occurs under the guise of legality. A great example is Vladimir Putin's (b. 1952) Russia.

KLEPTOCRATS – (*KLEP*-tow-crats) Legal professional thieves, government sanctioned thieves like banksters, brokers, and insurance company CEO's. Those allowed by law to embezzle from the common man are kleptocrats. No First Family in American History had profited in office more and more illegally that the family Trump.

KLEPTOMANIA – (klep-tow-*MAY*-nee-a) (Kleptomaniacs) A neurotic compulsion to steal. Like all defense mechanisms, kleptomania is a means to alleviate stress from elsewhere. A variation of kleptomania is *"kleptolagnia."* This is a sexual fetish in which one gets erotically aroused by sealing or witnessing theft take place. Even wealthy people who have no need to steel, like shoplifting can suffer from kleptomania. It is a neurotic compulsion, a defense mechanism that obfuscates some deeper subconscious stress or trauma.

KLEPTOPENIA – (klep-tow-*PEE*-nee-a) (Kleptopeniacs) An ink pen thief. One who casually, unconsciously walks off with borrowed ink pens. Kleptopenia is the reason why pens are tethered with string, chains, or rubber bands in banks, post offices, stores, everywhere.

KLISMAPHILIA – (klis-ma-*FEE*-lee-ah) (Klismaphiliac) A neurotic paraphilial disorder in which one is sexually aroused by enemas. A klismaphiliac may be on the giving or receiving end figuratively and literally).

KLUSKI – (*CLOO*-ski) Polish dumplings (also Silesian dumplings). Kluski is a general term which literally translates to *"noodles"* in English. Though thick dough dumplings are not noodles, they are called kluski. These Polish dumplings can be made with wheat or potato flour. They may be made into any shape or size. If the dough is scooped out with a spoon, like clay, it will take the flattened spoon shape and perfect size. Kluski dough is cooked by boiling. Then they can be added to soup or simply fried in butter (onions optional). Again, kluski literally means noodles. Indeed, thick egg kluski noodles are a heavenly match for chicken soup, or any soup. Kluski serve as a cheap food, very filling, full of carbohydrate energy. With kluski you can feed an army. They are absolutely *"smacznie,"* delicious.

KLUTZ – (*CLUTZ*) (also Klots) A Yiddishism for a clumsy, awkward person.

KNAPPING – (*NAP*-ping) The stone age art of chipping flint, chert, obsidian or any other glassy quartz in order to create a sharp tool. For thousands of years our ancient ancestors manufactured knives, spear points, arrowheads, and scrapers in this manner.

KNAVE – (*NAYV*) (Knavery) A rogue. A knave is an unprincipled, untrustworthy, dishonest person. This definition accurately, honestly, describes Donald Trump (b. 1946).

KNELLER – (*NEL*-ler) An archaic appellation for a chimney sweep, one who cleans the soot from chimneys. Incidentally: Soot is carbon and carbon can be a carcinogen. Knellers suffered a high incidence of cancer, especially testicular cancer.

K-NINE UNIT – (*KAY*-nyn *YOO*-nit) (usually K-9 Unit) Dogs employed by law enforcement. Dogs have been used by police forces since the Middle Ages. Dogs have senses of hearing, sight, and smell far superior to humans, and are far faster. This makes dogs valuable partners to police officers. But dogs are animals, not police officers, and should be treated as such. Dogs should be used for search and rescue, but not for apprehension and arrest. That's the police officer's job. Bloodhounds, for instance, should be used to track fugitive criminals, but not to seize and capture them. It is disgusting that the law considers attack dogs to be actual police officers. So to injure a police dog carries the same penalty as injuring a police officer. That's ridiculous! One must passively lay there and be mauled, maimed by the vicious animal, allowing it to tear pieces of flesh from one's body, without applying any self-defense, which is resisting arrest! The cruel torture will continue until the sadistic human police officer calls the dog off. This is indeed *"Cruel and Unjust Punishment"* outlawed by the 8th Amendment of the Constitution's Bill of Rights. Imagine having to watch one's loved one being chewed-up by a beast, and not being allowed to provide help. Police dogs as attack dogs should be illegal. Their employment is animalistic and inhumane. American police forces prefer the large, strong, and vicious German shepherd in their K-9 units. Why don't the police christen their remote control robots as police officers as well? Then what's next? Their patrol cars?

Incidentally: In Victorian England, the police, called Bobbies, used Bulldogs as their law enforcement companions. Originally bred for bull-baiting, bulldogs are tenacious to the extreme. Once they lock-on with a bite, they do not release. It's as if their jaws seize-up. Grabbing a fugitive's leg, they will remain, even after being killed. It is difficult to escape with a bulldog attached to one's leg. This tenacity won the bulldog the honor of being the totem of England, and her *Uncle Sam* counterpart named *John Bull* (after the <u>bull</u>dog). After Though: If you are lucky enough to strangle to death the police dog that is defacing you, did you legally commit murder? After all the dog is legally a police officer. But murder is the act of <u>Hom</u>icide (killing a <u>Homo</u> sapien). The police dog is not a Homo sapien but a *Canis familiaris.* I'd love to see this controversy play-out in court.

KNOT – (*NOT*) A measurement of speed, 1 knot equaling a little over 1.15 miles per hour. Therefore, 100 knots is 115 mph. Knots are used to measure maritime and aviation speed. Measurement by knots is typically used in non- metric countries. Curiously, the U.K. and U.S. utilize the knot system on sea, in the air, but not on land. The term knot derives from the Old English (West Saxon) *"cnotta,"* meaning *"intertwining ropes."* The nautical usage of knots as a measure of speed dates back to the 1630s. It derived from the practice of attaching <u>knot</u>ted string to the log line in the water at equal distances. The ship's speed could be calculated by the number of knots in the string that play out while being timed with a sand hour glass. This primitive, albeit ingenious method was effective.

KNOT – (*NOT*) In this case a knot is the collective name for an assemblage of toads. *"A knot of toads slithered over the mud."*

KNOWING HOW – (*NO*-ing *HOW*) In curriculum education, *"knowing how"* refers to performance capabilities, what we might call skills. Knowing how to ski or solve a quadratic equation for example. Knowing how is contrasted with *"knowing that,"* which refers to propositional knowledge, facts, concepts, and principles.

KNOWING THAT – (*NO*-ing *THAT*) In curriculum education, *"knowing that"* refers to propositional knowledge, or subject matter. In other words, knowledge of facts, concepts, and principles. Knowing that is contrasted with *"knowing how,"* which refers to performance capabilities, what we might call skills. Knowing how to sew, or write a persuasive essay are examples of knowing how.

KNOWLEGDE – (*NOL*-lej) Recall and recognition of useful information, skills, ideas, material and phenomena. Knowledge is not wisdom, which is knowing when to apply your knowledge. Knowledge is accumulated through formal education (schooling) and incidental experience (living). Knowledge is naturally acquired with time. Age refines raw knowledge into wisdom, as raw juice is refined into fine wine. When one mature in age fails to exercise wisdom, it is said that *"There is no fool like an old fool."* *"Knowledge is not intelligence.* – Heraclitus (535 – 475 BCE).

KNOWLEDGE ACQUISITION – (*NOL*-lej ac-kwis-*SISH*-shun) Not acquiring education, in this case, but an innocuous sounding euphemism for *"Train Your Replacement."* This is a new capitalist scheme to boost profits, to hell with the employee. Knowledge acquisition refers to endowing the man who will take your job with all you know about your job. Your company wants him to acquire your knowledge. They want from him the same fine performance as you have given for decades, but at half your salary. You are ordered to work cordially with Saheeb from Mumbai for one month, with pay, then you must evacuate the premises, never to return. If you refuse to endure the humiliation, you can quit on the spot. But you will have to sacrifice your severance pay and pension. Too, *"Don't let the door hit you in the ass on the way out!"* Consenting to a knowledge acquisition program is tantamount to having to dig your own grave. Understand that capitalism does not understand patriotism, loyalty, decency. All capitalism understands is capital, profits. The worker is an interchangeable nut or bolt in the corporate capitalist machine. The company will relegate you to the trash bin if it saves them money. Saheeb represents the future of American labor under capitalism. Do you still wonder why we need unions? Do you still wonder why we need Socialism?

KNUCKLEBALL – (*NUK*-cul-ball) (also Knuckler) A baseball pitch designed to confuse and deceive batters. A knuckleball is difficult to throw and more difficult to hit. When a batter does make solid contact, it is sheer luck. Few pitchers have mastered the difficult knuckler. The ball is not held by the fingers and thrown like a fastball. Instead it is gripped by the knuckles and pushed toward the batter rather than thrown. This is to minimize speed and spin. A knuckleball is a very slow pitch, minimally 50 mph, no faster than 70 mph. Consider that a fastball travels over 100 mph. The knuckler flies with almost no rotation. It zigzags randomly. The ball can veer to the right, then left, then drop, all on the same 60 foot, 6 inch journey to the plate. Each pitch behaves uniquely unpredictably. The batter, catcher nor pitcher knows what the ball will do. What is the aerodynamic physics behind the knuckleball? The erratic movement is influenced by the ball's seams. A baseball has 108 double stitches in a continuous course throughout the ball. If the ball was a perfectly smooth, round, seamless sphere, the knuckleball effect would not be possible. It is the combination of seams and smooth surfaces that makes the ball's flight so capricious. A knuckler will rotate only once every 2 seconds. The ball slowly turns either clockwise or counterclockwise. And the airflow behind the ball deviates left and right. The air-stream movements are caused by the ball's slightly raised seams. As the ball travels, the air strikes the ball's raised seams causing air turbulence on the ball's side, which sticks to the ball's surface, impeding the air. On the other side, the airflow striking the smooth part of the ball quickly slides by, uninhibitedly. When the 2 airflows, moving at different speeds merge behind the ball, the airflow is deflected. The knuckleball's deviation depends on the orientation of this air deflection. The ball is pushed to the left or to the right. If the air-stream behind the ball deviates toward the right, so does the ball. Likewise, the ball curves to the left, when the air-stream tilts left. Predicting the movement is quite futile, for pitcher, catcher, and batter. That's what makes the knuckler so effective. Incidentally: Some catches switch to an over-sized catcher's mit, when catching a knuckleball pitcher.

KOAN – (*CO*-in) (Koanistic, Koanistically) In Zen Buddhism, a baffling statement or verbal conundrum intended to confound logical reasoning and point to ultimate truth. A koan is a statement couched in irrational language which cannot be solved by intellectual processes, but whose meaning must burst on the mind directly. Koans are used as exercises in breaking the patterns of so- called thought, developing instead deep intuition and achieving a state of awareness beyond that of duality, to awakening. To figure out a koan, one must go beyond cognition to affection, beyond thinking to feeling out the answer or solution. Often, it is the simplicity of a koan that is so very complicated. A koan devised by Philosopher Dr. Gary J. Pasieka (b. 1951) asserts: *"Explain color to a blind man."* "You know the sound of two hands clapping; tell me, what is the sound of one hand?" "If only you hear the sound of snow." – Hakuin Ekaku (1686 – 1769). Incidentally: Jesus was responsible for many koanistic statements recorded in the Lost [read: *censored, suppressed*] Gospels, like that of the Gospel of Thomas. There Jesus declares: *"Blessed is the lion which becomes man when consumed by man; and cursed is the man whom the lion consumes, and the lion becomes man."*

KOBA – (*CO*-ba) Joseph Stalin's (1878 – 1953) adult nickname, used only by intimates.

KOHLBERG'S TAXONOMY – (*COL*-bergs taks-*ON*-om-mee) The stages of moral development as defined by psychologist Lawrence Kohlberg (1927 – 1987). LEVEL I (Pre-Conventional): 1. Obedience and Punishment Orientation. (*"How can I avoid punishment?"*) 2. Self-Interest Orientation. (*"How much will this benefit or cost me?"*) LEVEL II (Conventional): 3. Interpersonal Accord and Conformity. (*"What do people expect?"*) (*"Am I a good boy/girl?"*) 4. Authority and Social-Order Maintaining Orientation. (*"Is it legal or against the law?"*) LEVEL III (Post-Conventional): 5. Social Contract Orientation. (*"Have I done to others as I would have done to me?"*) 6. Universal Ethical Principles. (*"Would I want everyone in the world to behave this way?"*) Republicans/Capitalists are on a lower moral level than Democrats/Socialists. Republicans and capitalists think in terms of *"I, me, mine."* Democrats and Socialists think in terms of *"us, we, ours."* Republicans and capitalists ask *"What's in it for me?"* and declare, *"I got mine, to hell with you."* Democrats and Socialists ask *"How can we all benefit?"*

KOINE – (koy-*NAY*) An amalgam of Greek dialects, chiefly Attic and Ionic, that replaced the classical Greek dialect in the Hellenistic period and flourished under the Roman Empire. Koine became the common Greek spoken throughout the eastern Mediterranean region at the beginning of the Christian Era. The New Testament of the Bible was first written in Koine.

KOINONIA – (koy-*NO*-nee-a) A Greek term meaning *"communion, fellowship."* It derives from the Greek *"koinos,"* meaning *"in common."* Koinonia was the term applied to the Socialistic nature of early Christendom. The original Christian communities shared their wealth in common, very Communistically.

KOKOLOGY – (ko-*KOL*-lo-jee) A term derived from the Japanese word *"kokoro,"* meaning *"mind"* or *"spirit."* Kokology is a psychological exercise based on Freudian and Jungian theories. Through a series of guided questions, insights into one's deep psyche are revealed. Kokology is an exploration of self- discovery. Hidden attitudes about sex, love, family, work, race, religion can be unveiled. Kokology was introduced in a series of books by Tadahiko Nagao and Professor Isamu Saito in Japan (1998).

KOLYMA – (ko-*LEE*-ma) Notorious Stalinist gulag in Siberia. Kolyma was a forced-labor camp, primarily a goldmine. Over 3 million died at the camp – criminals, dissidents, prisoners of war, and innocent victims of Stalin's paranoia. Bear in mind that Kolyma and all the other gulags were the product of *"Stalinism,"* not *Communism* or *Socialism*.

KOMODO DRAGON – (ko-*MO*-do *DRA*-gon) Perhaps the most gruesome creature alive, the closest cousin to the extinct dinosaur. The Komodo dragon is a monitor lizard, the world's largest lizard, and the biggest venomous animal in the world. It can grow to 10 feet in length and weigh up to 300 pounds. The Komodo dragons (now becoming rare) inhabit 5 Indonesian islands east of Java, including Komodo

Island. It has vicious claws and are able to climb trees. The lizard's skin is reinforced with armor which contains tiny bones (*osteoderms*) that function as a form of natural chain-mail. Its 1 inch teeth are serrated like steak knives. Too, its teeth are covered with *gingival* (gum tissue) which lacerates and bleeds when the creature bites down. This produces the perfect incubation culture for bacterial growth. About 50 strains of bacteria infect the dragon's saliva. With its toxic saliva, the Komodo dragon will blood-poison a victim with a minor bite. Now it waits for the creature to weaken and die, perhaps in 24 hours. Incapacitated prey is often eaten alive by the Komodo dragon. This fearsome creature can eat 80% of its body weight at one feeding. Incidentally: Thousands of years ago, the first inhabitants of Australia encountered the *"Megalavia,"* a *"Mega-Komodo Dragon"* which was twice the size of today's creatures. The Megalavia was indeed the last living dinosaur.

KOMPROMAT – (*KOM*-pro-mot) Blackmail. A Russian political term which is a combination of the words *"compromising material."* Kompromat is taught in *Espionage 101* of Russia KGB School. Money, sex, hubris, resentment or scandal are used to ensnare a dupe into becoming a traitor or spy. Kompromat also involves the collection of damaging information about a politician or other public figure used to create negative publicity. Kompromat is used to control or destroy a political career. Russian intelligence had used kompromat to damage Hillary Clinton's (b. 1947) presidential run and elevate Donald Trump (b. 1946) to the White House in 2016. Russian Intelligence has proof of Trump and family selling American foreign policy for personal profit. They certainly have salacious video of bare-ass Trump with Russian prostitutes. The Russians can make Trump the laughing stock of his cellblock. Presently (2018), Russian kompromat is blackmailing U.S. President Trump into serving as Vladimir Putin's (b. 1952) Russian lapdog.

KNOW – (*NOH*) (Knowing, Known, Knowable, Knew) To understand, perceive, realize, and recognize. What you have been taught and learned you know. To know is to apprehend a truth or information with clarity and certainty. To know is to grasp reality from fantasy, veracity from falsity. One who knows is a believer. Of course, one can know, yet deny the truth out of expediency or fear. In other words, pretend that you don't know. Educated Republican legislators and government officials know that Donald Trump (b. 1946) is a dangerous fascist fool, an uneducated buffoon. Nevertheless, they deny what they know and support him, to maintain what they have and to get what they want. "*We know you know you perfidious cowards!*"

KORAN – (kor-*RON*) (Quran) The Arabic word *"Quran"* comes from the root word *"qara'a"* or *"qa-ra-a"* which means to *read, recite, proclaim.* The Koran is the holy book of Islam, said to have been inspired by Allah (God), and dictated by the Angel Gabriel to the Prophet Mohammed (c. 570 – 632 CE). The book was compiled between 609 to 633 CE. The Koran serves as the Muslim Bible. Much of the Koran is based on the Hebrew Bible. It is the foundation of the Islamic religion, but also the basis of Muslim law, politics, and culture. The Koran creates Muslim identity and unity. It consists of 6,000 verses in 114 suras or chapters. Mohammed, the author of the Koran was a warrior-prophet. Therefore, the book and the religion based on it are the most aggressive, even violent, of all major faiths. This should not present a problem today. Because like the Bible, much of the Koran is *time contingent* – written for an exclusive group, in a particular setting, at a unique time in history. However Fundamentalist Muslims accept the readings fundamentally or literally, resulting in violence. Incidentally: Christian Fundamentalists are no different.

KORANIC JESUS – (kor-*RON*-nic *JEE*-sus) Jesus as perceived by Muslims. Jesus (called *Isa* in Arabic) is regarded as a great Islamic Prophet, born of a virgin (*Maryam*), but not the Son of God, or a manifestation of God. (Neither is Mohammad so regarded.) Jesus, of course, stands below Mohammad, as does all humanity. The Koran (*Quran*) relates that the Prophet Mohammad smashed the 360 idols in the Kaaba (*Ka'ba*). However, he spared the idols of Jesus and Mary. That indicates Islamic reverence for Jesus and his mother. The Koran denies that Jesus was crucified. Muslims believe that God had swept Jesus up to heaven before he could be nailed on the cross. The followers of Jesus faked the crucifixion. It was Judas who died on the cross. Too, Jesus had 3 wives, Mary Magdalen, and the sisters Mary and Martha. Incidentally: Mohammad admired Jesus and emulated the miracles Jesus had performed, (as Jesus had emulated Buddha's miracles).

KOREAN SOLUTION – (kor-*REE*-an sol-*LOO*-shun) The answer to the problem of North Korean dictator Kim Jong Un (b. ca. 1983) and his nuclear arsenal. China must secretly be encouraged to take control of North Korea. China should install a puppet government in the country (after eliminating Kim Jong Un). Kim's generals would be delighted with bribes and very much relieved. North Korea can become a Chinese client state, as Puerto Rico is to America. The addition of North Korea to China would not in the least upset the global balance of power. China can disband North Korea's nuclear program. The U.S., China, and the Koreas can formally end the Korean War. As an incentive, Taiwan (Formosa) should be given back to China. This would be a symbolic gesture, closing the last chapter of the Sino-American Cold War. (Consider that Britain had returned Hong Kong to China without any dramatic conflict.) South Korea will just have to give up its pipe dream of a unified peninsula. That was a mid- 20th century notion. History had changed the geopolitical map. Today, South Koreans live very well. Tomorrow, they will live even better without a nuclear threat hanging over their heads. So will the world at large. Incidentally: Kim Jong Un had killed his uncle and half-brother. He should have killed his barber and tailor!

KOREAN WAR – (kor-*REE*-an *WAR*) (1950 – 1953) The *"Forgotten War."* At the end of World War Two, American forces occupied southern Korea and Russian forces occupied northern Korea. With the cold war, Korea solidified into Communist North and capitalist South. President Harry Truman's (1884 – 1972) Secretary of State, Dean Acheson (1893 – 1971) had made a speech that did not include South Korea in the American defense sphere. This may have emboldened North Korea to cross the 38th Parallel and invade South Korea on June 25, 1950. American and South Korean forces were pushed back to the small coastal port of Pusan. General Douglas MacArthur (1880 – 1964) (who did not believe the North Koreans would attack) staged an amphibious invasion at Inchon, far behind enemy lines. The U.S (and U.N.) forces gained the momentum and were on the attack. MacArthur pushed the Northerners out of South Korea, and against orders invaded the North. The U.S./U.N. forces were soon overlooking China. MacArthur did not believe that the Chinese would attack. In November, 1951, over 150,000 Chinese troops attacked. The Americans were routed and fell back in the greatest retreat in U.S. military history. With massive reinforcements and total air superiority, the U.S. pushed the Chinese and North Koreans back across the 38th Parallel, into North Korea. The war became a stalemate, which frustrated MacArthur. He wanted to deploy 50 atomic bombs, reunite the Koreas, and invade China. MacArthur insubordinately criticized President Truman and was fired and retired. The new President Dwight D. Eisenhower (1890 – 1969) secretly asked India's Prime Minister Jawaharlal Nehru (1889 – 1964) to leak to the Russians that

Eisenhower would soon use nuclear weapons in Korea. The bluff worked. Russia and China persuaded North Korea to sign an armistice which ended hostilities but not the war, in July 1953. Over 10% of Koreans were killed in the war. The Koreas are still divided by the 38th Parallel. However in 2017, North Korea become a nuclear power.

KORZYBSKI'S CLEAVER – (kor-*ZSHIB*-skees *CLEE*-ver) *"The map is not the territory."* So admonished Polish scholar Alfred Korzybski (1879 – 1950), the *"Father of Modern Semantics."* Korzybski warned us not to confuse symbols with reality. Maps, charts, and especially words are merely symbols for what they represent. The flag, for instance, is just a symbol for the nation. Defending that colorful piece of cloth, is not defending the country. So fighting or dying for the flag is plain stupid.

KOSHER – (CO-*sher*) Dietary laws governing Judaism. Kosher laws go back thousands of years to the Biblical Book of Leviticus. The approved foods are blessed by a Rabbi and prepared according to Jewish religious law. Kosher is comparable to Islamic Halal.

KOSOVO – (co-*SO*-vo) (Kosovo-Metohija) An autonomous province of southwestern Serbia, primarily populated by Albanians since the 13th century. The region is mainly plateau. Kosovo is small in area (4,203 sq. mi.) much smaller than Connecticut. Its population stands at about 1,950,000. The capital city is Pristina. Kosovo, like Serbia, was a part of greater Yugoslavia (South Slavia). But Albanians are not Slavonic. Too, where Serbs are Orthodox, Albanians are mostly Muslims, with others being Roman Catholic. The Communist partisan hero, Josip Broz Tito (1892 – 1980) re-established Yugoslavia after World War Two. Marshal Tito was a benevolent despot. Like a strict father, Tito held the ethnic and religious factions together, suppressing ethnic hostility and separatist movements. Socialist Yugoslavia prospered. But with Tito's death, all hell broke loose. All the parts of Serbian-dominated Yugoslavia began to secede from the union. The Serbs tried to arrest the separatist movements by force. Kosovonian Albanians too sought independence. The Serbs retaliated with brutality. Rape and mass murder prevailed. Serbian *"ethnic cleansing"* of Albanians was so atrocious that in 1998, the U.S. launched a bombing campaign, striking Belgrade, Serbia. The Albanian Muslim paramilitary force, the KLA (Kosovo Liberation Army) retaliated with rape and mass murder of Serbs. The line between villain and victim was blurred. In 1999, U.N. forces entered Kosovo and declared the province independent in 2008.

KOWTOW – (*KOU*-tou) (Kowtowing, Kowtowed) The supreme act of *"ass- lickery."* To kowtow is to act in an extremely obsequious manner, showing slavish servile deference. The term *"kowtow"* is an Anglicized corruption of the Chinese word *"ketou."* The term *"ke"* means *"knock"* and *"tou"* means *"head."* To kowtow is to submissively kneel before some master, arms spread outward, knocking one's head on the ground in humiliating prostration. One's face must kiss the ground or floor. All individuals, both Chinese and foreigners, were required to kowtow before the emperor and other high ranking officials. Kowtowing was a great humiliation to European diplomats and businessmen, especially the arrogant British. However, business is business, and capitalists are capitalists who would readily sell their dignity to make a profit. The term kowtow was first recorded in English in 1795. The term has been used time and again in American politics after 2016 with the emergence of Donald Trump (b. 1946). Most conservative Republicans have kowtowed to their guru Trump, creating the cult of *"Trumpublicanism."* Incidentally: The master of the kowtow *"de-testicled"* Mike Pence (b. 1959). Pence holds a black belt is the humiliating art of kowtow. There is no limit to the extent that Pence will grovel in obeisance to Trump.

KRAIT – (*KRAYT*) (also Bungarus) A venomous snake of the Indian Subcontinent and SouthEast Asia, which is neither a viper nor an adder. Kraits are nocturnal snakes averaging about 3 feet in length. Kraits are black or bluish-black in color with about 40 thin white crossbars along the body. Kraits are very dangerous. Their venom is neurotoxic. A bitten human will feel abdominal pain, then progressive paralysis. Within 4 to 8 hours, respiratory failure occurs, causing death by suffocation. All venomous creatures reserve their venom for food hunting. They do not appreciate wasting their venom on people or aggressive animals. Snakes and other creature bite in self-defense.

KRAKATOA – (crak-ka-*TOW*-a) Indonesian island, 2/3 of which exploded in a series of volcanic eruptions (August 27, 28, 1883). Krakatoa produced the greatest explosion, and the loudest sound ever experienced on Earth in historic times. As the island collapsed into the magma chamber, the explosive force released was equivalent to 200 megatons of TNT (4 times greater than the most powerful nuclear device, Russia's *"Czar Bomba,"* 1960). The sound of the explosions were the loudest noise ever to be heard on Earth! It was estimated at 180 decibels. The sound was heard 3,000 miles away. Krakatoa was the most fatal volcanic eruption, killing over 36,417 oblivious people. One of the many pressure waves radiated from the doomed island at 675 mph, rupturing sailor's eardrums 40 miles away. A searing pyroclastic flow boiled for 25 miles from the island on a cushion of super-heated steam. The flow cooked the seabed for 9.3 miles from the eruption. Several tsunamis of 98 feet, one of 151 feet drowned distant shores. High-water waves were recorded in the English Channel. A great volume of smoke and ash were released into the atmosphere including 20 million tons of sulfur. The haze reduced the intensity of sunlight. This lowered the temperature of the planet by 2.2 degrees Fahrenheit for 5 years, conditions approaching a *"volcanic winter."* The debris in the atmosphere made for brilliant red, orange, and purple sunrises and sunsets for about 5 years, after Krakatoa.

KRAKEN – (CRAK-en) A legendary sea monster that attacks boats and causes whirlpools in the Atlantic off the Norwegian coast. Although cryptozoologists do not dismiss the possibility of monstrous creatures in the sea, conventional biologists suggest that the Kraken was and still is a cephalopod of the genus *Architeuthis* – a giant squid. These monsters can grow to 50 feet in length. Tales of a Kraken date back to the Vikings. Since then stories of similar sea monsters have been reported by Scandinavian merchant mariners and fishermen. Giant squid have been seen in the frigid North Atlantic. There have been reports of these creatures attacking boats. In 1874, the French warship *"Alecton,"* reported a squid attack. Jules Verne (1828 – 1905) wrote about aKraken in this novel, <u>*Twenty Thousand Leagues Under the Sea*</u> (1970). In Norwegian, the word *"krake"* (minus the suffix "n," krake<u>n</u>) means, among other things, a *"crooked tree."* One can picture such a tree bearing wild branches in all directions. This is similar to a squid's tentacles. Furthermore, a *"krake"* is a marine grapnel anchor, similar to a grappling iron with hooks protruding in all direction. This too recalls a squid's tentacles, or the mythical Kraken.

KRIO – (*KREE*-o) The African creole. The pidgin patois of Africa. Krio is about 80% English, with an admixture of Portuguese, French, and West African Yoruba. It serves as a neutral language useful in commerce among diverse populations.

KRISHNA – (*KRISH*-na) The most popular manifestation of almighty Brahma (God) in Hinduism and related religions. Krishna is the beautiful wise man-god with the blue corpulence. Devout Hindus consider Krishna their leader, hero, teacher, protector, and friend. *Krishnaism* (krish-*NAY*-ism) has had a profound influence on Hindu religion, philosophy, and culture. *"Hare Krishna, Hare Rama."*

KRONA – (*KRO*-na) Name for the currency in use in Sweden.

KRONE – (*KRO*-na) Name for the currency in use in Denmark and Norway.

KRYPTON – (*KRIP*-ton) (Kr) The name derives from the Greek *kryptos* meaning *"hidden."* The 36 protons in its nucleus give krypton its atomic number. Krypton is an inert, monoatomic gaseous element, present as a trace element in the atmosphere. Krypton is used in fluorescent lights, lasers, and in high-power, tungsten-filament light bulbs.

KRYPTONITE – (*KRIP*-ton-nyt) A fictional element or mineral from an imagined alien planet that has the property of depriving *"Superman"* of his supernatural powers. The term kryptonite has been adopted into the popular parlance to mean anything that can seriously weaken or harm a particular person, project, or thing. *"Those obscene emails were kryptonite to his political career."* Incidentally: Krypton is a real element (Kr). The term is taken from the Greek *"kryptos,"* meaning *"hidden."* *"The facts are kryptonite to the Republicans."* – Journalist David Rothkopf (b. 1955).

K STREET – (*KAY STREET*) An avenue in Washington D.C. where the corporate lobbyists congregate, accumulate, like maggots on a rotting carcass. It is the capitol's rogue gallery of thieves. It is from K Street that professional bribers corrupt our elected congressmen with corporate capitalist dollars and have undermined our democratic government. No streets in the poorest, roughest ghettoes of America can match the corruption of K Street in the nation's capital.

K-T BOUNDARY – (kay tee *BOUND*-dree) A geological/paleontological point of time (about 65 million years ago) when the Cretaceous Period ended and the Tertiary Period began. The K-T Boundary marked the transition from the reign of the dinosaurs to the emergence of the mammals. The boundary was created in a flash, with the collision of the asteroid Chicxulub. The K-T Boundary is identified in the Earth's geology by a band of the element iridium, which is very rare on Earth, but plentiful in asteroids. The iridium marks an actual boundary line.

KUDOS – (*KOO*-dows) Honor, glory, acclaim, a form of congratulations. One may say: *"Many kudos on your fine accomplishment."* The term is taken from the Greek *"kydos,"* meaning *"glory, fame"* especially in battle. Kudos were first given in about 1799 at English universities, as a slang term.

KUDZU – (*KOOD*-zoo) An invasive vine brought to the U.S. South from Japan in 1876 as animal fodder. Big mistake! It can grow a foot a day and has enveloped much of Georgia, including the city of Atlanta. It will blanket everything in its reach with a green shroud. Kudzu chokes all other foliage, and eats its way inro buildings, everything. It is an instant jungle maker. The City of Atlanta has to pay for a special unit in the sanitation department just to irradicate kudzu. *"What havoc do invasive species wreak, before the native creatures learn to adjust to the invader."* – Charles Darwin (1809 - 1882).

KUIPER BELT – (*KY*-per *BELT*) A cloud of drifting icebergs. The Kuiper belt is alternately known as the *"Oort Cloud."* The Kuiper Belt is a region of the solar system far beyond the orbit of the dwarf planet Pluto in which billions of comets move in nearly circular orbits unless pulled out of orbit by the sun's gravity. The Kuiper Belt is the source of most of our comets. The Kuiper Belt marks the outer limits our solar system.

KUMBAYA – (koom-by-*YA*) The term derives from *Gullah,* the African-American slave creole meaning *"Come by here."* Kumbaya is a simple appeal to God to come to those in need. It evolved into a popular spiritual song.

KUMQUAT – (*CUM*-kwat) A small, round or oblong citrus fruit having a sweet rind and acidic pulp. Kumquats are used primarily for preserves.

KUNDALINI AWAKENING – (kun-da-*LEE*-nee a-*WAKE*-ken-ing) *"The Yoga of Awareness."* Kundalini Awakening aims to cultivate the creative spiritual potential of a human to uphold values, speak truth, and focus on the compassion and consciousness needed to serve and heal others. Bliss and enlightenment are the blessings of a Kundalini Yoga Awakening. Kundalini is a Hindi word for *"coiled one."* Kundalini is a form of primal energy, centered at a chakra point at the base of the spine. The religion scholar Joseph Campbell (1904 – 1987) described the concept of Kundalini as: *"The figure of a coiled female serpent goddess...residing in a subtle, slumbering state...near the base of the spine. The aim of Kundalini Yoga is to arouse the serpent to lift her head. This will bring her up the nerve channel of the spine to the crown of the head. Kundalini will awaken all the lotus centers or chakras [along the way]. With each waking, the psychology and personality of the practitioner will be altogether and fundamentally transformed."*

KUNG FLU – (kung *FLOO*) President Donald Trump's (b. 1946) bigoted slander, racial slur at China, blaming the Chinese for the 2020 Coronavirus pandemic. Indeed, the virus had originated and mutated, naturally in China. The Chinese were the first victims of the disease. But President Trump's inactivity and ineptitude made America the epicenter of the outbreak. King flu was a Trump attempt to distract and deflect justifiable blame off of Trump. Footnote: We may never know is the virus was incubated in unsanitary outdoor markets, or an accidental escape from a Chinese military weapons lab.

KUNG FU – (kung *FOO*) A Chinese martial art that involves directing blows at vulnerable areas of an attacker's body. Kung Fu relies on fluid body motion of the hands and legs. Incidentally: The martial arts were devised in Japan by peaceful Zen Buddhist Monks. After the Samurai (knights) disarmed the peasantry in order to exploit them, the monks created techniques to fight with common farm implements, and their hands and feet. In fact, the high kick was devised to knock a Samurai off his high horse.

KUNYAZA – (coon-*YOZ*-za) A sexual technique performed by a man in order to bring a woman to a profound orgasm. Kunyaza is actually a foreplay maneuver. It seems elemental although it is quite effective. Before penetration, the male rubs his mate's labia, clitoris, and vaginal entrance with his penis. This is purported to excite the lady, sometimes to the point of climax. *"Kunyaza"* is a Rwanda-Rundi word from the Great Lakes region of East Africa. The term derives from *"kunyaar,"* meaning *"to urinate."* It is said that kunyaza so excites, so stimulates these African women that they gush or squirt from the *"Skene's Gland"* during orgasm. It is important for women to ejaculate during sex in this manner, in order to be considered a worthy lover and wife. Kunyaza helps to attain this goal. It should be noted that African women from that region perform *"labial stretching."* Their large, floppy pussy lips are very sensitive, making kunyaza even more effective. Kunyaza has a salacious history. The story is told that about 100 years ago in the Kingdom of Rwanda's Third Dynasty, the king went off to war. The queen had grown horny. So she ordered one of her guards to make love to her. The guard was so nervous that he could not develop an erection. In a panic he slapped and rubbed his limp dick against Her Majesty's royal pussy, hoping that his dick would grow hard. The sensation so excited the queen that she experienced an explosive orgasm and gushed or squirted for the first time. The kunyaza technique was serendipitously discovered. *"A woman's orgasm is such a fragile thing."* – Novelist Megan Hart (b. 1971).

KURDS – (*KERDS*) (Kurdish, Kurdistan) A large ethnic group in Southwestern Asia that has occupied a vague region (not nation) called *Kurdistan,* located in Turkey, Iraq, Syria, and Iran for over a thousand years. With a population as high as 45 million, the Kurds are the largest ethnic group in the world without their own state. Racially the Kurds are Caucasians, ethnically they are Iranians (Persians), not Arabs. They are an ancient people from Northern Mesopotamia. They are mentioned in ancient Sumerian clay tablets as dwelling in *"The Land of Karda"* or Kurd. The Kurds came to be associated with the ancient Medes, who established an empire in Mesopotamia. Kurdish fortunes had risen and fallen several times in the tumultuous Middle East. They have always played a central role in the politics and history of the region. The people have been weaned on warfare, involved is clashes with Turks, Iraqis, Syrians, and Iranians throughout the 20th and 21st centuries. The Kurds are a courageous people, the only reliable fighting force against fanatical Islam (ISIS). The Kurds have a tradition of religious tolerance, subscribing to many faiths. Technically, most Kurds are Sunni Muslims, with large contingencies of Shiites. More fundamentalist Muslims quip that *"Compared to the unbeliever, the Kurd is a Muslim."* Outside the Middle East, the Kurdish Diaspora encompasses at least 21 nations, especially Germany (1.5 million). Incidentally: In October, 2019, the perfidious President Donald Trump (b. 1946) made a diabolical deal with Turkish dictator Recap Erdogan (b. 1954). Trump promised to extricate U.S. forces allied with the Kurds in Syria, south of Turkey. This would give Turkey a free hand to remove, and perhaps exterminate their Kurdish enemy. Why Trump chose to abandon America's only trustworthy ally in the region is mystifying to all. The only possible reason why rapacious, avaricious Trump would betray the Kurds, is for lucrative business opportunities in Turkey. The Kurds may be condemned to genocide, as were the Armenians (1.5 million killed) at the hands of the Turks during World War One. Kurd it happen again?

KURSK – (*KERSK*) City in Western Russia, an industrial center in an agricultural region. In July through August, 1943, Kursk witnessed the greatest mechanized tank battle in history. About 2,928 German tanks engaged 5,128 Russian tanks in an inferno of steel. After the great victory at Stalingrad, the Russian Red Army was surging, pushing the Wehrmacht westward. The Russians advanced on a 500 mile front. They were especially successful near Kursk where they created a bulge, the *Kursk Salient.* This is where the Germans planned to stage a counteroffensive, to pinch the bulge and surround a good part of the Russian army. However, Soviet intelligence learned of the impending attack, and an army of Russian civilians dug anti-tank defenses. These were the heaviest, most impenetrable defensive positions in the history of warfare. If the Russian anti- tank ditches and defenses were strung together, they would have stretched from Moscow to Madrid. About 941,000 German soldiers attacked, supported by 2,110 aircraft and their tanks. The Russians poured 2,500,000 soldiers against them supported by 3,500 aircraft. Never before or since have so many machines battled at one time in one place. The Germans lost about 198,000 soldiers at Kursk, while the Russian losses were 254,470. The battle was a tactical draw, but a strategic victory for Russia. The Germans were forced to retreat. Unlike the Russians, the German loses could not be replaced. The Germans resumed their retreat toward Poland and Germany. Never again would Germany launch an offensive in the East after Kursk.

KVETCH – (*KVECH*) (Kvetcher, Kvetching, Kvetched) A Yiddishism meaning to chronically complain. A kvetch or kvetcher is also the complainer, a perpetual whiner.

KWANZAA – (*KWAN*-za) A Swahili word that has come to represent an African- American festival. Kwanzaa is a harvest holiday which runs from December 26 to January first. It celebrates family, community, and culture. Kwanzaa is regarded as an Afrocentric counterpart to Christmas. Kwanzaa was created by African Studies Scholar Maulana Karenga (b. 1941), (born: Ronald McKinley Everett). Karenga devised Kwanzaa, with its multiple ceremonies in 1961. Kwanzaa is an alternative to <u>Christ</u>mas. There is no <u>Christ</u> in Kwanzaa.

KWEYOL – (*KWAY*-ol) The French-African creole language of Haiti, Martinique, Dominica, Guadalupe, and St. Lucia in the Caribbean.

KYRIARCHY – (ky-*REE*-are-kee) (Kyriarichal) In feminist theory, a social system built around domination, exploitation, oppression, and submission of women. Kyriarchy embraces bigotry beyond misogyny like sexism, racism, speciesism, and homophobia.

L

L – (*EL*) The 12th letter in the English alphabet, a consonant. L is also the Roman numeral for the number 50 (fifty).

LABELS – (*LAY*-buls) Designations describing a person's character, ethnicity, race, sexuality, religion, ideology, affiliations, or social status. Labels are often condescending, pejorative, or opprobrious. Labels can harm and hurt. The Danish philosopher and theologian, Soren Kierkegaard (1813 – 1855) proclaimed: *"Once you label me, you negate me."* Indeed, sticks and stone can break my bones, but labels can break my heart. The Dutch humanist theologian Desiderius Erasmus (1466 – 1536) professed that *"Stupid names* [read: *labels*] *have separated humankind more than Jesus was ever able to bring it together."* The Taoist avatar, Lao Tzu (c. 604 – c. 531) wrote: *"Those who are highly evolved, maintain an undiscriminating perception. Seeing everything, labeling nothing, they maintain their awareness of the Great Oneness. Thus they are supported by it."*

LABIA – (*LAB*-bee-ah) (Labial) Latin for *"lips."* In medical terms, the labia refers to the female genital. *"Labia majora"* is the outer lips, *"labia minora"* is the inner lips. The labia is the lips on tha vaginal mouth. The labia is sexually sensitive with nerve ending and hugs the penis during intercourse.

LABIAPLASTY – (*LAB*-bee-ah-plas-tee) (also Labioplasty) A specific form of *"vaginoplasty,"* (vaginal surgery). Labiaplasty is plastic surgery on the *"labia majora"* (outer lips) and *"labia minora"* (inner lips) of the vulva. These folds of skin form the lips lining the vaginal mouth. A labiaplasty operation is performed to reconstruct the organ after accident or cancer. Alternately, it may be cosmetic genital surgery to alter the organ to the lady's desire.

LABOR – (*LAY*-ber) Productive toil, work in order to attain sustenance. Labor may be skilled or unskilled, of physical or mental nature. No honest labor is lowly, shameful, embarrassing, or humiliating. *"Let us not be ashamed or slow to do humble work,"* admonished Mother Teresa (1910 – 1997). Every task or chore can be consecrated, made holy as a sacrament, if offered as a prayer. This the Buddhists call *"Naikan."* As the Zen Masters say: *"I draw water, I carry wood. That's my miracle."* Mohandas Gandhi (1869 – 1948) taught that: *"Each man's labor is as important as another's. In fact, while you're doing it, cleaning the toilet is far more important than [practicing] the law."* As the Hindu Yogi and Guru Paramahansa Yogananda (1893 – 1952) had prayed: *"O Infinite Creator... I know that all work is Thy work, and that no task is too difficult or too menial when offered to Thee in loving service."*

LABOR – (*LAY*-ber) (The Human Workforce.) The most essential factor in production. Labor is the workforce, the power that completes the job. In order for labor to be effective, it must be contented and motivate. That's why slave labor is the least efficient brand. The worker must be healthy. That means she must have good healthcare. The worker must be skilled, well trained. He must be well compensated for his service. She must be treated with dignity and appreciation. Together, these factors will provide an enthusiastic and productive labor force. Profit-driven capitalist corporationists are instinctively anti-labor. To capitalists, labor is a necessary nuisance, a means to the end – profits. That's why labor must be organized into unions. *"There is no hope for the workingman outside of organization."* – Labor Leader Peter J. McGuire (1852 – 1906). Abolitionist Wendell Phillips (1811 – 1884) explained that: *"The labor movement means just this: it is the last noble protest of the American people against the power of incorporated wealth."*

LABORATORY SCHOOL – (lab-*BOR*-ra-tor-ree *SKOOL*) In education, a model school or classroom in a university's College of Education for experimentation and application of Progressive innovations.

LABOR PAINS – (*LAY*-ber *PAYNS*) This entry does not refer to birth, but rather to death – the death of the labor movement. Worker's unions reached the peak of their strength in 1956-1957. This was the height of the Cold War. American corporate capitalists feared the workers would side with the *Socialists* in the Union of Soviet *Socialist* Republics. So capitalist management was much more willing to share more with labor. The decline in organized labor was apparent by 1980. The 80's was a decade of management. The anti-labor Republican President Ronald Reagan (1911 – 2004) was elected. Foreign competition lessened the demand for U.S. goods, manufactured by American workers. Automation, robotics robbed workers of many jobs. The baby boom produced a surplus of workers vying for fewer jobs. This lowered wages and weakened the labor force. Corporate capitalists outsourced jobs abroad to take advantage of cheap child and slave labor. Republican state governments passed anti-labor legislation which further crippled organized labor. The pains of labor continue today. Indeed, labor will suffer as long as the worker stands alone against corporate power. Unionization is the cure for labor ailments.

LABOR RELATIONS – (*LAY*-ber ree-*LAY*-shuns) The interaction, attitude, and degree of rapport between boss and worker. In a capitalist setting, it is confrontational. In a Socialist setting, it is collegial, for there is no oppressive boss. The manager of a project is a colleague, a teammate striving toward a common goal. In 1951, a British industrialist, a Quaker member of the Roundtree Family gave the following address to an association of corporate capitalists. The message is perfectly pertinent today. *"It is important that industry should be efficient and waste should be reduced to a minimum. The greatest source of waste arises through lack of cordial cooperation between employers and employed. Our aim should be to induce all to work as hard and as intelligently as if they were working for themselves.... Remember there is no such thing as 'Labor.' The working force is made up of a number of individuals each having a personality different from the rest. They are sensitive as we are to encouragement and discouragement, as easily aroused to anger and suspicion, to loyalty and to effort. One may deal with things without love; but one cannot deal with men without it, just as one cannot deal with bees without being careful. If you deal carelessly with bees, you will injure them, and you will yourself be injured. And so with men."*

LABRADOR – (*LAB*-bra-door) A Canadian peninsula in northeast North America surrounded by the Hudson Bay, the Atlantic, and the Gulf of St. Lawrence, containing the Canadian provinces of Newfoundland and Quebec. Also, Labrador refers to the eastern part of the peninsula specifically. This is Labrador, the continental part of the Newfoundland province. Labrador is a cold, rocky, barren landscape. It is far north in latitude and licked by the cold Labrador Current from the Arctic. Labrador is a great place to view icebergs.

L'CHAIM – (la-*HY*-im) Means *"To Health."* L'chaim is a Jewish toast when sharing a drink.

LACHRYMOSE – (*LACK*-rim-mose) (Lachrymal) Tearful. Producing tears, indicative of weeping. *"We found her in a lachrymose condition."*

LACK – (*LAK*) The false perception of insufficiency due to distributive injustice. Capitalism excites a fear of lack which generates competition and greed. In a fair share Socialist economy the perception of lack is supplanted by the realization of plenty. Abundance is realized. Cooperation supersedes competition. The result is plenty for all. *"I lack nothing. I only needed myself."* – Franz Kafka (1883 – 1924).

LACKADAISICAL – (lak-a-*DAY*-si-cal) Listless, lethargic, lacking ambition, enthusiasm or pep. A lackadaisical person is a sluggish schmo.

LACKLUSTER – (*LAK*-lus-ter) Dull, without sparkle, boring, not exciting. A lackluster performance in entertainment, sports, anything is uninteresting and not worth watching. *"Their lackluster effort cost them the game."*

LACONIC – (la-*CON*-nic) Brief, concise, succinct, a man of few words. A laconic speech is short, terse, and curt in nature.

LACTIC ACID – (*LAK*-tic *ASS*-sid) ($C_3H_6O_3$) A colorless or yellowish carbolic acid, a water-soluble syrupy liquid which exists in 3 isomeric forms. One is found in sour milk, wine, and many fruits. Another form is manufactured for use in flavoring and preserving foods and beverages, producing pharmaceuticals, and in textile printing. Thirdly, the body produces lactic acid in the muscle tissues. It is a waste product of anaerobic metabolism of glucose. Muscle cells are living entities. They breathe, eat, work, and must rest and excrete waste. The waste that muscle tissue discharges after exercise is lactic acid. In a sense, muscle cells urinate lactic acid. With over exercise or over exertion, the lactic acid accumulates in the muscles. If it cannot be excreted fast enough, the muscles will become sore, aching, and painful. Only with rest, allowing the muscles time to *"pee-out"* the lactic acid, will the hurt subside.

LACUNA – (la-*COON*-na) A gap or missing section in a manuscript, collection, series, or in a logical argument.

LADINO – (la-*DEE*-no) A Sephardic Jewish dialect based primarily on Spanish, written in Hebrew. Ladino is the Sephardic counterpart to Ashkenazic Yiddish.

LAGNIAPPE – (lan-*YEP*) A tip, bonus, or gratuity. A lagniappe is a small gift given with a purchase to a customer, by way of compliment or for good measure. Lagniappe is primarily a regionalism prevalent in Louisiana and South Texas.

LAGOON – (la-*GOON*) A body of shallow water cut-off from the open sea by coral reef, sandbars, or barrier islands.

LAHAR – (la-*HAR*) A debris flow of mud, boulders, trees caused by a volcanic eruption, when fire meets ice. The intense volcanic heat instantly melts the glacial ice and snow of the mountain, triggering a lahar.

LAICIZATION – (lay-i-sy-ZAY-shun) To be "*de-priested.*" To be laicized is to be defrocked or stripped of the priesthood. To be demoted from a priest to a *lay* person.

LAICIZE – (*LAY*-i-size) To be defrocked as a priest. To be drummed-out of the priesthood.

LAIKA – (*LY*-ka) (c. 1954 – 1957) The first living creature in space. On November 3, 1957, the Russians launched this female dog into Earth orbit. Laika was a 3 year old mutt (part-husky, part-terrier), a Moscow street dog. Her mission was a success, though she did perish. Her spacecraft, Sputnik II, was not designed to bring her back. Animal rights organizations were up-in-arms over her demise. Laika is honored with a "*Monument to the Conquerors of Space*" in Moscow.

LIAR – (*LY*-er) (Lying, Lie, Lied) One who continuingly espoused untruths. In rare cases a pathological liar suffers from some mental condition. In most cases, a liar is an unscrupulous individual, devoid of honor, integrity, or shame. To be called a liar is, or at least was, a grievous insult. In bygone days, such a defamation would trigger a duel. Not today. Lying, especially in politics, has become an artform, a political strategy. This is particularly true of the Republican Party as it metastasized into the Trumpublican Party. Donald Trump (b. 1946) is the incomparable "*Prince of Liars.*" <u>The Washington Post</u> had recorded 30,573 lies spit out of the mouth of Trump during his 4 years in the White House. Trump is more twisted and vile today. Trump's sycophant advisor Corey Lewandowski (b. 1973) boasted that: "*Its not illegal to lie to the press.*" Much of Donald Trump's life had been a lie. Trump is such a brash, vociferous liar that many believe him to be a pathological mythomaniac. A liar is usually a cheater, and a cheater is usually a thief. Trump has proven to be all three. To have a liar as the leader of the nation would make all that America stands for, into a lie.

LAISSEZ FAIRE – (*LAY*-say *FAIR*) French which literally means, "*Let [people] do [as they think best].*" Government hands-off of business. Laissez faire is the heartbeat of capitalism. It advocates no restrictions, regulations, oversight over corporate capitalism. Laissez Faire gives capitalism a free hand to exploit and profit at free will. In a laissez faire economic environment, big business need not worry about health and safety measures, environmental restrictions, illegal business practices. A laissez faire economy is a corpocracy, a government run by corporations. "*The tail is wagging the dog.*" Capitalists cannot be trusted. They must be watched and they must be punished when they become hyper- greedy. Laissez-faire pertains to other facets of government and society. The Trump administration is taking a laissez faire approach to the Coronavirus pandemic. They call their approach "*herd Immunity.*" Actually, it is no approach. It is laissez-faire, hands-off, come-what-may, "*Social Darwinism.*" If employed, 2.1 million Americans will die. Actually, 1.3 million Americans succumbed to the virus.

LAKE-EFFECT SNOW – (layk ef-fekt *SNOH*) Exceptionally heavy snowfall in regions adjacent to large lakes like the Great Lakes. Lake-effect snow is produced during cooler atmospheric conditions when a cold air mass moves across long expanses of warmer lake water. The lower layer of air, heated by the lake water, picks up water vapor from the lake and rises through colder air. The vapor then freezes and is deposited on the leeward (downwind) shore. The snowiest region in the U.S.A. is Michigan's Northern Peninsula. The U P (<u>U</u>pper <u>P</u>eninsula) faces Lake Superior to the north, Lake Michigan on most of the south, and Lake Huron to the southeast. Most of the Upper Peninsula is wild, with no urban areas. The largest city,

Marquette hosts only 20,629 Michiganians. Therefore, the snowiest large U.S. city, due to lake-effect snow, is Buffalo, New York, downwind of Lake Erie, (as football fans know).

LAKE ERIE BATTLE – (*LAYK EAR*-ree *BAT'l*) (The Battle of Lake Erie, September 10, 1913). The Battle of Lake Erie was part of the *War of 1812* (1812 – 1814). Captain Oliver Hazard Perry's (1785 – 1819) carpenters and engineers built a fleet of 9 ships from raw timber in northern Ohio. They soundly defeated the British fleet (6 vessels) at Put-In-Bay, Ohio. For the proud British Navy, this was the first unqualified defeat of a British naval squadron in history. Twenty-seven U.S. seamen were killed, 96 wounded. The British lost 40 killed and 94 wounded. After the victory, Captain Perry sent his famous message to General William Henry Harrison (1773 – 1841): *"We have met the enemy, and they are ours."* The victory in the Battle of Lake Erie forced the British to abandon Detroit, ensuring U.S. control over Lake Erie and the Territorial Northwest.

LAKES – (*LAYKS*) Fresh bodies of inland water. Lakes cover 1.8% of the Earth's surface. There are 117 million lakes in the world. Lakes are fresh because they're flushed. All fresh water lakes have some outlet and recycles its water so it doesn't become mineral impregnated and salty. Geographers generally consider saltwater lakes to be inland seas (like the Caspian Sea). The relatively small Dead Sea is called a sea and not a lake because it is salty. Its water has no outlet. Lake Superior (North America) is the largest lake in area. Lake Victoria (Africa) is the largest of the tropical lakes. Lake Baikal (Russia) is the oldest, deepest lake. Baikal alone holds 20% of the plant's fresh water. Lake Baikal is so deep because it is a tectonic fissure, or crack in the Earth's crust. In fact, the world's lakes hold 20 times more fresh water than all the rivers combined. Lake Malawi in Africa has a greater variety of fish than any other lake in the world. Lake Vostok is a huge freshwater lake, buried under Antarctica's glacial ice. Incidentally: Glaciers have blessed Canada with more lakes than all the rest of the world combined.

LAKOTA PRAYER – (la-*CO*-ta *PRAY*-yer) *"Oh Great Spirit whose voice I hear in the winds, and whose breath gives life to all the world, hear me, I am small and weak, I need your strength and wisdom. Let me walk in beauty and make my eyes ever behold the red and purple sunset. Make my hands respect the things you have made and my ears sharp to hear your voice. Make me wise so that I may understand the things you have taught my people. Let me learn the lessons you have hidden in every leaf and rock. I seek strength, not to be greater than my brother, but to fight my greatest enemy – myself. Make me always ready to come to you with clean hands and straight eyes, so when life fades, as the fading sunset, my Spirit may come to you without shame."* – Lakota Sioux Chief Yellow Lark (1887).

LALLAPALOOZA – (la-la-pa-*LOO*-za) An early Americanism meaning an extraordinary person or thing.

LALOCHEZIA – (la-loh-*KEE*-zee-ah) Literally *"shity talk."* The use of vulgar, obscene language to gain emotional relief from stress, anger, or pain. This awkward term derives from two Greek words meaning *"speech,"* and *"to defecate."* Lalochezia is venting, blowing-off steam by swearing. For example, you hit your thumb with a hammer and yell-out: *"Oh Fuck!"* It was autonomic. You just employed lalochezia. When the project collapses before your eyes, you may unconsciously blurt out *"Son of a bitch!"* Again, lalochezia. Vulgar words are aggressive, while obscene words are sexual. Vulgar swear words are usually curses like: *"Damn you!" "Drop dead!" "Go to hell!"* Obscene swear words threaten sexual violence like *"Fuck you!" "Up your ass!" "You bloody cunt!"* It's popular to call an insufferable opponent a *"bitch"* or *"bastard."* These too carry indirect sexual allusions. Incidentally, most English swear words are of Germanic origin. The wise Mark Twain (1835 – 1910) understood the psychology. He said: *"Under certain circumstances, profanity provides a relief denied even to prayer."* Furthermore, an elementary school teacher in Detroit had a sign hung in the classroom that read: *"Don't hit or swear. But if you're going to hit, swear."* Lalochezia is usually a catharsis. However, in the culture of exotic erotica, lalochezia is used as a sexual stimulant. *"Talk dirty to me."* Some people are sexually aroused by obscene speech. *"Bend over you filthy slut!"* may turn the lady on.

LAMA – (*LA*-ma) A Tibetan term for a prominent, high-ranking Buddhist monk. The foremost Lama is the is the Tibetan Dalai Lama, Tenzin Gyatso (b. 1935), the 14th in line.

LAMARCKISM – (la-*MARK*-is-um) The evolutionary theory set forth by Jean- Baptiste Lamarck (1744 – 1829) that characteristics acquired by habit, use, or disuse may be passed on to future generations through inheritance. For instance, the giraffe's long neck resulted from generations of stretching to reach the leaves in the high branches. Lamarckism has been supplanted by Darwinism and Mendelian genetics.

LAMAISM – (*LA*-ma-is-um) The mystic rendition of Mahayana Buddhism, as practiced in Tibet and Mongolia. Lamaism includes elements of Hinduism and pre-Buddhist shamanism or *"Bon"* (pronounced *bain*).

LAMASERY – (la-*MAS*-er-ree) A Buddhist monastic college. A school for Buddhist monks.

LAMBASTE – (*LAM*-beyst) (also Lambast) (Lambasted, Lambasting) To beat or whip severely. Alternately, to excoriate, berate, reprimand harshly. The term is of Old Norse origin (c. 1590's). *"Lemja"* means *"to beat,"* or *"to lame,"* while *"baste"* means *"to thrash."*

LAMBDA – (*LAM*-da) The Greek letter "L." In a socio-political sense, Lambda is an American civil rights organization that focuses on lesbian, gay, bisexual, transgender (LGBT) communities, as well as people with aids (PWA's). The Lambda Legal Defense and Education Fund provides legal aid, impact litigation, societal education, and public policy work. Lambda was founded in 1971 by William J. Thom (b. 1941), New York City's first openly gay judge.

LAMBENT – (*LAM*-bent) (Lambency) Floating lightly over the surface. To be lambent is to deal gently, gracefully, lightly with a person or topic, the soft touch. A soft light is lambently radiant.

LAME DUCK – (*LAYM* duk) A politician who has served the maximum terms or has not been re-elected and is waiting out her tenure in office. The term suggests that the official is powerless, for he will soon be out of power. However, the elected official still has all the constitutional powers of the office. A politician becomes a lame duck only if she chooses to coast without making waves. In this case, political exhaustion may account for lame duck impotence. In a sense, a lame duck politician may be more powerful, for he is not beholding to anyone for re-election support. For the first time in her career, she can speek her mind. Many cowardly Republican legislators condemned Donald Trump (b. 1946) only after they had become lame ducks. In 2016, President Barrack Obama (b. 1961) was constitutionally obliged to appoint a Supreme Court Justice. The Republicans were incensed and expected President Obama to sit on his hands for the balance of his lame duck presidency. The Republicans filibustered, robbing President Obama the opportunity to make the appointment. In 2017, Donald Trump (b. 1946) became the first U.S. President in history to become a lame duck in his first 120 days. Trump's lies, racketeering, intrigue, incompetency and the numerous investigations into his loyalty had cost Trump all credibility.

LAME DUCK SESSION – (*LAYM DUCK SESH*-shon) The condition of Congress after an election. This is the period from the November election, to the day the newly elected Congress is seated. In the interim, many incumbent Congressmen who were not re-elected remain in power. The majority and power may have shifted to the other party in the election. The embittered losers, still in the majority for a short while, have an opportunity to wreak havoc. The lame duck session was originally from November to March. It took a long time in the late 18th century to get to Washington on horseback. The 20th Amendment (1933) shortened the lame duck session from November to January. With one-day air travel, even this is needlessly too long. Incidentally: After the great Democratic victory in the 2018 Congressional election, the lame duck Republicans maliciously took *"prevenge."* They knew that the upcoming Democratic Committees would hold hearings into Trump/Republican illegality/criminality. The Democrats would take *"revenge."* Therefore, the lame duck wanted to get their last nasty punches in, with their prevenge. They displayed their nature as the party of *NO!*

LAMINAE – (*LAM*-in-ay) (Laminate) Being in a series of thin layers. Laminated material like plywood is made of thin layers fused together. It is incredibly strong.

LANAI – (lan-*EYE*) A veranda, piazza. Lanai is a Hawaiian word for a large, roofed, encloses porch, often screened and fully furnished, which serves as a reading, meditating, relaxing room, semi-outdoors.

LAND – (*LAND*) Terra Firma. The good Earth. The rock on which we live. Heavy igneous basalt rock sank, forming the ocean floor. Some basalt pushed deep into the Earth, melting and mixing with water. It metamorphosized into lighter granite. The granite rose to form the platform for the continents. Rock ground by erosion produced soil. We were bequeathed with land.

LANDLINE – (*LAND*-lyn) Originally, the old fashion telephone. This communication device was called a *"POTS,"* which is a retronym acronym for Plain Old Telephone Service. Initially, historically, POTS stood for Post Office Telephone System, because the master switchboard was usually at the local post office. The common telephone came to be called a *"landline"* only with the ubiquitous emergence of the *"cellphone."* Original landline phones rested on a table or was mounted on the wall. A physical cord or phone line connected the handset to the base unit, which is plugged into the telephone wall jack. Another line from the phone jack in the house connects to the main phone line outside on the telephone pole. These phones are simple, and simplicity is a characteristic of efficiency. They do not require expensive batteries nor do they need charging. So landlines are reliable, serviceable even during a power outage. Of course, one's mobility is limited to the length of the phone cord on the handset. Thirty-foot cords are available. So, you have enough cord to reach the toilet, and the reception is perfect. Then, in 1963, the first cordless landline was offered. These phones do not have a physical cord connecting the handset to the wall jack. Instead, they communicate wirelessly with the base mechanism in the house by radio. They are far more complex requiring expensive batteries and charging, and have a limited range from the base mechanism in the house. Telephony is always clearer than radio. Radio is plagued with static, radio-electrical interference, and unreliable signals. Dense walls or floors can block the radio reception. Actually, the term *"cordless landline"* is a false misnomer, for there is no line at all. Everything is radio operated. Storms, power cuts, internet failures will cut off your phone service. Again we see that all novelty, all progress is not always progressive. Old fashion landline telephones do not drop calls. Incidentally: The word *"telephone"* came from the French in 1835. The term *"tele"* is Greek for *"far,"* and *"phone"* is Greek for *"voice."*

LANDLORDSHIP – (land-*LAWRD*-ship) (Land lord) The landed gentry. A landlord is an aristocrat or capitalist who controls more than his share of space on planet Earth. She is a member of the landed gentry. He has made himself master of the land which belongs to all. Landlords lord over the land and the people that occupy it. Landlordship is an archaic vestigial remain of Medieval Feudalism. It creates a lord-serf relationship. Landlords maintain their power through force, financed by wealth, accrued from the land they control. They dominate and abuse the poor through rent. Landlordship is a pillar of capitalist exploitation, inequality, and oppression. It supports the capitalist class system by maintaining the disparity of wealth and power. In fact, man is the only animal on Earth who must pay rent, for a spot to lay his head. Historically, expropriating and avenging landlords has been the first reform measure in revolutions. In Socialism, landlordship becomes an historical footnote. *"The interest of the landlords is always opposed to the interest of every other class in the community."* – British Political Economist David Ricardo (1772 – 1823). Incidentally: The Old English (West Saxon) word for lord was *"hlafweard,"* literally meaning *"keeper of the loaf"* – translation: *"controller of our bread,"* meaning sustenance.

LAND LUBBER – (*LAND LUHB*-ber) A lubber is a big, clumsy, stupid person. The term *"land lubber"* was originally a contemptuous sailor's designation for a landsman. Later, the term was expanded to include an incompetent boatman or one who dislikes sailing. Keeping a great ship asail was a complicated and dangerous task. Incompetent seamen who didn't *"know the ropes"* were despised, because they were dangerous at sea. Therefore, to be considered a land lubber was a serious insult. In <u>*A New Dictionary of the Terms Ancient and Modern of the Canting Crew*</u> (1699), the anonymous author, B.E. Gent wrote: *"Land-lopers or Land-lubbers, Fresh-water Seamen so called by the true Tarrs."* In his 1847 novel, <u>*Omoo*</u>, Herman Melville (1819 – 1891) captures the contempt good sailors had for land lubbers: *"Now, nobody is so heartily despised as a pusillanimous, lazy, good-for-nothing land-lubber; a sailor has no bowels of compassion for him.... Whenever there is any plain, hard work to be done, he is put to it like a lever."*

LANDMINE – (*LAND*-myn) A vile, heinous killing/maiming device, more a cowardly instrument of terror, than a bold weapon of war. Landmines are explosive devices buried hidden in the ground. Any vehicle and person who treads on the triggering mechanism is blown apart. Now then, large powerful anti-tank/truck mines are arguably justifiable, (if one can make a good argument for conducting war). Blowing up a combat vehicle by landmine is not different than destroying the same with artillery or air strike. But there is no moral justification for planting anti-personnel landmines. Why? Because a landmine is totally indiscriminate. Its victims are arbitrary. It cannot distinguish friend from foe, enemy from innocent. An anti-personnel landmine is a modern day mantrap. A weapon like a rifle can target an enemy combatant. There are eyes behind the gun. But a landmine is blind to its victims. Soldiers, farmers, men, women, children, cows, sheep, horses are all capriciously victimized. When the war is over and the fighting ceases, the rifle, tank, and bomber depart. The landmine lingers, forever, unless it is removed or it explodes under someone's body. Landmines are so morally repugnant that 164 nations have signed a treaty banning them in warfare. However the world's three greatest powers, the United States, Russia, and China have refused to abandon them. Astoundingly, someone is killed by a landmine every 20 minutes in the world. Research reveals that 78 countries are presently contaminated with landmines from previous wars. As many as 20,000 people are killed annually by landmines, 80% being civilians, primarily children. Survivors lose limbs, maimed for life. One might as well poison the soil, for the fields and pastures are totally inaccessible. Incidentally: Diana, Princess of Wales (1961 – 1997) campaigned passionately against landmines. In fact, she intended to expose the names of prominent powerful Brits, capitalists who were invested in the profitable manufacture of landmines. Diana never got the chance. She was mysteriously killed in an auto crash. Very curios.

LANDMINE – (*LAND*-myn) In social psychology, a totally unforeseen incident, or statement that ignites a major confrontation. The person who steps on the hidden landmine is oblivious of the impending explosion. The victim is innocent, with no intensions of setting the other party into a tirade. Husbands of overly critical and sensitive wives are often landmine casualties. The innocent wrong choice of words, a forgotten occasion, an unheard appeal, are concealed landmines, the detonation of which can trigger World War III in the household. Wives that maintain emotional minefields are subconsciously and consciously directing their husbands to avoid the area. They may soon avoid communication altogether.

LAND RECLAMATION – (*LAND* rec-clam-*MAY*-shun) Restoration of the environment after the wealth has been extracted. Land reclamation is a method used after mining to prevent erosion, clean the water sources, and plant native trees. The area is to be returned to its original contours, its natural state. This is a major thorn in the corporate capitalist side. Land reclamation takes time, and costs money. It cuts into the precious profits, which is *"counter- capitalistic."* The mining industry would prefer to just take and make their break. Strick laws and regulatory oversight by honest officials must force the corporate capitalists to meet their responsibilities.

LAND/SEA BREEZE – (land see *BREEZ*) The daily inward and outward winds on the seacoast. It is due to high and low pressure systems because the land and sea heat at different rates. During the day, the land heats up more and quicker than the water. Warm air rises over the land, allowing cool sea air to rush in below. The breeze comes from the sea. As the day progresses toward evening, the land cools, while the sea heats up. The cool land air sinks producing high pressure. The land air blows as wind toward the warmer sea. Nature insists on harmony. The land/sea breeze assures that temperature balance is maintained.

LANGUAGE – (*LANG*-gwij) Agreed-upon nonsensical sounds, to which sense and meaning was attributed. The first and original communication internet. Language is a code. Language is a system of linguistic sounds, signs, gestures, and symbols used in common by a community of people to facilitate communication. Language was a game changer, that elevated us above other mammals. A common language is an essential ingredient in forming a culture. Cultural anthropologists believe that language differences were triggered by minute discrepancies in pronunciation among neighboring tribes. For instance, tribal leaders long ago met to trade. One may have called the hand-ax an *"aga."* The other corrected him, insisting that the tool was an *"oga."* The discussion heated into an argument. Disgusted with each other's perceived ignorance, they departed, maintaining and perpetuating their linguistic differences. Though not as dramatic as the Biblical story of the *Tower of Babel,* this is how accents, then different languages evolved. *"The whole earth had one language and the same words."* – Genesis 11:1. *"Let us confuse their language, so that they may not understand one another's speech."* – Genesis 11:7.

LANGUID – (*LANG*-gwid) Lackadaisical, ambitionless. A languid individual lacks vigor, vitality, interest, and spirit.

LANGUISH – (*LANG*-gwish) To become weak, feeble, lose vigor and vitality. One suffering from neglect, hardship, and inactivity will languish, as in prison.

LANGUOR – (*LANG*-gor) (Languid, Languorous) Sluggishness, listlessness, physical weakness. A languorous person lacks energy, vitality, enthusiasm, and ambition. To languor is to stagnate.

LANIAKEA SUPERCLUSTER – (luh-nay-uh-*KEE*-uh *SOO*-per-clus-ter) A partition of the observable universe. The Laniakea Supercluster is a supercluster of superclusters of stars, over 100,000 galaxies like the Virgo Supercluster. Laniakea Supercluster is about 520 million light years across. Nevertheless, it is but a tiny bit of the observable universe. Furthermore, the observable universe is a small portion of the unobservable unknown universe beyond.

LANTHANIDES – (*LAN*-than-nides) The *"Rare-Earth"* elements. Lanthanides are the metallic elements with atomic numbers (proton counts) of 57 through 71. They include: cerium (Ce), dysprosium (Dy), erbium (Er), europium (Eu), gadolinium (Gd), holmium (Ho), lanthanum (La), lutetium (Lu), neodymium (Nd), praseodymium (Pr), promethium (Pm), samarium (Sm), scandium (Sc), terbium (Tb), thulium, ytterbium (Yb), and yttrium (Y). Despite the name *"rare-earth,"* the lanthanides (with the exception of radioactive promethium) are not rare, but rather plentiful. Rare-earth is an archaic appellation. In the past, many of these metals were difficult to find. Too, when found, they were difficult to separate from their ores. They appeared to be hidden [read: *rare*] in the Earth. In fact the name lanthanide derives from the Greek *lanthanein,* meaning *"to lie hidden."*

LANTHANUM – (*LAN*-than-num) (La) The name derives from the Greek *lanthanein* meaning *"to lie hidden."* The 57 protons in its nucleus give lanthanum its atomic number. Lanthanum is a silvery-white ductile metallic element. Lanthanum is used in pyrophoric alloys (that spark when struck). Too, lanthanum is used in glass for lenses, electronic devices, and lights for movie or television studios.

LAO TZU'S ADMONITION – (lauw *TSOOS* ad-mon-*NISH*-shuhn) The pious Chinese sage and avatar, Lao Tzu (c. 604 – c. 531 BCE) authored the sacred philosophical- spiritual book, <u>*Tao Te Ching*</u> (<u>*Book of the Way*</u>). He admonished us in the right way to live. *"In dwelling. Live close to the ground. In thinking, keep to the simple. In conflict, be fair and generous. In governing, don't try to control. In work, do what you enjoy. In family life, be completely present."* Incidentally: Lao Tzu once met the great philosopher and sage Confucius (551 – 479 BCE). Lao Tzu cautioned Confucius about being too outspoken to powerful people, saying his intelligence would not save him.

LAPA – (*LA*-pa) A Polish-American slang term for an airhead, a dufus, a schmo. A lapa is a good-spirited, though befuddled soul. He is perpetually dumbfounded. Of a lapa one would say, *"He doesn't have a clue."*

LA PALMA – (la-*PAL*-ma) The north-westerly most island in the Atlantic's Canary Islands. La Palma is site of Cumbre Vieja a 6,394 foot volcano, a *"ticking time bomb."* Rising magma in the volcano is heating water trapped within the structure of the island. This is like a herculean steam boiler begging to explode. When it blows, the western flank of Cumbre Vieja will slide into the Atlantic. A track of land almost twice the size of the Isle of Man will crash, splash into the ocean creating a mega-tsunami, the size of which the Earth has not seen since the *Storegga Slide* off the coast of Norway, which drowned *Doggerland,* about 8,400 years ago. The block of land, 16 miles long, 9 miles wide, 4,593 feet thick will tumble into the sea. Computer calculations put the initial splash wave at 2,950 feet high, traveling at 450 mph. In 1 hour it would swamp the African coast. Britain would be inundated in 3.5 hours, and Western Europe in four. In about 6 hours the 200 foot mega-tsunami would slam into the Canadian and U.S. East Coast, drowning the great population centers. In 7 hours, the Caribbean, in 8 hours, the northern coast of South America would be under water. The La Palm Slide could result in a casualty count equal to that of World War Two.

LAP DANCE – (*LAP* dahns) (Lap Dancer, Lap Dancing) An erotic physical performance made a stripteaser against the body of a seated patron. Lap dancing is common in topless titty bars. The dancer is usually a gorgeous young female but may be a male in a gay bar. The performer rubs her/his private parts in the lap, and against the chest and face of the designated recipient in a sexually seductive manner, simulating copulation. The lap dance is considered *"adult entertainment."*

LAPIDARY – (*LAP*-pi-dar-ree) An expert in precious stones. A lapidary or lapidarist cuts, polishes, and engraves precious stones or jewels.

LAPIS LAZULI – (la-*PEES* la-*ZOO*-lee) Azure or deep-blue in color. Lapis lazuli is a deep-blue mineral composed primarily of lazurite with traces of other minerals, used mainly as a gem or as a pigment.

LAPPS – (*LAPS*) Laplanders. The most northerly dwelling Caucasians, the simplest, most archaic cultural group in Europe. In their native Uralic language, the Lapps call themselves *Sami* or the *Saami* people. These Finno-Ugric people live in the Arctic reaches of Scandinavia (Norway, Sweden, Finland), and the Kola Peninsula of Russia (Lapland). They are the only example of *"indigenous"* white people, true Caucasian *"natives."* In other words, on a cultural level, the Lapps are to all other Europeans, what the American Indians were to the white population. According to Jacob Bronowski (1908 – 1974), in *The Ascent of Man* (1973) *"The ancestors of the Lapps may have come north from the Franco- Cantabrian cave area of the Pyrenees in the wake of the reindeer as the last icecaps retreated from southern Europe 12,000 years ago."* There may be 100,000 Laplanders in Arctic Europe. Their transhumance lifestyle makes them the most primitive Caucasian culture in the world. The Lapps are dependent on the reindeer, as the Sioux were dependent on the bison. The Lapps don't drive the reindeer, they are driven by the reindeer. Like the Amerindians of the past, the Lapps today remain technologically primitive, but by choice, living close to nature. The Lapps are not herdsmen. The reindeer run wild. The people move with the herd, crossing international borders with no visas or passports. (There are no government officials in Lapland to check on them.) The Lapps eat about a pound of venison (dear meat) a day, and drink reindeer milk. They use the hides, sinews, bones, and antlers of the animals as well. On the migration, they dwell in teepee-like tents made of hides. Different groups or clans of Lapps are officially citizens of different nations (Norway, Sweden, Finland, or Russia). That's a mere technicality to them. Their primitive simplicity makes them the freest people in Europe.

LAPSE – (*LAPS*) An accidental or temporary decline or deviation from an expected or accepted condition or state. To lapse is a falling or slipping from a previous standard. In a religious sense, a lapse is a moral fall, as from virtue or orthodoxy. The Romans considered the Christian heresy blasphemous. Indeed Christians were martyred, but only the most obdurate or faithful [read: *fanatical*]. The Romans made it easy for a wayward Christian to save her life. All he had to do was to perform a *"revoco,"* meaning *"I recant."* Too, they had to sign an official document renouncing Christianity and profess devotion to the Roman gods and declare so 3 times in public. The official document was called a *"lapsus."* The reformed Christian had lapsed. Incidentally: At times, a hysteria had gripped the early Christians communities. Many desired to experience martyrdom, a quick ticket to heaven. (Radical jihadists express this desire today.) One of the late Roman emperors tired of these Christians had lamented: *"There are plenty of cliffs to jump, and plenty of tree from which to hang yourself. Do stop troubling me."*

LAPSUS CALAMI – (*LAP*-sus ca-*LOM*-mee) Latin for a *"slip of the pen."*

LAPSUS LINGUAE – (*LAP*-sus *LING*-way) Latin for a *"slip of the tongue."*

LARCENY – (*LAR*-sen-nee) (Larcenous) Theft, stealing. The wrongful, illegal confiscation of another's property, taken as one's own. Burglary is a larceny, as in breaking and entry. No violence is involved. Too, robbery, is larceny that involves lethal weapons or assault. It is therefore a major felonry. (A robbery suspect would not be charged with larceny, for robbery is the more serious crime.) Stealing cheap property as in much shoplifting is misdemeanor larceny. If the theft is $500 to $1,000 dollars (depending on the jurisdiction), it will be considered felonious or felony larceny. Incidentally: Larceny can be viewed as a transfer of wealth from the prosperous, to the indigent who need it. In this sense, the larceny may be a divine redistribution, a Karmic occurrence, balancing of the books.

LARD – (*LAHRD*) Melted animal fat used as a lubricant and for frying food. Lard was once called *"pigbutter."* Fat pigs yield the best lard. Lard and butter are used primarily in Northern European cooking, while olive oil is used in Southern Europe. Lard, being fat, is concentrated, reserved energy. That's why lard burns 4 times hotter than wood, the stored energy is released as heat in the burning. Incidentally: Montego Bay, Jamaica was an exporter of lard made from wild pigs (released by the first Spanish). In fact, the name *"Montego"* is an English corruption of the Spanish word *"manteca"* meaning lard. Footnote: During the fire-bombing of Hamburg and Dresden, Germany in World War Two, families sheltered in basements. There, they were cooked alive. Their bodies melted, leaving the floors coated with thick human lard. *"For they sowed the wind and had reaped the whirlwind."* – Hosea 8:7.

LARGESSE – (*LAR*-jes) The generous bestowal of gifts, favors, but especially money. Charities such as donations, endowments, philanthropies qualify as largesse. The term largesse entered English in about 1200, directly from Old French meaning *"a bounty, munificence."*

LARIAT – (*LAR*-ree-at) A lasso. A long noosed rope used to catch horses, cattle, or other livestock. The lariat is an essential accoutrement of cowboys and ranchers.

LARK – (*LAHRK*) An innocent, good-natured prank. A lark is also a whimsical, casual suggestion. It is an idea or chance proposal that's not put forth very seriously, almost an afterthought. A lark can be considered a long shot. *"I didn't devout too much thought to the proposition. I just threw it out as a lark."*

LARPING – (*LAR*-ping) LARP is an acronym for *Live Role Plating*. Enthusiasts act- out the life of a historical epoch in costume, speech, behavior, for instance Medieval Days, Colonial period, Civil War Battles. The British-American plumbing engineer and body-builder, Nicholas Alexander Pasieka (b. 1993) of Dover, England is a renowned larping specialist.

LASER – (*LAY*-zer) An acronym for *LIGHT AMPLIFICATION* by *STIMULATED EMISSIONS* of *RADIATION*. A laser is a device that produces a very narrow, highly concentrated and powerful beam of electromagnetic light. The laser light is a source of high-intensity optical, infrared, or ultraviolet radiation produced as a result of stimulated emissions maintained within a solid, liquid, or gaseous medium. The light photons involved in the emission process all have the same energy and phase so that the laser beam is monochromatic and coherent, allowing it to be brought to a fine focus. The first laser was built in 1960 by Theodore Maiman (1927 – 2007) at the *Hughes Aircraft Research Laboratories* in Malibu, California. The laser is a magnificently useful tool. In medicine, it is replacing the scalpel in many types of surgery. Lasers can burn away tumors, remove fat cells, scars, and tattoos. Laser beams can cut through the hardest metals, and the most delicate substances. Lasers are used to weld metals. They are utilized in microscopic photography. They can establish perfectly straight lines in geographical surveying. The laser reads the data from compact discs. Unfortunately, the laser is also becoming a magnificently powerful weapon. It can detect and mark targets precisely. Its beam can incinerate, explode, and vaporize a target, machine or man. Lasers are certain to replace metallic solid and explosive projectiles on the future battlefields.

LASSITUDE – (*LAS*-si-tood) Physical and mental fatigue, weariness, and strain from oppressive work and weather. Lassitude results in depletion of energy, weakness, and indifference.

LAST SUPPER – (*LAST SUP*-per) Late 15th century mural by Leonardo da Vinci (1452 – 1519), one of the world's most famous paintings. It depicts the Passover meal of Jesus and his disciples, just before his passion. The masterpiece is not a fresco painted on wet plaster. It was painted on wood (15 by 29 feet) at the convent of Santa Maria delle Grazie, Milan, between 1494 – 1499. Leonardo had mixed egg yolk into his paint pigments. The picture is perpetually flaking away. The innovative genius Leonardo introduced depth perception to painting in the background of this masterpiece. Tragically, the paint composition, humidity and time have ravaged this treasure. French Revolutionary troops had thrown rocks and food at the mural. Furthermore, the convent was bombed during World War Two. The Last Supper is a psychological study by Leonardo of the Apostle's reaction when Jesus said: *"On this night, one of you will betray me!"* The Last Supper is commemorated in the Communion banquet of the Mass. Therefore, from the Last Supper on, the central rite of Christianity is the distribution of food to all. The great Leonardo painted for a living. His passion was engineering. Incidentally: When DaVinci was commissioned to paint the Last Supper, he sat before the wall for days in meditation. The abbot became frustrated and harassed DaVinci to get on with the job. DaVinci got his revenge by using the abbot as his model for Judas.

LAST STRAW – (last *STRAW*) A reference to the proverbial final stalk or stem of grain which added weight had collectively broke the camel's back. Used in popular parlance, the last straw is the final of a succession of irritations, incidents, insults that leads to a loss of patience, disaster, or violent action. This idiom traces back to an Oriental Proverb of 1799: *"It is the last straw that overloads the camel."*

LAST WORDS – (last *WERDS*) Following is a long, but interesting list of the brief dying words of famous people. Some are mundane, others profound, still others delirious. The group is confined to those who have passed in the 20th and 21st centuries. Queen Victoria (1901) said *"Bertie."* Mark Twain (1910) *"Give me my glasses."* Leo Tolstoy (1910) *"How do the peasants die?"* Jack Daniel (1911) *"One last drink, please."* Clara Barton (1912) *"Let me go!"* J.P. Morgan (1913) *"Don't baby me so!"* Mata Hari (1917) *"It is unbelievable!"* Theodore Roosevelt (1919) *"Please put out the light, James."* Alexander Graham Bell (1922) *"No."* Marcel Proust (1922) *"Yes, my dear Robert, you are."* Warren G. Harding (1923) *"That's good. Go on, read some more."* Vladimir Lenin (1924) *"Good dog."* Woodrow Wilson (1924) *"I am ready."* Anatole France (1924) *"So this is what it is like to die – it takes a long time!"* Rainer Maria Rilke (1926) *"I don't want a doctor's death. I want to have my own freedom."* Arthur Conan Doyle (1930) *"You are wonderful."* Anna Pavlova (1931) *"Get my Swan Costume ready."* Thomas Edison (1931) *"It's very beautiful over there."* Calvin Coolidge (1933) *"Good morning, Robert."* Marie Curie (1934) *"I don't want it."* James Joyce (1941) *"Does nobody understand?"* John Barrymore (1942) *"You heard me, Mike."* Benito Mussolini (1945) *"Shoot me in the chest."* Theodore Dreiser (1945) *"Shakespeare, I come."* Mohandas Gandhi (1948) *"Oh God!"* Babe Ruth (1948) *"I'm going over the valley."* Al Jolson (1950) *"This is it. I'm going."* Andre Gide (1951) *"It is well."* Albert Einstein (1955) *"I have done my share, it is time to go. I will do it elegantly."* Humphrey Bogart (1957) *"Goodbye, kid. Hurry back."* Ernest Hemmingway (1957) *"Goodnight my kitten."* Lee Harvey Oswald (1963) *"Ugh. Fuck!"* Malcolm X (1965) *"Brothers please! This is a house of peace."* Margaret Sanger (1966) *"A party! Let's have a party."* Che Guevara (1967) *"Shoot coward, you are only killing a man."* Sharon Tate (1969) *"Please don't kill me. I don't want to die. I want to have my baby."* Jimi Hendrix (1970) *"I need help bad, man."* Coco Chanel (1971) *"You see, this is how you die."* Noel Coward (1973) *"Good night my darlings. I'll see you tomorrow."* Elvis Presley (1977) *"I'm going to the bathroom to read."* Bob Marley (1981) *"Money can't buy life."* Natalie Wood (1981) *"Help me, someone please help me, I'm drowning!"* John Belushi (1982) *"Just don't leave me alone."* Truman Capote (1984) *"Mama - Mama - Mama."* Abbie Hoffman (1989) *"It's too late. We can't win, they've gotten too powerful."* Jim Henson (1990) *"See you later, I feel like I'm in good hands."* Michael Landon (1991) *"You're right. It's time. I love you all."* Richard Nixon (1994) *"Help."* Jacqueline Kennedy (1994) *"Don't cry for me. I'm going to be with your father."* Timothy Leary (1996) *"Why? Why not?"* Princess Diana (1997) *"My God, what's happened?"* Frank Sinatra (1998) *"I'm losing it."* George Harrison (2001) *"Love one another."* Richard Harris (2002) *"I was the food."* Johnny Cash (2003) *"It's time."* Pope John Paul II (2005) *"Let me go to the house of the Father."* Michael Jackson (2009) *"More milk."* Steve Jobs (2011) *"Oh wow. Oh wow. Oh wow!"* Whitney Houston (2011) *"I'm going to see Jesus, I want to see Jesus."* Robin Williams (2014) *"Goodnight, my love."* Gene Wilder (2016) *"I trust You."* Tony Bennett (2023) *"Thank you."* Jimmy Buffett (2023) *"Have fun."*

LAS VEGAS – (lahs *VAY*-guhs) Spanish for *"the meadows."* With a population of 641,903, Las Vegas is the largest city in Nevada, 25th largest in the U.S.A. Las Vegas roasts in the Mohave Desert. With global warming, the summer temperatures soar to over 1000F for scorching weeks on end. The community was founded in 1905, and incorporated as a small city in 1911. In his book *America: A Personal History of the United States* (1972), British-American journalist Alistair Cooke (1908 – 2004) said that: *"During the Depression, Las Vegas was a dusty little place with dirt roads and hotels with cockroaches the size of turtles."* In the 1950s, Havana, Cuba was the gambling capital of North America. Cuba was governed by the fascist dictator, Fulgencio Batista (1901 – 1973). Havana was ruled by Batista's partner, the Mafia. But after years of guerrilla warfare, in 1959, the Socialist Fidel Castro (1926 – 2016) overthrew Batista, who was exiled to Spain. The Mafia tried to bribe Castro, but he expelled these gangsters from Cuba. Their hotels and gambling casinos became hospitals, schools, and apartment housing. Mafia Don Lucky Luciano (1897 – 1962) had to find a safe haven for the Mafia's gambling enterprises. Obscure Las Vegas was perfect. Pouring many laundered millions into the small city, Las Vegas succeeded Havana as the gambling capital. With law-and-order crackdowns, the capitalists supplanted the Mafia in Las Vegas in the mid-1980s. History aside, Las Vegas is the most useless city in America. Las Vegas is the U.S. city that America can most afford to lose with the least repercussions. That's because Las Vegas produces nothing materially – no cars, no food, no commodities, – nothing, but misery. Its gambling has destroyed millions. Homes have been lost, families fractured. Las Vegas does produce plenty of divorces and suicides. It is the pawnshop capital of America. Las Vegas' legalized prostitution has lured young girls from across the nation into the flesh trade. It is advertised that the industry of Las Vegas is fun. The city promoters like to brag: *"What happens in Las Vegas, stays in Las Vegas."* Translation: *"Don't worry. Your wife will not find out that you screwed hookers your daughter's age."* Furthermore, if you awaken with a blinding hangover next to a stranger who you had married, chances are good that you are in Las Vegas. Indeed, Las Vegas has contributed no redeeming qualities to society. From the air, the city resembles a toppled, decorated Christmas tree. It is indeed, *"The City of Lights."* In fact, just one high-rise hotel/casino gluts an amount of electricity equal to a normal city of 60,000. Utter waste of precious energy! Furthermore, without air conditioning, Las Vedas would be uninhabitable. Where does all this power come from? Hoover Dam and the Colorado River. But Nevada must share the Colorado's water with Utah, Wyoming, Arizona, California, Colorado, and New Mexico. Other regions need this water for human consumption, domestic use, industrial and agricultural applications. Las Vegas needs the water to party. To whom do you think the courts will allocate the water? To make matters worse, global warming is evaporating the life- sustaining Colorado River. Las Vegas is living on borrowed time! *"All go to one place. All are from the dust, and to dust all return."* – Ecclesiastes 3:20.

LATCHKEY KIDS – (*LACH*-kee *KIDS*) Not *Stanley* and *Stella Latchkey* from St. Florian High School in Hamtramck, Michigan, but the children who must let themselves into an unsupervised house after school. This opens the door to all sorts of mischief and peril. Under capitalism, both parents must work to remain above the poverty level. That's why there are latchkey kids. Too, American capitalism does not provide daycare as other western nations do. That's why more than 1 out of 3 American children are latchkey kids.

LATENT – (*LAY*-tent) Hidden. Present but not visible, apparent, or actualized. Anything in a latent state is not obvious or explicit but exists as potential.

LATENT ENERGY – (*LAY*-tent *EN*-ner-jee) Hidden heat released when water vapor condenses into water drops or turns directly into ice high in the atmosphere. This latent energy supplies most of the fuel, power, for hurricanes.

LATENT MEANING – (*LAY*-tent *MEE*-ning) The hidden meaning. According to Psychoanalyst Sigmund Freud (1856 – 1939), the latent meaning is the actual, albeit hidden meaning of dreams. The latent meaning is shrouded in symbolism, myth, and analogy. The *manifest meaning,* the verbatim enactments in the dream obscure the latent meaning from understanding.

LATERITE – (*LAT*-ter-rite) A reddish ferruginous (iron-bearing) soil formed in tropical regions by the decomposition of underlying rocks. Laterite is a thick infertile soil. Incessant tropical rainstorms leach much of the nutrients out of the laterite soil.

LATIFUNDIUM – (la-ti-*FUN*-dee-um) (plural, Latifundia) A great agricultural plantation, especially one worked by slaves in ancient Rome. Today, a latifundium is just a great estate.

LATIN – (*LAT*-tin) Language spoken by the ancient Romans. Latin is the parent of all the Romance languages (Italian, Spanish, Portuguese, Romanian). Too, Latin has contributed a vast vocabulary to all European languages. Latin was once the lingua franca of educated Europeans and remains the liturgical tongue of the Catholic Church. *"I don't see how the Romans had time to conquer the world, if they first had to learn Latin,"* lamented the scholarly philosopher Heinrich Heine (1797 – 1856). Nevertheless, Latin is still taught in some isolated academic circles. In fact, Latin remains the longest lasting educational tradition in the West. Conservative Secretary of Education William Bennett (b. 1943) was an ultra-rigorist. Bennett insisted that *"I suffered through Latin, today's students should suffer too."*

LATIN AMERICA – (*LAT*-tin a-*MER*-ri-ca) A region of the Western Hemisphere which includes Mexico, much of the Caribbean, and Central and South America. Latin America was conquered and settled by the Spanish. Today, the language of these regions is the Latin based Spanish (or Portuguese in Brazil).

LATIN GRAMMAR SCHOOL – (*LAT*-tin *GRAM*-mer skool) America's earliest secondary school, dating back to colonial times. The Latin Grammar School emphasized the study of literature, history, mathematics, music, dialectics, and Latin. It was an elite, college preparatory institution. The Latin Grammar School was supplanted by the Academy, which was supplanted by the elite, later comprehensive High School.

LATINX – (lah-*TEE*-neks) (plural Latinxs = lah-*TEE*-neks-siz) Of or relating to people of Latin American origin or descent, especially those living in the United States. Latinx is a gender-neutral term applying to both male Latino and female Latina.

LATITUDE – (*LAT*-ti-tood) Imaginary lines running east and west on the globe, which measures the distance north and south from the equator to the poles. The equator is the zero degree mark, both poles are the 90 degree marks, north and south. For every 300 miles north in latitude the temperature drops 3.5 degrees Fahrenheit. This is comparable to climbing 1,000 feet in elevation. Incidentally: The terms latitude and longitude were coined by the Egyptian astronomer Ptolemy (c. 100 – c. 170 CE).

LATITUDINARIANISM – (la-ti-tood-in-*AIR*-ree-in-is-um) (Latitudinarian), Tolerating, encouraging latitude of opinion, freedom of thought, especially in religious matters.

LAUDANUM – (*LAW*-dan-um) Opium juice, formerly used as an anesthetic. When mixed with rum the soporific cocktail was called grog. Groggy soldiers were more patient on the operating table when being amputated.

LAUDATION – (law-*DAY*-shuhn) (Lauding) A tribute, encomium. To extol praise is a laudation. *"His laudation was long, loud, and enthusiastic."*

LAUGHTER – (*LAF*-ter) (Laugh, Laughing, Laughed) The physical expression of amusement, delight, and merriment. Humans are the only animals that laugh. It is a readily recognized emotion in every culture. Laughter is a primary stress reliever, combating depression. People who laugh regularly have 40% fewer heart attacks. Laughter stimulates the immune system to fight-off illness and stimulates the right side of the brain increasing creativity. Children laugh on average 150 times a day, 4 times more than adults. The vitality of laughter was captured by the author Og Mandino (1923 – 1996). *"Laugh at yourself and at life. Not in the spirit of derision or whining self-pity, but as a remedy, a miracle drug, that will ease your pain, cure your depression, and help you to put in perspective that seemingly terrible defeat and worry with laughter at your predicaments, thus freeing your mind to think clearly toward the solution that is certain to come. Never take yourself too seriously."* Incidentally: If you can't laugh together, you can't work together either. Footnote: Comedian David Sedaris (b. 1956) was asked by TV journalist Ari Melbar (b. 1980) what was the greatest compliment he had ever received. Concerning one of his jokes, a woman once told Sedaris: *"I read your joke to my mother who was dying, and she laughed."* *"When anybody laughs, he has no mind, no thought, no problem, no suffering."* – H. W. L. Poonja (1910 – 1997).

LAURASIA – (law-*RAY*-shee-a) The great northern landmass that broke away from the global super-continent Pangaea 200 million years ago. Laurasia consisted of North America and Eurasia. Its southern counterpart was *Gondwanaland* (South America, Africa, India, Australia, and Antarctica). Laurasia was created by perpetual continental drift driven by plate tectonics.

LAUREATE – (*LOR*-ree-at) A distinguished talent in a particular field. A laureate achieves distinction and is granted coveted honors and awards. An example is the Poet Laureate.

LAUS DEO – (*LAUS DAY*-o) Latin for *"Praise to God."*

LAVA – (*LA*-va) Magma that has broken through the Earth's crust, usually from volcanoes. Being magma, the lava consists of molten rock, minerals, metals (mostly iron). Lava is the hottest natural substance on Earth. Hawaiian lava is basaltic lava (2,000 degrees Fahrenheit) the hottest and most fluid on Earth. Silica (sand) impregnated lava is thick and sticky. It can block-up a volcanic vent, trapping the gas, heat and magma under excruciating pressure. Eventually, when it does blow, it will be a catastrophic disaster.

LAVA BOMB – (*LA*-va *BOM*) (also Volcanic Bomb) A blob of molten rock (lava) ejected from a volcano. The lava bomb is 2.5 inches in diameter or larger. It cools in the air, solidifies, and falls to the ground as a solid igneous rock.

LAW – (*LAW*) Regulations established by the ruling class to protect their wealth and superior status. Laws are made by the rich and powerful in order to keep the poor and weak under control. Laws are encouraged by the poor and weak in order to keep the rich and strong from oppressing them. Supreme Court Justice Louis D. Brandeis (1856 – 1941) admonished that *"If we desire respect for the law, we must first make the law respectable."* However law is established to maintain order [read: *status quo*] and suppress change. Law and order is enforced with punishment by police and military controlled by the rich. It is morally immoral to obey unjust laws. As Henry David Thoreau (1817 – 1862) exclaimed: *"It is not desirable to cultivate a respect for the law, so much as for the right."* Equality under the law, blind justice is a jurisprudential axiom. It is also a myth. As Anatole France (1844 – 1924) so very ironically stated in <u>Le Lys Rouge</u> (1894) (<u>The Red Lily</u>): *"The majestic equality of the law…forbids the rich as well as the poor to sleep under bridges, to beg in the streets, and to steal bread."*

LAW AND ORDER – (*LAW* and *OR*-der) Euphemism for *"Protect my wealth from the poor."* Law and order maintains the peace, and the status quo. Law and order is paramount in the Republican political platform. Republicans represent the rich. The rich want to protect their wealth. They are happy with a status quo which finds them in a privileged position. Disruption in the status quo [read: *"breakdown in law and order"*] is bad for business and can only jeopardize their wealth and privilege. The converse of law and order is change. Change in the extreme is revolution. It is the assignment of the police (and military) to suppress change [read: *"maintain law and order"*] and protect the capitalist system. This makes the police the mercenaries of the rich. Incidentally: Notice how in a capitalist society, when the police kill Socialist protestors demonstrating for economic justice, it is called re-establishing *"law- and-order."* But in a Socialist society, when the police kill capitalist counter- revolutionaries, out to re-establish economic disparity, it is called *"tyranny."*

LAWFARE – (*LAW*-fair) <u>Law</u>ful war<u>fare</u>. To weaponize the legal system to work (legally, albeit unethically) to one's advantage. As nuclear warfare is the exclusive domain of rich nations, lawfare is the exclusive domain of rich individuals. When a rich bitch like Donald Trump (b. 1946) declares war on a little man, expect him to employ lawfare. He will throw an army of highly-paid attorneys into the battle. The poor are always outnumbered. Too, the wealthy will employ Special Forces in the form of expert lawyers and professional witnesses in the attack. A fundamental strategy of lawfare is *"war of attrition."* Who can bear the financial casualties the longest? Lawfare like warfare is expensive. But the wealthy can fight on forever. Hostilities will last for years, exhausting the resources of the common litigant, bankrupting his economy. Might makes right in lawfare. Even if the poor plaintiff or defendant is initially declared victorious, the case will be appealed, and re-appealed, until the poor party can fight no more, and must surrender. Legal technicalities are decisive weapons employed by the rich in lawfare. A wealthy defendant can afford to manipulate lawfare until the statute of limitation runs out, exonerating him of crimes. Few notorious figures have used lawfare more effectively, to destroy the innocent, and protect himself as has Donald Trump (b. 1946). *"When you're rich, all is fair in love and war and law."*

LAWN – (*LAWN*) A stretch of open grass-covered land, especially one closely mowed, around a house, an estate, or a park. A lawn is cultivated, ornamental grass. There are many varieties for different soil and climactic conditions. Some people are fanatically meticulous [read: *anal retentive*] about cultivating and manicuring their lawns. This is particularly true in the suburbs. Their lawns represent suburban prosperity and exceptionalism. In fact, the boundary between the inner-city and suburbs has been called the *"crabgrass border."* (In Detroit, it is 8 Mile Road.) Too, many refugees from the city protect their lawns with maniacal fervency. To step on their lawn is a personal affront that will elicit a violent response or attack. *"Dammit! Get off the grass!"* is a threatening command familiar to most suburban kids. Private lawns are nonfunctional turf. These ornamental lawns on which one may gaze but not tread are a silly waste of precious space. A lawn is a homogeneous ecosystem, in which all plants other than grass is poisoned. Too, they are labor-intensive and expensive, requiring fertilizer, weed-killer, and lots of water. (Some people devote more time to their lawns, than to their children.) Lawns consume a selfish glut of water, which is an arrogant waste in arid areas. That's why in April 2021, the *Southern Nevada Water Authority* proposed to prohibit the use of dwindling Colorado River water to irrigate nonfunctional ornamental lawns. (Unfortunately, the new ordinances goes into effect on January 1, 2027.) Metro Las Vegas has a combined area of 8 square miles of useless private lawn, especially in the affluent suburbs that suck-up 12 billion gallons of life-giving water annually. The prohibition does not include public parks, picnic grounds, golf courses, or athletic fields that are the property of all. Fussy homeowners will have to plant native desert flora instead of imported grass. Incidentally: Not surprisingly, at the *Las Vegas Substance Abuse Rehab Center,* the sign on the lawn warns: *"KEEP OFF THE GRASS!"*

LAWN JOCKEY – (*LAWN JOCK*-key) A racist Jim Crow stereotype of African- American men. Lawn jockeys were/are pejorative statues of Black men, dressed in red-and-white uniforms as horse-racing riders. These statutes are displayed by oblivious, insensitive, bigoted, or racist homeowners in their gardens or front lawns. Lawn jockeys are about 3 feet tall and are usually holding a lantern. Originally, they may have been larger, anchored into the ground, and held out an iron ring on which to tether a horse. In the spirit of Jim Crow, lawn jockeys reinforced the subservient, servile social position of African-Americans as menial stableboys. There were several varieties of lawn jockey, some more demeaning than others. All were inhumanly jet-black-faced. *"Cavalier Spirit"* was the tall, *dignified rendition. "Jocko"* was the short *niggrified rendition.* Jocko is squat, bent forward, with big white bug-eyes, and inflated red lips. Both versions are designed to send the message that African-Americans have a lowly place in society, and should stay in their place. In ironic Karmic Justice, some Black homeowners have painted their lawn jockeys as Caucasians.

LAWRENTIAN – (lar-*REN*-tee-an) Reminiscent of D.H. Lawrence's (1885 – 1930) literary works. Hatred of technology, instinct over intellect, agrarian over urban, sex over prudishness are characteristic Lawentian attributes.

LAWRENCIUM – (lar-*REN*-see-um) (Lr) A transuranic element (# 103) named after Ernest O. Lawrence, an American physicist best known for developing the cyclotron [read: *atom smasher*]. Lawrence is the person for whom the Lawrence Livermore National Laboratory and the Lawrence Berkeley National Laboratory are named. Lawrencium was discovered in 1961. Lawrencium has a half-life of 11 hours maximum, before it decays. It is used in nuclear research.

LAWYER – (*LAW*-yer) An attorney (solicitor or barrister in Britain). A professional scholar of the law. Because the rules of society have been made so complicated, abstruse, esoteric, an elite class of interpreters have emerged to make sense of it all. These are lawyers. The complexity of the law has made society dependent on lawyers. Even the language of the law (*legalese*) precludes most of us from serving as our own legal counselors. Lawyers take full advantage of their essential position by charging obscene fees. Often, only the wealthy can afford to retain a lawyer, giving the lie to the platitude: *"Equal justice under the law."* In a sense, lawyers are professional liars. They are licensed to mangle the truth in court, in order to win their case. Some would say that most lawyers are *"full of shit!"* These are the crooked *"shyster lawyers"* who are mostly concerned with self-enrichment. In fact, the word shyster (originally *scheisser*) means *"shitter"* in German. Lawyers are mercenaries of the law. They will serve the plaintiff or defendant, as defense attorney or prosecuting attorney, whatever pays more. This is why of all professions listed, lawyers (and politicians) are the least respected. Most politicians are lawyers, by the way. As gangster James "Whitey" Bulger (1929 – 2018) would say: *"If you want to make crime pay – go to law school."* *"I think we may class the lawyer in the natural history of monsters."* – John Keats (1795 – 1821). Incidentally: An ancient Chinese curse declared: *"May your life be filled with many lawyers!"*

LAWYER/CLIENT PRIVILEDGE – (*LAW*-yer *KLY*-ent *PRIV*-lej) A priviledge is a benefit or immunity enjoyed by certain people under certain circumstances. In a court of law, a lawyer is one's spokesman and advocate. One's official attorney is legally an alterego of oneself. In America, one cannot be forced to testify against oneself (pleading the 5th Amendment). Likewise, neither can your lawyer be forced to testify against you. Only if your lawyer colluded with you in a crime, will he be subpoenaed to testify as a witness against you. In this case, the lawyer/client privilege is suspended. At this point, your lawyer needs a lawyer. Incidentally: Donald Trump (b. 1946) defiles everyone with whom he associates. So many of Trump's lawyers have gone bad that Trump's MAGA campaign has come to mean: *"Make Attorneys Get Attorneys."*

LAWYER'S CREDO – (*LAW*-yers *CRAY*-dow) *"If you can't beat the law, beat the table."*

LAWYER-UP – (*LAW*-yer *UP*) A popular reference to seek legal counsel, to retain an attorney in a crisis. When law enforcement investigators come knocking at a guilty man's door, he will promptly lawyer-up. An apprehensive, fearful conscience induces one to lawyer-up. The term became prominent during the *"Trump/Russiagate Scandal"* (2017, 2018). President Donald Trump's (b. 1946) campaign staff, White House staff, and family members all speedily lawyered-up.

LAX – (*LAKS*) (Laxity) Carless, negligent, slack, neither strict nor severe.

LAYABOUT – (*LAY*-ah-bout) Chiefly a British term for a loafer, a lazy idle person.

LAYAWAY – (*LAY*-a-way) A pre-creditcard capitalist scheme to assure a sale and purchase. With the layaway program, the store puts aside an item the customer desires. The customer pays for the item over time, in instalments. When the item is fully paid-off, the customer retrieves her purchase. Both the seller and consumer must be patient – the seller for the profit, and the consumer for the purchased product. The disadvantage of layaway is lack of instant gratification. The benefit of layaway is lack of debt. With the credit card, one would be hard pressed to find a layaway program anywhere today.

LAZARUS EFFECT – (*LAZ*-are-us ef-*FECT*) When a species thought to be extinct is found. Scientists call that the Lazarus effect. This alludes to Jesus resurrecting his friend (perhaps brother-in-law) Lazarus from the dead.

LEACHING – (*LEECH*-ing) The process in which water carries dissolved minerals to lower layers of rock. Incessant rains as in the tropics leaches the soil of vital nutrients leaving it infertile. One such infertile tropical soil is called *laterite*.

LEAD – (*LED*) (Pb) *Lead* is the Old English (West Saxon) name for the metal. The Latin word for lead is *plumbum,* which accounts for its chemical symbol. The 82 protons in its nucleus give lead its atomic number. Lead is a soft, heavy, malleable, toxic, bluish-gray metallic element, often found in its natural state as galena ore. All radioactive elements will ultimately, naturally, break-down to lead, the dead end. Lead is used in alloys, paints, solder, weights, bullets, batteries, cable sheaths, and as radiation shields. Incidentally: Everything floats on heavy molten lead except uranium.

LEADER – (*LEE*-der) The person in charge, with authority. With authority comes responsibility and accountability. A leader can never be a *"boss."* A boss governs with intimidation. A leader governs with inspiration. Corporate capitalist leaders tend to be bosses. There are many ways to characterize a leader. She is a problem solver, obstacle mover, peace maker, consensus producer, harmonizer, confidence builder, expeditor, and information disseminator.

LEADERSHIP – (*LEE*-der-ship) (Leader) An action rather than a position. Leadership is causing others to want what you are doing, in order to accomplish the goals of your project or organization. Leadership is sharing the vision and enthusiasm. A leader is never a boss, because a boss is a bully. There is no place for intimidation in leadership. Such leaders will covertly (through sabotage) or overtly (through revolt), be rejected. Acting as the group's primary servant, the leader is the chief problem solver, obstacle remover, resource procurer, and expeditor. The leader makes it easy for the employees to do their jobs. The leader is the only official information disseminator. Therefore, he must be trusted implicitly. When confidence wanes, the leader is the enthusiasm encourager. She is the primary peace maker, arbitrator, mediator, and harmonizer. The entire organization acquires the temperament and personality of its leader. This is why Donald Trump (b. 1946) will never be a successful leader. Too, this is why the vile, vulgar, mean-spiritedness of government and politics is, what it is today. The ship of state is adrift in polluted waters due to Trump's lack of leadership.

LEADERSHIP CREDO – (*LEE*-der-ship *CRAY*-doe) *"The Buck Stops Here."*

LEAF OF LIFE – (*Kalanchoe pinnata*) A succulent herb native to Madagascar Island, Africa, with extraordinary curative properties. Leaf of Life has been naturalized throughout the tropical/subtropical world. It can grow to almost 5 feet tall with a thick reddish tinged stem. Its thick crunchy leaves have indented edges, from which new plants propagate, once the leaf falls onto soil. When mature, the Leaf of Life bears clusters of bell-shaped flowers. Its name alludes to its health-supporting properties. A virtual pharmaceutical factory, the Leaf of Life produces antibacterial, antimicrobial, antifungal, and antiviral chemicals. Brewed into a tea, it is a traditional remedy for colds, coughs, bronchitis, and hypertension. The juice from the leaves contain antihistamine and anaphylactic properties, beneficial in soothing stings, insect bites, and asthma attacks. The Leaf of Life is involved in cancer research as well.

LEAGUE – (*LEEG*) According to the Imperial or English System of measures, a distance equivalent to 3 miles or 15,840 feet. Therefore Jules Verne's (1828 – 1905) *Twenty Thousand Leagues Under the Sea* (1870) would be 60,000 miles down, and quite impossible. There is no such ocean depth. The deepest ocean depth in the Marians Trench is almost 7 miles (36,070 feet). Verne's fictional submarine descended over 53,000 miles deeper than actually exists. If his sub had rocketed up, instead of sinking down, he would have been in space.

LEAKS – (*LEEKS*) (Leakers) Classified government information disclosed, *"leaked"* to the public via the press. Leaking secret information is a criminal offense on the part of an individual with a security clearance. Are they heroes or villains, patriots or traitors? Government officials leak information when they know that the government is doing wrong. Officials with faith in the government do not leak. *Leakers,* like *whistleblowers* have the greater interests of the citizenry at heart. Even former FBI Director James Comey (b. 1960) leaked information concerning President Trump's (b. 1946) obstruction of justice (June, 2017). We are a democracy. We have a right to know. If the government is clandestine, withholding information from the people, we need more and more conscientious leakers. We are a republic. The people we elect don't *rule* us, they merely *represent* us. Again, we the people have the right to know. Leakers uncover corruption. It was leakers who brought down the perfidious Republican, Richard Nixon (1913 – 2004) in the *Watergate Scandal* (1972 – 1974). (Nixon's C.I.A. henchmen were secretly called *"plumbers"* to stop leaks. Corroded [read: *corrupted*] pipes always leak.) It may be courageous leakers who will bring down the rapacious Republican Donald Trump (b. 1946) in the *Trump-Russiagate Scandal* (2016, 2017, 2018 – present). Indeed, leakers are heroes and patriots.

LEAP – (*LEEP*) The collective name for an assemblage of leopards. *"A leap of leopards terrorized the countryside."*

LEAP YEAR – (*LEEP* yeer) A year in which an extra day is added to the end of February (the 29th day) every four years. This is done to coordinate our monthly calendar with the solar calendar.

LEARNED – (*LURND* or *LUR*-nid) To be erudite, knowledgeable, scholarly, educated. This adjective is pronounced two different ways, depending on its usage. Learned (*LURND*) behavior is acquired by study or experience. For example: *"Racism is a learned (LURND) behavior." "I learned (LURND) to play baseball at school." "He learned (LURND) his lesson."* However, having much knowledge or involved in a scholarly pursuit is of a learned (*LUR*-nid) nature. For Example: *"A group of learned (LUR-nid) professors." "She is learned (LUR- nid) in the ways of the world." "The evidence is taken from a learned (LUR-nid) journal."*

LEARNED HELPLESSNESS – (*LURND HELP*-less-ness) A depressed state when a person feels that no matter what he or she does, it will have no influence on important life events. The weight of poverty can crush one into a condition of learned helplessness. Repeated disappointment will eventually make the most persistent person throw his hands up in despair. Learned helplessness is a social-psychological term. Incidentally: The flip side of learned helplessness is learned laziness.

LEARNED LAZINESS – (*LURND LAY*-zee-ness) A social-psychological term for the inability to function because of having everything done for you. This is not a condition of the poor, who must be very resourceful to scratch-out a living, but an ailment of the rich. Learned laziness is handicap of the opulent affluent, whose every bodily function is tended to by servants. Those who had learned laziness are hopelessly helpless when on their own. As the astonished English squire exclaimed in his Oxford accent: *"Me? Work at a job?"* Learned laziness can prove fatal in an emergency. This was witnessed at the Jamestown Colony when the English dandies nearly all starved to death. They were saved by Captain John Smith (1580 – 1631) who decreed: *"Those who do not work, neither shall they eat!"* – 2 Thessalonians 3: 10. Incidentally: The flip side of learned laziness is learned helplessness.

LEARNING – (*LURN*-ing) An alteration or addition in mentation. A change in thought and behavior that modifies a person's capabilities. Simply put, learning is going from the familiar to the unfamiliar until it becomes familiar. Learning involves the acquisition of new information or knowledge through study. Learning involves thinking, but learning and thinking are not the same. Learning is purposeful, methodological concentrated thinking [read: *study*] in order to gain, retain, and apply new information when needed. Learning requires concentration and concept formation or discovering new concepts. The engine of learning is study. The fuel for that engine is teaching. Educationist William Glasser (1925 – 2013) maintained that: *"We learn 10% of what we read; 20% of what we hear; 30% of what we see; 50% of what we see and hear; 70% of what we discuss; 80% of what we experience; and 95% of what we teach others."* Learning is enjoyable work but work none the less. *"The price of achievement is toil; and the gods have ruled that you must pay in advance,"* declared the Greek poet Hesiod (c. 750 – 650 BCE). Incidentally: Physiologically, learning entails the creation of new neural connections in the brain. Somehow, it has been estimated that we learn about 15 trillion binary digits (bits) of information in a lifetime. *"When your mind expands joy comes."* – St. Thomas Aquinas (1225 – 1274). *"Learning is the only thing the mind never exhausts, never fears, and never regrets."* – Leonardo da Vinci (1452 – 1519).

LEARNING STYLE – (*LURN*-ing *STILE*) In educational psychology, the set of cognitive, affective, and physiological behaviors through which an individual learns most effectively. Learning style is determined by a combination of hereditary and environmental influences. *"Why is it that we remember with difficulty, and without difficulty forget? Learn with difficulty and without difficulty remain ignorant?"* – St. Augustine of Hippo (354 – 430 CE).

LEASH – (*LEESH*) (also Skulk) The collective name for an assemblage of foxes. *"A leash of foxes overran the hound."*

LEATHER – (*LETH*-er) Tanned animal hide. Leather is hairless animal skin prepared by tanning to preserve it against decay and making it pliable or supple when dry. Any animal skin can be turned into leather. The raw skin is tanned, meaning it is pickled, marinated in a solution of tannin, a compound from tree bark. In the West, the Romans were first to prepare leather for their army's use. Shoes, clothing, belts, harnesses and shields all required leather. During the Middle Ages, it was discovered that ammonia from human urine was a beneficial additive in the leather solution soup. Poor families would collect their urine and sell it to the tanner or leatherier. They collected the pee in a family piss pot. Some families were so poor, they didn't even have a pot to piss in. At any rate, all skin can be leatherized, even human. Some demonic German Nazis in World War Two concentration camps skinned the tattooed flesh from dead prisoners and converted it to leather handbags and lampshades.

LEAVEN – (*LEV*-uhn) (Leavening, Leavened, Unleavened) A substance such as yeast or baking powder, that causes fermentation and expansion of dough or batter. A leavening agent like the fungus yeast produces gas (flatulence) as it consumes the carbohydrate (sugar). This gas creates bubbles that makes bread rise. Unleavened bread remains a cracker.

LEBENSBORN – (*LAY*-bens-born) Adolf Hitler's (1889 – 1945) program to breed a Germanic master race (*ubermenschen*). The Lebensborn eugenics program goes to the heart of Nazism. Hitler hoped that Germany would give birth to a million babies a year. About 700,000 to 800,000 were expected to be culled [read: *killed*] in order to improve the racial stock. Fair, blue-eyed Nordic type were to be propagated by SS studs on breeding farms. The sickly, handicapped, homosexuals, Gypsies, Jews, and Slavs were to be exterminated, purifying the human race. Babies and children from occupied lands that fit the pseudo-racial profile were kidnapped and brought to Germany. Much of this fiendish enterprise was conducted by the "*Brown Sisters,*" Nazi women who posed as nuns. Only 40,000 of the 200,000 Polish children and infants stolen in the Lebensborn program were ever to return to Poland.

LECHAIM – (leh-*HY*-im) (also L'chaim) Hebrew meaning, *"To Life!"* Lechaim is a drinking toast. Too, it is sometimes regarded as the small drink (a shot), with which to toast.

LECHERY – (*LECH*-er-ree) (Lecher, Lecherous) Lewd, lustful, lascivious, lubricious behavior. There has never been a greater lecher, occupying the White House, than Donald Trump (b. 1946), an admitted lecher.

LECTERN/PODIUM – (*LEC*-tern *PO*-dee-um) Two devices to facilitate public speaking, lecturing. A lectern is a simple, portable box with a slanted top to accommodate a book, notes, or a written speech. A lectern is placed on a table or desk before an audience. A podium is a large, permanent structure. It may be elevated above the audience. One stands on the podium, whereas one stands at the lectern. The podium is furnished with a built-in lectern.

LECTION – (*LEC*-shun) (Lectionary) A reading of a passage from a larger text. For example, the reading of a Gospel verse during a sermon is a lection.

LECTIONARY – (*LEC*-shun-air-ree) A prayerbook containing readings (lections) like Gospel verses for religious services.

LECTURE – (*LEC*-chur) To share one's expertise, knowledge, and experience with a group of learners. Lecture is the oldest, most common teaching method. A lecturer has been disparagingly called *"The sage on the stage."* Nevertheless, lecturing is the most efficient way to transmit the greatest amount of information in the least amount of time. The Prophet Muhammad (c. 570 – 632 CE) taught: *"To listen to the words of the learned, and to instill into others the lesson of science, is better than religious exercises."* Lecturing requires a great deal of knowledge, and successful communication skills. Those who criticize lecturing the most are those who can't do it. Still, as efficacious as lecturing is, *"You cannot, by all the lecturing in the world enable a man to make a shoe."* – Samuel Johnson (1709 – 1784) English writer and lexicographer.

LEEWARD – (*LEE*-ward) A geographical position sheltered from the wind. The leeward side of a landmass does not get the moist winds and is therefore dry. Mountain ranges blocking the wind from blowing rain clouds can produce a desert on the leeward side.

LEEWARD ISLANDS – (lee-*WARD EYE*-lands) A group of Caribbean Islands in the northern part of the Lesser Antilles. The Leeward Islands include: Puerto Rico, Virgin Islands, Anguilla, Saba, Saint Barthelemy, Sint Eustatius, Sint Kitts, Nevis, Barbuda, Antigua, Redonda, Montserrat, Guadeloupe, and Saint Martin/Sint Maarten.

LEFTCOAST – (left-*COAST*) A corruption of the term *"Westcoast,"* of the United States on the Pacific Ocean. This region consists of the Liberal States of Washington, Oregon, and California. The citizens of these coastal States are Progressive, Liberal, Left-wing, ergo *"Leftcoast."* (Too, looking on a map, the Westcoast is on the left.) Leftcoasters are Liberal because they have a *"Window on the World,"* peering out onto Asia. They are not insulated, isolated, like the citizens of Nebraska, Oklahoma, or Kansas. Furthermore, they are educated.

LEFT IN THE LURCH – (left in thuh *LERCH*) To be abandoned in a difficult position without help. The origin of this phrase begs the question: What is a lurch? The word *"lurch"* is a corruption of the English word *"lych,"* which derived from the Old English (West Saxon) *"lich,"* meaning corps. Many old English churchyard cemeteries had a small roofed structure at the entrance. This was called the *"lych-gate."* During funeral services, coffins would be rested at the lych-gate, while waiting for the clergyman to escort it into the church. If the minister was late, or failed to arrive, the funeral party was *"left in the lurch,"* a desperate condition for all, except for the deceased.

LEFT/RIGHT ATTITUDES – (left ryht *AT*-ti-toods) The Left refers to liberal, progressive, Democratic, Socialistic. Right refers to conservative, reactionary, fascistic, Republican, capitalistic. The Left advocates distribution, dissemination, cooperation. The Right advocates acquisition, accumulation, competition. The Left is concerned with the public welfare. The Right is concerned with private property. The Left believes in sharing, need; *"There's plenty for everyone."* The Right believes in hoarding, greed; *"I got mine, to hell with you!"* People on the Left and Right differ in other ways. Following are six categories in which Left and Right attitudes differ. <u>FOOD</u>: Left – Vegetarian, low fat, tofu, sushi, health foods, exotic foreign goods, wine. Right – Traditional Western meals, meat and potatoes, high fat, fast foods, beer. <u>CLOTHES</u>: Left – Casual, street-wear, bright colors, revealing, unexpected. Right – Formal, traditional, modest, dark colors. <u>WORSHIP</u>: Left – Religious experience comes through furthering progressive causes for oppressed groups in the public sphere. Non-sectarian, ecumenical. Right – Comes from traditional organized religions, Fundamentalist. <u>SEX/LOVE</u>: Left – Kinky, non-heteronormative, equality between male and female, consent very important. Right – Vanilla variety, non-explorative, heteronormative, follows traditional male-female gender roles. <u>ART</u>: Left – Often non-representational, exists to challenge social assumptions. Purposely offensive to challenge worldviews. Right – Representational. Art exists to fulfill traditional expectations of beauty.

TEACHING: Left – Teachers exist to empower their students. They will teach them how to change the world in a positive way and engineer them to be better people. Right – Teaching exists to prepare students to be stable members of society, knowing about their societies, ethics, and useful skills. Granted, this generalized observation is stereotypical. However, there is a kernel of truth in every stereotype.

LEFTWING – (left-*WING*) Refers to Progressives, Liberals, Democrats, Socialists, the people's interests, and the coalition encouraging socio-economic change for justice. At the start of the French Revolution (1789), the Liberals sat on the left wing of the assembly hall, while the conservatives sat on the right wing. Coincidentally, about 2,550 years ago, the Sacred Sage Lao Tzu (c. 604 – c. 531 BCE) wrote in *Tao Te Ching* (The Book of the Way): *"The wise man prefers the left. The man of war prefers the right.… On happy occasions precedence is given to the left, on sad occasions to the right."* *"I think a good Left is a party that always thinks about the future and doesn't care much about our past sins."* – Philosopher Richard Rorty (1931 – 2007). *"If you are truly on the Left, if you reject ideas of power and hierarchy, what you want is equality. Otherwise, it won't work at all.* – Simone de Beauvoir (1908 – 1986). The leftwing is always the way of the future.

LEGACY – (*LEH*-uh-see) A bequest. A gift of property or money handed down to a legatee. Legacy has also come to mean one's reputation, image, historic standing, as a President's lasting legacy. Not everyone is concerned with their legacy. Trump sycophant, Attorney General William Barr (b. 1950) was confirmed as the nation's and people's chief lawyer. Instead, he acts as Donald Trump's (b. 1946) personal lawyer against the nation and people. When asked about his legacy, Barr responded: *"I am at the end of my career. Everybody dies.…"* (Translation: *"I don't give a damn!"*) Another Trump ass-licker, attorney Rudy Giuliani (b. 1944) said: *"I don't care about my legacy. I'll be dead."* *"There will be many a dry eye at their funerals."* – Irish Proverb.

LEGACY MEDIA – (*LEG*-uh-see *MEE*-dee-uh) A legacy can be anything handed down from the past. The legacy media is the old, original institutions of mass information communication. Newspapers, books, advertising, radio, television, music, film are all included in the legacy media. The legacy media dominated news disseminated before the dawn of the *"Information Age,"* the proliferation of computers and the internet. The legacy media is now being challenged by online websites, blogs, and social platforms that can reach millions in minutes. with unknown consequences.

LEGACY RECRUITMENT – (*LEG*-uh-see ree-*KROOT*-ment) (also Legacy Admission) Legacy is a gift, especially money. A legacy is also a privilege handed down or received from a parent, ancestor, or predecessor. Recruitment refers to the enlistment of chosen individuals. Elite schools, particularly prestigious Ivy League Universities practice unfair, discriminatory legacy recruitment. They enthusiastically admit students who are the children of wealthy alumni. This is true for 42% of elite private colleges. Though often unqualified, these students are admitted with their parents' legacy – a fat donation to the school. Legacy recruitment perpetuates the family legacy by welcoming the unworthy wealthy, and also perpetuates the plutocracy. The sole requirement of the recruits is to belong to the *"Lucky Sperm Club."* Incapable rich kids are legacied behind the ivy-covered walls, not to study and learn, but to network and conspire with other rich kids. The connections they forge benefits them later on Wall Street. Being associated with an esteemed school serves as an awesome asset. Perception becomes reality. Legacy recruitment reinforces the capitalist oligarchy. It is undemocratic, it is un-American, it is *"Boola-Boola-Bullshit!"*

LEGALISM – (*LEE*-gall-is-um) (Legalist, Legalistic) Strict adherence to the law. A legalist puts more credence in the letter of the law than the spirit of the law. Legalism is obsession with the law, inundated by regulations, overrun by rules. In theology, legalism is the judging of conduct, and seeking salvation by the strict adherence to religious laws. Jewish and Muslim dietary laws, for example. Jesus was criticized by the Jewish legalists for healing a man on the Sabbath. *"And Jesus said to them, 'The Sabbath is made for man, not man for the Sabbath'."* – Mark 2:27. God gave the Hebrews 10 Commandments. They changed them to over 2,000 laws. Jesus reduced them to two: *"Love God. Then go and love your neighbor as yourself."* – Mark 12:31. Incidentally: An incredible, somewhat hilarious example of religious legalism had emerged at St. Anastasia Catholic Church is Troy, Michigan, outside of Detroit. A deacon (para- priest) performed a Baptism ritual saying *"We Baptize you,"* instead of *"I Baptize you."* Later it was discovered that the two terms were used unconsciously, interchangeably for years at the Church. The same oversight was made in Arizona. So what? Well, the Vatican at Rome declared all the Baptisms performed with the *"We Baptize"* phrase are invalid! The reasoning is that *"I"* refers to Jesus. It is Jesus who is Baptizing, through the priest or deacon. Those Baptized incorrectly, if they die, are not eligible for Heaven, according to the Catholic Church. Many people panicked because of this legalistic Canon sophistry. A good <u>Christ</u>ian will simply follow the words and deeds of Jesus the <u>Christ</u> and ignore the legalistic Catholic Ecclesiastics. Jesus railed against such legalism of the Pharisees in his day. Furthermore, Jesus said: *"For where two or three are gathered in my name, there am I among you."* – Matthew 18:20. Therefore, at the Baptism ritual, the term *"We"* included Jesus as well, which compensates for not saying *"I"*. This sort of legalism belongs in a court of law, not a divine place of worship.

LEGATE – (*LEHG*-gate) An ecclesiastic delegated by the Pope as his representative.

LEGATION – (lehg-*GAY*-shun) A diplomatic minister and staff in a foreign mission. The legation includes the headquarters, being an embassy or consulate.

LEGEND – (*LEJ*-jend) In cartography, the key to the map. The legend is the place on the map listing the map symbols, their meanings, and the distance key.

LEGERDEMAIN – (*LEJ*-er-da-main) Stage magic, clever trickery, sleight-of-hand. Legerdemain sows seeds of disbelief in the real magic of miracles. Even Jesus (c. 7-2 BCE – 30-33 CE) was mocked as a wonder worker, a magician, a practitioner of legerdemain.

LEGGINESS – (*LAY*-gee-nes) Literally, having tall, skinny legs. In horticulture, legginess is a danger sign that the newly germinated sprouts are in trouble. When the seedlings exhibit tall, spindly, weak stems or stalks, they are suffering legginess. These plants are desperate, starving for light. They are stretching to an area where the light is stronger. Becoming too top-heavy, they will fall onto their sides. These seedlings are doomed.

LEGUME – (*LEH*-gewm) A large family of plants that produce pods that bear the seeds. Many legumes are valuable vegetables, high in protein, including beans, peas, and peanuts.

LEGUMINOUS – (le-*GEWM*-min-us) Any plant or tree that bears seed pods or legumes.

LEHRFREIHEIT – (*LER*-fry-hyt) German for academic or educational freedom. It is the right of teachers and professors to teach what they perceive to be the truth, without administrative censorship or interference. Tenure was designed in part to protect lehfreiheit. The formal concept of academic freedom traces back to Germany's University of Leiden (founded in 1575). There, the concept of *"Lehrfreiheit"* (freedom to teach) and *"Lehnfreiheit"* (freedom to learn) was established as academic imperatives.

LEHRNFREIHEIT – (*LERN*-fry-hyt) German for academic freedom, the right to learn. Lernfreiheit refers to academic freedom on the part of the student. Students have the Lernfreiheit to question conventional beliefs and to agree or disagree with what they are taught. The formal concept of academic freedom traces back to Germany's University of Leiden (founded in 1575). There, the concept of *"Lehrfreiheit"* (freedom to teach) and *"Lehnfreiheit"* (freedom to learn) was established as academic imperatives.

LEI – (*LAY*-ee) The traditional flower garland worn in Hawaii. The Frangipani bush that provides the flowers that have a milky poisonous sap, and is native to Central America and the Caribbean, not Hawaii.

LEIGHTONWARD – (*LY*-ton-wawrd) An archaic appellation for a gardener.

LEITMOTIF – (*LYT*-moh-teef) A unifying or dominant theme, plot, style, subject, or idea, especially in an artistic, musical, or literary genre. A school of art is established by its common leitmotif.

LEMMINGS – (*LEM*-mings) Small but aggressive mouselike rodents of northern Norway and Sweden. Lemmings are noted for their periodic mass migrations when the population swells and the food supply diminishes. The migrations sometimes result in mass drownings, once mistakenly thought to be suicide. Much knowledge of lemming behavior is attributed to the English entomologist and zoologist, William Duppa Crotch, M.A., F.L.S. (1831 – 1903). (Died on August 25, 1903.) Duppa wrote <u>*On the Migration and Habit of the Norwegian Lemming*</u> in the *"Journal of the Linnaean Society of London,"* 1876.

LEMUR – (*LEE*-mur) Tiny primitive primate of Madagascar with ape-like hands. It is the world's smallest primate. A lemur is an evolutionary link between a mouse and a monkey. Too, the lemur is an evolutionary ancestor of man.

LENINISM – (*LEN*-nin-is-um) Marxist Socialism customized to meet Russian conditions. Leninism was an alteration of Marxism by Vladimir Lenin (1870 – 1924), Father of the Russian Communist Revolution. Because Russia was mostly an unsophisticated peasant country, Lenin concluded the people must be led into revolution. Leninism asserts that a small cadre of professional revolutionaries must be in the vanguard of the Socialist revolution.

LENITY – (*LEN*-ni-tee) The state or quality of being lenient. An authority figure who exercises lenity is mild and gentle with subordinates. Display lenity toward the weak.

LEPORINE – (*LEP*-por-ryn) Relating to or resembling a rabbit or hare. The term derives from the Latin *"lepus,"* meaning *"hare."* Leporine entered the English language in the mid-17th century.

LEPROSY – (*LEP*-pro-see) (Leper) A leper was considered to be a cursed individual, a societal pariah. Leprosy was and still is a horrible scourge, almost a Biblical curse. Leprosy is a bacterial disease that kills nerve endings resulting in localized anesthesia. The victim feels no pain in the infected area. Injuries will go unnoticed and untreated. Infections set in. Leprosy still runs rampant in poverty stricken regions like India. At night, rats gnaw the appendages of lepers who are senseless and oblivious. In the morning, they wake up without fingers and toes, or disfigured faces. Incidentally: a sanatorium that tends to invalid lepers is a leprosarium. Incidentally: There are about 200 cases of leprosy diagnosed in America annually. Strangely, the creature most responsible for transmitting leprosy is the armadillo. The leprosy bacteria thrives in the animal's blood. One of the Texas State animals is the armadillo.

LEPROSARIUM – (lep-pour-*SARE*-ree-um) A colony or hospital that cares for contagious lepers victims/ patients. The idea of being consigned to a leprosarium was a condemnation to hell. *"He's a pariah, about as welcomed as a leper."*

LESBIAN – (*LES*-bee-an) (Lesbianism) A female homosexual. A lesbian is a woman with a sexual preference for females. She is more comfortable loving women rather than men. The term is taken from the Isle of Lesbos off the coast of Greece. In ancient times, only women were allowed on the island. Lesbianism is the only sex act never mentioned anywhere in the Bible. All cultures have been far more tolerant of lesbianism than male homosexuality. Gay women have not suffered the vile persecution as gay men. This is probably due to the prurient nature of most men. Lesbianism is sexually titillating. In *The Passionate Pilgrim*, IV, 47, William Shakespeare (1564 – 1616) wrote: *"Were kisses all the joys of bed, one women would another wed."* In the *Black Iris* (2015) Leah Raeder (b. 1982) revealed: *"Girls love each other like animals. There is something ferocious and unself-conscious about it. We love with claws and teeth and the blood is just proof of how much. It's feral. And it's relentless."* Incidentally: Jesus apparently had no problem with lesbianism. In the last surviving words of *The Gospel of Thomas*, Jesus said: *"I say unto you, every woman who makes herself male will enter the Kingdom of Heaven."* No wonder the Church Fathers disregarded this Gospel.

LESBOLICIOUS – (lez-boh-*LISH*-uhs) A blend of two words, *"lesbian"* and *"delicious."* Lesbolicious is an enjoyable, gratifying, pleasurable sexual encounter with a gay lady, either in the flesh, or virtually on the screen. A lesbolicious experience may be in watching lesbian sex, or participating as a lesbian or a *"lesbro,"* a guy who enjoys sex with lesbians. Whatever the arrangement, it is sure to be lesbolicious. *"The only unnatural sex act is that which you cannot perform."* – Sexologist Alfred Kinsey (1894 – 1956).

LESBOPHILIA – (lez-boh-*FEE*-lee-ah) (Lesbophiliac) One committed to lesbophilia is a lesbian lover. It is a male who becomes exceptionally aroused by watching woman make love. Watching a sexual congress, be it heterosexual, homosexual, whatever, is erotically exciting. But a lesbophiliac is a voyeuristic connoisseur of gay female sex. *"The only unnatural sex act is that which you cannot perform."* – Sexologist Dr. Alfred Kinsey (1894 – 1956).

LESBOPHOBIA – (lez-boh-*FO*-bee-a) (Lesbophobiac) Phobic fear of gay women, lesbians. It would seem that an insecure male, questioning his own virility, who needs to dominate weak women, would fear strong, aggressive, gay ladies.

LESBRO – (*LEZ*-broh) A blend of two words: *"lesbian"* and *"brother,"* (*bro* being a truncation of brother). Lesbro has two meanings. First, it is a guy who has many lesbian friends. The alternate meaning is a guy who tries to seduce lesbians for sex. This designation of lesbro depicts a man who regards seducing lesbians as a sport. He is challenged to put his sexual prowess to the test. Winning over a woman-lover is a victory, an ego trip.

LESION – (*LEE*-shun) A wound or injury. A lesion is a localized pathological change in an organ or tissue. It can be an abrasion, infection, or disease on a small patch of skin.

LESSER ANTILLES – (*LES*-ser an-*TIL*-lees) A group of Caribbean islands southeast of Puerto Rico. The Lesser Antilles are divided into the Leeward Islands and Windward Islands. The Lesser Antilles include: Barbados, Dominica, Grenada, Saint Lucia, Saint Kitts and Nevis, Antigua and Barbuda, Trinidad and Tobago, Saint Vincent and the Grenadines.

LESSER LIGHTS – (*LES*-ser *LYTS*) Those of secondary fame, honor, and importance. Philosophers and religious leaders not of first rank are the lesser lights. Though their light shines, it is not as bright as the major representatives. The prophets of the Old Testament are divided into the major and minor prophets. That latter are the lesser lights.

LESSON PLANS – (*LES*-son *PLANS*) What and how the teacher intends to do. A lesson plan is an outline of a teacher's educational priorities. To a novice teacher, the lesson plan is a detailed road map. To the veteran teacher, the lesson plan is a casual reminder.

LET'S GO BRANDON – (lets goh *BRAN*-duhn) A banal, low-brow euphemism for *"Fuck You Biden!"* *"Let's go Brandon"* is becoming a rallying cry for the minimally-educated and nasty Trumpublicans who despise President Joe Biden (b. 1942). The sentence was conceived on October 2, 2021, at the NASCAR Talladega Superspeedway in Alabama – *"of course! Where else?"* Racer Brandon Brown (b. 1993) was celebrating his upset victory. While being interviewed by an NBC Sports reporter, the throng of rednecks chanted, what the reporter interpreted as *"Let's go Brandon."* He was mistaken, perhaps intentionally. For the horde of hillbillies were really chanting: *"Fuck You Biden!"* It didn't take long for the crude euphemism to go viral among America's stupids. Right-wing politicians had jumped on the bandwagon too. Texas Senator Ted Cruz (b. 1970), Kentucky Senator Mitch McConnell (b. 1942), South Carolina Representative Jeff Duncan (b. 1966), Florida Representative Bill Posey (b. 1947), Texas Governor Greg Abbott (b. 1957) and many more red state racists have repeated the silly slur. The passengers on a Southwest Airline flight out of Houston gasped when their pilot greeted them with *"Let's go Brandon!"* Never at a loss to make a cheap easy buck, the Trump Organization printed *"Let's go Brandon"* T-shirts for sale, of course. Incidentally: On Christmas Eve 2021, President Joe Biden (b. 1942) and the First Lady were speaking with families around the country who had called into the North American Defense Command (NORAD) to receive an update on Santa's location. One of the parents ended the conversation by saying, *"Let's go Brandon."* The President did not appear to recognize that the phrase is used by right wing nasties as a euphemism for *"Fuck You Biden."* President Biden agreed with the parent saying *"Let's go Brandon, I agree."*

LETTING GO – (*LET*-ing *GOH*) (Let Go) To release, relinquish, abandon. Spiritually speaking, letting go is surrendering to a Higher Power. It is letting go and letting God. One who lets go, goes with the flow of life. She does not force her will on God's will. Of course, letting go requires strong faith. It acknowledges that we are not ultimately in change, and therefore cannot ultimately be at fault. This eliminates guilt. It is not shirking responsibility, but rather allowing God to take responsibility for us. Letting go is tremendously liberating. *"The greatest step towards a life of happiness and simplicity is to let go. Trust in the power that is already taking care of you spontaneously without effort."* – Mooji (b. 1954). *"Breath by breath, let go of fear, expectation, anger, regret, cravings, frustration, fatigue. Let go the need for approval." "Forgiveness means letting go of the hope for a better past."* – Lama Surya Das (b. 1950). *"When I let go of what I am, I become what I might be." "By letting go, it all gets done. The world is won by those who let it go. But when you try and try, the world is beyond winning."* – Lao Tzu (c. 604 – c. 531 BCE). *"We must let go of the life we have planned, so as to accept the one that is waiting for us. The old skin has to be shed before the new one can come."* – Joseph Campbell (1904 – 1987). *"Life is a balance of holding on and letting go."* – Rumi (1207 – 1273). *"Let go of what has passed. Let go of what is happening now. Don't try to figure anything out. Don't try to make anything happen. Relax, right now and rest."* – Tilopa (988 – 1069 CE). *"Sometimes letting go is an act of far greater power than defending or hanging on."* – Eckhart Tolle (b. 1948). *"Learn to let go. That is the key to happiness."* – Buddha (c. 563 – c. 483 BCE). *"Letting go means to come to the realization that some people are a part of your history, but not a part of your destiny."* – Steve Maraboli (b. 1975). *"Sometimes the hardest part isn't letting go but rather learning to start over."* – Nicole Sobon. *"Anything you can't control is teaching you how to let go."* – Jackson Kiddard (d. 1901). *"You only struggle because you're ready to grow but aren't willing to let go.* – Drew Gerald. Remember: You did the best you could, with who you were, and what you knew, at those points in time, space, and life.

LEUKOCYTES – (*LOO*-co-sites) White blood cells, the soldiers in the body's immunizational army. Leukocytes are hunters, flowing with the blood, seeking out foreign enemies live bacteria. Like an amoeba, the leukocyte ingests the bacterium. At an infection site, the dead white blood cells (leukocytes) may ooze from the wound as white pus.

LEVANT – (le-*VANT*) The former French name for the Eastern Mediterranean, now occupied by Lebanon, Syria, and Israel.

LEVEE – (*LEV*-vee) A ridge made of compacted dirt along a river bank intended to hold back the water and prevent flooding.

LEVIATHAN – (le-*VY*-a-than) A Biblical sea monster. Leviathan had come to represent any gigantic marine animal, like a whale. The meaning of the word expanded to include anything of immense size. The term was popularized in 1651 by Thomas Hobbes' (1588 – 1679) philosophical book *Leviathan.*

LEVITY – (*LEV*-vit-tee) A sense of lightheartedness, playfulness, in a less than serious manner. A little levity is a bit of fun, as with a joke.

LEWD – (*LOOD*) (Lewdly, Lewdness) Lascivious, salacious, lecherous, lustful behavior. To act lewdly is offensive to different people to various degrees. What constitutes lewdness is relative, a social construct, a customary more.

LEXEME – (*LEK*-seem) (Lexemes) In linguistics, a lexeme is a basic word in the vocabulary of a language. A lexeme is an essential, fundamental unit of the lexicon or word stock. Elemental lexemes are the simplest building blocks of the language. For example: the nouns *dog* and *man*; the verbs *talk* and *walk*; the adjectives *good* and *bad* are lexemes. There is nothing fancy about a lexeme. Lexemes enable basic communication. A toddler learning to speak is armed only with lexemes, as is a person learning a foreign language. Lexemes are also called lexical units, terms, or words. For example: in English, the Anglo- Saxon word *"king"* qualifies as a lexeme, whereas the Anglo-French *"monarch"* may not.

LEXICAL – (*LEK*-si-kuhl) Relating or referring to words or the vocabulary of a language, especially distinguished from its grammatical and syntactical aspects.

LEXICAL OVERLAP – (*LEX*-si-kuhl *OH*-ver-lap) Lexical refers to the vocabulary of a language, the words in use. Lexical overlap refers to the number or percentage of words that are the same in related languages. The following is a sampling of lexical overlaps: Spanish & Italian = 82%; Spanish & French = 75%; French & Italian = 89%; Portuguese & Spanish = 89%; Polish & Slovakian = 60%; Polish & Russian = 38%; Russian & Bulgarian = 73%; Russian & Ukrainian = 60%; Ukrainian & Belarusian = 84%; English & German = 56%: English & French = 29%.

LEXICON – (*LEKS*-i-con) A dictionary. Also the vocabulary of a particular language, field, social class or person. This publication is *THE LIBERAL LEXICON*.

LEXICOGRAPHER – (leks-i-COG-graf-er) (Lexicography) A scholar who comprises dictionaries, or encyclodictionaries.

LEX LOCI – (leks *LO*-chee) Latin for the *"law of the place"*.

LEX NON SCRIPTA – (leks non *SCRIP*-ta) Latin for the *"unwritten, common law."*

LEX SCRIPTA – (leks *SCRIP*-ta) Latin for the *"written law."*

LEYTE GULF – (ly-*TEE GUHLF*) A partially enclosed part of the Pacific Ocean by the Philippine Islands of Samar and Leyte. On October 23 – 26, 1944, Leyte Gulf was the site of the greatest naval battle in history, between the U.S. and Japanese navies. The sea battle was a prelude to the U.S. invasion of the Philippines (The Battle of Leyte). The desperate Japanese threw every warship they had left against the American fleet. This greatest of naval battles was fought primarily by aircraft. The Japanese lost 28 warships, to the American loss of six. About 200 U.S. planes were lost, compared to Japan's loss of 300. The 3,000 American casualties seem light compared to Japan's 12,500 killed. The Battle of Leyte Gulf destroyed the Japanese navy and assured an invasion of the Philippine Islands.

LGBTQ+ – (el-jee-bee-tee-kyoo-*PLUS*) An initialism for *Lesbians*, *Gays*, *Bisexuals*, *Transgenders Queer Plus* collectively. The plus sign (+) indicates the tolerant inclusion of all others not aforementioned. LGBTQ+

represents and supports freedom, sexual liberty and privacy within the bounds of legality and propriety. We do not need morality police or sex gendarmes as in some fundamentalist Muslin countries.

LIABILITY – (ly-a-*BIL*-li-tee) Accountability. Being held responsible. Being expected to act in a certain manner, deemed appropriate. In law, a legal responsibility. One who is liable is bound or obligated by law. A liable party is responsible for actions that may involve restitution.

LIAISON – (lee-*AY*-sohn) French for a union. A contact and communication maintained by individuals or organizations that must ensure concerted action, coordination, and cooperation, for example, a military air strikes.

LIAR'S CREDO – (*LY*-yers *KRAY*-doh) *"Watch what we do, not what we say."* Attorney General John Mitchell (1913 – 1988) in the Watergate Scandal. The most shameless, unabashed liar in American political history was Donald J. Trump (b. 1946). During 4 years in office, Trump told at least 30,573 lies. Trump's defenders and apologists applied the liar's credo constantly concerning Trump. They literally told the public not to take President Trump seriously.

LIBATION – (ly-*BAY*-shun) A beverage poured out as an offering to a deity, spirit, or beloved dead with a ritual context as a form of communion or to give honor or thanks. Libations vary by tradition. They may consist of water, wine, milk, oil, honey, or alcoholic spirits. A libation may be ceremonially poured into a *"patera,"* a libation bowl, or onto a sacred object, altar, statue of a deity, gravestone, or into the Earth.

LIBBERISH – (*LIB*-ber-ish) A pejorative designation by conservatives for Progressive, Liberal language, terminology, ideas, and principles. The term libberish is a combination of the words *"Liberal"* and *"rubbish,"* or *"gibberish."*

LIBEL – (*LY*-bel) In law, written defamation. To destroy someone's reputation, good name, with the written word. Libel must be intentional, malicious, published, and untrue in order to be an offense.

LIBELANT – (*LY*-bel-lant) In law, a person who initiates a libel suit, believing she has been libeled, slandered in writing. *"I don't care what is written about me so long as it isn't true."* – Actress Katherine Hepburn (1907 – 2003).

LIBELEE – (ly-bel-*LEE*) In law, a person against whom a libel has been filed in court. A libelee is the accused, the defendant in a libel suit.

LIBERAL – (*LIB*-bral) (Liberalism) A Progressive, Left-winger. One who welcomes socio-economic, political change. Liberals are Socialistic, seeking distributive justice, on the side of righteousness. Liberalism is in the interests of the poor and middling classes. Democrats tend to be Liberal, and Socialists moreso. Liberals exhibit compassion, empathy for the less fortunate. All the great Avatars, religious leaders throughout history preached liberality, sharing the fruits of the Earth. *"If Jesus was alive today, we would kill him with lethal injection. I call that progress. We would have to kill him for the same reason he was killed the first time. His ideas are just too liberal."* – Kurt Vonnegut (1922 – 2007).

LIBERAL ARTS – (*LIB*-bral *ARTS*) Today, the liberal arts refer to the purely academic disciplines (humanities, history, and literature) that produce knowledge for knowledge's sake. Liberal arts are the polar opposite of vocational education. Where vocational education is concerned with things and products, the Liberal Arts are concerned with thoughts and ideas. The liberal arts do not produce anything tangible, other than better human beings.

LIBERAL BASHING – (*LIB*-bral *BASH*-ing) The apparently unreasonable disdain that many in the working class harbor for Progressives or Liberals. After all, Liberals desire an equitable distribution of the wealth which would benefit the working class. So why do the under-paid vote against their economic interests, and support the rich capitalist Republicans? In a word, envy. Liberals [read: *"open-minded"*] became Liberal through education. The *"low-information"* [read: *"unschooled"*] are subconsciously envious of the educated Progressives, even though the Progressives are on their side. Therefore, Liberal bashing is rooted in an inferiority complex. Low-information voters certainly can't admit this fact. They euphemistically refer to the *"educated"* as the *"elite."* They cannot very well say, *"we hate the educated."* Many in the working class accuse Liberals of *"arrogance,"* when it is actually *"envy"* that they are projecting. Many low-come citizens still believe the capitalist slander of Socialism. They still hold fast to the mythical *"American Dream."* They don't want to bring down the rich, they want to join them. They are not educated in the fact that it is by sharing the wealth, not hoarding it, that they will prosper. Because Donald Trump (b. 1946) is uneducated and wealthy, he serves as their ideal role model. He sounds like the uneducated, and he is rich. They therefore support Trump and bash the Liberals who deplore the conman.

LIBERAL COALITION – (*LIB*-bral co-a-*LISH*-shun) The union of diverse Progressive constituencies for socio-economic justice. The Liberal coalition consists primarily of the "have-littles," and "have-nots." They include the poor, ethnics, Blacks, Hispanics, workers, and unionists. Much of the middle class, Hollywood celebrities and highly educated are Liberal. Remember that most came from humble families. An important component of the Liberal coalition are enlightened elderly, and all dependent on social entitlement programs.

LIBERALITY – (lib-ber-*RAL*-li-tee) Generosity, being of a charitable spirit. One expressing liberality is pleased to share her abundance with those who are deficient. Liberals, who are liberal with their resources exercise liberality. Conservatives conserve [read: *"hoard"*] their resources. Liberality goes to the heart of Liberal Socialism and is the antithesis of conservative capitalism. Capitalism promotes greedy individualism: *"Every man for himself." "Posted: Keep Out!" "I got mine, to hell with you!"* Every great avatar of every great religion demanded liberality. Lao Tzu (c. 604 – c. 531) wrote in the <u>*Tao Te Ching*</u>: *"The Tao of Heaven is to take from those who have too much and give to those who do not have enough."* Jesus said: *"For of those to whom much has been given, much is expected,"* (Luke 12:48). Furthermore, Jesus asserted: *"Peter, if you love me, feed my lambs, feed my sheep,"* (John 21:15). Liberality is one characteristic that elevates us above the brute beasts.

LIBERAL LEXICON – (*LIB*-ber-al *LEX*-i-con) *A Socialistic, Spiritualistic Encyclodictionary* authored by philosopher Dr. Gary J. Pasieka (b. 1951). The first edition of the <u>*Liberal Lexicon*</u> was published in 2018. This pansophic tome is a compendium of valuable, fascinating information. Like the Bible, it is contentiously controversial, and presents something for everyone. The <u>Liberal</u> <u>Lexicon</u> is Progressive and zealously left-wing. The <u>Liberal Lexicon</u> is deeply metaphysical. It champions the causes of labor, the poor, the oppressed, the exploited, the helpless. The text endorses, encourages, demands the implementation of Jesus' *"Social Gospel,"* as written in Matthew 25: 35 – 40. The ax being grind in this publication is meant to decapitate capitalism, fascism, and the perfidious Donald Trump (1946 – XXX?). *"Now step I forth to whip hypocrisy."* – William Shakespeare (1564 – 1616), <u>Love's Labour's Lost</u> (c. 1598).

LIBERALTARIAN – (lib-er-al-*TAR*-ree-an) A type of Progressive, a Liberal/Libertarian hybrid. A Liberaltarian has mixed emotions concerning government regulation. He's a Liberal Socialist who demands a command economy controlled by the government. However she is also a *conservative* libertarian who intends to *conserve* personal liberties. A Liberaltarian expects government regulation in the boardroom, but not in the bedroom. Private personal issues like sexual preference, abortion rights, recreational drug use is not the state's business. The Liberaltarian believes that people should be free to do as they please, as long as they are not exploiting others. *"Love, then do as you will."* – St. Augustine (345 – 430 CE).

LIBERATION MOVEMENTS – (lib-ber-*RAY*-shun *MOOV*-ments) Wars of liberation throughout Asia and Africa in the 20th century, to free themselves from the colonial capitalist yoke. The imperialist colonial powers were raging capitalists all. It was therefore natural that the freedom fighters, the independence partisans would turn to Communist, anti-capitalist Socialist nations like Russia, China, and Cuba for help. After all, how could they have turned to their oppressors, other capitalists? Too, these revolutionary leaders knew that after centuries of capitalist exploitation, only a Socialist economy would provide distributive justice and prosperity for all.

LIBERATION THEOLOGY – (lib-ber-*RAY*-shun thee-*OL*-lo-jee) -Theosocialism, the melding of Marx and Jesus. Liberation Theology is a hybrid of Christianity and Marxism. Liberation theology takes Jesus' *"Social Gospel"* seriously, as Jesus intended. For centuries, the Church had sided with the monarchy and aristocracy against the peasantry, in order to maintain its privileged social position. Those few priests who supported the poor became martyrs and saints. With Liberation Theology, the meek, the poor shall inherit the Earth. Liberation theology is most active among Socialist Catholic priests in the squalid barrios of Latin American cities. Its ultimate goal is distributive justice, the fair redistribution of wealth. The spiritual founder of Liberation Theology was none other than Jesus, the Socialist. Therefore, *Liberation Theology = Catholicism + Marxism = Jesusism* (or true Christianity). The great martyr of Liberation Theology was the Theosocialist Fr. Oscar Romero (1917 – 1980), Bishop of San Salvador. Fr. Romero was murdered in Church by a capitalist, C.I.A. sponsored death squad. The saintly Fr. Romero said: *"When I fed the poor, I was called a saint. When I asked why they were poor, I was called a Communist."* Today, we have our first Theosocialist Pope, Francis the First (b. 1936). Being an Argentinean priest, Pope Francis is a compassionate proponent of Liberation Theology.

LIBERTARDS – (*LIB*-ber-tards) A silly pejorative name used by the Trumpsters to describe Liberals. Libertard is a combination of <u>Liber</u>al and <u>retard</u>. Ironically, the Liberals are the highly educated constituency, whereas the Trumpster are the *"low-information voter,"* [read: *stupids*]. The hillbillies, red necks, bigots, racists, skinheads, neo-Nazis call the sophisticated Liberals libertards.

LIBERTARIAN – (lib-ber-*TAIR*-ree-an) A laissez-faire conservative who advocates minimal government interference in economic or personal life. They are against any moral dictates in the boardroom or bedroom. Libertarians are *"rugged individualists"* [read: *anti-welfare*]. Libertarians oppose legislation restricting social behavior which angers conservatives. And Libertarians oppose legislation restricting economic behavior, which angers the Liberals. Therefore, libertarians present a bad compromise to both left and right. Traditionally, in a two party system, libertarians leaned toward the conservatives or Republicans.

LIBERTARIAN CREDO – (lib-ber-*TAR*-ree-an *CRAY*-dow) *"Every man for himself."*

LIBERTINE – (*LIB*-ber-teen) A person who is morally or sexually unrestrained, especially a dissolute man. A libertine takes anti-social, contra-cultural liberties, ignoring all conventional mores. He is a profligate rake.

LIBERTY – (*LIB*-ber-tee) Having unrestricted choice of movement, contrasted with freedom which is having unrestricted choice of thought. Liberty is external, environmental, whereas freedom is internal, attitudinal. The servile jailer at liberty in a dictatorship, is less free than his free-thinking prisoner.

LIBIDO – (ly-*BEE*-dow) All the instinctual energies and desires geared toward pleasure. Libido pertains to the sexual drive or instinct particularly. Much of Freudian psychoanalysis concerns the libido.

LIBRA – (*LEE*-brah) Latin for *"pound."* The letters L and B in libra gave us our abbreviation for pound (lb.) and gave the British their L-like symbol for pound currency.

LIBRARY – (*LY*-brar-ree) Society's most spiritual public facility, a Socialist municipal cathedral. It is a totem of the totality of human knowledge. The library is a repository of the living minds of dead scholars. The library is the *"Sanctum Sanctorum"* (Holy of Holies) of the Academe. It is the ultimate symbol of civilization. That's why barbarians always burned libraries. The library is the only institution in society that trusts people to take valuable property without capitalistic collateral or security deposits. The public library is Socialism in action. *"The death of a library, any library, suggests that the community has lost its soul."* – Kurt Vonnegut (1922 – 2007). *"The America I love still exists at the front desks of our public libraries."* – Kurt Vonnegut.

LIBRARY OF ALEXANDRIA – (*LY*-brar-ree of al-lex-*AND*-ree-a) A true academic, intellectual wonder of the ancient world. The Library was the greatest depository of knowledge, information, and wisdom of antiquity, and perhaps of history, located in Alexandria, Egypt. The Library was established during the reign of Ptolemy II Philadelphus (308 – 246 BCE) between the years 285 to 246 BCE. From that time it grew exponentially. The Library's location put it at the crossroads of the ancient world, Africa-Asia-Europe. It was once obligatory of every merchant, dignitary, diplomat, or scholar to contribute at least one book (educational scroll) from anywhere on Earth to the Library as a tax, in order to enter the City of Alexandria. The scholars of Alexandria consciously set out to acquire a written record of every piece of human knowledge up to their time. They lovingly referred to the great Library most accurately as *"The World's Memory."* But man's memory of antiquity would be lost in the ashes of war, bigotry, and ignorance. Two Roman soldiers, General Julius Caesar (100 – 44 BCE) in 48 BCE, and Emperor Aurelian (214 – 275 CE) in about 273 CE accidentally set fire to the Library during attacks on the city. Later, two religious fanatics, one Christian, the other Muslim finished the destruction of the Library. The bloody Coptic Pope and Patriarch of Alexandria, Theophilus (d. 412 CE) set fire to the surviving *"pagan"* manuscripts in 391 CE. Finally, zealous Muslims completed the destruction in 642 CE, in order to cleanse the city of *"infidel"* literature (ISIS-like). They also cleansed themselves, for it is said that the burning books provided fuel for 4,000 hot public baths for 6 months! (Anti- intellectuals would view this as putting education to practical use.) A universe of ancient knowledge was lost at Alexandria. The loss of the Library was an unperceived turning point in world history. There may not have been a *"Dark Ages"* if the Library had survived. All the knowledge of antiquity would not have to be re-discovered, re-invented. As a matter of fact, if the Library of Alexandria had survived fully intact, and had continued to accumulate and expand knowledge, Christopher Columbus (1451 - 1506) would not have sailed for America, Columbus would have sailed for Mars!

LIBRARY OF CONGRESS – (*LY*-brar-ree of *CON*-gress) One of the world's greatest libraries located in Washington D.C. It is unofficially considered to be the national library of the U.S.A. The Library was established by Congress in 1800 for service to its members, but the original building was burned by the British in the War of 1812. Today, the Library also serves government agencies, other libraries, and the public. With over 132 million items on 650 miles of shelves, the Library of Congress is a research gold mine. The United States Copyright Office of the Library of Congress is the official government body that maintains records of copyright registration in the U.S., including a Copyright Catalog.

LIBRETTO – (li-*BRET*-to) The text, words, lyrics of an opera or similar musical composition, as well as the book in which it is recorded by the librettist.

LICENSE – (*LY*-sens) A legal permit issued by the state which attests that one meets standards designed to protect the public. Licenses are issued by the government the state not by a school. (Schools issue diplomas.) A license can apply to a plumber, doctor, lawyer, bar owner or an automobile driver. Licenses are not free of charge. They are a permission tax. Many see it as a governmental extortion scheme. Practically everything you do requires a license. You even need a license (permit) to repair, beautify your private home. Which begs the question: Why would the government *"fine"* you for improving the neighborhood? Licenses are essential to maintain quality from practioners, and as a source of government income.

LICENSEE – (ly-sens-*SEE*) A person or company that is granted a license. In law, a person granted the privilege to enter into property by action or implied consent for her own purpose rather than the purpose of the one who owns the property.

LICENTIOUS – (li-*SENT*-chee-us) Lewd, lascivious, promiscuous, sexually immoral and unrestrained. A licentious person feels as though he has license to do as he pleases. *"His Piggishness,"* President Donald Trump (b. 1946) has proven himself to be licentious through his own words and actions. *"I like to grab them by the pussy. When you're a star, they let you do it, you can get away with anything."* – Donald Trump.

LICENTIOUS LIBERTARIANS – (li-*SENT*-chee-us lib-ber-*TAIR*-ree-ans) Those who advocate legal lasciviousness, particularly permissible pedophilia. A libertarian advocates liberty, freedom of conduct, minimal restraints. Licentious is being sexually uninhibited or unrestrained. Therefore, libertarian licentiousness is being unrestricted in one's sexual appetite. There are laws governing the age of sexual consent. This is where licentious libertarians take issue. It is the definition, the parameters of pedophilia

613

that they dispute. There are many with the burning desire to partake of the forbidden fruit. Few act on it. Fewer still are as honestly candid as the renowned M.I.T. Computer Scientist Richard Stallman (b. 1953). Stallman defended child molester Jeffrey Epstein (1953 – 2019) and child pornography in general. *"Epstein was not apparently a pedophile, since the people he raped seemed to have been postpuberal. Epstein was a serial rapist,"* Stallman insisted. Stallman wrote that: *"It is morally absurd to define 'rape' in a way that depends on minor details such as which country it was in or whether the victim was 18 years old or 17."* This high-tech genius favors legalization of pedophilia and child pornography. *"This 'child pornography' might be a photo of yourself or your lover that the two of you shared. It might be an image of a sexually mature teenager that any normal adult would find attractive. What's heinous about having such a photo?"* Stallman declared that: *"I think that everyone age 14 or above ought to take part in sex, though not indiscriminately. (Some people are ready earlier.)"* Harvard Law Professor and Libertarian Alan Dershowitz (b. 1938) was a friend and guest of Jeffrey Epstein, at Epstein's Caribbean fleshpot, *"Pedophilia Island."* Dershowitz wrote that *"Statutory rape is an outdated concept."* Too, he insisted that any 16 year-old should have the *"Constitutional Right"* to consensual sex. The controversial Stallman proclaimed that: *"I am skeptical of the claim that voluntary pedophilia harms children. The arguments that it causes harm seem to be based on cases which aren't voluntary, which are then stretched by parents who are horrified by the idea that their little baby is maturing. There is little evidence to justify the widespread assumption that willing participants in pedophilia hurts children."* Professor Richard Stallman is an extreme licentious libertarian. He wrote that: *"Prostitution, adultery, necrophilia, bestiality, possession of child pornography, and even incest and pedophilia – all of these acts should be legal as long as no one is coerced. They are illegal only because of prejudice and narrow-mindedness."* Bear in mind that neither the brilliant Stallman nor Dershowitz are Child Developmental Psychologists.

LICHEN – (*LY*-kin) A symbiotic union of fungus and alga. Lichens have a greenish, gray, yellow, brown, or blackish thallus that grows in leaf like, crust like, or branched forms on rocks, trees, walls, tombstones.

LICORICE – (*LICK*-or-ish) (*Glycyrrhiza glabra*) A Eurasian plant of the legume family. The dried roots of this plant yields a bitter-sweet extract that is used in medicine and as a candy flavoring.

LIE – (*LYH*) (Lies, Lied, Lying, Liar) An intentionally stated untruth. A false statement with the deliberate intent to deceive. Presenting false facts as true. One who constantly lies is considered a liar. Far and away, the greatest Presidential liar, the most notorious liar in American political history has been Donald J. Trump (b. 1946). According to the <u>Washington Post</u>, in his 4 years as President, from January 20, 2017 to January 20, 2021, Trump told the public 30,573 lies. This does not count all the lies that his subordinates and lackeys were forced to tell. *"To lie to the media is not illegal."* – Cory Lewandowski (b. 1973) Trump political advisor. Distorting the facts may constitute an outright lie. Trump's political consultant, Kellyanne Conway (b. 1967) tried to sanitize the administration's lies by labelling them *"alternative facts,"* some sort of optional truth. Lies by influential people carry consequences. Trump's *"Big Lie,"* that the Presidential victory was stolen from him in 2020 has torn the nation apart. Some people are better liars than others. The less conscientious a person is, the more skilled he'll be at lying. Donald Trump has no conscience. He is therefore a master liar. Trump is so proficient, that political pundits, politician observers cannot determine if Trump believes his falsehoods or not. Some had called Trump a pathological liar, which would make him a *"mythomaniac."* Normal people feel guilty when lying, and it shows on their faces. Not so Trump.

He will lie into the TV camera with impunity

He will lie into the TV camera with impunity, and then contradict his lie with another lie in the same interview! That's why his lawyers have tried every legal/political trick to keep Trump off the witness stand. Lying is not easy for basically honest people. Physiological changes take place in normal people when lying. One should be on the look-out for these signs of deception. Lying is stressful and stress causing sweating. A liar will tend to squint and blink her eyes continually. The tension of lying makes the nose itch. The liar will rub his nose often. The nervousness caused by lying will make the large muscles of the buttocks twitch, the *"gluteus maximus,"* resulting in squirming. A liar will tend to cross her arms over her chest. He is subconsciously covering his heart, so the truth he knows in his heart is not visible. The police are well aware of these telltale physiological clues. Donald Trump (b. 1946) is the unrivaled *"Prince of Liars."* *"People need good lies. There are too many bad ones."* – Kurt Vonnegut (1922 – 2007).

LIEGE – (*LEEJ*) Originally, the allegiance and service a vassal owed to his feudal lord. Today, liege means loyalty and faithfulness in general.

LIE/MISTAKE – (*LHY* mis-*TAYK*) (Lying versus Mistaken) A lie and a mistake are related – both are untruths. The difference is in intension, motivation. A lie is an intentional deception. A mistake is a misinformed belief. The *"Costanza Defense"* against being accused of lying is: *"It's not a lie if you believe it's true."* That is true for the reasoning stated above. A mistaken person is wrong, but not lying. The Costanza Defense is taken from the fictional character, George Costanza, from the TV comedy *"Seinfeld Show."* The moment the mistaken person is informed of his mistake, and still maintains his wrong point, he is lying. For example: A MAGA election denier may truly believe the falsehood that Trump won the 2020 election. So when he says the election was rigged, he is not lying because he believes it. However, when he is presented with the facts, and he still maintains that Trump won, he has become a liar.

LIEN – (*LEEN*) The legal claim of one person upon the property of another person to secure the payment of a debt or satisfaction of an obligation. The party slapping the lien has the right to retain possession of the property until the obligation is satisfied.

LIEU – (*LOO*) *In lieu* means instead, *in lieu of* means in place of. *"We will fry with butter, in lieu of olive oil."*

LIEUTENANT – (loo-*TEN*-ant) A Second Lieutenant is the lowest ranking commissioned officer in the U.S. army. She wears a single gold bar (called a "butter bar"). Second Lieutenants are promoted to First Lieutenants and switch to a single silver bar.

LIEUTENANT COLONEL – (loo-*TEN*-nant *KER*-nal) The 6th highest ranking officer in the U.S. army. A Lieutenant Colonel is promoted to a Full Colonel and is above a Major. A Lieutenant Colonel wears a silver oak leaf.

LIEUTENANT GENERAL – (loo-*TEN*-nant *JEN*-ner-al) The Second highest officer in the U.S. army. The Lieutenant General is promoted to a full General and is above a Major General. The Lieutenant General wears 3 silver stars.

LIFE – (*LYF*) (Alive, Live) Life is the Breath of God. The state of being alive with the power of sentience. It is the greatest miracle and mystery in the universe. A state of existence experienced by plants and animals, mysteriously different from the existence of rocks and minerals. With life, chemistry becomes biology. Living entities are metaphysically created from non-living chemicals. What is life? There are philosophical and theological definitions, but no scientific definitions (none adequate anyway). All Life, to some degree, is self-aware, apparently appreciative of the privilege of living, and defensive to protect its Life. We cannot create Life technologically or scientifically. Life can be destroyed, but not created. Though we can bring Life to death, we cannot bring death to Life. Only Life can create Life. We cannot bring Life back, once it departs. We cannot prove or disprove if Life returns as Life in another form, after it had departed in death. A tree, a rock, a man, a rat, and a pot can be ground-up, analyzed, and separated into their chemical constituents. All will contain many of the same common chemical elements. But only the tree (a plant) and the man and rat (animals) were once alive. What is this *"aliveness"* that we cannot find in the chemical residue? If it isn't physical or material, it must have be metaphysical or spiritual. It must be a spirit or a soul that provides Life to the person, the rat, and tree, but not to the rock or pot. Therefore, Life is spirit, a spirit we can call soul. Therefore, all living creatures, plants and animals, are endowed with a soul, which provides them with Life. Indeed, Life is the greatest mystery in the universe. *"We will never know the essence* [meaning: *life force*] *of even a single fly."* – St. Thomas Aquinas (1225 – 1274). Incidentally: The only force proven more powerful than Life is Love. Though we Love Life, many would sacrifice, surrender their Life, to preserve the Life of those we love.

LIFEKIND – (*LYF*-kind) All sentient people, creatures, beings, animals, plants, microbes or combination of all, that reside anywhere throughout the great cosmos. Lifekind acknowledges lifeforms other and beyond mankind or humankind. Lifekind may be great, small, or infinitesimal. As diverse as life is on Planet Earth, from a single-celled amoeba to mankind, so is lifekind infinitely more diversified throughout the universe. Too, creatures with a humanoid level of intelligence may be very low on the evolutionary scale in other worlds. Extraterrestrial lifeforms may seem alien, bizarre, or grotesque to us Earthlings, as we may look to them. Nevertheless, being alive, they have had life breathed into them by the One, Universal God. With God as our Mother/Father, we are all part of the universal family. Incidentally: When praying for all sentient beings, include your cosmic kin, the lifekind throughout the universe as well.

LIFE'S NECESSITIES – (*LYS* nes-*SES*-sit-tees) What is required for a fulfilling life. The necessities are: 1. *Health* – physical, mental, and spiritual; 2. *Food* – basic nutritious sustenance; 3. *Shelter* – a home; 4. *Income* – more in than out; 5. *Love* – the companionship of a mate, family, and friends; 6. *Adventure* – stimulating interests for the body and mind; 7. *Civil Rights* – liberty, freedom, safety; 8. *Education* – knowledge and the opportunity for unlimited learning; 9. *Work* – a meaningful life-purpose, a chance to be of service; 10. *Distributive Justice* – knowledge that all others are cared for in like manner. These necessities of life are the Socialist agenda.

LIFESPAN – (*LYF*-span) Genetically programmed period of existence. Both plants and animals have a designated lifespan. As that time limit is approached, *entropy* is set into motion. Energy level drops, growth and healing diminish, tissues breakdown, old age has arrived. Lifespans terminate with death. In general, a mammal will live for as long as it takes its heart to beat to a billion. The smaller the animal, the faster the heart rate, the shorter the lifespan. Humans are an exception to this rule, because humans can control their environment [read: *lifestyle*]. People can increase their lifespan through healthy living.

LIFE PARTNER – (*LYF PART*-ner) (Life Partnership) A loving relationship between two individuals of different or the same gender who dedicate their lives to each other. A life partnership may entail formal matrimony or not. Usually, the term life partner is applied to one's marital mate of the same gender. Life partner is less awkward than referring to each other as the husband or both as the wife. Therefore, the term life partner familiarly refers to one's homosexual spouse.

LIFE'S PUROPSE – (lyfs *PUR*-pos) Our reason, the justification for being. Our mission on this planetary plane is to generate light, to enlighten. Light is life, light is love. We all have unique gifts and powers to accomplish this purpose. Even an impaired homeless beggar has the power to elicit our compassion. This may be his life's purpose. Everyone's purpose in life is to enlighten our soulmates with love, in any, every way. A purposeful life is the deep desire of compassionate, altruistic people. Life's purpose is to accomplish, make a mark, and leave a legacy. To have lived, rather than just to have existed is the purpose of life. Service to others endows life with purpose. To leave your world a better place because you had lived is life's purpose. Emily Dickinson (1830 – 1886) put it most poetically: *"If I can stop one heart from breaking, I shall not live in vain. If I can ease one life from aching, or cool one pain. Or help one fainting robin unto his nest again, I shall not live in vain."*

LIFE STAGES – (*LYF STAY*-jes) The various rungs up then down the professional ladder, as describe by actor Hugh O'Brian (1925 - 2016). Mr. O'Brian was famous, particularly in Western films in the 1950s, into the 1970s. He wrote a simple but profound list of 5 stages in an actor's career. 1. *Who is Hugh O'Brian?* 2. *Get me Hugh O'Brian.* 3. *Get me a younger Hugh O'Brian.* 4. *Get me Hugh O'Brian type.* 5. *Who is Hugh O'Brian?*

LIGAMENT – (*LIG*-ga-ment) Sinew. A tough band of fibrous tissue that connects bone to bone and holds organs in place. In contrast, a tendon connects muscle to muscle, and muscle to bone.

LIGHT – (*LYT*) Scientifically speaking, light consists of various wavelengths of energy. Matter is congealed light. Conversely, light is diluted matter. Therefore, everything and everyone is light. The universe is different states of light energy. With light, the physical and metaphysical realms converge. The first words God spoke in Genesis [meaning: *the beginning*] were *"Let there be light."* Then the Big Bang occurred, which was an explosion of light. Incidentally: The speed of light is 186,282 miles per second. At that speed, a beam of light could circle the Earth 7 times in one second.

LIGHT – (*LYT*) Metaphysically speaking, God said: *"I am the Light of the world."* In the beginning there was God, and there was Light and God is Light. The further one is from the source of Light, the deeper one descends into the darkness. God is the Light of the world, the universal source of energy and life. Enlightenment is nearness to God. God is love and so is Light – soul illumination. Light is energy, power, heat, matter, everything, as is God. All matter is congealed Light. Light is omnipresent, as is God. We too are matter, we too are Light, therefore we too are one with God, in atonement [read: *at- one-ment*]. So everyone and everything is part of God. We may not understand that we are Godly. As we come to that realization, we become en*lightened*, filled with Light, filled with God, as was Buddha and Jesus. The mystic Muslim Sufi, Fakhruddin Araqi (1213 – 1289) put it splendidly: *"I am light itself, reflected in the heart of everyone; I am the treasure of the Divine Name, the shining Essence of all things. I am every light that* *shines, every ray that illuminates the world. From the highest heavens to the bedrock of the earth all is but a shadow of my splendor." "To the light I have attained, to the light I live,"* declared the Prophet Muhammad (c. 570 – 632 CE). *"I am a child of the light. I love the light. I serve the light. I live the light. I am protected, illuminated, supplied and sustained by the light and I bless the light."* – Comte de St. Germain (d. 1784?).

LIGHTBULB MEMORY – (*LYT*-bulb *MEM*-mor-ree) An interesting recall phenomenon, when one can remember exactly where they were, and what they were doing, when they had learned of a great event. Most people of the proper age have vivid lightbulb memory of the 9/11 attack, for instance. Traumas or spectacular events will be videotaped in our lightbulb memory.

LIGHTHEARTED – (*LYT*-hart-ted) Living a carefree, cheerful, stressless existence. The opposite of lighthearted is heavyhearted – living a burdened life. Lighthearted people are always warmhearted people. Conversely, heavyhearted people tend to be coldhearted as well. Lighthearted people take life and themselves less seriously. They tend to laugh easily. Lighthearted people are optimistic. They have faith that God is good, all the time. Lighthearted people live in a good world, despite all the injustices. And they live longer. A lighthearted person is seldomly attacked by her own heart. In fact, lighthearted people have a 40% less chance of suffering a heart attack. It is enlightening to live lightheartedly.

LIGHTNING – (*LYT*-ning) Atmospheric electricity that strikes the Earth about 6,000 times a minute. Worldwide, there are about 60 million lightning storms a year, resulting in about 24,000 deaths. Nowhere on Earth is struck by more lightning bolts than the Congo Rain Forest (about 100 million strikes a year). Only the tropical Lake Maracaibo may be hit by more lightning strikes. A lightning bolt can be as thin as a pencil or as thick as a large tree trunk, 5 miles long, packing a shocking 100 million volts of electricity. The bolt can reach 50,000 degrees Fahrenheit, 5 times hotter than the surface of the sun. Each strike yields the power of a ton of TNT. When lightning strikes, negatively charged electrons in the cloud race to Earth on the invisible *"stepped leader"* (not ladder). Positively charged particles on Earth flash up the stepped leader to the cloud. That is the flash we see, going up. So the visible lightning bolt is actually traveling from the ground up to the cloud. Incidentally: Lightening is a vital fertilizer. Lighting infuses vital nitrogen from the atmosphere into the soil, essential for plant growth.

LIGHTNING ALLEY – (*LYT*-ning *AL*-lee) A belt running across central Florida from St. Petersburg on the Gulf of Mexico to Daytona Beach on the Atlantic (sea to sea) experiencing more lighting strikes and deaths than anywhere else in America. This area includes the cities of St. Petersburg, Tampa, Winter Haven, Orlando, Daytona Beach. Nationwide, there are about 40 million lightning strikes yearly. Incidentally: Lake Maracaibo (5,100 square miles) in northern Venezuela is the lightning capital of the world. For 140 to 160 nights a year, for 10 hours, the Lake will experience up to 280 lightning strikes per hour. This ancient lake is in a great bowl rimmed by mountains. Actually, the narrow outlet to the Caribbean in the north turns Lake Maracaibo into a brackish bay. Warm moist air (storm clouds) enters the Lake from the Sea. It is trapped in the Lake's basin and churned into tropical storms. So spectacular thunder/lightning storms are concentrated over Lake Maracaibo.

LIGHTNING ROD – (*LYT*-ning *ROD*) A metal rod high atop a building or structure to protect it from lighting strikes. A wire is connected to the rod that runs down into the ground. The structure or building is therefore *grounded*. If lightning strikes, it will hit the highest point, which should be the metal rod. The current will run down the wire, into the ground. The building or structure will be saved. The lightning rod was invented by Ben Franklin (1706 – 1790), a pioneer in lightning research in 1749. Franklin insisted that the rod have a sharp point. The British Royal Society of Science insisted that the rod bear a rounded top (a metal ball). Of course, King George III (1738 – 1820) supported his Royal Society. A hot dispute ensued, a real tempest in a tea pot. Earlier (1726) Jonathan Swift (1667 – 1745) had written *Gulliver's Travels.* Later, several sequel editions were published. In one of them, the controversy concerning the lightning rod is satirically alluded to. The empires of *Lilliput* and *Blefuscu* debate, dispute, and battle over what side of the egg should be broken, the pointed or the rounded. Actually, the lightning rod configuration didn't matter (much like the egg imbroglio). The entire controversy was strictly academic, scholastic snobbery.

LIGHT WORKER – (*LYT WERK*-er) (also Light Bearer) One who has become "enlightened." Through meditation, contemplation and spiritual edification, a light worker has reached a higher level of consciousness. He is in atonement [read: *at-one-ment*] with God. She understands that she is *"Not a human being having a spiritual experience, but a spiritual being having a human experience."* – Fr. Pierre Teilhard de Chardin (1881 – 1955). Though light workers have given up the human sense of being, they have not given up on their fellow human beings. They live to serve, making this planet a better place. They strive to uplift other people to a higher, spiritual level of consciousness. Light workers work to enlighten humanity.

LIGHTYEAR – (*LYT*-year) The distance light traveling at 186,282 miles per second, will travel in one year (about 6 trillion miles). If a light year was reduced to 1 mile, then a mile in relations would be reduced to 1 inch. Incidentally: Theoretical physics predicts astounding phenomena when approaching the speed of light. Objects are said to shrink, and time slows, then stops, then reverses! This scientific theory is parodied in the *"Relativity Limerick." "There was a young lady named Bright. Whose speed was faster than light. She went out one day, in a relative way, and came back the previous night."*

LIGNEOUS – (*LIG*-nee-us) (Lignin, Lignification) Xyloid, woody or made to resemble wood, as some synthetic floors.

LIGNIFICATION – (lig-ni-fi-*KAY*-shun) (Lignin, Ligneous) The chemical transformation of soft plant tissue to wood. Particle board or any wood-like substance made from wood shredding or pulp has been processed by lignification.

LIGNIN – (*LIG*-nin) (Ligneous, Lignification) In botany, lignin is an organic polymer (complex molecule) consisting of various aromatic alcohols. Lignin is the chief non-carbohydrate constituent of wood. Lignin binds to cellulose fibers and hardens, strengthens the plant wall. So lignin turns a soft plant to wood.

LIGNITE – (*LIG*-nite) Lowest quality coal, dark brown with a distinct wood-like texture, and intermediate in density and carbon content between bituminous coal and peat. One may still see the decaying wood grain in samples of lignite. Lignite is younger coal. It would need several millions more years to season in the ground under great pressure to become high quality anthracite coal.

LIGNUM VITAE – (*LIG*-num *VEE*-tay) (*"Tree of Life"*) A tree native to tropical America and the Caribbean yielding one of the *heaviest* wood in the world. It is so dense that it will not float. Too, it takes forever for the wood to rot. Lignum Vitae is the world's 4th *hardest* wood just behind 2 South American varieties and #1 Australian Buloke. A lignum vitae healthy tree with its vivid green foliage and mushroom shape resembles a giant stalk of broccoli. The tree has light-blue blossoms that attract swarms of pale yellow butterflies. The pale blue blossoms of the Lignum Vitae tree provides is Jamaica's National Flower. The tree bears small orange-yellow, heart-shaped fruit which further decorates the plant. The crown of the tree has round, dense foliage. The smooth bark on the trunk is light beige with a darker dappled pattern. The dense hard wood has long been prized for tools, mallets, pulleys, batons, mortars-and-pestles, and the sturdiest furniture. Its nature to sink disqualifies it for ship building, except crucial propeller shaft bearings. Lignum vitae, came to be called the *"Tree of Life"* for its medicinal qualities. The Taino Indians used all parts of the plant to cure various ailments. In the 16th century, *gum guaiac* obtained from the tree's resin was used in a syphilis medicine (a Caribbean disease). Today, the inner bark of the lignum Vitae is made into a liniment for sprains and pains due to arthritis. Too, a tea is brewed from the leaves as a soothing eye wash. Incidentally: The preservative quality of the lignum vitae wood encouraged Princess Diana Spencer's (1961 – 1997) family to line her coffin with its wood. This would serve to preserve the body longer – but for what?

LIKE – (*LYK*) A feeling of approval. A gratifying emotion less intense than *love* or *lust*. We tend to like people who bolster our self-esteem. Too, we tend to like people like ourselves. When someone says *"I don't like you,"* what they are really saying is *"You are not like me."* The subliminal implication is *"Become more like me and I'll like you more."* In other words, adopt my opinions, beliefs, prejudices, bigotries, personality, and <u>likes</u>, then I'll <u>like</u> you. We will be a<u>like</u>. These are conditions, and we know that conditional love is no love at all. The same applies to like. Therefore dismiss the silly statement: *"I love you, but I don't like you."* It's hypocritical, it's invalid, it's a lie. That's the coward's way of saying *"Stay out of my life."* Actually, like is the fuel for the fire of love. No fuel, no fire; no like, no love. *"I have no notion of loving people by halves, it is not my nature. My attachments are always excessively strong."* – Jane Austen (1775 – 1817), <u>Northanger Abbey</u> (1803). Incidentally: *"It is better to be disliked for who you are than to be liked for who you are not."* – Judith Ann Parsons.

LIKERT SCALE – (*LYK*-ert *SCALE*) A five-point scale with linked options: strongly agree, agree, undecided, disagree, and strongly disagree.

LILAPSOPHOBIA – (lil-lap-so-*FO*-bee-a) (Lilapsophobiac) Phobic fear of tornadoes and hurricanes. It is normal to feel some amount of fear in the face of dangerous situations. Tornadoes and hurricanes certain qualify as dangerous, so some amount of fear is warranted. But lilapsophobia is an unreasonable neurosis. A victim is obsessed with the weather. She over-stocks with survival supplies. Living with lilapsophobia is a perpetual stress. This phobia is a defense mechanism, masquerading some deeper subconscious trauma or fear. Alternately, the sufferer many have been traumatized by one of these storms in infancy.

LILITH – (*LIL*-lith) According to Jewish tradition, Adam's first wife (prior to Eve). Lilith was the prototype for the insufferable wife. She insisted on domineering, even being on top during sexual congress. After Adam abandoned her, Lilith became a demon tormenting couples by killing their infants. Mysterious crib death had been attributed to Lilith from ancient times. It has been said that a mother's *"lullaby"* to her baby originated as a corruption of the term *"Lilith-go- bye,"* a charm to protect the baby by warding-off Lilith.

LILLIPUTIAN – (lil-li-*PU*-shun) Tiny, diminutive, very small. The term was coined by Jonathan Swift (1667 – 1745) in his 1726 novel, <u>Gulliver's Travels.</u> Swift described the island of Lilliput, populated by inhabitants only 6 inches tall.

LIMB CATALEPSY – (lim *CAT*-tal-lep-see) The paralysis of the arms and legs, frozen in a rigid position, which can be induced through hypnotic suggestion. Traumatic hysteria can, under specific conditions, result in limb catalepsy. Limb catalepsy is a form of hysteria. It can occur when one is frightened to death but does not die. However, the person wishes he was dead to alleviate the stress. In stead of dying, the body goes numb. For example, a person suffering from neurotic stage fright may be struck with limb catalepsy. The subconscious mind will no longer tolerate the stress of the upcoming speech. So it shuts the body down. This had happened to rookie athletes who had to perform before a national television audience. Though limb catalepsy may make no sense to observers, the mind knows what's best for the body.

LIMBERDICKLE – (lim-*BER*-di-cal) (Limberdick) An exceedingly wimpy male. A Limberdickle guy a whiner, sniveler, unmanly, a weak wuss, (a real *"limber dick"*).

LIMBIC SYSTEM – (*LIM*-bic *SIS*-tem) The mammalian part of the human brain. The limbic system governs basic emotions, hunger, and the sex-drive. Evolutionary lower animals like the reptiles do not possess a limbic system.

LIMBO – (*LIM*-bo) An intermediate, transitional, or midway place or state. In Roman Catholic Theology, limbo is an intermediate region between heaven and hell. It is neither a place of punishment, nor ecstasy. Limbo serves as the abode after death of unbaptized infants, and of the righteous that had died before coming to Christ. Righteous people like isolated natives who had not been introduced to Christianity could not be sent to hell. For what? They would go to limbo, and supposedly be Christianized, prepared for heaven. So limbo is a sort of spiritual waiting room. Limbo is an archaic doctrine for an illiterate medieval peasantry. It is kept out of sight in the Catholic closet. Alternately, the term limbo has come to mean in a state of indecision, neither here nor there, in the gray area. *"I found myself in a state of limbo, not knowing what to do next."*

LIMBO – (*LIM*-bo) A Jamaican term for a dance-game from the West Indies, in which the dancer bends backward from the knees and moves with a shuffling step under a horizontal bar that is lowered after each successive pass. Limbo requires athletic acuity. Limbo originated in Africa as a ritual practiced at wakes and funerals. Limbo proved to be a therapeutic exercise to *limber* up slaves who had been shackled for long periods, especially on the slave ships. The name derives from the Jamaican term *"limba,"* meaning *to bend.* Limbo today is most commonly associated with Trinidad.

LIMERENCE – (*LIM*-er-uhns) (Limerent) The state of being obsessively infatuated with someone, usually accompanied by delusions of or desire for an intense romantic relationship with that person. Neurotic limerence may degenerate into pathologic stalking.

LIMERICK – (*LIM*-mer-rik) A kind of humorous, clever verse of 5 lines, in which the first, second, and fifth lines rhyme with each other, and the third and fourth lines, which are shorter, form a rhymed couplet. For Example: *"There was a young lady from Ryde; Who ate a green apple and died. The apple fermented; inside the lamented; and made cider inside her inside."* Alternately: *"There was a young lady named Bright; whose speed was faster than light. She went out one day; in a relative way; and came back the previous night."* The term Limerick is an Irish place name. That's not surprising. The Irish have a long history of being clever with language.

LIMESTONE – (*LYM*-stone) The calcareous remains of coral polyps (calcium carbonate), forming 1/10 of the Earth's surface rock. Calcareous ooze made from seashells hardened into limestone. Chalky karst or limestone absorbs carbon dioxide ($CO2$) in the atmosphere (a greenhouse gas), stabilizing the planet's temperature. Limestone is an important building material and an ingredient in the production of cements and concretes. Limestone is burned in a kiln. It gives off carbon dioxide and becomes quicklime. It mixes with wood ash to produce white lime. Adding water to while lime creates whitewash. Incidentally: Limestone produces hard water (mineral rich), good for bass and perch. Limestone-free soft water is good for trout.

LIMINAL – (*LIM*-min-nal) (Limen) In psychology, the point at which a stimulus is of sufficient intensity to begin to produce an effect. Sub-liminal means unconscious, or below the limen of consciousness.

LIMITATION STATUTE – (lim-mih-*TAY*-shun *STACH*-oot) (Statute of Limitation) The finite period of time in which to bring lawsuits or criminal prosecutions for many categories of crime. The statute of limitation does not apply to: murder, involuntary manslaughter, reckless homicide, arson, forgery, or treason. Till this day, Nazi war criminals in their late 90s are occasionally arrested. Donald Trump (b. 1946) had committed a plethora of crimes from business corruption, election fraud, sedition, to treason. But as President, he was untouchable, above the law. That accounts for Trump's desperation to be elected for 4 more years, to allow the statute of limitation to run out on most of his crimes.

LIMN – (*LIM*) (Limned) To represent in drawing or painting. To describe or portray in words. *"I limned the crime scene on my sketch pad." "His paintings is a limn of 19th century rural life."*

LIMOUSINE LIBERALS – (lim-mo-*SEEN LIB*-er-als) Affluent Socialists who *"talk the talk, but don't walk the walk,"* so to speak. When not chauffeured, limousine liberals may be *"Lexus liberals,"* at least. Publicly, these spurious Socialists *virtue signal* when among Progressives. They lament the plight of the poor, oppressed, and exploited, while enjoying their lives of luxury and opulence. Limousine Liberals are hypocrites, left-wing liars. They are the Pharisees who Jesus condemned, who made a grand show of their meager charity. Limousine Liberals are always *"politically correct."* In fact, the designation *politically correct* was originally a pejorative term first used by Liberals to describe hypocritical Liberals, Socialists, and Progressives – Limousine Liberals.

LIMPID – (*LIM*-pid) Lucid, clear, pellucid, transparent as limpid crystal, air, or water. *I could see the lake floor through the limpid ice."*

LINCHPIN – (*LINCH*-pin) (also a Cotter pin) A pin inserted through the end of an axletree to keep the wheel on. The linchpin is an ancient device, as old as the wheel. Therefore, linchpin has been expanded to apply to anything or anyone that holds the various elements of a complicated structure together. *"Our engineer departed, the linchpin of the project."*

LINCON'S DREAM – (*LINK*-cons *DREEM*) President Abraham Lincoln (1809 – 1865) was mystically spiritual, a staunch believer in the efficacy of dreams. Just before his murder, Lincoln dreamt of the tragedy. Only days before his death, Lincoln related the following story to his wife Mary Todd (1818 - 1882). *"About ten days ago, I retired very late. I had been up waiting for important dispatches from the front. I could not have been long in bed when I fell into a slumber, for I was weary. I soon began to dream. There seemed to be a death-like stillness about me. Then I heard subdued sobs, as if a number of people were weeping. I thought I left my bed and wandered downstairs. There the silence was broken by the same pitiful sobbing, but the mourners were invisible. I went from room to room; no living person was in sight, but the same mournful sounds of distress met me as I passed along. It was light in all the rooms; every object was familiar to me; but where were all the people who were grieving as if their hearts would break? I was puzzled and alarmed. What could be the meaning of all this? Determined to find the cause of a state of things so mysterious and so shocking, I kept on until I arrived at the East Room, which I entered. There I was met with a sickening surprise. Before me was a catafalque, on which rested a corpse wrapped in funeral vestments. Around it were stationed soldiers who were acting as guards; and there was a throng of people, some gazing mournfully upon the corpse whose face was covered, others weeping pitifully. 'Who is dead in the White House?' I demanded of one of the soldiers. 'The President' was his answer; 'he was killed by an assassin!' Then came a loud burst of grief from the crowd, which awoke me from my dream."* *"There are stranger things in heaven and earth, than are dreamt of in your philosophy."* – William Shakespeare (1564 - 1616), *"Hamlet"* (c. 1600).

LINCOLN'S MAGNANIMOUS MISTAKE – (*LINK*-cons mag-*NAN*-ni-mus mis-*TAYK*) Abraham Lincoln (1809 – 1865) was the American President who preserved the Union by winning the Civil War (1861 – 1865). To be magnanimous is to be compassionately forgiving. A mistake is something that, if you could do over, you'd do differently. Lincoln's magnanimous mistake was not punishing the treasonous Confederate leaders who rebelled, and made war against the United States, resulting in over 700,000 deaths, millions and millions in destruction. The ringleaders of the confederate coup should have been hanged, as the *"Radical Republicans"* had intended. This included the top political and military leaders: Jefferson Davis (1808 – 1889); Alexander Stephens (1812 – 1883); Robert E. Lee (1807 – 1870); George Pickett (1825 – 1875); John Bell Hood (1831 – 1879); Joe Johnston (1807 – 1891); P.G.T. Beauregard (1823 – 1893) Simon Buckner (1823 – 1914); James Longstreet (1821 – 1904); Nathan Bedford Forrest (1821 – 1877), and many, many more. Any other country in the world would have executed these traitors. Britain and Germany would have hanged them. Spain would have shot them. France would have guillotined them. God knows what Russia would have done to them. There was no accountability, with no one held responsible. Rather than punished, the insurrectionists were lionized with memorials, statues, and glowing biographies. (Unlike the Nazi swastika, the Confederate flag became a symbol of honorable rebellion.) Lincoln's love could not overcome the rebel's hate. The rebellious spirit simmered into defiance to this present day. Slavery morphed into discrimination/segregation and racism. The Ku Klux Klan emerged, followed by today's white supremacist groups. The virus of hate was never eradicated by Lincoln's magnanimity in 1861. That's why it re-emerged on January 6, 2020 with the failed coup to overthrow the legitimate American government.

Hopefully, President Joe Biden (b. 1942) will not make President Lincoln's great mistake. If the leaders of this revolt, starting with Donald Trump (b. 1946) are not punished, today's fascist *"Radical Republicans"* will be so emboldened, we may be heading toward the *Second American Civil War.*

LINCOLN'S POLICY – (*LINK*-cons *POL*-li-see) *"My policy is to have no policy."* – Abraham Lincoln (1809 – 1865). Lincoln was very pragmatic and flexible. He kept all options open.

LINEAMENT – (*LIN*-ee-ah-ment) Distinctive characteristics, especially facial features. A big mole on one's nose would qualify as an unfortunate lineament.

LINE-AND-STAFF – (*LYN* and *STAFF*) The two types of personnel arrangements in an organization. In a line representation, the employee or officer is directly subordinate to a supervisor. A line organization is strictly hierarchical, proceeding through a chain of command. In a staff representation, the employee or officer is not under the direct control or authority of a supervisor above him. He is somewhat of a freelancer in the organization.

LINE FIRE – (*LYN FY*-er) (also Backfire) A controlled fire intentionally set along the inner edge of a fireline to consume the fuel in the path of a wildfire. The line fire can change the direction or force of the wildfire's convection column. A line fire is literally fighting fire with fire.

LINE-ITEM VETO – (*LYN EYE*-tem *VEE*-to) The ability to cancel specific budget items without rejecting the entire budget. The line-item veto also permits an executive (governor or the president) to veto a rider in a bill while approving the rest of the bill. The Congressional Line Item Veto Act of 1996 was held to be unconstitutional by the Supreme Court in a 1998 ruling, Clinton v. City of New York. Every executive from every political party desires the line-item veto. It would help trim the wasteful fat off bills cutting off unrelated spending proposals.

LINEN – (*LIN*-nen) Yarn and cloth made from the fibers of the flax plant. Linen was our most valuable plant fiber until cotton surpassed its usage. Linen is a durable, hard-wearing fabric. It may be the strongest natural fiber in popular used. Linen has long been used for clothes, sheets, bedding, bandages, and tablecloths. Wild flax fibers (linen) that were spun, dyed, and knotted were found in caves in the Republic of Georgia, dating back 30,000 years. The flax plant with its brilliant blue flowers was domesticated and cultivated for linen in the Fertile Crescent 9,000 years ago. The ancient Egyptians wrapped their mummies in strips of linen that survive today. Until the mid-Middle Ages, linen was the fabric of Europe. In the 12th/13th centuries, wool replaced linen as the fabric of choice in Europe. Wool was replaced by cotton in the 18th century. Synthetics, test tube fabrics have taken over today.

LINGAM – (*LING*-gam) (also Shiva Linga) An aniconic or abstract representation of the Hindu deity Shiva. Lingam means *"evidence"* or *"proof"* of God's existence. The Shiva Linga or Lingam is a stone or metal pillar with a rounded head. It is set on a disc-shaped platform. For the longest time, Western archeologists thought the Lingam to be a phallic symbol, which was plausible, but incorrect. Water is poured on the head of the pillar as a symbolic sacrifice, reminiscent of Christian baptism.

LINGERIE – (lahn-zhuh-*RAY*) A French term for sexy female sleepwear or nightgown. Lingerie is lacy and skimpy, erotically alluring. It is a seductive garment intended to excite a man to participate in intercourse. Lingerie is worn by brides and newlyweds. Some time after the honeymoon, the sexy lingerie gives way to stodgy pajamas.

LINGERIE FOOTBALL – (lahn-zhuh-*RAY FOOT*-bawl) The sport of football as played in the female (LFL) Lingerie Football League. The young ladies are clad in bikini-like uniforms. It is a salacious display of athleticism. Lingerie football is a hybrid of sport and soft-porn. The players are gorgeous, sexy, tough athletes, like female fighters and wrestlers. They take their beatings, as do all football players. Tempers often flare, which results in fights and the tearing off of clothing – to the delight of the fans. These altercations can prove to be quite *"EmBARE-ASSing."* One never knows when he'll be treated to as ass shot, or nipple peek. Watching nearly-naked women gang-tackle each other is very erotic – which accounts for the sport's popularity. Incidentally: The success of lingerie football has spurred the formation of lingerie basketball as well. These sports can only be topped by naked gymnastics.

LINGUA FRANCA – (*LING*-gwa *FRANK*-ka) Latin literally for *"free tongue,"* or language spoke freely throughout the world. There have been a few prominent lingua frankas in the history of civilization. Alexander the Great hoped to make Greek the universal tongue in the spreading of Hellenic *Homonoia*. Jesus spoke Aramaic because that had been the lingua franca of the Persian empire. For the longest time, the Romans had made Latin the universal language, and it remained so, especially in the academe and Church. Muslims worldwide study the Koran in Arabic, the lingua franca of Islam. Today, English is the universal language due the extent of the British empire, and the influence of the U.S.A. If you hope to succeed at any trade, occupation, or profession, anywhere in the world, you better learn English. You cannot be licensed to fly any plane anywhere if you can't speak English, the lingua franca of international flight.

LINGUIST – (*LING*-goo-ist) A language specialist. A professional scholar in language mechanics and evolution.

LINGUONYM – (*LING*-gwon-nim) (also Glossonym or Glottonym) A name for a language. For example: French for France, Polish for Poland, Manx for the Isle of Man.

LINK – According to the Imperial or English System of measurement, a link is almost 8 inches in length.

LINIMENT – (*LIN*-uh-ment) (also Embrocation) A medical preparation, usually an oily substance, topically applied to the skin and rubbed into the muscles. Liniments sooth the pain of sprains, bruises, arthritis and sore muscles. They usually contain alcohol, camphor, balms, and herbal oils. Adding capsicum (the ingredient in hot peppers) will produce a heat rub liniment. The term liniment derives from the Latin *"linere,"* meaning *"to anoint."*

LINO – (*LYN*-oh) An acronym for Liberal In Name Only. (Also, DINO, or Democrat In Name Only.) A perfect example is West Virginia Senator Joe *"Judas"* Manchin (b. 1947). Though elected a Democrat, Manchin votes with the Republicans, and sabotages chances for the advancement of Democratic legislation to help the poor. Manchin is bought by Republican Big Business, particularly the coal industry. Manchin is a disgusting LINO. Another LINO is the perfidious bitch, Arizona Senator Kyrsten Sinema (b. 1976).

She too sold her soul to the Republican corporate capitalists. Both Manchin and Sinema have sabotaged the Democratic agenda, which amounts to a better life for the poor and middle classes. Too, they've greatly aided the Republican chance of winning over both houses of Congress in 2022. Furthermore, these Democrats or Liberals In Name Only have fortified the Republican for the 2024 Presidential Election by tarnishing Democratic President Joe Biden's (b. 1942) legacy.

LION/MAN ENIGMA – (*LY*-on *MAN* en-*NIG*-ma) The strange, conundrum Jesus presents in the <u>*Gospel of Thomas.*</u> *"Blessed is the lion which becomes man when consumed by man; and cursed is the man whom the lion consumes, and the lion becomes man."* This koanistic statement has perplexed scholars for over two millennia. The interpretation taken by the <u>*Liberal Lexicon*</u> reads as follows: The lion represents a beast (a dictator). The man represents the population. The beast or dictator is only blessed when consumed (conquered) by the populous. But the populous is cursed when consumed (conquered) by the beast (dictator). In this case, the populous becomes beastly as well. On a more spiritual level, the beastly lion can symbolize the ego, carnal in man. Man represents the spiritual, divine nature. Blessed is the egoistic lion when consumed by man's spirit and becomes spirit. Conversely, cursed is the spirit of man when consumed by the ego, and the ego (lion) becomes man (beastly). Another perspective of this cryptic pronouncement may have to do with Fascism versus Democracy, Capitalism versus Socialism. If the lion (Fascism, Capitalism) is consumed by man (Democracy, Socialism) the lion becomes blessed. But if the man (Democracy, Socialism) is consumed by the lion (Fascism, Capitalism), the man is cursed. Therefore, when fascistic capitalism is converted into Democratic Socialism, the lion will lay with the lamb, and the man will lay with the lion.

LIPOPHOBIA – (ly-po-*FO*-bee-a) (Lipophobiac) Phobic fear or aversion to fatty foods. Granted, fatty foods, in excess, is unhealthy. So it's prudent to limit the intake of fatty foods. But a lipophobiac is neurotically fearful of fat in her diet. This may have originated from a repulsive experience when a small child with fat. At any rate, if lipophobia interferes with normal daily, professional help must be sought.

LIPOMA – (ly-*PO*-ma) A benign (non-cancerous) tumor consisting of fatty tissues. Lipomas are common and harmless. They are routinely removed. Have them checked out. Never ignore a growth on the body.

LIPOSUCTION – (*LY*-poh-suk-shun) (Liposuck, Liposucked) Adipose removal. Liposuction is the surgical withdrawal of excessive fat from local areas under the skin by means of a small incision and vacuum suctioning. *"Lipos"* is Greek for *"fat"* or *"grease."* Beginning in 1983, liposuction had become a popular form of cosmetic surgery for the affluent obese. Liposuction is a quick-fix solution that successfully trims the body – sometimes, for a while. Understand that adults have a finite compliment of fat cells that formed during youth. New fat cells are not created. The original fat cells simply enlarge. Liposuction physically extracts the fat cells from a localized area of the body. That part of the body will not increase in size without fat cells. But other parts of the body will enlarge, even faster. Excessive calories that are not burned must be stored as fat somewhere. So if the belly had been liposucked, the calories will be deposited as fat on the thighs, breasts, buttocks, even face. Other fat cells will compensate as warehouses for those fat cells that were removed. So with liposuction, you will lose your beer belly. But if you continue to guzzle beer, you will inflate your spare tire, pack your saddle bags, and fatten your fat ass. Then liposuck me all over! Can't do, you'll die. Fat, like blood and skin is a vital component of the organism. A Caveat: The only real way to trim and slim the body is to burn more calories than you store, [read: eat less, exercise more].

LIQUESCENT – (lick-*KWES*-sent) (Liquescence) Melting, or liquefying. Rendering a solid to a liquid state.

LIQUEUR – (li-*KUR*) An alcoholic beverage made from a distilled spirit that has been flavored with fruit, cream, herbs, spices, nuts, or flowers, along with a sweetener. Liqueurs are traditionally served as an after dinner cordial. They are moderately alcoholic, more than wine but less that hard liquor. Brandy is the base for many liqueurs.

LIQUID – (*LIK*-kwid) A watery substance. Liquid has a definite volume but no definite shape. It takes on the shape of the container that contains it. A liquid is a state of matter in which the molecular structure is moderately packed in moderate motion. It is the moderate motion of the molecules that keeps the substance fluid. A liquid is the mid-point between solid and gas. Enough heat added to a solid will ment it, turning it into a liquid. Cool a gas adequately, and you condense it to a liquid.

LIQUID CRYSTALS – (*LIK*-kwid *CRIS*-tals) A state of matter between solid and liquid. A gel or a wax, for instance s a liquid crystal. Glass too is a hard wax, and a liquid crystal.

LIQUIFACTION – (li-kwi-*FAC*-shun) The process by which sediment that is wet starts to behave like a liquid. Coastal communities (like San Francisco) or those with a high water table (like Mexico City) are in particular peril during earthquakes. The churning Earth mixes with water forming a muddy slurry like pudding. Structures collapse readily on a foundation of slurry, caused by liquefaction.

LIRA – (*LIR*-ra) Name of the currency formerly used in Italy, having been withdrawn in favor of the Euro.

LISSOME – (*LIS*-som) (also Lissom) Being lithe, supple, pliable, flexible, limber in body as are ballerinas or acrobats.

LISTENING – (*LIS*-ning) Devoting undivided, concentrated attention to the speaker. Listening is 50% of communication. A good listener is patient and never finishes the speaker's sentence. All too often, a poor listener is rehearsing a response before the entire message is communicated. A good listener acknowledges understanding with assent by utterance (aha) or gesture (a nod). Listening is a courtesy and a communicative skill.

LITANY – (lit-*TAN*-nee) Within a spiritual context, a litany is a long, repetitious series of short prayers, invocations, and supplications often led by a priest or priestess with responses from the group. These are usually rhythmic chant-like pronouncements. The monotonous rhythm can produce a mild hypnotic effect. The Catholic rosary is a litany of prayers.

LITERACY – (*LIT*-er-uh-see) Being literate or able to read and write. One who cannot read or write is illiterate. One who has no concept of reading and writing is alliterate. Literacy, along with numeracy, oracy, and courtesy are the *4C's* of fundamental education. To be considered minimally literate is to read and write on a 4th grade level (as would a 9 year old). Most Americans read at a 6th grade level (age 11). Too, this is the reading level of most U.S. newspapers. To not have acquired literacy in today's world is almost tantamount to blindness. Incidentally: The literacy rate should serve as a gage of the society's level of advancement. But this has proved to not always be the case. Germany was the most literate nation, per capita, in the world, when it turned to Adolf Hitler (1889 – 1945) and the Nazis. Apparently, literacy or education is not necessarily wisdom and compassion.

LITERACY RATE – (*LIT*-er-uh-see *RAYT*) The percentage of a nation's adult, mentally able population, that can read and write. The literacy rate indicates the sophistication of the country's people. Too, it's a report card on the nation's educational system. A literate populous speaks volumes about a nation's priorities. What a government spends its taxes on, is what a government deems important. So nations with high literacy rates put great stock in the welfare of its people. One would expect the richest nation in the world, The United States of America, to have the top literacy rate. Prepare to have your expectations dashes. In 2022, 121 nations have a literacy rate higher than the U.S.A. America's 86% literacy rate ties it with Oman. Fourteen percent of the American population cannot read or write! Arrogant American exceptionalism is, in truth, American mediocrity. In order to curb American hubris, the entire list of nations with a higher literacy rates than America is presented here. At 100%: Poland, Russia, Ukraine, Belarus, Slovakia, Slovenia, Cuba, Andorra, Finland, Liechtenstein, Luxembourg, Norway, North Korea, Latvia, Estonia, Lithuania, Azerbaijan, Tajikistan, Georgia, Armenia, Kazakhstan, Barbados, Turkmenistan, Palau, Uzbekistan; At 99%: Kyrgyzstan, Tonga, Moldova, Croatia, Italy, Hungary, Australia, Belgium, Canada, Czech Republic, Denmark, France, Germany, Iceland, Japan, Monaco, Netherlands, New Zealand, Sweden, Switzerland, Tuvalu, United Kingdom, Samoa, Antigua & Barbuda, Trinidad & Tobago, Micronesia, Cyprus, Romania; At 98%: Montenegro, Maldives, Bulgaria, Marshall Islands, Bosnia & Herzegovina, Mongolia, Uruguay, Austria, Argentina, Serbia, South Korea, Grenada, Israel, Spain, Macedonia; At 97%: Greece, Costa Rica, St. Kitts & Nevis, Albania, Chile; At 96%: Thailand, Qatar, Brunei Darussalam, St, Vincent & Grenadines, San Marino, Singapore, Kuwait, Bahamas; At 95%: Philippines, Nauru, China, Cook Islands, Palestine, Equatorial Guinea, Venezuela, Suriname, Bahrain; At 94%: Saudi Arabia, Panama, Seychelles, Paraguay, Peru, Portugal, Fiji, Vietnam; At 93%: Columbia, Malta, Malaysia, Mexico, South Africa, Indonesia, Myanmar, Turkey, Jordan; At 92%: Bolivia, Ecuador, Dominica; At 91%: Sri Lanka; At 90%: Brazil, Libya, United Arab Emirates, Lebanon, Dominican Republic, St. Lucia; At 89%: Mauritius; At 88%: Jamaica; At 87%: Botswana, Burundi; At 86%: Oman and *The United States of America*. There you have it, the shameful facts. Why is American education lagging so far behind? Economic disparity. *"America has the meanest form of capitalism in the world,"* Professor Robert Reich (b. 1946) reminds us. America ranks #1 in military spending, but 17 nations spend a higher percentage of their GDP (G̲ross D̲omestic P̲roduct) than the U.S.A. on education. The fault lies with the Republican Party, the lackeys of the wealthy. They refuse to spend money on public education, because their handlers have their elite private and charter schools. *"I got mine, to hell with you!"* – Republican Capitalist Credo. Of course, the Republicans blame America's appalling literacy rate on Teacher Unions and bad teachers. The truth is: *"There are bad schools with good teachers, but no good schools with bad teachers."* Indeed, there are very few bad teachers. Teaching is too grueling for a bad teacher to survive very long. Every teacher is an innate missionary.

LITERATI – (lit-ter-*ROT*-tee) Latin for *"Men of letters."* Literati refers to writers. *"Any one who chooses will set up for a literary critic, though he cannot tell us where he went to school, or how much time was spent in his education, and knows nothing about letters at all."* – St. Basil (330 – 379 CE).

LITERATIM – (Lit-ter-*ROT*-tim) Latin for *"letter for letter,"* or *"word for word"*, literally.

LITEROTICA – (lit-ter-*ROT*-ti-ca) Erotic literature or pornographic stories in print. *Playboy, Hustler,* or *Penthouse* magazines qualify as literotica.

LITHE – (*LYTH*) (Lithesome) Being flexible, pliable nimble, limber in body as an acrobat or ballerina.

LITHIC REDUCTION – (*LITH*-ik ree-*DUK*-shuhn) A fancy term for stone chipping, the technology of the Stone Age. Lithic refers to stone. Reduction means to break down in size (reduce), in this case to re-fashion. Lithic reduction refers to the working of stone into handy tools and weapons. Particularly, glassy stone like flint, chert, chalcedony, and especially obsidian (volcanic glass) will chip predictably into razor-sharp flakes. By knapping these stones in a specifically skillful way, one can create rudimentary blades, knives, scrapers, choppers, axes, spear and arrow heads. For roughly 3.4 million years, our ancestors (human and proto-human) the world over utilized lithic reduction at some point in their history. (Some small, isolated groups in Amazonia, and in Indo-Oceania still do.) The advent of metalworking between 4,000 to 2,000 BCE marked the end of the Stone Age and lithic reduction. (The Indians of North America were dependent on lithic reduction at the time of first contact (1492). For 99.9% of human/proto-human history, wood, bone, and stone had served and assured our survival. Incidentally: A flake of obsidian (volcanic glass) produces the sharpest blade in the world, sharper than the finest scalpel. The blade can be a molecule in thickness. In fact, tiny chips of obsidian are used today in microscopic eye surgery. A Stone Age tool used in modern medicine.

LITHIUM – (*LITH*-thee-um) (Li) Named from the Greek *lithos* meaning *"stone."* The 3 protons in its nucleus give lithium its atomic number. It is the 3rd simplest element on the periodic table. Lithium is a soft silvery-white alkali metal, with a black oxidation coating. Lithium is the lightest of all metals, the lightest (least dense) solid element. It will float in water (before it ignites). Lithium is found combined in other minerals. About 25% of lithium was created in the Big Bang (along with hydrogen, helium and beryllium). But unlike the heavy elements, lithium is not cooked up in the stars. The remainder of all the lithium is created in space by collisions. Particles from cosmic explosions like supernovas hit heavier elements, re-arranging their atomic structures, sometimes resulting in lithium. Lithium is used as an alloy hardener, as a reducing agent, and in lithium batteries. *Lithium compounds* impregnated waters were long known as health spas. The water had mysterious curative properties for nervous disorders. That's why people would *"go to take the waters."* It was the natural lithium that calmed their nerves and reduced anxiety. Pharmacological research had discovered that *lithium carbonate* or *citrate* succeed in treating mania and bipolar disorders. Lithium ion batteries have become popular for their light weight, high energy density, and their ability to be recharged. But why do TSA (T̲ransportation S̲afety A̲dministration) officers ask if you are carrying lithium batteries before you board a plane? Because pure metallic lithium can be dangerous. In contact with water, lithium will explode in flames. It will quickly burn and crackle, in a very hot pink-red flame with white smoke. It will give off sparks and burn away in an explosion. The heat can melt the surface on which it burns. Lithium batteries contain a thin ribbon of lithium, wrapped in protective plastic, encased in a small metal cylinder. They should be safe, but keep them dry, away from moisture. On a plane 33,000 feet in the sky, it is better not to take risks. That's why you can't fly with lithium batteries. Incidentally: Lithium has been detected on the surface of the sun. This indicates that a gas giant planet like Jupiter must have crashed into the sun eons ago.

LITHOMETEORS – (*LITH*-o-meet-tee-ors) In meteorology, solid gray particles like dust in the air.

LITHOSPHERE – (*LITH*-o- sfear) Part of the Earth that includes the crust and the rigid upper mantle. Therefore, the lithosphere consists of the solid rock portion of the planet.

LITHUANIAN – (lith-thu-*AY*-nee-a) Oldest *"National"* language in Europe, quite close to the proto-language Sanskrit. (Gaelic is also an ancient tongue. Gaelic is still spoken in isolated parts of Brittany, France and Great Britain, but as a secondary or academic language.)

LITIGATION – (lit-ti-*GAY*-shun) (Litigate, Litigious, Litigator) A lawsuit. Formal challenge, contesting, or trial in a court of law.

LITIGIOUS – (lit-*TIJ*-ee-us) (Litigate, Litigator, Litigation, Litigiousness) Exceedingly ready to litigate or go to court. Litigious individuals are sue-crazy. A litigious individual may be a schemer and scammer who expects to make a living by setting up phony law suits. Incidentally: Perhaps the world record for litigiousness is held by Donald J. Trump (b. 1946). In his book: *Plaintiff in Chief: A Portrait of Donald Trump in 3,500 Lawsuits* (2019) lawyer and author James D. Zirin (b. 1940) traced Trump's 45 years of suing people. In his research Zirin had met hundreds of people of modest or humble means who Trump had destroyed. Plumbers, carpenters, electricians, masons, painters, landscapers, every sort of trade had fallen victim to Trump's deceitful, demonic duplicity. Hundreds testified that Trump owes them thousands. Family businesses have been destroyed by Trump, and the swine is proud of his unscrupulousness. Trump is never pleased with work he had hired and insists on paying only 10 cents on the dollar. When sub-contractors object, Trump's stock reply is always *"Sue me!"* Trump's litigation strategy has always been *"delay, delay, delay,"* until the aggrieved party can no longer afford to pursue the case. Trump wins, the little guy is destroyed. This vile scoundrel wants to be President of the United States, the nation's top cop? See you in court Trump, at one of your own trials.

LITMUS TEST – (*LIT*-mus *TEST*) Litmus is a substance obtained from the *Roccella tinctoria* lichen. In an alkaline environment, litmus turns blue. In an acidic environment, it turns red. This makes litmus the perfect catalyst to indicate the pH level of substances. So in chemistry a litmus test is a simple trial to determine the acidity or alkalinity of a solution. The term litmus test has been adopted by political pundits. In politics, a litmus test is a proof of identity, cohesiveness, and loyalty. For example, voting one way or another on a particular bill may be considered the litmus test of party unity. President Donald Trump (b. 1946) has pushed the litmus test to the realm of paranoia. Inorder to stay in Trump's good graces, all must accept and expound the *"BIG LIE,"* that Trump really won the 2020 Presidential election. Trump's litmus test for subordinates is the sacrifice of their integrity and honor in support of Trump. Trump appointees must lie and cheat for him, and publicly praise him ad nauseum. Frequent *"ass kissing"* is the litmus test for a loyal Trump employee.

LITTERATEUR – (lit-tur-*ROT*-tur) French for one occupied with literature, a literary man.

LITTLE ICE AGE – (*LIT*-tul *EYS AYJ*) The period from the mid-14th century to the mid-19th century during which average global temperatures were lower than during previous and subsequent periods, by at least 2 degrees or more. A drop of a few degrees results in more snow and ice which reflects more solar heat, which makes the planet colder – the *Albedo Effect*. The Little Ice age has been attributed to sunspot activity, lessening solar heat; an increase in volcanism worldwide which blocked solar heat; and disruption of ocean circulation. Whatever its cause, the Little Ice Age had profound historical effects. The cold prevented the Vikings from establishing Scandinavian culture in North America. It produced great rainstorms in Asia, resulting in an explosion of the rat population which spread the Black Death (Bubonic Plague). It caused drought in MesoAmerica that may have done-in the Mayan Civilization. It caused crop failures, famine, revolts and revolutions in Europe. The year 1818 was known as the *"Year without Summer."* In New England, some snow was visible on the ground in every month of the year.

LITTLE TRUMP – (*LIT*-tul *TRUMP*) One who is considered to be a political copy, substitute, or surrogate for Donald J. Trump (b. 1946). Internationally, the Dictopresident of Brazil, Jair Bolsonaro (b. 1955) is called *"Little Trump"* in his country. On the home front, many ass-licking Trumpublican politicians hope to serve as a *"Little Trump,"* inorder to gain Trump's popularity and power. As of August, 2022, the Little Trump leader is Florida's racist Governor Ron DeSantis (b. 1978). Political commentator Joy Reid (b. 1968) perfectly characterized DeSantis as *"Trump with a brain."* That makes DeSantis so very dangerous. It was DeSantis' embrace of Trump, and Trump's reciprocal support, that won DeSantis the governorship in 2018. DeSantis won by a measly 14,000 votes out of millions. Otherwise, he would have been facing political oblivion. Indeed, as he brags, Trump did make DeSantis. DeSantis had studied and modeled himself after Trump, hoping to benefit from Trump's successes. Split-screen comparisons of Trump's and DeSantis' gestures, hand movements, speaking style, phraseology reveals that DeSantis is remaking himself into a Little Trump. It is most embarrassing to watch. DeSantis even now signs bills with a big black marker, as did Trump. Since 2018, DeSantis had consolidated his power and has become emboldened. With Trump's multiple legal problems, Little Trump feels strong enough to challenge Big Trump. In fact, political pundits have referred to DeSantis as *"Trump without the baggage."* DeSantis is an Ivy League lawyer and a fascist. He had suppressed the vote, banned books, and attacked opponents in Florida. He has ruled the state like his personal fiefdom. He has used the culture war like Trump, to rile up the uneducated. DeSantis knows how to sound stupid inorder to appeal to the stupid supporters. If Florida is a template for the nation as a whole, democracy and America are in dire peril. As of today, Little Trump DeSantis is the most dangerous man in America. Update: Little Trump Ron DeSantis deflated. He proved to be a cold, humorless, unlikeable manikin, devoid of personality. DeSantis was forced to drop out of the Republican Presidential Campaign of 2024.

LITTORAL – (lit-*TOR*-ral) The oceanographic name for the seashore of the ocean or a lake.

LIVE PROJECT – (*LIV PRUH*-jekt) Actually, the *"I Want to Live Project"* (*Khochu zhit'* in Russian). The *I Want to Live Project*, established on September 18, 2022, is a surrender hotline operated by the *Main Directorate of Intelligence of Ukraine*. It is designed to help humane Russian soldiers escape the war unharmed. Many Russian soldiers are conscientious objectors to the criminal invasion of the Ukraine. The *I Want to Live* hotline enables them to surrender with honor to the *Ukrainian Armed Forces* in accordance with the protections of the Geneva Convention (1949). Most of the Russian soldiers are ill-trained forced conscripts. Many of them know that this is *"Putin's War,"* not a defense of Russia. According to the *Ukrainian Department of Prisoners of War*, a phone, website and app are available to communicate with Ukrainian forces on the battlefield. After the initial contact, the Russian soldiers must fulfill the conditions. They must cross into Ukrainian-held territory. They must put down their weapons and raise their hands in the air. A mini-drone is sent to the area where the Russian soldiers are located. The soldiers are asked to follow the drone to an *I Want to Live Team*. The entire process is monitored by cameras on the drone. The Ukrainian Team escorts the Russians to a safe zone. Millions of soldiers' relatives have contacted the *I Want to Live* hotline from Russia. To January 2023, over 7,000 Russian soldiers have safely surrendered through the project. The number of defections increase daily. This is a grave and humiliating concern to Vladimir Putin (b. 1952) and the Russian Military.

LIVERPUDLIAN – (liv-er-*PUD*-lee-an) The English dialect of the Liverpudlians, the Irish Brits of Liverpool. Incidentally: The Beatles: John Lennon (1940 – 1980), Paul McCartney (b. 1942), George Harrison (1943 – 2001), Ringo Star (b. 1940), were/are famous Liverpudlians.

LIVERMORIUM – (liv-er-*MOR*-ee-um) (Lv) A transuranic element (#116) named after the Lawrence Livermore National Laboratory in California. Livermorium was discovered in 2000. Livermorium is high radioactive, therefore dangerous. Its life span is instantaneously brief, 56 to 60 milliseconds. Its only use is in nuclear research.

LIVESTREAM – (*LYV*-streem) (Livestreamed, Livestreaming, Livestreamer) A verb meaning to transmit or receive video of an event, especially with commentary on the internet while the event id taking place in real time. Interviews, sporting events, breaking news, most anything can be livestreamed.

LIVID – (*LIV*-id) Discolored completion, usually bluish. However livid also means enraged, incensed, so infuriated that one's face flushes red. *Russian Dictopresident Vladimir Putin went livid, when the warship Moskva blew up and sank."*

LIVING CONSTITUTION – (*LIV*-ing con-sti-*TOO*-shun) Progressive, Liberal philosophy that the U.S. Constitution is not a static dead document. The basic law of the land is a dynamic, growing, living organism. It must change to meet changing conditions in changing times. This has been known as *"loose construction,"* not a tight, word-for-word interpretation. The living Constitution is based on the *"elastic clause,"* (Article I, Section 8), also known as the *"necessary and proper clause."* It states that *"Congress shall have the power to make all laws necessary and proper."* The elastic clause enables the Constitution to stretch beyond its wording to meet any eventuality to assure justice. This scares conservatives fearful for their wealth.

LIVITY – (*LIV*-vi-tee) The Rastafarian concept of righteous, everliving livity. The essence of livity is the realization of the life-force, the energy conferred by *"Jah"* (God). This energy flows through all people and living creatures. This energy is God dwelling within us and is represented by the invocation: *"I and I."* The first I represents God, the second I represents oneself. With livity, Rastafarians meditate on the awareness of I and I. The primary goal of a Rasta's life is to expand his or her livity. This is achieved through prayer, meditation, natural living, which includes a special vegetarian diet, uncut hair, *"ganja":* sacramental marijuana usage, and abiding by the concept of *"One Love,"* for all sentient creatures. This is living livity. Incidentally: Livity, One Love, Rastafarianism practiced worldwide originated on the Island of Jamaica.

LLAMA – (*LA*-ma) A South American animal, the New World camel. The llama is native to the Andes Mountains. It is the largest domesticated animal native to the Americas. (The horse was brought to the New World by the Spanish.). The llama is the only large animal domesticated by the Native Americans as a beast of burden (prior to contact). However, the llama cannot be saddled or harnessed to a plow. It serves as a valuable source of meat and wool and can carry burdens. Llama wool is, in fact, warmer than wool from sheep. The other large American animals like the bison, deer, moose, and antelope are not suitable for domestication.

LLANOS – (*LAH*-nohs) A large, grassy, treeless area of South America, used for grazing and farming. Most of the llanos is located in southern Columbia and Venezuela. – (el el *EL*) An initialism for *"Live Life in Love."*

LO – (*LOH*) An archaic interjection meaning *"look! see!"* The term is frequently found in Biblical expressions. *"And Abram said, Behold, to me thou has given no seed: and, lo, one born in my house is mine heir."* – Genesis 15:3. *"Lo"* dates back to Old English (West Saxon) and was perhaps an abbreviated version of *"lok"* (look). The term appears in the epic poem *"Beowulf."* Today it is usually used as an expression of surprise, as in the phrase *"lo and behold"* (1779). *"And lo, he died of his wounds."*

LOADED DEFINITION – (*LOW*-did def-fin-*NISH*-shun) A propaganda technique of giving a definition to a word in a biases or prejudicial way. The capitalists, for example, would define Socialism as *"A Communist dictatorship where people are not free to own property."* That is a false, loaded definition.

LOADED QUESTION – (*LOW*-did *KWES*-chun) The logical *Fallacy of Complex Question.* A loaded question is a form of sophistry in which a complex question containing falsehoods or the assumption or unfounded presumption of guilt is inferred. In Latin, a loaded question is called *"plurium interrogationum,"* meaning *"of many questions."* A typical loaded question from a MAGAmaniac is: *"Do you believe that crooked Hillary could have received more votes than Trump?"* Another rendition of the loaded question is asking a question for which either a *Yes* or a *No* answer will incriminate the respondent. This loaded question is a verbal trap. The desired answer is already tacitly assumed in the question and no qualification of the simple answer is allowed. For example: *"Have you stopped beating your wife?"* *"Have you quit smoking crack?"* *"Have you stopped soliciting prostitutes?"* *"Answer "YES' or 'NO'."* You're damned with a yes, you're damned with a no. (Incidentally: To a yes-or-no question reply: "I'm to a witness in a court of law.") An alternate form of the loaded question is the *"leading question."* In this case, the question guides the person to respond to a desired answer or answer in a specific way. In other words, the question is framed to elicit the answer desired. Lawyers are expertly trained in asking loaded and leading questions.

LOAM – (*LOME*) A rich friable soil containing a relatively equal mixture of sand, silt, humus, and a somewhat smaller portion of clay. Loam is productive farming soil, perhaps the world's best.

LOAN SHARKING – (*LONE SHARK*-ing) Heartless usury. Loan sharking is a brutal manipulation of a desperate person. It profits off a person in dire need of money, by providing a loan at monstrous interest, perhaps 50%, 80%, or 100%. Loan sharking is a crime practiced by organized crime. Gangsters loan shark, because banksters refuse legal loans. Collateral on a sharked loan can be one's body or life. Broken kneecaps have served as traditional incentive to pay the loan shark.

LOANWORDS – (*LONE*-words) Terms borrowed from another language, and usually naturalized without translation. English has always readily incorporated loanwords. French officially limits foreign words. Though French remains somewhat pure, English is wonderfully rich. For example, *"Café"* was adopted from the French; *"Macho"* was adopted from Spanish; *"Vodka"* was adopted from Russian; *"Khaki"* was adopted from Persian; *"Kielbasa"* was adopted from Polish; *"Pizza"* was adopted from Italian. *"Hotdog"* has been adopted from AmerEnglish. Food terms are readily loaned and barrowed.

LOATH – (*LOHTH*) Unwilling, reluctant, averse, disinclined. *"Donald Trump (b. 1946) is loath to admit that he's a loser."*

LOATHSOME – (*LOHTH*-sum) Disgusting, revolting, repugnant, repulsive, Trumpistic, abhorrent.

LOBBYNG – (*LOB*-bee-ing) (Lobbyist) Legal bribery of government officials by the rich. Lobbying is unethical and should be illegal. Under any other circumstances, lobbying would be considered bribery. However it is too profitable to politicians, so it remains legal. Lobby a cop or judge and you go to jail. Lobby a congressman, and you get a favor. It is lobbying by the rich, which has turned our elected officials into *political prostitutes.* Through lobbying, the de facto capital of the U.S.A. has been transferred from Washington to Wall Street. There are at least 5 lobbyists for each member of Congress, from the banking industry alone. That amounts to 2,700 professional bribers sent to Congress by the banks to corrupt the lawmakers. Billions of dollars have been paid to perfidious politicians. And it all remains legal. Being the party of big business, the lion's share of lobbied loot goes to the Republicans. Corporate money has deafened Congress to the voice of the electorate. Corporate lobbyists have stuffed so much money into Congressional pockets, fists, and ears they cannot hear the electorate. Money has been stuffed in Congressional mouths, so they cannot speak-up for the citizen-consumer. Money has been stuffed in every Congressional orifice by lobbyists. Incidentally: If lobbying was eliminated, the guarantee of dirty lucre would be eliminated, and corrupt legislators would be eliminated. We would be blessed with lawmakers dedicated to the people, not to the corporate capitalists and their personal self- aggrandizement. *"Washington is dominated by big money."* – Socialist Senator Bernie Sanders (b. 1941). *"The universe is not rich enough to buy the vote of an honest man."* – Pope Gregory I (540 – 604 CE). *"An advocate who has been well paid in advance will find the cause he is pleading all the more just."* – Blaise Pascal (1623 – 1662).

LOBOTOMY – (lo-*BOT*-tom-mee) (Also called a *"Prefrontal Leucotomy."*) A lobotomy is a surgical procedure that cuts and interrupts nerve tracts in the frontal lobe of the brain. A lobotomy is a radical, last-option operation. It is rarely performed today, only on patients with intractable psychiatric disorders, or debilitating seizures. A lobotomy patient/victim becomes docile, dull, personality-less. Decades ago, lobotomies were routine in prisons and mental institutions to make inmates easy to manage. Because of the devastating side- effects, *"I'd rather have a bottle in front of me, than a frontal lobotomy."* Incidentally: A ghastly lobotomy incident occurred within the Kennedy family. The beautiful Maryrose Kennedy (1918 – 2005) was born with a learning disability. She was intellectually slow. As a young lady she was vivacious and very popular with the boys. Dad Joseph P. Kennedy Sr. (1888 – 1969) was ashamed of her. He feared that daughter Maryrose would become pregnant. That may have negatively impacted the family's political ambitions. So 1941, Joseph arranged for Maryrose to undergo a lobotomy! She was asked to sing, while the doctor cut into her brain. When she lost the capacity to sing, the surgery was completed. Maryrose also lost the capacity to speak and was rendered mentally retarded. She was institutionalized for the rest of her life. Maryrose died in 2005 at the age of 86.

LOCAL GROUP – (*LO*-cal *GROOP*) A partition of the observable universe. The local group is a congregation of 54 galaxies, including our Milky Way. The local group is 10 million light years across. The local group is 5 million times bigger than our solar system. The local group itself is part of the greater partition, the Virgo Supercluster, (which is 11 times bigger than the local group).

LOCH – (*LOCK*) Scottish Gaelic for *lake.* A loch is a long, deep lake carved by a glacier (a kettle lake). The most famous is the 23 mile long Loch Ness, in northwest Scotland near Inverness. It is purported to be the home of the prehistoric *Loch Ness Monster.*

LOCKDOWN – (LOK-*doun*) (Locked-down) An emergency measure or condition in which people are temporarily prevented from entering or leaving a restricted area or building during a threat or danger. Prisons are locked-down during riots, schools, workplaces, stores, banks, malls, are locked-sown during some terrorist attack. Entire cities can be locked-down during a revolt of the poor. During the Coronavirus pandemic of 2020, entire nations were locked-down. People were required to *shelter-in-place* and maintain *social-distancing.* Business activity ceased. Work stopped. Jobs were lost. The lockdown was an extreme and painful operation to stop the spread of the disease. Incidentally: The lockdown, shelter-in-place, stay-at-home, has transformed *"couch potatoes"* into patriots.

LOCK-DOWN KIDS – (*LOK* doun kids) The present generation of American school children endangered by random shootings. A lock-down drill consists of bolting the classroom doors to protect the students from a crazed gunman. This drill has become as common as a fire drill. It would have been unthinkable a generation or two ago, when the most dangerous weapon in school was a knife. Today's *"lock-down"* generation is reminiscent of the *"duck-and-cover"* generation of the early cold war years. Duck-and-cover represented a foreign threat. Lock-down represents a domestic threat. Too, no one ever got killed ducking and covering. The lock-down crisis is due to the proliferation and easy access to guns, especially military-grade mass murder machines. Guns can be eliminated. However gutless politicians, bribed and fearful of the NRA (N̲ational R̲ifle A̲ssociation) do not have the balls to save the children. This is particularly true of the *"testicularly deficient"* Republicans.

LOCKED-N-LOADED – (*LOCKD* en *LOW*-ded) A threatening expression borrowed from the gun lobby. It indicates that one is armed, capable, and anxious to kill. The phrase was introduced by right-wing, failed politician-cum-celebrity Sarah Palin (b. 1964). Conservative [read: *Republican*] gun advocates love the machoism of this veiled threat. In April, 2018, the Republican UN Representative Nicki Haley (b. 1972) disinterred the phrase warning Syria and Russia that the United States is *"Locked-N-Loaded."*

LOCK EM' UP – (*LOK* em up)A nasty litany from nasty Donald Trump's (b. 1946) 2016 Presidential campaign. The persecutory cry served as *"bloody red meat"* thrown to the vicious animals who attended Trump's beastly campaign rallies. It created a feeding frenzy. This sinister threat was precisely *"Lock Her Up,"* in reference to Trump's Democratic political opponent, Hillary Clinton (b. 1947). It was first inaugurated by Trump sycophant, General Michael Flynn (b. 1958). *"Lock Her Up!"* repeated again and again turned the audience into a frenzied lynch mob,(like *"Seig Heil! Seig Heil!"*). There were attacks and acts of violence on the auditorium floor. The *"Low-Information Voters"* [read: *stupids*] who attended Trump's rallies became the kernel of his base. But Karmic Justice will prevail. Perfidious Michael Flynn soon pleaded guilty to a variety of crimes associated with the Trump campaign. Whenever in public, disgraced Flynn is met with a chorus of *"Lock Him Up!"* Too, it seems more likely each day that the same refrain will follow loathsome Donald Trump. *"Lock Him Up!"* *"Those who dig pits under others, will surely fall into them themselves."* – Psalm 7:15.

LOCKOUT – (*LOK*-out) A company initiated strike. In a lockout, it's the company, management that halts production and worker's paychecks. Management refuses to let employees work until company demands are met. Like a conventional strike staged by the workers, a lockout is a test of endurance. Which side can stand the pain longest, the company's loss of profits, or the worker's loss of wages?

LOCUS – (*LOH*-kus) A place, location, locality. Locus also refers to a center or source, as of activities or power. The term *"locus"* entered English circa 1525. It derived from the Latin *"stlocus,"* meaning *"a place."* *"The locus of power had always been in Moscow."*

LOCUS OF CONTROL – (*LO*-kus of kon-*TROLE*) Locus is Latin for *"location."* Locus of control refers to the location of one's control center, either the internal or external. A person with an internal locus of control is self-disciplined. She does not need an authority figure directing her behavior. A person with an external locus of control requires supervision, to oversight his behavior. The concept of Locus of Control was introduced by Psychologist Julian R. Rotter (1916 – 2014) in 1954.

LODESTONE – (*LODE*-stone) A variety of the mineral magnetite that possesses magnetic polarity and attracts iron. The loadstone was man's first natural magnet.

LOESS – (*LOWS*) A fertile, calcareous, loamy soil, found in Europe, Asia (China), and North America (Mississippi Valley). This light, fertile, yellowish-brown soil is easily displaced and deposited by the wind. Loess is productive farming soil.

LOGGERHEADS – (*LAWG*-ger-heds) Not thick-headed stupid people (like Trump's *MAGAs*). Nor the *Caretta caretta,* or large-headed sea turtle. In this case, being at loggerheads is being in an intransigent, stubborn dispute, disagreement. Parties at loggerheads are not budging, far from compromise. Democratic legislators and MAGA Republicans are at perpetual loggerheads.

LOGIC – (*LOJ*-jic) Branch of philosophy that deals with the nature of reasoning. Logic involves the study of inferences. Logic was formerly called *dialectic* and is presently called *critical thinking*. During the early 20th century, logic made a move out of the realm of philosophy, into that of mathematics (symbolic logic). The philosophic theories of logic are today the purview of semantics. Logic is a left-brain function. As such, it presents only half the picture and answer. Intuition is the right-brain counterpart to logic. Logic is linear, formulaic thinking, in algorithms. Logic is not creative, innovative, and imaginative. These are right-brain functions. Albert Einstein (1879 – 1955) admitted that *"Logic will get you from A to B. Imagination will take you everywhere."*

LOGICAL POSITIVISM – (*LOJ*-ji-cal *POS*-si-tiv-is-um) A school or movement of philosophy developed from the contributions of Auguste Comte (1798 – 1857), John Stuart Mill (1806 – 1873), and Wilhelm Ostwald (1853 – 1931). The base for logical positivism is the belief that knowledge should be restricted to the *"positive"* facts of experience. These three philosophers applied methods of science. They were interested in the prediction of data and used hypotheses and theories as their tools. In the 1920s and 1930s, the logical positivists felt that language was misused, and that much of the language used had no meaning to people. They argued that many academic logical arguments had no meaning because they could neither be verified nor falsified.

LOGICISM – (*LOJ*-ji-siz-um) The theory that mathematics is an extension of logic. Too, only mathematics can relate logical concepts accurately. Words are too vague and imprecise to be logical. The logisists like philosopher Bertrand Russell (1872 – 1970) unsuccessfully tried to make logic into a branch of mathematics.

LOGICOMATHEMATICAL – (lo-ji-co-math-e-*MAT*-I-cal) Relating to the inductive, scientific method of problem solving. Logicomathematical reasoning requires precision, a systematic approach, and proofs.

LOGISTICS – (lah-*JIS*-tiks) (Logistical, Logistician) The planning, coordinating, supplying, and implementing of a plan, program, or operation. Logistics is usually associated with the equipping, supplying of an army in the field. *"An army crawls on its stomach,"* Napoleon Bonaparte (1769 – 1821) declared. That has always been the case and is today. If a general cannot feed his army, it degenerate into a huge, mutinous, armed mob. (That's what happened to the Russian army in World War One, 1917.) Indeed soldiers need food, water, weapons, ammunition, clothing, medicine and transportation. Furthermore, equipment needs to be serviced and repaired. Field hospitals have to be maintained. The wounded must be evacuated. This is all the purview of logistics. In fact, logistics is what professionalizes an army. At present (early May, 2023) the Russo-Ukrainian War rages in the Ukraine. The war disclosed Russia's logistical incapacity. Incompetence, corruption, economic sanctions have impeded the Russian army from supplying their troops with everything necessary to fight. Though the Russian invaders have many more soldiers (albeit demoralized), the Ukrainians have U.S./NATO logistical support. That's why the vastly, outnumbered Ukrainians are winning the war – logistics. They have unlimited supplies and the most modern precision, high-tech weapons available, delivered to them. Incidentally: America supplied the Russian Army the same way in World War Two (1939 – 1945), in order to defeat the German Nazis. *"If it wasn't for American Spam and trucks from Detroit, we would not have been able to win the Great Patriotic War."* – Nikita Khrushchev (1894 – 1971), *Khrushchev Remembers* (1971). Footnote: The ferocious battle, the meat-grinder that was

Stalingrad (August 22, 1942 – February 2, 1943) marked the beginning of the end of Nazi Germany. Logistics was desperate, perilous, on both sides. Low-flying Russian planes had to drop food, medicine, ammunition, crashing to the ground onto their troops. Only the precious vodka came gently floating down on mini-parachutes. *"Amateurs study tactics. Professionals study logistics."* – Military Maxim.

LOGOGRAM – (*LO*-go-gram) A single symbol representing a word or phrase. For Example: % symbolizes percent; # symbolizes number; $ symbolizes dollar; & symbolizes and; < symbolizes less than; > symbolizes more than. All are logograms.

LOGOS – (*LO*-gose) In philosophy and theology the divine reason, the creative thought or plan of the universe. Logos is the word of God.

LOGOTHERAPY – (Lo-go-*THER*-a-pee) An existential psychotherapy predicated on finding meaning in life. It puts high credence in the power of attitude, the last free will. Logotherapy was founded by psychiatrist and Holocaust survivor Viktor Frankl (1905 – 1997).

LOGWOOD – (*LOG*-wood) (Haematoxylon campechianum) A leguminous (pod- bearing) tree of the Caribbean and Central America. The heavy reddish-brown wood yields the dye haematoxylin. This red dye is used as a biological stain. Incidentally: Logwood and fustic dyes were so important in days before the development of Osynthetic dyes that even the ermine robes of English Lords were stained in logwood. Until the 1950's, Jamaica was a major source of logwood.

LOINS – (*LOYNS*) (also Lumbus) The genitals, the pelvic or crotch region. In days of yore, one's offspring were called *"the fruit of my loins."*

LOL – (LOL) An initialism for L̲aughing O̲ut L̲oud. An expression of amusement. LOL is used chiefly in electronic correspondence to draw attention to a joke or amusing statement.

LOLITA SYNDROME – (lo-*LEE*-ta *SIN*-drome) Middle-aged man's lust for a seductive teenage nymphet. The term derives from Vladimir Nabokov's (1899 – 1977) novel <u>*Lolita*</u>, (1955). Perhaps the Lolita Syndrome indicates a covert subliminal pedophilia in many men, the temptation to bite into the forbidden fruit. Incidentally: Wall Street billionaire investment banker and pedophile, Jeffrey Epstein (1953 - 2019) had his *"pimpress,"* Ghislaine Maxwell (b. 1961) procured tender young Lolitas for Epstein's enjoyment. Many were flown to his *"Orgy Island"* (also *"Pedophilia Island"*) in the Caribbean on his private plane named *"The Lolita Express." "There she stood, part shadow, part light. A sight to make an old man young."* Alfred Lord Tennyson's (1809 – 1892) reaction to seeing his gardener's young, gorgeous daughter.

LONELINESS – (*LONE*-lee-ness) A negative emotion not to be confused with *alone* ("all one") which is a positive emotion. Theologian and philosopher Paul Tillich (1886 – 1965) explained that: *"Language has created the word loneliness to express the pain of being alone. And it has created the word solitude to express the glory of being alone."* Loneliness produces depressing lonesomeness. One yearns for human companionship. To be lonely is an empty state of isolation. Spiritual teacher Marc Gafni (b. 1960) maintains that *"Loneliness is the inability to share the essence of who I am, my soul print, with another."*

LONER'S CREDO – (*LONE*-ners *CRAY*-dow) *"Familiarity breeds contempt."* – Quintilian (c. 35 – c. 100 CE).

LONE WOLF – (lohn *WOLF*) In sociology and criminology, a radicalized convert to an extremist religion, cult, or ideology. Though adopting the terrorist organization's mission, the lone wolf works alone in implementing his terrorist agenda. In Medieval England there was a bounty on wolves. Outlaws also had a bounty on their heads. Many outlaws, like wolves, ran in packs or gangs. A good example is Robin Hood (c. 13th century) and his gang of Socialists who robbed the rich and gave to the poor. Solitary outlaws who worked independently were lone wolves.

LONGANIMITY – (long-gan-*NIM*-mit-tee) (Longanimitous) Forbearance. Longanimity is patient endurance of hardship, offense, or injury. The term entered English after 1400 from the late Middle English *"longamimyte,"* which derived from the Latin *"longanimitas,"* meaning *"patience."*

LONG BUBBY SUSAN – (*LONG BOO*-bee *SOO*-san) A mythical, magical Jamaican and Guyanese woman, with breasts that hung below her knees. When threatened, she would flip her breasts over her shoulders and run. The legend of Long Bubby Susan is of African origin.

LONGEST DAY – (*LAWNG*-est *DAY*) June 6, 1944, the day the Allied forces invaded the four beaches of Normandy France from England. The amphibious attack was against Nazi Germany's *"Western Wall"* during World War Two (1939 – 1945). The Longest Day was officially *"Operation Overlord,"* though popularly called *"D-Day,"* for Debarkation Day. The primary Allies were the British, Americans, and Canadians, accompanied by French, Polish, Australian, Czech, Belgian, Dutch, Norwegian, Greek, and New Zealandic forces. The Allied victory on the Longest Day marked the beginning of the end For Adolf Hitler's (1889 – 1945) Nazi empire and regime. The leading commanders on D-Day were U.S. General Dwight D. Eisenhower (1890 – 1969), British General Bernard Montgomery (1887 – 1976), and U.S. General Omar Bradley (1893 – 1981). The German defenders were led by General Gerd von Rundstedt (1875 – 1953), and General Erwin Rommel (1891 – 1944). It was Rommel who coined the term, *"Longest Day."* He had said: *"When the Allies invade, the first 24 hours will be crucial. They must be stopped on the beaches. Those first 24 hours will be the 'Longest Day'."* The Allies were not stopped. They gained a beachhead on June 6, 1944. From there they advanced inland through France, the Low Countries, into Germany. With the Russian juggernaut rolling in from the east, Germany was doomed, and the Second World War concluded.

LONGEVITY CURSE – (lawn-*JEV*-vi-tee *KURS*) The often overlooked curse of living an extraordinarily long life. A centenarian lives to be 100 years of age or longer. A supercentenarian lives to be over 110 years old. Only 1 in 1,000 centenarians gain super status. There are not more than 450 in the world. Is such longevity a blessing or a curse? Much depends on one's physical and mental capacity. To be writhing in pain or a vegetable is no life. But be careful what you wish for because even if one is very healthy and lucid, such an extraordinarily long life has great drawbacks. What joy is there in having to bury all of your children, who had died of old age? All of your friends are long gone too. To your great- great-grandchildren, you are a vague curiosity. You lost any family resemblance decades ago. The technological world around you is as foreign as another planet. The only visitor is the occasional newspaper reporter on a slow news day. Living extremely long may not prove to be a happy way to pass on.

LONG-FORM JOURNALISM – A branch of journalism dedicated to lengthy articles with a great amount of content. Typically, this will be between 1,000 to 20,000 words. Long-form journalism often takes the form of creative nonfiction, documentaries, or narrative journalism. Great historical events are related in long-form journalistic style, like the <u>New York Times</u> *"1619 Project"* of August 2019.

LONG HAIRED ARMY – (*LONG HARED AR*-mee) The many thousands of heroic women who fought the French, then Americans in the two Vietnam Wars (1946 – 1973, then on to 1975). Patriotic women carried supplies and weapons, nursed the wounded, manufactured homemade weapons and booby traps. They suffered from the heat, rain, snakes, leeches, and insects of the Vietnamese jungle. Most North Vietnamese soldiers and Vietcong partisans were city-dwellers as terrified of the jungle as were the French or Americans. The dedicated long haired army may have suffered more than most. *"We killed many American today. They are giants! I don't know why they came here to fight us. Maybe they think we are rich?"* – Vietnamese farmer-cum-soldier.

LONG ISLAND ICE TEA – (*LONG EYE*-land *EYS* tee) A cocktail concoction made with vodka, tequila, rum, gin, triple sec, and a splash of cola. The cola provides the amber color that resembles tea. Long Island icetea has a much higher alcohol content than most cocktails, at least 22%. This is due to the small amount of mixer. The drink was invented by Robert "Rosebud" Butt, employed at the Oak Beach Inn on Long Island. Butt insisted: *"This drink will kick yo butt!"* (a conficta). The cocktail was an entry in a contest to create a new drink using triple sec. Actually, the mishmash called Long Island ice tea could have been made at a college frat party as a pot luck, communal inebriation concoction.

LONGITUDE – (*LAWN*-ji-tood) Imaginary lines running north and south on the globe, which measures the distance east and west. Greenwich, England is the zero degree mark. West from Greenwich to the International Date Line (180 degree mark), is west longitude. East from Greenwich to the Date line is east longitude. Being a sphere, the Earth is 360 degrees around. Since the sunshine rounds the Earth in 24 hours, each of the 360 degrees of longitude occupies 4 minutes of time. A sailor who compares noon on his ship (the highest position of the sun) with noon on a clock that keeps Greenwich time therefore knows that every 4 minutes of difference place him one degree further away from the Greenwich meridian (0 degrees).

LONGITUDINAL – (lawn-ja-*TOO*-din-al) Taking place over a long period. A longitudinal study may take years. Data is collected over a great deal of time, in order to prove valid. In climatology for instance, at least 30 years of observation must be invested for accurate results. Longitudinal studies in sociology may follow a control group through childhood, adolescence, into adulthood.

LONG PORK – (*LAWNG* pohrk) (also Long Pig) Not a reference to the *"male member"* exclusively, but indeed to the male member inclusively. For the term *"long pork"* means human flesh. It is probably a euphemism of anthropological origin. Anthropologists studying cannibals have attested that human flesh is said to taste like pig meat or pork. To the cannibals, the male member can be considered a *"tube steak,"* literally.

LOOSE CANNON – (*LOOS CAN*-non) An unpredictable, unbalanced, and dangerous person, in a position of authority and power. It is no coincident that this term has military implications. Most loose cannons are high ranking military officers. General Douglas MacArthur (1880 – 1964) wanted to invade Communist China with atomic bombs during the Korean War. He was fired by President Harry Truman (1884 – 1972) for being a loose cannon. The quintessential loose cannon was General Curtis LeMay, U.S. Air Force. He said: *"The difference between peace and war is where we put our bombs."* But by far, the most perilous loose cannon is erratic President Donald Trump (b. 1946). Trump is tantrum prone. With his finger on the nuclear button, Trump is a dire threat to world peace, civilization, and human life on Earth.

LOOSE CONSTRUCTION – (*LOOS* con-*STRUCT*-shun) A Liberal or Progressive interpretation of the Constitution. Loose constructionists rely heavily on Article I, Section 8, Clause 18, the *"elastic"* or *"necessary and proper clause"* in the Constitution. It reads: *"Congress shall have the power to make all laws necessary and proper...."* This provision enables Congress to pass laws to meet unexpected contingencies that are not mentioned in the Constitution but are implied by the clause. With implied powers, Liberals stretch the Constitution like elastic to do what is deemed necessary and proper (like eliminating poverty). This scares conservatives who are *"strict constructionists."* They fear that a loose interpretation of the Constitution will enable Progressives to re- distribute their wealth fairly to all. Our Progressive President Theodore Roosevelt (1858 – 1919) declared that *"The Constitution was made for the people, and not the people for the Constitution.... The president has a moral duty to the American people which is higher than his Constitutional duty...."*

LOOTING – (*LOO*-ting) (Looted, Looter) Legally defined as robbery because the rich and powerful control the law (and the loot). In fact, looting is the most efficient form of levelling the wealth and realizing distributive justice. It is instant gratification, relief, justice for the desperately deprived. To the wealthy, looting is a crime. The poor, looting is a compensation for decades of exploitation and oppression. Traditionally, looting has been an accepted aspect of international warfare. *"To the victor goes the spoils,"* (1832) – William Marcy *"Boss Tweed,"* (1823 - 1878), New York Political Boss. Likewise, looting is encouraged as an accepted aspect of class warfare. Looting is a vital contributor to the *"underground economy,"* when the capitalist economy is closed to the poor. *"When the looting starts the shooting starts."* – President Donald Trump's (b. 1946) deadly warning. For capitalist Republicans, protecting property always trumps protecting lives.

LOQUACIOUS – (lo-*KWAY*-shus) Garrulous, over-talkative, babbling non-stop. Incidentally: Research indicates that women are 3 times (300%) more loquacious than are men.

LORD – (*LAWRD*) (Lordly, Lordship, Landlord) An aristocrat, nobleman, duke, baron, count in control of a county and all who reside within. The original Old English (West Saxon) word for lord was *"hlafweard,"* literally meaning *"keeper of the loaf"* – translation: *"controller of our bread."* The term hlafweard reduced to *"hlaford"* meaning *"ruler,"* which evolved by the mid-13th century to *"laverd,"* then *"loverd,"* finally to lord. The Lord of the land [read: *Landlord*] had life-or-death power over his serfs. Their tenancy rested on the Lord's pleasure. The peasants, villeins, commoners were obliged to pay homage to his Lordship.

Lords were treated with deference, reverence under pain of punishment. *"Aye me Lord,"* head bowed, hat in hand became customary. Lordships were hereditary. They were passed down from father to son. To be a lord was an accident of birth (a member of the *"lucky sperm club"*). The Lord's son, that pudgy little shit, is *"His Lordship"* as well. *"Because you are a great nobleman, you think you are a great genius. You have taken trouble with nothing, except to be born."* – Pierre de Beaumarchais (1772 – 1799), in <u>The Marriage of Figaro</u> (1786). The original lords were bullies who became tribal chiefs and their henchmen. They carved out exclusive territory and extorted produce from the weak who dwelled in it. (*"Steal a loaf and you're put in prison. Steal a land and you're made a lord,"* – Polish Proverb.) Eventually, the most ruthless lord, the lord-of-lords came to be called king. The king reserved the power to create lords of those who would help secure his power. Medieval lordship was based on land ownership, the source of wealth. Modern lordship is based on corporate ownership, the source of wealth. Today, we pay homage directly (or indirectly through our *"lobbied"* legislators) to Lord Bezos (b. 1964) of Amazon, Lord Musk (b. 1971) of Tesla, Lord Gates (b. 1955) of Microsoft, and Lord Zuckerberg (1984) of Facebook. These centibillionaires will continue to lord over us because: *"Who controls the money controls the world."* – Henry Kissinger (b. 1923).

LORD'S PRAYER – (*LAWDS PRAY*-yer) The *"Our Father."* The Lord's Prayer is an abridgement of Jesus' (c. 7-2 BCE – 30-33 CE) Sermon on the Mount. It is Christianity in a nutshell. The Lord's Prayer is the only ritual uniting all Christian sects and denominations. It reads: *"Our Father, who art in heaven, hallow be Thy name. Thy kingdom come, Thy will be done on Earth as it is in heaven. Give us this day our daily bread and forgive us trespasses. As we forgive those who trespassed against us. And lead us not into temptation. But deliver us from evil. For Thine is the kingdom, the power, and the glory. Amen."* In December, 2017, Pope Francis I (b. 1936) suggested to change a line in the Lord's Prayer. *"Lead us not into temptation"* would be changed to *"Do not let us fall into temptation."* The original version *"Is not a good translation"* the Pope said. It incorrectly suggests that God leads us to sin. The French Catholic Church already uses the revised rendition.

LORD'S PRAYER – (*LAWDS PRAY*-yer) The following is a modernized rendition of the *"Our Father,"* influenced by *"New Thought Christianity."* *"Our Father, who art within us, hallow be our name. Our kingdom come, our will be done, in the heavenly state that resides within us. Give us this day our eternal grace, blessing us with love, as we bless those who You love as well as us. And lead us only into peace, by delivering us from our selfish ego. For ours's is the kingdom of unity, holiness, and love, for ever and ever. So mote it be."* – Dr. Gary J. Pasieka (b. 1951), June 8, 2016.

LORD'S PRAYER – (*LAWDS PRAY*-yer) Popularly known as the *"Our Father."* This prayer is the only ritual uniting all Christian denominations and sects. The Lord's Prayer was first pronounced by Jesus in his famous *"Sermon on the Mount."* It has been translated into every major language on Earth. As with any prayer, it makes no difference in what language it is uttered. Being Jewish, Jesus spoke Aramaic in that place at that time. According to Luke 11: 1-2, and Matthew 6: 7-8, *"One of his disciples asked: 'Lord, teach us to pray.' And Jesus said to them: 'When you pray, say': "Abun D-bashmayo* (Our Father in Heaven) *Neth Qadash Smokh* (Hallowed be your name). *Tithe Malkuthokh* (Your kingdom come) *Nehwe Sebyonokh* (Your will be done) *Aykano D-bashmayo* (As in heaven) *Oph Bar 'O* (So on earth). *Hab_lan lah mon D-sunqonan Yowmono* (Give us the bread we need today) *Wa-sbuq lan Hawbayb wa-htohayn* (and forgive us our sins and debits), *Aykano dof hnan* (As we too forgive those), *Sbaquan l-hayobayn* (who sin against us). *Lo ta 'alan l-nestuno* (Do not bring us to trial) *Ela faso lan Men biso* (But deliver us from evil). *Metul d'dilokh hi malkutho* (For yours the Kingdom) *W-haylo W-thes 'buhto* (The power, and the glory) *L 'olam 'olmin.* (To the ages of ages). *Amin.* (Amen)."

LORD PROTECTOR – (*LAWD* pro-*TEK*-ter) The title issued to Oliver Cromwell (1599 – 1658), the Puritan autocratic dictator of England (1653 – 1658). It is human nature to desire a strong leader in time of peril. In times of troubles, people will unwisely trade liberty for security. *"Those who would give up essential liberty, to purchase a little temporary safety, deserve neither liberty nor safety,"* declared Benjamin Franklin (1706 – 1790). Thomas Jefferson (1743 – 1826) declared that *"A society that will trade a little liberty for a little order will lose both and deserve neither."* Bill Clinton (b. 1946) observed that *"When people are uncertain, they'd rather have leaders who are strong and wrong, than right and weak."* Frightened, confused people will pray to the Lord for a protector – a Lord Protector. He is always an autocrat, despot, tyrant, dictator. This occurred time and again throughout history. In modern times, we saw this happen in Italy with Benito Mussolini (1883 – 1945), in Germany with Adolf Hitler (1889 – 1945), and in America with Donald Trump (b. 1946). Back in the 7th century BCE, the people of Israel asked their Prophet Samuel (c. 1070 – c. 1012) for a Lord Protector. *"Appoint for us a king to judge us like all the nations"* (1 Samuel 8:22). Samuel warned his people to beware of what they wished for! Samuel said: *"This will be the manner of the king that will reign over you: He shall take your sons, and appoint them for himself, for his chariots, and to be his horsemen; and some shall run before the chariots. And he will appoint them captains over thousands, and captains over fifties; and he will set them to ear his ground, and to reap his harvest, and to make his instruments of war, and instruments of chariots. And he will take your daughters to be confectionaries, and to be cooks, and to be bakers. And he will take your fields, and your vineyards, and your olive yards, even the best of them, and give them to his servants. And he will take the tenth of your seed, and of your vineyards, and give to his officers, and to his servants. And he will take your menservants and your maidservants, and your goodliest young men, and your asses, and put them to his work. He will take a tenth of your sheep: and ye shall be his servants."* – (1 Samuel 8:10-18). Nevertheless, the Israelites got their king. And in about 106 years, their nation was divided between Israel and Judah. The lesson: *"Beware of false messiahs."* – Psychiatrist Wilhelm Reich (1897 – 1957).

LOSING WEIGHT – (*LOOS*-ing *WAYT*) Lightening the body by reducing its size. Bone cannot be reduced, and muscle must not be reduced. Only fat can be reduced in a weight loss program. Remember: *"You only put on, what you put in; and lose what you use."* Losing weight is somewhat like accounting or banking. In this case, you are counting calories. You make deposits and withdrawals, but in fat units (calories). Eat more (deposits) and you'll have greater fat deposits. Eat less (withdrawals) and you'll deplete your account of fat deposits. Weight gain is like interest accrued on deposits. In this case however, the intension is to spend, not save fat deposits. Staying with the financial analogy, if you increase your expenditures (of energy) you will lose fat and weight. You must exercise. Too bad accumulating wealth isn't as easy as accumulating weight. Conversely, too bad losing weight isn't as easy as losing wealth. Incidentally: The record for losing weight has to be held by Russian Cosmonaut Alexei Leonov (1934 – 2019) on March 18, 1965. On that day, Leonov became the first human being to *"walk in space."* It was both an historic and hysteric day. After 10 minutes floating outside the space capsule, the cosmonaut was ordered back in. However pressure change caused his spacesuit to blow up like a balloon. He couldn't fit through the opening of the spacecraft. In 5 minutes, Leonov would be in the total darkness of Earth's shadow. So he released the gas from his suit, deflating himself. But the interior of the suit began to heat up. Leonov was cooking and profusely sweating. His boots were filling up with body sweat. Thankfully, he squeezed back into the spacecraft. However, Alexei Leonov had lost 13 pounds in 10 minutes, about 10% of his total body weight.

LOS PEPES – (los *PEP*-pees) Los is Spanish for *"The."* Pepes is a contrived term derived from the Spanish "PEseguidos POr Pablo EScobar," (*"People persecuted by Pablo Escobar"*). Los Pepes was a Columbian governmental/vigilante group composed of police, military, and enemies of drug lord Pablo Escobar (1949 – 1993). Los Pepes was supported by the U.S. Delta Force. Escobar was the *"King of Cocaine,"* Lord of the Medellin Drug Cartel. Escobar was a ruthless killer. Therefore, Los Pepes operated just as mercilessly. They performed as a secret, extra-legal terrorist organization. With American help, they intercepted the 10 most frequent phone communications made by Escobar. Then Los Pepes intercepted the 10 most frequent calls made by each of the first ten. In this way, they got a good picture of the cartel's organizational chart. Now, to find the Drug Lord. Los Pepes targeted everyone associated with Escobar. Chauffeurs, butlers, bookkeepers, attorneys, bodyguards, business associates and their families were killed. It was a systematic reign of terror. Escobar was deserted, isolated, and on the run. In 1993, Pablo Escobar was located, wounded, and executed by Los Pepes on the roof of a building. Law and order can be achieved at the cost of democracy and humanity.

LOSS – (*LAUS*) (Lost, Losing) Experiencing a hurtful feeling of deprivation, associated with losing something precious. We suffer 3 types of experiences that generates this ill feeling: loss of love, loss of control, and loss of self- esteem. Too, if the loss is anticipated in the future, it is felt as fear. If the loss is taking place in the present, it is perceived as pain. If the loss has occurred in the past, it can manifest as anger. Absorbing the loss of material goods is a painful experience. Even in the case of theft, the loss may be Karmic, a Divine redistribution of the wealth. Jesus instructed us that *"If someone takes your shirt, let him have your coat as well."* – (Matthew 5: 38 – 42). The great 13th century Sufi philosopher Rumi (1207 – 1273) consoled us about loss. *"Don't grieve. Anything you lose comes back in another form."* *"You possess only whatever will not be lost in a ship wreck."* – Persian Philosopher Al-Ghazali (1058 – 1111).

LOST – (*LAWST*) Having missed the way or gone astray. A lost person is bewildered as to direction or place. The lost have consulted the wrong map – the wrong material, emotional, or spiritual map. Nevertheless, *"Not all those who wander are lost."* – J.R.R. Tolkien (1892 – 1973). Sometimes, the only way to find ourselves is to get lost. Wandering in the wilderness has long been the mystic's means of acquiring enlightenment. Both John the Baptist and Jesus wandered the wilderness. *"Not until we are lost do we begin to understand ourselves."* – Henry David Thoreau (1917 – 1862).

LOST GENERATION – (*LAWST* jen-er-*RAY*-shun) In Western culture, the population cohort born between the years 1883 – 1900. The Lost Generation was in early adulthood during World War One (1914 – 1918). Many suffered the horror of fighting that war. They were a generation *"lost"* in the sense of being disoriented, directionless, wandering spirits in the early postwar period. It was as if the youth who had survived the war suffered from a collective post- traumatic neurosis. The term *"Lost Generation"* is also applied to a group of disillusioned American expatriate writers who congregated in Paris in the 1920s. One of the most prominent was Gertrude Stein (1874 – 1946) who coined the term *"Lost Generation."* Another lost soul was the writer and Great War veteran Ernest Hemingway (1899 – 1961). He popularized the term in the epigraph for his novel, *The Sun Also Rises* (1926): *"You are all a lost generation."* The postwar peace did not bring relief, but rather further death with the outbreak of the Spanish Flu pandemic. Those who survived the disease went on a collective crazy spell during the Roaring Twenties. But the Great Depression silenced the roar and crashed the party for the Lost Generation in 1929. The Lost Generation was succeeded by the *"Greatest Generation"* (1901 – 1927) who resumed the Great War by definitively winning the Greater War. Incidentally: Harry Truman (1884 – 1972) was the first and only President from the Lost Generation. The last surviving member of the Lost Generation, known to have been born during the 19th century died in 2018.

LOST WAX PROCESS – (*LAWST WAKS PROS*-ses) Ingenious ancient sculpture technique. An intricate wax sculpture in molded. It is encased in a block of clay. The clay takes the form of the wax sculpture. The clay is fired, hardening it into a hollow cast or mold of the sculpture. The *wax* vaporizes and evaporates and so is *lost* in the *process*. Molten metal is poured into the clay caste or mold. When the metal cools, the clay is chipped away, leaving the metal sculpture. This process has persisted for millennia. It created the marvelous bronzes of Benin/Dahomey Africa.

LOST YEARS (of Jesus) – (*LAWST YEERS*) The period between the ages of 12 and 30, of which we know nothing about Jesus. These were his educational years, when he learned the *"Social Gospel,"* and *"Noetic Arts."* Many believe that Jesus travelled and studied in Asia (India and Tibet). At the feet of Lamas, Brahmans, and Yogis, Jesus became a mystic. Like Buddha, Jesus was worshiped by Magi, wise men at birth. When a Buddha dies, it is customary that a delegation of wise men search the world for the infant destined to be the new Buddha. When the baby matures to boyhood, he is taken from his parents to the Far East, to be educated and dedicated to God as the Buddha. This may account for Jesus' Lost Years, and Buddhistic philosophy. Like the Great Buddha 500 years earlier, Jesus commenced his public ministry at age 30.

LOTHARIO – (low-*THAR*-ree-o) A compulsive womanizer. A lothario is a man who obsessively seduces and deceives women. *"Love 'em and leave 'em"* is his credo. A lothario is a libertine who approaches winning-over females as a game, a sport, *"a hunt for cunt"* in the vulgar vernacular. Originally, the term was the name of a notorious character in a play by Nicholas Rowe (1674 – 1718) *The Fair Penitent* (1703). Since the 18th century, lothario has been synonymous for a foppish, unscrupulous rake.

LOTTERY – (*LOT*-ter-ree) A gamble at the numbers game. Numbered tickets are sold. The ticket with the winning number is awarded the prize. The term lottery first appeared in English in the 1560's. The term was taken from the Italian *"lotteria,"* which derived from *"lotto,"* meaning *"lot, portion, share."* Playing the lottery is participating in a game of chance, like casting lots (dice). In fact, the term *"lot"* is taken from the Old English (West Saxon) *"hlot"* meaning *"what falls to a person by lot or chance."* In a sense, the lottery is a desperation tax, a regressive tax voluntarily assumed by those least able to afford it. In this respect, the lottery is a poverty tax. Devout Muslims do not play the lottery. This form of gambling is prohibited by

Islam, because one wins at the cost of thousands losing. Incidentally: In 2017, Americans spent more on lotteries than on books, videos, magazines, and movie shows combined. This speaks volumes concerning people's faith in the economy and future. Only an act of God will provide prosperity in this capitalist economy. Furthermore, by the year 2022, the average American lottery hopeful spent $285 dollars annually. At $2.00 a ticket, that's 142 tickets. Foot Note: With the obscene transfer of wealth to the top, the American dream has been reduced to winning the lottery!

LOTTERY PRAYER – (*LOT*-ter-ree *PRAY*-er) An invocation to God, to enable you to win the lottery. *"Mother/Father God, Bless this lottery ticket. Enable me to win this contest, not for self-indulgence or self-aggrandizement, but so I will be able to serve as an Angel Agent, and feed the poor, as did my Socialist Brother, Jesus. So mote it be!"*

LOTUS – (*LO*-tus) The water lily. An aquatic plant having shield-like leaves and large, magnificent, multi-colored flowers that protrude from the water. The delicate unfurling of the lotus petals serves as a profound symbol, representing the continuous expansion of the soul and its inherent capacity for spiritual growth. The lotus has long served as a Buddhist symbol of divinity, purity, spiritual enlightenment, and of Buddhism. The Buddha (c. 563 – c. 483 BCE) instructed us to live like the lotus. It is clean, fragrant, and beautiful, though it dwells in a pond of mud. The Buddha taught: *"As a lotus flower is born in water and rises out of water to stand above it unsoiled, so I, born in the world, raised in the world having overcome the world, live unsoiled by the world." "As the lotus rises on its stalk unsoiled by the mud and water, so the wise one speaks of peace and is unstained by the opinions of the world." "Om mani padme hum,"* (Hail to the Jewel in the Lotus), Buddhist Prayer.

LOUISIANA PURCHASE – (loo-*WEES*-see-ana *Pur*-chas) (1803) The greatest real estate deal in world history. The young United States bought 828,000 square miles of North America from France for $15 million dollars ($254,922,773 in 2017 dollars). That amounted to 3 cents an acre (about $9.24 in 2017 dollars). The transaction was concluded between President Thomas Jefferson (1743 – 1826) and General Napoleon Bonaparte (1769 – 1821). The Purchase consisted of all the land from the Mississippi River to the Rocky Mountains, from Canada to the Gulf of Mexico. This included the territory of 15 states: Arkansas, Missouri, Iowa, Oklahoma, Kansas, Nebraska, parts of Minnesota, North Dakota, South Dakota, New Mexico, Texas, Montana, Wyoming, Colorado, and Louisiana, with its great port of New Orleans. With the sweep of a pen, the size of the United States was doubled (a 140% increase, to be exact). The non- Native population was only about 60,000 (half of whom were slaves) in this vast region. Why did Napoleon do it? Because he had just lost his Caribbean colony of Santo Domingo (Haiti) in a great slave rebellion. Without his vital Caribbean naval port, Napoleon could not defend French interests in the Western Hemisphere. He would either sell Louisiana cheaply to the Americans for something or lose it to the Americans for nothing. Incidentally: The entire Louisiana Purchase was illegal, unconstitutional. The President cannot conclude a treaty with a foreign nation without the approval of the Senate. Jefferson approved the purchase himself. As Jefferson put it: *"The Executive, in seizing the fugitive occurrence which so much advances the good of their country, have done an act beyond the Constitution…. It is the case of the guardian investing the money of his ward in purchasing an important adjacent territory, and saying to him when of age, I did this for your good!"*

LOUT – (*LOUT*) (Loutish, Louting, Louted) As a noun, a lout is an oaf – a stupid, awkward, clumsy person. As a verb, to lout is to treat someone with scorn, contempt. The term *"lout"* entered English in the 1540s meaning *"an awkward fellow, a boor or bumpkin."* The term may have derived from the Middle English *"louten,"* meaning to *"bow down"* (c. 1300) which in turn derived from the Old English (West Saxon) *"lutan,"* meaning *"bow low."*

LOVE – (*LUHV*) A form of electromagnetic energy, as are all thoughts and emotions. Love is a power source, a vibratory frequency that can be felt like the sun's radiation. Therefore, love, like everything else in the universe is light. So to love is to be literally enlightened. Love is the life-force that animates us all. It is the sense of union among all creatures at the soulful level. *"Anyone who does not love does not know God, because God is love."* – 1 John 4:8. A sign of love is wanting someone to be happy, even if you are not a part of it. Love is seeing yourself in another. In fact, Love is the strongest force in the universe. Though we all Love Life, most will sacrifice their Life, in Love for our Loved ones. However, *"Love is granting another the space to be the way they are and the way they are not."* – Werner Erhard (b. 1935). Love is recognizing the Christ in you, and in others too. Different personalities have different love priorities. Liberals love mankind and good works. Conservatives love industry and tradition. Nevertheless, everyone must feel loved. The Swedish proverb says, *"Love me when I least deserve it, because that's when I really need it."* Love is not confined only to people. All of nature deserves our love. The Buddha said: *"I have love for the footless, for the bipeds too I have love; I have love for those with four feet, for the many footed I have love."* Incidentally: Love is defined in the dictionary. It is listed somewhere between Like and Lust. Incidentally: Romantic love lasts a year, after that attachment love sets in. *"Love is not a sentimental attachment to a human being. Love is a mode of conduct that comes from the heart."* – Ma Jaya (1940 – 2012). *"Love on its essence is spiritual fire."* – Emanuel Swedenborg (1688 – 1772).

LOVE CHILD – (*LUHV CHILD*) A baby born out of wedlock. A love child is usually the result of an unwanted pregnancy, the progeny of a love affair. Therefore, a love child is usually fatherless.

LOVE HANDLE – (*LUHV HAN*-dal) An affectionate appellation for a ring of fat around the midsection, along both sides. Love handle usually applies to men. It is less affectionately called the *"spare tire."*

LOVE LEVELS – (*LUHV LEV*-vels) Looking for *love?* It's to be found in the dictionary between *like* and *lust*. The dictionary will provide the different levels of love. *Philia* is fondness or showing an affinity toward something. For example: *"I love Philosophy, History."* *Eros* refers to sexual love, and lust. For example, *"I love Suzanne's breasts."* Agape (a-*GOP*-pay) is spiritual love for God and mankind. For Example, *"I love the human family." Ordinary love is selfish, darkly rooted in desires and satisfactions. Divine love is without condition, without boundary, without change. The flux of the human heart is gone forever at the transfixing touch of pure love."* – Sri Yukteswar Giri (1855 – 1936).

LOVELORN – (*LUHV*-lorn) Loveless. Being without love or a lover. Having been forsaken by one's lover. Lovelorn is a miserable condition. It's not just the absence of a sex partner, masturbation can ease that tension. To be lovelorn is to feel absolutely uncared-for. Everyone needs someone, at least one person, who recognizes their existence, and care about their wellbeing. Please find a lovelorn person. Grant them a little attention, recognition, time, and appreciation. This is what Jesus would do. *"Truly, I say unto you, as you did it to one of the least of these my brothers, you did it to me."* – Jesus, in Matthew 25:40. "Forgive a sinner, and wink your eye at a homely girl." – H. L. Mencken's (1880 - 1956) epitaph.

LOVEMAP – (*LUHV*-map) One's secret sexual wish-list. The concept of lovemap was originated by sexologist John Money (1921 – 2006) in his book: *Love and Lovesickness: the Science of Sex, Gender Differences and Pairbonding* (1980). Dr. Money defined the lovemap as: *"A developmental representation or template in the mind and in the brain depicting the idealized lover and the idealized program of sexual and erotic activity projected in imaginary or actually engaged in with that lover."* The lovemap need not be a graphic recorded on paper. It is a serious consideration of one's sexual personality, identity. When lovemapping, one must be candidly honest, uninhibited. It is a confession, a declaration of one's erotic desires. It maps-out one's covert fantasies, fetishes, and expectations. The love map defines what you want from a lover. It may prevent your mate from freaking-out in bed. (*"Oh my God! who's that naked couple in our bedroom!?" "Oh Honey, I didn't tell you…."*) Sex is a vital link in a successful marriage. A lovemap will assure compatibility. *"There were maps that lived, maps that one could study, from over, and add to: maps, in short, that really meant something."* – Naturalist Gerald Durrell (1925 – 1995).

LOVE TRIANGLE – (*LUHV TRY*-ang-gal) A romantic relationship involving 3 people. Like the geometrical figure, there are 3 sides to the relationship which can only accommodate two. Therefore, a love triangle is a complicated conflict. Two men love one woman; Two women love 1 man; One woman loves 2 men; or One man loves 2 women. A love triangle is heartbreaking in any case, infinitely more when marriage is involved in the mix. Indeed, love is blind. Too, love can blind one to all propriety. Love triangles often are broken by murder. *"My heart is a great mansion of many rooms."* It is perfectly normal to dear love more than one person at a time. Unfortunately, society and human nature cannot tolerate this degree of sharing.

LOW BLOW – (low *BLOW*) A boxing expression for an illegal punch below the belt, unfair, unsportsmanlike. The term has been expanded to mean an exceedingly unscrupulous attack or insult. A low blow goes far beyond the pale and is totally uncalled for. *"That racial slur was a low blow."*

LOWBROW – (*LOW*-brow) A lowly-educated, bigoted, easily duped individual. The press has generously designated lowbrows as *"low-information voters."* Lowbrows constitute the base of President Donald Trump's (b. 1946) support. They are poor, uneducated disgruntled individuals, as id Trump. They see themselves in Trump and fanaticize on his wealth). Lowbrows populate the Trumpublicans, the MEGAmaniacs.

LOW HANGING FRUIT – (loh *HANG*-ing *FROOT*) Literally, edible produce suspended from a tree but near the ground for easy picking. Low hanging fruit is readily accessible, so is usually gathered first without difficulty. As an idiomatic cliché, *"low hanging fruit"* means anything that proves to be easy pickings. The simplest, most effortless task in any project or job is the low hanging fruit. It is often completed first. For example: *"The army closed the salient, and the enemy soldiers trapped inside were low hanging fruit."*

LOW-INFORMATION VOTER – (low *IN*-for-*MAY*-shun *VOH*-ter) A kind appellation for an unschooled, uneducated, ignorant, often stupid member of the electorate. Due to their lack of learning, most low-information individuals tend to be conservative, closed-minded, prejudiced, bigoted, even racist. Low-information voters are easily duped. They readily fall for right-wing propaganda. The low-information electorate is white and poor. Nevertheless, they enthusiastically vote against their own economic interests, because of their stupidity. They fanatically supported the fascist demagogue, Republican Donald Trump (b. 1946) in the 2016 Presidential campaign. Low-information voters frustrated Winston Churchill (1874 – 1965). The Prime Minister maintained that *"The best argument against democracy is a 5 minute conversation with the average voter."* The French Socialist Louis Auguste Blanqui (1805 – 1881) was kinder to the low-information voter. *"The poor do not know the source of their miseries. Ignorance, the daughter of bondage, makes them a docile instrument of the privileged...."*

LOW-INTENSITY VOTERS – (low in-*TEN*-si-tee *VOH*-ters) Constituents with weak enthusiasm and ambition for voting. Actually, the term *"low-intensity voters"* is a tepid political euphemism for *"lazy citizens."* A low-intensity voter is a rung above a no participating voter, but a rung below a *"low-information voter."* The ability to vote is the soul of democracy, or people rule. To display low intensity for voting is to display low intensity for democracy and liberty.

LOW PRESSURE – (low *PRESH*-shur) In meteorology, low barometric pressure (L). The uneven heating and cooling of the ground produces air pressure differences. With low pressure, the weight of the air weighs less heavily on the ground. Lighter air rises, cools, forming clouds which produce rain and snow. A low pressure trough will produce cloudy, humid, rainy, snowy, stormy weather. Tornadoes and hurricanes are ultra-low pressure systems.

LOW-TECH ADVANTAGE – (low-*TEK* ad-*VAN*-taj) Low-tech implies simplicity. What is simple is easy, which, in turn is efficient. This entry considers the advantages of low-tech weaponry. Guerrilla warfare, partisan combat is inherently low-tech, albeit highly successful. What is truly low-tech is home made. The classic example of a low-tech weapon is the Molotov cocktail, a gasoline bottle firebomb. The Viet Cong demonstrated the efficacy of low-tech booby traps against the high-tech U.S. Army in the Vietnam War (c. 1963 – 1973). In the Iraqi conflicts (2003 – 2011), low-tech IEDs (Improvised Explosive Devices) succeeded in injuring the dominate Americans from the shadows. Much of low-tech weaponry is improvised, makeshift. So low-tech is low-cost. Actually, the ultimate smart-bomb is the low-tech suicide bomber. Today (May 2024) the vastly outnumbered Ukrainian forces are holding back and defeating the superior Russians with cheap, toy-like drones. Patriotic Ukrainians who cannot fight are being trained to manufacture drones as a cottage industry. A small hand-held helicopter drone costing about $100 dollars can blow up a tank costing hundreds-of-thousands of dollars with a grenade bomb. Drones the size of large kites or small planes, made of plastic or wood can carry an explosive payload that can destroy a building. This low-tech weapon may cost a couple thousands of dollars. The enemy will be required to expend a high-tech guided missile costing millions to shoot down the cheap drone. Low-tech weaponry is cheap and simple to operate. They don't require extensive, expensive training. Low-tech weaponry evens the playing field (or rather the battlefield) for a poor man's army. Remember: Wars are won by men and by money. If an army runs out of men, it loses. However, if an army runs out of money, it also loses.

LOX – (*LOCKS*) Brine-cured salmon, having either a salt cure (Scandinavian lox) or a sugar cure (Nova Scotia lox) often eaten with cream cheese on a bagel. Lox is particularly a Jewish delicacy cuisine.

LUBBER – (*LUHB*-ber) (Lubberly) A big, clumsy, stupid person. A lubber is a real lout. Originally, a lubber was an awkward, incompetent sailor.

LUAU – (*LOO*-au) A traditional Hawaiian feast, usually held outdoors, accompanied by Hawaiian entertainment. The traditional cuisine served at the luau includes: *"kalua pua'a"* – whole roast pig cooked in an underground oven (buried in the sand); *"poi"* – a thick pudding made from cooked breadfruit, taro, or plantain; *"poke"* – diced raw fish; *"lomi salmon"* – a tomato and salmon salad; *"opihi"* – sea snails or limpets; *"laulau"* – cooked taro leaves filled with chopped pork, fish, and coconut cream; *"kulolo"* – grated taro root baked with coconut meat and milk; *"squid lu'au"* – taro leaves cooked with onions and garlic in coconut milk with diced octopus added; *"haupia"* – a coconut milk- based gelatin desert; *"tropical fruits"*; and *"beer."* Having become the 50th state in the United States, this luau menu is all-American food.

LUBRICIOUS – (loo-*BRISH*-us) (Lubricity) Sebaceous. Greasy, slimy, oily, slippery. A lubricious person is a devious, underhanded individual. He may be lewd, lascivious, lecherous, prurient, a grease ball in all manner. *"His Lubriciousness,"* Donald Trump (b. 1946), is a text-book example.

LUCID – (*LOO*-sid) (Lucidly, Lucidness) Clearly comprehensible, intelligible, easily understood. *"Trump's fascism is perfectly lucid."*

LUCID DREAMING – (*LOO*-sid *DREE*-ming) Active, semi-conscious dreaming. In a lucid dream, one knows that she is dreaming and takes an active role in the dream drama. In lucid dreaming, one is not a mere spectator, but a participant. One can control the outcome of a lucid dream. A lucid dream is akin to a revery. A lucid dream is like actually participating in a living episode, but in another dimension.

LUCIFER – (*LOO*-sif-fer) One of many names for Satan, the devil. The name Lucifer is taken from two Latin terms, *"lux"* meaning *"light,"* and *"ferre"* meaning *"to carry,"* *"to bear."* Therefore, Lucifer literally means *"light bearer."* Actually, Lucifer was the name for the planet Venus, the *"Morning Star,"* (which is the brightest object in the early morning sky, after the moon). In about 742 BCE, the Prophet Isaiah compared the fall of the Babylonian King like the rapid fading of Venus in the morning sky. He referred to the planet as Lucifer. *"How art thou fallen from Heaven, O Lucifer, son of the morning"* – Isaiah 14:12. Later Christians compared Isaiah's comment with one made by Jesus: *"I beheld Satan as lighting fall from heaven"* (Luke 10:18). The names Lucifer and Satan were conflated. These Christians then interpreted Isaiah's description of the downfall of Babylon as an allegory for the fall from heaven of the rebel Archangel Satan. Lucifer, they concluded, must have been the devil's (Satan's) original name when he reigned in heaven as an Archangel. In this manner, the *"Bearer of Light,"* became the *"Prince of Darkness."*

LUCIFEROUS – (loo-*SIFF*-er-us) Bringing or providing light, enlightenment or insight. The term luciferous comes from the Latin name Lucifer, meaning *"light- bearer."* *"His luciferous explanation enlightened us all."*

LUCK – (*LUHK*) (Lucky, Luckless) Karma, good or bad, God's Divine justice. One's good luck or bad luck, may simply be a case of reaping what we had sown, in this life or in some past incarnation. We make our luck by how we treat others. Simply put, if you want to succeed, help others to succeed. Though luck can be positive or negative, to be *"lucky"* is always a good think, a blessing. *"Luckless,"* on the other hand, means never being blessed with good luck.

LUCKY SPERM CLUB – (*LUHK*-kee *SPERM CLUB*) *Cornucopia Kids*. Children born to filthy rich parents, who develop filthy abhorrent personalities. They display an arrogance of superiority toward those who have less. Having been given everything, members of the lucky sperm club have nothing to hope for. This is a common symptom of *affluenza*. They turn to carnal pleasures and material acquisition for fulfillment. Their shallow characters attract equally shallow acquaintances that are just out for what they can get. It can be lonely in the lucky sperm club. Drugs are often the inevitable escape from a boring life of over-abundance. To have nothing to strive for results in a barren, sterile life. Members of the lucky sperm club don't always end up so lucky. Note how many children of rich and famous celebrities are ib drug rehab.

LUCKY UNFORTUNATES – (*LUHK*-kee un-*FOR*-choon-nats) A contradiction in terms, symptomatic of a contradiction in economics. *"Dog-eat-dog"* capitalism is designed to produce a small ring of winners, and a huge legion of losers – the rich and the rest. On the very bottom are the unfortunates – the starving, naked homeless. Occasionally, an unfortunate gets lucky, and is provided a surprise lunch by a compassionate soul. These recipients are the *lucky unfortunates*. Of course, the charitable parcels are not donated by a capitalist millionaire or billionaire. They're too busy protecting their wealth from those who need it. The compassionate people are the poor, or near-poor who can empathize, relate to the pain of want and need. (Incidentally, Jesus would serve as a free lunch distributor today. Too, Jesus would expel the money-changers from Wall Street.) The way to change the fortunes of the unfortunates is to eradicate, outlaw poverty. The means is the redistribution of the wealth. The problem is capitalism. The solution is Socialism. *"Charity is no substitute for justice withheld."* – St. Augustine of Hippo (354 – 430 CE), a Father of your Church. *"There, but for the grace of God, go I."* – Writer John Bunyan (1628 - 1688).

LUCRE – (*LOO*-ker) Money, wealth, monetary reward or gain. Lucre is usually applied in a pejorative sense as in *"filthy lucre."* Illegal or unethical remuneration is lucre.

LUCUBRATION – (loo-cue-*BRAY*-shun) A laborious study, intense thought, often continuing long into the night. Too, a lucubration is a solemn literary tome, dissertation, or written speech. *"Her doctoral lucubration won her a Ph.D."*

LUCULLAN – (loo-*CUL*-lan) A lavish, sumptuous, opulent banquet. Lucullan also referrers to obscenely wealthy people who enjoy extravagant ostentatious entertainment. The lifestyles of the rich and famous tend to be lucullan. The term is taken from the name Lucius Licinius Lucullus (117 – 56 BCE), wealthy Roman general. Lucullus was renowned for his vulgarly luxurious parties. By the 1890's, the term lucullan had become an eponym and attained its present day meaning. *"Tonight, Lucullus hosts Lucullus."* – Lucius Licinius Lucullus. This quote is used to indicate vulgar self-indulgence.

LUDDITES – (*LUD*-dites) A pejorative term coined by *"technonerds"* for those who resist every new technological innovation. The term, an eponym, comes from the name, *Ned Ludd*, a fictitious character. The Luddites were English workers in the woolen and cotton industries (1811 - 1816) who sabotaged the new machines (technology) that were stealing their jobs. They blamed one Ned Ludd for the vandalism, providing the anti-technology movement with its name. Luddite today is a pejorative term. It connotes backwardness and close- mindedness. This is unfair and unfounded. All progress is not Progressive. Change for change-sake is unnecessary, change for profit is criminal. The Sacred Sage Lao Tzu (c. 604 – c. 531

BCE) wrote in <u>*Tao Te Ching*</u> (Book of The Way) *"Though there are machines that can work 10 to 100 times faster than man, they are not needed."* Before accepting any technological innovation, a good luddite will ask: *"What is the problem, for which this new technology is the solution?"* Of course, if the innovator cannot name a problem, there is no need to the solution.

LUDDITE'S CREDO – (*LUD*-dites *CRAY*-dow) *"What is the problem for which this new technology is the solution?"*

LUFTWAFFLE – (*LOOFT*-waf-ful) A German Air Force type of pancake, (*"a conficta"*). The *"Luftwaffe"* is the German air Force. A *"waffle"* is a gridlike pancake. Conflate the two produced *"Luftwaffle,"* a joke.

LUMINARY – (*LOO*-min-air-ree) Originally, a celestial body, as the sun or moon. The term was extended to anybody or object that emits light. Today, a luminary also includes a person of eminence in her field who serves as an inspiration to others.

LUMPENPROLETARIANS – (loom-pen-pro-let-*TER*-ree-ans) (Lumpenproletariat) A German term for the poorest of the poor. The homeless street people, vagrants, vagabonds, handicapped, dispossessed, deserted, addicts, retarded, insane, unemployable, and bag ladies prostitutes comprise this group. The lumpenproletariat are often mentally challenged or addicted. They are the forgotten, neglected, throwaway people. Out of options, and out of desperation, they may resort to prostitution or burglary, mugging. Capitalist greed and indifference had stripped the lumpenproletariat of their dignity, their humanity. Many have become animalistic predators. *"If the misery of the poor be caused not by the laws of nature, but by our institutions, great is out sin."* – Charles Darwin (1809 – 1882). The Russian Anarchist Mikhail Bakunin (1814 – 1876) called the lumpenproletarians: *"The millions of uncivilized, the disinherited, the miserable and the illiterate."* These *"untouchables"* are the people that Jesus (d. ca. 30 – 33 CE) and Gandhi (1869 – 1948) embraced and loved the most. *"When you give a feast,"* Jesus said, *"invite the poor, the maimed, the lame, the blind. And you will be blessed, because they cannot repay you."* – Luke 14: 13-14. Incidentally: Seeing a lumpenproletarian about to be hanged inspired English write John Bunyan (1628 – 1688) to pen: *"There, but for the grace of God go I."* Furthermore, one day in Paris, a wealthy lady approached St. Vincent DePaul (1581 – 1660) complaining: *"Father, the poor frighten me."* *"Yes,"* replied St. Vincent, *"the poor are frightening – as frightening as God's justice."*

LUNAR ARK – (*LOON*-ner *AHRK*) A depository of human and animal sperm and eggs, as well as seeds of all kind from all species to be preserved on the moon. Ark is a reference to *Noah's Ark,* the huge boat that saved Noah and his family, and specimens of life on Earth from the disastrous flood, as recorded in the Bible's Book of Genesis 6-9. Scientists have proposed hiding samples of frozen Earth-life in lunar lava tubes. The Lunar Ark would serve as an Earthly gene bank preserving cryogenetically preserved material from over 6.7 million species of plants, animals, and fungi on Earth. The purpose of the Lunar Ark is to save Earthly life (again?), in case of an existential cataclysm, an Armageddon event. Perhaps some celestial entity will discover the Lunar Ark and repopulate a suitable planet creating another Earth. If this occurred, the inhabitants would consider the celestial creator God.

LUNAR ECLIPSE – (*LOON*-ner *EE*-clips) An astronomical phenomenon when the Earth passes between the moon and the sun during which the Earth's shadow crosses the lighted half of the moon, shrouding it in darkness. This can only occur when the sun, Earth, and full moon are in perfect alignment called *"syzygy."* Such eclipses terrified our ancient ancestors, as it does to primitive people today.

LUNAR LIBRARY – (*LOON*-ner *LY*-brer-ree) A nano-technological assemblage of information and knowledge deposited on the moon for future reference, ours's and our galactic neighbor's. The Lunar Library is a history of Planet Earth, Humanity, and Human Civilization. Pessimistically speaking, if humanity goes extinct, our Extraterrestrial cousins will have a record of our existence. This is no joke. In April, 2019, the *"Arch Mission Foundation"* had landed the Lunar Library on the moon with a *SpaceIL "Beresheet" Lunar Lander.* The information in the Library covers all subjects: history, science, cultures, nations, languages, along with thousands of photographs, illustrations, diagrams, maps, and documents – the story of life on Earth. It is equivalent to over 30 million book pages. The Library is housed within a 100 gram nanotechology device that resembles a 120mm DVD. This contains 25 nickel discs, the size of a dime, only 40 microns thick. This information is designed to survive for billions of years. Any advanced civilization will easily be able to read about us. *"When I'm dead, I hope it's said: 'His sins were scarlet, but his books were read'."*

LUNATIC – (*LOON*-a-tic) An insane person, sadly unsound of mind. The word *luna* is Latin for moon. The ancient Romans believed that some people's minds and behavior were affected by the different phases of the moon. In the medical and legal literature of the 18th and 19th centuries a distinction was often made between the lunatic and the insane. The insane person was crazy all the time, while the lunatic went crazy only during certain phases of the moon. Today, the term lunatic describes a crazy person, or one who is wildly foolish. Nevertheless, many police officers testify that crime escalates during a full moon. Incidentally: On February 2, 2019, right-wing commentator Ann Coulter (b. 1961), a vociferous Donald Trump (b. 1946) supporter said, concerning Trump: *"We put a lunatic in the White House."* A day earlier, Coulter had called Trump *"lazy and incompetent."*

LUNATIC FRINGE – (*LOON*-a-tik *FRINJ*) The Republican crazies. Originally, the lunatic fringe was only the extreme right-wing of the Republican Party, on the border, the border of insanity. However, after 4 years of exposure to Donald Trump (b. 1946) the lunatic fringe had moved beyond conservatism toward reactionism, into the realm of fascism. Today, the lunatics no longer infest the fringe of the Republican Party, they have commandeered the center. All present day Republicans are lunatics. Initially, the lunatics hoped to undo all the Progressive social legislation enacted in the last 120 years. Their most visible representative was the *"Tea Party,"* (later the *"Freedom Caucus"*). In fact, the lunatic Donald Trump began his nasty political career on the fringe as a vocal *"birther"* (2011). He treacherously tried to undermine President Barack Obama's (b. 1961) Presidency by denying Obama's American citizenship. This was blatant racism, a dominant force of the lunatic fringe. In his revelatory memoir, *A Promised Land* (2020) President Barack Obama (b. 1961) contends that the abduction of the Republican Party by the lunatic fringe commenced with the selection of Alaska Governor Sarah Palin (b. 1964) by Senator John McCain (1936 – 2018) as his Vice-Presidential running-mate. Obama wrote: *"Through Palin, it seemed as if dark spirits that had long been lurking on the edges [fringe] of the modern Republican Party – xenophobia, anti- intellectualism, paranoid conspiracy theories, an antipathy toward Black and brown folks – were finding their way to center stage…. I'd like to think that given the chance to do it over again, [McCain] might have chosen differently. I believe he really put his country first."* From his birther conspiracy days, Trump came to believe that he would be rewarded with media attention by being outrageous. *"In this sense,"* Obama wrote: *"There wasn't much difference between Trump and [former Speaker] John Boehner (b. 1949) or [Senate Majority Leader] Mitch McConnell (b. 1942). They too understood that it didn't matter whether what they said was true. In fact, the only difference between Trump's style of politics and theirs was Trump's lack of inhibition."* After the 2020 electoral defeat, Trump and his Republican sycophants cried *"rigged election."* The Republican insanity may prove terminal. The GOP may shrink into the delusional fringe again. The bulk of the Party may emerge as a fascist, anti-Socialist, neo-Nazi movement. *"The inmates are running the asylum!"*

LUNCHEN – (*LUN*-chin) An inner-city slang term originated in the drug culture. Lunchen is the intentional inhaling of secondary marihuana or crack cocaine smoke. It is practiced by addicts who have exhausted their funds and cannot purchase their own dope. The secondary smoke is that exhaled by the addict lucky enough to be getting high. Lunchen is a desperation measure of desperate people.

LUNGFISH – (*LUHNG*-fish) A variety of air-breathing, fresh-water fish of Africa, Australia, and South America. All lungfish dwell in the Southern Hemisphere. This bizarre creature has a lung-like air bladder from which it can breathe air, as well as gills. If the water becomes too deoxygenated, the lungfish will crawl out on its fins, and seek a more accommodating water supply. Like whales and dolphins, the lungfish was an ancient land animal that reverted back into the water, fresh water. The lungfish is an omnivorous animal feeding on fish, frogs, snails, crustaceans, mollusks, worms, insects and plant matter. Some species can grow from 3 to 6 feet in length. *"Yea, slimy things did crawl with legs upon the slimy sea."* – Samuel Tayler Coleridge (1772 – 1834) in *The Rime of the Ancient Mariner.*

LUPUS – (*LOO*-pus) Technically, *Systemic Lupus Erythematosus,* (SLE). (*Erythematosus* refers to inflamed redness of the skin.) Lupus is Latin for *"wolf."* Since the late 14th century, the term was used for several diseases that caused ulcerations of the skin. The choice of the name apparently indicates how the disease *"devoured"* the affected area. Lupus is a heinous autoimmune disease in which the body's defensive immune system mistakenly attacks healthy tissue. Why the body turns on itself is not understood. Lupus probably has a genetic proclivity triggered by environmental factors like diet, pollution, stress. Lupus is a diabolically debilitating disease with a series of painful, symptoms. They include fatigue, hair loss, skin rashes, fever, painful swollen joints, mouth ulcers, chest pain, and swollen lymph nodes. Lupus diminishes one's life and may terminate it. The disease destroys the skin, joints, kidneys, heart, and brain.

LURCH – (*LERCH*) An abrupt swaying of a ship or the awkward staggering of an intoxicated man. *"The wave made the ship lurch drastically starboard."*

LURID – (*LUR*-rid) Gruesome, shockingly horrible. Slasher films are lurid. Too, a lurid pallor presents a wan, pallid countenance [translation: sickly completion].

LUSATANIA – (loo-sa-*TAIN*-nee-a) The ancient Roman Province now Portugal. More recently, the British luxury liner sunk by a German submarine, 11 miles off the coast of Ireland (May 7, 1915). The sinking killed 1,198 people including 128 Americans. Before the Lusitania sail out of New York, the German embassy took out a full page ad in the New York newspapers warning Americans not to sail on British Ships. After all, Germany was at war with Britain, and Britain was sinking German Ships. America was neutral at the time. Nevertheless, at least 5,000 crates of ammunition were illegally being shipped to Britain on the passenger liner. That is illegal and reprehensible. Chances are that the exploding munitions helped sink the ship. The sinking of the Lusitania and unrestricted submarine warfare would contribute in propelling the U.S. into war against Germany (1917-1918). This was the primary factor in Germany's defeat.

LUST – (*LUST*) (Natural, normal lust.) A passionate, intense sexual appetite or desire. When you gawk at the stewardess on the plane and your ego yells out: *"I want her!"* that's lust. Leonardo da Vinci (1452 – 1519) recognized that: *"Lust is the cause of generation,"* [read: procreation]. The word *lust* is found in the dictionary far beyond *like* and *love.* Lust tempered with love is ideal sex, or love-making. However lust is regarded as a vice, even a sin by religions. Actually, lust, [read: *sex drive*] is a natural condition that nature (God) had hard- wired into the male brain. Research indicates that men think of sex 33 times (*not percent but times*) more often than women. This is a defense mechanism to assure that males do not become bored with sex, procreation, so that the species continues. Monogamy is a socio-religious restriction that is contrary to biology. Monogamy is the victory of nurture over nature. That is why, even with the most loyal of husbands, *"An erect penis has no conscience."* Ask unfaithful faithless President Donald Trump (b. 1946). Alternately, ask the faithful faithfilled President Jimmy Carter (b. 1924). In a 1976 Playboy Magazine interview, even Fundamentalist Jimmy admitted that *"I look on a lot of women with lust…. I committed adultery in my heart many times."* *"In love the other is important; in lust you are important."* – Rajneesh (1931 – 1990*). "There is no disease so destructive as lust."* – Chanakya (370 – 283 B.C.E.).

LUST – (*LUST*) (Salacious, lecherous lust.) Sexual hunger, dire desire, passionate obsession. This form of lust is sex minus care. It is selfish desire that only takes, in a give-and-take sexual encounter. It is recreational sex. Unlike humanistic love, lust is an animalistic crave. One need not care for the object of lust. In fact, lust objectifies the subject of desire. It turns the person into an object, a sex toy with which to play. Lust is purely of the flesh. It is carnal, not Spiritual, it is physical, not emotional. Copulating with a stranger, a prostitute constitutes lust fulfillment. Incidentally: Satisfying sexual lust is the only pleasure not enhanced by wealth. Prince and peasant are indistinguishable when stripped naked. Sexual passion is not augment through affluence. Lust is absolutely egalitarian. It observes no class boundaries and is racially neutral. *"Disharmony prevails when you confuse lust with love, while the distance between the two is endless!"* – Persian Poet Rumi (1207 – 1273). *"Beware of lust; it corrupteth both the body and the mind."* – The Prophet Zoroaster (c. fl. 1300 BCE).

LUSTER – (*LUS*-ter) Glitter, sparkle, sheen, gloss caused by the reflection of light from the surface of a mineral. Metals, metallic substances readily reflect luster.

LUSTRUM – (*LUHS*-truhm) A period of five (5) years. Lustrum is a Latin term for an ancient ceremonial purifying the Roman people every five years. With time, the term simply came to mean 5 years.

LUTETIUM – (loo-*TET*-tee-um) (Lu) Named after Lutetia, the Latin name for "Paris." The 71 protons in its nucleus give lutetium its atomic number. Lutetium is a silvery-white metallic element. It is used in cracking (petroleum distillation) alkylation (gasoline production) and polymerization (creating complex molecules).

LUXURIATE – (luks-*ZHUR*-ree-ayt) (Luxuriating, Luxuriated, Luxuriation) To thrive. To luxuriate is to flourish extensively, to grow profusely, to live abundantly, sumptuously. One who luxuriates lives in luxury. Of course, in a capitalist society, only the wealthy few are enabled to luxuriate. Luxuriation is reserved for the rich. Socialism democratizes Luxuriation for all.

LYCANTHROPY – (ly-*CAN*-tho-pee) A variety of zoanthropy in which a person transforms into a wolf and back. Lycanthropy involves the legendary werewolf.

LYCEUM – (*LIS*-see-um) An institution for popular public education, providing movies, documentaries, lectures, discussions, and concerts. The lyceum movement was an important educational institution in 19th century America. The original Lyceum was Aristotle's (384 - 322 BCE) school of philosophy.

LYCHEE – (*LIE*-chee) A sweet fruit native to China now grown on trees throughout the Caribbean. It is similar in structure to *"guinep."* Lychee grows in bunches like grapes, though larger. The outside is covered by a pink-red, roughly-textured rind that is inedible, but easily broken and removed with the teeth. The fruit consists of a layer of sweet translucent white flesh, rich in vitamin C, with a texture somewhat similar to that of a grape. It resembles a scallop. In Jamaica, lychee is popularly called *"chiny guinep,"* due to its Chinese origin.

LYME DISEASE – (*LIME* dis-*EES*) (Lyme borreliosis) An infectious bacterial disease carried by ticks. An infected bite results in a rash, fatigue, head and muscle ache, neck stiffness, and heart palpitations. If unchecked, the Borrelia bacteria can spread throughout the body. An advanced stage of Lyme disease results in paralysis, cognitive difficulties, brain and nervous system complications, speech and vision impairment, and death. Lyme disease is an ancient ailment transmitted by deer ticks throughout the Northern Hemisphere (Europe, Asia, North America). Its symptoms had always been confused or attributed to other diseases, until 1975. In that year, Lyme disease was diagnosed as a separate condition, when an outbreak occurred in Old Lyme, Connecticut (ergo, the name). This is where the story becomes sinister. The U.S. Army knew about Lyme disease 30 years earlier, and the Nazi German Army even longer. Nine miles from Old Lyme in Long Island Sound lies Plumb Island. It served as a secret army biowarfare research facility. After World War Two, over 1,500 Nazi scientists were exonerated and brought to America to continue their often nefarious research. Among them was bacteriologist, Nazi SS Dr. Erich Traub (1906 – 1985). He was sent to Plumb Island. During the war in Germany, Traub investigated Lyme disease. He fortified this ancient nuisance and turned it into a plague. Lyme Borrelia ticks were sprayed from planes over Russia. The research continued on Plumb Island, Long Island Sound. Infected ticks were released on the island. Diseased animals died or had to be killed. Seabirds carried the infected ticks to Old Lyme, Connecticut. Today, most of the cases of Lyme disease occurs in the New England region, radiating from Connecticut.

LYNCHING – (*LIN*-ching) (Lynch) Execution, death by hanging. Lynching usually was conducted by illegal, unauthorized mob, vigilantes making it murder. Lynching was a popular murder technique of blacks by white racists throughout the southern Bible belt. Often a fire was set beneath the feet of the victim while being hanged. There is a significant correlation between the drop in cotton prices and the rise in lynchings. There were over 3,200 lynchings of Blacks in the South between 1882 and 1927. The last public lynching of a White man in the South was in 1957. The last Black man was lynched on March 21, 1981. The victim was 19-year-old Michael Donald (1962 - 1981) in Mobile, Alabama by the KKK.

LYONNAISE – (lie-on-*NEYZ*) French for simply fried potatoes and onions. Incidentally: Will Rogers (1879 – 1935) was once handed a menu in an exclusive French restaurant. Of course, Will, a Cherokee Indian was unable to read the selections. When asked which dish he desired, Will replied: *"It doesn't matter. After all, once you get under the gravy, it has to be meat and potatoes."*